ENCYCLOPEDIA OF ASIAN PHILOSOPHY

ENCYCLOPEDIA OF ASIAN PHILOSOPHY

Edited by Oliver Leaman

London and New York

First published 2001
by Routledge
11 New Fetter Lane, London EC4P 4EE

Simultaneously published in the USA and Canada
by Routledge
29 West 35th Street, New York, NY 10001

Routledge is an imprint of the Taylor & Francis Group
©2001 Routledge

Typeset in Baskerville by Taylor & Francis Books Ltd
Printed and bound in Great Britain by TJ International, Padstow, Cornwall

British Library Cataloguing in Publication Data
A catalogue record for this book is available from the British Library

Library of Congress Cataloging in Publication Data
Encyclopedia of Asian philosophy/edited by Oliver Leaman.
Includes bibliographical references and index.
1. Philosophy, Asian–Encyclopedias. 2. Asia–Religion–Encyclopedias.
I. Leaman, Oliver.
B121 .E53
2001
181'.003–dc21
00-032836

ISBN 0–415–17281–0

Contents

Authors and editors

Consulting editors and authors

Chris Bartley is an Honorary Research Fellow in the Department of Philosophy, University of Liverpool and teaches Sanskrit and Pali at the University of Manchester.

Thupten Jinpa is the President of the Institute of Tibetan Classics, Montreal, Canada, and the principal translator of the Dalai Lama.

Yong-choon Kim is Professor of Philosophy, University of Rhode Island, USA, and has written extensively on Korean philosophy and religions.

Whalen Lai is Professor in the Religious Studies Program and East Asian Languages and Culture at the University of California at Davis and the author of many works on Chinese philosophy.

Oliver Leaman is Professor of Philosophy at the University of Kentucky and writes on Islamic and Jewish philosophy.

Gregor Paul is Professor in the Department of Philosophy, University of Karlsruhe, Germany, and writes on Chinese and Japanese philosophy.

Mark Teeuwen is Professor of Japanese, University of Oslo, and writes on Japanese intellectual culture.

Alan Williams is Senior Lecturer in Comparative Religion, University of Manchester, and writes on Iranian religions.

Authors

Greg Bailey is Reader in the Department of Asian Studies, La Trobe University, Australia. He has published widely on Sanskrit and Tamil literature and poetry, and on the social and economic history of early Buddhism.

James Benson is a Fellow of Wolfson College Oxford and University Lecturer in Sanskrit.

Eivind Kahrs is Lecturer in Sanskrit at the University of Cambridge and a Fellow of Queens' College.

David Lea is Senior Lecturer in Philosophy, Department of Humanities, University of Papua New Guinea.

Azim Nanji is Director of the Institute of Ismaili Studies, London.

John Williamson is Lecturer in Philosophy, University of Liverpool.

Acknowledgements

I should like to thank my colleagues on this project, which has survived all sorts of major problems and minor disasters to be completed in a reasonably efficient manner. The authors of the entries are of course to be thanked for them, and the students with whom we have worked closely are to be thanked for their advice and suggestions. I hope that all those who have been involved in the volume feel that their efforts have been worthwhile when they see the final product.

As always, I am grateful to the skilled team at Routledge for their work on this volume. It has, as always, been a pleasure to work with Morgen Witzel on the production team and I would like to thank Mike Solomons for his work on the index.

Oliver Leaman
February 2000

Introduction

For a long time, Asian philosophy inhabited a rather ambiguous role in philosophy. It was clearly a fringe activity in most of the Anglo-Saxon and continental philosophical worlds, regarded often more as a scholarly pursuit for philologists and cultural historians than as serious philosophy. Sometimes Asian philosophy was not even regarded this positively, but has been identified with mystical rambling and vague personal advice, not really a part of 'serious' philosophy at all. Interestingly, even those working in one area of Asian philosophy sometimes have rather negative attitudes to those working in different areas, which just goes to show how difficult it is to think without stereotypes. For many years I have been working in Islamic and Jewish philosophy, but thought not at all about Indian philosophy, which I suspected was not really worthy of philosphical attention, at least not from an analytical philosopher.

Then I worked on a couple of projects which changed my mind. One was the *Companion Encyclopedia of Asian Philosophy*, edited by Indira Mahalingam and Indira Carr, and published by Routledge in 1997, and the other was the huge *Routledge Encyclopedia of Philosophy*, edited by Edward Craig and published the year after. These collaborative efforts brought me into contact for the first time with many people working on topics and thinkers which I had never come across before, and much to my surprise I discovered that they shared many of the same concerns and interests as I did. Not only was that the case, but also the ideas themselves produced in the various traditions which come under the rubric of Asian philosophy came to seem to me to be extremely interesting, sometimes exactly the same as those with which I was familiar, and sometimes intriguingly distinct. I started teaching in the area, and wrote a couple of short books designed to help my students find their way around this diverse series of topics and thinkers, and these appeared in 1999 (*Key Concepts in Eastern Philosophy*) and 2000 (*Eastern Philosophy: Key Readings*).

One reason why there is a need for more reference material on Asian philosophy is that the general reference works on philosophy often have very little information on it (the *Routledge Encyclopedia of Philosophy* is a worthy exception here). I thought it would be interesting to have a reference work which looked at some of the most important thinkers and ideas in Asian philosophy, written by just a few people, and in a format which allows them to express themselves at some length. Although some of the entries are long, many are short, and readers should be aware that most of the entries here have a large literature devoted to them; all we can supply is a relatively restricted discussion. Also, the fact that some topics have become entries and others not does not mean that there is nothing worth saying on the excluded topics. For example, under the entry 'sage' there is only discussion of the Chinese notion of the sage. There are of course discussions of this role in the other Asian traditions, but we felt that it is most central to Chinese philosophy and so only have an entry on it with respect to the latter.

I thought a lot about whether it would be better to have a great number of short entries, covering as much of Asian philosophy as possible, or whether we should have just a few long entries. The advantage of the former is that it enables a comprehensive description of the area to be undertaken, but of course does not enable much discussion of individual aspects of the area. The advantage of having relatively few large entries is that one would be able to display some of the complexity in argument and structure of Asian philosophy, but would be severely restricted in the number of entries which could be included. I decided on a compromise, and so readers will find quite a few brief entries, together with some long ones, where we felt that a fairly extended discussion was appropriate. I am sure that there will be readers who disagree with the decisions which have been made, but those decisions were taken on the basis of advice from teachers and students of Asian philosophy, with the intention of producing the most useful and appropriate sort of volume.

Another interesting debate was over the amount of space which should be devoted to the discussion of the religions on which the philosophy reposes, since there appears to be a much closer link between religion and philosophy in Asian philosophy than in many of the other traditions of world philosophy. In my two earlier books on Asian philosphy, I did not have that much material on religion, being severely constrained in terms of space, but here we felt that there was room to write at some length about the religions and systems of thought so closely linked with the various Asian philosophies, and we have used that space accordingly. On the other hand, readers should be aware that we discuss religion only in so far as it relates to philosophy, and this is not a book on Asian religion. Those interested in exploring Asian religions will have to look elsewhere for detailed and comprehensive material on this topic. However, we have interpreted 'philosophy' here in a wide sense, and have included what might be regarded as inessential topics when it was felt that they gave useful information on the context within which Asian philosophy took place.

Whether we have got the balance right is an issue for the reader to decide. The success of this volume will lie entirely on whether it is found to be useful in explaining the main topics and thinkers in the area. If readers are enabled to continue their study of Asian philosophy by using this book and then moving onto more specific and specialized works, the authors will have achieved their aims.

How to use this book

I have attempted to transliterate all terms in a way which will give the reader some grasp of how they are pronounced. Terms have not always been transliterated in such a way as to reproduce them as scholars would tend to do it, i.e. in a way which would make it easy to reproduce the term in its original language. But that is not our concern here, and I hope those who do understand some of the original Eastern languages will not mind the liberties I have taken. I have done away with all macrons and diacritics (signs which indicate the length of vowels over the vowel, and signs under letters which indicate the precise letter in the original language which is being used).

Dates

Dates are given in terms of before the Christian Era (BCE) and Christian Era (CE). For Islamic philosophers, *hijri* dates are given also (AH).

Transliteration

Chinese

There are two systems in popular use, the rather older Wade-Giles system, and the newer pinyin system. In general most names and terms have been reproduced here in terms of both systems, since they are used as often as each other, and the Wade-Giles system is rather ubiquitous. The Wade-Giles system here omits the diaresis. When the term is the same in both systems, generally only the pinyin has been used. Pinyin is used to specify where entries appear alphabetically, and there is cross-referencing to the Wade-Giles term. Sometimes pinyin terms are expressed as just one word,

and sometimes as more, and both forms are used here. So, for example, the thinker Chuang-tzu is sometimes presented as Zhuangzi and sometimes as Zhuang Zi. All three forms are frequently to be found in the literature. The Index has all the varieties, so it should be easy to find any reference if one has any of the approved forms of the name.

Tibetan

The system which has been used is not the official scholarly one, since this gives no guidance on pronunciation.

Sanskrit/Pali

Most of the terms from Indian philosophy are given in Sanskrit, sometimes with their Pali equivalents, and it should be clear which is which from the context. The letter p after a term means it is Pali. The order is generally Sanskrit/Pali.

Arabic

The normal system of transliteration is used, minus macrons and diacritics.

Japanese

I have followed the standard system here, without macrons.

Korean

I have followed the style which comes closest to modern pronunciation.

Ancient Persian Languages

I have omitted macrons but otherwise used the standard form.

Order of names

The names of authors and thinkers are placed in alphabetical order, with the exception of Japanese, Korean and Chinese names, where it is less obvious which name should be regarded as the surname. These have generally been reproduced in full, and there has been no attempt to specify a particular surname. The intention here is to make it easier to find these names. Cross-referencing of the entries will provide details of where the entry is to be found under various versions of a name or term. For Arabic the prefix 'al' is ignored when deciding on order, but the prefix 'ibn' is used.

Cross-referencing

Terms and names which occur in one entry and yet which have entries of their own are highlighted in **bold**. This has not been done in entries of a general survey nature. Other entries which are not specifically mentioned but which are relevant are introduced at the end of each entry by the phrase 'See also . . .'. Some terms are so ubiquitous that they are not always cross-referenced, and these include the names of the main religions (e.g. Buddhism, Daoism) and some of the most frequently mentioned movements (e.g. Huayan, Madhyamaka, *yin–yang*, Yogachara) as well as some terms which are very commonly used (*dao, dharma*).

Terms which have in many ways really entered the English language are not always italicized (e.g. yoga). In the short survey entries (such as Islamic philosophy), none of the terms are cross-referenced.

In the list of entries I have sometimes put terms together if they are linked as parts of a system (e.g. Daoism and some of the major Daoist thinkers) but these terms also appear in the text in their proper alphabetical place with a cross reference to where the entry is to be found.

References

An indicative list of references follows many of the entries, and a general list is available at the end of the book. There are in general no specific references to other works of reference, since it should be obvious to the reader that information is available on many of the entries here in such works of reference. A list of relevant reference texts is provided in the bibliographical section.

The dates which are provided are of course the date of publication, not an indication of when the work was actually written.

Index

There are two indices, one for persons and one for concepts, and there is extensive cross-referencing here to the variety of different forms of transliteration which readers may find both here and elsewhere.

A reference chart of the Chinese dynasties

Owing to the important role imperial patronage played in setting the style of culture among the elite, Chinese philosophy, art and literature did tend to coalesce in and around the capital and then emanate outward from that axis of her centralized bureaucratic rule. As the dynasty changed, the products of intellectual life also underwent notable shifts such that it is still customary and meaningful to date various cultural styles by their ties to dynasties.

Shang (1751–1112 BCE): end with Change of Mandate
Zhou (1111–249 BCE): Duke of Chou, Rites and Music
Spring and Autumn (722–481 BCE): Confucius, Laozi
Warring States (493–222 BCE): Age of Philosophers

Qin (221–206 BCE): pre-eminence of Legalism
Han (206 BCE–220 CE): *yin–yang* Confucianism
Wei (220–265): Neo-Daoism
Jin (265–420): Neo-Daoism and Buddhism
Northern and Southern Dynasty (320–589): Buddhism (learning phase)
Sui (581–618): Tiantai and Pure Land
Tang (618–907): Huayan and Chan
Five Dynasties (907–960): Chan pre-eminence
Song (960–1279): Neo-Confucian revival
Yuan (Mongol) (1271–1368): first full foreign rule
Ming (1368–1644): Neo-Confucian orthodoxy
Qing (Manchu) (1644–1912): Pre-modern thought
Republic (1912–): May Fourth liberalism
People's Republic (1949–): Maoist communism

WHALEN LAI

References and further reading

General texts

The following list contains compilations of relevant material, some of which are introductory, and some of which involve translations of key texts. Since there is so much relevant material in all these volumes, there are no references in the text to such material. It would be necessary to mention almost all of these works of reference for each entry, and that would not be helpful.

Of particular value is the *Routledge Encyclopedia of Philosophy*, edited by Edward Craig, with its extensive discussion of key concepts in Eastern philosophy along with philosophy as a whole. This has a wide coverage of the traditions in Eastern philosophy and is without doubt the leading source of information on philosophy today.

A guide to the main terms and concepts in the area is available in Oliver Leaman, *Key Concepts in Eastern Philosophy*, and a selection of some of the most important short passages can be found in his *Eastern Philosophy: Key Readings*. The thinkers themselves are often nicely discussed in *A Companion to the Philosophers*, edited by Robert Arrington, and the whole of world philosophy is remarkably outlined by Ninian Smart in his *World Philosophy*. In the *Companion Encyclopedia of Asian Philosophy* (ed. I. Mahalingam and B. Carr, Routledge, 1997), readers will find a very substantial discussion of the topics listed here.

Those interested in pursuing topics in Islamic philosophy in more depth are recommended to consult the *History of Islamic Philosophy*, edited by S.H. Nasr and O. Leaman.

Arrington, R. (ed.) (1999) *A Companion to the Philosophers*, Oxford: Blackwell.

Audi, R. (ed.) (1995) *The Cambridge Dictionary of Philosophy*, Cambridge: Cambridge University Press.

Billington, R. (1997) *Understanding Eastern Philosophy*, London: Routledge.

Carr, B. and Mahalingam, I. (eds) (1997) *Companion Encyclopedia of Asian Philosophy*, London: Routledge.

Chan, Wing-tsit (1972) *A Source Book in Chinese Philosophy*, Princeton, NJ: Princeton University Press.

Clarke, J. (1997) *Oriental Enlightenment: The Encounter between Asian and Western Thought*, London: Routledge.

Collinson, D. and Wilkinson, R. (eds) (1994) *Thirty-Five Oriental Philosophers*, London: Routledge.

Cooper, D. (1996) *World Philosophers: An Historical Introduction*, Oxford: Blackwell.

Craig, E. (ed.) (1998) *Routledge Encyclopedia of Philosophy*, London: Routledge.

Dasgupta, S. (1922–55) *A History of Indian Philosophy*, 5 vols, Cambridge: Cambridge University Press.

de Bary, W., Embree, A. and Heinrich, A. (eds) (1989) *A Guide to Oriental Classics*, New York: Columbia University Press.

de Bary, W.T. *et al.* (1964) *Sources of Japanese Tradition: Introduction to Oriental Civilizations*, New York: Columbia University Press.

—— (1966) *Sources of Chinese Tradition: Introduction to Oriental Civilizations*, New York: Columbia University Press.

—— (1988) *Sources of Indian Tradition: Introduction to Oriental Civilizations*, New York: Columbia University Press.

Deutsch, E. and Bontekoe, R. (eds) (1997) *A Companion to World Philosophies*, Oxford: Blackwell.

Eliade, M. (1987) *The Encyclopedia of Religions*, 16 vols, New York: Macmillan.

Fakhry, M. (1983) *A History of Islamic Philosophy*, New York: Columbia University Press.

Leaman, O. (ed.) (1998) *The Future of Philosophy*, London: Routledge.

—— (1999) *Key Concepts in Eastern Philosophy*, London: Routledge.

—— (1999) *A Brief Introduction to Islamic Philosophy*, Oxford: Polity.

—— (2000) *Eastern Philosophy: Key Readings*, London: Routledge.

McGreal, I. (ed.) (1995) *Great Thinkers of the Eastern World*, New York: HarperCollins.

Nasr, S. and Leaman, O. (eds) (1996) *History of Islamic Philosophy*, London: Routledge.

Potter, K. (1977–) *The Encyclopaedia of Indian Philosophies*, Delhi: Motilal Banarsidass; Princeton, NJ: Princeton University Press.

Radhakrishnan, S. and Moore, C. (1957) *A Source Book in Indian Philosophy*: Princeton, NJ: Princeton University Press.

(1989) *The Rider Encyclopedia of Eastern Philosophy and Religion*, London: Hutchinson.

Scharfstein, B.-A. *et al.* (1978) *Philosophy East/ Philosophy West: A Critical Comparison of Indian, Chinese, Islamic and European Philosophy*, Oxford: Oxford University Press.

Smart, N. (1999) *World Philosophy*, London: Routldge.

Solomon, R. and Higgins, K. (eds) (1993) *From Africa to Zen: An Introduction to World Philosophy*, Lanham: Rowman and Littlefield.

Tsunoda, R., de Bary, W.T. and Keene, D. *et al.* (1964) *Sources of Japanese Tradition*, New York: Columbia University Press.

Further reading

Abe, M. (1985) *Zen and Western Thought*, Basingstoke: Macmillan.

—— (1992) *A Study of Dogen: His Philosophy and Religion*, ed. S. Heine, Albany, NY: State University of New York Press.

Adelmann, F. (1982) *Contemporary Chinese Philosophy*, The Hague: Nijhoff.

Allinson, R. (1989) *Chuang Tzu for Spiritual Transformation*, Albany, NY: State University of New York Press.

—— (ed.) (1989) *Understanding the Chinese Mind: The Philosophical Roots*, Oxford: Oxford University Press.

Ames, R. (1994) *Self as Person in Asian Theory and Practice*, Albany, NY: State University of New York Press.

Ames, R. and Callicott, J. (1989) *Nature in Asian Traditions of Thought*, Albany, NY: State University of New York Press.

Angel, L. (1994) *Enlightenment East and West*, Albany, NY: State University of New York Press.

Armstrong, R. (1914) *Light from the East: Studies in Japanese Confucianism*, Toronto: University of Toronto Press.

Aronson, H. (1980) *Love and Sympathy in Theravada Buddhism*, Delhi: Motilal Banarsidass.

Aston, W. (1964) *Sources of Japanese Tradition*, compiled by R. Tsunoda, W. de Bary and D. Keene, New York: Columbia University Press.

Aurobindo (1987) *The Essential Aurobindo*, ed. R. McDermott, Great Barrington, MA: Lindisfarne Press.

Basham, A. (1951) *History and Doctrines of the Ajivikas*, Delhi: Motilal Banarsidass.

Beidler, W. (1975) *The Vision of Self in Early Vedanta*, Delhi: Motilal Banarsidass.

The Bhagavad Gita (1994), trans. W. Johnson, Oxford: Oxford University Press.

Bhatt, S. (1975) *Studies in Ramanuja Vedanta*, New Delhi: Heritage Publishers.

Billington, R. (1990) *East of Existentialism: The Tao of the West*, London: Unwin Hyman.

Bishop, P. (1993) *Dreams of Power: Tibetan Buddhism and the Western Imagination*, London: Athlone.

Bloom, A. (1965) *Shinran's Gospel of Pure Grace*, Tucson: University of Arizona Press.

Bloom, I. (ed.) (1996) *Meeting of Minds: Intellectual and Religious Interaction in East Asian Traditions of Thought*, New York: Columbia University Press.

Bondurant, J. (1965) *Conquest of Violence*, Berkeley, CA: University of California Press.

Bowes, P. (1977) *The Hindu Religious Tradition: A Philosophical Approach*, London: Routledge and Kegan Paul.

Bowker, J. (1991) *The Meanings of Death*, Cambridge: Cambridge University Press.

Boyce, M. (1975) *A History of Zoroastrianism: The Early Period*, Leiden: Brill.

—— (1984) *Textual Sources for the Study of Zoroastrianism*, Manchester: Manchester University Press.

Brinkman, J. (1996) *Simplicity: A Distinctive Quality of Japanese Spirituality*, New York: Peter Lang.

Brockington, J. (1996) *The Sacred Thread: Hinduism in its Continuity and Diversity*, Edinburgh: Edinburgh University Press.

Buddhaghosa (1976) *The Path of Purification: Visuddhimagga*, trans. b. Nyanamoli, Berkeley, CA: Shambhala.

Burch, G. (1976) *Search for the Absolute in Neo-Vedanta*, Honolulu, HA: University of Hawaii Press.

Buswell, R. (trans. and ed.) (1983) *The Korean Approach to Zen: The Collected Works of Chinul*, Honolulu, HA: University of Hawaii Press.

Buswell, R. and Gimello, R. (eds) (1992) *Paths to Liberation: The Marga and its Transformations in Buddhist Thought*, Honolulu, HA: University of Hawaii Press.

Cabezon, J. (1994) *Buddhism and Language*, Albany, NY: State University of New York Press.

Capra, F. (1976) *The Tao of Physics: An Exploration of Parallels between Modern Physics and Eastern Mysticism*, London: Fontana.

Carman, J. (1974) *The Theology of Ramanuja: An Essay in Interreligious Understanding*, New Haven, CN: Yale University Press.

Carter, R. (1989) *The Nothingness beyond God: An Introduction to the Philosophy of Nishida Kitaro*, New York: Paragon House.

Chakraborty, A. (ed.) (1961) *A Tagore Reader*, New York: Macmillan.

—— (1996) *Mind-Body Dualism*, New Delhi: D.K. Printworld.

Chambliss, J. (ed.) (1996) *Philosophy of Education: An Encyclopedia*, New York: Garland.

Chan, Wing-tsit (1963) *A Source Book in Chinese Philosophy*, Princeton, NJ: Princeton University Press.

Chapple, C. (1993) *Nonviolence to Animals, Earth, and Self in Asian Traditions*, Albany, NY: State University of New York Press.

Chapple, C. and Viraj, Y. (eds) (1990) *The Yoga Sutras of Patanjali*, Delhi: Sri Satguru Publications.

Chatterjee, M. (1983) *Gandhi's Religious Thought*, Notre Dame, IN: Notre Dame University Press.

—— (1996) *Studies in Modern Jewish and Hindu Thought*, London: Athlone Press.

Chatterjee, S. (1965) *The Nyaya Theory of Knowledge*, Calcutta: Calcutta University Press.

Cheng, C. (ed.) (1989) *Sun Yat-sen's Doctrine in the Modern World*, Boulder, CO: Westview Press.

Chi, R. (1969) *Buddhist Formal Logic*, Delhi: Motilal Banarsidass.

Ching, J. (1976) *To Acquire Wisdom: The Way of Yang Wang-ming*, New York: Columbia University Press.

Chittick, W. (1997) *Imaginal Worlds: Ibn al-'Arabi and the Problem of Religious Diversity*, Albany, NY: State University of New York Press.

Chung, B. (1992) *Zhuangzi Speaks!*, Princeton, NJ: Princeton University Press.

Chung, E. (1995) *The Korean Neo-Confucianism of Yi T'oegye and Yi Yulgok*, Albany, NY: State University of New York Press.

Cleary, T. (1991) *The Essential Tao*, San Francisco: HarperCollins.

—— (ed.) (1991) *The Art of Worldly Wisdom: Confucian Teachings of the Mind Dynasty*, Boston: Shambhala.

Collins, S. (1982) *Selfless Persons: Imagery and Thought in Theravada Buddhism*, Cambridge: Cambridge University Press.

Confucius (1993) *The Analects*, trans. R. Dawson, Oxford: Oxford University Press.

Conze, E. (1962) *Buddhist Thought in India*, London: Allen and Unwin.

Cook, F. (1977) *Hua-yen Buddhism: The Jewel Net of Indra*, University Park, PA: Pennsylvania State University Press.

Coward, H. and Raja, K. (eds) (1990) *The Philosophy of Indian Grammarians: Encyclopedia of Indian Philosophies*, vol. V, Princeton, NJ: Princeton University Press.

Creel, H. (1953) *Chinese Thought: From Confucius to Mao Tse-Tung*, Chicago: University of Chicago Press.

Dainian, F. and Cohen, S. (ed.) (1996) *History and Philosophy of Science and Technology*, Dordrecht: Kluwer.

Daizhen (1990) *Tai Chen on Mencius: Explorations in Words and Meaning*, trans. A. Chin and M. Freeman, New Haven, CN: Yale University Press.

Dasgupta, S. (1922) *A History of Indian Philosophy*, Cambridge: Cambridge University Press; repr. Delhi: Motilal Banarsidass, 1975.

Dasgupta, S.B. (1974) *An Introduction to Tantric Buddhism*, Berkeley, CA: Shambhala.

Datta. D. (1972) *Six Ways of Knowing*, Calcutta: University of Calcutta Press.

Davidson, H. (1992) *Alfarabi, Avicenna, and Averroes on Intellect: Their Cosmologies, Theories of Active Intellect and Theories of the Human Intellect*, New York: Oxford University Press.

de Bary, W. (ed.) (1958) *Sources of Japanese Tradition*, New York: Columbia University Press.

—— (1988) *The Message of the Mind*, New York: Columbia University Press.

—— (1996) *The Trouble with Confucianism*, Cambridge, MA: Harvard University Press.

de Bary, W. T. and Haboush, J. (eds) (1985) *The Rise of Neo-Confucianism in Korea*, New York: Columbia University Press.

Deutsch, E. (1968) *Advaita Vedanta: A Philosophical Reconstruction*, Honolulu, HA: University of Hawaii Press.

—— (1975) *Comparative Aesthetics*, Honolulu, HA: University of Hawaii Press.

Deutsch, E. and Van Buitenen, J. (1971) *A Source Book of Advaita Vedanta*, Honolulu, HA: University of Hawaii Press.

Dilworth, D. and Viglielmo, V. (1998) *Sourcebook for Modern Japanese Philosophy: Selected Documents*, London: Greenwood Press.

Dravida, R. (1972) *The Problem of Universals in Indian Philosophy*, Delhi: Motilal Banarsidass.

Dreyfus, G. (1997) *Recognizing Reality: Dharmakirti's Philosophy and its Tibetan Interpretations*, Albany, NY: State University of New York Press.

Dundas, P. (1992) *The Jains*, London: Routledge.

Eckel, M. (1992) *To See the Buddha: A Philosopher's Quest for the Meaning of Emptiness*, San Francisco: HarperCollins.

Elberfeld, R. (1999) *Moderne japanische Philologie und die Frage nach der Interkulturalität*, Amsterdam: Editions Rodopi.

Eliade, M. (1958) *Yoga: Immortality and Freedom*, Princeton, NJ: Princeton University Press.

—— (1969) *Patanjali and Yoga*, New York: Schocken.

Fakhry, M. (1983) *A History of Islamic Philosophy*, London: Longman.

—— (1997) *A Short Introduction to Islamic Philosophy, Theology and Mysticism*, Oxford: Oneworld.

al-Farabi (1961) *The Fusul al-Madani of al-Farabi (Aphorisms of the Statesman)*, ed. and tr. D. Dunlop, Cambridge: Cambridge University Press.

Faure, B. (1993) *Chan Insights and Oversights: An Epistemological Critique of the Chan Tradition*, Princeton, NJ: Princeton University Press.

Feuerstein, G. (1980) *The Philosophy of Classical Yoga*, Manchester: Manchester University Press.

—— (1989) *The Yoga-Sutra of Patanjali: A New Translation and Commentary*, Rochester, VT: Inner Traditions International.

Filippi, G. (1996) *Mrtyu: Concept of Death in Indian Traditions*, New Delhi: D.K. Printworld.

Fingarette, H. (1972) *Confucius: The Secular as Sacred* New York: Harper and Row.

Fontana, D. (1992) *The Meditator's Handbook: A Comprehensive Guide to Eastern and Western Meditation Techniques*, Shaftesbury: Element.

Franco, E. and Preisendanz (eds) (1997) *Beyond Orientalism: The Work of Wilhelm Halbfass and its impact on Indian and Cross-Cultural Studies*, Amsterdam: Editions Rodopi.

Fung, Yu-lan (1948) *A Short History of Chinese Philosophy*, New York: Free Press.

—— (1970) *The Spirit of Chinese Philosophy*, trans. E. Hughes, Westport, CN: Greenwood Press.

—— (1983) *A History of Chinese Philosophy*, trans. D. Bodde, Princeton, NJ: Princeton University Press.

Gandhi, M. (1969) *The Collected Works of Mahatma Gandhi*, Delhi: Government of India Publications.

Gardner, D. (1986) *Chu Hsi and the Ta-Hsueh*, Cambridge, MA: Harvard University Press.

Garfield, J. (ed.) (1995) *The Fundamental Wisdom of the Middle Way*, New York: Oxford University Press.

Gombrich, R. (1971) *Precept and Practice*, Oxford: Clarendon Press.

—— (1988) *Theravada Buddhism: A Social History from Ancient Benares to Modern Colombo*, London: Routledge.

—— (1997) *How Buddhism began: The Conditioned Genesis of the Early Teachings*, London: Athlone Press.

Gonda, J. (1970) *Visnuism and Sivaism*, London, Athlone Press.

Goodman, L. (1992) *Avicenna*, London: Routledge.

Graham, A. (1958) *Two Chinese Philosophers: Ch'eng*

Ming-tao and Ch'eng Yi-ch'uan, London: Lund Humphries.

—— (1978) *Later Mohist Logic, Ethics and Science*, Hong Kong: The Chinese University Press.

—— (1981) *Chuang-tzu: The Inner Chapters*, London: George Allen and Unwin.

—— (1989) *Disputers of the Tao: Philosophical Argument in Ancient China*, La Salle, IL: Open Court Press.

Gregory, P. (ed.) (1987) *Sudden and Gradual: Approaches to Enlightenment in Chinese Thought*, Honolulu, HA: University of Hawaii Press.

Griffiths, P. (1986) *On Being Mindless: Buddhist Meditation and the Mind-Body Problem*, La Salle, IL: Open Court.

—— (1994) *On Being Buddha: The Classical Doctrine of Buddhahood*, Albany, NY: State University of New York Press.

Gross, R. (1993) *Buddhism after Patriarchy*, Albany, NY: State University of New York Press.

Gudmunsen, C. (1977) *Wittgenstein and Buddhism*, London: Macmillan.

Guenther, H. (1972) *Buddhist Philosophy in Theory and Practice*, Harmondsworth: Penguin Books.

—— (1976) *Philosophy and Psychology of the Abhidharma*, Berkeley, CA: Shambhala.

Guenther, H. and Trungpa (1975) *The Dawn of Tantra*, ed. M. Kohn, Berkeley: Shambhala.

Gyatso, J. (ed.) (1992) *In the Mirror of Memory: Reflections on Mindfulness and Remembrance in Indian and Tibetan Buddhism*, Albany, NY: State University of New York Press.

Ha'iri Yazdi, M. (1992) *The Principles of Epistemology in Islamic Philosophy: Knowledge by Presence*, Albany, NY: State University of New York Press.

Hakeda, Y. (1972) *Kukai: Major Works*, New York: Columbia University Press.

Han Fei (1964) *Han Fei Tzu: Basic Writings*, trans. B. Watson, New York: Columbia University Press.

Hansen, C. (1983) *Language and Logic in Ancient China*, Ann Arbor, MI: University of Michigan Press.

Harvey, P. (1990) *Introduction to Buddhism*, Cambridge: Cambridge University Press.

—— (1995) *The Selfless Mind: Personality, Consciousness and Nirvana in Early Buddhism*, Richmond: Curzon.

Hatano, S. (1988) *Time and Eternity*, trans. I. Suzuki, Westport, CN: Greenwood.

Heine, S. (1985) *Existential and Ontological Dimensions of Time: Heidegger and Dogen*, Albany, NY: State University of New York Press.

—— (1989) *A Blade of Grass: Japanese Poetry and Aesthetics in Dogen Zen*, New York: Peter Lang.

—— (1991) *A Dream within a Dream: Studies in Japanese Thought*, New York: Peter Lang.

—— (1993) *Dogen and the Koan Tradition: A Tale of Two Shobogenzo Texts*, Albany, NY: State University of New York Press.

Heisig, J. and Maraldo, J. (eds) (1995) *Rude Awakenings: Zen, the Kyoto School and the Question of Nationalism*, Honolulu, HA: University of Hawaii Press.

Henderson, J. (1998) *The Construction of Orthodoxy and Heresy: Neo-Confucian, Islamic, Jewish, and Early Christian Patterns*, Albany, NY: State University of New York Press.

Hick, J. (1997) *God and the Universe of Faiths*, Oxford: Oneworld.

Hinnells, J. (1978) *Spanning East and West*, Milton Keynes: Open University Press.

Hirikawa, A. (1990) *A History of Indian Buddhism: From Sakyamuni to Early Mahayana*, trans. and ed. P. Groner, Honolulu, HA: University of Hawaii Press.

Hiriyanna, M. (1932) *Outlines of Indian Philosophy*, London: George Allen and Unwin.

—— (1985) *Essentials of Indian Philosophy*, London: George Allen and Unwin.

Hoffman, F. (1987) *Rationality and Mind in Early Buddhism*, Delhi: Motilal Banarsidass.

Hoshino, K. (ed.) (1997) *Japanese and Western Bioethics*, Dordrecht: Kluwer.

Hourani, G. (1985) *Reason and Tradition in Islamic Ethics*, Cambridge: Cambridge University Press.

Hubbard, J, and Swanson, P. (eds) (1997) *Pruning the Bodhi Tree: The Storm over Critical Buddhism*, Honolulu, HA: University of Hawaii Press.

Huntington, C. (1989) *The Emptiness of Emptiness*, Honolulu, HA: University of Hawaii Press.

Inada, K. (1970) *Nagarjuna: A Translation of his Mulamadhyamaka-karika with an introductory essay*, Tokyo: Hokuseido Press.

Inada, K. and Jacobsen, N. (eds) (1984) *Buddhism and American Thinkers*, Albany, NY: State University of New York Press.

Izutsu, T. (1984) *Sufism and Taoism*, Berkeley, CA: University of California Press.

Jackson, R. (1993) *Is Enlightenment Possible?*

Dharmakirti and rGyal-tshab-rje on Mind and Body, No-Self and Freedom, Ithaca, NY: Snow Lion Publications.

Jayatilleke, K. (1986) *Early Buddhist Theory of Knowledge*, Delhi: Motilal Banarsidass.

Jinpa, Thupten (1997) 'Self, Persons and Madhyamaka Dialectics: A Study of Tsongkhapa's Middle Way Philosophy', Ph.D. thesis, University of Cambridge.

Kaltenmark, M. (1969) *Lao Tzu and Taoism*, Stanford, CA: Stanford University Press.

Kalton, M. (1998) *To Become a Sage: The Ten Diagrams on Sage Learning by Yi T'oegye*, New York: Columbia University Press.

Kalupahana, D. (1975) *Causality: The Central Philosophy of Buddhism*, Honolulu, HA: University of Hawaii Press.

—— (1976) *Buddhist Philosophy: A Historical Introduction*, Honolulu, HA: University of Hawaii Press.

—— (1986) *Nagarjuna: The Philosophy of the Middle Way*, Albany, NY: State University of New York Press.

Karmay, S. (1988) *The Great Perfection: A Philosophical and Meditative Teaching of Tibetan Buddhism*, Leiden: Brill.

Kemal, S. (1991) *The Poetics of Alfarabi and Avicenna*, Leiden: Brill.

Kendall, L. (1985) *Shamans, Housewives, and Other Restless Spirits*, Honolulu, HA: University of Hawaii Press.

Keown, D. (1992) *The Nature of Buddhist Ethics*, New York: Curzon.

King, S. (1991) *Buddha Nature*, Albany, NY: State University of New York Press.

Kitagawa, J. (1966) *Religion in Japanese History*, New York: Columbia University Press.

Kraemer, J. (1986) *Philosophy in the Renaissance of Islam: Abu Sulayman al-Sijistani and his Circle*, Leiden: Brill.

Krishna, D. (1991) *Indian Philosophy: A Counter Perspective*, Delhi: Oxford University Press.

Kukai (1972) *Kukai: Major Works*, New York: Columbia University Press.

LaFleur, W. (1983) *The Karma of Words: Buddhism and the Literary Arts in Medieval Japan*, Los Angeles: University of California Press.

—— (ed.) (1985) *Dogen Studies*, Honolulu, HA: University of Hawaii Press.

—— (1992) *Liquid Life: Abortion and Buddhism in Japan*, Princeton, NJ: Princeton University Press.

Lal, B. (1973) *Contemporary Indian Philosophy*, Delhi: Motilal Banarsidass.

Laozi, (1989) *Lao-Tzu: Te Tao Ching*, trans. R. Henricks, New York: Ballantine.

Larson, G. (1969) *Classical Samkhya: An Interpretation of its History and Meaning*, Delhi: Motilal Banarsidass.

Lau, D. (1963) *Lao-Tzu: Tao Te Ching*, Harmondsworth: Penguin.

—— (1970) *Mencius*, Harmondsworth: Penguin.

—— (1979) *Confucius: The Analects*, Harmondsworth: Penguin.

Leaman, O. (1985) *An Introduction to Medieval Islamic Philosophy*, Cambridge: Cambridge University Press.

—— (ed.) (1996) *Friendship East and West: Philosophical Perspectives*, Richmond, Curzon.

—— (1997) *Averroes and his Philosophy*, Richmond: Curzon Press.

Lee, P. (ed.) (1993) *Sourcebook of Korean Civilization*, New York: Columbia University Press.

Ling, T. (ed.) (1981) *The Buddha's Philosophy of Man*, London: Dent.

—— (1997) *Buddhism and the Mythology of Evil*, Oxford: Oneworld.

Lipner, J. (1986) *The Face of Truth: A Study of Meaning and Metaphysics in the Vedantic Theology of Ramanuja*, Basingstoke: Macmillan.

Lopez, D. (ed.) (1988) *Buddhist Hermeneutics*, Honolulu, HA: University of Hawaii Press.

Lopez, D. and Rockefeller, S. (eds) (1987) *The Christ and the Bodhisattva*, Albany, NY: State University of New York Press.

Macey, J. (1991) *Mutual Causality in Buddhism and General Systems Theory: The Dharma of Natural Systems*, Albany, NY: State University of New York Press.

Mao, Tse-tung (1961–77) *Selected Works of Mao Tse-tung*, Peking: Foreign Languages Press.

Martin, R. and Woodward, M. (1997) *Defenders of Reason in Islam: Mu'tazilism from Medieval School to Modern Symbol*, Oxford: Oneworld.

Maruyama, M. (1974) *Studies in the Intellectual History of Tokugawa Japan*, trans. M. Hane, Princeton, NJ: Princeton University Press.

Ma'sumian, F. (1997) *Life after Death: A Study of the Afterlife in World Religions*, Oxford: Oneworld.

Matilal, B. (1968) *The Navya-Nyaya Doctrine of Negation*, Cambridge, MA: Harvard University Press.

—— (1971) *Epistemology, Logic and Grammar in Indian Philosophical Analysis*, The Hague: Mouton.

—— (1986) *Perception: An Essay on Classical Indian Theories of Knowledge*, Oxford: Clarendon Press.

Matilal, B. and Evans, R. (eds) (1986) *Buddhist Logic and Epistemology: Studies in the Buddhist Analysis of Inference and Language*, Dordrecht: Kluwer.

May, R. (1996) *Heidegger's Hidden Sources: East-Asian Influences on his Work*, trans. G. Parkes, London: Routledge.

McDermott, R. (ed.) (1987) *The Essential Aurobindo*, Great Barrington, MA: Lindisfarne Press.

McRae, J. (1986) *The Northern School and the Formation of Early Ch'an Buddhism*, Honolulu, HA: University of Hawaii Press.

Minor, R. (1978) *Sri Aurobindo: The Perfect and the Good*, Columbia, MO: South Asian Books.

Mohanty, J. (1993) *Essays on Indian Philosophy, Traditional and Modern*, ed. P. Bilimoria, Delhi: Oxford University Press.

Moore, C. (ed.) (1968) *Philosophy and Culture: East and West*, Honolulu, HA: University of Hawaii Press.

Morewedge, P. (ed.) (1979) *Islamic Political Theology*, Albany, NY: State University of New York Press.

—— (ed.) (1992) *Neoplatonism and Islamic Thought*, Albany, NY: State University of New York Press.

Mozi (1974) *The Ethical and Political Works of Motse*, trans. Y.-P. Mei, Taipei: Ch'eng Wen Publishing Company.

Murti, T. (1960) *The Central Philosophy of Buddhism: A Study of the Madhyamika System*, London: Allen and Unwin.

Murty, K. (1959) *Revelation and Reason in Advaita Vedanta*, San Francisco: Harper Row.

Nagao, G. (1991) *Madhyamaka and Yogacara: A Study of Mahayana Philosophies*, Albany, NY: State University of New York Press.

Nakamura, H. (1983) *A History of Early Vedanta Philosophy*, Delhi: Motilal Banarsidass.

Nasr, S. (1981) *Islamic Life and Thought*, Albany, NY: State University of New York Press.

—— (ed.) (1989) *Islamic Spirituality: Foundations*, London: SCM Press.

—— (1993) *The Need for a Sacred Science*, Albany, NY: State University of New York Press.

—— (1993) *An Introduction to Islamic Cosmological Doctrines*, Albany, NY: State University of New York Press.

—— (1996) *The Islamic Intellectual Tradition in Persia*, ed. M. Amin Razavi, Richmond: Curzon.

Netton, I. (1991) *Muslim Neoplatonists: An Introduction to the Thought of the Brethren of Purity (Ikhwan al-Safa')*, Edinburgh: Edinburgh University Press.

Nichiren (1990) *Selected Writings of Nichiren*, trans. B. Watson *et al.*, New York: Columbia University Press.

Nishida, Kitaro (1990) *An Inquiry into the Good*, trans. M. Abe and C. Ives, New Haven, CN: Yale University Press.

Nishitani, Keiji (1982) *Religion and Nothingness*, trans. J. van Bragt, Berkeley, CA: University of California Press.

Nishitani, K. (1991) *Nishida Kitaro*, trans. Y. Seisaku and J. Heisig, Berkeley, CA: University of California Press.

Nivison, D. and Wright, A. (ed.) (1959) *Confucianism in Action*, Stanford, CA: Stanford University Press.

Odin, S. (1982) *Process Metaphysics and Hua-yen Buddhism: A Critical Study of Cumulative Penetration vs. Interpenetration*, Albany, NY: State University of New York Press.

Park Sung Bae (1983) *Buddhist Faith and Sudden Enlightenment*. Albany, NY: State University of New York Press.

Parrinder, G. (1997) *Avatar and Incarnation: The Divine in Human Form in the World's Religions*, Oxford: Oneworld.

Patnaik, P. (1994) *Shabda: A Study of Bhartrihari's Philosophy of Language*, New Delhi: D.K. Printworld.

—— (1997) *Rasa in Aesthetics*, New Delhi: D.K. Printworld.

Paul, G. (1991) *Aspects of Confucianism: A Study of the Relationship between Rationality and Humaneness*, New York: Peter Lang.

Peerenboom, R. (1993) *Law and Morality in Ancient China*, Albany, NY: State University of New York.

Pereira, J. (1976) *Hindu Theology: A Reader*, Garden City, NY: Doubleday.

Piovesana, G. (1997) *Recent Japanese Philosophical Thought 1862–1996: A Survey*, Richmond: Curzon.

Potter, K. (1972) *Presuppositions of India's Philosophies*, Westport, CN: Greenwood Press.

—— (1988) *Guide to Indian Philosophy*, Boston: G.K. Hall.

Pruden, L. (trans.) (1988–90) *Abhidharma Kosa Bhasyam*, Berkeley, CA: Asian Humanities Press.

Puligandla, R. (1975) *Fundamentals of Indian Philosophy*, New York: Abingdon Press; 2nd edn, New Delhi: D.K. Printworld, 1997.

—— (1997) *Jnana-Yoga: The Way of Knowledge*, New Delhi: D.K. Printworld.

Pye, M. (1978) *Skilful Means*, London: Duckworth.

Radhakrishnan, S. (1953) *The Principal Upanishads*, New York: Harper and Brothers.

—— (1966) *Indian Philosophy*, London: George Allen and Unwin.

Radhakrishan, S. and Moore, C. (eds) (1957) *A Source Book in Indian Philosophy*, Princeton, NJ: Princeton University Press.

Rahman, F. (1958) *Prophecy in Islam*, London: George Allen and Unwin.

Raju, P. (1985) *Structural Depths of Indian Thought*, New Delhi: South Asian Publishers.

Ramamurty, A. (1996) *Advaita: A Conceptual Analysis*, New Delhi: D.K. Printworld.

Randle, H. (1930) *Indian Logic in the Early Schools: A Study of the Nyayadarsana in its Relation to the Early Logic and Other Schools*, London: Oxford University Press.

Ro Young-chan (1989). *The Korean Neo-Confucianism of Yi Yulgok*, Albany, NY: State University of New York Press.

Rodd, L. (1980) *Nichiren: Selected Writings*, Honolulu, HA: University of Hawaii Press.

Rosemont, H. (ed.) (1991) *Chinese Texts and Philosophical Contexts*, La Salle, IL: Open Court Press.

Rosenthal, E. (1958) *Political Thought in Medieval Islam*, Cambridge: Cambridge University Press.

Said, E. (1985) *Orientalism*, Harmondsworth: Penguin.

Sambhava, P. (1994) *The Tibetan Book of the Dead*, trans. R. Thurman, London: Aquarian/Thorsons.

Saran, P. (1997) *Tantra: Hedonism in Indian Culture*, New Delhi: D.K. Printworld.

Schilpp, P. (ed.) (1952) *The Philosophy of Sarvepalli Radhakrishnan*, New York: Tudor Publishing Company.

Schram, S. (1989) *The Thought of Mao Tse-tung*, New York: Cambridge University Press.

Sen, A. (1997) 'Indian Traditions and the Western Imagination', *Daedalus* 126(2): 1–26.

Sharma, C. (1964) *A Critical Survey of Indian Philosophy*, Delhi: Motilal Banarsidass.

Shun, Kwong-loi (1997) *Mencius and Early Chinese Thought*, Stanford, CA: Stanford University Press.

Smart, N. (1964) *Doctrine and Argument in Indian Philosophy*, Princeton, NJ: Humanities Press.

Stcherbatsky, F. (1962) *Buddhist Logic*, New York: Dover.

Streng, F. (1967) *Emptiness: A Study in Religious Meaning*, New York: Abingdon Press.

Suzuki, D.T. (1956) *Zen Buddhism*, ed. W. Barrett, New York: Doubleday.

—— (1973) *Zen and Japanese Culture*, Princeton, NJ: Princeton University Press.

Swanson, P. (1989) *Foundations of T'ien-t'ai Philosophy*, Berkeley, CA: Asian Humanities Press.

Tai Chen (1990) *Tai Chen on Mencius: Explorations in Words and Meaning*, trans. Ann-ping Chin and M. Freeman, New Haven, CN: Yale University Press.

Tanabe, G. (1992) *Myoe the Dreamkeeper*, Cambridge, MA: Harvard University Press.

(1995) *The Thirteen Principal Upanishads*, trans. R. Ume and G. Haas, Oxford: Oxford University Press.

Thurman, R. (1984) *Tsong Khapa's Speech of Gold in the 'Essence of True Eloquence'*, Princeton, NJ: Princeton University Press.

—— (1991) *The Central Philosophy of Tibet*, Princeton, NJ: Princeton University Press.

Tominaga, N. (1990) *Emerging from Meditation*, trans. M. Pye, London: Duckworth.

Tu Wei-Ming (1988) *Centrality and Commonality: An Essay on Confucian Religiousness*, Albany, NY: State University of New York Press.

Tuck, A. (1990) *Comparative Philosophy and the Philosophy of Scholarship: On the Western Interpretation of Nagarjuna*, New York: Oxford University Press.

Tyler, R. (1977) *Selected Writings of Suzuki Shosan*, Ithaca, NY: Cornell University Press.

Ueda, Y. and Hirota, D. (1989) *Shinran: An Introduction to his Thought*, Kyoto: Hongwanji International Center.

Upanisads (1996) trans. P. Olivelle, Oxford: Oxford University Press.

Vatsyayan, K. (ed.) (1995) *Prakriti: The Integral Vision*, 5 vols, New Delhi: D.K. Printworld.

Vivekananda, S. (1959) *Bhakti-Yoga*, Calcutta: Advaita Ashrama.

—— (1960) *Karma-Yoga*, Calcutta: Advaita Ashrama.

—— (1961) *Jnana-Yoga*, Calcutta: Advaita Ashrama.

Ward, K. (1998) *Concepts of God*, Oxford: Oneworld.

Warder, A. (1980) *Indian Buddhism*, Delhi: Motilal Banarsidass.

Watson, B. (1967) *Basic Writings of Mo Tzu, Hsun Tzu, and Han Fei Tzu*, New York: Columbia University Press.

Wei-Ming, T. (1985) *Confucian Thought: Selfhood as Creative Transformation*, Albany, NY: State University of New York Press.

Wilhelm, R. (trans.) (1967) *The I Ching or Book of Changes: The Richard Wilhelm translation rendered into English by Cary F. Baynes*, Princeton, NJ: Princeton University Press.

Williams, P. (1989) *Mahayana Buddhism: The Doctrinal Foundations*, London: Routledge.

Wu, J. (1963) *Lao Tzu*, New York: St John's University Press.

Yamasaki, T. (1988) *Shingon: Japanese Esoteric Buddhism*, Boston: Shambala.

Yampolsky, P. (ed.) (1990) *Selected Writings of Nichiren*, New York: Columbia University Press.

Yoshida Kenko (1967) *Tsurezure-gusa, Essays in Idleness*, trans D. Keene, New York: Columbia University Press.

Yu, C. (1988) *Shamanism: The Spirit World of Korea*, Fremont: Asian Humanities Press.

Yuasa, Y. (1987) *The Body: Towards an Eastern Mind-Body Theory*, trans. N. Shigenori and T. Kasulis, ed. T. Kasulis, Albany, NY: State University of New York Press.

Zaehner, R. (1955) *Zurvan: A Zoroastrian Dilemma*, New York: Biblio and Tanven.

—— (1958) *At Sundry Times: An Essay in the Comparison of Religions*, London: Faber.

—— (1969) *The Bhagavad Gita, with Commentaries based on original sources*, London: Oxford Univesity Press.

—— (1975) *The Dawn and Twilight of Zoroastrianism*, London: Weidenfeld and Nicolson.

—— (1997) *Hindu and Muslim Mysticism*, Oxford: Oneworld.

Zhuangzi (1968) *The Complete Works of Chuang Tzu*, trans. B. Watson, New York: Columbia University Press.

Thematic entry list

The concepts and individuals are here organized in accordance with their national origin or application. It should be stressed that many of the entries cross national boundaries and apply to several of the national categories, and so the organization here should be taken as indicative and not in any way final.

Australasia

Australian philosophy
New Zealand philosophy

China

abortion, infanticide and murder in Chinese
  philosophy
accident
action and knowledge in Chinese philosophy
acts of omission
aesthetics, Chinese: beauty
aesthetics, Chinese: landscape art
aesthetics, Chinese: mountains and waters
afterlife, Chinese: hell
afterlife, Chinese: hungry ghosts
afterlife, Chinese: hunpo
afterlife, Chinese: immortals
afterlife, Chinese: inferno
afterlife, Chinese: kuishen
afterlife, Chinese: purgatory
afterlife, Chinese: wandering ghosts
afterlife in Chinese thought
agrarianism
animals
atheism, modern Chinese
atomism and occasionalism
Awakening of Faith in Mahayana

Baizhang
barbarians
Beidu
beyond the square
Bodhidharma
bodies, problems with
body
Body, Shadow, and Soul
body and soul in pre-Buddhist China
Buddhism, late Ming
Buddhism in China, origins and development
Buddhist Chinese hermeneutics
Buddhist scholasticism
Buddhist thought, late Qing
causality, theory of
chaos
character
character, left and right
characterology and the occult
chastity
child
China, Middle Kingdom
Chinese philosophy
Chinese philosophy, pre-modern and Marxist
Chiyou
Christianity in China
Chunqiu and Lushi Chunqiu
civil religion
Classics and Books
common sense
comparative philosophy, Chinese
confession
Confucian spirituality
Confucius and Confucianism
conscience
correlative thinking
correlative thinking: macrocosm, microcosm

Abhidharma

This philosophical literary genre known as Abhidharma (in Pali, Abhidhamma) appears to have flourished amongst some of the conservative Buddhist schools, especially the Sarvastivadin Vaibhashikas and the Theravadins, between 250 BCE and 100 CE with further scholastic elaborations in succeeding centuries. Abhidharma texts are in essence lists (*matrika*) and analytical catalogues of what are considered to be types of irreducibly existent mental and material elements (*dharma*: *dhamma* (p)) and taxonomic presentations of the doctrines of particular **Hinayana** Buddhist schools. They specify the ultimate constituents out of which the macroscopic environment and its observers are constructed. These works demarcate the genuinely existent (*dravya-sat/paramartha-satya*), namely the types of *dharma*s whose conditioned (*samskrita*), interdependently originating (**pratitya-samutpada**) tokens are instantaneous occurrences, from that which is nominally or conceptually existent (*prajnapti-sat/samvriti-satya*). The philosophical stance is a realism about the microscopic combined with reductionism about the macroscopic.

The **Sautrantika** tradition eschewed the Abhidharma enterprise, confining its scriptural authorities to the canonical sutras which are believed to embody the teachings of the Buddha. But other Sarvastivadin and Theravada (now the Buddhism of Shri Lanka, Burma and Thailand) schools ascribed canonical status to their Abhidharmas along with the Pali *Sutta* texts and the moral and monastic codes (*Vinaya*) to form the three baskets (*Tripitaka*) of doctrine and praxis which were committed to writing in the first century BCE after a long process of oral transmission. This third section of the **Pali Canon** consists of schematizations of material presented more discursively elsewhere.

The Theravadin tradition recognises eighty-one conditioned (*sankhata*) *dharma*s and an unconditioned one (**nirvana**: *nibbana*). Everything comprised of conditioned *dharma*s is impermanent, unsatisfactory and lacking in essential identity. The conditioned *dharma*s receive a tripartite classification: materiality (*rupa*), mental factors (*chetasika*) and thought (*chitta*).

The primary constituents of the material *dharma*s are earth, water, fire and wind. From them derive the five physical sense-organs (*indriya*) which are the internal bases of awareness; five corresponding types of objects (*vishaya*) constituting the external supports (*ayatana*) of awareness; male and female characteristics; the heart, which is the physical basis of mental processes; physical and vocal expressions of intentional actions; physical vitality or animation; space as forming the boundary of physical bodies; the properties of lightness, softness and malleability; and the three marks of conditioned realities, namely growth, continuity and aging-and-impermanence, and nutrition.

There are fifty-two mental factors (*chetasika*) underlying morally good (*kushala*), bad (*akushula*) and ethically neutral attitudes, sensations, perceptions and conceptions and momentary conscious acts. Attitudes manifested in actions are negative or destructive (*akushula*) when associated with one of the three root poisons that are craving (*lobha*), aversion (*dosha*) or delusion (*moha*). They are morally neutral when they are simply the consequences of prior acts. Finally, thought (*chitta/vinnana*) is the causal substrate of all transitory acts of consciousness. In everyday life, it only ever occurs in association with other *dharma*s.

The skilled meditator develops a facility to analyse his experiences into their fleeting components, thereby dissolving the objects of attachment and extirpating desires for them. Eliminating ignorance about the true nature of reality, the *arhat* ('perfected one') attains *nirvana*, the extinction of the fires of grasping, hatred and delusion.

The Vaibhashikas recognise seventy-two conditioned and three unconditioned and changeless *dharma*s. Conditioned elements arise and cease as parts of coherent, continuous processes regulated by the synthetic causal sequence of interdependent genesis (*pratitya-samutpada*). Each type of element is self-existent (*sa-svabhava*): its tokens have determinate identities. The former are classified into four major categories:

1 Material (*rupa*); five sense organs and corresponding sense-data plus subtle matter which is the repository of karmic potencies (*avijnapti-rupa*).
2 Contentless mind or awareness (*chitta*).
3 Forty-six mental elements or faculties (*chaitta-dharma*) which can be combined with *chitta* and which receive a sixfold classification:

Class A: Feelings, perceptions, intentions, sensations, desires, intelligence, memory, attention, ascertainment, concentration.
Class B: Virtues of faith, courage in performing good actions, equanimity, modesty, remorse, lack of greed, non-malevolence, non-violence, practical wisdom, attentiveness.
Class C: Defects of delusion, negligence, intellectual idleness, unbelief, apathetic sloth, addiction to pleasure.
Class D: Disrespect to the virtuous and lack of remorse.
Class E: Secondary defects of anger, hypocrisy, meanness, jealousy, emulation, violence, resentment, deceit, fraudulence, complacency.
Class F: Faculties of remorse, deliberation, reflectiveness, investigation, determination, mental attachment, hatred, arrogance.

4 Fourteen forces (*chitta-viprayukta-samskara*, 'conditioned factors dissociated from mind') which elude classification as physical or mental: (1) a force governing the aggregation of particular types of *dharma* and linking experiences with their substrata (*prapti*, or 'acquisition'); (2) another preventing such aggregation; (3) a force producing homogeneity of existences; (4) a force transporting an individual into unconscious trance; (5) a force stopping consciousness and producing the annihilation trance; (6) another producing the non-ideational supreme trance state; (7) life energy; (8) the force of origination; (9) the force of stasis; (10) the force of decay; (11) the force of extinction; (12) the force of naming; (13) the force conferring meaning on sentences; and (14) the force conferring meaning on phonemes.

The three immutable, unconditioned factors are space, the extinction (*nirvana*) of the manifestations of elements through discriminative knowledge, and extinction through lack of productive causes, not through discriminative knowledge.

Further reading

Frauwallner, E. (1995) *Studies in Abhidharma Literature and the Origins of Buddhist Philosophical Systems*, trans. S. Kidd, under the supervision of E. Steinkellner, Albany, NY: State University of New York Press.

Lamotte, E. (1988) *History of Indian Buddhism: From the Origins to the Shaka Era*, trans. S. Webb-Boin, Louvain: Université Catholique de Louvain.

Potter, K. (1996) *Encyclopedia of Indian Philosophies, Vol. VII: Abhidharma Buddhism to 150 A.D.*, Delhi: Motilal Banarsidass.

Warder, A. (1991) *Indian Buddhism*, Delhi: Motilal Banarsidass.

CHRIS BARTLEY

Abhinavagupta

b. 970; d. 1025

Theologian and aesthetician

A Kashmiri theologian and aesthetician, Abhinavagupta was a votary of the Kala-samkarshini ('Devourer of Time') form of the goddess and thus a follower of tantric or non-Vedic traditions of scriptural exegesis and ritual (see **Tantra**). In the massive *Tantraloka*, condensed as the *Tantrasara*, he expounded the theoretical, yogic and ritual aspects of the syncretistic Trika cult (see **Trika Shaivism**). His major philosophical works are the *Ishvarapratyabhijnavimarshini* on the *Pratyabhijnakarika* of his teacher's teacher Utpaladeva and the *Ishvarapratyabhijnavivritivimarshini*. These works present non-dualist critiques of the dualism of the **Shaiva Siddhanta** ritualism, Vedantic illusionism maintaining that the world of human ·experience is a product of a force called *maya* or **avidya** and the anti-essentialism of the various phenomenalist, representationalist and idealist Buddhist reductionist theories. Abhinavagupta propounded a form of absolute idealism which equates the world with a single universal, autonomous (*svatantrya*) and dynamic consciousness (*para-samvit*) refracting (reflecting) itself into an infinite variety of forms.

This outlook is distinct from subjective idealism's solipsistic (exclusively first-personal) reduction of the world to the personal and individual stream of consciousness. Abhinavagupta takes it as axiomatic that the mind-independence of matter (accepted by the various realist schools: Purva Mimamsakas, Nyaya-Vaisheshikas, Shaiva Siddhantins and dualist Vedantins) is impossible. He is an anti-realist: whatever is inaccessible to human subjective standpoints cannot be spoken of as existent. What is mind-independent cannot be represented by consciousness, because as soon as something is represented by consciousness it is no longer mind-independent. There can be no proof of the non-experiential. Only that which enters the content of consciousness can be considered real. The unreal does not enter the content of consciousness. The mind-independent is non-existent.

What appear as external, physical objects are really constituted by consciousness because consciousness bears no relation to the insentient. If objectivity is defined in terms of independence of consciousness, how can it be experienced? Trans-individual consciousness (*samvit*) causes phenomenal objects of awareness (*abhasa*) to appear as if distinct from the subjects of experience which are aspects of its own autonomous self-contraction.

The cause-effect relation (*karya-karana-bhava*) obtains only between agents and the objects of action (*kartri-karma-bhava*). Causality is exclusively a property of conscious agents capable of volition. Thus causality and creativity on the part of the material or physical is impossible. Moreover, Abhinavagupta maintains that experience is intelligible without the presupposition of a world of objects different in kind from consciousness. So, according to him, everything is experiential and phenomena bear real relations to one another. The concept of a real relation is experienced-based. Everything we encounter is an aspect of a whole, and a constituent of a single field of consciousness.

Abhinavagupta's theory of ultimate non-dualism defines the all-inclusive supreme reality as inherently active, self-determining (*svatantra*), reflexive, trans-individual consciousness (*samvit*). It is not to be understood in static terms, but as self-conscious activity and will positing itself as other than itself. It operates through projective manifestation (*abhasa*) which may also be a form of self-limitation. It is characterized as a pulsating dynamism (*spanda*) which spontaneously expresses itself through its innate powers of cognition (*jnana-shakti*) and action (*kriya-shakti*) as individual subjects, acts and data of consciousness in a causally ordered and unified spatio-temporal framework, simultaneously and successively experienced by embodied selves as external, objective and differentiated. The universe of worlds is the emanative self-differentiation of this trans-individual consciousness, which is the efficient cause of everything. In theological language, reality is the self-expression of divinity who in each instant revitalizes a constantly active creation, not only *for* the subject but *including* the subject. This is not the thesis that empirical objects are illusions; the phenomena are as real as their transcendental basis. Individual selves, permanent backgrounds to their experiences in specific environments, are contracted and condensed modes of the universal consciousness.

The subjectivity of the self and the objectivity of the universe are contained in the supreme divinity, variously named Shiva, Bhairava and Kali. In relation to the manifold of phenomenal projections, the divinity is said to unify the knowing subjects like spectators at a play. Abhinavagupta argues that in manifesting subjects and their experiences of externality, trans-individual consciousness continually oscillates between its dual aspects, illumination or manifestation of the phenomena that appear as other than itself (*prakasha*), and reflexivity or self-awareness (*vimarsha*), which is also the stimulus to action. Were reflexive consciousness not thus dynamically constituted, it would be inert, like a crystal that receives reflections although itself insentient. In the absence of reflexivity, the internal synthesis of different experiences in which the constant subject relates them to itself would not be possible.

Two models are deployed to express the manifestation of the cosmos as the contraction of trans-individual consciousness: an emanationist schema comprising thirty-six categories of realities (*tattva*) and an account centring on the expansion of sonic resonance and pulsating consciousness. The logical – atemporal or pre-temporal – process of cosmic emanation is:

1 a plenitude of pure reflexive subjective energy characterized as the inexpressible void of being and consciousness (microcosmically realised in ecstatic experience – sexual and aesthetic);
2 an initial pre-cognitive impulse (*iccha*) to expand and contract;
3 internal polarization of consciousness into 'I' and 'this', subject and object;
4 affirmation of the 'this' aspect of contracted self-positing awareness;
5 oscillation between reflexivity and the activity of extroversion.

We now enter a realm of secondary causality in which through the instrumentality of what is termed the *maya-shakti* (creative power), embodied individual subjects, the permanent backgrounds to experience, and spheres of experience occur. As an aspect of its spontaneous self-contraction, trans-individual consciousness manifests itself as enduring individual centres of experience.

All forms of Buddhism reduce personal identity to a series of transitory, discrete and impersonal psycho-physical events. Abhinavagupta adduces the phenomena of memory, recognition, apperception or the interconnectedness of thought which is the formal condition of experience, and the synthetic and analytic unity of experience, to prove that there is an enduring integral subject which is the grounds of the possibility of cognitive unification. The self-conscious subject (**atman**), the permanent background to experience, persisting as a stable unity through space and time, synthesizes mental states. Without such a stable spatio-temporal continuant, there would only be momentary, self-contained, unrelated and chaotic mental episodes.

So Abhinavagupta assimilates the two seemingly opposed spheres of subject and object to aspects of a single creative consciousness which provides the data of ordinary awareness, ensures the coherence of experience and guarantees correspondences between acts and contents of awareness. The key to understanding his philosophy is to be found in his critique of the dualist's notion of conscious representation. What is mind-independent cannot be represented by consciousness because as soon as something is represented by consciousness it is no longer mind-independent. There is no proof of the non-experiential. He takes it as axiomatic that consciousness cannot illuminate, manifest or represent objects if they are external to it.

The dualistic traditions of Indian philosophical realism oppose two categorically different domains. Consciousness, a property of enduring subjects, is homogenous, formless, passive and receptive. It confronts an objective, mind-independent sphere of things, facts and values pre-arranged in accordance with the karmic dispositions of individuals. The orthodox soteriologies (methods of salvation) presuppose this ideology. According to this family of views, consciousness is intrinsically undifferentiated. But experience is complex and dynamic. This immediately raises the issue of the source of experiential variety. The simple claim that the experiences of blue and yellow are intrinsic features (*amsha*) of consciousness involves the abandonment of dualism or representation of the extra-mental. Now, suppose that blue and yellow are extra-mental objects (*vishaya*). How are we to understand the claim that by the same consciousness by which blue is cognized as blue, yellow is cognized as yellow? Perhaps one is caused by a blue patch, the other by a yellow patch. But this begs the question in that the appeal to causality assumes real differences between yellow and blue and awareness. Moreover, the realists cannot provide a coherent description of the extra-mental. The realistic Buddhist phenomenalists reduce macroscopic objects to collections of atoms. But if the atoms combine, they must have parts. The realists maintain that the whole exists in its parts by the internal relation of inherence. Abhinavagupta rejects inherence. It is supposed to be real in its own right. In that case an additional factor is required to connect it with the instances which are its relata, and an infinite regress results. The whole cannot be something over and above its parts.

The Buddhist representationalists (Sautrantikas) define reality as causally effective point-instants. It is fleetingly given only in immediate pre-perceptual and pre-conceptual sensation. They claim to establish the existence of the mind-independent sphere of momentary (*kshanika*) atoms inaccessible to perception by inference. Forms in perceptual awareness are representations that are causally related to ephemeral configurations of atoms. Perception involves the occurrence of representations that stand in a relation of conformity or isomorphism (*sarupya*) to their causal basis. The representationalist argues:

> The cause of successive variety in undifferentiated consciousness is reflection. The extramental blue patch is conformable to the reflection. Blue is inferable but conventionally treated as perceptible. Consciousness is really undifferentiated. If blue is identical with awareness, how could there be consciousness of yellow? If consciousness' essential nature is to appear successively as blue and yellow, there would be no intuition of pure subjectivity void of representations. This consciousness cannot be the cause of different representations because where the cause is undifferentiated, there can be no variety in its effect. Therefore the variety of manifestations leads to the inference of the extra-mental which produces representations in consciousness. The inferred is similar to its reflection. It comprises diversity corresponding

to the reflections successively falling on the light of consciousness from which it differs.

Abhinavagupta's reply is a straightforward appeal to a basic Indian philosophical tenet: inference depends upon the deliverances of perception. Inferential proof of the extra-mental is impossible since inference depends upon perceptual data for its operation.

The Buddhist idealist (Yogachara) denies the existence of a consciousness-independent domain and accounts for experiential variety by reference to residual traces preserved in an unconscious 'storehouse consciousness' (**tathagatagarbha**). Abhinavagupta admits this category: it is called memory. But we are looking for the cause of variety in present experience. If the traces which are claimed to be the causes of representations differ from consciousness and are real, then idealism is realism under another name. If they are taken as less than fully real (*samvriti-sat*), they cannot be causes. Since there is nothing other than consciousness such as time, space and circumstantial environments that might serve as different reawakeners of the traces, experience would be total and simultaneous.

Perhaps other mental episodes in a given stream of experiences may serve as stimulants. But since all differences, whether between internal sensations, external objects, earlier and later time and place are in essence consciousness and essence is indivisible, diversity in awareness is unintelligible. Moreover, the Buddhist idealist cannot account for the separate existences of individual persons.

All of these problems about experiential variety can be avoided if we abandon reference to the problematic extra-mental and the dualist dogma that intrinsically undifferentiated consciousness – homogenous, formless, passive and receptive – is different in kind from an objective, mind-independent sphere of things, facts and values. The appearance of diverse objects as different from the individual subject is intelligible if they are contained in a single inherently creative universal subject which manifests contracted centres of consciousness which are its modal expressions and the multifarious universe 'within' its own being. He says that all entities are internal to the absolute subject. All-encompassing reflexive subjectivity externalises the objects of awareness simultaneously and successively. The projection of distinct individual subjects occurs first. What are experienced as subjectivity and objectivity are included in trans-individual consciousness as aspects of its self-expression. The world exists only as its representation in consciousness.

The Divinity objectifies itself via its reflexive capacity, its capacity to understand itself. Abhinavagupta deploys a form of *reductio ad absurdum* (*prasanga*) to show that nothing can exist apart from awareness. If the objects of awareness were mind-independent, the self's attention to cognitive objects, which is indubitably given, would be impossible. This is because attention to mind-independent objects implies the subject's dependence upon them. But independence is a defining characteristic of the self. A dependent self is a contradiction. Whatever is dependently attentive to anything extraneous would be not-Self. There follows the undesirable implication that the insentient not-self could not attend to the cognizable. By reversing the implication, it follows that the autonomous self is attentive to that which is not separate from consciousness and that it creates its own objects of awareness.

In a spirit of absorbed quietism, orthodox Brahminical non-dualism (**Advaita** Vedanta), the philosophical articulation of the outlook of the person who has renounced his caste-based social role and participation in the public religion of the group conceives of the Absolute – *Brahman* – as featureless pure Is-ness, non-agentive, static consciousness; an abstract, uncharacterizable, empty unity; a state of transcendental repose. The *atman*, one's ordinarily misidentified 'inner self', is identical with the *Brahman* thus conceived. Release from the cycle of births is an individuality obliterating gnostic intuition of inherent non-agency on the part of a transcendental subject; an insight variously regarded as produced either in an immediate inspirational flash or gradually produced by reflection upon scriptural statements conveying the identity of the individual and supreme selves.

Abhinavagupta rejects this account of the Absolute on the grounds that reflexivity, supposedly integral to awareness, involves intrinsic activity. Given the non-active nature of its Absolute,

Advaita reduces it to the status of the inert and uncreative. All plurality of persons, mental states, actions and objects, claim the Advaitins, is due to a substrative causal force called *avidya*. *Avidya* veils one's true nature, generating the illusion of an individual agent subject to ritual duties and transmigration. But what is the subject of *avidya*? To whom does it belong? It cannot be *Brahman*, which is pure consciousness. It cannot be the individual subject because originally there are no individual subjects which it might afflict.

It is a tenet of Advaita that the real is unnegatable, in the sense that no experience could eliminate it. Duality, though it appears in the character of our experience, is said to be negated if we use the sort of intuition which sees everything as one whole, thus obliterating individuality. But by the same token non-duality is contradicted by experience of duality. Vedic scripture (the Upanishadic statements such as 'That thou Art') is held to be the cognitive authority (**pramana**) for non-duality. But scripture, qua differentiated, is unreal and so is the division of subject, acts and objects of knowledge.

If Absolute consciousness is void of internal distinctions, it cannot assume or project diverse forms. But everything makes sense if the ultimate possesses autonomy consisting in self-conscious volitional activity. Shiva manifests the complex real universe in an unbroken act of conscious will.

For Abhinavagupta and his school, bondage to cyclical existence is a state of ignorant self-limitation which regards the values of purity and impurity, central to the **caste** ideology of mainstream orthodoxy, as objectively inherent in a consciousness-independent sphere. But trans-individual consciousness is a plenitude of which individual subjects are contracted expressions. This is what we have lost sight of and must recognize. The enlightened person realises that the data of consciousness are non-different from one another and from the subject. They all appear in his consciousness as distilled into unity. The opposite is the case with the unenlightened, who are immersed in and untroubled by the experiences of diversity and externality. Anxious concern with caste and related values such as one's Vedic learning, family's status, conventional conduct, virtues and wealth, all sanctioned by orthodoxy, are aspects of a false identity. Fears of participation in non-Vedic rites, Tantric mantras, forbidden substances and types of people, deeds, places and dangerous supernatural forces, all represent limitations of an identity that is potentially infinite in its fullest expansion. The highest human good (*moksha* or liberation from cyclical existence) consists in the recognition, typically through yogic and meditational means, of one's identity as a mode of contracted self-expression of the infinite consciousness. According to this outlook, liberation consists in this awareness, it is not a separate phenomenon produced by knowledge. Liberation is the revelation of one's identity and that identity is self-expressive consciousness. One is said to become the divinity by the revelation that within one's own identity as the inexpressible void of consciousness one is causing the universe to appear and that in creating it, one is it.

Abhinavagupta's tradition has been one of remarkable durability. By *c.*1050 it had supplanted the dualist and Veda-conformist Shaiva Siddhanta ritualism as the dominant religion in Kashmir. Part of its success was due to its allowing the votary to conceive of himself as an actor assuming different roles, one of which is his inherited social and religious status. Recognition of one's identity as Shiva was thus compatible with sincere enactment of one's prescribed orthodox social role. Moreover, initiation into the cult is effectively open to all, not restricted to the intellectual elite. One could be in public an upholder of the Vedically sanctioned caste-based social order (*varna-ashrama-dharma*), in religion a Shaiva, but privately a Kaula; that is to say, an initiate into an esoteric cult practising salvific ritual and gnosis.

See also: aesthetics, Indian theories of; tat tvam asi

Further reading

Dyczkowski, M. (1992) *The Stanzas on Vibration*, Albany, NY: State University of New York Press.
Gnoli, R. (1956) *The Aesthetic Experience according to Abhinavagupta*, Rome: Serie Orientale.
—— (trans.) (1972) *Luce delle Sacre Scritture (Tantraloka) di Abhinavagupta*, Turin: Unione Tipografico-Editrice Torinese.
Iyer, K. and Pandey, K. (1986) *Isvarapratyabhijnavi-marshini: Doctrine of Divine Recognition*, 3 vols, Delhi: Motilal Banarsidass.
Padoux, A. (1990) *Vac: The Concept of the Word in Selected Hindu Tantras*, Albany, NY: State University of New York Press.
Pandey, K. (1963) *Abhinavagupta: An Historical and Philosophical Study*, Varanasi: Chowkhamba Sanskrit Series Office.
Sanderson, A. (1986) 'Mandala and Agamic Identity in the Trika of Kashmir', in A. Padoux (ed.), *Mantra et Diagrammes Rituels dans l'Hindouisme*, Paris: Centre National de la Recherche Scientifique.
Silburn, L. (1957) *Le Paramarthasara*, Paris: Publications de l'Institut de civilisation indienne.
Singh, J. (1989) *A Trident of Wisdom*, Albany: State University of New York Press (translation of *Paratrimshika-vivarana*).
—— (1991) *Pratyabhijnahrdayam*, Delhi: Motilal Banarsidass.

CHRIS BARTLEY

abortion, infanticide and murder in Chinese philosophy

Confucianism, Daoism and Buddhism all endorse the sacred nature of life, but popular practice has often gone against theory on this issue. Since the patrilineal system prevents daughters from being true bearers of the family surname, the female has always been marginalized in Chinese society. Female infanticide is widely practiced among the poorer families for economic reasons; the newborn is drowned in a bucket of water and is said to have died of natural causes. The Daoist *Taipingjing* (*Tai-p'ing Ching*) (Scripture of the Great Peace) in Han times noted and condemned this practice as opposed to the Daoist reverence for life. Religious Daoists abhorred killing and hated bloodshed, and initially Daoists were vegetarians. However, more than compassion for female infants is involved here. In Daoist thought, as there should be two of *yin* to every one of *yang*, there should be two wives for every man; thus saving female infants helps to ensure the cosmic balance.

The Buddhists are committed to **ahimsa** (non-violence), and Buddhist monasteries traditionally take in orphans and abandoned children that others would not care for. Both Buddhist and Daoist hells would identify the abortionist as drowning in a 'pool of blood', a hell not found in the Indian original set of hells. Abortion initially involved less guilt in China than Japan, although there is now a complex set of beliefs and practices in Japan surrounding abortion (La Fleur 1992). Drugs to induce abortion were apparently widely available in the late Qing dynasty (nineteenth century), but they were also avoided because they were deemed very risky for the mother.

The current Western debate on when life officially begins and ends is less of an issue in Buddhism. Coming from a past life, a new life begins at conception. Newborn children in China are also seen as coming from the *yin* world, and could easily slip back into it. A baby is only relatively secured in *yang* life after a full twelve months, and even then death while young would involve no formal mourning or ritual burial. Only with the ritual passage into maturity via the capping ceremony (an initiation rite indicating adulthood) would a male be registered into the clan lineage.

As to suicide, all three traditions are also against taking one's own life as much as that of another. However, justifications for exceptions exist. **Mencius** would forego life for the sake of **righteousness**. The Neo-Confucian cult of loyalty and **chastity** led several Ming officials to choose martyrdom during the Manchu takeover, and many women killed themselves rather than risk dishonour. Among religious Daoists, the Taiping Dao members flogged themselves during penance in Han times. The Buddhists criticized them for such immoderation, but later they also sliced and burnt themselves in yogic impassivity in defence of the *dharma*; in the 1960s, the Vietnamese monk who set himself on fire in protest against war did so to empower his cause and offset the evil of an age in decline. The pious also leapt off trees or cliffs in hope of a quicker birth in the Pure Land. Though denounced as folly by more discerning monks, the Pure Land patriarch Shandao (Shan-tao) was honoured with such a dramatic end in the hagiographies of his life.

Further reading

La Fleur, W. (1992) *Liquid Life: Abortion and Buddhism in Japan*, Princeton, NJ: Princeton University Press.

Lai, W. (1990) 'Ch'an Ch'a Ch'ing: Magic and Religion in Medieval China', in W. Buswell (ed.), *Chinese Buddhist Apocrypha*, Honolulu, HA: University of Hawaii Press, 175–206.

WHALEN LAI

ABSTRACT AND ABSTRACTION *see* nominalism and realism: abstract, abstraction

accident

The Chinese term for 'accident' is literally 'beyond (one's) understanding'. Referring to the 'unexpected', in modern usage it is usually associated with negative accidents, like being hit by a car. In classical and medieval times, however, it usually described an unexpected event. For the classical thinkers, something can be *shenyi* (demonic and out of the ordinary) but few would consider that an 'accident' or as 'unthinkable'. Indeed, classical thinking generally assumes that everything is thinkable; if it is unthinkable, it probably does not exist. This is not philosophical idealism, but has to do with the belief that there has to be a name for everything, known later as the 'ontological theory of language'. If there is in a reputable text a mention of a nine-headed dragon (like the Greek Hydra), then it must exist in some sense. To have a word and not the thing is 'unthinkable'.

The word 'unthinkable' in Buddhism came into vogue when Mahayana Buddhism introduced the Transcendental as the 'unthinkable' (*achintya*). It proclaims a reality beyond human comprehension. This term, rooted in *chitta* (mind), was in earlier use in **Hinayana**, but in the **Abhidharma** it meant only 'what does not accord with the categories of mind/thought'. It is not the pretext for proclaiming some transcendental reality, however, and Hinayana does not use *achintya* to describe **nirvana**. (*Nirvana* comes under the category of the noncomposite; realities of matter, mind, mental functions and so on fall under the composite.) Abhidharma rationality does not recognize such a totalistic category as the inconceivable that could in effect abolish and invalidate all rational reflection.

It is precisely in this way that Mahayana *sutras* would use this term freely to describe especially the 'unthinkable' glory and power of the transmundane Buddha. In the **tathagatagarbha (buddha nature**) corpus, *achintya* became a virtual excuse not to think or talk clearly. Under the pretext or under the cover of the inconceivable, legitimate mystery as well as confused thinking has been introduced into the area of enquiry. **Nagarjuna** had better sense: in his view, the less said about the ineffable (highest truth) the better. But it is the mark of the *tathagatagarbha* corpus to wax poetic; when it cannot explain how the pure buddha nature could ever get itself so tainted as to be involved in persistent **samsara**, it resorts to lines like: 'Such is the nature of the Inconceiveable Perfumation of the pure by the impure'. 'Perfumation' is a technical term in Yogachara philosophy: A has an effect on B subtly but leaves behind a near-immaterial trace like perfume or smell. How the 'innately pure mind' (buddha nature) can lose its lustre is here attributed to the incomprehensible (i.e. mysterious) impact of ignorance (the dark, the impure) on its purity. So, even though we are in essence enlightened, we may not know on a particular occasion. This gives enlightenment the status of the miraculous and fosters the identification of the transcendental as the unthinkable.

The term 'accident' and the issue of 'miracle' take two other forms. For Aristotle, 'accidents' are less than 'necessary' and far inferior to the 'essential'. Man as *homo sapiens* is essentially wise; he needs the necessities of life to exist, but his colour and race are accidental. The Chinese do not define 'human nature' in the Greek essentialist manner; the 'white' in 'White Horse is not a Horse' is clearly not thought of as accidental to some essential horse. In theory, **karma** in Buddhism disallows accidents. In fact, accidents exist and are recognized by the finer points of its law. One can 'accidentally' (without intention) step on an ant whose death may itself be an 'accident' (not a payback for past sin). A Buddhist would no more regard a 'falling brick' bruising his forehead, a result of material circumstance, as *karma* than a Christian would regard 'rain on a parade' an act of God.

WHALEN LAI

action and agency, Brahminical Hindu ideas

The central concepts here are the self (**atman**) as freely choosing agent (*karta*), cognition (*jnana*), wanting-in-general (*iccha*) and activity (*pravritti*). The agent is defined as that which is independent (*svatantra*) in an event or causal complex. He possesses the intention (*kriti*) that is appropriate to the action (*kriya*). Cognition relates to identification of the desideratum and the means to the end. Wanting arises in the self and the framing of specific intention proceeds from wanting. From intention follows physical effort (*cheshta*) and the action is consequent to effort. Intention transforms wants and desires into actual effort.

All philosophers would have been familiar with Panini's grammar, which formed part of the Brahminical educational curriculum. Every discussion of agency would have been conducted against a background of his semantic definitions of the factors (*karaka*) connected with an action in Book I of the grammar:

1.4.24   *dhruvam apaye'padanam*: that which is the fixed point of departure is called 'starting point' (standardly inanimate and non-volitional).

1.4.32   *karmana yam abhipraiti sa sampradanam*: he whom one aims at as the (standardly animate) object of one's action is called 'recipient'.

1.4.42   *sadhakatamam karanam*: that which is most effective is called 'instrument' (standardly inanimate and non-volitional).

1.4.45   *adharo'dhikaranam*: sub-stratum which is called 'locus' (standardly inanimate and non-volitional).

1.4.49   *kartur ipsitatamam karma*: what the agent most desires is called 'object'.

1.4.54   *svatantrah karta*: the agent is independent relative to the other aspects of his action;

the agent is standardly but not necessarily animate.

The *karaka*s are not identical with grammatical cases. There is no mention of the genitive or possessive relation which normally expresses a relation between two nouns rather than a feature connected directly with the verb. Rather, the *karaka* relations specify the conditions under which suffixes are added to verbal bases and nominal stems. The six categories may be related to the types of participants in Vedic ritual whose agent must be a volitional human being, whose recipients are divinities or priests and whose instruments and oblations are all inanimate objects.

Buddhist philosophy, which denies the existence of any form of enduring soul, does not ascribe any special significance to individual agency, reducing what is ordinarily and mistakenly understood as the agent to just another factor in a causal complex. This invites the objection from the Brahminical camp that there would be no principle of differentiation between the perpetrator and the victim of an evil deed.

Further reading

Mohanty, J. (1991) *Reason and Tradition in Indian Thought*, Oxford: Clarendon Press.

CHRIS BARTLEY

action and knowledge in Chinese philosophy

Action played an important role in early Chinese philosophy. **Confucius** demands that 'deeds' match 'speech', and thus kept alive the early pre-legal, pre-literary tradition that a 'man is as good as his word'. **Mozi** assumed that a rational discourse would lead to rational action, and both he and Confucius assume that language leads to action. There is taken to be no basic difference between theory and practice. After the Logicians pointed to the significance of the gap between speech and reality, **Mencius** shifted the discourse: deeds do not flow automatically from words. This is because regularly people lie and break their word. Sincerity

thus became an issue. For Mencius, right deeds can flow only from a sincere heart. His moral idealism privileges 'knowing one's heart', but goodness can also emerge without one even knowing it. Theory and practice remain one in the sense that only continual moral action would bring the heart in line with the will of **Heaven**.

For the Daoist, all human actions being *wei* (artificial, false), it is best not to act (**wuwei**) and repudiate the human intention (that is, return to nature). For the Buddhist, action is **karma**; its cessation is the prerequisite for **nirvana**. Both Daoists and Buddhists are suspicious of the point of acting, and seem often to be in favour of inaction.

The Neo-Confucians revisited this familiar problem. **Zhu Xi** trusted 'the course of study and enquiry', appearing to put theory ahead of practice. For granting priority to 'letting the virtue shine', Lu Xiangshan advocates letting the emanation of the good take its natural path. Wang Yangming followed Lu and made a point of proposing the 'unity of knowledge and action'. The 'mind that knows good and evil' can and will do the good, as surely as **filial piety** will care for parents and sexual desire will seek gratification. The 'left-wing' disciples of Wang were in favour of action as a means to bringing about desirable ends, and the 'Zen wing' was also in favour of spontaneity as a positive step on the route to enlightenment.

In general, it can be said that, similar to the West, the classical thinkers in China were committed to both theoria and praxis (knowledge and action) but by Han times, human action was confined to conforming with nature and with the natural course of a yin–yang cosmology. The medieval Buddhists were generally Idealists; for them, salvific gnosis liberates but that acts only to lift man above nature. After the Song Neo-Confucians turned their attention back to bettering this world, Zhu Xi still grounded praxis on theory. Rational knowledge guides premeditated action. It was Wang Yangming who recalled the Mencian moral impulse to act and revived a kind of Daoist spontaneity. Some of his disciples then increasingly put 'practical reason' ahead of 'theoretical reason'. The passion to 'change the world' outweighs simply passively 'understanding the world'.

See also: Sun Yat-sen

WHALEN LAI

active intellect

Active or agent intellect is in Arabic *al-'aql al-fa"al* and in Greek *nous poetikos*. The term comes originally from a particular argument to be found in Aristotle's *De Anima*. The active intellect is often represented as an immaterial being on the same level as the sphere of the moon, which acts as an intermediary between the divine mind and the human intellect, between transcendental reality and our ordinary world. Our intellect can achieve a state of relative perfection by becoming the acquired intellect, which involves understanding the logical and abstract principles behind what appears to us as reality, it receives from the active intellect an emanation from heaven. The active intellect in fact makes the acquired intellect possible, by transmitting from the higher world the force which links it with the sublunary world. The active intellect represents the highest level of thought which we human beings can attain, and it makes possible a whole variety of different ways of thinking and acting. For philosophers, it results in the ability to understand the nature of reality rationally, and for the prophet it means the ability to express oneself in ways which are capable of resonating with the widest possible audience. One should recall that the active intellect is the lowest of the stages of emanation, a theory in accordance with which divine grace overflows and gradually becomes less and less perfect, ending up eventually in this world; the active intellect is the last of these emanations, participating as it does partly in the intellectual due to its rational content and partly in the material, since it is accessible to material creatures like us. For the *falasifa* (philosophers), the active intellect is the highest stage that our thinking can reach, and sometimes looks like a rather secular representative for the deity.

See also: falsafa

Further reading

Leaman, O. (1985) *Introduction to Medieval Islamic*
Philosophy, Cambridge: Cambridge University Press.

—— (1999) *Brief Introduction to Islamic Philosophy*, Oxford: Polity Press.

OLIVER LEAMAN

acts of omission

Sins of omissions are relevant in any moral discourse. These can be specific according to law, or general to accord with principle. A conscientious disciple of **Confucius** will re-examine his or her conduct fairly to see if they had, on principle, 'failed' their friends. A conscientious disciple of Confucius will re-examine his conduct in three areas daily to see if they had, on principle, 'failed' their friends, asking three questions: 'In my dealings with others, have I been truthful? Towards my friends, have I been loyal? And do I practice what I transmit or teach?'

The Confucian standard of virtue is based on a principle of excellence, and the duty of the individual is 'to be what you can best be'. The Legalists detested such vague standards, and specified not only 'acts of commission and of omission' but also 'transgressions of (doing more than) the assigned duty'. A guard posted at the door who put back the bed cover that had fallen off the slumbering First Emperor was dismissed, for leaving his post outside the door. Later, this severe interdict almost cost the Emperor his life, when an assassin chased him around the elevated platform and the imperial guards dared not ascend the steps without his permission.

The cult of moral introspection insisted upon by the Neo-Confucians was due to a call to sagehood, a demand for **perfection** also emphasized in Mahayana Buddhism. The Six Perfections (*paramitas*) required of the **bodhisattva** outweigh the Eight Noble Paths needed for becoming a **Hinayana** *arhat*. This demand for self-perfection was later inherited by the Neo-Confucians.

See also: Noble Eightfold Path

Further reading

Lee, L. and Lai, W. (1979) 'The Chinese Concept

of Law: Confucian, Legalist, and Buddhist', *The Hastings Law Journal* 29(6): 1307–29.

WHALEN LAI

Advaita (non-dualist) Vedanta, post-Shankara

Advaita Vedanta is an Indian tradition of scriptural exegesis maintaining that the burden of the teaching of the **Upanishads** is that all forms of difference are ultimately unreal products of ignorance (**avidya**) and illusion (*maya*). Advaita is the philosophy of the radical renouncer (**samnyasa**). The sole authentic reality is held to be the Absolute *Brahman*, which is undifferentiated, relationless, static, contentless consciousness and bliss. The self-revealing (*sva-samvedana*) and self-established (*svatah siddha*) 'inner self' or soul (**atman**/*pratyagatman*) which is the constant witness (*sakshin*) of all conscious states is essentially identical with *Brahman* thus understood.

All plurality of selves, mental events, objects, causes and effects is a function of original ignorance or misconception (*avidya*) generating the misapprehension of the self as a personalized individual agent and experiencing subject to Vedic social and ritual duties (*varnashramadharma*) and transmigration (*samsara*). The human person is a composite of spirit (*atman*) and matter (non-*atman*). Such a composite has experiences and is subject to the illusion that it is an agent due to an ultimately unreal centre of individual awareness, a congenital conflation of spirit and the dynamic material sphere.

Misconception or ignorance of the true identity of the soul and the nature of reality as undifferentiated is the root cause of bondage to the series of births (**samsara**). Non-discursive, gnostic insight (*jnana*), preceded by the radical renunciation (*samnyasa*) of all the ritual actions (*karman*) and caste duties prescribed in the scriptures recognized as binding on and by the orthodox, into the identity of the non-acting core self and *Brahman* negates *avidya* and is a necessary and sufficient condition of release (*mukti* or *moksha* (both Sanskrit terms)) from the series of births propelled by intentional and motivated actions.

Salvific knowledge concerning the nature of the *Brahman-atman* state can only be derived from some of the accredited scriptures (**shruti**) which are the only means of knowledge about trans-empirical realities. Liberating insight is expressed in Upanishadic major statements (*mahavakyas*) such as 'That thou art' (**Tat tvam asi**), allegedly asserting the identity of the individual self (*jiva*) and the Absolute.

Ritual action (*karman*) and devotion (*bhakti*), while purifying the mind, cannot of themselves produce release since they presuppose that differences are real and thus belong in the sphere of ignorance. In short, since actions bind one to *samsara*, renunciation is a necessary condition of release from rebirth.

The most important early theorists whose works are extant are **Gaudapada** (450–500 CE), **Mandana Mishra** and **Shankara**, the latter two of whom probably flourished in the second half of the seventh century CE. Sureshvara probably belongs to the generation after Shankara and Mandana Mishra. His major works are the *Naishkarmyasiddhi* and an exposition of Shankara's commentary on the *Brihadaranyaka Upanishad*. He interprets *avidya* as the non-realization of the identity of one's inner self with the Absolute. This lack of knowledge leads to bondage, to the series of births, and the destruction of ignorance is release.

Some theorists of **Purva Mimamsa** ritualism hold that by abstaining from desire-based (*kamya*) and prohibited actions while continuing to perform disinterested and thus *karma*-exempt obligatory ones, then in the natural course of things accumulated past **karma** will decrease over time. Once the entire *karma*-stock has been exhausted the depersonalised individual will be released from rebirth. Sureshvara denies a direct connection between the performance of Vedically enjoined actions and release. Ignorance of the identity of the pure, immutable inner self with the static Absolute is removed by understanding the Vedanta texts. This understanding is identical with release and renders the performance of related actions, which presupposes beliefs in the reality of difference and individual agency, superfluous.

Padmapada, the author of the *Panchapadika*, also probably belongs to the generation after Shankara. Whereas Shankara identifies *avidya* with misconception (*mithya-jnana*) and the confusion of the self and not-self, Padmapada maintained that it is the cause of misconception and misidentification. He described *avidya* as a material (*jada*) force that is the substrative cause of the world-appearance. He held that *avidya* veiled the intact nature of *Brahman* and in association with the workings of *karma* and memory traces of previous cognitions produced the illusion of limited selfhood which is the substrate of individualised conscious experience and agency. He upheld the theory that the limited self is a reflection (*pratibimba*).

The polymath Vachaspati Mishra (*fl.* either 841 or 976 CE) wrote the Bhamati commentary on Shankara's commentary on the *Brahma-Sutras*. His definition of reality as undeniable self-revelation means that only the transcendental inner self can be considered real. He claims that there are two forms of *avidya*: a subjective psychological affliction and the objective indescribable substrative cause of limited personality and what is experienced as the material realm. The limited self is the substrate (*ashraya*) of *avidya* and the *Brahman*, understood as purely reflexive consciousness, its object. The content of the illusory experience of duality derives from the objective *avidya*. The content of illusory experiences can neither be described as real nor as unreal; they persist for a time but are eventually negated by other experiences.

Prakashatman (900–75), author of the *Panchapadikavivarana*, held that the substrative cause of experienced diversity is *Brahman* qualified by an ontologically indeterminable (*anirvachaniya*) power called *maya* or *avidya*. This *avidya* is a positive entity (*bhava-rupa*), since it differs from the mere prior absence of knowledge or blank ignorance. *Avidya* is characterized as 'indeterminable as being or non-being' because in the everyday sphere the content of a false cognition is a misrepresentation of a real external reality. Since it is a misrepresentation that is eliminable by knowledge, the content of such a cognition cannot be real. But the false cognition bears some relation to the reality which it distorts, and the subjective experience of a snake mistaken for a rope, for example, has practical consequences. Thus it cannot be categorized as wholly unreal like absolute fictions such as the 'hare's horn'. So it is held that it is neither determinately real or unreal. The same reasoning is applied when *avidya* is

treated as a power that is the substrative cause of pluriformity in that it generates the limited subjects that mistake the true nature of reality. According to the *satkarya* theory of causation, the substrative cause is of the same order of being as its effects. Thus causal *avidya* is also ontically indeterminable.

Against the view of Vachaspati Mishra that *Brahman* is the object of *avidya* and the limited self its substrate, Prakashatman held *Brahman* is both the substrate and object of *avidya* in that differentiated subjects, acts and objects of cognition are superimposed upon immutable, self-luminous pure consciousness. It is of crucial significance that error has an objective ground: it is a false awareness of something and not of nothing. Were it otherwise, the conclusion would follow that reality is **emptiness** (*shunyata*). He agreed with Padmapada in upholding the theory that the limited self is a reflection (*pratibimba*) of *Brahman*.

Sarvajnatman (*c.*900–50 CE) was the author of the *Samkshepashariraka* and the *Panchaprakriya*. He held that *Brahman* is the universal cause via the instrumentality of *avidya*, understood as a positive force, which has the pure self both as its substrate and its object. It both obscures the nature of the transcendental self and projects the illusion of diversity. *Avidya*-removing direct insight into the nature of the *Brahman* that underlies all appearances is derived from the *Upanishads*.

Vimuktatman (950–1000 CE) wrote the *Ishtasiddhi*, in which he characterized the Absolute as pure intuitive awareness (*anubhuti*). Indivisible, non-objectifiable subjectivity which is always reflexively given is the only beginningless, immutable and eternal reality. It is real because it is never negated. He is significant for his critique of the concept of difference that contributed to the arguments of **Shri Harsha**. Were difference identical with the essential nature (*svarupa*) of an entity, there would be the undesirable implication (*prasanga*) that on the apprehension of the essence there would also be experience of its difference from everything else as well as experience of the entity itself. One cannot argue that as well as the apprehension of the proper form of the entity there is a cognition of difference which depends on awareness of correlatives, because the person who strictly identifies essence and difference cannot appeal to the dependence of difference on correlatives if proper form and difference are essentially identical and synonymous. Just as cognition of essence does not depend upon correlatives, nor does cognition of difference.

Nor can difference be a property (*dharma*). Were it a property, it would be necessary to postulate another difference between it and the proper form. Given this difference, there would be another which applied to it and which would be its attribute and so on *ad infinitum*. Moreover, there would be the fallacy of mutual dependence or circularity: there would be cognition of difference when there is cognition of an entity qualified by properties such as the universal and there would be cognition of an entity qualified by properties when there is cognition of difference.

The same reasoning applies if difference is construed as the mutual non-existence (*anyonya-abhava*) of entities. Moreover, the self-luminous subject can never be categorised as an absence negated by something else. A straightforward denial that the universe existed would mean that the means of knowledge (*pramana*), including the Vedic scriptures from which knowledge of *Brahman* derives, would not only be invalid since lacking in objects but also would be non-existent. If independent reality is attributed to the world, it would either be different from *Brahman* (= pure awareness) or identical with *Brahman* or both. But given the impossibility of an adequate account of difference, the relation between pure subjectivity and what is experienced as the objectified world cannot be specified. Since the constant and immutable perceiver can be neither identical with nor different from the manifest sphere of mutable and differentiated phenomena, the latter must lack determinate identity. It is for this reason that Vimuktatman says that the world derives from a causal principle called *maya* which is indeterminable (*anirvachaniya*) as real or unreal. The sphere of manifest phenomena is like a magical illusion (*maya*) or dreams, neither substantial nor utterly non-substantial. Since it is not substantial, monism is not compromised. But since it is not wholly non-substantial, the occurrence of ordinary experience is intelligible and the problem about the status of the means of knowledge does not arise.

Vimuktatman draws distinctions between (i) the absolutely non-existent, the impossible, the purely fictitious and the contents of false cognitions, all of which are termed *pratibhasika-sat*; (ii) the conventionally or provisionally existent which we encounter through everyday valid cognitions, the *vyavaharika-sat*; and (iii) the absolute, unnegatable, unchanging reality or truth (*paramartha-sat*) relative to which the conventional world of human experience is unreal. It is within this framework that his claim that the sphere of manifest phenomena is describable neither as being nor as non-being nor as both and nor as neither must be understood.

Knowledge of *Brahman* destroys *maya* and its products for the enlightened individual who understands the ontologically indeterminable nature of the world. The removal of the veils obscuring the blissful pure luminosity of consciousness is the same as liberation from rebirth. The world as characterized by a variety of forms continues to be experienced by the enlightened person until death just as recollected cognitions of perceptual errors and dreams ordinarily remain in the memory.

Further reading

Cammann, K. (1965) *Das System des Advaita nach der Lehre Prakasatmans*, Wiesbaden: Otto Harrassowitz.

Dasgupta, S. (1922) *History of Indian Philosophy, Vol.1*, Cambridge: Cambridge University Press.

Hacker, P. (1978) *Kleine Schriften*, ed. L. Schmithausen, Wiesbaden: Steiner.

Halbfass, W. (ed.) (1995) *Philology and Confrontation: Paul Hacker on Traditional and Modern Vedanta*, Albany, NY: State University of New York Press.

Thrasher, A. (1993) *The Advaita Vedanta of the Brahma-siddhi*, Delhi: Motilal Banarsidass.

CHRIS BARTLEY

aesthetics, Chinese: beauty

Beauty is not particularly identified as an object of philosophical appreciation in China. The term 'aesthetics' is of recent coinage: traditionally, the topic was covered under the individual arts, such as 'poetics' for poetry and the standards of calligraphy and painting (the two are related by virtue of brushwork). Beauty in the sense of order (as implied by 'cosmos') was subdivided into the order of nature which is given, and the order of rule that comes with government. The two should mesh at some point, as the ideal design is that the individual should be integrated into society and society should be integrated into the natural order of things. Contemplation of this comes under the rubric of the concepts of *dao* (Way) and *li* (principle). The Neo-Confucians who devoted themselves to the 'study of principle' (the original designation of Neo-Confucianism) brought this art to perfection. Their moral system is based on a moral aesthetics, a contemplation of the beauty in the order and design innate in all things, in order to derive rules of conduct that would bring humanity into harmony with the grand cosmic plan.

Then there is the area of feminine beauty, the love of which **Confucius** considered to be instinctual. He lamented only that humans do not love humaneness (goodness) with the same zeal as they would love 'colour' (the term for 'sex' and 'feminine beauty', and what appears in **Gaozi**'s definition of human nature as 'food and sex'). That well-circumscribed and negative reading of sexual attraction also means that the Platonic metaphor of Eros as the power that draws one upwards for a reunion with the Good cannot be replicated by the word 'colour', even when that psychology of reunion through natural attraction is very much present in the Daoist art of nurturing life, sexual yoga, alchemy and metaphysics. There Eros is present as the lateral 'union of *yin* and *yang*' and subsequent upward (or downward) '**return to the root**' and 'reversal to the apex or the origin'. The Greek cult of homosexuality among men which rises to the heights of Platonic love has no similar position in China. There was, especially in late dynastic theatre circles, a cult of 'male colour' or male homosexuality, but it was looked down upon.

Since 'colour' as the object of sight is the term used to translate the Sanskrit term *rupa* (form: physical form in the case of *namarupa*, name-and-form or elements somatic and psychic), the Mahayana wisdom formula of 'form is emptiness and emptiness is form' implies in Chinese the lesson of life: the gratification of the sexual desires will in the end come to nothing, but also the

realization of life's futility can serve as the **trigger** to enlightenment.

See also: Dream of the Red Chambers

WHALEN LAI

aesthetics, Chinese: landscape art

Zong Ping (Tsung Ping), the first theorist on landscape painting, envisaged an empathy of *qi* between painter and object, a correspondence of *lei* (sameness in kind), a telescoping or condensation of form seen from a distance into the limited space of a canvas, and the ability of art to capture the *shen* (spirit) of the object so as to evoke the same experience in the twice-removed observer. Though highly visual, Chinese art is unlike the visual mode of Greek art's presentation of humanity and god. The paintings are not meant to reproduce an exact objective similitude, nor are they designed to glorify the rational proportions. Instead, the aim is to capture the *qi* of the mountain and water with a 'spirit' that moves through nature as well as man. Art is not 'a copy of a copy' or an intimation of the 'perfect nude that is never found in reality'. Rather, it is an encapsulation of a union of painter and environment, artist and nature, humanity and **Heaven**.

A new aesthetic note was struck later in the Song period for both painting and poetry, namely the ideal we associate with Chan Buddhism of the 'ordinary', as in the subject matter, and the 'insipid', rather like drinking very light green tea. In general, though, art suffered under the Neo-Confucian puritans who regarded theatre, music and even poetry to be frivolous, self-indulgent and not conducive to rational moral cultivation. However, there are interesting developments among some later 'literati painters', a category established in opposition to the 'academic paintings' that grew out of the courtly style under Song imperial patronage, in a shift from the impressionistic to the expressionistic. Overhanging gigantic boulders telling of the inner turmoils of the painter's soul can be anything but 'ordinary and insipid'. This style is individualistic and broke away from the school of

Ming–Qing painting, which is one in which the literati scholars emulated the great masters of the Song–Yuan era. Sometimes, the painters literally copied a previous painting instead of painting from nature directly. For this, literati painting was mocked as amateurish and non-professional, lacking in originality and a pastime of the leisurely, text-fixated class.

See also: music

Further reading

Bush, S. and Hsio-yen Shih (eds) (1985) *Early Chinese Texts on Painting*, Cambridge, MA: Published for the Harvard-Yenching Institute by Harvard University Press.

WHALEN LAI

aesthetics, Chinese: mountains and waters

'Mountains and streams' are cardinal *yang* and *yin* ideas. The regular refuge from life in the city, they also stand for nature. Nature poetry and painting is known as 'mountain and water' poetry and painting; painters juxtaposed the pair to create tension and harmony. The ink brush moving from left to right, being harder, is *yang*; from right to left, being weaker, it conveys *yin*.

In the *Book of Changes* (see **Yijing**), however, water is set against fire as mountain is set against marshes. In literature, mountains are associated with reclusive ascetics, while waters have erotic nymphs along their edge. During the Han period, mountains and waters were actually represented as more mythical than natural; paintings showed unicorns in hills, and poets encountered rain maidens at lakes, concurring with what is described in the *Classic of Mountains and Seas*. People saw what they were expected to see.

Buddhism helped to demythologize the mountains and waters, and nature became for the first time 'natural'. Nature painting and nature poetry then appeared as genres. The Buddhist analysis of the senses and perception is reflected in the first treatise on landscape painting by Zong Bing in the early fifth century CE. With monks, recluses, even whole peoples now moving away from war-ravaged cities, the hills and streams, once wild, alien, uncanny and monster-infested, became instead refuges, habitats and soulmates for people.

See also: friendship; recluse in Islam

Further reading

Allan, S. (1997) *The Power of Water*, Albany, NY: State University of New York Press.
Birbaum, R. (1986) 'The Manifestation of a Monastery: Shen-ying's Experiences on Mount Wu-t'ai in T'ang Dynasty', *Journal of the American Oriental Society* 106(1): 119–37.

WHALEN LAI

aesthetics, Indian theories of

The Kashmiri aesthetician Anandavardhana (*c*.850 CE), who enjoyed the patronage of King Avantivarman (855–883 CE), wrote the *Dhvanyaloka* which, with its Lochana commentary by the theologian and philosopher **Abhinavagupta** (970–1025 CE), is the most influential Indian work on the theory and practice of literary criticism. Their ideas are reproduced in a more accessible form in Mammata's (*fl.* 1050 CE) *Kavyaprakasha*.

Earlier writers tended to concentrate on studies of rhetoric and understood the nature of poetry as ornamented language (*alamkara*), describing it in terms of the external properties of the work of art produced by a technically skilled poet. Anandavardhana controversially proposed the suggestive capacity (*dhvani*) of poetic literature as a semantic power and source of beauty in its own right over and above features such as alliteration and assonance, metrical sophistication and figures of speech. There was a consensus among Indian thinkers that the semantic power of words was twofold: the power of literal meaning or direct denotation (*abhidha*) and a supervenient power of indirect expression (**lakshana**, *gunavritti*, *bhakti*, *upachara*). When the term *agni* (fire) is applied to something that is hot and burns brightly, it is being used in its primary, literal sense (*mukhya-artha*), but when it is used to describe an energetic and passionate individual as 'fiery', it has a transferred, non-literal or figurative sense (*lakshana-artha*). This semantic transference arises when the primary meanings are obstructed. The supervenient power may be evoked through a relationship of similarity between two objects, or it may be prompted by another relation such as that between property and property-possessor; as in, 'The umbrellas are coming', when what is meant is that people with umbrellas are approaching. Later writers say that there are three types of transferred, indirect predication:

(a) *Jahallakshana* (total secondary predication). For example, 'There is a village on the Ganges', where the primary sense of Ganges is wholly elided and replaced by the sense 'bank of the Ganges'.
(b) *Ajahallakshana* (retention of the primary sense plus adoption of a secondary sense). For example, 'The spears are coming', where 'spear' refers to both spears and their carriers.
(c) *Jahadajahallakshana* (partial secondary predication). For example, 'The boy is a lion'. Such properties as ferocity, etc. which he shares with the lion are attributed to the boy, while those leonine characteristics of which he is obviously devoid are eliminated from the sense of 'lion'.

Some writers such as **Kumarila Bhatta**, who subscribed to the 'harmony after designation' (*abhihita-anvaya*) theory of language functioning, propose another semantic capacity, called the 'purportive power' (*tatparya-shakti*). According to this theory, individual words are the primary units of meaning. When they have serially and separately expressed their own direct senses (*abhidha*), which are understood as *per se* expressive of generic features, there is produced a further syntactically connected whole which is the sentential meaning which refers to something specific.

Anandavardhana says that there is a type of semantic power in addition to the literal (*abhidha*) and transferred (*lakshana*) senses that is most appropriate to poetic expression. This is suggestion (*vyanjakatva*) which he also calls *dhvani*. Here is a case where the suggestion is the opposite of what is prima facie directly expressed:

Mother in law sleeps here, I there;
look, traveller, while it is light.
For at night when you cannot see,
you must not fall into my bed.

(Ingalls *et al*. 1990: 98)

Abhinavagupta comments on Valmiki's characterisation of winter:

The sun has stolen our affection for the moon,
whose circle now is dull with frost
and like a mirror blinded by one's breath
shines no more.

(Ingalls *et al*. 1990: 209)

The word 'blinded' must have a suggestive sense, since only sentient creatures can be literally blind and the sort of relationship that could serve as the basis of semantic transference is lacking between mirrors and the blindness that afflicts creatures. The purpose of this oblique usage is to suggest the innumerable properties of the moon in winter such as otioseness, loss of beauty and so on. The use of suggestion increases the semantic range of words beyond their narrow denotations and those supervenient, secondary senses which extend only to things that are closely related.

Hitherto we have been describing a rhetorical device which exploits semantic possibilities by going beyond the literal sense of words. But there is another type of suggestion where the literal sense is intended but only as leading to 'something further'. Here the 'something further' is a taste, mood or flavour (*rasa*); this is the soul or essence of poetry, and it cannot be directly expressed. It is an emotional experience, but differs from experience of the corresponding emotion in everyday life.

The ultimate aim of art is the production of *rasa*, which is the flavour enjoyed by the audience of a play if the author and actors are successful and the property of poetic expression which evokes aesthetic enjoyment in a reader. It is the translation of feelings into taste. The actor imitates the emotion supposedly felt by the character and communicates it to a sympathetic audience for the delight of the latter. Bharata's *Natya-Shastra* lists eight types of *rasa*: the erotic (*shringara*), the comic (*hasya*), the tragic (*karuna*), the cruel (*raudra*), the heroic (*vira*), the fearful (*bhayanaka*), the loathsome (*bibhatsa*) and the wonderful (*adbhuta*). These flavours are related to various basic (*sthayibhava*) human emotions portrayed by the actors: sexual desire (*rati*), laughter (*hasa*), grief (*shoka*), anger (*krodha*), heroic effort (*utsaha*), fear (*bhaya*), disgust (*jugupsa*) and wonder (*vismaya*).

Anandavardhana introduces a ninth *rasa*, that of tranquillity (*shanta*), whose status is controversial in that it seems to involve the suppression of the basic emotions to which the other *rasas* correspond. As we shall see, Abhinavagupta provides a rationale for this mode of aesthetic experience.

In a drama, *rasa* is produced by the combination of what are termed the determinants (*vibhavas*), the consequents (*anubhavas*) and the thirty-three transient states of mind (*vyabhicharibhava*). The determinants are those features which are the grounds of the possibility of the realisation of the emotion and the *rasa*. They are either objective (*alambana-vibhava*) or stimulative (*uddipanabhava*). The former are the *dramatis personae* towards whom the emotions are directed. The stimulative determinants in, for instance, the erotic mode will be factors such as springtime, gardens or the nuptial couch. The consequents of the emotions are seen by the audience as their symptoms; in the erotic mode they will include sidelong glances, smiles and gracious movements. The thirty-three transient states of mind portrayed as subsidiary to the basic emotions include discouragement, apprehension, jealousy, embarrassment, intoxication, impatience, contentedness and dissimulation. There are also eight involuntary states (*sattvikabhavas*) which a good actor can mimic at will, such as perspiration, horripilation, trembling and fainting.

Anandavardhana says that *rasa* is a basic emotion that is elevated in the consciousness of the spectator. The erotic form of aesthetic pleasure (*shringara-rasa*) deriving from reading love poetry differs from everyday feelings of sexual arousal. But the writer must be under the influence of the heightened state of emotion before he can produce the suggestive poetry that will transfer the *rasa* to his audience. Anandavardhana denies that *rasa* can be literally expressed: it can only be empathetically evoked by suggestion (*dhvani*). By means of *dhvani*, the *rasa* arises without any conscious realisation that the experience has been preceded by perceptions of the determinants, consequents and transi-

tory states of mind. If *rasa* is the goal of poetry, suggestion is the means to it.

The non-purely subjective criteria for the successful achievement of *rasa* include the appropriateness (*auchitya*) of the plot to emotions intended to be evoked and the association of the *rasas* with their peculiar ornaments, such as sweetness with love and strength with fury. Features of linguistic style such as metre, embellishment (*alamkara*), assonance, rhyme, the use of figures of speech such as simile and metaphor, lightness of touch, the use of long compound words and the relations between the stanzas are also significant.

In his *Lochana* on the *Dhvanyaloka*, Abhinavagupta accepted the literal (*abhidha*), transferred (*lakshana*, where the literal sense is impossible) and purportive (*tatparya*) modes of meaning, and reinforced Anandavardhana's arguments for the existence of *dhvani* as a fourth mode in its own right. The following passage summarizes his understanding of the relationship between literal expressiveness, purportive power and semantic transference:

The operation of denotation (*abhidha*) conveys senses that are of a general nature, for denotation is a semantic power which depends on convention, and convention is tied to the general; it lacks reference to the specific individual, for otherwise there would be no end [to the conventions that would have to be made for each word] and there would be failure of a word connected with one [individual to other individuals of the same class]. After literal expression, the purportive power conveys the sentential meaning, in which [the general and unconnected] word senses are particularised and mutually connected according to the maxim. The general senses [of the words] lead to a particularised sense, for if that were not the case, no effect could ensue... For semantic transference takes place when there is blocking of the primary sense. This blocking takes the form of an apprehension of inconsistency... Now there can be no apprehension of this inconsistency until the syntax is understood, and the understanding of the syntax does not come about through the literal meaning, for that exhausts itself in conveying the individual word meanings and has no power to function further. Our understanding of the syntax comes about only through the purportive power...In the example, 'the boy is a lion', there arises a third power called semantic transference, which is different from both the literal and purportive powers of expression. It arises immediately after the emergence of the factors repugnant to the syntactical connection conveyed by the purportive power belonging to the second stage and it is able to neutralise those repugnant factors...So then: the power of denotation is the power, regulated by convention, to convey the literal sense of the individual words; the power of sentence operation is the power to convey a sense of the whole, a power which is aided by the impossibility of the literal sense without it; the power of semantic transference is the power to reveal a sense as regulated by such cooperating factors as the blocking of the primary sense; the suggestive power is the power to suggest, a power which has its origin in one's understanding of the objects revealed by the first three powers, and which is then assisted by the imagination of the listener which has been prepared by these revelations...This suggestive power, this suggestive operation, overshadows the three operations which precede it and is the very soul of poetry.

(*Lochana on Anandavardhana's Dhvanyaloka* 1.4.b, in Ingalls *et al.* 1990)

In the *Abhinavabharati*, Abhinavagupta developed a theory of the aesthetic experience of sensitive readers or spectators as a distinct mode of cognition lying between ordinary awareness and the blissful interiority of enlightened consciousness. This theory is consonant with an aspect of the nondualist Shaiva meditational tradition, which sees enlightenment not in suppression of extroverted attention to the external but in contemplation of the radiant, self-projective consciousness that is the source of all appearances.

Abhinavagupta discerned a problem in the received *rasa* theory in so far as it implied that the audience would sympathetically experience the emotion appropriate to the flavour: an audience actually terrified or overcome by grief would leave the theatre. He held that there must be a difference in kind between the basic form of emotion (*sthayibhava*) and the flavour if it is to be intelligible that the tragic *rasa* or the *rasa* of fear can be relished. If we perceived the *rasa* as belonging to someone else, we would be unmoved. On the other hand, it is perceived by the spectator as belonging to him, albeit not in the mode of sense-perception. Neither the actor nor the character portrayed enjoys the flavour. What the character is depicted as experiencing is the basic emotion. If the actor experienced either the basic emotion or the *rasa*, he would forget his lines. Abhinavagupta sees in the suggestive power of *rasa* a force which transforms the spectator's consciousness. He responds to sorrow on stage by identifying that grief with his own recollected griefs. *Rasa* is not just the apprehension of another person's mental state but a sense of relish based on empathy. *Rasa* is an experience of emotion abstracted from the contingent features of actual situations. Aesthesis evokes general experiential possibilities. In art we do not experience, for example, love for a particular individual but love *per se* as an aspect of the human condition. One's own emotional experiences are assimilated to and felt in a wider context. *Rasa* is not an object to be enjoyed but enjoyment itself, characterized by rapture, melting and radiance and comparable to the blissful expansion of consciousness that is the realization of one's identity as the transindividual consciousness that is named Shiva.

Abhinavagupta's treatment of the *rasa* of tranquillity (*shanta-rasa*) links his aesthetics and soteriological metaphysics. He propounded a form of absolute idealism which equates the world with a single universal autonomous consciousness (*parasamvit*) refracting itself into an infinite variety of forms. He argues that the stable experience (*bhava*) on which this *rasa* depends is the radiant experience of the essentially reflexive self (*atman*) which is the permanent transcendental background on which all transient experiences are projected and which is the ultimate dynamic source of all experience of multiplicity. The *shanta-rasa* is the aesthetic relish on the part of blissful expanded, enlightened consciousness (*chamatkara*), annihilating the confining self-centredness of everyday life, of the drama that is the universe as the self-manifestation of the trans-individual consciousness with which one is essentially identical. The rapturous appreciation of the beautiful in nature and in art reflects the state of release and can be the means to it.

Further reading

Brough, J. (1953) 'Some Indian Theories of Meaning', *Transactions of the Philological Society*, 161–76; repr. in M. Hara and J.C. Wright (eds) (1996), *John Brough: Collected Papers*, London: School of Oriental and African Studies.
—— (1968) *Poems from the Sanskrit*, Harmondsworth: Penguin.
Gnoli, R. (1956) *The Aesthetic Experience According to Abhinavagupta*, Rome: Serie Orientale Roma.
Ingalls, D. *et al.* (trans.) (1990) *The Dhvanyaloka of Anandavardhana with the Locana of Abhinavagupta*, Cambridge, MA: Harvard University Press.
Masson, J. and Patwardhan, M. (1969) *Santarasa and Abhinavagupta's Philosophy of Aesthetics*, Poona: Bhandarkar Oriental Research Institute.
Matilal, B. (1990) *The Word and the World*, Delhi: Oxford University Press.

CHRIS BARTLEY

aesthetics in Islamic philosophy

Most of the early accounts of aesthetics in Islamic philosophy follow Neoplatonic lines of interpretation. Beauty is linked with perfection, and so God, as the most perfect being, possesses the most beauty. His beauty is part of his essence while for us the contemplation of beauty is an accidental aspect of the physical properties of the objects of contemplation. Similarly, the pleasure we take in contemplating beauty is intermittent, by contrast with God's constant self-contemplation. Ibn Sina develops this basically Farabian typology (see **al-Farabi**) by suggesting that there is scope even for human beings to perfect their physical faculties through imagination into something higher and purer. We have a choice as to how to proceed with our ideas on what we find attractive. We may limit them to the corporeal and get from them purely physical satisfaction, or we can use them as starting

points from which to move on to more abstract and perfect forms of thought.

Much of the discussion of aesthetics dealt with the role of poetic and rhetorical language in order to move an audience to action, and there was much use of Aristotle's *Poetics* in order to analyse instances of Arabic verse. In fact, all forms of expression were seen as examples of particular kinds of reasoning, and poetry is by far the lowest in demonstrative force, yet still important in carrying out an instructive role for those who are incapable of understanding theoretical approaches to the truth. What is crucial here is the faculty of imagination, which both characterizes the figurative nature of poetry and the ability of that material to be appreciated by an audience. Imagination is a mixture of the spiritual and the corporeal; it uses material images and refers to the experiences of physical beings, and yet extends those material ideas in new and intriguing ways. An entirely rational consciousness would not require the use of imagination. Concepts which make a direct reference to the emotional side of humanity only get in the way of rational thought, and should be avoided if at all possible. But for most people this is not possible, and images have to be employed in order to bring the message firmly into the mind of its audience.

Further reading

Black, D. (1990) *Logic and Aristotle's Rhetoric and Poetics in Medieval Arabic Philosophy*, Leiden: Brill.
Heath, P. (1992) *Allegory and Philosophy in Avicenna (Ibn Sina)*, Philadelphia: University of Pennsylvania Press.
Kemal, S. (1991) *The Poetics of Alfarabi and Avicenna*, Leiden: Brill.

OLIVER LEAMAN

aesthetics in Japan, post-Meiji

By contrast with art theory and literary criticism, philosophical aesthetics is not limited to investigations about art or particular kinds of art, but also deals with aesthetic features of nature. In principle, it is concerned with all kinds of aesthetic objects, aesthetic judgement and aesthetic production. One of the main problems of every philosophical aesthetics is, of course, to explain its notion of 'aesthetic'. In both European and Japanese history, explicitly comprehensive or general philosophical aesthetics appeared rather late. In Europe, Baumgarten (1714–62) and Kant (1724–1804) were among the first thinkers who advanced theories of aesthetics. In Japan, general philosophical aesthetics were introduced in Meiji times (1868–1912).

In 1874, **Nishi** Amane (1829–97) published his *Hyakuichi shinron* (A New Theory of the Unity of the Hundred [Sciences]) in which he stated that aesthetics is a philosophical discipline. Even earlier, around 1872, Nishi had written *Bimyo gakusetsu* (Theory of Beauty), defining aesthetics as a kind of philosophy that 'investigates the principles of the so-called fine arts'. But this treatise was not published before 1907. Around 1883, Nakae Chomin (1847–1901) translated Eugène Véron's (1825–89) *L'esthétique* of 1878 as *Ishi bigaku* (The Aesthetics of Véron). Though *bigaku* literally means 'theory of beauty', it became the standard Japanese term for aesthetics. The famous writer Mori Ogai (1862–1922) also contributed significantly to the establishment of philosophical aesthetics in Japan. Ogai, who studied and lived in Germany from 1884 to 1888, was strongly influenced by German aesthetics, and particularly the *Ästhetik* (Aesthetics) (1887) of Eduard von Hartmann (1842–1906). In his *Shimbiron* (Discourses on Beauty), which are mainly translations of Hartmann published between 1892 and 1895, Ogai introduced many key concepts of philosophical aesthetics. Also, from 1892, he lectured on aesthetics at **Fukuzawa** Yukichi's (1834–1901) Keio-gijuku, the later Keio University. Finally, Ogai engaged in many scholarly disputes on aesthetics, especially aesthetic principles of literature.

After Nishi, Nakae and Ogai, **Onishi** Hajime (1864–1901) was perhaps most important in introducing general philosophical aesthetics to Japan. Onishi published several studies on European aesthetics, and delivered respective lectures. He was a mentor of Otsuka Yasuji (1868–1931), who became the first to hold the chair for aesthetics which was finally established at Toyko University in 1899.

Not expressly concerned with general philosophical aesthetics but rather focusing on particular kinds of art, works like Tsubouchi Shoyo's (1859–1935) *Shosetsu shinzui* (The Essence of the Novel), published in sections between 1885 and 1886, also contributed to philosophical aesthetics. Like Aristotle's *Poetics*, they include theories and concepts which are applicable to (almost) all kinds of art, or even to aesthetic objects and judgements in general. For instance, Tsubouchi's view that, in the novel, 'rigid verisimilitude is as unappealing as total lack of realism', can be interpreted as (also) indicating general principles of art. Natsume Soseki's (1867–1916) studies on literature are of even greater philosophical relevance. Further, certain Japanese novels include contributions to philosophical aesthetics. Soseki's *Kusa makura* (Pillows of Grass) (1906, trans. A. Turner as *The Three-Cornered World*), is probably the most striking example, advancing such theories as that nature is beautiful only if it looks like art, or that one must take the position of a 'third person' (*daisan sha*), that is, an uninterested onlooker to be able to adequately appreciate beauty, or to arrive at an adequate aesthetic judgement. To what extent Soseki was influenced by Kant's *Critique of (Aesthetic) Judgement* and Kant's doctrine that impartial and inter-subjectively valid aesthetic judgement presupposes a kind of disinterestedness (particularly in morality, truth, and profit), and that an object of nature is (judged) beautiful if it looks like a piece of art, is difficult to decide.

Whereas treatises such as those by Nishi, Ogai, Onishi, Tsubouchi and Soseki, though taking into account cultural particularities, provided a basis for an aesthetics comparatively independent of cultural prejudice, other works laid the foundation for a more culturalist tradition of modern Japanese philosophical aesthetics. Actually, this tradition was mainly inaugurated by a Westerner, the American Ernest Fenollosa (1853–1908) who from 1878 to 1890 taught philosophy, economics and politics at Tokyo University. Fenollosa admired traditional Japanese art, particularly architecture, sculpture and painting, and vehemently argued for its protection. One of his students, Okakura Kakuzo (or Okakura Tenshin, 1862–1913), became one of the most influential advocates of specifically Japanese aesthetics. In his works *The*

Ideals of the East with Special Reference to the Art of Japan and *The Book of Tea*, published in the United States in 1904 and 1906 respectively, he argued that 'Asia is one', and that 'the history of Japanese art [is] the history of Asiatic ideals', thus making a sweeping distinction between 'the East' and 'the West', and maintaining that Japanese art is an expression of general Eastern values. Okakura conceived of these values as, primarily, characteristics of Daoism and 'Zennism', and regarded 'Teaism' and the tea ceremony as the most important art reflecting them. For instance, he emphasized that 'tea is a work of art' and 'a religion of the art of life', that 'Teaism [is] Daoism in disguise', and that 'Teaism is a result of the Zen conception of greatness' in everyday life. Also indicating that Zen meditation is a 'means to attain supreme enlightenment', Okakura conveyed the idea that Teaism achieves the same. Okakura further interpreted Daoism and Zennism as doctrines of peace, individuality and individual freedom, and implied that 'Teaism', especially the architecture of the tea room, expressed these values too.

In his booklet *Bushido: The Soul of Japan*, published in 1905, Nitobe Inazo (1862–1933) also extolled the tea ceremony as 'an art and... spiritual culture' that reflects 'calmness of mind' and a kind of inner purity. Okakura's and Nitobe's basic ideas were taken over and developed further by many Japanese – and Western – scholars. Members of the **Kyoto school** like Hisamatsu Shin'ichi (1889–1981), and similarly minded scholars, stressed that the tea ceremony is a way of practising Zen, and that it even expresses Buddhist, or Oriental, nothingness (*mu*). In 1986, Ohashi Ryosuke (born 1944) published *Kire no kozo* (The Structure of *Kire*) which includes a chapter on the aesthetics of *chado*, the way of tea. *Kire* means a 'cut' or 'fragment', and is interpreted by Ohashi as a more or less general principle of Japanese art indicating a methodical break, discontinuity, incompleteness, and individuality. For Ohashi, too, every perfect tea ceremony expresses Buddhist purity, but is also, he holds, a unique, unrepeatable encounter, and in this sense represents discontinuity and individuality.

As well as the tea ceremony, *ikebana* (flower arrangement), and the composition of *haiku* – poems of three lines of 5, 7, 5 morae (not syllables)

respectively – have been elevated to exemplarily Japanese ways of art and Japanese aesthetics. Also, these three traditions have been regarded as proof for the hypothesis that Japanese arts and aesthetics cannot be isolated from Japanese conceptions and forms of everyday life, and in this regard too differs significantly from its Western counterparts. Another attempt at advancing a somewhat culturalist aesthetics was Kuki Shuzo's (1888–1941) *Iki no kozo* (The Structure of *Iki*), published in 1930. *Iki* means primarily a kind of elegant and refined behaviour, or life style. Kuki explains it as a combination of coquetry, chic and resignation. Though this concept of *iki* was strongly influenced by the French, or Parisian, ideal of flaneurism – Kuki spent a considerable time in France – and a reflection of Edo life style, Kuki held that it indicates an aesthetic view of life distinctively traditional Japanese. The tea hut (*chaya*), he maintained, is an 'objectivation' of '*iki* architecture'. Tanizaki Jun'ichiro (1886–1965), in his brilliant essay *In'ei raisan* (In Praise of Shadows) (1933), compared Western and Japanese rooms, particularly toilets, and concluded that while Westerners aesthetically appreciated brightness and sharp contrasts, Japanese favoured shadows and more or less soft changes between light and dark zones. All such views result from insufficiently differentiating between different forms of Japanese arts and aesthetics, from over-estimating the metaphysical implications of the tea ceremony, *ikebana* and *haiku* poetry, and from over-generalizing particular characteristics. In spite of these methodological shortcomings, Japanese aesthetics has remained influential in Japan as well as in the West.

As indicated, the basic questions of philosophical aesthetics can be framed as follows. (1) What are the characteristics of aesthetic experience, or, more precisely, of aesthetic objects, aesthetic judgement, and aesthetic production? (2) Is aesthetic experience a realization of truth, morality, and/or pleasure? And if a realization of truth, is it a perception of an accordance with a particular spatio-temporal reality and/or (original) ideas? Is it a realization of pleasure, something similar to sexual pleasure and/or enjoyment of beauty? (3) Should art aim at expressing and conveying truth, at moral instruction, and/or at expressing and conveying (pleasant) feelings? Should artistic freedom be limited? (4) Can aesthetic experience be universally valid? Or is it always an individual or culturally distinctive experience that cannot be generalized? Answers to these questions imply explanations of how the term 'aesthetic' – as well as related terms – is, or should be, understood and used.

As already mentioned, most contributions to philosophical aesthetics treat only some of these problems focusing for example on art, or even a particular kind of art. Except for the writings of such scholars as Nishi Amane, Mori Ogai, or **Nishida** Kitaro who were well acquainted with systematic European aesthetics, and for the works of Japanese professional philosophers – that is, university teachers of philosophy who had to study, and lecture on, philosophical aesthetics – almost all Japanese contributions to philosophical aesthetics focus on art, especially literature and theatre. Even explicit and systematic comparisons between the aesthetic experience of nature and of art are comparatively rare. Soseki's respective remarks that a scenery looks beautiful only if we perceive it as if it were a painting, striking as they are, are brief and part of a novel. Professional or university aesthetics, however, is often rather uninteresting. In Japan, as elsewhere, it is primarily business routine, concerned with the interpretation and explanation of classics.

However, whether comprehensive and expressly philosophical, or as parts, and implications, of art theory, modern Japanese philosophical aesthetics provides clear answers to the basic questions of philosophical aesthetics. Moreover, these answers are rather uniform, and in most cases compatible with, and often influenced by, traditional doctrines the beginnings of which date back to Heian times (795–1185), namely, the theories of literature advanced for example by Ki no Tsurayuki (872?–945) and Murasaki Shikibu (9th–10th century), and – with regard to their central points – re-affirmed by Zeami Motokiyo (1363–1443), Chikamatsu Monzaemon (1653–1724), Keichu (1640–1701), Ogyu Sorai (1666–1728), Kada no Arimori (1706–51), Motoori Norinaga (1730–1801) and many others.

According to these theories, the main goal of literature, and art in general, is to express and convey human emotions. That is to say, what

makes a judgement an aesthetic judgement is that it expresses a feeling, such as pleasure, displeasure, and so on. Though art may also convey some truth, or provide moral instruction, this is not the main, and perhaps not even a necessary, aim of art. Employing the distinction between didactic and non-didactic aesthetics, all these theories belong to the second kind. Often, they explicitly argue against didactic aesthetics, especially rigid Confucianism according to which literature should encourage virtue and castigate vice, but also against the traditional Buddhist notion that it should facilitate enlightenment. As in pre-Meiji Japan, such didactic theories continued to play a role in modern Japanese aesthetics, for example, in respective views advanced by the Kyoto school. According to such views, perfect Zen art expresses an ontological and soteriologically relevant truth, namely, a realisation of nothingness, and permits the recipient to enter into this truth. Of course, the numerous Japanese contributions to Marxist art theory are also examples of didacticism.

Most great works of Japanese literature are primarily of a non-didactic nature, reflecting an aesthetic approach. But there are exceptions, as for instance a considerable number of Buddhist poems and No pieces. Most Buddhists who commissioned artists to create Buddhist pictures and sculptures probably intended the works to serve some soteriological purpose, sometimes their own salvation, but as with Christian art, the actual results very much depended on the artists' views and abilities.

Among those modern Japanese theoreticians who held that aesthetic experience is primarily emotional experience, and who maintained that art should, first of all, express, communicate, and invoke emotions, were philosophers like Nakae Chomin, writers like Yano Ryukai (1850–1931), Tsubouchi Shoyo, Ogai Mori, Natsume Soseki, Kitamura Tokoku (1868–94), and Tanizaki Jun'ichiro; critics like the young Shimamura Hogetsu (1891–1918), Masamune Hakucho (1879–1962), Kobayashi Hideo (1902–83); and the famous painter and friend of Okakura, Hashimoto Gaho (1834–1908). These scholars also basically agreed on the points that art should be original but not completely irregular, that it should appear natural and plausible without just imitating or copying nature and human life. Though convincing in its depiction of reality, art should remain identifiable as art. Also, though all these theoreticians defended the supremacy of aesthetic standards, they believed that concern for morality and social order should limit artistic freedom. There was, of course, much disagreement with regard to more specific theoretical questions, especially with respect to the goals and means of literature. For instance, between about 1880 and 1920, there were schools and periods called Naturalism (*shizenshugi*), Romanticism (*romanshugi*) and Realism (*jissaishugi* or *shajitsushugi*). Yano Ryukai emphasised that the 'novel [is a] vessel for simple enjoyment like other realms of art such as music and painting'. Tsubouchi, though certainly not in favour of artistic imitation, is often labelled a realist. Hogetsu, who, in his *Biteki seikatsu o ronzu* (On Aesthetic Life) (1901) and *Torawaretaru bungaku* (Literature in Shackles) (1906) argued against naturalism, defended it later in his *Shizenshugi no kachi* (The Value of Naturalism) (1908). But such differences are a matter of literary theory and criticism rather than of philosophical aesthetics which, in principle, represents a more general and abstract level of argument and discourse. Tsubouchi held that 'to arouse in the beholder by its sublime beauty emotions...that is [the] proper objective [of art], and that is what makes it art'. Improvement of moral nature, he continued, 'is an incidental effect and not its true aim'. Or: 'Moral instruction is not the first aim'. To indicate human feelings, Tsubouchi even used the traditional term *aware* (human emotion), so prominent in Norinaga. In his *Ebungaku keishiki ron* (Lecture on the Form of English Literature) (1903) Soseki characterized literature as 'what should appeal to taste – not in a difficult, philosophical sense of the word, but in the sense of like or dislike'. In *Bungakuron* (A Study of Literature) (1907), his basic view is that literature should appeal to emotion. However, he also expressed himself in a more qualified way, saying that the 'exclusion of the moral sense is an essential condition for appreciating *some part* of literature'. In an attempt to describe Japanese literature, Soseki, in his *Bungaku hyoron* (A Criticism of Literature) (1909) stated approvingly, 'if we remove [the] customary philosophy from Japanese literature, all that is left is an extremely simple expression of

natural beauty and human feelings'. As indicated, however, his most interesting remarks on aesthetic issues are in *Kusa makura*, expressing in essence the view that to appreciate natural and artistic beauty and thus experience a state of carefree pleasure, one must judge, or perceive, the object in a disinterested way, with no ideas whatever about improving one's knowledge, receiving moral instruction, or gaining material profit. Further, the object must be perceived as being different from reality, namely, as a kind of as-if-reality, or, as Kant would have said, aesthetic illusion. Well acquainted as he was with Western aesthetics, Soseki often expressly mentioned both nature and human feelings as adequate objects of art. Hogetsu demanded that 'literature must...be set completely free from the bonds of knowledge, and allowed to wander over the great sea of the emotions... May literature find...liberty'. Kobayashi Hideo emphasized that the success of a work of literature is not due to its ideological content but results from its being a convincing and moving expression of the author's feelings. Advocating aesthetic didacticism is but one way of advocating a heteronomy of aesthetic reflection, and of art in particular. For instance, as with Western naturalists, Japanese naturalists emphasized that art should be determined by, among other things, the results of natural science, and the idea of truth, representing not only what is beautiful, but also what is ugly. Though this view is compatible with the idea that art should express emotions, it can restrict their range.

In contrast to many artists, some influential philosophers interpreted aesthetic value, especially beauty, as a function of morality and truth. Similar to Plato and Hegel, they held that what is aesthetically valuable must also be good and true, or at least an expression of goodness and truth. Abe Jiro (1883–1959) who, in 1917, published a book entitled *Bigaku* (Aesthetics) was inclined to identify the beautiful with the good. Nishida Kitaro devoted a comprehensive study to analysing the relationship between art and morality. His *Geijutsu to dotoku* (Art and Morality), which appeared in 1923, includes such chapters as on 'the beautiful and the good' and 'the true and the beautiful'. Dissatisfied with, and unconvinced by Kant's sharp distinctions between the epistemological, practical (moral and useful), and aesthetic, he argued that the true, good and beautiful are closely connected. As in most of his writings, Nishida thereby employed a concept of truth that markedly differs from Kant's, namely a notion of ontological and existentially relevant truth. For instance, Nishida wrote that in 'the content of pure life there is nothing beautiful that is not good and nothing good that is not beautiful', and maintained that 'our moral society is the aesthetic creation of God'. Though, judged on a very abstract level, Nishida, in his interest in the ontological and soteriological significance of art, displayed a similar interest as Buddhist, and particularly Zen, scholars, in *Art and Morality* he made almost no mention of Buddhism and Zen. Imamichi Tomunobu (born 1922), who was professor of aesthetics at Tokyo University, in his *Betrachtungen über das Eine* (Reflections on the One) (1968), described aesthetic experience as an ecstasy comparable to that of a *unio mystica*, and grounded in a recognition of indications of eternity. Imamichi then proposed that theory of beauty should develop into ontodicy, a defence of being. For him, beauty is 'a prayer to god'.

Tsubunobu also discussed the 'aesthetics of Confucius', emphasizing the Confucian interest in the beautiful, especially beautiful customs, conventions and rituals, and the art of music, as means of aesthetic and ultimately social and moral education. In another essay, also included in *Betrachtungen*, he compared this Confucian approach to Plato's view of music as a means of education, and pointed out that such concepts called into question 'the independence of aesthetics'. After having demanded that the independence of aesthetics should be defended, however, he again argues in favour of an ontodicy, namely, an aesthetics which assures man of the value of being, and its existential relevance.

In comparative philosophy, Confucian aesthetics as a theory of a social order achieved by aesthetic means – art, ritual, refined convention – has gained much attention. Influential scholars from both East Asia and the West even regard this theory as a viable alternative to what they conceive of as inhumanely unemotional Western rationality. Some scholars also speak of a Shintoist aesthetics, but what they are actually referring to are rather long standing traditions of practice, such as the architecture of Shinto shrines, than specific aesthetic theories. At best, they provide subsequent interpretations of these traditional practices. Apart from this, it is anyway problematic to employ categories such as Confucian, Buddhist, Daoist, or Shintoist aesthetics, for they are too broad and vague to convey significant information. Though the culturalist aspects of much of modern Japanese aesthetics may lessen their relevance, it would be wrong to surmise that the respective theories are completely, or for the most part, worthless and uninteresting.

Determined by a strong interest in traditional Japanese arts and aesthetics, Japanese aesthetics includes many valuable interpretations of classic Japanese aesthetic categories, especially such notions as *okashii* (interesting; amusing, witty), *yugen* ([mysterious] elegance), *aware*, *wabi* (patina; withering, unobtrusive beauty), *iki*, and of course *utsukushii* (beautiful). Also, often the answers they give to the basic questions of philosophical aesthetics are completely independent of their culturalist perspectives. For instance, Okakura Kakuzo not only pointed out what he regarded as cultural particularities but also vehemently defended the universality of art, emphasising that 'art is common to all the world', and that 'there can be no distinction between East and West in this regard'. Okakura was thus more of a universalist than Soseki, who believed that the Japanese were principally unable to appreciate adequately English literature. As indicated, Okakura also stressed that art should be original. Further, in his *Book of Tea*, he was one of the first who dared to write that 'the Westerner' regarded 'Japan as barbarous while she indulged in the gentle arts of peace', yet called 'her civilised when she began to commit wholesale slaughter on Manchurian battlefields'. This kind of clear-minded and apt criticism of supposedly great cultural achievements which are actually regressions was very rare indeed. Okakura, by such a critique, wanted to suggest that – in contrast to the West – traditional, un-Westernized, Japan valued peace. Though this suggestion needed qualification, it made the point that art should be a culture of peace.

See also: philosophy of human rights, Japanese; Shinto

Further reading

Anesaki Masaharu (1916) *Buddhist Art in its Relation to Buddhist Ideals*, Boston: Houghton-Mifflin.

—— (1973) *Art, Life, and Nature in Japan*, Tokyo: Tuttle.

de Bary, W. (ed.) (1958) *Sources of Japanese Tradition*, New York: Columbia University Press.

Imamichi Tomonobu (1968) *Betrachtungen über das Eine – Gedanken aus der Begegnung der Antipoden*, Tokyo: Tokyo University, Institut der Aesthetik.

Kato Shuichi (1981) *Form, Style, Tradition: Reflections on Japanese Art and Society*, trans. J. Bester, Toyko: Tuttle.

Kuki Shuzo (1997) *Iki no kozo (Reflections on Japanese Taste: The Structure of Iki)*, trans. J. Clark, ed. Sakuko Matsui and J. Clark, Sydney: Power Publications.

Matsui Sakuko (1975) *Natsume Soseki as a Critic of English Literature*, Tokyo: The Centre for East Asian Cultural Studies.

Natsume Soseki (1968) *Kusa makura (The Three-Cornered World)*, trans. A. Turney, Tokyo: Tuttle

Nishida Kitaro (1973) *Geijutsu to dotoku* (Art and Morality), trans. D. Dilworth and V. Viglielmo, Honolulu: The University Press of Hawaii.

Okakura Kakuzo [Okakura Tenshin] (1922) *The Awakening of Japan*, London: John Murray.

—— (1956) *The Book of Tea* with foreword and biographical sketch by E. Grilli, Tokyo: Tuttle.

—— (1970) *The Ideals of the East*, Tokyo: Tuttle

Tanizaki Junichiro (1977) *In'ei raisan* (In Praise of Shadows), trans. E. Seidensticker and T. Harper, New Haven: Leete's Island Books.

Tsubouchi Shoyo (1981) 'Shosetsu shinzui (The Essence of the Novel)', trans. N. Twine, University of Queensland, Dept. of Japanese, Occasional Papers No. 11.

GREGOR PAUL

afterlife, Chinese: hell

Hell as a place of torture and pain is the opposite of the promise of salvation that came with the historic religions. Before that, hell was often a shady underground for the forlorn dead. In classical China, it was called the Yellow Spring, possibly a conflation of 'digging deep into the earth (yellow)' so as to reach 'the (black) waters', the latter being associated with the 'dark city' of the dead in the north. This is a subterranean land where no sun ever penetrates and where in theory, the *yang* soul of man cannot exist. By the time of the Han dynasty, the 'earth prisons' under Mount Tai in the east, a major nexus linking heaven, earth and the netherworld, gained prominence as the head-quarters of all local hells, and the administration of hell was as bureaucratized as the Chinese state on earth. Buddhism then introduced a variety of tortures to fit the various crimes.

Further reading

Tatz, M. and Kent, J. (1977) *Rebirth*, New York: Doubleday.

WHALEN LAI

afterlife, Chinese: hungry ghosts

One of the six paths of rebirth, the term 'hungry ghosts' originally described those who died without heir to provide them with food. The deceased then wandered on or under the earth looking for food. In Sanskrit *preta* refers back to a term for ancestors. When Buddhism made asceticism a virtue, gluttony in turn became a vice. The glutton and those who did not spare food for monks typically became hungry ghosts. With tiny necks but insatiably large stomachs, they go about forever hungry. Worse, everything they eat also turns into burning coal. Late dynastic Buddhists used a Tantric rite called 'Opening the Burning Mouth' to help them. Hungry ghosts are fed especially on the Ghost Festival, the Chinese 'All Souls' Day'. Growing fear of hungry ghosts parallels the growing number of the displaced poor in the city, for there is a saying that 'a beggar in this life, a hungry ghost in the next'.

See also: samsara

Further reading

Teiser, S. (1988) *The Ghost Festival in Medieval China*, Princeton, NJ: Princeton University Press.

Wolf, A. (1978) 'Gods, Ghosts, and Ancestors', in A. Wolf (ed.), *Studies in Chinese Society*, Stanford, CA: Stanford University Press.

WHALEN LAI

afterlife, Chinese: hunpo

The concept of *hunpo* refers to the Chinese theory of two souls: the *hun* or *yang* soul that goes with the higher mental functions and which at death ascends to heaven, and the *po* or *yin* soul that is closely tied to the body which at death is housed within or hangs around the grave on earth. One becomes a luminous 'god', the other a malicious 'ghost'. The Chinese imagine the former as 'clouds' (vapour, air, the breath leaving the body) and the other as 'white' (like the bleached bones). Neolithic burials show vents drilled to allow the former to escape, and also weights (a stone) to keep the latter confined. When *yin–yang* numbers were introduced, the number of souls rose to ten (because three goes with *yang* and six goes with *yin*). A tenth soul sometimes goes with the salvific drama about whether the person's spirit goes to heaven or to hell.

WHALEN LAI

afterlife, Chinese: immortals

Immortality is the Daoist ideal. The concept began with a promise of longevity, that is, a prolonging of the lifespan and the postponing of the hour of death. Life was deemed natural, and death was unnatural. Increasingly, the promise became one of a plain 'non-death' or life eternal in special paradises, east or west, over water (on islands) or on land (cosmic mountains). **Religious Daoism** eventually distinguished three classes of immortals: of heaven, earth and man. Individuals can ascend to heaven to become heavenly immortals. Sometimes the whole household – rooms, dogs and chickens – can come along. Aided by some magical dust, this happened to Huainanzi: he went straight to heaven in broad daylight.

Earthly immortals live in grottos, caves and mountains. The lowlier human immortals are those who live among men, work and finally are able to discard their bodies for good. That includes those who take drugs (of cinnabar and mercury) and 'left their cocoon' of a body, and those who actually die and are interred but then mysteriously disappear, leaving behind an empty tomb with a sandal or some other token of the presence which was once there.

Further reading

Bauer, W. (1976) *China and the Search for Happiness*, New York: Seabury.

Cahill, S. (1993) *Transcendence and Divine Passion: The Queen Mother of the West in Medieval China*, Stanford, CA: Stanford University Press.

Yu Ying-shih (1964) 'Life and Immortality in the Mind of Han-China', *Harvard Journal of Asiatic Studies* 25: 80–122.

WHALEN LAI

afterlife, Chinese: inferno

The layout of Dante's Inferno, with different hells for different sins and with a degree of rational complexity not visible in early Christian writings, is possibly influenced by Buddhist conceptions. Buddhist hells were all meant to be purgatories, not locations of eternal damnation and hopelessness. Those hells underwent some modification in Chinese thinking. By the time of the Ming dynasty, the Chinese pre-Buddhist notion of 'earth prisons' also overwhelmed the more rational Buddhist conception of purgatories. The new chambers of torture under the Ten Kings (magistrates of hell) took into account less the power of prayers and contrition and more the power of paper money, paper gold and paper silver sent down to bribe the minor hell officials, although not the impartial ten kings themselves. As the underground bureaucracy is fallible like the earthly one and likewise the incarceration is meant to punish and not to rehabilitate, those recent hells lost their educational (purifying, redeeming) function. These hells were now the very antithesis of the paradises.

Further reading

Matsunaga, D. and Matsunaga, A. (1971) *The Buddhist Concept of Hell*, New York: Philosophical Library.

WHALEN LAI

afterlife, Chinese: kuishen

Kuishen is the term for spirits, usually linked through the principles of *yin–yang* with the two souls in man. But the meanings of the words seem to have shifted historically. God or *shen* once referred to heavenly spirits who were never men, while ghost or *kui* is simply the human dead. One script shows 'light' and 'thunder/lightning', and the other 'a man with a death mask'. But this distinction became blurred because, in the Shang and early Zhou dynasties, the nobles (as in Homeric Greece) were descended from gods so that the ancestral dead of the elite might claim that higher heavenly destiny. It is doubtful that the ordinary people, who had no surnames, were not even allowed a decent burial and had no ancestral shrine, could then become gods. This class distinction, when extended to *post mortem* fates, was in turn blurred. By the time of **Confucius**, some would argue, the two soul theory was democratically applied to all men. The idea of the two souls could not help but remain naively anthropomorphic: both souls have the appearance of the deceased, although the god is more like light and the ghost is quasi-material (it can knock over tea cups). They eat different food: gods relish the aroma of the burnt fat of the sacrificial animal, while ghosts dine on blood and meat or worse.

To avoid such crude realism and to adjust the spirituality to fit the naturalism of Song Neo-Confucian thought (see **Neo-Confucianism, concepts**), Zhang Cai reduced 'gods and ghosts' by way of homophones in the Chinese language to the 'stretching' and the 'contracting' of the *qi* (material force, vital energy). That calculated rationalization might be opposed to superstition, but it did little to change ritual practice or common sentiment.

WHALEN LAI

afterlife, Chinese: purgatory

The cult of purgatory is of interest to moral philosophy, for in both East and West it accentuates the mutual dependence of the living and the dead. In China, the cult of the Ten Kings (tenth century CE) defined the Chinese purgatory cult for the last millennium. This tribunal of ten judges, each overseeing a hell, displaced the singular authority of Yama, the India Buddhist lord of the underworld, now made fifth of the ten. This may reflect the Tang state policy of replacing a single Leader of the Sangha (Buddhist community) with a board of Ten Worthies (monk prelates). The vacancies being not always filled, local monasteries ended up under the control of the civil authorities. The Ten Kings cult is distinct from the canonical cults in that it allows family members to bypass clerical help and make direct appeal to these judges in the hell bureaucracy. Paper money to oil the sluggish machine of justice became the currency of salvation even before paper money became the currency in Song society.

Having the cultic practice tied to the ancestral cult revived the concept of corporate responsibility. This undermined the Buddhist teaching of individualized **karma**, but contributed to the ethos of 'mutual dependence between the living and the dead'. Though never replacing the older mortuary service, it coincided with the spread of the money economy. No respectable Buddhist monk would touch those ubiquitous 'paper gold ingots and silver bullion', and many Confucian moralists inveighed against the gross commercialization of salvation. Yet this pay-off mentality informed also the 'moral ledgers', balance sheets of personal merits and demerits, which also needed no ecclesiastical overseership and which are credited by some thinkers with indicating an advance in moral autonomy.

Further reading

Teiser, S. (1997) *The Scripture of the Ten Kings*, Honolulu, HA: University of Hawaii Press.

WHALEN LAI

afterlife, Chinese: wandering ghosts

Wandering ghosts are another category of unmourned and unquiet dead. Urbanization in the late Ming period burdened the cities with an uprooted, urban working poor who often died unclaimed, unburied and unmourned. Guilds, charities, and sectarian religions took care of some; the local deities' beggars graves took care of others. Buddhist charity in particular supports feeding the hungry, clothing the naked, and tending to the sick and the dying. But there were enough left to fuel a new wave of ghost stories. Luo Rufang, a 'left-wing' disciple of Wang Yangming, believed in reported encounters with ghosts.

Meanwhile, as the segmented clan-based society still left many dead strangers unattended, the cult of the Eternal Parents, who claimed all mankind as their offspring, flourished. The Eternal Parents were believed to be calling back every lost and forgetful soul. Similar cults grew up elsewhere. In prewar Japan, a mission to take care of the nameless dead started the Reiyukai (Friends of the [Dispossessed] Dead), which has now grown into the Rissho Kosei Kai. In postwar Korea, the Eternal Parents have reappeared in Reverend and Mrs Moon and their nativistic Unification Church (see **new religions in Korea**).

Shape-shifters are survivals from early chthonic (underworld) demigods, gods of nature who change with the seasons. The classic shape-shifter in Greece is Proteus, a minor sea god, water being essentially 'free form'. Quite a number of ghosts named in early China are variants of the same murky, shapeless, mutable phantom. A later famous shape-shifter is the Monkey King in the novel *Journey to the West*. A beast of the forest, converted to protecting the pilgrim Tripitaka, the shape-shifting Monkey became the all-round guardian of the faithful and a ubiquitous demon-queller.

WHALEN LAI

afterlife in Chinese thought

In early China, the dead ended up in a gloomy underground called the Yellow Spring (yellow is the colour of earth). Together with the sky above it and water beneath it, this was a model of a three-tiered division of the universe. 'The Yellow Spring' itself refers to some subterranean fountain or source. At the same time, the souls (of the elite, at least) rose up skyward to a court of the Lord on High around the polar star. This is schematized into the theory of the two souls, with the *yang* soul going up and the *yin* soul staying under.

By the time of the Han, an underground bureaucracy had arisen similar to the one on earth. Its headquarters were under Mount Tai in the east, headed by a magistrate who receives petitions. Hells called 'earth prisons' also appeared. On the bright side, blessed souls could go to the paradises, east to the Isles of Immortals or west to the Peach Garden of the Queen Mother. Cultic practices show how different afterlife destinies ran concurrently. The elite had tombs designed as permanent homes and shrines like mansions, even though the tomb paintings might also show the dead journeying to some paradise. Meanwhile the use of guardian figures and pre-burial exorcism plus buried documents show how the burial plot was cleared of evil spirits. But the buried dead are also confined; they were not meant to come back to haunt the living.

At the time of **Confucius** there were held to be two souls to each man. One goes up to heaven as 'god' and is invited down to dwell in the ancestral tablet during worship. The other remains around the grave to haunt people, and requires food lest it become a hungry ghost. Ancestors were once thought to live in a court around the polar star, where they mediated on their descendants' behalf before the Lord on High. Grave goods of Shang and Zhou show that the elite dead needed material comfort, and that they were believed to live inside the well-sealed tombs, but there is also Han tomb iconography depicting the dead making their skyward journey to the sun or the moon, perhaps on their way to become some god, immortal or cosmogonic figure. Tomb icons and figures included guardians to keep the dead in place and instructions to guide the soul to the other world.

Immortality was the goal, but was not dependent on an afterlife after death. Some men simply did not die, and some were given the elixir of immortality while alive. The First Emperor and the early Han rulers sought personal access to the immortal isles in the sea to the east before they died. The later Han turned more to the paradise of the Queen Mother in the west; **Laozi** (Lao-tzu) supposedly went west to such a place

Originally, the grave was for the disposition of the polluted dead. A friend or a lover might thus weep privately at the grave; they would not do so at the ancestral shrine. The shrine is set away from the polluted tomb; it is where family and clan keep up the living memory of the departed ancestor. However, the Han Emperor Wu changed that spiritual geography when he combined his royal shrine and his royal grave. Before his death, he built a shrine directly on top of his grave. This was meant to ensure a continual glorification of his earthly life and career. Others followed suit, creating the idea that the tomb is the permanent home of the deceased. This conflated the confinement of the polluted dead with the soul's passage to the beyond, and also conflated the celebration of the earthly achievement of the dead with the affirmation of life originally meant for the bereaving. By the time of the later Han, the tomb murals had become more secular. They are not about the destiny in store in the other world; they recall instead the man's life and times on earth with scenes from his estate and farm. Some scenes are for the dead; some are for public display in the shrine. How all these were supposed to affect the concept of soul or souls and the afterlife is not yet entirely clear.

The first **geomancy** (divination) text appeared after the Han, but the practice may well predate this time. The use of geomancy would show how both the tomb and the home are equally real 'residences' (geomancy is used for both) and why the tomb deserves as auspicious a site as the home above ground. Unease below might affect the living above. But another set of post-Han evidence – documents to keep the tomb suppressed and the dead in place – tells another story. The texts seem to assume there is just one soul (not two) and they are preoccupied with the negative dead, i.e. keeping the dead from wandering off. Buddhism was then spreading, and it would change the concept of the afterlife, of souls and burial practices. There are still later (non-Buddhist) practices that involve buying up underground land

leases to ensure that the dead man's residence would not be disturbed.

Further reading

Feuchtwang, S. (1992) *The Imperial Metaphor: Popular Religion in China*, London: Routledge.

Goodrich, A. (1981) *Chinese Hells*, St Augustine, FL: Monumenta Serica Monography.

Lai, W. (1994) 'From Protean Ape to Handsome Saint: The Monkey King', *Asian Folklore Studies* 53(1): 29–65.

—— (1997) 'Rethinking the Chinese Family: Wandering Ghosts and Eternal Parents', in R. Carter and S. Isenberg (eds), *The Ideal in the World's Religions: Essays on the Person, Family, Society and the Environment*, St Paul, MN: Paragon House, 253–71.

Loewe, M. (1982) *Chinese Ideas of Life and Death: Myth, Faith and Reason in the Han Period (202 BC–AD 220)*, London: George Allen and Unwin

Overmyer, D. (1976) *Buddhist Folk Religion*, Cambridge, MA: Harvard University Press.

Watson, J. and Rawski, E. (eds) (1988) *Death Ritual in Late Imperial and Modern China*, Berkeley, CA: University of California Press.

WHALEN LAI

AFTERLIFE IN INDIAN THOUGHT *see* karma; atman; samsara

afterlife in Islamic philosophy

The basic objection with the notion of a personal afterlife by many of the *falasifa* is that they could not see what could be meant by personal identity on the disappearance of the body. The idea that both body and soul are resurrected on the day of judgement, that the body which rots can be resuscitated, as it were, is to go against the laws of nature. But could not God do this in the form of a miracle? Again, many of the philosophers would have problems with this, in that the laws of nature are assumed to be equivalent to the principles of reason, and were God to go against them he would be contravening the laws of reason itself. If a soul, but not a body, survives the death of the body, something which was accepted by many *falasifa*, we have the difficulty of working out whose soul it is. It is not at all obvious that the surviving soul is the soul of the person whose body has perished. This is because the principle of identity of persons and their souls is the body which that soul originally belonged to, and also the specific and unique memories, thoughts and experiences of that soul, and so on death the particular soul cannot continue in existence with its mental history unaffected by the demise of the body. Souls require matter, and if resurrection is only spiritual, there is nothing for the form of the person, the soul, to inform and shape. It is worth noting that the specific objection which **al-Ghazali** makes to the *falasifa* on the nature of the afterlife is not that they deny an afterlife, but that they deny it is physical, and he agrees that something has to be said about the nature of matter in that afterlife, as is recognized by the Qur'an when it describes in highly corporeal terms the nature of the afterlife. The problem which remains, though, is that while we may imagine dying, and then our physical resurrection through divine intervention, this does not according to philosophers like **ibn Rushd** prove that such an event is possible even for the Almighty.

Further reading

Leaman, O. (1997) *Averroes and his Philosophy*, Richmond: Curzon.

OLIVER LEAMAN

agrarianism

With over 95 per cent of its population working on farms, traditional China ascribed to a farm-based economy and an agrarian ideology. The basis of society was agricultural. The farmer was rated second only to the **scholar** in the official hierarchy of the four classes: scholar, farmer, artisan and merchant. Basic self-sufficiency was an ideal. 'Men plough and woman weave' was the basic dictum.

Trade in luxury goods was frowned upon; interest in things curious or new was deemed uncalled for. In some measure, this influenced the Ming decision to close the nation, discourage foreign trade, and even scrap its ocean-going fleet. The technological know-how for building those large vessels was subsequently lost; but the advance in commerce could not be stemmed as merchants gained prominence by the late Ming period (seventeenth century).

'In the morning I go out to till the field; in the evening I come home. Heaven is high and the ruler is remote – what care do I have for them?' This ditty captures the hope of the Chinese peasantry, who longed for a simple, self-contained life with not even a tax collector to bother them. In the time of **Confucius**, a 'school' called Agriculturalist had existed. Confucius encountered two such early hermit farmers who judged the Master's agenda for changing the world to be futile. **Mozi** also debated with a man who lived solely by farming and making pots. The First Emperor, during the burning of books, excluded the practical writings of this school.

The Agriculturalist school envisaged a utopian society that has a king but no ministers or scholar officials. The king farmed his plot of land like everybody else, while the queen wove like any other wife would. The king ruled by example of virtue, not with force; on merit, not through inheritance. His only real duty seems to be inspecting the fields and setting up a granary to take care of lean years. Built on total trust, society knows no crime and no punishment. Luxury is uncalled for, useless things are ignored and even the food should taste bland. The ideal size is a 'small community with few people'. The ***Laozi***, describing a similar system, paints such a self-contented picture that people do not even feel the need to visit a neighbouring village over the hill. Even if the society has carriages, it has no urge to use them; it has arms but never employs them, possesses troops but does not go to war. It does not even keep written records; people just tie knots to aid memory. These face-to-face communes frown upon 'making vows', a requisite of any pact sealed between strangers. Vows only show a basic lack of trust.

The figurehead of the Agriculturalist school is Shen Nong, the Divine Farmer. Agriculturist teachings were attributed to him in the fourth century BCE. He was placed in high antiquity above the sage-king Yao, Shun and Yu (see **sage-king**), and soon after Fu Xi, the first man. The three Sage-Kings are the trio who supposedly would abdicate their rule so that it might be passed on to the new man of virtue (the **sage**) instead of a dynastic heir (the son). This idea of 'philosopher kings' rose in the Age of the Philosophers (the Warring States period) as a criticism against dynastic succession (private reign instead of truly public-spirited reign). The three sage-king rule assumes class distinction and social hierarchy (a ruler, a court of ministers, the ruled). To project a more egalitarian reign, the Divine Peasant (the agrarian utopia) has to be put ahead of the trio. He supposedly came after the so-called First Man, a mythical figure who with the First Woman procreates humanity. Sometimes he appears as the Fiery Emperor ahead of his brother, the **Yellow Emperor**. The Yellow Emperor superseded or defeated him in war, then instituted centralized rule and championed cultural advancement.

Outstripped and outdated by the march of civilization, this romantic agrarian ideal survived well into the Han, being kept alive by legend of one such idyllic community surviving in some hidden valley among the hills. A visitor chanced upon this shangri-la at the end of the Peach Blossom Stream. He stayed, then returned with a report, but was unable to find his way back there again. Such reports helped keep the ideal of a perfect simple agricultural community fresh in people's minds.

In their rejection of civilization and its artifice (falsehood), Daoists seek to return to a natural state and romanticize the primitive society. Thus Laozi called for a 'doing away with humaneness and righteousness' and a 'return to compassion and filiality'. Humaneness and righteousness are urban, civic values; compassion and filiality are ideas of a simpler time. He called also for 'emptying the mind and filling the stomach', which is another critique of high culture and a return to the basics. Social fashions only breed social ills: 'Treasure gold and silver and there are suddenly more robbers; value beauty and there is suddenly this perception of

ugliness.' So abandon the sophisticated, he argued, and embrace the unadorned. The learning of the Way is to unlearn what civilization has taught; it is daily attrition of what had been a daily growth in human knowledge.

If Laozi idealized the 'small state with few men' and villages so self-sufficient as 'not even bothering to visit another one close by', then **Zhuangzi** went even further back, to the forest of hunters and gatherers, with footprints from unknown others, a time with no writing and no records. Sometimes only total regress to the time of chaos would appear to result in a satisfactory rediscovery of the simple life which ought to be lived by human beings. In the twentieth century, **Mao Zedong** aroused the peasant masses and mobilized them for the Communist Revolution.

Further reading

Graham, A. (1989) *Disputers of the Tao*, La Salle, IL: Open Court, 64–74.

WHALEN LAI

ahimsa

Ahimsa is a term from Hindu, especially important in Jain, thought, which means 'non-violence' or not harming. It has had a significant role in Buddhist thought. Jain thought advocates avoiding harm to any form of life whatsoever. Non-violence became an ideal of Hindu life, leading to the low status of those who were left with the **caste** role (**dharma**) of killing or working with dead animals. Non-violence was turned into an important political principle in the twentieth century by Gandhi, who advocated its application to economic life through what he called 'bread labour', the participation of everyone in simple productive work, preferably involving the production of food. This brings out what is the positive side of non-violence for Gandhi, which is charity and love for all. It involves three vows, the vow of self-control, fearlessness and universal social equality, including untouchables. Gandhi spends a lot of time in his writings explicating the notion of *ahimsa*, and arguing that in certain situations one would be permitted to cause some harm to prevent greater consequent harm.

See also: karma

Further reading

Bondurant, J. (1965) *Conquest of Violence*, Berkeley, CA: University of California Press.

Chapple, C. (1993) *Nonviolence to Animals, Earth, and Self in Asian Traditions*, Albany, NY: State University of New York Press.

Chatterjee, M. (1983) *Gandhi's Religious Thought*, Notre Dame, IN: Notre Dame University Press.

—— (1996) *Studies in Modern Jewish and Hindu Thought*, London: Athlone Press.

Gandhi, M. (1989) *The Collected Works of Mahatma Gandhi*, Delhi: Government of India Publications.

OLIVER LEAMAN

Ajivikas

The Ajivikas were an Indian renunciatory movement practising extreme asceticism, founded in the fifth century BCE in the vicinity of the Gangetic plain by Makkhali Gosala who, according to the **Pali Canon** scriptures of Theravada Buddhism, was an approximate contemporary of both the Buddha Gautama (*c.*450–400 BCE) and Mahavira, the founder of **Jainism**.

The naked monks who followed Gosala endured exacting penances, finally starving themselves to death. They were believed to possess thaumaturgical and predictive powers. Their most significant support derived from wealthy merchants. Both Buddhists and Jains regarded them as competitors for religious patronage. In the Seventh Pillar Edict, the North Indian Mauryan emperor Ashoka (268–232 BCE) ranked them third after Buddhists and Brahmins in the list of groups which he supported. After the end of the Mauryan dynasty in 185 BCE they seem to have entered a terminal decline, perhaps connected with the Buddhists' more manageable approach to soteriological praxis.

According to the *Samanna-phala-sutta* of the Theravadin Buddhist Digha Nikaya, the Avjivikas held that:

There is neither cause nor basis for the moral faults of living beings; they become corrupt without cause or basis. Neither is there cause or basis for the purity of living beings; they become pure without cause or basis. There is no action, no strength, no courage, no human endurance or prowess (that can affect one's future in this or later lives). All beings that breathe, are born and live are without power, strength and virtue, but are developed by destiny (*niyati*), chance and nature and experience joy and sorrow... There are 8,400,000 aeons of time through which unenlightened and wise alike will take their course and make an end to sorrow. There is no question of bringing unripe *karma* to fruition, nor of exhausting *karma* already ripened, by virtuous conduct, by vows, by penance or by chastity. Transmigratory existence is measured as with a bushel, with its joy and sorrow and its appointed end. It can neither be lessened nor increased, nor is there any excess or deficiency of it. Just as a ball of wool will, when thrown, unwind to its full length, so fool and wise alike will take their course and make an end of sorrow.

Clearly the Ajivikas believed in strict determinism by natural causality, thus differing from the Brahminical, Buddhist and Jaina approaches to moral responsibility and consequentiality which, for all their metaphysical differences, agree in recognizing the significance of human efforts, intentions and the reality of free will. They were not physicalist reductionists about the mental and it is the case that their conception of **nirvana** was of a state of blissful isolation of the soul disconnected from matter and divorced from other souls.

Further reading

Basham, A. (1981) *History and Doctrine of the Ajivikas*, Delhi: Motilal Banarsidass.

CHRIS BARTLEY

akasha

Akasha, the Sanskrit concept for space, is sometimes counted as one of the uncompounded *dharma*s in

Hinayana Abhidharma. It is thus regarded not so much because pure extension has no limit (that describes the trance state of infinite space, another uncompounded *dharma*), but because space cannot be subdivided into any multiple components. Because Chinese Buddhists took *akasha* to be like the Daoist 'vacuous **emptiness**' and because Daoists loved a potent but shadowy being, the Bodhisattva Akashagarbha (space-womb) won a cult following in East Asia as it would not in Central Asia or India. Northern Zen **meditation** used the metaphor of empty space for realizing emptiness. Southern style Chinese landscape painting turns the common 'fear of the void' (as in 'nature abhors a void') into a love affair with the mists and clouds.

See also: space and time, Indian theories of

WHALEN LAI

alaya-vijnana

Early Buddhism analyses human lives into five constituents: matter, sensations, perceptions, volitions and conscious acts. Consciousness is of six types, five involving the sense-organs and a sixth (*mano-vijnana*) concerned with their deliverances. Consciousness is not a unitary and permanent principle but a series of momentary episodes, each conditioned by its immediate predecessor. It is a cardinal tenet of early Buddhism that the enduring soul (*atman*) postulated by the Brahminical Upanishadic traditions as the core of individuality and principle of continuity through the series of lives is a fiction. Nevertheless, they uphold the morally retributive *karma* theory to the effect that motivated and intentional actions generate good and bad latent potencies that must be exhausted in future spheres of experience. In the absence of a soul, some other principle must be invoked to serve as the vehicle of those potentialities. The Theravadin tradition posits a category called the '*Bhavanga* mind' which is a subliminal mode of consciousness. At the initial instant of a new existence, what is termed *patisandhi* consciousness, which is not substantially identical with consciousness belonging to the previous life, arises as conditioned by past actions, intentions, dispositions

and memories. *Bhavanga* immediately succeeds *patisandhi* and replicates its content which is relative to the previous life but neither identical to nor totally distinct from it.

Theorists of the idealist Yogachara school postulated a 'storehouse consciousness' (*alaya-vijnana*) as the receptacle for the latent energies ('seeds': in Sanskrit, *bija*) produced by morally significant actions. Although it is anachronistic to call the *alaya-vijnana* 'the subconscious', this characterization has the merit of explicitly differentiating it from the ordinary category of mental awareness (*mano-vijnana*).

CHRIS BARTLEY

anatta

The term **anatta** represents the Buddhist denial that the subject of thoughts, feelings, actions and their consequences is a permanent, changeless, unified and eternal substance. While it is not disputed that thinking is going on, emotions are being felt, deeds are being performed and their consequences experienced, these events should not be interpreted as implying the existence of a thinker, agent and experiencer understood as a further fact over and above the stream of experiences, a constant, stable subject in the final analysis separable from cognitive and affective states and intentional and non-intentional actions. The supreme goal of Buddhist praxis is the discovery that there is no substantial enduring Self or Soul (*atman/atta* (p)). The tranquility of **nirvana**, that is, liberation from the ultimately meaningless and unsatisfactory series of births after the extinction of the fires of craving, hatred and delusion, consists in living in accordance with this realization.

Buddhists recognize that we are individuals with characters, interests, desires and projects, all of which are the products of past motivated and intentional actions and habits (**karma**) and structured by the factors comprising the synthetic causal nexus of interdependent origination (**pratitya-samutpada**/*paticcha-samuppada* (p)) which is held to account for predictable ethical consequentiality, causal regularities and the relative coherence of personality in the absence of any constant, transcendental entity that might otherwise be considered as serving as a principle of continuity persisting through a series of births in different environments. Those rare individuals who have realized the truth and attained *nirvana* live without craving, hostilities and delusions and are continuously suffused with lovingkindness, compassion, sympathetic joy and equanimity.

Early Buddhism may be seen as philosophically conservative in that it perpetuates a tradition present in some **Upanishads** of analysing the human being into impersonal constituents. It reduces individual personality to a stream of five causally interdependent psycho-physical components (*skandhas*) – matter, feelings, perceptions, dispositions and consciousness (**Four Noble Truths**) – which neither collectively nor singly amount to an enduring substantial self or soul. The latter items and the proper names supposedly designating them may be understood as abbreviated definite descriptions for bundles of causally related transitory experiences.

Enduring selfhood is regarded as a fiction which the experiential fluxes conventionally called persons mistakenly superimpose upon themselves. Acceptance of the 'Soul-doctrine', central to mainstream Brahminical orthodoxy, is criticized as a form of grasping that leads to suffering and anxiety. The postulation of the Soul is uneconomical since the facts of experience may be exhaustively described and adequately accounted for in terms of the fivefold componential analysis of personality which has just been described, coupled with the interdependent origination view of causation.

From the ethical point of view, recognition that there is no abiding self whose interests are in need of protection and promotion leads to a radical reorientation of perspective, a 'decentring' and concomitant diminution of self-concern. Thus the cultivation of a quasi-objective, more impersonal outlook upon experience is encouraged. According to the Brahminical renunciatory traditions (with which early Buddhism is linked despite the differences between the two) disinterested, detached, desireless, unmotivated actions will not generate *karma* and will thus be instrumental in producing a depersonalization. According to this family of views, the process of depersonalization

leaves some sort of integral, independent entity, usually understood as an isolated, featureless and inactive centre of self-awareness, intact. Buddhism, by contrast, sees any concept of individuality 'beyond' the 'I' of everyday experience as a pointlessly speculative view, a product of the conditioning factors such as desire and ignorance, the cessation of whose co-operation is the goal of its morality, meditative techniques and developed insight. Depersonalization, the exhaustion of karmic potency and cessation of individual experience, leaves no residue.

The dominant Brahminical traditions locate identity (*atman*) in transcendental consciousness, construed either as monadic or universal. Buddhists deny that consciousness is unitary and homogeneous. They define it in accordance with the conditions through which it arises; conditioned by the eye and external material objects, it is visual; by ideas and the mind, mental. But an independent real category, the conscious, cannot be abstracted from occurrent transitory conscious states.

Further reading

Bechert, H. and Gombrich, R. (1984) *The World of Buddhism*, London: Thames and Hudson.

Bhattacharya, K. (1973) *L'Atman-Brahman dans le Bouddhisme ancien*, Paris: Publications de l'Institut Civilisation Indienne.

Collins, S. (1982) *Selfless Persons: Imagery and Thought in Theravada Buddhism*, Cambridge: Cambridge University Press

Harvey, P. (1990) *An Introduction to Buddhism*, Cambridge: Cambridge University Press.

Rahula, W. (1969) *What the Buddha Taught*, London: Gordon Fraser.

CHRIS BARTLEY

animals

Animals in Chinese thought are classified as wild or as domesticated. Of the standard 'six domesticated kinds', the first four – fowl, dog, sheep, pig – are like the spirited animals also placed in the four cardinal directions.

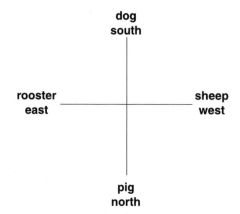

The remaining two species – ox and horse – were domesticated later, and are placed east and west. There are actual socio-economic and culturo-totemic ties to the four regions. The rooster awakes the sun in the east, and the eastern Yi people worshipped the sun-bird. They later became the Shang rulers, and one of their remote ancestors, King Hai, domesticated the ox. The dog is the ancestor to the southern Miao or Yao people; they worship a Dog-King who wedded a Chinese princess. The Yao still wear 'dog-tails' in their gowns. The western Jiang people were shepherds; the script for *jiang* is 'sheep + man', and they worshipped the Divine Goat on a sacred, central mountain. The northern Tungus (the word means 'pig') tribe had a pig totem; the Manchu dynast who later ruled China forced the Chinese to wear their hair in 'pigtails'. The nomads further to the west tamed the horse, and horse-drawn war chariots appeared in late Shang dynasty. The first six days of the Chinese New Year are still dedicated to these six domesticated animals; on the first day, eating chicken is taboo, and so on. The seventh day, called the 'day of man', is dedicated to Man himself.

Barbarians living on the fringe of China are 'fringe humans'. As a class, they are all sub-human canines. Being farmers and not hunters, Chinese cannot understand how the Europeans love their hounds and call the dogs their best friends. Dogs in Chinese villages are basically scavengers; they can be killed and eaten for food (except among the Yao). Man's best friend in China is the ox or the water buffalo. Grateful for their years of service, they are cared for, allowed to age and to die a natural death.

Wild animals have an important place in Chinese thought. Although *homo sapiens* is regularly referred to as 'the most spirited of all species', this was actually a later opinion. Initially in China, the four representatives of the 'spirited species', traditionally placed in the four cardinal directions, were as follows:

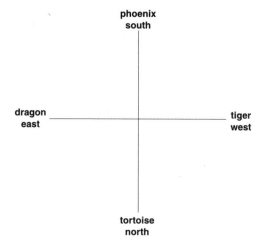

Chinese maps traditionally place the sunny south on top. The four directions are aligned with the four colours, the four seasons, and so on. The species classification is based on the body coverings the four types have. Their locations are based on the structure of the Chinese cosmography: coastal sea to the east, high sky to the south, rising hills to the west, and abyssal water (underground) to the north. *Homo sapiens* in fact is not represented in this set: the **dragon**, not man, is the most spirited of species, being capable of seasonal transformations (into the other species). Only in the Han period is a fifth species with just one member in that class added: the 'naked' species, or man.

The prime members of the four spirited species made regular appearances in China. The Emperor is a living dragon, and may revert to that form when asleep. The Chinese unicorn supersedes the tiger as the favourite icon of the West. The most 'humane' of animals, this long-haired, deer-like animal was sighted by the mother of **Confucius** before she gave birth to this most humane of all men. The fabulous fire bird of the south is frequently blamed for fire storms. Because of its hard armour, the black turtle of the north is called the Dark Warrior, patron god of soldiers in late dynastic China. It once appeared as a tall warrior in black armour to protect Peking (Beijing), the Northern Capital, from invaders.

WHALEN LAI

apoha

Apoha, 'exclusion of the other', is a Buddhist nominalist view of language which dispenses with universals and other properties as the meanings of general terms and substantial individuality, and which does without individual essences as the referents of proper names. The denial by Buddhists such as **Dignaga** and **Dharmakirti** of the mind-independent reality of universals, other properties and relations in addition to their rejection of essential identities raises the question of how general terms apply. According to the *apoha* theory, a natural kind term such as 'cow' does not refer on the basis of the real universal feature 'cowness' (the view of realists such as the Mimamsakas and Nyaya-Vaisheshikas but by excluding everything that is not a cow. The feature common to cows that serves as the grounds for the application of the term 'cow' is simply difference from all those things that are not conventionally designated as cows. Realists such as the Mimamsaka **Kumarila Bhatta** object that the differences require some basis and that objective general features appear to be the best candidates. But for Dignaga and Dharmakirti it is axiomatic that there are no such generalities: the fluid process of instantaneous reality is indeterminate and originally unarticulated relative to human modes of understanding. Thus any human conceptual scheme will be to an extent arbitrary. For Dignaga and Dharmakirti, conceptualization involves a process of dichotomization (*vikalpa*). To posit something is to exclude something else. The linguistic articulation of reality will involve purely conventional stipulations of differences organized in accordance with what is humanly convenient.

This interpretation is consonant with that of the eighth-century Buddhist philosopher Shantarak-shita. According to the *apoha* theory, a word functions by excluding whatever is not the referent. The Indian grammarians distinguish two types of negation:

1 Nominal negation (*paryudasa*), which has positive implications in addition to its negative import. For example, 'One should bring non-Brahmins' means that one is not to bring Brahmins but should bring members of other castes. Moreover, it is here suggested that the other entities significantly share some properties with Brahmins for the sentence clearly means that one should bring human beings who are not Brahmins, not cats and dogs.
2 Verbal negation (*prasajya-pratisheda*) has a purely negative force as in, 'One should not bring Brahmins'.

Shantarakshita appeals to this type of negation in formulating the *apoha* doctrine. It permits him to say that the word cow is meaningful without imputing a positive property common to every cow. His procedure can be illustrated as follows (the example comes from B.K. Matilal). Take a possible world populated by three cows, two horses and a cat, for each of which there is a mental representation for which an exclusion class can be formulated. In respect of the three cows, the exclusion class consists of the two equine representations and the feline representation. Given the extensional identity of the three bovine representations, they could be understood as three tokens of one type of mental representation. *Apoha* theorists such as Shantarakshita deny that the sameness of type derives from the presence of an identical common property in the three individual cows but ascribe it to the fact that they share the same exclusion class. Shantarakshita mentions three plants which reduce fever. He says that this does not mean that 'reducing fever' is a single common property. The mental representation 'reduces fever' arises simply due to the identity of the exclusion class – the class of all properties that do not reduce fever. The three plants may reduce fever for three completely different reasons. 'Reducing fever' is thus a conventional mental representation that is a feature of our human conceptual system.

Further reading

Hattori, M. (1980) 'Apoha and Pratibha', in Nagatomi, M. *et al.* (eds), *Sanskrit and Indian Studies: Essays in Honour of D.H.H. Ingalls*, Dordrecht: Reidel.

Matilal, B. (1986) *Perception: An Essay on Classical Indian Theories of Knowledge*, Oxford: Clarendon Press.

Matilal, B. and Evans, R. (1986) (eds) *Buddhist Logic and Epistemology*, Dordrecht: Reidel.

Sharma, D. (1969) *The Differentiation Theory of Meaning in Indian Logic*, The Hague: Mouton.

CHRIS BARTLEY

AL-'AQL AL-FA''L *see* active intellect

Arya Samaj

Arya Samaj is a traditionalist Hindu organization founded by the Gujarati Brahmin Dayananda Sarasvati (1824–1883) in Bombay in 1875. The movement was fundamentalist in that it insisted upon a return to the ancient religious beliefs and practices found in the Vedas, at the expense of subsequent developments which he identified as distorting accretions to a pure message. Originally an initiate into a cult devoted to the god Shiva, Dayananda reacted against what he regarded as idolatrous customs and renounced conventional society as a young man to devote himself to the individual pursuit of spiritual truth and liberation from rebirth. Returning to the world, he argued that the infallible Vedas alone are the definitive revelation of the one true formless and omnipresent divinity, and denounced most post-Vedic forms of Hinduism, but he accepted the authority of the principle of the Veda-derived *Dharmashastras*, the normative statements of orthodox **caste** Hinduism. He rejected the traditional interpretation of caste as an inherited essential property of the body, like the Buddha Gotama, seeing it as referring to different types of individuals. The Arya Samaj even invented a system of 'purification', allowing the transformation of outcastes into members of the higher 'twice-born' castes. Dayananda opposed the customs of ar-

ranged marriages and the marriage of young girls to older men, which inevitably resulted in a large number of widows. He recommended universal education, with an emphasis on the Sanskritic tradition. The fundamentalism represented by the return to Vedic beliefs and values is consonant with a militant extreme form of northwest Indian Hindu nationalism intolerant of Islam and Christianity.

CHRIS BARTLEY

asatkaryavada

Asatkaryavada is the theory of causation propounded by the Vaisheshika school of Indian philosophy. This is the denial that an effect pre-exists in a causal substrate from which it emerges as a modification or transformation (*Satkaryavada*). The effect is held to arise from its antecedent causal conditions as a whole (*avayavin*) new product over and above its constituent parts. The combination of homogeneous types of substance (*dravya*: earth, water, fire, air) by both the relations of conjunction (*samyoga*) and inherence (*samavaya*) brings about a novel product (for example, a cloth). The relation of conjunction on its own simply yields an aggregate (for example, a bundle of threads). The effect is defined as the counterpart of its own prior absence (*prag-abhava-pratiyogin*). Effects inhere in their parts and substrative causes whose aggregation produces them. This is contrary to the view that production or creation is *ex nihilo*, but it is not the idea that realities can arise from absolute non-existence. It is also clear that the emergence of the effect does not involve the annihilation of the causal factors but rather the termination of their co-operation.

A cause is defined as an invariably concomitant, temporally immediate and indispensable antecedent condition of an effect. There are three factors in a causal complex (*karana-samagri*): the substrative or inherent (*upadana* or *samavayi-karana*) which is always a substance (*dravya*), for example, the threads (parts, *avayava*) comprising the cloth (the whole, *avayavin*); the non-inherent (*asamavayi*) which is always a quality (*guna*) or activity (*karma*), for example, the weaving and colour of the threads; and the efficient or instrumental (*nimitta*), for example, the shuttle and other instruments. The weaver is the agentive cause (*kartri*). Similarly, in the case of pots which were made from the melding of two halves, the instrumental cause is the potter's stick, the inherent cause is the two halves and the non-inherent cause is their conjunction. The potter is the agentive cause.

Among the factors, one cause is singled out as special (*asadharana-karana*) if its operation involves some subsidiary or accessory activity (*vyapara*). A potter's stick is a special cause in that it brings about the accessory activity of the wheel's revolving. A sense-organ is a special cause in that through the exercise of the intermediate *vyapara* of its relation to the object it produces veridical perception (*pratyaksha-prama*). The later Navya-Naiyayikas (agreeing with the mainstream grammatical definition of *karana* as the most effective causal factor (*sadhakatamam karana*)) define it counterfactually as that in the absence of which the effect would not be produced despite the presence of the other causal factors.

Further reading

Halbfass, W. (1992) *On Being and What There Is*, Albany, NY: State University of New York Press.

CHRIS BARTLEY

Ash'ariyya and Mu'tazila

The Ash'arites and the Mu'tazailites were two theological schools in Islam which came to have a significant and longstanding impact on Islamic philosophy. Mu'tazila came from Basra around the beginning of the second *hijri* century (800 CE) and lasted for many succeeding centuries. The main opposition to it was provided by al-Ash'ari (d. 324 AH/935 CE) who turned on Mu'tazilism with all the fervour of a previous follower. He gathered a good deal of support for his claim that the rationalism of the Mu'tazilites needed to be countered by a reassertion of Islamic orthodoxy. Both schools shared a belief in atomism, which the Ash'arites used to emphasize the role of God in bringing whatever happens into existence at every moment.

A major point of contention lay in the appro-

priate interpretation of God's attributes. For the Mu'tazilites, this is to be understood in terms of metaphor, for the Ash'arites in terms of *bi-la kayfa*, i.e. without understanding how those attributes apply to God. The Mu'tazilites understand the Qur'an to be in time and so not eternal, since there would be no point in its preceeding the creatures to which it is addressed. Al-Ash'ari argues in opposition to this view that the Qur'an must be part of the eternal essence of God. It could not have been created since this would make it part of the contingent flow of existence, which would seriously detract from its stature as the word of God.

Much of the Qur'an imples that our actions are predetermined, but the Mu'tazilites interpret this to refer to the afterlife. In this life we must be free to act or not in accordance with virtue, which they understand in objective terms. God has to act justly, and so he must make available to everyone what is in their interests. What it means to say that God is just is that his actions accord with the basic laws of morality. The Ash'arites opposed this view, seeing God as creating himself the principles of justice, so that justice actually means whatever God orders, and evil what he forbids.

Further reading

Hourani, G. (1985) *Reason and Tradition in Islamic Ethics*, Cambridge: Cambridge University Press.

OLIVER LEAMAN

atheism, modern Chinese

Not a term native to Chinese discourse, atheism ('no-god/spirit-thesis') is a typology brought in by Chinese Marxists in their review of China's philosophical discourse. In this view, atheists are perceived as materialists lined up as progressives against the conservative theism of the idealists. **Wang Chong** and **Fan Zhen** became correspondingly the Marxists' favourite materialist and atheist, although both admittedly fell far short of Marx's 'scientific materialism'.

The first modern treatise on atheism was Chang Taiyan's *Wu-shen-lun* (No-God/Spirit-ism), a classic Buddhist critique of Hindu *satkaryavada* (that

the world somehow came from Brahman) rede-
signed for refuting a theistic West (the biblical faith
in a Creator God). Chang's arguments are not new,
being an eclectic combination of Kant and
Nagarjuna aimed at exposing the antinomies in
the doctrine of a Creator God. It includes
challenges to creation within or outside time,
God's omniscient knowledge of the changeable,
His goodness and His flawed creation, His self-
sufficiency and yet His relationship to the world as
the Other, and His omnipotence and man's
freedom to sin. These represent the stock arguments against traditional theism.

Chang listed the three basic options for religious
worldviews: theism, materialism and idealism. He
is a Buddhist atheist who sides with the idealism of
Mahayana **Yogachara** that reduces outer reality
to being a state of the mind. The Marxists
honoured his revolutionary career, but criticized
him for turning to idealism instead of materialism.

Further reading

Lai, W. (1989) 'The Buddhist-Christian Dialogue in
   China', in C. Fu and G. Spiegler (eds), *Religious
   Issues and Interreligious Dialogue*, New York: Greenwood, 613–31 (the appendix contains a translation of the *Wu-shen-lun*).

WHALEN LAI

atman

Atman is the widespread Indian conviction that the
soul or centre of consciousness is an immaterial,
integral and eternal further fact over and above the
series of psycho-somatic experiences that feature in
life in the here and now. It is the endurance,
meaning its wholly present persistence through
time, of this transcendent entity that guarantees the
continuity of an individual through a series of lives.
The *atman* is somehow the vehicle of the good and
bad karmic residues left by prior actions.

All forms of Buddhism deny the existence a
substantial soul, reducing identity to the interplay
of five impermanent constituents of personality
(*skandha*: in Pali, *khandha*); matter, sensation, perception, dispositions and consciousness. Neither collectively nor singly do the components amount to
an enduring, substantial self or soul. The latter
terms, and the proper names supposedly designating them, may be understood as abbreviated
definite descriptions for bundles of causally related
momentary experiences. Enduring selfhood is a
fiction which the experiential fluxes conventionally
called persons superimpose upon themselves.

CHRIS BARTLEY

atomism and occasionalism

Occasionalism interprets reality as a succession of
moment-to-moment occasions. It is found in
Islamic philosophy, in particular in theories and
arguments designed to refute Peripatetic thought,
with the latter's belief in the rationality and
necessity of the structure of the universe. The
value of occasionalism lies in its relating the way in
which the world is to the direct effects of divine
action, something which we do not on the whole
appreciate. Just because we see the world in terms
of subjects and objects, substances and their
predicates, we are not entitled to conclude that
the world is really like that. It is God who provides
us with the ability to see the world in this way; he
helps us find our way around the world by letting
us perceive regularities which reflect ways in which
he is happy for the world to operate. But we must
not ignore his influence on everything, since what
in fact exists are just his own momentary creations,
which we link together in particular ways but
which have in themselves no metaphysical glue
apart from that provided by the Almighty.

The link with atomism is evident here, in that
since reality is basically atomic, it requires someone
to hold these momentary states together to make
objects out of them. It is we who hold them
together by thinking in the right sorts of ways, and
it is the Almighty who makes it possible for us to
think in this way, since he organizes the world,
purely out of his grace, in ways which do not on the
whole go against our way of thinking about it.

Ironically, atheistic Buddhism developed its own
version of occasionalism. Theravada in the south
did not press this issue, but **Sarvastivada** in the
north developed *kshanavada*, a radical position that

breaks all appearances into being a string of *kshana* split-seconds. Because it held that 'everything exists', it avoided ontological positivism with its new reading of the doctrine of impermanence. All things might have a real base, but nothing lasts longer than a split second. Elements come together to form a seeming entity and then immediately disintegrate, leaving sufficient causal eddies for the next split-second configuration to rise and perpetuate this illusion of a continual identity through time.

Chinese Buddhists inherited enough of that sense of momentariness to speak of life-and-death (a synonym for **samsara**) as being from 'moment-to-moment'. Since the Chinese word for 'moment' (*nien*) doubles for 'thought', cessation of momentary thoughts is equated with the cessation of *samsara*. The state of 'no-thought' then recalls the pure mind of a priori enlightenment. This ideology of 'no-thought' appears in a sixth-century Chinese compiled text, the **Awakening of Faith in Mahayana**.

Atomism in China has its most important source in the later Buddhist Abhidharmic system acquired from India. Called 'atomistic' by some, **Abhidharma** is very different from the materialism of Democritus. The Chinese theory of the **Five Elements** is not atomistic: it does not reduce reality to invariable particles, but is a system of correlations mapping out a pattern of change. For this reason, it has also been referred to as five dynamic paths, phases or processes.

Further reading

Lai, W. (1980) 'A Clue to the Authorship of the Awakening of Faith: Siksananda's Redaction of the Word "Nien"', *Journal of the International Association for Buddhist Studies* 2(2): 34–52.

WHALEN LAI

Aurobindo

b. 1872; d. 1950

Political activist and spiritual thinker

Shri Aurobindo Ghose (1872–1950) was a Bengali political activist who became a spiritual thinker and leader. He was educated in England at St Paul's School and Kings College, Cambridge, where he read Classics. To escape the attention of the British authorities, by whom he was incarcerated for sedition and acquitted in 1909, he moved to the French enclave of Pondicherry in Southeast India, where he established an *ashram* which flourishes to this day and devoted himself to writing (in English), yoga and **meditation**. A prolific author, he produced works on philosophy, spirituality, psychology, politics, ethics, culture and yoga. His importance lies in his attempted synthesis of religion and modern science through the interweaving of various strands in classical Indian (especially **Advaita** Vedanta) and Western European thought.

Aurobindo's realist metaphysics was polarized in terms of an ultimately unknowable and ineffable God or Brahman and a mind-independent domain of physical objects. His epistemology is empiricist and directly realistic, but mystical and yogic experience may intimate the existence and nature of divinity. Brahman, understood as Perfect Being, Conscious-Will and Bliss evolves itself into a realm of finitude terminating in material energies. The emergence of limited centres of consciousness follows from the nature of Brahman. Imperfections and limitations implicit in matter are destined to disappear as evolution progresses and matter is more and more integrated with spirit. Human individuals, developing increasingly higher forms of awareness through a series of births, will eventually approximate to the divine perfection. 'Integral yoga' elevates the psychosomatic individual to an 'overmind' capable of communion with the 'supermind' and eventually merging with the Absolute Existence-Conscious-Bliss. Apparent here is the influence of Bergson's anti-materialistic and anti-mechanical theory of emergent evolution, according to which a process of constant change and development governed by a lifeforce overcomes the resistance of matter though effort and subtlety.

Further reading

Aurobindo Ghose (1921–8), *Essays on the Gita*, Pondicherry: Sri Aurobindo Ashram Trust.

—— (1943–4) *The Life Divine*, Pondicherry: Sri Aurobindo Ashram Trust.

—— (1951) *Savitri*, Pondicherry: Sri Aurobindo Ashram Trust.

—— (1971) *The Synthesis of Yoga*, Pondicherry: Sri Aurobindo Ashram Trust.

—— (1973) *Sri Aurobindo Birth Centenary Library*, Pondicherry: Sri Aurobindo Ashram Trust.

—— (1973) *The Foundations of Indian Culture*, Pondicherry: Sri Aurobindo Ashram Trust.

Hechs, P. (1989) *Sri Aurobindo: A Brief Biography*, Delhi: Oxford University Press.

Phillips, S. (1986) *Aurobindo's Philosophy of Brahman*, Leiden: Brill.

Singh, S. (1972) *Sri Aurobindo and Whitehead on the Nature of God*, Aligarh: Vidyan Prakashan.

CHRIS BARTLEY

Australian philosophy

The ancient people of Australia and New Guinea have occupied their homeland for 60,000 years – possibly as long as 100,000 years according to some recent views – and were originally migrants from Asia. Their modern descendants have many languages, little studied at present. Their verbal culture, doctrines about death and legends of the Dream Time are not philosophy in the modern sense, but are not unlike it if philosophy can be considered a cousin of poetry and religion. **New Zealand** seems to have been uninhabited until about 1000 CE when the Maori arrived. The European immigration to Australia began in 1788, and Europeans soon outnumbered the Aboriginals. This immigration was largely Anglo-Irish at first, with various tiny minorities including Chinese, Germans and Polynesians. Since 1945 it has become more cosmopolitan, but still largely European.

Modern philosophy began in the universities that flourished from 1870, notably in Melbourne, Sydney and Adelaide. Unlike India, China, Iran, the Arab world or Israel, Australia has no ancient indigenous written tradition, and there are few classicists or medievalists. Australian philosophy had certain typical themes in its early days, notably anti-idealism and idealism conflicts, but since 1945

it has become quite eclectic, a patch of international philosophy, if a bright and active one. The main cultural contacts are with North America and Europe (very little with the Hispano-Portuguese world), but in recent years not only has Australian trade shifted to Asia, there has also been philosophical contact. Many Asian students have taken Australian degrees, various Asian philosophers have taught in Australian universities, and there is a Jewish community. Authors from Malaysia, India, Sri Lanka and Hong Kong have published in the Australasian journals and East–West philosophy conferences have frequently been held.

Samuel Alexander was the first Australian philosopher of note. He was born in Sydney in 1859, moved to Melbourne in childhood, and was educated at Wesley College and for two years at Melbourne University. He sailed round the Horn to England in 1877 and never returned. He had first-class results at Melbourne and Balliol in classics and mathematics. After periods at Oxford, London and Fribourg-am-Breisgau, he settled in Manchester as professor of philosophy. His father died before he was born, and his mother and aunt migrated to join him in Manchester after twenty-five years' separation.

Alexander's first book, *Moral Order and Progress* (1889), was quite successful, though he later disowned it. His position was of the kind labelled evolutionist, influenced by Green and Sidgwick but critical of them, being drawn rather to Darwinism extended from animals to human society, and to Spencer and Lesley Stephen. His main interests later turned to psychology, metaphysics and aesthetics in such papers as 'The Nature of Mental Activity', 'Mental Activity in Willing and in Ideas', 'On Sensations and Images' and 'Freedom' in the Aristotelian Society (1908–13). His main book was *Space, Time and Deity* (1920). A Jew, his views had much in common with Spinoza, though were not derived from that source. Spinoza had a certain vogue at that time, though Alexander objected that he had an inadequate conception of the importance of time in metaphysics. Alexander took religious emotion seriously, but regarded doctrines as exploratory. The world has evolved and 'emerged', driven by a 'nisus' or striving, from initially bare space and time. These are real, *contra*

MacTaggart, but unintelligible by themselves, and they are aspects of composite space-time. World evolution leads on to matter, then organic life, mind and Deity, these things emerging in a sense similar to that of Lloyd Morgan's *Emergent Evolution*. The theory resembles the vitalism of the day, such as the literary versions of Butler and Bernard Shaw, or Bergson's *Creative Evolution*.

By this time Alexander, never a lover of Oxford idealism, was influenced by Moore's 'Refutation of Idealism' and *The New Realism* (1912), an American essay collection. The externality of relations was held to be important, an object never being constituted by its relations, and especially, what is known is not constituted by the knower, nor by its being known. Alexander published various journal articles and books, including 'Locke' (1908), 'Beauty and Other Forms of Value' (1933), 'Spinoza' (1933) and 'Philosophical and Literary Pieces' (1939). He never married, and had a reputation for being friendly, unpretentious and fond of conversation. There is a statue of him by Epstein in the Arts Faculty of the University of Manchester, and he received the Order of Merit in 1930.

An early Sydney institution was the Australian College founded 1831, and the first Australian published philosophy book was probably *Intellectual Sciences: Outline Lectures Delivered Chiefly at the Australian College 1850–51* by the Reverend Barzillai Quaife, mainly about Sir William Hamilton. The first three philosophy professors were from Scotland. Henry Laurie went to Melbourne in 1882 and was professor 1886–1911. Francis Anderson went to Sydney 1888, where he was professor from 1890–1921, and William (later Sir William) Mitchell was professor at Adelaide from 1894–1923. Mitchell became Vice-chancellor and Chancellor at Adelaide, and died aged 101 in 1962. His were among the first notable books in Australian philosophy, notably *The Structure and Growth of the Mind* (1907) and *The Place of Minds in the World* (1933).

These were the first three philosophy departments. Prior to that, philosophy was linked to other subjects: Classics at Sydney, English at Adelaide. By 1922 there were 1,000 philosophy students at Sydney and Melbourne. The *Australasian Journal of Psychology and Philosophy* (*AJPP*) was founded in 1923, edited by the newly retired Anderson, carrying short pieces by Bertrand Russell ('On Vagueness') and Norbert Wiener ('On the Nature of Mathematical Thinking'). For twenty years it was mainly a vehicle for Australians and New Zealanders, but after 1945 it quickly became an internationally prestigious journal.

W.R. Boyce Gibson (1869–1935) published some books before moving to Australia, but none thereafter, this being the Australian fashion until 1955. He was born in Paris, moved to Bath when aged 13, and studied mathematics at Queen's College Oxford. He taught mathematics at Clifton College, then moved to Jena and Glasgow. He lectured at London colleges from 1897–1907, at Liverpool from 1910–11, and then became Professor of Philosophy at Melbourne in 1912. His books include *The Problem of Freedom in its Relation to Psychology* (1902), *A Philosophical Introduction to Ethics* (1904), *R. Eucken's Philosophy of Life* (1906), *The Problem of Logic* (1908) and *God With Us* (1909).

Between the wars, the leading figure was John Anderson (1893–1962). Professor at Sydney from 1927–58, he edited the *AJPP* (1935–46). His published work was articles, some of which have been collected in *Studies in Empirical Philosophy* (1962) and *Anderson's Social Philosophy* (1979). He had a strong influence on many students, some later more notable than him, but it is not easy now to see where the magic lay. His literary style was gentle, generalized polemic (never personal), and he was said to have a vehement personality. His themes are not now much reconsidered and his theses not very clear. He uses labels a lot, and the modern reader gropes for what lay under them. Bad things were rationalism, idealism, relationalism and dualism; good were empiricism, realism, naturalism, materialism, pluralism, determinism, positivism, and one almost gets the impression they were much the same thing. Mackie, discussing his 'Empiricism' (1927) and 'Empiricism and Logic' (1961), in a paper entitled 'Rationalism and Empiricism' (published in the *AJPP* in 1965) suggests that he did not use the labels in what has become the traditional way, so that, for example, Locke, Berkeley and Hume are rationalists in his view, and so was sensationalism.

What argument there is is occasionally atrocious. For example, 'If there were in me a knowledge of the moon, then the moon would be in me', and 'If there were in A a power to produce B, then B would be in A, and no production would take place' (from 'Realism and Some of its Critics', published in *AJPP* in 1930). So, if a potter could make pots, the pots would be in the potter, and he would therefore fail to make pots. In part there is a strange opinion here, having a connection with Alexander. There is no knowledge in anyone, of the moon or whatever, because there is no containing self. A way into this system is by way of the Stout connection.

This is brought out in Passmore's 'G.F. Stout: 1860–1944' (published in *AJPP* in 1944). Passmore says that Stout and Alexander became personal friends about 1884. Stout succeeded Croom Robertson as editor of *Mind*, handing over to Moore. In 1939, his son A.K. Stout became professor at Sydney, and his redoubtable father migrated with him, having retired from St Andrews in 1936. The senior Stout's last few Australian years were active, with articles including 'Things, Predicates and Relations' (*AJPP* 1940), 'The Philosophy of Samuel Alexander' (*Mind* 1940) and 'A Criticism of Alexander's Theory of Mind and Knowledge' (*AJPP* 1944). The last piece brings out one issue from the earlier period.

Anderson approved of Alexander's realism, but took issue with its conceding too much to idealism in a remarkable short piece, 'The Non-existence of Consciousness' (*AJPP* 1929). Stout objected to both of them, which brought one old wheel full circle for Alexander's doctrines were 'founded on Mr Stout's treatment of perception in connection with impulse or instinctive action' (*Space, Time and Deity* II: 119; Stout's doctrine is in *Manual of Psychology* 3: i–ii). Alexander held that knowledge is a binary relation from a 'conation' to an object. The self does not come into it 'except in a secondary sense'. A hungry man's perceiving food is a hunger impulse perceiving food. Likewise, Anderson says, 'The motive believes that that state of affairs has occurred' ('Determinism and Ethics', *AJPP* 1930). Anderson says that whereas Alexander thinks that the relation of perceiving is the conation relation, so there are just two things, he himself thinks there are three; the conation, the perceiving relation and the thing perceived. Alexander needs a technical notion of 'togetherness' the joining of a relation R

to an object, but Anderson has not a self, but a conation having R to O. One motivation for this curious no-ego theory is to avoid Cartesian egos, which leads to idealism by a short route. The ancient materialist theory of the self as body seems not noticed, though in reviewing the 1927 reprint of *Space, Time and Deity* with a new preface, Anderson attributes to Alexander the view that 'mental processes are those brain processes which have the quality, consciousness' (in 'The Non-existence of Consciousness'). If Anderson is denying consciousness, his variant seems to be that mental processes are simply brain processes, yet apparently without any self at all.

The view common to Alexander and Anderson is that there is nothing whose nature is to know, and nothing whose nature is to be known. *Esse est percipi* is the target here, no doubt, but combined with the view that what knows is not a mind or person as whole, but some particular mental process, which is always a conation.

Anderson built up a more complex position than this between the wars. Realism in contrast to various idealisms such as Berkeley's or Bradley's was part of it. Determinism was rather casually taken for granted, together with incompatibilism ('Determinism and Ethics'), and a theory of ethics ensued that verges on fatalistic non-ethics. It is not the business of moral theory to issue policies or imperatives, but to discover facts, moral facts being no different in kind from those of science. There are no generalizations, since each individual works out his own destiny differently. Not only is there no supernatural, transcendental or moral order, but no mathematical world. There is just one uniform world. Geometry is empirical. The only comment Anderson made when reviewing Ramsey's *Foundation of Mathematics* was that if Ramsey had worked for longer he might have given up the errors of his 'rationalistic' mathematics. Anderson's empiricism recognised only one kind of fact, particular states of affairs found by scientific methods. Philosophy has no subject matter different from natural science. There is only one kind of truth, namely, natural observable particular fact. There is no moral truth and no necessary truth except natural necessity. As Ryle put it, there are only brass tacks ('Logic and Professor Anderson', *AJPP* 1950). Ryle's main criticism was directed at his mathematical and logical theory, claiming that it was too simplified: 'Anderson seems oblivious to any logical differences save the difference between qualities and relations'.

The world of philosophy changed everywhere during the Second World War , and amazingly so in Australia. Between the wars the European and North American world was led by the German-speaking philosophers, together with the new ideas of logic and physics. Little was then known overseas of the debates in the *AJPP*, and the Australian philosophers paid little attention to the new logic or to the new developments in Euro-American philosophy. The war changed that completely.

The *AJPP* continued intermittently through the war, hampered by paper restrictions. After the war there were new editors (Passmore and later Stout). It became the *Australian Journal of Philosophy* (*AJP*), dropping the psychology without really changing focus, since the old psychology had always been what is now called philosophy of mind.

The German language collapsed temporarily as a vehicle for philosophy, as Hitler drove many of his own philosophers as well as the Poles into the anglophone world. Some went to Australia, and part of the new climate included papers such as Falk's 'Morality and Nature' (*AJP* 1950), Baier's 'The Point of View of Morality' (*AJP* 1954) and 'pains' (*AJP* 1954 and 1961) and Herbst's 'The Nature of Facts' (*AJP* 1952). There was also a more peaceful immigration by choice of philosophers of renown, together with the achievement of renown by various Australians. The old insulation had already quite broken down by the time of Ryle's article. The whole world became keen to publish in the *AJP*, and the philosophical world became the village it now is.

J.P. Passmore was an Andersonian student who established a local reputation with 'Logical positivism, I, II and III' (*AJP* 1943–8). This was a close critical study of its subject, with sources documented in detail, doctrines clearly stated, the grilling of them meticulous and merciless, the objections forceful. Here was a performer of world class. Passmore went on to be largely a historian of philosophy, arguably among the best this century, for his *A Hundred Years of Philosophy* (1957) has no match within that period for scholarship, detail, accuracy, sympathy and penetration. Curiously,

Alexander is called an English philosopher, though Passmore does not usually put nationality labels on his subjects, and Anderson is accorded nothing but a bibliography. It was part of the Anderson ethos, not to be patriotic. Passmore's first book was *Ralph Cudmore: An Interpretation* (1951). *Hume's Intentions* (1952) is an incisive brief study of Hume's epistemology. Hume was always famous enough, but little appreciated in respect of the detail, depth, connectedness and ambiguity during the nineteenth century. Careful studies began only in the 1930s, and while Kemp Smith's contribution was a major work, it by no means sorted out the problems, and Passmore quite rightly renewed the attack. Numbers of such books have emerged since, and Passmore's is among the better ones.

Philosophical Reasoning has a historical approach, but Passmore was never 'just a historian'. It is a survey of argument kinds that have been used in philosophical argument since Plato. The topics include 'Catch-22' arguments to show that something could not be done unless it had already been done. Hume's induction argument might be taken that way: you cannot justify induction unless you have already done so. Infinite regress arguments are a related kind, such as the Third Man of the Parmenides or Ryle's regress of volitions. Self-refuting acts of speech or thought, and what to make of them is another theme, as also are ways of proving meaninglessness, paradigm case arguments and arguments about related opposites or polarities. One question discussed is whether there is a distinctive species of philosophical reasoning. Mathematicians deduce B from A to prove it true if A is a truism or has been proved true already. Physicists prove A is false by deducing B from A and adducing experiments to show that B is false. Often neither of these applies in philosophy.

More recently, Passmore's *The Perfectibility of Man* (1970) elicited an amusing review by Monro (*AJP* 1971). It has 'the qualities of the best type of encyclopaedia article', which I trust the reader will now be familiar with. 'Perfectibilism is dehumanising' says Passmore, having distinguished eight different kinds, beginning with ancients who exhorted people to imitate gods or goddesses who were either reprehensible, difficult or logically impossible to imitate. Ploughing on into Christian asceticism and mysticism, we come 'with relief all round' to the Enlightenment, with its governmentalists (who make people virtuous by good laws) and its anarchists, recommending small communities so that people can grasp the results of their actions and understand the people they have to deal with. Then we come to 'inevitable progress' theories, utopias and dystopias. Dystopias give you nightmare societies which should be avoided. Finally, there are the hippies, who have some of the worst features of Christian mystics. Both recommend freedom from care by ceasing to care for anyone. This book, says Monro, 'makes a considerable contribution to the history of ideas'.

J.L. Mackie was born in Sydney (1917) and graduated there in 1938, another Andersonian, though in accord with Andersonism he did not agree with him. He took Greats at Oriel (1938–40) and served in the army. He lectured in philosophy at Sydney (1946–54) and was professor at Otago (1955–9), Sydney (1959–63) and York (1963–7). He was a Fellow at University College Oxford from 1967. His early papers in *AJP* (1947–54) include 'Scientific Method in Textual Criticism', 'The Logical Status of Grammatical Rules' and discussions of Prior's *Logic and the Basis of Ethics*, Herbst on facts and Passmore on Hume.

After the Oxford fellowship he wrote a number of books. *Truth, Probability and Paradox* (1973) is a miscellany of loosely related separate papers. *The Cement of the Universe* (1974) is an intensive close study of questions about causation. Singular causal statements are said to be conceptually and epistemologically prior to generalizations. Counterfactual conditionals are said to be neither true nor false, but to be assertible according to subjectively variable matters such as the availability of evidence. A certain account of the form of causal regularities 'in the objects' is offered, deriving in part from Mill, in terms of incomplete 'gappy' generalizations. In response to Russell's disparagement of causal talk as scientifically obsolete, and his preference for functional laws (roughly, equations concerning mathematically expressed functions of variables), Mackie welcomes the mathematics as developing causal ideas. About the asymmetry of 'direction' of causation, Mackie introduces the ideas of fixity and unfixity to propose an explanation of it, related to the asymmetry of time, the dispersal of order or entropy, and the 'direction' of

explanation. The vexed old question of the necessary connection is treated as needing several distinctions. There is in causation no logical or a priori necessity, and laws do not differ in form or content from 'accidental' generalizations. However, something like a necessary connection is proposed in terms of a distinction of 'laws of working' and 'collocations', the former being associated with continuity and persistence in event sequences. The Kantian claim that all events need to follow rules is replaced by the claim that some do if there is not to be scepticism. There is some discussion of special questions about statistics, legal causation and finally final causes. Some surprising points have emerged. One is that Mackie himself notes that determinism implies on his account of causal priority, that there is no causal priority and a reviewer (Reid, in *AJP* in 1976) claims that this implies there is no causation at all, so determinism is inconsistent. A second is that Mackie's account of necessity in terms of persistence and continuity fails to explain what causation is especially invoked to explain, viz. change.

Ethics: Inventing Right and Wrong (1977) has puzzled many readers, for Mackie seems to attack by queer arguments what had never occurred to anyone. 'There are no objective values', which in some form is familiar enough when construed as subjectivism, non-cognitivism or moral scepticism seems to be taken as 'there are no value objects'. Such an object is that whose existence validates whatever satisfies the vague phrase 'some of the subjective concern which people have for things' (1977: 22). He seems to take seriously the argument that something does not exist because if it did it would be queer.

These objects are said to have the power to make people act, and nothing does. It is obvious that various things such as hunger, greed, lust and need have such a power, so he must be speaking of some special kind of object, but it is not clear what. Mackie maintains that there is no reason to obey a categorical imperative, because by definition no desire of the addressee of it is a reason for that person's obeying it, and this implies there is no reason to obey it.

Mackie was particularly good as a commentator on older philosophers. *Problems from Locke* (1976) is a collection of small scale but incisive essays on the

Essays of the Human Understanding. Hume's Moral Theory (1980) is a careful and detailed study of the third volume of Hume's *Treatise of Human Nature*, similar in scope and subject to J. Harrison's *Hume's Moral Epistemology*.

A number of able and influential philosophers in Australia have published little or even nothing. In 1944 a meeting at Sydney had papers by D. Taylor, D.A.T. Gasking and A.C. Jackson. All later held chairs, Taylor in New Zealand, the others in Melbourne. Gasking and Jackson were students of Wittgenstein, and along with George Paul brought his ideas to Melbourne. Gasking in 'Anderson and the *Tractatus Logico-philosophicus*' (*AJP* 1949) offered an account of some *Tractatus* doctrines in 'Sydney', i.e. the language of the Andersonians, having detected as Ryle was to say later, that they had a lot in common, though not in everything. For example, the positivist account of ethics as not statement-making conflicted with Anderson's view. However, it was wasted effort, as the neo-Andersonians were not committed to defending his views, and things quickly moved on. Gasking published a few more papers, on mathematical truth, cluster concepts and causation, and he and Jackson became the leading figures in Melbourne for some time.

D.H. Monro was a New Zealand teacher of English Literature. Imprisoned for pacifism during the war by his government, he moved into Andersonian Sydney, having written a book on humour (*Argument of Laughter*) and another on Godwin. He became the inaugural professor of philosophy at Monash. Ethics was his only subject, on which he wrote 'Archbishop Fenelon Versus my Mother' (*AJP* 1950) and 'Empiricism and Ethics' (1967). According to his views, a person's morality is a guilt system related to a specific policy complex selected by that individual. It centres on a choice of relatively settled preferences of certain actions over others, lapses from which produce guilty feelings. Nothing imposes uniformity on these individual moralities. One person judges another person wrong in doing something if the first would feel guilt in so doing. No questions of fact are at stake in differences of individual morality. Much disagreement concerning morality so-called is over matters of fact, but may also arise over not knowing one's own views. Monro calls his position naturalistic and

subjectivistic, but where empiricism comes in is not clear.

The university system expanded fast and considerably from 1960. Every large town had an older university, many of which were already large, and now the number more or less doubled with the arrival of Monash and LaTrobe in Melbourne, and Macquarie in Sydney, Flinders in Adelaide, Murdoch at Perth. Hobart was held back by an eight-year dispute over the dismissal of Orr, the chair being blackballed in 1956 and remaining vacant during the dispute. Joske resumed normal activity from mid-1960s, and was the author of *Material Objects*. S.A. Grave was a historian of philosophy, beginning with papers on Aristotle and on Butler (*AJP* 1950 and 1952); his main book was *The Scottish Philosophy of Common Sense* (1960), a study of Thomas Reid and his subsequent influence on Victorian Scotland. Passmore suggests that the American New Realism may owe something to that from their Scottish imports such as M'Cosh. Grave later wrote *A History of Philosophy in Australia* (1984). Two earlier sources of Australia's philosophical past are 'The Beginnings of Philosophy in Australia, and the Work of Henry Laurie' and 'The Beginnings of Philosophy in Australia', both by E. Morris Miller (*AJPP* 1929 and 1930).

A major contributor to the new atmosphere in Australia after the war was J.J.C. Smart. After an MA at Glasgow and the new BPhil at Oxford, he moved to Australia in the late 1940s and immediately began writing short pieces in the *AJP* such as 'Excogitation and Induction' (1950). *An Outline of a System of Utilitarian Ethics* (1961) is a revival of a variant of Benthamism, taking note of the then apparently new distinction of act and rule utilitarianism. (Mackie remarks that the rule utilitarian position was first formulated in the last century by Austin in *The Province of Jurisprudence Determined*.) Smart attracted some attention, and the debate resumed in *Utilitarianism For and Against* (1973) by Smart and B. Williams, Smart still defending the act utilitarian position.

Smart was mainly known as a philosopher of science. His papers on the metaphysics of time, such as 'The Moving "Now"' (*AJP* 1953) established a reputation in that particular area, and he edited a collection, *Problems of Space and Time*, that is still useful for students. He and Armstrong became

the prominent front runners in the 1960s movement known as Australian materialism. In *Philosophy and Scientific Realism* (1963), he maintains that
physicalism is true; phenomenalism is false about
perceptible objects; reductionist doctrines about
the elementary or theoretical entities of physics are
false; spatio-temporal concepts are generally and
mistakenly anthropocentric; science and philosophy together afford a reasonable world view; and
the secondary qualities are powers in objects.

On the secondary qualities, colour is his central
example. Colour is the power of coloured objects to
produce colour discriminations revealed in sorting
behaviour, but not on the basis of... (there then
follows a list of things which are not colours). But
'we must not become too behaviourist about it'
because of a problem raised by C.B. Martin,
namely that the same discriminations could be
made after an overnight total change of colours. To
account for this we must add that we would then
have different colour experiences, which is problematic if experiences are not brain processes. To
meet this, Smart introduces topic neutrality. A
description of a colour experience such as an after
image is topic neutral if it is stated in terms of
stimulus conditions and nothing expressly non-
physical. For example, 'what is happening in me is
like what goes on when...' and then follows
physical stimulus conditions, for example 'when my
eyes are open and the light is normal and there
really is a green thing...etc'. Then from two
claims physicalism is said to follow: (1) that topic
neutral descriptions of subjective experience are
always available; and (2) what goes on in me in
various stimulus situations is a question of fact, to
be settled by plausible reasoning and Occam's
Razor. Dualism and physicalism are seen as the
main alternatives, and physicalism is the best.

Smart's *Between Science and Philosophy* (1968) is a
student textbook, having no unifying thesis. It
discusses chapter by chapter various fairly recent
topics personally selected. There were many such
books after Feigl and Brodbeck's *Readings in the
Philosophy of Science* (1953). The topics include
explanations, laws and theories, induction, space
and time, determinism and machine intelligence.
Smart had no interest in Kuhn or theories about,
as distinct from knowledge of the history of science.

C.B. Martin was an American who arrived in

Australia in the 1950s. He wrote 'The Perfect
Good' (*AJP* 1955), a well-known paper on memory
with M. Deutscher, and *Religious Belief* (1959). This
argues that Christian religious statements (and
perhaps also those of other religions) are in radical
conceptual disorder. The difficulty is not truth, but
the difficulty or even impossibility of understanding
them. Religious language is riddled with conceptual confusion. It is a work of 'meta-theology', so to
speak. For example, 'God' is used both as a proper
name, and as a description of a particular, and this
he says is inconsistent. There is some discussion of
reductionist accounts of religious belief, such as in
Wisdom's 'Gods'. These he thinks make such
beliefs uncontroversial because given the analysis,
the beliefs make no claims about the world, and
make no reference to anything over and above the
world, whereas believers really do believe more
than that. The 'more' is what leads to impasses.

K.W. Rankin was a Scot who moved to Monash
in 1960, and later moved on to a Canadian chair.
Choice and Chance (1961) is according to one
reviewer (Franklin) 'a fine example of constructive
metaphysics in the traditional manner... in sophisticated modern dress'. It is a defence of free will
against determinism. A different view of the matter
from Rankin's is as two empirical matters (the will
is free, all events are determined) and a question of
logic (they are incompatible). The 'traditional' view
is that all three are more amorphous mixtures
where fact and logic have little application, and the
battlefield belongs to conceptual analyses of
responsibility, voluntary action, chance, causation,
substance, personal identity and notably time. Why
time should come into the matter is not obvious,
and this has been thought to be the most original
element of the book. Roughly, the line of argument
is that for causal connection to be applicable to the
world at all, we need the concept of events, which
essentially require time (or perhaps he should have
said metaphysical tense, as distinct from linguistic
tense), and this requires the change from potentiality to actuality. This in turn requires purpose or
intention, and therefore finally indeterminism.

D.M. Armstrong, a product of Geelong Grammar, lectured at Melbourne for some years, then
became professor at Sydney where he was at first a
member of the philosophy department and then of
one of the new departments that emerged following

the former's split. He was the first of the 'book-prolific' Australian philosophers. In *Berkeley's Theory of Vision* (1960) he attempts to show that distance is immediately seen, contrary to Berkeley; that the immediate objects of vision and touch are not distinct; and, against various commentators, the 'new theory of vision' is not a half way house to the doctrines of the *Principles*. If Berkeley were right, we could not have the picture of the world that we do. It has been questioned whether Armstrong and Berkeley use the same vocabulary in respect of the distinction of mediate and immediate perception, neither of them being all that explicit about its meaning. The question crops up again in *Perception and the Physical World* (1961).

The phrase 'naive realism' was introduced by Dewey (1916) to refer to a view of perception not implying knowledge, but it has been changed since to refer to several different theories, usually in recent years the view that what is perceived is always an element of the physical world. Armstrong defends this thesis, modified as that which is immediately perceived, this being taken to rule out immediate perception of sense data if these are understood as essentially mental and not physical. Berkeley's use of 'mediate perception' is in a casual remark about hearing a coach outside the house. Armstrong takes the 'argument from illusion' to be powerful, and to show that 'the immediate object of perception is a sense impression'. The representative realist response is then faced, by him, with a number of objections, even the claim that it is inconsistent. Phenomenalism is similarly objected to. Having sense impressions is not the immediate perception of mental objects or sense data. The only further alternative is direct realism, as he prefers to call it, so that is his view. Sensory illusion is to have a false belief, or at least an inclination to one, that we are perceiving some physical object or state of affairs. To have a sense impression is so to believe or be inclined to believe.

The theme develops further in *Bodily Sensations* (1962). Here, a sense impression is stipulated to be a seeming to perceive something, but declared not to be any kind of object. Sensations, however, do have objects and so are called transitive. Generally their objects are properties, as in the sensation of warmth, or else of facts, as when the sensation of motion in a train is the sensation that the train is moving. Intransitive sensations are those with no object but themselves, such as aches and tickles. Bodily sensations are sense impressions of one's bodily states, combined with attitudes towards them, such as dislike of pain. The motivation for the book seems to be to complete the direct realist view of perception. For that the key thesis is that the objects of sensation are never essentially mental and non-physical, and so experience is claimed to be cognitive, seeming to perceive oneself, together with attitudes.

A Materialist Theory of Mind (1968) resembles Ryle's *Concept of Mind* in structure, in running a general over-thesis about mind in general in tandem with an otherwise compendial structure, its seventeen chapters ranging over miscellaneous special topics in psychology. Mind-brain materialism is the general thesis, but whereas Ryle's dispositional behaviourism was a meaning thesis, and so affected his detailed analyses of various mental things, the identity thesis is said to be factual, and so need lead to no specific opinions about, say, purpose or belief. So the book is a spreadeagled miscellany of variously interesting essays of on the whole a traditional kind. Sometimes it seems to be baseless empirical assertion, as when he says that inference is one belief causing a second. There are no data given about causation, but if it is meant as a truism it seems to lack a provenance, in a theory of meaning.

In *Belief, Truth and Knowledge*, Armstrong offers 'a contribution to a naturalistic account of the nature of man' according to his concluding remarks. His main theses appear to be that belief is a representation of reality; truth is the content of a possible belief that, were it believed, would correspond to reality, and that knowledge is reliable true belief. Belief is at first said to be like a map, then to be a map. Since a map is a literal exact picture of a landscape, this sounds like Humean imagism, but little is said about old objections to that view, about various belief contents that are unpicturable, such as beliefs about meaning, evidence, infinity, numbers and so on, not a few. Then there are conditional, negative, disjunctive contents – it would be hard to have a map that was of something that was either Norway or Paraguay. One class of general facts of this kind is dismissed as non-existent, replaced by dispositions to make inferences. A dispositional analysis would imply the existence of what is analysed, presumably, whereas to claim non-existence puzzlingly abolished mathematics, logic and most of science. There is an echo of the metaphysics of the *Tractatus* in the account of ideas and concepts, which are said to be different (without reference to Kant or Frege, who also said this). The project of Chapter 5 is to analyse the parts of belief, and resolve the complex into its simples. The simple elements of a particular belief are ideas in various relations to each other, both the ideas and the relations representing other things and their relations. Concepts are common to different beliefs. Ideas and concepts are in turn complex and their elements have 'directedness'.

In *Universals and 'Scientific Realism'* (1978), Armstrong recognizes five kinds of nominalism, transcendental realism about universals, identification of properties and relations with particulars, and identification of particulars with collocations of universals. The first volume expounds all these views, and gives reasons for rejecting them. His own view is 'immanent realism', which says that particulars, properties and relations (both higher and lower order) all exist, this constituting an adequate ontology, and this realist claim is a posteriori. Which universals there are is empirical, the 'business of science'. Mathematics, then, is either empirical or does not discuss particulars or universals.

The second volume deals with various questions, one being the relevance of language. Armstrong thinks there is no simple correlation between predicates and universals, since there are predicates unconnected with any one genuine universal, and there may be universals to which no predicate corresponds. There are conjunctive but no negative or disjunctive universals. There are no 'substantial forms'. There are no reflexive relations. Law is second order relation between universals.

This is traditional metaphysics, done with immense thoroughness. The survey of views is wide indeed, the arguments careful and clear, and there is no padding or rambling. Most recent books on these topics are introductions for undergraduates, but this is a treatise for the grown-ups, a treat, and a rare one. Armstrong continues to write, his latest book being *A World of States of Affairs* (1997), which is a survey of constituents of the world,

taking facts or states of affairs as the fundamental constituents.

D.C. Stove of Sydney began publishing in the early 1960s, and subsequently published several books. *Probability and Hume's Inductive Scepticism* is about what in a sense does not exist. In the *Treatise* is a formula about reason not determining belief, that induces modern commentators to 'elucidate' it. This has been done in various incompatible ways, and there is no way to decide which is right. Stove takes it as exclusively about probability explained in what seems a Keynesian way, and Hume drops almost out of sight. He first argues, following Von Thun, that the probability of a conjunction of observables given one of the conjuncts conjoined to a tautology is greater than given just the tautology alone. This is then said to refute Hume's inductive scepticism. It is one way to interpret Hume's elegantly obscure language, but there are other ways, and it is a fact that Hume actually said nothing of this sort. Stove's writing has generally been in epistemology or philosophy of science, and is always argumentative and often amusing, as in *Popper and After*, which is an engaging work of disparagement.

In *Perception* (1977), Frank Jackson presents a substantial new defence of the representative theory of perception, almost entirely about vision. His view centres on five main theses, all variants of traditional positions: the distinction of mediate/immediate is accepted; all immediate objects of vision are mental; physical objects exist but none is immediately seen; they have only primary qualities; and mediate vision is to be in a visual state caused by the seen object. The route to these unoriginal views is original. The mental entities are said to be coloured patches, and are in reality, as they seem to be, and are called sense data. That there are some sense data sometimes immediately seen is more readily accepted than that nothing else is immediately seen, which his realist critics think is a weak point, or rather, the implausible thesis in representative realism. The question raised is what the mediate-immediate distinction is. If it is the distinction between inferential and non-inferential perception, it seems that clear cases of each are found among things not sense data. To see a red reflection in a shop window in a curving road approaching a hidden traffic light looks a plain case of mediate perception of the real traffic light, for you infer the real colour from the reflected image, but seeing your own hands is non-inferential seeing of a non-sense datum. In Berkeley's case, if we concede that clip-clop sounds are sense data, and that the also-heard coach outside is not, it remains a question what the relation is, but inference seems not the key.

Another Jackson view is that sense data are not only in the mind, but also are in real space, having size, shape and position. There seem problems here about privacy and perspective. A palace is the same height at both ends, but a sense datum is not, so they are not the same shape, and so do not occupy the same space by traditional criteria of shape sameness. If so, where is the sense datum in relation to where the palace is? Not, it would seem, in the same place.

The subject of conditionals took a Stoic turn in Frege's work, and then changed direction in 1945 with the new work of Goodman and Chisholm, and later Lewis, Stalnaker and Adams. The major Australian players in the more recent developments were Jackson and Vic Dudman, the second known from various scattered incisive and original papers. Jackson accepts the widely accepted division of conditionals in English into 'indicative' and 'subjunctive', and the problem of giving either or both their truth conditions or assertibility conditions. The standard approaches at present are probability theory for indicatives and possible world semantics for subjunctives. Jackson defends the view, deriving in part from Grice, on conversational implicature, that in indicative cases the truth conditions are those of the Stoic material conditional, and high assertibility is high probability of the antecedent.

Dudman was more radical and sceptical about the way the general problems are set up. Does English have moods? Perhaps there are no subjunctives. That might not matter in itself, but the great open question seems to be what to make of the 'deep' syntax of conditionals, and its relation to logical and philosophical questions, which seem more intricate and diverse than had earlier been recognized. It cannot be, for example, simply a matter of truth or assertibility conditions, if 'if' links what can neither be true nor asserted. One example is conditional imperatives, for example, 'shoot him if he pulls a gun'; the conditional

linkage of verbs, as in 'your house of cards will collapse if pushed'; and more theoretically, the analysis of 'if anyone should push my button, my doorbell will ring', as 'if (anyone push my button) will (my bell ring)', where 'if' is alleged to connect a tenseless protosentence with a tensed one. What should we say, for example, about the tense of conditionals, bearing in mind that in European languages the indications of tense are typically borne by inflections of the main verb, and conditionals do not have one? The work of that greatest New Zealand philosopher, Prior, must come to mind in these matters. One might suggest that the past tense of a conditional, when my doorbell becomes derelict from corrosion of terminals, flat battery, etc., be expressed by a Priorean sentence operator: 'Was ((if anyone push my button) will (my bell ring))'. For example, you used to be able to ring my bell, but at the moment it does not work.

The philosophers of Australia are Australasians, and have interacted internationally extensively and non-parochially with those of New Zealand. Not only is their journal a common property, but their communities have routinely intermingled and developed profitable interrelations. To mention some, we have interactions between Hughes, Londey and Cresswell in the field of modal and other logic.

Deductive logic became a standard element in the teaching of philosophy in 1945, without being in Australia a very prominent research preoccupation. One exception was Richard Routley (later called Sylvan). He worked at New England with Len Goddard from about 1966. Goddard, then a professor, wrote a first-year textbook, *Philosophical Problems*. Together they published *The Logic of Significance and Context Vol. I* (1973), a work of 641 pages, developing the earlier themes of Russell's theory of types, verifications, Carnap and Ryle on category mistakes, and so on. Its object was to produce a formal, consistent, complete theory of the logic of meaning. There is no well-known result in it, and it is virtually unread. Both authors moved on, Goddard to St Andrews and Melbourne, Routley to establish a major reputation by papers in the field variously called relevance or relevant or paraconsistent logic. This began with the dissatisfaction of Anderson and Belnap about 1970 with the thesis of classical logic, first noted by Russell, Lewis and Wittgenstein (in the *Tractatus*) that contradictions imply any arbitrary conclusion. But, the worry goes, there ought to be in reasoning a relevant connection of ideas. Routley co-authored a great deal, with for example Val Routley, R.K. Meyer and David Bennett. Among other writings he edited *Metaphysics and Morality* in honour of Smart, and wrote on green politics (with Bennett) in *The Greening of Ethics* (1994). The theme of paraconsistency continues in the work of Graham Priest of Queensland, such as *Beyond the Limits of Thought*, concerning paradoxes. Paradox has been quite an Australasian theme, considering Passmore, Hamblin's 'Fallacies' and Hughes's edition of Buridan on the liar paradox.

The problems of resource management are of world-wide concern these days, and not of course restricted to philosophers. A major classic on the special spectacular problems of Australia in that respect is by a palaeobiologist, *The Future Eaters* by Tim Flannery. The country has different types of region, much land is managed by few people, and there are diverse threats from powerful influences on the land, such as mining, agriculture and pollution, and in the sea there is the coral disaster and the threats to the Great Barrier Reef. The government has not recently been very green for the usual reason, that green costs money; the people want the money; and their leaders want their votes. Flannery takes the long perspective of the palaeobiologist, and reviews ancient themes such as the 'firestick' forest fire policies of early aboriginals, the unhappy intrusion of European farming methods, the continuing threat from imported pests, combining the antiquarian interest with a political writer's eye for the dangers in the future. Of related interest are the many publications of Peter Singer, one of the founders of the movement to defend the rights of animals and a staunch defender of utilitarianism.

The early *AJPP* carried occasional papers on philosophy of science, and after the war almost every philosophy department had someone active in that field: Smart in Adelaide; Ellis and Clendinnen at Melbourne, where the degree in history and philosophy of science attracted many students; Stove at Sydney; Presley in Brisbane. Ellis published *The Basic Concepts of Measurement*. Another

interesting work in the area is *The Existence of Space and Time* by Ian Hinkfuss (1975). The six topics are: the absolutism-relationism debate of Newton and Leibniz (and Clarke); the properties of space; geometry; spacetime; the peculiarity of the present; and the asymmetry of time. Four paradoxes are said at the end to have been what the book was about, which may be doubted, but they are certainly interesting:

P1: necessarily everywhere there is something, but it is not necessary.

P2: necessarily never does nothing exist, but it is not necessary.

P3: necessarily space and time cause nothing, in which case, beliefs being dependent on causation, we can know nothing of space or time, yet we do.

P4: necessarily time flows 'with respect to itself', but it cannot do this.

The book is directed at philosophy students, but it is also a work of research.

Two topics in epistemology that have in the past been somewhat neglected but have recently attracted attention are evidence from human testimony, and knowledge of one's inner states of mind. *Testimony* (1992) by C.A.J. Coady is a rather diffusely discursive exploration of topics relating to the giving of verbal evidence by witnesses. Various things said about it by past philosophers are reviewed, notably Hume, Reid and Clifford, and various recent views are discussed. The special case of evidence within the constraints of a legal system get close attention as Coady has some knowledge of the law. He gives an analysis of the speech act of testifying (arguably not a very central problem of philosophy). There is an assessment of some general arguments about the general justifiability of accepting testimony, or for thinking it is frequently reliable, such as that if people were not generally reliable, it would be impossible to learn a language, or that people could never understand other people. It is not easy to find decisive arguments about these questions.

In *The World Without, the Mind Within* (1996), André Gallois discusses the nature of a person's knowledge of his own mental or intentional states. This is a modern question with little historical background, but recently has received much attention. The problem is generally that since self-knowledge does not fit the usual kinds of accounts of justification that apply to a sensory knowledge, memory, evidence of a priori knowledge, we have to find some special account of how self-knowledge is possible. Gallois discusses the views of Davidson, Burge, Wright and others, maintaining that we are justified in thinking what we do about, broadly, what we are thinking about. He has recently moved from Australia to UK and published *Occasions of Identity* (1998).

The overlap of epistemology with philosophy of practical things such as action, intention and the will has emerged as a major theme recently. Since Davidson we have, for example, Brian O'Shaughnessy's *The Will: a Dual Aspect Theory* (1980). He distinguishes that which is psychological and mental from that which is psychological and not mental, the second being the domain of the will, and also of sensations and some appetites. One test for this is primitiveness; another is a difference of epistemic relation of the person to these states. These primitive things are objects of consciousness, but not constituents of the stream of consciousness. A test of this is the Dream Test. If a dream occurrence of an experience really is that experience, then the experience is mental and a constituent of consciousness. Strivings in dreams are not real strivings, dreams of pain are not real pain, so they fail the test. Sensations and acts of will are 'quasi-enmattered', whereas what is mental is not embodied in any substance. Sensations involve the physical because they are located in a sense-field or body image, that we are continually if subliminally aware of, and which is part of ourselves. To act purposively we need this, and it also needs to be veridical.

We cannot imagine the body without our having a will. Our experience of agency (the main examples are generally of physical acts) occurs in bodily striving. Acts of will are identified with bodily strivings or tryings. The truth conditions for trying differ from their speech conditions, such as conditions which make it appropriate to say 'I tried'. Trying and succeeding are the same thing. Acts of will are not purely mental volitions, as in

some older theories, and they are not mediated by concepts. This work, of over 600 pages, is the most substantial work on philosophy of action since Davidson. O'Shaughnessy has since turned his attention to perception, and is recently described as one of the major figures in this area. He is making his career mainly in the UK, and some other Australians have done likewise, rather mingling the distinctions of nationality, characteristic of Australian history. As well as Gallois, we have Jenny Teichmann, born in Melbourne, taught at Monash and living in Cambridge, writing books on subjects such as just wars and illegitimacy. Another case is Ray Gaita (*Good and Evil: an Absolute Conception* (1991) and *Value and Understanding: Essays for P. Winch* (1990)).

Political philosophy is debated day by day in Australia with as much vigour as anywhere, the press and various Parliaments being long accustomed to free and blunt speech. Academically, it is taught mainly in politics departments, but Canberra has a strong philosophy tradition, beginning in the postwar period with Partridge. The moral philosophers have said their political say *inter alia*, including as well as people mentioned earlier, McCloskey and Kovesi. Recently the Canberra team has Philip Pettit (*Not Just Desserts* with J. Braithwaite (1993) and various papers) and Robert Goodin (*Motivating Political Morality* (1992), *Utilitarianism as a Public Philosophy* (1995) and with Pettit *Companion to Contemporary Political Philosophy* (1996).

Further reading

Baker, A. (1986) *Australian Realism: the Systematic Realism of John Anderson*, Cambridge: Cambridge University Press.

Brown, R. (1988) 'Recent Australian Work in Philosophy', *Canadian Journal of Philosophy* 18(3): 545–78.

Brown, R. and Rollins, C. (eds) (1969) *Contemporary Philosophy in Australia*, London: Allen & Unwin.

Grave, S. (1984) *A History of Philosophy in Australia*, St Lucia: University of Queensland Press.

Mackie, J.L. (1977) *Ethics: Inventing Right and Wrong*, Harmondsworth: Penguin.

Sylvan, R. (1985) 'Prospects for Regional Philosophy in Australia', *Australasian Journal of Philosophy* 63(2): 188–204.

JOHN WILLIAMSON

AVERROES *see* Ibn Rushd

Averroism

The death of **Ibn Rushd** (Averroes) in 1198 saw the end of Peripatetic (*falsafa*) thought in the Islamic world for many centuries, until the Islamic Renaissance of the nineteenth century. But the thought of Ibn Rushd came to have great importance in Jewish and Christian philosophical circles, initially because of Ibn Rushd's great skill as an interpreter of Aristotle. Aristotle was held to be the most important philosopher (the *shaykh al-ra'is* in Arabic, or 'first master'; interestingly, in present-day Iran, this is a term used for **Ibn Sina**) in both Christian and Jewish philosophy, and Averroes was irreplaceable as a clear and consistent interpreter of Aristotle's views. The role of al-Andalus, Islamic Iberia, as a link between West and East was important here as well. In al-Andalus there existed three religious communities who lived in close proximity to each other and who of necessity had a good grasp of Arabic, which for a long time was the main language of scholarly activity and science. When Latin and Hebrew speakers wanted to know what Aristotle's theories were, they found it relatively easy to use translators from al-Andalus to transform the Arabic text of Averroes into Hebrew and Latin. The number of such translations which were commissioned shows how popular Averroes was as an interpreter, and how much demand there was for explanations of Aristotle's thought.

The return of Greek philosophy to the West represents an interesting paralleling of the original translations of Greek philosophy into Arabic in 'Abbasid Baghdad in the ninth century. Then these translations were officially made, often via Syriac by Christians, while in the thirteenth century they were sponsored by Archbishop Raymond of Toledo and Frederick II of Sicily, often via Hebrew by Jews. Although the main direction of the translation movement was on the commentaries on Aristotle, these of course involved a good deal of Averroes' own philosophy, and they led to the identification of Aristotle with particular controversial philosophical theses, such as the denial of the creation of the world out of nothing, the impossibility of individual existence after death and the relatively brisk dismissal of the role of theology and theologians.

The apparent views of Averroes quickly came to be condemned, and in 1270 and 1277 the Bishop of Paris, Etienne Tempier, banned thirteen propositions which were identified with Averroes. The object of the criticism was Latin Averroism, the theory which came to develop an extreme fideism, the thesis that there are different logics involved in religion and philosophy, and that there is no difficulty in accepting that they contradict each other. This came to be known as the 'double truth' theory, which suggested that religion and philosophy could both be true, and yet result in contrary conclusions. Such a theory was held to be controversial, since it meant that religious truths could not be rationally justified, while philosophical truths are irrefutable.

Averroes continued to have his supporters and critics in the medieval period, and philosophers of the status of Aquinas, Albert and Bonaventure regarded him of sufficient significance that they were obliged to deal with his views in their works. With the arrival of Greek texts in the European Renaissance one might have expected that the writings of Averroes would have fallen into obscurity; but the opposite was the case, since the renewed interest in the Greek Aristotle led to renewed interest in his interpreters, and in the Italian universities in the sixteenth centuries there was a revival of Averroism through the debates between Agostino Nifo (d. 1538) and Pietro Pomponazzi (d. 1525). The radical aspects of the thought of Averroes thus went on to play an important part in the philosophical curriculum of the West through the medieval and Renaissance periods, and provided the essential backdrop for the development of modern philosophy in the West.

Within the Jewish communities Averroes came to have an important place, in particular based on his accounts of the links between religion and reason. The translations which took place into Hebrew were often of his independent works as opposed to his commentaries, and so the discussions in Hebrew tended to be more accurate representations of Averroes' real philosophical views. Averroes continued to fashion the curriculum of the Jewish and Christian intellectual worlds long after he fell into obscurity in the Islamic world. The effect of his thought was to prepare the way for the complete separation of religion and philosophy, which allowed Western philosophy to develop into its characteristic form of modernity.

The significant principle established by Ibn Rushd which becomes the central idea of Averroism is that it is possible to come to the same truth in a variety of different ways. Ibn Rushd argued that religion and philosophy, by which he meant a rational way of establishing truth which is not based on revelation, are two paths to the same destination. They are two different ways of doing the same thing, as it were, and the differences are important in that they are appropriate to different kinds of people. For those who are capable of reasoning theoretically, philosophy is an appropriate way of seeking to establish the truth. For those who are less gifted theoretically, or perhaps not interested in working in that way, religion is the right method to follow. This is not to disparage religion, but to point out that (in Ibn Rushd's view) religion is available to everyone, while philosophy is only available to a minority, those who can understand it.

We tend to identify this sort of argument with Ibn Rushd, but in a different form it was also used by a very different thinker, **Ibn al-'Arabi**. The latter argued that we tend to think of the notion of *tawhid* (unity) in ways which do not really make it impinge on our own lives. But if the notion of *tawhid* is taken seriously, it implies that we do not really exist apart from God, that there is not really any us at all, there is just God. When we look around the world we see what we take to be different and discrete things, but really there is nothing except God, given the doctrine of the radical unity of everything, and Ibn al-'Arabi goes into great detail on how we might acquire the ability to see both ourselves and the rest of the world (as we say) as part of God. So we can see the

world both as it normally appears, and as an aspect of God. Both ways of seeing the world are correct, in the sense that there is truth in both these positions. Although in reality there only exists one thing, God, it is not the case that we are mistaken in experiencing the world as existing separately from God, or in a differentiated way. We can experience the world in this way, God has made this possible, and we do not get it wrong if we think of ourselves as separate from God, since to a degree we are separate from God. We are separate in the sense that we can regard ourselves as separate, and indeed it is difficult for us to regard ourselves as really part of the deity. Here again we have the idea of there being different routes to the same truth. What the ordinary person believes in his unreflective way is not wrong, but it is not a complete description of the truth either. It embodies the complete truth in a way which makes it possible for him to live his ordinary life, but the philosopher and the mystic know of another way of attaining the truth which is more remote from our notion of the ordinary life. What is important is the idea that there are different ways of doing the same thing, and different paths to the same destination, an idea which has been refined over a long period in Islamic philosophy.

Further reading

Leaman, O. (1996) 'Jewish Averroism', in S. Nasr and O. Leaman (eds), *History of Islamic Philosophy*, London: Routledge, 769–80.

—— (1997) *Averroes and His Philosophy*, Richmond: Curzon Press.

Schmitt, C. (1979) 'Renaissance Averroism Studied Through the Venetian Editions of Aristotle-Averroes', *L'Averroismo in Italia*, Rome: Atti dei Convegni Lincei, 122–42.

Wolfson, H. (1961) 'The Twice-revealed Averroes', *Speculum*, 373–92.

OLIVER LEAMAN

avidya

Avidya (in Pali, *avijja*), or 'ignorance', marks the absence of knowledge (*vidya*). The Chinese render it as *wuming*, which can double as 'absence of light or illumination' and thus 'darkness'. Darkness has however a positive meaning in Chinese. *Xuan* connotes the 'dark mysteries', and the Neo-Daoists were known as the 'dark scholars' (see **Neo-Daoism**). In the West, mystical insight has just as often been compared to darkness as to light, the Cloud of the Unknowing being one example. In the tradition of Sengzhou, who wrote on the indescribability of wisdom, the Japanese writer D.T. Suzuki can speak easily of Zen as the 'knowing of not-knowing'. Non-dual wisdom is not cognitive knowledge, and it may often look like ignorance and be rejected by those who are not able to grasp its deeper meaning.

The Buddhist twelvefold chains of causation leading to 'old age and death' begin with ignorance. Attaining **nirvana** requires the removal not just of **karma** but also of ignorance by wisdom. But ignorance is not some Aristotelian 'first cause'; privation (*avidya*) disqualifies it from that role, not that the Buddha approves of a single cause or of a substance at the basis of reality. So when ignorance is said to be 'beginningless', it implies anything but cosmogony. Yet that is how the **Awakening of Faith in Mahayana** would treat its key concept of a 'beginningless ignorance'.

WHALEN LAI

Awakening of Faith in Mahayana

A summation of the essentials of Mahayana teachings, the *Awakening of Faith* is not about a devotional faith. It is about the arousing of a confidence in one's innate Buddhahood or Original Enlightenment. Attributed to Ashvaghosa, the text appeared in China *c.*550 CE to influence all future Chinese Buddhist schools. Since no Sanskrit text or reference to it exists, the work has long been suspected to be a Chinese compilation. Known to contain Chinese innovations, it is organized along a numerical sequence: there is One Mind that encompasses the Two Aspects of Suchness (basis of **nirvana**) and **samsara**; subsumes the Three Greatnesses (the Three Bodies of the Buddha); and endorses the Four Faiths (taking refuge in the Three Jewels plus Suchness itself) and the Five Practices (the 'six perfections' of the **bodhisattva** minus the last one, wisdom, which is already assumed). Suchness or the nature of things such as it is (free from illusion) is the Buddhist goal.

The text also traces the devolution of the pure Suchness (i.e. enlightened) Mind, through nine steps, into becoming the deluded subject-object consciousness. It rewrites a key metaphor of 'water and wave' taken over from the *Lankavatara Sutra* so that the phenomenal world that we now see is said to be created by the inconceiveable perfumation (interaction) between the innate enlightenment and the beginningless ignorance. The *Lankavatara Sutra* is a late Mahayana sutra combining the ideas of the storehouse-consciousness and the Buddha-nature. Since deluded consciousness is by its nature changing 'moment to moment', the cessation of that momentary thought process characterized as 'no-thought' (or 'no-mind') is a sure way of recovering one's True Mind. These ideas are responsible for freeing Sinitic Mahayana philosophy from certain basic Indian Mahayana assumptions.

The structure of the text, which is attributed to Ashvaghosha (first/second century CE, although this is highly doubtful) follows a perspicuous path. It starts off by talking about the point of the text itself, which is to free all living things from suffering, to disseminate the true teaching, to support those on the path, to awaken the faith of those just starting, to show how to avoid evil, to instruct in the best forms of **meditation**, and it argues for the practice of reciting the name of Amitabha. There follows a fairly close analysis of the main technical terms of Mahayana Buddhism, and then on the main lines of that path. The mind is shown to consist of three parts, a distinction is made between enlightenment and non-enlightenment, ignorance is discussed, as are the varieties of false teaching available, and their competitors, the appropriate methods to reach enlightenment. Finally, the Mahayana understanding of the *bodhisattva* is explained, and this leads to an extensive discussion of the virtues of Mahayana praxis.

Further reading

Hakeda, Y. (trans.) (1967) *The Awakening of Faith*

attributed to Asvaghosa, New York: Columbia University Press.

Lai, W. (1980) 'Hu-jen nien-ch'i (Suddenly a Thought Rose): Chinese Understanding of Mind and Consciousness', *Journal of the International Association of Buddhist Studies* 3(1): 42–59.

WHALEN LAI
OLIVER LEAMAN

B

Baizhang

b. 749; d. 814

Buddhist philosopher

Baizhang (Pai-chang), a disciple of the Zen patriarch **Mazu Daoyi** (Ma-tsu Tao-i) (709–88), is responsible for the Zen monastic rules which displaced for good the monastic code of canonical Indian Buddhism. Mazu argued that the development of such rules of conduct are important, even though he adhered to a radical 'sudden cultivation, sudden enlightenment' mode. The Zen rules are very strict by modern standards but, when compared with the Indian set, are less austere and more relaxed, less individualistic and more communal. Designed for a self-sustaining order of meditative monks, they blend activity and quietude, making physical labour a part of mental training and circulating the various tasks around even for the abbot. They are perhaps best remembered for the rule, often compared with the Benedictine code, that says: 'no daily work, no daily meal'.

Among the classic *koans* (see **koan**), Baizhang supposedly contributed the one on the 'Wild Fox', which goes as follows. Whenever the master lectured at the Dharma hall, an old man would attend. One day he stayed behind, and revealed to the master that he was a fox in human guise. He was the superior on this mountain retreat aeons ago under Buddha Kasyapa, but was punished with animal rebirth for all time because, when a novitiate had asked, 'Does a great man of spiritual cultivation come under karmic causation?' he had answered, 'No'. The wild fox then asked the master to help free him with a 'turning phrase'. He then posed the same question, and Baizhang answered: 'Such a person does not obstruct the working of *karma*'. Enlightened, the old man thanked the master and requested a proper burial. Later, the master took his disciples to the other side of the mountain where he uncovered the carcass of a fox and gave it a monk's burial. When he related the whole incident during the evening talk, Huangbo (d. 850), the leading disciple, asked: 'What would have happened had the man way back then given the right answer?' The master said: 'Come up here and I will tell you.' After hesitating, Huangbo approached and slapped the master, who clapped and, laughing, exclaimed: 'I thought the barbarian (Bodhidharma from India) had a red beard. But here is another red-bearded barbarian!'

What is the meaning of this story? As with any *koan*, there is no one answer. But, staying close to the narrative and its structure, one may note how the wild fox (a Zen metaphor for a fake or a heretic), being often a lone predator living on the margin, could very well stand for the *pratyekabuddha* (the self-enlightened type). This type desires and achieves liberation (from karmic rebirth) but falls short of being the **bodhisattva** (the other-delivering kind) due to a lack of compassion. The latter, free from *karma*, can move freely in **samsara**, unobstructed by its *karma* as he sought aid for others. The final exchange is a replay of the earlier exchange in a Zen deconstructive reversal of master/disciple roles.

Further reading

Heine, S. (1996) 'Putting the Fox back in the Wild Fox Koan: The Intersection of Philosophical and Popular Religious Elements in the Ch'an/Zen Koan Tradition', *Harvard Journal of Asian Studies* 56(2): 257–317.

WHALEN LAI

barbarians

'Barbarians' is a Chinese term for the uncivilized people on the periphery of the Middle Kingdom. Though obviously sinocentric, it is not based on race; it is culturo-centric, the assumption being that once civilized by the Han way, the barbarians would become part of the larger Chinese family. Barbarians are divided into the cooked and the raw class, often placed rather neatly in terms of the four directions. The latter class, farther away, are closer to the beasts who ate their food raw. The use of fire is a sign of cultural advance. (Compared with the Japanese, Chinese cuisine generally shuns the uncooked. Gods and ancestors are given cooked food; ghosts and goblins eat raw food.)

Most names for barbarians carry a canine radical, signalling that they are sub-human (though dogs, having been domesticated, are one rank better than wolves and tigers that are truly wild). In the Han cosmography of the 'five zones' (marked by conquest) built around concentric circles, the royal domain is the centre; the lord's domain is next, the pacified domain is the third. Then come the barbarians, the ones in the fourth controlled zone and the ones in the outermost wild zone. The southern and eastern barbarians (the Yi and Man) fall into the former; the hostile, warlike western Rong and northern Di are in the latter. The barbarians, of course, did not necessarily see things the Chinese way: from the South came the legend that the Dog-King who carried off a Chinese princess who served him on her knees, while from the West came the legend of the Horse similarly kidnapping the Silkworm Lady.

Further reading

Yu Ying-shih (1986) 'Han Foreign Relations', in D.

Twitchet and M. Loewe (eds), *The Cambridge History of China. Volume 1: The Ch'in and Han Empires 221 B.C.–A.D. 220*, Cambridge: Cambridge University Press.

WHALEN LAI

Beidu

A mysterious foreign monk, name unknown, arrived in China and landed near present day Hong Kong around 315 CE. He was remembered as 'Cup Ferrying' for having crossed the Yangtze (Yangzi), the Long River, several times by riding on a cup. That is the hagiographic myth: the word 'cup' should be emended to 'bowl' for the monk's begging bowl, a symbol of the mendicant order. The river-crossing is symbolic of crossing over to the other shore. The 'cup' that ferries stands for the raft of the **dharma** that the Buddha has entrusted to the *sangha* (the Buddhist monastic community). The legend of this early figure took in other Daoist features that were also later popular with Zen Buddhists. This monk ate meat, drank wine, talked in riddles, carried a gourd (his wine bottle, symbol of the 'empty' *dao*), worked miracles and died twice, once leaving a sandal in an empty grave (a Daoist motif) and the other time dying of food poisoning (like the Buddha) only to be seen alive afterwards. His begging bowl (again like that of the Buddha) performed more *post mortem* miracles. Parts of his lore rubbed off onto **Bodhidharma**, the Zen patriarch who also crossed the river, riding on a twig, and was poisoned by his enemies only to be sighted on the Silk Road, walking back to India with just one sandal (the other one being later found in his empty grave). The archaeology of the myth of Bodhidharma ran much deeper and farther back than even the recent deconstructive reading of it set around the fractured persona of the early sixth century.

Further reading

Lai, W. (1997) 'A Minor Legend of Hong Kong; The Monk Pei-tu', a reflection on the return of

Hong Kong to China for the 40th anniversary volume of *Cheng Feng* 40(2): 81–92.

WHALEN LAI

BEING, CHINESE *see* non-being

beyond the square

In the early fifth century, the eminent monk Huiyuan (Hui-yuan) won the right not to have to pay homage to the king. This was common for *sannyasins* in India, but was not yet a recognized right for monks in China. Previously, hermits in China had sometimes received special, individual and specific dispensations from the ruler, but by law hermits still lived under the rule of the king, as described in the legend of Bo Yi and Shu Qi. Huiyuan made his case partially on the basis of the 'foreign' (Buddhist) theory of the Two Wheels of the *Dharma*. The Two Wheels of the *Dharma* in Buddhism refers to the Law of the Buddha and the Law of the Land, that is, the transmundane and the mundane *Dharma*. He appealed to traditional sentiment and presented the monk as a **sage** whose ministration of men is beneficial to the state. But he also characterized the otherworldly monk as a 'man beyond the square'. Daoist magicians known as 'men of the square' had served in the Han court. Their art might claim to tap into the power and directions of the earth 'square'. By characterizing the Buddhist monk thus, Huiyuan placed him 'beyond the world (square)' and 'above the Daoist powers'. This designation also says something about the imagination of the structure of medieval utopias.

Spiritual cosmography like that of the Buddhists tends to emphasize the vertical in order to emphasize qualitative transcendence. But imperial geography, like that of Han China, expands laterally. A newly imagined world was emerging. Now, far beyond the **barbarians** living on the fringes of the Middle Kingdom, there were being imagined in the outlands fabulous kingdoms of monsters or of sages, or both. For China, beyond the square of the human world there were havens of immortals and utopias of strange one-legged, or three-eyed, or shared-wing, or other fabulous beings. The anatomical anomalies were there to help develop the idea of the then prevailing 'classificatory imperialism' that stopped short of sliding into the colourless 'ineffables' and 'non-beings' of the post-Han Neo-Daoist metaphysicians (see **Neo-Daoism**). There is, for example, a kingdom of Confucian gentlemen to the far East and an entirely different type of person in the far West. These lands 'beyond the (regular) square' are deemed outside the jurisdiction of China. Citizens there do not have to pay homage or tribute to the Chinese emperor. It follows that neither should Buddhist monks pay homage, since they also are 'living beyond the square [i.e. beyond the boundaries] of the (Emperor's) world'.

See also: magic squares

WHALEN LAI

Bhagavad Gita

The *Bhagavad Gita* (Song of the Lord) is a self-contained episode of seven hundred verses embedded in a single book (the *Bhishmaparvan*) of the vast Sanskrit epic, the *Mahabharata*, whose central theme is the struggle for control of the kingdom of Bharata (northern India). Since that work was the product of many centuries of accretion and redaction, perhaps originating in oral traditions beginning as early as the eighth century BCE, questions of dating are otiose. The *Gita* was probably composed in the two centuries prior to the Christian era. The text regarded as standard is that commented upon by the non-dualist Vedantin theologian **Shankara** (650–700 CE). Within mainstream Hinduism, the *Gita*, which is classified as *smriti* or traditional literature whose function is that of elucidating and corroborating the Vedic revelation, is a constituent of the 'Triple Standard' (*prasthana-traya*) of **Vedanta**, along with the **Brahma-Sutras** and **Upanishads**, and was the subject of commentaries by the great theistic Vedantins **Ramanuja** and **Madhva** as well as Shankara. Its synthesis of different soteriologies lends it to many alternative interpretations. In recent times the militant nationalist B.G. Tilak (1856–1920) while imprisoned for sedition interpreted the text as a revolutionary manifesto calling upon the Indian people to engage in violent insurrection against the British. By contrast, **Gandhi** claimed that the *Gita* taught non-violence (*ahimsa*).

The protagonists in the *Mahabharata* are cousins, the offspring of a pair of royal brothers. The elder, Dhritarashtra, was born blind, and the younger, Pandu, ruled in his place. When Pandu died he left five sons from two wives; Yudhisthira, Bhima and Arjuna from one and Nakula and Sahadeva from another. They are known as 'Pandavas'. On Pandu's death, Dhritarashtra ascended the throne and produced a hundred sons known as 'Kauravas', of whom the eldest was Duryodhana. To avert civil war between Pandavas and Kauravas, Dhritarashtra divided the kingdom between righteous Yudhisthira and Duryodhana. In a crooked game of dice, the former lost everything, including his brothers and their joint wife Draupadi, to the latter, whose degradation of the lady ensures that no quarter will be given in the ensuing merciless strife. Yudhisthira tried his luck again in a last throw of the dice. This time the losers are to be banished to the forest for twelve years and to spend a thirteenth incognito before they can return and recover their domain. Yudhisthira lost again and the Pandavas went into exile. On their return after the expiry of the term of expulsion, Duryodhana reneged and refused to restore their due sovereignty. War follows. Each side mustered its allies numbered among whom was Krishna, the monarch of Dvaraka who has connections with both sides. Having delegated his armed forces to the Kaurava cause, he himself joined the Pandavas as Arjuna's charioteer. King Dhritarashtra requests the royal bard Sanjaya to narrate the events of the conflict, and the *Gita* is part of that story.

The two armies stand opposed. The great warrior Arjuna has mounted his chariot which is driven by Krishna. Arjuna is suddenly overcome by a paralysing crisis of conscience. How can he kill his relations and destroy the eternal laws of the family? He refuses to engage in combat and sinks into his chariot at which point Krishna comes to the fore and addresses the despondent soldier with a battery of reasons why he must fight; principally because it is his natural duty (*sva-dharma*) and it is better to perform one's own duty badly than that of another well. Human beings are immortal in that they have an everlasting and immutable transmigratory soul (*atman*) which is their true identity. Self-identification with the psychosomatic complex located in an external environment subject to natural forces from which finite agency derives is a form of misconception. In the course of his 700 verse discourse Krishna reveals that he is in fact the supreme deity, Vishnu who is the creator, preserver and destroyer of the worlds whose periodic 'descents' (*avatara*) restore righteousness (**dharma**) when it is in a state of decline. Instructed and enlightened, Arjuna regains his courage and determination. At this point, the *Gita* concludes. The bloody battle is won by the Pandavas and Yudhisthira becomes king.

Arjuna's dilemma illustrates the tension in Brahmanism between duty and individual conscience (rather than inclination), between a life guided by considerations of self-determination and self-constitution and a life whose every aspect is governed by the vast corpus of rules derived from the infallible Veda. Arjuna is a *Kshatriya*, a member of the warrior **caste** (*varna*), one of whose natural duties (*dharma*) and functions is warfare. What is specifically depicted is the conflict between the values of non-violence (*ahimsa*) and what is ordained by the normative Vedic tradition. More generally, he represents the aspirations of those who chose to renounce (**samnyasa**) their prescribed social and ritual duties and status in favour of a life of solitary homelessness and spiritual discipline and gnosis whose goal was the final transcendence (*moksha*) of the sphere of rebirth, repetition, becoming and suffering (**samsara**). The active religion of the householder generating wealth, producing children and co-operating in the maintenance of social (and cosmic) order (*pravritti-dharma*) is inextricably involved in purposive action which inevitably binds one to *samsara* in accordance with the principle of **karma** according to which motivated and intentional actions generate a residue which inheres in the agent and which must be depotentiated in future modes of experience. One of the questions which the *Gita* tries to answer is that of how one may continue to live and act in the world, obeying one's prescribed social and ritual duties, without generating the *karma* which propels one through the series of births in the here and now. It rejects the path of radical renunciation (*samnyasa*) of social and ritual role, teaching that, given the dynamic nature of matter, in the embodied state one cannot escape the necessity of acting and that what one should renounce is desire for the fruits of action, not actions themselves. Disinterested (*vairagya*) and disciplined (yogic) action, action without a desire for its fruits, will not generate *karma*. Understanding (*jnana*) is in itself insufficient for salvation, for embodied conditions make activity inevitable. This internalized renunciatory attitude conditioning the quality of one's actions is called *karma-yoga*.

Crucially superadded to these considerations is the notion of the discipline of attachment to God (*bhakti-yoga*). The Gita is a monotheistic text and Krishna portrays himself as a creator god who has also ordained the social order. Since he is the source of all, the appropriate human response is the dedication of actions and their results to him in a spirit of worship (*bhakti*). Moreover, God is the ultimate agent and humans merely instruments of what are in fact his actions. Realising that one is not an autonomous agent (*svatantra karta*) and then performing all one's actions, prescribed and non-prescribed, in a spirit of detachment and devotion prompts salvific divine grace (*prasada*) conducing to liberation. Some later interpreters characterise this combination of understanding, action and theistic devotion as the *jnana-karma-samucchaya-vada*.

Further reading

Buitenen, J. van (1953) *Ramanuja on the Bhagavad Gita*, The Hague: Smits.

Edgerton, F. (1944) *The Bhagavad Gita*, 2 vols, Cambridge, MA: Harvard University Press.

Johnson, W. (trans.) (1994) *The Bhagavad Gita*, Oxford: Oxford University Press.

Lipner, J. (ed.) (1997) *The Fruits of Our Desiring*, Calgary: Bayeaux.

Radhakrishnan, S. (1949) *The Bhagavad Gita* with an introductory essay, Sanskrit text, English translation and notes, London: George Allen and Unwin.

Sadhale, G. (1935*) The Bhagavad Gita with Eleven Commentaries*, Bombay: Gujarati Printing Press.

Zaehner, R.C. (trans.) (1969) *The Bhagavad Gita*, Oxford: Oxford University Press.

CHRIS BARTLEY

Bhartrihari

b. *c*.430 CE; d. 480 CE

Grammarian

Author of the *Vakyapadiya*, Bhartrihari was primarily an influential and original Sanskrit grammarian. He was also an exponent of a form of philosophical monism which identified the Absolute (*Brahman*) underlying the manifest cosmos with the essence (*tattva*) of transcendental Logos or Sound (*shabda*; *vak*) and meaning (*sphota*; literally 'the bursting forth (of meaning)'). Whereas most philosophers of monistic persuasion identified the Absolute with pure consciousness, for Bhartrihari thought and language are intrinsically identical on the level of the Ultimate. Sound and meaning originally coexist as undifferentiated and without sequence. Their differentiation into the serial diversity of subjects, acts and objects of awareness ('names and forms') in time and space is an emanation of the Absolute. Language and consciousness are inextricably intertwined, language being the creative 'vibration' (**spanda**) of consciousness. The distinction between signifier and signified has a conventional value: reality as meaning is indivisible. The sequential audible phonemes are the public manifestations of the impartite and atemporal *sphota* which is the essence and real medium of linguistic meaning and communication. Categories such as sentence and word are artificially superimposed upon this fundamental uniform meaning-bearer for the purpose of grammatical analysis. Similarly, a *sphota*-expressive word or sentence is formally analysable as a concatenation of phonemes in a particular sequence for the purposes of morphemic and phonetic description.

Bhartrihari discerned that it is sentences rather than individual words that are the actual vehicles of linguistic communication. Just as understanding of a word does not result from hearing the final phoneme and then combining it with memory traces of the sounds of the preceding elements, so we do not gradually understand a series of individual words and then mentally combine them to generate the sentential meaning. Rather, the latter is grasped immediately and instantaneously as a whole (*pratibha*, or 'flash of insight') and not as the result of a combinatory mental process. According to Bhartrihari, the sequential audible sounds (*dhvani*) forming a single word and the individual words themselves are only grammatical abstractions. It is the sentence that is the fundamental linguistic fact, words being abstractions from sentences. They are both convenient grammatical fictions and of utility in teaching the language.

Reconstructing Bhartrihari's thought, it can be seen that there is a natural progression from the view that it is the sentence rather than the individual words that is the primary vehicle of meaning or understanding to the idea that it is the paragraph or chapter or whole text (in modern terms) that is determinative and that these larger contexts are themselves to be understood in the context of the whole of language. This holistic concept of meaning is then identified as the Absolute. Reversing the sequence, the contexts, sentences, words and letters can be see as progressive fragmentary emanations of a Semantic Absolute.

Although *sphota* is unitary, it is commonly misunderstood as having parts and temporal sequence due to the sequential and compositional nature of the language (*nada*) in which it is communicated. Thought and language are non-differentiated (the 'Semantic Absolute') prior to the process of explicit verbalization. The Self is identical with this undifferentiated awareness understood as pre-linguistic meaning. Bhartrihari thinks that there are three stages of metaphysical and linguistic evolution (this is an ancient conceptuality traceable to *Rig Veda* 1.164.45) from the undifferentiated and transcendent 'Semantic-Absolute' which is identical with the essence of language (*shabda-tattva*). This first principle from which the diverse universe emanates is called *pashyanti*: it is the pre-verbal stage of language at which it is identical with thought. There is an intermediate (*madhyama*) stage at which particular objects are determinately separated but not yet sensible. In terms of linguistic evolution, the words are fully formed as successions of phonemes but the physical apparatus necessary for articulation is lacking. Language and thought are still one. Finally there is the physically manifested speech (*vaikhari*) that is the medium of mundane communication. Metaphysically, the objects comprising the macroscopic world have become sensible.

Bhartrihari understands time (*kala*) as the principal autonomous power (*svatantrya-shakti*) of the Absolute. It is the efficient cause (*nimitta-karana*) and instigating agent (*prayojaka-karta*) in the sequential development of the cosmos of name and form, the appearance of the pluriformity of phenomena from the original unity. Due to the workings of ignorance (**avidya**), hypostatised as a power (*shakti*) of the Absolute, finite subjects of experience, whose consciousness is a reflection of that of the Absolute, fail to realize that the cosmic diversity is the self-manifestation of the Absolute and assume that serial multiplicity is real in its own right. Once the unenlightened individual, which has misidentified itself with its embodied circumstances, intuitively realizes the identity of everything, including itself, with the Absolute, it is said to have achieved liberation from rebirth (*moksha*).

Bhartrihari describes time as a single, eternal, all-pervading reality (*dravya*), independent of processes (*vyapara*), the measure (*parimana*) of entities involved in actions. It is the cause of the origin, perdurance and destruction of finite entities and of sequential order through its self-differentiation. It is the wire-puller (*sutra-dharah*) of the world machine, differentiating and regulating the universe. This means that the supreme reality (*satta*) which is eternal activity (*kriya*) is manifested in lower universals which are the prototypes of particular modes of existence (*vyakti*). In this process, time is the principle regulative power. Although immutable, time appears to acquire the characteristics of past, present and future and divisions into moments, hours, days, months, seasons and so on, and to participate in the processes that it controls due to the actions associated with time. Incidentally, he rejects the cyclical view that reality will repeat itself.

Further reading

Brough, J. (1951) 'Theories of General Linguistics in the Sanskrit Grammarians', *Transactions of the Philological Society*, 27–46; repr. in M. Hara and J. Wright (eds), *John Brough: Collected Papers*, London: School of Oriental and African Studies, 1996.

—— (1953) 'Some Indian Theories of Meaning', *Transactions of the Philological Society*, 161–76; repr.

in M. Hara and J. Wright (eds), *John Brough: Collected Papers*, London: School of Oriental and African Studies, 1996.

Herzberger, R. (1986) *Bhartrihari and the Buddhists*, Dordrecht: Reidel.

Iyer, K. (1969) *Bhartrihari*, Poona: University of Poona.

Scharfe, H. (1977) *Grammatical Literature*, Wiesbaden: Otto Harrassowitz.

—— (1980) *A Study in the Dialectics of Sphota*, Delhi: Motilal Banarsidass.

—— (1991) *The Philosophy of Bhartrihari*, Delhi: Motilal Banarsidass.

Shastri, G. (1959) *The Philosophy of Word and Meaning*, Calcutta: Sanskrit College.

CHRIS BARTLEY

Bhaskara

*fl. c.*750 CE

Vedantin commentator

A realist Vedantin commentator on the **Brahma-Sutras** and **Bhagavad Gita**, Bhaskara propounded a dualistic and theistic interpretation of those Hindu scriptures in opposition to non-dualist **Advaita** Vedanta. He subscribed to the **satkaryavada** theory of causation according to which an effect pre-exists in subtle form in its causal substrate as a germinal modality of a future state prior to its manifestation as an identifiable entity with determinate name and form. He understood the cosmos of souls and matter as the real rather than apparent transformation (*parinama*) of an aspect of the Absolute *Brahman* conditioned by limiting conditions (*upadhi*). The *Brahman* is both the substrative (*upadana-karana*) and instrumental (*nimitta-karana*) causes of the universe. His philosophy is called *bheda-abheda-vada*; the theory of difference (the cosmos) and non-difference from the transcendent source. In terms of a favourite analogy, from one point of view, the waves are different from the sea but from another perspective, they are identical with it. On this view, reality is a single but complex, and internally differentiated, process.

Individual selves, subject to restricted awareness, the workings of **karma** and transmigration are held to be emanations of the Absolute, comparable to sparks from fire. In defence of his position against the charge that conditioning by limiting adjuncts renders the Absolute relative and imperfect, Bhaskara uses an unconvincing simile: just as atmosphere contained in a jar is different from the whole atmosphere in that the former is limited and the latter unrestricted and unconnected with the properties in the jar; similarly, defects occurrent in the embodied soul differentiated and conditioned by limiting adjuncts do not affect the unconditioned Supreme Brahman.

Against non-dualist Vedanta, he argues that if experience of duality and agency are false in that they are products of beginningless, primal ignorance (*anadi-avidya*), then we have no grounds for supposing that belief in monism is true since it arises in the sphere of **avidya**. If monism contradicts duality, duality also contradicts monism and we have no means of adjudicating the truth. The scriptures that are alleged to convey knowledge of non-duality themselves consist of differentiated phonemes.

On the question of the ontological status of *avidya*, Bhaskara says that if it is beginningless, it must be eternal with the result that release from rebirth is impossible. It cannot be both real and unreal on pain of contradiction. Were it a form of non-being, it could not cause bondage to transmigratory existence. If it causes bondage, it must be a positive entity, co-existent with *Brahman* which is claimed to be the sole reality. Desire for mundane things on the part of individual souls which are emanations of the Absolute causes their bondage to transmigration, whereas reorientation of desire (*raga*), in the form of devotional meditation (*bhakti*; *dhyana*), towards the transcendent, formless *Brahman* which has the qualities of infinite being and intelligence brings about liberation.

The agency of the embodied soul is real, although 'borrowed' from *Brahman*, its ultimate source. Against the renunciatory (**samnyasa**) outlook characteristic of Advaita Vedanta, Bhaskara conservatively maintains that the duties (*dharma*) appropriate to **caste** and stage of life as prescribed in the scriptures are inescapable even for the enlightened. A combination of the performance of enjoined ritual duties with understandings of the natures of the soul as an agent in a derivative sense and *Brahman* as the source of all is a necessary condition for attainment of the *summum bonum*, a state of felicity in which the omnipotent and omniscient soul may choose whether or not to be associated with a body.

Further reading

Dasgupta, S. (1940) *A History of Indian Philosophy,* Vol. III, Cambridge: Cambridge University Press.

Rocher, L. (ed.) (1988) *Studies in Indian Literature and Philosophy: Collected Articles of J.A.B. van Buitenen*, Delhi: Motilal Banarsidass.

Srinivasachari, P. (1934) *The Philosophy of Bhedab-heda*, Madras: Adyar Library and Research Centre.

CHRIS BARTLEY

Bo Yi and Shu Qi

The brothers Bo Yi (Po Yi) and Shu Qi (Shu Ch'i) opposed King Wu's attack on the declining Shang dynasty. They supposedly sang this song:

> (We) climb that western mountain
> And pick there the herb.
> They only substitute tyranny with tyranny
> Without knowing the wrong done
> Forgetting Shen Nong, Shun, and Xia.
> So who deserves our allegiance now?
> Alas! Away we go – now that
> The Mandate had dwindled away.

Legends of Bo Yi and Shu Qi as sages and as recluses abound. **Mencius** found them 'pure and aloof', in contrast to **Confucius**, whom he called 'timely'. This is because Confucius knew when it was appropriate to leave society and when it was right to start to teach others in a social setting. Confucius had previously come across two hermits who judged his goal high but futile, for there was no way it could be realized. The pair then went back to ploughing their field. Confucius also considered them to be 'aloof and pure' (apolitical), but reckoned that he had to do what he had to do. From that came the Mencian appraisal of Confucius as an idealist committed to 'doing what he knew full well could

not be done' except in a timely fashion; knowing when to advance his ideas and when his advice was not heeded, to withdraw and retire (to teach).

In later tradition, Bo Yi and Shu Qi were said to be two princely brothers who declined to rule and ended up as hermits. They opposed the Zhou campaign and turned down an offer of office, starving themselves to death because they would not even dine on ferns belonging now to the Zhou king. But there is another way to read the myth. The pair were of the Jiang ethnic group, shepherds who lived once on the Central Plains but were pushed further west by the expanding Shang. When the Zhou revolted and rallied other lords to join in an attack on the Shang, this pair stood in their way. For this, they were misread by the Grand Historian Sima Qian (author of the *Historical Records*) as Shang loyalists. When they later refused the generous emolument from the victorious Zhou and retired to Mount Shouyang, the story is really about their going back to 'rearing sheep' (*shouyang*). The Jiang shepherds traditionally lived on higher pasture grounds above the fields of the river-bed farmers. Because they moved back and forth with their herds, they did not count themselves subjects of either Shang or Zhou and did not join the fighting over permanent homesteads. When told that every blade of grass now belonged to the new king, the pair as herder and gatherer refused to be so indebted. The story then has them starving to death, but the political reality is that the Zhou encroachment on the hills 'killed' them. They were driven further west from where they had once reared their sheep and gathered their wild grain.

Further reading

Shirakawa Shizuka (1983) *Chung-kuo shen-hua* (Chinese Mythology), translated into Chinese by Wang Hsiao-lien, Taipei: Ch'ang-an.

WHALEN LAI

bodhichitta

One of the principles of Mahayana Buddhism's ethics is that actions must be carried out with the correct motivation. This is called *bodhichitta* or the awakened mind. This type of consciousness is a result of a deep compassion for the suffering of others. This is the most significant principle of action of the **bodhisattva** (the enlightened individual), and is extended to everything in existence. This is not a form of motivation or thought with which we can easily begin. After all, we are naturally concerned with our own interests and ambitions, and we have to use **meditation** to achieve liberation from this world, from **samsara**, by following a route with a number of stages. Firstly, one meditates on the difficulty and value of human rebirth if it is accompanied by the ability to practise the *dharma*. Then the meditator considers death and the mutability of everything, and this leads to a real commitment to virtue which will lead to positive future rebirths, and a higher moral and spiritual general attitude. Then one thinks about the varieties of rebirth and suffering which are available to creatures, which emphasizes the problematic nature of rebirth for the individual. Such a process of meditation needs to be frequently repeated, and could lead to a genuine renunciation of all rebirth in *samsara* and a reasonable ambition to develop *bodhichitta*.

There is a kind of meditation which is very helpful to reaching this state. It is where we visualize people and situations which produced strong passions in us, and we are encouraged to develop an attitude of equanimity towards them, to detach ourselves from those passions which often otherwise overwhelm us. In this way we realize that friends can become enemies, and vice versa, so it might be argued that there is no difference between a friend and an enemy. Since we have spent an infinite amount of time in *samsara*, at some stage or another we have been looked after by low creatures, or we have even been such creatures ourselves, which is a thought designed to suggest that there is no essential distinction between different levels of sentient being and we should reverence anything which might have been our parent or protector in a past life. Hence the need for a general compassion and the motivation to help others, all others, in so far as one can. The most help that one can provide is through becoming a Buddha oneself, and this is the aim of *bodhichitta*, the attainment of enlightenment out of a sincere desire to work for the welfare of all sentient beings. The process of **meditation** produces the *bodhichitta*, and has the capacity to perfect us.

Further reading

Griffiths, P. (1986) *On Being Mindless: Buddhist Meditation and the Mind-Body Problem*, La Salle, IL: Open Court Press.

Hoffman, F. (1987) *Rationality and Mind in Early Buddhism*, Delhi: Motilal Banarsidass.

Tominaga, N. (1990) *Emerging from Meditation*, trans. M. Pye, London: Duckworth.

OLIVER LEAMAN

Bodhidharma

fl. 460–534

Buddhist thinker

The fabled founder of Chan (Zen) Buddhism, Bodhidharma is said to be the twenty-eighth patriarch in an unbroken line of transmission from the Buddha. He arrived by sea, and chided Emperor Wu of the Liang dynasty for all the vain glory of the many temples there. 'No merit whatsoever', he charged, and left with a parting riddle, 'Great Emptiness'. He retired to a cave, sat gazing at the wall for years and transmitted the **Dharma** eventually to Huike. Whatever the historical facts might be, early Chan represented the tradition of forest monks, extreme ascetics protesting against the lax and worldly piety in the cities. It recapitulates the heroic dynamics of the *Emptiness Sutra* where the Buddha entrusted this Mahayana wisdom to Subhuti, one of his disciples who is said to have understood how to expound the notion of emptiness, and who 'loved the quietude of the forest' and mocked Sariputra. The latter was one of the leading disciples of the Buddha, a leader of the 'village settled monastic' mainstream and later associated with the **Hinayana** scholastic or **Abhidharma** tradition. He stood in opposition to the 'forest hermits' who put **meditation** and personal liberation above taking care of (ministering to) the lay villagers. Sariputra represented the monks who 'served the villagers' and Sariputra was credited with the Abhidharmic learning of the urban *Sangha* (monastic community).

Further reading

Ray, R. (1994) *Buddhist Saints in India: A Study in Buddhist Values and Orientations*, Oxford: Oxford University Press, 131–6.

WHALEN LAI

bodhisattva

A *bodhisattva* is someone who has taken the vow to become a perfect Buddha and who takes the appropriate actions. The *bodhisattva* (*bodhisatta* in Pali) renounces entry into **nirvana** until all other beings have become enlightened. This notion is given different interpretations in different forms of Buddhism. In Mahayana Buddhism becoming a *bodhisattva* is to be strictly distinguished from becoming an *arahat*, which latter was criticized for being selfish and limited in scope. The real *bodhisattva*, according to the Mahayana school, wants everyone to become *bodhisattvas*, and not only himself or herself. Indeed, the Mahayana *bodhisattva* rejects the possibility of any individual reaching a genuine enlightenment without taking everything else along, as it were. Nothing has its own nature and so everything is empty. *Nirvana* is also empty, and can be grasped through the empty consciousness of the meditator (see **meditation**). It follows that we can all reach *nirvana*, we can all reach the ultimate truth, and we all have the **buddha nature**. We all should have the ambition of being *bodhisattvas*, we should all seek to realize our buddha natures. The normal virtues of Buddhism are present in the Mahayana conception of *bodhisattva*, such as charity, moral behaviour, patience, energy, meditation and wisdom. The Mahayana teaching insists that *bodhisattvas* are very much involved in the world, and yet are able to reach a high level of personal spiritual development. It is not easy to see how some of the characteristics of the *bodhisattva* can really be attained by those who are not living a monastic and ascetic life.

Further reading

Griffiths, P. (1994) *On Being Buddha: The Classical Doctrine of Buddhahood*, Albany, NY: State University of New York Press.

Guenther, H. (1972) *Buddhist Philosophy in Theory and Practice*, Harmondsworth: Penguin.

Murti, T. (1960) *The Central Philosophy of Buddhism: A Study of the Madhyamika*, London: Allen & Unwin.

Williams, P. (1989) *Mahayana Buddhism: The Doctrinal Foundations*, London: Routledge.

OLIVER LEAMAN

bodies, problems with

Deformities are considered in most traditional societies as abominations, and birth defects are deemed divine punishment for the sin of the fathers. The special place given to blind seers, epileptic shamans and literary heroes like the Hunchback of Notre Dame notwithstanding, the fact is that cripples are shunned and ostracized. Even today in Japan the *hibakusha*, those affected by the atom bombs dropped on Nagasaki and Hiroshima in 1945, attract a certain stigma. Few philosophers have valued deformities, but **Zhuangzi** is an exception. Around Chapter 5 of his book is displayed a host of savants who are one-legged, leg-less, lame, crippled, hunchbacked, lip-less, toeless or otherwise deformed. These unwholesome beings are paraded as paradigms of supernal beauty who put the world to shame. More than just a product of an iconoclastic imagination, these sacred cripples are survivals from an ancient mythic lore, the most famous being that of the one-legged Kui **dragon**. When asked whether Kui was one-legged, Confucius supposedly said no: 'He is just so virtuous that one of him is enough.' (The word 'leg' also means 'enough'.) In fact, we are dealing here with a chthonic figure comparable to the deformed Cyclops. These are mythic lunar figures. As the moon that waxes and wanes is 'incomplete', so physical incompleteness stands for lunar becoming and endless metamorphosis. The incomplete moon being potent (with *de*), the cripple is likewise 'replete with *de* (virtue)'. Thus this chapter in the *Zhuangzi* was later titled 'Tallies of Complete Virtue'.

With the rise of the sky gods, however, the lunar deities became demonized. As the sun came to represent virtue, virtue in turn was associated with solar constancy rather than lunar metamorphosis. The changing moon was now called fickle, and incomplete cripples became abominations. If the cult of celestial **Heaven** reached its apogee under the Zhou dynasty, then perhaps it is not accidental that Zhuangzi came from the state of Song, home of the Shang remnant, known for keeping alive an archaic myth and lore.

The naked human body is not an object of artistic depiction in China. There are late dynastic writings on feminine beauty which go into physical details, but Neo-Confucian morality disallows the exposure of the female flesh to the wanton gaze of men. Women covered their bodies completely in Late Dynastic China. Nudes appear in 'spring pictures' (erotic prints), but such erotic art is more common in Japan than in China. In traditional China, the social self is identified with name. Classical norm dictates that there be no portraiture of the deceased at the ancestral hall, just the name written on the spirit tablet, plus any official titles and ranks. For most of the famous early historical personages, then, we have good prose descriptions but not real-life portraits. That was not due to any inability to produce actual facsimiles. Tomb paintings from Han shows the dead going to the world beyond but these are not exact portraitures. Likewise tomb paintings of the Seven Worthies of the Bamboo Grove – Neo-Daoists, each one an aesthetic individualist – remain stylized, more idealized memories than 'death mask' replicas.

Further reading

Lai, W. (1985) 'The One-Legged and the Three-Legged: A Chinese Answer to the Riddle of the Sphinx', *Asian Cultural Studies* 15: 49–66.

Todeschini, M. (1999) 'Illegitimate sufferers: A-Bomb Victims, Medical Science, and the Government', *Daedalus* 128(2): 67–100.

WHALEN LAI

body

Among Chinese schools of thinking, it is the Confucians who have the most corporeal reading of the self. Whereas the Chan Buddhist would 'cultivate the mind', the Neo-Confucians would 'cultivate the body'. Following the usage in *The Great Learning*, this in turn means 'cultivating the self'. 'Body' here is the psychosomatic unity, a corporeal self that is inherently social and moral; it is a body that can be extended outwards into larger bodies, such as family, clan, state, and the world under **Heaven**. That bodily self has a past and a future. A gift of the parents and placed in our charge, it should, says the *Analects*, not be allowed to come to harm. So it is 'better to travel in a carriage than walk, better make a boat trip than swim'. For that reason, the Chinese **scholar**, unlike the Japanese *samurai*, is physically untrained. From the Song period, the unarmed gentry no longer carried swords, not even a ceremonial one as the Tang poet Li Bo once did.

A corporeal self is inevitably tied to food. A regular feeding of the dead is required by the ritual classics; animal sacrifice is standard. If unfed, the dead became hungry ghosts, a major Chinese concern (see **afterlife in Chinese thought**). But above the material self there is the psychic self. Within the body cavity, the mind (meaning the heart) is the central control over the senses. The mind-heart ideally integrates reason and emotion. So **Mencius** considers feeling a 'natural condition' not contrary to the nature of the heart; but **Xunzi** seeks to read the word *qing* as 'emotion' (to be controlled by reason), and Buddhist thinking polarized the concept further. This shift complicates attempts at retrieving the Mencian discussion on the priority of will and of the passions (*zhi* and *qi*). Once the Buddhists made a radical distinction between reason and emotion (the ascetic needs to control desires), it is easy to miss the point that the heart, for Mencius, encompasses both reason and emotion (and thus emotions like **filial piety** cannot be deemed 'bad' or contrary to reason) and will. Passion is also **ether**, breath, *élan vital* and material force.

The centre of gravity of the bodily self is however lower than the heart; it rests with the 'cinnabar field' in the lower abdomen. This is the seat of the 'deep breathing' in the Daoist *qigong* exercise. **Laozi** knew its priority. As a ruler, he would 'empty the people's mind but fill up their stomachs'. More than food may be involved. The mind can be bewitched by the senses and ideas, but the cinnabar field is the imperturbable anchor of one's being. Filling it may mean letting it settle down. Whole books have been written on this *hara* (abdomen) in Japanese psychology, and much of this discussion has roots in China. Chinese also use body metaphors to classify social relationships. Brothers are like limbs to one another; the family is the torso. Treat a servant as if he is your 'arms and legs' and he will become as trustworthy as your 'heart and abdomen'. Torso or *ti* is featured in the paradigm of '**substance and function**'; the moving limbs are its function. **Face** also has to do with social status, like putting up a front and having a doorman to screen visitors.

The Daoist concept of the body is more complicated, but the rudiments are shared with the Confucians. The body is a microcosm of the macrocosmic universe. There are 365 joints to the body, complementing the 365 days of the solar year, there are five organs or orbs to go with the five planets, and so on. An interior landscape replicates the sacred topography. So the head or the navel is the *axis mundi* Mount Gunlun. An adept can travel through the sacred mountains or make a galactic journey inside the body. He may breathe in the fresh vapours of dawn (most *yang*) and lodge the five ethers in their proper orbs inside him. Visualization can bring deities to take up residence in a divine bureaucracy within. Chinese medicine depends on such mapping of the inner court with its chambers and passageways, and Daoist yoga works at mating the Dragon and the Tiger or other encrypted pairs like Yellow and White – primal *yin* and *yang* – to return to the one root. Pairs like Dragon and Tiger, or Red and White, are code names for the elemental cinnabar and mercury (*yin–yang*) poles which require unification. Unity is represented by Laozi, who is the *dao* incarnate, the primal ether congealing, or the dismembered giant who became everything. Self-cultivation then means bringing the physical body in line with the spiritual one. The 'body' plays host to many vexations, but the pure 'form' (*xing*) of that body does not. Ridding the vexations frees the form that is isomorphic with the macrocosm.

The end is to become an immortal and to free the spirit (*shen*), which is more than the physical organ of the mind-heart. In one proto-Tantric exercise, semen acts as the congealed 'essence' in the lower abdomen. It needs to be changed into the **qi**, the fluid 'vital force' that then circulates up the spine until it is refined into the non-material 'spirit' on the crown of the head. This spirit embryo, sometimes pictured as a second self, a new child, then leaves behind the gross body. The Daoist canon (divided into three 'grottos') is itself such a 'body' also, being a sacred corpus like the Buddhist *Tripitaka*. The latter is called 'store', the same word for the five 'organs' that actually marks circuits or 'orbs'.

Chinese Buddhists retain the Indian Buddhist understanding of the body as an impermanent composite. Death is just the dispersal of the five great elements. In Buddhism, they are earth, water, fire, wind and space. The body is made up of these; at death, the elements disperse. (Sometimes a sixth is added, consciousness, but this is the one that may go on to the next rebirth.) But for the enlightened ones, there are 'physical' remains – the relics – that are more than just physical. At the end of time, they will come back together to reconstitute one cosmic body of the transcendental Buddha.

Further reading

Kohn, L. (1987) *Seven Steps to the Tao: Sima Chengzhen's Zuowanlun*, St Augustine/Nettetal: Monumenta Serica Monograph XX.

Porkert, M. (1974) *The Theoretical Foundations of Chinese Medicine: Systems of Correspondence*, Cambridge, MA: MIT Press.

Schafer, E. (1977) *The Void: T'ang Approaches to the Stars*, Berkeley, CA: University of California Press.

Schipper, K. (1992) *The Taoist Body*, Berkeley, CA: University of California Press.

Yuasa Yasuo (1983) *The Body, Self-cultivation and ki-Energy*, Albany, NY: State University of New York Press.

WHALEN LAI

Body, Shadow, and Soul

'Body, Shadow, and Soul' is the title of a poem by **Tao Qian** or Tao Yuanming (365–427). It captures the then current quest for finding the true self. The poem is as follows:

> [Body to Shadow:] Heaven and earth endure forever
> Mountain and stream do not change
> Plants follow a constant course
> To wither by frost, to revive by dew
> But, alas, Man the most intelligent of the lot
> Is not equal to them
> Alive here today
> Gone soon to return no more
> No one notices his absence
> Not even relatives or friends
> Only the things he used remain
> Reminders to move them to tears
> With no way to avoid the inevitable
> What must be must be
> So pray my advice to take
> When wine is offered, don't hesitate.

> [Shadow to Body:] No use talking about immortality
> Keeping alive is hard enough
> Of course I desire paradise
> But it is far and the way is forgotten
> Ever since I met up with you
> We share our grief and our joy
> At night we might part awhile
> By day we are together again
> But this union does not last forever
> Together we dissipate into the dark
> When the body dies, so die too name and fame
> A fearful prospect it is
> But do good and it will outlive you
> Surely that is worth the effort
> For though wine might drown our sorrow
> It is not as good as [a legacy of fame].

> [Soul Explaining All:] The Great Potter is impartial
> All things churn by themselves
> That Man should unite Heaven and Earth

> Is that not due to me (Spirit)?
> You and I are of different paths
> Though in life we be conjoined
> Bound together for good and ill
> How can I not tell you what I know?
> The Three August Rulers were all sages
> But where are they today?
> [A Chinese Zarathustra] lived a long life
> Still even he was not ready to let go
> But die old or young, it is all the same
> Wise or foolish, it makes no difference
> Wine might make you forget
> But only to hasten death along
> Doing good is its own reward
> Why even ponder the public acclaim
> Too much thinking only hurts the *élan vitale*
> Better to go along with the preordained
> To ride the great waves of change
> Neither happy nor anguished be
> What ought to end will naturally end
> There is no cause for further ado.

The poem represents Chinese thought in late antiquity: it lists the body's Epicurean solution, the shadow's Socratic hope for a social legacy, and the soul's Stoic reunion with the cosmos. It stops short of a medieval quest for personal immortality or acosmic transcendence.

Further reading

Hightower, J. (1970) *The Poetry of T'ao Ch'ien*, Oxford: Clarendon Press.
Liebenthal, W. (1952) 'The Immortality of the Soul in Chinese Thought', *Monumenta Nipponica* 8: 327–92.

WHALEN LAI

body and soul in pre-Buddhist China

Body and soul translates into '(physical) form and (psychic) spirit' in Chinese. Three classical positions may be isolated:

1 Spirit above Body: mind oversees the body form, and is the master in control of the senses like Plato's charioteer in control of the horses.
2 Spirit is born of Form: intelligence is consequent to sensation, as 'When the form is replete, the spirit is born.'
3 Spirit and Form are interdependent: 'What animates is spirit; what embodies is form. Use the mind to excess and it tires; burden the body to excess and it weakens. Death is when these two separate. The dead cannot live again; what has been torn asunder cannot reunite.'

These three views are within the bounds of classical humanist assumptions. They presume a physical base, sensate inputs and an intelligent faculty. These make up a functioning whole: the chariot driver and the horses – mind and body – are a team. As the third position would put it, the soul is like fire; the body is like wood. The moment the wood is consumed by the fire, the fire itself also dies out. But in the Han period, the chapter on the 'quintessential spirit' (the English translation of a Chinese compound word, the 'most refined/essence' of the 'spirit/psyche') in the *Huainanzi* tied the human soul to the world spirit. Its view spans the classical and the medieval, the humanistic and the spiritualistic:

> Before Heaven and Earth rose, there was neither shape nor form, so dark and profound [was this chaos] that no one knows whence it came. Within it were born two spirits, which took charge of Heaven and Earth, so profound that no one knows their limits. Thereafter Yin and Yang separated and the eight cardinal directions emerged. The hard and the pliant then congealed, and the myriad things took form. The gross ether became animals, the fine ether became men. Therefore is the spirit of Heaven as the bones are of Earth. (In time) the spirit will return to its origin as the bones would revert to its root.

This became the *locus classicus* around which the medieval debate on the immortality of the soul raged. The Confucian, denying personal immortality, argued that at death a person disintegrates; with his *yang* soul returning to heaven and his *yin* soul to earth, the individual as a distinct entity is no more. The Daoist seeking immortality countered with a different reading, arguing that as the sublime *yang* soul may rise above the gross and corruptible *yin* body, it may reunite with the *dao*, live on indefinitely, and/or rejoin that cosmogonic world-soul that existed prior to the differentiation of the One via the two into the myriad things. Despite the early canonical teaching about there being no-soul, the Chinese Buddhists sided with but also went beyond the Daoists. There is a higher life beyond, but it is more than the lowly Daoist heavens. In the process, on this issue of body and soul, the Buddhists subdivide the classical psyche into two, not totally unlike the Christian development of a triad of 'body, soul, and spirit'. The psyche is differentiated into (1) a mundane subject-object consciousness caught up in a bind with the objects of this world that it knows; and (2) a transmundane **buddha nature** or buddha mind that has a higher home and is in unison with the absolute or Suchness (*tathata*).

See also: Fan Zhen; gnosticism

Further reading

Lai, W. (1981) 'Beyond the Debate on the "Immortality of the Soul": Recovering an Essay by Shen Yueh', *Oriental Culture* 19(2): 138–57.

WHALEN LAI

BOOK OF CHANGES *see* Yijing

Brahma-Sutras

The *Brahma-Sutras* are aphoristic summaries, intended as aids to memory, of the sense of the **Upanishads**, ascribed to Badarayana and probably composed around the beginning of the common era. With the *Upanishads* and **Bhagavad Gita**, they comprise the triple basis (*prasthana-traya*) of the **Vedanta** school of systematic exegesis. Any thinker aspiring to the ascription 'Vedantin' wrote a commentary explaining these pithy and frequently ambiguous statements. Classified in terms of literary styles, a *Bhashya* is an extensive explanation, a *Vritti* a brief explanation and a

Varttika is a critical treatment of a *Bhashya*. The earliest extant *bhashya* on the *Brahma-Sutras* is that by the non-dualist (**Advaita**) Vedantin **Shankara** (650–700 CE). Although he refers to predecessors, nothing further is known of them. The anti-Advaitic theistic theologian **Ramanuja**'s commentary is called the *Shri Bhashya*.

CHRIS BARTLEY

Brahmo Samaj

The Brahmo Samaj is a Hindu organization which has exerted a considerable influence on the social and religious affairs of modern India. It was founded in Calcutta 1828 by the Bengali thinker and social reformist **Rammohan Roy** and his followers to promote belief in and worship of *Brahman*, the one true God, 'the Eternal Unsearchable and Immutable Being who is the author and preserver of the universe'. Rammohan Roy was the first Indian whose thought was significantly influenced by exposure to post-enlightenment Western European culture. His influence has been formative of the self-understanding of many educated modern Indians. After a remarkably comprehensive education which involved exposure to aniconic Islamic monotheism, in 1803 he entered the East India Company, where he attained high rank. Having retired at the age of forty-two, a substantial private income enabled him to found and edit English, Bengali and Persian newspapers, to establish academies in which English was the medium of instruction, to campaign for the introduction of modern Western European education and to mount opposition to the practice of forcible widow-burning (*sati*, anglicized as suttee).

From 1843, under the leadership of Debendranath Tagore (1817–1905), the Brahmo Samaj attracted many young men of the Brahmin caste united in their desire to propagate brotherly love, the good of mankind and the aniconic devotional worship of the one true spiritual universal deity, the impersonal absolute proclaimed by the *Upanishads*, in opposition to what they considered the idolatrous polytheistic practices and beliefs of most Hindus and the endeavours of Christian missionaries:

> We base our faith on the fundamental truths of religion, attested by reason and conscience and refuse to permit man, book or image to stand in the way of the direct communion of our soul with the Supreme Spirit. This message of the Brahmo Samaj in the abstract does not materially differ from the doctrine of the pure theistic bodies all the world over. Viewed historically and socially, however, the Brahmo Samaj has the further distinction of being the bearer of this message to the Hindu people.

Keshab Chandra Sen (1838–84) advanced the Samajist cause in and beyond Bengal before ultimately destroying it. He founded discussion groups and schools, organized famine relief and defended the remarriage of widows and the education of women. He understood monotheism as a principle in accordance with which Hindus, Muslims and Christian could unite. In 1865 he adopted the radically anti-caste policy of telling Brahmins to abandon their sacred threads, which led to a schism. As a consequence Sen set up a rival organization, the Brahmo Samaj of India. In 1878, supposing himself to be the subject of divine guidance, he permitted the marriage of his thirteen-year-old daughter to a Hindu prince contrary to previously espoused principle. Most of his followers defected to form the General Brahmo Samaj. In later life he attempted a synthesis of what he considered the finest elements in every world religion, drawing heavily on Christianity. In 1879 he proclaimed a New Dispensation involving Christian notions of divine revelation, apostolate, mission, monasticism, sin, salvation and the divinity of Jesus:

> In Christ we see not only the exaltedness of humanity, but also the grandeur of which Asiatic nature is susceptible. To us Asiatics, therefore, Christ is doubly interesting, and his religion is entitled to our peculiar regard as an altogether Oriental affair...And thus in Christ, Europe and Asia, the East and the West, may learn to find harmony and unity.

Sen's vision of commodious Hindu tolerance as the inclusivist catalyst for the convergence of conflicting creeds is echoed in the thought of many subsequent neo-Hindus.

Further reading

Killingley, D. (1993) *Rammohun Roy in Hindu and Christian Tradition*, Newcastle: Grevatt and Grevatt.

Kopf, D. (1978) *The Brahmo Samaj and the Shaping of the Modern Indian Mind*, Princeton, NJ: Princeton University Press.

CHRIS BARTLEY

Buddha-nature, theory of

The theory of 'Buddha-nature', or ***tathagatagarhba*** as it is known in Sanskrit, is one of the fundamental concepts of Mahayana Buddhism. The theory pertains to a notion of an 'embryo-essence' that is described in some texts as 'permanent', 'immutable', 'blissful' and 'eternal'. It is the presence of such an essence that is said to allow the possibility of purifying one's mind of its pollutants such as ignorance, desire and hatred, and enable it to 'express' its basic nature which is held to be pure. Insofar as it is Buddha-nature, which opens the possibility for full awakening and liberation, it is likened to a 'germinal seed'. In that it is the 'basis' upon which the process of realization takes place, it is also described as a 'causal sphere'. Thus the essential nature of mind is said to be pure and all mental pollutants like lust, hatred, jealousy and so on are adventitious; that is, removable from the essential mind. All sentient beings are thought to possess this nature.

Tibetan Buddhist schools, on the whole, accept the theory of Buddha-nature and also that its principal classical Indian source lies in Maitreya's *Ratnagotravibhaga* and the Mahayana scripture known as *Tathagatagarbhasutra*. However, there is a great divergence of opinions on whether the theory should be accepted as literal or interpreted as metaphorical. The crux of the dispute pertains to the problem of description of the ultimate nature of reality. Those who accept the theory literally tend to adopt an affirmative language in their description of the ultimate truth and on the whole believe

the Buddha-nature to be some kind of an absolute. For their opponents, however, the acceptance of such an absolute entity is tantamount to resuscitating the notion of ***atman*** (eternal soul), the rejection of which is central to the pan-Buddhist doctrine of no-self (*anatman*). Thus, from their point of view, it is the **emptiness** of mind, the absence of mind's intrinsic existence, which must be identified as Buddha-nature. It is this openness or non-subtantiality that is said to allow the possibility for awakening. The dispute also reflects a difference of soteriological views. For the literalist, 'awakening' is a process of 'uncovering' for the Buddha literally exists within the individual, albeit veiled. In contrast, for the non-literalist, 'awakening' is both a process of cleansing the mind of its pollutants and also a process of perfecting the positive potentials inherent to mind.

Predictably, the dispute reflects a hermeneutical difference between the two sides. For the proponents of the literal interpretation of the theory, Maitreya's works represent the epitome of Mahayana philosophical thinking, while for others it is **Nagarjuna**'s Madhyamaka writings that represent the culmination of Buddhist philosophical thought. Although the two opposing trends broadly correspond to the two sides of what is known as the 'intrinsic emptiness' (*rang tong*) versus 'extrinsic emptiness' (*shen tong*) debate, the literal theorists are not always the followers of the Shentong school (see **Shentong philosophy**). For example, Taktsang Lotsawa (b. 1405 CE) refers to a school called 'Mentalist Madhyamaka' (*nam rik u ma*) which shares all the key elements of the literal theorist, yet is distinct from the Shentong school. Principal proponents of the nonliteralists include **Chapa Chokyi Senge**, **Buton Rinchen Drup**, **Tsongkhapa** and **Gyaltsap Dharma Rinchen**.

See also: accident

Further reading

Ruegg, D. (1989) *Buddha-Nature, Mind and the Problem of Gradualism in a Comparative Perspective: On the Transmission and Reception of Buddhism in India and Tibet*, The Jordan Lectures in Comparative Religion, vol. 13, London: School of Oriental and African Studies, ch. 1.

Williams, P. (1989), *Mahayana Buddhism*, London: Routledge, ch. 5.

THUPTEN JINPA

Buddhism, Chinese hermeneutics

Chinese Buddhist hermeneutics or 'theory of interpretation' includes the *panjiao* system of tenet classification. Faced with the confusing array of disparate Buddhist teachings arriving from India and trusting that they were ultimately about the same *dharma*, the Chinese Buddhists worked hard to make sense of these teachings and place them in an appropriate theoretical context. Building on paradigms in use already in India, they refined and remade them for new ends. The best known scheme came from Zhiyi of the Tiantai school. Called the 'Five Periods and Eight Teachings', it claims to date exactly when different types of scripture were taught by the Buddha in his life time on earth. It follows a logic of progression in the unfolding of the *dharma* as it was being adjusted to the audience, the capacity, the time and the place. It places the sudden teaching of the *Avatamsaka Sutra* immediately after the Buddha's enlightenment, and reserves the *Parinirvana Sutra* for his last day on earth. In between, the Buddha adjusted his teaching by gradual and expanding steps. The *Lotus Sutra* is given the honour of being the consummate gospel that subsumes all other teaching within itself.

The Huayan school has its own system of classifying the Ten Schools based more on the commentatorial divisions, and other schools and other individual masters had their own teleological orderings of the teachings. A common sequence is this:

> Hinayana Abhidharma (teaches) the phenomenal many;
> Madhyamika (teaches) universal emptiness of all phenomena;
> Ekayana (One Vehicle) of the *Lotus Sutra* (teaches) the all-inclusive transcendental one;
> Dharmadhatu (Realm of *dharma*) of the *Huayan Sutra* (teaches) infinity: all is one, one is all.

This set up in effect a progression of Many, Zero, One and Infinite, which favours a Huayan teleology. It starts with (1) the facts of the many in this seemingly fragmented world of **samsara**. It then advances to (2), realizing the universal emptiness of all worldly things. After that negative dialectical form of reasoning, it takes (3) a positive turn and affirms a transcendental unity. This is the One (Vehicle) associated with the *Lotus Sutra* that then absolves all the phenomenal particulars and draws them all up into itself. This is then topped by the Huayan insight (4) into the infinite nature of the All: every part of the universe is now at once the total universe, generating everything and being generated by each and every part, in an endless, moment to moment, celebration of this perfection of all perfections. Between (2) and (3) one can insert the non-dual teaching of the *Vimalakirti Sutra* and the doctrine of a permanent **buddha nature** from the *Nirvana Sutra*.

Further reading

Chappell, D. (ed.) (1983) *T'ien-t'ai Buddhism: An Outline of its Fourfold Teachings*, Tokyo: Daiichi Shobo.
Lopez, D. (ed.) (1988) *Buddhist Hermeneutics*, Honolulu, HA: University of Hawaii Press.

WHALEN LAI

Buddhism, Korean

Buddhism, which originated in India in the sixth century BCE and was introduced to China in the first century CE, arrived in Korea in the fourth century CE. It was introduced first to Koguryo, the northern part of the Three Kingdoms, in 372 CE, where the Chinese monk Sundo brought Buddhist images and scriptures. Soon thereafter, Buddhist temples were built in Pyongyang and Buddhism was promoted by the king of Koguryo.

The Paekche kingdom in the southwestern part of the Three Kingdoms received Buddhism in 384 CE, when the Indian monk Mararant'a arrived at the kingdom. He was well received by the king, who was interested in Buddhism. In the sixth century, the Paekche kingdom sent Buddha images and scriptures to Japan, marking the beginning of Japanese Buddhism. Later, many Buddhist monks and artists went to Japan.

The Silla kingdom in the southeastern part of the Three Kingdoms received Buddhism in 527 CE. Silla society was conservative, and at the beginning it reacted negatively to Buddhism. But after the martyrdom of Ich'adon in 528, Buddhism grew rapidly in Silla and produced famous monks such as Wongwang, **Uisang** and **Wonhyo**, and built great temples. Buddhism was an important spiritual aspect of Hwarangdo (the Way of Flower Youth), the military academy of elite youth in Silla, which produced the leaders of the Silla kingdom who became the major force in unifying the Three Kingdoms.

Silla Buddhism was transformed from an aristocrat-centered religion to the religion of the masses. This was its main strength. Compared with this, Buddhism of Koguryo and Paekche were weak, because they were mainly the religion of the privileged upper class and did not appeal to the masses. In the Silla kingdom, a belief in Maitreya, the Future Buddha, played an important role in connecting the rulers and the commoners. Buddhism was a popular belief among the masses, one which led them to identify their king with a Buddhist deity.

The golden age of Silla Buddhist culture was around the 7th–8th centuries CE. By then, through the strong support of Silla kings, Buddhism was firmly rooted in Korea. Hwangyong-sa temple, Punhwang-sa temple, the famous Pulguk-sa temple, Sokgul-am temple and other great temples were built during this period. Wongwang, Chajang, Uisang and other great monks returned after studies in China, and their scholarly works enlightened and advanced Silla Buddhism.

The primary reason for the great achievements of Silla Buddhism is its powerful idea of one vehicle, the essential idea of Mahayana Buddhism. Silla not only unified the Three Kingdoms by military force but also unified the Buddhism of the Three Kingdoms through the idea of one vehicle, and achieved a universal and common national Buddhism. However, Silla Buddhism began to decline as it gradually became divided among different schools, neglecting its great universal idea

of one vehicle. This factor in turn was a primary cause of the fall of the Silla kingdom.

Buddhism was again the state religion during the Koryo dynasty (10th–14th century). By this time, however, Buddhism was divided into many schools. Among them, the Son (Zen, **meditation**) School and the Doctrinal School were equally strong. Koryo Buddhism was superstitious, incorporating ideas such as **geomancy** (*feng-sui*) and emphasizing rituals for good fortune and wealth in this life, neglecting the authentic Buddhist way of meditation and spiritual training. Such phenomena were rightly criticized by Confucian scholars at the end of the Koryo dynasty.

However, there were some bright developments during the Koryo period. The most brilliant and glorious achievement of Koryo Buddhism was the production of the *Tripitaka Koreana* (the Korean compilation of Buddhist texts) with the most advanced woodblock printing technique available at that time in the world. The *Tripitaka*, totalling 81,340 woodblocks, which exists today in Haeinsa Temple, was carved in the thirteenth century CE. It is called *P'alman Taejang-gyong* (Eighty Thousand Tripitaka), and is a national treasure of Korea. It is the world's oldest extant and most precise set of Mahayana Buddhist texts. Another important event that developed in this time was the founding of the Chogye School of Buddhism by a great monk, Pojoguksa, or **Chinul** (1158–1210). He established the Chogye Order by unifying the Son (Meditation) and Doctrinal schools, and thereby popularized Buddhism and provided the means of completing the monumental Tripitaka project.

One of the main reasons for the fall of the Koryo dynasty was the corruption and wasteful spending of the national treasury by Buddhist leaders and rulers. At the end of the dynasty, Confucian scholars like Chong Mong-ju advocated the rejection of Buddhism, and Neo-Confucianism, which was introduced from China, became a powerful philosophical force. As Buddhism began to lose its credibility, so Confucianism was ascending. The Choson dynasty (14th–20th century), founded by Yi Song-gye, rejected Buddhism and adopted Confucianism as the state religion and philosophy. Gradually Buddhism was suppressed during the Choson dynasty, and monks fled into the mountains as persecutions against them grew.

During the Japanese invasion in the sixteenth century the great Buddhist masters, Sosan, Samyong and other Buddhist monks, rose with their followers and organized military forces against the invaders and defended the nation in crisis. This is regarded as the continuation of the spirit of Hwarang in the Silla period, who unified the Three Kingdoms following Buddhist ideals. Masters Sosan and Samyong contributed also significantly to the revival of the Son (Zen) tradition in Korean Buddhism. Nevertheless, the Choson rulers continued the persecution of Buddhism. While in hiding, many Buddhists found an opportunity for self-examination and self-cultivation. As a result, great Buddhist masters were produced during the Choson dynasty, and they made significant contributions to Buddhism and to the nation with their demonstration of patriotic spirit.

During Japanese imperial rule in Korea (1910–45), Korean Buddhism was reshaped under Japanese colonialism. The modern period was a time of critical self-examination for Korean Buddhism. One of the pioneering thinkers in modern Korean Buddhism was Han Yong-un, who advocated the reformation of Korean Buddhism by restructuring and removing all the negative and superstitious elements. He also advocated the independence of Korean Buddhism from government control and interference. He wanted to make Buddhism progressive, modern and appealing to the masses. He was also a great leader of the independence movement, fighting against Japanese colonialism in Korea.

Since 1945, the year of liberation of Korea from Japanese colonialism, the Chogye School has maintained its central headquarters in Seoul, overseeing the thirty-one main temples of the country. The Chogye Order is the largest body of Buddhism in Korea. There are also many other relatively small schools of Buddhism in Korea. Nominally, Buddhism is one of the largest religions in Korea today. However, it is weaker than Christianity in terms of activities and vitality in areas such as attendance at regular meetings, educational programmes, financial resources, and influence in society and politics.

See also: new religions in Korea

Further reading

Buswell, E.R. (1989) *The Formation of Ch'an Ideology in China and Korea*, Princeton, NJ: Princeton University Press.

Chung Byong-jo (1996) 'Korean Buddhism: Harmonizing the Contradictory', *Korean Cultural Heritage, Vol. II: Thought and Religion*, ed. J. Kim, Seoul: Korea Foundation, 50ff.

Keel Hee-sung (1993) 'Word and Wordlessness: The Spirit of Korean Buddhism', *Korea Journal* Autumn: 11–22.

Korean Buddhist Research Institute (ed.) (1993) *The History and Culture of Buddhism in Korea*, Seoul: Dongguk University Press.

Lancaster L. and Yu C. (eds) (1993) *Introduction of Buddhism to Korea*, Berkeley, CA: Asian Humanities Press.

—— (eds) (1996) *Buddhism in Koryo: A Royal Religion*, Berkeley, CA: Institute of East Asian Studies, University of California at Berkeley.

—— (eds) (1996) *Buddhism in the Early Choson: Suppression and Transformation*, Berkeley, CA: Institute of East Asian Studies, University of California at Berkeley.

Lee, P. (eds) (1993) *Sourcebook of Korean Civilization, Vol. I*, New York: Columbia University Press, 62–99; 384–428.

Park Sung Bae (1983) *Buddhist Faith and Sudden Enlightenment*, Albany, NY: State University of New York Press.

YONG-CHOON KIM

Buddhism, late Ming

Buddhism declined after the Song dynasty. By the Ming period, most monks were involved only in providing funeral services, partly because the state prohibited the two other groups of monks – the meditational and the philosophical – from active contact with the laity. The late Ming period does however boast four grand masters: Zuhung (1535–1615), who brought about reform within the *Sangha*, Zhenke (1543–1603), Deqing (1545–1623) and Zhixu (1599–1655). Zhuhung combined Chan and Pure Land Buddhism, and turned the chanting of Amitabha Buddha's name into a **koan**, 'Who is chanting the name?' Deqing harmonized Chan and Huayan. Zhixu, of Tiantai affiliation, reconciled Faxing and Faxiang (that is, Huayan and Weishi). The four grand masters came after Wang Yangming, who was inspired by Chan and who in turn revived that school.

WHALEN LAI

Buddhism in China, origins and development

Chinese Buddhism is an extension of the Pan-Asian Buddhist tradition and should be seen as an organic part of it. Buddhism in China can be divided into three major periods: (1) the time for incorporating the essentials, lasting up to the advent of the Sui dynasty; (2) the time of mature growth and the establishment of the independent Sinitic Mahayana schools in the Sui and Tang dynasties (up to the persecution of 845); and (3) the retrenchment thereafter that saw the fusion of schools and the consolidating of styles. This stage reached its peak in the Song dynasty. By the Ming dynasty, the classical renaissance that was Song Neo-Confucianism had outpaced and undercut the Buddhists. The Neo-Confucians maligned Buddhism, as an unwanted, un-Chinese, alien tradition.

Buddhism first came into China around the first century CE during the Han dynasty. Its meditative technique was absorbed through the then current Daoist vocabulary of refining the **qi** (breath, vital force), keeping guard over the *i* (the active thoughts) and actualizing the *shen* (the immortal soul). Deeper philosophical exchange came in the Wei–Jin period when the Mahayana concept of *shunyata* (**emptiness**) found resonance with Wang Bi's **non-being**, just as the notion with which it is associated, *tathata* (suchness), came to be linked with Guo Xiang's being-as-is. Such a concept matching exercise is natural to any initial cultural exchange. The possibility of distortion did not sink in until Dao'an became aware of it, and was not exposed until Kumarajiva tutored Sengzhao (384–414) on the full import of Mahayana emptiness as formulated in the Madhyamika philosophy of **Nagarjuna**. Emptiness is not non-being; it is the

eternal neither/nor, the emptying of both being and non-being.

But no sooner did that negative dialectics sink in than the *Mahaparinirvana Sutra* arrived in China and reinstated a positive-sounding, higher self or **atman** called the **buddha nature**. Chinese Buddhists spent the next century looking for this buddha-essence and working out a discourse on the **Two Truths**. The emptying of worldly reality was seen as a step leading to the attainment of the transmundane truth of a real Buddhahood. **Yogachara** or Mahayana idealism then arrived in the early sixth century. By about 550, a text compiled or authored in China called *The Awakening of Faith in Mahayana* attempted a bold synthesis and set down a dense digest of the essentials of Mahayana. This had an impact on all the major independent Chinese schools.

In the Sui–Tang period, under a China reunited and with strong imperial support, four major Sinitic Mahayana schools rose:

Tiantai of the *Lotus Sutra*, in Sui;
Pure Land of the *Pure Land Sutra*, by early Tang;
Huayan of the *Avatamshaka Sutra*, under Chou Empress Wu (700 CE);
Chan, at around the same time.

Of these four, Tientai defended a Chinese reading of the Three Truths thesis in Madhyamika that is influenced by *yin–yang* harmony. Pure Land built a cult of devotion to Amitabha in the West that conflated with the Daoist myth of the Queen Mother of the West. Huayan came to the defence of the 'Mind Only' Idealism of the *Awakening of Faith* then being challenged by the new 'Consciousness Only' school which Xuanzong had brought back from India. And just as Indian Buddhism faded from its homeland and could offer little further inspiration to China, Chan made a point of forsaking all reliance on (Sanskrit) scriptures and evolving a new, native genre. The Sinicization of Buddhism was by design or by default complete.

See also: Keyi Buddhism

Further reading

Chen, K. (1964) *Buddhism in China*, Princeton, NJ: Princeton University Press.

Hakeda, Y. (1967) *The Awakening of Faith*, New York: Columbia University Press.

Zurcher, E. (1959) *The Buddhist Conquest of China*, 2 vols, Leiden: Brill.

WHALEN LAI

Buddhist philosophy in Japan

Early Japanese Buddhism and the Nara schools

The arrival of Buddhism in sixth-century Japan occurred under conditions radically different from those in China, where Buddhism was introduced in the first and second centuries CE. In Japan, Buddhism was not confronted with a sophisticated native tradition of philosophical reflection. Perhaps even more significantly, the Japanese never felt the need to translate the Buddhist canon; Buddhist scriptures came to the Japanese (as to the Koreans) in Chinese translation, as part of the influx of Chinese culture and civilization that served as the model for the formation of the Japanese state in the sixth and seventh centuries. While in China great effort was put into the translation and thus Sinification of Buddhist scriptures, these same scriptures came to the Japanese *prêt-à-porter*, in a language that was understood and with an abundance of exegetical commentaries, ritual guidebooks and examples for institutional implementation. For better or worse, the Japanese were spared the great efforts made in China to domesticate the religion.

This is not to say, of course, that Buddhism arrived in a cultural vacuum. Buddhism was introduced in the context of pre-existing *kami* cults, and at first found a niche in Japan as a new *kami* cult, differing from traditional cults only in that it focused on a foreign deity and employed a dazzling repertoire of exotic ritual forms. This cult was conducted first by the Soga clan, who dominated the clan alliance around the Yamato (imperial) clan until 645, and later also by other leading clans, including the imperial clan itself. From the second half of the seventh century onwards, Buddhist rites (the chanting and copying of *sutras*, ceremonial lectures on sutras, penances, retreats of monks in the palace, vegetarian banquets, bans on hunting) were conducted at the court as a means of generating merit (good **karma**) to be transferred to the imperial lineage for the benefit and protection of the nation. This Buddhist ritual system functioned alongside a reformed system of *kami* rituals. In the event of a drought, for example, imperial envoys would be sent to *kami* shrines while monks were ordered to chant appropriate *sutras* at the ever-growing network of state temples.

Until *c.*750, the policy of the court was to monopolise the merit created by the Buddhist clergy. Monks and nuns were forbidden from engaging in religious activity outside their temples, and the ordination of monks was a state prerogative. Buddhist practices did, however, exert an influence on popular religion, even as early as the early eighth century. Ascetics known as 'privately ordained monks', who practised austerities in the mountains (which were traditionally regarded as the abode of the dead, and of the *kami*), adopted a wide variety of Buddhist rites and terms. Their practice became the source of an amalgamated *kami*–Buddhist religion that dominated most of popular religious life in Japan until at least the late nineteenth century.

Court policy regarding Buddhism changed slightly in the second half of the eighth century. In the 740s, Emperor Shomu (r. 724–49) undertook to build a temple of unprecedented size in the capital of Nara, containing a large image of Dainichi (in Sanskrit, Vairochana (Great Sun)), the buddha of the Avatamshaka (in Japanese, Kegon) or Flower Garland *sutra*. This temple (later known as Todaiji) functioned as the centrepiece of a nationwide network of provincial temples, all raising merit for the protection of the nation. To make this large-scale building project possible, the court pardoned and recruited popular 'privately ordained monks'. The concept of this national network of temples, focusing on the Dainichi image at the capital, cast the emperor in the role of head priest of a national cult (not coincidentally similar to the *kami* cult to yet another sun deity, the imperial ancestor Amaterasu), which formed part of the imperial project of transforming Japan into a centralized state along Chinese lines.

While doctrinal study was of secondary importance to ritual practice, it was certainly not neglected. In Nara, there were six main schools (*shu*) of Buddhist thought. These were not mutually exclusive sects; rather, they represented specializations within Buddhist scholarship that were thought to reinforce and complement each other. The most important among these six schools were the Sanron, Hosso and Kegon schools.

The first was based (via the Chinese Sanlun school) on the Indian 'Middle Path' or Madhyamika school, and offered a systematic method of attaining *prajna* or insight through the analytic investigation of all objects and concepts in **meditation**. The aim of this meditation was to realise that no object or concept, when analysed by this method, does 'really exist': all prove to be the result of karmic causes, which in turn have their origin in the mind. Lacking in 'inherent existence', they are all 'empty' and thus 'equal'.

The Hosso school was the Japanese representative of the Indian Chittamatra or **Yogachara** school, often translated as 'Mind Only'. In subtle contrast to the Sanron school, this school did believe in the 'inherent existence' of something at least: a causal flow that exists in our minds as a sort of substratum. This flow constitutes the deepest level of consciousness in our minds, known as our 'storehouse consciousness'. It is an ever-changing stream containing what Hosso scholars called 'seeds', sown by our personal *karma* and waiting to be activated by our conceptualizing minds. These seeds trigger our senses, and thus relay to us a steady flow of perceptions. To these, our 'tainted mind' attaches itself, and construes distinctions and conceptualizations that are ultimately unreal, and that are the cause of our suffering. The distant aim of practice, which could be achieved only after many lifetimes, was to purify our storehouse consciousness and eventually make its causal flow cease altogether. Importantly, this aim could not be achieved by all: the Hosso school distinguished between five categories of human beings, with different potentials for enlightenment. The highest three could aim to become 'listeners' (disciples of the Buddha), *pratyekabuddhas* (ascetics who attain enlightenment by themselves), and *bodhisattvas* (see **bodhisattva**). Others' 'seeds' were unstable, or in the case of the lowest category, simply too coarse to allow advancement on the Buddhist path. This last point led to prolonged disputes with the Sanron, and later the Kegon and Tendai schools, all of which insisted that all sentient beings had the potential to attain enlightenment.

The Kegon school was the Japanese equivalent of the Chinese Huayan school, systematized by Fazang (643–712). As mentioned above, it focused on the Flower Garland *sutra*. This large *sutra* describes the universe as seen by a buddha, from the viewpoint of the enlightened: as a single flow in which everything penetrates everything else, in which all things are one and yet are clearly distinguishable. This state of multiplicity within unity is personified in the buddha Dainichi, the 'World-Buddha' who is, in fact, the universe itself. The total interpenetration of all phenomena that characterizes the 'world as it really is' accounts for the real possibility of miracle-working: the ultimate reality of the world lies in the enlightened mind, and as the mind moves, the world moves with it. As mentioned above, the introduction of this school, with its doctrine of multiplicity within unity, inspired the imperial project of the building of the Todaiji temple in Nara.

Tendai and Shingon

A second wave of Buddhist scholarship entered Japan in the early ninth century with the founding of the Tendai and Shingon schools by Saicho (767–822) and Kukai (774–835), respectively. These schools soon overshadowed the Nara schools, and they and their offshoots have dominated Japanese Buddhism to this day.

Tendai was an imported version of the Chinese Tiantai school, established by Zhiyi (538–97) at Mount Tiantai in modern Zhejiang, where Saicho studied for eight months (804–5) as a monk-student sponsored by the Japanese court. Zhiyi attempted to classify the Buddhist canon, with its countless and often contradicting scriptures, by dividing the main *sutra*s into five groups, each of which, he argued, was preached by the Buddha during different periods of his life. During the first period, immediately after his attainment of enlightenment, the Buddha preached the Flower Garland *sutra*; but he soon found that this teaching was too advanced and pure for his audience to grasp, and for many years afterwards, he preached a succession of simpler, more relative teachings. The last and ultimate teaching to be taught by the Buddha was the Lotus *sutra* (*Saddharma-pundarika sutra*; in Japanese, *Myoho renge-kyo* or *Hoke-kyo*).

Interpretations of the Lotus *sutra*, then, constituted the core of Tiantai thought. This sutra is a complicated work consisting of many component layers, but perhaps the key point it makes is that every sentient being has the capacity to become a fully-fledged buddha. The distinctions between the 'three vehicles' or religious ideals of 'listener', *pratyekabuddha* and *bodhisattva* (as stressed, for example, by the Hosso school) are negated at length, and instead the *sutra* puts forward the 'one vehicle', in which all others are subsumed, and which enables all to attain full buddhahood. The Buddha of the Lotus *sutra*, moreover, is a cosmic figure, of which the historical Buddha was but an emanation. As already suggested by the position of the Flower Garland *sutra* in Zhiyi's *sutra* classification, Tiantai shared many of the characteristics of the (slightly later) Huayan school; perhaps most importantly the notion of a 'World-Buddha' who constitutes the universe, and the related idea that since all phenomena (or, more accurately, *dharma*s) interpenetrate, all sentient beings partake of the **'buddha nature'** that pervades the universe.

The ramifications of this notion become clear when we consider Tiantai's position on another topic that had already inspired debates between the Sanron and Hosso schools (as well as their Chinese predecessors): the question of inherent existence. Are all *dharma*s 'empty', as argued by the Sanron school, or is there a causal flow that 'really exists' as a substratum in our minds, as Hosso scholars believed? Tiantai/Tendai's view of this problem is summed up in the phrase 'the threefold truth'. The first of these 'truths' states that all *dharma*s are empty; the second says that in spite of that fact, *dharma*s do enjoy temporary existence, and as such trigger our senses. The first truth shows the universe as a single, uniform, undifferentiated whole; the second recognizes that it appears to our senses as a multitude of particular, distinct phenomena. The third (and highest) 'truth', finally, reveals that all *dharma*s are empty and temporarily existent at the same time. In the final analysis, the universe is both 'one' and 'many'; it is a realm in which the whole and its parts are identical. Being ultimately 'one', all its parts interpenetrate, and every fragment of it, every grain of sand or even

every thought that occurs to our minds, contains the whole of the universe in its ultimate unity. This ultimate unity is then defined as the enlightenment of the World-Buddha, or the buddha nature with which all *dharma*s are endowed.

Another perhaps less lofty but historically very important aspect of the Lotus *sutra* is that it contains references to the possibility of rebirth in the Western Paradise of the buddha Amida (in Sanskrit, Amitayus or Amitabha), and devotes a chapter to the great compassion of the *bodhisattva* Kannon (Avalotiteshvara), who saves even the staunchest sinners. These divine figures became important focuses of religious faith both among the monastic community and the laity.

While in China Tiantai was soon overshadowed by Huayan, the reverse occurred in Japan, where Tendai arrived some sixty years later than Kegon. Saicho established his headquarters on Mount Hiei, overlooking the new capital of Heiankyo (Kyoto, founded 794), and spent much of his energy struggling with the Nara Buddhist establishment. Most famous is his debate with the Hosso monk Tokuitsu (*fl. c.*820), who argued against the Tendai tenet that the teaching of the 'three vehicles' is no more than a provisional one, aimed at those who are unable to grasp the ultimate teaching of the 'one vehicle' according to which every sentient being can attain full buddhahood. Tokuitsu argued that not the teachings of the 'three vehicles', but that of the 'one vehicle' is provisional – intended only for those with 'unstable seeds'. Politically, however, the more significant battle was Saicho's struggle to gain imperial permission for the institution of an independent 'ordination platform' at Mount Hiei. At this time, all monks were ordained at Todaiji in Nara (or at two dependencies in the north and south), according to a 'Hinayana' monastic code of discipline (in Sanskrit, *vinaya*) known in its Chinese recension as *Sifenlü* (Precepts in Four Parts); Saicho applied for permission to ordain Tendai monks at Mount Hiei according to the 'Mahayana' bodhisattva precepts laid down in the *Bonmokyo* (*Brahmajala*, or 'Net of Brahma' *sutra*), which were intended for lay believers rather than the monastic community. The establishment of the Hiei ordination platform in 822 marked the beginning of two important trends in Japanese Buddhism: progressive sectarianism, and a narrowing of the distance between monastic clergy and lay believers. The establishment of the first sectarian ordination platform was an important step in the development of schools into sects, and soon it became less common for monks to look beyond their own Buddhist lineage. Moreover, while the Buddhism of the Nara schools was almost exclusively a state cult, Tendai (and Shingon) Buddhism also played an important role in the lives of the laity, albeit at first among aristocratic circles alone.

Like Tiantai, Tendai was an extremely broad church, including a wide variety of teachings and scriptures as at least relative truths and therefore valuable as steps leading to the ultimate teaching of Lotus *sutra*. Moreover, the 'perfect teaching' (*engyo*) of the Lotus *sutra* was but one of four fields of Tendai study and practice; the others were the precepts (*kai*), meditation (*zen*), and 'esoteric' or 'tantric' teachings (*mikkyo*). The last two were to play a major role in subsequent centuries. The intricate repertoire of esoteric rituals for a broad range of magical purposes was of more interest to the court than Buddhist philosophy; after all, the court sponsored monks' study in China precisely with a view to importing such rituals for the protection of the nation. Much to his detriment, Saicho's knowledge of esoteric teaching and ritual was scant; the esoteric expert of his age was his contemporary Kukai, the founder of the Shingon school.

Esoteric Buddhism differs from Theravada and Mahayana varieties of Buddhism to the extent that it is often set apart from these as a 'vehicle' of its own: Vajrayana, or the 'Diamond Vehicle'. Indeed, Kukai's esoteric Buddhism was built on premises radically different from those of all other schools that had entered Japan up to this time. All of these, including Kegon and Tendai, view the phenomena of this world as 'empty', produced by and in our minds alone, due to karmic causes. Esoteric Buddhism, in contrast, argues that both the world and the 'World-Buddha' Dainichi consist of the same six 'great elements' (earth, water, fire, wind, space and consciousness), and that these elements are no less than the concrete matter of enlightenment itself. The universe, then, is seen as a single, compassionate being, in which all parts consist of the same matter of enlightenment that is

symbolically personified as Dainichi. The term 'emptiness' is also used in esoteric Buddhist thought, but in a different meaning, referring to the absence of obstructions that could prevent any constituting part of the universe from realizing and sharing in the unitary source of that same universe: Dainichi's universal enlightenment.

The main practice of esoteric Buddhism is not to attain enlightenment (since being of this universe, one is already inherently enlightened), but rather to realise or gain access to the enlightenment out of which one's own body and mind are made. This is possible by attaining union with Dainichi or one of the numerous divinities that represent aspects of Dainichi. These divinities and their relation to each other and Dainichi are depicted in *mandala*s. There are numerous kinds of *mandala*s, and in fact each practitioner can compose his own *mandala*s on the basis of his personal insights, but the two *mandala*s that define Shingon's view of the universe are the Taizo or 'Womb' and Kongokai or 'Diamond Realm' *mandala*s, based on Shingon's two fundamental *sutra*s, the Great Vairochana *sutra* (in Sanskrit, *Mahavairocana sutra*; in Japanese, *Dainichi-kyo*) and the Diamond Peak *sutra* (in Sanskrit, *Vajrashekhara sutra*; in Japanese, *Kongocho-gyo*). Both feature Dainichi in the centre, and depict aspects of his/her existence and activity. The Womb *mandala* is thought to stress the quiescent presence of Dainichi's compassion, and the Diamond Realm *mandala* Dainichi's penetrating wisdom.

Attaining union with the divinities in these *mandala*s is possible through the practice of the 'three secrets' – the secrets of body, speech and mind. Forming the correct hand-posture or 'seal' (in Sansrkit, *mudra*; in Japanese, *in*), chanting the correct spell (*dharani* or *mantra*; *darani*, *shingon* or other terms), and meditating by means of the correct visualization practice (*samadhi*; *sanmai*) leads to union, and allows the practitioner to access and activate specific divinities. Knowledge about these secrets is transmitted in elaborate initiation ceremonies, called *kanjo* (in Sanskrit, *abhisheka*). Ultimately, this practice leads to the realization of the union of the twin aspects of Dainichi as depicted in the Womb and Diamond Realm *mandala*s, giving the practitioner free access to the enlightenment that constitutes both the universe and his own body. Mostly, however, practice of union through performance of the 'three secrets' of a divinity (known as *kaji*) also had more direct aims – notably the fulfilment of the this-worldly wishes of the ritual's sponsor. *Kaji* was to become the dominant format of ritualized prayer for centuries to come, not only in Buddhist but also in Shinto traditions.

Perhaps most central to the esoteric 'three secrets' is the second, speech. Shingon is firmly based on a particular, tantric view on language, and, more specifically, on syllables and spells laden with magical meaning. Such syllables and spells are not to be regarded as mere symbols or signs, referring to realities beyond them. In Shingon, these linguistic elements constitute reality itself in its purest form. Thus, the chanting of these spells, or the meditation on their written forms, gives direct access to the absolute language of ultimate reality. The syllable A, for example, does not refer to Dainichi as depicted in the Womb *mandala*, or teach that all *dharma*s form the body of Dainichi and as such exist independent of causation; rather, this syllable forms the essence of these truths, and allows those who meditate on it to grasp and realize them instantaneously.

Kukai, the founder of Shingon, spent most of his early years as a mountain ascetic. He acquired his systematic knowledge of esoteric thought and practice in China, where he studied for two years (804–6) and was initiated in the Zhenyan (Shingon) tradition by Huiguo (746–805). After his return, he proved the worth of his newly-acquired Chinese knowledge by successfully performing esoteric rituals for the imperial court. In contrast to Saicho, Kukai maintained good relations with the Nara Buddhist establishment; importantly, Shingon monks were ordained at Todaiji. He was able to build up a solid power base during the early decades of the ninth century, founding head-quarters for ascetic practice on Mount Koya in the mountains south of Nara, taking over the Toji temple in the capital, and even founding a Shingon chapel within the imperial palace.

Perhaps the most important contribution Kukai made to Japanese Buddhism was the introduction of a distinction between exoteric or 'open' teachings on the one hand, and esoteric or 'secret' ones on the other. Kukai labelled the existing Buddhist teachings known in Japan as exoteric teachings,

open to all, but because of that very fact rather superficial and containing only relative, provisional truths. The esoteric, secret teaching of Shingon, however, contained the absolute truth hidden beyond the various exoteric teachings, as revealed by Dainichi's '*dharma* body' itself. The distinction between open, conventional and superficial teachings on the one hand, and secret, exclusive and profoundly fundamental ones on the other, developed into a paradigm that provided the basic pattern of much of Japan's later religious thought.

Esoteric practice soon dominated court and state Buddhism, and also exerted a profound influence on the popular Buddhism of mountain ascetics. It must be noted that esoteric practices had been part and parcel in Japanese asceticism already long before Shingon's establishment, and Kukai's role was not so much to introduce esoteric Buddhism to Japan, as to systematize and institutionalize it. Moreover, even after Kukai, Shingon did not constitute a 'sect' but took the form of multiple, loosely connected lineages or branches, based at sub-centres scattered across the country. Kukai was, however, instrumental in establishing esoteric Buddhism firmly at the centre of court ritual. Both the Nara schools and Tendai jumped on the bandwagon of his success, and this led to what is often described as the 'esoterization' or 'tantrization' of Japanese Buddhism. Of particular importance is the esoterization of Tendai in the late ninth century, under Saicho's successors Ennin (794–864), Enchin (814–91) and Annen (b. 841), who all spent long periods of time in China and brought back a detailed knowledge of Tiantai esotericism. Tendai soon became Shingon's equal in the field of esoteric practice, and esoteric notions gradually came to dominate Tendai thought as well. This led to an increasing emphasis on the unity of the universe in Dainichi, and a de-emphasis of dualistic distinctions of all kinds. This esoterization of Tendai and, indeed, Kegon was achieved with remarkable ease, and did not lead to heated debates. One reason for this was the fact that the notion that all *dharma*s interpenetrate and are ultimately one in the 'World-Buddha', which was at the heart of Tendai (and Kegon) thought, was regarded as consistent with esoteric thought and practice.

Amidism

Rituals performed by Buddhist temples and monks during the Heian period (794–1192) can be largely grouped under two headings: rituals for the protection of the state and for this-worldly benefits on the one hand, and rituals for individual salvation in the afterlife on the other. The latter had been central from a very early date, and in fact provided the rationale for the founding of most temples, which were built expressly to transfer merit to a deceased relative. The hope was that the merit raised by the building of the temple and the ritual practice of the monks would allow the deceased to be reborn in one of the paradises created through the religious practice of particular *bodhisattvas* or buddhas: the paradises of the *bodhisattvas* Miroku (Maitreya) and Kannon (Avalokiteshvara), or of the buddhas Yakushi (Bhaishajyaguru), Ashuku (Akshobhya) and, most important of all, Amida (Amitayus or Amitabha). A particularly Japanese twist to this practice, inspired by native beliefs, was that the 'saved' ancestor would protect his descendants for generations to come.

The theological foundation for the belief in Buddhist paradises was the notion that the universe consists of countless 'buddha-fields', each the sphere of activity of one buddha. In the course of their practice as *bodhisattvas*, the compassion of such buddhas was thought to have 'purified' their sphere, rendering it a more amenable place for the attainment of enlightenment. Our *saha* (in Japanese, *shaba*) world is Shakyamuni's buddha-field, but is in fact very impure; one explanation suggested for this was that Shakyamuni is actually an 'emanation' of a buddha who has his buddha-field elsewhere. The impurity of our world renders it difficult (if not impossible) to attain enlightenment and salvation in it; therefore, our only option is to escape to another buddha-field by relying on the compassion of its buddha.

Despair of conditions in the *saha* world was further intensified by an eschatological view of history, which defined the age as the 'Latter Days of the Law' (*mappo*). This was based on a theory developed by Chinese (mostly Tiantai) monks in the course of the sixth century, stating that Buddhism would degenerate in three stages: from True Law, through Counterfeit Law to Degenerate

Law. In Japan, this last stage was widely thought to have begun in 1052 (which, according to a Chinese tradition, was 2,000 years after Shakyamuni's death). Under these circumstances, many thought traditional Buddhist practice had lost its salvific capacity, and saw no other possibility than to place their faith in buddhas such as Amida.

Amida and his 'Pure Land' in the distant west not only feature in the Lotus *sutra*, but are also the subject of a group of three *sutra*s. These describe Amida's paradise and his vows to save all sentient beings, as well as various methods to invoke him. Amidist practices were popular in China as early as the sixth century, and the invocation and visualization of Amida formed part of standard Tendai practice in Japan from an early date. Rituals focusing on Amida were first performed at the deathbed of court aristocrats, and spread from there to the general populace. Rising numbers of begging monks even performed Amida rituals for corpses left by the roadside, and spread Amida devotion among the general populace.

Gradually, Amidist practice changed from visualization and meditation to invocation. Thirteen visualization practices of Amida and the Pure Land are described in the (at least largely) Chinese 'Visualization of Amitayus' *sutra* (in Chinese, *Guanwuliangshou-jing*, in Japanese, *Kanmuryoju-kyo*); such practices also continued to form the mainstream of Amidist practice in Japan until the late Heian period. The most well-known Japanese text on such visualization practices is the influential *Essays on Rebirth into Paradise* (*Ojo yoshu*) (985), by the Tendai monk Genshin (942–1017). The meditation practices described in these works demand much religious training and effort on the part of the believer, and rely on his own powers to achieve the desired result. Others, however, argued that such complicated exercises are unnecessary, and that the invocation of Amida's name alone is sufficient to ensure rebirth in the Pure Land. Advocates of this practice argued that one should renounce one's belief in one's 'own power' (*jiriki*), and rely completely on the 'other power' (*tariki*) of Amida for salvation. An important scriptural basis for this was offered by the so-called 'Larger Sukhavati-vyuha' *sutra* (*Muryoju-kyo*), an Indian sutra that dates back at least to the second century and which records 48 (or 46) vows made by Amida during his practice as a *bodhisattva*. The eighteenth of these vows in particular promises that 'those who believe in Amida and sincerely wish to be reborn in his Pure Land need invoke his name (or think of him) only ten times', excepting only those who have committed one of the five most serious offences. The practice of incantation of Amida's name was given added impetus by the esoteric view on language: invoking Amida's name was the same as realizing the reality of Amida and his compassion.

These ideas can already be encountered in the writings of the first Chinese patriarch of Pure Land Buddhism, Tanluan (476–542); in Japan, they came to the fore only in the twelfth and thirteenth centuries, with the appearance of Honen (1133–1212) and Shinran (1173–1262), who will be discussed further below.

Kamakura Buddhism

Japanese Buddhism went through a new period of transformation during the late twelfth and thirteenth centuries. This period saw the origin of some of the sects that dominate modern Japanese Buddhism: Pure Land Buddhism (Jodo-shu), True Pure Land Buddhism (Jodo Shin-shu), Zen (notably Soto-shu and Rinzai-shu) and Nichiren Buddhism (Nichiren-shu). All of these new sects, which are often referred to collectively as Kamakura Buddhism because of their origin in the Kamakura period (1192–1333), were inspired by the lives and works of Tendai monks who broke away from Mount Hiei and established their own following. At the time, however, these new sects were still in a seminal stage, and the age was thoroughly dominated by Tendai, Shingon and some of the old Nara schools (notably Hosso and Kegon). These schools too went through great changes, and produced many innovators in the fields of both thought and ritual.

The foundation for these developments was laid during a period of great political turmoil, which led to the demise of imperial court rule and the establishment of the first *bakufu* or shogunate in 1192. During the latter half of the twelfth century, court aristocrats lost control over the country to a rapidly rising warrior class, in a painful process of successive wars that, perhaps most traumatically, saw the repeated destruction of the capital of Kyoto, the burning of the Todaiji, and the death by drowning of the child-emperor Antoku. The establishment of a separate power structure headed by a military leader with the title of *shogun* in Kamakura inaugurated a new era in Japan's political history, and established a political pattern that endured until 1868, when the third and last shogunate collapsed.

This period also brought great turmoil to the Buddhist world. The Buddhist monastic establishment depended on court patronage and private estates for its income; but both were threatened by the country's state of virtual or real warfare during much of the late twelfth century. Monasteries developed large armies and formed a formidable party in many of the power conflicts fought out during this period. As a result, precepts were increasingly ignored and practice became lax, leaving Japanese Buddhism increasingly ritualistic. This again confirmed and strengthened *mappo* pessimism.

These developments went hand in hand with the above-mentioned 'esoterization' of Japanese Buddhism, and the increasing emphasis on the unity of the universe as the realm of Dainichi's universal enlightenment. Statements such as 'life-and-death are the same as *nirvana*', or 'ignorance is the same as enlightenment', which can be encountered throughout Mahayana literature, took on a new literalness. While before, these statements had been intended as tentative descriptions of the enlightened insights attained as the result of prolonged and strenuous religious practice, they now came to be advocated as increasingly literal truths. The most radical argued that since all sentient beings, or indeed non-sentient beings including 'plants and trees', are enlightened just as they are, there is no need to practise anything at all. Since all possess a superior, natural 'inherent enlightenment' (*hongaku*) from birth, there is no need to exert oneself on the 'exoteric' path, that can only lead to an inferior form of 'acquired enlightenment' (*shigaku*). Less radical (and perhaps more common) varieties of this notion, that is widely referred to as '*hongaku* thought', argued that one's inherent enlightenment had to be 'realized' through the practice of union. All varieties of *hongaku* thought served to explain the age's relaxed attitude to the precepts and religious practice, and sought to kindle renewed hope in what was generally regarded as an age of terminal decline of the Buddhist Way.

Hongaku thought had its scriptural basis in the Chinese ***Awakening of Faith in Mahayana*** (*Dacheng Qixinlun*) and a commentary on this text, entitled *Shi Moheyanlun*. Both were basic textbooks of Tiantai/Tendai thought, and argued that all sentient beings possess the 'buddha nature' and are therefore able to attain full buddhahood. It was only in twelfth century Japan, however, that these texts were first interpreted in the way described above.

The history of Buddhism in the Kamakura period has been described as the history of the further development of *hongaku* thought, and of reactions against it. Such reactions took two forms: attempts at reviving the precepts and restoring religious practice either within or outside established Buddhism; and attempts at opening up new ways to salvation, based on a rejection of established Buddhism as it existed at the time. Both reactions contributed to the development of what is now commonly known as Kamakura Buddhism.

The most well-known figures in the early development of Kamakura Buddhism are Honen and Eisai (or Yosai, 1141–1215). Their thought was developed further by Shinran and Dogen (1200–53). The last major figurehead of Kamakura Buddhism was Nichiren (1222–82). Of these, Honen and Shinran were advocates of Amidism, Eisai and Dogen of Zen, and Nichiren of devotion to the Lotus *sutra*. This brief list alone may suffice to throw up the legitimate question why these disparate thinkers are so often brought together under one label.

Pure Land Buddhism: Honen and Shinran

Honen was a Tendai monk trained in Tendai Amidist theology and ritual. Inspired by his reading of the Chinese Pure Land patriarch Shandao (613–81), Honen rejected the various Amidist practices described in Genshin's *Essays on Rebirth into Paradise* and other similar works, and argued that the only necessary practice for rebirth in the Pure Land is the recitation of Amida's name (*nenbutsu*) with complete trust in his (eighteenth) vow to save all. This position was much criticised by contemporary monks (foremost among whom was the Kegon monk Myoe, 1173–1232), who accused him of neglecting the fundamental Mahayana quest for enlightenment by concentrating solely on rebirth in the Pure Land, and for that reason rejected his teaching as non-Buddhist. Honen retorted that rebirth in the Pure Land constituted the only realistic way of attaining enlightenment. Another accusation levelled against him was that his teaching negated the precepts: after all, it promised salvation even to the worst sinners. Honen answered that while he was convinced that even the most evil would be saved by Amida, this did not mean that evil deeds should be encouraged, and he promised that he and his followers would abstain from 'even the smallest sins'. A scandal caused by some of Honen's disciples eventually led to the persecution of Honen's group. Honen was defrocked, exiled, and eventually pardoned, but his group grew regardless of this repression.

Shinran was also a Tendai monk, and a disciple of Honen, defrocked and exiled at the same time (though to another province) as his master. Shinran took Honen's teaching of total reliance on Amida one step further. Shinran rejected all practices based on one's 'own power' as mere obstacles to the one path to salvation: wholehearted surrender to Amida's eighteenth vow. To achieve this, we must let go of our Selves; practice, however, comes forth from the Self and is in the final analysis always an egoistic enterprise, carried out for egoistic reasons. Our passport to salvation, therefore, is not practice (not even the practice of invoking Amida's name), but faith. This faith, however, should not be an act of volition, something we 'do' ourselves. Faith comes forth from Amida's compassion and not from our Selves. It is innate in us, and will shine forth if only we surrender our Selves. It is, in other words, an inherent quality with which the Buddha in his compassion has endowed us, and which we must realize – a notion strikingly similar to the buddha nature of mainstream Japanese Buddhism. If only one allows one's innate faith to shine forth, one is saved instantaneously. The Pure Land, then, is not so much a physical realm located in the distant west, as a pure, Self-less state of mind, or buddhahood itself. It can be achieved during this life, on this earth; after it has been achieved, reciting the *nenbutsu* is simply an act of gratitude to Amida.

Seen in this light, Shinran's thought can perhaps be characterized as an Amidist version of an idea that dominated Japanese Buddhism, and lies at the core of *hongaku* thought: the notion that salvation or enlightenment can be attained by realising one's innate buddha nature. This same notion was also at the heart of the Zen thought of Eisai and Dogen.

Zen: Eisai and Dogen

Zen is the Japanese equivalent of Chinese Chan, which in turn derives from Sanskrit *dhyana* (meditation). Chan claimed that the essence of Shakyamuni's experience of enlightenment was contained not in the *sutra*s, but in a secret transmission, passed on directly and non-verbally from mind to mind since the age of Shakyamuni himself. This transmission allowed the Chan practitioner to experience for himself the enlightenment of Shakyamuni. Chan, then, was more concerned with direct experience than philosophical reflection, and indeed argued that in order to experience enlightenment, it is necessary to rid one's mind of all discursive thought. Methods for achieving this varied widely among the many Chan schools that arose in China from the seventh century onwards. A premise shared by all, however, was that enlightenment consists of an experience of the fundamental unity that pervades the universe in all its apparent multiplicity. This unity is the buddha mind, and it is inherent in all sentient beings as their buddha nature.

Some form of Zen had been introduced in Japan already in the seventh century, and Zen had formed an integral part of Tendai practice since this school's inception. It was only in the Kamakura period, however, that Zen became established as an independent Buddhist school. An important impulse for this was given by Eisai.

The twelfth century saw renewed Japanese efforts to learn and benefit from contacts with China, after a long period of relative isolation that had begun in the late ninth century. Eisai was one of many monks who went to China with the aim of restoring and reinvigorating Japanese Buddhism,

which, as noted above, was generally thought to be in disarray. In China (where the Southern Song dynasty, 1125–79, was just beginning to feel the Mongol threat), Chan dominated the Buddhist world at this time. Naturally, Eisai came into close contact with it during his two stays at Mounts Tiantai and Tiantong (1168 and 1187–91), and he saw its rigorous discipline and practice as a way to breathe new life into Tendai at home. In contrast to some slightly earlier pioneers of Japanese Zen, Eisai's Zen was not purist to the extent of rejecting non-Zen practices; rather, he intended Zen practice to function as the spiritual essence of a reformed Tendai Buddhism. Nevertheless, after his return Eisai met with opposition from the Tendai headquarters at Mount Hiei; his prospects brightened only after the establishment of the Kamakura shogunate, whose patronage allowed him to build up a modest but active Zen community in Kamakura. Eisai's lineage, known as the Rinzai school (equivalent to the Chinese Linji school) was to flourish under the patronage of subsequent shogunates.

If Eisai's brand of Zen was accommodating, Dogen's was exclusive. Dogen was a Tendai monk who also spent some years studying under one of Eisai's disciples. He spent five years on Mount Tiantong in China (1223–7), where he attained enlightenment under the Chan master Rujing (1163–1228) of the Caodong (in Japanese, Soto) school. Under the influence of Rujing, Dogen rejected all practices other than silent sitting (*zazen*, or *shikan taza*). Even this practice, though, is not to be seen as a means of attaining enlightenment. Practice is worthless if it is perceived as a goal-oriented activity, carried out in order to achieve something other than the practice itself. To Dogen, the practice of silent sitting was nothing more than a way to remember that sitting is enlightenment – as are all acts of all sentient beings. This view of practice was based on a particular interpretation of buddha nature, that is very similar to *hongaku* thought. Dogen argued that all sentient beings, or indeed all *dharmas*, do not have buddha nature, but are buddha nature, just as they are. Buddha nature is not something hidden in man, that has to be developed; buddha nature means that the universe, when seen as it really is, is enlightenment; or, to put it the other way around, that enlightenment is none other than the daily reality in which we all live. Zen practice is no more than a superior way to savour this truth.

Dogen's purist stance and critical tongue soon brought the wrath of the Buddhist establishment upon him. In contrast to Eisai, or indeed to most of Japanese Buddhism, Dogen did not see it as his role to serve and protect the state. Eventually, Dogen succeeded in founding a small monastic community (later called Eiheiji) in the mountains north of Kyoto. It was only in the fourteenth century, after Dogen's austere ideals had been watered down, and prayer meetings, esoteric rites and lay funerals had been developed, that Soto Zen grew into one of the major sects of Japanese Buddhism.

Nichiren Buddhism

Even more purist than Dogen was the Tendai monk Nichiren (1222–82). Nichiren built his thought on the Tendai belief that the Lotus *sutra* is the scripture containing Shakyamuni's ultimate teaching. His prime concerns were to design a practice based on this *sutra* that was suitable for the 'Latter Days of the Law' in which he lived, and to make sure that the 'true teaching' of this *sutra* was taken on by the rulers of the day as the basis of their government.

Nichiren was born in a humble fishing village in eastern Japan, and entered a local Tendai temple at the age of eleven. He spent his late teens in the shogunal seat of Kamakura, and his twenties studying at Mount Hiei, where he acquired a broad knowledge of a wide range of Buddhist schools. Nichiren came to the conclusion that only one was of real value: Shakyamuni's teaching of the 'one vehicle' contained in the Lotus *sutra*. He criticized all other schools for failing to pay due honour to this teaching. Nichiren saved his harshest criticism for Honen's Pure Land sect, arguing that the Buddha of this *saha* world is Shakyamuni and not Amida, and that Honen's followers were wrong to seek salvation outside this world. Moreover, he pointed to passages in various *sutra*s predicting that a state which fails to propagate true Buddhism will suffer seven kinds of calamities. In a petition to the shogunate, Nichiren stated that of these seven, five had already occurred, and he prophesied that unless the government adopted the Lotus teaching

to the exclusion of all others, the remaining two, internal chaos and foreign invasion, would soon be upon it. If the government would accept the true teaching, however, Japan would be transformed into a Buddha land, a fountainhead from which the teaching of the Lotus would spread throughout the world.

Nichiren's strong language angered other Buddhists, and Nichiren and his followers suffered a string of attacks. Nichiren was exiled twice, and once came very close to being executed. He was also pardoned twice, but ended his life in a remote mountain temple while harassment of his followers continued. Nichiren regarded this persecution as the inevitable result of practising the Lotus *sutra* in the Latter Days of the Law. He increasingly identified himself with the *bodhisattva* Vishishtacharitra (Perfect Practice), to whom he believed Shakyamuni had given the special mission of spreading the Lotus teaching in the Latter Days of the Law. As Japan suffered internal disorder (in 1272) and two Mongol invasions (in 1274 and 1281), and as Nichiren himself suffered relentless persecution, his sense of being on a divine mission became ever stronger, and in the end he severed even his ties with the Tendai sect.

The practice propagated by Nichiren was faith in the Lotus *sutra*, realized by chanting this sutra's title, which, as argued already by the Tiantai patriarch Zhiyi, embodies the essence of its teachings. When one chants '*Namu* (or *Nam*) *myoho renge-kyo*' (I place my faith in the Lotus *sutra* of the Wonderful Law), even without an understanding of the *sutra*'s teachings, the salvific power of the scripture will be called forth and one will be saved here and now, in this world and this life. As the three pillars of practice, Nichiren identified this formula (called the *daimoku*), the World-Buddha Shakyamuni (which he depicted in *mandala*s, and called the *gohonzon*) and the 'ordination platform' (*kaidan*). Nichiren spoke of this platform either as a grand ordination hall that would be erected in a future age once the true teaching had spread throughout the world, or as the place (any place) where the *daimoku* is chanted, and that thus becomes a Buddha land. Enlightenment comes with the realization that the three are one: the formula is the World-Buddha, and the place where the practitioner finds himself is the Buddha land –

or will be, once the true teaching has been universally established and all heresies have been eradicated. Finally, and perhaps most importantly, the practitioner is the World-Buddha: 'The Buddha ... is anyone in any of the Ten Worlds who manifests his inherent buddha nature.'

Nichiren leaves the Tendai mould only in his stress on chanting the *daimoku* as the only viable method of practice in the Latter Days of the Law, and in his sense of having inherited not only the Tiantai/Tendai lineage, but also a direct, mind-to-mind tradition from Shakyamuni via Vishishta-charitra. Tendai concepts such as the three truths, interpenetration, and the buddha nature remained central to Nichiren's thought, as was his perception (shared by nearly all contemporary Buddhist schools) of Buddhism's role in protecting the state.

Buddhism in the Muromachi (1336–1600) and Edo (1600–1868) periods

As noted above, the new sects based on the legacies of monks like Honen, Shinran, Eisai, Dogen and Nichiren remained of marginal importance during the Kamakura period, and the older schools wielded far more influence in both secular and intellectual terms. The old schools (Tendai, Shingon, Hosso, Kegon) held large areas of land, and dominated imperial court ritual.

The first challenge to this dominance came from Eisai's Rinzai Zen school, which found a powerful sponsor in the shogunate. As the Kamakura period drew to a close, Zen also increased its influence at the imperial court, and a network of shogunally and imperially sponsored Zen temples arose, patterned on contemporary Chinese examples. Until the early fourteenth century there was a steady coming and going of Chinese and Japanese monks in both directions, and Zen temples functioned as the main window on Chinese culture. They were centres not only of Zen practice in a narrow sense, but also of the study of Chinese literature, Chinese thought (Daoism, Confucianism), and Chinese arts; this proved a valuable asset in attracting powerful patrons. Zen (as well as elements of Chinese culture mediated by Zen monasteries) was a major influence in the development of Japanese theatre (especially Noh),

architecture, painting, calligraphy and martial arts, and inspired the development of the tea ceremony.

The Soto Zen, Pure Land, True Pure Land and Nichiren schools also built up solid power bases in the course of the medieval period, while older schools such as Tendai and Shingon made progress by establishing themselves firmly in eastern Japan. As Japan entered a prolonged period of division and warfare (1482–1590), the major temples further increased their secular (and military) power, some even ruling their own territories in complete independence. Temples controlled lands, markets and guilds, were involved in money-lending, and performed rituals for this-worldly purposes for lay patrons. A practice that was to become of prime importance later also gained currency during this period: the performance of lay funerals. However, the reunification of the country (1568–90) broke the military power of Buddhism, and the new Tokugawa shogunate (1603–1868) moved to impose strict controls on Buddhism and to incorporate it in the fabric of government. A strict system of centralized sectarian control was instituted, and even more importantly, registration at Buddhist temples and the performance of Buddhist funerals became obligatory by law. This gave temples a secure base of parishioners, who were tied to their temple by secular law.

This system further strengthened the sectarian nature of Japanese Buddhism. It was at this point that loosely organized schools developed into mutually exclusive sects. It also stripped Buddhism of much of its former vitality: theological disputes were forbidden, and the headquarters of the various schools were expected to suppress heterodoxy within their ranks. On the other hand, new sectarian training institutes for monks (many of which were called *danrin*) became centres for Buddhist study, leading to a blossoming of Buddhist scholarship. Danrin scholarship concentrated on the lives and works of the founders of the various schools and their Chinese examples; the general thrust of *danrin* studies was to 'restore' a purer Buddhism by rejecting medieval *hongaku*-inspired ideas of the more radical sort. This took the form, for example, of a new stress on practice and on observance of the precepts; within Tendai, it even led to the restoration (in 1693) of the *Sifenlü* monastic code, and the abandonment of the less strict precepts based on the *Bonmokyo*, introduced by Saicho (see above).

On the other hand, Edo-period Buddhism was also characterized by a further laicization. Buddhism was replaced by Confucianism (and Confucianized schools of Shinto) as the dominant philosophical framework of the age, and was widely criticized by Confucian writers of being concerned only with the 'other world', and of ignoring or even denying lay morality. In reaction, Buddhists of all sects incorporated Confucian ethics in their teachings, arguing that filial piety, exertion in one's given occupation and loyalty to one's lord are at the core of Buddhist practice. From such Buddhist–Confucian teachings sprouted popular religious movements such as Shingaku.

Further reading

Dobbins, J. (1989) *Jodo Shinshu: Shin Buddhism in Medieval Japan*, Bloomington, IN: Indiana University Press.

Eliot, C. (1994) *Japanese Buddhism*, Richmond: Curzon Press.

Faure, B. (1996), *Visions of Power: Imagining Medieval Japanese Buddhism*, Princeton, NJ: Princeton University Press.

Kashiwahara, Y. and Sonoda, K. (eds) (1994) *Shapers of Japanese Buddhism*, trans. G. Sekimori, Tokyo: Kosei Publishing Company.

McMullin, N. (1985) *Buddhism and the State in 16th Century Japan*, Princeton, NJ: Princeton University Press.

Morrell, R. (1987) *Early Kamakura Buddhism: A Minority Report*, Berkeley, CA: Asian Humanities Press.

Paul, G. (1993) *Philosophie in Japan: Von den Anfängen bis zur Heian-Zeit*, Munich: Jiudicium.

Payne, R. (1998) *Revisioning 'Kamakura' Buddhism*, Honolulu, HA: University of Hawaii Press.

Ryuchi Abe (1999) *The Weaving of Mantra: Kukai and the Construction of Esoteric Buddhist Discourse*, New York: Columbia University Press.

Stone, J. (1999) *Original Enlightenment and the Transformation of Medieval Japanese Buddhism*, Honolulu, HA: University of Hawaii Press.

Ueda Y. and Hirota, D. (1989) *Shinran: An Introduction to his Thought*, Kyoto: Hongwanji International Center.

Visser, M. de (1935) *Ancient Buddhism in Japan: Sutras and Ceremonies in Use in the Seventh and Eighth Centuries A.D. and Their History in Later Times*, 2 vols, Leiden: Brill.

Yamasaki, Taiko (1988) *Shingon: Japanese Esoteric Buddhism*, trans R. Petersen and C. Petersen, Boston: Shambhala.

Yampolsky, P. (1990) *Selected Writings of Nichiren*, New York: Columbia University Press.

MARK TEEUWEN

Buddhist philosophy in Japan, post-Meiji

If one speaks of Buddhist philosophy, one presupposes that there are other kinds of Buddhist thought significantly lacking in philosophical character, namely, Buddhist convictions based on faith rather than reason, and comparatively indifferent to problems of logical validity and causal explanation. Popular Japanese belief in the existence of Amida Buddha's paradise provides an example of such convictions. Further, speaking of Buddhist philosophy indicates a possible difference between theory and practice. Since Buddhist arguments against the existence of gods on the one hand, and Buddhist belief in, and cult of, for example, the godlike Buddha of the *Lotus Sutra* (*Hokkekyo*) on the other differ fundamentally from each other, the distinction between philosophical and non-philosophical Buddhism seems justified. However, some scholars dispute this arguing that Buddhism equally includes philosophical, religious, and practical components, or that Buddhism is essentially practice. To refute this argument, proponents of the first view respond that, though all kinds of Buddhism are concerned with the question of how to end suffering, they greatly differ in their understanding of suffering and – as for example the various theories of gods indicate – their methods and answers. Hence, if one refuses to differentiate between Buddhist philosophy and Buddhist faith, one must also refuse to call Kantian ethics philosophy and to distinguish it from the Christian doctrine to venerate God, for both – Kantian ethics and Christian religion – answer the identical question of how man should lead his life.

As to the difference between Buddhist philosophy before and since Meiji times, it can be characterized as follows. (1) Since Meiji times, Japanese Buddhist studies were increasingly influenced by Western Buddhology. (2) Because of this influence, they became more positivist, linguistic and historical, and less apologetic. (3) This implied in particular that, on the scholarly level, Japanese Mahayana ideology (according to which Mahayana Buddhism was the only 'true' Buddhism, and the uniqueness and superiority of Japan was due to its being a 'Mahayana land') was severely questioned. (4) Also, the encounter with the West instigated attempts to develop respective eclectic and synthetic philosophies. (5) Even before Meiji times, Buddhist studies dealt with a large number of different doctrines and movements. With the influence of Western Buddhology, these studies became even more diversified also including, as indicated, extensive and thorough investigations and discussions, for example of the 'Hinayanist' Pali Buddhism. (6) Since Meiji, Buddhist studies no longer remained a domain solely of temples and private academies but eventually also became a field of research in public institutions, especially universities. As in other countries, however, Buddhist studies in Japan are not regular objectives of philosophy departments. They are almost always conducted within departments of Indology, Sinology, and so on, though there exist some universities such as Ryukoku daiguku in Kyoto which almost exclusively focus on Buddhology.

With the studies of A. Johnston, Christian Lassen (1800–78) and Eugène Burnouf (1801–52, who wrote *Introduction à l'histoire de Bouddhisme indien*), Buddhology in the West had reached a high scholarly level. Burnouf's disciple and successor at Oxford University, Max Müller (1823–1900), who is famous for having edited the series *Sacred Books of the East* became the teacher of several Japanese scholars, among them Nanjo Bun'yu (1849–1927) and Takakusu Junjiro (1866–1945). Other European scholars who strongly influenced Japanese Buddhist studies were Thomas W. Rhys Davids (1843–1922), Hermann Oldenberg (1854–1920), and Louis de la Vallée-Poussin (1869–1937). Rhys Davids greatly promoted the study of Pali Buddhism, Oldenberg wrote a pioneering book on the historical Buddha, and De la Vallée-Poussin

published an annotated French translation of the most important treatise of scholastic Buddhism, the *Abhidharmakosha* (Jap. *Kusharon*). The *Kusharon* has been fundamental for scholastic Japanese Buddhism since Nara times. De la Vallée-Poussin also translated Xuan Zang's (600?–64; known in Japan as Genjo) *Cheng wei shi lun* (Jap. *Joyuishikiron*), the fundamental treatise of the Sino-Japanese *School of Mere Consciousness* (*Joyuishiki shu*). This school taught that (with regard to man) everything is a function of consciousness, thus conceiving of consciousness as a kind of necessary transcendental condition. Under the influence of Western scholarship, scholars like Nanjo, Takakusu and Ui Hakuju (1882–1963) turned to the study of Pali and Sanskrit sources, and even translated important Buddhist works into English. Because of their knowledge of classic Chinese, they were also able to utilize, edit and translate from Chinese texts, and finally established themselves among the world's leading Buddhist scholars. Others like Inoue Enryo (1859–1919) and Anezaki Masaharu (1873–1949) became interested in comparative philosophy and religious history, and tried to reconstruct Buddhist doctrines from respective points of view.

Some exemplary achievements of this generation of Japanese Buddhologists should be mentioned. Nanjo compiled the bilingual *Catalogue of the Chinese Translations of the Buddhist Tripitaka: The Sacred Canon of the Buddhists in China and Japan*, first printed in Oxford in 1888. Takakusu co-edited the monumental *Taisho Tripitaka* (*Taisho shinshu daizokyo*), a 100-volume series of basic Sino-Japanese Buddhist texts (a series which became itself a canon), and other equally voluminous series. He also wrote *The Essentials of Buddhist Philosophy*. Ui Hakuju published important studies on Indian philosophy (*Indo tetsugaku*), the history of Buddhist thought (particularly in India, China and Japan), and Buddhist theories of logic (entitled *Bukkyo ronrigaku*). As early as in 1917, while in Cambridge, he translated a Chinese version of an important **Vaisheshika** treatise (*shastra*) into English.

Thus, from about 1890, with their editions, dictionary-like compilations, annotated translations, and studies, Japanese scholars contributed considerably to securing and broadening the basis for serious philosophical interpretations of Buddhist texts. Further, as exemplified by the English work of Takakusu, they also offered their own reconstructions of Buddhist philosophy. As indicated, most of them at first distanced themselves from the traditional Japanese Mahayana ideology, though later they became more conciliatory. But there were great differences. Takakusu, sympathizing with Tendai, was inclined to emphasize what he regarded as the value of what may be called a concept of all-comprising and dialectical ontological identity, whereas Ui attributed more importance to Buddhist studies on logical consistency so characteristic of followers of the School of Mere Consciousness (**Yogachara**).

Inoue Enryo's and Anezaki's reconstructions were more general. Also, Inoue's ideas were less determined by rigorous philological and historical analysis. In his *Bukkyo katsuron joron* (On the Vitality of Buddhism), he attacked Christianity as self-contradictory and irrational, and asserted that Buddhist schools such as Kegon and Tendai advanced doctrines of 'pure reason' as an absolute and universal principle similar to Hegel's (1770–1831) philosophy and in keeping with modern evolutionism. Enryo formulated even more speculative ideas of dialectical ontological identity than Takakusu. Because of his willful speculations he was strongly criticized by **Onishi** Hajime (1864–1900). Anezaki, who was interested in pointing out similarities between Buddhism and Christianity, published such English works as *Buddhist and Christian Gospels, Nichiren: the Buddhist Prophet* and *History of Japanese Religion*. They appeared in 1905, 1916 and 1930, respectively, and the first one was published in co-operation with Albert J. Edmunds.

The differences in interests and methods characteristic to the approaches exemplified by Ui, Enryo and Anesaki, may be called exemplary for the whole of Buddhist philosophy since Meiji times. Also, except for the time of the Second World War, communication and co-operation between Japanese and European scholars interested in Buddhist philosophy remained frequent and strong.

Through the twentieth century, many Japanese scholars devoted themselves to painstaking philological and historical research, with a considerable number of them focusing on studying texts primarily concerned with epistemological and logical problems, namely *hetuvidya* (in Japanese,

immyo) treatises. In this field, the Japanese contributions to **Dignaga** (*c.*480–*c.*540) and **Dharmakirti** (*c.*600-60) studies are outstanding. Also, co-operation between Western and Japanese scholars has been particularly close. For instance, since about 1960, Japanese scholars have been working in close contact with the Vienna school of Buddhism shaped by Erich Frauwallner. Among them are Kajiyama Yuichi, Tachikawa Musashi, Katsura Shoryu, and Erich Steinkellner and Lambert Schmithausen. However, the philological and historical approach is also characteristic of Japanese scholars who specialized in other fields. Takasaki Jikido (born 1926) has contributed fundamental studies and translations to the Mahayanist *tathagatagarbha* theory, the doctrine that everything, at least every living being, is endowed with **Buddha nature**, and hence originally capable of gaining salvation. Takasaki also published one of the best short surveys on Buddhism ever produced. Its English version, *An Introduction to Buddhism*, appeared in 1987. Inagaki Hisao has specialized in the study of Jodo shinshu (The True School of the Pure Land) which comprises philosophical as well as religious and even popular movements. He has contributed important translations and interpretations of respective texts, and also edited some English Buddhist dictionaries. Nakamura Hajime (1912–99) can be called a specialist in many fields but may be more appropriately characterized as having a comprehensive knowledge of Buddhism. His publications are numerous.

What makes the *hetuvidya* studies, and those of Takasaki, Inagaki and many others philosophical investigations, is the attempt at consistent reconstruction, and the critical analyses of argumentative validity. As indicated, some studies also explicitly deal with, and contribute to, philosophy. For instance, Kajiyama entitled one of his investigations on *hetuvidya*, *An Introduction to Buddhist Philosophy*. An annotated translation of a classic written in the eleventh or twelfth century, it also explicitly affirms the philosophical character of important traditional Buddhist problems, thus documenting the continuity of Buddhist philosophy. Further, it is a critical investigation of some of these problems. Among other philosophical problems, Kajiyama mentions the questions of whether a god (in

Sansrkit, *Ishvara*) exists, and of whether the fundamental components of entities exist only momentarily. Kajiyama also belongs to those Buddhist scholars who view the social history of Buddhism in Japan rather critically. In particular, he has criticized the fact that for many centuries Japanese Buddhists used the idea of karmic retribution to discriminate against outcasts and the poor.

Most *hetuvidya* scholars are critical about the views which representatives of the **Kyoto school**, and scholars related to this school, such as Suzuki Daisetz (1870–1966), have on Buddhism. They hold that these views cannot be justified philologically, and are often irrational. Also, they argue that – contrary to what many followers of the Kyoto school believe – Zen is no exemplary Buddhism but only one branch among many others.

Nishida Kitaro (1870–1945), who is called the founder of the Kyoto school, and most representatives of the school itself belong to that line of Japanese thinkers since Meiji who – like Inoue Enryo – were interested in Buddhism as a traditional means of correcting Western philosophy. Much impressed and influenced by Western philosophy, but critical with regard to what they viewed as unjustified and dangerous logocentrism and anthropomorphism, they tried to combine elements from Western and Buddhist teachings to create a new and – in their view – truly universal thought or philosophy. As to Western philosophy, perhaps Hegel and Heidegger (1889–1976) had the greatest influence on their thought, though Nietzsche (1844–1900), Husserl (1859–1938), Kant (1724–1804) and others also played a role. As to Buddhism, they regarded Zen as most important, though Tendai (in Chinese, Tiantai) also had a great impact. The more scholastic traditions such as **Abhidharma**, the School of Mere Consiousness, and *hetuvidya* were of only marginal, if any, influence. Nagarjuna (*c.*150–200), the founder of the Middle Way (in Japanese *chugan*), is often mentioned but always understood as a dialectician and originator of a distinctively Eastern logic different from Aristotelian logic and the logical doctrines of *hetuvidya*. Suzuki, who sharply and fundamentally contrasts what he calls Western logicalness and Eastern indifference to logicalness,

never takes into account that Japanese *hetuvidya* scholars (*immyo gakusha*) wrote thousands of pages on problems of logical validity.

Very roughly speaking, the Kyoto school and related thinkers used Buddhism as a source for developing and supporting the following views. (1) Western logocentrism, scientific orientation, and technology are no means to grasp the absolute or reality as such. Understanding this reality, however, is essential for being able to lead a life how it becomes man. Further, an understanding of the absolute is possible, for example by means of 'direct experience' and mystic union. (2) Western logocentrism, scientific orientation and technology are dangerous for they may lead to man's self-destruction. (3) They testify to an – unjustified – anthropomorphism for they are employed to enslave nature. Man ought to live in harmony with nature. (4) The notion of nothingness (in Japanese, *mu*) and/or emptiness (in Japanese, *ku*) is more fundamental, and more adequate to reality as such, than the notion of being. (5) A kind of dialectical logic is a better means to solve important problems than formal logic. Formal contradictions are no real obstacles for deep thought. These points were also supported by referring to respective Western sources as for example Martin Heidegger and Master Eckhart (*c.*1260–1327), but the application and mentioning of such Buddhist names and key terms as Nagarjuna, Zen, emptiness, non-self (in Japanese, *muga*) and enlightenment gave them a Buddhist touch.

In 1905, Anesaki Masaharu founded at Tokyo Imperial University the first university department for the study of religion in Japan. Like Takakusu in his early studies, Ui Hakuju, and the later *hetuvidya* scholars, he advocated a rational and historically critical approach to Buddhist studies, severely criticizing traditional Japanese Mahayana ideology. In his studies on the historical and eternal Buddha and on early Buddhism, he tried to separate facts from unfounded beliefs and pointed out that, after all, Theravada Buddhism is fundamental to Mahayana too. As indicated, Anesaki was also interested in detecting a kind of eternal truth common to Buddhism and Christianity, and in this respect was a pioneer too, though many of the respective writings by later Japanese scholars do not live up to his critical standards.

There have appeared numerous comparisons between Luther's concept that, to be saved, man must rely on God's mercy, and the Jodo shinshu's notion that man can only be rescued by relying on *tariki* (the saving power of the other, namely Amida). Also, numerous publications deal with Zen, Master Eckhart and Jakob Böhme (1575–1624). In his study *Mushinron* (Atheism), Hisamatsu Shin'ichi (1889–1980) discusses Buddhism to argue in favour of a general concept of religion that includes atheism. Nishitani Keiji (1900–90), in his book *Shukyo to wa nanika?* (What is Religion?), discusses Christianity, nihilism and Buddhism to answer the question of how to formulate a general notion of religion. Hisamatsu and Nishitani were members of the Kyoto school. As far as Japanese comparative studies in religion informed by Buddhism analyse and describe religious experience, or investigate questions of validity of religious convictions, they contribute to philosophy of religion.

Apart from the given examples of what could still be called (1) scholastic Buddhism – best exemplified by *hetuvidya*; (2) highly speculative comparative ontology informed by Zen and notions of nothingness and emptiness – best exemplified by the Kyoto school – and (3) comparative studies relevant to a philosophy of religion, some other examples of Japanese Buddhist philosophy may be mentioned. They belong to the first kind, though not to *hetuvidya*, and they include more speculative and ontological concepts. One of the most influential of these contributions is Nagao Gadjin's *Chugkan to yuishiki* (Madhyamika and Yogachara), which tries to refute simple distinctions between the two philosophical traditions. Nagao shares the common opinion that the two represent 'the apex of Mahayana philosophy' but argues against the view that only the first was 'established on the foundation of the thought of *shunyata* (non-being or emptiness)'. This view was often voiced by Japanese Madhyamika (Chugan-ha) adherents who opposed Yogachara (Yugagyo-ha), another name for the School of Mere Consciousness.

One of the most important questions of philosophy, the problem of how to formulate an adequate concept of causation, has always been a central question of Buddhist philosophy as well.

Since Meiji times, Japanese scholars have published numerous studies on Buddhist concepts of causation. Doi Torakuzu, who translated the *Avatamsaka-sutra* (*Kegon-kyo*, *Flower Garland Sutra*) into German, in his interpretation of this *sutra* advanced a notion of causation as an all-comprising system of mutual, or interdependent, causal relations. Tachikawa Musashi, in his *An Introduction to the Philosophy of Nagarjuna*, argues that Nagarjuna's notion of causality implies both profane and sacred truth; that is, it can be adequately understood as both a notion of causal relations as we know and must employ it in everyday life and as a notion that may help us ultimately to free ourselves from suffering.

As indicated, some Japanese scholars have taken a critical stance toward what they characterize as irrational distortions of Buddhist thought, and as irrational Buddhist faith and ideology in Japanese scholarly tradition and political history. From about 1980, they have advanced what they call *hihan bukkyo* (critical Buddhism). In particular, they criticize the Kyoto school and certain interpretations of Zen. In 1990, Hakamaya Noriaki (born 1943) published his book *Hihan bukkyo* (Critical Buddhism) in which he summarized the main points of this critical Buddhologist approach, pointing out that Buddhism should and can be rational and critical. Hakamaya expressly speaks of a 'critical [Buddhist] philosophy' as opposed to what is often named 'topical philosophy'. In the Japanese context, 'topical philosophy', among other things, indicates the Kyoto school's concepts of *basho* (place), and *basho no ronri* (logic of place). Another representative of critical Buddhism is Metsumoto Shiu (1950–), while Sueki Fumihiko is quite critical of the existing trends in 'critical' Buddhism. As indicated, most scholars of *hetuvidya* can also be regarded as critical Buddhologists, but their interest in the socio-political implications of Buddhist doctrines is usually less explicit than that of Hakamaya or Matsumoto.

Though Japanese Buddhologist contributions to philosophy are countless, it is in the interest of developing a general – though necessarily incomplete and fragmentary – picture of philosophy, or at least of getting a glimpse of what kinds of philosophy are pursued in the world of the twentieth and twenty-first centuries, that one has an idea of Japanese Buddhist philosophy too, be it only vague. This is the more so since Buddhist philosophy has already influenced Western university philosophy, and because this influence will increase. Further, what has often been called comparative philosophy is continuously gaining ground.

See also: logic

Further reading

Anesaki Masaharu (1916) *Buddhist Art in its Relation to Buddhist Ideals*, Boston: Houghton-Mifflin.
—— (1916) *Nichiren: the Buddhist Prophet*, Cambridge, MA: Harvard University Press.
—— (1923) *The Religious and Moral Problems of the Orient*, New York: Macmillan.
—— (1963) *History of Japanese Religion*, Tokyo: Tuttle.
—— (1973) *Art, Life, and Nature in Japan*, Tokyo: Tuttle.
Brüll, L. (1989) *Die japanische Philosophie*, Darmstadt: Wissenschaftliche Buchgesellschaft.
The Cambridge History of Japan (1989) vols 5 (*The Nineteenth Century*) and 6 (*The Twentieth Century*), Cambridge: Cambridge University Press.
de Bary, W.T. (ed.) (1958) *Sources of Japanese Tradition*, New York: Columbia University Press.
Dilworth, D. and Viglielmo, V. (eds and trans) (1998) *Sourcebook for Modern Japanese Philosophy: Selected Documents*, Westport, CT: Greenwood Press.
Hamada Junko (1994) *Japanische Philosophie nach 1868*, Leiden: Brill.
Heisig, J. and Maraldo, J. (eds) (1994) *Rude Awakenings: Zen, the Kyoto School, and the Question of Nationalism*, Nanzan Studies in Religion and Culture, Honolulu, HA: University of Hawaii Press.
Hisamatsu Shin'ichi (1990) *Philosophie des Erwachens, Satori und Atheismus (Satori – kokindaiteki [postmodern] nigenzo, Mushinron)*, trans. N. Klein *et al.*, Zurich: Theseus Verlag
Hubbard, J. and Swanson, P (eds) (1997) *Pruning the Bodhi Tree: The Storm over Critical Buddhism*, Honolulu: University of Hawaii Press (includes contributions by Hakamaya Noriaki, Matsumoto Shiro and other representives of *hihan bukkyo* (critical Buddhism) that emphasize the relevance of rational and critical Buddhism, while pointing out problems of Buddhist faith and Buddhist ideology).
Irokawa, D. (1985) *The Culture of the Meiji Period*, Princeton, NJ: Princeton University Press.
Jansen, M. (ed.) (1982) *Changing Japanese Attitudes toward Modernization*, Tokyo: Tuttle.
Japanese Culture in the Meiji Era (1955), Centenary Culture Council Series, 10 vols, Tokyo.
Japanese Religion, A Survey by the Agency for Cultural Affairs (1981), Tokyo: Kodansha International.
Kajiyama Yuichi (1998) *An Introduction to Buddhist Philosophy: An Annotated Translation of the Tarkabhasa of Moksakaragupta*, Vienna: Arbeitskreis für tibetische und buddhitsische Studien der Universität Wien.
—— (1999) *The Antarvyaptisamarthana of Ratnakarasanti*, Tokyo: The International Research Institute for Advanced Buddhology, Soka University.
Kato Shuichi (1990) *A History of Japanese Literature 3, The Modern Years*, Tokyo and London: Kodansha International.
Kisimoto Hideo (1956) *Japanese religion in the Meiji Era* (Vol. II of *Japanese Culture in the Meiji Era*), ed. and trans. J. Howes, Tokyo: The Toyo Bunko.
Kitagawa, J. (1966) *Religion in Japanese History*, New York: Columbia University Press.
Kosaka Masaaki (1958) *Japanese Thought in the Meiji Era* (Vol. VIII of *Japanese Culture in the Meiji Era*), ed. and trans. D. Abosch, Tokyo: The Toyo Bunko.
Nagao Gadjin M. (1991) *Madhyamika and Yogacara (Chugkan to yuishiki)*, trans. L. Kawamura, Albany, NY: State University of New York Press.
Nakamura Hajime (1968) *Ways of Thinking of Eastern Peoples*, ed. P. Wiener, Honolulu, HA: University of Hawaii Press.
—— (1969) *A History of the Development of Japanese Thought*, 2 vols, Tokyo: Japan Cultural Society.
—— (1980) *Indian Buddhism*, Tokyo: Kufs Publication.
—— (1982) *Ansätze modernen Denkens in den Religionen Japans (Nihon shukyo no kindaisei)*, trans. S. Schultz and A. Schomaker-Huett, Leiden: Brill.
—— (1992) *A Comparative History of Ideas*, Delhi: Motilal Banarsidass.
Paul, G. (1993) *Philosophie in Japan: Von den Anfängen bis zur Heian-Zeit*, München: iudicium.

Piovesana, G. (1997) *Recent Japanese Philosophical Thought 1862–1996: A Survey*, with a New Survey (1963–96) by Yamawaki Naoshi, Richmond: Japan Library, Curzon Press.

Pörtner, P. and Heise, J. (1995) *Die Philosophie Japans*, Stuttgart: Kröner.

Schinzinger, R. (1983) *Japanisches Denken*, Berlin: Erich Schmidt Verlag.

Tachikawa Musashi (1997) *An Introduction to the Philosophy of Nagarjuna*, trans. R. Giebel, Delhi: Motilal Banarsidass.

Takakusu Junjiro (1947) *The Essentials of Buddhist Philosophy*, Honolulu, HA: University of Hawaii Press.

Tsuchida Kyoson (1927) *Contemporary Thought of Japan and China*, London.

GREGOR PAUL

Buddhist scholasticism

Buddhist scholasticism is rooted in the **Abhidharma**, and is committed to a rational analysis of reality. Theistic faith is not involved. In **Vasubandhu**'s *Abhidharmakosha*, we may see how the creation of complex conceptual distinctions comes out of a need to rationalize the transcendental. In the Buddhist scheme of the Three Realms (desire, where we are; form, which is physically real and where the gods free from desires are found; and the realm of formlessness, which is non-physical – largely trance or meditative states of mind), gods who live in heavens astride the realm of desires, and the realm of form, where divine impassivity is the rule, can be rationally graded. In the ascending heavens, the gods increasingly shed the last shreds of their form. But in this dematerializing process of being 'thinned out', as it were, they grow in size, becoming less dense, ballooning like heated gas, such that the higher the god, the more space he actually takes up. Vasubandhu even has actual mathematical calculations for the sizes of these various gods. The logic is apparently the reverse of the one presumed in the question about the size of angels. It seems that angels as spiritual entities are thought to have still some minimal substantiality. In the Great Chain of Being, God as pure Spirit is omnipresent. Angels, being of a lower rank in that

chain, could conceivably have some amount of substantiality as to take up a tiny space, a fraction of a pinhead. So in theory, one can also calculate their size.

In Chinese Buddhism, there evolved schools which are built on the *sutras* and which make a point of speculating on the *achintya* (inconceivable) mystery of the Buddha. For the Tiantai school, based on the *Lotus Sutra* 'which argues for the *Triyana* (Three Vehicles) being absorbed now into its own *Ekayana* (One Vehicle)', the triune formula of 'Three is One' is found quite generally. For the Huayan school of the *Flower Garland Sutra*, it is the full, round number ten, and there is accordingly no end to sets of ten. Some of these schemata can become very complicated. Much of scriptural exegesis is not based on logical analysis; instead it falls back on Chinese **correlative thinking** which caters more to creating syncretic wholes.

Such schemata peaked with the Huayan philosophy around 700 CE, which helped to celebrate the Maitreyan reign of Empress Wu. In seeing the noumenal present in full in the phenomenal, the reality behind the world of appearances in those appearances, Huayan philosophy resembles theological realism that finds the presence of the universal in all particulars. The effect in China is that the world, so to say, is lifted *en masse* heavenwards and made to merge into the Lotus Womb of the Great Sun Buddha Vairochana (just like Sudhana the pilgrim in the *Gandhavyuha* chapter in Huayan (*Avatamsaka*) *sutra*).

The Lotus Womb of the Great Sun Buddha, like so much in the Mahayana spiritual sphere, is a poetic name to describe an 'enlightened matrix'. In Tantric Buddhist iconography, this Buddha (the most magnificent, being the brilliant Sun) reigns over this *mandala* realm and there are specific Buddhas placed in specific quadrants. The pilgrim – you and I by extension – finally walks straight into the body of Samantabhadra (a cosmic Wisdom-Buddha) and suddenly becomes the Buddha himself. The one becomes the all; the phenomena merged into the noumena.

When this grandiose vision, China's equivalent of high medieval scholasticism, collapsed, then naturalism (nascent Neo-Confucianism), mysticism (Chan) and fideism (Pure Land) came to flourish. What brought the Huayan system down was the over-extension of those perfect correlations of three, four, five, six, ten and fifty-two. For example, take the total count of fifty-two stages in the bodhisattvic ascent to Buddhahood. This is based on the *Huayan Sutra*, and is the culmination of reconciling a number of different series of spiritual ascents. But do we need to pass through all fifty-two stages? Like the counting of angels or the size of gods, it made good sense at one time but it was becoming tiresome and looked arbitrary to many. Cutting through the fine details came the impatient Zen call for sudden and total enlightenment. Pure Land faith also short-circuited the steps to salvation: a single practice of calling on the name of Amitabha can deliver the faithful. The Neo-Confucians went so far as to question the reality of the higher worlds, as they called for a return to this world of human beings living in the natural surrounding of heaven and earth.

See also: bodhisattva; spiritual ladders

Further reading

Lovejoy, A. (1964) *The Great Chain of Being*, Cambridge, MA: Harvard University Press.
Odin, S. (1982) *Process Metaphysics and Hua-Yen Buddhism*, Albany, NY: State University of New York Press.
Schuon, F. (1968) *In the Tracks of Buddhism*, trans. M. Pallis, London: Allen & Unwin.

WHALEN LAI

Buddhist thought, late Qing

Late Ming Buddhism claimed 'four grand masters', monks who mingled well with the gentry who returned from court to build their own local temple bases. By the early Qing dynasty, there was a dearth of learned monks and leadership went often to the lay gentry Buddhists themselves. In the late Qing period, the layman Yang Renhui (1837–1911) almost single-handedly rebuilt the tradition. An official of some standing, he devoted more and more time simply to re-issuing nothing but Buddhist works and gave them out free of charge to anyone for the asking. From his small publishing venture at Nanjing (which still exists today) came

all the major texts of the tradition. Well travelled, he had a key contact in Japan, Nanjo Bun'yu (1866–1945), and through the latter Yang was able to re-import the Weishi tradition from the Hosso temple at Nara.

The three leaders of the 1898 (constitutional monarchy) reform movement were all beneficiaries of Yang's publications. The 'Consciousness Only' philosophy was revived by layman Ouyang Jingwu at his Inner Learning Academy in 1922, and presented as the 'inner learning' to compete with Europe's 'external science'. An entire modern generation of Buddhist idealists came from this movement. The most outstanding was **Xiong Shili** (1883–1968), who later fashioned a self-styled 'New Consciousness Only' philosophy. Ironically, this least 'Chinese' of the Buddhist schools was revived as pure theory and outside monastic practice. It is **Yogachara** without the yoga or the monk *acharya*. Presented as a totally self-sufficient system, it leaves little room for cross-fertilization with the 'inner science' of Western psychology, for unlike the Sinhalese Buddhist Jayatilleke, who offered the West a similar dose of rational, abhidharmic psychology, this Chinese group does not have a ready Western sponsor.

Further reading

Chan Sin-wei (1985) *Buddhism in Late Ch'ing Political Thought*, Hong Kong: Hong Kong University Press.
Welch, H. (1968) *The Buddhist Revival in China*. Cambridge, MA: Harvard University Press.

WHALEN LAI

Buton Rinchen Drup

Within the Tibetan scholarly world, Buton (1290–1364) is perhaps best-known as a great encyclopedist. He edited what later became the standard version of the Tibetan Buddhist canon, *kan gyur* (translation of scriptures attributed to the Buddha) and *tan gyur* (translation of primarily Indian commentaries). Buton wrote extensively on many topics of traditional Buddhist scholarship and his works remain, to this day, highly influential.

Buton's greatest contributions in Tibetan philosophy lies perhaps in his highly articulate attack on the literal interpretation of the **buddha nature** theory and its attendant, the Shentong view (see **Shentong philosophy**), and in developing an alternative reading of the Buddha-nature theory. His work *An Ornament Beautifying the Buddha-Essence* set a new standard of scholarship on the hermeneutics of the Mahayana doctrine of the Buddha-nature and its relation to other Mahayana Buddhist concepts, including the Madhyamaka theory of **emptiness**. Buton's teachings came to be institutionalized in the emergence of the Shalu school, named after the monastic seat of learning that became closely associated with Buton's legacy.

THUPTEN JINPA

C

caste

The Brahminical Hindu system of the hierarchical classification of the human world into four ideal estates: Brahmins, who are intellectuals and priests; Kshatriyas, who are warriors and secular rulers; Vaishyas, who are farmers and merchants; and Shudras, who provide various services to members of the higher three estates. Only members of the first three estates, who are termed 'twice-born' because they have undergone the caste initiation ceremony (*upanayana*) entitling them to wear the sacred thread, have the qualification (*adhikara*) to participate in the normative Vedic religion of ritual. But in addition to the members of the lowest *Shudra-varna* there is the remainder of the population, who are classified as 'outcaste' or 'untouchable'. Each estate, as well as the outcastes, is divided into what are termed *jatis* (literally 'birth'), which are the actual units of social organisation. *Jatis* are endogamous social networks bound by ties of commensality. They are tied to hereditary trades and professions, thus effectively guaranteeing gainful employment for those born into them. While inequality is essential to the system, it must be stressed that the hierarchical arrangement is cohesive rather than divisive. The system is one of interdependence and reciprocity; that is to say, in a non-monetary economy, a Brahmin might provide religious offices in exchange for goods and other services.

Jatis may be understood as 'natural kinds'; *jati* means 'birth' or 'biological species' as well as hereditary social grouping. One's social status is an inalienable, essential property of one's body. Birth into a particular *jati* is thought of as determined by the quality of one's ***karma*** that has been accumulated as a consequence of good and bad deeds performed in an infinite series of past lives. The hierarchy is determined by considerations of spiritual purity, and the focal point of the system is the prestige accorded to Brahmins, who sustain their supreme position by strict observance of the vast catalogue of rules, held to derive from the infallible Vedic scriptures and codified in the **Dharma-Shastra** literature. These prescriptions apply to every aspect of life, and extricate the pure (*shuddha*) from the omnipresent spiritually polluting or impure, which tends to be associated with anything organic. The maintenance of purity involves keeping the company of other Brahmins, studying the Vedic literature, various daily and occasional religious observances and the avoidance of polluting physical contact with members of lower castes as far as possible. The notion of an essentialist caste hierarchy often conflicts with the tenets of theistic faiths according to which all are identical in the sight of God.

Buddhism is often described as 'anti-caste'. But the Buddha Gotama did not deny the reality of caste as a social phenomenon. He did, however, deny that it was something essential given at birth. The Buddha re-interpreted the fourfold classification in ethical terms relating to particular types of character and conduct. The twenty-sixth chapter of the *Dhammapada* is a classic statement of the Buddhist re-evaluation of the concept of Brahminhood, an inherited ascribed status in Hinduism, in strictly prescriptive, ethical terms: 'By whom no evil is done in body, mind and voice, him, restrained in these three respects, I call a Brahman' (Norman trans., 391). 'Not by matted locks, not by clan, not by birth, does one become a Brahman. In whom is truth and righteousness, he is pure and he is a Brahman' (393). 'But I do not call one born in a (Brahman) womb a Brahman, having his origin in a (Brahman) mother. ...One without possessions and without attachments, him I call a Brahman' (396).

Further reading

Dumont, L. (1979) *Homo Hierarchicus: The Caste System and its Implications*, trans. M. Sainsbury, L. Dumont and B. Gulati, Chicago: University of Chicago Press.

Norman, K.R. (trans.) (1997) *The Word of the Doctrine (Dhammapada)*, Oxford: Pali Text Society Translation Series No.46.

CHRIS BARTLEY

category

The classical Chinese debate on category surrounds the term *lei* (kind, class, genus). This is the basic topic in early Chinese logic. There were three basic positions:

1 categories are logical and real;
2 categories are not logical and not real;
3 categories are real but overlapping and extendible.

Mohists followed their founder and trusted logical categories to be real and have substance (see **Mohism: moral logic**). Universal love (concern for others) is possible and imperative because we are of the same kind as the rest of mankind and the number of men is finite and involves a real number. Gongsun Long accepted that categories are real but preferred to define them, as Buddhists would, in reductionist and negative or non-substantive terms. X and non-X being mutually exclusive, Gongsun Long argues that 'White Horse is not Horse' because what excludes the non-horse and the non-white is more than that which just excludes the non-horse. To that, the Neo-Mohists responded by using the

substantialist argument: since white horse and horse take up the same amount of space – like hardness and whiteness would take up the same space in a piece of marble – then what is coextensive must be materially the same thing. Even if one locates a horse geographically in the state of Qi (i.e., far away in a different place or space), the horse still takes up the same amount of space (space being homogeneous everywhere). Location does not change that materialist argument; therefore, a Qi horse is still a horse. The Mohists were no Platonists; they grounded their logic not in idealist abstractions (universals) but in real and concrete particulars.

Hui Shi judged categories like large and small, black and white, horse and dog to be all relative. They are not real and not substantive, being just very loose linguistic conventions. Thus if you ask for a white horse, you might get, in the middle of the night, a black dog. (Think of it as a large dark greyhound.) With nothing being ultimately logically distinct, he drew the conclusion, a substantialist one, that all things are, in their 'non-descript' base as 'thing,' fundamentally one. **Zhuangzi**, his friend, followed suit in also charging that all standards are relative and the myriad things are of 'one pointing' (that is, come under the same base category as thing). Both thinkers, by finding categorical distinctions to be unreal, are able to feel a substantialist communion with all things. The Neo-Mohists naturally disagreed; they find such fuzzy or badly conceived thinking a betrayal of the whole purpose of **logic**.

Mencius accepted the logical distinctions as real and he is known also for realizing a similar sense of being one with all things. That sense of communion with all is achieved by 'existentially' crossing various boundaries in the categorization of his being. He is not bound by the 'essentialist' assumption that ruled Aristotle. In the moral sphere, this means that for the Mencian, man is not an animal, but he can degenerate into an animal if he loses his humanity. '**Humaneness**' is his nature, but not in a fixed or definite amount. It can be small or big, it can shrink or expand, just enough to serve one's parents or sufficient to love everyone. Man can thus rise to god-like status and even touch **Heaven** within the highest reach of his humanity. The mind-heart (*xin*) of humaneness is commiseration. This 'commiseration among members of the same kind' is natural. We pity others, especially children, who suffer. But humane commiseration can be extended beyond our specific human species to a larger genus and still larger family to which we belong. We feel pity for animals being slaughtered; we even feel uneasy and regretful at the sight of broken tiles. This empathy, when maximized, would bring us into communion with all; man then becomes one with, or, it is better to say, he actively unites as one, heaven (above) and earth (below).

Xunzi sided with the Mohists in insisting on clear thinking: categories are real. But he would not remake society on the Mohist pretext of pure logic. Tradition, convention and usage matter. He agreed that things are classified together by their similarity and classified apart by their differences. A nominalist, he argued that the conventions of usage need to be assessed in relation to their practical utility. Given human nature (as he saw it), universal love as a logical construct is neither true or wise, nor prudent or practical. A rationalist through and through, he finds fault with Mencius's enthusiasm for this mystical oneness with all things. That is fine as poetry, he suggests, but such 'monistic pathos' is nothing more than feeling, not actual fact. It confuses the 'ought' of warm sentiment with the 'is' of cool reason. Stones and tiles, being inanimate objects, suffer no pain to deserve evoking our imaginary commiseration and regret.

Xunzi had the last word on how names should be applied to reality. His pragmatic approach served to rein in any excess of idealist abstraction in China, but Mencian sentiments ruled the Chinese realm of feeling while Daoist poetics came to organize the culture's flight of the spirit. By late dynastic China, these came together in the planning of her encyclopedia called *leishu* or 'book of categories', reference works with entries organized under a standard list of categories. There is no hierarchic Aristotelian structure as such; it is not so impersonally arranged. There is an imperial agenda, since the collections were sponsored by the ruler. The structure generally follows the Chinese life-world, with the king and the court in the centre and then extending by concentric circles outwards.

See also: Five Elements; Neo-Mohists

Further reading

Graham, A. (1989) *Disputers of the Tao: Philosophical Argument in Ancient China*, La Salle, IL: Open Court.

WHALEN LAI

causality, theory of

Despite the widespread espousal of the Madhyamaka ontology of **Nagarjuna**, which includes a thorough deconstruction of the concept of causality, Tibetan philosophers on the whole accept a rather realist account of causation. For the Tibetan thinkers, cause and effects are not a mere sequence of events; rather, there must exist a natural relation between the two. In fact, a cause is defined as 'that which brings into being its effect'; while, an 'effect' is 'that which is brought into being by its cause'. Thus, 'cause', according to Tibetan philosophy, literally means an 'efficient cause'. In contrast, explanatory causes are characterized more as 'evidence' or 'proof'. Furthermore, Tibetan thinkers reject the notion of a 'simultaneous' causation. Thus, the following appear to be principal features of causation: (1) causality is a part of the natural principles of the world; (2) cause and effects are necessarily sequential; (3) cause and effects must possess a relationship of commensurability; and finally, (4) a cause is necessarily a transient phenomenon.

Every event is believed to result from a multitude of causes; but these causes can be broadly divided into two classes, 'substantial' or 'material' cause and 'contributory' cause. In the case of, say, a clay pot, the clay is the substantial cause for it is the 'stuff' that turns into a pot, while factors such as the potter, the wheel, water and so on are contributory causes. The latter together create the conditions, which enables the clay to become the resultant effect, namely the pot. Although in a general sense there is no difference between a cause and a condition, in specific contexts, often 'cause' refers to the substantial cause and 'conditions' refer to the contributory factors.

This principle of substantial causation is said to hold even in the realm of mental phenomena. In fact, it is on the basis of a beginningless continuum of the 'substantial' cause of consciousness that the Tibetan thinkers argue for the existence of past lives. Various theories about how such a continuum is maintained during what in ordinary terms would be recognized as mindless states – fainting, deep sleep – are entertained. However, it seems unclear how the theory of 'substantial' cause is supposed to be understood in the context of what are clearly abstract but, from the Buddhist point of view, impermanent phenomena such as the properties of 'transience', 'contingency', 'unsatisfactoriness' and so on.

Like the Indian Buddhist epistemologists, the Tibetan realist theorists accept that the relation between cause and events is a mental construct. It exists neither in the cause, nor in the effect. It can be cognitively ascertained only from a perspective that embraces the temporal stages of both the cause and its effects. However, unlike Indian epistemologists the Tibetans reject any ontological status of ultimacy to the elementary constituents of both objects and events. For them, not only the objects and events (that is, the physical and mental worlds which they constitute) but also the laws of causality exist only on the level of the conventional truth. In other words, theory and propositions about causality can be valid only within the framework of conventional existence and thus can never be absolute. Principal Tibetan theorists of causality are the Shakya and **Geluk school** commentators on **Dharmakirti**.

Further reading

Dreyfus, G. (1997). *Dharmakarti's Philosophy and its Tibetan Interpretations*, Albany, NY: State University of New York, chaps 2, 5.

THUPTEN JINPA

causality in Islamic philosophy

According to much of the Peripatetic tradition in Islamic philosophy, causality is imbued with natural necessity. For Ibn Sina, for example, everything which occurs in the world of generation and corruption is necessitated by something else, and this is true as we go progressively higher in the range of reality, until we reach God who is the only

thing which is not brought about by something else. The principle of emanation which is so popular emphasizes the connections between everything in the universe, and the non-arbitrary nature of that connectivity. There is a reason for everything which takes place, and that reason is modelled on the rules of logical derivation. Of course, this made it look as though God had no significant role in the world, since whatever happens happens because it had to happen. **Al-Ghazali** criticizes the philosophers from a religious perspective for this theory, but he also criticizes the theory itself, arguing that God could alter the customary order of nature were he to wish such changes to take place. He sometimes adhered to an Ash'arite view that interprets reality in terms of atoms, where God is the only cause of anything taking place since the atoms do not in themselves have any ability to combine at all. This view also has the advantage, from a religious point of view, of allowing for the possibility of miracles. The Ash'arites developed a doctrine of *kasb* or acquisition, by which we acquire actions and powers from God, who is the creator of those actions which are then, in a sense, made available to us.

Further reading

Fakhry, M. (1958) *Islamic Occasionalism*, London: Allen & Unwin.

OLIVER LEAMAN

cause, condition and effect

China generally employed a biological model for understanding changes in life and in reality, so the mechanical model of cause and effect was unfamiliar. The Chinese did not even have any words ready to render a 'cause' and its distinct 'effect' when Buddhism first introduced this form of causal analysis. This does not mean China had no idea of precedents and consequents, or that the Mohist engineers had no mechanical knowledge, but it does mean that China had to come up with words for *hetu* (reason), *pratyaya* (condition) and *phala* (fruit, i.e. effect). The result was 'base/reason for' for cause, 'edge/running alongside' for condition and 'fruit/fruition' for effect.

Buddhists did not teach simply a straight cause and effect which would privilege some sort of Brahman as the first cause. Instead, they taught 'conditioned co-arising'. This means, if there is A, there is B. As there is not A, there is not B. When condition is added, the full causal sequence reads, 'cause, condition and effect'. Interpolating condition is one way to avoid the **Vedanta** thesis of 'the effect being pre-existing in the cause (*satkaryavada*)'. Perhaps because mechanical 'cause and effect' was less attractive to the Chinese, this idea of a concomitant 'condition' (something running alongside another) seems to justify aborting a cause–effect temporal sequence for some type of simultaneity. Though synchronicity is not unknown in India (it arose over the question whether the classic chains of causation all work at once or whether they span three life times), it made more of an impact in China. China rated the instantaneous causation as the highest notion of causation. And despite **Nagarjuna**'s equation of **emptiness** with causality, China took emptiness to negate cause and effect in such a way that emptiness is virtually synonymous with the non-causative. For that reason, emptiness is not listed in the structure of the four theories of causation. The four theories as Chinese philosophy saw them are:

1 karmic causation
2 *alaya-vijnana* causation
3 *tathagatagarbha* causation
4 *dharmadhatu* causation

The first traces the cause of events to past karmic conditions, which the second then roots in the (deluded) 'storehouse consciousness' in the subject. The third in turn roots that storehouse consciousness in the still deeper 'buddha-matrix'. Everything is seen then as being generated out of this pure buddha-mind. The fourth and last goes one step further and roots **buddha nature** in the infinite realm of the Dharma Reality such that the universe, parts as well as the whole, would generate itself out of itself by itself. This is when every cause and effect becomes instantaneously effect and cause to all others in an auto-genetic whole. The whole set of theories is evidence of a traditional Chinese interest in cosmogonic 'origin'. Since

emptiness is regarded as anti-causative, the Tiantai school which built itself on that form of reasoning billed itself as a *shixiang* (real form) philosophy which is opposed to and set apart from the *yuanqi* (conditioned co-arising) theory.

Further reading

Lai, W. (1977) 'Chinese Buddhist Causation Theories: An Analysis of Sinitic Mahayana Understanding of Pratitya-samutpada', *Philosophy East and West* 27(3): 241–64.

Takakusu, J. (1947) *The Essentials of Buddhist Philosophy*, Honolulu, HA: University of Hawaii Press

WHALEN LAI

Chang Taiyan

b. 1868; d. 1936

Buddhist philosopher and political activist

Chang Taiyan (Ch'ang T'ai-yen) was a supporter of the monarchist experiment of 1898 before being converted to the republican cause. Jailed for his political activity, Chang discovered Buddhism. He later wrote a commentary on the 'equalization of things' thesis in the *Zhuangzi*.

See also: atheism, modern Chinese

WHALEN LAI

chaos

There are two Chinese words that might be translated into English as 'chaos': *luan* for social chaos, as contrasted with political rule, and *hundun*, which is the cosmogonic chaos before the emergence of form. The latter appears in an anecdote in **Zhuangzi**. Two friends called Sudden of the South Sea and Swift of the North Sea decided to give this 'shapeless blob' of the Central Sea the seven orifices that all humans have. Having done this, they duly killed this natural Know-Nothing with their human kindness. *Hundun* is better known to us as the shapeless meat dumplings called *wonton* in Chinese restaurants. The unformed is potent even as a dish. From this appropriately obscure concept, the whole of Daoist philosophy, it is sometimes argued, can be understood.

Further reading

Girardot, N. (1974) *Myth and Meaning in Early Taoism: The Theme of Chaos*, Berkeley, CA: University of California Press.

WHALEN LAI

Chapa Chokyi Senge

Chapa Chokyi Senge (1109–69) can be seen as one of the founders of the logico-epistemological tradition of Tibetan Buddhism. He is specially known for his 'collected topics' system of intellectual training that emphasizes clarity and precision through the use of definition and bipolar argumentation. 'Collected topics' refer to a set of texts, which contain a selection of key logical and epistemological themes extracted from **Dharmakirti**'s *Pramanavarttika*. The presentation of the themes is designed specifically for a highly sophisticated form of debate and argumentation, which is used extensively to this day in the major Tibetan monastic colleges. Although Chapa's own original works on 'collected topics' are no longer extant, today the term is used to cover a specific genre of writing that not only deals with the topics chosen by Chapa but also approaches the themes in a unique style. This training in the 'collected topics' is most widespread in the **Geluk school** academic colleges.

On a number of key questions such as the problem of universals Chapa seems to have diverged from Dharmakirti, at least according to critics like **Shakya Pandita**. Chapa's views represent a more realist approach to epistemology, which has been inherited and further developed by Geluk thinkers like **Gyaltsap Dharma Rinchen** and Khedrup. Chapa is also one of the few Tibetan thinkers who have taken issue with Chandrakirti's interpretation of **Nagarjuna**. According to some Tibetan accounts, Chapa is reported to have won a debate (or debates) with the Indian scholar

Jayananda, who defended Chandrakirti's philosophy.

Further reading

Dreyfus, G. (1997) *Recognising Reality: Dharmakirti's Philosophy and its Tibetan Interpretations*, Albany, NY: State University of New York Press, ch. 23.

Kuijp, L. (1978) 'Phya-pa Chos-kyi-seng-ge's Impact on Tibetan Epistemology', *Journal of Indian Philosophy* 5: 355–69.

THUPTEN JINPA

character

Confucian humanism is grounded, not upon rational individualism, but ultimately on the linking and mutual identification of self, society and cosmos. For **Mencius**, the fully-flourishing human personality finds in its heart-mind a sincere empathy with the moral directive of the universe. By the time of the Han dynasty, this had become the idea of a 'Unity of Man and Heaven'. After the ensuing Buddhist era, the Song Neo-Confucians adopted Buddhism's 'ascetic' or yogic self-control but redirected it to 'inner-worldly' ends. Taking the view that a little suffering is good for the soul, they believed in character building by leading a self-imposed 'pure and simple life'. Character (*renge*) requires scrutiny (*gewu*). 'Plain and insipid' became a new aesthetic value.

Unlike the Song dynasty Neo-Confucians, the Han dynasty Confucians did not believe that everyone can and should 'learn to be a **sage**'. Sages were then a rare commodity: they were regarded as born rather than made, and sagehood was not achievable through effort alone. So, whereas the Song project at character building presumed universality and a homogeneous view of humanity, the Han recognized specific varieties and did not insist on a single theory of human nature. Human beings were usually classified good, bad, or some combination of both. The 'three grades' were applied also to political office, where adding the 'birth' (family background) factor (3×3) meant there were a total of nine 'grades'. A person could be recommended for office by these regional 'impartial adjudicators' of his moral character.

By the late Han period, this personality assessment had become an art. A few pithy but well-chosen words of praise or censure could well promote or demote a candidate. Called 'pure criticism', this evolved later into the 'pure conversation' among the Neo-Daoists (see **Neo-Daoism**), whose flair for personal self-expression – they were the first 'aesthetic individualists' – in turn inspired a new phrase in character appreciation. A debate then rose over what matters more: nature or talent, birth or merit? The conservative Confucians picked nature/birth, for they assumed that the highborn are more good-natured than the lowborn. The Neo-Daoists picked talent/merit, for they were aligned with the Neo-Legalist rulers of the Wei who promoted men of ability, caring less about birth rights or issues of morality. The Wei was founded by the general Cao Cao who had usurped Han rule, a master at Machiavellian machination and manipulation who was considered an evil genius. The words 'genius' and 'hero' came into vogue in this period, as political chaos fanned a cult of the 'extraordinary' man (great man, superman), a title some openly cultivated and even proudly claimed for themselves.

The *Renwuzhi* is one such 'Study of Human Abilities' from this era. With aesthetic objectivity, it assessed human personality. It described Cao Cao as 'heroic in talent and remarkable in foresight, one able to decide when to strike – and doing so with no second thought'. This work tried to turn character appreciation into a science, but was unable to shake loose from the correlative mindset of Han thought. It used the **Five Elements** scheme, as the Indians used the three *gunas* in **Samkhya**, to typecast people, fitting men with the fire or metal element to fill positions requiring such temperaments. The other work of the period, one that perhaps better captures the kaleidoscope of aesthetic individualism, is the *Shishuo Xinyu* (New Accounts of the Tales of World). A 'talk of the town' collection about the 'beautiful people' of the time, its anecdotal tales were classified under various virtues and vices such as affairs of state, cultivated tolerance, precocious intelligence, self-renewal, grieving for the departed, living in retirement, worthy beauties, the free and unrest-rained, stinginess and meanness, blind infatuations, hostility and alienation, and so on. A person could make a 'name' for himself by getting himself included in this register of manners. This 'aesthetic' individualism, however, lacks (to use a Kierkegaardian standard) 'ethical' consistency. The catalogue of virtues and vices lacks a social teleology; they do not add up to a unitary whole. One son famous for his inordinately long and tearful mourning – he 'mourned unto death', instead of 'unto life' as the rites would prescribe – appeared in another chapter as a stingy miser. It shows how he, emotionally extravagant in one sphere of life, could just as well be tight-fisted in another.

Although that is all too human, such inconsistency would have been discouraged and curtailed by the later Neo-Confucian project (see **Neo-Confucianism, concepts**) at 'character building'. Ethical individualism was then identified as involving greater communal conformity; it enforced a more integrated code of conduct, and required personal vigilance at all times. The Neo-Confucians had acquired the art of ascetic self-control from the Buddhist mores that flourished in that period; Buddhist monks who left their old samsaric selves behind had to learn to remake themselves into new beings. Later, there was a shift in the Neo-Confucian rhetoric of moral self-cultivation. Besides speaking of 'being' and 'becoming humane', they talked also in engineering terms of 'molding, making, crafting' their sagehood and destiny. That sense of learning as a vocation that calls for diligent effort as sanctification underwrote the Neo-Confucian anthropology that with destiny (*ming*) being in your heart or hand, you are what you should make of yourself.

There is a continuation of an earlier post-Han debate on nature and talent or 'ascription versus achievement'. This later debate, on virtue versus talent, arose in the Song period. Mencius had blamed moral failure on a 'lack of effort'. To him, 'I cannot' masks only 'I will not'. Mencius did not charge the failure to the material make-up of the person, but Cheng Yi did at one point consider human 'nature' to be good and blamed evil (or deviation from that good) on the material make-up or talent. Etymologically, 'talent' is 'raw timber'. This relegation of evil to material 'talent' was deemed a mistake. In the seventeenth-century debate, this mistake is likened to **Gaozi**'s thesis about 'bending wood (raw material) to make good (useful utensils)' that Mencius had defeated.

For Aristotle, virtue is what one acquires through habit. Thus honesty is born of the habit of not telling a lie. A child who regularly avoids telling lies grows into an honest man. In China, before Mencius turned all Confucian virtues into the issuing forth of an inner good, the *Analects* open with 'to learn and habituate oneself to what is learned – what joy!' Virtue results from habit becoming self-perpetuating. It is when the act is now self-gratifying, an end in itself, a joy. And emulation means simply, in Confucius' words: 'See not, hear not, speak not what is contrary to the rites'. Confucius did not say, 'think no evil'. That he reserved for describing the intent of the *Book of Songs*. Thoughts being invisible, you cannot emulate what you cannot see. But by avoiding, say, watching violence on television, a child is less likely to start sounding like what he or she saw and heard. Wild talk leads to wild action. The Chinese expression 'habit makes natural' is about good habits becoming a person's 'second nature'. Confucius knew this as 'polishing jade'; Gaozi knew it as 'coaxing wood'. But because Mencius so disparaged him, and because **Xunzi** used the metaphor of bending wood 'against its grain' to serve a different philosophical end, it was not until the anti-metaphysical thinkers of the seventeenth century that this classic debate on habituation into virtue was resurrected.

Further reading

Mather, R. (trans.) (1976) *Shih-shuo Hsin-yu: A New Account of the Tales of the World*, Minneapolis, MN: University of Minnesota Press.

Shryock, J. (trans.) (1966) *The Study of Human Abilities; The Jen-Wu Chih by Liu Shao*, New Haven, CN: Yale University Press.

WHALEN LAI

character, left and right

To be left-handed is to stand out as odd and evil while to be dexterous is to be gifted. The term 'left-handed' retains that semantic ambiguity in **Tantra**: suspect by the mainstream but doubly powerful to its adherents. Sex, alcohol and meat are normally taboo to the ascetic, but Buddhist Tantra claims the pure lotus flower blossoms only because of these poisons in the form of nutrients supplied by the muddy pond bottom (**samsara**). The strong *siddhi*, like the 'strong Christian', can afford to 'resist no evil'.

China is also in two minds about the metaphor of the left. The male, as *yang*, is to the left as the female, as *yin*, is to the right – possibly because, while facing south, the Chinese associate left with sunrise and right with dusk. Yet one term to describe 'heresy' is the 'way of the left'. Cultural encounters wrought other confusions. Some early Chinese translators of the Bible felt it necessary to move Christ, who was standing to the right of God, to the left. Some early Daoists charged Buddhists with drinking urine and eating faeces, probably because Chinese ate with chopsticks and not with their hands while Indians used the right hand for eating and the left for their ablutions. The Daoist observers probably conflated the two uses of the two hands.

Further reading

Kohn, L. (1995) *Laughing at the Tao: Debates Among Buddhists and Taoists in Medieval China*, Princeton, NJ: Princeton University Press.

WHALEN LAI

characterology and the occult

As early as **Mencius**, who claimed he could tell a person's moral character by observing his neck (that is, how he holds up his head), there has been an interest in China in physiognomy. This science of characterology can be based on the time of birth (the astrology of the 'eight lunar/solar characters' for year, month, day and hour), facial features, posture, palmistry or the anagrams of a Chinese person's name. Birth under one of the twelve zodiac animals types one's character. The 'eight characters' may decide if two persons should or should not join in marriage. With the greater social mobility since the Song dynasty, there has been heightened interest in knowing one's fate and bettering one's circumstances. Fate cannot be changed, but fortune or circumstance can be manipulated to one's advantage. India supplied some of these occult arts, but 'animalian physiognomy' (classifying human character according to some allegedly observable animal trait in the subject) appears to be due less to an Indian notion of animal rebirths than to a vestige of ancient Chinese beliefs in zoomorphic ancestors and totemic typologies. Late Dynastic fatalism went with a concurrent cynicism, and reliance on fortune-telling grew among the people even as the **correlative** cosmology of old was being abandoned by the progressive minds of the seventeenth century.

See also: animals

Further reading

Smith, R. (1991) *Fortune-Tellers and Philosophers: Divination in Traditional China*, Boulder, CO: Westview Press.

WHALEN LAI

charity

Buddhists and Christians alike place emphasis on works of charity, such as feeding the hungry, clothing the naked, nursing the sick, tending to the imprisoned and burying the dead. Such charities are expressions of Christian love and Buddhist friendliness or compassion. The terms *agape*, *metta* and *karuna* are quite close in meaning. For taking care of the poor and the needy, the early Christian church ran into trouble with the Roman authorities; likewise a Chinese minister, citing **Confucius** lodged a similar charge in 717 CE against Buddhist temples sponsoring free hospital care, claiming that they were usurping the prerogative of the state. In Rome as in Han China, feeding the hungry and burying the unclaimed dead were functions of the city or the state; the poor and the dead, as wards of the state, then owed their loyalty to the state. Christians and Buddhists undermined that loyalty by obeying a higher law to help the needy and the dead.

Even in sedentary China, kinship-based Confucians were committed to a brotherhood of all men 'within the four seas'. But Christian 'hospitality' and the European 'hospital' came out of institutional hospice care provided by the church to pilgrims who had fallen sick. Likewise, Buddhist temples in medieval China and Japan provided the first free clinics and hospital care for the same clientele. These were called 'compassion wards'. The term was taken over from a Buddhist text compiled in China between 517–20, seeking explicitly to 'aid the widowed and the orphaned' (i.e., the kin-deprived and thus most helpless). This text calls for generous donation to the 'field of compassion' to help the needy. That is judged better than showering more wealth on the 'field of reverence', the already well endowed Three Jewels (*Triratna*: the Buddha, the *Dharma* (his teaching) and the *Sangha* (his community of followers). This is based on a Mahayana reversal of a Hinayana principle in calculating merit. In Theravada, a charitable deed is measured not just by the goodness of the intention (the Kantian good will) but also by the good of the end the act may produce (Benthamite utility). When grafted onto the two-tiered structure of **Hinayana** Buddhist spirituality, it is then always better to give to a pure monk than a less reputable one; but better any monk than a more needy beggar. The monk, spiritually more pure than the layman, could do more spiritual good. This is a sound principle, but the unintended consequence is that monks in an urban temple are usually better fed than the beggars that gather outside seeking a pittance from the lay temple visitors. An early Mahayana preceptory text, the *Upasaka Shila Sutra*, spoke up first for a separate field of merit dedicated to aiding the poor. The Chinese renamed that 'poverty field' the 'compassion field'. The free hospital care that is the 'compassion ward' is an expression of that Mahayana ideal of charity.

See also: Buddhism in China, origins and development

Further reading

Demieville, P. (1985) *Buddhism and Healing: Demie-*

ville's Article on 'Byo' from Hobogirin, trans. M. Tatz, Lanham, MD: University Press of America.

Kalupahana, D. (1976) Buddhism: An Introduction, Honolulu, HA: University of Hawaii Press.

Lai, W. (1992) 'Chinese Buddhist and Christian Charities: A Historical Comparison', Buddhist-Christian Studies 12: 5–34.

Shih Heng-ching (trans.) (1991) The Sutra of Upasaka Precepts, Tokyo and Berkeley, CA: Bukkyo Dendo Kyokai.

WHALEN LAI

charvaka

Charvaka is an Indian atheistic and anti-ritualist outlook which maintains the radical empiricist doctrine that perception (pratyaksha) is the only authoritative source of knowledge (**pramana**). It rejects the validity of inference (anumana) as a pramana in its own right. A typical (simplified) inferential schema has the form:

There is fire (to be proved) on the mountain.
Because there is smoke (evidence).
Wherever there is smoke, there is fire (invariable concomitance).

The Charvakas deny that the relation of invariable concomitance between the evidence and what is to be proved can be satisfactorily established on the basis of observational evidence. Observed instances may lend support to a hypothesis or purported general rule, but since they represent only a finite sample they cannot prove it. If it is sought to avoid this problem by saying that the generality obtains not between particulars but between universals or essential properties, the Charvaka responds that it is with the particulars that inference is concerned. The universals are allegedly known already and there would be no need for inferential procedures. The associations which form the bases of inference merely reflect habits of mind and an assumption of natural uniformities.

The Charvakas recognize the existence of the four sensorily experienced gross, material elements of earth, fire, air and water. They deny the soul (**atman**), reducing personal identity in

material terms to bodily continuity. Consciousness is an emergent property of physical processes. Feelings are reductively identical with their bodily expressions. The post mortem decomposition of the body is the absolute and final dissolution of selfhood.

Of the four legitimate goals of life (**Purush-artha**), they recognize only economic prosperity (artha) and aesthetic and sexual enjoyment (kama), rejecting social and religious duty (**dharma**) and irreversible release from the series of births (moksha). They propose a mild hedonism: 'enjoy yourself while you are alive'. Charvakas reject the morally retributive **karma** theory, regarding the operation of causality as restricted to the natural and observable.

The sole surviving Charvaka text is Jayarashi's (770–830 CE) Tattvopaplavasimha. This work expounds a radical scepticism about the nature of the realities (tattva) identified in the ontological schemes of other schools on the grounds that there are no coherent definitions (**lakshana**) of the authoritative means of knowledge (pramana). Jayarashi subjects **Nyaya**, **Purva Mimamsa**, Buddhist and **Samkhya** definitions of valid cognition and perception to destructive criticisms. He also assails the Nyaya and Buddhist theories of inference, the inference of the soul and the theory that scriptural or for that matter, any other sort of language (shabda) is an authoritative means of knowledge.

Further reading

Franco, E. (1994) Perception, Knowledge and Disbelief: A Study of Jayarashi's Scepticism, Delhi: Motilal Banarsidass.

CHRIS BARTLEY

chastity

Chastity is a virtue often demanded of woman, usually in the context of a patriarchal society. In China, the demand for chastity was aggravated by the medieval Buddhist asceticism. Women were blamed for distracting the male ascetic, since erotic desire was deemed a powerful craving and cause of suffering, while at the same time the cult of asceticism also idealized the nun. Buddhist culture, however, was kinder to women than that of the Neo-Confucians, who exacted further demands: chastity now meant loyalty to a spouse for life. Remarriage of widows was attacked, and it was suggested that it is better for a woman to commit suicide than to be raped – or even touched. Horrendous cases of such exemplary acts were included in the education of women which was meant to prepare them for their roles.

After the expulsion of the Mongol Yuan dynasty, Ming society equated female chastity with (male) official loyalty. A chaste woman is loyal; a loyal official is chaste. Yet this mentality came out of a society where the male was increasingly emasculated into an effeminate 'pale-faced' **scholar** and women were outwardly desexualized (wearing the shapeless gowns that covered all their skin except for the face and the hands). Femininity became associated with willowy weakness: as Victorian ladies swooned easily, Chinese ones tragically spit blood.

As in other patriarchal societies, the Chinese woman was subordinated to man. It was decreed that she should obey the father before marriage, the husband when married and the grown child if widowed. There was also a set of four feminine virtues, but when the number of educated women actually increased in late dynastic China, enough men felt threatened that a proverb was born: 'A woman without talent is virtuous enough.'

Further reading

Paul, D. (1979) *Women in Buddhism: Images of the Feminine in Mahayana Tradition*, Berkeley, CA: Asian Humanities Press.

Cao Xueqin (1973–80) *The Story of the Stone (Dream of the Red Chambers)* vols 1–3, trans. D. Hawkes, in five volumes, Harmondsworth: Penguin.

Ishihara, A. and Levy, H. (1970) *The Tao of Sex*, New York: Harper & Row.

WHALEN LAI

CH'I *see* qi

CHI *see* trigger

CHI-TSANG *see* Jizang

CHIA I *see* Jia Yi

child

A child is usually a metaphor of innocence (St Augustine's reading of its inherent sinfulness notwithstanding). A child of nature may be a barbarian (and vice versa) for **Xunzi**, but it is also an anti-culture symbol. In early and classical societies, teachings are meant for the adult male. Thus women and children were often barred from tribal initiation **rites**.

In China, the *Analects* of **Confucius** have little to say about children. Only in later legend would the Master be outwitted by some wise child and admit that 'deference is due no less to the very young'. In Daoism, however, with nature being valued over nurture, **Laozi** prized the newborn. The babe is pliant and full of life, as the aged is bound for a stiff death. **Mencius** also compared the 'innate good' in man to 'the heart of a newborn'. When catching sight suddenly of a small child about to fall into a well, we are moved to compassion; it is the innocence of the endangered child out there that touches off this empathy from the 'child in us'. We feel differently if it is a horrible person about to fall into the well. **Mozi** loved the young no less than the mature, but Mohist rationality had little use for a metaphor of an unthinking child. Yizi, a Mohist, did try to reconcile Mohist 'universal love' with the **sage** having a 'child's mind', but the passage he cited from the *Book of History* did not get beyond paternalism: the former rulers treated their subjects like children. **Zhuangzi**, in his role as the urbane dialectician, did not use the child metaphor as much as he did when discussing **meditation**.

Interest in precocious children went back to the Han dynasty or even further, but interest in heaven-endowed talent meant that the post-Han Neo-Daoists were drawn to child prodigies. The Buddha was born with his faculties fully developed; as karmic merit or demerit is carried over from prior lives, so Buddhists do not have to presume all newborns to be equally innocent or dumb. Later records show the Sixth Patriarch **Huineng** as younger and younger, in the end a mere child, and one famous Chan **koan** looks back to the prenatal 'face you had before you were born'. The Song period Neo-Confucians did not go so far; as upholders of patriarchy, they did not consider the child to be the father of the man. Wang Yangming had more sympathy with Chan, and one of his disciples, the iconoclast Li Zhi, who dressed in monk's garb and was known for keeping up a correspondence with a nun, devoted an essay on the Mencian 'heart-mind of a child'. He also openly considered girls to be equal to boys, a concept which would make Confucius and perhaps even Mencius sit up in their graves.

Care should be exercised in the use of the child metaphor. A child cannot be said to be in possession of the virtue of wisdom; wisdom comes with age, around fifty for both Confucius and Aristotle. Also, the Mencian parable of being roused to concern by the sight of a child in peril does not apply to another child. Two children crawl towards a well: one falls in, and the other could be innocent enough to follow laughingly after.

Further reading

Kinney, A. (1995) 'The Theme of the Precocious Child in Early Chinese Literature', *T'oung Pao* 81: 1–24.

WHALEN LAI

China, Middle Kingdom

The word 'China' came from the Roman encounter with the Qin Empire (Rome was also known to China as the Great Qin). Chinese names for the country include the Central Plain, the Middle Kingdom, the Middle Flower, the Bloom of Xia (the first dynasty) and Central Xia. In the idealized world map, China occupies the centre box of a nine-square (3 × 3) cosmos based on the Magic Square of Three (see **magic squares**). Those nine continents are separated by water or waterways. Since China knew sea to the south and

to the west, she has also been placed in the southeast box instead of the central box. According to Chinese mythology, the country is surrounded by the uncivilized, the **barbarians** of the four directions, sometimes in two rings.

Myth overlaps reality to some extent. Politically Sinocentric, China has always expected others to come to her bearing gifts, to pay tribute and acknowledge her cultural superiority. In times of peace, that meant exotic gifts for which the giver got more than equal gifts in return and, in reciprocal recognition, a kingly title. China had her share of expansionism and imperial conquest but never really developed a system of deputized or stable indirect rule, unlike the Persian, the Macedonian and the Roman empires.

See also: beyond the square

WHALEN LAI

Chinese philosophy

There are three predominant schools in Chinese philosophy: Confucianism, Daoism and Buddhism. All three had religious versions, of course, but one of the distinct aspects of Chinese philosophy and religion is its syncretism, the fact that followers of one school and religion often had little difficulty in accepting many of the principles of the other or others.

The earliest thinker was Master Kong, better known as Confucius, who lived in the 6th century BCE, but even at that time he was able to look back on long periods of previous Chinese history to illustrate his arguments. He claims that he considered himself as nothing more than a mouthpiece of the classical Chinese tradition which encapsulated the principles of how to live. He defended the idea that the ruler has the sanction of heaven if he is righteous, and has it taken away from him if he behaves badly, although his conception of heaven is very different from that of a religious believer from the traditions of Judaism, Christianity and Islam. Although Confucius spends a good deal of time praising earlier customs and events, he is certainly not a conservative. On the other hand, he did use the idea of fixed social relations as the basic constituents of society, and emphasized the significance of respect for those in such relationships, but what makes his theory intriguing is that he does not just say that a society should stick to traditional ideas. These ideas need to be revived, he argues, because they symbolize the rules of the good society as such, the rules of social harmony which remain the same throughout all time. Those rules strengthen personal integrity and also rest on such integrity, and the cultivated individual, the sort of person we should try to become, is not just someone who is born a member of an educated and privileged class, but is someone who seeks to be wise and benevolent, and who submits himself to authority where such submission is justified. Education is impossible without respect for the past and for those superior to oneself, but once it has been achieved one ought to progress socially to whichever position one is most appropriate to fill on the basis of one's own talents and efforts. This idea led to the theory of the rectification of names, according to which it is necessary for those who are acting out a particular role to work in accordance with the real nature of those roles or names. If the reality 'out there' is accurately described by our language, then we shall know what the nature of reality is and we shall take care to describe it properly, leading us to deal with it and everything else in a rational, calm and appropriate manner.

Confucius may well have contributed to some of the Classics, and the *Analects* is a collection of his sayings and ideas. There are other books which incorporate Confucian ideas, especially that of Mencius, the *Mencius* (*Mengzi*), and a large number of commentaries on his thought have appeared over time. What might be regarded as the philosophical curriculum also included the *Book of Changes* (*Yi jing*), which deals with the principles controlling change and which is also based on the idea of the significance of harmony.

Tradition has it that the founder of Daoism (Taoism), Laozi, was a contemporary of Confucius, and the main text of this school is the *Dao De Jing*, or the 'Account of the Dao (Way) and its Power'. This is a text with an often highly mystical orientation, advocating the advantages of the quiet and contemplative life, yet it also presents political advice and ideas. It deals with the notion of the *dao*

or the Way, which structures and describes the life and operations of the universe. Ultimate reality cannot be described, yet we can make some reasonable statements about the operation of the Way. It acts spontaneously and without intention, and so in a sense acts without acting, because it does not set out to achieve anything. Through being as it is, other things are brought into existence, but not through anything it sets out to do. For example, the valley makes possible the mountain, but it does not do anything directly to bring about the mountain. It is just there, and since it is there it defines the mountain. Human beings should do the same sort of thing, i.e. align their activity in similar ways; we should act through not acting, and unite through contemplation with the harmony of the Way. The notion that the microcosm which is us can become identical with the macrocosm, and that the ultimate aim is harmony is strengthened by the use of the concepts of *yin* and *yang*, the two contrasting forces in the universe which pull in opposite directions and which have to be reconciled for balance to be achieved.

Before the arrival and development of Buddhism in China a number of other schools of philosophy, including Mohism and Legalism, arose. Mozi lived around 400 BCE during a very turbulent period, and opposed the Confucian emphasis on tradition and ritual. He advocated a form of universal benevolence and the equality of all humanity, with the implication that he directly drew for the abandonment of the elaborate rituals and sacrifices which characterized so much Chinese formal worship. The Legalists argued for the important of law or *fa* as the central guiding principle of the state, since anything less strong than force and the authority of law would not do as a method of social control. This became the official doctrine of the Qin dynasty between 221 and 206 BCE.

The leading schools of Confucianism and Daoism were subjected to a great deal of commentary and creative development by later thinkers, and the theories of Neo-Confucianism and Neo-Daoism arose as result. At the same time Buddhism arrived in North China from India from the second century CE, and gradually came to have a strong effect on Chinese philosophy. It had a stronger initial influence in north China, and it is only with the reunification of China between the sixth and the tenth centuries that it really established a solid grip on China as a whole. The Tiantai school emphasized the significance of the *Lotus Sutra*, and particularly its use of the idea of skilful means, *upaya*, in order to show how the Buddha adapted his teaching to the ways of thinking of his audience. This can be generalized to think of the different periods of the Buddha's life as being those in which he produced different messages for different audiences. That is why we get a variety of different Buddhist schools, but they are all encapsulated in the *Lotus Sutra*, the greatest of the teachings. The most characteristic view of the theory is that everything already possesses buddha nature, so enlightenment is a matter of rediscovering our original nature. Naturally, there was much discussion about precisely how we are to reach that original pure buddha nature.

The Huayan school in the fifth century used the theory of dependent origination to argue that the universe is a system of interlinked *dharmas* or events. Each particular event is able to represent every other, although in itself it is completely empty and lacking in solidity, only able to reflect others. Like the Tiantai school, the Huayan presented an account of the variety of Buddhist schools which explained and justified that variety. The Hinayana or Lesser Vehicle school was correct to defend the emptiness of everything, but wrong in their account of the emptiness of the whole system of *dharmas*. The Mahayana are right to defend emptiness and attack the ordinary ideas people have of what constitutes reality, but do not understand that the mind contains considerable possibilities for knowledge. The *tathagatagarbha* school correctly point out that the buddha nature is present in everything sentient, but use it to devalue the events of the everyday world which is regarded by it as of importance only in so far as it is symbolically representative of a deeper reality. Finally, those who think that enlightenment can come about suddenly are right to be wary of the ideas which are implicit in our concepts and language, but they do not understand the importance of language and appropriate (gradual) preparation for the approach to enlightenment. The Huayan sees itself as positioned in the middle of all these various interpretations, defending both the particular and the universal, the empty and the real, the sudden and the gradual, the duplicity and yet the necessity of language, and the basic unreality of the world along with the necessity to regard it as real to a certain extent.

The Chan/Zen form of Buddhism argued that it is possible to achieve enlightenment through sudden experience, without a long and slow system of preparation, and in this aligns itself closer to Daoism than to Confucianism. The latter was not at all sympathetic to the idea of a philosophy which sought to exclude rituals, tradition and all the trappings of religion. The idea of Chan is that all that one needs is a direct experience of reality, which can lead to sudden enlightenment, and it is not difficult to understand this given the ubiquity of the *tathagatagarbha* or buddha nature in us. The language of Chan is frequently paradoxical, since it describes an experience which is literally indescribable, and uses language to account for what cannot be said. The point of this use of paradoxes is to startle and awaken the mind, to bring it back to its original awakened state. There is a use of riddles, the *kongan*, which stimulates our concepts so that we are forced to go beyond them. This form of Buddhism, known as Zen in Japanese, became especially significant in Japan, as did the Pure Land school, which identified *nirvana* with a particular heaven and argued that salvation is attainable through worship and the grace of divine beings.

There have been changes in fashion as to which school is more in favour at particular times, of course, and it has been argued that Chinese philosophy includes two distinctive features. Firstly, it has a practical orientation, and is far more interested in social and moral issues than many other systems of philosophy, in particular the Indian philosophy which is so important to the principles of Buddhism. Secondly, and connected to this, is the fact that Chinese philosophy often finds it difficult to take seriously the idea that this world is not the real world.

Further reading

Adelmann, F. (1982) *Contemporary Chinese Philosophy*, The Hague: Nijhoff.

Allinson, R. (1989) *Chuang Tzu for Spiritual Transfor-*

mation, Albany, NY: State University of New York Press.

—— (ed.) (1989) *Understanding the Chinese Mind: The Philosophical Roots*, Oxford: Oxford University Press.

Cheng, C. (ed.) (1989) *Sun Yat-sen's Doctrine in the Modern World*, Boulder, CO: Westview Press.

Creel, H. (1953) *Chinese Thought: From Confucius to Mao Tse-Tung*, Chicago: University of Chicago Press.

Fung Yu-lan (1970) *The Spirit of Chinese Philosophy*, trans. E. Hughes, Westport, CN: Greenwood Press.

—— (1983) *A History of Chinese Philosophy*, trans. D. Bodde, Princeton, NJ: Princeton University Press.

Gregory, P. (ed.) (1987) *Sudden and Gradual*, Honolulu, HA: University of Hawaii Press.

McRae, J. (1986) *The Northern School and the Formation of Early Ch'an Buddhism*, Honolulu, HA: University of Hawaii Press.

Peerenboom, R. (1993) *Law and Morality in Ancient China*, Albany, NY: State University of New York Press.

Wei-Ming Tu (1985) *Confucian Thought: Selfhood as Creative Transformation*, Albany, NY: State University of New York Press.

OLIVER LEAMAN

Chinese philosophy, pre-modern and Marxist

The collapse of the Ming dynasty and the subsequent Qing dynasty's suppression of intellectual protest meant a setback for Chinese philosophy. Knowledge of the West brought in by the Jesuits eroded the faith in the old cosmology. The new currents in Qing thought were anti-metaphysical. The rationalist camp of Neo-Confucianism had formerly charged the intuitive camp with being too Chan-ist; now, the whole of Song–Ming Neo-Confucian scholarship was being criticized as proto-Buddhist. The a priori reality of the principle was questioned; the material reality of the **ether** was embraced. The call for a return to a ritual orthodoxy, to practical learning and to concrete utility, went out in the mid-seventeenth century. A return to Han textual study, classical

philology, and evidential historiography rose a century later and disguised a new, socio-political criticism. Western imperialism impacted on China in the nineteenth century, and Confucianism took a last stand with Kang Yuwei leading the 1898 constitutional monarchy reforms before the 1911 Revolution, Japanese invasion and the Second World War drew China into the stark reality of modern nation-state building in the post-colonial Far East.

Under **Mao Zedong**, there was a concerted effort to review and rewrite the history of Chinese philosophy. A committee under Ho Weilu produced the well-documented volumes in the series titled (in Chinese) 'A General History of Chinese Philosophy' that includes new findings and critical insights. The whole of history is divided according to the classifications of materialists and idealists, feudal conservatives and progressive pre-moderns. The series includes painstaking attention to proving the iron link between class background, clique formation and the ideological stand taken as a result of these factors. It is an impressive exercise in the inevitable progress of historical materialism; at its best, it is good solid Marxist scholarship. At its worst, there is much doctrinnaire name-calling and inappropriate debates such as whether **Laozi** should be counted a materialist or an idealist, or to what extent. Although the Mao era has passed, official Marxist scholarship remains, especially in the state-funded research institutes. The social sciences toe the official line more often than (so far) the softer disciplines like the humanities and the arts. Philosophy is ideology sensitive; the academic discipline of religious studies or comparative religion remains an oddity, with only a small programme at Beijing University.

WHALEN LAI

Chinul

b. 1158; d. 1210

Buddhist philosopher

Chinul is the founder of the native Son (Zen in Japanese) Buddhism and one of the two most important philosophers in Korean Buddhist history, together with **Wonhyo**. Korean Buddhism of his time was divided between the scholastic school (Kyohak), which emphasized the doctrinal study of the Buddhist scriptures, and the **meditation** school (Son), which emphasized meditation and a special transmission of truth outside the scriptures and doctrines. Chinul was interested in both meditation and the scriptural studies and integrated both traditions, which became the foundation of the Chogye order, the largest and main school of Buddhism in Korea today.

Chinul laid the philosophical foundation of the Korean Son tradition and tried to develop a unified system of doctrinal study and the practice of meditation. He found a great similarity between the basic idea of the *Flower Garland Sutra* and the idea of Son meditation. Through the reading of the *Flower Garland Sutra* he realized that the words of the Buddha became the doctrines of Buddhism, while the mind of the Buddha evolved into meditation. He understood that as the words of the Buddha reflected what was in his mind, the doctrinal teachings of Buddhism reflected the mystical knowledge derived from meditation. Thus, Chinul found a basis for synthesizing the Flower Garland and the meditation schools into a harmonious system of Buddhist thought and practice, which had a great influence on the shaping of Korean Buddhism. Chinul's essential conviction was that there is a basic unity between the truth described in the Buddhist scriptures and the truth experienced through meditation.

Chinul believed that the truth which is taught in the Doctrinal school and the truth which is experienced in the Meditation school have a single, common source, that is, the true mind. For Chinul, the true mind is the buddha mind or buddhahood. According to Chinul, all sentient beings have the **buddha nature** or the buddha mind. When one recognizes one's innate Buddha nature, that is the moment of realizing the absolute truth, the moment of enlightenment. One must have faith to accept the fact that one's original mind is the buddha nature.

Chinul developed a highly original theory of 'sudden enlightenment and gradual practice' (*tonochomsu*). Ordinarily, one might think that enlightenment is attained after gradual practice of meditation. However, according to Chinul, sudden enlightenment precedes gradual practice. According to the theory, practice is true practice only after

enlightenment is attained. Chinul stated that the practice of meditation before enlightenment is still the continuation of the dualistic mental discipline, discriminating between buddhas and sentient beings, and therefore, it is not true practice.

Chinul's idea of enlightenment has two levels; initial insight and ultimate wisdom. Initial insight is considered as immature enlightenment. However, true practice is possible only after this sudden flash of initial insight. The ultimate wisdom is the final enlightenment, in which one attains the full and perfect wisdom of realizing the absolute truth. Thus, one must continue to practice meditation after the sudden initial enlightenment, because the newly enlightened one is like an infant who needs to grow and mature. Through gradual cultivation, one should eliminate bad habits and develop wholesome qualities; and when one's wisdom and action become fully mature and holy, then one is a buddha in reality.

With regard to cultivation, Chinul emphasized a balance between meditation and doctrinal study. He said that those who emphasize the doctrinal study are so focused on the analytic knowledge of various issues, neglecting meditation for attaining buddhahood, while those who meditate on the direct mystical transmission of truth often sit and waste time, lose their sanity, and do not know the difference between a shallow and a deep understanding. Thus, he warned against one-sided views and approaches to truth. Chinul made a unique and significant contribution to the development of Korean Buddhism by synthesizing conflicting views and practices.

Further reading

Buswell, R. (1983) *The Korean Approach to Zen: The Collected Works of Chinul*, Honolulu, HA: University of Hawaii Press.

Keel, Hee-sung (1984) *Chinul: The Founder of the Korean Son Tradition*, Seoul: Pochinjae.

Lee, P. (ed.) (1993) *The Sourcebook of Korean Civilization*, vol. I, New York: Columbia University Press, 408–21.

Park Sung-bae (1983) *Buddhist Faith and Sudden Enlightenment*, Albany, NY: State University of New York Press.

YONG-CHOON KIM

Chiyou

A mythical figure, Chiyou (Ch'ih-yu) is of historic significance as the arch-enemy of the **Yellow Emperor**. By defeating him in a cosmogonic battle, the Yellow Emperor united the country, founded the first (mythic) dynasty, created culture and fathered all Chinese. Through the Song dynasty, the imperial court observed the Great Exorcism, a year-end ritual that purges all the evils of the old year so one can begin a New Year with nothing but good influences. The exorcist who performs that ritual is known as 'Square Face', the square being the sacred space, the cosmos to be restored. The accounts are seemingly confusing, since it can be either the Yellow Emperor who exorcized this Chiyou monster or the latter the square-faced one who is the exorcist, or he just exorcized himself. As the yearly round is often symbolized by a 'snake biting its own tail', so it is appropriate to have the eaters being the eaten, the exorcized being the exorcist, or the sacrificer being the sacrificed (and, in the Christian mystery, being the recipient of sacrifice, God himself). This helps to explain how the Yellow Emperor was also 'four faced'. He did not have exactly 'four faces' as alleged; rather he faced (stared down) his enemies in the four directions.

See also: Five Elements; magic squares

Further reading

Bodde, D. (1975) *Festivals in Classical China: New Year and Other Annual Observances during the Han Dynasty, 206 B.C.–A.D. 220*, Princeton, NJ: Princeton University Press.

WHALEN LAI

Ch'oe Han-ki

b. 1803; d. 1879

Sirhak philosopher

Ch'oe Han-ki was a brilliant Korean philosopher of the nineteenth century, whose thought belongs to **Sirhak** (the school of Practical Learning). He developed a unique '*ki*-only philosophy', influenced by the natural science of the West. The term *ki* here may be translated as material force or matter (*qi* in Chinese). Ch'oe wrote many volumes on Western science and his own ideas of philosophy.

Ch'oe's ontology is *ki*-monism or pure materialism. According to him, the essence of all things in the universe is *ki*. It is in everything, both things that coalesce and disintegrate and things that neither coalesce nor disintegrate. Before one is born, there was only *ki* in heaven and earth. When one is born, there is the *ki* of one's body. After one's death, his *ki* returns to the *ki* of heaven and earth. The *ki* of **heaven** and earth is large and everlasting, while the *ki* of one's body is small and can be obliterated. The *li* (principle) has no form, but *ki* has form and traces. *Li* is found in *ki*. Therefore *ki* alone is real.

Ch'oe was also an empiricist. According to him, the sense experience is the basis of all knowledge. He explained that all knowledge is a product of experience, denying innate knowledge. He said: 'We know what a bell sounds like even if we don't strike it. Because we have heard and seen a bell, we know that if we strike one, it emits a sound. If we had never seen or heard a bell, how could we know what its sound would be like?' Ch'oe claimed that children learn compassion and respect from their elders and practice them in relation to their parents and elder brother. Thus, even moral knowledge is based on experience, and not on innate knowledge.

According to Ch'oe, the essence of the mind is clear and clean. The way that the principle of new things comes to be known in the mind is by seeing and hearing things, which forms an experiential habit. Ch'oe divided the conditions for forming experience into three; the subject of experience, the medium which connects the internal with external, and the object of experience. The subject of experience was called *shin-ki* or divine energy, and the object was called the things of the outside world, and the medium which connects the subject and object was called the sense organs of body, namely, eyes, ears, mouth, nose and skin.

Ch'oe Han-ki also developed an interesting and unique idea of government. According to him, when a ruler's conduct is righteous and proper, his authority brings peace to the nation and the world. Proper government and the peace of a nation mean putting man and things in harmony with the will of heaven. He also interpreted the idea of value in a very original way, as follows: it is *ren* (Chinese) or **humaneness** that makes man manage his life well; *ui* (*yi* in Chinese) or **righteousness** makes man conduct his life in a proper way; *ye* (*li* in Chinese) or ceremony puts order into our lives; and *chi* (*ji* in Chinese) or wisdom enables man to choose between what is necessary for our lives and what is unnecessary. Ch'oe denied that these traditional Confucian virtues are innate and absolute standards for judging good and evil, arguing that what is good for one person is not necessarily good for another. He claimed that the criterion of good and evil should always be decided by majority opinion.

Ch'oe had a democratic and empirical vision of value. In his view, the ability to determine good and evil belonged not only to the aristocratic class but also to the humble commoners. He believed that it was immoral for a small group of a certain class to hold power, where the majority of the people must submit. He stated that the authority of judging right and wrong was not given to man by divine will, but depended on what is helpful for, or a hindrance to, human life. He stressed that the nation cannot exist without the people and the state cannot survive if it neglects the wellbeing of its citizens. Ch'oe's view was a bold one, considering that Korea in the nineteenth century was a semi-feudalistic society governed by the minority aristocratic class called *yangban*, who often mistreated the commoners.

Further reading

Choi Min-hong (1980) *A Modern History of Korean Philosophy*, Seoul: Seongmoon Sa, 203ff.

Lee, P. (ed.) (1993) *Sourcebook of Korean Civilization*, vol. 2, New York: Columbia University Press, 174ff.

YONG-CHOON KIM

Chong Che-du

b. 1649; d. 1736

Neo-Confucian philosopher

Chong Che-du is known as the founder of the Yangming school of Neo-Confucianism in Korea. He was an outstanding thinker, who systematically interpreted the philosophy of the famous Chinese Neo-Confucian philosopher Wang Yangming in a distinctive way. He is often known by his pen name, Hagok. He was a descendant of Chong Mong-jun (1337–92), who was called the father of Neo-Confucianism in Korea.

Chong Hagok's contribution to the Yangming school in Korea is unique, because Korean Confucianism was dominated by the **Zhu Xi** school of Neo-Confucianism. Zhu Xi's Neo-Confucianism was the orthodox philosophy of Korea between the fourteenth and nineteenth centuries, and it dominated not only the political system but also the thought and life of people. The orthodox Neo-Confucians in Korea considered any philosophy and religion other than the Zhu Xi school as heresy or heterodoxy in Hagok's time.

In spite of personal risk and danger, Hagok pursued learning and advocating Wang Yangming's Neo-Confucianism. He was deeply impressed by Wang Yangming's writings. Hagok's teachers and friends advised him against the study of Yangming's philosophy, because they considered it heretical and dangerous for him. However, Hagok defended himself and Wang Yangming by stating that many ideas of Wang Yangming were identical with those of Zhu Xi, especially the goal of becoming a **sage**, even though their methods for becoming a sage were different. Hagok's motivation for studying Wang Yangming's philosophy was to become a sage. He believed that the philosophy of Yangming was essentially Sage Learning, which is Mind Learning. Like Wang Yangming, Hagok was interested in understanding and attaining *dao* in his own mind. He believed that the *dao*, which is the ultimate criterion of right and wrong, is inside a person's mind. Thus, he was an idealist, following Wang Yangming's tradition.

Like Wang Yangming also, Hagok maintained that the mind is the principle (*i* in Korean; **li** in Chinese), never separating nature from the concrete function of mind. According to Hagok, the principle (*li*) as the substance and the material force (*ki* in Korean; **qi** in Chinese) as function are inseparable in mind. He followed Yangming's idea that there is no principle outside of the mind and there are no things outside of the mind. He regarded the principle as a pattern. However, unlike Wang Yangming, Hagok divided *i* into two kinds of pattern. One has a spiritual penetration, which is called the vital principle, and the other has nothing, being an empty pattern. The vital principle is the spiritual force, which penetrates all things.

Hagok also conceived that there are two aspects of vital force (*qi*). One becomes principle and the other becomes material force, depending on whether the spiritual force resides in it or not. When the vital force is able to penetrate the spiritual aspect or moves toward the spiritual aspect, it becomes identified with the principle (*li*). Like Wang Yangming and **Yi Yulgok**, Hagok maintained that the principle and vital force are inseparable.

One of the most important ideas in Wang Yangming's philosophy is the theory of 'innate knowledge of the good', which also became important in Hagok's thought. Based on Yangming's view, Hagok stressed that the innate knowledge of the good is not a perception, but a substance of the mind, and it is identical with benevolence, a key Confucian virtue. He also identified the innate knowledge of the good with the vital principle and with the four beginnings of the mind, that is, the feeling of commiseration, the feelings of shame and dislike, the feeling of modesty, and the feeling of discerning right and wrong. Furthermore, Hagok stated that the five constant virtues of Confucianism, namely, benevolence, **righteousness**, propriety, wisdom and trust, are the essential content of human nature and the essential substance of mind.

Further reading

Choi Min-hong (1980) *A Modern History of Korean Philosophy*, Seoul: Seongmoon Sa, 136–8.

Chung In-chai (1996) 'Chong Che-du (Hagok): The Father of Yang-ming School in Korea', in H. Choung and H. Han (eds), *Confucian Philosophy in Korea*, Songnam: The Academy of Korean Studies, 169–212.

Lee, P. (ed.) (1996) *Sourcebook of Korean Civilization*, vol. 2, New York: Columbia University Press, 281–5.

YONG-CHOON KIM

Chong Yag-yong (Tasan)

b. 1762; d. 1836

Sirhak philosopher

Among the scholars of **Sirhak** (the school of Practical Learning) in Korea, Chong Yag-yong is the greatest and best known. He is usually known by his pen name, Tasan (Tea Mountain). He was influenced by Western Learning, including its scientific technology and Roman Catholicism. He interpreted Confucianism in a new way, incorporating some Western views. He developed his own theoretical system of ethics, politics, and religion with emphasis on practicality. Tasan, like other scholars of the school of Practical Learning, had encyclopedic knowledge of the Confucian Classics (see **Classics and Books**), politics, economics, natural science and agriculture.

On the whole Tasan was Confucian, as he took the Confucian Classics as the authoritative norm of truth. But he refused to identify Confucian philosophy with that of **Zhu Xi**. He thought that the Neo-Confucian ideas of principle (*i*) and material force (*ki*) were overly abstract theories without practical value. He tried to change the metaphysical emphasis of Neo-Confucianism to a practical one.

Tasan incorporated into his thought Western Learning, including its science, philosophy, and religion. His idea of human nature was influenced by the Western idea of individual freedom and equality of people. His idea of **Heaven** or God was also influenced by Western ideas. Tasan emphasized the personal aspect of Heaven (Supreme Being) who knows and rewards man according his deeds. He also stressed the transcendent and unfathomable God, who is beyond man and the world. According to Tasan, knowing Heaven has a practical value for both self-cultivation and a moral government.

Tasan rejected Zhu Xi's dualistic distinction between the original nature of man as good and the psycho-physical nature of man as both good and evil. According to Tasan, there is no essential difference between human beings and the material world, because the entire universe is bound by the same principle. Differences between man and animals and plants are only in varying degrees of purity of endowment. Thus, by rejecting the Neo-Confucian formula of the principle and material force, Tasan developed his own idea of human nature in terms of tendencies and exercise of will.

Tasan also developed his own ethical theory based on the moral freedom of an individual. He believed that a human being has freedom to make a moral choice. Such an ability of self-determination is a basis of realizing sagehood. He thought that every person is endowed with the knowledge of good and evil as well as the ability to choose between virtue and vice, and therefore has a responsibility for self-cultivation to become a sage, who is morally perfect and knows Heaven. According to Tasan, the four moral virtues of **humaneness**, **righteousness**, propriety and knowledge are not given to man by birth, but they are the goal which man has to attain by practice of his spiritual tendencies. Here too, Tasan was distinguishing his ethical view from that of Neo-Confucianism.

Heaven or God was an important concept in Tasan's thought. According to Tasan, Heaven is the ultimate reference for human nature and the ultimate standard for the conduct of individuals and government. He emphasized that man should have a religious fear and piety for moral living. Knowing Heaven and the way of Heaven is a prerequisite for self-understanding, and after self-understanding, moral cultivation comes, according to Tasan. In other words, by knowing the will of Heaven, one can choose between good and evil. For Tasan, the way of Heaven is following one's conscience in concrete situations.

Tasan also had a wide interest in politics, law and economics. He not only set out to present the way of self-cultivation through the Confucian Classics, but also provided practical guidance on how to govern the nation through his works, the *Last Memorial for Governing the State*, the *Heart Book for Looking After People* and the *New Book on Human Law*.

Tasan attempted to construct a synthesis of Eastern and Western ideas by developing new ways of understanding and interpreting the nature of man, ethics, Heaven or God, and human values. He expanded the Confucian vision of man and the universe by incorporating the Western ideas of God, individual freedom, and modern science.

Thus, Tasan made a unique contribution to the development of Korean philosophy.

Further reading

Choi Min-hong (1980) *A Modern History of Korean Philosophy*, Seoul: Seongmoon Sa, 180ff.

Kim, S. (1996) 'Chong Yagyong (Tasan): Creative Bridge between the East and the West', in H. Choung and H. Han (eds), *Confucian Philosophy in Korea*, Seongnam: Academy of Korean Studies, 216ff.

Lee Eul-ho (1985) 'Tasan's View of Man', *Korea Journal* (September): 4–16.

Lee, P. (ed.) (1993) *Sourcebook of Korean Civilization*, vol. 2, New York: Columbia University Press, 29ff, 64ff, 100ff.

YONG-CHOON KIM

Christianity, Korean

Roman Catholicism

In Korea, the Roman Catholic Church is called Ch'onjugyo (Religion of the Heavenly Lord) or the Catholic Church as it is known in China and Japan. *Ch'onju* (T'ienju in Chinese) means Heavenly Lord, the Catholic term for God, which is similar to the Chinese idea of *t'ien/tian* (*ch'on* in Korean), meaning **Heaven**, the Supreme Being or the ruler of the universe. *Ch'onju* was first used in China as the Catholic term for God around 1583, and spread in the Far East mainly through Matteo **Ricci**'s book, *Ch'onju Sirui* (The Real Meaning of Catholicism), published in 1593. This book and other Catholic and Western books were brought to Korea and stimulated the minds of Korean intellectuals, who were interested in Western thought.

Korean Catholicism was founded in Korea in 1784, when Yi Sung-hun began to hold Catholic meetings with his friends in Seoul. He was converted to Catholicism in Beijing, and upon returning home he began to teach Catholicism to his friends. Thus, Korean Catholicism was founded not by foreign missionaries but by Korean intellecual laymen who were interested in Catholicism.

Around this time Jesuit missionaries were active in China, translating and publishing books on Christianity and Western thought. Korean tributary missions to China brought these books to Korea, and many young Confucian literati became interested in them and learned Western ideas, including Catholicism. The Korean intellectuals were highly stimulated by the Western ideas, which were in contrast to much of the Confucian worldview.

Korean society since the seventeenth century had experienced great difficulties stemming from the Japanese invasion, and there was political and social corruption, especially within the aristocratic ruling class. In the midst of these situations, there were some scholars who wanted to rebuild the nation and society, provide help to the masses and develop the kind of learning which would revive the nation. The result was the birth of **Sirhak**, the school of Practical Learning.

Scholars belonging to the Sirhak movement wanted to restore the real Confucianism based on the original thought of **Confucius** and **Mencius** and the classical texts of Confucianism rather than the abstract theories of Neo-Confucianism, which had no practical value. They rediscovered and re-emphasized the traditional, classical idea of *t'ien/tian* (Heaven), the Supreme Being, which in their opinion was similar to the Catholic idea of God. Since they could easily make a connection between the Confucian idea of Heaven and the Catholic idea of God, they could easily accept Catholic thought. On the basis of scholarly search and research, some of these Confucian intellectuals became the founding members of Korean Catholicism. Some of them were outwardly Confucian but inwardly Catholic.

Gradually Catholicism moved and spread to the middle and lower classes of Korean society throughout the nation. Peasants and women especially joined Catholicism, because they found in it a hope for a better future. They saw Catholicism as a new, fresh and powerful idea of equality and love in this world, which no other traditional religions and philosophies or rulers offered. Catholicism also provided the masses with the message of eternal and blessed life beyond the earthly life, where suffering was often unbearable.

Korean Catholics experienced approximately one hundred years of persecution by the Choson rulers until 1887, when freedom of religion was granted by the Korean–French treaty of that year. During the long period of severe persecution, there were approximately ten thousands martyrs in the Korean Catholic church. Philosophical and religious as well as political and social factors led to the persecution. The philosophical and religious reason behind the persecution was the idea of 'rejecting heresy and protecting orthodoxy', which was the governing principle of the ruling class during the Choson dynasty. Orthodoxy in that period was Confucianism, especially Neo-Confucianism, and all other philosophies and religions were considered heretical. Thus, Buddhism was rejected from the beginning of the Choson dynasty; when the Western Learning and Catholicism arrived, they were persecuted; and when Tonghak (Eastern Learning) developed, it too was oppressed. Some Confucian scholars attempted to develop rational arguments against the Catholic ideas of soul, salvation, heaven and hell, asceticism and miracles. They claimed Catholicism was an unethical religion, not respecting and honouring parents and rulers, weakening human relationships, and bringing chaos into society. Some Confucians claimed that Catholicism was a dangerous forerunner of the invasion of the Western powers and therefore to be rejected. Many Confucian scholars of that period were ignorant about world affairs, and had no clear knowledge about the relation between Catholicism and Western powers.

A cultural reason for the rejection of Catholicism in the Korean society during the Choson dynasty was the Catholic stand regarding ancestor worship. At that time, Catholics regarded ancestor worship as a violation of the divine commandments. The Confucian rulers of the Choson dynasty thought that the Catholic rejection of ancestor worship and the Catholic idea of gender equality were destructive of the social order and undermined the value system of the nation. Within the Catholic church, there was a long period of theological controversy regarding whether ancestor worship was heretical or not. In 1939, the Catholic church finally decided that ancestor worship is just a folk custom in Asian society to memorialize ancestors with respect and honour, and therefore poses no difficulties with respect to Catholicism.

Despite the persecution, Catholicism in Korea continued to grow. Father Zhou Wen-mu, a Chinese priest, came to Korea in 1794 and was martyred after six years of work. Pope Gregory XVI ordered the establishment of a Korean diocese in 1831, and French missionaries entered Korea and educated Korean priests. Several young Koreans were sent abroad for education. One of these was Kim Tae-gon, who was ordained as the first Korean priest in 1845. In 1866, alarmed at the growth of Christianity, King Taewon'gun ordered a further harsh persecution of Catholics. Foreign priests and many laymen were killed. After the treaty with France brought freedom of religious activities, foreign missionaries resumed their work and Catholicism grew still further; churches as well as schools were built in many cities. In 1906 the Catholic Church started to publish a weekly newspaper, *Kyonghyang Shinmun*, which later became a popular and major daily newspaper.

Many Korean Catholics participated in the patriotic movement against the Japanese colonialism in Korea. Under Japanese rule, Korean Catholics suffered much along with the rest of the nation. The Catholic church, however, continued to grow and to serve the masses with its educational and medical programmes. When the Japanese government imposed Shinto shrine worship, many Korean Catholics first refused it, but when they were told that Shinto was only a national ceremony, the Catholic church yielded to the demand.

In 1945, when Korea was liberated from Japanese colonialism, the Catholic church gained full religious freedom in South Korea, although in North Korea under Communism darkness fell upon all religions, including Catholicism. In South Korea, many new Catholic schools were built and many new programmes were developed, and the Catholic church has grown rapidly.

The Second Vatican Council, which began in 1962, had a great impact on the Korean Catholic church to initiate reforms. The Mass and other Catholic ceremonies began to be performed in the Korean language. Archbishop Kim Su-hwan was elected the first Korean cardinal in history. In 1984

Pope John Paul II came to Korea and canonized 103 martyrs in celebration of the bicentennial of the Korean Catholic church. Recently, many Korean Catholics have been active in works of social and economic justice, influenced in part by the liberation theology movement which developed in Central and South America (see the comments on *minjung sinhak*, below).

Protestantism

In Korea, Protestantism is called Kaesin'gyo (The Reformed Church) or Kidokgyo (Christianity). Protestantism emphasizes the authority of the Bible, the priesthood of all believers, and the church as the community governed by its members. There are many denominations within Protestantism in Korea, the largest of which is the Presbyterian Church, itself split into many groups.

In 1873, John Ross of Scotland, who was in Manchuria, met So Sang-ryun and other Korean young men. In 1876 he baptized them, and began to translate the Bible through them. This is the beginning of Protestantism in Korea. In 1882, this group published the Korean translation of the Gospel according to Luke and in 1887 the whole New Testament. So Sang-ryun built a church in Songch'on in Hwanghae-to Province in 1884, the first Protestant church in Korea.

The Presbyterian Church in the USA sent the first American medical missionary, Horace Allen, to Korea in 1884. At the end of that year he cured Min Yong-ik, an important government official. Because of this, he was well treated by the Korean government and the door for missionary work was opened wide. The American Presbyterian missionary Horace G. Underwood and the American Methodist missionary Henry Appenzeller arrived in 1885, and many other missionaries followed thereafter.

Because of the early and diligent works by the able missionaries from Presbyterian and Methodist denominations, today they are the strongest and largest denominations in Korea. Many missionaries from these denominations were highly educated intellectuals, and they introduced a Western-style modern educational system to Korea, establishing fine institutions on the high school and college levels where the leaders of modern Korean society were produced. Among those institutions, Yonse University and Ewha Womans University are particularly renowned today. The Western missionaries also contributed significantly to the enhancement of women's position in society, medical work and social service.

Christianity grew rapidly in Korean society, because many Koreans embraced Christianity as a saving grace not only for their spiritual destiny but also for their earthly destiny. In Christianity, many Koreans found a solution for their personal education as well as national problems. As the Choson dynasty was falling under Japanese aggression, many Koreans found refuge and guidance in Christianity. The Western missionaries showed Koreans not just the age-old Christian gospel, but also the new educational, political, social and scientific ideas of the West, by which both their individual and national lives could be revitalized and improved. Christianity made a significant contribution to the modernization of Korea by establishing modern educational institutes, hospitals, and publishing facilities. Through the publication of the Korean Bible, Han'gul, the Korean alphabet, was more widely learned; and through the establishment of the schools of higher learning for both men and women, important leaders of modern Korea have been trained.

It was not long after the introduction of Christianity to Korea that imperial Japan colonized Korea, and the oppressive policy of the Japanese government was applied to the Korean church. The Japanese rulers regarded the leaders of the Korean church as the leaders of an anti-Japan and independence movement. Many Korean Protestant leaders were arrested and imprisoned in 1912 and thereafter in order to pressure and harass them to cooperate with the Japanese policy of colonialism.

In the famous nationwide March First independence movement of 1919 against Japanese colonialism, the Korean Protestant Church played a major role. Of the thirty-three signers of the Declaration of Independence on 1 March 1919, which encompassed all the major religions of Korea, sixteen were Protestant ministers and lay leaders. The Declaration of Independence emphasized the sovereign right of the Korean people for self-government and opposition to foreign colonialism, as well as the basic human rights of freedom, equality, and justice. These ideas were influenced by the ideals of Western democracy, which many Korean Christian leaders learned from Western missionaries and Western philosophy.

The Japanese government also applied a cultural policy to the Korean church as well as to the entire Korean population. It required Koreans to use Japanese as the official language in schools, and pressured Koreans to change their names to Japanese. This was a policy to Japanize Koreans and to destroy Korean nationhood and culture. From 1932 onward the Japanese government further imposed Shinto shrine worship on Korean churches as well as on the entire Korean population; this became more intensive and severe when the Second World War started. The Japanese government required Korean churches to recite the declaration of loyalty to the Japanese emperor during Christian worship, and demanded all Christians practice Shinto shrine worship. This policy was enforced in order to destroy Korean Christianity.

Many Korean Christian ministers and laymen refused to participate in the Shinto shrine worship, because they believed that it was the violation of the divine commandment against idol worship. Because of this, many of them were imprisoned, approximately fifty were martyred in prison, and several hundred churches were closed. In 1942 all foreign missionaries were expelled from Korea. The persecution by the Japanese government of the Korean church came to an end on 15 August 1945, when the Second World War ended. However, as soon as Korea and the Korean church gained liberation from Japanese imperial rule, the country was divided between north and south at the 38th parallel, and the division brought another tragedy for the Korean people and the Korean church. Although the Protestant churches in South Korea have enjoyed complete religious freedom, in North Korea under communism they have been persecuted, and virtually all churches were closed. Many Christians were killed by the communists, while millions of others escaped to South Korea, especially during the Korean War (1950–3).

Since 1945, the Protestant Church in South Korea has grown tremendously, and its membership constitutes approximately one-quarter of the South Korean population; it is three times larger than the Roman Catholic Church. Christianity, including both Roman Catholics and Protestants, is probably the largest and definitely the strongest religion in Korea today in terms of its financial resources, educational programmes and impact on modern Korean society. The Protestant Church has been the fastest growing major religion in Korea in the last century, and has made significant contributions to Korean society through its educational, medical and social programmes.

New developments

Since 1945, there have been two new and major theological developments in Korea. One is *t'och'ak sinhak*, which may be translated as 'nativistic theology' or 'indigenous theology'. Another is *minjung sinhak*, which may be translated as 'people's theology' or 'the theology of the masses'. Yun Song-bom and Pyon Son-hwan, both former professors of Methodist Theological Seminary in Seoul, and Professor Yu Tong-sik of Yonsei University are the representative thinkers of the 'nativistic theology'. They attempted to de-Westernize Korean Christianity and Koreanize Christianity, because they believed that Christianity introduced to Korea by the Western missionaries has a Western cultural background and basis, and is not quite suitable to the Korean cultural situation. These scholars believed that Western theology is conditioned by Western culture, especially Western philosophy, and Korean Christian theology should be shaped in the context of Korean culture, especially Korean philosophies and religions. Yun Song-bom attempted to interpret Christian theology in the context of and in comparison with the Confucian ideas of Heaven and reverence. Pyon Son-hwan attempted to interpret Christian theology in comparison with Buddhist philosophy. Yu Tong-sik interpreted Christian thought in relation to shamanism. Thus, the result was a synthesis of Christianity and traditional Korean thought.

Minjung sinhak is very similar to the 'liberation theology' of Central and South America. *Minjung* theology was invented and advocated by the faculty members of Han'guk Theological Seminary and University. The main thinkers of this movement are Suh Nam-dong, An Pyong-mu, Mun Ik-hwan and Mun Tong-hwan.

Minjung may be translated as the common people or masses and it means the oppressed people with a long history of struggle against the oppressive government or class. *Minjung* theologians claim that Jesus Christ was the liberator of the oppressed, alienated and underprivileged masses. They emphasize that Christ came, preached, taught and died for the liberation of the poor and oppressed class of the society. *Minjung* theologians refer to the liberation movement of the masses as the movement of the kingdom of God.

Minjung theologians were very active in the democratic movement of Korea, when there was a virtual dictatorship in Korea for a few decades since the independence of the nation in 1945. They have also actively advocated and promoted the unification of Korea. They claim that it is necessary for *minjung* theology to analyse and criticize the oppressive politico-socio-economic system in order to achieve the unification of Korea. Furthermore, *minjung* theologians have been advocating positive dialogues between South Korean Christians and *chuch'e* philosophers of the Communist North Korea for the advancement of the unification of Korea. *Minjung* theologians are willing to accept the Marxist criticism of religion as the opium of the masses, since Christianity in the past has often been a tool of the ruling class to exploit the masses. *Minjung* theologians consider the **chuch'e philosophy** of North Korea as the Koreanized version of Marxism, and they believe that both *minjung* theology and *chuch'e* philosophy have the common goal of fighting against the oppressive class system of society and achieving the liberation of the oppressed masses.

Minjung theology is a somewhat unique and interesting development in Korea, and it has been popular among the liberal theologians and students. However, it is not widely accepted among Korean Christians, because the majority of Korean Christians are conservative and evangelical, and they have had a tendency not to be political activists. In the Korean Protestant Church, the Presbyterian, Reformed or Calvinistic denominations remain strongest thanks to the influence of the early Presbyterian missionaries from the United States, who were well-trained in traditional Calvinistic theology. Korean Presbyterians who have studied in the conservative theologial schools in the United States have taken the key leadership positions in the Korean Church, and they constitute today the majority of leaders in the Korean Protestant Church and its theological schools.

Further reading

Baker, D. (1997) 'From Pottery to Politics: The Transformation of Korean Catholicism', in L. Lancaster and R. Payne (eds), *Religion and Society in Contemporary Korea*, Berkeley, CA: Institute of East Asian Studies, University of California, Berkeley, 127–68.

Ch'oi Suk-woo (1982) *Han'guk Ch'onju Kyohoe-ui Yoksa* (A History of the Korean Catholic Church), Seoul: Han'guk Kyohoesa Yon'guso Ch'ulp'anbu.

—— (1984) 'Korean Catholicism Yesterday and Today', *Korea Journal* (August): 4–13.

Clark, D. (1986) *Christianity in Modern Korea*, Lanham, MD: University Press of America.

—— (1997) 'History and Religion in Modern Korea: The Case of Protestant Christianity', in L. Lancaster and R. Payne (eds), *Religion and Society in Contemporary Korea*, Berkeley, CA: Institute of East Asian Studies, University of California, Berkeley, 169–214.

Lee, P. (ed.) (1996) *Sourcebook of Korean Civilization*, vol. 2, New York: Columbia University Press, 131ff.

Min Kyong-bae (1986) *Han'guk Kidokkyohoe Sa* (History of Korean Protestantism), Seoul: Taehan Kidokkyo Ch'ulp'ansa.

Moon Tong-hwan (1982) 'Korean Minjung Theology', in Wonmo Dong (ed.), *Korean-American Relations at Crossroads*, Princeton, NJ: The Association of Korean Christian Scholars in North America, Inc., 12–34.

Mun Hui-sok (1985) *A Korean Minjung Theology: An Old Testament Perspective*, New York: Orbis Books.

Paik, L.G. (1980) *The History of Protestant Missions in Korea, 1832–1910*, Seoul: Yonsei University Press.

Palmer, S. (1967) *Korea and Christianity: The Problem of Identification with Tradition*, Seoul: Royal Asiatic Society, Korea Branch.

So Kwang-son (1991) *The Korean Minjung in Christ*, Hong Kong: Christian Conference of Asia, Commission on Theological Concerns.

Yu Chai-shin (ed.) (1996) *Korea and Christianity*, Seoul: Korean Scholars Press.

YONG-CHOON KIM

Christianity in China

Buddho-Christian encounters began with the Nestorians in the Tang dynasty, but the Jesuit mission in the late Ming dynasty put the relationship on a new footing. Matteo Ricci at first dressed as a monk, but then put on a scholar's garb in order to pass himself off as a Western Confucian. His third major disciple, Yang Tingyun, became Ricci's conduit for confronting the Buddhists. Between 1550 and 1650 there lived the four Buddhist 'grand masters', the best known of whom was Zuhung (1535–1615), who spread Buddhist piety among the gentry in Hanzhou.

How Buddhist was Yang Tingyun? Ming Buddhism itself had diluted scriptural study, and a Buddhist from the gentry such as Yang Tingyun probably knew only the practical side of the faith. Yang, who had a **bodhisattva** statue and so was obviously a devotee, probably of Guanyin (Avalokiteshvara – the compassionate *bodhisattva*), who attends the Buddha Amitabha. As an act of compassion, the pious would buy up animals, birds, fish caught by hunters or fishermen and then free them. 'Release of life' is 'freeing living things from captivity', in accordance with the traditional stories of the activities of the *bodhisattva*.

Some of the parables in the *Lotus Sutra* can be read in a surprisingly familiar way, the story of the prodigal son in particular. The Christian critic however faults the Buddhist father for not running ahead with open arms to welcome back the lost sheep in unconditional *agape* (love). The Buddhist defender responded with the argument that the point of the story is that the son has to be advanced in wisdom. A closer look would reveal that reading it either from the point of view of **faith** or of wisdom overlooks the real meaning of the story. Unique and crucial to the Buddhist parable is that the son could not recognize his father. In the interim fifty years the father had relocated himself and become like a king. That is in reference to the idealization of the Buddha. The son who left home as a Hinayana ascetic left a father, a Shakyamuni Buddha who in his teaching career (of about fifty years) was himself a mendicant. The ascetic son who chanced upon this regal figure years later chanced upon a Mahayana, transmundane Buddha whose estate (*stupa* reliquary, a building holding important Buddhist remains) dazzled the Hinayanist with the luxury of many an object of sensual delight. The point of educating the son is to bring this Hinayanist ascetic – of low self-esteem with his imposed self-denial – around to accepting the princely heirlooms from his regal and 'prodigal' father. If, in that parable, the *Lotus Sutra* here does not confirm exactly to Christian faith, the following parable does not exactly replicate the Gnostic 'Song of the Pearl' either, however similar it might at first appear:

It is like this case of a destitute man
visiting a close friend in his home.
The man's house is grand and luxurious,
and well stocked with delicacies.
Taking a precious jewel, [the rich friend]
puts it inside the man's garment,
Doing so without a word and then goes off.
The man asleep at the time knows nothing.
Awoke, he rises
and travels to another country,
Seeking food and clothing, doing so alone by
himself
In what amounts to a very hard life.
But he is contented with the little he has,
Never wishing for the good things of life,
And utterly unaware that inside his garment
Is this priceless jewel.
The dear friend who gave him that jewel
Later sees this poor man and,
Having sternly rebuked him,
Shows him the jewel sewed inside his coat.
The poor man, seeing it at last,
is overjoyed. With his new found wealth,
He comes to own many precious objects,
well able to gratify his five senses too.

In the 'Song of the Pearl', the pearl is a symbol of the soul from the upper world trapped in the material universe here below (represented symbolically by Egypt). The Song tells of a search and a recovery of this lost 'divine spark.'

Had the passage cited above from the *Lotus Sutra* been a Gnostic parable, the man would have had the jewel (prenatal divine spark) at birth; he would have lost it – not given it – during sleep (ignorance). The garment (matter) would be a curse; the trip to an alien country would mark a fall (into a lower realm). Although the tale does involve a messenger (the return of the rich friend) and a revelation (the hidden pearl), there is no implication of a cosmic dualism. If it is copied off a Gnostic parable, then it is reinscribed to evoke the same message as that of its own parable of the prodigal son (better, father). Both serve to absorb and absolve the earlier Hinayana tradition of ascetic denial into this newer, higher, and opulent celebration of a regal gift from this rich friend, the Mahayana Buddha.

Further reading

Gernet, J. (1985) *China and the Christian Missions: A Conflict of Cultures*, trans. J. Lloyd, Cambridge: Cambridge University Press

Hurvitz, L. (trans.) (1976) *The Lotus Blossom of the Fine Dharma*, New York: Columbia University Press.

Standaert, N. (1988) *Yang Tingyun: Confucian and Christian in Late Ming China*, Leiden: Brill.

WHALEN LAI

Chu Si-kyong

b. 1876; d. 1914

Linguist and philosoper

Chu Si-kyong was a significant Korean analyst of language and enlightenment thinker in modern times. Many of his writings on Korean language and literature became important tools for the ideas of democracy and the independence movement. He thought that the spread of a systematic language and literature was essential for eliminating the feudalistic system. For many centuries the ruling aristocratic class used Chinese characters for writing, having restricted the use of the native Korean language. Chu Si-kyong contributed to the wide use of the Korean language for and by the masses, and thereby speeded up the progress of a modern democratic Korean society.

Chu Si-kyong believed also that the political independence and autonomy of Korean people rested upon an independent and autonomous national language. During Japanese colonialism in Korea, especially during the early 1940s until the end of the Second World War, when Korea gained independence, the Japanese government enforced the use of Japanese as the official language in Korea in an attempt to destroy Korean cultural identity. Therefore, Chu's research and promotion of the Korean language became an effective force in opposing the repressive cultural policy of Japan.

Chu Si-kyong conceived the idea of the ultimate reality of the universe as the foundation of all concepts and language. According to him, there is an infinite 'One' in the universe, which has no beginning and no end. It is the origin and lord of all things. It is called by various names such as Heaven, God or principle. This One is similar to the idea of 'Han', the unique representative idea of Korea from ancient times, which means greatness and totality. The Korean language is called 'Hangul', which means great language.

For Chu Si-kyong, this idea of One or unity became the metaphysical basis of his philosophical thought. In application it means that there must be unity between government and people. It was the basis of his idea of democracy, in contrast to the class system of feudalism. He advocated a democratic system of ethics of equality and human rights. Along with other enlightenment thinkers, Chu Si-kyong made a significant contribution to the modernization of Korean society.

Further reading

Choi Min-hong (1980) *A Modern History of Korean Philosophy*, Seoul: Seongmoon Sa, 231–6.
Lee, P. (ed.) (1996) *Sourcebook of Korean Civilization*, Vol. 2, New York: Columbia University Press, 418–22, 426ff.

YONG-CHOON KIM

chuch'e philosophy

After the division of Korea into North and South Korea in 1945 with the end of the Second World War, North Korea adopted communism as its politico-socio-economic philosophy, while South Korea adopted democracy and capitalism. In North Korea the long-time ruler, Kim Il-sung, through the assistance of scholars under his rule, developed the so-called *chuch'e* philosophy, which means the philosophy of self-identity or philosophy of subject. It was intended to be the unique philosophy of Korean communism, and it has also been called Kim Il-sung's philosophy. In reality, it is a reformulation of Marxism or dialectical materialism with a vision of a classless society. Because of the iron rule of Kim Il-sung and then of his son, Kim Chong-il, there has been no freedom of alternative views in philosophy or religion in North Korea.

Chuch'e philosophy or ideology implies a rejection of foreign ideology and establishment of North Korea's own subjective philosophy. It implies that North Koreans are not accepting even Marxism-Leninism without modification. *Chuch'e* means subject, and it has a special and unique meaning. In *chuch'e* philosophy, Korean people, especially the working class or the masses, are the subject or centre of thought. The implication of this philosophy is that communism must be Koreanized.

Although *chuch'e* philosophy started soon after 1945, it developed gradually. Until 1972, *chuch'e* philosophy was basically Marxism-Leninism. From 1973, however, it developed as a distinctive and unique philosophical system different from Marxism-Leninism. The *chuch'e* philosophy emphasizes a radically man-centered worldview, which is much stronger than Marxist Leninism. In 1978 North Korean philosophers developed more substantial new theories regarding humanity, society and history, and in 1985 they published ten volumes of *Widaehan Chuch'e Sasang Ch'ongso* (Collections of Great Chuch'e Ideology). After 1986, most of the articles in *Ch'orhak Yon'gu* (Philosophical Study), the main journal of philosophy in North Korea include many references to the sayings of Kim Il-sung and Kim Chong-il, but references to Marx and Lenin almost disappear. In other words, *chuch'e* philosophy as the philosophy of Kim Il-sung and Kim Chong-il replaced Marxism-Leninism as the communist philosophy of North Korea.

Pak Sung-dok, who is the president of the Institute of the Study of Chuch'e Ideology and the leading thinker of *chuch'e* philosophy in North Korea, claims that *chuch'e* ideology is superior to Marxism-Leninism. He states that Marx and Lenin dealt with the relation of matter and consciousness as the central issue in their philosophy, and they claimed that matter is primary and consciousness is secondary. According to Pak Sung-dok, this is the basic materialistic philosophy of Marxism-Leninism. In contrast, the main issue in *chuch'e* philosophy is the question of human destiny and finding the right answer to it.

Pak quotes the teaching of Kim Il-sung, which is as follows: 'The human being is the master of his own destiny; this is the heart of chuch'e ideology and the essence of the revolutionary ideology' (Pak Sung-dok 1993: 163). Pak elaborates this idea further by claiming that the most important thing for an individual human being or nation is to develop the destiny of the individual or nation. He states that destiny includes the present and future conditions, and human destiny develops in relation to the world. In the *chuch'e* worldview, man is the subject and master, who determines the destiny of himself and the world. Thus, in this system of thought, there is no room for God, and it is clear that *chuch'e* ideology is atheistic. Furthermore, Pak Sung-dok claims that *chuch'e* ideology is a revolutionary philosophy. When the people, especially the working class masses realize that they are the subject and master of the world, they can elevate their social positions by fighting against any discriminatory class system. Pak states that North Korea has achieved an ideal socialist revolution and built an ideal communist society based on *chuch'e* philosophy.

Another important difference, according to Pak, between *chuch'e* philosophy and Marxism-Leninism is the view of life. He claims that viewing life as an immaterial spiritual reality or as a mere material entity is wrong, and even Marxism-Leninist philosophy, which regarded life as a mere biological substance, has a limitation. *Chuch'e* philosophy was the first in human history to develop the idea that life is basically social, and this philosophy unified the individual and community life.

Pak quotes the statement of Kim Chong-il, the son of Kim Il-song, as follows: 'Life is the most precious thing to the human being. With regard to life, social and political life is more important than physical life, and social group life is more important than individual life. Individual life exists only after social life' (Pak Sung-dok 1993: 168). This statement clearly shows that *chuch'e* philosophy is communism, as it places a priority of value on communist social life. According to Pak, man is the subject and master of history, and thus overcomes the limitation of the materialistic view of history in Marxism-Leninism. Pak claims that the *chuch'e* worldview provides a unique and right explanation concerning the central position and role of the working class in the development of social movement and social history.

Kim Il-sung taught as follows: 'The reformation of nature, the reformation of man, and the reformation of society are the three great areas of the creative action of the people in order to establish the humanistic, socialist, and communist society' (Pak Sung-dok 1993: 179). Pak Sung-dok elaborates this idea by stating that man is the subject and master of this reformation movement, in which the ideological reform must take place first, followed by an economic and cultural revolution, in order to overcome the social and economic inequality of capitalistic society. According to Pak, after this process, the true socialist and communist society will be realized in Korea.

Further reading

Hab'guk Ch'orhak Sasang Yon'guhoe (ed.) (1995) *Kangchwa Han'guk Ch'orhak* (Lecture on Korean Philosophy), Seoul: Yemoon Seowon, 301–16.

Pak Sung-dok (1993) 'Chuch'e sang ui chemunje (Several Issues of Chuch'e Thought)', in *Kiddokkyo wa Chuch'e Sasang* (Christianity and Chuch'e Philosophy) and *The Proceedings of 1989–92 Annual Conferences*, Seoul: Sinang kwa Chisongsa.

Pak Yong-kon (1990) *Chuch'e ui Segyekwan* (The Chuch'e Worldview), Tokyo: Kuwolsobang.

YONG-CHOON KIM

Chunqiu and Lushi Chunqiu

Literally 'spring and autumn', the Lushi *Chunqiu* is an annal or year-by-year court chronicle from the state of Lu attributed to Confucius (551–479 BCE) himself, and thus the sole Confucian classic that the Master did not merely transmit. Since the chronicle is extremely terse or cryptic, tradition alleged that Confucius hid his moral judgments on the 'matter-of-fact' events by a subtle choice of words 'rich in meaning'. For example, different verbs for 'to die' are supposed to hint at different causes from the natural to the treacherous. The period covered by the chronicle was also known as the Spring and Autumn period (722–481 BCE). In early China there were counted only two seasons, spring and autumn, to mark the active and inactive farming seasons.

A commentary on the Lushi *Chunqiu* was written by Lu Buwei, the powerful prime minister to the First Emperor of China (Qin). Counted as an 'eclectic' text, it shows an interest in cosmological thought, its chapters being divided into **Heaven**, Earth and the **Five Elements**. An interest in cosmology went with an interest in destiny, with men then seeking for signs from heaven which would indicate their future fate. This persisted through the Qin and Han dynasties as the new empires worked at grafting their regimes onto the structure of the universe.

Further reading

Loewe, M. (ed.) (1993) *Early Chinese Texts: A Bibliographical Guide*, Berkeley, CA: Institute of East Asian Studies, University of California.

WHALEN LAI

civil religion

Confucianism may be counted as China's 'civil religion', in that it makes duties to this world a priority. It provides the legitimacy to rule; it underwrites the social ethos, and it also holds up society to a higher critique. The loyal and righteous Confucian minister risks his life admonishing the ruler; the literati staffing the civil service system observe what amounts to a professional ethics; and the ideology of virtue (the mandate of **heaven**) allows protest from the people. When the reign 'has lost its Way', the people may presume to carry out – as rebels are wont to say – the Way on behalf of Heaven. In 1898, not even a candidate at the examination in the capital and so with no prospect of an official position, Kang Yuwei submitted a petition to the throne proposing political reform. He rallied the candidates in the capital and the scholarly communities in the provinces protesting at the Japanese incursion, won the ear of the young emperor, and initiated a constitutional monarchy reform. The last stand of Confucianism adjusting to modernity, it exemplifies civil religion in action. It ended when the Empress Dowager called in the army, and the pen once again was defeated by the sword.

Further reading

Davis, M. (ed.) (1995) *Human Rights and Chinese Values: Legal, Philosophical, and Political Perspectives*, Oxford: Hong Kong University.

WHALEN LAI

Classics and Books

The Han rule canonized Five Classics as guides to how to rule, while the Song dynasty Neo-Confucians canonized the Four Books for personal cultivation. The Five Classics are the Classics of Songs, History, Rites, Changes and the Spring and Autumn Annal. The Classic of Music is lost; that of Changes is the **Yijing**, better known as *Book of Changes*.

The suffix *jing* (classic) was added in Han times; it means 'what is permanent', since the Classics provide the invariable norms to bring order to society. The word also means the warp of a fabric, running lengthwise. The Han commentaries are called *wei*, which is the 'woof' that runs sideways. Putting the two together, the commentary provides the *yin–yang* prognostications for uncovering the hidden design of the Classics.

The Four Books are the *Analects* of Confucius, the *Book of Mencius*, the *Great Learning* and the *Doctrine of the Mean*. Although these are also loosely called 'classics', an underlying distinction should be maintained. The Five Classics supposedly edited by Confucius came from a model society and represented the collective wisdom of the ancients, not the ideas of any one single man. The Four Books are the teachings of individual thinkers from the later age of the philosophers after the passing of that golden age. As such, they do not measure up to the collective wisdom of old. We now prize their original thinking and individual authorship, but that is a modern myopia. The Classics are for 'managing' the world, and the later revival of Han learning would make that its agenda.

The word *jing* has of course been extended to the *Filial Classic*, *Daodejing*, *Taipingjing* and others. Yang Xiong titled his major work the *Taixuanjing* (Classic of the Great Mystery) and the Buddhists used the term to name their *sutras*.

Further reading

Most of the works mentioned above are available in translations by James Legge in seven volumes (1961–1872). Five have been reissued by the University of Hong Kong Press in 1970 as 'The Chinese Classics' in five volumes:

Vol. 1 Confucian *Analects* with *The Great Learning* and *Doctrine of the Mean*
Vol. 2 *The Works of Mencius*
Vol. 3 *The Shoo King: The Book of History*
Vol. 4 *The She King: The Book of Poetry*
Vol. 5 *The Ch'un Ts'ew: Spring and Autumn Annal*

James Legge's translation of *Li Kï: the Book of Rites* was in M. Müller (ed.), *The Sacred Books of the East* series (1885); it was not included in the above set. It can be found as:

Legge, J. (trans.) (1967) *The Book of Rites*, New York: University Books.

For the *Book of Changes*, see:

Wilhelm, R. (trans.) (1967) *The I Ching*, Princeton, NJ: Princeton University Press.

Shaughnessy, E. (1996) *I Ching*, New York: Ballantine.

Arthur Waley has also translated a number of the Classics and Books:
(1928) *The Book of Songs*, London: Allen & Unwin.
(1933) *The Book of Changes*, Bulletin for the Museum of Far Eastern Antiquities No. 5.
(1938) *The Analects of Confucius*, London: Allen & Unwin.
(1958) *The Way and its Power*, New York: Grove Paperback.

WHALEN LAI

cognition, sevenfold typology of

The study of cognition in terms of what is known as the 'sevenfold typology of cognition' (*lo rig dun*) is popular in the educational curriculum of many Tibetan monastic colleges, especially in the early stages of a student's training in Buddhist epistemology. Though based on Indian Buddhist epistemological writings, the classification itself and the manner in which it is used as an educational device appear to be entirely Tibetan innovations. It was probably **Chapa Chokyi Senge** who first formulated the sevenfold typology of cognition. The following are the seven classes of cognition with their brief individual definitions.

Perception: a cognitive event that is devoid of conceptualization and is unmistaken with respect to its object.
Inferential cognition: a cognitive event that is veridical with regard to a non-evident object and which arises in dependence upon the application of a valid reasoning.
Subsequent cognition: a cognition that takes place subsequent to a valid cognition that precedes it and causes the succeeding instances to come into being.
Correct assumption: a single-pointed apprehension of an object, which is not dependent upon either direct experience or valid reasoning.
Inattentive perception: a cognitive event in which although the object is perceived clearly, there is no capacity for ascertainment to take place.
Wavering thought (doubt): a cognition that engages with its object in an indecisive manner.

False cognition: a cognitive event that is distorted with regard to its object.

Though distinct, these seven classes are not seen as mutually exclusive of each other. For example, there will be common locus between 1 and 3, 2 and 3, 1 and 5. **Shakya Pandita** has taken issue with the idea of 'correct assumption' (or true belief) as a valid, separate class of cognition. He has argued that there is no real basis within the Indian epistemological writings for identifying such a category of cognition.

Further reading

Dreyfus, G. (1997) *Dharmakarti's Philosophy and its Tibetan Interpretations*, Albany, NY: State University of New York, chaps 22 and 24.
Napper, E. (1981) *Mind in Tibetan Buddhism*, Ithaca, NY: Snow Lion.

THUPTEN JINPA

cognitive error, classical Indian theories

There are five types of theory of cognitive error (*vibhrama, bhrama*) proposed by different philosophical schools. They are as follows:

(1)   *Anyatha-khyati*. This is the standard direct realist account of the misapprehension of one object as another espoused by Naiyayikas and Bhatta Mimamsakas for whom awareness is always and only of objects external to the knowing mind. The initial sensory stage of the perceptual process (*nirvikalpaka-pratyaksha*) is always veridical. While cognitive errors may result from defects in the sense-organs, they are more usually attributable to environmental factors such as when a limpid crystal is misidentified as red due to reflections from proximate red objects. It is a crucial feature of the Naiyayika's direct realism that he rejects attempts to analyse perceptual illusions by appeals to entities such as sense-data intervening between consciousness and what is given.

In the case of shell mistaken for silver, there is visual perception of a shiny white surface upon which revived memory traces of silver from another context of experience are superimposed due to similarity of the surfaces of the objects. That this is possible is illustrated by cases such as awareness of a seen but untouched piece of ice as cold. The content of erroneous cognition always derives from experience of something real and has an objective basis. Error results from a miscombination of what have been data of awareness with the immediate objective support of the present experience. Non-correspondence to immediate reality is manifested in unsuccessful activity and valid cognition in success.

(2)   *Atma-khyati*, self-apprehension. This is the theory of the idealist **Yogachara** (Vijnanavada) Buddhists, who explain cognitive error as consisting in consciousness inappropriately projecting its own intrinsic forms which appear as external objects. Accordingly, all cognitions that purport to be of mind-independent objects are false.

(3)   *Asat-khyati*, the apprehension of non-being. This is the theory of the Madhyamika Buddhists for whom awareness is innately formless. They maintain that the content of false perception is an unreal (*asat*) item since it is neither mental nor material and neither internal nor external.

(4)   *Akhyati*, 'no-illusion'. This is the theory of the direct realist Prabhakara Mimamsakas who maintain that all cognitions are veridical simply in virtue of their occurrence. In the mistaking of shell for silver, there are two awareness events of different types: a primary, direct sensation of shell as a substantive 'this' which has a causal, supportive role (*alambana*) and a recollection, prompted by the similarity of surface appearances, of silver that has been cognized at a different time and place. Cognitive error and consequent behaviour results from the confusion of the two modes of awareness. In the case of visual perception of a white shell as yellow, the error results from the perception of bilious matter in the visual organ symptomatic of jaundice.

Ramanuja and his followers in the **Vishishtadvaita** school also deny the possibility of cognitive error. All cognitions correspond to existent realities. Appealing to the ancient theory of quintuplication (*panchi-karana*) according to which material things have a compounded constitution containing all the five elements (*bhuta*: earth, water, fire, air and the atmosphere) in different proportions, Ramanuja says that in the case of a mirage, we really do perceive water in the sands of the desert. When shell is mistaken for silver, we are actually apprehending traces of silver present in the shell manifested in the lustrous similarity of their surfaces.

(5) *Anirvachaniya-khyati*, indefinable apprehension. According to this theory, associated with post-**Shankara Advaita** Vedanta, the fact that since cognitive errors occur and have practical consequences means that they cannot be classified as unreal *tout court*. On the other hand, the fact they are annulled by a correcting awareness means that they cannot be real. The content of misconception is thus indefinable as real or unreal; a formulation which perhaps attempts to avoid the contradiction implicit in calling it both.

See also: Nyaya

Further reading

Hiriyanna, M. (1993) *Outlines of Indian Philosophy*, Delhi: Motilal Banarsidass.
Matilal, B. (1986) *Perception: An Essay in Indian Theories of Knowledge*, Oxford: Clarendon Press.

CHRIS BARTLEY

common sense

An appeal to 'common sense' in settling issues is now a standard practice. The 'sense' in question is deemed so common that no proof is necessary. But not everything which represents common sense is rational or sensible; what is common sense in one culture may be very different in another. It is only common sense in the West 'not talk with one's mouth full', but at a Chinese banquet, the common rule is 'the noisier (and merrier) the better'. What in English is called 'common sense' the Chinese usually call 'general knowledge'.

In China, a time came when the nobility of old had long gone and cultural taste was set by the arts in the capital. The Neo-Confucians examined these forms of cultural refinement, criticized them as superficial and repackaged them for a common standard of ritual decorum (see **Neo-Confucianism, concepts**). They set the new

norm of good sense in their production of conduct books. A collection of such books meant for mass consumption was later produced in the Ming–Qing popular press. These came under the class of guide books for 'daily use in households' that covered all kinds of topics, and upgraded public morality and spread accepted modes of behaviour as part of that stock of 'general knowledge' required for clean living. A lack of acquaintance with such self-evident truths is then routinely charged to a lack of 'general knowledge' or 'common sense'.

WHALEN LAI

comparative philosophy, Chinese

The fact that Confucianism, Daoism and Buddhism existed side by side in China made for sustained exchanges, debates and assessment of their relative worth. The contentions, once heated, had become more relaxed by the time of the Ming dynasty when the thesis of 'unity of the three teachings' and religious syncretism as a whole became almost commonplace. With Neo-Confucianism being the state ideology, Buddhists and Daoists were eager to show their compatibility with that state orthodoxy. Neo-Confucianism itself masked a synthesis of Daoist cosmology, Buddhist psychology and Confucian morality. Following in their footsteps, the Ming syncretists all tend to reduce the essence of the three teachings to the same central concern for 'self-cultivation'; they all focused on issues of Mind and Nature, presented a common, puritanical moral front, and claimed the ultimate personal communion with the absolute to be the same or very much alike. This 'essentialism' may be the Song–Ming contribution to the three-party exchange; but that is hardly the only premise (there are wider ones) upon which the exchange can be conducted.

This in turn affects how the 'unity of the three teachings' may be assessed. Some scholars might look to the co-existence of the three teachings in China and their ability at reaching some consensus as a model for doing comparative philosophy or even for an ecumenism of world religions. Others, however, doubt whether that dialogue was so open at all. It could be charged that the alleged harmony was very far from supportive of a modern pluralistic society, or even less of a world ethics.

Further reading

Berling, J. (1980) *The Syncretic Religion of Lin Chao-en*, New York: Columbia University Press.

Kohn, L. (1995) *Laughing at the Tao: Debates Among Buddhists and Taoists in Medieval China*, Princeton: Princeton University Press.

WHALEN LAI

comparative philosophy, Japanese

Since Meiji times (1868–1912), Japanese philosophy has almost inevitably been comparative philosophy. Shushigaku doctrines of nature and principle (*ri*) could not but be contrasted with Western philosophy of nature, science and technology, which had proved a much more successful means of knowledge and technology. This paved the way for empiricist and pragmatic epistemologies. Also, it seriously called into question traditional holistic philosophies which failed to distinguish between the social (or moral) realm and the realm of nature, or between norms and facts. In ethics and socio-political philosophy, ideas of human rights and democracy challenged traditional notions of human inequality and hierarchical order. Both theoretical and practical philosophy were also philosophy of culture. They reflected such questions as whether their particular characteristics resulted from something distinctively 'Western', 'Eastern', or 'Japanese'. In other words, the following questions almost inevitably entered, or even guided, the comparisons. (1) Is there something like cultural identity? (2) Is it of intrinsic value? Is it worth preserving? (3) What are the characteristics of Japanese identity? (4) Should culture be modelled according to universal laws of theory and practice (if there are such laws)? These questions were mixed with questions of national and international politics. (5) Has a state – perhaps because of its value as an embodiment of superior

culture and traditional morality – the right, or even the obligation, to conquer other states?

If one analyzes such questions from strictly logical and empirical points of view, they prove meaningless in almost every respect. For (1), the mere existence of a tradition or culture does not imply that it ought to exist. (2) The value and validity of doctrines is principally independent of their genesis, particularly the place and time of their origin. (3) Cultures are not unalterable essences. They are the work of human beings. They change, and can be changed. (4) All cultures comprise within themselves theoretical and practical forces of change. Classic Confucianism, too, included such anti-traditional doctrines as, for example, the norm to promote humanity and the justification of tyrannicide. In other words, seen from the perspective of classic Confucianism, culture ought be modelled according to the idea of humanity, and not vice versa. (5) Cultures comprise within themselves different, and often antagonistic, value traditions. For instance, the ethics of classic Confucianism and Shushigaku are basically incompatible for the first emphasizes commonsensical humanity, while the letter advances an ontologicalized and highly speculative notion of humanity that leaves almost no room for individual freedom. The whole question of so-called cultural identity is relevant only with regard to two respects. First, it is of great psychological relevance. That is, to give meaning to their existence, and to feel comforted, human beings need something to identify with. Thereby, the goal of identification is conceived of as a source of value. Second, sometimes the preservation of a cultural identity – though of no intrinsic value – is a prerequisite for dignified human life.

The changes that took place, and often were consciously inaugurated, since Meiji times created enormous psychological pressure. For example, the *samurai*, losing their traditional privileges, also lost traditional social security. Industrialization produced a labour surplus, and hence again social insecurity. The 'Manchester capitalism' of the first decade of the twentieth century seemed to replace altruist morality by egoistically motivated competition. For many Japanese, Japanese imperialism was a source of national pride. For others, it was a grave violation of universal morality. The history and success of Western imperialism and colonialism seemed to prove the correctness, or at least effectiveness, of cultural chauvinism.

Hence, since almost all philosophical comparisons required value judgements, and since these judgements somehow reflected an estimation of traditional Japanese culture and, even more problematic, actual politics, the results were often artificial, namely, determined by an interest to show that there existed a distinctively Japanese traditional culture and ethics, and that this traditional culture and ethics was superior to Western alternatives. In most cases, this interest led to simplified pictures of 'the West', 'the East' and 'Japanese culture', namely clichés, caricatures, overgeneralizations and one-sidedness. Especially worthless were contrasts formulated in such general terms as 'Confucianism', 'Buddhism' and 'Christianity', or 'Western logic' and (Eastern) Zen. Even more sophisticated approaches like that of **Nishimura** Shigeki (1828–1902), who compared particular 'Western' and 'Confucian' virtues, remain questionable since they do not take into sufficient account the traditions of critical Confucianism. Recurrent contrasts were those of Western logocentrism and Eastern/Japanese indifference to logicalness, Western interest in abstract and general concepts and Eastern interest in 'the concrete', Western anthropomorphism and Eastern 'oneness of man and nature', Western distinctions between subject and object and, again, Eastern 'non-duality', Western individualism, egoism and materialism and Eastern communitarianism, altruism and spiritualism, Western interest in competition and strife and Eastern interest in harmony, and so on. Such distinctions which have remained influential throughout the twentieth century were worked out by Okakura Kakuzo (1862–1913), Nitobe Inazo (1862–1933), **Nishida** Kitaro (1870–1945), **Watsuji Tetsuro** (1889–1960), Suzuki Daisetz (1870–1966), members of the **Kyoto school**, Kuki Shuzo (1888–1943), Yamauchi Tokuryu (1890–1982), Nishimura Shigeki, **Inoue** Tetsujiro (1855–1944), Yuasa Yasuo (born 1925) and many others.

The attempts to identify a unique, and uniquely valuable, Japanese culture culminated in the development of kokutai ideology (see **kokutai ideology since Meiji times**). Critique of these

culturalist views came from more scientific minded philosophers, such as for instance **Nishi** Amane (1829–97), from ethical universalists like human rights advocates, critical Kantians, socialists and Marxists, and from scholars who simply had a broader and deeper knowledge of cultures, most notably Nakamura Hajime (1912–99), Maruyama Masao (1914–96) and Kato Shuichi (1919–). They did not fall prey to the temptation to equate the traditionalist features of Japanese history of thought with the whole of this history, but also pointed out the more rational, logical and critical ideas in Japanese thought. Also, they did not view 'the West' as a monolithic block of rationality, logocentrism and modernity. Most important, however, they refused to be influenced by political ideology. Though even Nakamura and Kato sympathize with ideas of an Eastern disinterest in logic, they do not go so far as to regard such disinterest as indicative of a particular Eastern ethics.

Nakamura Hajime – one of the world's outstanding Indologists, Buddhologists and philosophers of culture – has pointed out many universalist, rational and proto-democratic features in early Japanese thought, particularly in the Nara (710–94) philosophy of state. Also, he has made it clear that what he calls Japanese 'this-worldliness' and a lack of interest in religious belief actually reflects a kind of critical empiricism and pragmatism, that is, something quite rational. Maruyama has directed attention to the fact that, in Japanese history, the *Mencius* and its doctrines of critical loyalty and tyrannicide were by no means without influence, and that Ito Jinsai (1627–1705) and Ogyu Sorai (1666–1728) were philosophers much interested in logical consistency and empiricalness. Kato has contributed to our understanding of such rational and critical minds as Tominaga Nakamoto (1715–46), Nakae Chomin (1847–1901) and **Kotoku** Shusui (1871–1911).

See also: logic; philosophy of human rights, Japanese; Japanese philosophy, post-Meiji

Further reading

Nakamura Hajime (1968) *Ways of Thinking of Eastern Peoples*, ed. P. Wiener, Honolulu, HA: University of Hawaii Press

—— (1969) *A History of the Development of Japanese Thought*, 2 vols, Tokyo: Japan Cultural Society.

—— (1980) *Indian Buddhism*, Tokyo: Kufs Publication.

—— (1982) *Ansätze modernen Denkens in den Religionen Japans (Nihon shukyo no kindaisei)*, trans. S. Schultz and A. Schomaker-Huett, Leiden: Brill.

—— (1992) *A Comparative History of Ideas*, Delhi: Motilal Banarsidass.

Suzuki Daisetz (1959) *Zen and Japanese Culture*, London: Routledge & Kegan Paul.

Yuasa Yasuo (1987) *The Body: Toward an Eastern-Mind-Body Theory (Shintai – toyoteki shinshinron no kokoromi)*, trans. Nagatomo Shigenori and T.P. Kasulis, Albany, NY: State University of New York Press.

GREGOR PAUL

confession

Confession of sin has a special place in ethical monotheism, but is not absent in other traditions. The Confucian gentleman daily reviews in private his actions of the day, to see if he had done anything or anyone wrong in public. The archaic rite of confession preserved in religious Daoism is before the Three Officials – Heaven, Earth and Water – for any violations, knowing or unknowing. This is to be accompanied by formal sacrifice, sent up in smoke to heaven, buried under ground for earth or thrown into the river for water. Driven by fear of taboos, the rite was largely exorcistic, but the *Taiping Dao* movement in the late Han dynasty gave it a more moral content. Members sat up all night in 'quiet rooms' to 'reflect and repent'. Contrition might now involve self-flagellation, which was credited with the power to eradicate evil.

Buddhist ethics, being universal, rational and taboo-free, marked another advance. Apart for being atheistic, Buddhist confession is communal, conducted at the fortnight recitation of the precepts, one on one, between fellow monks. Except for grave transgressions deserving expulsion, the penitent rejoins the community after having carried out prescribed tasks. The will to confess and the promise to make good are deemed auto-therapeutic. But in the Pure Land faith, confession of personal inadequacy comes close to being theistic, that is, cleansed by grace for it may trigger that transference of merit from the salvific Buddha to the undeserving sinner. Coming after the Buddhist period, Neo-Confucians took over some of that 'communal confession' aspect. For mutual edification, 'companions of the Way' (close friends) passed around their personal diaries or moral records and made resolutions together. Simpler people kept 'records of merits and demerits' and direct confessions to various gods, to **Heaven** or the Most High. It has been said that unlike Stalinist Russia, Maoist China early on invested much time and energy in public confessions and re-education campaigns, as if this is a Confucian legacy. But such forced self-transformation was more harsh in the south than in the north and later turned confrontational with open struggles, coerced confessions and mock trials.

See also: Buddhist philosophy in Japan; Confucianism in Japan

Further reading

Lai, W. (1990) 'The Ch'an-ch'a-ching: Religion and Magic in Medieval China', *Chinese Buddhist Apocrypha*, ed. R.E. Buswell, Jr, Honolulu, HA: University of Hawaii Press: 175–206.

WHALEN LAI

Confucian spirituality

Confucianism was presented negatively in the modern period by its critics in the May Fourth Movement (the liberal movement started by Beijing University students, which rose in 4 May 1919, condemning China's past as entirely feudalistic and opting for a total Westernization and embrace of science and democracy). It was seen by these critics as dated and superstitious. However, modern defenders view Confucianism positively as timely, humanistic and this-worldly. The latter view dissociates it from any hint of being 'religious'. Among American Confucian scholars, there is more recently a move to reverse both modern readings and to retrieve traditional Confucian 'spirituality'. Some spokesmen also use Confucian spirituality to develop a postmodern critique of the Enlightenment, presenting a new Neo-Confucianism as a third wave and a world philosophy for the third (Christian) millennium.

Confucian spirituality is not secular 'humanism'; it is 'cosmo-humanism', a rephrasing of the Han 'unity of man and heaven'. It is 'religious' but not in the theocentric sense, its 'spirituality' being attested to by reports of 'awakening to sagehood' that involves a sense of the sacred, of inner reverence, of ultimate concern and transformation. Discussion always goes back to **Mencius**'s experience of a union with the Dao, his moral empathy with a cosmic righteousness, spelled out later in the *Doctrine of the Mean*. This sort of 'spirituality' is always traced through Wang Yangming and his school, although **Zhu Xi** is also influential on this issue. The scholarship, in that sense, has a 'spiritual lineage'.

The Transmission of the Dao is being rekindled

'Transmission of the Dao' is a Neo-Confucian phrase; it claims that the Dao had been transmitted from Confucius, through Mencius, leapfrogging to Han Yu and to the Song Masters. This was obviously copied from the Chan term 'transmission of mind', but was used to defend the notion of a Han Chinese orthodoxy against the barbaric teachings of a Buddhist India. If the May Fourth 'westernizing' liberals saw only the dark side of China's material past, some of these 'postmodern' neo-traditionalists seem to paint only the spiritual best. They are also in part a specific product of American academic culture.

Confucianism is enjoying a creative vogue at the moment within American academia. The 'old school' led by John Fairbank at Harvard holds that Confucian China needs Western challenge to modernize, and that the Christian missions had had a positive input. Study of Confucian philosophy is centred on the classical period; Neo-Confucian writings were virtually inaccessible until Wing-tsit Chan included a selection in his *Source Book of Chinese Philosophy*. A new focus on Song and Ming thought then arose under Theodore de Bary at Columbia University. A Catholic (as Fairbank is Protestant), de Bary appreciated the spirituality in the Song masters and worked at presenting a 'liberal' side to this tradition: a moral individualism with the potential to bring China into the modern era. Meanwhile in Hong Kong, proponents of a 'New Confucianism' were reinterpreting Neo-Confucianism for a new age at the New Asia College, founded with that agenda. Tang Junyi and Mou Zongsan spearheaded that effort. Tu Weiming (who worked predominantly at Harvard) later brought that zealous reading of a living tradition to the United States and heralded a Third Age for a Mencian vision appropriate for the whole world. Independently, Thomas Metzger applied the Mou–Tang reading to repeal Max Weber's understanding of China. Weber contrasted the Puritan as the 'innerworldly ascetic' with a mission to change the world, with the Confucian gentleman as somone who, in his worldliness, seeks only to accommodate himself to the world, to be mystically in tune with nature.

More recently, Roger Ames and David Hall have teamed up and reinterpreted Chinese thought through the approach of thinkers such as Whitehead and Mead. It is not always easy to reconcile these highly idyllic readings of Confucian ideals with the reality of China's past as described by social historians like Patricia Ebrey. The prospect of Confucianism being the world philosophy for a new millennium seems both improbable and undesirable.

Further reading

Chou Tse-tsung (1960) *The May Fourth Movement: Intellectual Revolution in Modern China*, Cambridge, MA: Harvard University Press.

de Bary, W. (ed.) (1970) *Self and Society in Ming Thought*, New York: Columbia University Press.

—— (ed.) (1975) *The Unfolding of Neo-Confucianism*, New York: Columbia University Press.

—— (1981) *Neo-Confucian Orthodoxy and the Learning of Mind-and-Heart*, New York: Columbia University Press.

—— (1989) *The Message of the Mind in Neo-Confucianism*, New York: Columbia University Press.

—— (1991) *Learning for One's Self: Essays on the Individual in Neo-Confucian Thought*, New York: Columbia University Press.

—— (1991) *The Trouble with Neo-Confucianism*, Cambridge: Harvard University Press.

Ebrey, P. (1984) *Family and Property in Sung China: Yuan Ts'ai's Precept for Social Life*, Princeton, NJ: Princeton University Press.

Lai, W. (1991) 'The Spirituality of Confucian Humanism', *Journal of Humanism and Ethical Religion* 4(1): 63–76.

Sawada, J. (1993) *Confucian Values and Popular Zen: Sekimon Shingaku in Eighteenth-Century Japan*, Honolulu, HA: University of Hawaii Press.

Taylor, R. (1990) *The Religious Dimension of Confucianism*, Albany, NY: State University of New York Press.

Thomas, M. (1977) *Neo-Confucianism and China's Evolving Political Culture*, New York: Columbia University Press.

Weber, M. (1951) *The Religions of China*, New York: Free Press.

WHALEN LAI

Confucianism in Japan

The ancient and classical periods

Regular contacts between Japan and China began around 100 BCE. At this time, state examinations in the Confucian classics to recruit government officials (instituted by the Han dynasty in 124 BCE) were already in use in China. These examinations, and the state college that ran them, had a chequered history in the next few centuries, but were restored on a grand scale during the Sui (589–618) and Tang (618–907) dynasties. Mastering the Confucian classics was a prerequisite for a career in the bureacracy, and Confucian ideals (such as rule by moral example, and self-cultivation through the study of classical rites, poetry and music, and through the perfection of moral virtues such as filial piety, loyalty and benevolence) pervaded élite Chinese culture.

As diplomatic contacts with China (and, of course, Sinified Korea) intensified in the course of the fifth through the seventh centuries, so did Japanese interest in Confucian studies. The seventh century saw the emergence of a centralized, imperial state in Japan, whose institutions were designed on the basis of Tang examples. Knowl-

edge of the Confucian classics was actively imported from China during this period, and Confucian institutions and ideas pressed their stamp on the Japanese court. Confucian rhetoric formed part of the language of Japanese emperorship right from its origin in this century, alongside more traditional lines of argument based on *kami* myth. This rhetoric was employed in imperial pronouncements, exhortations to officials, and, perhaps most prominently, in the first Japanese attempts at the Confucian art of history-writing. The recording of history, and the drawing of moral lessons from historical events, was a core activity of Confucians in China. This Chinese example inspired the compilation on imperial orders of, first, the 'Record of Ancient Matters' (*Kojiki*, 712), and then a series of six dynastic histories, starting with the 'Chronicles of Japan' (*Nihon shoki*, 720). Imperial history writing continued for some two centuries: the last of this series was finished in 901. These histories display a mixture of native Japanese and Confucian notions of emperorship. While the emperor's position of power was legitimized first of all on the basis of his descent from the sun-goddess Amaterasu, individual emperors were also depicted as moral rulers possessing Confucian virtues.

As this already suggests, the Japanese attitude to Confucianism was somewhat ambiguous. The Confucian ideal of rule by a morally superior meritocracy was adopted as a form of political discourse, but did not displace the notion that access to power was the prerogative of hereditary lineages with roots in the Age of the Gods. In this environment, the Chinese examination system was unlikely to prosper, although a serious attempt was made to emulate the Tang in this respect, too. A first Confucian university was founded in the capital (Otsu) in *c*.670, and in the course of the following century a nation-wide network of state academies developed whose functioning was firmly embedded in the law. The curriculum was patterned on that of the Tang universities, and focused on the *Analects*, the *Classic of Filial Piety*, the *Books of Songs*, *Odes*, *Documents*, the *Rites*, the *Rites of Zhou*, the *Rites of Yi*, and the *Zuo Zhuan Commentary on the Spring and Autumn Annals*. These Classics (see **Classics and Books**) were studied with the help of Han and post-Han commentaries. Graduates who passed the state examination with good results were rewarded with a court rank and office.

However, this Japanese version of the Chinese institution of state examinations was to remain a peripheral phenomenon. Those born in aristocratic lineages were automatically promoted to ranks that were out of bounds for even the most brilliant of university graduates, and the university functioned mainly to educate lower-ranking bureaucrats who had to be competent in reading and writing Chinese, the language of the bureaucracy. A literary course to train students more effectively in these skills was introduced in 728, and soon became more prestigious than the traditional Confucian course itself. In time, positions within the university itself became hereditary, and Confucian scholarship became the exclusive province of a few court families (notably the Kiyowara), who transmitted their knowledge of the classics privately and derived an income from this as their traditional family pursuit. After a long period of slow decline, the university in the capital ceased to exist after a fire in 1177.

This is not to say that Confucianism did not have a lasting impact on Japanese thought, even during this early period. Perhaps the Confucian notion that took root most successfully in the Japan of the classical period was the view that human society and nature form part of a single, precariously balanced system. Imbalance in the human realm was believed to cause a similar imbalance in the natural world, and it was the task of the emperor to maintain a cosmic equilibrium throughout the realm. Natural phenomena were interpreted as portents, good or bad, predicting illness or political upheavals in the human world, and an elaborate system of divination had been developed to pinpoint potential trouble, based on the binary opposition between *yin* and *yang*, as well as the cycle of the Five Phases of matter (wood, fire, earth, metal and water). In Japan, a 'Yin-Yang Bureau' (On'yoryo) functioned as a state office for such divination between 718 and 820. Many of its techniques were subsequently absorbed by esoteric Buddhism and survived in Buddhist garb after its demise. Moreover, speculation on *yin* and *yang* and the Five Phases continued to play a central role in Japanese thought throughout the medieval and early modern periods.

The medieval period

A new chapter in Japanese Confucianism began with the introduction to Japan of the so-called Neo-Confucianism that developed during the Song dynasty (960–1279) in China. The founders of this school were the two brothers Cheng Hao (1032–85) and Cheng Yi (1033–1107), and **Zhu Xi** (1130–1200); it became established as the basis for the Chinese state examinations in 1314. This school of Confucianism added a metaphysical layer to the Confucianism of the Han and Tang, partly under the influence of Daoism and Buddhism. Its cosmological speculations focused on the concepts of *li* (in Japanese, *ri*), the formless 'principle' that imposes order on both natural and human affairs, and *qi* (in Japanese, *ki*), a gaseous 'matter' or 'energy' that, governed by *li*, condenses to take on physical shape. The material world consists of *qi*, which alternates between *yin* and *yang* and takes on the forms of the Five Phases, and this *qi* also constitutes our bodies; *li* is present as the ordering principle behind all matter, and exists in man as his human nature (*xing*; in Japanese, *sei*). *Qi* can be either pure or impure. If it is the latter, evil arises; but all human beings can overcome the evil of their bodily *qi* by returning to their pure human nature, which dwells in their hearts or minds, and so become sages in harmony with *li*. This can be achieved through the study of *li* as it manifests itself in the world, moral effort, and silent sitting in contemplation.

Neo-Confucianism was introduced to Japan more or less simultaneously by the Confucian specialists who had their roots in the state university (the Kiyowara) and by Zen monks, of which the latter, perhaps, were the most influential. Zen monasteries, which flourished under shogunal patronage during the thirteenth and fourteenth centuries, functioned as the main gateways to Chinese learning and culture during the medieval period. At these monasteries, Neo-Confucianism was taught more or less as a lay version of Zen itself. 'Human nature' was an obvious equivalent to '**buddha nature**', and *li* to the universal enlightenment which, as the Zen, Tendai, Shingon and many other contemporary Buddhist schools believed, constituted the universe itself. Even the practice of silent sitting corresponded to Buddhist

Zen practice. Neo-Confucianism offered a practical lay morality that was compatible with Zen, and moreover had the prestige of being the official orthodoxy of contemporary China. It was through the medium of 'Confucian monks' (*juso*) that Neo-Confucian ideas spread among the military élite during the course of the medieval period.

At the same time, Neo-Confucianism also blended with the newly-emerging Shinto tradition. Confucian principles were utilized to explain and interpret *kami* myths and rituals. The most influential work in this genre was the 'Chronicle of the Direct Descent of Gods and Sovereigns' (*Jinno Shotoki*, 1339, revised 1343) by Kitabatake Chikafusa (1293–1354). This work was written during a fifty-six-year struggle between two rival imperial courts (1336–92), and sets out to prove the legitimacy of the Southern Court. To this end, Chikafusa, a figure of great importance within the Southern Court, wrote a history of the imperial line stretching back to the Age of the Gods. While stressing that imperial legitimacy was ultimately based on the mandate of the imperial ancestress Amaterasu, Chikafusa explained the frequent shifts of the succession from one branch of the imperial house to another by measuring up the relative amounts of 'virtue' possessed by these branches. Also, he incorporated earlier theories that interpreted the three imperial regalia (mirror, jewel and sword) bequeathed to the imperial line by Amaterasu as symbols of sovereignty, as wellsprings of the virtues of uprightness, compassion and wisdom, respectively. The divine mandate embodied by these regalia rendered Japan a 'divine country' superior even to China; this superiority was clear above all from the fact that the imperial line had never been broken and was guaranteed by the gods for all eternity. The combination of Shinto and Confucian elements in Chikafusa's work, and his stress on absolute loyalty to the imperial lineage, were to become recurrent themes in centuries to come.

During the medieval period, Confucian ideas functioned as components of a system that was at bottom dominated by a Buddhist or Shinto world view. Zen-Confucian and Shinto-Confucian syncretism found the patronage of many military leaders, and left traces in their house laws and in the education of their retainers. Arguably, such amalgamated traditions continued to dominate Japanese Confucian thought throughout its premodern history, at least at a semi-intellectual level, although a purer Confucianism did emerge during the early modern period.

The early modern period

The period immediately following Japan's reunification in 1590 and the establishment of the Tokugawa shogunate (1603–1867) saw a rise in the number of scholars of Chinese studies, and thus also of Confucianism. The main reasons for this were the economic boom that followed the establishment of peace, and the growth of bureaucracy both at the shogunal and the domainal level, which offered opportunities for those competent in Chinese. These circumstances gave rise to a new self-consciousness among Chinese scholars, expressed perhaps most strikingly in an anti-Buddhist stance that formed a marked contrast with the Confucian monks of the medieval period.

Confucianism flourished during this period, both in depth and breadth. The emergence of a class of Confucian specialists who made their living teaching Chinese and the Confucian classics at both private and official schools contributed both to the growth of Confucian expertise, and to the spread of Confucian teachings among wider segments of the populace. Official patronage of Confucianism further reinforced its impact, especially towards the end of this period. Hayashi Razan (1583–1657), a Confucianist employed by the shogunate as an advisor and clerk since 1607, was given money and land to found a private Confucian academy in 1630, and in 1644 was ordered to compile a Confucian-style history of Japan (*Honcho tsugan* (A Comprehensive Mirror of Our State), completed by Razan's son Gaho in 1670). Also, the shogunate built an official Confucian shrine next to the Razan academy where the shogun attended Confucian rituals, although it must be stressed that such occasions were rare. Several Confucian advisors rose to positions of influence in the late seventeenth and early eighteenth centuries; but Neo-Confucianism began to benefit significantly from state support only in the late eighteenth century, after the so-called Kansei reforms (1787–93). As part of these reforms (which were designed to deal with an economic, social and diplomatic crisis compounded by financial mismanagement, large-scale famine, frequent peasant revolts and Russian encroachment in the north), the shogunate prohibited the teaching of other schools of Confucianism at the Hayashi academy, and so in effect recognised Neo-Confucianism as the nation's only orthodox school of learning, although no attempts were made to impose Neo-Confucian orthodoxy beyond this one academy. From 1792 onwards, regular state examinations were held at the Hayashi academy, and the academy itself was in 1797 taken over by the shogunate and has since been run as an official training college for *bakufu* retainers. Now known as the Shoheizaka Gakumonjo, the academy also organized public lectures open to commoners, and published some two hundred books, including a running history of the Tokugawa shogunate entitled *Tokugawa jikki* (True Records of the Tokugawa), completed in 1849. In addition to this college, the shogunate also established schools teaching Neo-Confucian ethics to commoners in shogunal lands, and supported popular Neo-Confucian groups such as the **Shingaku** movement.

The second half of the eighteenth century also saw the spread of domainal schools, maintained by the domain authorities for the education of the retainers of the various *daimyo*. By the end of the period there were some 280 such schools, most of which had a curriculum that combined Confucian studies with martial arts. Some of these schools, such as the domain school in Kaga, also admitted commoners; many schools published Confucian texts and historical works.

The real dynamism of early modern Japanese Confucianism, however, did not arise from shogunal and domainal schools, but rather from the private 'academies' of commoner Confucian teachers. Such academies, which were mostly one-man enterprises, first became popular among *samurai* and merchants alike in the cities of the late seventeenth and early eighteenth centuries. At the centre of their curriculum was the study of the Chinese classics and the composition of Chinese prose and poetry. These academies recruited a new audience for Confucian thought outside the ruling class. This fact alone inspired new interpretations

of the Confucian classics, interpretations that were relevant to social groups for whom traditional Confucianism had a low regard, such as merchants.

During the second half of the seventeenth century, when Confucianism was beginning to broaden its audience among the ruling class and commoners alike, two trends in Confucian studies became prominent almost simultaneously. One was concerned with the establishment of a pure and up-to-date Neo-Confucianism – in contrast to the eclecticism of the medieval Confucianists who had used both 'old' (Han and Tang) and 'new' (Neo-Confucian) commentaries to establish the meaning of the Confucian classics. Central figures representing this trend were the afore-mentioned Hayashi Razan, who laid the foundations for the later shogunal patronage of Neo-Confucianism, and Yamazaki Ansai (1618–82), who ran a highly successful private academy in Kyoto and played a major role in giving Neo-Confucianism a new popular appeal. Whether Razan's and Ansai's Confucianism were in fact pure reflections of contemporary Chinese Neo-Confucianism is another matter. Aspects that clearly make both scholars stand apart from their Chinese examples are their concern with Shinto, and the stress on self-sacrificing loyalty to the Japanese imperial state that was especially strong in Ansai's thought – both notions that had emerged already in medieval thinkers such as Kitabatake Chikafusa. Also, it should be kept in mind that the Neo-Confucian tradition on which Japanese thinkers from this era drew was not a monolithic orthodoxy. Thinkers such as Razan were widely read not only in the works of the Cheng brothers and Zhu Xi, but were also familiar with a wide range of Neo-Confucian thinkers from Ming China (1368–1644) and Yi dynasty Korea (1392–1910), such as Luo Qinshun (1465–1547) and **Yi T'oegye** (1501–70). Between scholars such as these, interpretations of fundamental Neo-Confucian issues varied considerably. Where Luo, for example, emphasized that principle (*li*) could not exist apart from matter (*qi*), and therefore stressed the 'investigation of principle as it manifests itself in things and affairs', Yi emphasized the importance of the practice of quiet sitting, and argued that only by 'stilling one's mind' can one allow one's innate virtues to shine forth unobstructed by the various 'emotions' that arise from one's bodily *qi*. These two ways of nurturing virtue – through the investigation of the 'things and affairs' of the world, and through quiet contemplation of the workings of 'principle' within one's own mind – were both part of China's Neo-Confucian tradition. While Razan and Ansai can both be described as orthodox Neo-Confucians, their preferences for interpretations of Neo-Confucianism here exemplified by Luo and Yi respectively, gave their thought a radically different character.

While Razan's and Ansai's brands of Neo-Confucian orthodoxy were taking shape, a school that was critical of Neo-Confucian metaphysics arose in the second half of the seventeenth century. The Confucianists of this school, known as Kogaku (Ancient Learning), were convinced that the Neo-Confucian commentaries on the Confucian classics obscured rather than illuminated the original teaching of Confucius. Therefore, they strove to reinterpret the ancient texts without depending on the later commentaries. A pioneer of this school was Yamaga Soko (1622–85), who started his career as a student of Razan. Soko rejected the metaphysical Neo-Confucian view of morality as an innate quality with which all human beings are endowed; rather, he stressed that moral norms were historical creations first set out by Confucius in his *Analects*, that have to be actively taught and studied by every generation. Even more influential than Soko was Ito Jinsai (1627–1705), who ran the most successful private academy of his age in Kyoto. Jinsai rejected the Neo-Confucian teaching that one must return to one's original human nature by extinguishing one's *qi*-based emotions through constant 'reverence', as argued by Yamazaki Ansai. Referring to Mencius, he taught that, quite to the contrary, these feelings and emotions are at the core of human nature. They should be regarded as inborn impulses to do good, and be developed into virtues such as humanity and righteousness. These virtues he too regarded as historical creations, first enunciated in ancient China, and to be mastered by subsequent generations through study of the classics and even the sheer language of that land.

Somewhat later, the Edo scholar Ogyu Sorai (1666–1728) went one step further. Jinsai had rejected the notion that a static cosmic 'principle' is present in man as his human nature, and instead looked at human emotions as the seeds of historically created virtues; Sorai rejected not only the Neo-Confucian idea of a cosmic 'principle', but also the very existence of seeds of virtue in human nature. He dismissed as 'Buddhist and syncretic' the notion that there is anything to be gained from exploring one's own mind, and rejected all introspection as irrelevant to the true Way. According to Sorai, the Way deals not with the improvement of individual minds, but with the regulation of society as a whole. In Sorai's definition, the Way was not a set of cosmic principles or inborn virtues, but a historical body of rules and institutions, invented by the 'Early Kings' of China (the primeval rulers Fu Xi, Shennong and Huangdi, and the founders of the earliest dynasties, Yao, Shun, Yu, Tang, King Wen, King Wu and the Duke of Zhou), and laid down in the Six Classics (the Books of *Documents*, *Songs*, *Rites*, *Music* and *Changes*, and the *Spring and Autumn Annals*). Not only do these classics give us information about the Way of the Early Kings, but the very words and style in which they are written are an expression of that Way. Therefore, Sorai placed great importance on the study of the language of the classics, and he argued that this language was to be mastered by emulating it: students should compose their own prose and poetry in the style of the Classics.

Sorai's school of Confucianism was at the height of its popularity between the late 1730s and the early 1750s; Jinsai's during the decades immediately preceding that period, when his school was led by his son Ito Togai (1670–1736). During the first half of the eighteenth century, Kogaku was a serious rival of Neo-Confucianism, and the discussion between the two schools set the perimeters for the further development of Confucian thought in Japan. The question whether virtue is rooted in a natural, cosmic 'principle' or in history remained a central issue. Direct results of the appearance of Kogaku on the Confucian scene were the decline and eventual demise of Confucian Shinto, and the rise of the Kokugaku school, which during the second half of the eighteenth century supplanted Neo-Confucianism as the main framework for the conceptualization of Shinto. Also, Kogaku's formulation of an interpretation of the Chinese classics that was radically different from Neo-Confucian orthodoxy had the liberating effect of inspiring others to be equally adventurous.

In the school's wake, a wide range of Confucian schools of thought flourished. The philological and historical stand of Kogaku scholars inspired a tendency towards rationality and empiricism even among Neo-Confucians. Under the banner of 'investigating principle as it manifests itself in things and affairs', Confucianists studied not only history but also natural sciences such as botany and astrology, laying a basis for the acceptance of Western science. Some, inspired both by Kogaku and a contemporary Chinese school known as 'Investigations Based on Evidence' (*Kaozheng-xue*; in Japanese, *Kosho-gakuha*) or 'Han Learning', concerned themselves with textual criticism and philology; others, such as the so-called 'Eclectic school' (*Setchu-gakuha*) cast their nets wider than orthodox Neo-Confucianism would have allowed, taking on board not only the philological methods developed by Kogaku scholars but also a variety of Han, Tang, Song and Ming commentaries. At the same time, moreover, Neo-Confucianism itself was given a new impulse by the shogunal seal of approval attached to it by the Kansei reforms mentioned above.

During the last century of the Edo period (1600–1868), Neo-Confucianists tended to stress the practical application of Confucian morality in everyday life rather than 'book-learning', and turned increasingly to Ming and Qing (1644–1912) commentaries, which showed a similar trend. To make such practice possible, a thorough understanding of the mind, as the innate source of the Way, was thought to be essential, and introspection while sitting quietly was regarded as a key element both of self-improvement and of social and political action. In this climate, study of the works of Wang Yangming (1472–1529) also gained in popularity. This Ming thinker had rejected the Neo-Confucian dichotomy of human nature (thought to arise from *li*) versus body and 'emotions' (consisting of, or arising from impure *qi*). He taught that 'good knowledge' (*liangzhi*; in Japanese, *ryochi*) is innate in man and can be realised through **meditation** and introspection, leading to a Zen-like experience of 'insight' in which *li* is realised. This insight allows one to achieve 'unity of thought and practice', and to act morally in the world. In Japan, the school of Wang Yangming (in Japanese, Yomeigaku) had isolated followers already in the seventeenth century (for example, Kumazawa Banzan, 1619–91), and it expanded its influence in the turmoil of the last decades of the Edo period, when it provided a philosophical basis for the actions of political activists such as Oshio Heihachiro (1793–1837), who led an uprising during the disastrous famines of 1833–7, and Yoshida Shoin (1830–59), who fought for the restoration of imperial rule.

However, during this period Japanese Confucianism developed not just through debates between different Confucian schools, but perhaps to an even greater extent also in dialogue with the rapidly rising Kokugaku school. To the Japanese, Confucianism remained a hallmark of Chinese culture, and therefore foreign. The foreignness of Confucianism was problematic because Sinocentrism was a prominent element of Confucian thought. From the point of view of the 'Middle Kingdom', Japan was a land of barbarians, no better than other peripheral nations. The **Shinto-**Confucian teachings of the seventeenth century constituted an attempt to domesticate Confucianism, but were discredited by the rise of the Kogaku school. This school's belief that the Way was created by the Early Kings of China, and its conclusion that there had existed no Way, and therefore no morals in Japan prior to the arrival of Chinese learning, were widely seen as unpatriotic and spurred on the development of a school of 'Ancient Japanese Studies', the Kokugaku school. The accusation that Kogaku scholars showed 'disrespect for the land that fed them' was not entirely justified: many Kogaku thinkers insisted that since Japan abided by the ritual and ethical standards set by the Early Kings more closely than contemporary China, Japan could now lay claim to the title of Middle Kingdom with more justification than China itself. Kokugaku, however, insisted that

Japan was superior on its own terms, and not because of its success at internalizing Chinese norms. Kokugaku scholars such as Motoori Norinaga (1730–1801) and Hirata Atsutane (1776–1843) argued that Japan is superior first of all because of its divine origins, personified to this day by the reign of an unbroken imperial dynasty of divine descent.

A synthesis of Kokugaku nationalism with Confucian thought was construed by the so-called Mito school. This school originated in 1657, when the *daimyo* of the Mito domain, Tokugawa Mitsukuni, established an office charged with the compilation of a historical work, entitled *Dainihonshi*, 'History of Great Japan', and finally offered to the shogun in 1720. This project threw up many awkward questions, such as the legitimacy of the Northern and Southern branches of the imperial line in the fourteenth century, and the position of the shogun himself as a ruler in the name of the emperor. *Dainihonshi* emphasized that possession of the three regalia was the decisive criterion in deciding the question of legitimacy, and narrowly avoided the crass substitution of virtue by the possession of these regalia as a condition for legitimate rule by stating that the regalia were 'spiritual entities' which would automatically find their way to the most appropriate, i.e. virtuous recipient. These questions demanded new answers during the last decades of the Edo period, when Mitogaku flourished once more under the Mito *daimyo* Tokugawa Nariaki. Thinkers such as Fujita Yukoku (1774–1826), Fujita Toko (1806–55) and Aizawa Seishisai (1782–1863) combined the idea of a sacred imperial lineage, 'divinely bestowed with virtue' by Heaven itself, with a stress on the need for practical application of the virtues of loyalty and filial piety on the part of the emperor's subjects. Seishisai in particular refined the notion that Japan possesses a unique 'national essence' (see **kokutai ideology since Meiji times**), consisting of a sacrosanct imperial lineage and a naturally loyal populace. In the last years of the Tokugawa shogunate, the arguments of Mitogaku and Kokugaku scholars served to legitimate the overthrow of the shogun and the 'restoration' of imperial rule, and had a great impact on the formation of Japanese nationalism during the late nineteenth and twentieth centuries.

See also: Buddhist philosophy in Japan; Shinto; Shinto, Confucian

Further reading

Bock, F. (1985) *Classical Learning and Taoist Practices in Early Japan*, Tucson, AZ: Arizona State University Press.

Kracht, K. (1986) *Studien zur Geschichte des Denkens im Japan des 17. bis 19. Jahrhunderts. Chu-Hsi-konfuzianische Geist-Diskurse*, Wiesbaden: Harrassowitz.

Maruyama Masao (1974) *Studies in the Intellectual History of Japan*, trans. Mikiso Hane, Tokyo: University of Tokyo Press.

McMullen, I. (1996) 'The Worship of Confucius in Ancient Japan', in *Japanese Religion: Arrows to Heaven and Earth*, Cambridge: Cambridge University Press.

Nakai, K.W. (1980) 'The Naturalization of Confucianism in Tokugawa Japan: The Problem of Sinocentrism', *Harvard Journal of Asiatic Studies* 40 (June).

Nosco, P. (ed.) (1984) *Confucianism and Tokugawa Culture*, Princeton, NJ: Princeton University Press.

Wakabayashi, B. (1991), *Anti-foreignism and Western Learning in Early-Modern Japan: The New Theses of 1825*, Cambridge, MA: Harvard University Press.

Yoshikawa Kojiro (1983) *Jinsai, Sorai, Norinaga: Three Classical Philologists of Mid-Tokugawa Japan*, trans. Kikuchi Yuji, Tokyo: The Institute of Eastern Culture.

MARK TEEUWEN

Confucianism in Japan, post-Meiji

The term 'Confucian philosophy' is used to distinguish philosophical Confucianism from State Confucianism and Confucianism as a way of life. While State Confucianism refers to an official, rather oppressive ideology supportive of state power, Confucianism as a way of life means a mix of everyday morality and popular Confucius cult. State Confucianism originated in Han times (206 BCE–220 CE). Popular Confucianism reflects

State Confucianism in its emphasis on role ethics and unconditional obedience.

As to Confucian philosophy, one must distinguish different schools, teachings, movements and personalities. Often the respective teachings contradict each other even on a fundamental level. This is especially true with regard to classic Confucianism (which developed between approximately 520 and 230 BCE) and the Neo-Confucian School of Principle formed by **Zhu Xi** (known in Japan as Shushi, 1130–1200). In Tokugawa times (1600–1868) these two directions were reflected by the Kogaku-ha, the School of Ancient Learning, of Ito Jinsai (1627–1705) and Ogyu Sorai (1666–1728) on the one side, and Hayashi Razan's (1583–1657) Shushigaku on the other. While classic philosophy and the Kogaku-ha can be understood as rational and critical humanism, favourable to human rights ideas, Shushigaku is characterized by rather conservative and metaphysical doctrines. Instead of critical loyalty and critical **filial piety**, it supported unconditional obedience. While according to classical Confucianism, *dao* (in Japanese, *do* or *michi*, the Way) and *ren* (in Japanese, *jin*, humanity) are more important than a subject's loyalty toward his sovereign or government, and more important than unconditional filial piety, the Shushigaku was inclined to the opposite view. Also, because of its doctrine that man and his behaviour ought to be a perfect realization of *li* (in Japanese, *ri*, principle), with *li* being a fixed though rather elusive ontological and cosmological concept, Shushigaku was a hindrance to socio-political change. Finally, whereas classic Confucianism, as put forward in the *Lunyu* (known in Japan as *Rongo*, the *Analects*, or *Words of Confucius*), the *Mencius* (*Moshi*), and especially the *Xunzi* (*Junshi*), distinguished between the way of nature and the way of man, and between is and ought, Shushigaku did not, and thus again favoured the status quo and totalitarian government. It was because of such characteristics that philosophers like **Nishi** Amane (1829–97) and **Fukuzawa** Yukichi (1834–1901) regarded Shushigaku as responsible for what they called Japanese servility, and sharply condemned it. They also realized that the abstruse metaphysics of Shushigaku was incompatible with modern science. Accordingly, during the first years of the Meiji era, Shushigaku played no important role.

Even with regard to the idea that a 'Japanese morality' should be preserved, up till about 1890, the declaration of the *Imperial Edict on Education*, classic Confucian ethics proved more influential. In particular, it strengthened the inclinations toward an affirmative **philosophy of human rights**.

The decline of Shushigaku was especially apparent from the following developments. Official Shushigaku schools and institutions were abolished; until 1917, no further *sekiten*, or traditional Confucian ceremonies, were performed, and for several years Confucian teachings played no role at all in official educational curricula. However, when the view became influential that Westernization, and hence egoism, material interests and liberalism, had gained undue strength, the ideas of unconditional loyalty and piety came to the fore again, though no notable efforts were made to revive Shushigaku ontology, cosmology and epistemology. This approach reflected the maxim of 'Eastern morality, Western technology'. As has been pointed out, it also followed 'the general pattern of the retreat of religion [belief] before science in the West'. Part of this development was the foundation of new Confucian societies, the first of which, the Shibunkai, was established in 1880. This society was supported by members of the imperial family. Finally, in 1882, a department for Chinese classics was established at Toyko University.

From Meiji times, Confucian philosophy as ontology and philosophy of nature became obsolete, while it continued to play a role as a resource for ethical and political theory. Whereas in the years up to about 1890, classic Confucianism, especially the *Mencius*, was influential, later Shushigaku-like thought and the norm of unconditional loyalty were emphasized once more. With the victory of kokutai ideology in the 1930s (see **kokutai ideology since Meiji times**), classical Confucianism could no longer openly exert any influence. Throughout Japanese philosophical and political history, the justification by Mencius (372?–289? BCE) of tyrannicide was a hotly debated issue. Mostly, this justification was condemned as Chinese, foreign and non-Japanese, but there were also cases of approval. Thus, developments since Meiji did not significantly deviate from traditional positions. What was particular about Confucian ethics and political theory since Meiji times were the following features.

First, Confucian ethics served as an additional, quasi-indigenous motive for the defence of human rights and the quasi- or proto-democratic idea that the people are the foundation (though not the ruler) of the nation. The last idea figures prominently in the *Mencius* and *Xunzi*. During Meiji and Taisho times (1912–26), Yoshino Sakuzo (1878–1933) and others formulated a distinction between *minshushugi* and *minponshugi*, with the former term meaning 'government *by* the people', and the latter 'government *for* the people', or more precisely, 'government which takes [the interest of] the people as a basis'. Only the latter was regarded as compatible with the idea that all sovereignty rests with the *tenno*. Yoshino also pointed out that 'the way' (*do* or *michi*) is 'a sort of limitation on the free exercise of sovereignty'. By saying this, Yoshino meant that the rules of universal morality and humanity (as formulated within classic Confucianism) restrict the freedom of governments and rulers.

Second, in its Shushigaku version, Confucianism was utilized as an alternative to what was denounced as Western immorality and decadence, namely individualism (which was equated with egoism), disputatiousness and lack of spiritualism. This approach often implied a wilful identification of the neo-Confucian notion of humane government (*wang dao*; in Japanese, *odo*, the 'way of the [ancient] kings') with the 'Japanese' way of the gods (*shinto*) and the 'Japanese' way of the emperor (*kodo*), and finally even with the traditional 'Japanese spirit' (*Nihon seishin, Yamato damashii*) and *kokutai*. Among those who followed, or sympathized with, the first line of thought were Nishi Amane, **Tsuda Mamichi** (1821–1903) and **Nishimura** Shigeki (1828–1902), though the latter in particular was by no means in favour of 'Westernization'. As to the second line of Confucian thought, a revival of a Shushigaku-like conservative ethics, Motoda Eifu (1818–91), who lectured to the Meiji emperor, and **Inoue** Tetsujiro (1855–1944) were particularly influential. Among those who conceived of themselves as Confucians but explicitly denounced the 'Chinese revolutionary theory' (*Shina kakumei ron*) as incompatible with *kokutai* and the Japanese way of

government, were Shionoya On (1878–), Nakamura Kyushiro and Iijima Tadao (1875–1954).

Other Confucian scholars like Hattori Unokochi (1867–1939), Ichimura Sanjiro (1868–1947) and Uno Tetsuto tried to develop a Confucian middle way between human rights thought and democracy on the one hand, and Shushigaku ethics on the other, emphasizing for instance traditional Confucian humanity, but also communitarism, familiarism and role ethics.

In the years after the Second World War, Confucian philosophy did not play a significant role. Confucian studies were primarily carried out by university sinologists focusing on historical and philological investigations. Though they produced fine editions, translations and interpretations of, for example, the *Lunyu*, *Mencius*, and *Xunzi* which are valuable material for philosophical discussion, it was perhaps only with the world-wide success of modern Neo-Confucianism which started in the 1980s that Confucian ethics became a prominent issue again. Respective discussions again focus on such questions as whether Confucian ethics constitute a set of distinctively Asian values, whether such values provide a viable alternative to Western ethics, or whether they are compatible with the idea of universal human rights. As elsewhere, in Japan all kinds of answers are given.

See also: Japanese philosophy, post-Meiji times

Further reading

Motoda Eifu (1912) *Lectures Delivered in the Presence of His Imperial Majesty the Emperor of Japan by the Late Baron Motoda*, extracts from a translation by N. Asaji and J. Pringle, *Transactions of the Asiatic Society of Japan*, Vol. XL.

Shively, D. (1959) *Motoda Eifu: Confucian Lecturer to the Meiji Emperor: Confucianism in Action*, ed. D. Nivison and A. Wright, Stanford, CA: Stanford University Press, 302–33.

Smith, W. (1973) *Confucianism in Modern Japan: A Study of Conservatism in Japanese Intellectual History*, Tokyo: Hokuseido Press.

GREGOR PAUL

Confucianism in Korea

History

The historical origin of the arrival of Confucianism in Korea is not certain. In Koguryo, T'aehak, the National Academy of Confucianism, was established in the fourth century CE, which signifies that Confucianism was highly advanced by then. In Silla, the National Academy was established in the seventh century CE, and the Confucian classics were the main texts of study. Hwarang, the elite youth corps of Silla, learned the Confucian virtues of **humaneness**, **righteousness**, propriety, filial piety and loyalty from the Confucian classics.

In ancient Confucianism, **filial piety** was more important than loyalty. But when filial piety, which is the key virtue in family ethics, is expanded to the nation, it becomes loyalty. Hwarang embraced the Buddhist and Daoist ideas as well, but the Confucian ideas of filial piety and loyalty were also essential aspects of the Hwarang ideology, which became the powerful spirit in unifying the Three Kingdoms.

Since Buddhism was the main religion during the Koryo dynasty, Confucianism was not promoted. But during the Choson dynasty, Confucianism, especially Neo-Confucianism, became the official philosophy and religion of the state and the Confucian virtues, especially filial piety and loyalty, were promoted. And there was a great emphasis on the Five Human Relationships, that is, ideal, orderly and harmonious relationships between father and son, between ruler and minister, between husband and wife, between elder brother and younger brother, and between friends. The theory of human nature advanced by the great Neo-Confucian philosophers of the sixteenth century, especially Yi Hwang (**Yi T'oegye**) and Yi I (**Yi Yulgok**), became the metaphysical basis of the above ethical ideas.

The Confucian ethical ideas such as filial piety, loyalty, propriety and rituals were social and political in nature, practice, and implications. Violations of these ethical principles and ideals were often considered as criminal acts and resulted in punishments. The rulers of the Choson dynasty embraced the Confucian moral ideals of benevolence, justice, propriety and wisdom, and adopted

them as the governing principles of the nation. By instituting the examination system for the government officials, the idea of just government was promoted. The ideal of the scholar-official, who dedicates his life for the nation's public service with virtue and knowledge, was the standard tradition in Korean Confucianism. In Korea during the Koryo and Choson periods, there had also been the beautiful and lofty ideal of the *sonbi*, the virtuous **scholar** for public service without government positions.

Some Korean Confucians thought that the rituals of Shamanism and Daoism were superstitious and harmful to the people. The fourteenth-century Confucian scholar Chong To-jon claimed that Buddhism neglected and undermined family, ethics and national values, especially filial piety and loyalty. During the eighteenth and nineteenth centuries, Korean Confucian philosophers and the government regarded Roman Catholicism as a heretical religion, mainly because of its alien idea regarding ancestor worship. The Catholic teaching of the equality of all men before God was also contrary to the Confucian idea of the Five Human Relationships, which is basically hierarchical.

The political mood of the Choson government under Taewon'gun, King Kojong's father, was strongly anti-Catholic, because Roman Catholicism was linked to the military force of Western powers and extremely dangerous to national security. The prevailing attitude of the Choson rulers was 'defending orthodoxy and rejecting heterodoxy'. In this case, orthodoxy meant Confucianism and heterodoxy was Catholicism. When the Choson dynasty collapsed under the Imperial Japanese conquest and the Koreans lost national sovereignty, the national spirit of loyalty cultivated by Confucianism was exercised by all Koreans. Many patriots fought against Imperial Japan as their expression of loyalty for the preservation of the nation. Thus, Confucianism contributed to the development of the consciousness of national self-identity and national value.

The impact of Confucian ethics has been very significant in Korean history. Even today the Confucian ideas of the Five Human Relationships and ancestor worship constitute an important part of Korean culture. These ideas and practices have been weakened significantly because of Western influences, including the democratic ideas of equality and freedom, and the Christian idea of prohibiting or discouraging ancestor worship. The Confucian value system, based on the ideas of humaneness, justice, propriety and wisdom, and on the ideals of filial piety and loyalty, is still an important part of the value system for many Koreans.

The political and social idea of democracy has brought a revolutionary change in modern Korean society. Thus, the traditional hierarchical idea of the Five Human Relationships is undoubtedly weakened and needs a modified interpretation in the light of the principle of equality inherent in democracy. However, even under democracy, parents are to be respected and honoured by their children. Even today there should be humaneness, justice and propriety within all types and all levels of human relationships. The positive spirit of Confucian ethics transcends time and space and cultures, although social and political systems may change and the concrete application of these ethical ideals may need modifications according to time, place and cultures.

See also: Christianity, Korean

Further reading

Choung, H. and Han, H. (ed.) (1996) *Confucian Philosophy in Korea*, Seongnam: The Academy of Korean Studies.

de Bary, W. and Haboush, J. (eds) (1985) *The Rise of Neo-Confucianism in Korea*, New York: Columbia University Press.

Deuchler, M. (1992) *The Confucian Transformation of Korea*, Cambridge, MA: Council on East Asian Studies, Harvard University.

Lee, P. (ed.) (1993) *Sourcebook of Korean Civilization*, Vol. 2, New York: Columbia University Press, 113–17, 272ff, 306ff, 551ff.

YONG-CHOON KIM

Confucius and Confucianism

Confucianism traces itself back to **Confucius** (551–479 BCE) and was known as the tradition of the *ru* (**scholar**), a term which once had the meaning of 'weakling'. Born into the then disintegrating Zhou feudal rule, Confucius was the defender of the ideal of the classical Zhou against the potential threat of barbarism, as the nomads from the west were again knocking at the gates. Confucius extended Zhou enlightenment, especially the call by **Heaven** for virtue beyond the ruler to all humanity. The golden age of early Zhou rule was based on the institutions of '**rites** and **music**' set down by the Duke of Zhou during his regency. To these, Confucius added the Zhou collection of songs and documents – the Classics of Rites, Music, Odes and History – which became the cornerstones of his curriculum (see **Classics and Books**). In releasing this knowledge, once meant only for the sons of nobles (*junzi*, the gentleman), to anyone desiring to learn, Confucius remade the Way of the nobles (called *ren*, as distinct from the commoners called *min*) into a life of virtue for all. *Ren* (the excellence that comes with being a man, i.e. **humaneness**) became the concept of the highest good. Confucius also extended the notion of ritual life – once the *noblesse oblige* that is not required of the common people who were to be ruled by the threat of punishment instead – so that all of life is to be an arena, a theatre, for all to perfect the proper deportment so as to bring forth the highest good. Thus was born China's classical humanism, an ethos of truthful moderation that is not reliant on a faith in the gods or some fear of the spirits. It is not a secular humanism because the good that man does is moved by the Will of Heaven and tied to the structure of a moral universe.

Confucius's life also changed the way in which that will was perceived and how the Way should be implemented. Of low noble birth and with no imperial claim or design, Confucius nonetheless felt personally called by Heaven and put on a mission to rectify the world. As a result, he toured the various states in hope of gaining patronage to re-enact what his role model, the Duke of Zhou had done before: to counsel, advise, and institute anew a rite-based order. Failing to be heard, Confucius returned home and retired into a life of teaching, becoming the first teacher and popular educator to found a school of thought that heralded the age of the philosophers. His life became a paradigmatic life for his followers; it marked the beginning of a new, existential understanding of human nature and destiny. Born with a gift from a moral heaven, human duty is to be truthful to our innermost being: to bring accord to our family and step by step, to society at large; to be a man of letters, a vessel of culture, and a counsel to rulers; and, in the footsteps of the master, be a teacher of the Way and a member of an academy. Following Confucius in the Warring States period were **Mencius** (371–289? BCE) and **Xunzi** (*fl.* 298–238 BCE), each giving his own distinct interpretation to Confucius's legacy.

Of the hundred schools of thought that flowered in that age of the philosophers, Confucianism like others suffered the 'burning of the books' under the Qin. Instigated by the Legalists, that policy was meant to ensure ideological consensus under the First Emperor. Enough Confucian scholars survived that purge to allow the Classics to be orally retrieved during the next dynasty. The Han Emperor Wu had professors (those well versed in the texts) of the Five Classics summoned, tested and appointed to official posts as the 'scholar officials' in the imperial administration. By then, Han Confucianism had taken in much of the cosmological speculations of the *yin–yang* and **Five Elements** school founded previously by **Zou Yan** (305–240 BCE). Such prognostic arts had not been banned during the burning of the books. Wedding that *yin–yang* cosmocentrism to the Confucian homocentrism was the achievement of **Dong Zhongshu** (*c.*179–104 BCE). This *yin–yang* Confucianist worked out a system of cosmo-ethical correspondence between Man and Heaven. With that 'law of nature' decoded, he could offer reasons for the succession of dynasties and derive moral lessons from the omens or auspices of nature, and justify the institutions for ordering society.

Dong became the ideologue of the new Han rule. He also set into motion the commentary tradition known as the *wei* apocrypha to go with the ching of the classics. The word *jing*, for 'classics', is literally the 'warp' of a fabric; the 'woof' that crisscross the 'warp' in a woven cloth is called *wei*. So when these early writings were called or given the status of *jing*, the assumption is that there is a set of commentaries (*wei*) to go along with it. Dong tapped the *yin–yang* Five Elements cosmology to help 'make sense' of the (hidden meanings in the) Classic-s. This opened the door to the *wei* (now called apocrypha) to flourish as a growing body of elemental and prognostication commentaries on the **Classics**. Yang Xiong (53 BCE–18 CE) later offered an innovative reading of this Han Confucian cosmology and Wang Chong (b. 27 CE) became the outspoken critic of the many unfounded superstitions within the system. In becoming the official religion or state ideology, *yin–yang* Confucianism also courted its own collapse when the order it supported itself faltered and ended in 220 CE. Not until the Song dynasty did the Neo-Confucians effect a classical revival and renaissance of sorts.

Further reading

Creel, H. (1949) *Confucius: The Man and the Myth*, New York: J. Day.
Fingarette, H. (1972) *Confucius: The Secular as Sacred*, New York: Harper & Row.
Henderson, J. (1984) *The Development and Decline of Chinese Cosmology*, New York: Columbia University Press.

WHALEN LAI

conscience

Mencius argued that man has an innate knowledge of what is right and wrong. No socialization is required; even a recluse in the hills when he witnesses good knows it is good. The Northern Song masters Zhang Zai (1020–77) and the Cheng brothers honoured this innate sense of virtue. After **Zhu Xi** stressed the analytical function of mind and focused on acquiring knowledge and accumulating learning, it was left to Wang Yangming in the Ming dynasty to underscore that innate moral sense once more. Out of the four beginnings of the mind in Mencius, Wang took above all to the mind of wisdom. For him, this 'mind that knows right from wrong' would also act instinctively to do good. Zhu Xi's reading of *kewu* as 'investigation of things' became in Wang the 'rectification of human affairs'; the goal is not to 'acquire objective knowledge' about the principle of things but to 'extend that precognition of the good'. That inborn moral sense is conscience.

Following Wang, the left-wing Taizhou school chose as its first order of business to awake this 'good mind'. It brought the message to the unlettered (literally the 'foolish') men and women as part of its programme to reach the masses, but also to demonstrate how that moral sense is inborn and requires no elite learning. Since Wang's favourite term, 'knowledge of the good', still sounded too cerebral, the school popularized the expression the 'good heart'. It is not some 'moral reason' but rather a 'moral passion' that can move even the unlettered to this spontaneous outpouring of a heart-felt concern. Following Wang Yangming's advice in a short treatise on education to the effect that children and the young in general should not be overly restrained by **rites** but rather be induced into appropriate action by ditties and rhymes, the Taizhou school spread its teaching by drawing on simple, everyday analogies, often accompanied by folk music and song, including Chan-like antics. This emotionally charged pedagogy evoked the same in kind from the awoken 'conscience' of the audience. Tears and joy marked some of these open-air evangelical meetings held in open fields.

See also: education in China, philosophy of

Further reading

Ching, J. (1972) *Philosophical Letters of Wang Yang-ming/Wang Yangming*, Camberra: Australian National University Press.

WHALEN LAI

conventional existence

What is a conventional existence, and what are its criteria? **Tsongkhapa** felt that the grounding of the conventional world, i.e. the world of everyday experience, within a valid framework is critical for the Madhyamika if he is to be successful in not falling into ontological nihilism. On this view, although one rejects any absolute status to such a system of validity, it does not entail that anything goes. The principles of **logic** such as consistency and empirical laws such as causality must be accorded a status of validity that is defensible within a framework that may ultimately be revealed to be provisional. Thus Tsongkhapa developed the following three criteria of conventional existence: (1) that the thing in question is an object of a conventional knowledge; (2) that the object thus known is not liable to be invalidated by some other valid conventional knowledge; and finally (3) the object thus known must not be negated by any reasoning that probes into the way things really are, that is, at the ultimate level. For example, a snake is an object of a valid cognition; unlike the perception of a coiled rope as a snake, the perception of snake is not invalidated by another instance of a valid cognition. Furthermore, the analysis that searches into the snake's ultimate existential status – whether or not the snake exists by means of its intrinsic being – does not negate the snake's existence.

In his latter works Tsongkhapa has chosen to use an 'eliminative argument' rather than the above three criteria to establish the validity of conventional existence. He has argued that existence could make sense either on the ultimate level, where things and events can be thought to possess some intrinsic being, or on the conventional level, where things and events are found to possess an ontological status that is constructed by language and thought. By eliminating the first position on the grounds that any notion of ultimacy to existence is untenable, Tsongkhapa concludes that the only notion of existence that can be made sensible must remain 'conventional'. One could thus say that Tsongkhapa's ontological theory is a form of 'conventional realism' in that it accords a high degree of reality to the world of everyday experience, yet that reality remains firmly limited to a framework which ultimately remains conventional. Tsongkhapa's conventional realism has been an object of major criticism by subsequent Tibetan thinkers such as Taktsang Lotsawa (b. 1405), Karmapa Mikyo Dorje and **Gendun Chophel**.

Further reading

Tauscher, H. (1992). 'Controversies in Tibetan Madhyamaka Exegesis: sTag stan Lotsaba's Critique of Tsoukhapa's Assertions of Validly Established Phenomena', *Etudes Asiatiques* 46(1): 297–306.

THUPTEN JINPA

correlative thinking

Western rational analysis has been contrasted with Chinese correlative thinking, the sort of thinking which involves comparing different kinds of ideas as opposed to deriving conclusions from a set of premises. Correlative thinking is based on the idea of a set of cosmic correlations among things classified under the same categories within the system of the **Five Elements**. For example, the five internal organs of the body are spleen (wood), lung (fire), heart (earth), liver (metal), kidney (water); for the five grains, the corresponding set would be wheat, beans, panicled millet, hemp and millet; and for the five virtues, benevolence, wisdom, faith, righteousness and decorum. Based on the principle of like/dislike or attraction/repulsion, the lungs in theory would be strengthed by a diet of beans and weakened by excess millet consumption, even to the benefit or detriment of a person's moral fibre. It is the same principle as that in the pre-science of Alchemy. Mars and Venus (stars) would affect male and female (humanity) because of their correlative (male/female, water/fire) alignment. Correlative thinking allows such (unscientific) liberal crossings (interactions) between different classes or species of entities: there is, to us today, no necessary link between the green wood of spring and how that might affect our spleen and our sense of benevolence (**humaneness**). The correlative linkages are merely 'metaphorical', like feeling greater well-being towards our fellows on a rosy spring day after a harsh winter.

Since much of medieval European thought (in particular, theology and alchemy) was also correlational, that East/West contrast of traditional versus modern thought is rather suspect. There are two issues here: continuity and departure. To what extent did correlative thinking contribute to, and at what point did it impede the development of certain areas of modern science? It is clear that Chinese science was at one point more advanced, that empirical experiments and verifications mattered, and that certain areas of Chinese science are still of value. It is also clear that the correlative paradigm has its limitations; it works well up to a point, but if it remains unchanged then it is an obstacle to further developments. The other issue has to do with differences in correlative systems

and the different ends they are made to serve. By itself, correlative thinking could be mechanistic, atomistic and pluralistic (for example, **Samkhya** and **Abhidharma**) or it could be organic, dynamic and monistic. Chinese correlative thinking inclines more towards the fluid synthesis of the latter.

A case in point is **Mencius**'s peculiar use of 'deduction' at retrieving the hidden 'major premise' in Chinese thought. Deduction is translated into Chinese as 'pushing forward the principle'. In Mencius, that goes not just forward but also upward. The sight of broken tiles, notes Mencius, stirs men to pity. Why? Because 'likeness in kind stirs pity'. But we are not like tiles; they do not even suffer when broken. Yet oneness with all things, which is a principle defended by Mencius, meant that it is also not in the original nature of the tile to be broken (not one). Reality is one Whole. Fragmentation is contrary to nature. Therefore, a broken tile saddens our heart. From that sadness, Mencius deduces; that is, he pushes the principle forward and upward, which is to be contrasted with concluding in a gross materialist way that we are dead matter like tiles, but which rather leaves us on a moral high ground. When **Heaven** gives birth to all things, it intends them to be all good. It is man's task to see to it that it be made whole. Mencian deduction backtracks; it serves to retrieve the cosmogonic Oneness.

Mencius's peculiar use of deduction (extending the principle or rationale) relies on poetic metaphor, so incidents in nature can be cited to support a moral norm and projected upwards so as to end up in Heaven. An example would be 'water naturally seeks its own level'; in the same way, human nature (which is naturally sympathetic to the suffering of other men) should also be allowed to flourish naturally for its end (the teleology of humaneness). This is how Heaven (which gives birth to all things) would intend it to be.

The discourse of Mencius is poetic; it is a rhetoric that stirs hearts and moves minds, not a Mohist logic in dry prose, not clear definitions and unambiguous signs. For all the Abhidharmic analyticity Indian Buddhism would later teach China, Chinese Buddhists eventually fell back on a correlative logic and an argument via analogy, so that the Neo-Confucians who came after would also 'investigate things so as to extend knowledge'. They investigated the principle of things and extended moral knowledge by deducing, as Mencius did, that there is only One Principle (of morality) informing the world of the multiple manifestations (of the facts).

One should note that Mencius predated the systematization of the theory of the Five Elements. He used analogies to cut across the categories of kind and the hierarchies of genus, species and family; he did not schematize these into correlative sets. Yet, despite recent doubts to the contrary, the allegation that the Mencian school inspired the correlative mapping of the five virtues may not be groundless. Mencius did deduce moral lessons from nature. He prefers organic (nurture) metaphors over mechanical (constructive) ones favoured by Mohists and **Xunzi**. He compared cultivating the self to cultivating young seedlings: it is foolish to hasten maturation, that is like tugging at a plant to make it taller. By conjoining Man and Heaven – the goodwill of Heaven is the innate good in Man – Mencius assumes a macrocosmic/microcosmic correspondence that is basic to the operation of the Five Elements. Analogical argument fuels correlative thinking even as the latter, by trying to be overly schematic, also erodes the poetic power of its original rhetoric.

correlative thinking: macrocosm, microcosm

A basic element in any correlative system of thought, macrocosm and microcosm sets up a correspondence between the two cosmic ends. There are, for example, 365 bones in the body to go with the 365 days of the year, suporting the Han cosmo-humanism or the ideal 'unity of heaven and man'. The medieval counterpart to that Han ideal would be the cosmo-buddhism of Huayan philosophy. The telescoping of the All into the One may make for spiritual liberation, but in social philosophy, that usually translates into the 'sacrificing of the lesser self in order to complete the greater self'. An example would be sacrificing oneself for the family; or the family for the state. In that case, the individual self is the lesser self, the family is the larger self; so being a son to a father who is greater than one has precedence over duty to oneself. In English, this would be a self sacrifice 'for the

greater good'. The European Enlightenment undercut both traditional options.

Further reading

Wu Kuang-ming (1997) *On Chinese Body Thinking: A Cultural Hermeneutic*, Leiden: Brill.
Yearley, L.(1990) *Mencius and Aquinas: Theories of Virtue and Conceptions of Courage*, Albany, NY: State University of New York Press.

WHALEN LAI

cosmology: creation

Does China have the idea of a Creator? **Zhuangzi** suggests at one point that there is a 'creator' who 'made things' the way things are. There are also myths about a creatrix who fashioned men out of mud on a potter's wheel; about a primeval chaos that slowly congealed into visible shapes; about a primeval giant being sacrificed and dissected in order to make up different parts of the world; or the same giant incubating inside a World Egg which he then pushed apart, one half up into what became heaven and one half down into what become earth. In the search for a metaphysical root metaphor that would account for the difference between China and the West, there are recent attempts to make the emergence of form from a formless but potent **chaos** the Chinese distinction. This positive survival of chaos into order has then been contrasted with creation *ex nihilo* to yield a refinement of an earlier characterization of China knowing an 'aesthetic continuum' of dynamic Becoming.

China is sometimes characterized as stressing dynamic Becoming instead of static Being. Becoming is common to 'lunar' worldviews. The poem 'Questions to Heaven' (found in the collection called *Songs of the South*), asks: 'What virtue (*de*) has the moon, the bright of night, that waxes and wanes?' The answer is: precisely as it changes, it claims that potency. The query however came from a time when solar values became dominant. The sun is constant; and virtue comes to be identified with constancy. The moon is then deemed fickle: if so, what virtue may it claim? This episode shows that China knew as much about the constancy of the sun (Being) as she did the potent mutability of the moon (Becoming). It is how that juxtaposition was handled that may distinguish her metaphysics. For those intrigued more by the liminal, her mystique lies not so much in Becoming or Chaos (as contrasted to Being and Order) but what is inbetween: the myth of the One-Legged and the crux and pivot that is *ji*, the **trigger** point.

But is cosmogony really definitive as a root metaphor for a culture? Some thinkers (like Mircea Eliade) regard cosmogonic myths to be fundamental; others (like Claude Lévi-Strauss) are more concerned with how the world is classified. Speculative cosmic beginnings (systematizations like Hesiod's *Theogony*) came late. But systems of classification affect actual daily social behaviour. The relative weight given to that affects how Chinese cosmogony is read. Interest in misty beginnings seems to come from South China, the home of the chaos myth. It appears only once in the classical texts, in the *Zhuangzi*. The only other reference is to a king who puffed up with pride shot at a blood sack hung on a tree. Is that a symbol of a prior Heaven – as chaos – or a token of a fetus?

Astrology in North China puts more energy into developing a **logic** as compared with a system of classification. The two systems – cosmogony and classification – then came together in Han times. When systematized, we have an evolutionary scheme: from the One (Great Ultimate) came the Two (*yin–yang*) and then the Three or the Four, or Eight, and eventually all things. A notion of the continuum ensures that the primal One is embedded somewhere still in the Many. Often before the One there is a notion of a prior nebulous chaos. The degree of materiality assigned to the origin depends on the commentatorial tradition. Han thought favoured the One as **ether**; **Neo-Daoism** introduced the One as **non-being** and as principle; the Buddhists took to the One and introduced the Pleroma, the notion of the fullness of being. Once properly qualified, a general East/West contrast is not impossible.

Further reading

Eliade, M. (1959) *Cosmos and History: The Myth of the Eternal Return*, trans. W. Trask, New York: Harper.

Hawkes, D. (trans.) (1985) *Ch'u Tz'u: The Songs of the South: An Ancient Chinese Anthology*, Harmondsworth: Penguin.

WHALEN LAI

cosmology: the flood

The deluge is not a philosophical topic but it touches on the structure of the cosmos, the image of the **sage** or hero, and the measure for space and time, enough to play an important role in Chinese thought. Chinese cosmography assumes that the land mass is resting precariously on a bottomless body of primeval waters, such that the threat of flooding came not so much from torrential rain falling from above (as in the Bible, though there is a motif of water cascading from lunar mountains) but rather from water oozing up from below to above ground.

This in turn is tied to the nature of the earth diver myth, found around the Pacific from where it then spreads into continental Eurasia and into the inland lakes of the Native Americans. Earth divers were gods, animals or humans who dived into the primeval ocean to fish up a bit of mud that then grew into the first land in the middle of overwhelming waters. In China, the Sage-King Yu ('fish, dragon') became the Chinese Noah, while his father Gun ('Ur-fish, turtle') was the earth diver. This demigod of a turtle failed only because, at the last minute, the Lord of Heaven snatched back the magical earth he allegedly stole (with a swallow from on high). This turtle and its accomplice, a bird, have survived in Han tomb decorations as an owl riding on the back of a serpentine turtle amidst rolling waves. (In Japan, the creative couple Izanagi and Izanami dipped instead of dived for earth to create the divine islands.) The earth so created may then rest on a turtle (India adds an elephant) or, in Japan, on a giant, slumbering catfish (which causes earthquakes when it tosses in its sleep). Earth divers often die for their effort: Gun was executed, while the misbehaving raven in native northwestern American myths (it flapped its wings and ruffled flat land into mountains) was killed.

As aspects of the Great Goddess, turtles, frogs, snakes, birds, and fish decorated prehistoric pottery in China and elsewhere. Such chthonic demigods then receded to the background with the rise of sky gods such as the cult of Heaven in China. The first chapter of the **Zhuangzi**, entitled 'Free and Easy Wandering', recalls that a giant fish called Kun (an alias of Gun) in the North Sea transformed itself into a giant roc ('companion of the wind', an alias of the owl). It rose and flew all the way to the South Sea. In the full myth, the bird, after diving into the South Sea, would turn back into that giant fish, which would swim underground all the way to the north in order to complete a cycle. This makes up a dance-in-the-round of dragon (fish) and phoenix (bird). Zhuangzi turned his abbreviated version of the myth into an analogy of expansive freedom, the Daoist 'true man' can rove with ease in the cosmos, travelling far. He contrasted it with the tiny hop of the cicada or the petty world of an owl or the tunnel vision of a frog at the bottom of a well (i.e. the turtle in the subterranean sea). Elsewhere though, this free-spirited thinker turned down an offer of office, saying that he would rather be like the turtle dragging its tail in the mud, a hidden reference to the earth diver Gun.

The flood myth in China has local variants. The giant Gong Gong (an alias of Gun) was the hero in the North or West, but was vilified for his pride in the Chinese Centre, while in the East, the flood was tied to a solar child orphaned in a hollow mulberry, and in the South to a cult of a second creation of mankind under a female creatrix. The Chinese Classic preserves the version of the Centre. **Mozi** idealized Sage-King Yu, son of Gun. A people's hero, this tireless Noah battled the Flood on behalf of all mankind. In the nine years of his Herculean labour, he passed by his home thrice but never once went inside. A clear violation of Confucian etiquette, this probably egged Mencius on to champion Shun, the Confucian **Sage-King** who lived at an earlier time. Exemplary in his **filial piety** and brotherly love, Shun never blamed his evil father or punished his murderous half-brother even though the pair plotted to kill him.

Further reading

Boltz, W. (1981) 'Kung Kung and the Flood: Reversed Euhemerism in the Yao Tien', *T'oung Pao* 67: 3–5.

Dundee, A. (ed.) (1984) *Sacred Narratives*, Berkeley, CA: University of California Press.

Gimbutas, M. (1982) *The Goddesses And Gods Of Old Europe: Myths And Cult Images 6500–3500 B.C.*, Berkeley, CA and Los Angeles: University of California Press.

Girardot, N. (1983) *Myth and Meaning in Early Taoism/Daoism*, Berkeley, CA: University of California Press.

WHALEN LAI

cosmology: myths of sun, moon and star

Before there was philosophy, there was myth. Some early Chinese myths of sun, moon and stars had a great influence on later philosophy. For example, the sage-king Shun is famous for his **filial piety**. His devotion was put to the test by an evil father and a murderous half-brother. His father, the Blind Man, sent Shun up the barn which was then set on fire. Shun escaped by flying down to safety, using his bamboo hat as wings. Then his evil brother Xiang (Elephant) tricked him into going down the well, the exit of which he then blocked with stones. Shun somehow discovered an underground passageway and made it back home just when Xiang was about to take possession of his goods and his two wives. This is a disguised solar myth. Shun ('eminent and beautiful') is the Sun. His father, the Blind Man, is Night; Night chasing Day translates into the Blind Man (north) pushing Shun, the morning sun (east), to climb up the sky. By high noon (south) the sun sets the world (the barn) ablaze, and in the afternoon, the sun as a winged sun-bird sets down (in the west). Sinking below the horizon (going down the well) by dusk, the sun reaches the subterranean ocean which it crossed (midnight, north) in order to reappear above ground (return home) the next morning. **Mencius** had to dispose of other versions of this myth – involving vengeance – to preserve the orthodox one advocating filial piety.

Lunar myths abound in early China. The waxing and the waning of the moon has been said to be the inspiration behind the *Book of Changes*, the word 'change' (*yi*) being possibly a combination of 'sun + moon'. The classic Chinese myth of *hubris* involves the giant Guafu, who chased the sun. He came so close to it that in his thirst, he drank first from the Yellow River and then the Wei River, and was heading for the Great Pool when he died. His walking stick, which he discarded, later turned into a peach forest. This giant has been mocked for 'not knowing the limits of his strength' (his overstepping his bounds) ever since. Upon a closer look, he is a Chinese lunar Icarus. His name suggests a lunar giant, Gua meaning both 'to cut, to diminish' as well as 'to expand, to boast': he waxes and wanes like the moon. In chasing the sun, he went from the Yellow River delta (east), upstream (south), reaching the Wei at the river bend (west), before turning towards the Great Pool (north), which is the daily path of the sun and the moon. He died in the northwest, where monthly the moon shrinks down to a crescent, disappearing from the night sky for three nights (in due north), only to reappear in the northeast as the new moon. Northwest is the site of a mountain called 'Failing to Complete the Round' (the dying moon); northeast is the site of a small hillock called 'Inauspicious Bovine' (the new moon, moon being bovine). The resurrection of the crippled (incomplete) moon is suggested by his walking stick (a dead branch) blooming anew into peach (solar) forest. But in the end, unlike the Christian West, China played down the sin of *hubris* and emphasized instead the flip side of this lunar myth, the tale of the Foolish Old Man who Moved Mountains. This tireless fellow defied and scared the gods by deciding to remove a mountain that blocked his way, scoop by scoop, generation after generation. Mao later rallied the people with this slogan of the 'Foolish Old Man who Moved Mountains' for his 'Great Leap Forward' to rapid industrialization, a costly failure.

The best loved stellar myth in China involves the Weaver and the Cowherd, the star-crossed lovers of Altair and Vega, two stellar constellations seen in the night sky on either side of the Milky Way. They move closer to one another on the night the Chinese celebrate the annual reunion of the pair as the Oxherd and the Weaver Stars. Separated by the Lord of Heaven for neglecting their chores (axiomatic for all Chinese peasantry),

they were allowed to meet once a year on the seventh night or the seventh moon when Altar and Vega move closest to one another. This celebration of 'love and work', a basic requirement for all healthy cultures, appears in Japan as the flawed marriage between Amaterasu the Sun Goddess, alias the Divine Weaver and her brother Susa-no-o, the God of Storm and of Husbandry which ended in a divorce. The covert conflict there between farmers and nomads in Japan does have or draw on a counterpart myth in the northwest Chinese frontier: the myth of the Silkworm Lady kidnapped by a Horse (Man) after it has been skinned.

For encoding a Chinese science of the heavens, the myth of another lunar giant Gong Gong is most telling. A God of Water (his name is of a raging flood; tides are lunar), he battled his nemesis, the God of Fire. Losing the fight, he knocked down the cosmic mountain holding up the sky in the northwest. As earth (floating on a subterranean ocean) was elevated to meet the fallen sky in that corner, the land also dipped downwards in the southeast (into the China Sea). Henceforth, the heavenly bodies all slide down towards the northwest while the rivers of China all flow down towards the southeast. The myth is based on a knowledge of geography and of how (in our terms) the tilt of the earth's axis influences the planes of rotations for the sun (around which the earth rotates), the moon (which rotates around the earth), and the stars (the galaxy that forms the backdrop to those movements).

See also: Five Elements; Yijing

Further reading

Birrell, A. (1993) *Chinese Mythology: An Introduction*, Baltimore, MD: John Hopkins University Press.
Girardot, N. and Major, J. (eds) (1985–6) 'Symposium Issue: Myth and Symbolism in Chinese Tradition', *Journal of Chinese Religions*, vols 13–14.
Lai, W. (1995) 'Unmasking the Filial Sage-King Shun: Oedipus at Anyang', *History of Religions* 33(2): 163–84.

WHALEN LAI

courage

Courage was the hallmark of the warrior in a heroic age, but was replaced by 'moral courage' as city mores replaced military ethics. Moral courage was championed by the demilitarized knights who became Confucian men of letters, but not so among the swordsmen or professional assassins. Some of these roving knights were given the prefix 'Mo' (from **Mohism**) as champions of the people. They were banned in the new order of the Han dynasty.

The magnate families that retained power down to the early part of the Tang dynasty still wore harmless ceremonial swords, but in the tenth century the founder of the Sung dynasty rewarded his generals with land grants but also stripped them of arms. A civil service examination targeting aspirants from the new gentry class was put in place, but from that time the literati (higher class) and the military (lower class) parted company. There developed two distinct career paths, with the military being drawn from mercenaries and increasingly from the rougher edges of society – one reason why the once noble *haofang* spirit was diluted by more self-serving partisanship. Later China produced the emasculated bookworm or 'white-faced' **scholar** civilians on the one hand, who were useful in times of peace, and on the other hand a potentially unruly military (thoroughly dangerous in times of chaos).

The code of the four classes lists first the *shi*, which denotes the scholar-official in China but the warrior *samurai* in Japan. (The *samurai* class later staffed governing posts under the peaceful Tokugawa regime.) But *shi* also described a class of knights during the Zhou dynasty, and the word *junzi/chun-tzu* (gentleman) referred to these well-armed sons of aristocrats. Courage in battle was also a primary virtue, like the virtue of *andrea* befitting the warrior in Homer's epics of war and conflict (*agon*). But with peace established in the city states, Greece trained bodies for the Olympic Games and China allocated the kill to the imperial hunt. When later the philosophers and their views became significant, a still higher Good was envisaged, and heroic courage was conceived as moral courage. The Confucian gentleman was still trained in 'archery and chariot driving', two of the six arts of the nobility. But Confucius put learning the *Odes* and the *Documents* (*Songs and History*) first, and helped transform the knight into a scholar, a man of culture committed to *ren* as the universal Good.

By the time of **Mencius**, the *shi* class looked forward to serving in government, becoming by the Han dynasty the career bureaucrats and scholar officials. For that, the Confucians were called *ru*, which meant 'weaklings'. Although Confucius once counted courage in a list of three virtues, it took a back seat to wisdom and humaneness. Prizing the wisdom of mind over the courage of physical strength, he dismissed feats of strength, noting how 'the man of humaneness will naturally possess courage', but not necessarily the other way around. He referred instead to moral courage. In the standard list of the five virtues that went with five human relationships, courage that would go with comrades in arms is not listed. Critical of his disciple Zilu, who 'loved *yung*' (courage, being prone to fight), Confucius predicted that Zilu would die a violent end (and he did). In contrast, the disciple who exemplified moral courage was Zengzi, whom Mencius classified as the bravest of all men, even though Zengzi was no fighter and would even cower before a lowborn nobody.

There is a Chinese tradition of valiant swordsmen living by a personal code of honour and dedicated to the public cause of justice. Called Mo Xia, they are loosely connected with the Mohist tradition, at least in spirit. It could be that Confucians were *déclassé* knights who traded the sword for a brush, whereas other *déclassé* knights kept their swords and played out new roles as personal retainers, paid assassins or these roving Mohist defenders of the weak. But when order returned, they were judged unruly and were duly banned by the Han state. They resurfaced, however, in later periods of **chaos**. The *Record of the Three Kingdoms* provided the setting for the later military saga, the *Romance of the Three Kingdoms*. The civil war of the Five Dynasties (the half-century between the Tang and the Song dynasty, 907–60) added a Buddhist touch; this is the time when Zen supposedly inspired various schools of the fighting arts. The weakened Song state that ended with the Mongolian conquest of China saw the last flowering of robust heroics that was reflected in the literature.

The favourite Chinese 'Robin Hood'-style tale is the *Water Margin*, which is set in that period and setting. Ming–Qing society was administered by scholar officials who had more brain than brawn. The vogue for 'swordsmen tales' in this period grew increasingly unrealistic, apolitical and escapist, and this persists into the modern kung-fu movies and the cult of Bruce Lee. But the *Water Margin* captures well the alternative ethos of this armed band. This brotherhood, made up of a displaced population turned bandits, held up a system of cultural values which was opposed to the orthodox Confucian ideology. Instead of hierarchic **filial piety** and loyalty defended by officials who were enthusiastic literati, it endorsed the sworn brotherhood of outlaws and swordsmen and their ethics of **humaneness** and **righteousness**: doing good and being just to one another, one for all, all for one.

The immovable mind in Mencius

In an exchange with **Gaozi** on the steadfastness that comes with having an 'immovable mind', **Mencius** cited three cases of courage showing the distribution of reason, passion and will in a subtle analysis of mind comparable to Plato's discourse on the tripartite psyche. First, there is courage due to passion. There is the case of Bokong Yu who would not accept a slight from anyone, be he of high or low status. Upon hearing of any reported injustice, he would rise up and strike out at that offensive party. So fired up was he with indignation that his courage came in the form of an irrepressible passion, a passion for righteousness that would not wait to act. That is bravery without a second thought, never pausing for rational reflection.

Second, there is the courage of will. Meng Shishe, another exemplary man of valour, also refused to weigh rationally the advantage and disadvantage of war. To do so before going into battle amounts to cowardice, for true courage is a matter of being indifferent to victory or defeat. So Meng would just 'psych' himself up into a singleness of intent for battle. This is a courage of the will which recognizes the real enemy is the enemy within.

For Mencius, these two men exemplified the courage of passion and the courage of will. The Chinese language indeed routinely connects 'courage' with either 'passion' or 'will': *yongqi* and *yongzhi*. In one, a singleness of passion for justice moved the person into action, overriding the deliberating function of the mind ('without thinking'). In the other, a singleness of will pulled the passions along behind it. This will lacks all trepidation; it suspends all need for rational calculation of winning or losing. Such calculations (say, in face of a whole army) would only be self-defeating; they would weaken the will. So whereas Bokong Yu had the valour of a 'raging bull', the cool Meng Shishe had the fearlessness of stoic *apatheia*. Mencius found it hard to judge who was better, but if he had to pick, he would side with the courage of singular will over the courage of blind passion. This discourse grew out of his exchange with Gaozi in *Mencius* 2A:2. It is based on a model of the mind comparable to the Platonic one: the mind is the charioteer in control of the two horses of the passions. The challenge facing the charioteer (reason) is one of how to bring in line these two horses, one of the lower passion ('food and sex' in Gaozi) and the other the higher social passions ('speech and deed' in Confucius). Faced with that problem, Gaozi would rely on a cool deliberation of the pros and cons. He had a courage guided by the reasoning of the mind. The problem is that in his scheme, he would side with the horse of the higher passions: do what society requires of oneself. Mencius agreed that normally the mind should be in control of the passions, but then he cited the first case to show how a singleness of passion for justice can also move the mind, and then how a singleness of will (intentionally refusing to weigh the pros and cons) can also move the passions. The Mencian analysis of the working of the mind as reason, emotion and the will is more subtle than the thinking of Gaozi, but his ultimate intention is to subvert an ethics of a 'public good' (what society requires) with an absolute good, a personal response to Transcendence (**Heaven**) that would not be swayed one way or the other by what current society and common sense might dictate. For that, he cited the third example, that of Zengzi.

An introvert, Zengzi was no warrior. Daily he reflected on three things: Has he been honest in all his dealings? Had he been truthful to his friends?

And did he practice what he preached? Mencius, who prided himself in being a man 'who labours with his mind' instead of one who labours with his body, sided with the moral rectitude of this man of letters who would challenge an army ten thousand strong if he knew he alone was in the right. This readiness to die for what one believes in (for righteousness' sake) outpaced Gaozi, whose courage would only do so much as his peers would reasonably require of him. The crowning touch in the parable is that Zengzi could also appear a coward. If he knew that he was in the wrong, he would cower in fear before even the lowest riffraff of society. Such seeming cowardice is utterly contrary to the old standard of heroic courage in war. This earned Confucians the negative attribute of *ju* or weaklings. Yet such was the nature of the moral Good that a moral man should stand in fear of its judgment.

See also: conscience; scholar

Further reading

Hsia Chih-tsing (1968) *The Classic Chinese Novel: A Critical Introduction*, New York: Columbia University Press.

Lewis, M. (1990) *Sanctioned Violence in Ancient China*, Albany, NY: State University of New York Press.

Liu, J. (1967) *The Chinese Knight Errant*, Chicago: University of Chicago Press.

MacIntyre, A. (1966) *A Short History of Ethics*, New York: Macmillan.

WHALEN LAI

creation and redemption, Nestorian

The Biblical tradition distinguished itself by a faith in a creator God. Creation *ex nihilo* suggests a God who is everything and a nature which by comparison is little or nothing. The Nestorians, who arrived in China in 635, had to make the argument to the Chinese that nature is not 'simply so'. If we see an arrow flying, we may assume there is an archer. If we see it following a trajectory and not falling straight down, it is because some force is sustaining it. That someone who shot and sustains the flight of the arrow is God. The Jesuit missions in the seventeenth century had to produce the same argument again, this time to the Neo-Confucians. If there is a natural order, a heavenly principle to nature, that design points to a designer. Thus above **Heaven**, which is only an abode, there is a Lord of Heaven (God). Writing in the Tang dynasty, amid Buddhists who knew such gory self-sacrifice as the **bodhisattva** feeding himself to a hungry tigress, the Nestorians did not shun telling the story of the Cross. The later Jesuits preached the Lord of Heaven openly, but reserved the more gruesome death of Christ for the initiated.

Further reading

Oppenheim, R. (1963) *The First Nestorian Mission in China*, Berkeley, CA: University of California Press.

Yoshio, S. (1928) *The Nestorian Monument in China*, New York: Macmillan.

WHALEN LAI

critique of 'autonomous syllogism'

Tibetan traditions on the whole perceive Chandrakirti's critique of Bhavya's acceptance of 'autonomous syllogism' as the principal basis of division between two major schools of interpretation of **Nagarjuna** in India. Contemporary scholars have argued that the names of the two schools, Svatantrika-Madhyamaka and Prasangika-Madhyamaka, and the sharp division suggested by these labels are probably Tibetan constructs. Tibetan Madhyamikas generally maintain that Chandrakirti's Prasangika reading represents the highest interpretation of Nagarjuna's Madhyamaka thought.

Ostensibly, Prasangika's critique of the 'autonomous syllogism' deals with a methodological point about whether the use of 'consequential reasoning', i.e. *reductio ad absurdum*, is adequate for generating inference in the context of a discourse on the ultimate nature of reality, or whether it is necessary to apply syllogistic argument as well. Prasangikas argue that their opponent's insistence on the use of syllogism reflects a theory of inference that is highly problematic. It implies a metaphysical belief in what could be called the 'autonomy of reason' which suggests that the capacity for drawing inferences is intrinsic to logical forms. An essential part of seeking this 'correct' form is to ensure that all the key elements of an argument such as the subject, predicate, the inferring sign and the illustration, must all be incontrovertibly established for both parties involved. So long as this condition is not met, the argument cannot have the power to give correct inference for there is not enough common ground to initiate a serious discourse. For the Prasangika, this is an impossible condition.

There is a variety of opinions among Tibetan interpreters of Madhyamaka philosophy as to what exactly this critique of autonomous syllogism consists of. What follows is a brief summary of the reading of **Tsongkhapa**, perhaps the most influential of the Tibetan Madhyamaka philosophers. Tsongkhapa follows Chandrakirti very closely on this critique and one can detect three key elements in his critique. First, Tsongkhapa demonstrates the untenability of the premise that all the essential elements of the syllogism must be incontrovertibly established for both parties. He argues that this requirement is too stringent and can never be fully met. To expect such a consensus between the opposing parties is like putting the cart before the horse. Such consensus can only be reached, if at all, when the debate is over, not before the argument has even begun!

The second element in Tsongkhapa's critique is to demonstrate an internal contradiction in Bhavya's belief in 'autonomy of reason'. The crux of the argument is this. If the subject of the syllogism is to be established on the basis of a consensus between a Madhyamika and his opponent, this entails that the subject is established by a cognition that is veridical with regard to its intrinsic nature. However this would directly contradict the Madhyamaka's basic premise that objects are, in the final analysis, deceptive realities. Third, Tsongkhapa seeks to demonstrate the possibility of developing a form of argument that does not entail any belief in the autonomy of logic. Such types of argument are said to be based on 'conventions familiar to the other', the essential

import of which is to suggest that inferences take place within the context of a complex interplay of many factors. In brief, one could say that the Prasangika's critique of 'autonomous syllogism' reflects a systematic attempt to relativize logic so that reason too cannot be seen as providing a haven for the belief in the notion of intrinsic existence.

Further reading

Hopkins, J. (1983) *Meditation on Emptiness*, London: Wisdom Publications, part V, 441–99.

Thurman, R. (1984) *Tsongkhapa's Speech of Gold in the Essence of True Eloquence*, Princeton, NJ: Princeton University Press.

THUPTEN JINPA

cynicism in Late Dynastic China

High expectations and dashed hopes make for cynicism. The Confucian faith in a moral universe has meant that it foregoes what other major world religions had opted for, a theodicy of redress: justice in the next world in exchange for all the injustices in this one. By trusting in sufficient redress in this world, Confucianism exudes a certain degree of moral high-mindedness which, when frustrated, often turns rather sour.

Such cynicism has a long history. After the founder of the Han dynasty rose from peasant rebel to become the Son of **Heaven** – he won the throne even as his rival, another peasant rebel, lost – it was deemed that winning is everything. As the idiom went, 'the victor is declared king; the loser an outlaw forever'. But by the Later Han, the consolidation of power by the magnate families ended any such drastic change of fortune. And as long as that conservative social order functioned well enough, there was more acceptance of the given (fate) and less call for cynical discontent. Popular literature then escaped into the ghostly fantasy which later evolved into the Tang dynasty 'romance', tales of the extraordinary interrupting the routine life of this world. But this happened so rarely that the romance genre hardly served as a form of social protest.

The Song dynasty changed that. With the civil examination promising officialdom to anyone who could by dint of effort prove himself merit-worthy, expectation ran high. The work ethic seemed vindicated when the new gentry class became the circulating elite. Neo-Confucianism bolstered this optimism by holding that sagehood is acquired by learning; that is, it is achieved and not ascribed. Since the **sage** should hold influential office, a Chinese version of the myth of 'from the log cabin to the White House' spread. This idea became the staple of popular novels and theatre, featuring poor, young, diligent scholars winning top honours in the examinations at the capital and winning the hands of and marrying the girls of their dreams, even into the imperial family. But by the early Qing dynasty, the pool of talent had grown large while the number of official posts stayed virtually unchanged, so that the chance of success was minuscule. (By 1800, out of a population of 300 million, only 500,000 could earn the first degree; out of those, only 300 to 350 with higher degrees would be eligible for office.) As high hopes were dashed, faith in just deserts eroded.

In his own day, an unemployed **Confucius** stayed on his moral course; it is the times that failed the Way. Late dynastic literati learned to blame the system and social satire flourished. Valued now for realism, their exposé of social mores and manners was ineffective and the discontent could not be translated into protest nor into reform. A folk saying about what matters in life – 'Of what counts, first, fate; second, luck; third, divination; fourth, accumulating merit (good **karma**); fifth, study' – utterly reversed the Neo-Confucian priority. Resignation to one's lot (fate), seeking to change one's fortune (luck) and hoping for a godsend (consequent to finding a good site for ancestral burial) take higher billing.

It is precisely this competitive discontent, not some lofty 'Asian Values', that is now fuelling the economic entrepreneurship in China. But the idea that greed is good and winning is everything is not helping to build a much-needed civic society. Frustrated aspirants may have the luxury of being cynical, but a different mood prevails in the permanent underclass: fatalism.

Further reading

Bond, M. (1991) *Beyond the Chinese Face: Insights from Psychology*, Hong Kong: Oxford University Press.

WHALEN LAI

D

Dai Zhen

b. 1724; d. 1777

Philosopher

Followng the assumption of power by the Qing dynasty, the Manchu rulers continued the state support of **Zhu Xi**'s orthodoxy, arid textual scholarship and comprehensive but uncritical encyclopedias. This spurred Dai Zhen (Tai Chen) to strike out on a new path. Declaring the Six Classics (see **Classics and Books**) to be a part of history, he relativized the once timeless 'classics' and used early historiography to criticize current historiography, which resulted in reviving Han philology to undercut Song metaphysics. The word *ren*, for example, refers to 'two men' in a concrete setting; it is not an abstract principle in the mind. When the *Analects* says 'discipline the self with rituals', it is not about the rational self controlling the emotional self (the selfish feelings). Since that task 'begins with oneself', the self cannot be divided against itself. With that, he threw out the dualism that pits the principle nature (man's rational being/essence, his *li*) against the fallible passions (*qi*, ether). If **ether** is fallible, nature is fallible; if nature is good, ether is good. Instead of relying on an abstract principle (accessed by the self through the mind) to control the emotions, that role should be given back to the rites. So, it is not the psycho-metaphysics of the Song but historical research into the institutions of ritual that should have the overriding priority.

Dai Zhen is the outstanding mid-eighteenth century thinker, coming at a turning point in Qing rule. The 'practical learning' of the Ming loyalists during the early Qing had abandoned the intuitionism of the School of Mind. The later followers of Wang Yangming had devolved into 'empty talk'. The practical thinkers now attended to concrete affairs and opted for breadth in learning. At the time, the new rulers had responded to the subtle use of literary innuendoes to mock the Manchus measure by measure, i.e. by instituting a ruthless 'literary inquisition'. But state support of Song Neo-Confucian orthodoxy continued: Zhu Xi's commentaries remained the standard for the civil examinations. By the mid-eighteenth century, peace and prosperity under strong Qing rule had allayed much Han discontent. Many scholars of the Han Learning welcomed being recruited into the Encyclopedia projects and serving their royal, now well-sinicized patrons. Textual scholarship was then pursued often just for its own sake. Dai Zhen, versed in phonetics, linguistics, astronomy, mathematics, geography and hydrology, was recruited into that imperial project, but he and his lineage preserved a more critical stand in their scholarship.

In the later half of his life, Dai Zhen was openly critical of Zhu Xi. He disputed the separation of Principle from Ether and the contraries of heavenly principle and human passion. He grounded the *dao* in man in daily activity, in the dynamics of 'daily renewal', in the observable patterns of change, the concrete and the static. None of these correctives to Song–Ming idealism were new, but Dai Zhen completed what his early Qing predecessors had more loosely registered. He framed his final argument in a treatise, *Probing the Meaning of Words in the Book of Mencius*. His was a diligent philological retrieval of Mencius' original discourse. He marshalled evidence to prove what others had suspected to be a medieval Buddhist distortion. His textual criticism supported his charge that the word 'principle' had been misused for legitimizing social inequities. Dai Zhen is however better remembered for his 'evidential scholarship' and despite the conservative use the Qing state had made of Han Learning, such textual criticism laid the foundation for more progressive readings and possibilities

WHALEN LAI

dao

Probably the most important term in Chinese thought, *dao* (*tao*) means the Way, a path to be walked on; it is as much *praxis* as *theoria*. In early discourse, *dao* is usually prefixed: it is the Way of **Heaven**, or that of Man, or that of Kings. Rarely was the term used as the Way by itself. **Laozi**'s ***Daodejing*** was the first to do so. This work begins with a crisp couplet: 'The *dao* that can be talked about (*dao*) is no longer the eternal *dao*/The Name that can be named is no longer the invariable Name.' Embedded within it are already (a) the superseding of *dao* over the Heaven of Zhou; (b) the repudiation of the thesis that name does correspond to reality; and (c) a plea for a new mode of discourse. The two lines do not exactly run parallel. Not only is that because the *dao* is Nameless, but also because *dao* has at least two meanings. Where the language of signs (names) fails, a language of metaphors (poetry), may succeed. Both **Mencius** and **Zhuangzi** would discourse on the *dao* in that mode.

The meaning of *dao* varies. It is the course of change; the source of things; the rationale of beings; the moral norm of society; the guideline for rule; the pattern of nature; and so on. All those can be found in the *Daodejing*. Whether the *dao* is transcendental or immanent, material or immaterial, above or internal to things, these are all topics in the current debate. Those issues were also debated by the Neo-Daoists after the Han (see **Neo-Daoism**). Some held the *dao* to be above things and others in things; before being or within being; prior to nature or synonymous with nature, promoting change in others or just their principle of creation. The Neo-Confucians (see **Neo-**

Confucianism, concepts) in the Song dynasty equated *dao* with **li** (principle) and for ethical reasons preferred to discourse more on the Heavenly Principle than on the *dao* of Nature. They also shifted the focus away from *dao* and its *de* (virtue, power) to the divide between *dao* and Vessel (above and below form). The *dao* is the 'non-physical' Principle while the Vessel (utensil) is of the 'physical' world; it is what contains or possesses the particular Principle. The material 'car' would have or is molded by the principle of the 'car-ness'. Principle is what is 'above form' or antecedent to form (a material shape); vessel is what is 'below form' (what has to have a material shape). Form mediates the formless that went before and the materialized that comes after.

Further reading

Csikszentmihalyi, M. and Ivanhoe, P. (eds) (1999) *Religious and Philosophical Aspects of the Laozi*, Albany, NY: State University of New York Press.

WHALEN LAI

dao as nameless

It has been standard practice since the Han commentaries to equate the *dao* with the Nameless on the basis of the opening lines of the **Laozi**, which says: 'The *dao* that can be spoken of is not the invariable *dao*; the Name that can be named is not the invariable Name.' In fact, one can read the first line as: 'The Course that can be Discoursed is an extraordinary Dis/Course' which is more than registering simply that 'The Name that can be named is not the invariable Name'. Coming after the debate on whether a name truly describes the thing it names, this amounts not just to a denial of the 'correspondence theory of names' (viz. the language of signs) but in addition an endorsement of a discourse built around the power of dis/semblance basic to the language of metaphor. It is the 'clash of symbols' and the intentional 'abuse of reference' – viz. the 'excess of meaning' – that holds the key to the poetic power of the *Laozi*. Unlike learning the Name that names or fails to name, the *dao* invites one to 'course the dis/course', to embody the Way, to Talk the Walk and Walk the Talk in a fully performative speech.

WHALEN LAI

Daodejing

A book in 5,000 characters attributed to **Laozi**, the *Daodejing* (*Tao Te Ching*) was also known from the Han period onward as the *Classic of the Way and Its Power*. The text opens with a chapter that supposedly summarizes the whole book.

> The *Dao* (Way) that can be spoken of (*dao*)
> Is not the eternal Way.
> The Name that can be named
> Is not the invariable Name.
> The Nameless is the origin of heaven and earth
> The Named is the mother of all things.
> Therefore should we observe without desires its quintessence;
> And with desires its manifestations.
> These two which rose at the same time are given different names.
> For that, they are the gate to mystery.
> (Behold) mystery of mysteries,
> The gate to various wondrous subtleties.

Because of its dense summation, this chapter might be later than other chapters. It was known to the Legalist **Han Fei**, who gave us the first commentary on this passage:

Dao is that through which all things become what they are. It is that with which all principles are commensurable. By principle is meant the pattern by which all things came into being as the *dao* causes that to be. Everything has its own principle that does not interfere with that of another. (That is how) principles are the controlling factor in all things . . . and the *dao* is commensurable with them all.

Han Fei sees the *dao* not as some transcendental ineffable principle but rather as an immanent factor in all things. The book was a guide for princely rule; and it was so treated in the Huang–Lao tradition down to early Han. Recent discovery of two Han versions of the text have raised new questions for specialists. Later, among the religious Daoists, the 'double mystery' commentators would collapse the distinction between being and **non-being** just as the Buddhists would remove the distinction between form and **emptiness**.

See also: Keyi Buddhism

Further reading

Lau, D.C. (trans.) (1943) *Tao Te Ching*, Harmondsworth: Penguin.

WHALEN LAI

Daoism in Korea

In contrast to Buddhism, Confucianism and Christianity in Korea today, Daoism is not a major philosophy or religion. However, Daoist ideas have permeated Korean ways of thinking in various ways throughout Korean history. The *Laozi* or **Daodejing** (*Lao Tzu/ Tao Te Ching*) and *Zhuangzi* (*Chuang Tzu*), the two most important philosophical classics of Daoism, have been widely read in Korea since the seventh century CE. The essential Daoist ideas such as *dao*, **wuwei** (natural life), nature and **sage**, appealed to the speculative minds of Korean people for many centuries. The idea of *dao* in particular has been a central philosophical and religious idea throughout Korean history, due probably to the influence of Daoism, although the meaning of *dao* as understood by most people in Korea is broader and more varied than in Daoism.

According to some scholars, Daoist nature mysticism and Tan'gun mythology surrounding the origin of Korea are interrelated. The story of Tan'gun, the legendary founder of Korea, is interconnected with the idea of *sinson*, which can be translated as immortal nature mystic. Sinson also means a divine-human being living in a beautiful setting of nature, or paradise. According to legend, Tan'gun became a mountain god and lived for nearly two thousand years. In this legend, Tan'gun is a *sinson*, an immortal nature mystic, which is very much a Daoist idea.

The idea of *sinson* has continued as a tradition of nature mysticism throughout Korean history, including the Silla, Koryo and Choson dynasties. However, many who belonged to this tradition were hermits. They had their own view of history and tried to build their own way of life. Their influence on Korean history and culture was very limited.

According to a Korean history contained in *Samguk yusa* (Events of the Three Kingdoms), in 624 CE, the emperor of the Chinese Tang dynasty sent to Koguryo, the northern kingdom during the period of Three Kingdoms, a Daoist priest with an image of a Daoist god. Upon arrival, the Daoist priest lectured on *Daodejing* to King Yongryu and the people of Koguryo. In 643, eight Daoist priests and the *Daodejing* arrived from China, and Daoism became the national religion of Koguryo, taking a higher position than Confucianism and Buddhism for a short time.

Daoism also played some role in the Silla kingdom, which was in the southeastern part of the Three Kingdoms. During the ninth century CE, several Silla scholars, including Kim Ka-gi, went to Tang China and brought Daoism to Silla. They studied mainly **religious Daoism** in the famous temples in Chinese mountains. They brought to Korea various Daoist books. After several years of study, these Korean scholars achieved *tan* (cinnabar), which is a high level of physical and spiritual maturity in Daoist alchemy. It does not mean that they acquired the technique of making a drug to become immortal, but it means that they arrived at the level of realization through prescribed physical and spiritual training. According to a legend, Kim Ka-gi became an immortal mystic in 858, and later transmitted the oral teaching to Ch'oe Ch'i-won, a famous scholar in the Silla kingdom. Such stories of mystics and mystical experiences in Daoism caused interest among Silla scholars regarding the serious academic study of Daoism.

The mystical tradition of Daoism continued in the Koryo dynasty (918–1392). During the Silla dynasty, Daoist ritual was not a national affair. Only in the Koryo kingdom were Daoist rituals widely performed to prevent harm and to bring blessing upon the nation. The kinds of rituals practiced included reverence for many objects of heaven such as the Heavenly Lord and stars, and prayers for rain. During the Koryo dynasty, Daoist books were widely read among some intellectuals. Several left the secular world and trained themselves spiritually and studied Daoist medicine and practiced curing people. Yi Chung-yak was one of the most able Daoist scholars, who studied Daoist medicine and became an expert practitioner, successfully curing King Sukjong (r. 1095–1105). For this he was greatly revered and given a place of honour in the palace. Later, Yi Chung-yak went to Song China to receive Daoist instructions from a famous Chinese master, Hwang Tae-ch'ung, and returned to Korea with a deeper knowledge of Daoism. He requested that King Yejong (r. 1105–22) build a Daoist temple and make it a national centre for ceremonies and blessings. According to the request, a large temple was erected and it became a centre of Daoist rituals and of learning the essence of Daoism. In 1118, several Chinese medicine doctors came to the Koryo kingdom and taught the principles of Daoist medicine, which were incorporated with those of Korean medicine.

During the Choson dynasty (1392–1910), Confucianism was the official philosophy of the kingdom. Some royal persons still believed in Daoism, but because of opposition by strong Confucian ministers and scholars, Daoist rituals on the national level decreased gradually. During Chungjong's reign (1506–44), Confucian scholars strongly insisted on the destruction of Sogyokso, the main Daoist temple, and discontinuance of the king's ceremony for the god of heaven and earth, and in 1518 the temple was destroyed. The Confucian scholars claimed that Daoism was evil, heretical, nonsensical and destructive. They promoted Confucianism as the right philosophy and religion. After the Japanese invasion of Korea in 1592, Daoism declined and the Neo-Confucian scholars condemned Daoism as an evil heresy. The Daoist religion was persecuted and destroyed in Korea in the last several centuries by strong Confucian opposition.

In the history of Korean Daoism, the religious aspect has been strong. However, Korean Daoism was really a mixture of philosophical and religious aspects, incorporating the philosophical ideas of *Dao*, *yin–yang*, the **five elements** and natural life, as well as the religious ideas of nature mysticism and medicine. Korean Daoism was also mixed with native shamanism. The idea of immortality was important in Korean Daoism as in Chinese Daoism. Both external alchemy and spiritual training were important aspects of *kumdan* (the pill of immortality).

Compared with Buddhism and Confucianism, Daoism has never been a major philosophy and religion. However, the essential philosophical ideas of Daoism such as *dao* and natural life have had a significant impact on the Korean way of thinking throughout history. One can find the impact of

Daoism in the *Hwarangdo* (the way of the elite young knights) of the Silla dynasty. *Hwarang* (young knights) embodied the Daoist idea of love of nature and nature mysticism together with some Buddhist and Confucian virtues. The influence of Daoism is also evident in Tonghak (Eastern Learning) thought, which developed in the nineteenth century.

Further reading

Ch'a Chu-hwan (1978) *Ha'guk Togyo Sasang Yon'gu* (A Study of Korean Taoism), Seoul: Seoul National University Press.

Lee, P. (ed.) (1993) *Sourcebook of Korean Civilization*, Vol. I, New York: Columbia University Press, 131ff, 444ff, 454ff.

Nam, S. (1993) 'Taoismus in Korea', in G. Floistad (ed.), *Contemporary Philosophy*, Vol. 7, *Asian Philosophy*, Dordrecht: Kluwer Academic Publishers, 239–52.

Yu Chai-shin (1977) 'Korean Taoism', in C. Yu (ed.), *Korean and Asian Religious Tradition*, Toronto: Korean and Related Studies Press, 189–96.

Fung Yu-lan (1948) *A Short History of Chinese Philosophy*, trans. D. Bodde, New York: Macmillan.

YONG-CHOON KIM

Daosheng

b. *c*.390; d. 434

Buddhist philosopher

Daosheng (Tao-sheng) was an early fifth-century Buddhist thinker who shocked his contemporaries with new (unconventional) theories, first by proposing 'sudden enlightenment' and then by proposing universal **buddha nature** (the essence or seed of enlightenment, present in all sentient creatures). Gradual enlightenment is enlightenment achieved via a series of steps, while the sudden variety is not graded but is rather one-step, total enlightenment. The two theses were thought to be related but a closer look would reveal they come together only towards the end. The *Lotus Sutra* turns out to be a key catalyst. Gradual enlightenment was the prevalent assumption for both Indian and Tibetan Buddhism. But Daosheng built on the **Hinayana Abhidharma** tradition, which recognizes that in the 'last step' marked by the 'diamond trance' (*vajra-samadhi*) state, the stepping out from **sam-**

sara into **nirvana** is total, taking just one step, with no gradations. The diamond trance is the highest trance state before enlightenment itself. Being hard, the diamond is a metaphor for the ability to cut through or sever all obstructions and mental defilements.

It was recognized that, among the enlightened, there are the Three Vehicles with clear rankings of the higher and the lower. The Three Vehicles or Triyana is the standard set of three paths of enlightenment: the *arhat* who attains it after learning from the Buddha's teaching; the *pratyekabuddha* or the solitary, self-enlightened one who is untaught; and finally the Mahayana **bodhisattva** who attains his own enlightenment and also seeks to enlighten others. The idea is that the single Buddha vehicle, the Ekeyana, can be presented in three different ways, depending on the capabilities of the students. The Ekeyana or One Vehicle is a doctrine of the *Lotus Sutra*, which declares the Three Vehicles to be just an expedient teaching. The real and final truth is that there is only One Vehicle, namely, that everyone would one day become Buddha. This is the Buddhayana of the *Lotus Sutra*. However, One Vehicle is now deemed synonymous with Mahayana, and the distinction between the Bodhisattvayana of wisdom and the Buddayana of faith is long blurred.

The *Nirvana Sutra* reverses the Hinayana doctrine of 'no-self' and qualifies the early Mahayana of 'universal **emptiness**'. There is a 'buddha nature' in all sentient beings; it is called a '**self**' (*atman*), and though empty it is also lasting, pure and blissful. When that Triyana distinction was raised by the Ekayana (One Vehicle) doctrine of the *Lotus Sutra*, Daosheng (*c*.360–434) drew the further conclusion that enlightenment into that One Reality has to be unitary, total and sudden. That thesis stirred up a controversy but there was no one clear canonical pronouncement to help settle the debate. This is very different from the case of his proposal of the existence of a 'universal buddha nature'. The *Nirvana Sutra* has initially declared a class of people to be devoid of sound possibilities for future enlightenment. Only in the final chapters does the scripture reverse itself and accept everyone into buddhahood.

Without knowing that final judgment, Daosheng proposed his thesis. For contradicting the words of the Buddha, he was banished from his community of monks and had to take refuge at Lushan under

Huiyuan, the famous scholar turned monk who retired to Mount Lu and refused to cross the Tiger Creek again to return to the world and successfully defended the monk's right not to bow before the temporal ruler. Those final chapters of the scripture then arrived and proved Daosheng prophetically correct. But only in a preface he contributed to a collective commentary on the *Nirvana Sutra* did he conjoin his two theses, that because of the presence of the buddha nature in man, his awakening to buddhahood in full is guaranteed.

See also: enlightenment, sudden

Further reading

Lai, W. (1987) 'Tao-sheng's Theory of Sudden Enlightenment Re-examined', in P. Gregory (ed.), *Sudden and Gradual: Approaches to Enlightenment in Chinese Buddhist Thought*, Honolulu, HA: University of Hawaii Press, 169–200.

WHALEN LAI

darshana

The term *darshana* or 'view' is applied to the six mainstream orthodox schools of Indian philosophy: **Samkhya**, **Yoga**, **Purva Mimamsa**, **Vedanta**, **Nyaya** and **Vaisheshika**. Each has a variously conceived soteriological intent and each claims to be faithfully expounding an original canonical message summarized in aphoristic collections of *sutras*. The literary style is primarily commentatorial and the stance frequently adversarial given the importance of refuting opposing views.

CHRIS BARTLEY

deference

The mind of deference, says **Mencius**, is the beginning of propriety. Out of this innate quality of mind came supposedly the **rites**. For Mencius, it is natural that inferiors defer to superiors just as a younger brother would naturally respect his elder brother. In society, among equals, deference is a show of courtesy. If deference is performed by a superior, it is grace. The Jesuits who witnessed Chinese social conduct in late Ming China were impressed by this civility, especially the decorum of the **scholar** officials.

Other classical thinkers assessed this matter of deference differently from Mencius. **Laozi** prized non-contention and regarded deference as one strategy for avoiding conflict. It may even be the yielding way of the winsome *dao*. **Mozi** also hated contention, but he would not yield to the powerful; he preached 'non-aggression' to the aggressor and helped arm the weak state for its self-defence. **Xunzi** saw how men fought over limited resources, and did not consider deference to be at all ingrained; it is a virtue acquired from without, and involves learning the rites which the sages had instituted as a check on man's natural greed. The Legalists built on that: you cannot teach deference, instead you must enforce compliance. The most famous form of *yang* as deference is *chanyang*, the voluntary abdication of rule by one **Sage-King** to the next. It is an ideal mode of rule lodged in high antiquity. Mencians endorsed it but Xunzi found it highly questionable, or at least not applicable in more recent history.

A related but lesser virtue, often paired with deference, is forbearance. Forbearance, however, comes more under prudential ethics. It is what you need to be geared up with in the absence of others showing you deference: namely, grin (or grimace) and bear it. A Chinese emperor once enquired of the head of a large, extended household how the patriarch was able to sustain (a semblance of) **harmony** in what would normally be a contentious household. In response, the stoic old man wrote down a single magic word to secure peace in the household: forbearance.

See also: courage

WHALEN LAI

DEFINITION *see* lakshana; logic and Islamic philosophy

demons in Zoroastrianism

The concept of 'demon' (in Avestan, *daeva*-; in Pahlavi, *dew*) was for many centuries central to both the theology and ritual practice of **Zoroastrianism**, and figures largely in the Avestan, Pahlavi and

Persian texts of the ancient and medieval tradition. As in other religions which arose in prehistoric antiquity, modern Zoroastrians have in the course of the last century mostly desisted from using demonological terms in their current theology and ethical philosophy, yet the liturgical rites, and of course the scriptures, continue to make constant reference to demons. However in the past the faithful Zoroastrian was actually defined by the Avestan term *vi daeva* (against the *daevas*), just as he was *mazdayasna-* (Mazda-worshipper) and *zarathush-tri-* (Zoroastrian). In his own revelations, in the *Gatha*s, Zarathushtra explicitly renounced the old gods of the Indo-Iranian religion as *daeva*s who chose to follow the Hostile Spirit Angra Mainyu. Later Zoroastrian texts mention demons which personify every imaginable notion of evil. They are often referred to collectively in the plural, even when the singular noun is used, along with the term *druz* (lesser demons) and other terms for evil spirits and wicked human beings.

Demons play a central role in the cosmogonic drama of Zoroastrian religious mythology, in texts such as the Pahlavi *Bundahishn* (Creation), a ninth century CE text which preserves much more ancient Zoroastrian lore. After Ohrmazd (Ahura Mazda) created the good spiritual beings, the Blessed Immortals (*amahraspands*), the Evil Spirit Ahreman 'miscreated' his demons from the demonic essence in retaliation. Each of these demons is the exact antithesis of the *amahraspand*s, by which Ahreman is said to 'make himself worse'. Ahreman produced his miscreation in that form, and from that miscreation he became 'useless' (in Pahlavi, *akar*). This refers to the ignorant and ultimately self-destructive demonic nature: as is so often said in the texts, the will of Ahreman and the demons is to smite, and ultimately they will turn their destructiveness upon themselves. In their simplest and most graphic representations, in the *Bundahishn*, and in other mythological texts, the demons are devils of varying powers, ranging from the six arch-demons (*kamaligan dewan*) who oppose the *amahraspand*s, to the myriad, minor, nameless demons who, when the sun sets, rush out from hell for the destruction of the world. They are responsible for all corruption and destructiveness: cosmic, celestial, terrestrial, elemental, corporeal, moral and social. The present world is a state of mixture just because the demons have entered it at every level: they are even present in the bodies of men, in the form of disease, pain, grief and so on. Some demons are graphically depicted as having claws, faces, hair and feet, and as producing demonic semen. There are stories of some demons having had sexual intercourse with humans, as in the tale of Jam and his sister Jamag with a male and female demon, whereby certain noxious creatures were brought into being. By contrast, they can also take the form of abstract notions (heresy, denial) or climatic disorders (whirlwinds, lightning, drought).

There is some question as to what was understood to be the ontological status of Ahreman and the demons, for, since they were all said to be devoid of any truth, it was logical that even their existence was denied. This line of thought occurs several times, both in the philosophical compendium, the *Denkard*, and also in more popular texts. The non-existence of the demons refers to the doctrine that Ahreman and the demons have no physical (*getig*) form of their own (Shaked 1967: 228ff). The presence of demons in the physical world is thus entirely parasitic upon the existence of forms created by Ohrmazd. Being itself is considered to be good in origin, and therefore may only be stolen by the demons from good creatures. Their reality in this world is therefore an intrusion, an outrage and a lie. According to a well-known text, as long as in this world even a small demon has his dwelling in the body of a single man, Ahreman is in the world (*Denkard* VI: 264). Ahreman and his demons are thus a force of evil will in the physical world, but have no being (*astih, sti*) of their own. The evil of Ahreman and the demons was felt, however, to be utterly real producing catastrophic effects on the world if left unrestrained. Zoroastrian priests seem not to have written about the demons to instil fear into the reader, except in a particular genre of admonitory texts such as the *Book of the Righteous Wiraz* (*Arda Wiraz Namag*), which warns of dire punishments to be meted out by demons in Hell.

Demons were believed to be a present reality in the mixed state of this world. They could be dealt with more easily than in the spiritual world, and this is said to be one of the chief reasons the physical world was brought into existence by Ohrmazd, that is, in order to trap the Evil Spirit and his demons into limited time and the physical state where they could be easily destroyed. For example they can be smitten by kindling fire in the night; cursing the demons (*nifrin kunish*) is a religious act (*Denkard* VI: 123); man's daily duty and eschatological duty is to smite demons, through good action and through prayer. Fire (along with prayer) is the most powerful weapon against the demons, for they shrink from its very presence: fire is to be kept burning in a house where there is a pregnant woman, for fire is said to have protected Zarathushtra's own mother from the onslaught of demons when they tried to destroy the unborn prophet in her womb. Demons are particularly attracted to the results of organic processes in human life, in particular those of excretion, reproduction and sexuality in general. Two of the most powerful demons are the female whore, Jeh, who attacks men and women, and the *druj i nasush*, the demon of pollution. Much of the text called the *Vendidad* (Law Against the Demons) warns of the preventative and punitive measures associated with the attacks of such moral and physical pollution. In the philosophical texts, however, which attempt a rationalization and analysis of religious values, it is the demon Az ('Lust', or perhaps better 'Concupiscence') who is said to be most dangerously opposed to true human nature, for Az is capable of destroying the innate wisdom of man.

In this spiritual sense, and elsewhere in a moral and ritual context, the demons may win a temporary victory for Ahreman. Death itself is demonized in the form of the demon Astwihad, who casts a noose around the necks of mortal men from birth. However, the religion is at heart optimistic, in spite of all its strategies for countering demons. Evil in Zoroastrianism can only be viewed as negative; it has no being in its own right and is secondary in the cosmic order, implying the priority and ontological superiority of the good power.

See also: Zoroastrian philosophy in the *Denkard*

Further reading

Christensen, A. (1941) *Essai sur la démonologie iranienne*, Copenhagen: Det Kgl. Danske Videnskabernes Selskab. Historisk-filologiske Meddelelser 27.1

Shaked, S. (1967) *Studies in Mysticism and Religion presented to G. Scholem*, Jerusalem: Magnes Press.

ALAN WILLIAMS

dependent origination in Tibetan philosophy

The theory of dependent origination is, as in the case of Indian Buddhism, central to the thoughts of all schools of Tibetan Buddhism. Tibetan philosophers, however, make a distinction between what they see as three distinct senses of the meaning of dependence: (1) dependence in terms of causation, (2) dependence in terms of constituents and the constituted, and (3) dependence in terms of mutuality of concepts. These three senses are argued as corresponding to progressively increasing levels of subtlety in the understanding of the theory of dependent origination. In the first sense, all things and events are said to be 'dependently originated' in that they come into being as a result of the aggregation of multiple causes and conditions. This sense of dependence is intimately related to the theory of causation; in fact, it could be argued that it refers to the same principle. In this sense, the idea of dependence is understood strictly in terms of the 'material' or the 'factual' existence of things and events. It is this meaning of causal dependence which is thought to underlie the basic Buddhist doctrine of the twelve links (in the chain of) dependent origination, which seeks to give an account of our unenlightened existence. This causal theory also underlies the Buddhist rejection of any creation theories.

The second sense of dependence, in terms of constituents and the constituted, relates both to existence and identity of things and events. According to this view, all things, events, acts, objects and so on come into being not only in dependence on their causes, but there is also dependence between the constituted and the constituents. All material objects from tangible objects to the minute atoms are composed of their constitutive parts, such as particles, and mental events, constituted by their temporal stages. Nothing can exist in isolation of its constitutive parts. On this view, even abstract entities like universals are thought to have 'parts' or 'aspects' that make them dependently originated as well.

The third sense of dependence, dependence in terms of mutuality of concepts, is considered to represent the highest understanding of the principle of dependent origination. On this reading, the principle is understood in terms of dependence between designations, designating mind and designative bases. Here the sense of dependence is more related to the problems of identity in that the identities of things and events are asserted to be, in a profound sense, 'derivative'. Nothing can be said to possess intrinsic reality and intrinsic identity for everything is dependently originated. Thus at this level, the meaning of dependent origination becomes equivalent to the meaning of emptiness. In fact, **Tsongkhapa** argues that the heart of Prasangika's interpretation of Madhyamaka philosophy is to equate the principle of dependent origination with the principle of emptiness. This is, as he puts it, to understand emptiness in terms of dependent origination. **Shentong** philosophers, however, assert that there is one exception to the principle of dependent origination. In their view, **emptiness** is not dependently originated for it is the absolute and thus lies beyond the bounds of the law of dependence.

See also: pratitya-samutpada

Further reading

Hopkins, J. (1983) *Meditation on Emptiness*, London: Wisdom Publications, part VI, 659–77.
Napper, E. (1989). *Dependent Arising and Emptiness*, London: Wisdom Publications, part III, 339–60.

THUPTEN JINPA

designation, theory of

Some kind of a theory of 'designation' appears to be crucial if the Tibetan Madhyamaka philosophers are to succeed in formulating their nominalist ontology. At least, this is what **Tsongkhapa** seems to think. According to Tsongkhapa, the theory of designation is best described in terms of the process of 'appropriation'. This is the idea which **Nagarjuna** calls *upadana*, literally meaning 'to grasp' or 'to appropriate', as presented in his *Mulamadhyamakakarika*.

According to this view, the physical and mental states of the person are said to be designative bases

and the 'self' or person, the 'designation'. In what sense can we maintain that, say, the eye organs are 'appropriated' by the person? Tsongkhapa suggests that when the person engages in the act of looking at an object it is the eye organs that make the individual a 'looker', i.e. an agent. Because of this, the act of seeing could immediately give rise to the natural thought, 'I am seeing'. This illustrates how 'I'-consciousness can spontaneously arise due to reliance upon the visual organs. So, the argument goes, it is true of many other physical and mental constituents. This theory of designation suggests a relativistic ontology whereby existence and identity of things and events are understood within a complex network of interrelations.

This theory of designation can be also seen as the third level of the principle of dependent origination, that is, all things and events come into being through a process of mutual dependence between designations, designating mind and the bases of designation. On one level of reading, the theory of designation can be seen as a form of conceptualism, namely that reality or unreality is determined on the basis of thoughts and concepts. Thus the Madhyamikas can be charged with proposing an ontology whereby everything is perceived to be nothing but constructs of the mind. Tsongkhapa is certainly sensitive to such a criticism and takes great care in attempting to demonstrate that the Madhyamaka ontology is not a form of mere conceptualism. His strategy is to ground the reality of the everyday world of experience within a framework, which can be shown to have a high degree of validity.

Further reading

Napper, E. (1989) *Dependent Arising and Emptiness*, London: Wisdom Publications, part III, 339–60.

THUPTEN JINPA

Dhammapada

The *Dhammapada* is an extremely popular Theravada Buddhist text, written in the Pali language and belonging to the Khuddaka Nikaya of the Sutta Pitaka portion of the **Pali Canon**. Broadly concerned with morality, it is an assemblage of 423 verses arranged in twenty-six chapters, some of which are not originally specific to Buddhism but drawn from the well of pan-Indian wisdom sayings.

The *Dhammapada* belongs to the Dharmapada genre, which also includes a version in the Gandhari Prakrit language which has been assigned to the Dharmaguptaka sub-sect of the 'Doctrine of the Elders' (*Sthavira-vada*) tradition of non-Mahayana Buddhism. The *Patna Dharmapada* is a version in a form of Prakrit highly influenced by Sanskrit and may belong to the **Mahasamghika**. There is a corresponding Sanskrit text belonging to the Sarvastivadins or Mulasarvastivadins called the *Udanavarga*. Dharmapada material also appears in the *Mahavastu* of the Lokottaravadin Mahasamghikas.

The text (from Norman's translation, pp. 1–2) begins with a mentalistic interpretation of the doctrine of retributive action (*kamma*):

1 Mental phenomena are preceded by mind, have mind as their leader, are made by mind. If one acts or speaks with an evil mind, from that sorrow follows him, as the wheel follows the foot of the ox.

2 Mental phenomena . . . . . . If one acts or speaks with a pure mind, from that happiness follows him, like a shadow not going away.

3 'He abused me, he struck me, he overcame me, he robbed me.' Of those who wrap themselves up in it, hatred is not quenched.

4 'He abused me, he struck me, he overcame me, he robbed me.' Of those who do not wrap themselves up in it, hatred is quenched.

5 For not by hatred are hatreds ever quenched here, but they are quenched by non-hatred. This is the ancient rule.

9 The impure person who will put on a yellow robe, without self-control and truth, he is not worthy of the yellow robe.

10 But whoever would be devoid of impurity, well-concentrated in virtues, possessed of self-control and truth, he is indeed worthy of the yellow robe.

13 Just as rain penetrates a badly thatched house, so passion penetrates an undeveloped mind.

The text continues to recommend a disciplined mind, detachment from possessions, constant mental vigilance, emotional self-control, the eradication of craving, hatred and delusion and moderation in all things as preliminaries to the achievement of *nibbana* in this life and ultimately the end of rebirth.

The twenty-sixth and final chapter is a classic statement of the Buddhist re-evaluation of the concept of Brahminhood, an inherited ascribed status in Hinduism whose maintenance is partly tied to ritual observances, in strictly predictive, ethical terms: 'By whom no evil is done in body, mind and voice, him, restrained in these three respects, I call a Brahman' (Norman's translation, 391). 'Not by matted locks, not by clan, not by birth, does one become a Brahman. In whom is truth and righteousness, he is pure and he is a Brahman' (393). 'But I do not call one born in a (Brahman) womb a Brahman, having his origin in a (Brahman) mother. . . . One without possessions and without attachments, him I call a Brahman' (396).

See also: caste, karma, nirvana

Further reading

Brough, J. (1962) *The Gandhari Dharmapada*, London: Oxford University Press.

Cone, M. (1986) 'The Patna Dharmapada', unpublished Ph.D. dissertation, Cambridge University.

—— (1989) 'The Patna Dharmapada. Part I: Text', *Journal of the Pali Text Society* 13: 101–217.

Hinuber, O. and Norman, K.R. (1994) (eds) *Dhammapada*, Oxford: Pali Text Society.

Norman, K.R. (trans.) (1997) *The Word of the Doctrine (Dhammapada)*, Oxford: Pali Text Society Translation Series No. 46.

CHRIS BARTLEY

dharma

Dharma is a fundamental Brahminical (Hindu) concept held to be revealed by the infallible Vedas (see **Veda**). The term is variously translated as 'natural cosmic order', 'social and religious duty', 'religion', 'law' and 'morality'. It is both an ethically normative and a descriptive concept: it is the *dharma* of grass to grow and of the sun to shine. Analogously, it is the *dharma* of members of the Brahmin class (*varna*) to study and teach the Veda, and the *dharma* of Vaishyas to engage in agriculture or commerce. *Dharma* would be unknown were it not taught by the unauthored, non-personal (*apaurusheya*) Veda, whose unconditional authority is restricted to matters transcending sensory perception and inference. This ethic is thoroughly deontological. Utilitarian criteria such as welfare, pleasure and pain or the biddings of conscience are irrelevant in determining what is right and wrong which are exclusively defined by Vedic injunctions and prohibitions and manifested in the 'conduct of the virtuous' which derives from strict observance of Vedic sanction: the vast corpus of rules extricating the pure from the potentially pollutant.

According to the earliest known traditions, the observance of *dharma* chiefly involved the performance and patronage of elaborate and expensive ritual acts generating merit (*punya*) realized in mundane prosperity (*bhoga*) and temporary post-mortem enjoyment in a heaven (*svarga*), while its neglect has all sorts of deleterious consequences ranging from personal misfortunes to the collapse of the universe into chaos.

For the later Purva Mimamsaka theorists of ritual and social duty (see **Purva Mimamsa**), the punctiliously accurate performance of both the Vedic public rituals (*shrauta*) by Brahmin priests and the domestic (*grihya*) rituals by twice-born house-holders of the highest three castes, in addition to observance of the obligations appropriate to one's caste and stage of life, transcends the achievement of benefits and rather controls, maintains and perpetuates dharmic order and stability in the universe. There is no place for an absolute, autonomous divinity in this ideology. Divinities exist, but only in so far as their names are mentioned in the ritual mechanisms. A properly performed rite automatically produces its result. To account for cases where the rite is not observed to deliver its promised result, the Mimamsakas introduced a special form of supernormal causality called *apurva* (new), which is a latent power specific to properly performed ritual acts which brings about their results at a later time. According to **Kumarila Bhatta**, the potency lies dormant in its substrate which is the soul of the patron of the sacrifice (*yajamana*) and it may be actualized in future lives. It is thought of as overriding 'normal' causal and retributive karmic conditions. This notion of retributive causality which is tied to ritual performances by the Purva-Mimamsakas is extended to moral conduct in general by other Hindu schools, most notably Vedanta.

Dharma is not a 'universal' ethic in that its prescriptions vary according to the character of circumstances and agents belonging to the three highest castes (Brahmin, Kshatriya and Vaishya) and are not reducible to a single basic principle. One and the same type of action might be right for one person (*sva-dharma* = 'own *dharma*') and wrong for another. There was a widespread recognition of the principle that it is better to perform one's own *dharma* badly than that of another well. Conflicts within the sphere of *dharma*, for example between the duty to kill in certain circumstances and the value of non-violence (**ahimsa**), are the themes of literature such as the *Mahabharata* and **Puranas**.

The life of a member of one of the three higher castes ideally has four stages (*ashrama*); that of the celibate student; that of the householder whose duty is to produce children, patronize rituals and generate prosperity; 'retirement' as a forest-dweller (*vana-prastha*); renunciation (**samnyasa**) of social role and participation in the public religion of the group. The legitimate goals of human life (**purushartha**) were initially conceived as social and religious duty (*dharma*) from which flow economic prosperity (*artha*) which is a consequence of the householder's following his proper occupation and sensual pleasure (*kama*) whose ultimate aim is procreation. This formulation prescribes what a man must do if he is to live in harmony with natural law and thus help to perpetuate the universal order. Later versions added ultimate liberation (*moksha*) from bondage to negatively evaluated cyclical existence as an individual in the here and now (*samsara*). This obviously consorts ill with the other three values, in that it represents their cancellation in respect of the released individual. The conception was successfully integrated into the dominant ideology by specifying *moksha* as the *dharma* of the renouncer (*samnyasin*) who had fulfilled his duties as a member of the religion of the group. This negative form of duty was termed '*nivritti-dharma*' in contradistinction from the active *pravritti-dharma* of the man in the world and the tension between the two has been seen by some as one of the enduring features of Hinduism.

The *Dharma-Shastras* (see **Dharma-Shastra**) are catalogues of rules defining a path of purity by the exhaustive and detailed specification of right actions for members of the different castes (although the law books are chiefly concerned with the obligations of Brahmins). The conduct of every aspect of life is rule-governed. Conformity to *dharma* which involves the exacting performance of ritual and social duties is understood as a prophylactic against pollution by the contaminant.

In Buddhist contexts the term is used quite differently, to mean either 'atomic constituent' or the universal moral and metaphysical truth discovered by the Buddha (in Pali, *dhamma*). In philosophical usage, the terms *dharma* and *dharmin* are frequently used neutral expressions translatable as 'attribute' and 'substrate'.

See also: caste

Further reading

Flood, G. (1996) *An Introduction to Hinduism*, Cambridge: Cambridge University Press.

Halbfass, W. (1991) *Tradition and Reflection*, Albany, NY: State University of New York Press.

Olivelle, P. (1993) *The Asrama System: The History and Hermeneutics of a Religious Institution*, New York: Oxford University Press.

CHRIS BARTLEY

Dharma-Shastra

The Sanskrit word *'shastra'* means 'educational treatise', and is applied across the range of arts, sciences and technologies. The Dharma-Shastra literature is concerned with the three goals (*trivarga*) whose pursuit is incumbent on Hindus: *dharma* (social and religious duties), *artha* (political stability and economic prosperity) and *kama* (aesthetic and sensual pleasure). It centres upon the duties of the four castes (*varna*) (see **caste**). The most important text is the Laws of Manu (*Manava-dharmashastra*), datable to the period 200 BCE–100 CE, and followed by the *Dharmashastras* attributed to Yajnavalkya, Vishnu, Narada, Brihaspati and Katyayana. Where their authority is concerned, they are classified as *Smriti* ('remembered', 'traditional') literature of human origin which is regarded as derived from the ultimately authoritative preterhuman Vedic **Shruti** texts.

The *Manu-smriti* or *Manava-dharmashastra* opens with an account of cyclical natural creation including the origin of the four castes: Priests (*Brahmin*), Warriors (*Kshatriya*), Agriculturalists (*Vaishya*) and Servants (*Shudra*) and the duties, benefits and occupations specific to each. To the Brahmins, the Lord assigned the teaching and study of the Veda, the performing of sacrifices for oneself and for others, the giving and receiving of gifts; the Kshatriyas he ordered to protect the people, to give, sacrifice and study; he ordered the Vaishyas to raise cattle, give, sacrifice, study, trade, lend money and cultivate the ground; finally he ordered the Shudras to serve the other three classes.

The *Manu-smriti* provides descriptions of the ritual performances (*samskara*) or *rites de passage* that mark the successive periods in a Hindu's life from cradle to funeral pyre and of the duties to be performed in each of the four stages (*ashrama*) of studentship (*brahmacharya*), being a householder (*grihastha*), forest-dweller (*vanaprastha*) and renunciation (*samnyasa*). It exhaustively specifies the sources of contamination that are to be avoided and the ritual mechanisms (*prayashchitta*) by which violated purity may be restored. The proper exercise of duly consecrated monarchy is delineated in terms of protecting the realm, inflicting punishment, raising taxes, appointing ministers and embassies, making donations to Brahmins, military strategy and tactics, and the civil and criminal judicial systems. The duties of women are focused on fidelity and obedience to the husbands upon whom they are dependent. The treatise concludes with an explanation of the ways in which actions performed in the present life condition specific forms of rebirth.

The *Arthashastra* is a text on polity attributed to Kautilya, a minister of the Mauryan king Chandragupta at the end of the fourth century BCE. The text probably belongs to the first centuries CE. This is a manual for successful royal administration. As well as describing bureaucratic offices and functions, it deals with the foreign policy to be pursued by a monarch with expansionist ambitions. Kautilya proposes the Machiavellian policy of forming alliances with one's neighbour's (that is, one's enemy's) neighbour in an effort, reinforced by the wiles of espionage, to defeat him.

Further reading

Derrett, J. (1973) *Dharmasutras and Juridical Literature*, Wiesbaden: Otto Harrassowitz.

Doniger, W. (1991) *The Laws of Manu*, Harmondsworth: Penguin.

Kane, P. (1968) *History of the Dharmasastra*, 5 vols, Poona: Bhandarkar Oriental Research Institute.

Leslie, J. (1989) *The Perfect Wife: The Orthodox Hindu Woman According to the Stridharmapaddhati of Tryambakayajvan*, Delhi: Oxford University Press.

CHRIS BARTLEY

Dharmakirti

b. 600; d. 660

Buddhist philosopher

Dharmakirti was an Indian Buddhist philosopher who expounded and developed the ideas of **Dignaga**. In his writings, he wavers somewhat between the critical realism or epistemological representationalism of the Sautrantikas and the idealism of the 'mind-only' **Yogachara** school, ultimately favouring the latter. His major works are the *Pramanavarttika* and *Pramanavinishchaya*, which deal with issues of perception, inference and proof. The *Nyayabindu* (an abstract of the *Pramanavinishchaya*), *Hetubindu* and *Vadanyaya* are logical treatises. In the *Santanantarasiddhi*, he refuted solipsism and rejected the ultimate reality of all types of relation in the *Sambandhapariksha*.

For Dharmakirti, like Dignaga, perception (*pratyaksha*), understood as pure sensation, which grasps the real momentary particular instances (*svalakshana*), and inference (*anumana*), which deals with conceptually constructed generalities, are the only two modes of valid cognition (*pramana*). Verbal cognition deriving either from authorities or the Buddhist scriptures is included under inference. He defined reality, which for him is the momentary, as actual (as opposed to potential) efficacy (*arthakriya-karitva*) rather than in terms of the definitions as temporal presence, substantial stability, spatio-temporal duration or susceptibility to valid cognition as canvassed by various Brahminical Hindu opponents. Later commentators extend this idea to the epistemological sphere and construe knowledge as the manifestation of things capable of efficacy. The capacity to produce a particular effect is one which must be discharged immediately. An entity ceases to exist as soon as it has generated its specific effect. A putative enduring substance would,

having the property of immutability, lack efficacy and thus fail to satisfy the criterion of existence.

Perception alone grasps the instantaneous mind-independent reality. Inference operates in the sphere of what is conceptually constructed by human minds. This conventional inter-subjective matrix of representations may be more or less adequate to the reality which it articulates. It also admits of degrees of consistency. The function of inference is the improvement of adequacy and internal consistency within the world-view or conceptual system.

A typical (simplified) inferential schema has the form:

> There is fire (probandum) on the mountain.
> Because there is smoke (warrant).
> Wherever there is smoke, there is fire (invariable concomitance).

Dignaga specified the conditions under which the warrant or reason (*hetu*), for example, the smoke that signifies the unseen presence of fire in an inference is valid: it must be wholly present in the case under consideration; it must be present in similar instances and it must be constantly absent in dissimilar cases. Dharmakirti elaborates Dignaga's theory of inference by providing a metaphysical justification of the three characteristics of the warrant that are the necessary conditions of logical certainty. The necessary logical relation (*vyapti*) between warrant and probandum (*sadhya*) is either one of natural causality or one of identity of essence (*tadatmya*), which may perhaps be construed as a type of analyticity. A general principle is a genuine case of invariable concomitance when the relation between warrant and probandum is causal (e.g. smoke and fire) or analytic, that is, if I know that something is an oak then I know that it is a tree. An oak has essence-identity with a tree because the property treeness pervades it. Here, 'pervades' means that the property occurs in every locus where oakness occurs. The conditions for invariable concomitance are thus more exigent than in the **Nyaya** tradition where an unfalsified inductive generalization would usually suffice.

The key concepts where inference is concerned are those of essential property (*svabhava*), effect (*karya*) and non-perception of something perceivable (*drshya-anupalabdhi*) which operates in inferences such as 'Had the visible object been present, its non-perception would not have occurred'.

Dharmakirti's nominalistic theory of **apoha** explains a concept as the difference from all other things that is common to a group of individual entities. Unique particulars cause the same judgments because the experience of them differs from experience of others. The resultant concept does not have a real referent but through the process of interpersonal communication there develops a pragmatic system of conventional relations between the unarticulated sphere of indeterminate momentary particulars that is reality and the realm of linguistic constructs that is the fabric of everyday, unenlightened life. While perception directly grasps what is real, inference is only intra-systematic valid cognition since it is essentially conceptual.

In an idealist vein, Dharmakirti formulated the principle of co-apprehension (*sahopalambha-niyama*) or the invariable association of cognition and its object or content. Thoughts and things always occur together and never separately. Consequently, there are no grounds for assuming their distinctness and they may be understood as two aspects of a single factor. In the *Sambandhapariksha*, Dharmakirti challenged the realist claim that relations are real, cognizable entities independent of their relata. His conclusion is that the relations of cause and effect, conjunction and inherence are human conceptual constructions and not actualities.

Further reading

Bijlert, V. van (1989) *Epistemology and Spiritual Authority*, Vienna: Arbeitskreis für Tibetische und Buddhistische Studien: Universität Wien.

Franco, E. (1997) *Dharmakirti on Compassion and Rebirth*, Vienna: Arbeitskreis für Tibetische und Buddhistische Studien: Universität Wien.

Matilal, B. and Evans, R. (eds) (1986) *Buddhist Logic and Epistemology*, Dordrecht: Reidel.

Stcherbatsky, T. (1992) *Buddhist Logic*, 2 vols, Delhi: Motilal Banarsidass.

Vetter, T. (1969) *Erkenntnisprobleme bei Dharmakirti*, Vienna: Hermann Bohlaus.

—— (1990) *Der Buddha und seine Lehre in Dharmakirti's Pramanavarttikam*, Vienna: Arbeitskreis für Tibetische und Buddhistische Studien: Universität Wien.

Warder, A. (1991) *Indian Buddhism*, Delhi: Motilal Banarsidass.

CHRIS BARTLEY

Dharmapala

b. 530; d. 601

Buddhist philosopher

A Buddhist idealist (**Yogachara**) philosopher, whose major work is a commentary on **Vasubandhu**'s *Vijnaptimatratasiddhi*, Dharmapala systematized Dignaga's view that the forms of subject and object are intrinsic to consciousness (*Sa-akara-vijnana-vada*). He distinguished four aspects of consciousness: subjective; objective; self-conscious; and self-self conscious. Interpreting the Buddhist theory of causation (**pratitya-samutpada**), he developed the Yogachara account of the karmic mechanism, maintaining that every action generates a latent potentiality for future action. These so-called 'seeds' (*bija*) are deposited in a subconscious 'storehouse consciousness' (**alaya-vijnana**) from which they manifest themselves under appropriate future conditions. The 'storehouse' serves as a repository of retributive karmic potentials maintaining the continuity of previous actions in the stream that is an individual series of lives. Experiences are synthesized by the mind (*manas*) so that they form an integrated totality. But the existence of the storehouse somehow generates the misconception of the substantial endurance of a soul (**atman**). The contents of consciousness do not refer to a mind-independent sphere, but are the products of prior actions and episodes of awareness arising from the storehouse surfacing in consciousness and appearing as if external.

Like other Yogacharins, he interprets experience as having a threefold nature (*trisvabhava*):

(1) everything experiential is a mental construct (*parikalpita-svabhava*).
(2) everything lacks essential identity because it is dependently originated and ontically interdependent (*paratantra-svabhava*).
(3) the real is undistorted by conceptualization and is empty (*shunya*) of essence (*svabhava*) (*parinishpanna-svabhava*).

CHRIS BARTLEY

Diagram of the Great Ultimate

Adopted from the Daoist diagram of the Former Heaven, this diagram is used by the Neo Confucians to show how the Great Ultimate evolved into the myriad things without it (the one Principle) being diminished even in the many manifestations (see **Neo-Confucianism, concepts**). The diagram is basically a series of five: the topmost is a blank circle symbolizing the Great Ultimate; the second is the same diagram divided left and right into *yin* passivity and *yang* activity. This evolved later into the *yin–yang* circle. The third shows how this pair evolved into the **Five Elements**; it contains the mutual conquest and birth series of that five. The fourth, another blank circle, shows the five being telescoped back into the set of **Heaven** above and Earth below; this in a way marks the beginning of the world. (The above/below division is spatial as the left/right split in the second diagram is temporal.) The intercourse of Heaven and Earth then produced the myriad things, the target depicted by the fifth circle.

See also: meditation; *qi*; trigger

First circle showing the Great Ultimate

Second circle showing movement and rest due to Yang and Yin halves. [The cross-over shows how movement and passivity alternate, linking it to the next diagram.]

Fire · Water

Third set of circles showing the further emanation of the two of Yin-yang into the five of the Five Elements.

Earth

Note the succession of Wood, Fire, Earth, Metal and Water. [Thus the leapfrogging.]

Wood · Metal

The five are telescoped back into the small blank circle at the bottom. [I use the dotted lines to show that re-union.]

Which becomes the pair of Heaven (above) and Earth (below).

From out of their intercourse, the myriad things are said to evolve.

Further reading

Chan Wing-tsit (trans.) (1967) *Reflections on Things at Hand: The Neo-Confucian Anthology*, compiled by Chu Hsi and Lu Tsu-ch'ien, New York: Columbia University Press.

WHALEN LAI

Dignaga

b. 480; d. 540

Buddhist philosopher

According to tradition, the Indian Buddhist philosopher Dignaga was a native of Kanci who mastered **Yogachara** idealism and **Sautrantika** representationalist critical realism under **Vasubandhu**'s influence. His most important work is the *Pramanasamucchaya* upon which he also composed a commentary. He produced commentaries on Vasubandhu's *Abhidharmakosha* and *Vadavidhana* and composed an independent logical work, the *Nyayamukha*. The *Alambanapariksha* forms the basis of the epistemology expounded in the *Pramanasamucchaya*.

About ontological issues Dignaga is an extreme nominalist for whom unarticulated reality, including human experience, consists of momentary particular instances (*svalakshanas*) which are in a state of perpetual flux. In epistemological terms, he may be characterised as a phenomenalist. In the first chapter of the *Pramanasamucchaya* he adumbrates his definition of perception (*pratyaksha*) as pure sensory awareness free from conceptualisation and judgment (*kalpana; vikalpa*). A cognition has two aspects: one relating to the ineffable particular (*svalakshana*) and another to the universal (*samanyalakshana*). The former is the object of sensation, and the latter the province of a conceptualising process. Conceptualization (*kalpana; vikalpa*) is a constructive act of the intellect at one remove from the given involving the association of a proper name, classproperty, quality, action and substance with a percept. It crucially involves verbal designation (*avyapadesha*). According to Dignaga, conceptual construction is inseparable from language. The distinction may be expressed as that between the immediate sensation of blue and the propositional judgment that something is blue which implies a belief about the appearance of the percept.

Dignaga follows Buddhist tradition in asserting that in addition to awareness involving the external sense organs (eye, ear, etc.) there is also concept-free mental sensation which is twofold: (1) awareness based on the percept in the form of immediate experience (*anubhava*) which is best interpreted as referring to the self-aware character of every mental event (later commentators describe this as a transitional stage between sensation and conceptual construction); and (2) the immediate, introspective self-awareness of inner states such as desires, anger, feelings of pleasure and pain which is not dependent upon sense-organs. These 'raw feels' are individuated by their intrinsic qualities experienced by the subject whereas sensations of external objects are identified by reference to how external objects look, sound, feel, taste and smell.

Discrete but extremely rapid cognitive episodes are tied by causal links in a series possessing a relative continuity sufficient to generate the illusion of enduring substantial personal identity. Those episodes are intrinsically reflexive or self-aware (*svasamvitti*). Each cognition has two aspects: its content – the appearance of, for example, the blue object (*artha-abhasa*) – and its own form: itself as subject (*sva-abhasa*). Each act of awareness acquires an intrinsic content or object-form (*sa-akara*) which differentiates it from other acts of awareness and which is immediately given. Dignaga draws the conclusion that cognition, whether perceptual or inferential, simultaneously and in virtue of the same act cognizes itself while cognizing the object. Self-awareness is to be distinguished from the formal cognition aspect in that the former identifies the latter as characterized by the content or blue-aspect while the cognition aspect involves only the blue-aspect. If awareness had only one aspect, then the reflexive awareness would be indistinguishable from the awareness itself. If the cognition involved only the blue aspect which was the object of self-awareness, the distinction between awareness and self-awareness would vanish:

The cognition that cognizes the object, a thing of colour, etc., has (a two-fold appearance, namely) the appearance of the object and the appearance of itself (as subject). But the cognition which cognises this cognition of the object has (on the one hand) the appearance of that cognition which is in conformity with the object and (on the other hand) the appearance of itself. Otherwise, if the cognition of the object had only the form of the object, or if it had only the form of itself, then the cognition of cognition would be indistinguishable from the cognition of the object.

(trans. in Hattori 1968: 29–30)

Sometimes a previously cognized object appears in a later cognition. This is a problem for the Sautrantika Buddhists, who think that the mind-independent sphere consists of a transitory flux of point instants. But, claims Dignaga, the experience is intelligible in terms of the dual-aspect theory:

At Time 1, Cognition 1 grasps object A
At Time 2, Cognition 2 grasps Cognition 1 as an event with a dual aspect.
Cognition 2 grasps the A-content aspect of Cognition 1. It does not grasp A directly.

Recollection is not only of the object previously cognized, but also of the cognition itself. This proves not only that a cognitive event has a dual-aspect, but also that it is reflexive since one cannot recall something without previous experience of it. The Naiyayikas (see **Nyaya**) reject the view that awareness is intrinsically reflexive and claim that cognitions are only sometimes cognized by a separate, subsequent cognitive event (*anuvyavasaya*). Dignaga says that this would result in an infinite regress and that there would be no movement of thought from one cognition to another.

According to Dignaga's economical formulation of the widely accepted Indian theory, a typical valid inference has the form:

1 There is fire (probandum: *sadhya*) on the mountain (the subject: *paksha*).
2 Because there is smoke (warrant: *hetu*).
3 Whatever has smoke has fire (invariable concomitance: *vyapti*).
   As in a kitchen (positive supporting example: *sapaksha*). Unlike in a lake (*vipaksha*).

A valid form of inference requires that there be an invariable concomitance (*vyapti*) between the *hetu*, variously translatable as warrant, reason or sign and what is sought to be established (*sadhya*). The *vyapti* is an evidence-based inductive generalization which must satisfy three conditions:

1 The warrant must be really present in the subject under consideration (*paksha*).
2 The warrant must be present in at least one case similar to the subject (*sapaksha*).
3 The warrant must be absent from dissimilar cases (*vipaksha*).

The second condition exemplifies the evidence for the generalization. The third, apart from indicating the lack of falsifying counter-example, shows that the generalization is not a truism.

As a logician, Dignaga is chiefly noted for the *hetu-chakra* or table of reasons which shows the nine possible relations between the warrant (*hetu*) and the probandum (*sadhya*) demonstrating the cases in which the warrant is either valid or invalid. A valid warrant has to be a property of the subject (*dharmin*) of the thesis under consideration (*pakshadharmatva*); it must exist in all or some similar instances (*sapaksha*); it must never exist in dissimilar instances (*vipaksha*). Of the nine possible combinations between warrant, similar instance and dissimilar instance, only two yield valid inferences: that in which the warrant is absent from all *vipakshas* and present in all *sapakshas* and that in which the warrant is absent from all *vipakshas* and present in some *sapakshas*.

The instantaneous propertyless unique particular (*svalakshana*) given in purely sensory awareness is strictly inexpressible. Our conceptual and linguistic processes which are at one remove from pure sensation operate by means of exclusions or dichotomies (*vikalpa*). The constructive act involving the association of a proper name, universal, quality, action or substance with a percept is a conventional articulation of the experienced sphere of indeterminate and fluid particulars in terms of what are purely human concepts. We impose order, classify and interpret via the application of conceptual and linguistic schemes. On this view, objects and universals, properties and relations in which the given is articulated are functions of conceptual schemes. They do not exist objectively or independently of human minds.

In Chapter 5 of the *Pramanasamucchaya*, Dignaga develops the **apoha** theory that a word relates to its referent or object through the exclusion of other dissimilar objects. A purported essence such as cowness is reduced to exclusion from the mixed set of non-bovine particulars and this difference serves

as the common feature that is the grounds for the application of the term 'cow'. In consonance with his rejection of essences and generalities as conceptual constructions, Dignaga denies that a word signifies either a real universal or individual essence. The word 'cow' distinguishes its referent from everything else comprising the network of conventional classifications. It is in this context that his cryptic statement that everything has multiple forms should be construed.

The apprehension of an object through the exclusion of other objects is not a perceptual but an inferential procedure. To explain: the presence of smoke generates knowledge of the presence of fire in a particular locus by excluding loci, such as bodies of water where fire is absent (*vipaksha*). Awareness of other loci (*sapaksha*, such as a kitchen) where the invariable concomitance of smoke and fire obtains serves a confirmatory purpose. The word 'cow' generates cognition of a cow by excluding non-bovine individuals and this is assisted by our shared linguistic practice of applying the word. A consequence of this is that language (*shabda*) is not an authoritative means of knowledge (**pramana**) in its own right. Perception (*pratyaksha*) which grasps the momentary particulars (*svalakshana*) and inference (*anumana*), which only deals with conceptually constructed generalities, are the only two modes of valid cognition (*pramana*).

In the *Alambanapariksha* Dignaga attacked realist theories, maintaining that a cognition cannot have as its object an external or mind-independent item whether an atom or an aggregate of atoms. For realism to be intelligible, the objective support (*alambana*) of awareness must satisfy two conditions: it must exercise a causal role and it must have the same form (*akara*) as the manifest content of cognition. To satisfy these conditions, the object must be real (*dravya-sat*) and possess gross form (*sthula-akara*). Since no form of realism passes the test, Dignaga draws the conclusion that what is conventionally considered as the object of cognition is nothing other than the internal content or form (*akara*) of cognition.

Further reading

Hattori, M. (1968) *Dignaga, on Perception*, Cambridge, MA: Harvard University Press.

Hayes, R. (1988) *Dignaga on the Interpretation of Signs*, Dordrecht: Reidel.

Matilal, B. (1986) *Perception*, Oxford: Clarendon Press.

Matilal, B. and Evans, R. (eds) (1986) *Buddhist Logic and Epistemology*, Dordrecht: Reidel.

Shastri, D. (1980) *Critique of Indian Realism*, Delhi: Bharatiya Vidya Prakasana.

Warder, A. (1980) *Indian Buddhism*, Delhi: Motilal Banarsidass.

CHRIS BARTLEY

divination

Divination was a major preoccupation of Shang kings and has had a lasting legacy. There is hardly a well-visited temple in China that does not offer fortune telling. This mantric art is canonized in the Confucian Classic, the *Yijing* (Book of Changes) attributed to the Zhou King Wen. A line in the *Analects* has **Confucius** saying that if he had more time in his waning years, he would devote himself to studying the *Yi*. This has lent legitimacy to this Classic as being the most profound. (The line is now known to involve a homophone; re-read, it simply says, 'It is never too late to learn'.) **Zhu Xi** helped to demystify this text, long elevated to metaphysical heights, by openly noting that it was originally a manual for telling fortunes. He himself consulted it on a matter of high personal risk: should he or should he not send a memorial to the emperor criticizing certain recent reform policies? The answer came back 'no', and so he desisted.

Further reading

Keightley, D. (1986) 'Shang Divination and Metaphysics', *Philosophy East and West* 38: 367–97.

Smith, R. (1991) *Fortune-tellers and Philosophers: Divination in Traditional Chinese Society*, Boulder, CO: Westview.

WHALEN LAI

DOGEN *see* Buddhist philosophy in Japan

Dolpopa Sherap Gyaltsen

b. 1292; d. 1361

Buddhist philosopher

Dolpopa began his early education as a Shakya, but later changed his sectarian affiliation to the **Jonang school** after his visit to Jonang monastery at the age of thirty-one. Recognized as a great master of the Kalachakra Tantra, Dolpopa played a major role in the establishment of the study and practice of this **tantra** in Tibet. However, he is best known for his philosophical treatise *The Ocean of Definitive Meaning*, which presented a heterodoxical interpretation of the Madhyamaka philosophy of **emptiness**. Dolpopa argued for an affirmative conception of the ultimate truth and suggested that the aphophatic discourse of **Nagarjuna**'s *Fundamentals of the Middle Way* does not represent the definitive standpoint. In contrast, he suggested, it is Nagarjuna's collection of hymns that present his final views about the ultimate nature of reality. Dolpopa's views became institutionalized as **Shentong philosophy**, and have been an object of vehement criticism by various thinkers including **Buton Rinchen Drup**, Rendawa and **Tsongkhapa**.

Further reading

Stearns, C. (1996). *The Buddha from Dol po: The Study of the Life and Thought of the Tibetan master Dolpopa Sherab Gyaltsen*, Albany, NY: State University of New York Press.

THUPTEN JINPA

Dong Zhongshu

b. 195 BCE; d. 115 BCE

Confucian philosopher

A major figure in Han Emperor Wu's court, Dong Zhongshu (Tung Chung-shu) was responsible for making *yin–yang* Confucianism the state ideology. A New Text scholar – 'New' refers to the Classics (see **Classics and Books**) being written down from memory in the current, 'new' script after the 'burning of books' under the First Emperor – he presented **Confucius** as an uncrowned **sage-king** who prophesied the rise and helped design the institutions of Han rule. In order to unify China, the First Emperor of the Qin dynasty sought ideological conformity. (According to legend, spread by Confucians, he followed Legalist advice and supposedly destroyed all records of the other schools of thought, except those in the imperial library.) This is spelled out in Dong's commentary on the *Spring and Autumn Annals*. His New Text scholarship endorsed the theory of three historical ages and the succession of dynasties based on their place in the scheme of the **Five Elements**.

Against the cult of the 'Great Unity' personally favoured by the Emperor, Dong asserted the primacy of the Confucian cult of **Heaven**. The Great Unity or Ultimate One is a monistic principle, the number one that oversees and runs through the myriad realities (all the other numbers) in the **magic square**. Although he considered the ruler the indispensable pillar who united Heaven, Man and Earth, he also held the ruler answerable to the omens and auspices sent by Heaven. That is based on a faith in a 'correspondence between man and Heaven'. It means that moral events in the human realm would stimulate the moral universe to respond with these signs of heavenly pleasure and displeasure. In his *yin–yang* anthropology, he assigned humaneness to the *yang* half and greed to the *yin* half. Though he made the 'three pillars and five relationships' the Confucian orthopraxy, this professor at the imperial academy did not consider women, slaves or **barbarians** (*yin* social inferiors) any less able to do good. The five cardinal human relationships in Confucianism are 'ruler/minister', 'father/son', 'husband/wife', 'elder brother/ younger brother' and 'friend/friend'. These are supposed to be reciprocal relationships. The three pillars take the first three and make the first member (ruler, father, husband) the pillar upon which the subordinate (minister, son, wife) would lean or rely.

WHALEN LAI

dragon

A mythical animal, usually considered evil and chthonic (linked with the underworld) in the West, the dragon is deemed auspicious and highly valued in China. It is associated with water below (ground) and water above (rain clouds). As a result, it is not an evil figure but a celestial and an imperial symbol, the Emperor being supposedly a living dragon in his regal dragon robe. Legends abound of emperors turning into dragons when asleep. The last to have that auspicious sign told of him is President Yuan Shikai, first president of the Chinese Republic. Medieval China incorporated the Indian tradition of the *nagas* (sea snakes), and better accommodated the 'evil (other side of the) dragon' linguistically by having a second term for the malicious type. As a symbol of **chaos**, it is often sighted by travellers in rivers, lakes, and wilds.

The prototype is a pig-nosed dragon in the round (biting its own tail) carved on a jade disc going back to a prehistoric 'jade age' in northeast China. Associated with the mythic Sage-King Yu (for fish, thus dragon) of the Xia dynasty, it appears in the art of the historic Shang dynasty, being found on the bottom of the 'spring libation' dish, a ritual bronze, in the form of a coiled serpent. On a frieze running below the rim of the dish run the icons for fish, bird and tiger; on the underside is a turtle. A structuralist analysis shows the dragon not as a mythical animal, but as the sum of all animals. The spring libation rite (water poured into the dish) awakes the coiled serpent from its wintry hibernation. This ur-dragon then mutates into the fish (of spring), the bird (of summer) and the tiger (of autumn) before (all these species) withdraw into the turtle (of winter). The turtle (in its shell) is an inanimate rock (dead) until its dragonic rebirth next spring. This explains why the dragon is said to be 'the most *yang* (potent) of all beings' and 'capable of infinite mutation'. What the Bible kept separate, namely birds of the air, fishes of the waters, and beasts of the forests and regarded their species distinction as 'good', the Chinese considered as mutable and deemed the mixed forms 'potent'. As an example of this, it is worth noting that traditional Jewish diets thus prohibit shrimps while the Chinese love dragon-shrimps (lobsters).

Within the Classics (see **Classics and Books**), the dragon is most prominently featured in the 'Heaven' hexagram in the *Book of Changes*. The six unbroken (*yang*) lines are said to be 'six dragons'. To ride these six dragons – a shamanic flight – is to have total control of the universe. The explanation given to the six lines (six dragons) is of philosophical interest. It goes as follows:

1 Hidden Dragon in the deep.
   Do not disturb.

2 Dragon appearing in the field.
   It advances one to see the great man.

3 All day long the superior man is creative and
   active.
   By night his mind is beset by cares.
   Danger. No blame.

4 Wavering flight over the abyss [separating earth
   and sky].
   No blame.

5 Flying dragon in the sky.
   It advances one to see the gentleman.

6 Arrogant dragon [overshoots].
   Will have cause to regret.

The overall judgment of all six lines: 'A band of (six)
dragons with no leader: Auspicious.'

Upon a closer look, 'no leader' (no head) points to
its having no beginning and no end. That refers to
the form of the carved jade dragon noted earlier: it is
a circular dragon, a snake biting its own tail. Hidden
in the six lines is a description of a yearly change.
Translated in sequence, the six animal forms are:

1 The dragon in the deep is the turtle (north);
2 The dragon coming onto the rice fields or
   marshes is the amphibious frog (east);
3 The dragon labouring hard all day is making its
   trip from east to west and shore to hill, mutating
   into;
4 The dragon in hesitant flight, meaning a tiger in
   the hills (west) leaping into the air;
5 The dragon in confident flight is its changing
   into the winged bird (south);
6 The dragon overshooting its target is the bird
   falling down and turning back into the turtle in
   the deep.

This annual tour of the dragon runs thus: north,
east, west, south, north. It forms an endlessly
twirling helix. Translated into the five elements, the
sequence is water, wood, metal, fire [plus earth].
This accords with the 'conquest series' of the **Five
Elements**. Fire (south, fire) is dampened/put out
by Water (winter) that follows it. Wood (spring) is
overcome/chopped up by Metal (an axe: autumn)

that comes after. Earth interrupts the series in the
northeast corner, i.e. at the turn of the New Year.

Further reading

Douglas, M. (1966) *Purity and Danger. An Analysis of
the Concepts of Pollution and Taboo*, London:
Routledge & Kegan Paul.
Lai, W. (1984) 'Symbolism of Evil in China: the
K'ung-chia Myth Analyzed', *History of Religions*
23(4): 316–43.
Ricoeur, P. (1967) *The Symbolism of Evil*, New York:
Harper & Row.

WHALEN LAI

dream and illusion

Dreams were a medium for communication with
the dead and the spiritual world long before
philosophers turned them into metaphors of
illusion. Thus at one point **Confucius** still
regretted that he had not had recent dreams of
the Duke of Zhou, his spiritual mentor. **Zhuangzi**
used dreams to cast doubt on the waking state. He
dreamt himself a butterfly. Unsure if he was in or
out of a dream, he then wondered if he was a man
or a butterfly. Early China produced reports of
dream divination and of dream journeys. But it is
the Buddha who compares insubstantiality to
dreams, the Mahayana which equates **emptiness**
with *maya* (illusion), and that had some early
Chinese Buddhists reading the statement 'Form is
emptiness, emptiness is form' as describing 'illusory
transformation'. The empty dream looks formally
real: until one wakes up.

The heightened awareness to the world as an
illusion was applied to a tale of worldly fame and
fortune in a well-known story. A man fell asleep
and dreamed he was summoned to become a
prime minister and to marry into the royal family,
only to wake up to find that he had fallen asleep
next to an anthill. His fabled career was due to his
being transported to that kingdom. It was a literary
samsara. Under a confident Tang dynasty,
Buddhists turned to celebrating suchness over
emptiness, reality over illusion; that is, until
Chan once more preferred the negative dialectics.
Chan favoured the Chinese-edited *Surangama Sutra*
and the Chinese-compiled *Perfect Enlightenment Sutra*.

Both highlighted the frailty of life; it is like 'a flower [conjured up by a magician] in mid-air'. Beautiful to behold, it masks its own emptiness.

That and similar metaphors allowed the Neo-Confucian **Zhu Xi** to charge Buddhism with being nihilist, as he called for a return to the real duties of social living. But by the late Ming period, that realism had become so humdrum that people flocked to watch a famous set of four 'dream plays' on the stage, of which *Peony Pavilion* and *Anthill Dream* are the most famous. Dreams could also turn nightmarish; in the early Qing dynasty, people dined on the nightmare tales from the Leisure Studio. Dreams also were cultivated for revelations. Many manuals of dream analysis were circulated, the most popular being titled *Queries on Dreams to the Duke of Zhou*. Phonocentric and picturocentric, the interpretations relied heavily on puns and dissection of the Chinese scripts.

Further reading

Lai, W. (1978) 'Illusionism (Mayavada) in Late T'ang Buddhism', *Philosophy East and West* 28(1): 39–51.

Li Wei-yee (1993) *Enchantment and Disenchantment: Love and Illusion in Chinese Literature*, Princeton, NJ: Princeton University Press.

Lu K'uan-yu (Charles Luk) (1962) *Ch'an and Zen Teachings*, Part III, 'The Sutra of Complete Enlightenment', London: Rider, 149–278.

—— (1996) *The Surangama Sutra*, London: Rider.

Wu Kuang-ming (1982) *Chuang Tzu: World Philosopher at Play*, Chico, CA: Scholars Press.

Zeitlin, J. (1993) *Historian of the Strange: Pu Songling and the Classical Chinese Tale*, Stanford, CA: Stanford University Press.

WHALEN LAI

Dream of the Red Chamber

Perhaps the greatest masterpiece of Chinese literature, *Dream of the Red Chambers*, a Chinese novel from the mid-Qing period, describes life in a Chinese family which, however extraordinary in terms of wealth, is nonetheless identifiable with the tensions and dynamics in most Chinese family settings. The story is of philosophical importance because it shows clearly the socialization into the virtues and the

traditions. A Chinese person enjoys a carefree, happy, natural, guile-less Daoist childhood; which ends rather abruptly at age six when he has to adjust fully to the requirement of Confucian etiquette; to which he is bound until, as a grandparent at age sixty, he is allowed to have his second childhood (hold hands with his spouse in public and spoil his grandchildren) even as he prepares for a Buddhist retirement and final deliverance. By depicting the tragic loss of childhood on the part of the main character and the loss of the love of his life, the novel also teaches the Mahayana lesson that 'Form (eros) is **emptiness**; emptiness is form'.

Further reading

Hawkes, D. (trans.) (1973–82) *The Story of the Stone*, Harmondsworth: Penguin.

Knoerle, J. (1972) *The Dream of the Red Chamber: A Critical Study*, foreword by Liu Wu-chi, Bloomington, IN: Indiana University Press.

WHALEN LAI

Dvaita

Dvaita was a strongly dualistic school of Vedanta philosophically articulating a rigorously monotheistic Vishnu cult (which was originally Shaiva). This tradition was inaugurated in Southwest India in the thirteenth century by **Madhva** in reaction to the ultimately anti-theistic non-dualism of **Advaita** and as a response to the *Vishishthadvaita* of **Ramanuja**, whose intimate association relation of God and the soul he regarded as compromising the latter's transcendent perfection. He departed from the tenets of mainstream Vedanta by denying that God is both the material and the efficient cause of the world which he creates from an independent material principle subject to his governance. Other exponents are Jayatirtha (1345–88) and Vyasatirtha (1460–1539), both of whom commented on Madhva's expositions of the *Upanishads*, *Bhagavad Gita* and *Brahma-Sutras* and who are chiefly notable as logicians.

Dvaitins uphold the existence of a plurality of individual selves and the mind-independence of the physical world, each of which spheres is existentially dependent upon Vishnu who is the only truly independent and self-sufficient reality sustaining the finite and contingent realm. Devotion (*bhakti*) to the personal deity is held to be the necessary and sufficient condition of liberation from the series of births in the here and now.

Further reading

Dasgupta, S. (1949) *A History of Indian Philosophy*, Vol. IV, Cambridge: Cambridge University Press.

Sharma, B. (1981) *History of the Dvaita School of Vedanta and its Literature*, Delhi: Motilal Banarsidass.

—— (1986) *Philosophy of Sri Madhvacharya*, Delhi: Motilal Banarsidass.

CHRIS BARTLEY

Dzokchen thought

According to the **Nyingma school** of Tibetan Buddhism, Dzokchen (literally, Great Perfection) represents the apex of the Buddhist path to enlightenment. It is the 'highest' and the last within the so-called nine *yana*s or vehicles. The historical sources of Dzokchen teachings remain somewhat uncertain. Although the tradition traces its origin to the teachings brought from India by the great eighth-century Tibetan translator Vairochana, and maintains that Dzokchen is a revealed tradition with autonomous Indian roots and some Tibetan roots, modern scholars have detected unmistakable characteristics of Chan/Ch'an influence in some of its basic tenets. **Yogachara** doctrines also appear to exert significant influence on the development of Dzokchen thought. It was, however, in the fourteenth century that Dzokchen became systematized by **Longchen Rabjampa** as representing a cohesive philosophical viewpoint.

The central issue in Dzokchen thought is the nature of mind and the possibility of its recognition. It is the 'mind' (*sem*; spelled *sems*), which is said to be different from 'pristine awareness' (*rik pa*) that creates the world of appearance and through its activities has obscured its own real nature from beginningless time. Yet, it is maintained that the real nature of mind is primordially pure and this purity is our spiritual basis. It has always been in a state of perfection and nothing more is required. Hence the name 'great perfection'. This pure awareness or *rikpa* is said to be free of any conceptualization and also that it is 'unborn' and cannot be modified. It is pure and infinite from the very beginning and always perfect in its totality. Though indescribable both in cataphatic or aphophatic terms, this primordial basis is said to be fundamentally positive and is conceived in terms of cognition. It has three principal characteristics: (1) its status is pure from the beginning; (2) its nature is spontaneous and luminous; and (3) its true being is the primeval cognition that pervades all. This embodiment of the three attributes is the transcendent state of mind and is also called *Dharmakaya*, the Buddha body of reality, sometimes depicted in a personified form as Samandrabadra ('He who is entirely good').

It is unclear whether the Dzokchen doctrine of primordial purity is to be taken as an ontological theory or whether it is primarily a meditative perspective. Also the question of the theory's relation with the Madhyamaka central tenet of the **emptiness** of intrinsic existence remains open. Traditionally, Dzokchen thinkers have attempted to address this question by harmonizing the two perspectives by turning the Madhyamaka standpoint into representing an important preliminary to Dzokchen thought.

Further reading

Karmay, S. (1988) *The Great Perfection: A Philosophical and Meditative Teaching of Tibetan Buddhism*, Leiden: Brill, ch. 7.

THUPTEN JINPA

E

education in China, philosophy of

The Chinese consider their philosophies to be 'teachings' or 'learnings'. Such a teaching or learning is affected by an explicit anthropology or view of man. If children are seen as being born evil, you are less likely to spare the cane. If human nature is viewed as basically good, you work to draw it out. And schooling style and method is affected by how knowledge is organized and how psychological growth is assessed. For ruling the world, a Han scholar focused on the objective institutes of the Classics; for cultivating the self, a Song student discerned, step by step, a personal ascent towards the good.

Pedagogy is at the centre of **Xunzi**'s essay on 'Inducement to Learn'. To learn is to become civilized; education which changes nature into culture is what separates man from beast, a child of nature from a civilized adult, and Chinese from **barbarians**. Education involves employing 'artifice' to develop the 'humane', as when one needs to ride a horse to cover a long distance faster, or take a boat to cross large oceans. Focus and perseverance are required. The goal is to polish a rough encrusted gem stone into fine jade, to make beautiful (as the Greeks would say) the form of the self. A more Mencian mode of pedagogy appears in the chapter 'On Learning' in *The Book of Rites*. It is better to be tutored into virtue, not by formal rules but through a positive, living exemplar, a good teacher. Reverence for a master and

honouring the Way is what moral schooling truly means.

By the time of the Han dynasty, **Dong Zhongshu** had schematized the rule by **rites** and the rule by law, as follows: *yang* goes with virtue, *yin* goes with punishment. Education into virtue is the positive *yang* means; the interdicts of law are the negative *yin* means. That two-pronged approach went with the new imperium of Legalist statecraft as tamed by the Confucian family values. But if we look at the Family Teaching of the Yan Clan that came after that synthesis was lost along with the Han rule, we see how the learning of the Classics (see **Classics and Books**) had devolved into rather arid footnoting on words and sentences. That 'attention to details' had lost sight of the 'larger meaning'. Those two themes used to be one. Meanwhile, Tao Qian had aired a new attitude. He confessed that he as 'Mr Five Willows' (he named himself after nature) loved 'reading books but did not particularly care to understand (the details)'. But whenever an idea or insight struck him, he would be so enthralled as to forego food and forget sleep. This delight in seeing the larger picture meant giving up on the tedious details. These two approaches, however, did not seem to mesh or meet.

The Buddhists in the same period, namely the Six Dynasties (420–581), were caught up in the same struggle. They appended notations to the *sutras*, sentence by sentence, and they pondered how all these many and varied words of the Buddha could possibly be addressing the one *dharma*. Finally, by the end of the sixth century,

Zhiyi made a historic breakthrough. He uncovered, after working through 'the words and sentences' of the *Lotus Sutra* and grasping its hidden meaning, a perspicuous structure to this and all other *sutras*. A system of grading and then a means of integrating the many and varied *sutras* was created. (The modern Buddhist canon – Japan's Taisho Daizokyo set – still employs that system to help catalogue and make sense of the mass and confusion of Mahayana texts.) This solution to the problem was learned by the Neo-Confucians from the Buddhists.

Before the Song dynasty, there was no idea of schooling children according to age and grades. Grading was developed when the principle behind the Five Classics of the Han was seen somehow to be embedded in the new canon and the sequence of the Four Books. These could then be graded, starting with short dialogues of the *Analects*, then going on to the longer conversations in **Mencius**, proceeding on to the essay of the *Great Learning*, and capping it all with the philosophically most complex, the *Doctrine of the Mean*. For good measure, **Zhu Xi** compiled the *Small Learning* for youngsters. Other popular primers for children like the *Three Character Classic* appeared later. Zhu Xi also set down six rules for book learning: follow the steps and proceed slowly; commit to memory and reflect keenly; empty the mind and let the truth sink in; submit it to a close scrutiny and personal verification; with a sense of urgency, exert effort; and dwell in reverence with a mind ever so attentive. We are not talking here about learning new facts about new worlds; we are talking about spiritual growth. Such is the Way, the goal of which is nothing less than sagehood.

With Neo-Confucianism becoming the state orthodoxy in Ming China and the competition in civil service examinations growing ever more fierce, the schooling schedule started now at an increasingly earlier age; the number of texts to be memorized became more and more mechanical, and soon the quest for a career identity overshadowed the quest for sagehood and the Way. Schools became 'no fun' for the pressured young, and so Wang Yangming revoked the overly intellectualist approach and worked to elicit the goodness of the child's mind by games and songs. This more emotive approach was extended by the Taizhou school to involve peasants and womenfolk with ditties, dance and popular theatre. Although in the early Qing dynasty there was a revival of philology and of Han learning and a criticism of the Song philosophical principles, that venture back into the Classics and to the historical particulars, though important, touched only a small circle and did not affect education in general, which continued in the Ming style up until 1911.

To the list of five cardinal human relationships, Han Confucians added one more sacred tie: the honouring of the teacher by the student. Buddhists strengthen this concept, since one's master mentors one into the holy life. He mediates – even intercedes – for the novitiate before the Buddha. Neo-Confucianism inherited that Buddhist model: a true teacher initiates the student into a quest of sagehood. The student moves away from home, stays with and serves the master like a second (spiritual) father and owes him filial mourning at death. He marries the master's daughter, too, if that can be arranged. Under despotic Ming rule, Neo-Confucian moral idealists protested by following Han Yu (768–824) who in an essay 'On Teachers' recalled a legend in the *Book of Rites* in which a **sage** ruler of virtue would revere and defer to his teacher. Like **Confucius**, the 'teacher of kings', the teacher presumes a moral authority that places him above one who employs him. This actually works with even poor private tutors, who can demand satisfaction for an affront. (In one biographical account, the doorman put on the master's gown and apologized to the tutor, saving face all around.)

See also: friendship

Further reading

Chaffee, J. (1985) *The Thorny Gates of Learning in Sung China: A Social History of the Examinations*, Cambridge: Cambridge University Press.

de Bary, W. (ed.) (1970) *Self and Society in Ming Thought*, New York: Columbia University Press.

—— (1983) *The Liberal Tradition in China*, Hong Kong and New York: Chinese University of Hong Kong and Columbia University Press.

Lai, W. (1987) 'The Earliest Folk Buddhist Religion in China: The Ti-wei Po-li ching and its

Historical Significance', in D. Chappell (ed.), *Buddhist and Taoist Studies II: Buddhist and Taoist Practice in Medieval Chinese Society*, Honolulu, HA: University of Hawaii, 11 35.

WHALEN LAI

EISAI *see* Buddhist philosophy in Japan

emptiness

Ever since the introduction of Madhyamaka thought to Tibet there has been a broad consensus that emptiness (*shunyata*) is the highest truth and is thus the ultimate nature of reality. However, as to what exactly is emptiness, there is a great divergence of opinions among Tibetan thinkers. For **Tsongkhapa**, emptiness is the final truth that we arrive at when we subject all things and events, including our own selves to critical analysis as presented in the Madhyamaka discourse. It is the total absence of the intrinsic existence and intrinsic identity. This truth, though 'unborn', 'unceasing' and 'thoroughly pacifying', can only be conceptualized in terms of a negation. In other words, in the ultimate sense, we can describe the nature of reality definitively only through the language of negation. In fact, Tsongkhapa argues that any attempt to conceptualize emptiness in affirmative terms would entail reification thus leading to further obscuration. Hence, according to Tsongkhapa, emptiness is a mere negation that does not imply anything affirmative in the wake of its negation of intrinsic existence.

For others, like Taktshang Lotsawa, Gorampa, **Shakya Chokden** and Karmapa Mikyo Dorje, the emptiness of intrinsic existence is only a step towards the final truth, which according to them transcends all conceptual elaboration. Final emptiness, in their view, is said to be free of all four dichotomies, namely existence, nonexistence, both and neither. It is literally both ineffable and nonconceptualizable. Such truth can only be directly 'experienced' but never 'cognized' by an intellect through a rational approach. Thus we have no recourse to emptiness through language and thought. According to these Tibetan thinkers,

by understanding emptiness in terms of the absolute negation of intrinsic existence, Tsongkhapa has fallen into nihilism. Among them, however, Taktshang and Gorampa accept Tsongkhapa's point about the dangers of conceptualizing emptiness in terms of an affirmation. However Shakya Chokden and Karmapa Mikyo Dorje take issue with this. They attempt to develop a cataphatic description of the ultimate nature of reality thus sharing the basic standpoint of **Shentong philosophy** on the issue of the description of ultimate reality. Related to this question of description is the issue of whether or not final emptiness is a non-implicative negation or an 'implicative negation'. This debate remains to this day one of the most enduring and contested questions of Madhyamaka discourse in Tibet.

Further reading

Jinpa, T. (1998). 'Delineating Reason's Scope for Negation: Tsongkhapa's Contribution to Madhyamaka's Dialectical Method', *Journal of Indian Philosophy* 26: 275–308.

Napper, E. (1989) *Dependent Arising and Emptiness*, London: Wisdom Publications, I, 39–143.

THUPTEN JINPA

Enlightenment, Korean

Enlightenment thought known as *Kaehwa sasang* developed in Korea during the period 1876–1910, which is also known as the period of modernization or enlightenment in Korea. By the end of the nineteenth century, Korea was being greatly influenced by Western culture, its education, philosophy, religion, politics, economics and scientific technology. As a result of this influence, the traditional control of society by the Neo-Confucian philosophy was significantly shaken and weakened. A growing number of intellectuals advocated modernization of the political, social and economic systems of Korea by emulating modern Western systems. They championed enlightenment and reform through the process of learning and adopting Western ideas, especially Western science and technology. Hence, this movment was called the modernization or enlightenment movement. This movement was a successor of the spirit of **Sirhak** (the school of Practical Learning), which was important between the seventeenth and nineteenth centuries, and which began to challenge the sterile orthodoxy of Neo-Confucianism and offered an alternative world-view by reforming the social and economic conditions of the masses.

There was a severe conflict between this progressive modernization movement and the conservative traditionalist group, which wanted to maintain the orthodoxy of Neo-Confucianism and opposed Western ideas. The *yangban* (aristocratic) class which controlled politics and society wanted to preserve its positions and power by maintaining traditional ways. However, the masses were not interested in the Neo-Confucian tradition and began to reject the power structure of the *yangban* class, which discriminated against the commoners.

Thinkers of this modernization and enlightenment movement were keenly aware that Western technology and Western political and economic systems were more advanced than the ones in Korea, and they realized that Japan was learning and adopting the Western systems rapidly. They wanted to reform the political, social, and economic systems of Korea to make the nation strong. They wanted to change the feudalistic system of Korean government into a modern system of government. They had a progressive, modernistic spirit of enlightenment, and made significant contributions to the reform of Korea and its transformation into a modern society. The representative thinkers of the modern enlightenment in Korea were **Kim Ok-kyun**, **Pak Un-sik** and **Chu Si-kyong**.

Further reading

Lee, P. (ed.) (1996) *Sourcebook of Korean Civilization*, Vol. 2, New York: Columbia University Press, 337ff.

YONG-CHOON KIM

enlightenment, sudden

Sudden enlightenment was a famous doctrine of the Southern School of Zen, championed by Shenhui, disciple of the Sixth Patriarch who employed the 'northern gradualism, southern subitism' formula against the deviant path of the Northern – actually then the mainstream – school. D.T. Suzuki introduced it as part of the Zen mystique to the West, he himself being of the Rinzai school that has considered its own *koan* method to be the sudden style, compared against the quietism of the Soto school. This school was founded by Linji, who taught through 'dialectical' formulae, and his very strong personality is remembered through his 'recorded sayings'. Since both Rinzai and Soto considered themselves heirs of the Southern School, this raises the question what sort of theory subitism truly entails and whether such 'name-calling' serves a purpose.

Historically, **Daosheng** first proposed 'sudden enlightenment' in the early fifth century; by tying the pre-existent **buddha nature** to sudden awakening, he anticipated the Chan/Zen position. However, up to the sixth century the presumption even among the members of the Nirvana School is one of 'gradual cultivation (leading to) sudden enlightenment'. Buddha nature remains the 'seed of enlightenment' requiring nurture to become fully grown. By around 550, a distinction was being made between 'principal buddha nature' which is replete in itself, and 'active buddha nature' which pertains to deeds and process. This pair of concepts appeared also in a treatise attributed to **Bodhidharma**. This is also the time when the *Awakening of Faith in Mahayana* made its appearance. From this point on, the formula is reversed: 'gradual cultivation is predicated upon sudden enlightenment (or full endowment of enlightenment)'. Zongmi later considered this to be the correct essence of the Southern Zen school.

Further reading

Gregory, P. (ed.) (1987) *Sudden and Gradual: Approaches to Enlightenment in Chinese Buddhist Thought*, Honolulu, HA: University of Hawaii Press.

WHALEN LAI

enlightenment experience and religious biography

An interesting example to consider is the case of Wang Yangming (1472–1529), the major Chinese thinker of the late Ming dynasty who successfully challenged the **Zhu Xi** orthodoxy. Wang argued that the principle does not so much rest in the nature of things as it is fully present already in the mind. This idea that the 'Mind is Principle' came to him while, in disgrace, he was exiled to a non-Han location, when he heard it whispered into his ears during sleep. Psychological history is of relevance in studying the place of religious biography in intellectual history only when we have such narratives of personal enlightenment. Chan had made the enlightenment experience into a cult of its own before and Wang is known to have been influenced by Chan. Not every detail in a religious biography needs to be true to fact in order to be real. All memories, after all, are constructed out of a past that is being continually re-interpreted by us. Some famous Chan encounters of great import are demonstrably fictive. To do a good 'narrative analysis', we must take the whole structure of the full narrative into account. Wang affords us an intriguing 'full' case, although some earlier efforts have fallen short.

Wang was born with a speech impediment; he could not talk or speak well until age six. He regained the power of speech at that point when his given name (or milk name) was changed from Shouyun to Shouren. The former has connotations of Daoist 'cloud' where the latter has Confucian 'benevolence'. At eleven, Wang surprised his tutor by saying that the purpose of learning is not to win an official post; it is to become a **sage**. Being schooled in the Zhu Xi orthodoxy, at eighteen he literally went about *gewu* or 'investigating things' so he might 'access the knowledge' of the moral principle. He and a friend lined up side by side (*ge*) these bamboo strips. They looked and looked intensely at them. His friend fell sick; Wang persisted for a few more days but could not find any principle in them. All these were forgotten or put aside when Wang succeeded on the 'career' route. It was only when that faltered and he was exiled that the old quest was revived – and enlightenment came.

At the simplest level, Wang was facing a cultural shock. An erudite individual, he was living among aboriginals who could not even speak proper Chinese. In that situation – like an American tourist in Paris – old values unhinged from its supporting culture (now absent) either fall apart (into anomie) or they could be positively reconfirmed through radical interiorization. Wang took the latter route; he realized that the (moral) principle is within irrespective of a change in environment. But in terms of psychohistory, it is telling that he heard that truth whispered into his ears. Speech was the medium of his awakening, just as a speech impediment at birth once held him back in apparent ignorance. Children learn initially by do's and don'ts, commands they heard spoken (given by the father) and taken as true before the child could think for himself. This, says Freud, is the root of 'the small voice of conscience', and in Wang's philosophy this comes out indeed as his principle of the Innate Good, an immediate (precognitive or intuitive) knowledge of good and evil. This auditory mode occupies a central place in the otherwise visual metaphor of the enlightenment. The visual goes with outward shame (shame-faced-ness) at a naive level, but also with full awareness (personal in-sight) at a more mature stage. Wang had failed visually before, foolishly looking out at the bamboo strips and expecting the principle to emerge from the things without, as suggested by Zhu Xi. He now discovered, in an insight, that the Truth is replete within. In short, he discovered his 'true self' or identity during exile when a series of previously unsolved crises and existential quests encompassing his total being – body, mind and spirit – postponed by his outward success, came to a head and were suddenly overcome. From discovering sagehood as a social nobody in uncivilized environs, Wang would tutor others to see their own sagehood irrespective of class, learning, race or place.

Further reading

Ching, J. (1976) *To Acquire Wisdom: The Way of Wang Yang-ming*, New York: Columbia University Press.

Henderson, J. (1998) *The Construction of Orthodoxy and Heresy: Neo-Confucian, Islamic, Jewish, and Early Christian Patterns*, Albany, NY: State University of New York Press.

Ivanhoe, P. (1990) *Ethics in the Confucian Tradition: The Thought of Mencius and Wang Yang-ming*, Atlanta, GA: Scholars Press.

Lai, W. (1991) 'Wang Yang-ming's Enlightenment Experience and Hung Hsiu-ch'uan's Dream: A Psychological Interpretation', *Cheng Feng* 35: 3–4, 200–12.

Tu Wei-ming (1976) *Neo-Confucian Thought in Action: Wang Yang-ming's Youth (1472–1509)*, Berkeley, CA: University of California Press.

Wang Yang-ming (1963) *Instructions for Practical Living, and Other Neo-Confucian Writings*, trans. with notes by Wing-tsit Chan, New York: Columbia University Press.

WHALEN LAI

ether

Mencius provides an account of a moral and mystical union, as follows:

> [This flood-like ether] as breath goes, is most expansive and strong. Nourish it naturally without harming [its innate tendency] and it will fill the space between Heaven and Earth. Otherwise this breath – being that which unites [man's inner] righteousness and the *dao* or Way – would collapse. Born [only] of patiently integrating righteousness, it is acquired not by snatching at random some [outer] right. Actions beneath the standard of the mind would deflate it … So whatever rises [naturally] out of [the goodness] of the heart, do not block it [or do not seek to correct it]. Just do not let [that good] out of your mind, and do not ever forcibly hasten it either.
>
> (*Mencius* 2A2)

There is a story and controversy behind this view. Around the time of Mencius, the ideology of *qi* (breath, ether, vital force, psychosomatic material) gained currency; it also surfaced in Song Xing and **Zhuangzi**. Two major views existed: one that associates this vital breath with a finite allotment that rests inside man, which should not be exposed

or wasted since health and life depend on its safe-keeping; and one that finds this breath to be filling the whole universe and trusts that there is a way for man to tap into this external spring of energy for his own cosmic well-being. *Mencius* 2A2 brought the views – loosely called 'Daoist' – into the Confucian fold and gave them a distinctively moral stamp. The mode of passive receptivity – letting this mind be – is 'Daoistic'; the emphasis on its being a strong moral force is 'Confucian'; the negative judgement against 'random snatching' is directed at **Gaozi**, whom Mencius charged with mistaking 'righteousness to be external', i.e. thinking that it comes from outside of us.

This passage, now deemed the most elevated of Mencius's moral discourse, went virtually unnoticed in the Han; it was rediscovered by the Song Neo-Confucians. However, the reading (and the English translation) of it varies. The more mystically inclined register the vital breath as a force larger than man and sweeping the moral agent off his feet, as it were. The more rationally inclined, on the contrary, follow **Zhu Xi** in seeing a more self-directed 'accumulation of righteousness' that matures into a comprehensive understanding of self and world.

Further reading

Lau, D. (1970) 'Introduction' to his translation of *Mencius*, Harmondsworth: Penguin.

WHALEN LAI

ethics in Islamic philosophy

The original debate in Islamic philosophy over the nature of ethics took place within a largely theological context, and dealt with the conflict between the Mu'tazilites and Ash'arites over the objectivity of ethics (see **Ash'ariyya amd Mu'-tazila**). The former argued that if some action is good then it will be ordained by God as a law for us, while the Ash'arites countered that what 'good' means is 'that which God orders'. Much early ethics was obviously heavily influenced by Stoicism, and Socrates was often seen as a major spiritual and ascetic figure. Al-Kindi, often called the first Islamic philosopher, went into great detail on how important it is for us to bear unfortunate situations, Many other philosophers criticized the idea that there is anything worrying about death, which is merely a necessary aspect of being human and mortal. In any case, there is nothing very important about this world, and it is only to our advantage to exchange it for the next world, a far purer and elevated realm of existence.

The ethical views of Plato and Aristotle had a significant impact on Islamic philosophy, and all the major thinkers in the classical period were very interested in the ideas of their Greek predecessors. The notion of an ordered and just society often follows from Plato's *Republic*, while the analysis of morality as consisting of dispositions to act in particular ways and as representing a mean between extremes comes from Aristotle. But the ways in which these ideas were combined with Islamic ideas are far more than merely mixtures of originally Greek ideas. In particular, the Islamic thinkers had to provide an account of human happiness which made it generally available to everyone who was prepared to behave well, as opposed to those who were intelligent. Islam offers salvation to all those who are virtuous, and it is not limited to those who are philosophically acute. So the debate in Aristotle as to whether the social and moral life, or the intellectual life, represents the highest form of life for human beings, had a particular poignancy in Islamic philosophy. Some thinkers like **al-Farabi** and **Ibn Sina** seem to imply that it is only the philosophers who can really reach the highest levels of happiness, and the masses can approach this end through religion but are unable to attain it completely. **Ibn Rushd**, by contrast, argues that the philosophical and the religious route to truth are merely two different routes to the same end, although many interpreters have suspected the genuineness of this view as his real opinion. Was he merely saying it in order to avoid trouble from the religious authorities? An important line of interpretation of Islamic philosophy is built around this question, and Leo Strauss and his followers have sought to distinguish between the real views of the philosophers and their apparent views.

It was Persian thinkers who produced the most concentrated work on ethics, in particular Ibn Miskawayh (d. 421 AH/1030 CE) and Nasir al-Din al-Tusi (d. 672/1274). The former argued that we have a threefold duty, to God, to our superiors and equals and to our ancestors. It is just that we obey God, since he is the epitome of the religious law on which both spiritual and physical welfare depend. God's representatives are also to be obeyed as are those who are superior to us morally. The notion of human beings as the representatives of God on earth (as his *khalifa*; see surah 2:30 in the Qur'an) is made much of by subsequent *shi'i* thinkers, who can then identify the *imam* or spiritual and some-times temporal ruler with the qualities of the deity.

Al-Ghazali provides an account of ethics which describes the sort of ordinary social behaviour which is available to everyone, and yet urges us to perfect our personal contact with the deity which can only be really established through mysticism or **Sufism**. He has an interesting argument against much of Ibn Miskawayh's ethics, in that he criticizes the latter's thesis of the rationality of much religious morality. Ibn Miskawayh claims that we can find reasons for what the *shari'a* (religious law) prescribes if we ask ourselves what the point of that law is. Although at first glance the particular rules may appear to be arbitrary, on closer examination they have the role of strength-ening faith, or linking the community together, or some other desirable quality from a religious point of view. Al-Ghazali counters this with the Ash'arite argument that the point of such laws is that they have no point apart from being religious laws. What gives these laws their point is the fact that they are religious laws, and no other reason can be plausibly connected with them. To interpret religious law as rational is to misunderstand its nature entirely.

See also: orientalism

Further reading

Fakhry, M. (1994) *Ethical Theories in Islam*, Leiden: Brill.

Hourani, G. (1985) *Reason and Tradition in Islamic Ethics*, Cambridge: Cambridge University Press.

Leaman, O. (1995) 'Christian Ethics in the Light of Muslim Ethics', in C. Rodd (ed.), *New Occasions Teach New Duties?*, Edinburgh: T & T Clark, 219–31.

—— (1999) *Brief Introduction to Islamic Philosophy*, see chapter on 'Ethics', Oxford: Polity Press.

OLIVER LEAMAN

ethics in Korean philosophy

Certain essential values in Korean tradition have a long history, and most of them have been shaped by various religions and philosophies of the Korean people. Many values of mankind including Korean values have universal characteristics. From the fourth century CE, Buddhism has taught Korean people certain important values such as desirelessness, egolessness, non-violence, respect for all living beings, the harmonization of disputes and peace. It has taught that one should perform good **karma** (action, works) in thought, speech, and conduct. One's *karma* should be without egoistic and materialistic desire. Compassion and wisdom are high spiritual and moral values in Buddhism. The idea of a **bodhisattva** (*posal* in Korean), who makes a vow to remain in this world or to return to the world repeatedly to help everyone so that they may all reach **nirvana** together, is a lofty and popular ideal in Korean Buddhism.

The concept of **emptiness** (*shunyata*) is also a lofty value in Buddhist spirituality and morality. Its central meaning is to view all things with a non-dualistic and non-discriminatory mind and to see all things in totality with the insight of the great one vehicle. The emptiness-mind is the Buddha mind, the state of enlightenment. Buddhism was the state religion of Korea during the Silla and Koryo dynasties, and these ideas and values had a great impact on the minds and lives of Korean people at that time. Even today, Buddhism is one of the two largest religions in Korea, and therefore these values have great influence still on the way of thinking of Korean people.

Confucianism was the state philosophy and religion of Korea during the Choson dynasty, and its moral value largely shaped the Korean way of thinking and life since the fourteenth century. The Confucian idea of the four essential virtues – **humaneness**, **righteousness**, propriety and wisdom – and related ideas of **filial piety** and

loyalty have been the paramount moral values for the Korean people for the last several centuries.

The Confucian idea of the Five Human Relationships (*oryun*) has been a central ethical value in Korea for many centuries. This is as follows: between father and son there should be affection; between ruler and minister, there should be righteousness; between husband and wife, there should be attention to their separate functions; between elder brother and younger brother, there should be a proper order; and between friends, there should be faithfulness. This idea of the Five Human Relationships has been a most important ethical principle governing Korean family and Korean society. Order and harmony are the key virtues in this idea. Three of the Five Relationships are the relationships within the family, which demonstrate the high value that Confucianism places upon family.

Influenced by the Confucian ethics, Korean people have valued the stable family, affectionate parents, filial children, benevolent elders, superiors, and employers, loyal juniors and employees, and faithful friends. These interpersonal values of the Korean people have been shaped primarily by Confucian ethics. Confucian influence in the Korean value system is also clearly seen in the familiar, common and popular terms of value that Koreans use. Examples are *hyo*, which means filial piety or filial duty, *yeui*, proper manner and conduct, and *tori*, the way or truth that people ought to follow. These terms and ideas have constituted an important part of the Korean value system for a long time.

The idea of filial piety has been especially important in the Korean value system. It is primarily Confucian ethics which have shaped this idea in the Korean mind. It is reverence and respect for and honouring parents, whether children are young or old. Filial piety is the root of all virtues in Confucianism, for children learn virtues from parents and by obeying and respecting parents. It is the basic virtue which brings solidarity, harmony and continuity to the family.

Confucianism has also taught the Korean people the value of education. Success in the Choson dynasty meant taking a government position by passing the civil service examination, which was based on the Confucian Classics (see

Classics and Books). This tradition became an important link to modern education, which is highly valued by Koreans, for even today a good education usually ensures a good job and success.

The Confucian value system is basically this-worldly and pragmatic. It emphasizes the following levels of human values: first, the moral cultivation of self; then governing one's home with virtue; next ruling the nation morally; and finally achieving peace in the world. With the idea of the four virtues of humaneness, righteousness, propriety and wisdom, and with the idea of the Five Human Relationships and especially through the ideals of filial piety and loyalty, Confucianism has contributed more to the development of moral values in Korean society than any other religions and philosophies.

However, some of these values, especially the ideas of the Five Human Relationships, filial piety to parents and loyalty to rulers have been changing gradually in modern Korean society due to the influence of Western democratic values, which emphasize equality and freedom. The order in the Five Human Relationships presupposes hierarchy; that is, parents are above children, rulers are higher than ministers and husband is above wife. Modern democratic ideas of equality pose problems and conflict with at least some aspects of the traditional idea of the Five Human Relationships. There has been increasing tension and conflict between the traditional values and the contemporary values in Korean society, especially between spouses and between parents and children. Human beings and human society need to ask serious questions. Is not order necessary for **harmony** and peace, and is not some kind of hierarchy of authority necessary for order? To what extent should equality be allowed in all types of human relationships, especially in the home? These are urgent questions facing Korean society today.

Another related issue is the conflict between modern individualism and the traditional Confucian value which is family-centered, which may be called 'familyism'. Due to Western influence, Korean society has become increasingly individualistic, neglecting the traditional values of family. In the contemporary democratic society of Korea, individual rights are highly regarded values which were hardly considered in the traditional society.

Since Christianity arrived in Korea in the eighteenth century, its impact has been enormous. It is the fastest growing major religion and one of the two largest religions in Korea approximately equal in size with Buddhism. Its value system has influenced at least 30 per cent of the Korean population in the last century. Among all religions, Christianity has the largest numbers of educational institutions in all levels, which may be ten times more than the educational institutes of all other religions combined. Its medical and other charitable organizations also are much more in number than those of other religions. These facts indicate the extent of Christian influence on the modern Korean value system.

Christianity was one of the major forces which brought Western democratic values to Korea. The Christian missionaries from the West, mostly from the United States of America, introduced to Korea the idea of equality in all areas of society. By establishing high schools and colleges for both males and females, they taught Christian as well as Western values to the future leaders of Korea and contributed to the modernization of Korean society.

Christianity teaches the values of love and righteousness, which have universal characteristics common to most or all religions and philosophies. Jesus's teaching of moral values includes love for one's neighbour as an essential part of Christianity. He taught that one ought to love one's neighbour as oneself and that one ought to love even one's enemy. As far as the interhuman moral values are concerned, there is a great similarity between those of Christianity and those of other religions. However, the value system of Christianity has a fundamentally different starting point and foundation from that of Buddhism and Confucianism. The Christian value system begins with God and ends with God. It is a theocentric or God-centred system. God is the moral law giver and judge of human conduct. Both Buddhism and Confucianism are basically humanistic religions and philosophies. Buddha is the enlightened man, who is the source and standard of the absolute truth. Confucianism is basically a humanistic ethical philosophy, although the super-moral value of Heaven and the oneness of man with Heaven is also occasionally emphasized as a high ideal. In the Christian value system, God is the ultimate value. He is the Creator and Redeemer. The ultimate purpose of man is to glorify God forever. God created man in His own image, which means that man is like God in rational, moral and spiritual consciousness, although there is an infinite gap between God and man, for God is infinite in His being, knowledge and power, while man is finite in these respects. The image of God also includes the dignity, freedom and value of man in general. Men are also called the children of God to have fellowship with Him for eternity. Thus, Christianity gives a very high value to man as a spiritual and moral being.

The idea of salvation or redemption has a central value in Christianity. Men lost in sin are saved by the grace of God and through faith in Jesus Christ. In other words, salvation in Christianity for the lost man is granted only through God's grace of redemption accomplished by Christ on the cross and when the person accepts grace by faith. This gospel of salvation has been overwhelmingly popular among Koreans, which is a main reason for the rapid growth of Christianity in Korea. In Christianity, this spiritual value of salvation is higher than moral values, for morality cannot bring salvation. However, Christianity teaches that after salvation, good works, such as charitable and missionary works, must follow.

In modern Korean society, there are several competing moral and spiritual values based on different religions and philosophies, since Korea is religiously and ideologically a pluralistic society. There are also secular, materialistic and individualistic values among non-religious people. With regard to contemporary political and social values, South Korea follows democratic values of freedom and equality. In economics, it follows capitalism as the value system. These contemporary political, social and economic values are adopted from the West.

It would be difficult to find any single or several common spiritual and moral values which can be accepted by all Koreans without qualification. There is serious tension and conflict between the traditional Confucian oriented values and the modern democratic and often individualistic values. The Tan'gun ideology and *hanol* (Korean or one spirit) ideology are promoted by some Koreans

as the unifying ideology of Korea, but were mainly promoted by the new religions associated with Tan'gun ideology and were not accepted by Christians.

The traditional Confucian idea of the four virtues of love, righteousness, propriety and wisdom, along with the ideals of filial piety and loyalty, have commonality and universality, which are also important values in Buddhism and Christianity, although not in exactly the same sense. Broadly speaking, these values are acceptable and agreeable among all religions and philosophies. Korean society should continue to emphasize them as an important heritage of Korean values, although some changes may be inevitable due to continuing Western influence.

See also: Buddhism, Korean; Christianity, Korean; Confucianism in Korea

Further reading

Duncan, J. (1997) 'Confucian Social Values in Contemporary South Korea', in L. Lancaster and R. Payne (eds), *Religion and Society in Contemporary Korea*, Berkeley, CA: Institute of East Asian Studies, University of California, 49–74.

Kim Yong-choon (1995) 'Ethics in Korean Society', *Korean Culture* (Fall): 8–10.

Yun Sung-bom (1977) *Ethics East and West*, Seoul: Christian Literature Society.

YONG-CHOON KIM

European Enlightenment and China

The European perception of China did an about-turn between the eighteenth and the nineteenth centuries. The Enlightenment thinkers were inspired by the Jesuit reports of China. The binaries in the *Book of Changes* inspired Leibniz's work on calculus, and the (wrong) idea that Chinese words actually represent quite perspicuously the objects which they name was part of a long and enthusiastic project by Leibniz and other European thinkers. The naturalist philosophy of **Zhu Xi** struck a chord with Spinoza. The irony is that the

Jesuits were Thomists who argued that China had once known God, and that her current Neo-Confucian philosophy was due to a later Buddhist corruption. China needed only to acknowledge God and incorporate a particular hierarchy of ideas, in particular those of the supernatural and grace, into her naturalist philosophy. The Enlightenment thinkers, on the other hand, rather appreciated a China without God or Revelation, with no meddling Church nor clergy. A China which saw God in Nature (Heaven) came closer to Deism and was judged more enlightened.

This view of China was to change sharply. After the French Revolution removed the Old Regime and Kant welcomed that break with a dark past, Hegel was sure that the historical march of Being attained consciousness in a modern Christian Europe while China still lagged behind in the gloom of a pre-conscious Spirit. China was no longer considered to be enlightened.

See also: orientalism

Further reading

Clarke, J.J. (2000) *Tao of the West*, London: Routledge.

WHALEN LAI

expediency

Quan (*Ch'uan*), or expediency, is the antonym to *jing* (*ching*), which means permanent and invariable. In the *Analects* of **Confucius**, *quan* means 'to weigh'. In response to Mohist utilitarianism, **Mencius** also 'weighed the heavy and the light' in deciding what course of action to take. He allowed for special circumstances when norms can be suspended. To save a drowning sister-in-law, the taboo of physical contact may be suspended expediently. Legalists link the term to 'power and authority'. *The Book of Lord Shang* recognizes that there are 'three things by which a country is ruled – Law, Trust, and Power. Law is what ruler and ministers both exercise (over the ruled); trust is what they both count on (among themselves); but power is what the ruler alone would possess (over his ministers)'. The term was later used to render the Sanskrit *upayakaushalya*

(skillful means, expediencies), but probably because it rather self-consciously embodied the amoral Legalist usage (see **Legalism**). Kumarajiva (344–413) coined a new term, 'convenient device', that became the standard.

The idea that enlightenment is available to everyone is defining of Mahayana Buddhism, although the different schools and thinkers differ on how precisely this aim may be attained and how we can be helped to reach it. It is crucial that people are addressed in ways which make sense to them, since only such methods will be effective. Skilful means (*upayakaushalya* in Sanskrit, *hoben* in Japanese) are used to bring about enlightenment, and those who are most advanced themselves will seek to help others along the way. This is one of the differences which the Mahayana see between themselves and the Theravada, who they accuse of only being interested in the personal salvation of particular individuals, in particular monks and those entirely devoted to the religious and contemplative life. In fact, it is so important from the Mahayana point of view that one speaks to those who are potentially on the road to *nirvana* (i.e. everyone) in the right sort of way that the literal truth of what one says is not so important. This even goes for the nature of moral action, what is significant here is more the motive out of which that action takes place rather than the action itself. If the action emerges out of a genuine feeling of compassion, then the precise physical deed which is selected is far less significant than that motive. This gives considerable scope for skilful means since almost any action which is likely to be effective may be selected in order to help people achieve salvation, there are no actions which are ruled out a priori, that is, in principle.

It is this significance of motive which makes it feasible for Mahayana Buddhists to undertake actions which in themselves are questionable, provided that they are done for the right end. That can lead to an antinomianism, to a disinclination to be confined by laws, rules and rituals. It was certainly helpful to the integration of other, non-Buddhist, ideas into the religion, or into the way in which the religion was presented in China, where there are often particularly strong links between the three approaches of Confucianism, Daoism and Buddhism. There is no reason why a Buddhist should feel embarrassed at using ideas from the other two ideologies if it is likely that such use will help in bringing people around to the correct way of thinking, and eventually attaining *nirvana*.

It is this discussion about what is expedient which makes the debate between the subitists and gradualists on the nature of enlightenment rather beside the point. Some, the subitists, argue that enlightenment is sudden and total, and is best attainable by dramatic techniques. The gradualists emphasize the significance of operating slowly and gradually, allowing the individual to travel along the path to enlightenment in an orderly and careful manner. What makes the contrast misleading is that expediency suggests that different approaches are suitable for different kinds of people, and there is likely to be no grand formula for enlightenment which is likely to be effective for everyone.

See also: trigger

Further reading

Pye, M. (1978) *Skilful Means*, London: Duckworth.

WHALEN LAI
OLIVER LEAMAN

F

face

Often used to describe the social mores of the Chinese and Japanese, 'face' or 'body and face' is never regarded as a moral issue by China's ethicists. A true gentleman does not operate with such superficial values. Face has to do with status, negotiations and as such is hardly limited to the Confucian East; it just seems more obvious to modern outside observers. The rule is that a social inferior has little face to begin with, so he cannot 'give face' to another. With enough status or face to spare, a high-born individual can better afford to be generous. So 'the higher (nobler) a person, the broader (the more magnanimous)', for in 'giving face' a high-born person gains even more face (status) – and puts the recipient in greater debt to him. This can devolve into an interminable ritual of mutual deference.

The reason 'face management' is more notice-able in China is that China lacks a real aristocracy, compared with Japan, or even a stable gentry class, compared with Korea. The nobility had disap-peared under the First Emperor and the gentry families regularly rose and fell (in four generation cycles), so status-seeking had long been a Chinese preoccupation. But because the social unit was not the individual, face is corporate. Being shared, face has to be kept up by the corporate members and sustained very often by conspicuous display and consumption. Thus a family of high standing has to have a doorman to screen the visitors, keep the master inaccessible and turn away unwanted solicitations. In the same way the emperor is hidden, elevated and made to inspire awe. The arrangement unfortunately leads to institutiona-lized bribery, be it with the eunuchs at court or a doorman before a grand mansion. As an extension of the master's corporate 'face', the doorman deserves his graft. To fail to respect the doorman can be taken as a slap on his master's face. A good master, an impartial official, a benevolent emperor would not stand for such abuse of face.

Moralists have decried this, and popular Ming–Qing novels satirized it thoroughly. But without a modern rule of law, men in power may reassert their status distinction and salvage any public 'loss of face' simply by a show of force. Lin Yutang likes to tell the story of how a worthless son of a powerful general could misbehave in a bar and be chastised by an indignant, ordinary person. A good son would take that as a lesson, and a moral father would insist that he does. But a no-good son and a no-better father would count this as a 'loss of face' and an affront to their corporate standing in society so that, to save face, the general might send his private army in to beat up the ordinary person. In this way he would silence a public challenge to his authority.

See also: deference

Further reading

Eberhard, W. (1967) *Guilt and Sin in Traditional China*, Berkeley, CA: University of California Press.
Lin Yutang (1959) *The Chinese Way of Life*, Cleveland, OH: World Publishing Company.

WHALEN LAI

faith

Faith as trust among friends

Xin, 'faith' or 'belief', is written as 'man + speech' and denotes 'trust' and 'trustworthiness'. Traditionally equated with *cheng* (sincerity, written as 'speech + to complete'), it implies a validation of speech by deed. Neither word denotes religious 'belief', but rather the basic virtue of 'truth-telling' and 'promise-keeping', upon which all social intercourse depends. Listed last in the Confucian set of five virtues, after **humaneness**, **righteousness**, propriety and wisdom, it is aligned with 'friends' when the set is paired to the five human relationships. Being fifth and last, it was cut out from **Mencius**'s set of the Four Beginnings or **Four Germs**. Ritual **friendship** among these non-kin was sealed by speech before there were any written contracts or *wen* (the word also for 'culture') in the age of peace. A classic tale of 'promise keeping' goes as follows: a man vowed to join his friend again one year later at the spot where they were saying good-bye. He kept his word, not moving from under the bridge as he waited for his companion even as flood waters rose. Sidelined in times of peace, trust and courage re-surfaced as primary virtues in subsequent ages of **chaos** and persisted on the social margin, beyond family and state, being the code of outlaws and honour among thieves.

It has however been noted that, comparatively speaking, violence is the underside of Greek civilization that valued *agon* (war) relative to a clan-based China that valued more genteel harmony and peace. Bruce Brooks has registered *xin* as a necessary virtue of leaders in the early Warring States period; the leaders needed to win and earn the trust of the people conscripted into the new large armies.

Faith as belief in a higher power

In the classical period, *xin* is not used to describe faith in gods and spirits. The pictogram for 'trust' is 'human + speech', so meaning 'trusting in a report'. With **Heaven** being 'speechless', one cannot *xin* Heaven either. (The word when so used glosses for *xun* or 'going along with the will of

heaven'.) Reports can be disbelieved. **Mencius** warned, 'If you believe (literally) everything (told you) in *The Book of History*, it would be better not to have this book (at all)'. The classical use of this verb is directed at the reportage, not at the truth of the proposition as such. *Xin* usage, however, did change in the medieval period; it came to stand for religious belief, not unlike the tone of Christian *pistis*. China also had to believe in the report of this 'foreign immortal', called the Buddha. One must first 'believe' before one truly 'sees' the Buddha. That change is phrased as: 'One enters the stream in faith; one crosses it in wisdom' (**Nagarjuna**).

The initial *shraddha* (faith) is tentative; the final *prajna* (wisdom) is definite. Seeing through the glass darkly thus precedes seeing clearly. Trying to find the right words for rendering that psychology, the Chinese monk Huiyuan used a clumsy expression, 'registering in the dark', for that uncertain faith. Zong Bing did better; in his essay on 'Elucidating Enlightenment', this lay Buddhist used *xin* and compared such trust to gazing at a moon temporarily hidden behind some clouds. The moon, a symbol of the Buddha and the light of enlightenment, is truly there. That preliminary trust is valid; enlightenment verifies it when the clouds move away and the moon shines through. That this involves a turnaround, a metanoia, is captured in the line, 'I did not find the light; the light (the Buddha) found me'.

In time, the word *xin* deepened into being a part of the wisdom formula. China embraced enthusiastically the Mahayana gnostic teaching of a **'buddha nature'** in all man. So faith is not in a higher power beyond, but simply this awakening of wisdom (**bodhichitta**) within, which, once aroused, would remove all doubts and ensure enlightenment. This is the intended message in the title of a key Chinese-compiled text, *Awakening of Faith in Mahayana*. Here, the word 'faith' really means 'confidence, surety'. This text impacted on all Chinese Buddhist schools. In Chan, it is the 'great conviction' behind the 'sudden enlightenment'. That is because 'Faith (read: truth) and Mind are not two; not-two (read: unwavering) is this Mind of Faith (Truth)'. This Chan spirit of 'great confidence' later backfired. Just as free grace can become 'cheap grace', truth can devolve into truism. To rekindle the original insight, **Koan**

Chan made not the 'great faith' but the 'great doubt' into the key to the Great Awakening.

See also: enlightenment, sudden; Neo-Confucianism, concepts

Further reading

Burkert, W., Girard, R. and Smith, J. (1987) *Violent Origin: Ritual Killing and Cultural Formation*, Stanford, CA: Stanford University Press.

Shim Jae-ryong (1987) 'Faith and Practice in Hua-yen Buddhism: A Critique of Fa-tsang (645–712) by Li T'ung-shan (646–740)', in D. Chappell (ed.), *Buddhist and Taoist Studies II*, Honolulu, HA: University of Hawaii, 109–24.

Smith, W. (1979) *Faith and Belief*, Princeton, NJ: Princeton University Press.

WHALEN LAI

faith and Buddhism

In Buddhism the conflict between faith and reason is only really present in Pure Land and some forms of Zen Buddhism. For many forms of Buddhism there is no need for faith, since there is no real notion of transcendental truth which we need to leave our ordinary ways of thinking behind in order to grasp. That is not to say that it is easy to achieve enlightenment – quite the contrary – but it is hardly faith which can bring it about. Faith in a teacher is important in some forms of Zen, however, and the rituals and rationale of Pure Land are clearly dependent on a religious formula which does involve a commitment very different from that which is a part of everyday life.

Further reading

de Bary, W., Chan Wing-Tsit and Watson, B. (1960) *Sources of Chinese Tradition: Introduction to Oriental Civilizations*, New York: Columbia University Press.

Hick, J. (1997) *God and the Universe of Faiths*, Oxford: Oneworld.

Yampolsky, P. (ed.) (1990) *Selected writings of Nichiren*, New York: Columbia University Press.

OLIVER LEAMAN

faith versus reason in Islamic philosophy

The idea that faith is in conflict with reason is much discussed in Islamic philosophy, and has formed the main basis of interpretation of that thought in recent scholarship, perhaps in ways which have been rather overdone. Many of the *falasifa* argued that there was no incompatibility between philosophy and faith, since these are merely two different ways of looking at the same truth. In addition, it was often argued that the apparent incompatibility between reason and religion was only apparent, and that once one really understood what faith meant, it was not necessarily different from the conclusions which reason provides. The advantage of faith is that it appeals to everyone, and provides access to the nature of the truth for everyone, while reason is restricted to those capable of using it.

One should not overemphasize the difference between faith and reason, however. The Qur'an is itself a profoundly rational work, and it calls on its readers to use their reason to develop faith, since it presents arguments on the basis of which the religion should be accepted.

Further reading

Leaman, O. (1999) *A Brief Introduction to Islamic Philosophy*, Oxford: Polity.

OLIVER LEAMAN

falsafa

Falsafa, an Arabic version of the Greek *philosophia*, represents the orientation of a type of Islamic philosophy towards Greek thought. The term which is normally used for philosophy is **hikma**, or wisdom, but this is sometimes used to describe philosophy in the sense of a wider understanding of the meaning of the universe as compared with an analytical and technical investigation of theoretical problems.

OLIVER LEAMAN

Fan Zhen

fl. early 5th century

Philosopher

The Buddha accepted the reality of **karma** and **samsara**, but taught an anti-Upanishadic doctrine of no-soul. Nothing transmigrates from one life to the next, and no self or soul goes to **nirvana**. The early Chinese Buddhists, however, wrongly assumed that if there is rebirth and *nirvana*, there must be something reborn and something that enters *nirvana*. Following the lead of the Daoists, they argued for the existence of an immortal soul. Even after Kumarajiva cleared up that mistake, Buddhist apologists still agreed with the Daoists against the Confucians on this point. However, they criticized the Daoists for stressing only physical longevity and realizing only the rebirth path of the heavens of the gods, far short of Buddhist *nirvana*.

Within that long-running debate, Fan Zhen (Fan Chen) in the early fifth century is perhaps the most able of the anti-Buddhist critics. He argued that the soul (meaning for him, the mind) depends on the body to be; they function together; and that at death, both would disintegrate with nothing surviving. Before this, others had compared the mutual dependence of body and soul to the firewood and the fire. The body as wood fuels the fire as the soul; when the wood is consumed, the fire also dies, so there is no soul (fire) ever surviving the body (wood). But Buddhism knew a similar analogy of flame and candle, which is used to explain not the soul but how *karma* is transferred from one life to the next. Rebirth is like a flame being transferred from one candle to another. The Chinese Buddhists had used this metaphor to subvert the firewood analogy.

Fan Zhen responded by using a new and a sharper analogy. He likened the substance of the body to the knife and the function of the mind to the keenness of the blade. **Substance and function** are inseparable; who has ever heard of the sharp blade (the keen wit of the soul) surviving when the body of the knife is destroyed? So daunting was this thesis that he forced the pro-Buddhist court of Emperor Wu of the Liang dynasty to respond. The Emperor convened his court and headed a concerted defence of **faith**. Familiar with Daoism, the emperor wrote an essay that equated the (Daoist) immortal soul with the (Buddhist) seed of enlightenment or **buddha nature**. He then turned Fan Zhen's materialist thesis on its head. In his idealist reinterpretation, the soul or buddha nature is the abiding substance; the body is its derivative and mutable function. The essence is eternal, even as its physical form may come and go. This substance of enlightenment then functions to (a) carry over the *karma* between rebirths; (b) point ahead to eventual enlightenment; being (c) a paradoxical mix of wisdom and ignorance, with (d) wisdom being granted ontological priority to and forming the basis of the accidental ignorance responsible for trapping us in the cycles of rebirth.

The poet Shen Yue, a court official, wrote in support of the Emperor, answering another aspect of Fan Zhen's challenge. If life is the congealing of elements and death is their dispersal, then indeed reality is in a ceaseless state of flux. Flux amounts to a minute-to-minute momentariness. With momentary reality out there being correlated to momentary streams of consciousness within, then indeed nothing appears permanent. But if as the Emperor had shown, namely, that there is this permanent substance behind these mutable functions, then, argues Shen Yue, if we sever the train of momentary thoughts (perhaps in a flash of realizing 'no-thought') a person may recover that nirvanic Buddha mind behind the samsaric consciousness. The thesis has conflated the Daoist state of 'no-mind' and the Buddhist idea of 'erasing deluded thought coverings'. That term 'no-mind' or 'no-thought' would later appear as the principal teaching of the southern Chan school in the *Platform Sutra* of the Sixth Patriarch.

See also: Awakening of Faith in Mahayana; Huineng

Further reading

Lai, W. (1981) 'Emperor Wu of Liang on the Immortality of the Soul', *Journal of the American Oriental Society* 101(2): 167–75.

WHALEN LAI

Al-Farabi

b. *c.*257 AH/870 CE; d. 380 AH/950 CE

Philosopher, logician and musician

Abu Nasr Muhammad ibn Muhammad ibn Tarkhan ibn Awzalagh al-Farabi was born in Turkestan, and died in Damascus. He is well-known not only as a writer on philosophy and logic but also on the theory of music, and indeed as a composer. He is often known as the 'second teacher' (second, that is, to Aristotle), an appropriate title since it is really to al-Farabi that the whole traditon of Peripatetic philosophy in the Islamic world owes its structure. He set out the main theoretical framework of *mashsha'i* (Peripatetic) thought and established a real role for that philosophy in the Islamic world.

The basis of this theory is the notion of emanation in the hierarchy of being. At the summit of the hierarchy is God, labelled as 'the First'. From this a second being emanates, which is the First Intellect and the Second Being. In sum, ten intellects emanate from the First Being. Emanation is an entirely intellectual process which results in the production of multiplicity out of unity. The First Intellect comes to an understanding of God, and as a result produces a third being which is the Second Intellect. The First Intellect also thinks about itself, and as a result produces the body and soul of the First Heaven. The chain of emanated Intellects are linked with the generation of other celestial things such as the Fixed Stars, the planets, the sun and the moon. The Tenth Intellect is the intermediary between the celestial and the terrestial worlds. This Intellect, which is the Aristotelian *nous poietikos*, is often known as the Active or Agent Intellect, or the **'aql al-fa'l**, and is a crucial notion in Islamic philosophy. It has the role of making human thought actual and providing form to humanity and the sublunary world. An interesting feature of this notion is that it rather abstracts us from God, in that there is a type of intellectual growth which we can acquire without any direct divine intervention, and which appears to operate automatically on the basis of individual human effort and merit.

Al-Farabi distinguishes between four different kinds of intellect. The potential intellect represents the ability to abstract the forms of an object and separate them from its sensible nature. As we abstract our understanding of the form, we move to the stage of the actual intellect, and when this is perfected (only available to a few) the stage of the acquired intellect is attained. At this level the intellect is completely actualized and the individual human intellect becomes the same as the other immaterial intellect, the active intellect. It can now not only understand itself and the intelligibles it has abstracted from material things, but can even grasp the active intellect and the immaterial substances. This is the highest level of knowledge available to human beings, and represents ultimate happiness. Although al-Farabi does compare such a state with immortality, it is clearly not personal immortality, since in such a state the body has disappeared, so the criterion of identity for the individual is no longer present. This is a persisting theological problem which al-Farabi left for Islamic philosophy, an account of immortality and the afterlife which no longer paid much attention to the literal meaning of religious texts.

Al-Farabi followed Plato in political philosophy, as did many Islamic thinkers, and the highly hierarchical nature of Plato's *Republic* fitted in nicely both with Islam itself and the elitism of Islamic philosophy. The political ruler must have both intellectual and personal strengths, and he can organize the state into the best possible structure by helping everyone to reach that level of understanding and happiness which is appropriate to them. The inhabitants of the virtuous city enjoy both salvation and happiness, but these are differently organized for different people. Happiness is available to the philosophers through their pursuit of intellectual knowledge, but it is also available to everyone through religious and moral practices. The philosopher-king, who in al-Farabi's theory is also a prophet or spiritual leader (*imam*), is precisely the person who is able to construct a political system in which the community as a whole will be able to participate in happiness and salvation.

The ruler finds out how to act politically through his contact with the Active Intellect. The philosopher contacts the Active Intellect using his intellect alone. The prophet uses his imagination, and it is this faculty which is the source of revelation, inspiration and prophecy. The advantage of using imagination is that he is able to express that knowledge in ways which are accessible to the public at large, since he can illustrate that message with vivid and compelling images. Prophecy is the result of the combination of the intellect and the imagination, and it produces in symbolic form precisely the same truths available through philosophy. The perfected imaginative skills of the prophet lead him to receive an emanation from the Active Intellect. The prophet as a consequence has political skills not shared by the philosopher, who only has intellectual skills.

Al-Farabi not only provided the agenda for most subsequent political philosophy, but he also established the nature of ontology in Islamic philosophy. He regarded existence as a predicate of essence, rather than as an inherent quality of essence. This led to his construction of the distinction between two basic kinds of being, being which is necessary in itself since it cannot not be (i.e. God) and everything else, being which is necessary through the action of something else, but contingent in itself. Such a distinction came to be a basic presupposition of Islamic metaphysics.

Al-Farabi's work on the nature of logic led to the eventual acceptance in the Islamic world that the rules of logic and grammar are distinct. He argued that logic is the deep structure of all language, and as such it is important to study it if we are to be able to understand the nature of the arguments which appear in linguistic forms. In this way he provided a significant role for philosophy and distinguished it from grammar and all those thinkers who wished to use the Islamic sciences such as the grammar of the Arabic language in order to resolve theoretical difficulties.

Al-Farabi is perhaps the least generally known of the main Islamic philosophers, although some of his works were translated into Latin, and many became very important in Jewish philosophy (the outstanding thinker within that tradition, Maimonides, praised him unreservedly). Although he was believed to be a sufi, there are no extant works on mysticism, and from the evidence of his writings it is only justifiable to think of him as an analytic thinker.

See also: logic in Islamic philosophy

Further reading

Black, D. (1990) *Logic and Aristotle's 'Rhetoric' and 'Poetics' in Medieval Islamic Philosophy*, Leiden: Brill.

Corbin, H. (1993) *History of Islamic Philosophy*, London: Kegan Paul International, 158–65.

Al-Farabi (1981) *Al-Farabi's Commentary and Short Treatise on Aristotle's De Interpretatione*, trans. F. Zimmermann, London: British Academy.

—— (1985) *Al-Farabi on the Perfect State*, trans. R. Walzer, Oxford: Clarendon Press.

Galston, M. (1990) *Politics and Excellence: The Political Philosophy of Alfarabi*, Princeton, NJ: Princeton University Press.

Netton, I. (1989) *Allah Transcendent: Studies in the Structure and Semiotics of Islamic Philosophy*, London: Routledge, 99–148.

—— (1992) *Alfarabi and his School*, London: Routledge.

OLIVER LEAMAN

fatalism in Chinese philosophy

In the Chinese language, the word *ming* as in *Tianming* (Mandate of **Heaven**) covers everything from a command (a moral imperative, an ought) to one's given lot (what simply is). What in English would be divine providence, inherent destiny or blind fate are all subsumed under that one word. What appears to be Chinese 'fatalism' is the tendency to assign everything to what Heaven wills and which ascribes the most passive of possible responses to *ming*. Within Chinese fortune-telling, which presumes a high degree of determinism, a distinction is made between fate and fortune. Fate cannot be changed; it is set before birth. But fortune is amenable to manipulation. Bad luck can be avoided and good fortune be made to flow your way. The tradition of divination in China ran deep;

it went back to the Shang dynasty, and was canonized in the Zhou dynasty in the *Book of Changes*. Confucius did not indulge in prognostication, but even **Zhu Xi** once consulted this work, when he pondered whether he should risk petitioning the emperor against the new policies. (He desisted.) Still, there is evidence that fatalism (and cynicism) grew in late imperial China. People consulted fortune tellers more often, the profession flourished, and most of the compendia and handbooks on this esoteric art appeared then. These later works also drew a good deal on Indian practices.

See also: Yijing

Further reading

Eno, R. (1990) *The Confucian Creation of Heaven*, New York: State University of New York Press.

Smith, R. (1991) *Fortune-Tellers and Philosophers: Divination in Traditional Chinese Society*, Oxford: Westview Press.

WHALEN LAI

fatalism in Indian philosophy

In Indian philosophy there are a variety of thoroughly fatalistic schools, in particular the **Ajivikas**, for whom fate (*niyati*) is overwhelmingly powerful, making it impossible to try to take control of one's life. Despite this view, they argued for an extreme form of asceticism as a lifestyle, which might be thought to be unnecessary given the idea that everything which is likely to happen is not influenced by us and our actions. Some materialists tended to emphasize the significance of fate also, arguing for a determinism which makes the world turn out in the way which it does. It might be thought that the concept of **karma** is fatalistic, since it implies that one's fate in the future is determined by one's past, and yet it is not really fatalistic, since it is always possible for the individual to change the future by behaving in a suitable way in this life. That is, although what is happening to us may be thought to be a reflection of what we have done in previous lives, it provides us with the possibility of affecting future lives on the basis of our present actions.

It is this point which is picked up by Buddhism, particularly the Madhyamaka school, which saw itself as taking up a middle position on the question of fatalism, as it saw itself as taking up a middle position in general. We are subject to causality through our participation as physical creatures in the world, and we are also causally affected by what precedes us, what we have done in previous lives and what is done to us. Our role in this life is characterized by dependent cooorigination (**pratitya-samutpada**), which brings out the importance of the past in structuring the present. But this should not make us think that there is no point to acting, since that very view would itself be causally created. What we need to do is take control of our lives by transcending the world of causes and effects by seeking enlightenment, and in so far as we liberate ourselves from the world, we rise above its fatalism. After all, although when we examine the world we see that it is governed by causality, we should be aware that this impression is merely a reflection of **avidya**, ignorance, because the world itself is unreal in the sense that it is replete with changing and insubstantial phenomena.

Further reading

Basham, A. (1971) *History and Doctrines of the Ajivikas*, Delhi: Motilal Banarsidass.

Conze, E. (1962) *Buddhist Thought in India*, London: Allen & Unwin.

Dundas, P. (1992) *The Jains*, London: Routledge.

LaFleur, W. (1983) *The Karma of Words: Buddhism and the Literary Arts in Medieval Japan*, Los Angeles: University of California Press.

Nagao, G. (1991) *Madhyamaka and Yogacara: A Study of Mahayana Philosophies*, Albany: State University of New York Press.

OLIVER LEAMAN

filial piety

Endorsed by **Confucius** and elevated by his disciple Youzi to being the root of all virtues, filial piety has been a cornerstone of Confucian morality. It entailed a 'three-year mourning' of the parents, a standard not current even in

Confucius's home state. Judged excessive by **Mozi**, it was made by **Mencius** into a litmus test of filial devotion. The Legalists would have liked to reduce familial favouritism and nepotism, but Han support for Confucianism canonized filial piety for good. In theory, the state distributed to every (elite) household the *Filial Classic*, a work that openly made filial piety the rafter of the cosmos and the pillar of rule. That may have to do with the nature of the Han 'family-state', in which the central authorities had to negotiate power-sharing with the local magnate clans. In concert, the family inculcated loyalty even as the state sanctioned filial piety. The organic homology of family and state leaves little room, it would seem, for the development of civil society. In the twentieth century, to undermine the family in pursuit of the policy of building the new state, **Mao Zedong** worked to reverse the classic rule that Confucian sons do not testify against fathers.

Further readng

Freedman, M. (1958) *Lineage Organization in South-eastern China*, London: Athlone Press.

Hsu, F. (1981) *Under the Ancestor's Shadow: Kinship, Personality and Social Mobility in China*, Stanford, CA: Stanford University Press.

WHALEN LAI

Five Elements

The theory of *yin–yang* and of the Five Elements (five processes, five phases) is fundamental to premodern Chinese **correlative thinking**. The rudiments may already have been in place at the Shang court, where Chinese astrology seems to have been highly developed. One radical reading argues that the astrological aspect to the myth of **Sage-King** Yu (a **dragon**) and his father Gun (a turtle) might involve a knowledge of the displacement of the Corona Australis from the night sky, i.e. its sinking beneath the horizon as a result of the 'procession of the equinoxes'. In the historical records, however, **Zou Yan** (305–240? BCE) is usually credited with codifying these two systems into one, and with offering it as a system of elemental conquests that could both explain and forecast the rise and fall of kingdoms. The true reigns are accorded one of the five elemental virtues. This thesis supposedly 'drove fear into the hearts of the nobles and kings of the time' (the same wording was later used to describe the impact of the Buddhist teaching of **karma**). Zou Yan thus uncovered more than just a system of natural law, which was already known to court astrologers. Rather, he claimed to have found a moral necessity and a theodicy of cosmic rule.

According to the theory of the Five Elements, everything in the universe can be classified under one of the five. Recent scholarship criticizes and dispenses with the old use of the term 'elements' (used here for ease of comparative reference), since the theory does not seek to reduce reality to a fixed set of invariable atoms like that of Democritus. The word *xing* (picture of a path, a cross road) describes a process of becoming, and thus the preferred term is Five Processes. In a further internal development, restricted to the Han dynasty, it may better be rendered as Five Phases, that is, five moments in one continuous process. One might prefer to see it as involving two interlocking, counter-balancing paths. In any case, the system is not static (as in the term 'element') but correlated (using 'relationship') and dynamic ('action/reaction'). The two key patterns for their cyclical displacement are by mutual succession (or birth) and via mutual conquest (or overcoming). To explain them, we start with the correlation of the five elements and the four seasons (plus an interregnal fifth). That is, there are four seasons to go with the four directions, and so to accomodate the fifth element – Earth in the centre – in the year; the mid-year point (between summer and autumn) is the fifth season given over to Earth

The birth series is relatively simple to explain; it follows the course of the sun or of the seasons, east for spring and morning, south for summer and noon, and so on. Accordingly, spring (wood) gives birth to summer (fire), followed by fall (metal) and winter (water). Earth is allowed to come in between summer (fire) and fall (metal). The pretext for inserting earth there is a break in mid-year dividing the *yang* ascendancy (spring and summer) and the *yin* ascendancy (fall and winter). This 'birth series' is based on the sun's movement along the equator;

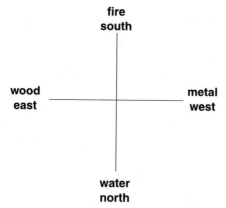

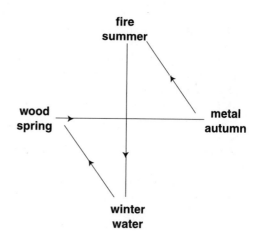

the 'conquest series' is based on the lunar path as it is affected by the tilt of the earth's axis.

The rationale for the latter series has baffled scholars. It is this conquest series that Zou Yan used to explain the law of the succession of dynasties: the succeeding dynasty follows but then overthrows the one that went before. The standard explanation relies on relational analogies, viz. Water overcomes Fire by putting out the flames; Metal conquers Wood as with an axe cutting trees; a useless *post facto* rationalization. One can always come up with an analogy for any sequence, for example, the heat of the sun can bake dry a puddle of water and so on. The more satisfactory explanation involves numerology in the design of the 'magical diagrams' of the River Chart and the River Writing. But the root inspiration may lie with the movement of the heavenly bodies. The Shang court astrologers knew enough about the movements to have the royal tombs at Anyang lined up according to the north–south axis but at 12.5 degrees off due north (compensation for the tilt of the earth's axis). If so, they might even have had some inkling of the 'processsion of the equinoxes'. A slightly earlier occurrence of the equinoxes each year is caused by the differences in the rotations of the sun, moon and stars. Although a complete to-and-fro movement would take 25,800 terrestrial years to complete, the Shang seem to register some such displacements of the stellar houses in the night sky.

The 'conquest series' now reads Earth, Wood, Metal, Fire and Water. The conquest being in reverse, Chinese children memorize the sequence in reverse. Bracketing off Earth, the four other elements when mapped according to the four directions would zigzag as indicated below.

Earth interrupts the conquest series in the northeast as it interrupts the birth series in the southwest. The two key conquests are on the cross-bars – water over fire, metal over wood – where the *yin* element overruns the *yang* element that leads it. When the cross-bars are joined as shown, we have a complete loop, a helix. That three-dimensional tilted '8' figure, when compressed into a two-dimensional form, would yield on the top side the design for the *yin–yang* circle. The tilt compensates for the tilt of the earth. In a Chinese myth, this tilt of the heavens (towards the northwest) is caused by the giant Gong Gong knocking down the mountain holding up that corner of the sky.

See also: law, natural; magic squares

Further reading

Schwartz, B. (1985) *The World of Thought in Ancient China*, Cambridge, MA: Harvard University Press, especially ch. 9.

Henderson, J. (1984) *The Development and Decline of Chinese Cosmology*, New York: Columbia University Press.

WHALEN LAI

Folk Chan

Unlike Zen in Japan, which became the tradition of the *samurai* elite, Chan in China suffered under Song Neo-Confucian critique. Even though Chan inspired the military arts, the Song separated for good the military and literary careers such that 'no son of a good family ever joined the army'. In its decline, Chan merged with the folk tradition and evolved into Folk Chan. Folk wisdom had however made its mark in earlier periods. The story of the Sixth Patriarch told in the *Platform Sutra* is in part folklore, more of which appeared in the *Baolinzhuan*.

Folk Zen is often seen in popular literature, and several masterpieces of Chinese novel writing represent it well. Monkey in *Journey to the West* earned his name 'Awakening to Emptiness' after he studied magical arts under a Daoist master. That episode is in fact modelled after the story of the Sixth Patriarch, a 'southern barbarian' (literally 'monkey'). Monkey found his true nature when as a 'natural' creature, he said he had 'no nature' (no surname, no manners). This terrible simian infant then turned the world upside down as Zen iconoclasts would.

'Lay down the cleaver, sit in meditation and be a Buddha' is a Chan proverb that dramatizes the suddenness of enlightenment (see **enlightenment, sudden**). That teaching informs an episode in *Water Margin* (in Pearl Buck's translation, *All Men are Brothers*). A tale of Chinese Robin Hoods, it includes a Friar Tuck figure. Hiding from the law, this character joined the order but continued to indulge in meat and wine. His master had to send him away with a parting poem, saying 'You will know what it means when the time comes.' Years later, after a bloody battle, this warrior monk heard the chime of a distant temple bell. He recalled the poem. Laying down his weapon, he burnt himself up in yogic *tapas* (austerity), and rejoined his true, Buddhist destiny in a crowning Zen theodicy.

Dream of the Red Chambers – also known as *Story of the Stone* – is framed by a poem recalling the Mahayana saying 'form is emptiness, emptiness is form'. With 'form/colour' doubling for 'eros', the poem drives home the lesson that enlightenment comes to the hero only through the joys of love and the subsequent pain and disillusionment. The hero was protected by a pair of guardian angels who acted in the role of *deus ex machina*, Chan style: a crazed Buddhist monk and a childlike Daoist adept, talking in enigmas.

The Drunken Buddha, on the other hand, is not great literature. It grew out of the legend of the Chan monk Daoji, an incarnation of Maitreya and of Avalokiteshvara. A filthy, uncouth, drunken, homeless menace, he was everything the 'proper and prim' Ming dynasty Neo-Confucians were not. Sought after for his magical cures, he was able to make endless fun of the false modesty and hypocrisy of these Chinese puritans.

Folk Chan has one legendary legacy linking its military arts with the religio-political underground. Shaolin boxing monks supposedly helped the Manchus to fight off the equally well armed Tibetan forces, but the Manchus later betrayed the monks and burned their temple. Only two monks escaped, and it is believed that from them came the secret society of the Hung Brothers. The anti-Manchu Triad societies were in fact involved in some nationalistic causes, but they also organized criminal gangs.

See also: Huineng

Further reading

Hawkes, D. (1973) *The Story of the Stone*, Harmondsworth: Penguin.

Lai, W. (1994), 'From Protean Ape to Handsome Saint: The Monkey King', *Asian Folklore Studies* 53(1): 29–65.

Waley, A. (trans.) (1943) *Monkey: Folk Novel of China by Wu Cheng-en*, New York: John Day Company.

WHALEN LAI

forgiveness and grace

Forgiveness in Confucian China is tied to *shu* in *zhong shu*. Meaning 'of like minds', *shu* is extending to others the consideration one desires in turn from others. The term might have once been hierarchic and related to the magnanimity of *noblesse oblige*, but **Confucius** extended and applied it to associates or equals. As such, it does not mean baring one's soul before a high God and being forgiven for one's sins; the latter goes with faith while the Confucian tradition trusts in works, the assumption being that every man can recognize his mistake, ask for forgiveness from his fellowmen and take action to correct it thereafter. The gentleman is obliging and will forgive another – more easily than he would himself – but justice remains the norm. So when Confucius was asked about 'repaying grievance with virtue' (a wisdom saying found in **Laozi**), he rejected this because, if that is the case, then 'with what would one repay kindness?' Buddhists have less difficulty with the concept: the *Dharmapada* suggests that 'hatred is not conquered by hatred; it is conquered by love'.

God's grace in the Bible is transcendental, since God is an absolute monarch. Grace is super-natural. The closest in China is imperial *en* (grace), pardons meted out on special occasions as royal benevolence. Among men, the gift of *en* solicits gratitude and incurs obligation. The repaying of such 'debts' constitutes a general ethics of *bao en* and comes under the egalitarianism of *bao* (reciprocity) rooted ultimately in the timeless ethics of 'gift exchange', later blending into the Buddhist teaching of **karma**: 'The good will have good *bao*; the evil their like share'. In Buddhist lay ethics, *baoen* expands into a universal, communitarian ethics. It means considering all men and women as if they were one's father and mother or brother and sister, because in one's many past rebirths, one could well have been connected intimately with all others so as to incur beneficence and exact gratitude. (One of course does not repay injury or seek vengeance.)

See also: confession

Further reading

Lien-sheng Yang (1957) 'The Concept of "Pao" as a Basis for Social Relationship in China', in J. Fairbank (ed.), *Chinese Thought and Institutions*, Chicago: University of Chicago Press.

WHALEN LAI

foundational consciousness

Tibetan philosophers accept that the concept of foundational consciousness (**alaya-vijnana**; in Tibetan, *kun shi*, literally 'the basis of all') is central to the philosophy of mind of the Chittamatra (Mind Only) or **Yogachara** school of Indian Mahayana Buddhism. On this view, eight classes of consciousness are posited, namely the five sensory consciousnesses; the sixth, or mental consciousness; seventh, a deluded 'I'-consciousness; and the eighth which is called the 'foundational consciousness'. This foundational consciousnesses is characterized as (a) that which retains its continuum across time, (b) the repository of all the imprints of experience of the other consciousnesses, (c) the basic substratum from which arises the illusion of the external material world, and (d) neutral in itself, that is, neither positive nor negative. **Tsongkhapa** introduces an innovative distinction between the 'foundational consciousness as basis' and 'as based-on potentials'. The former is the substratum upon which are stored all the residual impressions and propensities, while the latter refers to the residual impressions themselves. The two are, according to Tsongkhapa, neither materially identical nor materially different, and to understand their relationship is to understand the world of dependent origination according to the Mind Only school.

However the question of whether or not the doctrine of foundational consciousness (the 'basis of all') is reconcilable within an ontology that is based on **Nagarjuna**'s philosophy of **emptiness** has a much more complex history within Tibetan thought. **Buton Rinchen Drup** and Tsongkhapa vehemently reject the doctrine and perceive it as a metaphysical postulate of Buddhist idealist schools, while thinkers like **Shakya Pandita**, **Dolpopa Sherap Gyaltsen**, Sasang Mati Panchen, Takt-sang Lotsawa, **Shakya Chokden** and the later **Nyingma school** thinker Ju Mipham accept the doctrine's validity even within their own Madhya-maka ontology. For example, according to Shakya Pandita and many pre-Tsongkhapa thinkers the concept of foundational consciousness belongs to the category of 'ordinary appearance' and is thus part of the 'lower truth', while the Madhyamaka doctrine of emptiness is associated with the 'ultimate truth'. Thus the concept is accepted on the level of conventional, relative truth.

For Dzokchen, however, 'foundational con-sciousness' has a much deeper meaning associated with an ultimate meditative perspective (see **Dzokchen thought**). For them, foundational consciousness refers to the real nature of mind, which is also the primordial basis, a nature that is said to be pure from the beginning. It is ever pure and in its true being, in a state of pure awareness (*rigs pa*). Sasang Mati Panchen associates 'foundational consciousness' with the concept of Buddhanature and suggests a distinction between a surface level, which is deluded and obscured, and the ultimate level which is that of non-dual wisdom. This view resonates with the view of **Shentong philosophy**, according to which the highest truth or the ultimate truth is the wisdom of non-duality. Tsongkhapa accepts that sometimes the term *alaya* (the basis of all) is used even in Madhyamaka writings and also in the Vajrayana texts. Nevertheless he argues that in the Madhyamaka texts the term is used as an epithet for emptiness, while in the Vajrayana contexts, it is used as a reference to the fundamental innate mind of inner radiance.

Further reading

Karmay, S. (1989) *The Great Perfection: A Philosophical and Meditative Teaching of Tibetan Buddhism*, Leiden: E.J. Brill, ch. 7.

Sparham, G. (trans.) (1993) *Ocean of Eloquence: Tsongkhapa's Commentary on the Yogacara Doctrine of Mind*, Albany, NY: State University of New York, introduction.

THUPTEN JINPA

FOUR BOOKS *see* Classics and Books

Four Germs

The Four Germs is a Mencian doctrine (see **Mencius**) that traces all good to the mind or heart of man:

> The heart of compassion is the germ of benevolence; the heart of shame, the germ of righteousness; the heart of courtesy and modesty, the germ of propriety; the heart of right and wrong, the germ of wisdom. Man has these four germs just as he has four limbs. For a man possessing these four germs to deny his own potentialities is to cripple himself....
>
> (*Mencius* 2A6)

Omitted from this set of four is the fifth virtue in the Five Permanents, **faith** or trustworthiness. It is sometimes explained that if one has the four virtues, this fifth virtue is automatic. The four (or five) being qualities of the One Mind, there is an assumption of a unity of the virtues.

For example, in the troubling case of whether one should break taboo and have physical contact with a sister-in-law in order to save her from drowning, the answer is of course, yes, you should reach out and save her. But if so, then **humaneness** apparently has overridden propriety and we may be presented with a case of conflicting virtues. However, a case can be made to show that the four germs were involved in working out what to do in that sort of situation: (a) humaneness provides the pre-reflective impulse; (b) propriety literally read raises momentarily the fear of a taboo; but (c) wisdom as sound judgment that comes with maturity could weigh the pros and cons; and in conclusion (d) rightness decides what is the fitting thing to do in this case.

That continuous response may even reconcile Daoist spontaneity, Confucian honour, Mohist deliberation and Realist action. It takes the form of (a) humaneness, (b) propriety, (c) wisdom, and (d) rightness which may even be paired with (a) Daoist spontaneity to love all life, (b) Confucian emphasis on the ritual of society, (c) Mohist rational deliberation on means and end, and (d) the realist or Legalist attention to what is fitting in a particular situation. Such a sequence gives each of the virtues its own due. But Song dynasty Neo-Confucians chose a different solution. They elevated *ren* or benevolence to a basic position, and considered the rest (including trust) to be a function of benevolence itself. Benevolence is here a cosmic power that penetrates everything. Lack of it (*buren*) causes an ailment which in Chinese medicine amounts to paralysis. Lack of humaneness leads to a moral blockage of the other virtues, since it amounts to an unnatural state of affairs which impedes the free flow of the natural being, and so prevents its free expression.

Further reading

Lai, W. (1991) 'In Defense of Graded Love: Three

Parables from Mencius', *Asian Philosophy* 1(1): 51–60.

WHALEN LAI

Four Noble Truths

The *Arya Satya* (Four Noble Truths) are the basic principles of the universal system of ethics, physics and metaphysics thought by Buddhists to have been discovered by Siddhartha Gotama (Shakyamuni), called the Buddha or 'Enlightened One' (*fl.* 450–400 BCE). The Truths are as follows:

1   All compounded and conditioned (*samskrita*, in Pali, *samkhara*) things are ultimately unsatisfactory (*duhkha*; in Pali, *dukkha*). This is the eternal round of existences (*samsara*). 'It is impossible to find any beginning from which beings steeped in ignorance and bound by the thirst for existence wander aimlessly from birth to birth' (*Samyutta Nikaya* II). Rebirth proceeds through the five destinies (hells, animals, ghosts, men and gods) and the 'three spheres':

Kama-dhatu: the plane of desire which includes the destinies of the hells, ghosts, humans as well as the six divinities presiding over the six worlds (*loka*) belonging to the sphere where the fruits of *karma* are experienced.
Rupa-dhatu: the plane of pure form inhabited by beings reborn in the heavens of the world of Brahma and who are distributed in terms of four kinds of meditative accomplishments called *dhyana*s (see **meditation**).
Arupya-dhatu: the plane of formlessness in which are reborn accomplished meditators purely as 'mental series' in four sectors of attainment (*samapatti*):

1   infinite space
2   infinite consciousness
3   infinite nothingness
4   beyond perception and non-perception.

The nature of future modes of existence is determined by the quality of the accumulated *karma* in a stream of experiences that temporarily forms a succession of lives. It appears that in the earliest forms of Buddhism, only deliberate, intentional (*chetana*) actions manifested in good or bad physical, verbal and mental events were regarded as automatically producing retributive potencies. While the originating action is good or bad, its future consequence, which occurs ineluctably in the appropriate stream of experiences and is inescapable for the 'originating agent', is morally neutral and thus does not itself yield further karmic consequences.

Universal unsatisfactoriness is attributed to the impermanence (*anitya*; *aniccha*) and non-substantiality (*anatma*; in Pali, *anatta*) of all conditioned entities. Buddhism propounds anti-essentialist and reductionist theories in its process or event ontologies. What appear to be stable and integral spatio-temporal continuants are reduced to temporary parts; human beings – to which the Upanishadic tradition (see **Upanishads**) attributes a separable essential, impermeable identity (**atman**) – are analysed into streams of causally interdependent psycho-physical components (*skandhas*, constituents of personality). These are matter, feelings, sense-perceptions, dispositions and conscious events and acts. Neither collectively nor singly do the components amount to an enduring, substantial self or soul. The latter terms, and the proper names supposedly designating them, may be understood as abbreviated definite descriptions for bundles of causally related momentary experiences. Enduring selfhood is a fiction which the experiential fluxes conventionally called persons superimpose upon themselves. Attempts to cling to the unstable and impermanent are bound to end in disappointed frustration.

The five psycho-physical components of personality are described as follows:

1   Form or corporeality (*rupa*): comprised of the four base elements, earth, water, fire and air and their derivatives which include the physical sense organs and their external objects.
2   Sensation or feeling (*vedana*): this may be physical or mental and is derived from contact between the six internal sense-organs (five plus mind (*manas*) which relates to mental phenomena or thinkables (*dharma*) and six types of sense data deriving from external objects.
3   Sense-perception (*samjna*): determinate perception involving recognition and naming and relating to the external objects.

4 Dispositions of character (*samskara*): accumulated **karma** and the volitions and intentions that derive from and are produced by it.
5 Consciousness (*vijnana*) grasps the characteristics of the six types of objects. It is of six kinds; visual, auditory, olfactory, gustatory, tactile and mental.

The five components are referred to as conditioned formations characterized by origination, disappearance, perdurance and change.

The interactions of phenomena are also analysed in two other classifications:

1 a 'twelve-base' (*ayatana*) account postulating the five sensory modalities plus synthesizing mind and six kinds of sensory and cognitive data that are their objective correlates.
2 a 'base-element' (*dhatu*) which adds to the twelve 'bases' six types of awareness; visual, auditory, olfactory, gustatory, tactile and non-sensory. The sense-organ (*indriya*) acting as a substrate (*ashraya*) and the external item (*vishaya*) acting as an intentional object (*alambana*) produce consciousness. 'Because of the eye and the visible, visual consciousness arises . . . because of the mind that the thinkables (*dharma*), mental consciousness arises' (*Samyutta Nikaya* II).

2   The second truth discovered by the Buddha is that there is a causal explanation (**pratitya-samutpada**; in Pali, *paticcha-samuppada*) for the arising of unsatisfactoriness (*duhkha-samudaya*) in terms of 'thirst' which serves as a metaphor for desire and attachment (*trishna*; in Pali, *tanha*) on the one hand and on the other ignorance of the way things really are as expressed in the four noble truths. Not only is there 'thirst' for pleasurable sensations, but also for more existences, more experience. Allowance is also made for the thirst for annihilation. All actions are motivated by craving (*raga*) or hatred (*dvesha*; in Pali, *dosha*) or delusion (*moha*).

The second truth is elaborated in terms of the twelve-fold causal nexus of interdependent genesis automatically ordering the factors of existence (*pratitya-samutpada*): spiritual ignorance (*avidya*) conditions karmic dispositions (*samskara*) which condition consciousness (*vijnana*) which conditions the psycho-physical matrix (*nama-rupa*) which condi-

tions the six bases of consciousness (*sad-ayatana*) which condition sense-object interactions (*sparsha*) which condition feelings (*vedana*) which condition 'thirst' (*trishna*) which conditions craving (*upadana*) which conditions repeated existences (*bhava*) which condition births (*jati*) which condition old age and death (*jara-maranam*) and all our woe.

This is proposed as an account of causal regularity, the repeatability of kinds and predictable ethical consequentiality given the absence of any persisting entity such as a soul (*atman*) that might serve as a principle of continuity. Ignorance and desire are the key factors propelling causal processes.

3   There is potentially an end to *duhkha*, called *nirvana* or in Pali *nibbana*. This is the end of the series of unsatisfactory existences (*samsara*) through the extinction of the fires of craving, hatred and delusion which generate rebirth-causing actions. It is a selfless and detached state beyond sensory pleasures and all forms of clinging. The enlightened person has a profound grasp of the truth about existence (*dharma*): to wit, everything is unsatisfactory (*duhkha*) because transitory (*anitya*) and lacking essential identity. All the transient phenomena constitutive of existence are said to be conditioned (*samskrita*): they are both causes and caused. *Nirvana* transcends the chain of being, becoming and causation and is said to be unconditioned.

According to the early Buddhist Sarvastivada realist traditions there are two types of existential transformation: (a) cessation of suffering due to knowledge (*pratisankhya-nirodha*) which is disjunction from impure *dharmas*, i.e. nirvana attained while alive through transformative insight (*prajna*) into the Four Noble Truths; and (b) cessation of suffering not due to knowledge (*apratisankhya-nirodha*) which is the prevention of the arising of future conditioned *dharmas* in a psycho-physical stream. It is so called because it is obtained not by the comprehension of the Truths, but by the impotency of the causes of arising. It is the attainment of ultimate extinction (*parinirvana*) at death. The idea is that the life in the world of the enlightened one (*arhat*) continues until the five constituents of personality (matter and form, feelings, perceptions, dispositions and conscious acts) are expended or 'burnt out'. After the death of the enlightened one, there is no rebirth.

Nirvana is the irreversible end of recognizable forms of human life.

The early traditions refer to the 'blowing out' or 'extinction' of the fires of clinging, hostility and delusion. The fires metaphor is not accidental. It refers to the three fires which the Hindu Brahminical householder was obliged to keep burning and which symbolized his life, responsibilities and attachments as a man in the world. The original sense of the metaphor was missed in developed Mahayana where craving, aversion and delusion are simply called the 'three defects'.

4   There is a path to the cessation of *duhkha* (the **Noble Eightfold Path**). The fourth truth states the Noble Eightfold Path of right views, right decisions, right speech, right action, right livelihood, right effort, right mindfulness and right concentration. They are classified as morality (*shila*), concentration (*samadhi*) and insight (*prajna*) into the transitory, unsatisfactory and non-substantial nature of the elements of conditioned existence. Morality consists in abstention from murder, theft, sexual misconduct, false speech, slander, harsh words, frivolous talk, covetousness, malice and false views. Normative Buddhist lay ethics involves abstention from theft, lies, injury, sexual malpractice and intoxicants which occasion heedlessness and lead to the other four. Concentration involves fixing the mind on a single point. It is the achievement of tranquility through avoidance of distractions and sensory withdrawal.

Further reading

Collins, S. (1982) *Selfless Persons: Imagery and Thought in Theravada Buddhism*, Cambridge: Cambridge University Press.

Conze, E. (1959) *Buddhist Scriptures*, Harmondsworth: Penguin.

Gethin, R. (1998) *Introduction to Buddhism*, Oxford: Oxford University Press.

Harvey, P. (1990) *An Introduction to Buddhism*, Cambridge: Cambridge University Press.

Rahula, W. (1969) *What the Buddha Taught*, London: Gordon Fraser.

Warder, A. (1991) *Indian Buddhism*, Delhi: Motilal Banarsidass.

CHRIS BARTLEY

free will

According to many Buddhist views, we are what we are by virtue of our past action. This can degenerate into karmic determinism. Although there is no Buddhist word for 'free will', the assumption is that knowledge of how **karma** works changes that equation. Henceforth, what we will be is due to how we now choose to act. In denying fatalism or predetermination, the Buddha fully acknowledges 'free will', without using or knowing that term. The fact that knowledge of *karma* makes us potentially free eventually from *karma* does raise the issue about the place, the status and the power of knowledge in the chain of causation. To the extent that the Buddha emphasized above all *chitta-karma* (mental action which slides into the momentum of *samskara*, a kind of blind will to be), the tradition would have to reckon with, at some point, the source of that will to change. But whether that ultimately involves a 'revulsion' (a total 'change of heart') or just a 'manifestation' (the 'same heart' that to date is deluded) is a matter for debate.

The Chinese discussion is a bit more complicated. Those who hold that human nature is good (**Mencius**) and those who regard it as evil (**Xunzi**) never disagree on human corrigibility. **Confucius** assumes that we can live up to our humanity; it is the way in which this should be done that was a matter for argument. **Mozi** argues that logic would guide us to change our behaviour. Mencius is not convinced by Mohist logic (see **Mohism: moral logic**), since he argues that it is not utilitarian calculation but a passion for righteousness that moves us to act. The first thinker to recognize a frequent 'failure of the will', he finally falls back on a flood-like **ether** (a cosmic-and-inner goodness) that, nursed by past habit of **righteousness**, would propel and guide us to a union with the ***dao***. Other thinkers offer other ways of ensuring the proper choice of action. Even the Legalists, who have a low opinion of human motivation (see **Legalism**), would hold up the carrot and the stick and assume that man would choose the right alternative. For the Daoists, the issue of a spirited freedom has to do with the renunciation of the human will. Within **religious Daoism**, there rose a concept of familial *karma* – the 'sins of the fathers' conceptualized now as a 'burden from the past' – but the new phraseology connotes a willingness to accept and a possibility of overcoming such an inherited legacy.

'Freedom' in English is tied to 'autonomy', and the freedoms guaranteed by modern democracies – of belief, association, the press, and so on – are meant to enhance individual autonomy. As we have seen, the modern term for 'freedom' in Chinese reads 'self-caused' or 'self-motivated', but it connotes, not 'self-rule' or 'self-determination', but 'being at ease' or feeling 'self-possessed'. It describes a state of 'self-being' which is the word for nature in Chinese. So that instead of polarizing freedom versus necessity or free will versus fate, the Chinese idea of freedom is being in **harmony** with the natural given (in Daoism) and bringing about an accord with the Mandate of **Heaven**. (The word for 'mandate' also serves as the word for 'fate'.)

See also: avidya; fatalism in Chinese philosophy

Further reading

Hendrischke. B. (1991) 'The Concept of Inherited Evil in the Taiping Jing', *East Asian History* 2: 1–30.

Kalupahana, D. (1975) *Causality: The Central Philosophy of Buddhism*, Honolulu, HA: University of Hawaii Press.

Nivison, D. (1996) *The Ways of Confucianism: Investigations in Chinese Philosophy*, LaSalle, IL: Open Court.

WHALEN LAI

freedom

Freedom understood as individual autonomy guaranteed by basic civil liberties is a recent development. Since the concept, created by the European Enlightenment, came to China in the nineteenth century, it is worth noting the existence of a wider range of historical 'freedoms' than just the modern ones. Confucian discourse of course recognizes moral autonomy and individual responsibility; otherwise, Zengzi would not have 'daily reflected on his actions in three areas', if it was not

presumed that he was free to act otherwise and that he could do better the next day. Three ideal-types of freedom may be isolated: Daoist *ziyou*, Hindu *moksha* and modern *liberté*. The first is a freedom that comes with being in tune with nature; this is the Daoist ideal. The second is a freedom that totally transcends nature; this is what much Indian philosophy seeks. They are different from the third, the social liberties upon which modern democracy rests. The modern Chinese term for 'freedom' reads 'self-originating'; it may capture the sense of 'autonomy', but it went back to a Daoist sense of losing oneself in nature.

Daoist freedom is not freedom as opposed to necessity; it is freedom that comes with immersion in the natural flow of things. Any sense of a 'self' would be in the sense of being self-contented or self-contained, a universe unto oneself (microcosm) by abiding with the Way of nature (macrocosm). It is not a freedom to dominate nature, it is the ease and calm that comes with being absorbed in the natural world. Cultural anthropologists might however recast that oneness with nature as 'being under nature', as when a farming community have to bend to the whims of the seasons and the weather.

Hindu *moksha* or liberation has the opposite goal. Its aim is totally to transcend nature. Judged as world-weary and world-denying by secular modernity, the Hindu standard could as well return the compliment and judge modern social liberties as being anything but free. They amount to being freedom only from a dozen or so restraints from among a thousand more. The 'thousand more' are what bind us to this earth – and they include the laws of nature, the law of necessity itself. In Hindu *moksha* or Buddhist **nirvana**, a person defies even the law of gravity. As with angels who are able to fly, the accomplished *yogi* could levitate, this being part of the hagiography of saints everywhere. Freedom from gravity was never featured as one of the goals listed in the French Revolution; but that is precisely the point. That revolution, through forsaking those spiritual freedoms from physical necessity, could then fight and succeed in wrestling those more 'limited' earthly freedoms like freedom of speech, of press, of assembly, etc. which in time changed our social world. If Daoist freedom goes with a natural economy, then Hindu *moksha* goes with superhuman *sannyasins* who live away from the social world, in hills and forest. For civil liberties, we expect the movers to be in the cities.

The three types of freedoms outlined above in spatial (regional) terms may also be mapped temporally. Classical traditions that consider the world to be fundamentally good seek to integrate the person into society and society into the cosmos. Medieval spirituality that sees the world subsequently as evil or corrupted worked hard to free the individual totally from it. If Weber is right, then modernity began with a translation of that 'otherworldly mystical' flight into an 'innerworldly ascetic' quest for more specific liberties in the here and now. That is, the 'otherworldly mystic' has to be converted into an 'innerworldly mystic'.

Further reading

Bellah, R. (1976) 'Religious Evolution', in R. Bellah, *Beyond Belief*, New York: Harper & Row.

Lai, W. (1980) 'Three Kinds of Freedom: Tzu-jan, Moksha, Conscience', *World Faith Insight* (formerly *Insight*) 1: 2–9.

Weber, M. (1930) *The Protestant Ethic and the Spirit of Capitalism*, London: Allen & Unwin.

WHALEN LAI

friendship

Fifth of the five cardinal human relationships in Confucianism, friendship is the one that makes possible an independence from the family and state that rule the other four. It is understandably held suspect by upholders of family priority, and popular conduct books warn against making commitments to strangers and against 'sworn brotherhood' that jeopardizes family loyalty. But the *Analects* opens with 'What pleasure to have a friend visit from afar', a testimony to how, by contrast with most people who only know their close neighbours, the **scholar** is a member of a far-flung community of like minds. The late Ming period saw a deepening of the understanding of the notion of friendship which, by the time of Ho Xinyin (1517–79), was often chosen over the other four human relationships. Li Zhi (1527–1602) wrote in memory of Ho,

and devoted ten chapters of his major work (1588) to a review of this topic.

Friendship, for **Confucius**, had always been morally defined. Like Aristotle, he held that only good men (gentlemen) can make true friends; inferior persons only lean on one another in partisan gangs (*dang*, which had the meaning of 'clique' in the past but is the word for 'political party' in our time). Beneficial friends edify; harmful friends corrupt; for a person is only as good as the company he keeps. Loyalty and trust are essential. But you can also befriend the ancients, through their writings. Drinking partners do not rank very high in that assessment, though it is clear that 'the pleasure of (a friend's) company' is a major factor in any friendship. Swordsmen and assassins made friends differently from peasants and literati. They are less tied to the soil or to the clan. So too were the more mobile artisans or the close-knitted band of the Mohists. The scheming Legalist, ever suspicious of both friend and foe, is sometimes painted as ready to betray a fellow Legalist, but that is an unkind caricature. **Recluses** made delightful company, like the later whimsical Chan pair of poets Hanshan and Shide.

The breakdown of political order after the Han freed lateral ties from hierarchic control. Some Neo-Daoists violated father–son bonds due to their different political ties. As a whole, the Neo-Daoists were famous for cultivating friendship; they gave feeling a free rein and this, with the aid of wine, nurtured a degree of 'romantic' friendship not seen before. Wine would induce the imbiber to drop into any wine house and mingle with other drunks, including the lowborn whom he would shun when sober. But there were also highly conscientious and impassive types among the Neo-Daoists. Sick of the political duplicity of the times, they valued the haven of like-minds but also, being sensitive to possible betrayal, would just as readily terminate friendship in open letters. As poets and musicians, they shared in a cult of aesthetic friendship. Their hearts and their music fully in tune, they read one another's minds without opening their mouths. The mutuality of these 'knowers of my heart and/ or tune' is legendary. Civil war and barbarian invasion also made this a prime time for hermits and monks to retreat from the world.

When that vocation for a few grew into a much

emulated lifestyle by the elite, what on paper was 'hiding away in peace and quiet' often meant in reality 'comfortable retirement'. The best-known figure in this lifestyle is Xie Lingyun, the 'mountain and water' poet who had enough money and political connections to buy up whole mountains in the south. The better and truer spirit of the era is a once-salaried scholar official, Tao Qian, who returned home to write poems on 'orchard and farm'. (Tao was virtually unknown and unsung, pale by comparison with Xie, until the mid-Tang dynasty when he was rediscovered.) A new compromise was reached when the poet Shen Yue, in the early sixth century, moved on his retirement back into the political capital to become an 'urban hermit'. The three above are not true hermits, but the first discovered companionship with mountains and waters; the second found it in the wine bottle drinking alone; and the third, unable to retire from politics, had to live with divided loyalties.

Friendship may cross class lines, but gender was a different matter. A Neo-Daoist zither player stopped a boat trip to go ashore to join a slave musician he heard playing a fine tune. Another stopped his boat in mid-water to listen to a female zither player, but in this case Confucian decorum kept in check any open friendship between the sexes. Even the admiration for the talented could not make easy any breach in the gender divide. The courtesan culture, similar to Kyoto's *geisha* quarter, came in the cosmopolitan Tang period. Friendship between men and women surfaced in that artificially refined culture. Female poets of humble background made the list of eligible companions of mind and soul, and woman's feelings, longings, complaints and wishes gained literary exposure. The disbanding of courtesan culture by the increasingly puritanical Song state and its devolution into the commercialized sex in the mercantile Ming cities ended the Tang romantic period. Less refined singing girls appeared, and concubinage became widespread. On the fringe of the new theatre, which had no female actors, friendship and romance of a different kind flourished, gender confusion notwithstanding. On the positive side, 'companion marriage' among literati couples fortunate enough to overcome the accidents of arranged marriages also appeared.

Further reading

Lai, W. (1996) 'Friendship in Confucian China', in O. Leaman (ed.), *Friendship East and West: Philosophical Perspectives*, London: Routledge, 215–50.
Mather, R. (1988) *The Poet Shen Yueh (441–513): The Retreat Marquis*, Princeton, NJ: Princeton University Press.

WHALEN LAI

friendship in Islamic philosophy

The notion of friendship in Islamic philosophy tends to follow the analysis of Aristotle, who devotes a considerable amount of space to the topic. He clearly sees it as a vital part of the good life as enjoyed by those living in society, and this emphasis on the significance of conviviality and life in a group is developed by ibn Miskawayh in his explanation of the point of many of the laws and practices of Islam. According to ibn Miskawayh, the excellence of Islam is evidenced, in part, by the ways in which it has created institutions and rituals which strengthen the ability of people to live and work together. For example, the requirement that people go to mosques to pray, if they can, encourages the ability of human beings to be together and uses a natural aspect of humanity (its collegiality) to increase enthusiasm for religion. Islam works with the human desire for friendship, not against it, in order to make it easier for human beings to carry out their religious obligations.

Further reading

Goodman, L. (1996) 'Friendship in Aristotle, Miskawayh and al-Ghazali', in O. Leaman (ed.), *Friendship East and West: Philosophical Perspectives*, Richmond: Curzon, 164–91.

OLIVER LEAMAN

frugality

Frugality is an aspect of the type of virtue praised by Neo-Confucians (see **Neo-Confucianism,**

concepts). This virtue has a complex history. Among the early thinkers, since **Confucius** was a *déclassé* of low nobility with limited means, he recognized a virtue of economy. He desired to economize on dress codes, and early Confucians in general were sticklers for form. However, in the matter of rites, Confucius was less thrifty, and the high level of expenditure on rites led the Mohists to urge cutting back on wasteful and non-utilitarian rites. However, the Confucian view prevailed.

The old aristocracy disappeared by the time of the Han dynasty, and China became the first major society of status-seekers. In classical China, generosity was required of the old feudal nobles. The magnate families that replaced them from the Han to Tang dynasties were still keen on social distinction; men of the 'grandiose gate' looked down on those from an 'unadorned gate' (the more wealthy and powerful a family, the more elaborately the entrance to their household would be decorated, so 'grandiose gate' became shorthand for a magnate). Men sought to enhance their stature by the proper amount of expenditure. The less secure, the more extravagant. Post-Han Neo-Daoists were nearly all from the magnate families.

It was Buddhism that first made poverty a virtue. The Han magnate family disappeared by the middle of Tang dynasty, and the Neo-Confucians that came in the Song dynasty were not of high-born stock, coming instead from the new land-owning gentry class. They made a moral life of material simplicity a virtue.

By the Ming dynasty, with competition for office growing, that virtue of 'the pure and austere' often translates into being a poor and incorruptible minor official, one who refuses bribes and the buying and selling of influence. They looked upon the new rich with moral contempt but also with increasing envy. This rising merchant class was prone to compensate for their lower status by conspicuous consumption. As they bought up land and titles, so the earlier ethic of frugality tended to be less respected.

Further reading

Lai, W. (1996) 'Puritanism and Neo-Confucianism: A Mutual Challenge', *Cheng Feng* 39(3): 149–72.

Tu Wei-ming (ed.) (1990) *Confucian Tradition in East Asian Modernity: Moral Education and Economic Culture in Japan and the Four Mini-Dragons*, Cambridge, MA: Harvard University Press.

Weber, M. (1951) *The Religion of China: Confucianism and Taoism*, ed. and trans. H. Gerth, Glencoe, IL: Free Press.

Yu Ying-shih (1955) 'Confucian Thought and Economic Development: Early Modern Religious Ethics in China and the Ethos of the Merchants', *Chih-shih feng-tzu* 2(2): 3–34 (in Chinese).

WHALEN LAI

Fukuzawa Yukichi

b. 1835; d. 1903

Scholar and educator

Fukuzawa's numerous writings include many philosophically relevant discourses, particularly on ethics, culture, politics, and education. He was born in Osaka, the son of a minor *samurai*. When he was about eighteen months old, his father died and his mother moved the family to Kyushu. Fukuzawa became extremely critical of feudalism even at an early age, and looked for a way to escape its restrictions. Arriving at the opinion that the reigning Confucian ideas were one of the main causes responsible for feudalism, he concluded that his education in Chinese classics was, after all, not of great help to achieve his goal. This led him to study the Dutch language and Western sciences, in Nagasaki (1854) and later in Osaka (1855). But after having studied Dutch, he realized that English was more important. Eager to learn and strong-willed, he then went to Edo and devoted himself to studying English. Only one year later, in 1860, he accompanied a Japanese delegation to the United States, and in 1862 joined a Japanese mission to Europe, serving as an interpreter. During his travels in Europe he visited France, England, Holland, Portugal and Russia. In 1887 he again went to America.

Back home, Fukuzawa settled down in Edo and, from 1866 to 1870, published his experiences in a series of three books, entitled *Seiyo jijo* (Conditions in the West), which became best-sellers. In 1874, he joined Meirokusha. Convinced that Japanese society and politics should be modelled on ideas of human freedom and dignity, and that education was the best means to achieve this goal, he founded a school and a newspaper, published numerous studies and articles, and delivered speeches. The school became the prestigious Keio University of today.

Perhaps the most important of his books is *Gakumon no susume* (An Encouragement of Learning). Its first section was published in 1872. The whole book was completed in 1876, and during Fukuzawa's lifetime went through seventeen printings, selling almost three and a half million copies. Probably, at least one in every 100 Japanese had read it, or parts of it. Even before he went abroad, Fukuzawa had also translated into Japanese several Western works relevant to a philosophy of socio-political and cultural progress, among them John Stuart Mill's *On Liberty*. These works were of a pragmatic, utilitarian and evolutionist bent, and thus belonged to those Western writings which most strongly influenced the first period of modern Japanese philosophy.

Keen to protect his independence and self-respect, Fukuzawa never accepted an official post. He died in 1903; some 15,000 people attended his funeral.

Fukuzawa combined ethics with social and political philosophy, and to a large extent his theories are also comparative philosophy of culture. He emphatically defended the idea of inborn human rights, especially human dignity, freedom and equality, and advocated education and enlightenment to realize them, and thus promote the process of civilization. The first sentence of *Gakumon no susume* – 'It is said that heaven does not create one man above or below another man' – became famous. However, since Fukuzawa believed that the actual differences between men were ultimately due to their education, or lack of education, he was inclined to look down on people and societies who did not try, or failed, to escape the conditions of ignorance, powerlessness and poverty, and hence also voiced elitist views. Perhaps his veneration for the spirit of independence contributed to this attitude. He further held that the Japanese people as a whole were not yet prepared for fully fledged democracy. Also, he had

serious reservations with regard to majority decisions and long and complicated democratic procedures.

As Fukuzawa himself observed, he tried to base his arguments on experience and logically consistent reasoning guided by a kind of methodical doubt. Accordingly, he rejected mere faith, particularly religious faith, and blind belief in tradition. With regard to his epistemology, Fukuzawa can be called a critical positivist or even critical rationalist, while his ethics can be characterized as a mixture of deontological and pragmatic liberalism and humanism. In his writings, he expressed himself in a concise and lucid manner.

As indicated, it was Fukuzawa's personal experience of social and political discrimination, oppression and exploitation in feudal Japan which, combined with his strong sense of independence and justice, led him to advocating human rights. He once remarked that, as a young man in Edo, he was treated 'as if... of a different race, like a worm', an object of 'contempt and humiliation'. Sharply condemning the Tokugawa shogunate, Fukuzawa pointed out that 'they enacted such notorious laws as that which gave the *samurai* the right to cut down a commoner'. Fukuzawa also mentioned other examples of what he called 'outrageous cases of "Might makes right"'. His determination to combat sexism, racism, imperialism and colonialism was a further motive for his struggles. Hence he addressed the individual as well as human communities and states, emphasizing individual as well as racial and national equality. Also, he strongly argued for an improvement of women's rights, and in particular for monogamy.

Following Henry Buckle's (1821–62) and F. Guizot's (1787–1874) theory that human progress led from savagery (nomadism) through barbarism (agricultural feudalism) to civilization (modern society), Fukuzawa characterized Japan as not yet fully civilized. In his *Bummeiron no gairyaku* (An Outline of a Theory of Civilization), he stressed the following points as crucial for a civilized country. First, there should be an awareness of the difference between the realms of nature and society, which enables man to recognize that he himself can design his social world. As an example, Fukuzawa mentions that the 'ruler–subject relationship... is not a natural principle' and can be 'reformed'. Second was the knowledge that traditionalism for its own sake is wrong: 'Merely being old does not make a thing valuable'. Men ought not to be 'slaves of custom'. In this connection, Fukuzawa deplored the fact that due to the long feudal rule, 'the minds of the Japanese [were] ossified'. He also pointed out that up to his time Confucian morality had proven unable to constitute satisfactory government. In his view, one must distinguish between a 'moralist's philosophy and a politician's political problems'. On the other hand, however, change should be enacted in a reasonable and humane way. Hence, Fukuzawa argued against revolution. 'A sudden blind upheaval can only replace violence by violence and stupidity by stupidity... there is nothing in the world as inhuman as civil disorder...' Third, civilization presupposes optimal education. Such education must include both scientific and moral education. As Fukuzawa poignantly remarked, 'the West has two advantages: a learning based on mathematics and reason and a spirit of independence'. He also indicated that people in the West have 'the courage to raise doubts'. Such remarks not only show what in Fukuzawa's mind was optimal education but again hint at the view that a scientific methodology and a sound awareness of one's individual dignity are the best guarantees of human life as it ought to be.

See also: comparative philosophy, Japanese; Japanese philosophy, post-Meiji; Meiroku Zasshi; philosophy of human rights, Japanese

Further reading

Fukuzawa Yukichi (1969) *An Encouragement of Learning (Gakumon no susume)*, trans. D. Dilworth and Umeyo Hirano, Tokyo: Sophia University.
—— (1973) *An Outline of a Theory of Civilization (Bummeiron no gairyaku)*, trans. D. Dilworth and C. Hurst, Tokyo: Sophia University.
—— (1982) *The Autobiography of Fukuzawa Yukichi*, trans. Kiyooka Eiichi, Tokyo: Hokuseido Press.
—— (1988) *Fukuzawa Yukichi on Japanese Women: Selected Works*, ed. and trans. Kiyooka Eiichi, introduction by Fujiwara Keiko, Tokyo: University of Tokyo Press.

Oxford, W. (1973) *The Speeches of Fukuzawa: A Translation and Critical Study*, Tokyo: Hokuseido Press.

GREGOR PAUL

fundamental innate mind

Some notion of a 'basic mind' as opposed to the conscious thoughts and sensory perceptions of an everyday waking life appears to be salient in the Buddhist philosophy, at least in the Mahayana tradition. **Yogachara**'s foundational consciousness and Bhavya's notion of mental consciousness as the real referent of first-person terms are examples of this. The notion of basic mind also seems to be associated with the concept of **buddha nature**. A key premise underlying this principle is the view that there must be a level of process which retains its continuum not only throughout an individual's life but also which connects the various lives of the same being. However, it is in the Vajrayana writings that we see a full development of this notion and the theory of mind that underpins the concept.

According to Vajrayana, various levels are posited to the mind or consciousness all sharing essentially the same nature of 'luminosity' and mere 'knowing'. Every mental event, on this view, is a composite of cognition and an 'energy' (*prana*). The grosser the level of energy, the grosser the level of mind; all our sensory perceptions, conceptual thoughts and strong emotions are said to belong to this level. In fact, our everyday, ordinary life of a waking consciousness represents the archetypal example of this gross level of existence. However what makes even these gross levels of experience 'mental' – that is, what makes these events cognitive rather than purely physical – is what the texts call 'innate mind of radiance' (*nyug mai o sel*). It is this basic luminosity and mere knowing that gives all our cognitive and emotional experience a quality of subjectivity. In itself, this basic nature of mind is said to be pure and untainted whose real nature becomes fully manifest only when all the gross levels of mental and 'energy' activity cease. Although it is only at the point of death that one is said to experience this basic radiance naturally there are nevertheless other occasions when we are said to have fleeting experiences of this, such as fainting, sneezing and sexual climax. Therefore a principal emphasis on religious praxis in Vajrayana is to engage in a systematic evocation of this experience within meditative states.

From a philosophical point of view, this notion of fundamental innate mind must raise certain conceptual problems. Given that all schools of Tibetan Buddhism perceive themselves as espousing Vajrayana, it becomes vital for them to be able to develop a theory of soteriology within which the concept of innate mind has a vital place. Yet if they wish to remain faithful to **Nagarjuna**'s Madhyamaka thought it is critical that this Vajrayana concept of the fundamental mind does not constitute a restoration of the ghost of the self or some metaphysical entity. In many ways, the problem posed by this concept resembles those raised by the theory of Buddha-nature.

Further reading

The Dalai Lama (1984) *Kindness, Clarity and Insight*, Ithaca, NY: Snow Lion, 168–82.

THUPTEN JINPA

funerals

A Mohist who appeared in *Mencius* 3A5, Yi Zhi had just given his parents a lavish funeral which was somewhat contrary to Mohist practice. In effect having reconciled Mohist 'universal love' and Confucian 'charity (that) begins at home', he expected to receive **Mencius**'s approval, since Mencius had showed a universal concern for any child in danger but also insisted upon lavish funerals for parents. But Mencius rejected him, coming back with the question:

Does Yi Zhi really believe that a man loves his brother's son no more than a neighbour's? He has misused the special case of a small child crawling toward a well (to possible death) due to no fault of its own. When Heaven gives birth to all things, it gives them a single basis or root; yet he has made that into two.

What that last line means is still being debated. Was Yi Zhi mixing a Mohist head and a Confucian heart? Or is it about Mohist ethics being in two minds from the start, proposing that one should love everyone because everyone then benefits, and also that one should love everyone because Heaven commands it? Or is something else meant? Staying with the narrative, it would appear that Mencius disputed the popular perception that he had offered a thesis that instinctually we love every child alike. We do not; we naturally love our own kin more. The idea that we naturally love everyone equally is wrong. We love our kin and by extension, we love others' kin and finally we love all mankind. The fact that we show concern for any child crawling towards a well involves special circumstances. The child is innocent; it does not know any better. The reference to the 'one root' to all things is not to some basic feeling of commiseration in all men. 'One root' is what the Logician Hui Shi had postulated, namely that at root, all things are one – and we should therefore love all things generously. The formula 'love the ten thousand things' originated with him, and was then adopted by Mencius and **Zhuangzi**. It became a standard expression in later moral discourse. That formula however makes no sense in Mohism: universal love is for one's kind, human kind, only. If you love a horse as you would a man, then you could have to give a man to a horse as you would a horse to a friend in order to benefit the beloved.

Mencius respected a unity of all things (the 'one root') that supports a concern for all things but he also intended to support and not contradict the idea of differentiated love. This is done by noting that it is through loving one's kin first that a person then, step by step by way of 'extension from the near to the far', comes to love all children and all men and then even things. This continuous process is the 'one root' that grows outward to include strangers. It is not a theory which starts from a universal notion of love, like a Mohist love for all humanity (as captured in the case of a child in peril), which then comes down to love for a peculiar individual. Mencius goes on to recall how in former times, people abandoned the dead in the hills. Then one day a son passed by and saw his parents' corpses being mauled by foxes and sucked at by flies. He was so horrified that he ran home and prepared a proper burial for his parents. That historical event supposedly then established the custom.

Mencius designed this imaginary tale to mock the Mohists who buried their own dead by 'wrapping them in mats' and 'dumping them into shallow ditches' (actually, not exposed but rather under three feet of dirt). In their cool rationality, Mohists had argued that 'the dead cannot feel as the living can' so that 'corpses are not men', and therefore offering lavish funerals or offering fine food to the dead is not part of the Mohist requirement of caring for parents or loving man. If so, then being gnawed at by foxes would not hurt the corpses at all. But it hurt the son who witnessed it. Why? Because, on account of his having had intimate ties with his parents, he imagined it and brought that sympathetic pain upon himself. He sensed and felt a horror at that perceived indignity. This is different from the case of the falling child who (through no fault of its own) courted death and whose innocent suffering touched us all. We would not have the same urge to run ahead if it was some well-paid stunt man, hanging off a cliff in front of a movie camera. (We feel the excitement but, presuming that it is all planned, we do not anticipate and feel the pain of an immanent death.) That special case of an innocent child in peril is different from the example of the corpse being mauled. Here the son was the one who abandoned the dead in the hill; his parents being gnawed at by foxes is due to his fault, his negligence. It is that sense of responsibility that caused the son (and all sons hence) to make the necessary sentimental amends, providing a proper burial for parents. Now we might also be horrified at seeing some unknown dead person being gnawed at in some paupers' graveyard, but to the degree that that corpse of a stranger is farther removed from us, to that degree we do not suffer the same sympathetic pain.

In classical Confucianism, a gentleman no more sacrifices to **Heaven** (unless he is the Son of Heaven) than he would honour the ancestral dead of another, burying an unknown dead subject being the duty and prerogative of the state. It is the Buddhist monk offering free mass for any and all dead that changed this norm in China, as Christianity did in Europe. The Mencian record here may not do the Mohists justice. Mohists allowed sons to bury parents and even make food offerings; that is the son's duty. They had no qualms about kings having large tombs which went with and matched the status of kings. In both cases, the restriction was only that the burial should not be so lavish as to cause public distress.

See also: afterlife in Chinese thought; logic in Chinese philosophy

Further reading

Lai, W. (1991) 'Of One Mind or Two? Query on the Innate Good in Mencius', *Religious Studies* 26: 237–55.

Nivison, D. (1996) 'Two Roots or One?', in D. Niven, *The Ways of Confucianism*, Chicago and La Salle, IL: Open Court.

Shun Kwong-loi (1997) 'Mencius' Criticism of Mohism: An Analysis of Meng Tzu 3A.5', in Shun Kwong-loi, *Mencius and Early Chinese Thought*, Stanford, CA: Stanford University Press.

WHALEN LAI

G

Gandhi, Mohandas Karamchand

b. 1869; d. 1948

Philosopher and political leader

Mohandas Karamchand Gandi was educated in India and studied for the Bar at the Inner Temple in London before returning to Bombay. From 1893 to 1914 he practised as a barrister in South Africa where he became a champion of the migrant Indian community in Natal. Returning to India in 1915, he became involved in the struggle for self-rule, becoming increasingly active after the Amritsar massacre of 1919. Identifying God, Truth and the true Inner self (**atman**), he came to believe that the force of truth (*satyagraha*) should be actualized in non-violent (**ahimsa**) passive resistance to the British. His principal inspiration came from the **Bhagavad Gita**'s teaching that one should engage in activity while selflessly renouncing the fruits of action. The adept of 'truth-force' should be a celibate vegetarian and immune to the ensnarements of passion in order to counter the force of untruth and promote justice in the interests of everyone. This included the out-castes or untouchables (see **caste**), whom he designated 'Harijans' or 'children of God'. Indeed, he claimed to 'believe in the essential unity of man and for that matter of all that lives'. A rare example of someone believing that moral conviction could successfully accomplish political changes, it is as a politician striving for Indian independence from British rule rather than as a philosopher that Gandhi is best understood. It has been observed that all political careers end in failure, and the partition of the sub-continent in 1947 marked the end of Gandhi's aspirations for the regeneration of India.

Further reading

Brown, J. (1972) *Gandhi's Rise to Power: Indian Politics 1915–1922*, Cambridge: Cambridge University Press.

—— (1977) *Gandhi and Civil Disobedience: The Mahatma in Indian Politics*, Cambridge: Cambridge University Press.

—— (1989) *Gandhi: Prisoner of Hope*, New Haven, CN: Yale University Press.

Chatterjee, M. (1983) *Gandhi's Religious Thought*, London: Macmillan.

Copley, A. (1987) *Gandhi: Against the Tide*, Oxford: Blackwell.

Gandhi, M.K. (1958) *The Collected Works of Mahatma Gandhi*, New Delhi: Ministry of Information and Broadcasting.

Woodcock, G. (1972) *Gandhi*, London: Fontana.

CHRIS BARTLEY

Gaozi

b. *c*.420 BC; d. *c*.350 BC

Philosopher

Human nature

Gaozi (Kao-tzu) instigated the first public debate on human nature. Defeated by **Mencius**, his position has been distorted by the Mencian reportage and misconstrued by those who accepted that report ever since. Coming after **Confucius**, who stressed the family, Yang Zhu, who prized the self, and **Mozi**, who loved everyone, Gaozi essentially combined their different views of humanity, internalized them, arranged them in a hierarchic order and came up with a dictum on how best to pursue the Good.

At the most basic level of human life lie the instincts for food and sex. This raw material of life is pre-moral but, like raw timber, it can be molded. At the next level, man as a family man 'loves his own kind'; this he called 'inner humaneness'. This is not blind instinct but it is a natural inclination. At the highest level, man as *homo politicus* answers to the duty required of him by society; this he called 'outer righteousness'. These three levels are derived from the egoism of Yang Zhu, the familism of Confucius and the altruism of Mozi. The rule of thumb is: duty to society overrides inclination to aid family, which overrides pure ego or instinct. The illustration he offered for this is a village feast. The raw instincts, unfeeling and unthinking, would have us grab the food for ourselves. But our inclination (due a love of kin) would have us willingly delay our own gratification and help feed a younger sibling first. This is 'inner humaneness'. But duty, which as Kant notes always has the potential to rub against inclination, dictates that we should, whether we like it or not, offer the food to the most elderly person present, even if he is not a kinsman, simply because he is by objective measure, the highest in age count. Seniority is 'outer righteousness'. So always do what is right first; follow your humane (familial) inclination next; and satisfy your own appetite (nature) last. To Mencius, and for Mencians thereafter who considered righteousness, **humaneness**, and human nature to be one and the same, Gaozi's stratification here makes no sense.

On moulding the raw material of the instincts

But far from seeing any innate conflict among duty, inclination and instinct, Gaozi believed in moulding the lower self into the higher self. Therefore he compared human nature – by which he meant the instincts – to whirling water in a pool. It is vital, and it moves; but how it flows – east or west – depends on how we breach (open up) the dykes. Or it is like a piece of willow, raw timber that can be bent and moulded into a bowl. Such a moulding of nature into culture was acknowledged by Confucius, when he compared a cultured gentleman to a piece of polished jade. (We still say in Chinese, 'An uncarved or unpolished jade does not a utensil make'. Only **Laozi** would desire to leave the *dao* as the literally uncarved block.)

Holding to a different premise about human nature, Mencius charged that water naturally flows downward, so that splashing it upward goes contrary to its nature, and going against its (good) nature cannot produce the Good. Likewise, bending the willow is going against its grain, and violating its (good) nature cannot be good. In Gaozi's defence, one may cite the Chinese proverb, 'Water may flow naturally down, but Man should always aspire high'. And Chinese has always associated 'flowing downward' (i.e. downstream) with the despicable behaviour of the lower class. As to the willow, the Chinese ideogram for 'talent or ability' is the picture for 'wood' with a limb chopped off. Any woodwright would testify that you have to coax wood into good form, and that there is a way of doing that without actually cracking it. In Gaozi, moulding instinct into inclination – turning 'grabbing the food for oneself' into 'willingly helping a younger brother first' – is not that different or that impossible an affair. Why? Because we always negotiate one kind of joy or happiness for another, eating alone or sharing it with a brother. This idea that joy is a basic criterion for what is good is found in the opening lines of the *Analects*; it is basic to Aristotle as well. We do not deny ourselves happiness by taking care of a younger brother. Joy is contagious among kin. The hurdle comes with duty: 'Offer food first to whosoever is eldest', even if he is not a kinsman. To do so is 'to his delight' (at his pleasure), not to ours.

That sense of civic Duty is where Mohist reason comes in to help override the Confucian inclination. For the communal good, Confucian family feelings like egoist appetites must be deferred. That is what 'outer righteousness' commands. Are we necessarily unhappy doing that? The response by Confucius is negative. 'To learn (the rites) and to practice frequently (what has been learned), is that not a joy!' Learning may not be fun at first compared with play; any child would know that. But when learning becomes a joy in itself is when the child becomes a good student and a little gentleman. That is when virtue, as with Aristotle's 'good habits' (habituation into the good), becomes self-gratifying and self-perpetuating. There is vicarious joy in the observance of etiquette; there is a logical progression from honouring a senior kinsman to then willingly honouring all non-kin elders.

The immovable mind of impartiality

Gaozi was the first to formulate a guideline for having an impartial mind. Out of consideration for the greater good, a person should not be moved by familial sentiments or his lower appetites. The rule reads:

> What does not accord with speech (*yan*, a gentleman's reputation or social repute), do not seek to resolve by the mind (**xin**, the inclination to take care of one's family first). What does not accord with mind (the love of family), do not seek to resolve with the lower passion (**qi**, the instinct for self-gratification).

Gaozi's claim to observe outer righteousness rests on this impartial commitment to 'doing the right thing'. It does require a cool-headed weighing of priorities. But Mencius would subvert his thesis by noting how people would rush forward to save a child about to fall into a well 'without first deliberating the pros and cons'. Mencius also came up with a different psychological model for understanding what constitutes true moral courage. It is not just doing what society says you should do; it is acting according to the **righteousness** that one believes in one's own heart, no matter what prudent society might say.

Kantian ethics stresses the moral intent (the good will) and opposes an ethics which is based on the beneficial end being the criterion of value. For Kant, a moral act must involve conscious choice. Doing good blindly 'by instinct' will not count. But then duty, doing what must be done, also naturally rubs against inclination. Instinct, inclination and duty are all one to Mencius, but Gaozi came closer

to Kant on this issue. He also suggests that duty is different from instinct and involves an exertion of a moral will that runs contrary to inclination. At a village banquet, our instinct might be to grab the food for ourselves; our inclination (our subjective family feeling) is to help feed a younger brother first; but we must observe duty and etiquette to offer food first to the most elderly member as judged by his objective age. In this, Gaozi overcame the instinct that guided the egoist Yang Zhu and the 'family first' inclination of the Confucians, and supported the call of duty, the higher civic rules, championed by the Mohists.

Further reading

Graham, A. (ed.) (1960) *The Book of Lieh Tzu*, New York: Columbia University Press, 135–57.
—— (1989) 'Retreat to Private Life: The Yangists', in A. Graham, *Disputers of the Tao*, La Salle, IL: Open Court, 133–43.
Lai, W. (1984) 'Kao-tzu/Gaozi and Mencius on Mind: Analyzing a Platonic Shift in Classical China', *Philosophy East and West* 34(2): 147–60.

WHALEN LAI

Gaudapada

b. *c*.450; d. *c*.500

Vedantist philosopher

An early non-dualist Vedantin of idealist persuasion (see **Vedanta**), Gaudapada was the author of the *Agama-Shastra* which is also known as the *Gaudapadiya-Karikas* or *Mandukya-Karikas*. Albeit a Vedantin, he was clearly influenced by the Buddhist Madhyamika dialectician **Nagarjuna** and the Buddhist idealist Yogacharins Asanga and **Vasubandhu** (see **Yogachara**).

According to Gaudapada, the goal of soteriological praxis, actions to bring about salvation, is manifestation and realization of the universal inner Self (called Brahman or **atman**) which is inactive, pure consciousness (*vijnana*) by a process of progressive interiorization. This *atman*-Self exists in the body in three forms corresponding to the states of orientation to an external environment or waking (*jagrat*), dream (*svapna*) and deep sleep (*sushupti*) in which it abides in its proper, original form. There is an inexpressible, all-pervasive ultimate fourth state (*turya*) beyond duality and changes whose realization is the *summum bonum*. Experience of duality is produced by a power of illusion (*maya*). But it is through the religious activities that are features of duality-based experience that we can be predisposed to an understanding of and attain the supreme non-dual state (*advaitam paramarthatah*). Non-duality is realizable through contemplation of the *atman* through the symbol *Pranava* or *Om*. That syllable is analysed into the sounds A (which stands for the waking state), U (the dream state) and M (deep sleep). The combined product of the sounds stands for the 'fourth state', which encapsulates and transcends the other three. Ignorance, which sees duality and activity as real, is removed by escaping the cosmic *maya* 'when the soul awakes from the sleep of beginningless delusion.'

Gaudapada thinks that waking experience is on a par with dream experience in that both are mental creations. The bifurcation of unitary awareness into the distinction between graspable cognitive object (*grahya*) and subject (*grahaka*) is imagined. It is an apparent vibration of the spirit which is in reality unmoved. Personal individuality is illusory. The universe is like a dream, a magical illusion or a city in the sky. There is neither origination nor destruction (*ajati-vada*): neither bondage to a series of births (**samsara**) nor release (*moksha*). Just as space (**akasha**) assumes the forms of the spaces occupied by limiting conditions (*upadhi*) such as pots which merge back into space when the pots are shattered, so the *atman* appears as individuals (*jiva-atman*) with distinct, private experiences due to illusory association with imagined bodies. When the latter perish, the individualised *jivas* merge into the *atman*. The forms, functions and names of the pots may be different, but space is the same. Likewise with the consciousness of the Self; as the space in a pot is neither a modification (*vikara*) nor a part (*avyayava*) of space, so the *jiva* is neither a part nor a transformation of the *atman*. Space only appears to be polluted: likewise in the case of the Self which seems polluted to the ignorant.

Origination or coming into being (*jati*) is an impossibility. According to different theories of causation, an entity arises from the existent (*sat*) or the non-existent (*asat*). Neither what already is nor what is not can come into being. If something really originates from the existent, a thing already originated originates again. Origination from the non-existent is impossible. An unborn thing cannot be born: there is an unbridgeable gulf between the non-existent and existent. He rejects the **satkaryavada** theory of the Samkhyas according to which effects pre-exist in their causal substrate prior to their actualization: there can be no production if the effect already exists in the cause. Spirit is beginningless and eternal.

When the mind withdraws from the imagined objects to which it is attached, when mental functioning ceases, it achieves stability and freedom from sorrow, desire and anxiety. The cessation of mental activity is release or spirit's recovery of its original form.

Further reading

Bhattacharya, V. (1943) *The Agamashastra of Gaudapada*, Calcutta: University of Calcutta.

Halbfass, W. (ed.) (1995) *Philology and Confrontation: Paul Hacker on Traditional and Modern Vedanta*, Albany, NY: State University of New York Press.

Potter, K.H. (ed.) (1981) *Encyclopedia of Indian Philosophies, Vol.III, Advaita Vedanta up to Samkara and His Pupils*, Delhi: Motilal Banarsidass.

CHRIS BARTLEY

Geluk school

Appearing in the early fifteenth century following the establishment of Ganden monastery by **Tsongkhapa** in central Tibet in 1410, the Geluk soon became the dominant school across the whole of Tibet. This dominance was strengthened further following the assumption of political power by the Fifth Dalai Lama in the seventeenth century, which led to the rule of the successive Dalai Lamas that continues to this day. Generally speaking, the delineation between the four principal schools of Tibetan Buddhism has more to do with allegiances to the lineage of individual masters than to different doctrinal and philosophical standpoints. There are, however, justifiable grounds to attribute different, and often opposing, philosophical and doctrinal standpoints that characterize these schools. At the core of Geluk philosophical thinking lies the study of **Nagarjuna**'s philosophy of **emptiness** as read by Chandrakirti and the logico-epistemological tradition of **Dharmakirti** and his Indian interpreters.

In the first realm, Tsongkhapa's influential Madhyamaka writings gave rise to an entirely novel appreciation of the Indian Madhyamaka philosophy. Key elements of this interpretation involve, amongst others, delineating the parameters of Madhyamaka dialectics so that they cannot be seen as negating everything, establishing a coherent status of reality to the world of everyday experience, emphasizing the use of non-implicative negation in Madhyamaka's deconstructive analysis, and developing a systematic Madhyamaka standpoint on issues of epistemology and ontology. In the realm of epistemology, the Geluk thinkers, especially **Gyaltsap Dharma Rinchen**, Khedrup and Gendun Drup, have developed a highly sophisticated and somewhat realist epistemology within the Buddhist epistemological tradition. This represents a counterpoint to the nonrealist epistemology of **Shakya Pandita**, which became the received view amongst the Shakya thinkers, especially following the influential works of Gorampa and **Shakya Chokden**. In this sense, the Geluk epistemologists can be seen as the heirs of Chapa's realism. Together with Shakya (see **Shakya school**), the school to which Tsongkhapa shared strong affiliations through his main teacher Rendawa, the Geluk school has been most active in what could be characterized, from the contemporary Western philosophical perspective, as substantive philosophical discourse.

Key figures in the development of Geluk philosophical thought are, in addition to Tsongkhapa, Gyaltsap Dharma Rinchen, Khedrup (1385–1438), Gendun Drup (1391–1474), Nyelton Paljor Lhundrup (1427–1514), Khedrup Norsang Gyatso (Jamyang Gawai Lodro) (1429–1503), (1423–1513), Gendun Gyatso (1476–1542), Jetsun Chokyi Gyaltsen (1469–1544), Panchen Sonam Drakpa (1478–1554) and Panchen Lobsang Chogyen (1570–1662).

Further reading

Cabezon, J. (1994) *Buddhism and Language: A Study of Tibetan Scholasticism*, Albany, NY: State University of New York, ch. 1.
Dreyfus, G. (1997) *Dharmakarti's Philosophy and its Tibetan Interpretations*, Albany, NY: State University of New York, introduction.

THUPTEN JINPA

Gendun Chophel
b. 1903; d. 1951
Poet, philosopher, historian and linguist

Gendun Chophel is one of the best-known Tibetan thinkers of the twentieth century. He began his education as a monk at Labrang Tashi Khyil monastery, and later joined the famous Drepung monastic university near Lhasa. During his years as a student, Gendun Chophel established his fame as an erudite debater with a sharp philosophical mind. It was however his encounter with the Indian scholar Ragu Vira, who had come to Tibet to search for lost Sanskrit manuscripts, that was to change the course of Gendun Chophel's life. As an assistant to Ragu Vira, Gendun Chophel left for India and Nepal. He embarked on a long journey which took him through much of the silk route through Afghanistan, modern Pakistan including the Swat valley, and various parts of Northern India.

Gendun Chophel's philosophical writing, though limited to the single work entitled *Ornament of Nagarjuna's Thought*, posthumously published and purported to be based on his lectures, has attracted considerable interest amongst Tibetan scholars. The work reinvokes Taktsang Lotsawa's critique of 'validly established convention' (*tha nye tse dup*) and develops a series of arguments that resonate with many of the sceptical arguments against the possibility of valid knowledge. A principal object of many of Gendun Chophel's arguments appears to be aimed at demonstrating that the so-called thesisless view of the early Tibetan understanding of Madhyamaka need not be read as irreconcilable with **Tsongkhapa**'s thought. The work is perceived by scholars of non-Geluk schools, especially the **Nyingma school** and **Shakya school**, as rescuing their understanding of Madhyamaka against the influential reading of Tsongkhapa and his followers. Amongst the various refutations of Gendun Chophel's text, the most comprehensive is that of Zemey Rinpoche Lobsang Palden (1927–96) entitled *A Critique of the Madhyamaka Work called 'Ornament of Nagarjuna's Thought'*.

Further reading

Stoddard, H. (1986) *Le mendiant de l'Amdo*, Paris: Société D'Ethnographie.

THUPTEN JINPA

geomancy

Literally 'wind and water', geomancy (*fengsui*) is the Chinese art of finding the most auspicious site for home and grave so that the occupant and the descendants would benefit from the flow of good fortune. The first known text on geomancy is supposed to come from the Six Dynasties, but the concern for proper placements of sites might be pre-Han or even Shang. By the Song dynasty, tomb geomancy had become all-pervasive. The cult reflects an increase in traffic between the living and the dead. Warmer family ties within the new agnatic (male) lineages meant that survivors missed the departed more deeply; this helped to increase mutual obligations and support between the two worlds. But tomb geomancy is also socially divisive, for competition for good burial sites can be fierce. There is no end to rumours of 'stealing (the flow of another's) geomancy'. Even railway lines have been re-routed to avoid cutting into some 'dragon vein'. This is because the landscape is taken to be alive and able to affect human fortunes and dispositions; running through it are the 'veins' or 'vital force'. The idea of a 'living landscape' is perhaps best seen in the macrocosmic/microcosmic parallel between the human body and sacred landscape, especially in the Daoist body where the bodily organs (including the veins) have geological counterparts.

WHALEN LAI

Al-Ghazali

b. 450 AH/1059 CE; d. 505 AH/1111 CE

Theologian and philosopher

Abu Hamid Muhammad ibn Muhammad al-Ghazali was born in Tus in Persia, and spent the first part of his life as a theologian in Baghdad. He both lectured in Islamic law there, but also set out to refute what he took to be heretical views. A spiritual crisis led to his ending that career and adopting the life of a wandering sufi until his death. Al-Ghazali is often seen as the chief enemy of Islamic philosophy, but he is a philosopher himself, and the basis of his critique is itself philosophical. He went through a large number of intellectual permutations throughout his life, something his critics latched onto with glee, and one of the appealing aspects of his work is the constant search for a personally and intellectually satisfying view of the world.

Al-Ghazali started off as an adherent of the Ash'arite theological school, which based itself on occasionalism, ethical subjectivism and atomism. This theory was established in opposition to the Mu'tazilites, who regarded human beings as the originators of their own actions; the Ash'arites understand both human and divine power as created ultimately by God (see **Ash'ariyya and Mu'tazila**). The Mu'tazilites argue that everything was created with the purpose of illustrating divine justice, so God must do the best he can for us and must reward us in accordance with our merit. Al-Ghazali accepted and developed the Ash'arite response to these views, arguing that it detracts from the greatness of God if he is obliged to follow any general principles of justice. God can do anything he wants, he can punish virtuous people and reward the wicked were he to wish to, he is under no obligation at all to his creatures. This is because God has no purposes and his actions cannot be described using human notions like justice at all, so whatever he may do to his creatures cannot be called either just or unjust. While this debate took the form of a theological struggle in accordance with the principles of Islamic theology (*kalam*), it resonates with the familiar philosophical debate as to whether moral judgements are subjective or objective. If the former, then it must be based on someone or some institution, and if the latter then it is based on nothing more than itself and the rationale of ethics alone.

Al-Ghazali's works were translated into Latin, and his *Intentions of the Philosophers* (*Maqasid al-falasifa*) was such a faithful description of the views of *mashsha'i* (Peripatetic) thought that he was believed to be a member of that school himself. Interestingly, this is a claim which has been made again recently after consideration of some of his theological works (see Frank 1994). This seems to be wrong of the *Maqasid* at least, and in this book he seeks to explain clearly the views of his opponents before undermining them, in his *Incoherence of the Philosophers*. In the latter he undertakes to overturn the main Neoplatonic and Aristotelian views of reality. The three most serious views to be refuted are the thesis that the world is eternal, that God cannot have knowledge of particulars, and that there is no such thing as individual physical resurrection. The philosophers argued that the emanation of the First Intellect and subsequent beings is the result of the necessary and constant causal power of God's essence. The implication is that the world is then co-eternal with him. He could not have created the world at a particular time, since this would imply change in him, which is impossible. In any case, since each moment of time is exactly the same as every other moment for God, why would he choose a particular moment as the right one to create the world? All times are the same for God. Al-Ghazali responds by suggesting that God's creation of the world was carried out before the start of time and so does not imply change in God, and he uses the notion of time established by his opponents. Time itself is an aspect of God's creation and started when God created the world. Again, even though one time is the same as any other time from our limited point of view, it is the nature of God to be able to distinguish through his will between similar things and choose one of them.

The philosophers reinterpreted the notion of God's knowledge of particulars since they argue that such knowledge would mean a change and plurality in the divine essence. As al-Ghazali points out, if God has complete knowledge of a thing there will be no change in his eternal knowledge, even though the thing changes. To deny that God can know, for example, whether Muhammad prophesied or how we had acted during this life struck Ghazali as highly problematic in a theory which claimed to be Islamic.

The third main objection he makes is to philosophical problems about any significant notion of physical resurrection. He agrees that individual resurrection goes against the principles of causality, but he describes these as merely customary ways of human thinking, which God may quite readily alter should he wish to. We may not understand how he could do this, but that is because we do not appreciate how God is really the ultimate cause of everything, and so could make possible what previously was naturally impossible.

What we should notice about al-Ghazali's critique of philosophy here is that he is antagonistic towards a particular form of philosophy, the specifically Neoplatonic curriculum, which he often attacks using Aristotelian logic. Al-Ghazali is frequently described as the person who brought Islamic philosophy to an end, and this is entirely inaccurate. But it is true that he marks the end of the type of *mashsha'i* thought which had been the leading way of operating up to his time, and his use of logic played a large part in the continuing enthusiasm for logic in theology circles.

After becoming convinced of the spiritual poverty of traditional philosophy, al-Ghazali became committed to **Sufism**. This seemed to him to be the most secure route to salvation, a route which permits the sufis to glimpse the world where God's decree is inscribed. Ordinary believers can experience this also through their dreams, and as a result the veil between that world and the soul is lifted. Al-Ghazali's Sufism is far from unphilosophical. Like the philosophers, he holds that the soul is the most important part of the individual person, and that it is liberated from the body by death. The human soul is a spiritual substance totally different from the body; it is divine and makes possible our knowledge of God. In his encyclopedic *Ihya' 'ulum al-din* (Revival of the Knowledge of Religion), he argues in detail for a particular understanding of our role in the universe and our path to salvation. The body is the vehicle of the soul on its way to the next life, and if we restrain our emotions, appetite and intellect we can acquire the virtues of temperance, courage, wisdom and justice. He argues in a rather Aristotelian way that we need to aim at the mean when operating with the body, and so transform ourselves through religion to imitate God, in so far as we can do this. Although Sufism is often seen as a private and subjective pursuit of a relationship with God, al-Ghazali argues that the traditional demands of Islamic life must be obeyed by the Sufi if salvation is to be attainable. There is not just one route to this end. One route is personal and can only be undertaken by the Sufi who has mastered the mystical path and who has undergone all the preparatory work which is necessary to achieve such an end. (Al-Ghazali is a bit coy about the role of the *shaykh*, which is held to be vital by most Sufis, but which seems to have been bypassed by him.) The other route is available to the ordinary believer, and it comprises an exacting obedience to the law and customs of religion, since this enables him to learn how to control himself and how to transform himself in such a way as to bring him as close to God as is possible within his less demanding interpretation of how to live.

See also: revival of Islam, theories of

Further reading

Frank, R. (1992) *Creation and the Cosmic System: Al-Ghazali and Avicenna*, Heidelberg: Carl Winter.

—— (1994) *Al-Ghazali and the Ash'arite School*, Durham, NC: Duke University Press.

Al-Ghazali (1964) *Incoherence of the Philosophers*, trans. S. Van den Bergh in his *Averroes' Tahafut al-Tahafut*, London: Luzac.

—— (1980) *Freedom and Fulfillment*, trans. R. McCarthy, Boston: Twayne.

—— (1989) *The Remembrance of Death and the Afterlife*, trans. T. Winter, Cambridge: Islamic Texts Society.

Leaman, O. (1985) *An Introduction to Medieval Islamic Philosophy*, Cambridge: Cambridge University Press.

—— (1996) 'Al-Ghazali and the Ash'arites', *Asian Philosophy* 6: 17–28,

—— (1997) *Averroes and his Philosophy*, Richmond: Curzon, 104–16.

Nakamura, K. (1993) 'Was Ghazali an Ash'arite?', *Memoirs of the Research Department of the Toyo Bunko* 51: 1–24.

OLIVER LEAMAN

gnosticism

Gnosticism, considered a heresy by the Christian Church, flourished on the Silk Road. Gnostics believed in, among other things, the entrapment of some divine spark – the spirit – in the material prison of the body. Plato might have used that metaphor, following Pythagoras who believed in metempsychosis; but in general, classical Greek thought did not so devalue the world as to consider the cosmos to be created by some evil Demiurge as a means for trapping these divine sparks that had fallen from a totally transcendental source of Light. Thus Plotinus wrote against the Gnostics to protect the classical view of the world as a sacred cosmos, not some tyrannical rule by blind fate.

China, in the transition from her classical to medieval era, also knew such a devaluation of the world and was able to entertain the idea of a disembodied soul fallen from some transcendental home. This broke the classical presumption of a natural harmony between man and cosmos. A world-pessimism that came with Buddhism enhanced that view. As Mahayana Buddhism developed through the Wisdom *sutras*, it also recognized a transcendental gnosis. It later embraced the doctrine of a **buddha nature**. As it came into China via Central Asia, Buddhism absorbed more Gnostic elements from the Silk Road. A standard set of metaphors for buddha nature as listed in the **Tathagatagarbha** (womb/embryo of the buddha) *Sutra* goes as follows:

Like a buddha inside an ugly lotus flower
honey covered by bees
the kernel of grain inside the husk
gold hidden among impurities
treasured buried underground
a sprout from a small fruit

a buddha-image in a worn garment
a future king in a poor woman's womb
a precious statue in a wooden cast –
so too is this (buddha) essence hidden by
accidental defilements inside every sentient
being.

All the metaphors paint a Gnostic dualism of
what is real and what is apparent with no
substantial connection between the two. (All
rebirths being self-propelled, the future king is
not an extension of the poor woman.) The
Buddha-nature is hidden. Obscured by accidental
defilements, it needs to be liberated so as to shine
forth on its own. Meanwhile, **religious Daoism**
was also evolving its own notion of a 'sage embryo',
a spiritual second self inside the body. These two
concepts later became mingled when the Chan
master Linji talked of this 'true man of no fixed
rank going in and out of the body'.

Further reading

Jonas, H. (1958) *The Gnostic Religion*, Boston:
  Beacon Press.
Pagels, E. (1979) *The Gnostic Gospels*, New York:
  Random House/Vintage Press.
Takasaki Jikido (1966) *A Study of the Ratnagotravibhaga
  (Utteratantra): Being a Treatise on the Tathatagarbha
  Theory of Mahayana Buddhism*, Rome: Istituto
  Italiano per il Medio ed Extremo Oriente 33.

WHALEN LAI

grammar and the philosophy of language in India

In India, grammar was considered a paradigm
science, and it had already attained a level of
brilliant sophistication in the centuries preceding
the Christian era. The earliest text to survive was
Panini's *Ashthadhyayi*, a description of Sanskrit
which eventually became the subject of hundreds
of commentaries and subcommentaries, and served
as the model for later grammars, both of Sanskrit
and of derivative Indo-Aryan languages. Panini's
date is unknown, but his work preceded that of
Katyayana, who wrote a lengthy annotation

(*varttika*) of the *Ashthadhyayi* and Patanjali, who
may well be datable to the second century BCE and
whose *Mahabhashya* (literally, 'Great Commentary')
is directed primarily to Katyayana, but also to
Panini. Legend places Panini in the far northwest
of India (modern Pakistan), and the ancient texts of
Vedic Sanskrit which he seems to know correspond
to those of that region. It is in the nature of Panini's
work that he tells us nothing directly about his
intention, but it is clear that he is describing a
language which is at the same time literary and
spoken. This is the language subsequently known
as classical Sanskrit. Although it is not his primary
focus, Panini also supplies a large number of
statements about the more archaic state of the
language, which is known as Vedic Sanskrit.
Panini, Katyayana and Patanjali were the three
great scholars who, according to tradition, witnessed the Sanskrit language and were able to
formulate rules to describe it. By contrast, later
scholars were able to check the correctness of
Sanskrit only through rules articulated by the early
grammarians.

The works of the three early grammarians
correspond to a pattern found in other systematic
sciences. Panini's *Ashthadhyayi* is a set of roughly
4,000 short rules, called *sutras*. Katyayana's *varttika*
is made up of approximately 5,000 comments
attached to 1,200 of Panini's rules, but with
implications for many more. Patanjali's *Mahabhashya* is not of the nature of distinct rules or single
sentence comments, but a mix of shorter and
longer discussions on the statements of his
predecessors. The primary cotence, such as words,
suffixes and bases, whether recognized by scholars
or ordinary people, were fictitious. However useful
such parts may be for analysis, they have no
ultimate reality. For the grammarians, the meaning
of the whole was not simply greater than that of the
parts, the latter did not in fact exist. Other systems
offered alternative explanations for the supposed
fact that the meaning of a sentence is not simply a
concatenation of the isolated meanings expressed
by the constituent elements. The concern for both
Katyayana and Patanjali is to evaluate the
adequacy and necessity of Panini's formulations.

Discussions of semantics and the philosophy of
language first appear in Patanjali's *Mahabhashya*,
and are typically based on statements by Panini

and Katyayana. The next important text for this subject is **Bhartrihari**'s *Vakyapadiya*. Bhartrihari seems to have lived in the fourth to fifth century CE, and he refers to a revival of grammatical studies in immediately preceding generations. In his book, he not only discusses the nature of language as a means of knowing about the world, with learned and careful discussions on topics such as the relation of words to sentences and the particular categories embedded in the Sanskrit language (uniquely or not), but he considers in detail the claims of other philosophical systems. Apart from the *Vakyapadiya*, he also wrote a commentary on at least part if not the whole *Mahabhashya*. Only a small part of this has survived. Within the tradition of grammatical literature, numerous commentaries on these and other texts continued the discussion of semantics and the philosophy of language, and these topics were also raised in the literature of other philosophical and speculative systems.

An important figure in the history of grammar was Bhattoji Dikshita, a southern scholar who studied in Benares in the sixteenth century. His *Shabdakaustubha*, nominally a commentary on Panini but in fact a voluminous treatise on a wide range of grammatical issues, both technical and philosophical, was perhaps the seminal work for a period of intense scholarship. The texts of earlier grammarians came under close scrutiny, as did the competing linguistic analyses of rival systems, namely, the Mimamsa and the **Nyaya** (roughly, the schools concerned with the exegesis of the Veda and with logic). Two authors in particular may be mentioned here, Kaunda Bhatta, the nephew of Bhattoji Dikshita, whose *Vaiyakaranabhushana* and *Vaiyakaranabhushanasara* have been the object of critical studies in recent years, and Nagesha Bhatta, the Maharashtrian author, many of whose books on grammar are considered to be of the highest authority and have themselves been the subject of lengthy commentary.

The texts listed above are only a very small fraction of the surviving literature on grammar. Panini's description of Sanskrit underlies this tradition, and so even a brief account of his work may provide a useful background for understanding the sorts of issues which were considered to be important. As stated above, the *Ashthadhyayi* is composed of 4,000 rules. These are arranged in eight books (*adhyayas*), with four chapters (*padas*) in each. A fundamental structure of the work is its tripartite division. Books 1–2 define the technical terms which are used in the work, teach the principles of operation which enable us to interpret the rules, classify grammatical forms which are met later, etc. Books 3–5 could be considered the core of the grammar. Here Panini teaches the addition of hundreds of suffixes to specific bases when various meanings are to be expressed. Finally, Books 6–8 teach operations which are directed to the sequences which have been formed by adding suffixes. This is only a rough description, to which many exceptions could be stated. However, it conforms in general with two principles underlying the grammar.

Firstly, all words are considered to be derived by the addition of suffixes to bases. The tradition views both of these as abstractions, in that outside grammatical analysis they exist only in combination with each other. They are also abstract in another way, in that Panini has followed a model of grammar in which distinct forms, which, in another descriptive model, could otherwise be recognized as a set, are in fact derived from a single underlying form. For instance, various (in fact thousands) of words are derived by adding suffixes to the verbal root listed by Panini as *kri* and which has the sense of 'to make' or 'to do'. These words all contain the segments *kri, kar, kar* or *kur*. Rather than listing this group as a basic set and adding statements specifying which particular form is used in any given formation, Panini derives *kar, kar* and *kur* from an initial form *kri*. In this way the root *kri* not only fails to exist independently outside grammatical texts, but even in many words derived from it, such as *karoti* (he/she makes) or *kurvanti* (they make), it exists only in a modified form.

A second principle underlying the grammar is that it operates so as to generate full sentences from the starting point of a number of semantic notions. Suffixes are added to bases in order to express whatever sense is intended to be expressed, and the sequence thus created will extend to the length of the desired sentence. The presence of certain suffixes enables sections of the sequence to be recognized as words, but this happens only after suffixes have been added. The grammar does not stop operating until the various rules of euphonic combination within words and between individual words have taken place, and also the rules of accent which depend on the order of complete words. In this way, Panini does not draw a sharp distinction between morphological rules, that is, those which describe the formation of words from meaningful elements, and syntactic rules, because his rules enjoin the formation of words are only in the context of the generation of a particular sentence.

Topics in Indian semantic theory often correspond closely to particular features of the Sanskrit language and its indigenous grammatical description. One such topic which has received special attention in recent scholarship is Panini's description of *karakas*. These may be described as six distinct features of activity which Sanskrit grammar systematically accounts for. The tradition views them as causes of an action in that they assist in bringing it about. They are identified as the agent, the object, the instrument, the locus, the fixed point when there is motion away, and the person or thing which is aimed at through an object or action. All six *karakas* need not be expressed in a given sentence. Panini defines them in Book 1 of the *Ashthadhyayi* and then uses them to teach operations. In his system, a finite verb (that is, one with a final suffix marking grammatical person and number) directly expresses one of two *karakas*, the agent or the object, or in the case of an intransitive root, the action itself. *Karakas* may also be expressed by the suffixes which are added to create nominal stems, as well as by the case suffixes which are added at the end of all nouns. In theory, the *karakas* are all agents in their own sphere of activity, and are all subordinate to the action denoted by a verbal root. For instance, in the sentence 'He cooks rice in the pot', the pot is the locus of the cooking, but it is an agent with regard to the action of holding the rice. If that action is to be emphasized, the speaker can base an alternative description of the same event on the agency of the pot and say 'The pot cooks'. It is the intention of the speaker which determines the expression of *karakas*.

The theory of the *karakas* as a set of features subordinate to the action which they help to effect can be related to the grammarians' view of the sentence as being primarily a description of an action. Various analytic schools in India produced rival accounts of how the various parts of a sentence are related to each other. For the grammarians, the action denoted by the root was the predominant element, and all the other meanings expressed by words and parts of words served to qualify it, directly or indirectly. In contrast, the Nyaya school held that the meaning of the word ending with the nominative case suffix (which in Sanskrit is used to mark the agent in a transitive sentence) was predominant. Although the grammarians had constructed a hugely complex analysis of Sanskrit grammar, they held that the only real conveyor of meaning was the unique sphota, literally, 'burst', which accompanied the understanding of a entire sentence. By contrast, writers in the Nyaya school argued that the intended meaning of the utterance itself enabled the meanings of individual words to combine into the sentence meaning. For writers in the Mimamsa tradition, the meanings of individual words had a secondary significative power which enabled them to join with one another, or, according to another school within the Mimamsa, the individual words could only denote meanings as related to others.

The question as to how words are denotative at all was discussed from an early date. Although recognizing that the meanings of words are learned by children from observing their elders in each successive generation, grammarians and followers of the Mimamsa tradition viewed the connection of word and meaning as without beginning in time. By contrast, the followers of the Nyaya held that the relation was established by a creator deity. For the grammarians, both words which are grammatically correct and those which are incorrect are equally meaningful, whereas the writers in the Nyaya and Mimamsa traditions held that incorrect words functioned only by reminding the hearer of the correct form. The question of whether a word primarily denotes an individual or a universal (roughly speaking, the feature common to all things to which a word might be applied), received various answers. Beyond the primary meaning, secondary or implied meanings were recognized and variously accounted for. Also, distinctions were drawn between meanings which followed a word's etymology as provided by grammar and those meanings which were recognized by convention, with or without any etymological foundation. This particular topic had arisen very early in the literature of the ritual exegetes who tried to analyse systematically the meanings of Vedic texts.

A few of the many other topics closely connected to particular features of Sanskrit may simply be listed. These include how the meanings of compounds were related to the meanings of the constituent words, which, in Panini's derivational system, preceded the formation of a compound, how indeclinable words such as prepositions and conjunctions contributed to the meaning of the utterance, how the suffix with which Panini taught the formation of injunctive verbs conveyed its particular sense, and how the particle used to express negation expresses its various meanings. These are just a few examples of a very rich tradition of linguistic investigation.

Further reading

Coward, H. and Kunjunni Raja, K. (1990) 'The Philosophy of the Grammarians', in *Encyclopedia of Indian Philosophies*, vol. 5, Delhi: Motilal Banarsidass.

Scharfe, H. (1977) *Grammatical Literature*, Wiesbaden: Otto Harrassowitz.

Staal, J. (ed.) (1973) *A Reader on the Sanskrit Grammarians*, Cambridge, MA: MIT Press.

EIVIND KAHRS

Great Learning

The *Great Learning* (*Daxue* or *Ta-Hsueh*) was one of the Four Books canonized by Song dynasty Neo-Confucians as the basis for moral self-cultivation (see **Classics and Books**). Originally a chapter in the *Book of Rites* and a Han thesis on the 'higher education' of ministerial rule, it was regarded as a self-sufficent treatise containing the words of **Confucius** and the commentary of his disciple Zengzi, transmitted through Confucius's grandson Zisi. The central thesis is that he who wishes to see bright Virtue shine everywhere under **Heaven** should first bring order to the state (towards which end) by first regulating the family (towards which end) by first cultivating himself. In that self-cultivation, he rectifies his mind by first making his will sincere. That is achieved by a diligent

'investigation of things' that would 'extend knowledge to its proper end'. The last line is critical: it was even taken to mean a Buddhist-like 'avoidance of things' of the world, before **Zhu Xi** canonized it as 'an investigation of things'. Later still, Wang Yangming would take it further into an activistic 'rectification of things'. Man, says Nietzsche, is an unfinished project; this text also urges that 'becoming a man' (an adult) involves 'bringing to completion one's humanity'.

Further reading

Tucker, M. (1989) *Moral and Spiritual Cultivation in Japanese Neo-Confucianism: The Life and Thought of Kaibara Ekken (1630–1714)*, Albany, NY: State University of New York Press.

WHALEN LAI

Guan Yu

Guan Yu was a general of the Three Kingdoms period (220–77) who became deified as the God of War. He died in battle and was beheaded, and his vengeful ghost haunted the site of his death. The Tiantai master Zhiyi (530–97) had pacified another such restless dead person killed in a war by giving the ghost a shrine when he built a Buddhist temple in its haunted site. The ghost of Guan Yu then visited Zhiyi, asking for his lost head. He was taught a karmic lesson: 'As you have beheaded others, you died likewise beheaded.' Converted to the **dharma**, the spirit became a guardian of the temple and a protector of faith, much as Indra had done in India before and Hachiman would later do in Japan. A shrine was set up and prayers were chanted to ensure his eventual deliverance.

Since Buddhist temples are protected by the Four Heavenly Kings stationed at the gate, it is possible that the iconography of these majestic demon-quellers rubbed off on this native guardian deity. Known for his devotion to his lord, Guan Yu was honoured by the Tang court for his 'righteous loyalty' but he did not make the roll of the ten virtuous men honoured in the Halls of Literary and Military Worthies. Rash and bad-tempered while alive, he was still 'all too human' to be fully godlike.

His cult grew in the Five Dynasties (907–60), when regional commanders ruled and when personal loyalty to a lord was a premium virtue. When the Song dynasty was threatened by new foreign invaders, this demon-queller protected so many cities from attack that he ended up as a city god in many municipalities. Regarded already in the Tang period as a duke, he rose to the rank of prince by the time of the Song and was finally given the title of king by the late Ming. By then, he had crossed over from the military to become also the patron of the literati, holding Confucius's *Spring and Autumn Annals* in one hand. But it is by way of the Yuan theatre and the Ming novels, especially *Romance of the Three Kingdoms*, that he was endeared to all, both high and low.

The philosophical justification for euhemerism is given in the preface to a collection of his miracles. 'Euhemerism' is named after Euhemerus, who lived at the time of Alexander the Great and chronicled an alleged practice by natives in an island off India who worshipped as gods prior kings and heroes. The term now refers to such cults of deified men. Because the First Emperor assumed the power to promote and demote gods, the term may be applied to Chinese practice, but the thesis has also been extended back to ancient China in a reversed form. It is alleged that China had few myths (stories about gods) because in a 'reversed euhemerism', she had remade gods into men and turned myth into history. This theory seems to accord with Confucian agnostic humanism. However, some historical perspective and caution is called for. Euhemerism appeared only with the rise of empires under Cyrus the Great, King of Kings in Persia and then under Alexander the Great of Macedonia, who claimed descent from the previously deified Hercules. Likewise, it is also most likely that only after the apotheosis of the First Emperor in China – who saw himself as the Black Emperor (of the North in the dawning of the Age of Aquarius [black waters]) and once presumed the power to punish a mountain – did the line between man and god become easier to cross.

The 'Song of Righteousness' speaks of this moral force animating the whole universe: 'Below it is manifested as rivers and mountains; above as sun and stars; and among men, as sages.' It is this moral force behind the 'moral universe' that empowers such men of exemplary virtue. Miracles are then seen as due to this law of 'stimulus and response'. Like the canonization of saints in the Catholic Church, strictly speaking it is not humanity that is being deified, but rather the person's superhuman virtue and saintliness.

Further reading

Allan, S. (1979) 'Shang Foundation of Modern Chinese Folk Religion', in S. Allan and A. Cohen (eds), *Legend, Lore, and Religion in China: Essays in Honor of Wolfram Eberhard on his Seventieth Birthday*, San Francisco: Chinese Materials Center, Inc.

Bodde, D. (1961) 'Myths of Ancient China', in S. Kramer (ed.), *Mythologies of the Ancient World*, Garden City, NY: Anchor Books.

Johnson, D. (1985) 'The City-God Cults of T'ang and Sung China', *Journal of the American Oriental Society* 43(2): 363–457.

WHALEN LAI

Guan Zhong

fl. 7th century BCE

Legalist philosopher

Guan Zhong (Kuan Chung) was an early, able administrator who was later counted as a Legalist thinker (see **Legalism**). A text under his name has survived, containing a wide variety of material including early reflections on the ways of government. Of the less Legalistic materials, the so-called 'psychic chapters' are thought to be from **Song Xing**, an early Daoist thinker. It is not without relevance to issues of government. Like 'Legalist', the description 'Daoist' is a later attribution.

WHALEN LAI

Gyaltsap Dharma Rinchen

b. 1364; d. 1432

Buddhist philosopher

Originally a member of the **Shakya school**,

Gyaltsap, as he is known by his abbreviated name, later became the first to succeed to the Chair of Ganden monastery following the death of **Tsongkhapa** in 1419. Together with Khedrup, the followers of the Geluk school regard Gyaltsap as the most authoritative interpreter of Tsongkhapa's thought. A prolific writer in many areas of classical Buddhist scholarship, Gyaltsap's greatest contributions to Tibetan philosophy lie perhaps in the fields of epistemology and the issues pertaining to the interpretation of the doctrine of **buddha nature**. In his in-depth studies of **Dharmakirti**'s *Pramanavarttika*, *Pramanavinishchaya* and *Nyayabindu*, Gyaltsap developed a highly sophisticated epistemological system that is consonant with Tsongkhapa's overall position on the question of universals. Contrary to the Shakya's literal reading of Dharmakirti, the views of Gyaltsap and his student and colleague Khedrup represent a realist interpretation of Dharmakirti's epistemology more along the lines of **Chapa Chokyi Senge**'s approach. A central dispute between the two opposing epistemological schools was the question of the ontological status of universals and their instantiation.

To this day Gyaltsap's commentary on *Pramanavarttika* entitled *Illumination on the Path to Liberation* is used as the primer on Buddhist logic and epistemology in many of the academic colleges of the Geluk school of Tibetan Buddhism. On the concept of buddha nature, Gyaltsap's commentary on Maitreya's *Ratnagotravibhaga* established an influential interpretation of the doctrine that develops a purely apophatic conception of buddha nature, which is in greater harmony with the Madhyamaka philosophy of **emptiness**.

THUPTEN JINPA

H

Han Fei

b. *c*.280 BCE; d. 233 BCE

Legalist philosopher

The major Legalist thinker, Han Fei was in favour of a strong, centralized state, well-armed to enrich the government with victory and rule the people with the strong arm of the law, ready to punish or to reward. A student of Xunzi, he carried his naturalist philosophy to an amoral Machiavellian conclusion. His book includes a chapter explicating Laozi, showing how under **Legalism** and Daoism the exercise of covert power under the disguise of overt non-action could and did co-exist.

See also: *wuwei*

Further reading

Liao, W.K. (trans.) (1939) *The Complete Works of Han Fei tzu*, London: Probsthain.

WHALEN LAI

Han and Hanunim

The idea of Han is a central one in the history of Korean thought. The term 'Han' implies one, great, total and bright being. This meaning is embedded in the idea of Han-in and Han-ung, the grandfather and father of Tan'gun, the founder of Korea. The present name of Korea is Han-guk (Han'guk), which means one, great and bright nation. The name of God, the supreme being of the universe, in Korean, is Hananim (Han-anim), Hanunim (Han-unim) or Hanullim (Han-ullim). The first one implies God as the One supreme being, and the second and the third terms imply God as the Heavenly being. All three are often interchangeably used by many people, for essentially they all mean God as the supreme being. All have the basic root meaning of Han.

The Korean idea of Hananim or God is quite personal compared with the Chinese idea of *tian*, which means **Heaven** or God. Although the early shamanistic religion of Korea was basically animistic and polytheistic, the ancient Koreans had also a vague and primitive notion of a monotheistic idea of one supreme being who is the Heavenly Lord of the universe. The Confucians and Buddhists in Korea also accepted this idea of Hanunim. When Christians translated the word 'God' into the Korean language, they used the term 'Hananim', which means one Supreme Being.

In the ideas of Han and Hanunim, one may find that Korean people have valued from very early times the ideas of One, Great, Total Reality and bright universe. The bright heavenly objects of the universe such as the sun, moon and stars were the objects of worship in the early shamanistic religion of the Korean people. These ideas were the basic and important aspects of the early Korean mind. In these terms and ideas, one may also find the worldview of the early Korean people, valuing oneness and totality, that is, the monistic universe.

Further Reading

Ch'oi Min-hong (1974) *Han'guk Ch'orhaksa* (History

of Korean Philosophy), Seoul: Songmunsa, 7–22.

—— (1984) *Han ch'orhak: Han minjok ui chongsinjok ppuri* (The Philosophy of Han: The Spiritual Root of Korean People), Seoul: Songmunsa.

Kim Sang-il (1984) *Hanism as Korean Mind: Interpretation of Han Philosophy*, Los Angeles: Eastern Academy of Human Sciences.

YONG-CHOON KIM

Han Learning

The term 'Han Learning', from the mid-eighteenth century, is used to describe an early Qing dynasty movement to repeal the 'Song Learning' of the Neo-Confucians. Judging the Song moral metaphysics to be quasi-Buddhist, these scholars sought to go back to the kind of solid, philological, textual scholarship of the Han scholars working on the Classics (see **Classics and Books**). Under the slogan, 'Six Classics are all History', which helped to move the classics from being metaphysical norms (the term 'classic' means 'eternal, permanent') to becoming texts solidly grounded in actual history, this evolved into antiquarian scholarship or 'evidential research' that used the rules of 'textual criticism' involving archaic linguistics and phonetics. This has been compared with modern, rational, Western critical scholarship, but it now appears that it was as much an extension of a conservative drive to retrieve the fundamentals of Chinese ritual culture as anything else.

This 'back to the Han' movement was in part an assertion of Han identity against the new Manchu rule. It was also a protest against the Western learning introduced by the Jesuits into late Ming China. The truth of the Classics was reconfirmed. The rule of the rites was recalled to help set up a new discourse concerning lineage and self-rule at the village level, where state administration had not reached. Unlike the Song learning which concentrated on 'human nature and mind', Han learning focussed on 'words and texts'. Hence the new interest in philology as a basic discipline with textual criticism as a major tool, both employed to help retrieve the norms of the distant past. Interestingly, this movement was co-opted by the

Manchus, who actively sought out these scholars and recruited them in the prestigious imperial-sponsored encyclopedia projects.

The Han Learning had exposed the Song myth of a claim to an esoteric 'transmission of the *dao*' based on a sixteen-character mantra (a formula of the mind), which had proved to be the borrowing of the **Diagram of the Great Ultimate** from the Daoists. These findings are now a part of how Chinese intellectual history is written. But soon, that confidence in rebuilding a Han standard also resurrected the Han disputes over the Classics in the 'new script' versus the 'old script'. Textual evidence to prove the precise forgery of this or that passage had to be found; a drawn-out debate followed. One political consequence came with the revival of the New Text school, whose archaic ideology was updated by Kang Yuwei (1858–1927) for the constitutional reform of 1898. Finally, the search for the norm of the Classics even opened up the Classics themselves to critiques. Just as 'higher criticism' of the Bible has unearthed layers of accretion to the scripture, works like the *Analects* of Confucius also came under higher textual criticism. With astounding acumen, Cui Shu (1740–1816) isolated layers in this Confucian Bible. (This enterprise is currently being continued by Bruce and Taeko Brooks, whose book *The Original Analects* (1998) is dedicated to Cui.)

Cui did not doubt the truth of the Classics but in the Republican period at the National University of Peking, the circle of Gu Jiegang known as 'antiquity-doubters' published seven volumes of the Chinese journal called *Antiquity Examined* (1926–41). This threw the whole Chinese prehistory – from the **Yellow Emperor** to the Xia dynasty, once deemed sacred and inviolable – into doubt. We usually do not count the 'evidential scholars' as philosophers, but to the extent that the early myths embedded philosophy and moral ideologies rooted in the Warring States period, the whole Han Learning that ended up undoing not just the Han authorities but also challenging China's founding myths, the historiography that rewrote Chinese history also affects our appreciation of Chinese philosophy.

In one sense, it was providential when the Han Learnng movement declared that 'The six Classics are all history'. The word for classics (*jing*) once stood for 'what is eternal'. During the Han, scholars saw the Classics as embodying the eternal norms of Heaven and Earth which they helped to map using *yin–yang* cosmology. Because 'Heaven does not change', so 'neither would the Way'. But the self-proclaimed Han scholars in the Qing dynasty no longer lived in the security of that Han cosmos. In part because of the Jesuits, Chinese cosmology had broken down by the eighteenth century. So the call of 'back to the Han' in order to recover the eternal way of the Classics was an oxymoron. The creed that confesses to 'The six Classics are all History' ended up like a snake that bites its own tail. History swallows up the Classics; the historical envelops the timeless. So the only way to recover the timeless truths now is to go through that baptism of history.

Further reading

Brooks, B. and Brooks, T. (1998) *The Original Analects*, New York: Columbia University Press.

Chow Kai-wing (1994) *The Rise of Confucian Ritualism in Late Dynastic China: Ethics, Classics, and Lineage Discourse*, Stanford, CA: Stanford University Press.

Elman, B. (1984) *From Philosophy to Philology: Intellectual and Social Aspects of Change in Late Imperial China*, Cambridge, MA: Harvard University Press.

—— (1990) *Classicism, Politics and Kinship: The Ch'ang-chou School of New Text Criticism in Late Imperial China*, Berkeley, CA: University of California Press.

Smith, R. and Kwok, D. (eds) (1993) *Cosmology, Ontology, and Human Efficacy: Essays in Chinese Thought*, Honolulu, HA: University of Hawaii Press.

WHALEN LAI

HANPO *see* afterlife in Chinese thought

Han Yu

b. 786; d. 824

Essayist and Confucian philosopher

A late Tang essayist famous for his clear classical

style, Han Yu influenced more than the literary circle, being counted as the reviver of Confucian orthodoxy and credited with calling attention to the *Great Learning* and the *Doctrine of the Mean*. In an essay 'On the *Dao*', he railed against the inroads made by Daoism and Buddhism which resulted in the corruption of orthodoxy. Firing the first volley at the foreign faith, he boldly protested against the royal reception of a Buddha relic in 803. He revived what he regarded as the classical ideal: that all writings should serve as the vehicle of the Way and not just be valued for their beauty of style and their expressiveness of private emotions. He resuscitated prose over verse, reason over emotion, the public over the private. His polemics against Buddhism as the principal cause of the corruption of society and state earned him exile. During his exile, he was not above writing poems or celebrating the local cult of crocodile deities. By leapfrogging the Han Confucians in order to return directly to **Confucius** and **Mencius**, he paved the way for the Neo-Confucian theory for a hidden 'transmission of the *dao*'. But in that process, he actually also demoted the status of Confucius from the Han perception of the Master as a **sage** and king, prophet and king-maker, and remade him into the Song perception as a depoliticized 'inner' sage, a 'spiritual' teacher of humanity, and a 'loyal' counsel of the sovereign.

Further reading

Hartman, C. (1986) *Han Yu and the T'ang Search for Unity*, Princeton, NJ: Princeton University Press.

Pulleyblank, E. (1980) 'Neo-Legalism and Neo-Confucianism in T'ang Intellectual Life, 755–805', in A.F. Wright (ed.), *The Confucian Persuasion*, Stanford, CA: Stanford University Press, 77–114.

WHALEN LAI

Haofang

Haofang, a virtue of the heroic and brave (*hao*), generous and free (*fang*), characterizes a form of open, masculine **friendship** that is possible everywhere but is more noticeable among artists and swordsmen. It describes largely male bonding, although some rare women might make it into the circle. It is a legacy of a bygone heroic age, being the camaraderie of men in arms bound by lateral ties and the exigency of war. Death being ever immanent, living in the present was all too necessary. Typically, celebration of hard-won battles is with war song and dance and a generous supply of red meat and strong wine. The last evil king of the Shang was vilified for such excess: he had 'pools filled with wine and boughs hung with meat'. The judgment came from a triumphant Zhou dynasty, who soon turned to a new instrument of rule, **rites** and **music**. But that old ethos survived on the margins, including the underclass. In all those circles, generosity is a must. Men share and share alike. Trust is paramount; loyalty is absolute; but partisanship ensures that cunning and deception in dealing with one's enemy is perfectly acceptable. The overall moral standard is **righteousness** (*yi*, justice), not some tedious rules but simply 'doing right to one's fellow men'.

A certain informality makes the friendship often quite physical; one jostles and cajoles, rubs shoulders and pats backs. Guided more by passion than by reason, men are easy to anger, ready to seek redress, but also at times able to forego and forgive. Forgiveness involves rites of surrender, individually or as a group. Talk is cheap; action is what counts. A lifetime of undying gratitude can result from one single act of **charity**. Among the economically hard-pressed, a quick loan of cash with no strings attached can mean the difference between life and death. This is the ethos of mutual aid basic to guilds and 'mutual aid' associations; and among the social outcast it is 'honour among thieves'. Because they lack normal social support and judicial guarantee, such friendships are usually sealed by a blood earth, in secret ceremonies if need be, before heaven and earth. Among the outlawed mafia, breaking the contract risks divine (and less than divine) retribution. The immediate ethos is to protect one's own; the grander goal (often just lip service) is to obey **Heaven**, serve the *dao* and right all wrongs. This transition among the socially displaced from hoodlum to Robin Hood to even Son of Heaven, occurs with some frequency in Chinese history.

Such open friendship may be admired by legitimate society. It usually attends painters, poets and musicians (zither players), but all the famous cases predated the Song dynasty when Neo-Confucian rational moralism put a damper on it. It re-emerged among the radical wing of the Wang Yangming school, but was sufficiently censored by the Cheng–Zhu orthodoxy to not be deemed a heroic model. Ho Xinyin, who rated friendship higher than family and state, was persecuted to death as a heretic. By Qing times, the pressure to succeed as a literate candidate at examinations led to romanticizing the exploits of the swordsman and the knight errant in an escapist literature that still captures an audience young and old. The tales became increasingly unrealistic, but they remained real enough that schoolchildren, tired of dreary book learning, sometimes ran away from home to look for such fighting masters in the hills. (The kung-fu movies today are only the latest extension of this vogue.) The true classics remain the period saga of *Romance of the Three Kingdoms* and the heroic outlaws of *Water Margin* from the Ming dynasty.

Haofang is about male bonding, and in that sense it is misogynist. There is another term, utilizing the metaphor of 'wind and current' or 'as easy-going as the waves' to describe the untrammelled lifestyle of the free spirits which can better capture the 'romantic' kind of friendship, and this type can freely include both sexes. It was first exemplified by the Neo-Daoists who, though high-born, so admired talent and appreciated beauty that they would befriend the gifted commoner and even slaves.

Further reading

Lai, W. (1997), 'Friendship in Confucian China', in O. Leaman (ed.), *Friendship East and West: Philophical Perspectives*, Richmond: Curzon, 215–50.

Shih Nai-an (1963) *Water Margin*, trans. J. Jackson, Hong Kong: Commercial Press.

WHALEN LAI

harmony

Chinese philosophy places considerable emphasis on harmony, and it is necessary to distinguish between Confucian and different versions of this principle. According to Confucius, the society of the Zhou dynasty was especially desirable since it was based on ritual and propriety (*li*, not to be confused with *li* or principle), and this meant that there was a system of activities available to everyone which would provide each individual with a particular route to living with everyone else, in such a way as to reflect specific natural and social abilities and interests. Of course, harmony is to be valued when it is compared with its opposite, when society is riven by conflict and instability, and Confucius emphasized the role of rituals in bringing about a satisfactory organization of a necessarily stratified society.

The whole working of the *yin–yang* philosophy is based on the search for harmony, since harmony is always there in the background. *Yin* and *yang* are different and contrasting aspects of balance, and it is important to establish an appropriate relationship between the two sets of forces, since otherwise one will be out of balance. Of course, for change to be possible there will have to be imbalance of one type or another, but this is acceptable provided that the actors know how to bring these forces eventually into a balance. The notion of **correlative thinking**, which is so important in Chinese thought, operates in accordance with the harmony which is implicit in the comparison and contrast between different levels of ideas and concepts. One might want to note here the ordinary linear notion of logic, as producing conclusions which extend an original set of premises and which takes the original ideas further, as it were, in the direction of new ideas and discoveries. This could be contrasted with the use of analogical reasoning, where ideas are set against each other and compared, and so preserve some kind of balance and harmony. One might even mention here the ways in which in Chinese thought so much effort has been expended to defend the compatibility of the different sorts of philosophy, as though it is more important to establish the harmony between these different ways of doing philosophy (all of which have corresponding religious principles as well, of course) rather than to determine which is the uniquely 'true' or 'valid' approach.

See also: expediency; li as morality

WHALEN LAI

harmony in the round

The philosophical quest for the Absolute is common the world over: it seeks Being in Greece, Brahman in the **Upanishads** and *dao* in China. But as an ontological Other, the Absolute tends to rob man of his subjectivity; it dissolves his 'lesser self' into its greater self. Even Buddhist **nirvana** initially has that same effect.

Philosophical idealism later rose to provide the concept of the mind with that creative subjectivity. However, instead of looking to a transcendental Absolute, **Zhuangzi** in China looked to affirming the here and now within the Round Perfection that encompasses all. The universe is one totalistic **harmony**; part and whole, high and low, here and there are providentially one. When Mahayana **Yogachara** restored to the self that creative subjectivity, Huayan joined that to this Chinese concern for harmony or perfection in the round. All the other philosophical schools are concerned with reaching the same end. Chinese Madhyamika realized a 'Roundness of Function' and all verbal mundane truths now point equally to the highest truth as a matter of procedure. Tiantai built on that and defended the 'Roundness of Essence'; it collapses even the distance between a finger and the moon. The verbal means which we normally employ become the ineffable end when the One Vehicle of Buddhism emerges from the Three Teachings. That is, the more complex ways of understanding the nature of enlightenment can be reduced to just one simple truth, the Oneness of reality which represents both the Buddha and the harmony of everything. Huayan idealism represented the 'roundness of one and all', while Chan (Zen) practices the 'roundness of activity'.

Further reading

Fok Tou-hui (1986) *Chueh-tui yu Yuan-yung* (Absolute and Perfect Harmony), Hong Kong: Tung-t'ai T'u-shu.

WHALEN LAI

heaven

The term for heaven in Chinese is *tian*, and it is frequently used by **Confucius**, yet without imply-ing anything specifically religious. **Mozi** came to criticize Confucius for his failure to assert that heaven plays a direct role in human events. According to Mozi heaven plays a direct interven-tionist role in the world, and this role should be acknowledged and identified clearly. There is more of an indirect role for Confucius in that the ruler is directed to align his will with the will of heaven, so that the state will be organized in accordance with the organization of nature.

OLIVER LEAMAN

heaven, former and later

Former and later heaven is a nuanced distinction associated with two circular diagrams that config-ure the hexagrams of the *Book of Changes* to accord with two modes of pristine nature, the post-natal Later Heaven and the pre-natal Former Heaven. The idea is that there is a distinction to be made between a former heaven, which is linked with a pre-natal self, the pure spirit, and later heaven which is the self one is born with, a self which is innately good. For the Daoists, the goal is to reverse the birth process. Viewed in the context of a history of ideas, the Confucians needed this distinction to combat the Buddhists. Buddhism held that every-one has **buddha nature**, but this describes a single, uniform, pre-natal essence or what Chan seeks to find, the so-called 'original face before you were born'. Neo-Confucians charged the Buddhists with claiming to know the one principle but not its emerging manifestations, the properties of nature The design of the former heaven and the later heaven is meant to capture that distinction: a perfectly balanced but static cosmos and the same thing which has emerged into rhythmic change, with inherent tension setting off that initial move-ment. That movement is well captured in the concept of the *yin–yang* circle. Human nature can be similarly divided into the pre-natal and post-natal. In Chinese palmistry, one palm denotes the former and the other the latter nature. The Daoist

diagram of the Former would be copied and adopted into the Neo-Confucian **Diagram of the Great Ultimate**.

Further reading

Birdwhistell, A. (1989) *Transition to Neo-Confucianism: Shao Yung on Knowledge and Symbols of Reality*, Stanford, CA: Stanford University Press.

Smith, K., Bol, P., Adler, J. and Wyatt, D. (1990) *Sung Dynasty Uses of the I Ching*, Princeton, NJ: Princeton University Press.

WHALEN LAI

HELL *see* afterlife, Chinese: hell

hermeneutics

Hermeneutics, especially textual, has a long history in Mahayana Buddhism. It was however the emergence of **Tsongkhapa**'s treatise *Essence of Eloquence* which seems to have given rise to the recognition of hermeneutics as a distinct philoso-phical enterprise in Tibet. Tsongkhapa's treatise gave birth to a whole new genre of philosophical literature, which came to be referred to simply as *drang nge* (spelled *drang nges*), 'the provisional and the definitive'. Thus the heart of the hermeneutic enterprise in the Tibetan context is the distinction between the 'provisional' and the 'definitive'. This act of distinguishing can take place on two levels, one at the textual level where the task is that of distinguishing between the provisional and definite meaning of the scriptures. The other is at the level of reality itself. In this latter context, the nature of reality is approached by means of drawing a distinction between the 'surface level' constituted by provisionality, temporality and multiplicity on the one hand, and the 'ultimate level' characterized by uniformity, stilling of conceptual elaboration, and emptying of all ontological characteristics on the other. This distinction of the two levels of hermeneutics reflects **Vasubandhu**'s notion of Buddha's doctrine as 'linguistic', i.e. scriptural, and his doctrine as 'realization'.

Briefly put, textual hermeneutics involves the application of certain interpretive techniques in one's reading of the scripture, all of which have their roots in classical Indian Buddhist works. This entails, amongst other things, (a) drawing a critical distinction between a provisional and definitive meaning of the texts, (b) the application of the principle of skilfulness in means which involve amongst others placing greater emphasis on the purpose over the letter of the scripture, and (c) distinguishing between four levels of meaning in texts: the literal, the common, the pregnant or hidden and the ultimate meaning. A typical hermeneutical approach to a scripture that is perceived as belonging to the provisional class, such as a scripture which propounds the notion of the self, would move along the following lines.

First, the basis of its intended meaning is identified. In the context of a *sutra* advocating the notion of the self, the intended meaning is said to be the denial of the existence of the self, which is thought to be actually the Buddha's ultimate standpoint. Second, it is acknowledged that the self is the actual subject matter of that particular scripture. Third, the purpose of advocating the existence of the self is identified, which is said to be to attend to those whose attachment to the concept of self is so strong that an explicit teaching of 'no-self' would only have a negative effect at this stage. Finally, objections are raised against accepting the scripture at its face value. It is through such a process that a scripture is shown to be not representing a definitive standpoint. The principal theme of this entire textual hermeneutical tradition is to underline the point that one should not adopt the scriptures in their literal form. It is also to underscore the basic point that between scripture and reason (and understanding derived through it) that it is the latter that must be seen as the higher source of authority in Buddhist philosophical and religious quest.

See also: Buddhism in China, origins and development; expediency

Further reading

Cabezon, J.I. (1994) *Buddhism and Language: A Study*

of Tibetan Scholasticism, Albany, NY: State University of New York, chaps 3–4.

Lopez, D.S., Jr (1988) *Buddhist Hermeneutics*, Honolulu, HA: University of Hawaii.

Thurman, R. (1984) *Tsongkhapa's Speech of Gold in the Essence of True Eloquence*, Princeton, NJ: Princeton University Press, introduction.

THUPTEN JINPA

hidden and manifest

This pair of concepts is a shade subtler than *yin* and *yang*, for whereas *yin* cannot be *yang* and vice versa, the hidden can become manifest and vice versa. Although *yin–yang* adds up to One (harmonious whole), *yin* is not *yang* and *yang* cannot be *yin*. However, the same reality can be hidden or manifest, and these may be regarded as two modes alternating in time, two sides of the same coin. (Some **Shinto** scholars in Japanese **Kokugaku** in fact used this to show how Japan has a still more permeable world of men and spirits, life and death, than China with its clearer *yin–yang* paradigm.) To sustain a more dynamic metaphysic (than the Han one) the Neo-Confucians (see **Neo-Confucianism, concepts**) speak of the relationship between the One and the Many in terms of 'substance and function being of one source'; there is no gap between the manifest and incipiency as such either. The word for 'to hide' (*yin*) is also the verb 'to become a recluse'.

See also: recluse in Islam; substance and function; yin–yang harmony

WHALEN LAI

hikma

Islamic philosophy, like many systems of philosophy, makes a basic distinction between two ways of working in philosophy, between *falsafa* and *hikma*, between Peripatetic (*mashsha'i*) and mystical thought. One way in which to make the distinction is to characterize the former type of reason as linear, while the latter is circular. Peripatetic reason is linear since it operates via syllogisms, through the analysis of premises and the development of the implications of those premises. If one sees the world as corresponding to a logical pattern, then in principle it would be possible to work out exactly what features the world would have if one had the basic axioms of the system and then followed their logical consequences. **Ibn Sina** considers this way of thinking when he talks about certain advanced thinkers grasping all the major premises which encapsulate the main rules by which the world works. These thinkers, on the whole prophets, are able to predict what is going to happen since they know what the general rules which govern everything are, and when they combine these rules with individual facts of experience they can work out what is going to happen. Mystical thought, by contrast, is not analytic but synthetic. It brings elements of reality together into a whole, as opposed to taking them apart, and it is circular in nature, in this way representing the circularity of reality. Of course, to claim that a reasoning is circular is to criticize it from a Peripatetic point of view, since it means that there is a hidden premise which illegitimately includes the conclusion. From the point of view of mysticism, however, such hidden premises are valuable, because they accurately describe an aspect of reality, that the end is in the beginning, as it were, or that events follow a particular pattern which is constant.

Although we have distinguished between *falsafa* and *hikma*, we must not take this distinction too strictly. Many of the *falasifa* referred to what they did as *hikma* and to themselves and their colleagues as *hukama'*. However, they were on the whole quite clear on the distinction, which was made perhaps most clearly by Ibn Sina in his original remarks on the distinction between *hikma mashriqiyya* (oriental/ Eastern wisdom) and *mashsha'i* thought.

Ibn Sina presents a rather unusual account of knowledge by contrast with the traditional distinction. **Al-Farabi** takes the normal line of arguing that knowledge can be seen as the progressively more abstract development of our experiences and ordinary ideas, and when we reach the level of the **active intellect**, we attain a position which represents the possibility of acquiring abstract ideas. For Ibn Sina, those abstract ideas are already in existence there, and any ability we have for

acquiring such ideas comes from the ideas themselves, not from developing and purifying our thought about the world. This theory suggests that he really does think that there are two approaches to knowledge, the philosophical approach and the mystical. It follows from his account of knowledge that the only sort of knowledge worth having is the knowledge of the abstract ideas which exist in the active intellect. Of course, this is no different from the views of most of the other Islamic philosophers, but for them the ideas are abstracted from the world of experience; for Ibn Sina they are not. So for Ibn Sina, any correspondence between the ideas and our ordinary notion of reality is haphazard, while for the other thinkers it is guaranteed to some extent by the common origin of objects and ideas in the material world. For Ibn Sina, acquiring knowledge means that we turn away from the world and concentrate on what is higher than the world. One is reminded of his distinction between two sorts of theoretical enquiry, one being Peripatetic philosophy (**falsafa**) to which he made such a distinguished contribution, and the other being what he called *hikma mashriqqiya* or 'oriental wisdom'. By the latter he meant a theory which not only sought to represent the objective truth, but which also did justice to the subjective need for the seekers after knowledge to find spiritual value in the objects of study.

There is a good deal of controversy as to whether Ibn Sina really thought, as he says, that this form of mystical philosophy is a profounder version of the Greek style of philosophy, or whether it is an entirely mystical and very different form of thought. The problem with this way of doing philosophy is that it appears to be rather subjective, and it is difficult to know what sort of criteria may be employed to decide between contrasting claims for truth when some of the evidence is in terms of individual feelings of spiritual authenticity. Yet what Ibn Sina nicely captures in his contrast betweeen these two ways of doing philosophy is that for most of the *falasifa* there was no conflict between their analytical work and their more mystical work. These merely represented two different ways of doing philosophy, ways which are often complementary since they address different concerns. Analytical philosophy addresses the problem of establishing deductive truth, and resolves theoretical issues finally if those issues can be formalized in terms of syllogisms. On the other hand, 'oriental wisdom' resolves more personal issues by exploring them through mystical and aesthetic techniques, and resolving them in some satisfying construction of a whole which resonates with a particular audience.

Further reading

Leaman, O. (1999) *A Brief Introduction to Islamic Philosophy*, Oxford: Polity.

OLIVER LEAMAN

Hinayana (Lesser Vehicle) Buddhism

The term 'Hinayana' (Lesser Vehicle) is actually derogatory and was applied by adherents of the later rival Mahayana traditions. It is used here purely as a matter of classificatory convenience. The term Theravada refers to the Buddhism of Sri Lanka, Thailand and Burma. In early Buddhism, the ideal of spiritual progress was represented in the person of the *arhat* (saint, or enlightened one) who has attained **nirvana**, expressed as the extinction of the 'fires' of craving, hostility and delusion, while still alive in this world. The Mahayanists regard this as a selfish aspiration cultivated by those who are only concerned with their own salvation, whereas their saints (*bodhisatta* or **bodhisattva**, 'future Buddhas') are compassionately dedicated to the well-being of all suffering, transmigrating beings.

Early Buddhism lacked central canonical and institutional sources of authority, with the consequence that it was a fragmented and sectarian movement embodying diverse interpretations, primarily in the area of monastic discipline, of what the teaching of the historical Buddha named Siddhartha Gotama (*fl.* 450–400 BCE) was believed to have been. The available sources of evidence are very late and usually biased. They do not permit a detailed and accurate account of the fragmentation of 'primitive Buddhism', but it is possible to identify

some of the doctrinal differences, although 'schisms' were more likely to have occurred over questions of practice rather than theory. According to most non-Theravadin sources, the first major division probably occurred at the Council of Vaishali or Vesali in the mid-fourth century BCE (assuming that the Buddha died towards the end of the fifth century). It is not known what brought this about. Later sources explain it in terms of doctrinal differences and disagreements about rules for the monks' lives. A group calling themselves the **Mahasamghika** are described as holding that the enlightened *arhats* retained some imperfections and were thus susceptible of 'falling away'. Their opponents called themselves Sthaviravadins or 'those who teach the doctrine of the elders'. The Singhalese and Southeast Asian Theravada Buddhists are their surviving successors. Of the original Mahasamghikas, little is known. The docetic (those who adhere to the thesis that the Buddha is really only spiritual) Lokottaravada (or Ekavyavaharika) sub-sect regarded the mundane careers of the Buddhas as only apparent phenomena (*nirmana-kaya*) emanating from the perfect, transcendent Buddha form (*dharma-kaya*, 'the body of doctrine'). These ideas form part of the background to the Mahayana traditions where they will be elaborated.

At the end of the third century BCE, the Vatsiputriyas broke away from the Sthaviravada. The Vatsiputriyas upheld the existence of a persisting, transmigrating self (*pudgala*) neither identical to nor different from the stream of five transient and causally interdependent psychophysical components (*skandhas*; matter, feelings, perceptions, dispositions and consciousness) that make up individual personality. Other schools regard the Vatsiputriyas as heretics re-introducing the Brahmanical soul (**atman**) doctrine to which mainstream Buddhism is a reaction. The Vatsiputriyas held that while all *dharmas* are impermanent (*anitya*), not all are absolutely momentary or instantaneous (*kshanika*). Duration is a necessary condition of movement, in particular the *karma*-expressive physical movements of the *pudgala*. *Dharma*s such as mental events, sounds and flames lack duration but entities such as wood, pots and physical matter last for the time being. At a later date, the Vatsiputriyas split into the Dharmottar-iyas, the Bhadrayaniyas, the Sannagarikas and the Sammatiyas.

There was an anti-Vatsiputriya school of the Sthaviravada called the Vibhajyavada, whose distinctive doctrine was that time (*kala*) is an eternal entity in its own right, conditioned states of affairs (*samskara*) passing through its stages (*adhvana*). This is opposed to the mainstream Sarvastivadin Abhidharmists, who do not include time as a real category in their ontologies. The latter regard temporal stages as reducible to relations between conditioned events, temporal succession thus being a form of human experience. According to **Vasubandhu**'s *Abhidharmakoshabhashya*, the Vibhajyavadins asserted both the reality of the present and an aspect of the past, viz. an action which has not yet borne fruit, and the non-existence of the future and of a part of the past, viz. an action which has borne fruit.

During the reign of the north Indian emperor Ashoka (268–231 BCE), the Sarvastivadins (see **Sarvastivada**) became the dominant Buddhist presence in northwest India from Mathura to Kashmir and Afghanistan and into Central Asia from about the middle of the third century BCE to the seventh century CE. They were divided into Vaibhashikas and Sautrantikas. The latter rejected the **Abhidharma** enterprise of philosophical systematization and restricted their scriptural authorities to the canonical sutras and monastic code. The distinctive cardinal tenet of the Vaibhashika sub-school is that the fundamental elements of existence (*dharma*) possess irreducible individual identities and subsist in past, present and future. On this basis they try to account for continuity within a stream of experiences and the accrual of appropriate consequences within the series in which a given action has occurred, thus ensuring the apportionment of just deserts through a succession of lives. The second-century CE Kashmiri work called the *Mahavibhasha* (whence 'Vaibhashika') is an encyclopedia of the doctrine of this tradition. The most informative opus here, epitomizing the *Mahavibhasha*, is the *Abhidharmakosha* (with auto-commentary), written by Vasubandhu probably towards the end of the fourth century CE. He was regarded as a Sautrantika heretic by the Kashmiri Vaibhashika, Samghabhadra. But he was writing from a Sautrantika point of view.

The Sautrantikas (also called Samkrantivadins) and the Mulasarvastivadins, who are known to have been present in Gilgit in western Central Asia in the sixth and seventh centuries CE broke away from the Sarvastivada sub-sect of the Sthaviravada. The Sautrantikas emphasized the radical momentariness doctrine (*kshanika-vada*) and rejected the view that the irreducible constituents of reality (*dharma*) subsist in past, present and future; a view which is condemned as an eternalist heresy. They held that reality consists of instantaneous, featureless particulars with unique causal efficacies. They reason that if a putative entity A endures (that is, persists by being wholly present at more than one time) for, say, three moments, it must be causally effective at each of them and thus productive of three effects because the same effect cannot be thrice generated. It follows that A has disintegrated into three momentary realities. But if we construe persistence as perdurance (the possession of different temporal parts or stages at different times with no one part being present for more than one time) and say that tri-momentary A lies dormant, awaiting auxiliary factors, for its first two moments and is causally effective at the third (as the seed in the granary awaits soil and rain), then it is only the terminal condition that is real, the previous temporal parts or stages being either non-entities or distinct entities, one generating the other.

The Singhalese Theravada (dating from *c.*250 BCE) 'tradition of the elders' (which is also the form of Buddhism found in Burma, Thailand and Cambodia) derives from the Vibhajyavadins. They used the originally north Indian Middle Indo-Aryan language called Pali. The **Pali Canon**, committed to writing in the first century BCE, is claimed to preserve the original discourses of the Buddha in what is called the *Sutta Pitaka*. The rules for monastic discipline binding on monks and nuns are collected in the *Vinaya Pitaka* and scholastic elaborations of the Doctrine in the *Abhidhamma Pitaka*. Most Hinayanist Buddhist schools, but not the Sautrantikas, developed their own systematic Abhidharma philosophical literature, while the substance of the books of Discourses (*Suttas*) and Discipline (*Vinaya*) are common to every tradition.

The structure of the Pali Canon is:

Vinaya-pitaka (The Basket of Discipline), regulations for monks and nuns, including:

1 *Sutta-vibhanga*. This is an analysis of violations of the basic codes of rules (*Patimokkha*) for monks (227 rules) and nuns (311 rules). Monks should avoid murder, larceny, sex, dishonesty, false claims to supernatural powers, alcohol, eating after noon, dancing, music and entertainment, garlands, perfumes and unguents, soft beds, and gold and silver.
2 *Khandaka*. Regulations (*kamma-vacana*) of organization of the monastic order (*sangha*).
3 Appendices including some history of the order.

Sutta-pitaka (The Basket of Discourses of Gotama Buddha), including:

1 *Digha-Nikaya* (Collection of Long Discourses).
2 *Majjhima Nikaya* (Collection of Middle Length Discourses).
3 *Samyutta Nikaya* (Collection of Connected Discourses).
4 *Anguttara Nikaya* (Various Discourses).
5 *Khuddaka Nikaya*; includes the **Dhammapada** (ethical treatise); *Suttanipata* (various verses); *Theragatha* (accounts of early monks' enlightenment); *Therigatha* (accounts of early nuns' enlightenment); *Jatakas* (547 edifying 'birth stories' of previous lives of the Buddha, exemplifying moral conduct; and the *Buddha-vamsa* about twenty-four previous Buddhas.

Abhidhamma-pitaka, systematizations of material presented more discursively in the *Sutta-pitaka*, including:

1 *Dhammasangani*.
2 *Vibhanga*.
3 *Dhatukatha*. The above refine the analysis of personality into the five components (*khandha*), listing and characterizing the basic elements (*dhammas*) of phenomenal existence.
4 *Puggala-pannatti*, which deals with character types and levels of spiritual development.
5 *Kathavatthu* (Points of Controversy), which defends orthodox views against over two hundred opinions held in other schools of Buddhism.
6 *Yamakas* (Book of Pairs), to prevent terminological ambiguity.
7 *Patthana*, which refines articulation of interdependent genesis (***pratitya-samutpada***) specifying the links between psycho-physical phenomena.

These texts represent the earliest layer of Theravada Buddhist writings and are claimed to be the actual words of the Buddha, Siddhartha Gotama. But since the Buddha probably lived in what is now Northeast India in the second half of the fifth century BCE and probably spoke another Middle Indo-Aryan Prakrit called Magadhi, and since the canonical texts were not committed to writing in Pali, and thus to an extent stabilized, until the first century in Sri Lanka, such claims must be treated with caution. The Pali texts appear archaic, and their often repetitive style is indicative of their origins in oral transmission of the teaching. But they are not truly primitive, and often seem to reflect puritanical, world-renunciatory trends followed by people afflicted by world-weariness and aspiring to an ideal of individual self-sufficiency. While some of the material is of considerable antiquity and may go back to the Buddha Gotama, much of it expresses the various interests and beliefs of later generations of monks who were charged with spreading the message.

It is not known how and when the north Indian language Pali came to Sri Lanka. It was perhaps brought by missionaries sent by the third king of the Mauryan dynasty, Ashoka (*c.*269–*c.*231 BCE), who ruled over a large area of North India from his capital Pataliputra which is now Patna in Bihar State.

Further reading

Bareau, A. (1955) *Les sectes bouddhiques du Petit Vehicule*, Saigon: Ecole Francaise d'Extreme-Orient.
Bechert, H. and Gombrich, R. (1984) *The World of Buddhism*, London: Thames and Hudson.
Collins, S. (1982) *Selfless Persons*, Cambridge: Cambridge University Press.
Conze, E. (1959) *Buddhist Scriptures*, Harmondsworth: Penguin.
Cousins, L. (1991) 'The "Five Points" and the Origins of the Buddhist Schools', in T. Skorupski (ed.), *The Buddhist Forum*, Vol. II, London: School of Oriental and African Studies.

—— (1996) 'The Dating of the Historical Buddha: A Review Article', *Journal of the Royal Asiatic Society* ser. 3, 6(1): 57–63.

Gombrich, R. (1988) *Theravada Buddhism: A Social History from Ancient Benares to Modern Colombo*, London: Routledge.

—— (1996) *How Buddhism Began: The Conditioned Genesis of the Early Teachings*, London: Athlone Press.

Lamotte, E. (1988) *History of Indian Buddhism: From the Origins to the Shaka Era*, trans. S. Webb-Boin, Louvain: Université Catholique de Louvain.

Rahula, W. (1969) *What the Buddha Taught*, London: Gordon Fraser.

Warder, A. (1980) *Indian Buddhism*, Delhi: Motilal Banarsidass.

CHRIS BARTLEY

historiography

There are basically four models of historiography in China. The *Historical Records* by the Grand Historian, Sima Qien, is considered the pinnacle and the model. Then there are the official dynastic histories. These are sponsored by the succeeding dynasty to register the rise and fall of the preceding dynasty. Finally, there are two ways to read Confucius' *Spring and Autumn Annals*: the Han style and the Song style. **Dong Zhongshu** turned Confucius into a prophet of Han rule who instituted the rites and music for the Han; this is a religio-mythopoeic reading, an interpretation which actually created an important influential story about the period in question. The Song historian Sima Guang offered the demythologized moral reading of it. He recaptured the original spirit of that historical criticism in his own work, *Comprehensive Mirror for Ruling the State*, an encyclopedic collection of events held up as mirrors for the edification of rulers and the world. It is not even chronological, history being reduced to or highlighted as moral case studies.

Further reading

Gardner, C. (1970) *Chinese Traditional Historiography*, Cambridge, MA: Harvard University Press.

Schneider, A. and Weigelin-Schwiedrzik, S. (eds) (1966) *Chinese Historiography in Comparative Perspective*, Middletown, CT: Wesleyan University.

WHALEN LAI

history, Chinese theories of

Tradition ascribes to **Zou Yan** (305–240 BCE) of the Warring States period the synthesis of the *yin–yang* and the **Five Elements** theory. The five can generate one another or overcome one another. The mutual conquest series goes: Earth, Wood, Metal, Fire and Water. The subsequent element conquers the preceding one. The 'conquest series' (i.e. where the Five Elements conquer or overcome each other, like water putting out fire and a metal axe cutting wood) was put to a new use to map the succession of dynasties yielding the sequence in the first column.

This turned the once moral ideology of the Mandate of Heaven into a kind of predictable 'natural law' of ruling. Working in the state of Qi in the northeast, Zou probably was courting his patron with the prospect of him being the Black Emperor to rise in the North. He would then end the **chaos** of that warring period. However, victory went instead to the King of Qin. The First Emperor duly adopted the colour Black for his reign, but that empire lasted not 500 years but only fifteen years. The Han dynasty that succeeded it ignored the Qin and claimed the Black colour and element for itself. Emperor Wu later sought higher status as a second Yellow Emperor, and changed the reign colour to earthly yellow. With a usurper

Earth	Yellow Emperor - - - - - - - - - - - -	ruling from the centre
Wood	Xia dynasty	colour green
Metal	Shang dynasty	colour white
Fire	Zhou dynasty	colour red
Water	Black Emperor - - - - - - - - - - - - -	soon to come from the north

founding the New Dynasty and the later Han having to find new colours, this scheme of cosmic kingship gradually fell into dispute.

Other theories of kingship – Buddhist and Daoist – rose in its place. The Daoist **Taiping** Scripture retained the expectation of a Black Emperor who was to rise in the North. The barbaric Wei dynasty was later touted as (and accepted) the prophesied Ruler of Great Peace. That period of barbaric rule in North China ended with another rumour that the 'black robed' would ascend the throne. As Buddhist monks were black robed, this was part of the cause of the Zhou Wu persecution of the *Sangha* (Buddhist community) in the North in 574. The Sui rulers banned the use of such fortune-telling apocrypha, and the tradition of elemental kingship finally died.

WHALEN LAI

history, concept of

China has a number of views on history. It is not true that there was only cyclical time, as Christian theologians have sometimes argued. Other concepts of history include the following:

1 A theory of decline, since the golden age of the Early Chou. This cultural conservatism may itself be a myth, created as a 'historical precedent' for reforming the present.
2 A theory of different standards for different times: the 'rites and music' of the Three Dynasties varied to serve three types of society. This cultural relativism opens up possibilities for new forms of socio-cosmic orders for new eras to come.
3 A theory of utility irrespective of time. Mohists eventually gave up, as a form of valid proof, 'historical precedent'. What works to man's benefit should work uniformly at all times. This encourages cultural activism that soon led to the next option.
4 A theory of positive progress: going beyond **Xunzi**, the Legalists gave up even the model of the 'later kings' (see **Legalism**). A new era needs new policies.
5 A theory of an upswing: the *Book of Rites* accepted an antiquity in which everybody loves

everybody's parents and children followed by a recent age of Lesser Prosperity. Now that **chaos** has superseded it, there may be an ascending peace and finally the Great Peace.

6 A theory of cycles: dynasties follow the conquest series of the **Five Elements**. Attributed to **Zou Yan**, the current age of Red Fire (the Zhou element) will be conquered by a Black Emperor to rise in the next ascending element in the age of Aquarius (Water).

7 A theory of case history and moral judgment: Confucius wrote the *Spring and Autumn Annals* to register his approval and condemnation of the human conduct told within it. The historian has the last word on history and what history is about.

8 A theory of an empire reborn: following the last model, the Grand Historian (Sima Qien) wrote the definitive *Historical Records* that covers, critically, emperors as well as commoners. But he also probably intended his work to mark the reign of Han Emperor Wu as the final and perfect regime. His chronicle begins with the reign of the Yellow Emperor; he was probably behind the Han ruler's decision in 104 BCE to change the reign colour to yellow to help mark the new empire. In China, the title 'emperor' came with the founding of the Qin empire by the First Emperor, who chose the title himself. Not satisfied with the proposal from his courtiers to be named 'emperor among men' (in a triad of emperors of heaven, earth and man), he coined the title *Shi* (meaning 'First') *Huangdi* (Emperor). The latter combines two royal epitaphs used in the set of 'three *huang* (august rulers) and five *di* (supreme lords)' that headed the Chinese mythic chronicle of kings. By subsuming these two epithets under one imperial title, the First Emperor elevated himself to being a cosmic king. With that, he assumed jurisdiction over even the gods of nature. Earlier kings worshipped mountains and rivers in awe; Qin was the first known ruler to punish a mountain god for failing in its duty at preventing flood. The (unwise) punishment is a deforesting of its hill slope. After this the Chinese rulers had the authority to promote and demote deities. From the Han dynasty on, the title *Di* denotes the 'Lord' on high, and is used in the posthumous name of the rulers.

9 A theory of 'alternating rule and chaos'. The presumption behind (5) to (8), this is the most mythless and most matter-of-fact view with no attempt at a teleology. There are just good times of rule followed by bad times of chaos followed by rule again.

There are Daoist and Buddhist views of history, but these are not included in this survey since they are strongly marked by the theories of those systems themselves.

Further reading

Watson, B. (trans.) (1961) *Records of the Grand Historian of China*, 2 vols, New York: Columbia University Press.

WHALEN LAI

played prophet to the Han dynasty, and inspired the constitutional monarchy reform of 1898.

Further reading

Eliade, M. (1959) *Cosmos and History: The Myth of the Eternal Return*, New York: Harper & Row.
Lai, W. (1991) 'Buddhism as a Historical Faith: Answer to John Cobb', *Pacific World, New Series* 7(1): 1–13.
Sponberg, A. and Hardacre, H. (eds) (1988) *Maitreya: the Future Buddha*, Cambridge: Cambridge University Press
Voegelin, E. (1981) *The Philosophy of Order: Essays on History, Consciousness and Politics*, ed. P. Opitz and G. Sebba, Stuttgart: Klett-Cota.

WHALEN LAI

history, sense of

The idea that only the Biblical tradition has a sense of history is not true. Other cultures are not doomed to be mired in a myth of the Eternal Return. All historical religions or philosophies that took that 'Leap of Being' in the Axial Age (fifth century BCE, when many of the major religious thinkers lived) broke away from bondage to nature; and if they celebrate a historicity of the founder, they surely then take on the burden of history. For example, Moses, Confucius and the Buddha all re-envisaged a new social order under God as King (*theo*-cracy) or **sage** as king (*arete*-cracy) or the world-renouncer as the world-conqueror (Buddho-cracy).

In each case, there is an interruption in profane time and a reorganization of the temporal horizons so that the past is reviewed in light of the hierophantic (explaining the deeper mysteries) event with the future seen as a project, a promise of fulfillment. History is re/written by that one history-making, earth-shaking event. In the Abrahamic traditions, the theophany marked a new age midway between Creation and final Consummation. In Buddhism, the enlightenment of Bodhgaya ended the reign of Mara, symbolizing the realm of desire, and opened up the future for the epiphany of Maitreya, the future Buddha. Confucius also

Hong Xiuquan

b. 1814; d. 1864

Revolutionary leader

Leader of the Taiping rebellion, Hong Xiuquan was a failed candidate for the civil service examinations who was converted to the Christian faith after a missionary tract helped reveal the meaning of a dream. He dreamed, after failing the examination for the third time, that he was summoned with honours to heaven, where an old woman washed clean his intestines (symbol of death and rebirth); then he met a fatherly figure (God), and together with an elder brother (Jesus) battled a demon (Satan) in heaven before it escaped to earth. He founded the God-Worshipping Society, exorcized demons, destroyed idols, and later identified those escaped demons with the Manchus and still later, the foreign devils. The missionaries at first supported this Christian movement but would later disown its nativistic colouring. The movement introduced social innovations such as the 'equality of the sexes' which was unheard of. The Taiping rebels destroyed land records and took Beijing.

See also: Taiping

Further reading

Boardman, E. (1952) *Christian Influence upon the Ideology of the Taiping Rebellion, 1851–1864*, Madison, WI: University of Wisconsin Press.

WHALEN LAI

Huainanzi

d. 122 BCE

Nobleman and philosopher

Prince Huainan, or Liu An, was the brother of Han Emperor Wu. The prince had gathered around himself in his own domain a school of eclectic thinkers who kept alive alternative traditions. For that and other reasons, he was put to death by the emperor who went on to make the Confucianism championed by **Dong Zhongshu** the state religion. A consortium of essays from the dissident camp has come down to us as the *Huainanzi Huainantzu*. This collection contains more than Daoist treatises, but it is remembered by many as a Daoist text and the prince himself would be deemed a Daoist immortal who ascended to **heaven** in broad daylight – with his whole household, building, dogs and poultry included. The text works out a full Daoist cosmological sequence: the famed 'Great Ultimate' (later deemed the basis of Song metaphysics) was just one of four dim and nebulous stages. The text also lays out, clearly for the first time, the two (*yin* and *yang*) gods lurking in the **chaos** that became the two souls in man. The two souls disperse at death and/or rejoin their two separate cosmic destinies, one heaven bound and one abiding in earth. That scheme informs both sides of the later debate on the 'immortality of the soul'.

See also: afterlife in Chinese thought

Further reading

Ames, R. (1983) *The Art of Rulership*, Honolulu, HA: University of Hawaii Press.
Morgan, E. (trans.) (1934) *Tao: The Great Luminant*, Shanghai: Kelly & Walsh.

WHALEN LAI

Huineng

b. 638; d 718

Buddhist patriarch

Huineng (638–713) is often regarded as the source of all the different zen schools, through his students, and his *Platform Sutra* (*Tanjing*) is full of extraordinary stylistic displays. He is said, probably apocryphally, to have recited the famous verse about the nature of the mind when competing with others to succeed Hongren, the fifth patriarch. The latter produced a verse comparing the human body to the bodhi-tree under which the Buddha had sat and the mind to a stand holding a mirror which ought to be kept completely clean of dust. Huineng replied that since the essence of everything is **emptiness**, these analogies with physical objects really tell us nothing of any value. His institution of the southern school of sudden enlightenment tried to bring into sharp focus his opposition to the idea that one should wrap up the truths of Buddhism in complex and sophisticated language and practices. Simplicity is sufficient to bring the aspirant to an understanding of the path to enlightenment, often through the production of a challenging and witty question (*koan*) or equally surprising and even shocking action. This view was opposed by the northern school of gradualism, but the latter school was defeated and sudden enlightenment became the more popular approach for a long time. Over time, however, it became as complex, if not more complex, than its northern rival, and many of the hermeneutical techniques required to unravel the *koans* of the southern 'sudden' school require far more than quick solutions.

Further reading

Huineng (1967) *The Platform Sutra of the Sixth Patriarch*, trans. P. Yampolsky, New York: Columbia University Press.

OLIVER LEAMAN

HUMAN NATURE *see* humaneness

human feelings, Confucian

The Confucians prize 'human feelings' (*renqing*). For **Mencius**, they are evidence of the innate sources of human goodness, which lie within us. For Neo-Confucians, *renqing* is what separates their school of thought from the Buddhists, whose denial of family life runs contrary to 'human feelings'. However, the openness of the term is such that it varies with the context. It can mean in Mencius simply 'what is genuine in man', while narrowing it down to 'feelings' is more how the rationalist **Xunzi** would read it (so that he might restrain it with reason). It can also describe the general 'human situation' in contrast to, say, 'the principle of things'. It can be so broad a social compass as to be synonymous with the English 'custom'; so to exchange gifts at New Year time is creating 'human feelings' (meaning, following 'custom'). Not to observe such basic courtesy shows a lack of 'human feeling'. In real life, some such social rituals are recognizably taxing and not very considerate: for example, it is customary for poor underlings to give expensive gifts to their rich master on his many happy occasions.

Many of the so-called 'human relationships' are so formalized that, by modern Western standards, they lack any spontaneity of feeling. The father–son relationship is cardinal, but never as warm as the secondary mother–son one. Yet precisely because of the ritual impersonality of the former, it is more eminently transferable to other figures of authority in the larger patriarchal system. For that, China regards that system of obligations called *yili* to be the embodiment of *renqing*.

In Japan, where feudal norms are recent and strict but where emotions are allowed freer expression, *giri* (the Japanese reading of *yili*; meaning duty) is often seen as being at odds with *ninjo* (Japanese for 'human feeling'). This conflict is found in many more Japanese stories and dramas, which are more emotionally expressive than their more formalistic Chinese counterparts. Repression can cut, it seems, both ways.

See also: face

Further reading

Ames, R. *et al.* (eds) (1994) *Self As Person in Asian Theory and Practice*, Albany, NY: State University of New York Press.

Cheng Chung-ying (1991) *New Dimensions in Confucian and Neo Confucian Philosophy*, Albany, NY: State University of New York Press.

Munro, D. (ed.) (1985) *Individualism and Holism: Studies in Confucianism and Taoist Values*, Ann Arbor, MI: University of Michigan Press.

WHALEN LAI

humaneness

The Chinese script for humaneness (*ren*) shows 'two men', and so connotes the 'interhuman'. Used to described the noble class, it was pitted against *min* for the commoners. Confucius selected out the term for designating the sum of noble virtues; it functions then as the *summum bonum* in Confucian ethics. In fact, it may not be the highest of status achievements possible: above humanity there is sagehood and even god-likeness, but neither sage nor god should be without this human-heartedness.

Religious Daoists sought to rise above humanity; they aspired to become immortals by imitating the eternity of Heaven and Earth. The *Laozi* aired a discordant note when it said: 'Heaven and Earth are not humane; they treated men as if they were (sacrificial) straw dogs.' Pious commentators had to get around this by interpreting the passage as 'Heaven and Earth is not partial as mortals would be.' In accordance with just such a divine impartiality, God has rained on the good and bad alike. In another attack on the ethics of the urbane nobility, Laozi also would like to see 'humaneness and **righteousness** put aside' so that the 'common people could return to the ethos of compassion and filiality'; meaning, it seems, the communal village duty of taking care of all the young and all the aged without regard to strict elite lineage distinctions.

Under the Han dynasty, **Dong Zhongshu**, the spokesman for Han Confucianism, aligned *ren* with *yang* and its opposite, greed with *yin*. It catered to a Han hierarchic metaphysics that undercut the Mencian ideal of *ren* as universal, common, essential and fundamental to all men. The social constraint placed on *ren* later led to the iconoclastic

Neo-Daoists revolting against 'humaneness and righteousness'; these non-conformists called for a return to spontaneity and naturalness. A fitting criticism of the abuse of a Later Han patronage system (when a person could win high office based on recommendation of their moral worth), it lapsed into libertinism and abandonment.

The Buddhist ascetics reined in the latter excesses. The Buddha was phonetically rendered in Han sometimes as *buren* (a different script) meaning, as with Mencius, one who 'cannot bear' (to see another suffer). Semantically, the name Buddha is about a being of *ren* (benevolence). His compassion is cosmic and all-pervasive or penetrating. It is probably from that cosmic sense that the Neo-Confucians would refashion the classical *ren* into a metaphysical reality that penetrates; it removes all obstruction and makes manifest the heavenly principle. With that, they elevated *ren* to being the substance of all other virtues; no longer a virtue among virtues or even just the sum of the virtues. The last major theoretician of *ren* came in the 1898 reform when **Tan Sitong** wrote a treatise on it and identified it with the notion of an invisible **ether** with which nineteenth century physics glues the galaxy together.

Further reading

Wing-tsit Chan (1955) 'The Evolution of the Confucian Concept Jen', *Philosophy East and West* 4: 295–319.

WHALEN LAI

HUNGRY GHOSTS *see* afterlife, Chinese: hungry ghosts

hypocrisy

A necessary vice in puritanical cultures, hypocrisy is the flip side of a publicly pure life. Puritan sanctification and Neo-Confucian sincerity assume that a person can will the good and do the good. As a Chinese proverb goes, 'Nothing in the world is so difficult that perseverance cannot overcome'. Those who fail should just try, try, and try again.

One does so by confessing in public, and for that one is welcomed with open arms. Even sages make mistakes, so 'to admit one's fault and to make the proper amends is tantamount to being a great worthy'. The problem is that God may be forever forgiving, but an avowed community of 'secular saints' and 'self-willed sages' is not that tolerant for long. Less extreme than the Puritans, Neo-Confucianism strengthened the Confucian demand that 'a father behaves like a father as a son a son'. An elder must live up to role expectation and, failing that, still put up the necessary front. Thus as the pillar of the family, a man is not supposed to appear so weak as to shed tears before his son. A model of virtue in public, he has to hide his failings in private. A son discovering the sins of the father can be devastated, but that American tragedy acted out in the play *Death of A Salesman* would probably not occur in China. With father and son being never 'on a level' in traditional China, sons are not supposed to judge fathers. Sons cannot even openly sympathize with their fathers. The battered youth in **Dream of the Red Chambers** learned to 'forgive' the harsh supervision he received from his father when he later realized that his father suffered the same caning in his younger days from his own father. But that private sympathy never grew into a public reconciliation between father and son, for inferiors cannot presume to sympathize and even less forgive their superiors – not in public.

Ming despotic rule further underwrote the absolute authority of the father at home, a trend that finally led to the massacre at Tiananmen several hundred years later. Modern students, presuming equality (as citizens), clashed with their seniors who felt 'a loss of face'. A 'shamed elder', as a proverb goes, 'retaliatory anger makes'. That is the Chinese tragedy, for whereas Puritanism erased feudalism, Neo-Confucianism did not. Non-theistic, it is less judgemental, but then by the same token it is a Puritanism without grace. This incidentally explains why evangelical Christianity has made many converts of those moral-minded Chinese who are haunted by the prospect of moral and/or social failure.

See also: moral failure

Further reading

Bertrong, J. (1994) *All Under Heaven: Transforming Paradigms in Confucian Christian Dialogue*, Albany, NY: State University of New York Press.

Hawkes, D. (trans.) (1985) *The Story of the Stone*, Harmondsworth: Penguin (the work is also known as the *Dream of the Red Chambers*).

Lai, W. (1990) 'Growing up Rational, Puritanical and Weaned of the Gods: Confucian Education of the Son after Age Six', *Cheng Feng* 33(4): 232–47.

—— (1996) 'Puritanism and Neo-Confucianism: A Mutual Challenge', *Cheng Feng* 39(3): 149–72.

WHALEN LAI

I *see* righteousness

Ibn al-'Arabi

b. 560 AH/1164 CE; d. 638 AH/1240 CE

Mystical thinker

Without doubt the greatest mystical thinker in the Islamic world, Ibn al-'Arabi was born in Murcia, Andalus, and died in Damascus. He is the author of hundreds of books, some of which have become very influential in the development of mystical thought in Islamic philosophy. He argued that rational thought and knowledge gained through sense experience is available to anyone, given the appropriate training and experiences. But there is also a type of knowledge called *ma'rifa*, a type of intuitive gnosis in which mysteries and secrets are revealed, and this is the type of knowledge which lies at the pinnacle of human achievement. In his celebrated debate with **Ibn Rushd**, Ibn al-'Arabi criticizes the Peripatetic thinker for glorifying knowledge through reason, and for failing to appreciate the significance of mystical thought.

Although Ibn al-'Arabi argues that rational thought is not the highest form of thought of which we are capable, he does argue rationally for this conclusion. God is in himself unattainable through reason and all that may be grasped are his names or properties, and God himself is everywhere. Like **Ibn Sina**, Ibn al-'Arabi distinguishes sharply between existence and essence, and possible things are only possible due to their dependency on God's will. Human beings have a special status among possible existents, since we as microcosms with consciousness can bring the divine names together in a special kind of unity. Only the **perfect man** (*al-insan al-kamil*), whose best example is the Prophet Muhammad, manages to balance all the divine names within himself perfectly. This gives Ibn al-'Arabi the opportunity to suggest that all the prophets are perfect men in a sense, but Muhammad as the final prophet is the most perfect of them all. They were limited in their message to a particular place and time, and hence were examples of the divine names in a way which does not exemplify complete equilibrium. Only Muhammad manages to achieve complete balance, and so remains relevant for all times and places.

One of the Qur'anic terms which Ibn al-'Arabi develops brilliantly is that of the *barzakh*, the isthmus or bridge between one level of reality and another. There are three distinct levels of reality, the realm of spirits, the realm of images and the realm of bodies. The latter is our ordinary world and the route to the higher realm of spirituality needs the mediation of imagination, since in imagination we are able to think about things being different from the ways in which they appear to be, and we can thus extend our understanding of the possible range of the world with which we are familiar. Much of the language to do with miracles and saints can be interpreted as imaginative language, as compared with accurate descriptions of facts. But we should not conclude from this that there is anything wrong with imaginative language; on the contrary it is often better able to provide information about reality than are the parochial and certain facts of the world of generation and corruption. We should be aware that our language is often systematically misleading, since it is based on the distinction between God and everything else, which is basically wrong. Essentially there is no distinction between God and his creation, and as we perfect our consciousness we come to realize progressively the emptiness of that distinction. On the other hand, there is no doubt but that our experience provides us with a good deal of evidence for such a distinction, and our whole conceptual vocabulary is based on it. Hence what we need to do as we improve in understanding is both to appreciate the way in which the world appears to us to be and how it is in reality.

Further reading

Chittick, W. (1989) *The Sufi Path of Knowledge: Ibn al-'Arabi's Metaphysics of Imagination*, Albany, NY: State University of New York Press.

Elmore, G. (1999) *Islamic Sainthood in the Fullness of Time: Ibn al-'Arabi's Book of the Fabulous Gryphon*, Leiden: Brill.

OLIVER LEAMAN

Ibn Khaldun

b. 732 AH/1332 CE; 808 AH/1406 CE

Philosopher and historian

Abu Zayd 'Abd al-Rahman ibn Khaldun was born in Tunis, and died in Cairo. He is the outstanding philosopher of history and the social sciences in the Islamic world. Much of his work deals with actual history and social science, but his *Muqaddima*, his introduction to those empirical works, is very interesting from a theoretical point of view. He created what he called the *'ilm al-'umran* or the science of culture, which provides historians with criteria for judging accounts of past events. This science distinguishes between the accidental and the essential in human society, the use of sources and the reliability of different kinds of evidence. Most important of all, it enables the social scientist

to discover the laws which govern the transformation of society from one state to another. One interesting feature of this approach is that Ibn Khaldun sees the individual as having very little power to affect social change. It is change in large quantity which brings about new kinds of state, and the individual, however heroic or impressive, can do little to prevent such change.

Although Ibn Khaldun accepts the importance of physical factors in explaining how nationalities act, the key to their understanding lies in their sociological constitution. History consists of constant cyclical change, and it is explicable in terms of the varying status of different social and economic groups. The basic contest is between the inhabitants of the town and the nomads. The former are cultured and wealthy but lacking in the martial arts, while the *'asabiya* or cohesiveness of the latter makes them powerful when eventually they come to confront the city dwellers. Luxury in the city leads to a decline in cohesiveness and solidarity, a disinclination to fight and so to their defeat at the hands of the stronger, but less cultured, nomads. The latter in turn become corrupted by the institutions of the city, coming to rely more and more on others to defend them and becoming progressively isolated from their original virtues and supporters.

Ibn Khaldun was antagonistic to much Peripatetic thought, and even to much **Sufism**, arguing as he did that one should adhere strictly to *shari'a* (religious law) and beware ecstatic fantasies. *Falsafa* is unsatisfactory because it emphasizes insufficiently the role of revelation in knowledge. Reason is not in itself capable of purifying and making more abstract the ideas which we receive through the senses. These ideas are incapable of being anything more than empirical, and if we are to grasp their wider significance only religion can be of use, not reason. He also criticized the abstractness of political philosophy, which he saw as too general in its arguments to apply to the actual state of affairs in existing and previous states. Despite his hostility to particular ways of doing philosophy, there is no doubt but that Ibn Khaldun was attracted to many of the basic theses of philosophy and used them in his remarkable theories of society.

Further reading

Al-Azmeh, A. (1990) *Ibn Khaldun: An Essay in Reinterpretation*, London: Routledge.

Ibn Khaldun (1967) *Muqaddima*, ed. and trans. F. Rosenthal, *The Muqaddima*, Princeton, NJ: Princeton University Press.

Issawi, C. (1986) *An Arab Philosophy of History*, Princeton, NJ: Princeton University Press.

Mahdi, M. (1957) *Ibn Khaldun's Philosophy of History*, London: Allen & Unwin.

OLIVER LEAMAN

Ibn Rushd

b. 520 AH/1126 CE; d. AH/1198 CE

Philosopher and physician

Abu'l Walid ibn Ahmad ibn Muhammad ibn Rushd, also known by his Latin name, Averroes, was born in Cordoba, Spain. Like so many of the Islamic philosophers, he played an important public role both as a physician and a judge. His political career was tempestuous, and by the time of his death he had suffered several periods of banishment. He is perhaps the outstanding thinker of the classical period of Islamic philosophy, beginning by commenting on the works of Aristotle but going on to produce very original and challenging works. He commented on Aristotle in various ways, in long, medium and short commentaries. The long commentary is a detailed explanation of the text suitable for philosophers, while the middle commentary deals with the main ideas but not all the text. The short commentaries are much freer, often allowing Ibn Rushd to express his own views on wider issues within the context of some attention to an Aristotelian theme. Ibn Rushd grasped all too well the corrupt nature of many Aristotelian texts through their translation from Greek into Arabic, often via some other language, and then the imposition on the text of Neoplatonism, the standard philosophical school in Islamic philosophy.

This attempt to distinguish his approach from Neoplatonism is made very clear in his *Tahafut al-tahafut* (Refutation of the Refutation), his critique of al-Ghazali's *Tahafut al-falasifa* (Refutation of the Philosophers). **Al-Ghazali** attacks the standard philosophical curriculum as presented by **Ibn Sina**, and Ibn Rushd tries to defend what he regards as authentic Aristotelian philosophy on the compatibility between religion and reason. The trouble with the critics of philosophy, he says, is that they do not sufficiently appreciate that we have to talk about God in very different ways from how we talk about ourselves. Al-Ghazali keeps on challenging the philosophers to show that God can really know what we are doing, that he can genuinely act and do anything he wants. When the philosophers talk of the divine activities they hedge them round with so many conditions that al-Ghazali is convinced that they do not really leave room for God to act at all. Ibn Rushd argues by contrast that al-Ghazali's view results in transforming God into someone too much like us and so not really God at all. What is the point of insisting that God creates the world at one particular time, since all times are the same for him? How could God create the world at a particular time, since before the world was created and motion started there was no time?

Al-Ghazali tried to emphasize the power of God by arguing for the radical contingency of the world – although some recent commentators have argued against this interpretation – so that whatever we think are stable essences are in fact nothing more than reflectiions of a stability which God himself creates, and could withdraw at any time. We can easily think of nature being different, so there is nothing in nature itself which has to be as it is. Ibn Rushd criticizes this account, agreeing that we can think of nature being very different, but that this does not show that it really could be different. On this point he links Ibn Sina with al-Ghazali, in that both make the world dependent upon something outside it. Ibn Rushd, like Aristotle, is a realist, regarding the world as having nothing mysterious about it. Existence and essence are ontologically linked, so that the meaning of a name is logically connected with its instantiation. In that case the sort of thought-experiments which al-Ghazali uses to try to throw doubt on the objectivity of the natural world fail to make sense. The familiar facts of the world are parts of the meanings which we apply to the world itself, so that if the facts are imagined to become very different, we should not know what meanings to apply. This seems to leave little scope for religion, since it gives great significance to the way nature is constructed, but then one could always argue, as Ibn Rushd did, that God would of course follow the most rational path in that creation. Given this fact, he is not going to bring about the sorts of arbitrary events which al-Ghazali insists he could.

Ibn Rushd follows Aristotle's uncertainty over the meaning of the supreme type of happiness for human beings. Is it intellectual, or is it some combination of the intellectual and the social? If it is the former, then it would be limited to a very small minority, and such people might feel that they could abandon their social and religious duties, since these are irrelevant to the attainment of intellectual excellence. The rules of behaviour are given to everyone through religion and prophecy, and the prophet is able to inspire people through his political understanding, in particular how to address different constituencies in such a way as will resonate with them. Prophecy is political, and revelation and miracles are themselves aspects of politics in serving to persuade the masses that they ought to behave in particular ways. The difference between philosophers and prophets is that only the latter have the legislative ability to embody their theoretical knowledge, which they share with the philosopher, in laws.

It is just because the philosopher and the prophet have the same knowledge that the apparent conflict between religion and philosophy is indeed only apparent. The philosopher is expert in intellectual matters to do with reason, and to him should follow the task of explaining difficult theoretical issues. Most people are not philosophers, and should listen to prophecy when it is a matter of knowing how to live and satisfy any doubts about faith which may occur to them, since most people would not understand the sorts of things which philosophers say in defence of their arguments. There are different routes to the truth, and they are equally valid. No successful religion would only establish one route to the truth, since this would be to exclude a part of the community from access. We need to understand that philosophy and religion express the same truth, albeit in different ways.

Ibn Rushd came to have a powerful impact on philosophy in Christian and Jewish Europe. In fact, his influence was so great as to lead to the school of **Averroism**, made up of those who considered themselves to be his followers.

Further reading

Fakhry, M. (1958) *Islamic Occasionalism and its Critique by Averroes and Aquinas*, London: Allen & Unwin.

Ibn Rushd (1954) *Averroes' Tahafut al-Tahafut (The Incoherence of the Incoherence)*, trans. S. Van den Bergh, London: Luzac.

—— (1961) *Averroes on the Harmony of Religion and Philosophy*, trans. G. Hourani, London: Luzac.

—— (1974) *Averroes on Plato's Republic*, trans. R. Lerner, Ithaca, NY: Cornell University Press.

—— (1984) *Ibn Rushd's Metaphysics*, trans. C. Genequand, Leiden: Brill.

Leaman, O. (1994) 'Is Averroes an Averroist?', in *Averroismus im Mittelalter und in der Renaissance*, ed. F. Niewoehner and L. Sturlese, Zurich: Spur, 9–22.

—— (1997) *Averroes and his Philosophy*, Richmond: Curzon Press.

Urvoy, D. (1991) *Ibn Rushd (Averroes)*, London: Routledge.

OLIVER LEAMAN

Ibn Sab'in

b. 614 AH/1217 CE; d. 669 AH/1270 CE

Sufi philosopher

'Abd al-Haqq ibn Ibrahim Muhammad ibn Nasr was a sufi philosopher of Andalusia, who became well known in Christian Europe for his replies to questions sent to him by Frederick II, ruler of Sicily. He is commonly called Ibn Sab'in, and sometimes Qutb al-Din (the pole of religion). He was born in Murcia, emigrating to North Africa with some of his disciples, and finally settling in Ceuta. While there he received Frederick's four philosophical queries concerning Aristotelianism. He later travelled to Egypt around 646 AH/1250 CE. He died in Mecca; some have suggested that he committed suicide, while others think that he was poisoned by the vizier.

Ibn Sab'in produced forty-one works, most of which are not extant. His greatest work is the *Budd* al-'arif (Idol of the Gnostic). His Rasa'il (Epistles) and his replies to Frederick II tell us much about his philosophical views. His style is highly esoteric and his reading was obviously very broad, covering Greek philosophy and ancient oriental philosophies such as hermeticism, Zoroastrianism and Hinduism. He was well-read in the works of **al-Farabi** and **Ibn Sina**, from the east of the Islamic world, and among Andalusian thinkers he was familiar with Ibn Bajjah, Ibn Tufayl and **Ibn Rushd**. He was familiar with the Rasa'il (Epistles) of the Brethren of Purity, and was well grounded in both the Islamic sciences and sufi thought.

Ibn Sab'in was a follower of the Shuzi sufi way, founded by al-Shuzi of Seville. This was a continuation of the school founded by Ibn Masarrah (269 AH/882 CE–319 AH/931 CE), which was especially influential among those sufis in Andalusia who had a philosophical tendency. But Ibn Sab'in was highly critical of much previous Sufi thought, as he was of **Ibn al-'Arabi**, whose thought he described as 'corrupted'. Ibn Sab'in founded a sufi group which came to be known as the Sab'iniyyun. They followed an eclectic path which combined Greek, Islamic and ancient oriental elements. This form of Sufism survived up to the time of Ibn Taymiyyah (d. 728 AH/1328 CE), who attacked it throughout much of his work.

The idea which caused so much anger was the pantheism of Ibn Sab'in, which is based on the concept of wahdat al-wujud, the idea that only God really exists and that there is no real basis to the distinction between the existence of God and of everything else. The existence of God should not be seen as a quality added to his essence, but his existence is rather an essentially permanent single reality. This interpretation is characterized by Ibn Sab'in as pure wahdat al-wujud, or comprehensiveness, by which the notion of anything existing separately from God is absolutely denied. Being is spiritual rather than material, and he goes on to compare existence with a circle, with a periphery that is absolute existence and controlled or limited existence (the ways in which existence seems to us ordinarily to be) which is within the circle. In reality there is no distinction between the two types of existence, they are essentially the same. He sometimes links the absolute existence of God and contingent beings as like the relationship between

form and matter, in that it is only when God infuses what appears to be matter that it takes on any form at all. Ibn Sab'in seeks support for his views in certain Qur'anic verses such as 'He is the First and the Last, and the Outward and the Inner' (57:3), and 'Everything will perish except his Face' (28:88).

Ibn Sab'in's pantheism is the basis of his concept of the genuine gnostic or 'arif. This concept is quite similar to that of other sufis such as Ibn al-'Arabi when describing the Muhammadan Reality (al-Haqiqat al-muhamaddiyyah) or the Pole (al-Qutb), and 'Abd al-Karim al-Jili when discussing the **perfect man** (al-insan al-kamil). The real gnostic, the person who really knows, is the most perfect of human beings. He combines the perfections of the jurist, the theologian, the philosopher and the sufi. He is superior to them in that he possesses his own special knowledge, real gnosis, which is the route to the Prophet from whom everything stems.

In his Idol of the Gnostic, he attacks Aristotelian logic and replaces it with a new 'illuminative' logic. The logic of the gnostic is not achieved through deductive reasoning but through intuition, and avoids the misleading multiplicity of Aristotelianism. This new logic leads to the conclusion that logical forms are innate, and that the six logical terms (genus, species, difference, property, accident and person) which give the impression of multiplicity are indeed illusory, as are the ten categories. Although these may be various, they really refer to the absolute unity of existence. He takes issue here with Ibn Rushd, who shares Aristotle's view that the categories cannot be identified as belonging to just one genus.

Ibn Sab'in extends his pantheism to other areas of sufi philosophical thought. For example, he argues that the soul and our rationality cannot have real existence as independent phenomena. Their existence derives from the One, and the One cannot be multiplied. Good and evil are identical from the point of view of existence. Since existence is One and is absolute Good, evil cannot really emerge. Evil is only a way in which we look at the world, a way which on closer examination turns out to be false. The real gnostic cannot be described as happy or good or perfect since he is Happiness itself, Goodness itself and Perfection itself. Ibn Sab'in's main criticism of other thinkers is that they do not sufficiently emphasize the unity of everything which is implied in the *wahdat al-wujud* principle, since if this principle is understood as he thinks it ought to be, the sorts of divisions and distinctions which we tend to make are unreal and should be regarded merely as indications of a greater and entirely unified reality. We can see this quite clearly when we look at the ways in which he analyses the concept of knowledge, which leads him to be highly critical of the approach of the *falasifa*. They suggest that the mind, and especially the intellect, is really just a means for the acquisition of knowledge. We can progressively purify our mind and gradually acquire more and more knowledge, eventually leading to contact with the **active intellect**, which represents the highest level of knowledge which the *falasifa* think can be realized.

Ibn Sab'in counters that the intellect is nothing more than a divine creation, and so should have no problems in actually uniting and knowing that which created it. There is no need to think of knowledge as consisting of the piecemeal process which the *falasifa* describe which may result in a gradual progress towards, but never actually to, God. We are divine creations, and it is natural to expect that it would be possible for us to understand the deity. The Qur'an says that God has taught Adam all the names (2:29) and has sent him to earth as a viceregent, so we are in possession of divine properties, and if we wish to come closer to God, we need to engage in the process of trying to understand the secret which he has given us. Although this sort of knowledge is not obvious, it is occluded by the multifarious nature of our experience, it is always possible for us to see the world correctly and convert our minds into something more like the thinking of the creator of the world and his Prophet.

See also: Ikhwan al-Safa'

Further reading

Ibn Sab'in (1965) *Rasa'il Ibn Sab'in* (Letters of Ibn Sab'in), ed. A. Badawi, Cairo.

—— (1978) *Budd al-'arif* (Idol of the Gnostic), ed. G. Kattura, Beirut.

Ibn Taymiyyah (1930) *Rasa'il wal Masa'il* (Letters and Issues), Cairo.

Kattora, G. (1977) *Das mystische und philosophische System des Ibn Sab'in*, Tübingen.

Lator, E. (1944) 'Ibn Sab'in de Murcia y su Budd al'Arif', *Al-Andalus* 9(?): 371–417.

Taftazani, A. (1973) *Ibn Sab'in and His Philosophical Sufism*, Beirut.

OLIVER LEAMAN

Ibn Sina

b. 370 AH/980 CE; d. 429 AH/1037 CE

Philosopher

Abu 'Ali al-Husayn ibn Sina, known in the West as Avicenna, was born near Bukhara and had a typically broad interest in a whole range of intellectual issues. He had a very active personal and political life, and produced a large number of logical, philosophical, medical, psychological, scientific and literary works by the time of his death.

Although it would be right to see **al-Farabi** as the thinker who created the philosophical curriculum of the Islamic world during the classical period, it was Ibn Sina who developed it into a set of novel and challenging theories. God is the principle behind existence, and as pure intellect is the necessary source of all other existing things. The universe is produced through emanation following the normal Neoplatonic model. God is at the summit of the hierarchy of being, and the highest that human beings can proceed along the hierarchy is towards the Active Intellect, the principle behind the formal organisation of everything in our world and the last of the ten cosmic intellects that exist below God. This notion of the Active Intellect corresponds to the development of Aristotle's concept of the *nous poietikos*, about which Aristotle has very little to say but which comes to have huge significance in Neoplatonism and Islamic philosophy. Our world appears to be contingent, but if we understand the way in which causes necessitate effects we will understand that once the cause is given, the effect proceeds inevitably, while only God is necessary in himself. We can grasp the nature of the **active intellect** by perfecting our rational abilities, and a prophet can do this perfectly since he has an entirely rational soul and is able to grasp the formal structure of reality.

Ibn Sina uses the theories of both Aristotle and Alexander of Aphrodisias in identifying the concept of the Active Intellect with the first cause of the universe. God's self-knowledge is eternal and results in three products, namely, a first intelligence which has as its object the necessity of God's existence, the necessity of its own existence as a result of its relationship with God, and its existence as possible in the sense that it is dependent upon God. From these thoughts other existing things are produced, until we reach the level of the Active Intellect which produces our world. As we descend down the hierarchy the intelligences become less powerful, and the Active Intellect is so far down the hierarchy that it cannot even emanate eternal beings, by contrast with what is above it. However, despite what this might be taken to imply, there is nothing really contingent about or in the universe, according to Ibn Sina. If something is possibly existent, then it must come to pass at some time; if something remains potentially existent but never comes about, then this is because it cannot come about. If a possible thing becomes actual, its existence is necessitated by its cause. It cannot not be. Its cause is itself necessitated by another cause, and so on, but not *ad infinitum*, since there is a being which is necessary through itself, God, who is both the beginning and the end of the hierarchy of causes and effects.

Logical reasoning is the route to human perfection. Those who are incapable of logic are entrapped in the sorts of experiences which the world of generation and corruption throws up, and seriously misunderstand the nature of reality. We can acquire some knowledge through sense perception, but it is limited by its particularity. The philosopher's task is to refine that experience and derive its formal features, which can then be progressively refined until we reach increasingly abstract and advanced forms of thinking. Ibn Sina gives an important role to imagination in human thought, which enables us to produce images of things we have not experienced and so broadens the scope of our thought. But there are dangers in imagination also, it tends to anchor our thought in the physical and the corporeal world. The more advanced thinker needs to rise above the material nature of our images. The appropriate refinement of our resulting ideas leads to the point where the Active Intellect is able to work with us to produce the rational universals. We can rise no further in our thought than the Active Intellect, which represents the basic structure of reality as emanated from God, the pure intellect. Even at this stage in the hierarchy of emanation, we reach a level of reality which is no longer powerful enough to generate an intelligence and soul. Instead, emanation generates from the Active Intellect a multiplicity of human beings and sublunary matter. Our souls emanate from the Active Intellect, and its illumination (*ishraq*) of our souls makes possible the kinds of knowledge which in turn can be orientated towards it.

Perhaps the most discussed aspect of Ibn Sina's philosophy is his distinction between essence and existence, typically an idea derived originally from al-Farabi but turned into a powerful theory by Ibn Sina. No essence must exist, with the sole exception of the essence of God, according to Ibn Sina. If there were no necessity about existence, then it could be that nothing apart from God would actually exist. Something must ultimately necessitate actual existence, yet that something cannot itself be merely possible since it would then require something necessary to bring it about if we are to avoid an infinite regress. Eventually we arrive at God as the necessitating cause of the universe, the only necessary being in itself. It follows from the essence or definition of God that he exists, and he is the only thing in existence of which that can be said.

The soul has to be unlimited by the body, according to Ibn Sina, since thought itself is indivisible and can transcend material limitations. It is also immortal, and its link with the body, important though it is, is accidental. The soul can quite easily exist without the body. Since the soul is not composite, it is not subject to dissolution. When we think of the next life, we should think of it as being experienced by the soul, not the body which just disintegrates on death. The eternal soul will suffer penalties and rewards in a life after death as a result of the behaviour of the individual during this life. Like most of the Islamic philosophers, Ibn Sina accepts a theory of the next life which can be understood by everyone. Those skilled intellectually understand salvation in terms of rational improvement, and will not need the dramatic and corporeal language of the afterlife to motivate them appropriately. On the other hand, those who are not intellectually gifted are provided by religion with a language which is capable of helping them to understand imaginatively that the consequences of their actions in this life have an extension which is not limited to this life entirely. The most effective way of instructing them is to make them think in terms of the next life being rather like this life.

As well as being one of the major figures in *mashsha'i* thought, Ibn Sina is often regarded as an important mystical thinker. He is sometimes seen as the originator of *ishraqi* or **illuminationist philosophy**, a form of philosophy which is one of the three major schools of thought in Islamic philosophy. This form of thought is something of a compromise between Peripatetic and Sufi thought, sharing with the former a respect for reason and with the latter a refusal to put reason on a pedestal. The 'Eastern philosophy' which he is taken to have regarded as far more significant than his other work is no longer extant, if it ever really existed, so it is difficult to know what the truth is on this issue. Whatever the truth may be about the putative 'Eastern' philosophy, there is no doubt that Ibn Sina did write some important mystical works and saw this as a valid and important way of doing philosophy, and his continuing influence in the Persian world has a great deal to do with his connection with *ishraqi* thought.

See also: afterlife in Islamic philosophy; hikma

Further reading

Ibn Sina (1952) *Avicenna's Psychology* trans. F. Rahman, Oxford: Oxford University Press.
—— (1984) *Remarks and Admonitions, Part One: Logic*, trans. S. Inati, Toronto: Pontifical Institute of Mediaeval Studies.
—— (1985) 'Essay on the Secret of Destiny', trans. G. Hourani, in his *Reason and Tradition in Islamic Ethics*, Cambridge: Cambridge University Press, 227–48.
Goodman, L. (1992) *Avicenna*, London: Routledge.
Gutas, D. (1988) *Avicenna and the Aristotelian Tradition*, Leiden: Brill.
Kemal, S. (1991) *The Poetics of Alfarabi and Avicenna*, Leiden: Brill.
Leaman, O. (1985) *An Introduction to Medieval Islamic Philosophy*, Cambridge: Cambridge University Press.

OLIVER LEAMAN

iconoclasts

A number of scholars in the early twentieth century, led by Gu Jiegang and involved in the path-breaking journal *Gushipien* (Antiquity) were the 'higher critics' of tradition in this century. They are called 'iconoclasts' because they debunked the history of China's high antiquity by questioning anything that predated the verified archaeological finds of the Shang dynasty. The Xia dynasty and, preceding that, the three Sage-Kings all the way up to the venerable Yellow Emperor are declared to be myths; they are ideological creations traceable to the age of the philosophers who looked to alleged precedents for pretexts to reform current society. Still regarded as too radical by many who hate to see sacred tradition pushed aside, even Peoples Republic of China scholars would like the Xia culture dated and located archaeologically to preserve China's claim to an unbroken ancient history, the group has opened up whole new avenues of bold, critical scholarship unimagined before.

Further reading

Schneider, L. (1971) *Ku Chieh-kang and China's New History: Nationalism and the Quest for Alternative Traditions*, Berkeley, CA: University of California Press.

WHALEN LAI

idealism, Chinese

The Mahayana school of **Yogachara** has been called idealist, although strictly speaking, *vijnaptimatrata* argues for 'representation only'. Reality is known only through mental representations which require meditative correction. Chinese Buddhism, however, traditionally reduced that into 'consciousness only', which it further distinguishes from 'mind only'. The former traces everything to the eighth *alaya-vijnana* or storehouse consciousness, which is currently deluded and falls slave to a subject–object duality. The latter assumes, behind that polluted consciousness, a deeper mind; this mind is pure and forms the basis of all the realities it generates. 'Mind Only' is represented by the Huayan school which accepts the universality of that **buddha nature** (mind). The thesis that the mind actually creates (instead of just provides representations of) the world is derived from a very loose translation of a line in the *Dashabhumika* (describing the **bodhisattva** path) which reads in Chinese: 'The three realms are only the creation of mind'.

The term 'mind only' is now used by Marxists to render idealism, and the expression 'things only' for materialism. It is doubtful the Chinese ever knew those European forms of idealism and materialism, though. For example, Song Xing (*fl.* 319–301 BCE) was probably the first 'Idealist', but what he said is: 'There is a mind within the mind. Intention is prior to speech. First intention, then form ... then thought ... then knowledge. Any time the forms of the mind moves beyond knowledge [i.e. bare awareness], it loses its vitality [due its entanglement with things of the world]'. Until Buddhism became popular, the Chinese never doubted that there is a world out there.

See also: Awakening of Faith in Mahayana; subject and object

Further reading

Lai, W. (1977) 'The Meaning of "Mind Only" (*wei-hsin*): An Analsysis of a Sinitic Mahayana Phenomenon', *Philosophy East and West* 27(1): 65–83.

WHALEN LAI

IDOLATRY *see* Christianity, Chinese

idols and anti-idolatry

The iconoclastic debate rose in the Eastern Church when the opponents to the icons coming from the Monophysites worried about a 'human' likeness for Christ, a single-nature divinity. The aniconic faction was also well aware of the stand taken against idol worship by Judaism and later Islam. China was seen as a nation of idol-worshippers by the Christian missionaries. However, the adoption of sculptured images in worship was largely a gift of the Buddhists; and Buddhism, originally aniconic, was introduced to the Apollo figure by the Alexandrine conquest of northwest India. The irony is that whereas Gnostic Christianity on the Silk Road objected to a human image or idols, Gnostic Mahayana could accept it because the artistry of the transmundane Buddha image is such that there is no way an image can be mistaken as a mundane human.

Whatever the missionaries might have seen, China has her own iconoclastic tradition, now best remembered by events during the Cultural Revolution when the Red Guards destroyed temples and toppled statues from altars. Just as eagerly, members of the God-Worshipping Society, the nativistic Christian movement that led to the **Taiping** Rebellion (1850–65), took the missionaries' teaching about graven idols to heart. But Dr **Sun Yat-sen**, leader of the Republican Revolution of 1911, also smashed idols in his youth, before he even heard of Christianity or was converted to it.

In fact, Confucianism is officially aniconic. It does not use images in its worship, only an inscribed name. Effigies might have existed in the distant past, but this has not been proven. The ritual Classics (see **Classics and Books**) dictate clearly that only 'spirit tablets' be used. It is Buddhism that popularized the use of the statue. Before that, Daoists had honoured a gourd on the altar as a symbol for the (empty) *dao* and a marker for **Laozi**. Images were soon accepted, however, and proliferated until the Song Neo-Confucians revived the classical norm. The Ming dynasty later purged all installed images from official altars. Though portraits may adorn Confucian temples and imperial shrines, only spirit tablets were officially allowed on the altar. This rule was circumvented by some city god temples that honour Guan Gong, and did not apply to popular places of worship where images of gods, buddhas and immortals often stood side by side.

WHALEN LAI

Ikhwan al-Safa'

The name Ikhwan al-Safa' has been translated as either 'Brethren of Sincerity' or 'Brethren of Purity', and refers to a group of Islamic philosophers who lived in the tenth or eleventh century CE in Basra. There is no certainty about who they were exactly and what sort of Muslims they were, but their work, which consists of fifty-two epistles, is encyclopedic in nature, dealing with mathematics, theology, magic and science as well as philosophy. It is a real product of syncretism, a mixture of Platonic, Aristotelian, Neoplatonic and Islamic ideas, and has ever since played an important role in Islamic culture. The book represents reality as consisting of a hierarchy of levels of being, ranging from the Creator, the Intellect, the Soul, Prime Matter, Nature, the Absolute Body, the Sphere, the Four Elements and the Beings of our world. As against the normal Neoplatonic view, matter is viewed positively, not as a force for limitation and evil. Our understanding of God is mediated through the different levels of being as he descends towards us, and is necessarily limited.

The point of the arguments of the epistles is to save their participants, to escape the claims of matter and join the 'ship of salvation' (an expression they use) through the practice of asceticism, cooperation and virtue. What is particularly interesting in their approach is their toleration of alternative systems of thought, many of which they tried to incorporate in their compendium of wisdom. Their work is representative of an important tradition in Islamic philosophy, the *adab* tradition, of presenting summaries of the thoughts and practices of a long line of great thinkers, and then discussing what relevance their ideas have to contemporary conditions.

Further reading

Netton, I. (1991) *Muslim Neoplatonists: An Introduction to the Thought of the Brethren of Sincerity (Ikhwan al-Safa')*, Edinburgh: Edinburgh University Press.

OLIVER LEAMAN

illuminationist philosophy

Illuminationist philosophy is a form of Islamic philosophy whose name comes from *ishraq*, which means 'rising (of the sun)' and which is also linked to the Arabic for 'east'. It is often contrasted with Peripatetic thought and the importance which the latter gives to deductive reason, and also with *tasawwuf* or **Sufism**. Illuminationist thought uses a notion of immediate and intuitive knowledge, and is often identified with **Ibn Sina**'s oriental or eastern philosophy, which may not actually have existed, but which is taken to be his deeper teaching as opposed to his work within the Aristotelian or Peripatetic tradition of philosophy. The trouble with *mashsha'i* (Peripatetic) thought from the *ishraqi* perspective is that it is too limited in its perception of what counts as knowledge, and also what counts as reasoning.

The real creator of illuminationism is **al-Suhrawardi**, a Persian thinker from the twelfth century CE. In his extensive work, he sets out to replace Peripatetic philosophy with an entirely new form of logic and ontology. He rejects the Aristotelian account of definition which is in terms of genus and differentia since he argues that it is a process of explaining something in terms of something else which is less well known than itself. The project of starting the whole process of scientific investigation with a definition, and working from there to develop more and more conclusions is essentially flawed, according to al-Suhrawardi, since the starting point is no more certain than the conclusion. If we really could know the definition of a proposition then we should not need to carry out the reasoning process, which in fact reveals some of the aspects of the definition. When we set on such a form of reasoning we are assuming that we understand the notion of definition, whereas in fact we do not have this sort of information.

Al-Suhrawardi also criticizes the list of categories defended by the Peripatetics, claiming that they can be reduced to five and still encompass the same conceptual range. The main epistemological notion is that of knowledge by presence (*al-'ilm al-huduri*) which is used to describe a form of knowledge which has such an immediate relationship to the truth that it supersedes propositional knowledge, and is far more perfect than it. It is knowledge about which one cannot be mistaken, and the light of our self brings to our awareness important aspects of the truth. This idea of light is used to replace the traditional philosophical vocabulary of Islamic philosophy. Light flows through the universe and brings to existence and awareness different levels of being, and the differences between distinct things lies in their degrees of luminosity, not in their essences. Some thinkers within the tradition identified God with the Light of Lights, the light from which all subsequent light emerges and which does not itself receive light, and which is completely one.

It may look as though this philosophy comes close to mysticism, but it is worth pointing out that a good deal of illuminationist philosophy deals with technical and analytical aspects of philosophy. In many ways, *ishraqi* philosophy lies between *mash-sha'i* thought and Sufism. It uses many of the same analytical methods as the former, albeit it defends the idea of a different form of logic. It does, it is true, replace the language of subject and object in terms of light and the gradations of light, but once the rules of that system are understood there is nothing especially mysterious about the process and its implications. Even the idea of knowledge by presence is defended in a perfectly rational manner, and there are good reasons for thinking that there are ways of knowing which are more immediate and certain than our propositional knowledge, i.e. knowledge which is about facts that are separate from us. On the other hand, there are mystical features of illuminationism, the very notion of light has itself a certain religious flavour, and the way in which spirituality flows through the universe as light passes over different levels of reality clearly has a link with much mystical language. This form of philosophy has been very popular in the Persian-speaking world, which has been the area in which Islamic philosophy has been most enthusiastically and consistently pursued, and it has developed in complex and contrasting ways to represent different approaches to the interpretation of its key ideas and concepts.

See also: imaginal realm

Further reading

Nasr, S. (1996) *The Islamic Intellectual Tradition in Persia*, ed. M. Amin Razavi, Richmond: Curzon.

OLIVER LEAMAN

imaginal realm

The notion of the imaginal world is largely a product of the thought of **Ibn al-'Arabi** and **al-Suhrawardi**. This world is there to connect the lower world, of our world of generation and corruption, with the higher levels of reality, where the perfect and pure ideas exist. What need is there to have such an ontological realm between the ordinary ideas of our world and the more abstract ideas of the world of ideas? After all, as I progressively refine my ideas, a stage is reached where I no longer need to make those ideas concrete. The point of talking about an imaginal realm is to note that there is a stage in human thought during which we play about with ideas in ways which are not entirely determined by our experiences, but also in ways which are not entirely unrelated to those experiences. We have private and personal experiences, and these often work their way into our more abstract speculations, so that, for example, if I think about the nature of love I may think first about the people whom I love myself. I may come to understand that the notion of love has a wider extension than is experienced by me, and some people love things and people which I should find difficult to love. How can I understand what it is for them to love those objects? Imagination, or the imaginal realm, is what is important here, since I work from my experience of love to what I take their experience of love to be, and this is not something which can be carried out in a flash of recognition. One has to work slowly to change the way one's ideas feel to make sense of this new and unusual idea of love. The imaginal realm is necessary for this sort of task; we have to use our ability to imagine what it is like to love in this new situation. This comes out in al-Suhrawardi's description of the imaginal world as linking our microcosmic reality (what is important for us) and the macrocosmic nature of objective reality. The forms of the imaginal world are material in the sense that they use physical imagery, but also abstract in the sense that they point to what is higher than it. It is more real than our world, but not as real as the higher world. In the imaginal world we have imaginal bodies (*al-jism al-khayali*) which differ from our physical bodies in that they can roam more freely across a range of ideas and experiences than our ordinary day-by-day bodies. When we use our imagination we are not limited by our personal experiences or the range of our bodies, but may extend our thinking and our very being in a variety of different and novel directions.

This suggests that the sorts of very mysterious types of expression which mystics use can often be given a more down-to-earth meaning. This is even true of the *wahdat al-wujud* doctrine, which often seems to be a mystical claim about the unity of existence and the necessity to develop some very special ways of understanding that unity. We need to note here the view of creation as emanation, so powerful a result of **Ibn Sina**'s continuing influence over Islamic philosophy, and the effect it has on the notion of being. The major contrast between Ibn Sina and Aristotle lies in the responsibility for matter which for the latter does not apply to God. Aristotle's God is indeed the cause of the world, but not of the matter of the world, so that there is something in existence apart from God and his effects, namely, matter. There is also the matter of whether this ultimate source of existence can be described in terms of substance and accident, in terms, that is, of the categories, which for Ibn Sina is impossible. It is impossible because whatever brings about the form and matter of the universe cannot be defined in the same terms as the things within that universe. The source of being serves as a limiting concept, and we should not expect to be able to use the same concepts when describing such a concept as we can when describing what that concept makes possible. The only route we have to grasp the nature of the source of being is through contemplation of what it is for a perfect thing to bring about another thing. The only proper analogy for this is the way in which a thinking thing brings about its thoughts, but it has to be in a pure and autonomous way, not as a result of the ordinary ways of thinking to which

we are subjected by our life as members of the world of generation and corruption. Those thoughts have to flow from our self as aspects of our contemplation of ourself, a contemplation which succeeds in picking out the most important aspects of our being.

According to Ibn Sina, we cannot talk about the world and God, as though these were two different entities. Without God there is no world, and the world is merely a result of God's self-contemplation, so that in a sense there is no God without the world either. Everything is one in the sense that it all originates with God, and plays a part in the rational structure of a reality which could not be otherwise, according to Ibn Sina. This is a point which is emphasized by **Mulla Sadra**, who claims that God is equivalent to existence itself. What this means is that the answer to the problem of why anything exists lies in the existence of God and his role as the source of the existence of everything in the world. Ordinary language is always going to find it difficult to explain how this is to be explained, since ordinary language rests on a form of existence which it itself cannot explain. Hence the need for mysticism. It might even be said that the move from the notion of the *wajib al-wujud*, the Necessary Existent, to the doctrine of *wahdat al-wujud*, the unity of being, is really quite clear. It is not difficult to accept, therefore, the need for the use of various intermediaries which bring together the different levels of our experience and our thinking in order to represent more appropriately the nature of reality, and it is precisely this which is made possible by the ideas in the imaginal realm.

Further reading

Leaman, O. (1999) *A Brief Introduction to Islamic Philosophy*, Oxford: Polity.

OLIVER LEAMAN

imagination and creativity

Imagination was the rallying cry of the European Romantics; it was a revolt against the Age of Reason and against the drab mimesis of social reality. The Chinese counterpart to that movement was the literary Gong'an school in the late Ming dynasty. This movement had none of that European romantic individualism, no Faustian egotism, no claim by elitist artists to a second creation of reality after God, but there was a comparable dissatisfaction with the drab imitation of reality. In revolt against reason, there was an idealization of emotion and a passionate escape into fantasy. The Chinese catchword here is not 'imagination' (the Chinese word for 'imagination' is 'recalling a semblance'; it does not suggest 'to project or create'), but rather 'illusion'. The rationale is that strong emotions create these illusory transformations and help open up a new vista of reality that defies reason. These new writers signed their names to their novels and plays they wrote. They did not apologize; they knew they were writing fiction. Ghost stories dominate the collection from the Leisure Studio. Dreams run through four famous Dream Plays, dramas including a goddess or a dream lover. *Record of Strange Happenings Compiled at the Leisure Studio* is the best-known collection of Chinese ghost stories and other such marvels from around 1700.

The European Romantics came from a cultured elite who looked down on the common men in the industrial age. The Chinese romantics came from the left-wing of the Wang Yangming school. They sought out ties with the people and with popular literature. Philosophers like Li Zhi, seeking a new freedom of expression, looked to vernacular speech, to folk wisdom and folk songs, to common life experiences so as to create a broader-based culture. That search for a *vox populi* in the seventeenth century to head a national literary renaissance continued into the twentieth century when the revolt against Mandarin (the officials' form of expression) led to adopting a 'plain or unadorned speech'. That became the 'national speech', and the basis for a new colloquial literature under the Republic. It has been renamed the 'common(er) speech' by the Peoples Republic of China. (All vernacular speech turns out, of course, to be manufactured out of a local speech for the whole nation.)

'Creativity' carries a modern flavour that was not high on the list of values in any traditional society. Only a daring few in China ever titled their treatise, their dynasty or their reform 'new'. When the monk **Daosheng** proposed 'sudden enlight-

enment', it was called by others a 'new' thesis, implying that he was being unnecessarily and excessively clever. Newness was however valued by the Neo-Daoist circle, and that spirit passed on later to Chan, which made a virtue (and a necessity) of giving novel twists to the **koan** system. That also rubbed off on some late Ming aesthetics, who praised the unconventional in painting style.

But 'creativity' is also a recent value held aloft during the Romantic revolt against the Enlightenment. The Age of Reason had left men with an empirical reality, tried and true but drab and dull, and the Romantics held that only a flight of 'creative imagination' could redeem modern humanity lost in a world of things. When the European Enlightenment came East, a number of Eastern thinkers inherited that Romantic ethos and pitted a dynamic, Oriental creativity against a mechanical Western rationality. As long as that romantic claim does not translate into disinheriting the West from its share of creativity, it can serve as an entrée into mutual self-discovery. Much of the presentation of Chinese creativity focuses on its metaphysics of dynamic change and aesthetic sense of a self-unfolding natural landscape and mood.

Some modern Chinese thinkers seeking to modernize China have made much of the formula of 'daily renewal'. Many thinkers made much of the **Yijing**'s idea of 'life giving birth to life' as denoting creativity. But concerning renewal, there is one actual historic innovation on the part of the Neo-Confucians that was indeed forward-looking, and this was the adoption of *The Great Learning* and the *Doctrine of the Mean* as part of the Four Books (see **Classics and Books**). These works are in fact chapters in the *Book of Rites* and were selected by **Zhu Xi**, who urged the moral ruler to 'be like a father to his people'. By amending that into a homophonic call to 'renew the people', the Neo-Confucians looked forward to creating a 'new man' for a 'new age'. That use of tradition for new ends set the precedent for similar calls to become a 'new citizen' in the new Republic in this century.

See also: orientalism

Further reading

Chan Wing-tsit (1963) *A Source Book of Chinese*

Philosophy, Princeton, NJ: Princeton University Press, 751–62.

Chang Chung-yuan (1963) *Creativity and Taoism*, New York: Julian Press.

Chaves, J. (1985) 'The Expression of the Self in the Kung-an School: Non-Romantic Individualism', in R. Hegel and R. Hessney (eds), *Expressions of Self in Chinese Literature*, New York: Columbia University, 123–50.

Fang, T. (1980) *Creativity in Man and Nature*, Taipei: Linking Publishing.

Frye, N. (1957) *Anatomy of Criticism: Four Essays*, Princeton, NJ: Princeton University Press.

Fung Yu-leng (1952–3) *A History of Chinese Philosophy*, 2 vols, Princeton, NJ: Princeton University Press.

Li Wei-yee (1993) *Enchantment and Disenchantment*, Princeton, NJ: Princeton University Press.

Mair, V. (1989) *T'ang Transformation Texts*, Cambridge, MA: Harvard University Press.

Zeitlin, J. (1993) *Historian of the Strange: Pu Songling and the Classical Chinese Tale*, Stanford, CA: Stanford University Press.

WHALEN LAI

immortality in Chinese philosophy

The search for immortality in China is associated generally with the Daoist tradition. 'Long life', 'not ageing' and 'non-death' describe that legitimate and possible goal in the writings of the Warring States period. Han Daoists worked to prolong life (*ming*); Song Daoists worked at realizing one's true nature (*xing*). But commentators on Daoism question that neat shift from 'material' longevity to 'spiritual' enlightenment.

Immortality more broadly considered may be divided into three major types: genetic, social and personal. The last type can be divided into the cosmic and the acosmic. Some very rough order may be assumed. Genetic immortality is the most archaic; it is living through one's descendants. In patriarchal society, this means passing down physically the male seed and socially the surname. In China, it goes with the rules of inheritance and the obligation to see to the upkeep of the ancestral temple and the feeding of the dead. Concern for the family line may overshadow concern for personal survival. But as city states rose, commitment to civic mores fostered the ideal of social immortality. Individuals die, but their achievement may live on through social memory and public commemoration. The dictum is that the good should outlive the person but that the evil men did should be 'interred with their bones'. (Mark Anthony reversed that dictum in Shakespeare's *Julius Caesar* for political ends.) The truly evil deserve no burial. Their remains should be scattered so that they would find no eternal rest. The *Book of Rites* supports this.

A gentleman should 'establish virtue, speech and deed'. 'Speech' refers to a teaching that may be vindicated in time. Socrates, accused of corrupting the young (a bad deed) and sentenced to death (an ill repute), refused the option of going into exile because this lover of the city Athens trusted that in time the truth of his teaching would be vindicated. He would then be recalled with honour. **Confucius**, who was unheeded in his life, won that public acclaim; he became the 'paradigmatic teacher for ten thousand generations'.

Plato, seeing the injustice Athens did to Socrates, constructed a perfect Republic ruled by a philosopher king. He also put in Socrates' mouth a teaching about the immortality of the soul. In China, **Mencius**, who came after Confucius, did not follow this strategy. Speculations on an immortal soul came from Daoist circles. **Laozi** hinted that man by imitating nature can last as long as Heaven and Earth. Religious Daoists traditionally trace their idea of personal survival to Laozi and to **Zhuangzi**, who recognized only an impersonal union with nature. The word *shen*, for spirit, meant among the classical thinkers the spirited part of the mind, but not yet an independent entity that can survive death. The theory and practice of personal immortality flourished in the Han. To the extent that Daoists then knew only the limit of **Heaven**, the term 'acosmic' denoting a transcending of that limit is best reserved for the **nirvana**-seeking Buddhists.

Further reading

Yu Ying-shih (1965) 'Life and Thought in the Mind

of Han China', *Harvard Journal of Asian Studies* 25: 80–122.

WHALEN LAI

IMMORTALS *see* afterlife, Chinese: mortals

Indian philosophy

The philosophy of the Indian subcontinent has played the leading role in the rest of the Asian world. Like much philosophy, it has its base in religion, in this case with the *Rig Veda*, an ancient hymn possibly as old as 1000 BCE, which defined the notion of the Brahmins, the priestly class. With the development of Vedic texts some of the characteristic ideas of Hinduism, such as reincarnation and the cycle of birth and rebirth, appeared. The *Upanishads*, which followed, began to raise issues about the meaning of religious ritual, and also created certain themes such as that of the *brahman* or sacred which is present in everything, the idea of an eternal self or *atman* both within us and within the universe as a whole, and the idea of liberation from the cycle of birth and rebirth.

The earliest philosophical Hindu school is that of Samkhya and analyses reality in terms of eternal souls which are spiritual (*purusha*) and a material (*prakriti*) world. The souls are constantly reborn unless they achieve liberation, which allows them to exit from the life of generation and corruption. It is worth escaping this life, since its main characteristics are suffering, and to escape this miserable cycle we need to achieve knowledge of the real nature of the world. This real knowledge is made up of an understanding of the distinctions which exist between soul and nature. The theory, like much Indian philosophy, is strongly dualistic, since there are two entirely different kinds of thing in existence, many souls and one nature. This school came later to be linked with Yoga, on the basis that the sort of understanding of the nature of reality could be best attained through the sorts of practices involved in yoga. That is, if we can access spirituality through physical training, we can bridge the gap between the radically different kinds of thing in existence. The other orthodox schools are the Mimamsa-Vedanta, which bases itself on the interpretation of the sacred texts, and the Nyaya-Vaisheshika, which concentrates on logic and adopts an atomistic view of reality. There are also a large number of what have come to be called unorthodox schools, largely those of Buddhism, Jainism and materialism. By 'orthodox' is meant basing one's thought on the authority of the Vedas, something which all the schools associated with Hinduism do.

One of the unorthodox schools is Jainism, which like Buddhism (but also like Sankhya) rejects the notion of God. This school thinks in terms of many souls dying and being reborn; these are not spiritual, but are things which enter the bodies they inhabit. The way to liberation is through an extreme form of asceticism and preventing harm, *ahimsa*. It had rather unusual views on the nature of different points of view, according to which there is no absolute perspective from which truth may be seen.

Another unorthodox school was the Charvaka or materialists, about whom very little is known except through reports from its enemies, which probably are not entirely reliable. Its main problem was analysing phenomena in materialist terms which do not seem to be material, such as consciousness, and it used the analogy of putting together material things and getting something entirely different to account for consciousness. By far the most significant of the unorthodox approaches is Buddhism, traditionally originated with the Buddha, who was born in Nepal in the sixth century BCE. His pursuit of the ultimate truth which would end suffering resulted in the doctrine that the source of suffering is craving, identified with suffering (*duhkha* [Sanskrit]/*dukkha* [Pali]), which may be brought to an end in *nirvana* which results in the ending of the cycle of birth and rebirth. A particularly important and perplexing doctrine was that there is no essential or eternal soul, which went right against the Sankhya theory, and which of course goes against our intuitions of a personality which lies within us in some way.. Buddhist thought became enormously creative, and split up into many different schools. The two main divisions are the Theravada, which predominates today in Sri Lanka and Southeast Asia, and the Mahayana, which spread throughout the rest of Asia. The Theravada were called Hinayana by their detractors, a term which means the Lesser Vehicle, since Hinayana emphasized the importance of the individual seeking enlightenment and seemed to be oriented very much towards the community of monks (*sangha*), which their opponents interpreted as a selfish and limited objective. The Mahayana, or Greater Vehicle, saw the enlightenment of everything sentient as the only appropriate aim. They came to discuss at considerable length the sorts of ways in which this could be brought about, spending a lot of time on the analysis of how enlightenment is feasible for anyone, and what could bring it about. From the tenth century Buddhism fell into decline in North India, when the Muslim invasions became significant, while the Theravada version continued to flourish in Sri Lanka. Buddhist philosophy moved to other parts of the Eastern world, and indeed latterly to the West, while the other schools of thought have continued to flourish in India and to be incorporated in more and more elaborate systems and theories.

Further reading

Conze, E. (1962) *Buddhist Thought in India*, London: Allen & Unwin.

Gonda, J. (1970) *Visnuism and Sivaism*, London: Athlone Press.

Hiriyanna, M. (1932) *Outline of Indian Philosophy*, London: Allen & Unwin.

Radhakrishnan, S. (1966) *Indian Philosophy*, London: George, Allen & Unwin.

OLIVER LEAMAN

INFERNO *see* afterlife, Chinese: inferno

innate apprehensions

The basic idea of apprehension or grasping, especially at the notion of self, is explicit in the Indian Buddhist philosophical literature. However, it is perhaps in Tibetan thought that we find systematically developed views about the various levels of apprehension including those which are said to be innate. Again it is in **Tsongkhapa**'s

works that we find a clear articulation of the distinction between those apprehensions that are 'acquired' or 'imputed' and those that are 'innate' or 'inborn'. The former refers to all reason-based thinking including all our philosophical views. They are 'imputed' in that these thoughts occur in us not as human beings, but rather as a result of some form of thinking or conditioning. This is especially true of all the metaphysical views that we may hold, for we hold these because of our philosophical, political or religious affiliations. However, Tsongkhapa sees all of these metaphysical views as ultimately aimed at affirming or justifying something that we naturally grasp at a deep level of our existence. According to Tsongkhapa, there is something in the very mechanism of our perception that makes us instinctually and naturally apprehend some kind of enduring nature both to our own existence and to the world. It is almost as if we are deeply conditioned to view the world in terms of independently existing entities possessing real beings. He argues that this 'positing' of an enduring objectivity takes place both at the level of perception and apprehension. And it is this inborn apprehension, which propels the whole complex and often confusing nexus of emotional entanglement. By 'believing' that the objects we desire possess a total quality of goodness, and those we abhor as possessing a total quality of badness, we tend to swing from one extreme emotional reaction to another. Thus we see that the concept of innate apprehensions is both a psychological theory and a philosophy of mind.

For example, in the case of a belief in the self, we can see varying levels of apprehensions. The paradigmatic self or the **atman** of the non-Buddhist ancient Indian schools is characterized as eternal, unitary, and autonomous. Yet the notion of self that is a composite of these characteristics is clearly a metaphysical postulate arrived at only through a process of thinking. Similarly there would be another level of a belief in the self, which although rejecting the above characterization continues to apprehend it as enjoying some kind of status as the controller of physical and mental constituents of the person. In this conception, there is still a residual belief in some kind of separateness between the self and the mind–body complex, which constitutes the existence of the person. This is still a conscious, acquired sense of self. Still further we can detect a deeper level of a sense of self, which may be largely unarticulated and yet which arises on the basis of an underlying belief in some kind of enduring entity that possesses a real nature of its own. This is what Tsongkhapa means by 'innate apprehension' of self.

The notion of innate apprehension is intimately connected to another critical aspect of Tsongkhapa's thought, namely the doctrine of 'identifying the object of negation'. Tsongkhapa argues that at the root of all our delusion and afflictions lies an innate apprehension of the intrinsic existence of the self and the world. It is therefore not adequate simply to reject only the metaphysical postulate of the others, what is more important is to eliminate one's own innate apprehensions. This, Tsongkhapa argues, can only be done if one has attained the highest understanding of the doctrine of **emptiness**, which according to Tsongkhapa is the absolute negation of intrinsic existence. All Madhyamaka analysis, including many of its complex arguments, must serve as a form of a 'self-critique'. The real object of critique is not external; rather it is one's innate apprehensions and their contents. Through chipping away at postulates by applying the Madhyamaka reasoning, one rejects all conceivable possibilities of expressing this belief in intrinsic being. The Madhyamaka critique of other schools is therefore only an aid along the path towards this ultimate goal.

Further reading

Hopkins, J. (1983) *Meditation on Emptiness*, II, London: Wisdom Publications, 175–96.

THUPTEN JINPA

Inner Classic of the Yellow Emperor

The *Inner Classic of the Yellow Emperor* is a major Han medical text that is crucial for understanding Chinese medicine. It also synthesized much of the Chinese conception of man and the cosmos. Among other things, in keeping with the medical assumption of a healthy psychosomatic whole, it

does not observe a body/mind divide. The mind, though housed in the heart, moves around the other four organs under its control (spleen, lung, kidney, liver), flows with the blood and the vital force and animates the bodily senses, thereby bridging the inner and the outer. A radiant mind has a radiant countenance. An inattentive mind causes people to have a dazed look, hearing but not registering. A fully alert mind ensures a keen edge to all the senses. A mind withdrawn into non-action or being unperturbed is naturally illuminating; the more it is vacuous within, the more penetrating without. This soul (mind) can be drawn out the body by an object; this causes temporary soul-loss. If the soul does not return, some other spirit might take over the non-animate body. A placement by Earth and by Heaven would assign the *yin* to 'essence' and the *yang* to 'spirit' (the two souls of *po* and *hun*) and locate these in two internal organs. Nascent intention (seminal mental thought) goes to the mind but the will (what begins to move ahead into action) adds physical momentum.

See also: afterlife in Chinese thought

Further reading

Lee, F. (1980) *The 'Silent Art' of Ancient China: Historical Analysis of the Intellectual and Philosophical Influences in the Earliest Medical Corpus–Ling Shu Ching*, Taipei: Linking Publishing.

Lu, H. (1978) *A Complete Translation of the Yellow Emperor's Classic of Internal Medicine and the Difficult Classic*, Vancouver: Academy of Chinese Heritage.

Sivin, N. (1995) *Medicine, Philosophy and Religion in Ancient China*, Aldershot: Variorum.

WHALEN LAI

inner peace

A psychology of inner peace presumes an inner self as microcosm feeling at home in the world as macrocosm, even if the actual world might be anything but peaceful. We may exclude such a sense of 'inner peace' from **Confucius** and **Mozi** to the extent that both operated largely on a part/ whole psychology (where the self is part in a larger whole) and not on the basis of a microcosmic–macrocosmic identity. Confucius lived a life of fear and trembling, as if walking on thin ice, and was ever more vigilant when alone. Mozi was too indignant about the injustice of the real world to retreat into some 'inner peace' and loss of self. The Egoist Yang Zhu was too much of a self-preservationist to relax his hold on his precious self. Song Xing's project to disentangle himself from the world is for the purpose of minimizing desires. Hui Shi realized finally a communion with all things, but there is little psychic depth in his logical paradoxes. Only with **Mencius** and **Zhuangzi** do we sense an 'inner peace' as they 'let the mind roam free' or 'wash it clean at the gate of mystery'. Among the Neo-Confucians, the *Western Inscription* of Zhang Zai captures that surety of inner peace well.

Further reading

Chang, C. (1957) *The Development of Neo-Confucian Thought*, New York: Bookman Associates.

WHALEN LAI

Inoue Tetsujiro

b. 1855; d. 1944

Philosopher

Inoue was born in Dazaifu, a small city on Kyushu island, and in his childhood attended a Confucian school. In 1871, he went to Nagasaki to study English and Western sciences. From 1875, he continued his studies in Tokyo where, two years later, he became one of the first students of philosophy at the newly founded Tokyo University. He graduated in 1880. From 1884 until 1890 Inoue studied and worked in Germany. After his return, he was appointed professor of philosophy at his old university. After a long and distinguished career, Inoue died in Tokyo.

Though he had stayed and studied in Europe for many years, Inoue remained critical of many features of Western culture, and his most important philosophical works are on Japanese Confucianism. In his life and thought, three periods can be distinguished. In his first period, Inoue seemed rather open to Western philosophy and 'civilisation and enlightenment', for instance contributing to the *Tetsugaku jii* (Philosophical Dictionary), published in 1881. However, beginning with his *Chokugo engi (Commentary on the Imperial Edict on Education)* of 1891, his political and ethical views became more and more traditionalist and conservative. Also, from about 1902 until 1908, his scholarly interest focused on Japanese Confucianism. Then he turned to Shinto studies of an ideological rather than philosophical character, and contributed to the development of kokutai ideology (see **kokutai ideology since Meiji times**). Finally, by the end of the 1930s, Inoue became an ultra-nationalist. Thus, Inoue's career almost perfectly reflects Japanese intellectual and socio-political history from Meiji times through to the end of the Second World War, and in this respect is both instructive and irritating. Inoue was a highly capable intellectual, well-educated and versed in both Western and Sino-Japanese philosophy, and also able – and through the first half of his life also inclined – to argue rationally and systematically. Further, for many years he sympathized with the classic Confucian idea of humanity. Hence, although **Fukuzawa** (1834–1901) called him a *goyo gakusha*, a government-serving and unprincipled scholar, it is difficult to believe that he turned Shintoist and ultra-nationalist simply because he was an opportunist.

As indicated, Inoue's most important philosophical works are his studies of Japanese Confucianism. They are no mere histories and anthologies but also express Inoue's own respective philosophical position. In 1900, he published *Nihon Yomeigakuha no tetsugaku* (The Philosophy of the School of Wang Yang Ming in Japan). Two years later, *Nihon kogakuha no tetsugaku* (The Philosophy of the School of Ancient Learning in Japan) appeared. 'Ancient Learning' refers to classic Confucianism, particularly the teachings of **Confucius** (551–479 BCE), **Mencius** (372?–289? BCE) and **Xunzi** (313?–238? BCE). In 1905, Inoue brought out the last book of his trilogy, *Nippon Shushigakuha no tetsugaku* (The Philosophy of the School of Zhu Xi in Japan). From 1901 until 1903, he published *Nihon rinri ihen* (Anthology of Japanese Ethics), a monumental collection of seventy-seven Confucian works from the Tokugawa period (1600–1868). Inoue concluded his monographs on Confucianism with *Jukyo* (Confucianism) published in 1908.

Generally speaking, during these years Inoue seems to have favoured a universal humanism based on, or in accordance with, the classic Confucian concept of humanity (*ren*, in Japanese, *jin*). In this connection, he argued that Confucianism 'transcends all religions', is free of superstition, and because of its rationality 'moves in perfect harmony with the principles of modern science'. To support his conviction that a convergence of Western and Sino-Japanese ethics was possible, he also drew parallels between Japanese and European philosophers, for example, between the ideas of Ito Jinsai (1627–1705) and Kant (1724–1804), Ogyu Sorai (1666–1728) and Thomas Hobbes (1588–1679).

Besides the works mentioned, Inoue published numerous other writings, including studies on Buddhism, Shintoism and Bushido. Since most of his later works, however, are actually ideological tracts about the alleged uniqueness and superiority of Japanese morality (*kokumin dotoku*), Japanese *kokutai* and 'Japanese spirit' (*Nihon seishin*), they are of less philosophical relevance.

See also: humaneness; Kokugaku; kokutai ideology since Meiji times; Meiroku zasshi; philosophical dictionaries and Japanese philosophy

Further reading

Dening, W. (1908) 'Confucian Philosophy in Japan: Reviews of Dr. Inoue Tetsujiro's Three Volumes on this Philosophy', *Transactions of the Asiatic Society of Japan* 36(2).

Inoue Tetsujiro (1897) *Kurze Übersicht über die Entwicklung der philosophischen Ideen in Japan*, trans. from French by A. Gramatzky, Berlin.

Nawrocki, J. (1998) *Inoue Tetsujiro (1855–1944) und die Ideologie des Götterlandes: Eine vergleichende Studie zur politischen Theologie des modernen Japan*, Hamburg: LIT (this book includes German translations from Inoue's writings on Japanese morality, Japanese spirit and on *kokutai*).

GREGOR PAUL

Iqbal, Muhammad

b. 1876; d. 1938

Philosopher and political theorist

One of the outstanding thinkers in modern times, Muhammad Iqbal was born in India. He continued the tradition in Islamic philosophy of trying to reconcile religion with modernity. Much of his work is actually poetry rather than philosophy, but there is no doubt that his contributions in the latter area are impressive and wide-ranging. Like **Mulla Sadra** and Henri Bergson, he was attracted to the idea of reality as fundamentally consisting of process, whereby the universe is in a process of constant change and alteration, with the implication that the individual has to continue making efforts in order to make progress, or even just to stand still. Iqbal even suggests that heaven is not a place of rest, but an environment in which the individual has to try to continue to perfect himself, just like the mortal world.

The individual self (*khudi*) exists within a theoretical and practical context, and has to decide on how it is going to develop, in which direction it is to go. Reality is seen as being neither entirely physical nor mental, but rather a continually creative form of activity. God himself represents the perfect form of activity, the sort of creativity which we should seek to emulate. Iqbal saw the implications of this to practical life as being that the Muslim should reject the idea of the existence of a permanent set of principles and rules which are completely unchanging. In fact, in the past Muslims were very open to science and technology, and Islam itself is a practical religion celebrating our understanding of the natural world, and also allowing considerable theological variety and debate. In recent times, however, Islam has become narrow and static, Iqbal argues, and what it requires is a revival which will succeed in aligning it appropriately in relation both to modern science and to traditional religious authority.

Iqbal is regarded as very much the theoretician behind the establishment of Pakistan as an Islamic state, although its actual implementation is unlikely to have been enthusiastically received by him. The point of an Islamic state is to reject both capitalism and communism and to distribute wealth fairly, while at the same time embodying religious principles in the structure of the state. One of the problems with a state which is based on nationality is that it contravenes the universality of the Islamic message, but that does not mean there should not be such a state. After all, for the time being it might well be better to have such a state than otherwise, as a stage on the route to the universal acceptance of the principles of Islam. What would distinguish an Islamic state from other kinds of polity is that the former would involve rules which accord with a general acceptance of the significance of God and the necessity to acknowledge his influence on the everyday events of the world.

See also: revival of Islam, theories of; space and time in Islamic philosophy

Further reading

Ahmad, A. (1967) *Islamic Modernism in India and Pakistan*, Oxford: Oxford University Press.

Iqbal, M. (1930) *The Reconstruction of Religious Thought in Islam*, Lahore: Ashraf.

Raschid, M. (1981) *Iqbal's Concept of God*, London: KPI Press.

OLIVER LEAMAN

ISHIDA BAIGUN *see* Shingaku

ISHRAQI *see* illuminationist philosophy

Islamic philosophy

Islamic philosophy grew out of the contact between Islam and Greek philosophy. The early rapid expansion of Islam brought it into a world which was strongly influenced by Greek culture in all its aspects, including philosophy. Some Muslims argued that Greek culture had nothing to contribute to the theoretical understanding of reality, and that Islam by itself is enough. Other Muslims were impressed by the technical and intellectual strengths of Greek thought and sought to incorporate them within Islamic culture itself. Initially the political authorities supported the latter view, and an extensive translation project was initiated,

which often went from Greek to Syriac and then to Arabic, and which brought into Arabic many of the current texts in the Neoplatonic curriculum then popular within the area. Many of the texts were of Aristotle's works, including those attributed to him but not really by him, and by his commentators within the Neoplatonic tradition. Plato was regarded as very much an earlier version of Aristotle and not really disagreeing with him on major issues.

It is important to stress the diversity of philosophical work which took place during the early years of Islamic philosophy. The Ikhwan al-Safa' (Brethren of Purity) produced an eclectic philosophy which combined personal spiritual liberation with philosophical perfection. Many writers came to combine philosophy with the literary arts, while others used philosophy to criticize religion (ibn ar-Rawandi and ibn Zakariyya' al-Razi). Most thinkers within Islamic philosophy had some commitment to sufism or mystical philosophy which is linked in rather complicated ways with their more analytical work. Although it is possible to distinguish between different schools of thought in Islamic philosophy, none of these schools is entirely exclusive and many thinkers straddle a number of ways of doing philosophy.

The Peripatetic (*mashsha'i*) tradition based itself on the Greek tradition in philosophy, and the main thinkers are al-Kindi, al-Farabi, Ibn Sina and the Andalusi (Iberian) school, whose most important member is Ibn Rushd. This whole way of doing philosophy, which on the whole was thoroughly based on Neoplatonic ideas, was criticized by al-Ghazali, who is often seen as the individual who brought this way of doing philosophy to an end. What made this sort of philosophy controversial was the way in which it describes a picture of reality which appears to give little role for the divine as ordinarily understood by religion. The Neoplatonic world is one in which one thing emerges from something else in a necessary and automatic way, and in which the structure of reality is linked with principles of rationality, not divine will. In addition, it tended to stress the significance of philosophy as a route to perfection, and to throw doubt on the customary understanding of the afterlife, which were hardly minor issues in Islam or any of what might be called the Abrahamic religions.

One of the unusual aspects of Islamic philosophy is its almost constant interest in mysticism or *tasawwuf*, sometimes in combination with Peripatetic thought and sometimes in opposition to it. Al-Ghazali did a great deal to make Sufism or mysticism respectable within the Islamic theological world, but like many sufis rejected Peripatetic philosophy as a feasible route to the truth. Despite his opposition to this sort of philosophy, he argued in favour of logic which he regarded as independent of philosophy and which came to be pursued within the Islamic intellectual world even where philosophy was rejected. The desire by many thinkers to combine analytical thought with mysticism led to a new and important way of doing philosophy, which came to be called illuminationist (*ishraqi*) philosophy. This replaces the principles of Aristotelian thought with a new metaphysics and logic based on the idea of light as the leading source of creation and knowledge. The *ishraqi* school was initiated by al-Suhrawardi and found its most fertile environment to be the Persian-speaking world and thinkers such as Mulla Sadra, Mir Damad and al-Sabzawari.

After the death of Ibn Rushd, Peripatetic (*mashsha'i*) philosophy fell under something of a cloud in the Islamic world until the nineteenth century, when it returned to participate in the debate about religion versus modernity. However, in the Middle Ages there was a considerable transmission of texts back to the non-Muslim world from which they had originally arrived, this time usually in the form of commentaries on Aristotle, who had become popular in Christian universities. Ibn Rushd himself came to be of particular importance as a commentator and the interpretation of his work as a radical critique of religion and defence of philosophy led to the creation of the movement known as **Averroism**, which came to be highly influential in both Christian and Jewish Europe. In the Islamic world the *ishraqi* school continued to be important in the Persian-speaking world, and in the Indian subcontinent, and mystical philosophy also continued to have many followers. Philosophical ideas came to influence contemporary political theory, providing a rationale for various fundamentalist critiques of the

modern secular state. Even *mashsha'i* thought played a part in the *Nahda*, the Islamic renaissance movement, which sought to bring about a genuine reconciliation between traditional Islamic culture and Western notions of modernity.

Further reading

Leaman, O. (1985) *An Introduction to Medieval Islamic Philosophy*, Cambridge: Cambridge University Press.
—— (1999) *A Brief Introduction to Islamic Philosophy*, Oxford: Polity.
Nasr, S.H. and Leaman, O. (eds) (1996) *A History of Islamic Philosophy*, London: Routledge.

OLIVER LEAMAN

Islamic science, distinctiveness of

There has been a tendency to contrast religion with science, in that the former is based on **faith** and consists of eternal truths, while the latter is achieved through experimentation and constantly changes. It is not surprising that the form of Islamic philosophy called ***falsafa*** should accept the truths of natural science, since *falsafa* tends to see the world as a basically comprehensible place which is appropriately investigated using scientific methodology. But philosophy needs to do more than this; it should create space for the development of our links with the spiritual, to help us understand what our place in the world is. An appropriate religious philosophy should impact on the actual operation of science, in that it makes a difference to what is done. There should be principles of Islamic science which differ in some way from the principles of non-Islamic science, and we need to be able to specify what they are. It might be argued that, by contrast with the monolithic structure of Western science, Islamic science is pluralistic and inclusive of different approaches to scientific work. That is, Western science is positivistic and insists on complete freedom to do as it wishes. The Islamic approach, by contrast, argues that science can and should be regarded as just a different form of worship; it operates within a social and spiritual context, and outside of that context it has no value. Given the principle of *tawhid*, the unity of God, there is no scope for claiming that a part of our lives, even our scientific lives, can be separated from considerations of the divine nature of the universe. We are in the position of *khilafa*, trustees for the welfare of the world as a result of our divinely-provided role. We are obliged to treat both the world and ourselves as parts of divine creation, and we must treat these possible objects of enquiry with the respect that this understanding requires. Knowledge is then not a neutral attempt to grasp an external object, by contrast with the situation for positivist science, but is rather an aspect of worship and perhaps we should conclude that there are forms of knowledge and varieties of science which are not worth pursuing.

Knowledge is not worth pursuing if it is spiritually and physically destructive of both humanity and faith. Such knowledge is opposed to the preservation of social justice, and to the preservation of the natural world itself, and should be discouraged from an Islamic perspective. Only knowledge which is useful is worth having, and so there is no justification of knowledge for knowledge's sake. But it is very difficult to say precisely how this distinction actually results in practical differences. One of the problems with laying down rules about how science should be done is that it is not possible to predict before research takes place what the consequences of that research might be for humanity. To take an example, there is a lively debate in many Western countries about how far we are justified in carrying out research on genetically modified crops to provide food. Some would argue that there is no such justification, since the consequences of such an intervention on ecology can have enormous and unpredictable dangers. Others argue that the risks are well-known and negligible. What would be the response from the Islamic approach to science? Some Muslims might argue that it is humanity which is specifically mentioned with respect to *khilafa*, as God's representatives on earth, so everything else in the world is a lower form of creation and is there for our use. Provided the crops are safe for us, it would not matter what their effects were on other sorts of organisms. Others might extend the meaning of the Qur'an to suggest that all living things are just

as much a part of God's creation as we are, and we are not entitled to exploit them for our welfare. It is difficult to see how one could argue that a specifically Islamic attitude to science would be clearly different from the ordinary variety of Western approaches. Neither system of thought is monolithic, of course, and it should not be assumed that an Islamic science has to have any particular form at all.

Further reading

Butt, N. (1991) *Science and Muslim Societies*, London: Grey Seal.

Leaman, O. (1999) *A Brief Introduction to Islamic Philosophy*, Oxford: Polity.

OLIVER LEAMAN

Ismaili philosophy

Ismailism belongs to the Shi'a branch of Islam. Its philosophical tradition grew out of an attempt at discursive reflection on foundational Qur'anic principles, based on the understanding that the truths embodied in divine revelation were to be explicated by human reason, which was regarded as a gift of God. The appropriate use of the intellect in the service of philosophical inquiry was thus regarded as both necessary and legitimate.

Early Ismaili philosophical works date back to the Fatimid period (tenth/twelfth centuries CE). The tradition was continued in Yemen and India, and in Iran and Syria in Arabic and Persian. The key themes of the tradition are as follows.

Revelation

Among the tools of interpretation of Scripture that are associated particularly with Shi'i and Ismaili philosophy is that of *ta'wil*. In Ismaili writings the purpose and goal of *ta'wil* is to arrive at an 'original' understanding of Scripture by going beyond the formal, literal meaning of the text. Such an approach neither limits the total significance, nor rejects entirely the validity of a formal reading, but affirms that the ultimate significance and totality of meaning of any text can only be grasped by the application of *ta'wil*. It attests to the divine use of language in multiple ways, particularly as exemplified in the Qur'anic verses that employ symbolic and figurative language. Ultimately, this process engages both the intellect and the spirit, functioning in an integral manner to illuminate and disclose truths.

The unity of God (*tawhid*)

In his writings the Fatimid philosopher Hamid al-Din al-Kirmani (d. *c*.412 AH/1021 CE) juxtaposes a discussion of language to his exposition of the concept of God. He argues that languages grow out of words which are composed of letters which allow words to signify specific meanings. But words as well as languages are contingent and relative. Since God is not contingent but absolute, language, by its very nature, cannot appropriately define Him in a non-contingent way and take account of that which makes God different from all that is contingent. Language, however, is a beginning, because it is the foremost tool for signifying and representing the possibility of what God is. The fact of being human and possessed of an intellect compels one to speak of and inquire about the agent from whom existentiation (or origination) comes forth. Thus when one speaks of God, one does not necessarily describe Him as He is, but one has affirmed that He is indeed the originator of all that we employ to understand and describe His creation.

Abu Ya'qub al-Sijistani (d. *c*.361 AH /971 CE), an earlier writer, located a similar discussion in the context of the larger debate in the fourth/tenth century among Muslim theologians and philosophers regarding the relation between God's attributes and essence. He maintained that if indeed one were to affirm that God could not be defined in terms of attributes, then it must be complete negation, denying that God has any attributes essential or otherwise and therefore He is beyond existence and non-existence.

Such a concept raises the question of how one might worship such a God and also, if God indeed so transcends His creation, how is it that it comes into existence? The 'grammar of divinity' affirming distinction now leads in Ismaili thought to the 'ladder of meaning', by which transcendence manifested through creation becomes 'knowable'.

Manifesting transcendence: knowledge of the cosmos

The starting point of Ismaili cosmology is the doctrine of *ibda* (derived from Qur'an 2:117). In its verbal form it is taken to mean 'eternal existentiation' to explain the notion in the Qur'an of God's timeless command (*Kun*, 'Be!'). *Ibda* therefore connotes not a specific act of creation but the dialogical mode through which a relationship between God and His creation can be affirmed: it articulates the process of beginning and sets the stage for developing a philosophy of the manifestation of transcendence in creation.

Ismaili thought distinguishes between multiplicity and diversity in the initial process symbolized by the First Intellect. Though the forms within it can be said to be multiple, they do not yet possess this aspect, since no diversity or differentiation exists within the First Intellect. The analogy is the Qur'anic symbol of the 'Pen', and of the potential intellect, the 'Tablet', which represents form and matter, respectively.

Accordingly creation can be said to take place at several levels. Origination represents the initial level; one transcends history, the other creates it. The spiritual and material realms are not dichotomous, since in the Ismaili formulation matter and spirit are united under a higher genus and each realm possesses its own hierarchy. Though they require linguistic and rational categories for definition, they represent elements of a whole, and a true understanding of God must also take account of His creation.

Within this cosmology human history operates cyclically. According to this typological view, the epoch of the great Qur'anic prophets mirrors the cosmological paradigm, unfolding to recover the equilibrium and harmony inherent in the divine pattern of creation. Prophets and, after them, their appointed successors the Imams have as their collective goal the establishment of a just society. The essence of governing in such a society is not mere judicial order but rather an integrated vision of equilibrium where individuals mature intellectually and spiritually, through right action and knowledge.

As Nasir-i-Khusraw, the best known of the Ismaili writers in Persian, states in a passage paraphrased by Corbin (1983):

Time is eternity measured by the movements
of the heavens,
whose name is day, night, month, year.
Eternity is Time not
measured, having neither beginning nor end –
The cause of Time
is the Soul of the World; it is not in time, for
time is
in the horizon of the soul as its instrument, as
the duration
of the living mortal who is 'the shadow of the
soul', while
eternity is the duration of the living immortal,
that is to
say of the Intelligence and of the Soul.

This synthesis of time as cycle and time as arrow, to
borrow a phrase from the scientist Stephen Jay
Gould, lies at the heart of an Ismaili philosophy of
active engagement in the world.

Further reading

Alibhai, M. (1992) 'The Transformation of Spiritual Substance into Bodily Substance in Isma'ili Neoplatonism', in P. Morewedge (ed.), *Neoplatonism and Islamic Thought*, Albany, NY: State University of New York Press, 167–77.

Corbin, H. (1983) *Cyclical Time and Isma'ili Gnosis*, trans. R. Mannheim and J. Morris, London.

Daftary, F. (1990) *The Isma'ilis*, Cambridge: Cambridge University Press.

Khusraw, N. (1998) *Knowledge and Liberation: a Treatise on Philosophical Theology*, trans. F. Hunzai, London: I.B. Tauris.

Nanji, A. (1990) 'Transcendence and Distinction: Metaphoric Process in Ismaili Muslim Thought', in D. Burrell and B. McGinn (eds), *God and Creation*, Notre Dame, IN: University of Notre Dame Press, 304–15.

Tusi, Nasir al-Din (1998) *Contemplation and Action*, trans. and ed. S. Badakhchani, London: I.B. Tauris.

Walker, P. (1993) *Early Philosophical Shiism: the Ismaili Neoplatonism of Abu Ya'qub al-Sijistani*, Cambridge: Cambridge University Press.

AZIM NANJI

J

Jainism

Jainism is an Indian renunciatory religious movement whose goal is individual self-perfection, traditionally held to have been founded by Vardhamana Mahavira in the latter half of the sixth century BCE in Magadha which is now northern Bihar. Mahavira (the '*Jina*' or 'Victor') is considered to be the successor to twenty-three previous teachers or ford-makers (*tirthankara*) who enable souls to cross the river of transmigratory existence. The movement's early history is obscure, and some scholars maintain that it actually began about a century later than the tradition maintains and that its original environment is comparable to that of early Buddhism, with which it shares the characteristic of being a renunciatory reaction against the Vedic ritualism of the Brahmin priesthood. By 79 CE, when the movement split into the Digambaras ('sky-clad', or naked) and the Shvetambaras ('white-clad'), its main doctrinal tenets had been established. Umasvati's *Tattvarthasutra* (fourth century CE) is an authoritative compendium of Jaina metaphysics. Another important work is the sixth century Mallavadin's 'Twelve-spoked Wheel of Perspectives' (*Dvadasharanayachakra*). There are approximately three million Jains in modern India: the Digambaras are present in Maharashtra and Karnataka, and the Shvetambaras in Panjab, Rajasthan and Gujarat. From a socio-economic point of view, they are chiefly notable for their involvement in commercial activities.

The Jaina community (*sangha*) comprises monks and nuns, laymen and laywomen who uphold the three principles of right faith in Jaina teachings, right knowledge and right conduct as the means to release from the series of births through the elimination via ascesis of binding and identity-permeating **karma**, which is understood as an automatic cosmic force. Monks and nuns, who have no possessions beyond the most basic necessities, vow to abstain from harming living creatures (**ahimsa**), lying, theft, sexual malpractice and attachment to mundane things. Although Mahavira was a solitary, monks and nuns live in communities. During the four months of the rainy season, monastic communities stay in one area where they are visited by householders soliciting advice and instruction. For the rest of the year, their austere life is peripatetic and their days divided into periods of study, **meditation** and self-examination, mendicancy and sleep. Consistently with the emphasis on non-violent conduct, only vegetarian food prepared specially for the monk is acceptable and there is a stress on fasting which may extend to total abstinence from nourishment.

The laity take vows which include non-injury (*ahimsa*), truthfulness and honesty in commercial dealings and charity to the monastic order. They are committed to avoiding illegitimate means of acquiring wealth, to the avoidance of sexual impropriety and to the renunciation of attachment to material prosperity. In addition, they are obliged to cultivate proper states of mind, undertake pilgrimages to sacred sites, meditate, fast and confess their failings and request forgiveness.

The cosmos is conceptualized as having three layers. The comparatively minuscule 'middle world', parts of which are inhabited by humans and where the law of karmic moral retribution operates, is the only sphere in which it is possible to aspire to and approach final liberation from rebirth. Perfected souls (*siddhas*) inhabit a region of the upper world. Deities are found in all three worlds, but Jainism does not recognise an absolute divinity. Jaina saints (*tirthankaras*), the 'ford-makers' across the ocean of rebirth, are born only in the human domain.

Jaina ontology is realistic, recognizing the existence of a mind-independent sphere, and pluralistic in holding that more than one kind of thing exists. There are two basic types of reality (*dravya*); the animate (*jiva*) and the inanimate (*ajiva*). The first comprises an infinity of individual eternal spiritual monads (*jivas*) one of whose essential properties is reflexive consciousness which is potentially infinite in its fullest expansion. The second comprises matter (gross or spatial and subtle or non-spatial), space, time, motion and stability. *Jivas* are contingently embodied and subject to a series of existences in the here and now due to their previous ethically significant physical, mental and verbal actions. Actions performed out of ignorance of ultimate truth and under the sway of the passions of anger, pride, self-deception and greed attract subtle matter in the form of karmic influxes (*asrava* or *asava*) into the previous *jivas* and restrict their potentialities. Consciousness and the physical are thus regarded as actually interrelated. The purpose of religious praxis is that of purging the *jiva* of the subtle matter in the form of karmic influxes that are thought of as having entered it. If karmic influxes remain at death, the *jiva* is reincarnated in karmically appropriate circumstances. Depersonalized selves free from *karma* recover their intrinsic non-physical nature as infinite intelligence and inactive tranquillity and inhabit the upper world.

Amongst the forms of the inanimate, infinite time which guarantees continuity is inclusive of cycles of moral improvement and decline. The whole of human history belongs to a period of decline. Space is conceived as twofold: a sphere in which movement is possible and another where it is not. Entities are contained in the former, the latter being an infinite void. Eternally existent matter basically consists of an infinity of identical atoms but is susceptible of association with the properties of touch, flavour, smell and colour. The in themselves indistinguishable atoms combine in association with the four properties which function as agents of differentiation to form earth, water, fire and earth which in turn constitute the spatially and temporally continuous substances belonging to the macroscopic environment. Since all the atoms share the same nature, it is possible for any one thing in the physical sphere to change into any other. The Jains are hylozoists: every atom contains a soul. What may be seen as the movement's mental-physical holism in the empirical sphere is expressed in the traditional verse, 'He who knows one entity completely, comprehends everything. He who comprehends every entity, knows any one thing completely.'

While Jaina philosophers accept the category of properties (*guna*), the concepts of individual substance (*dravya*) and modal change of state (*paryaya*) are fundamental in their metaphysical system. Entities or individual substances are defined as substrata of the states of origination (*utpada*), endurance (*dhrauvya*) for at least an instant and cessation (*vyaya*). Substances are continuants subject to modal changes of state which include entry *ab initio* into particular modes of existence and becoming finally dissociated from them, participation in episodes with beginnings and endings as well as changes in properties. The *jivas* are intrinsically spiritual monads and therefore non-spatial, immaterial simple substances which become material, because embodied, spatial substances albeit only non-intrinsically or contingently.

A central feature of Jaina logic and epistemology is the relativistic and anti-dogmatic tenet that every assertion in the empirical sphere is perspectival and provisional (*syad-vada* or *anekanta-vada*). This has been seen by some as an intellectually eirenic reflex of the movement's ethical emphasis on non-violence. It may also be understood as a consequence of on the one hand the thesis that physical reality, in so far as it ultimately consists of indistinguishable atoms, is indeterminate (it being possible for any one thing in the physical sphere to change into any other) and, on the other hand, the metaphysic of substances and modal changes of state. It follows that, reality as humanly experienced resists definitive, absolute conceptions and descriptions. Jains hold that the complexity (*anekanta*) of past, present and future reality is such that the standpoint of finite observers can only attain partial points of view. If reality is indeterminate and originally unarticulated, any conceptual scheme, systematic theory or metaphysical account will be to an extent arbitrary. In other words, while there is an objective reality, it is indeterminate relative to human modes of understanding.

Jaina theorists hold that of an entity, state of affairs or proposition, we can say:

Maybe, it is.
Maybe, it is not.
Maybe, it is and is not.
Maybe, it is indeterminate/undecidable (*avakta-vya*).
Maybe, it is and is indeterminate/undecidable.
Maybe, it is not and is indeterminate/undecidable.
Maybe, it is and is not and is indeterminate/undecidable.

For example, of a piece of clay we may say that it currently exists as a pot, but the constituent atoms may possibly exist in another form at some other time and place. The assertion that it is a pot is true only provisionally and for the time being. In one sense the clay is a pot and in another it is not. Accordingly, there is a sense in which it is strictly speaking indescribable as a pot. The individual self is permanent qua spiritual substance but may be regarded as impermanent in relation to its current embodied condition in the here and now. Similar considerations apply when it is asked whether the *jiva* is embodied or not.

In their quest for self-perfection and dissociation from gross and karmic forms of matter (*moksha*, liberation), monks undertake a rigorous discipline whose goal is the obstruction (*samvara*) of karmic infiltration (*asrava*) by the control of mental, verbal and physical acts; by taking care not to harm living creatures; by the exercise of the virtues of patience, humility, straightforwardness, purity, honesty, restraint, austerity, renunciation, chastity and obedience to elders in the community; by reflections on the impermanence of phenomena, human helplessness, transmigration, individual solitude, the difference between soul and body, physical impurity, the actuality of karmic influxes, the means to blocking karmic influxes, ascetic means to rid

oneself of karmic subtle matter, individual responsibility for salvation, the rarity of enlightenment and the truth of the teaching of the *jinas*. The elimination (*nirjara*) of already accumulated *karma* begins once the acquisition of fresh *karma* has been prevented by the discipline which is augmented by meditation and desireless action. The released soul is a featureless, actionless and isolated centre of awareness and calm.

Further reading

Dundas, P. (1992) *The Jains*, London: Routledge.

Jacobi, H. (1964) *Jaina Sutras*, Sacred Books of the East XXII & XLV, Delhi: Motilal Banarsidass.

Jaini, P. (1979) *The Jaina Path of Purification*, Berkeley, CA: University of California.

Matilal, B. (1981) *The Central Philosophy of Jainism*, Ahmedabad: L.D. Institute.

Radhakrishnan, S. and Moore, C. (1957) *A Source Book in Indian Philosophy*, Princeton, NJ: Princeton University Press and Oxford University Press (contains translations of the *Tattvarthadhigama Sutra* and *Syadvadamanjari*).

Schubring, W. (1992) *The Doctrine of the Jainas*, Delhi: Motilal Banarsidass.

CHRIS BARTLEY

Japanese philosophy

Japan has largely emerged as a result of cultural influences from China and Korea, and in recent centuries from the West. Buddhism arrived in the sixth century CE, and there were developed Japanese versions of Chinese philosophical schools, in particular Confucianism and Daoism, and also the Tendai (from the Chinese Tiantai) and Shingon (*tantra*), and later the Pure Land movements, Nichiren Buddhism, and two varieties of Zen, Rinzai and Soto. Confucian thought was also often important, and then of course there was the native Shinto tradition, which often managed to blend with other philosophies but sometimes tried to maintain its purity by self-consciously distinguishing itself from theories of foreign origin. Daoist theories and ideas were also often popular. Shintoism represents a view of the way of the gods, and could be readily integrated with other religious and philosophical views, and in popular thought there has been a good deal of intermingling of Shinto deities with important figures in Buddhism.

An unusually muscular variety of Buddhism was created by Nichiren, who valued the *Lotus Sutra* over all other texts. Salvation is attainable by reciting this and through worshipping the transcendental beings which it describes. Nichiren defended the use of force to defend Buddhism, and saw nothing strange in persecuting or killing those with different views, especially in the extreme conditions in which he found himself. Another form of Buddhism which especially flourished in Japan is Zen Buddhism, which entered Japan from China at around the same time as the other schools. Rinzai Zen was constructed by Eisai, and it puts the emphasis on the individual pursuit of enlightenment, as opposed to looking for it from elsewhere. Rinzai Zen adhered to the principles of sudden enlightenment, believing that we are already enlightened and possessors of the buddha nature and just have to come to realize this, often as a result of a shock or puzzle which awakens us to what we are. Dogen takes the opposite view, that enlightenment can only come about through a gradual process, in particular through sitting meditation (*zazen*). His Soto Zen school argued that the buddha nature is in fact a changing thing which is difficult to pin down and acknowledge. Anyone in principle can access the buddha nature, but it is only in reality accessible through long and difficult meditative processes, hardly surprising given the importance of what is being acquired and its distinctiveness from our ordinary ways of thinking. Both schools have had a powerful impact on Japanese philosophy, and might be seen to have taken a specifically Japanese orientation with their emphasis on austerity, aesthetic representation and the capacity of religion to merge with the practical aspects of life. However, the clash between these two forms of Zen really only replicates the earlier controversy in China between the Northern and Southern schools of sudden versus gradual enlightenment, but there is no doubt that the development of these schools in Japan came to acquire a rather distinct flavour and force.

An interesting feature of Japanese philosophy is its ability to combine different theoretical positions taken from a variety of theoretical traditions and combine them into a creative whole. Political events often led to the fashionability of some forms of philosophy among the ruling circles, and there were occasional nationalistic attempts to emphasize Shintoism at the expense of the rest and of the very special role of Japan as a cultural site. The modern Kyoto school has developed an interest in Nietzsche and Heidegger for apparently entirely metaphysical reasons, which goes against the platitude that Japanese philosophy is primarily concerned with taking a practical attitude to the world. The thinkers in this school offered what they saw as distinctly Eastern perspectives on traditional Western philosophical topics by using Buddhist concepts, and at the same time they tried to gain a new understanding of those Buddhist concepts by examining them through the techniques of Western philosophy.

Further reading

Dilworth, D. and Viglielmo, V. (1998) *Sourcebook for Modern Japanese Philosophy: Selected Documents*, London: Greenwood Press.

Heine, S. (1989) *A Blade of Grass: Japanese Poetry and Aesthetics in Dogen Zen*, New York: Peter Lang.

Heisig, J. and Maraldo, J. (eds) (1994) *Rude Awakenings: Zen, the Kyoto School, and the Question of Nationalism*, Honolulu, HA: University of Hawaii Press.

Hoshino, K. (ed.) (1997) *Japanese and Western Bioethics*, Dordrecht: Kluwer.

Piovesana, G. (1997) *Recent Japanese Philosophical Thought 1862–1996: A Survey*, Richmond: Curzon.

Tsunoda, R., de Bary, W. and Keene, D. (1964) *Sources of Japanese Tradition*, New York: Columbia University Press.

OLIVER LEAMAN

Japanese philosophy, post-Meiji

Socio-political conditions

By the middle of the nineteenth century, Japan was troubled by serious problems. Most of these problems resulted from internal developments, but others were simply the result of Western imperialism. Tokugawa Nariaki (1800–60), the head of the Mito domain and father of the last ruler of the Tokugawa or Edo period (1600–1868), characterized the situation as 'disaster at home and affliction abroad'.

After a long period of comparable peace, many *samurai* had lost their calling and become impoverished, while a considerable number of merchants in Osaka and Edo had amassed great wealth. The gap between rich landowners and poor peasants had widened considerably. From 1833 through 1836, the Tempo famine left about one hundred thousand people dead. From then on peasants frequently protested against high taxes and rents, and there occurred several peasant uprisings every year. The oppressive character of the traditional system of feudal military rule, the shogunate, increased the widespread dissatisfaction of the poor and powerless. The hierarchy and inflexibility of the system often severely restricted political freedom and social advancement. Foreign pressure added to these problems. In the 1850s, the United States and several European governments forced Japan to open its country and to engage in foreign trade and diplomatic exchange. Western colonialism in Southeast Asia, especially the Opium War in China (1840–2), as well as the obvious military and technological superiority of the West, made it clear that the Western powers posed a serious threat.

Both the problems of domestic and of foreign politics asked for a change of the traditional system of government with the goals of such a change being quite clear, namely prosperity and inner peace on the one hand, and national sovereignty, i.e., Japan's equality with Western nations, on the other hand. Theoretically, there existed the following possibilities to achieve this: (1) to reform the shogunate, or (2) to abolish the shogunate. Both could be done by giving in to Western demands and adopting Western ways, or by trying to reform on the basis of Japanese tradition. A mixed approach was also possible. Quite naturally, all kinds of respective suggestions were made. Some reformist parties were openly anti-foreign, attributing even Japan's self-made problems to foreign influence. Among them were agitators who, relying on ancient – though fabricated – mythology and

believing in – equally fabricated – ideas of a golden past, held that the emperor should be re-established to power.. Thus 'Revere the emperor, and repel the barbarians' (*sonno joi*) became a popular slogan (advocated for instance by Nariaki and Mito scholars). Though initially it was not meant to imply that the shogunate must be abolished but rather referred to a united government of emperor and *shogun*, it soon became used by xenophobic royalists who simply wanted to replace the ruling system by a kind of Tennoism. Others, like Sakuma Shozan (1811–64), believed that Japan must adopt Western technology to be able to deal successfully with Western imperialism and 'to repel the barbarians', while in the realm of morals and arts Japan should stick to her own tradition. Slogans such as 'Enrich the nation and strengthen the military' (*fukoku kyohei*), 'Eastern ethics and Western technology' (*toyo no dotoku, seiyo no gakugei*) or 'Japanese spirit, Western civilisation' (*wakon yosai*) expressed their goals. Another group called for wholesale Westernization.

From about 1850, Japanese philosophy reflected all these views and convictions. In view of the existent socio-political problems, and in the context of the encounter with the West, the answers to the basic questions of culture, ethics and politics ranged from ethical universalism, especially concepts of universal human rights, through the extremes of cultural relativism, namely chauvinism on the one side, and blind admiration for what were regarded as Western values on the other. Even epistemology and philosophy of science were pursued from the perspective of how to improve the situation of the Japanese people and nation. Thus many Japanese scholars felt themselves compelled to investigate, and make explicit, the presuppositions of Western politics, science and technology, some arriving at the conclusion that ethics and morals are independent of scientific and technological development, while others concluded that they are not.

When, in 1868, the Meiji Restoration (*Meiji ishin*) took place, the shogunate and feudalism were abolished and imperial rule re-established. Hence the name 'restoration'. While the re-introduction of imperial rule was primarily a consequence of traditionalism and culturalism, the end of feudalism was due to an interest in modernization –

aiming, on the one side, at an appropriation of Western mathematics, natural science and technology, and, on the other, at a greater equality and liberty of the people.

The term 'Meiji Restoration' must be understood in a qualified sense. Except for the years from about 660 until 850, real power was almost never in the hands of the emperors. Also, from the very beginning of his rule, the Meiji monarch was never able to wield unrestricted power.

The notion of modern Japanese philosophy

Often, Japanese philosophy since Meiji times is called 'modern Japanese philosophy'. This is to say that from about 1868, Japanese philosophy developed under the influence of Western culture, and that it was because of this influence that Japanese philosophy became modern, that is, it significantly departed from its traditional modes. There are, however, earlier examples of what could be called modern philosophy. Yamagata Banto (1748–1821), in his *Yume no shiro* (Instead of Dreams), argued in favour of empirical science and methodical doubt, while strongly criticizing superstition and religious belief. Like a number of other scholars, he was influenced by *rangaku*, 'Dutch learning', i.e., especially theories of natural, technical, and medical sciences as they were developed in the West and transmitted to Japan via Dutch companies in Nagasaki. *Rangaku* in turn was a version of 'Western learning' (*yogaku*), the beginnings of which date back to the sixteenth century when the Jesuits arrived in Japan, and which played a continuous though restricted role throughout Tokugawa times (1600–1868). Also, 'modern' must not be equated with 'Westernized'. There exists a modern Buddhist philosophy which, except for its philological and historical methodology, is independent of Western ideas, for example, modern reflection on ancient Buddhist treatises (Sanskrit *shastra*, Japanese *ron*). The same applies to Confucianism. Furthermore, Western influence did not mean mere acceptance of Western ideas. It rather meant critical appropriation or critical rejection.

On the other hand, the word 'Japanese' in (modern) Japanese philosophy must not be understood as indicating philosophies that are fundamentally or even mysteriously different from Western philosophy. The word indicates only the origin and, in most cases, the language in which the respective texts are written, namely Japanese, though some of the works written during the Meiji period are in Chinese, and a considerable number of works written in the twentieth century are in Western languages. Further, though many philosophical ideas were expressed in literary, or 'aesthetic', language, this again does not point to a fundamental difference between philosophy in Japan and the West. In particular, it does not imply that Japanese philosophy is less logically consistent than Western philosophy.

Some scholars hold that, before the influence of Western philosophy, no 'Japanese philosophy' existed at all. They maintain that what is called modern Japanese philosophy or Japanese philosophy since Meiji times so radically differs from pre-Meiji modes of thought that it would be inappropriate to call these earlier ways of thinking 'philosophy'. They claim that the nineteenth century influence of Western philosophy meant such a break with earlier ways of theorizing that it would be wrong to speak of any philosophical continuity. Such cultural relativism presupposes very specific and uncommon notions of philosophy. Since Japanese scholars of pre-Meiji times also discussed questions like 'What can we know?' or 'What should we do?' in a rational, logical and critical manner, and often arrived at similar conclusions as Western and post-Meiji scholars, these narrow notions of philosophy have been disputed. Among others, the following features have been pointed out. From Nara times (710–94), through the beginning of the twentieth century, Buddhist scholars engaged in studies of *immyo*, namely, theories of reasons that included concepts of formal logical consistency and valid logical reasoning. Also, there are too many similarities between such theories as the moral teachings of the Japanese school of classic Confucianism and the syncretistic ethics of **Nishimura** Shigeki (1828–1902) and **Inoue** Tetsujiro (1855–1944) to justify classifying the former as non-philosophical. Significantly, Inoue himself spoke of the philosophy of Japanese Confucianism. Arima Sukemasa (1873–1931), in his *Nihon tetsugaku yoron* (A Short Survey of Japanese Philosophy) (1902), and other contemporary Japanese scholars also described certain

Japanese traditions of thought as philosophy. When Nakae Chomin (1847–1901) spoke of a lack of philosophy in traditional Japanese culture, he actually meant a lack of principled critical and non-opportunist thinking and behaviour. In this sense, his diagnosis hints at a specific feature of the beginnings of modern Japanese philosophy: it was much more socio-politically critical than most – though not all – traditional Japanese philosophy.

In sum, the designation 'modern Japanese philosophy' refers to a way of thought which shares significant features with Western as well as traditional Japanese philosophy. Its modernity is due to its interest in ideas of liberty, equality and human rights on the one hand, and science and technology on the other, and the respective influence of contemporary Western philosophy.

Further characteristics of Japanese philosophy since Meiji times

Like earlier Japanese philosophy, philosophy since Meiji times focuses on ethical, social, political, aesthetic and ontological questions, and the problem of cultural identity. Similarly, philosophy of religion has continued to play a considerable role. In the early years of Meiji, philosophy of science and technology were also regarded as vital, while neo-positivist and analytic philosophy became important only after the Second World War.

In particular, the problem of cultural identity has been a highly charged subject. Like many thinkers from Nara through Tokugawa times, not a few modern philosophers became preoccupied with the question of how to define and evaluate what could be regarded as the uniquely Japanese character. Whereas the former tried to distance themselves from Indian, Chinese or Korean cultures, the latter searched for fundamental differences between Japan and the West. **Watsuji Tetsuro** (1889–1960) maintained that Westerners are rational and individualistic, and endeavour to conquer nature, while the Japanese are aesthetically minded, socially oriented, and prefer to live in **harmony** with nature. Watsuji's ideas have become widely accepted even in academic circles. Kuki Shuzo (1888–1941) maintained that *iki*, a kind of elegant life style displayed by men of Tokugawa Tokyo, was also an expression of the spirit of Yamato, or Japanese culture and state as it existed in the fifth and sixth centuries. **Nishida Kitaro** (1870–1945) advanced notions of a uniquely Oriental nothingness (*mu*) and a uniquely Oriental logic (*toyo no ronri*). Nishida, who was a professor of philosophy at Kyoto University, is regarded as the founder of the Kyoto school. Adherents of this school, such as Tanabe Hajime (1885–1962) and Nishitani Keiji (1900–90), continued spreading notions of uniqueness similar to those of Nishida.

For obvious reasons, such concepts were especially popular during the times of political chauvinism, or ultra-nationalism, such as from 1890 until 1913 and 1930 to 1945. However, some comparative philosophers also emphasize cross-cultural commonalities. Thus Nakamura Hajime (1921–99) points out that there exist significant traditions of rational philosophy in both Western and Japanese cultures.

As to philosophical aesthetics, novelists advanced the most convincing concepts. Their views resemble both traditional and Western notions. For instance, regarding arts, Mori Ogai (1862–1922), Natsume Soseki (1867–1916) and Tanizaki Jun'ichiro (1886–1965) stressed autonomy, and ideas of creativity that differ from imitation but aim at gestalt-like naturalness, thus concurring with Murasaki Shikibu (about 1000), Chikamatsu Monzaemon (1653–1724) and Motoori Norinaga (1730–1801), as well as Aristotle and Kant. Western theories such as naturalism and socialism became influential too, though only for short times. Naturalism flourished between 1900 and 1910, and socialism in the 1920s. Zennists and followers of the Kyoto school have asserted that there exists a distinctively Eastern or Japanese aesthetics, the artistic reflections of which express the ontological truth of Eastern nothingness.

Periods

For a general overview, the history of modern Japanese philosophy can be divided into three periods or lines of thought.

1 During the first decade of the Meiji era, the influence of positivism, pragmatism and utilitarianism prevailed. Many Japanese scholars who advocated such philosophy had spent some time in

Europe or the United States. In his plea for scientific methods and modernization, **Nishi** Amane (1829–97), who for two years studied at Leiden University, employed Auguste Comte's (1798–1857) classification of religious, metaphysical and scientific civilizations, and John Stuart Mill's (1806–73) inductive logic and utilitarian ethics, recommending as highest goals health, knowledge and wealth. In his reconstruction of Japanese history from positivist and utilitarian views, he concluded that unscientific features of the Shushigaku such as its confusion of 'is' and 'ought', its praise for contemporary events and its feudal ethics hindered modernization. Another representative of this period, **Fukuzawa** Yukichi (1835–1901), who visited the United States and Europe and was also influenced by Mill, held similar views. He argued that without recognizing the equality of men, individual dignity and independence, and a division of power, Japan would not be able to develop into a modern and fully civilized nation. However, in his view, modernity did not necessarily imply democracy. Fukuzawa particularly championed independence, regarding it as the most important source of man's interest in public and national affairs. He recommended that, in the first place, education should be improved, for it is the best way to awake in man a sense of self-esteem and eventually independence. According to Fukuzawa, almost all Japanese of his time still showed a 'worm-like servility'.

Nishi coined many of the technical terms of modern Japanese philosophy, notably the term for philosophy, *tetsugaku*. Also, in his *Encyclopedia* (*Hyakugaku renkan*), he introduced the full range of Western philosophy and, like many others in this first period, translated Western philosophical works.

In addition to such translations, a considerable number of **philosophical dictionaries** and surveys of Western philosophy appeared. When in 1874 the Meirokusha, the Society of Meiji, was established and devoted itself to the promotion of 'enlightenment and civilization' (*bummei kaika*), Nishi and Fukuzawa became leading members.

2   However, their positivism and egalitarianism did not remain unquestioned. In the early Meiji period, the drive for modernization often led to surprising ideas, for example, that Japanese should marry Westerners and/or adopt Christianity – a religion which many Confucian and Buddhist philosophers regarded as utterly irrational. This in turn gave rise to a growing traditionalism that eventually even viewed introducing notions of human rights and egalitarianism as Westernization. A widespread confusion of 'Western' with 'egoistic', 'materialist' and 'disputative' contributed to such views. At the same time, the influence of German philosophy rose which, in its irrational features, could be employed to support chauvinism. In 1890, the Imperial Edict on Education (Kyoiku chokugo) was proclaimed. This edict advocated the traditional state-Confucian notions of unconditional loyalty (*chu*) and **filial piety** (*ko*) and – albeit mildly – Tennoism. Contrary to the humane and critical teachings of classic Confucianism, as put forward in the books *Lunyu* (Japanese, *Rongo*), **Mencius** (in Japanese, *Moshi*) and **Xunzi** (in Japanese, *Junshi*), state Confucianism was an ideology of the powerful. The Japanese Neo-Confucian Shushigaku was strongly influenced by state Confucianism.

The political and ideological development that was officially inaugurated by the Imperial Edict culminated in imperialism and ultra-nationalism. In two wars, from 1894–5 and 1904–5, Japan defeated China and Russia. It annexed Korea (1910) and occupied other parts of the Asian continent, establishing colonies. Finally, Japan started the Sino-Japanese War (1937–45) and entered the Second World War. In 1937, the ultra-nationalist ideology was summed up in a pamphlet entitled *Kokutai no hongi* (*The Fundamental Principles of National Essence*). Though itself no philosophical work, it delineated the frame within which practical philosophy, particularly ethics, had to remain, thus severely restricting the possibility for critical philosophy. Besides conservative German political philosophy and reactionary state Confucianism, **Kokugaku** mythology was employed for respective ideological indoctrination.

Thus Hozumi Yatsuka (1860–1912) used German statism to revive Kokugaku Tennoism by giving it a pseudo-scientific guise. Similarly, Inoue Tetsujiro (1855–1944), though aware of many shortcomings of Neo-Confucianism, argued that positivism and egalitarianism neglected spiritual morality and failed to adequately appreciate such traditional Japanese values as loyalty and filial piety. Like Yatsuka and Inoue, **Onishi** Hajime (1864–1900) also studied in Germany and rejected positivism. However, in contrast to them he did not succumb to irrational idealism and statism, but rather followed Kant's critical methods. Kato Hiroyuki (1836–1916), in his later works, argued against egalitarianism and the universal validity of human rights from evolutionist points of view. He relied on Charles Darwin (1809–82), Herbert Spencer (1820–1903) and the German evolutionist Ernst Haeckel (1834–1919).

The influence of German philosophy, which is the general characteristic of the second period, culminated in Nishida's appropriation of idealism and mysticism, and the reception of Martin Heidegger (1889–1976) by the Kyoto school. Nishida and his school deserve particular attention, if only because of their fame. Nishida's main interest was in religion and ontological truth. His 'Oriental nothingness' designates true reality, as conceived by a religious experience that follows 'Oriental logic'. This 'logic' must not be confused with formal logic. It simply means a way of reflecting that is determined by the (allegedly) concrete character of true reality itself, a method exemplified by traditional Buddhist discourses of nothingness, and, paradoxically, Western mysticism. Perhaps, Nishida's thought should be called religious philosophy rather than philosophy of religion. Like Watsuji, Tanabe and Nishitani studied with Heidegger. They employed Heidegger's methods to further reflect on Nishida's notions of religion, nothingness and logic. The influence of German philosophy was also due to Raphael von Koeber (1841–1923) who had arrived in Japan in 1893 and until 1914 taught German and philosophy at Tokyo (Imperial) University. Nishida, Tanabe, Kuki and Watsuji were among his students.

It was not only opposition against 'Westernization' and interest in preserving a unique Japanese identity that led Japanese scholars to criticize the positivism, utilitarianism and philosophy of human rights so characteristic of the first period. Some arrived at the conclusion that this philosophy failed to cope with the existing social and political problems, such as for instance the lasting poverty and powerlessness of most people, and imperialism. The most famous among them was **Kotoku**

Shusui (1871–1911), who advocated a kind of activist socialism and anarchism and was executed because of his political engagement. The very short period of early socialist and anarchist philosophy between about 1905 and 1911 may be considered a radical consequence of the first phase of rational humanism. Christian philosophers, because of their esteem for spiritual values, also opposed positivism. Onishi Hajime was also influenced by Christianity. Especially during the early years of Meiji, Christian missionaries succeeded in winning some outstanding personalities for their faith.

3   After the Second World War, Japanese scholars, benefiting from the newly guaranteed freedom of thought, sharply criticized Japanese imperialism and nationalism. Accordingly, they attacked schools and teachings that, like the Kyoto school, had advanced statist and culturalist doctrines supportive of the imperialist and totalitarian system. Though the Kyoto school has continued to exist, it no longer prevails. Probably it is more influential outside Japan than at home. Even before 1945, critically minded and socially oriented Japanese philosophers had attacked the theories of Nishida and the Kyoto school as irrational and dangerous. Among them was Kuwaki Gen'yoku (1874–1946), a professor of philosophy at Tokyo University who adhered to the critical spirit of Kant. The impact of German idealism and mysticism so characteristic of the second period also remained a factor in Japanese professional philosophy, but only one among many others. Besides political and meta-ethical reasons, the encounter with a wealth of new philosophical ideas, and the renewed reception of traditional Western philosophy, was responsible for this; for with the end of the war, studies in Western philosophy intensified again. Many philosophical classics were translated or re-translated. Numerous interpretations of European philosophies appeared including both comprehensive surveys and highly specialized studies. Also, new dictionaries were brought out. Philosophical journals flourished. Between 1979 and 1985, Tanaka Michitaro (1902–85) published four volumes on Plato. Even European medieval philosophy became a topic as studies on Augustine, Anselm and Thomas Aquinas appeared. In 1972, Ishihara Ken (1882–1976) published his *Yoroppa kirisutokyo-shi* (History of

Christianity in Europe). In 1959, Nambara Shigeru (1889–1974) wrote *Fihite no seiji tetsugaku* (Fichte's Political Philosophy). Shimomura Torataro in his *Burukuharuto no sekai (The World of Burkhardt)* (1983), provided an interpretation of Burkhardt's art theory. Descartes and Pascal also became the focus of renewed interest. In 1950, Watanabe Kazuo (1901–75) published *Dekaruto* (Descartes). Bergson, Sartre and Marcel were translated. The widespread and deep postwar interest in existentialism is also documented by works on Kierkegaard, Nietzsche, Jaspers and Heidegger. Phenomenology, especially Husserl and Heidegger, continued to be influential. Similar to postwar interest in existentialism, the interest in Marxism and materialism led to numerous respective publications. For many years Marxism – which had already experienced a first surge after the Russian revolution – remained a powerful stream of thought. One of the most influential materialist thinkers was **Kawakami Hajime** (1879–1946), though his attempt to prove that materialism and religiousness are compatible was a rather unorthodox endeavour. Finally, American pragmatism and Anglo-Saxon analytical philosophy became part of professional philosophy in Japan. For example, in 1959 Nagai Shigeo (1921–) wrote *Bunseki tetsugaku* (Analytical Philosophy), and in 1976 Kameo Toshio (born 1926) published *Dyui no tetsugaku* (The Philosophy of Dewey).

By about 1970, Japanese university philosophy in many respects had become part and parcel of a worldwide, more or less uniform professional and institutionalized philosophy. Japanese philosophers organize and participate in numerous international philosophical conferences, join in international cooperative publications and write books in Western languages. Specific features of Japanese philosophical studies are in principle similar to the specific features of philosophical studies by Western philosophers, i.e., they concern rather specific issues of specific theories. As far as comparisons with philosophical doctrines from their own traditions shape Japanese studies, apart from philosophies of cultural identity, they do not lead to hypotheses that differ fundamentally from the results of Western studies. Moreover, there exist a number of Western works that characterize and evaluate 'Japanese identity' as Japanese cultural

studies do; for example, German investigations into 'the otherness' of Japan.

There are of course other, and also more detailed, attempts to divide Japanese philosophy since Meiji times into different periods. In 1932, Inoue Tetsujiro, in his *Meiji tetsugakukai no kaiko* (The Philosophy of the Meiji Era in Retrospect), distinguished three eras of Meiji philosophy, namely the years from 1868 to 1890 (the date of the Imperial Edict on Education), the years from 1890 to the end of the Russo-Japanese war in 1905, and finally the period until the end of the Meiji time. The victory over Russia marked a certain change in political philosophy, for it intensified the discussion about nationalism, imperialism and universal humanism. In another attempt, Kano Masanao (1931–), in an article *Kindai shiso* (Recent Thought), uses the following key words to distinguish different periods: (1) enlightenment, (2) liberty and people's rights, (3) monarchism and Christianity, (4) democracy and ethnical nationalism, (5) early socialism and anarchism, (6) Taisho democracy (1912–26), (7) socialism and Marxism, (8) fascism and (9) postwar democracy. As Kano explains, the third phase overlaps with the second and finds its marked expressions in the Imperial Edict on Education (which supports Tennoism) and **Uchimura Kanzo**'s (1861–1930) religiously motivated refusal to regard the Tenno as superior to (the Christian) god. In the fourth phase, which began in the late 1880s, Tokutomi Soho (1863–1957) advanced his notion of popular democracy, *heiminshugi*, while Miyake Setsurei (1860–1945) advocated an ethnical motivated nationalism, *kokusuishugi*. Kotoku Shusui is representative of early socialism and anarchism. Its later developments started after the Russian Revolution. The applicability of the notion of fascism to Japanese ultra-nationalism and imperialism has been disputed, though it is clear which phenomena it is intended to indicate. Most scholars agree that with the end of the Second World War a new epoch of Japanese philosophy started which, in its basic respects, still continues.

See also: aesthetics in Japan, post-Meiji; Buddhist philosophy in Japan, post-Meiji; Confucianism in Japan, post-Meiji; kokutai ideology since Meiji times; logic; philosophy of human rights, Japanese

GREGOR PAUL

JEN *see* humaneness

JI *see* trigger

Jia Yi

b. 201 BCE; d. 169 BCE

Poet and statesman

Jia Yi was a Han poet and statesman who wrote a florid-styled essay on the rise and fall of the First Empire. It shows how Qin rose by applying the Legalist statecraft; how its army was able to defeat the 'vertical alliance' of nine other feudal states; and how its 'horizontal alliance' swallowed up these enemies one by one. It notes the First Emperor then enforced a unification, disarmed the powerful, drafted the many in building the Great Wall, burned the books of other schools of thought and buried alive the Confucian literati. For all that, the empire collapsed soon after his death, its weakness exposed by two peasant rebels whose ragtag bands fell far short of the strength of the nine states that the rising Qin once routed, 'Because it (Ch'in/Qin) failed to rule with [Confucian] benevolence and righteousness and to understand that it is one thing to conquer by might and another to rule.' That moral judgment still receives endorsement from institutional historians. The Confucian bureaucracy with its claim to moral authority is said to be indispensable for any lasting rule in China and that problem soon faced the **barbarians** who swarmed into the Central Plain after the Han.

Further reading

Eberhard, W. (1952) *Conquerors and Rulers: Social Forces in Medieval China*, Leiden: Brill.

Hsiao Kung-ch'uan (1979) *A History of Chinese*

Political Thought, Princeton, NJ: Princeton University Press.

WHALEN LAI

Jizang

b. 549; d. 623

Buddhist monk and philosopher

Jizang (Chi-tsang) was the founder of the main Chinese Madhyamaka school – the School of the Three Treatises – which is called thus due to its adherence to the superiority of three texts, the *Madhyamakakarika Dvadashadvarashastra* by **Nagarjuna** and the *Shatashastra* by Aryadeva (all translated into Chinese and commented on by Kumarajiva in the fifth century). He demolished what he regarded as the Chinese mistake of considering the **Two Truths** to be two realities (that can be united into one). The Two Truths, Jizang reminded his audience, pertain to methods of teaching, not to aspects of reality. There is no One Truth hiding somewhere mysterious; the point is to realize that there is 'nothing to gain or ascertain', nothing but the freedom that comes with the denial of both the affirmative and negative claims which may be made about reality. Although he was committed to **emptiness**, however, he also theorized on the One Vehicle.

The two truths is based on the idea that there is a relative truth, which represents the reality of the everyday world with which we are normally familiar. Then there is a higher truth which does away with the sorts of distinctions we ordinarily make. What the Madhyamika needs to do is to live as though the world is real, but acknowledge that really it is not, and that its suffering is merely relative to a particular attitude which we take to the ordinary world. One route to this realization is by denying both what we can say positively about reality, and also what we can say negatively about it. So we can accept as part of the Two Truths the reality of existence and of non-existence as defining our ordinary and relative point of view. As defining a higher notion of reality, though, we can assert the contrary of all these notions. To set this out according to Jizang:

Ordinary point of view/ sophisticated point of view
we assert existence/we assert non-existence
we assert existence or non-existence/we deny
both existence and non-existence
we either assert or deny existence/we neither
assert nor deny existence

The result of this reasoning process is the ubiquity
of emptiness as a feature of reality, since nothing
can be either reasonably asserted nor denied.

WHALEN LAI
OLIVER LEAMAN

Jonang school

The Jonang school evolved following the founding
of a monastery by Kunpang Thukje Tsondru
(1243–1313) at Jonang, Lhatse in southern Tibet.
It was, however, **Dolpopa Sherap Gyaltsen**
who, through his extensive efforts at dissemination
of the Jonang teachings, appears to have developed
Jonang as a full-fledged, systematic school of
thought. At the core of this school of thought is
the so-called **Shentong philosophy**, or the
'emptiness of other' view, which the majority of
Tibetan thinkers have considered heretical. Another important characteristic of this school is its
emphasis on the study of the Kalachakra tantra,
and its association with the Shentong view of
emptiness. Hermeneutics of the 'three turnings
of the wheel' by the Buddha play a critical role in
the philosophical discourse of the Jonang school.

The Jonang school argues that there exists also
what could be called the 'fourth council' of the
Buddha, the teachings of which present the
Buddha's final and definitive standpoint on the
profound teachings on the ultimate nature of
reality. This, in their view, is the view of the
'emptiness of the other', that is called 'the great
middle way' (*u ma chen po*), and supersedes the
teachings of the Prasangika-Madhyamaka's view of
emptiness of intrinsic existence as a mere negation.
Key figures in the development of this school are,
in addition to Dolpopa himself, Jonang Chokle
Namgyal (1306–86), Nypon Kunga Pal (1345–
1439), Jonang Kunga Drolchok (1507–75) and the
historian Taranatha (1575–1634). Unfortunately,
the seventeenth century witnessed what is perhaps
one of the saddest episodes in the history of
Tibetan philosophy, namely a state-enforced pro-
scription on the activities of this school. This
involved the closure of Jonang's main monasteries
and libraries.

Further reading

Ruegg, D. (1963) 'The Jo nang pas: A School of
Buddhist Ontologists According to the Brub
mtha' shel gyi me long', *Journal of American
Oriental Society* 83: 73–91.

THUPTEN JINPA

JU *see* scholar

K

Kagyu school

The emergence of Kagyu as a distinct school with its identification with a specific Indian and Tibetan lineage is due perhaps to Gampopa (1079–1153), who was himself one of the principal disciples of the famous Milarepa (1052–1135). The principal doctrinal characteristic of this school is the development of the idea of **mahamudra** (the great seal) as representing a comprehensive philosophical and practical system. Although there are Madhyamika masters like Maitrepa and Naropada amongst the Indian masters that the Kagyu tradition lists in its lineage, the scholarly study of Madhyamaka philosophy of **emptiness** does not appear to have been an important part of the school's heritage. There are, however, notable exceptions such as Karmapa Mikyo Dorje (1507–54) and Druk Pema Karpo (1527–96). On the whole, many of the influential Kagyu masters appear to have espoused, in so far as their ontological views are concerned, what are effectively versions of the **Shentong philosophy** view of the **Jonang school**. There appeared to have also been not much interest shown in the Dharmakirtian epistemology (the notable exception being Karmapa Chodrak Gyatso), which had remained a major preoccupation among the philosophers of other Tibetan schools, especially the **Shakya school** and the **Geluk school**. Certainly, there must have been complex social, political and historical reasons for the Kagyu school's deliberate lack of serious interest in these issues that were of central importance to Indian Buddhist philosophers. Perhaps the central philo-sophical concern in Kagyu discourse appears to be the idea of 'many in single taste' (*du ma ro chik*), which can be seen as an extension of the Nagarjunian equation between **samsara** and **nirvana**. The key figures in the development of Kagyu schools are, in addition to Gampopa himself, Baram Dharma Wangchuk (twelfth century CE), Karmapa Dusum Khyenpa (1110–89), Phakmo Drupa (1110–70) and Shang Drowai Gonpo (1123–93), who are each accredited with the founding of the four main subdivisions of the Kagyu school.

THUPTEN JINPA

Kang Yuwei

b. 1858; d. 1927

Reformer

Leader of the 1898 constitutional monarchy Reform movement, Kang Yuwei (K'ang Yu-wei) was a New Text scholar going back to the Former Han tradition of **Dong Zhongshu**, who presented **Confucius** as a political prophet and a reformer. Ming Confucianism had so endorsed the 'closed country' policy of the Ming that China had lived in a kind of economic and intellectual self-sufficiency which meant that the country was ill-prepared for the advance of the West and the incursion of a modernized Japan. In his major work, *Utopia*, which was circulated only among an inner circle, Kang looked forward to the coming of the age of the Great Harmony following the current trial of **chaos**. An internationalist who believed in free trade and cooperation, he welcomed Huayan philosophy and its call to 'break through the many, varied and graduated boundaries' dividing minds as well as nations. He sought spiritual as well as political 'open borders' for realizing the idyllic 'One is All, All is One'. His autobiography shows how that vision came from an enlightenment experience during an unsupervised 'quiet sitting' that he willed himself to pursue. For the next year, he lived like a wild man in the hills practicing various yogic feats and writing a commentary on the *Laozi* that he later repudiated and destroyed.

His free reclusive days ended when his uncle cut off his allowance. A trip to Hong Kong and a first look at what a microscope revealed confirmed for him the Huayan interpretation of the mystery of life. Step by step, he enriched, rewrote and redirected the mystical experience he once had into the political reform he advocated. When the reform failed and his leading disciple gave up on the pro-monarchy party to join the revolutionaries, Kang would not, or probably could not, change. He saw himself as Confucius reborn: a prophet and a **sage** working for the edification of kings. There are no such ranks in a modern democracy.

See also: Liang Qichao

Further reading

Chan Wing-tsit (1963) 'K'ang Yu-wei's Philosophy of Great Unity', *A Source Book in Chinese Philosophy*, Princeton, NJ: Princeton University Press, 723–42.

Lai, W. (1983) 'K'ang Yu-wei and Buddhism: From Enlightenment to Sagehood', *Cheng Feng* 26(1): 14–34.

Thompson, L. (trans.) (1958) *The One-World Philosophy of K'ang Yu-wei*, London: Allen & Unwin.

WHALEN LAI

KAO-TZU *see* Gaozi

karma

Karma (literally 'action') refers to the widespread Indian presupposition that motivated and inten-

tional actions produce a residue or retributive potency (*bija-shakti*) that remains somehow latent in the soul until future circumstances are appropriate for its actualization or fruition (*vipaka*) in the experience (*bhoga*) of the original agent in whom it then becomes active. Karmic causality supervenes upon natural causality. The 'sowing of seeds' and the 'reaping of fruits' are the standard metaphors for the connection between ethically significant actions and their consequences. It is the operation of *karma* that personalizes individual souls (*jiva-atman*) and propels them through the series of births in the here and now (**samsara**). The accumulation of merit through the performance of right actions guarantees a superior status in one's next incarnation in either this or higher worlds and demerit ensures an inferior destiny. But many forms of religious praxis have as their ultimate goal the elimination of inherited *karma* and the prevention of the accretion of fresh *karma*.

The idea of *karma* can be invoked to explain the present uneven distribution of benefits, fortune and misfortunes and the separation of people into castes. In ritualistic Brahminism, the operation of the karmic mechanism was closely tied to sacrificial performance, although the notion of 'ethical' *karma* was not absent. The extension of supernatural karmic causality to behaviour in general is particularly apparent in the Buddhist identification of the intention (*chetana*) with which an action is performed as primarily determinative of its quality.

Within theistic contexts, there are controversies over whether God in re-creating the universe takes account of the prior *karma* of individuals. If it does (*karma-sapeksha-vada*), as justice seems to require, is the divine autonomy compromised? If an antinomianalistically conceived divinity does not organize the universe in accordance with accumulated *karma* (*karma-nirapeksha-vada*), it may be open to charges of cruelty and partiality. The theist **Ramanuja** resolves the problem by equating the operation of *karma* with the will of God, thus effectively abolishing *karma* as a category in its own right.

The reductionist materialist **Charvakas** (and also some medical writers) reject the ritualist and ethical versions of the *karma* theory, confining the operation of causality to the natural and observable.

Further reading

O'Flaherty, W. (1980) (ed.) *Karma and Rebirth in Classical Indian Traditions*, Berkeley, CA: University of California Press.

CHRIS BARTLEY

karma, Chinese

The Han **Taiping** Daoists in China discussed the idea of an 'inherited burden' from the family's past affecting future generations. Trying to link *karma* to the **Yijing** sentiment that a family that accumulates good deeds is sure to enjoy overflowing bliss (down the generations) does not really connect with the traditional notion of *karma*. Closer in concept to *karma* is actually *bao*, a system of moral retribution which occurs as a result of good and evil deeds performed in the past. Some early Chinese karmic stories confused karmic retribution with the deeds of vengeful ghosts; that confusion was later cleared up. The Song dynasty Neo-Confucians campaigned against *karma*; that iron law is too impersonal and unrelenting by their neo-classical standard. The religious Daoists co-opted *karma* in a popular record of **Laozi**'s 'response to stimuli', but later the idea of a corporate justice returned. A man who seduces or molests a woman is punished when he comes home by finding his wife or daughter has met the same fate.

See also: samsara in China

WHALEN LAI

Kawakami Hajime

b. 1879; d. 1946

Economist and Marxist philosopher

Born in Iwakuni, the son of a former *samurai*, Kawakami studied at Tokyo University. After graduating from the Department of Law in 1902, he taught economics at his *alma mater* before moving to Kyoto University. In 1913, Kawakami went to Europe but, due to the outbreak of the First World War, he stayed only for a short time. Back in Japan, he became a full professor at Kyoto University. In 1919, Kawakami founded his journal *Shakai mondai kenkyu* (Studies in Social Problems), which focused on materialist and Marxist thought. In 1928 his political convictions led to his resignation as a university teacher. After joining the Communist party in 1932, Kawakami was persecuted and was imprisoned from 1933–7. The remaining years until his death were spent in a type of self-seclusion.

Kawakami was sincerely interested in social justice. On several occasions, he wholeheartedly and without restraint threw himself into extremely altruistic projects. He even joined Pure Land and Zen movements in order to work for a more humane world. In Kawakami's view, economics should be conceived of as a means to promote social justice and humaneness. Similarly, in his understanding of Marxism he emphasized justice and humanity, and not dialectics and revolution. In other words, though a socialist, materialist, Marxist and communist, Kawakami throughout his life remained a basically humanist thinker, and this was probably one of the reasons for his success. His *Bimbo monogatari* (Tale of Poverty), published in 1917 and reflecting his encounter with poverty in Europe, was one of the most successful books of its time. Though his following works were written from Marxist points of view, they also followed the line of Kawakami's more fundamental humanism. In 1923 he wrote *Shihonshugi keizaigaku no shiteki hatten* (The Historical Development of Capitalist Economics). In 1928, *Keizaigaku* (An Outline of Economics) and *Shihonron nyumon* (An Introduction to Capitalism) appeared. Kawakami also initiated the translation of Marx's *Capital*, and produced his own translations from Marx, Lenin and Bukharin. When orthodox Marxist-Leninists criticized him because of what they regarded as a lack of scientific Marxism and actual political engagement, Kawakami attempted to amend his views. Together with his colleague **Miki** Kiyoshi (1897–1945), he studied Hegel. As mentioned, he also entered the Communist party. As is clear from *Gokuchu zeigo* (Prison Ramblings) and his *Jijoden* (Autobiography) (1947), however, Kawakami never completely abandoned what can be called his spiritual interests.

In *Gokuchu zeigo*, Kawakami tries to show that materialism and Marxism are compatible with religious belief or faith. He argues that the realms, goals and methods of both are different. While materialism and Marxism are concerned with the 'external world', particularly society, social justice and welfare, and with the technical mastery of nature, religious belief is radically private, concerned with the 'interior world', and has as its goal the 'realisation of the true meaning of [individual] human life'. In this connection, Kawakami also employs Buddhist notions of 'self' (*ga*) and 'non-self' (*muga*), indicating that religious truth consists in an awareness of the insubstantiality of the 'I' or 'self'. Whereas materialism and Marxism, as natural and/or social sciences, aim at scientific truth by means of knowledge, religious conviction is faith in religious truth. While knowledge of scientific truth makes feasible a humane social life, insight into religious truth leads to an untroubled individual mind. In his defence of religious truth, Kawakami takes pains to distance himself from any form of organized religion, from superstition, even from metaphysics, and from religion as an opiate for the people. He emphasizes that 'nature is primary and spirit secondary', and also stresses that 'outside the material world reflected in man's consciousness', no gods and buddhas exist. What Kawakami actually brings into confrontation with each other are (1) the objective science of nature and society, and (2) a private belief in the value or meaning of one's individual existence that remains absolutely private.

With his *Gokuchu zeigo*, Kawakami also wanted to ascertain the importance of principled thought and argument against an overpowering (Japanese) statism, and the kokutai ideology (see **kokutai ideology since Meiji times**). In doing so, Kawakami again remained true to an early conviction. As Kato Shuichi (1919–) has pointed out, Kawakami, in his comments on the execution of **Kotoku** Shusui (1871–1911) and other anarchists, explained that it was because the Japanese state feared men who believed that there are ideas more important than the idea of the Japanese state that the executions took place. 'The Japanese god is the state', Kawakami wrote in his *Nihon dokutoku no kokkashugi* (Japan's Distinctive Nationalism) of 1911, and for him this probably indicated an irrational and dangerous confusion.

Further reading

Bernstein, G. (1976) *Japanese Marxist: A Portrait of Kawakami Hajime, 1879–1946*, Cambridge, MA: Harvard University Press.

GREGOR PAUL

Keyi Buddhism

Keyi (Concept Matching) Buddhism refers to the early attempt on the part of the Chinese to understand the Buddhist teaching by way of 'concept-matching', that is, looking for Daoist terms in order to render Buddhist ones. The Buddha becomes a 'true man'; **nirvana** appears as 'non-action'; no-soul or no-self is now 'not of body'; **dharma** is rendered as '**dao**' and so on. An exciting record of an intercultural encounter and meeting of different mindsets, much – perhaps too much – has been made of the seeming misunderstandings and distortions involved. Recent scholarship on metaphor would argue that all interpersonal or intercultural encounter involves initially such 'concept-matching', and even that much understanding may initially be metaphorical. It is a matter of translating the unfamiliar into the familiar. That reliance on past concepts is how 'normal science' (in Thomas Kuhn's assessment) works in response to uncharted territories. The reliance will persist until it hits a wall, that is, a limit to and a failure at concept-matching, at which point one is forced to re-examine one's premises and perhaps by facing up to the new reality, find and shift to a new paradigm. Sometimes the very mix of metaphors allows a new model to emerge, and creative insight can rise out of that originary exploration; and sometimes, it is an impasse that reveals the chasm dividing one way of thinking from another, one era from the next.

However, in one sense, 'concept-matching' has never ended. It did not disappear even after the monk Dao'an in the late fourth century condemned the approach, having become aware of the risk of distortion, especially in the conflation of Buddhist **emptiness** and Daoist **non-being**. But in fact, the early Prajna-ists who were guilty of this abridgment were themselves, step by step, becoming sensitized to and challenged by the misalliance.

By later standards Dao'an, who offered an amended reading to 'original nothingness', himself would fall under that same censure of having an incomplete understanding. (He actually spent his final years building up a better foundation by backtracking; he moved away from Mahayana emptiness back into studying Hinayana **Abhidharma**.)

Keyi Buddhism of the third and fourth century makes a strange bedfellow with the renewed mixture of things Buddhist and things Daoist, known to us as Chan, that came at the end of the medieval Buddhist era. This was done not from a position of weakness or as a result of not knowing what the *dharma* is, but from a position of strength, of having digested the theory well. A case in point is the *Baozanglun*, a late work freely attributed to Sengzhao in the early fifth century, the opening verse of which is an unapologetic borrowing from **Laozi**:

> The Emptiness that can be emptied is not the true Emptiness
> The form that can be formed is not the True Form
> The True Form is without Form
> The True Emptiness is without name
> The nameless is the father of the named
> The formless is the mother of form
> (They are the) root and source of all things
> And the ultimate ancestor of Heaven and Earth
> Above, they organize the various (pre-material) forms
> Below they arrange the chambers of the dark realm
> The original ether is embedded in the great form
> The great form is hidden within the formless
> The spirit of the sentient and the insentient
> Within the spirit is the soul
> And within the soul the body...

The work matches or meshes Buddhist and Daoist ideas fairly well, doing it with verve and ease. But this interesting mix of ideas, though it found some favour in Chan circles, somehow lacks a creative tension and left no real legacy.

Further reading

Lai, W. (1979) 'Limit and Failure of ko-i (Concept-Matching) Buddhism', *History of Religions* 18(3): 238–57.

Zurcher, E. (1972) *The Buddhist Conquest of China: The Spread and Adaptation of Buddhism in Early Medieval China*, Leiden: Brill.

WHALEN LAI

Kim Ok-kyun

b. 1851; d. 1894

Modernizer and philosopher

Kim Ok-kyun was one of the main thinkers of the modernization movement in Korea at the end of Choson dynasty. At the age of thirty-one, he went to Japan and observed the rapid progress of the country due to the adoption of Western ideas by the Japanese. When he returned to Korea he became a strong advocate of the modernization of the country. In 1884, with the help of some of his friends, he tried to take over the government, but failed; later he was assassinated.

Kim Ok-kyun appealed to the King of Korea (Choson dynasty) to establish diplomatic relations with the Western nations, especially America, to reform the government, to develop technology and commerce, to get rid of the *yangban* (aristocratic) system, and to educate people by building many schools. Kim's goal was to build a strong modern nation. Kim also advocated freedom of religion, which meant allowing the free flow of foreign religions to Korea, including Christianity. He advocated the elimination of the class system and the establishment of equal rights. All these meant direct opposition to the feudalistic social system and the power structure built by the Neo-Confucian philosophers and the *yangban* class. Kim Ok-kyun's progressive ideas played an important role in the Korean enlightenment movement (see **Enlightenment, Korean**) and contributed significantly toward the development of modern Korean society.

Further reading

Choi Min-hong (1980) *A Modern History of Korean Philosophy*, Seoul: Seongmoon Sa, 219–22.

Lee, P. (ed.) (1996) *Sourcebook of Korean Civilization*, Vol. 2, New York: Columbia University Press, 347–54.

YONG-CHOON KIM

KO-I *see* Keyi Buddhism

koan

Koan (in Chinese, *gong'an*) are 'public cases', Zen puzzles used to trigger off enlightenment especially in Linji (in Japanese, Rinzai) training. A well-known example created by Hakuin is, 'What is the sound of one hand clapping?' Introduced to the West by D.T. Suzuki, *koan* was offered as a means to break down modern Western rational and dualistic thinking. Recent scholarship has moved beyond Suzuki's appeal to the irrational and/or the unconscious.

Among recent Chinese scholars, Bao Hutian works at solving *koan* by noting the recurrent patterns of meanings and linguistic allusions. For example, a wayfarer was criticized for spitting on a Buddha image. His reply was, 'Show me any spot where the Buddha is not.' His irreverent behaviour is meant to drive home the point about the Buddha's omnipresence. Another example involves a master wondering aloud which end of a halved but still wiggling earthworm is alive (has life). A respondent hit one end, then the other – in effect killing the earthworm – and then he hit the space in between the severed halves. Though not a very charitable story, this is his way of denying the two extremes ('neither end is alive') and demonstrating the Middle Path (the space between) as empty. Or take a master's advice to a monk: 'Go wash your bowl', after the morning porridge. Most of us would take it, like a Hasidic tale, as saying that every act can be uplifting and Zen. But cross-referencing with another *koan* involving sticky stuff may show the rice gruel to be another metaphor for the defilements clinging to the mind. So the instruction is: go cleanse your mind. Sometimes the key to a *koan* lies with a regional dialect or a local lore. For example, a puzzling line goes 'I am Hou White; you are Hou Black'. This is simply baffling. Reading it literally as being about a white and black monkey (*hou*) is traditional; but it turns out to be a spin-off from a local Fujien story about two tricksters surnamed Hou trying to outdo one another.

Another Chinese scholar, Wu Yi, follows Bao and offers a classification of 'ten types of *koan*'. Their anti-Suzuki (anti-irrational) reading typifies a Chinese Zen 'rationalism' which has existed before. Dogen knew it; in fact, this may be the kind of *koan* 'scholasticism' – careful study and cross-referencing of cases – that probably triggered off an antithetical irrationalism during the Song dynasty. Among current Zen scholars, it is William Powell that has moved the analysis beyond this obsession with content; he works at the cues hidden in the form of exchange instead. You do not have to know what a *koan* means; the key is to catch what is going on. The most simple example is this: we should learn to register a shift in the exchange. A conversation about facts (information) – like 'Where have you been?' and 'I just came back from Hunan' – can suddenly shift to a request for a demonstration of Zen wisdom. The next question, 'Is the *hu* (lake) full?', is not asking about the spring runoff. The respondent who came back with an unexpected answer like, 'When has it never been full', might win approval. That is not a sure bet, however, because once the issue of content is taken out, we as observers can only infer a 'right' answer by what happens next. Did the master approve the answer by, say, sending the student a cup of tea? An identical answer can earn kudos for one and a rebuttal for another.

Still more recently, Steven Heine weaves both form and content together again and re-presents the Koan tradition as one Derrida-esque train of texts deconstructing texts. But a historical approach is also possible. If so, then **Mazu Daoyi** might be the ultimate source and cause for the cult of *koan*. Skillful in his use of the Zen '**trigger**' to touch off enlightenment, he had relativized the *dharma*. He taught, after all, both 'Mind is Buddha' as well as 'No Mind, No Buddha'. Henceforth no fixed content is feasible. The master must improvise and use whatever opportunity that affords to him and his student. Looking over Mazu's recorded sayings, it is possible to register how a number of his *koan*-like exchanges have still decipherable meanings. At one time, he stopped an enquirer at the door with the question, 'When is the lion neither inside nor outside the den?' The point is getting the man to see that he – and not just the patriarch Ma – was the lion (the enlightened one). The threshold of a door is 'neither in nor outside' the room. When this exchange was 'fresh' and the answer was not widely known, form and content still meshed. When the answers became public knowledge, the *koan* system became formalized and form was cut loose from content, as Powell shows. When *koan* study became overly scholastic, then the exercise became very different. It is that seeming irrationality that Suzuki advocated, that Bao tried to reverse, that Heine deconstructs and which continues to fascinate modern readers.

An interesting twist in *koan* Zen is 'The greater the doubt, the greater the enlightenment' – as if it is not by faith but rather by doubt that one is delivered. The truth is the reverse. Early Zen is a Zen of certitude, derived in part from **The Awakening of Faith in Mahayana**. Due to the presence of a Suchness Mind (**buddha nature**) in all men, man may bring into being this certainty of enlightenment. The word '**faith**' in the title is not some uncertain 'belief' but self-assured 'confidence'. Early Zen utilized that to 'turn the mind' of its followers, to get an 'unwavering mind of faith' to realize 'that Mind and Faith (meaning Truth) are one'. But early Zen confidence can backfire when too many minds assume that they are already buddhas. This left the true seeker haunted by the irony: if I am already a Buddha, why don't I feel any more enlightened?

Song *koan* training, by posing these seemingly insolveable enigmas, has the effect of stripping the neophyte of any sense of surety. Swallowed in darkness (ignorance) and layers of 'clouds of doubt', he might have this sudden breakthrough into wisdom: 'the greater the doubt, the greater the enlightenment'. That does not mean there are different grades in enlightenment, nor that the Zen of Doubt is contrary to the Zen of Faith. And it is not even that the Awakening of Faith is only a matter of confidence. Though never explicit, this

work which rose in a dark hour evokes confidence when uncertainty about the continual presence of the **dharma** was prevalent. Such traumatic experience is part of the Zen 'sickness' during training. Episodes of 'bedevilment' (possession by Mara) have landed a number of trainees, including Japan's foremost Dada-ist poet (Takahashi Shinkichi (1901–)) temporarily in asylums.

Further reading

Chang Chung-yuan (1969) *Original Teachings of Ch'an Buddhism: Selected from the Transmission of the Lamp*, New York: Grove.

Heine, S. (1994) *Dogen and the Koan Tradition*, Albany, NY: State University of New York Press.

Lai, W. (1978) 'Innerworldly Asceticism: East and West', in H. Heifetz (ed.), *Zen and Hasidism*, Wheaton, IL: Theosophical Society, 186–207.

—— (1985) 'Ma-Tsu Tao-I And The Unfolding Of Southern Zen', *Japanese Journal of Religious Studies* 12(4): 173–202.

Pao Hu-t'ien (1972) *I-hai mi-lan [Ripples on a Literary Sea] also known as Ch'an yu shih [Zen and Poetry]*, Taipei: Kuang-wen: 127–44.

Wu Yi (1981) *Chung-kuo che-hsueh te sheng-ming ho fang-fa* (The Life and Method of Chinese Philosophy), Taipei: Tung-ta, 69–81.

WHALEN LAI

Kokugaku

Kokugaku, which is usually translated as 'National Learning' or 'Nativism', is a rather ambiguous term. Most commonly, modern scholarship uses it to refer to the writings of Motoori Norinaga (1730–1801) and Hirata Atsutane (1776–1843), as well as those scholars whom they regarded as their predecessors: Keichu (1640–1701), Kada no Azumamaro (1669–1736) and Kamo no Mabuchi (1697–1769). The term further refers to the writings of later students of the schools established by Norinaga and Atsutane, which were influential in the last decades of the Edo period (1600–1868) and extended their influence into the Meiji period (1868–1912) or even later. However, most of those identified as Kokugaku scholars in this definition preferred other terms for their scholarship, such as 'Japanese Learning', 'Ancient Learning', or 'Imperial Learning'. Moreover, the term 'Kokugaku' was widely used by scholars outside this tradition.

As indicated by its translation as 'National Learning', Kokugaku began as the study of the history, literature and ancient practices of Japan. It arose as a new branch of learning in the seventeenth century, modelled after the older study of the Chinese Classics (see **Classics and Books**). In spite of the fact that National Learning has by some scholars been characterized as a movement of 'Shinto revival', Shinto was but one of the interests of Kokugaku scholars, and many did not occupy themselves with it at all. In early Kokugaku, attention focused on poetry and literature rather than Shinto. Students studied under Kokugaku masters primarily because they enjoyed reading and writing poetry in classical Japanese, and only a few went on to develop an interest in historical or theological matters. As a general trend, this was gradually reversed in late Kokugaku. Whereas Keichu, who was a Buddhist monk, was uninterested in Shinto and concentrated on poetry, the reverse was true of Atsutane. On the other hand, most of Norinaga's students were less interested in the 'Way of the Gods' than their master had been, and concentrated on linguistic and literary studies. In spite of this fact, this outline of Kokugaku will focus on philosophical (or perhaps, more accurately, theological) ideas articulated and spread by Kokugaku scholars.

Like Chinese learning, National Learning was rooted in private academies. Such academies were pioneered by Confucian scholars in the late seventeenth century, most famously by the scholar of Ancient Learning Ito Jinsai and taught the reading and composition of Chinese prose and poetry. Inspired by the success of schools like Jinsai's, private academies for the study of classical Japanese prose and poetry sprung up in the larger cities soon afterwards. From the outset, the study of the Japanese classics was profoundly influenced by the ideas and methods of Kogaku scholars of Chinese, and especially the school of Ancient Learning.

Keichu, whom Motoori Norinaga regarded as the founding father of National Learning, was a contemporary of Ito Jinsai. Keichu's fame is based on one work, *A Stand-in's Chronicle of the Ten Thousand Leaves* (*Man'yo Daishoki*, 1687, revised in 1690), which is a commentary on the poetry in the *Collection of Ten Thousand Leaves* (*Man'yoshu*, *c*.759). Although his scholarship covered completely unrelated ground to Jinsai's, the two had much in common. Like Jinsai, Keichu rejected 'medieval' commentaries and endeavoured to recover the 'original meaning' of ancient texts (see **Confucianism in Japan**). Moreover, he shared with Jinsai a strong dislike for the moralistic rigorism of Neo-Confucianism, which also permeated the medieval commentaries on Japanese poetry. He stressed that Japan's ancient poems were simply expressions of emotions, rather than bearers of didactic messages.

In Keichu's works, the ancient world which is reflected in the poems from the Collection of Ten Thousand Leaves appears as an age of a primeval simplicity and natural political and social order. Keichu used the term 'Shinto' with reference to the 'oral traditions' on which ancient society was based, but stopped short of calling for a revival of this tradition, and the subject of Shinto was at most peripheral to his studies.

Shinto moved to the centre stage of National Learning in response to the development of Ogyu Sorai's school. In Sorai's scholarship, China's Classics and China's Early Kings were the one and only source of the Way, and Sorai regarded ancient Chinese as the language of the Way, superior to all others. As a result, his attitude towards the Japanese Classics and Shinto was at best one of indifference; it was fundamentally different to that of Neo-Confucian scholars (see **Neo-Confucianism, concepts**) such as Yamazaki Ansai, who had regarded Shinto as a native expression of the Way in its own right. Some of Sorai's students (most famously Dazai Shundai, 1680–1747) were more outspoken and rejected Shinto as a fraud, fabricated by self-serving priests in the Middle Ages to enhance their own status, and based on Buddhist fallacies about the 'human mind'. The position of Sorai's school was that since the Way was founded by the Chinese sages and recorded in the Chinese Classics, Japan was a country without any form of civilization until its adoption of Chinese culture. This included not only knowledge of Chinese rites, music and institutions of government, but also such basic rules of social propriety as **filial piety** between a son and his father, or loyalty between a 'minister' and his ruler. Before the Japanese were instructed in the Way of the Chinese sages, Sorai and his students argued, they killed those who were weaker than themselves, forgot their parents as soon as they grew up, had sexual intercourse with their children, fought with their brothers and were unfamiliar with the concept of **friendship**.

Shinto scholars were sensitive to Sorai's argument that introspective theories arguing that the Way is inborn in the human mind are essentially Buddhist and inferior. Anti-Buddhist rhetoric had formed an integral part of Shinto discourse since the early seventeenth century, and had roots that went back even further. At the same time, however, they were appalled by the derision with which scholars of Ancient Learning dismissed the Japanese tradition of Shinto. Scholars of Yamazaki Ansai's Suika school were confronted with a situation in which 'everyone stopped attending lectures given by scholars who relied on the commentaries of the Cheng brothers and Zhu Xi' (according to the Confucianist Nawa Rodo, writing about Kyoto in the 1740s), and they found it difficult to argue against the sophisticated philological arguments of Ancient Learning.

A Shinto scholar whose work reflects the influence of Ancient Learning was Yoshimi Yukikazu (1673–1761). Yukikazu was a priest at the Toshogu shrine in Nagoya, and a scholar of the Suika school. However, in the years after his retirement from active service (in 1728), his thought gradually moved away from Suika orthodoxy. Yukikazu was one of a number of scholars who did refer to their own scholarship as 'National Learning', but who are not included in the modern definition of the term. Yukikazu agreed with Sorai that teachings about the mind are Buddhist fallacies. Like Sorai, he insisted that the Way is not a method for improving the minds of individuals, but a concrete set of historical institutions and rites from a divine age in the distant past, created with the aim of regulating society. However, he located this Way not in the Chinese Classics, but in the Classics of Japan: the National Histories and official records. This body of texts included historical works such as the *Chronicles of*

Japan (Nihon shoki) (720), and works on shrine ritual such as the *Procedures of the Engi Period (Engishiki)* (927). Moreover, he agreed with Sorai that the Way was not a 'principle' that existed naturally, as held by Neo-Confucianists, but an invented, historical construct, created by sages of superior wisdom. However, while Sorai stated that there were no sages other than the Early Kings of China, Yukikazu gave Japan its own sages, in the form of the divine ancestors of the Imperial House. He defined Shinto as a body of divine institutions created by the imperial ancestors. In his *Outline of School Regulations (Gakki taiko)* (1743), he explained the principles of his scholarship as follows: 'The foremost task of National Learning is to establish the facts concerning the strict Way of ruler and minister and the correct performance of rites and government – facts which are based on the meritorious efforts of the gods who have ruled our country since the beginning of time – by reflecting on the National Histories and official records.'

A nearly identical view of Shinto was held by contemporary scholars who, unlike Yukikazu, are regarded as members of the lineage of National Learning: Kada no Azumamaro and Kamo no Mabuchi. Azumamaro, whom Hirata Atsutane regarded as the founder of National Learning, was a priest at the Fushimi Inari shrine in Kyoto. He is remembered not so much for his scholarship as for his initiative to found a private academy which specialized in National Learning. In 1728, he even petitioned Shogun Yoshimune (r. 1716–45) for a grant of land, on which to set up a new 'school for studies of the Imperial Land'. Even though this request was never granted, his existing school in Kyoto attracted a considerable number of students, some of whom became well-known scholars. Azumamaro's studies concentrated on ancient Japanese poetry, including that of the *Collection of Ten Thousand Leaves*, and on the *Chapter of the Age of the Gods in the Chronicles of Japan*. His petition to Yoshimune drew quite obviously on the concepts and terms of Ancient Learning. Azumamaro stated that it was his aim to restore 'the Way of the Early Kings', to which he also referred as 'the teachings of our Divine Emperors', by way of the philological study of Japan's Classics. Although his own works did not live up to this ideal, they did set out the way for later generations of students of National Learning.

The last decades of Azumamaro's life saw a growing popularity of 'Japanese Studies'. As mentioned above, the motor behind this movement was not the study of the 'Way', whether Japanese or Chinese, Shinto or Confucian, but the social activity of exchanging poems at 'poetry gatherings'. In the same way as the theories of Confucianists of Ancient Learning about the Way emerged from the more basic study of the reading and writing of ancient Chinese, students of National Learning were drawn into theories about the 'Way of the Gods' through the medium of their study of reading and writing ancient Japanese.

This was also true of Azumamaro's most prominent student, Kamo no Mabuchi. Mabuchi's first interest was in classical Japanese poetry, and when he joined Azumamaro's school in Kyoto he became interested in the ancient poetry of the *Collection of Ten Thousand Leaves*. Throughout his career as a scholar, his studies focused on the interpretation of poems from the *Collection*, and on the composition of poems in the style of this work. He did not develop his theories about Shinto until much later, and they followed naturally from his views on ancient poetry.

Mabuchi regarded the period in which the poems in the *Collection* were composed as a golden age, an era in which the country was 'naturally governed'. He found this era's 'natural order' expressed most eloquently in the poems of antiquity, which he saw as 'spontaneous expressions' of the human emotions of the men of old. According to Mabuchi, these poems displayed the 'sincerity' (*magokoro*) of the people of antiquity, and he argued that it was this natural truthfulness of the people that allowed the nation to remain in a state of natural harmony. In fact, these poems did not merely reflect the natural sincerity of the people of ancient Japan, but helped to bring it about. Mabuchi regarded the composition of poetry as a practice of divine origin, which served to vent human emotions that might otherwise damage social order.

The most prominent distinction in Mabuchi's scholarly writings is between the 'natural', which is at the same time 'divine' and 'sincere', and the 'artificial', which is 'human' (and therefore inferior to the divine) and 'conceited'. This distinction applied not only to antiquity versus the 'latter age' in which Mabuchi lived, but also to Japan versus China. Mabuchi argued that it was the encroachment of Chinese learning in Japan that caused the Japanese to lose their natural sincerity. Chinese theories were the product of Chinese minds, and in contrast to the Japanese, the Chinese were fundamentally insincere and given to disorder; this, he argued, was the very reason why they had to invent their 'artificial' teachings in the first place.

Mabuchi's theories occupied an unusual position within the power field between Neo-Confucianism and Ancient Learning that defined scholarship in the mid-eighteenth century. Ancient Learning was an obvious influence: Mabuchi's method of recovering the spirit of an idealized ancient world through its language was the same as Sorai's. However, Mabuchi's views on what constitutes the 'Way' were radically different from those of the scholars of Ancient Learning. Mabuchi did not regard the Way as something that had been 'invented', whether by humans (as argued by Sorai) or by the gods (as argued by, for example, Yoshimi Yukikazu). Instead, he regarded the Way of Japan as 'naturally present', and as superior to the Way of China for the very reason that the latter was a mere 'human invention'. As a result, Mabuchi's quest for the Way had more in common with Neo-Confucianist thought: it was a quest for something that was inborn in one's own mind. In Mabuchi's thought, the Way of Japan was a set of virtues, such as sincerity, truthfulness and manliness that were inborn in every Japanese and could be activated by the study of ancient poetry and history. These virtues were 'naturally present' in every Japanese, and it was possible to 'return' to them if one could purify oneself of the Chinese conceitedness that had come to pervade Japanese society in historical times. Although Mabuchi's stress on 'naturalness' was inspired by Daoism rather than Neo-Confucianism, the parallels between the return to one's 'original human mind' in Neo-Confucianism (and its Shinto equivalent, Suika Shinto), and the return to the 'natural sincerity of the Japanese mind' in Mabuchi's thought are clear.

Mabuchi was remarkably successful both in his contacts with the ruling elite and in his teaching to private students at his own academy in Edo. Many of his students in Edo and Totomi (his home province) gained wide recognition as scholars of National Learning. His best-known student, however, and according to many the defining figure in the history of National Learning, was the son of a merchant who lived in Matsusaka (Ise province): Motoori Norinaga.

Norinaga's interest in Japanese Studies had the same origin as Mabuchi's: an early fondness of poetry and an active participation in poetry gatherings. Parallel to this, however, Norinaga also held an early fascination for Shinto, and possibly as a result of this, his Shinto thought was not linked to his study of poetry as inextricably as Mabuchi's had been. Although Norinaga was formally Mabuchi's student, most of his ideas were already developed to a remarkable degree of maturity before he joined Mabuchi's school (in 1764). Before he met Mabuchi, Norinaga had spent a period of five and a half years in Kyoto (1752–7), where he studied medicine as well as Confucianism (both Neo-Confucianism and Sorai's Ancient Learning) and the Japanese Classics – among others, through the works of Keichu. At this time, he felt attracted to what he called 'natural Shinto', which he saw as the Way that had allowed ancient Japan to be naturally moral and harmonious, without knowledge of the Chinese 'Way of the Sages'. Moreover, Norinaga explained his preference for Japanese studies over Confucianism by stating that the latter is only of interest to those who 'have a country to rule'. As a common citizen and subject, without a nation to govern, Norinaga saw no use in the study of Confucianism, and instead concentrated on the reading and writing of Japanese poetry and literature. Both his adherence to 'natural Shinto' and his stated disinterest in the Confucian Way were reactions to Ancient Learning: they are responses to the arguments that Japan had no Way before it adopted the Way of the Chinese sages, and that the Way is a method for bringing order to society as a whole, rather than for improving the individual.

Norinaga's outlook on the Way from the standpoint of the ruled rather than the ruler stayed with him throughout his life, and was one of the defining traits of his scholarship. Acceptance of the status quo was the starting point of Norinaga's thought, and his ideas focused on self-improvement under circumstances that were given and unchangeable. To begin with, this self-improvement took the form of developing a sensitivity for the emotional quality of life through the reading and composition of Japanese poetry and literature. This sensitivity would allow one to grieve about sad matters and rejoice about happy matters in a wholehearted manner, without the duplicity inherent in the negative view of emotions propagated by Neo-Confucianism and Buddhism alike.

In contrast to Mabuchi, Norinaga preferred the 'medieval' poetry of the *New Collection of Old and New (Shin Kokinshu)* (1205) over the ancient poetry of the *Collection of Ten Thousand Leaves*. He further nurtured a special reverence for the equally 'medieval' *Tale of Genji (Genji Monogatari)* (early eleventh century). He regarded both works as prime examples of the attainment of emotional sensitivity. Needless to say, his ideal of emotional sensitivity was at variance with Mabuchi's ideal of primitive manliness, and it did not find favour in his teacher's eyes. Thus on the subject of poetry and literature Mabuchi's and Norinaga's views were largely incompatible.

Norinaga's admiration for medieval literature was also incompatible with his teachings on the 'Ancient Way'. Like Mabuchi, Norinaga regarded the age before the introduction of Chinese culture to Japan as a divine age, in which man was sincere and the nation was governed naturally. He echoed Mabuchi when he stated that the adoption of Chinese culture (which he dated to the mid-seventh century) corrupted the truthful minds of the ancient Japanese, and like Mabuchi, he called for a restoration of the Way of ancient Japan. It is difficult to reconcile Norinaga's admiration for 'medieval' literature with his description of that age as 'corrupted'. The one consistent element between his literary theory and his teaching of the Way appears to be the fact that both depart from the premise that man is born into circumstances that are given and unchangeable, and that both advocate graceful submission to a higher power as the essential virtue of man.

From 1764 onwards, Norinaga's studies focused on the *Record of Ancient Matters (Kojiki)* (712); his life work, the *Tradition of the Record of Ancient Matters (Kojiki-den)*, was a philological study of this text that took until 1798 to be completed. It was in the early years of working on this text that Norinaga's ideas about the Way took shape.

Norinaga's perception of the Way was different from Mabuchi's in a number of important aspects. In Mabuchi's thought, the Way was a state of mind, characterized by sincerity, and to be attained through the medium of the language of ancient Japanese poetry. In Norinaga's writings, however, the Way is described in rather more concrete terms. While Mabuchi argued that the Way 'exists naturally' in the Japanese mind, Norinaga stated that the Way was a product of actions of the gods who figure in the 'Chapters of the Age of the Gods' in the *Record of Ancient Matters*. Created by the deity Takami-musubi, the Way was inherited by Amaterasu and handed down by her to her descendants, the emperors of Japan. Moreover, in Norinaga's thought, the Way is not necessarily good: it is simply a word for the way things were in the divine age described in the *Record of Ancient Matters*. He argued that all matters, including human acts, are the result of the will of the gods, and those acts that are evil are simply the result of the will of evil gods. As the ultimate evil in this world, Norinaga mentioned death, and he stated that it is the will of the gods that after death, all humans go to an utterly evil place called Yomi, the Netherworld, as described in the *Record of Ancient Matters*. Thus the Way does not offer an escape from evil; evil is actually part of the Way of the Gods. In Norinaga's thought, the Way appears as an ultimately unintelligible reflection of the unfathomable will of the gods.

What then is the proper attitude of humans to this Way, to which we are all subjected? First of all, there is sincerity and truthfulness. Like Mabuchi, Norinaga stressed that Chinese-like conceitedness was detrimental to the sincere and 'natural' compliance with the Way which had characterized the ancient Japanese. But Norinaga asked for more. He also added faith as an important element of abiding by the Way. In order to follow the Way, one should study the Classics (and especially the *Record of Ancient Matters*) because they are our only source on the Way. Also, he emphasized reverence for the imperial succession. In Mabuchi's perception, the Way had ultimately been embedded in people's minds, and as a result, the gods and emperors of the National Histories performed only

a marginal function in his discussion of the Way. In Norinaga's thought, however, the gods were the very substance of the Way, and the imperial succession was the embodiment of the Way on earth. Carrying the mandate of Amaterasu, who is both the sun in the sky and a human-bodied imperial ancestor, the emperors pass the will of the gods on to the world, and, through their magistrates, rule over the people in accordance with the will of the gods. Therefore, it is the prime duty of the people, as subjects of the emperor, to comply with those who rule in his name with sincere and truthful minds.

Norinaga's views on the Way took the notion of Japanese superiority to new heights. Since Japan is the country where the gods originated (again, as described in the *Record of Ancient Matters*), Norinaga argued that Japan is the 'Land of Origin', to which the rest of the world is heavily indebted. Moreover, because Japan is ruled by an imperial succession that has a special mandate from the Sun Goddess, Amaterasu, all nations in the world owe allegiance to her. There is, after all, only one sun in the world, and all life depends on it.

While there was much that was new in Norinaga's thought, there are also obvious links with the past. The idea of sincerity, for example, had its roots in Mabuchi's thought. However, Norinaga's approach was much more in line with the principles of Ancient Learning than Mabuchi's had been. As in Ancient Learning, Norinaga defined the Way as a historical, concrete invention – in Norinaga's case, an invention of the gods. Moreover, we are told never to question the Way, or even try to understand it, but simply to learn about it from the Classics and have faith in it. Both these important features of Norinaga's thought, as well as his sophisticated philological methods, had their roots in Sorai's school of Ancient Learning.

Norinaga's school was even more successful than Mabuchi's had been. His fame spread throughout the country, and Norinaga had hundreds of students outside his home province, some from as far away as Kyushu and northern Honshu. Late in life, he also attracted the interest of the ruling class, and from 1792 onwards he received a small stipend from the *daimyo* of Kii (in whose domain he lived), allowing him to retire from his work as a physician. After Norinaga's death, his school continued to prosper under his adopted son Motoori Ohira (1756–1833) in Wakayama and his natural son Haruniwa (1763–1828) in Matsusaka. However, the study of Japanese poetry and literature and that of the Ancient Way, which had been only precariously linked in Norinaga's lifetime, tended to split into two separate fields, and the former proved incomparably more popular than the latter.

The dominant Kokugaku scholar in the study of the Ancient Way after Norinaga was Hirata Atsutane. Atsutane called himself a student of Norinaga, but he was not accepted as such by Norinaga's heirs. He was born in Akita (Dewa province), but left the domain for Edo, presumably after a difficult youth, and from the early 1810s onwards he made a name for himself as a teacher of National Learning there. His early writings reveal a familiarity with Norinaga's writings, and Norinaga's thought formed the point of departure of his scholarship.

As Norinaga before him, Atsutane regarded the National Histories as sacred depositories of the Way, and interpreted them in a fashion that has been described as 'fundamentalist': as literal, factual truths. However, while Norinaga selected one of the Histories, the *Record of Ancient Matters*, as the ultimate authority on the Ancient Way, and endeavoured to improve his understanding of that Way by the philological study of this work, Atsutane treated the ancient tradition in a rather more free manner. His largest work, the *Tradition of Ancient History* (*Koshi-den*), begun in 1812, and largely completed by 1825, was a commentary along the lines of Norinaga's *Tradition of the Record of Ancient Matters*; but Atsutane compiled his own 'Ancient History' as he went along, by making his own collage of (not infrequently, specially adapted) passages from the various national histories on the basis of his own ideas about the Way.

The aspect of Norinaga's thought that Atsutane felt least comfortable with was his idea that all human beings go to the evil place called Yomi after death. Reinterpreting the tradition of the Age of the Gods, Atsutane arrived at the view that there exists a 'hidden world' (*kakuriyo*), ruled by the deity Okuninushi, parallel to and intermingling with the 'visible world' (*utsushiyo*), which is ruled by Amaterasu's divine descendants. He posed that the dead are judged on their acts and rewarded or punished

by Okuninushi in their afterlife in the 'hidden world'. Atsutane made every effort to find out more about this world, not only through study of the ancient tradition, but also through mediums who claimed that they had visited this realm and returned to the land of the living.

Occasionally, Atsutane gave the impression that he regarded the 'hidden world' of the spirits as more important than the world of the living. However, in the final analysis, he maintained that knowledge about our fate after death is to be seen as a prerequisite to practice of the Way in this life: it is simply a means of finding the peace of mind that is needed if one is to maintain the sincere 'Japanese spirit', and abide by the Way of this world, which is embodied in Amaterasu and her descendants, the emperors. Thus the emphasis on absolute loyalty to the imperial succession, and the government of its magistrates, remained as central to Atsutane's thought as it had been to Norinaga's. Moreover, if anything, Atsutane reinforced the fundamentalist nationalism that was already present in Norinaga's thought. He further elaborated a cosmological model of the world that had been developed on the basis of the *Chapter of the Age of the Gods* by Norinaga's student Hattori Nakatsune (1756–1824) and appended to Norinaga's *Tradition of the Record of Ancient Matters*. In this model, Japan was placed literally on top of the world.

After Atsutane, very few new ideas were added to what one could call the theoretical basis of National Learning. In the last decades of the Edo period, the movement penetrated at a grassroots level throughout Japan. This period saw a flood of writings by scholars associated with National Learning, about subjects ranging from popular morals to agriculture and local politics. Although, naturally, these writings display a wide range of views and theories, loyalty to the imperial succession and sincere dedication to one's given profession run through them as a common theme.

Hirata Atsutane's school grew rapidly after his death, both among Shinto priests, lesser *samurai*, wealthy peasants and merchants. In the turbulent final years of the Edo period, many followers of the 'Hirata school' were active in the movement which under the rallying call 'revere the emperor and expel the barbarians' (*sonno joi*), contributed to the downfall of the Edo shogunate. However, members of the school failed to attain high positions in the Meiji government. Many made careers as 'National Evangelists' in the Great Promulgation Campaign, which lasted from 1870 until 1884. This government campaign (which has been described by Hardacre (1989)) had as its aim to spread 'Three Great Teachings', one of which was 'reverence for the emperor and obedience to the will of the court'. After the Campaign was discontinued, the Hirata school remained influential among Shinto priests.

Ideas that were central to (later) National Learning, such as reverence for the emperor, made a further career in the 'State Shinto' of the Meiji, Taisho and early Showa periods. They formed the theological basis for the efforts of governments to tie local shrines in with a national cult headed by the emperor. When Shinto ideologists founded the Institute for the Study of the Imperial Classics (Koten Kokyusho) in 1882, they regarded themselves as the guardians of the tradition of National Learning. Soon after, this Institute was charged with the education of Shinto priests by the Home Ministry, and it established the Pavilion of National Learning (Kokugakuin) for that purpose in 1890. This shows that during the prewar and war periods, when Shinto priests functioned as the performers of state ritual, 'National Learning' had the status of a state-sponsored ideology. However, it must be remembered that during this period, 'National Learning' tended to merge with the state-sponsored Shinto orthodoxy that was later termed State Shinto. State Shinto drew not only on the National Learning of the Edo period, but depended in equal measure on nationalist Confucian thought, such as that of Mitogaku (see **Confucianism in Japan**), and on the Western-inspired ideas of the movement of National Morality (*Kokumin dotokuron*).

See also: Shinto

Further reading

Hardacre, H. (1989) *Shinto and the State, 1868–1988*, Princeton, NJ: Princeton University Press.

Harootunian, H. (1988) *Things Seen and Unseen: Discourse and Ideology in Tokugawa Nativism*, Chicago: University of Chicago Press.

Matsumoto Shigeru (1970) *Motoori Norinaga, 1730–1801*, Cambridge: Cambridge University Press.

Nosco, P. (1990) *Remembering Paradise: Nativism and Nostalgia in Eighteenth-Century Japan*, Cambridge, MA: Harvard University Press.

Yoshikawa Kojiro (1983) *Jinsai, Sorai, Norinaga: Three Classical Philologists of Mid-Tokugawa Japan*, trans. Kikuchi Yuji, Tokyo: The Institute of Eastern Culture.

MARK TEEUWEN

kokutai ideology since Meiji times

The Japanese word *kokutai* has various meanings. However, as far as its usage since Meiji times (1868–1912) is concerned, and as far as this usage is important for an understanding of modern Japanese philosophy, the meaning 'national [i.e., Japanese] essence' is most relevant. This is true in spite of the fact that the word, when used in this sense, was not a philosophical term at all. From about 1890, the date of the *Kyoiku chokugo* (Imperial Edict on Education) through the end of the Second World War, *kokutai* denoted an ideological norm every Japanese scholar had to respect if he did not want to be attacked, persecuted or even imprisoned. After the World War, *kokutai* became a symbol for almost everything ideologically, morally and politically wrong. This is to say that, especially between 1890 and 1945, the *kokutai* ideology determined the possibilities and limits of (public) philosophical thought. While, in the years from 1890 to 1930, these limits varied considerably, from about 1933 they were extremely tight. After the government's publication of *Kokutai no hongi* (The Fundamental Principle of National [Japanese] Essence) in 1937, open criticism of Japanese nationalism, and imperialism, especially in its cultural forms, became virtually impossible.

The word *kokutai* was used to refer to what was declared Japanese uniqueness. This uniqueness was conceived of as a distinctive class of both descriptive and evaluative characteristics with most of the basic descriptive characteristics being speculative fabrications. In other words, *kokutai* designated a confused notion of largely fabricated 'facts' and norms. The alleged 'facts' and norms were:

1 The *tenno* is a descendent of the sun goddess Amaterasu omikami and thus himself divine (*aramikami*).
2 From the very beginning of her history, Japan has been ruled by an unbroken line of *tenno*.
3 Hence Japan is a divine country (*shinkoku, shinshu*).
4 The relationship between ordinary Japanese and the *tenno* is not only one of ruler and ruled but also of benevolent father and grateful child. The Japanese constitute one harmonious family. Japan is a 'family state' (*kazoku kokka*).
5 Hence the Japanese must serve the *tenno* with *unconditional* loyalty (*chu*) and (filial) piety (*ko*). Since the *tenno* is a god, he must never be opposed. If required, every Japanese should readily sacrifice his life for the *tenno*. Since loyalty and piety are a unity (*chuko ippon*), there can be no conflict between them.
6 Because of Japan's nature as a divine family state which developed in (comparative) isolation on an island, her people are untainted by exterior influences and thus pure and homogenous in character.
7 This in turn demonstrates that the Japanese value a peaceful, honest and harmonious way of life, and are naturally opposed to egoism and strife.
8 Divinity, purity, harmony and virtues like honesty, loyalty and piety testify to the fact that Japan and the Japanese are (not only unique but also) morally superior to all other nations, races and peoples.

Because the 'national essence' referred to by *kokutai* could be understood as a socio-political and ideological system centred around, and determined by, the *tenno*, government and polity based on *kokutai* ideology has been called Tennoism.

Though in most cases the concept of *kokutai* was not formulated in an express and comprehensive manner, its meaning was nevertheless quite clear for there existed many texts which were rather explicit at least with regard to some of the listed points. Further, whoever criticized one of these points was censored, if not persecuted. Finally, most of these points – though not their complete

combination – were known from traditional sources, namely Japanese myth (*Kojiki* and *Nihongi*), Shintoist ideology, Shushigaku and its ideology of loyalty and piety, **Kokugaku** (especially the teachings of Motoori Norinaga, 1730–1801), Bushido (the way of the *samurai* and of his readiness to die a loyal death) and Mitogaku.

The *Kyoiku chokugo* appears rather moderate in tune. Nevertheless, it strongly indicates that the 'Imperial Throne coeval to heaven and earth' is something divine, that loyalty and piety are the most important virtues, that in the situation of 'emergency' one should sacrifice one's life 'courageously to the State', and that all this is infallible and eternal truth and duty. Most interpretations of the *Kyoiku chokugo*, at least the most effective, emphasized this meaning and strengthened it by explicitly speaking, for example, of divinity, unbroken continuity of the imperial rule, Japanese purity and Japanese unconditional loyalty to the *tenno*. In the last case, following a long standing tradition, they often added that the Mencian doctrine of justified revolution was not valid in Japan, since – in contrast to Chinese rulers – the *tenno* was a divine being. They could further explain that since the *tenno* was also the father of the people, and all Japan nothing but one family, conflict between loyalty and filial piety was impossible. Whereas classic Confucianism advocated critical loyalty (which could permit tyrannicide) and – if *dao*, the highest moral norm, allowed for this – valued piety over loyalty, Tennoism thus tried to preclude all possible sources of conflict between individual and state, or government. Among the influential commentaries on the *Kyoiku chokugo* which helped to pave the way for totalitarianism, nationalism and imperialism was **Inoue** Tetsujiro's (1855–1944) *Chokugo engi* (Commentary on the Imperial Edict) of 1891. Though in many respects comparatively moderate, it already stressed obedience, familiarism, and the organic unity of state and people. At that time, however, such indoctrination could still be criticized, as for instance **Onishi** Hajime (1864–1900), in his *Kyoiku chokugo to rinri setsu* (The Imperial Edict on Education and Ethics), did in 1893.

When Japanese politics became more and more totalitarian and imperialistic, criticism became increasingly difficult. Though during the Taisho era (1912–26) there were still periods of considerable freedom of speech, finally, during the Sino-Japanese War and the Second World War, the government was vitally interested in ideological support. Since the *kokutai* ideology provided an excellent means against any kind of political opposition, it was elevated to a sacred teaching. The *Kokutai no hongi* stated, 'Our country is a divine country governed by an Emperor who is a deity incarnate'. In the first place, the *kokutai* ideology could be utilized to justify imperialism and cruel war as the moral obligation to let other countries and people participate in the superior achievements of divine Japan, the most perfect nation and society in the world. (Indeed, as has been pointed out, the Japanese general Matsui Iwane (1878–1948) justified the 'rape of Nanjing' (1937) as a punishment meted out by a loving elder brother to his obstreperous younger brother.) Then, in the name of the emperor, the government and military could ask for unconditional obedience and readiness to sacrifice one's life.

Many Japanese perhaps never believed in *kokutai* ideology, but pressure and fear prevented most of them openly stating this. Some did make their views known, and were executed or died in prison. The ideology was not easy to believe, for it was a crude mix of fabrications, impossibilities and rhetoric instead of rational argument. However, the rhetoric was suggestive, and often beautiful, and the elements of the ideology seemed like an old truth. Indoctrination began even before 1890, and – though considerably varying in strength – continued till 1945. While until the end of the 1920s there was also significant critical dissent, in the 1930s indoctrination became ubiquitous, comprehensive and intensive. Domestic and foreign political problems, as well as social pressure, made it even more difficult for an individual not to believe that there might be some truth in *kokutai* ideology. Nevertheless, it remains difficult to explain how even a philosopher like Inoue Tetsujiro, who was well versed in both European and Chinese philosophy, and able to argue rationally and systematically, in his last years produced grossly irrational texts supportive of radical *kokutai* ideology.

The implications *kokutai* ideology had for Japanese philosophy were as follows. In the first place, this ideology precluded acknowledgement of universally valid human rights. Since the *tenno* was regarded as divine, and his 'children' as superior to other people, men could not be called equal Because of the superiority of certain human beings, the freedom of others had to be restricted. Since the *tenno* and *kokutai* were all-overruling values, the right to life was of rather limited worth. The very notion of *individual* rights was rendered invalid, for man – and at least the ideal Japanese – had to be conceived of primarily as integral part, and function, of a quasi-organic whole. The element *tai* in the word *kokutai* itself had a connotation of (living) body. Since the whole ideology was infallible eternal truth, to argue against it was anyway impossible. In particular, any justification of a right to resist, or even revolt against, a *tenno* (i.e., a Japanese government) was ruled out, for this had meant to go against the divine and against eternal truth. In sum, the ideology virtually precluded any kind of critically rational and humane practical philosophy (ethics, socio-political philosophy, and so on).

Accordingly, European enlightened philosophy, Marxism, socialism and classic Confucianism were unacceptable, and only philosophies supportive of *kokutai* ideology permissible. Hence evolutionism and German theories of statism and familiarism became influential. As early as 1882, and independent of the *kokutai* debate, Kato Hiroyuki (1836–1916) had relied on Social Darwinism to defend the idea that the stronger rightly oppress the weaker. Hozumi Yatsuka (1860–1912) and Inoue Tetsujiro utilized theories such as Otto Gierke's (1841–1921) doctrine that the state is a kind of living organism that does not allow for plurality of thought and behaviour, for this would endanger the state's life. They strengthened this approach by developing their notion of Japan as a uniquely 'harmonious racial' and 'family state'. Arguing against what he condemned as Western individualism and unwelcome Westernization of Japanese law, Hozumi wrote his *Mimpo idete chuko horobu* (The Emergence of the Civil Law and the Annihilation of Loyalty and Filial Piety).

As to Confucianism, while the classic notions of critical loyalty and piety, and Mencius' (372?–289? BCE) and Xunzi's (313?–238? BCE) justifications of tyrannicide were attacked as foreign and un-

Japanese, Shushigaku's most reactionary doctrines of unconditioned obedience were revived. Only philosophy that was, or appeared to be, unrelated to ethics, morality, politics, society and culture remained free of the restrictions the *kokutai* ideology imposed on philosophical thinking. Except for the first twenty years of Meiji, and apart from certain versions of philosophical aesthetics, however, such philosophy did not play an important role before the end of the Second World War.

See also: Confucianism in Japan, post-Meiji; Japanese philosophy, post-Meiji; philosophy of human rights, Japanese

Further reading

Gauntlett, J. and Hall, R. (eds and trans.) (1949) *Kokutai no hongi: Cardinal Principles of the National Entity of Japan*, Cambridge, MA.: Harvard University Press (*Kokutai no hongi* is an ideological and indoctrinating pamphlet that expresses the political conditions and restrictions under which Japanese philosophy developed from about 1890 through the end of the Second World War).

Gluck, C. (1985) *Japan's Modern Myths: Ideology in the Making in Late Meiji Period*, Princeton, NJ: Princeton University Press.

Kato Hiroyuki (1894) *Der Kampf ums Recht des Stärkeren und seine Entwicklung*, Berlin: Friedländer.

Minear, R. (1970) *Japanese Tradition and Western Law: Emperor, State, and Law in the Thought of Hozumi Yatsuka*.

Najita Tetsuo and Koschmann, V. (eds) (1982) *Conflict in Modern Japanese History*, Princeton, NJ: Princeton University Press.

GREGOR PAUL

Korean philosophy

Korean philosophy has its roots in shamanism (see **shamanism in Korea**), which is the earliest religion of the Korean people. Around the fourth century CE, Buddhism and Confucianism arrived in Korea from China, and they have had a significant impact in shaping Korean ways of thinking. They have constituted large parts of Korean philosophy for nearly two thousand years.

As in the case of the whole of Asia, religion and philosophy have been closely interrelated in Korea. This is especially true in the cases of Buddhism and Confucianism.

With the arrival of Christianity and Western ideas in Korea around the eighteenth century, Western philosophy has been an important part of the philosophy curriculum in most colleges in Korea. Western educational, political and scientific ideas have reshaped much of the Korean way of thinking and living. Christianity was instrumental in bringing much of the Western educational system, including Western philosophy, to Korea. Today Korea is philosophically and religiously a pluralistic society.

In recent years, there has been some tension between tradition and modernity in religion and philosophy. Christianity represents the modern Western religion and a major challenge to the traditional religions. Christianity has been the fastest growing major religion in Korea, especially since the end of the Second World War in 1945, when Korea gained independence from Japanese colonialism. Christianity, both Roman Catholic and Protestant, is probably the largest religion in Korea today and is strongest in the areas of education, financial resources, and social and cultural programmes. However, Buddhism has been regaining some popularity and strength in recent years due to active propagation of their faith by the monks and renewed interest in the meditation of Buddhism among the general public.

Further reading

Choi Min-hong (1980) *A Modern History of Korean Philosophy*, Seoul: Sungmoon Sa.

Kim Joungwon (ed.) (1996) *Korean Cultural Heritage, Vol. II: Thought and Religion*, Seoul: Korea Foundation.

Korean National Commission for UNESCO (1983) *Main Currents of Korean Thought*, Seoul: Sisa yongo Sa.

Lee, P. (ed.) (1993, 1996) *Sourcebook of Korean Civilization*, 2 vols, New York: Columbia University Press.

YONG-CHOON KIM

Korean philosophy, contemporary

When Korea gained independence from Japanese colonial rule in 1945 at the end of the Second World War, Korea was divided by the superpowers into North Korea and South Korea. In North Korea, communism became the politico-socio-economic philosophy, while in South Korea democracy and capitalism became the basis of the political system and philosophy.

In South Korea, because of its democratic system, the free expression of philosophical and religious views has been allowed, and Korea has become increasingly a pluralistic society in philosophy and religion. At present, Buddhism and Christianity are the largest and strongest religions, and Confucian ethics still play a significant role in the Korean way of life.

In South Korean universities and colleges, both Western and Eastern philosophies are being taught almost equally. This fact indicates that Korean students have a more balanced education in philosophy than Western students in general, who are mostly acquainted with the Western philosophy, but relatively little exposed to the Eastern philosophy. Korean college students are generally familiar with the Korean and other Eastern philosophies.

Revitalization of the traditional philosophy

Since 1945, there have been debates concerning the value of the traditional philosophies of Korea. Some scholars thought that Korea lost vitality because of the extreme fundamentalistic adherence to the traditional philosophy of Confucianism. They blamed especially Neo-Confucian orthodoxy as the cause of the backwardness of the nation's politico-socio-economic system. However, many scholars began the revitalization of the traditional philosophies of Korea by interpreting them in a new historical and systematic method, which was influenced by Western philosophy.

The first Korean scholar, who revitalized the traditional Korean Confucianism as a contemporary living philosophy, was Hyon Sang-yun. Another philosopher, who made a similar contribution, was Yi Sang-eun. In 1949, Hyun Sang-yun published *Choson Yuhaksa* (History of Korean Confucianism) in Korean. This was the first book on Korean Confucianism written in a modern historical and systematic method. In this book, Hyun defined the Neo-Confucianism of **Yi T'oegye**, which was based on the Neo-Confucianism of Zhu Xi, as the representative philosophy of Korea. Hyun regarded T'oegye's philosophy as the highest achievement of Korean philosophy from a pure philosophical point of view. Because of Hyun's influence, many new scholars became interested in the study of T'oegye and other Confucian philosophers in Korea.

Since 1950 an increasing number of scholars have studied Korean philosophy. Pak Chong-hong, who was an eminent philosophy professor at Seoul National University, made a significant contribution to the revitalization of the study of Korean philosophy by publishing important books on Korean traditional philosophy. He was very knowledgeable in both Korean and Western philosophy, and his books were written systematically and historically, using Western philosophical methodology. Choi Min-hong, a former philosophy professor at Chungan University, also made a similar contribution to contemporary Korean philosophy.

With government support, scholars at the Academy of Korean Studies and various universities in Korea, have been actively engaged in research and have published many books and articles on Korean philosophies, including Buddhism, Confucianism and Sirhak (Practical Learning). Some scholars have concentrated on the distinctive aspects of Korean Neo-Confucianism and Korean Buddhism. There has also been strong interest in Sirhak as a unique development of Korean Confucianism, which is qualitatively different from Neo-Confucianism. Many scholars find in Sirhak a distinctive modern spirit of Korean philosophy.

Han philosophy

Among some scholars, students and the general public, there has been increasing interest in the unique philosophy of Korea. One reason for this interest is due to the overwhelming influence of Western culture in Korean society in the areas of politics, economics, education, science and religion. Another reason is due to the confusion caused by the introduction of many religions and philosophies that have come to Korea and have formed parts of Korean traditions. In the midst of these phenomena, some Koreans have been searching for the identity of the so called 'Korean philosophy' or 'Korean thought'.

Since 1945, some Korean scholars have attempted to develop a 'Korean philosophy', which they refer to as 'Han philosophy' or 'Han ideology'. This is a modern reformulation and a new interpretation of the ancient Korean philosophy rooted in the idea of 'Han', which means 'one', 'large', 'whole' or 'totality'. Choi Min-hong, one of the main contemporary philosophers in Korea, was responsible for developing the Han philosophy. According to him, the idea of knowledge in Han philosophy is non-dualism. It does not look at reality in a partial or dualistic way, but always looks at the reality in totality. It avoids dualistic thinking, which views reality in two separate ways. Choi claims that only by looking at things as a whole or a unity, can the whole truth be discovered. According to him, such a view was held by ancient Koreans. They did not look at life and death as two entirely separate realities, but rather as a continuing process and unified whole. A man may live and die, but he does not cease to be. Life on the earth continues after physical death. The dead person continues to communicate with the living. This idea is strongly expressed in the ancestor worship, which has been practiced in Korea as in other parts of Asia since ancient times.

With regard to Han ethics, Choi Min-hong claims that the traditional semi-feudalistic and hierarchical ethics had to change because of the democratic ethics of the modern world. Also Han ethics could not sanction the dualistic and discriminatory system of the traditional ethics based on class distinction. Choi claims that the modern Western ethical idea of valuing individual freedom is also contrary to Han ethics, since individual freedom often leads to extreme individualism, which does harm to the good of the whole. Han philosophy places the standard of the good in a unified, totalistic point of view without negating or neglecting individual freedom. Ideally,

it attempts to harmonize and unify the ruler and people.

One of the most important ideals at the time of the founding of Korea was the idea of 'benevolent man' (*hongik in'gan*). The benevolent man is one who always benefits and helps others. Self and others are not separate, but unified in the spirit of the benevolent man. Choi claims that the spirit of the benevolent man is the spirit of Han philosophy.

According to Choi Min-hong, this Han spirit was also manifested in Hwarangdo (the Way of the Flower Youth), an elite order of knights chosen from the nobility during Silla dynasty (57 BCE–935 CE). The purpose of Hwarangdo was to select the ablest young men in the nation and train them in the spirit of unity so that they might dedicate their lives for the protection and wellbeing of the nation. The value system of Hwarangdo included unity, harmony and the good of the whole country, transcending individual desires. The Hwarang (knights) embodied the spirit of Han philosophy, viewing and valuing the totality of life and the good of the whole. They studied and cultivated noble moral character based on the syncretism of the Confucian ideals of filial piety and loyalty to the king, the Daoist ideal of the love of nature and the Buddhist ideal of desirelessness. Through military training they developed and displayed their love for the nation and trust in their community. By doing so, they became the driving force in the unification of the Three Kingdoms into one kingdom of Silla (668 CE).

According to Choi Min-hong, this same spirit of Han philosophy has come down to modern Koreans and formed the basis of their life. The Korean philosophy of Han is in keeping with the progress of the value systems of the modern world, which also seek harmony in areas such as politics and economics, and between races and cultures. Choi claims that Han philosophy, as the philosophy of totality and unity, contains within itself the principle of harmony, because harmony means integration of various ideas into a complete whole. Through such a philosophy people can overcome provincialism, racial discrimination and bias to other cultures. However, the number of those who subsribe to this Han philosophy in Korea is limited.

Western philosophy in South Korea

Western philosophy was introduced to Korea first through the Christian missionaries around the nineteenth century. German philosophy was introduced to Korea through the influence of the Japanese, the colonial power. Among the philosophy articles published in Korea between 1931–68, German idealism and existentialism were dominant, and Kant, Hegel and Heidegger were most frequently studied philosophers.

In 1953 the Korean Society for Philosophy was organized, and after 1950 a substantial number of Korean students went abroad, especially to the United States and Germany. Upon return to Korea, these scholars began to teach and publish on logic, philosophy of science, existentialism, and other areas of the Western philosophy. Existentialism became very popular among Korean intellectuals especially during the 1950s, because the Korean War during 1950–3 brought much suffering and anxiety in Korean society. Pak Chonghong contributed significantly to the popular study of existentialism in Korea.

Gradually the influence of American philosophy has become dominant in Korea, because after 1950 a majority of Korean students, who went abroad for the study of philosophy and religion, went to the United States due to the close relationship between Korea and the USA. Thus, after the Second World War and especially the Korean War, Korean society has been greatly influenced by American culture, including philosophy and religion.

Since the 1960s, Korean philosophical societies have become more active. The Korean Kant Society and the Society for the Study of Korean Thought were organized. In the face of speedy and massive introduction of Western philosophy to Korea, many Korean philosophers began searching for the identity of Korean philosophy and began the work of rediscovery of the traditional thought of Korea. During the 1960s, the main concern of the majority of Korean scholars with regard to Western philosophy shifted from German philosophy to British and American philosophies, as Korea has become a capitalistic country like England and the United States. Analytic philosophy, phenomenology and social philosophy have

also become important areas of study during and since that time.

Today, both Western and Eastern philosophies are studied almost equally in Korea. In contrast to the most Western countries, where most scholars and students of philosophy are ignorant about Eastern philosophy, most or all of Korean philosophy students and scholars have a balanced knowledge of both Eastern and Western philosophies.

Further reading

Choi Min-hong (1980) *A Modern History of Korean Philosophy*, Seoul: Seongmoon Sa, 237–50.
—— (1990) *Han Philosophy and the 21st Century*, Seoul: Seongmoon Sa.
Han'guk ch'orhak sasang yon'guhoe (Korean Institute of Philosophical Thought) (ed.) (1995) *Kangchwa Han'guk Ch'orhak* (Lecture on Korean Philosophy), Seoul: Yemoon Seowon, 283ff.
Kim Sang-il (1984) *Hanism as Korean Mind: Interpretation of Han Philosophy*, Los Angeles: Eastern Academy of Human Sciences.
Lancaster, L. and Payne, R. (eds) (1997) *Religion and Society in Contemporary Korea*, Berkeley, CA: Institute of East Asian Studies, University of California.

YONG-CHOON KIM

Kotoku Shusui

b. 1871; d. 1911

Marxist and anarchist philosopher

Kotoku Shusui (real name Kotoku Denjiro) was a rigourous critic of autocracy and imperialism who was executed because of his convictions. He was one of the first Japanese Marxists and anarchists. He was born in Nakamura, a small city in Kochi prefecture, the son of a merchant. In his early youth, he studied at a local Confucian academy. In 1887, he went to Tokyo to intensify his English studies. Because of his engagement in the Freedom and Peoples Rights Movement, however, he was soon forced to leave the city. In Osaka he met Nakae Chomin (1847–1901) and became his disciple. Over the following years, Kotoku turned to socialism and Marxism. In 1903, together with his friend and fellow socialist Sakai Toshihiko (1871–1933), he founded the *Heimin shimbun* (Commoners' Newspaper). In 1904, the two published the first Japanese translation of the *Communist Manifesto*. At the same time, they protested against the Russo-Japanese war. Though Kotoku hoped to realize his goals by legal and parliamentary means, he was accused of having violated a press law and imprisoned for five months (1905). After his release, he went to the United States where he stayed for half a year. During that time, Kotoku became attracted by Peter Kropotkin's (1842–1921) anarchism, and came to the conclusion that only extra-parliamentary activism could change Japanese socio-political conditions. Back in Japan, he accordingly turned into a radical activist. In 1910, he was accused of having been involved in a plot to assassinate the emperor, and in January 1911 was hanged.

In an autobiographical note published in *Heimin shimbun*, Kotoku explained 'how he became a socialist'. 'From his childhood', he said, he 'was intoxicated with the ideas of freedom and equality'. Among the works he read as a youth and which influenced him most were not only European treatises and Chomin but also **Mencius** (372?–289? BCE). Though he became a socialist only several years later, it seems clear that in his case the *Mencius* facilitated understanding and acceptance of ideas of human rights.

Kotoku's most important philosophical contribution was his *Nijusseiki no kaibutsu teikokushugi* (The Monster of the Twentieth Century: Imperialism), published in 1901. According to his analysis, imperialism is characterized by patriotism, militarism and expansionism, or colonialism. Kotoku holds that patriotism results from hate of an enemy rather than from love for one's home country. It is 'hatred, scorn and vain pride . . . by nature brutish, superstitious' (i.e., an uncivilized 'love' for one's country that is not based on reason and sound argument), intent on war. Militarism is the result of 'greed and desire for fame'. Like patriotism, it is also 'superstitious', and contradicts universal reason and morality. Expansionism too results from greed. Kotoku compares imperialism to pestilence which destroys everything it touches. He concludes

optimistically that in the future 'fraternity and justice' will suppress (immoral) patriotism and 'destroy barbarous militarism'.

In a letter to Kotoku, Chomin remarked that imperialism is comparable to the politics of the first Chinese emperor Qin Shihuangdi (d. 210 BCE) and the Han emperor Wudi (r. 141–87 BCE), with the utilization of 'modern precision weapons based on science' added. In Chinese history, Qin Shihuangdi, who united the warring Chinese states by a long war, is notorious for his inhumane and totalitarian politics, while Wudi is primarily remembered for his relentlessly expansionist politics. Like a Confucian scholar, Chomin points to the alternative, namely, humaneness as exemplified in virtuous Chinese (but also Western) men, and hints at the idea of a unification of Asia by such moral leaders. As has been noted, this indicates that even such a rational moral universalist as Chomin could be influenced by contemporary Japanese ideology, and thus the letter helps to appreciate the originality of Kotoku's thought.

In 1903, Kotoku wrote *Shakaishugi shunzui* (The Quintessence of Socialism) in which he tried to explain socialism on the basis of historical materialism, and also attempted to show that capitalism was inconsistent and ultimately doomed to failure. The texts he referred to included the *Communist Manifesto* and Marx's *Capital*. Though Kotoku argued that human progress requires revolutions, he still also looked to the possibility of conciliating socialism and the Japanese governmental system. While in prison in 1910, Kotoku wrote *Kirisuto massatsu ron* (The Killing of Christ) which, as Kato Shuichi (1919–) remarked, 'can be read as a critique' of Tennoism.

See also: kokutai ideology since Meiji times; philosophy of human rights, Japanese

Further reading

Notehelfer, F. (1971) *Kotoku Shusui – Portrait of a Japanese Radical*, Cambridge: Cambridge University Press.

GREGOR PAUL

KUISHEN *see* afterlife in Chinese thought

Kumarila Bhatta

b. 625; d. 675

Hindu philosopher

A Hindu **Purva Mimamsa** theorist of ritual, Kumarila was a wide-ranging philosopher whose influence was considerable. His major works include the *Shlokavarttika* and *Tantravarttika* commentaries on Shabara's commentary on the Mimamsa Sutras of Jaimini.

In Kumarila's view the individual self (**atman**) is eternal and omnipresent, a centre of agency (*karta*) and experience (*bhokta*). His epistemology is a form of direct realism and empiricism: the non-creative mind is a blank slate, the passive recipient of sense-mediated data. No potentially distorting inner realm of ideas and language is allowed to intervene between awareness and the given. Cognitions are to be considered as intrinsically valid (*svatah pramana*) on pain of infinite regress (*anavastha*). The validity of the beginningless, unauthored and unfalsifiable Vedic mandates follows from the simple fact that they are perceived. Cognitions are acts (*kriya*) which are per se formless (*nirakara*) and they are individuated by their objects. In other words, the difference between cognitions is due to the difference between objects. Cognitive acts relate the self in a unique way to specific objects. Cognitions, qua transitory acts, produce in their objects the quality of being known (*jnatata*). We know that we know by hypothetical presumptive inference (*arthapatti*) from this effect but not reflexively or by introspection. (This position standardly invites the objection that everything would be cognized by every observer.) Consciousness, having no perspective upon itself, only has the power to manifest or reveal objects and is not reflexive or self-manifesting (*sva-prakasha*). It is argued that a cognition, while functioning to illuminate an object cannot function to illumine itself as one thing cannot possess two operations (*vyapara*) simultaneously. Where the perceptual process is concerned, he holds that a perceptual episode occurs in two successive stages: a pre-linguistic and pre-conceptual (*nirvikalpa*) undifferentiated observation (*alochana*), which is comparable to the awareness of babies and the mute, of the object as an undifferentiated whole; this is immediately followed by a determinate, analytical and propositional perceptual awareness involving an explicit grasp of the object in its individuality with its real properties including its generic form (*akriti*).

As a Mimamsaka concerned with the nature of ritual duty (**dharma**), he is committed to the thesis that the infallible Vedic scriptures are intrinsically valid and our only means of knowing about that which lies beyond the bounds of sense, revealing what would otherwise be unknown. The Vedas are simply given; they have no author either human or divine (*apaurusheya*). The relation between a Vedic word and its referent is direct, innate and constant. Words primarily stand for everlasting universals (*samanya*), natural kinds (*jati*) and generic structures (*akriti*), on the basis of which they may be applied to individual instantiations (*vyakti*). He says that there is an eternal mutual dependence between the universal and the particular. A universal does not exist without particulars, and the particulars would not exist without the universal. Thus there is no absolute difference between them.

Unlike his fellow Mimamsaka **Prabhakara Mishra** and his followers, Kumarila recognizes that language may express both facts (*siddha*) as well as things to be done or states of affairs to be brought about (*sadhya*). But he restricts the independent cognitive authority (*pramanya*) of language to Vedic ritual prescriptions (*vidhi*), the factual being already established by perception and inference. Kumarila's account of the mechanism of language functioning is less sophisticated than that of Prabhakara, who was an adherent of the view that it is only in the context of a sentence that a word has meaning. Kumarila's theory is labelled 'Abhihita-anvaya-vada' which is paraphrasable as the view that a sentence (*vakya*) is a series of already expressed word-meanings. A sentence is a string of individual words, each in isolation denoting or naming a pre-arranged universe of discrete objects which is the primary epistemological 'given', which separately and serially express their own direct senses (*abhidha*; *padartha*) which are in turn combined to produce a further syntactically connected whole which is the sentential meaning (*tatparya-shakti*; *vakyartha*). Kumarila held that the meanings of individual words are universals (*jati*) construed as generic structures (*akriti*) whereas the sentential meaning is specific and relative to circumstances.

In accordance with the maxim, 'Not even the stupid act without some end in view', Kumarila thinks that the Vedic imperatives (*vidhi*) are hypothetical and have motivational and reason-giving force only for people who have an interest in the promised results of enjoined actions, even if this is only the avoidance of the demerit that would be the consequence of their neglect. In this he differs from Prabhakara and his followers, who espouse the deontological view that the Vedic injunctions (*niyoga*) have an intrinsic and automatic reason-giving force when heard by those whose ritual duty they command. They may thus be compared to categorical imperatives that are held to move to action regardless of the desires and interests of the agent.

To account for cases where a rite is not observed to deliver its promised result, the Mimamsakas introduced a special form of supernormal causality called *apurva* ('new'), which is a latent power specific to properly performed ritual acts which brings about their results at a later time. According to Kumarila, the potency lies dormant in its substrate which is the soul of the sacrificer and it may be actualized in future lives. It is thought of as overriding 'normal' causal and retributive karmic conditions.

Further reading

Bhatt, G. (1962) *Epistemology of the Bhatta School of Purva Mimamsa*, Benares: Chowkhamba Sanskrit Series.

Biardeau, M. (1954) *Theories de la Connaissance et Philosophie de la Parole dans le Brahmanisme Classique*, Paris and The Hague: Mouton.

Hiriyanna, M. (1993) *Outlines Of Indian Philosophy*, Delhi: Motilal Banarsidass.

Matilal, B. (1986) *Perception*, Oxford: Clarendon Press.

CHRIS BARTLEY

Kyoto school

The name 'Kyoto school' (*Kyoto-[gaku]ha*) refers to a group of scholars who, in their lines of thought, followed **Nishida** Kitaro (1870–1945), or utilized his key concepts. Hence, the philosophy of this group is sometimes also referred to as *Nishida tetsugaku* (Nishida philosophy). The reference to Kyoto is due to the fact that Nishida and the most influential members of the group taught at Kyoto University. Though Nishida is often called the founder of the Kyoto school, he never intended to establish such a uniform group. Probably, the name was first used by Tosaka Jun (1900–45) in his article *Kyoto-gakuha no tetsugaku* (The Philosophy of the Kyoto School) in 1932. Though the Marxist Tosaka studied under Nishida, he himself cannot be regarded as a member of the school. In fact, the question as to who should be called a member of the school has been answered quite differently, although certain names are almost always included: these are Tanabe Hajime (1885–1962), Hisamatsu Shin'ichi (1889–1981), Yamauchi Tokuryu (1890–1982), Nishitani Keiji (1900–90), Kosaka Masaaki (1900–69), Shimomura Torataro, Tsujimura Koichi (1922–) and Ueda Shizuteru (1926–). Ohashi Ryosuke (born 1944) perhaps represents the youngest generation of followers. Whether scholars like Suzuki Daisetz (1870–1966) should be called members of the Kyoto school is an open question. Suzuki's views on Zen, logic, and nature were similar to those of most members but his early scholarly studies in Buddhism and his attempt to spread Zen in the West also qualify him as an independent figure.

Generally speaking, the thought of the Kyoto school focuses on ontological, religious (or soteriological) and ethical issues, and on respective comparisons between Eastern and Western ideas. It is strongly influenced by a specific understanding of Buddhism, especially Zen, according to which the knowledge of true or absolute reality enables men to free themselves from all suffering. Thereby, true reality is interpreted as *mu* (**nothingness**) and *ku* (**emptiness**). This is also to say that true reality is interpreted as something unsubstantial. (Since everything exists only by virtue of being an (integral) element in a net of interdependent 'entities' and conditions, there are no substantial 'entities', independent 'selves' or identifiable isolated 'entities'.) Though this true reality is conceived of as inaccessible by means of formal logic and rational conceptualization, it is regarded as realizable by other means, namely intuition, a logic of contradictions, sudden enlightenment, mystical union and so on. Realization of true reality, the Kyoto school holds, testifies to the fact that this absolute is without distinction, non-dual, and beyond affirmative verbal articulation. This view is then reflected in the conviction that formal logic, rational distinctions, differentiation between subject and object and man and nature, self-assertion, and the use of technology preclude a profound and soteriologically relevant human life. Since self-assertion and use of technology are interpreted as derivations from, or violations of, the true (original, authentic, non-dual) ontological and morally relevant condition of reality, and humanity in particular, such conclusions can be understood.

Such understanding, however, need not imply approval. Seen from epistemological and logical points of view, the ontology and ethics of the Kyoto school appear rather questionable, and have accordingly been criticized by many scholars, particularly neo-Kantians, analytical philosophers, political scientists and critical Buddhologists. Among others, the following objections have been raised: (1) the fact that we cannot realize the alleged absolute by means of logic, does not permit the conclusion that we can realize it by non-logical means. Whether or not it can be realized, cannot be decided by argument, and is thus a matter of soteriological practice rather than philosophy. (2) Also, the ontology and ethics of the Kyoto school widely ignore the distinction between is and ought. (3) The distinction between absolute reality and everyday reality is not clear. Further, the descriptions of absolute reality contradict the view that it is beyond logical verbalization.

Following Nishida, members of the Kyoto school often characterized reality, and the existence of man, as self-contradictory identities. Here the objection is that if this is meant in the sense of formal logic, it is nonsense, and that if it is not meant in the sense of formal logic but, summing up insights gained from different points of view, as a pregnant reference to one identical object, or issue, it is unclear and confusing. Further, if 'self-contradictory identity' refers to everyday reality, it must be meant in the second sense. If it refers to the alleged absolute, then the question arises how this knowledge could be gained at all.

Besides the influence of Buddhist, and in particular Zennist, ideas and Nishida's thought had on the Kyoto school, Heidegger's (1889–1976) philosophy had a great impact on some of the school's members, especially Tanabe, Nishitani and Tsujimura, who also studied with Heidegger. Further, Nietzsche (1844–1900) and Master Eckhart (1260?–1327) were the object of much attention. That, during the Second World War, most members succumbed to the influence of kokutai ideology (see **kokutai ideology since Meiji times**), was not only the result of political indoctrination and pressure but also a consequence of their cultural leanings.

As indicated, the ontology, soteriology and ethics of the Kyoto school are reflected in the school's comparative philosophy of culture and politics. Most members sharply confronted Eastern and Western culture, almost equating the former with Zen, non-duality, the norm of a unity between man and nature, a communitarian and spiritual orientation, intuitive reasoning, indifference toward logicality and rationality, while more or less identifying the latter with logocentrism, rationality, ontological dualism, anthropomorphism, individualism, materialism and the will to instrumentalize nature. Accordingly, during the high tide of nationalism, they argued against universal ethics and democracy.

The scholar usually regarded as the most important representative of the Kyoto school is Tanabe Hajime. Tanabe studied at Tokyo University and was first primarily interested in philosophy of science, publishing such works as *Saikin no shizenkagaku* (Recent Natural Science) and *Kagaku gairon* (Outline of Science), which appeared in 1915 and 1918 respectively. His major work in philosophy of science, namely *Suri-tetsugaku kenkyu* (A Study of the Philosophy of Mathematics), also earned him his doctoral degree. In 1919, Tanabe became assistant professor at Kyoto University, and later Nishida's successor. In 1945 he resigned from his post.

While his earlier works display a strong interest in, and influence of, neo-Kantianism, his later studies are strongly influenced by and primarily focus on Hegel's (1770–1831) dialectics and Nishida's concepts of nothingness and logic. Distancing himself from what he regarded as

Nishida's negligence of the notion of species, Tanabe advanced a *shu no ronri* (logic of species) as a *shakai sonzai no ronri* (a logic of social being), thus interpreting logic (*ronri*) as a set of laws of social structures and structural developments. More or less equating the individual man with a logical individual, and mankind with a logical genus, Tanabe characterized the state as the mediating species between both, and emphasized the importance of this function. In particular, he held that the species of man is determined by his nation. After the war, and because of the sharp attacks he earned for his statism, Tanabe again changed his convictions and entered into severe self-criticism. However, his *Zengedo toshite no tetsugaku* (Philosophy as Repentance), published in 1946, may be characterized as an expression of religious or soteriological views rather than a philosophical treatise.

Soteriological interest is also apparent in the publications of other members of the Kyoto school. Hisamatsu Shin'ichi, in his interpretation of Buddhism, defended a notion of atheist religion. Nishitani Keiji, in his *Shukyo to wa nanika?* (What is Religion?), argued that absolute truth is a matter of religion, and Ueda Shizuteru made a name for himself with his comparative studies on mysticism, Zen and Master Eckhart.

However, followers of the Kyoto school also have to their credit philosophical investigations of quite a different nature. Perhaps the most valuable among these achievements are critical surveys and anthologies of the history of modern Japanese philosophy. Kosaka Masaaki's *Japanese Thought in the Meiji Era* and Ohashi Ryosuke's *Die Philosophie der Kyoto Schule* (The Philosophy of the Kyoto School), published in 1956 and 1990 respectively, are examples of such works.

Some scholars distinguish between a right wing and a left wing of the Kyoto school, and accordingly include Mutai Risaku (1890–1974), **Miki** Kiyoshi (1897–1945) and Tosaka Jun among the leftists. But the differences between the 'rightists' on one side and Miki and Tosaka on the other are considerable and significant, the latter two being Marxists; Tosaka was moreover an express critic of Japanese nationalism, who in the 1930s wrote works such as *Ideorogii no ronrigaku* (The Logic of Ideology) and *Nihon no ideorogiiron* (On Japanese

Ideology). Hence, Ohashi has called their characterization as members of the Kyoto school inadequate.

The case of Mutai Risaku is different. After having studied under Nishida and the philosopher of religion Hatano Seiichi (1877–1950), he graduated from Kyoto University in 1918. The titles of such works as *Hyogen to ronri* (Expression and Logic) and *Basho no ronrigaku* (The Logic of Place), published in 1940 and 1944 respectively, document the influence of Nishida and Tanabe. Even in his later writings, Mutai utilizes Tanabe's quasi-logical terminology for the purpose of practical philosophy. What distinguished Mutai from Tanabe, Nishitani and other members of the Kyoto school who are regarded as constituting the right wing was his postwar pacifism and his philosophy of a new humanism formulated in his works *Daisan hyumanizumu to heiwa* (The Third Humanism and Peace) (1951) and *Gendai hyumanizumu* (The Humanism of the Present) (1961). Mutai argued for a new ethics of humanity as a criterion of political, social, scientific and technological developments. By using the expression 'third humanism' he wanted to distinguish his notion of humanism from the concepts of Renaissance and Kantian-like individualist humanism. Acknowledging the relevance of both existentialism and socialism, especially Kierkegaard (1813–55) and Marx (1818–83), but criticizing them as one-sided, Mutai, with his philosophy of a new humanism, aimed at a theory of the existential and social interests of the concrete and historical man. As indicated, he remained indebted to Tanabe as far as he employed the categories genus, species and individual to express his ideas. This remains true in spite of his criticism of Tanabe. Whereas, according to Tanabe, only the 'mediation' of the 'genus' of mankind works against totalitarianism, according to Mutai, such 'logical' operation must be complemented by the force of real historical humanity. This view of Mutai's perhaps indicates his position in, or relation to, the Kyoto school.

See also: logic in Japanese philosophy, post-Meiji

Further reading

Buchner, H. (ed.) (1989) *Japan and Heidegger*, Sigmaringen: Jan Thorbecke Verlag (includes German translations of studies by Tsujimuru Koichi, Tanabe Hajime, Kuki Shuzo, Keiji Nishitani, Suzuki Daisetsu, Hisamatsu Shin'ichi, Tezuka Tomio and others).

Ohashi Ryosuke (ed.) (1990) *Die Philosophie der Kyoto- Schule*, Freiburg: Alber (includes German translations of studies by the main representives of the Kyoto School).

Parkes, G (ed.) (1987) *Heidegger and Asian Thought*, Honolulu, HA: University of Hawaii Press (includes translations of studies by Nishitani Keiji and Yuasa Yasuo).

GREGOR PAUL

L

lakshana

Lakshana means 'definition' (generally, 'distinguishing mark'). In Indian philosophy, a satisfactory definition must cite a uniquely identifying characteristic (*asadharana-dharma*) of the definiendum: it is not a comprehensive enumeration of the properties of the object. For example, possession of the dew-lap is cited in the case of members of the class of cows.

A definition must avoid the defects of over-extension (*ativyapti*) where there is mention of a property present both in the definiendum as well as in cases exceeding the intended scope (for example, possession of horns where the class of cows is concerned), under-extension (*avyapti*) where the definition fails to apply to some of the definienda (for example, cows are brown) and inapplicability or impossibility (*asambhava*) where the definition misses the point altogether. The emphasis tends to be placed on the differentiating function; as **Shankara** says, 'an attributive expression specifies an entity in relation to members of the same class, but a definition demarcates it from everything else'.

Definitions of objects (*prameya*) and means (*pramana*) of knowledge propounded by various schools of realist persuasion are trenchantly criticized by the twelfth century non-dualist Vedantin **Shri Harsha**.

See also: aesthetics, Indian theories of

Further reading

Athalye, Y. and Bodas, M. (eds) (1974) *The Tarka-Samgraha of Annambhatta*, Poona: Bhandarkar Oriental Research Institute.
Granoff, P. (1978) *Philosophy and Argument in Late Vedanta*, Dordrecht: Reidel.

CHRIS BARTLEY

language, Chinese philosophy of

The Chinese language has provided a suggestive framework for the idea that language represents reality ever since Ezra Pound romanced about the pictographic quality of Chinese characters, so that every Chinese word is somehow a miniature picture. If that seems to confirm the fame of the poet-painter Wang Wei and his quip that there is a 'poem in every painting and a painting in every poem', that also goes counter to the statistics that Chinese graphs based on 'similitude to form' make up the smallest percentage of her characters. Then there is the further fact that spoken Chinese predated written Chinese, so that it is phones (sounds) and not graphics that lie at the root. Chinese writing came later; it just happened not to be structured around a phonetic alphabet.

But this opens the other flood gate: the use of homophones (words with the same or very similar sound) to explain the meaning of a word. This was very common even by the time of the Han. As with the pictographic exegesis, sometimes it works and sometimes it does not. Two classic examples are *yi* for righteousness and *gui* for ghost. The Doctrine of the Mean equates the former: righteousness is *yi* for 'what is appropriate to a situation'. This is still used today to defend the Mencian position that *ren* (**humaneness**) and *yi* (**righteousness**) are nearly synonymous and that both are (and not just the former, as **Gaozi** argued) 'inner'. This is because one is the universal Good and the other is its judicious application to 'fit a particular situation'. (This maligns and totally distorts the Mohist use of the objective standard of *yi* to show the harm that Confucian **rites** could do: rites that harm are not right.) The Neo-Confucians (see **Neo-Confucianism, concepts**) used the same phonetic pretext to reduce 'ghosts' to being *gui* for 'to return, withdraw'. Spirits, in the exegesis of the terms, are just the **ether** expanding (into gods) and contracting (into ghosts). It might qualify as the deism of the Song Enlightenment, but that was not how spirits were seen in early times.

The Chinese language has developed, over time, a large number of written characters but only a limited number of sounds, so that the challenge is not finding enough homophones; there are so many that Chinese actually make few jokes out of puns. The two cases related above show a creative use of selective homophones; they also demonstrate that what is at issue is not phonetics or semiotics but semantics and hermeneutics, not sound or reference but meaning and interpretation.

The density of the Chinese language is perhaps best illustrated by Broberg's hyper-meticulous translaton of the first line in the **Daodejing**, a virtual exegesis by itself. For fun, we can entertain a contemporary double entendre or a deconstructionist rendition, in which case we would have (a) 'The Walk that can Talk is the extraordinary Walk/Talk'; it will serve to remind us that to 'walk the talk and talk the walk' is a primal union of the Word and the Deed; and (b) 'The Course that can be Discoursed is not the invariable Dis/Course'. The density of the Chinese *langue* was in part an accident of history. There was, in Waley's words, a 'crisis of language' at the dawn of the age of philosophers for the simple reason that the written language was still evolving and there was a limited availability of words. The *Analects* could manage only short snippets of conversation.

Allegations that the Chinese did not think in terms of eidetic Being and discrete beings (as the transcendental Greeks allegedly did) led to a number of postulations about Chinese thinking in terms of process, or with a part/whole logic, or having not to deal with the problematic verb 'to be'. Some of the old East/West contrasts have, it seems, become *passé*. Other contrasts have stayed alive due to, for example, an infusion of Whitehead. There is the question of whether the Chinese debated on Being and **non-being**, if the words *yu* and *wu* do not involve the copula 'to be' and 'not to be' but rather 'there is, have' and 'there is not, have not'. Whether this can be resolved at the level of philology is questionable. The *Book of Changes* counts 'non-change' as one of its principles; Wang Bi knew the term *wu* as a virtual **nothingness**.

Perhaps the most powerful recent hypothesis concerns Chinese 'mass nouns' based on the fact that the Chinese language does not require articles or numerals before a word like 'horse'. Upon this, Chad Hansen has offered a solution to why 'White Horse is not Horse'. A foreign language always delights the speculative, but at some point we have to move into the larger units of speech. Single unique concepts are hard to translate, but sentences, paragraphs and whole essays provide enough internal context for making the overall meaning translatable. So it would seem more fruitful to move beyond the semiotics of signs to considering the larger structures of language and thought, and venture into correlative logic, parallel prose, analogies and metaphors where such cultural differences may often (not always) be diminished.

Finally, it is well to remember that language can change and new expressions are created all the time. There is no Greek basis for saying 'Logos becomes flesh', but a converted Europe would think otherwise. Many Chinese now do not blink an eye reading how the '*dao* became flesh'. It is not that Europe has one language that is providentially analytical and China has another language that is pre-eminently synthetic; the same language can be made to serve either or both ends, and Europe had to wean itself off the language of alchemic correlation. Everyday English and everyday Chinese are not that different. It is historical circumstance like the required 'eight-legged' style at the examinations that causes the Chinese to think in more complex syntactical forms than they had to or even wished to.

Further reading

Boltz, W. (1994) *The Origin and Early Development of the Chinese Writing System*, New Haven, CN: American Oriental Society.

Hansen, C. (1983) *Language and Thought in Ancient China*, Ann Arbor, MI: University of Michigan Press.

WHALEN LAI

language, Islamic philosophy of

In the early years of Islamic philosophy, there was a protracted debate over the role of language as a theoretical tool. Some thinkers argued that the best way to investigate difficult issues was by using logic which transcended particular languages, while others were convinced that the grammar of a language is what is required to investigate problems which arise within that language. The particular source of problems lay in religion, and in particular in understanding the meaning of the Qur'an, which sometimes is not entirely clear. Also, the other sources of authority in Islam, including the traditional sayings of the Prophet and his Companions (the *hadith*), the corpus of religious law and theology, and the practice of the community, the *sunna* (for the Sunnis) or the teaching of the *imams* (for the Shi'i) often presented divergent understandings of the meaning of religion. Those inclined to mysticism also tended to separate religious propositions into the *batin* (hidden) and the *zahir* (open), and offered a methodology for distinguishing between them. Clearly the issue of how religious language is to be understood, and the implications this has for language as such, is an important issue in Islamic philosophy.

There was a famous debate in Baghdad in 320 AH/932 CE between Abu Bishr Matta, a logician and translator and the theologian and grammarian Abu Sa'id al-Sirafi. Matta argued that language consists of meanings which are there regardless of the particular language, and we need to examine these meanings using logic and not the language itself. Language deals with the contingent and conventional, while logic is attuned to the general and the necessary. Al-Sirafi countered that it is not possible to separate logic from language, since logic is inevitably infected by the structure of the particular language in which it is expressed. To understand problems in Arabic texts we need to use the science of Arabic grammar; a logic which is based on Greek grammar is not going to be of much value here. Although on this particular occasion al-Sirafi was taken to have won the argument, logic did enter into the Islamic sciences quite powerfully, and even those theologians who disapproved of philosophy tended to use logic and argue for it in their texts (a particular example is **al-Ghazali**).

The history of Islamic philosophy often seems like a debate between different theories of meaning, one broadly Neoplatonic and developed by **Ibn Sina** and al-Ghazali, and one more Aristotelian and supported by **Ibn Rushd**. The ways in which they are characterized are often in terms of essence and existence. According to Ibn Sina, essence has priority over existence in the sense that what actually comes into existence is dependent upon a particular idea or notion being brought into existence. Ultimately the mover of ideas into existence is God, and in principle it is entirely up to him what he instantiates. Al-Ghazali uses this theory to good effect to argue that what could happen to the things of our world is entirely up to God, and we should not think that there is any natural or any other kind of necessity in existence. The implications for meaning are clear. If we can imagine one of our ideas changing in a particular way, then that shows that such a change is meaningful, provided it is logically possible. We can imagine being reunited with our bodies after death, we can imagine God creating the world out of nothing, we can imagine a ball of cotton coming into contact with fire without burning, and this shows that all these ideas are meaningful.

According to Ibn Rushd, for whom existence precedes essence, we cannot conclude that what may be imagined is therefore possible. The causes of events are part of the meaning of those events and cannot be separated from them. The fact that we can imagine changes to the customary pattern of nature does not show that we can really incorporate such changes in our conceptual scheme and the corresponding language. If the meaning of cotton involves something which is burnt when in contact with a flame, one cannot conclude that cotton could not burn merely by thinking of it not burning when in contact with a flame. How then should we understand language when it is given a religious use and seems to evade the normal constraints of meaning? According to al-Ghazali, this language must be understood literally, since any suggestion that the language describing God as an agent or as a knowing subject is ambiguous and does not do justice to the very real sense in which God acts and knows. Ibn Rushd takes an entirely different line, that we cannot use the same language for God as we do for ourselves. God cannot be defined in terms of genus or species, he cannot be thought of as containing a variety of attributes as we do. God can be described, but when properties are applied to him they are used perfectly and only applied to us derivatively, or *pros hen* as Aristotle would put it. There is nothing wrong with equivocation in language, Ibn Rushd argues, and insisting that language is used univocally runs the risk of treating God as very much someone like us, which is surely not appropriate.

The implication of Ibn Rushd's argument is that the best people to understand the theoretical difficulties of religious language are not the theologians but rather the philosophers, who are able to appreciate the subtlety of the language. One of the characteristics of the language is that it is rich enough to appeal to a number of different audiences, and it requires a philosopher to understand and explain how this works. The text will speak to those capable of understanding demonstrative argument in demonstrative ways, and to those only capable of lesser forms of thought (lesser in the sense of less rigorous) in appropriate ways for them. So, right at the bottom of the demonstrative scale poetry will be used to impress and enthuse those who are only capable of being moved by that sort of language. The problem with allowing the theologians and the jurisprudents to sort out these issues is that their demonstrative abilities are insufficiently developed to get a good grasp of the variety of forms of argument and language which exist. All they manage to do is to confuse the situation even more, perhaps even inspiring doubt in the individual with regard to his faith. This is something the philosopher always tries to avoid. He knows that philosophy and religion are merely two different ways of looking at the same issue, and would not talk philosophically to those who are incapable of benefitting from such language, and whose faith might indeed be harmed by it.

See also: logic and Islamic philosophy

Further reading

Ibn Rushd (1976) *Fasl al-maqal* (Decisive Treatise), ed. and trans. G. Hourani as *Averroes on the Harmony of Religion and Philosophy*, London: Luzac.
—— (1978) *Tahafut al-tahafut* (Incoherence of the Incoherence), trans. S. Van den Bergh, London: Luzac.

OLIVER LEAMAN

Laozi

Tradition assigns to the figure of Laozi (Lao-tzu) the honour of being the founder of the Daoist tradition. His text, the *Laozi* or **Daodejing**, is the first to elevate the *dao* above the particular 'ways' and to elaborate on it as the natural Way of all things. Laozi is sometimes said to be Li Er, an elder contemporary of **Confucius** whom Confucius supposedly consulted. But tracking down the true roots and real lineage of Daoism proves a much harder task. Tradition may count Laozi, **Zhuangzi** and Liezi as the three classical Daoist thinkers; but of the three, the book that bears Liezi's name is a fourth century CE text, and Zhuangzi (399–295 BCE) was not called a Daoist by the Grand Historian in Former Han. He was paired with Laozi, and the two were seen as philosophically linked really only by the Neo-Daoists who came after the Han dynasty. Before that, Laozi was regarded as a political theorist while Zhuangzi would have nothing to do with politics. Zhuangzi also accepted the natural course of death to such an extent that the religious Daoists who honoured Laozi and pursued **immortality** did not count Zhuangzi as a member of their group at all. They did not include his work, retitled the *Nanhuajing*, in the Daoist canon until rather later, in the sixth century CE. (Nanhua or 'southern flower' is in honour of Zhuangzi, who came from the south as the bloom among men.)

There might be earlier sayings of Laozi but the text of the *Laozi* as we have it today is most likely a work of the Warring States period. It first attracted the Legalists; **Han Fei** (d. 233) wrote the earliest commentary on the first chapter. The recent recovery of this text in a Han tomb verified the text's tie to politics of a Huang–Lao (Yellow Emperor and Laozi) school of thought that rose in the late Warring States period and impacted on the politics of the early Han dynasty. But after the Han, the text of the *Laozi* has been read with the Neo-Daoist text of Wang Bi. Most people now associate the *Laozi* with that more mystical interpretation. The roots of the Daoist tradition are equally elusive. Feng Yulan saw it as being derived in part from Yang Zhu, the egoist who treasured life and prized his self, a motif that can be found also among the Daoists. Sima Qian the Grand Historian in the Han period traced the Daoist tradition further back to the office of the court oracles. If that seems to point to an ancient religious root, then interestingly the *Laozi* does compare the *dao* to the 'mystic female'. The word 'female' is not just anti-patriarchal but also pre-anthropocentric: it is the 'female' of animals, a bovine creature.

The *dao* is the ineffable, the One behind the many, the **non-being** pregnant with *de* (potency, virtue, power). It is Nature in its spontaneity, the non-action doing nothing that nonetheless gets everything done, the **emptiness** in the centre, the motionless eye of the storm, the Valley nurturing all things. This *dao* frequently reverses the values of the world. It regards the weak as the strong, elevates the babe above the adult and the female over the male, as it mocks the mores of the world. It reacts as *yin* would, it seems, to the *yang* of the Confucians. The Daoist imitation of Nature fuelled the hopes of realizing physical longevity. Its praise of *wuwei* (non-action) led to a politics of *laissez-faire*. It hints at a diligent quest for the occult and an exploding pantheon of immortals, poetic metaphors to some but living reality to others. Zhuangzi, who waxed poetically on the text, dismissed the artificial quest for longevity, yet was himself turned into an immortal.

Although the *yin–yang* idea was ancient and sometimes characterized as Daoist, the *yin–yang* philosophy was in fact systematized by **Zou Yan** and had its own school in the age of philosophers. That organic, correlative philosophy became the basic Chinese worldview held in common by the Huang–Lao school, *yin–yang* Confucianism and an eclectic school (often called Daoist) that gathered around Prince Huainan, the brother of Han Emperor Wu. As Han rule and the Han Confucian ideology weakened, two organized 'religious Daoist' movements arose. One of them, the Way of the Heavenly Masters (which lineage of 'Daoist popes' lasts to this day) produced the Xiang'er commentary on the *Laozi*. But it is the Neo-Daoist movement of the Wei-Jin period that organized the text of the *Laozi* and the *Zhuangzi* as we now know it. **Neo-Daoism** is however a somewhat misleading English misnomer. The Neo-Daoists were scholar-officials drawn to what they called the 'dark learning'. They probed the three 'dark mysteries' of the *Yijing* (a Confucian Classic), the *Laozi* and, belatedly, the *Zhuangzi*. They might be inwardly Daoist but outwardly they were Confucian; and at the start of the movement, proud of it. Ho Yan (d. 239), the prime minister of Wei, turned to the wisdom of Laozi only after rating Confucius the better thinker: Confucius knew the *dao* and knew better than to speak openly of it. The lesser Laozi spoke.

Wang Bi (226–49) provided the definitive exegesis of the *dao* as non-being, the empty substance informing the concrete functions of all things. It is the One unused (useless, actionless) milfoil stalk being put aside to make it possible for the Many to move, although how is entirely mysterious. This conception of non-being lifted it to new transcendental heights and paved the way for the Chinese Buddhist reception of **Hinayana nirvana** as well as Mahayana emptiness. Later, Guo Xiang (d. 312) would in his commentary on the *Zhuangzi* oppose Wang Bi's thesis. He argued simply that something cannot come from nothing. He then offered the radical alternative to that of creation *ex nihilo*: things just are. Nature being by definition 'spontaneous', the myriad things come about in an instant. This reading however also eased the path to acceptance of the Chinese Buddhist understanding of *tathata*, seeing things-as-they-are or suchness.

Further reading

Hansen, C. (1992) *A Daoist Theory of Chinese Thought*, New York: Oxford University Press.

Laozi (1963) *Lao Tzu: Tao Te Ching*, trans. D. Lau, Harmondsworth: Penguin.

—— (1989) *Te-Tao Ching: A New Translation Based on the Recently Discovered Ma-wang-tui Texts*, trans. R. Hendriks, New York: Ballantine Books.

WHALEN LAI

Lateral and Longitudinal Alliance, School of

This name, sometimes called the School of Alliances, refers to two political strategies in the Warring States period. To oppose the rising power of Qin in the West spreading eastward, the 'longitudinal' defence was to have the states up and down (north to south) join force. Meanwhile, the Qin used a lateral truce and entered into a non-aggression pact with a power further east, and so the future First Emperor swallowed up his closer neighbour. Later in Buddhism, the vertical describes a gradual ascent (via various spiritual ladders) while the horizontal which cuts across refers to a sudden deliverance by single-minded faith in Amitabha. This is not to be confused with warp and woof, the criss-crossing threads on a loom which were used to characterize the inter-locking relationship between the Classics and the Apocrypha, woof and warp in Han exegesis.

WHALEN LAI

law, natural

To overcome the parochialism of the city states and the moral relativism, the Stoics as the first cosmopolitans (citizens of the universe) conjoined nature and law into 'natural law'. They were committed to a personal ethics that afforded them an 'inner peace' or *apatheia* well adapted for living in the new, mass society of the empire which had swallowed up the city states.

Classical China faced a similar dilemma when the Zhou rule by '**music** and **rites**' collapsed.

Music and rites were said to be composed by the Duke of Chou; they marked culture and its depature from nature. But moral relativism spread in the Warring States period. **Xunzi** tried to anchor the ritual codes, created by sages, on some principle in nature. But the Legalists supported only positive law; it was the Huang–Lao wing that looked to some natural principles. To combat the immorality of the Legalists and of the power politics they supported, **Zou Yan** came up with scientific rules about the succession of the elements and of dynasties. It is that cosmic law that alone could induce some fear among what otherwise would be ruthless men of destiny who lived by naked power alone. By the Han dynasty, natural principles were made to underwrite imperial law. So morality received a cosmic stamp of approval. The *Filial Classic* declared **filial piety** to be the basic support of the universe. The problem with equating human norms with cosmic principles is that any attack, say, on filial piety was then perceived as an attack on the cosmic law. Disobeying the father suddenly turns into a revolt in defiance of **Heaven** itself.

WHALEN LAI

Legalism

Han Fei actually appeared at the end of a variety of Legalist schools and produced the main statement of this school of thought. Legalism is interested mainly in the organization of the state, although not really in legal organization. Rather, it describes and justifies the principles of leadership and social control. There was a protracted debate in the school as to its leading principle, whether it is *shi* (power or authority), *fa* (law or regulation) or *shu* (the technique of making friends and influencing people). Han Fei produced a synthesis of these different points of view by arguing that all are criteria of effective government. The successful leader has authority, and uses it to establish a system of legislation, and because he knows how to impose this system of law in such a way that people do not even realize that they are being controlled by it, he is is an efficient political operator.

One of the interesting features of Legalism which serves to distinguish it from other forms of Chinese philosophy is its lack of respect for the past. The Legalists argued that in the past the precise mechanisms of social control were not so important, since there were few people around and a lot of resources, so there was not much scope for conflict; but during modern times the situation is very different. There exists a requirement for strong legislation to control the people and establish a community, and what the ruler chiefly needs is power, which could be very different from the capacity to lead by the example of his moral character (the Confucian model). The ruler does not need himself to incorporate the Confucian virtues, he will be able to get others to do this for him; and one of the political skills he can employ is making people think he has qualities which in fact he does not have. He can do this as a result of his political skills, and will be able to use punishment and reward to shape the thinking and behaviour of the citizens. He understands how people are affected by pleasure and pain, and through his awareness of human nature he can devise laws and institutions which build on it and direct the actions which stem from our nature in ways which are in both his and our interests. After all, it is in all our interests for harmony to prevail in the state.

One might have thought that the Daoists and the Legalists would have little in common, but the contrary is the case. The Daoists are in favour of a policy of doing nothing, yet with everything being done, the principle of *wuwei*. The Legalists take this to show that the best kind of ruler should follow the principles of non-action, allowing others to act for him without their even realizing that they are doing so. After all, we are part of the natural world, and so should be governed in accordance with the natural order of that world, the *dao*. The principles or *li* of reality reflect the principle of government by the clever ruler, who at his best controls everything by persuading others to behave in accordance with his wishes without them ever realizing that they have been persuaded. Part of his ability to control others is due to his ability to control himself, which he does by seeking to follow the *dao* and the *li* which represent for him the natural and appropriate way forward. It is in this alignment of the natural with the political that Legalism finds most support from Daoism.

The term 'legalist' makes explicit the principle of *fa* (law, method) as a means of rule, a rough designation of reflections on ways to govern the state. Traditionally, there are said to be three components, with Shang Yang (d. 338 BCE) teaching the overall importance of law and institutions, Shen Buhai (d. 337 BCE) the statecraft or the administrative means by which the ruler controls the ministers, and Shen Dao (350–275 BCE) the situational exercise of power that can take advantage of the specific circumstances. Han Fei (d. 233 BCE) is credited with the synthesis of the three. Legalism supports a strong, centralized state, bureaucratic rule, and clear and simple laws which are easy to understand and equally applicable to all with rewards and punishments well advertised before hand. No one, not even the old aristocracy with their privileges, is immune; none is above the law but the ruler.

The Legalists were political realists for whom the end – social order based on the power and wealth of the state – justified the means. To their critics, they were ruthless Machiavellians who respected no tradition. Since there could not be two sets of laws, they were also remembered for ruthless machinations. Fellow Legalist Li Si (d. 208 BCE) plotted the demise of Han Fei, forcing him to take his own life. In turn Li Si, fleeing from court, could have escaped but he died by a law that he himself instituted. The Marxists considered the Legalists the prime examples of materialist thinkers, and looked much more favourably on the achievements of the First Emperor who employed Legalism for conquest and rule.

The expression *xingming* appeared occasionally in classical Chinese philosophical literature. It has now been properly amended as being not about 'form and name' but 'punishment and name'. It is a stricture that came with the assignment of duties. A Legalist topic, it dovetails into the Daoist politics of the school of the 'Yellow Emperor and the *Laozi*'. The other side to the stick of punishment is the reward that is the carrot. But punishment connotes incarceration and torture, which does not speak highly of the Legalist view on how best to get people to comply with the law. Modern European visitors to imperial China found the Chinese use of torture to extract confession horrendous, and even now accused Chinese criminals do not have many rights.

Further reading

Chang, L. and Feng, Y. (trans.) (1998) *The Four Political Treatises of the Yellow Emperor*, Honolulu, HA: University of Hawaii Press (original Mawangdui texts with complete English translations and an introduction and with a foreword by B. Schwartz).

Creel, H. (1953) *Chinese Thought: From Confucius to Mao Tse-Tung*, Chicago: University of Chicago Press.

Graham, A. (1989) *Disputers of the Tao: Philosophical Argument in Ancient China*, La Salle, IL: Open Court Press.

Han Fei (1964) *Han Fei Tzu: Basic Writings*, trans. B. Watson, New York: Columbia University Press.

Hu Shih (1922) *The Development of the Logical Method in Ancient China*, Shanghai: The Oriental Book Company.

Peerenboom, R. (1993) *Law and Morality in Ancient China*, Albany, NY: State University of New York Press.

Wang, H. and Chang, I. (1986) *The Philosophical Foundations of Han Fei's Political Theory*, Honolulu, HA: University of Hawaii Press.

Watson, B. (1967) *Basic Writings of Mo Tzu, Hsun Tzu and Han Fei Tzu*, New York: Columbia University Press.

OLIVER LEAMAN
WHALEN LAI

Li Ao

fl. 789 CE

Confucian philosopher

A student of Han Yu, Li Ao might have influenced his teacher on the matter of the spiritual transmission of the *dao*. He also revived the debate on human nature. His master held a theory of a three-grade classification of man which falls short of the pristine Mencian ideal. The acceptance of gradations often means a concession to status distinction and a limit to permissible political advancement. Li Ao in his essay 'On Retrieving One's Nature' accepted a homogeneity of human nature, but he was not entirely free of the Buddhist ascetic attitude. He pitted the goodness of 'nature' against the evil inherent in 'feeling'. This vitiates the Mencian thesis where **filial piety** is as much 'human nature' and 'humane feeling'. The Song dynasty Neo-Confucians resolved this through a more nuanced reading of the Doctrine of the Mean (see **Neo-Confucianism, concepts**).

See also: Zhu Xi

Further reading

Barrett, T. (1992) *Li Ao: Buddhist, Taoist, or Neo-Confucian*, Oxford: Oxford University Press.

WHALEN LAI

li as morality

There are two concepts of *li* in Chinese, which must not be confused, since they have distinct characters. *Li* in one concept means 'principle', and may well have appeared first in the *Book of Changes*. The other means 'ritual' (and is linked with the word for 'sacrifice'). It has developed into 'religion' or 'morality', but its original meaning is 'rites of propriety' and it denoted part of the ritual of sacrifice. It brings out nicely the connection in much Chinese philosophy between the appropriate performance of ritual tasks with morality. The carrying out of rituals is taken to be representative of the various actions which are conducive to **harmony** and social stability, so *li* cannot just be seen as the public aspect of private morality. On the contrary, it is part and parcel of the development of moral dispositions and ways of thinking as well as acting. The Legalists attacked this idea, arguing that a notion of *li* is much too weak to serve as a means to instil rules of good behaviour in people (see **Legalism**).

Further reading

Chan Wing-tsit (1972) *A Source Book in Chinese Philosophy*, Princeton, NJ: Princeton University Press.

Confucius (1993) *The Analects*, trans. R. Dawson, Oxford: Oxford University Press.

Creel, H. (1953) *Chinese Thought: From Confucius to Mao Tse-Tung*, Chicago: University of Chicago Press.

Fung Yu-lan (1952) *A History of Chinese Philosophy*, trans. D. Bodde, Princeton, NJ: Princeton University Press.

Griffiths, P. (1994) *On Being Buddha: The Classical Doctrine of Buddhahood*, Albany, NY: State University of New York Press.

Kaltenmark, M. (1969) *Lao Tzu and Taoism*, Stanford, CA: Stanford University Press.

King, S. (1991) *Buddha Nature*, Albany, NY: State University of New York Press.

Tu Wei-ming (1985) *Confucian Thought: Selfhood as Creative Transformation*, Albany, NY: State University of New York Press.

Watson, B. (1967) *Basic Writings of Mo Tzu, Hsun Tzu, and Han Fei Tzu*, New York: Columbia University Press.

OLIVER LEAMAN

li as principle

Meaning principle or rationality, the word *li* describes the veins in marble stones; it suggests a pattern, a rationale, to the structure of reality. It became a near synonym for *dao*. But whereas *dao* retains a cosmogonic function, principle is simply the ever present rationale. It appears as such in some classical philosophers such as **Xunzi** and **Han Fei**. The early Buddhists, who had less use for a cosmogonic reference, freed principle as the transcendental norm from the world of matter. The Huayan school of Buddhism later postulated a *li* and *shi* (principle and face) distinction. That is, there is taken to be a clear line of connection between what appears to be real and what lies behind that appearance, the basis of reality. Along those lines, **Zhu Xi** distinguished principle and **ether**, the form 'above' and the form 'below'. The Neo-Confucians rejected the Huayan equation; their dictum has the One Principle present in the many differentiated particulars. As the Great Ultimate, the Principle is present in full in all things, and so remains undiminished despite its complete submersion in the world of our experience.

With its near synonym *dao* (Way), *daoli* as a compound functions like Logos and may denote Reason. *Lixie* (the study of principle) is the Chinese term for what in English is called Neo-Confucianism. It holds that everything has a *dao* and everything has a *li*; and that the mind can comprehend it (Zhu Xi) or the mind is it (Wang Yangming). Heaven imparts a *dao* to man; it embeds a *li* to things. A near synonym for *dao*, *li* is different from *dao* in one regard. *Dao* can be said to give birth to all things; it may have a cosmogonic function. Principle is the reason for things being what they are; it is usually not credited with their material creation. For that, *li* has the appeal of being a 'metaphysical' principle and was adopted by the Song Neo-Confucians to describe the Principle over and against the ether (**qi**, the materiality) of things.

The Neo-Confucians used the concept of *li* as the metaphysical essence of the world, and the significance of this idea is that there is something which is actually the basis to everything, perhaps something like gas, out of which everything else could be said to be made. Of course, this then leads to the problem that if everything is made out of some common stuff, what is there in such material which could produce different things? All there is originally is a common form of material. The answer is that the *li* takes on some of the qualities of the object into which it is developing, since the principle of each object is different from principles of other objects.

The Neo-Confucians could then use the concept of *li* to attack Buddhism. Buddhism attacks the notion of the reality of *li*, since the idea of a permanent and unchanging principle which underpins reality is not acceptable to a theory which argues that there is no such permanent basis to anything, since the only thing which might be said to describe the essence of the world is **emptiness**. But the Neo-Confucians responded that although it is true that the world of our experience is characterized by impermanence and change, there are good reasons to defend the existence of eternal and permanent principles which lie behind that world. Zhuxi and Wang Shuren argue that the very determination of the Buddhists to reject attachment to the world is itself a form of attachment, attachment to rejection of attachment. It is the Confucians who are able to relate to the world appropriately, since they can distinguish between what is important, what is essential and what is superficial, and so can insulate themselves from the negative consequences of attachment.

The Huayan Buddhists argue that matter lacks its own essence, since it can be transformed into anything at all by whomever has the power to affect it. When it is shaped into something it takes on a form or power, a *shi*, but as matter it is *li*, the basis out of which all forms are constructed. It is not difficult then to identify *li* with the dao as the absolute principle behind change, and also to identify it with the **buddha nature**, and to regard the latter as an essential transcendent entity. It might then seem that there is no point in strictly differentiating between different metaphysical levels of what brings about change and what the basis of change is, since whatever is material must have some shape, and whatever has some shape must have something material about it. So the notion of ultimate reality is not that distant from the world of experience, and should not be seen as something mysterious behind it, the ordinary world with which we are all familiar, and there is little difficulty in relating this conception with the Daoist conception of nature and enlightenment as living in **harmony** with nature and the natural processes of the changing world.

But although the *li* has to have some shape or another, it does not have to have a particular shape, so the matter is always matter, but it is only matter if it also has a shape. When the shape is constructed, the matter comes into existence, in the sense that it takes on a particular shape. We might say that the matter remains matter throughout, and this is true, but the matter has to be shaped into a particular form if it is going to remain matter. The matter itself as matter does not change, and in a sense it remains dormant, since unless something changes it will not change by itself. It seems to have a rather problematic status before it is informed by principle, and this leads to the idea that it is equivalent to emptiness, which is challenged by the possibility of identifying it with the buddha nature. It provides scope for the Madhyamaka idea that the buddha nature is

everything, in all sentient things at least. Since all the things in our world are just matter informed in a particular way, and the form does not really exist in the sense that without the matter it is literally ineffective, all things are the same. Matter, as matter, is the same and does not change; it is only when it is shaped in some way that it comes to seem to be different from other shapes. Since the matter itself does not change it remains the same throughout, and so all things which we experience are in themselves the same thing. In just the same way, although our experience of the world suggests that it consists of many different kinds of thing, in so far as they all contain, and are based, on buddha nature, everything is really the same.

Further reading

Chan Wing-tsit (ed. and trans.) (1986) *Ch'en, Ch'un, 1159–1223. Neo-Confucian Terms explained: the Pei-hsi tzu-i*, New York: Columbia University Press.
Graham, A. (1958) *Two Chinese Philosophers: Ch'eng Ming-tao and Ch'eng Yi-ch'uan*, London: Humphries Lund.

WHALEN LAI
OLIVER LEAMAN

LI XUE *see* Neo-Confucianism, concepts

Liang Fa

b. 1789; d. 1855

Chinese Christian

The first ordained Chinese Protestant preacher, Liang (also known as Liang Afa) was converted by William Milne (1789–1822), and he was the second Chinese to be baptized by the Morrison mission. His pamphlet 'Good Words to Admonish the World' converted Hong Xiuquan, the later leader of the **Taiping** Rebellion, to the Christian faith. Before his conversion, Liang had already a clear sense of sin. Tutored by a monk, he confessed regularly his wrongs in an open field and towards **heaven** on the first and fifteenth night of the month (new moon and full moon, time of Buddhist fortnight confessionals). Liang's 'theology' is simple. Aiming to save souls from the jaws of the 'evil wind' (Satan), he stressed man's distinction in having a God-given soul which knows good and evil; but it was corrupted by Adam's sin such that man now lives a life of physical desires. That psychology of reason and emotion resonates with Neo-Confucian morality (see **Neo-Confucianism, concepts**). God, above the world that he created, is unlike heaven, which only the Emperor could worship. Accessible to all, God should be worshipped by all. Those who have faith in his Son will be saved. Christ had chosen to be born by the 'good wind' (Holy Spirit) in a pure woman. He had triumphed ultimately over Satan. Liang looked forward to the soul's rebirth in the Kingdom of God and spoke of the Church, a public (civic) community, as the 'kingdom of God' on earth. This inspired Hong to set up his own 'God-Worshipping Society' that later sought to bring about the eschatological 'Heavenly Kingdom of the Great Peace' on earth.

Further reading

Lai, W. (1995) 'The First Chinese Christian Gospel: Liang A-fa's "Good Words to Admonish the World"', *Cheng Feng* 38(2): 83–105.

Powers, E. (1952) *Christian Influence upon the Ideology of the Taiping Rebellion 1851–1864*, Madison, WA: University of Wisconsin Press.

Wagner, R. (1982) *Reenacting the Heavenly Vision: The Role of Religion in the Taiping Rebellion*, Berkeley, CA: Institute of East Asian Studies, University of California Press.

Wu Pei-i (1979) 'Self-examination and Confession of Sin in Traditional China', *Harvard Journal of Asiatic Studies* 38(1): 5–38.

WHALEN LAI

Liang Qichao

b. 1873; d. 1929

Reformer

A disciple of Kang Yuwei and party to the 1898 Reform, Liang Qichao (Liang Ch'i-ch'ao) left the

monarchists and joined the revolutionaries. He championed the cause of liberty and wrote an essay that basically changed the Neo-Confucian formula of 'learning to become a **sage**' into just 'learning to become a man' (see **Neo-Confucianism, concepts**). By that he meant a citizen, a 'public person' where the word 'public' is used to mean the 'lord' or 'what belongs to the king'. The neologism is significant because it marked a change in both conception and perception. Civil society in Europe meant public society and public meant 'what does not belong to the king'. In place of traditional Confucian morality, the new Republic sought to inculcate classes in 'Civics'. Liang wrote on what it means to be a 'new citizen'. He also moved beyond the New Text ideology of his teachers into modern critical scholarship, being one of the first to apply that to the study of Buddhist texts and historiography.

Further reading

Chang Hao (1971) *Liang Ch'i-ch'ao and Intellectual Transition in China 1890–1907*, Cambridge, MA: Harvard University Press

WHALEN LAI

Liang Souji

b. 1893; d. 1962

Philosopher

Liang Souji (Liang Sou-chi) was a modern Chinese philosopher who managed to retain the respect due a grand old man even under Communist rule. Liang made his name with his study titled *The Culture and Philosophy of East and West*. A landmark from a time when China sought to define itself *vis-à-vis* the West, this quest for a digest of European and Indian culture depicts the Promethean West seeking to dominate the external world of nature and an introvert India probing the deeper reaches of the psyche. This leads to Liang taking pride in the Confucian way of being able to take the middle path that avoids the two extremes. Unlike the Japanese quest for an Oriental Philosophy, where Zen inspiration remains predominant, the Chinese quest of Liang and of **Xiong Shili** turned initially to **Yogachara** Buddhism, only to return to the Confucian mainstream. Although such condensation of cultural essences remains a pastime among some comparativists, any Europeanist or Indologist would find the generalizations myopic because they are based on highly selective and accentuated data, as if the West is just a culture summed up by recent 'science and democracy', while India is lost forever in the timeless fog of mystical introspection. Such generalizations often tell us more of the perception of author and the problems a culture faces at that juncture in history than anything about the actual facts.

See also: orientalism

Further reading

Alitto, G. (1986) *The Last Confucian: Liang Sou-ming and the Chinese Dilemma of Modernity*, Berkeley, CA: University of California Press.

WHALEN LAI

liberalism in China

The First World War weakened the European imperial powers economically, thus enabling China to make relative progress. As industry and commerce grew, a new urban population of ten million people developed. Unlike Japan, which modernized by extending its traditional social (household and village) structure, the Chinese urban class struggled more independently; for example, 'modern marriage' based on individual choice took root in the cities while Japan, even now, retains the custom of *omiai* (arranged marriages). Exposed to the world stage, this new class also spearheaded a movement to 'save the nation', especially against Japanese aggression. Students who studied abroad in Europe, America and Japan returned with progressive ideas. The National University of Peking (known in shorthand as Beida) became the hotbed of student protests, thanks to key appointments made in the new Republic. Cai Yuanpei (1876–1940), educated in Germany, became the chancellor in 1916; Chen Duxiu (1879–1942), educated in France, became dean of the college of letters in 1917; Hu Shi (1891–1962), educated in the United States, became professor of literature the same year. And under Li Dazhao, the head librarian appointed the year after, worked a young assistant named **Mao Zedong**.

Liberalism, socialism and pragmatism left their mark among the youth. Cai turned a traditional academy into a modern university by fostering critical thinking. Chen founded the journal *New Youth* and set down six modern principles to counter the weight of tradition: (a) to be independent and not servile; (b) progressive not conservative; (c) aggressive not retrogressive; (d) international not isolationist; (e) utilitarian not impractical; and (f) scientific not dreamy-eyed. In the modern urban, capitalist culture, Confucianism was considered outdated for (a) teaching superstition and servility; (b) placing the family above the individual; (c) supporting social inequality; (d) inducing dependence via **filial piety**; and (e) upholding orthodoxy at the expense of the freedom of expression. Hu, who was tutored in Huxley and Dewey, advocated writing in 'plain speech' and regarded the use of the vernacular as a means for fostering national identity and staging a cultural renaissance. Considering the Confucian tradition as wholesale feudal baggage, he urged total Westernization in a slogan that embraces 'Mr Science and Mr Democracy'.

The May Fourth Movement came about on 4 May 1919, when five thousand students from Beida staged a demonstration protesting against the twenty-one demands imposed by Japan upon China. They appealed to the Western powers in the League of Nations meeting at the Conference of Versailles. May Fourth marked the peak of the Liberal movement. When the appeal failed, disillusionment drove a number of Chinese intellectuals to the left, to look to the Russian Revolution for a model of radical change. Chen and Li had been translating Marx and Lenin; Li became the first famous convert to the Communist cause. Chen also became a powerful spokesman, and of course Mao would outstrip them and all in time. Hu defended the path of gradual reform; he argued for pragmatic study of issues and against the lure into ideological 'isms'. But the shift to the radical left would leave the liberals behind and labelled as being bourgeois and pro-capitalist West. Although Hu Shih was honoured in the Republican era, he was slighted in his later years in

Taiwan under the Republic of China. The Guomindang there had decided to honour the tradition of Confucius, whom Hu had maligned. In looking for 'science and democracy' in China, however, Hu has assisted in the rediscovery of **Mozi**. He wrote on Mohism in English and offered a modernist *Outline to a History of Chinese Philosophy* (in Chinese), though his later attention was turned more to literature. Among those who seek a current revival of Confucianism, Hu remains a traitor to that cause. (The New Asia College in Hong Kong was founded for the purpose of preserving and propagating this positive evaluation of Confucianism.)

Further reading

Chou Ts'e-tsung (1960) *The May Fourth Movement: Intellectual Revolution in Modern China*, Cambridge, MA: Harvard University Press.

Hsu, I. (1995) *The Rise of Modern China*, New York and Oxford: Oxford University Press.

Hu Shih (1922) *The Development of the Logical Method in Ancient China*, Shanghai: The Oriental Book Company.

WHALEN LAI

life and death, Chinese philosophy of

The *Book of History* recognized how life gives birth to life. The *Book of Changes* (*Yijing*) crowns that as the principle of change. For that reason, Chinese thought is said to embrace endless Becoming. **Confucius** wondered why 'If you do not yet know life, why ask what death is? One should stay faithful to this earth. He went on to ask 'if you cannot yet serve people, why talk of serving the spirits?' The proper service of man is man. But soon after, Yang Zhu noted the fact that life may generate other life, but he as a distinct self would die. He argued that life is good and natural but death is not. The religious Daoists agreed, and sought out ways to prolong life and postpone death. Life may be naturally perpetuated; it is *ming* (the allotted life span) that is artificial. So they nurtured *xing* or 'inborn nature, life' in order to modify fate or *ming*.

Confucius said that both 'life and death are mandated', and would no more tamper with that than seek out worldly success, 'for wealth and promotion (too) is due to **Heaven**'. **Mozi** advocated dying for the common good, trusting in the benefit of social immortality. For all his disagreements with Mozi, **Mencius** adopts very much the same attitude. **Zhuangzi** would not seek to prolong life artificially either, and as for life and death, there is no cause to rejoice just in one while trying to ignore the other. In death, one should be prepared to rejoin nature's 'great transformation'. Zhuangzi argues that life has a limit, knowledge has no limit, and it is folly to chase after the limitless with the limited.

Existential anxiety over death returned with the fall of the Han dynasty. Hedonism and fatalism surfaced side by side in the third-century work of Liezi. In real life, the Neo-Daoists led a precarious existence during the reign of their arch-foe, the conservative Jin. They wavered between a life of natural abandon and a cultivating of stoic *apathaia*. But with 'life and death' now equated with *samsara*, the Buddhists could offer a higher nirvanic transcendence, although at the cost of renouncing the instinctual life (passions and cravings), for the celibate. Inheriting that Buddhist rationality but re-embracing life, the Neo-Confucians as 'innerworldly ascetics' rediscovered the *Mencius* and returned China to a (neo-)classical norm.

Further reading

Marks, J. and Ames, R. (eds) (1995) *Emotions in Asian Thought: A Dialogue in Comparative Philosophy*, Albany, NY: State University of New York Press.

WHALEN LAI

logic

Logic in Indian philosophy has a long and distinguished history. Some extreme materialists and nominalists such as the Lokayata were suspicious of the whole enterprise of logic, based at it is upon the existence of universals and entirely general forms of reasoning. Any theory which emphasizes the significance of sense expeience is likely to be worried about forms of reasoning which seek to abstract from those individual experiences to produce far wider and grander conclusions The different philosophical schools were not in general so restrictive, though, and took different lines on what makes it possible to move from one premise to particular conclusions. The example which they often took would be classified today more as one of induction than deduction, since it starts with the phenomenon of smoke on a hill, and then moves to what we can conclude from that evidence, and how what we can conclude is linked with the original evidence. Contrary to the stereotype of Indian philosophy as largely being concerned with personal salvation and mystical formulae, it was fascinated with issues of what constitutes valid reasoning, and how we can repose confidence in conclusions which can be derived from initial propositions.

A similar point can be made about Buddhism, which often went in for elaborate analytical construction. One of the interesting areas of controversy in Buddhist logic lay with the law of excluded middle, the rule that a proposition must be either true or false. This is difficult to reconcile with the sorts of arguments that many Buddhists, in particular the Madhyamaka, produce. They often argue that when confronted with sets of contrary propositions (i.e. propositions which cannot be true at the same time) we should not seek to determine which propositions are true or false, but rather should appreciate that all these propositions are dubious, given the underlying **emptiness** of the world and what it includes. That is not to say that there is anything wrong with the law of excluded middle – it is a perfectly valid way of dealing with most propositions most of the time – but it does not capture correctly the fact that the world of our experience is full of conceptual problems which we cannot resolve and which point in the direction of reality. In fact, it is rather useful that we are not able to solve the problems neatly since it is that very failure which sends us in the right direction, that of looking behind our systems of reasoning and logic at the real nature of things. This tendency to value contradictions for what they can show explains the nature of many of the

statements produced by the Buddha and by his followers, especially those in the Zen movement.

Confucius's argument for the rectification of names, which was followed by many later Chinese thinkers, stressed the significance of obtaining a clear view of the meaning of names and their connections with other names. When this clear view is obtained then everyone knows where they are, as it were, and harmony and justice prevail. Many philosophers concentrated on the paradoxes which arise when we try to understand the nature of names, in particular when we use universals. The various paradoxes which arise in consequence reveal a thoroughgoing scepticism by many thinkers in the ability of logic to get us anywhere.

OLIVER LEAMAN

logic in Chinese philosophy: Buddhist logic

Chinese Buddhists had translations of the treatises on Buddhist logic, they studied them, but it never really took root. Fok Tou-hui argues that unlike formal logic, it is based on deduction from empirical evidence, not inductions from major and minor premises. 'All men are mortal; Socrates is a man; Socrates is mortal', is an acceptable syllogism. 'All gods are immortal; Apollo is a god; therefore Apollo is immortal' is not, because no proof of immortality has been established prior to the syllogism. Intent on controlling the causal outcome, Buddhist logic worked backward from 'effect to cause' and is quite satisfied with finding just the sufficient cause instead of the full 'necessary and sufficient' conditions. As long as suffering can be eliminated by removing its sufficient cause, that is all that matters. In the end, China prefers a logic of interrelatedness (dependent co-arising) and fused that to a Daoist sense of an organic whole to create the 'round and perfect' teaching.

Further reading

Fok Toh-hui (1985) *Fo-chiao Lo-chi* (Buddhist Logic), Hong Kong: Fa-chu Press.
Tucci, G. (trans.) (1929) *Pre-Dinnaga Buddhist Texts on*

Logic from Chinese Sources, Baroda: Oriental Institute.

WHALEN LAI

logic in Chinese philosophy: compound thinking

Chinese correlative logic (using the classification of the **Five Elements**) is well-known. Marcel Granet, in making much of Chinese ritual distinctions, has however observed the lack of generic terms like 'to carry': there are different terms for 'to carry' to go with different subjects and objects. Registering how Chinese thought is 'concrete' (versus abstract), Nakamura Hajime also shows how Chinese formed their generic words with compounds: the term for 'sibling' is 'elder brother, younger brother'. For generic length, the compound is 'long, short'. (But since you can also list a person's 'long' (i.e. strong) points and his 'short' comings, the same compound is a metaphor for 'gossip' or 'evaluation'.) All that would seem to hamper any classification similar to Aristotelian definition through classifying the meaning of terms by looking at their essential qualities.

For cattle or domesticated animals, the compound is 'horse sheep', but for reasons of taxonomy the word 'horse' can be compounded with 'deer' for a 'horse deer' class. Deer are seen as horned/antlered horses. Compound nouns like 'ox horse' forced Neo-Mohists to conclude that it is 'neither ox nor horse'. It also conflicts with the compound 'ox sheep' for describing a different kind of animal. 'Horse sheep' are not herded into a compound, while 'horse deer' describes a different kind of family of animal. By thus relying on types based on partial resemblance, such compounds in the Chinese language are more appropriately designed for metaphors and poetry than for formal signs and logic. Some sympathetic magic in Chinese medicine is a modern version of this way of thinking; one need only think of 'aphrodisiacs' like rhino horns, deer antler fuzz and erect penguin genitalia.

Further reading

Granet, M. (1930) *Chinese Civilization*, London: Kegan Paul, Trench, Trubner.
—— (1975) *The Religion of the Chinese People*, Oxford: Blackwell.

WHALEN LAI

logic in Chinese philosophy: paradox

Both **Confucius** and **Mozi** accepted that 'names' describe 'reality', at least in the sense that whether we realize it or not there is a close and accurate link between names and what they name, The thinker who subverted that confidence is Hui Shi, famous for a set of ten paradoxes. Life is death; long is short; north is south; yesterday is today; high is low; heaven is one with earth (and so we should love all things generously). But committed to logic and to moderation, his paradoxes remain logical paradoxes: there is almost no poetry, no depth, no soul in his writing. His friend **Zhuangzi**, who echoed some of those very same paradoxes, added poetry, depth and soul and moved the discourse inwards. The relativity of things became a function of different, subjective standards. Overcoming relativity is not possible through a blissful self-loss, a state of no-mind, or a dialectical 'forgetfulness of both' (subject and object). An acute thinker, it is difficult for anyone who came after Zhuangzi to outdo him in his play on the paradoxical.

The Buddhists added one subtle touch, as follows: **Laozi** knew that names cannot exhaust reality, so silence may also convey the ineffable. Zhuangzi exposed the relativity of names and transcended them. But **Nagarjuna** could, without resorting to the ineffable rise to a different level of discourse, stay with what is given him and turn a name (a thesis) against itself. As Sengzhao puts it, it is not that things turn out to be unreal and, for that, are called empty of reality. It is rather that reality is 'not true' to its claim; reality indicts itself, its untruth is what is meant by empty. So whereas **Xunzi** once accused Hui Shi with 'using names to create confusion of names', Madhyamika (or better, Prasangika) presents the test of 'using names to destroy names'. The other Buddhist contribution to paradoxes came at the end of the medieval period. The gymnastics of the Zen **koan** training is an advance; it is an exercise in perpetual troping, using words figuratively, that removes/exaggerates the whole pretence of means and ends, signifier and signified.

Further reading

Hansen, C. (1983) *Language and Logic in Ancient China*, Ann Arbor, MI: University of Michigan Press.

Kjellberg, P. and Ivanhoe, P. (eds) (1996) *Essays on Skepticism, Relativism, and Ethics in the Zhuangzi*, Albany, NY: State University of New York Press.

WHALEN LAI

logic in Chinese philosophy: 'separating hard and white'

There is in Chinese philosophy a well-known topic of debate on how categories like hard and white (as in a piece of marble) should be handled. The Mohists were substantialists who insisted on there being one hard and white being which is co-extensive with the marble. They insisted on that cohabitation in space (extension) to prove an absolute identity so as to distinguish their account from one based on identity in kind or a partial identity. A white horse is a single entity; another white horse somewhere else is similar in kind, and a white dog or a black horse has a partially similar identity. (Colour and shape are treated as co-equals, for 'there is no such thing as a colourless horse'.) Gongsun Long was the non-substantialist who emphasized the discreteness of the two categories. Whether 'horse' and 'white' are co-extensive or not is not an issue during an actual search for 'white horse'. Either way, you still have to count twice (discount the non-horse and then the non-white) and locate a 'white horse' in a barnyard of animals. For him, options within a category should mutually exclude each other: black should exclude white. Items from different sorts of

category do not have to: a horse could be white or black.

The substantialist argument is flawed: if hard and white take up the same space or if horse and white are coextensive and add up to 'one thing', then that would exclude horse from even conjoining with the reverse of white (black). In his essay titled 'Hard and White', Gongsun Long correlates hard to touch and white to sight, two separate sensations that the mind conjoins into one. The union is in the mind; it needs not be attributed to reality. To this non-substantialist thinker, only logical concepts are clear and their rule of exclusion is real.

The philosopher who did not agree with this view and who found all categories to be far from real is Hui Shi (380–305 BCE), the other logician, who recognizes only very rough 'family resemblances' as representing the ways in which concepts are linked with their qualities. He held the reverse of 'separating hardness from whiteness', the thesis known as 'conjoining similarity and dissimilarity'. He concluded that in the end we can say absolutely nothing discrete or distinct about anything, therefore, 'love all things generously (because even opposites are alike). Heaven and Earth are basically the same'. They are not so much 'alike' because that would assume attestable similarity but more like one undifferentiated shade of gray.

Further reading

Graham, A. (1978) *Late Mohist Logic, Ethics and Science*, Hong Kong: University of Hong Kong Press.

Lai, W. (1997) 'Kung-sun Lung and the Point of Pointing: The Moral Rhetoric of Names', *Asian Philsophy* 7(1): 47–58.

WHALEN LAI

logic in Chinese philosophy: a white horse is not a horse

In a famous debate authored by Gongsun Long (b. 380 BCE), the conclusion is reached that a white horse is not a horse. This surprising statement led to him being accused by **Xunzi** (*fl.* 298–238 BCE) of 'using names (logic) to confuse reality', since the plain fact is that white horses are very much horses. The proof sometimes looks as though it is based on the logic of the Chinese use of 'mass nouns', which compares 'white horse is not a horse' to what in English would be similar to 'white sand is not sand'. Sand is not countable; it is not a count noun but a mass noun. As such, it is a kind of stuff on the beach, so that white sand, a portion of the beach that is white, is not sand, i.e. the whole beach. This ignores the fact that when the occasion dictates, the Chinese could add a prefix and specify 'Give me one head of a horse'. Gongsun Long's original thesis assumes such a reasonable request. (No Chinese ask for *ma* and expect to get all the horses of the world.) The thesis does not involve a part/whole logic either; there is no abuse of a synecdoche like asking in English for a blade (=sword) and not being satisfied when handed just the blade portion. That is not translatable into asking for 'white horse' (whole) and not happy with just 'horse' (a part of it). The original thesis specifically notes how a person asking for 'horse' would be satisfied with a horse of any colour. Colour is a necessary attribute of the horse class; there is just no such thing as a colourless horse (essence). The right solution to the 'white horse is not a horse' thesis is to follow the Buddhist lead that holds that there being no positive essence (*atman*) to horse, a horse is best defined negatively. It is located when all the 'non-horse' shapes in a barn are excluded. What remains is 'horse'. For 'white horse', a double elimination (non-horse and non-white) is required. Therefore the term 'white horse' is not equivalent to the term 'horse'.

Further reading

Lai, W. (1995) 'White Horse Not Horse: Making Sense of a Negative Logic', *Asian Philosophy* 5(1): 59–74.

WHALEN LAI

logic and Islamic philosophy

Logic in the Islamic world employed the rich legacy of Greek logic to establish its early arguments and theories. The main source was undoubtedly Aristotle, but Stoic and Neoplatonic logic were also used. The most important idea which was taken from Aristotle was that of the all-pervasiveness of the syllogism in any form of reasoning, including even poetry. There was taken to be a hierarchy of reasoning, with demonstrative reasoning at the apex, employing as it does certain propositions, propositions which can only be known by the intellect, as its axioms and using exact reasoning to draw conclusions from such premises. Other lesser forms of reasoning also used exact argument processes, but their initial premises are less certain, and may use evidence based exclusively on sense experience or even imagination.

The first battle which logic had to fight was against the Islamic sciences such as Arabic grammar which also saw themselves as the appropriate technique in order to resolve difficult theoretical issues. An important debate arose in Baghdad in 932 CE between al-Sirafi, who criticized the use of Greek logic, and Ibn Matta, who defended it. Al-Sirafi wondered how the logic of one language could be applied to another, and argued that logic is limited in its scope to a particular language. Then the appropriate tool of analysis to use for Arabic texts such as the Qur'an must be Arabic itself. Ibn Matta, and **al-Farabi** after him, argued that logic represented the deep structure of all languages, and so could be applied to anything at all. This came to be the view which prevailed, even those thinkers who rejected philosophy usually accepted the significance and general applicability of logic, although some like Ibn Taymiyya had qualms about Aristotelian logic. Whereas al-Farabi and Yahya ibn 'Adi argued that logic deals with more general issues than grammar, they nonetheless linked logic with language in ways not acceptable to **Ibn Sina**. The latter points out that logic is only concerned with forms of argument, which may be expressed linguistically but may also be represented entirely formally.

Most of the logicians made a sharp distinction between *tasawwur* (conceptualization) and *tasdiq* (assent). The former is largely a matter of determining the sense of a proposition, while the latter relates to its reference, to whether it is true or otherwise. Demonstrative syllogisms consist of premises which require assent, including as they do necessary principles. Dialectical syllogisms include propositions which are generally accepted or assented for the sake of the argument, as it were. They typically examine propositions offered by opponents and see what they imply. Of course, if the propositions themselves are dubious, then whatever may be derived from them will only be of limited value as an item of knowledge. Rhetorical syllogisms are based on premises which are accepted without much thought, sophistical syllogisms use premises which resemble other kinds of premises, while poetry produces imaginative assent. They all share a common syllogistic form, albeit they all have very different theoretical rigour. This theory of the common form of argument came to play a large role in the protracted debate between religion and philosophy in the Islamic world. It came to be argued that religion was an imaginative and rhetorical form of demonstration, so that it came to the same conclusions as the more intellectual activity of philosophy, but it presented those conclusions in ways which are of more general accessibility.

Some commentators argue that **al-Ghazali**'s support for logic is really an indication of his general adherence to philosophy of which logic is a part or a tool. There was a long debate in Islamic philosophy as to whether logic is a part of philosophy or a tool to be used by it, and if the former is the case, then logic will be affected by the principles of philosophy itself. If it is a tool then it could always be argued that logic might be independent of that to which it is applied. Al-Ghazali seems to be arguing that while philosophy itself is replete with all sorts of problems, even on its own terms, logic transcends these problems since it is merely a neutral method, a methodology, one which formalizes patterns of reasoning which are found in all sorts of writing and in particular in scripture, anyway.

Ibn Taymiyya argues against al-Ghazali that there is no possibility of demarcating logic from philosophy, and that the use of logic brings with it the objectionable use of philosophical concepts also. A major influence on Ibn Taymiyya was the critique of Aristotelian logic provided by **al-Suhrawardi**. What is intriguing about the fact that Ibn Taymiyya and al-Suhrawardi share an antagonism to Aristotelian logic is that they both have radically different approaches to philosophy itself. Ishraqi (illuminationist) thought, as devel-

oped by al-Suhrawardi, horrified Ibn Taymiyya, especially its leading idea that the main principle of reality is linked to the world in much the same way that our perception of objects is linked to the source of light, ultimately the sun. The principles of reality exist in the shadowy world of the *'alam al-mithal*, the **imaginal realm**, and by perfecting our thought (and ourselves) we can approach the source of those principles. What is particularly troubling with these views, according to Ibn Taymiyya, is that they imply that there are certain principles which God must use in his creation of the world, as opposed to the correct state of affairs, in which there is nothing limiting his thought and activity.

Ibn Taymiyya is quite right in thinking that the Aristotelian notion of definition (*hadd*) presupposes the existence of a basic distinction between essential and accidental properties. The central idea here is that to understand what something is we need to be able to distinguish between those features of it which it has to have, and those which it can but need not have. This is a question about the properties of a concept, of course, not about whether it actually exists. This distinction between existence and essence proved to be a very rich source of philosophical distinctions between that which cannot but exist, i.e. God, and everything else. Ibn Taymiyya attacks this distinction, since it suggests that there is a basic connection between God and his creation, in that the one who has to exist is the source of the existence of everything else. This enabled the sufis (see **Sufism**) to develop their theory of the unity of existence, *wahdat al-wujud*, which leads to the view, according to Ibn Taymiyya, that there is no essential distinction between the issuer and the recipient of orders.

Interestingly, the notion of definition is also criticized by al-Suhrawardi and **Ibn Sab'in**, both thinkers whom Ibn Taymiyya sought to attack for their mystical views. Ibn Sab'in rejected the notion of definition since he argued that it does not sufficiently acknowledge the impact of God on everything in existence, including the nature of the concepts themselves. Aristotelian definition emphasizes analysis, our ability to split concepts up into their parts, while what we should be doing, Ibn Sab'in argues, is emphasizing synthesis, bringing parts together in order to help us appreciate the basic unity of being. Al-Suhrawardi argues that the trouble with definition is that it is not possible to list all the essential qualities of a thing. We can only seem to do this if we know how to define the term in the first place, but if we can do this then there is no point in trying to seek its definition. Also, if defining a thing is to list its essential properties, this sets up an infinite regress, since in order to know what each of those properties were one would have to define it, and so on.

Ibn Taymiyya's basic opposition to the theory of definition is that it separates the question of how to find out from the question of the existence of God. The notion of essential logical distinctions implies that God himself is constrained by such rules, and this is the source of a great deal of metaphysical mischief. It has led, in his view, to the development of Sufism and Ishraqi thought, both of which inappropriately link the world of generation and corruption with God. If logic could be used without importing such metaphysical distinctions then it would be acceptable, but logic is made up of such distinctions, and so should be treated with suspicion.

Further reading

Abed, S. (1991) *Aristotelian Logic and the Arabic Language in Alfarabi*, Albany, NY: State University of New York Press.

Abrahamov, B. (1998) *Islamic Theology: Traditionalism and Rationalism*, Edinburgh: Edinburgh University Press.

Al-Ghazali (1980) *Al-Qistas al-mustaqim* (The Correct Balance), trans. R. McCarthy as *Freedom and Fulfillment*, Boston: Twayne, 287–332.

Ibn Taymiyyah (1993) *Jahd al-qariha fi tajrid al-nasiha*, trans. W. Hallaq as *Ibn Taymiyya against the Greek Logicians*, Oxford: Clarendon Press.

Leaman, O. (1985) 'Introduction', *An Introduction to Medieval Islamic Philosophy*, Cambridge: Cambridge University Press, 1–21.

—— (1999) 'Philosophical and Scientific Achievements in Islamic History', in F. Daftary (ed.), *Intellectual Traditions in Islam*, London: I.B. Tauris, 31–42.

Rescher, N. (1964) *The Development of Arabic Logic*, Pittsburgh, PA: University of Pittsburgh Press.

OLIVER LEAMAN

logic in Japanese philosophy, post-Meiji

'Logic' in Japanese is *ronri* or *ronrigaku*. While the first term means 'logic' or 'theory of logic', the second means 'theory of logic' or 'study of logic'. In Japanese works which are conventionally considered philosophically relevant, the term *ronri* has been employed in various ways, referring for example to formal logic (*keishikiteki ronri*), transcendental logic (*senkenteki ronri*), dialectical logic (*benshohoteki ronri*), 'Buddhist logic' (*bukkyo no ronri[gaku]*), and most often to general methods of thought and (rules of) material structures.

'Transcendental logic' is used in a similar manner as in Kant (1724–1804). 'Dialectical logic' refers to Hegel's (1770–1831) theory of thesis, antithesis and synthesis, and to the laws of dialectical and historical Marxism, but is also used to characterize the structure of **Nagarjuna**'s Buddhism (about 150–250) and of Daoist thought. In the last case, the structure of the respective texts is interpreted as a form determined by principles incompatible with fundamental axioms of formal logic, particularly the law of excluded middle. This, then, is understood as indicating acknowledgement and application of logical laws distinctively different from the principles of 'Aristotelian', 'European' or two-valued formal logic. Conceiving of Nagarjuna's Buddhism and of Daoism as process ontologies, the structure of the respective texts is further understood as expression of continuous developments from As into non-As, and thus as a kind of dialectical evolution. Also, famous Buddhist phrases such as '*nirvana* is samsara', and 'form is emptiness', are taken as acknowledgment of a principle of *coincidentia oppositorum*, or negation of the laws of identity and non-contradiction. Finally, the *tetralemma* (Sanskrit, *chatushkoti*; Japanese, *shiku fumbetsu*) which functions prominently in Buddhist texts is often regarded as incompatible with the structure of 'Aristotelian' (or 'European') logical axioms. Thereby, the *tetralemma* is usually formalized as a sequence of four negations, namely (1) S is not P, (2) S is not non-P, (3) S is not P *and* non-P, and (4) S is not not P *and* non-P.

Many Japanese and Western scholars maintain that Buddhist and Daoist process ontology, Buddhist phrases which they interpret as identifications of opposites, and the Buddhist application of the tetralemma indicate the existence of a distinctively 'Eastern', 'Daoist' and/or 'Buddhist logic', the principles of which are incompatible with 'Western', 'European', 'Aristotelian' or two-valued logic. Perhaps the most influential Japanese scholar who was of this opinion was Suzuki Daisetz (1870–1966). Others were the followers of the **Kyoto school**. In his book *Rogusu to remma* (Logos and Lemma), published in 1974, Yamauchi Tokuryu (1890–1982) contrasted Western and Eastern thought by characterizing the first as being determined by *logos* and the latter as being structured by the principles of the *tetralemma*, thereby conceiving of *logos* as a method of exclusion and of *lemma* as a way of 'friendly' inclusion (even of 'the middle'). Even such competent Buddhologists as Takakusu Junjiro (1866–1945) and Nakamura Hajime (1912–99) were inclined to the view that the most profound Buddhist thought does not acknowledge the validity of the 'Aristotelian' axioms.

However, the hypotheses of a distinctively Eastern or Buddhist logic have long been refuted. As has been pointed out, theories of ontological structures, i.e., theories of the structure of reality, must not be confused with theories of formal logical laws. To formulate an ontology, one must apply principles of formal logic. Nagarjuna in particular is an example of strictly applying rules of formal logic and thus arriving at the conclusion that these rules are no determinants of reality as it is. As to such formulas as 'samsara is nirvana', it has been explained that the 'is' (*soku*) need not be understood as indicating total identity. As in the case of 'morning star' and 'evening star', it may designate the same entity without expressing the same meaning (intension). Finally, the *tetralemma* almost never occurs in the way it is generally formalized. As far as it simply expresses the conviction that a certain thing does not exist (in a certain sense of 'existence'), it is anyway logically consistent. For instance, Nagarjuna's famous *tetralemma* that (1) *dharma*s ('entities', 'things', 'elements of being') are not caused by themselves, (2) not caused by others, (3) not caused by a combination of themselves and others, but are nevertheless (4) not without cause and/or condition, simply implies

that *dharma*s are not caused or conditioned in the way they are supposed to be if the notions of 'cause' and 'condition' are understood and used as the opponent employs them. Also, as in this example, the 'and' in the third *lemma* usually means a non-exclusive logical 'or' (Latin *vel*). If it negates 'either A or non-A', it usually expresses views comparable to the proposition that neither a blue nor a non-blue pegasus exists. (A pegasus is neither blue nor non-blue, for there exists no pegasus.) Such arguments against the hypothesis of a distinctively Eastern or Buddhist logic have been advanced by Japanese and Western logicians and Buddhologists, particularly scholars of *hetuvidya* (Chinese *yinming*; Japanese *immyo*), among them Kajiyama Yuichi, Tachikawa Musashi and Gregor Paul. Suzuki and the adherents of the Kyoto school probably never studied the Buddhist theories of non-contradiction and valid conclusion, i.e., of formal logic, as they are included in *hetuvidya*.

Since Nara times (710–94) through to the twentieth century, many Japanese scholars have contributed to *hetuvidya*. This has been comprehensively documented by Takemura Shoho (1914–) in his *Immyo-gaku* (Studies in the Theory of Reasons). This book appeared in 1986, and is not only a survey of *immyo* studies in Japan but also an outstanding contribution to (the history of) logic in general. The Sanskrit term *hetuvidya* means 'theory/doctrine of logical and/or causal reason', and comprises epistemology, theory of argumentation and theory of non-contradiction and valid logical deduction. The Chinese rendering *yinming*, pronounced *immyo* in Japanese, means the same. The common translation of *hetuvidya* (*immyo*) as '(Buddhist) logic' is misleading, as would be a translation of the Aristotelian *Organon* (Tools) as *Logic*. Logic is only one part of *hetuvidya*, namely the part which deals with the question of what criteria a logical reason (*hetu*, *yin*, *in*) must fulfil to validate a proposition or conclusion. For example, in 'S is P because S is R', '[it is] R' is the logical reason. Among the necessary criteria this reason fulfils is the criterion that everything that is R, is (also) P.

In addition to its interpretation as a distinctively Buddhist (or Daoist) logic, the notion that there exists a uniquely Eastern logic is often understood as a hypothesis of **Nishida** Kitaro (1870–1945) and the Kyoto school. Nishida indeed spoke of an

'Eastern logic' (*toyo no ronri, toyoteki ronri*) and a 'logic of space' (*bashoteki ronri*); and Tanabe Hajime (1885–1962) coined the concept of a logic of species (*shu no ronri*). However, in all such cases, *ronri* does not refer to formal logic and laws of formal logic but again to ontological laws and ontological structures and the material way these structures are grasped or intuited. Tanabe, with his 'logic of species', actually develops a philosophy of state. Using *shu*, or 'species', as a metaphor for 'state', he maintains that the state plays a vital role as 'logical' mediator between the individual (the individual member of a state) and the genus-like mankind.

The preoccupation of nationalistic philosophers with material logic is a universal characteristic of philosophy. The allegedly unique 'laws of thought' in which nationalists believe can easily be employed as methods for justifying cultural and political elitarianism and particularism. Further, the preoccupation with material logic is a feature shared by mystics, Hegelians, Marxists and dialecticians in general. Also, except for nominalists, philosophers interested in ontology often maintain that material logic is a more appropriate instrument of knowledge than formal logic. Like Western scholars, Japanese scholars hotly debated the pros and cons of formal and material, especially dialectical, logic. This does not only apply to Buddhologists. In the 1950s and 1960s, there was a particularly sharp controversy between analytical and Marxist philosophers. In 1953, the materialist and student of Hegel Matsumura Kazuto published *Benshoho no hatten – Mao Takuto mujunron o chushin toshite* (The Development of Dialectics: On Mao Zedong's Theory of Contradiction), and in 1957 Terasawa Tsunenobu (1919–) published his *Benshohoteki ronrigaku shiron* (An Essay on Dialectical Logic).

Today in Japan, as elsewhere in the world, formal logic has become a highly specialized technical discipline of a comparatively small group of university mathematicians and philosophers, reflected in papers the understanding of which often presupposes years of detailed studies.

See also: Buddhist philosophy in Japan, post-Meiji; comparative philosophy, Japanese

Further reading

Nakamura Hajime (1968) *Ways of Thinking of Eastern Peoples*, ed. P. Wiener, Honolulu, HA: University of Hawaii Press.
—— (1969) *A History of the Development of Japanese Thought*, 2 vols, Tokyo: Japan Cultural Society.
—— (1980) *Indian Buddhism*, Tokyo: Kufs Publication.
—— (1982) *Ansätze modernen Denkens in den Religionen Japans* (*Nihon shUkyo no kindaisei*), trans. S. Schultz and A. Schomaker-Huett, Leiden: Brill.
—— (1992) *A Comparative History of Ideas*, Delhi: Motilal Banarsidass.
Suzuki Daisetz (1959) *Zen and Japanese Culture*, London: Routledge & Kegan Paul.
Tachikawa Musashi (1997) *An Introduction to the Philosophy of Nagarjuna*, trans. R. Giebel, Delhi: Motilal Banarsidass.
Takakusu Junjiro (1947) *The Essentials of Buddhist Philosophy*, Honolulu, HA: University of Hawaii Press.

GREGOR PAUL

LOKAYATA *see* charvaka

Longchen Rabjampa

b. 1308; d. 1363

Buddhist philosopher

Longchen Rabjampa studied many of the Indian Buddhist classical texts on logic and epistemology, middle way philosophy and other subjects at the monastery of Sangphu in central Tibet. It was in recognition of his great learning that the name *rabjampa* ('one who is in abundant in learning') was given to him. Longchenpa then embarked on a journey as a wandering mendicant. During one such journey, Longchenpa is said to have had a profound mystical experience leading to an early indication of the maturing of his destiny, which would lead him to encounter the teachings of the **Dzokchen thought**. So, at the age of twenty-nine, Longchenpa finally met with his guru Rikzin Kumaraja, who was to initiate him into the rich traditions of the Dzokchen meditative practice. Longchenpa's initiation into the practice of Dzokchen led him into a series of mystical experiences that culminated in the revelation of the Indian master Vimalamitra's secret writings on the essential practices of Dzokchen. Longchenpa thus became the authoritative medium and interpreter of this important Buddhist mystical tradition, which later became known as *Vima Nyingthik* (the Heartdrop of Vimalamitra). Longchenpa's works on Dzokchen, especially his trilogy known as the three cycles on Being at Ease, the seven Treasures, and his commentary on the *Guhyagarbhatantra*, remain to this day the authoritative source on the key doctrines of the Dzokchen teachings of the **Nyingma school** of Tibetan Buddhism.

See also: Vimalakirti

Further reading

Herbert, G. (1975) *Kindly Bend to Ease Us*, Emeryville: Dharma Publishing, Introduction.

THUPTEN JINPA

love in Chinese philosophy

The history of love in the West has examined the subject in a number of forms and mapped epochal shifts in taste and style. The full Chinese story has yet to be told. Love is *ai*. A man of *ren* (humaneness, benevolence) loves other men, says **Confucius**. **Mozi** took up this idea and spelled out a 'universal love' as a concern shown other members of the same class. It is logical for man to love men, not horses, and to seek out what is good (i.e. beneficial) for them and vice versa. Critics of Mohist utilitarianism depict that love as calculating and less than spontaneous. That is not the picture one gets from narratives about those hardy souls: Mohist camaraderie is open, masculine and impassioned. If anything, it is Confucian **friendship** that is (too well) circumscribed and (overly) deferential. There is little of the male bonding one sees among classical Greek men, and definitely nothing remotely homosexual. Greek *eros* in the physical or the metaphysical mode is strangely absent from the sedate Chinese texts; and when modern China looks for a translation of *agape*, the choice does not fall on *ren* but properly on 'love or

sentiment among friends'. Trust among friends being the last of the five human relationships, this seems to underscore *agape*'s peripheral status in the Confucius system of **rites**. This does not mean the Chinese did not know love in the *agape* form, but rather, it is captured in the kinship metaphor that attends *ren* at its most expansive. It is the sense that 'within the four seas, all men are brothers'. This is a form of fraternity that comes close to equality. (It falls slightly short because brothers always came as elder and younger brothers.) For a still wider 'oceanic feeling' of universal love, there is the line of 'being human to one's fellowmen (*renren*) and loving all things (*aiwu*) besides'.

In a patriarchal society where family always comes first, the issue of 'love' is about how it is translated. It is telling that both **Hinayana** *metta* and Mahayana *karuna*, which in the original Indian Buddhist context actually correspond fairly well to Christian *agape*, by the time they were acculturated into medieval China came out as more parental than fraternal. The Sanskrit terms came out in Chinese as paternal 'kindness' and maternal 'commiseration'. (The Chinese image of 'compassion' allowed the heroic Amitabha of India to slide gracefully into being a double of the Daoist Queen Mother of the West, a soft-hearted dowager of a saviour.) The economy of salvation in the Christian tradition and its gospel of love is triune: there is a Son between the Father and the feminine Holy Spirit. In China, the metaphor of love came through a dual relationship: a law that came through loud and clear from the father and a love that came through gently and softly from the mother.

Han Fei the Legalist philosopher knew best how that system would work. To ensure impartial justice, the ruler is warned against letting love (his personal likes and dislikes) ruin his policy. In the Chinese family, with a division of labour, the father canes and the mother soothes; he sternly commands and she softly coaxes. As Han Fei once told the rulers, Neo-Confucian 'conduct books' remind the family head: 'A strict father (makes for) a filial son', with an aside, 'a soft-hearted mother (brings up) a bad brood'. The same conduct books indict a recent proverb as utterly misguided, correcting it with a definite negative: no, a compassionate father does not create a filial son.

That 'recent' proverb however reveals changes in Chinese society and family since the seventeenth century. Late Ming thinkers and writers, novelists and dramatists began to glorify the life of feelings. If there were more family tensions between brothers reported in the eighteenth century, that could be as much a sign of the growing warmth and intimacy within the primary family. The increased number of break-ups of extended households into smaller units might well tell of that recent introversion. Among the educated, we find indications of a growth in 'companion marriages'. The rise of female education among the gentry allowed women to share a common interest with their spouses, making for a partnership of soulmates. That most tender husband–wife relationship and simple domestic bliss is told in the titles from an autobiographical *Six Chapters of a Floating Life*: 'wedded bliss', 'the little pleasures of life', 'sorrow' and 'joys of travel'. (The last two chapters are missing.) The work holds up a new domestic bliss that is a real and inspiring ideal, capturing a recent possibility and model to imitate.

Further reading

Birrell, A. (trans.) (1982) *New songs from a Jade Terrace: An Anthology of Early Chinese Love Poetry*, London: Allen & Unwin.

Chang Hen-shui (1991) *The Eternal Love: The Story of Liang Shanbo and Zhu Yingtai*, ed. and trans. S. Munro, Singapore: Federal Publications.

Clack, R. and Clack, D. (ed. and trans.) (1977) *The Herd Boy and the Weaver Maid: A Collection of Chinese Love Songs*, New York: Gordon Press.

Lin Yutang (trans.) (1942) *Six chapters of a Floating Life*, in Lin Yutang (ed.), *The Wisdom of India and China*, New York: Random House, 960–1050.

WHALEN LAI

Luo Qing

b. 1443; d. 1527

Religious sect founder

Luo Qing (Lo Ch'ing), known to his followers as Patriarch Luo, was a contemporary of Wang Yangming. He headed a major reformed sectarian religious movement in Late Dynastic China. A soldier guarding grain transport to the northern frontier via the Grand Canal, Luo had followed a devotion to Amitabha Buddha as the Unborn Mother, when he was further introduced to the Zen of the *Diamond Sutra*. In a momentous enlightenment, he realized that the true home of Pure Land was this **emptiness** of his mind; that his true nature was forever enlightened, beyond good and evil, and requiring no gradual cultivation, being itself the incarnation of a Sage Patriarch of the Great Ultimate. This blending of Pure Land and Chan, this celebration of the unity of the Three Teachings, was not new but his writings, now known as the 'precious scrolls' in Five Works in Six Volumes became scriptures to his followers. Basically a leader of a reformed (non-millenarian) White Lotus sect, this layman was denounced by leading Buddhist masters, Dejing and Zuhung, in the late Ming dynasty.

Further reading

Liu, K. and Shek, R. (eds) (forthcoming) *Heterodoxy*, Berkeley, CA: University of California Press.

Overmyer, D. (1976) *Buddhist Folk Religion*, Cambridge, MA: Harvard University Press.

WHALEN LAI

MACROCOSM *see* correlative thinking

Madhva

b. 1238; d. 1317

Theologian

Madhva, sometimes known as Anandatirtha, was a South Indian exclusivist Vaishnava theologian who, as a Vedantin, wrote commentaries on several *Upanishads*, the *Bhagavad Gita*, the *Brahma-Sutras* and the decidedly sectarian *Bhagavata Purana* as well as a non-commentatorial work, the *Anuvyakhyana* setting out his Vedantic doctrine. A resolute opponent of **Advaita** Vedanta, he is a realist and dualist insisting on an ontological gulf between two categories: the Self-determined (*svatantra*), i.e. Vishnu and the necessarily dependent (*paratantra*), i.e. everything else. Differences obtain between God (Vishnu) and the individual self (*jiva*); between the numerical infinity of souls; between God and matter; between souls and matter and between the material entities. The gulf between the absolute and finite realms is spanned by the divine will sustaining and supporting the contingent created order. Clearly, Madhva's Vedanta is not only anti-Advaitic, but also distanced from other theistic forms of Vedanta such as **Ramanuja**'s ***Vishishtadvaita*** (Integral Unity of a Complex Reality), which posits an ontic nexus between God and the world of conscious and non-conscious entities which constitute the divine body.

Individual entities are characterized by a particular essence, each possessing a uniquely individuating feature (*vishesha*). According to Ramanuja,

released souls are intrinsically qualitatively identical. This raises a problem about their individuation. Madhva may be seeking to avoid such a difficulty by postulating a distinguishing factor other than the working of accumulated ***karma***.

There are three categories of souls: those who are liberated; possible candidates for liberation; and those who are unsusceptible of salvation – the permanent transmigrators and the damned (including individuals of non-Vaishnava persuasion) and denizens of supernal realms. Liberation consists in the realization of a state of innate consciousness and bliss (*sacchidananda*) focused on the divinity and is unattainable without a combination of devotion (*bhakti*) and divine favour (*prasada*).

Exceptionally for a Vedantin but consistently with his dualistic emphasis, Madhva denies that God is both the efficient and the substrative cause of the universe. The conscious cannot become the unconscious, so God cannot be the material cause. Rather, God has recourse to eternal, subtle matter (*prakriti*) whose transformation he excites.

Further reading

Dasgupta, S. (1922) *A History of Indian Philosophy*, vol. IV, Cambridge: Cambridge University Press.

Sharma, B. (1981) *A History of the Dvaita School of Vedanta and Its Literature*, 2 vols, Bombay: Motilal Banarsidass.

Siauve, S. (1968) *La Doctrine de Madhva*, Pondichery: Publications de l'Institut Français de l'extrême orient.

CHRIS BARTLEY

Madhyamaka Buddhism

Madhyamaka is the 'middle way' school of Mahayana Buddhism whose most prominent theorist is **Nagarjuna** (*c*.150 CE), the author of many works including the *Madhyamaka-karikas* and the *Vigrahavyavartani*. Using a *reductio ad absurdum* style of argument, he was concerned to demonstrate fallacies in all theories (*drishti*) and did not claim to be propounding a doctrine of his own. His best-known disciple was Aryadeva, who wrote the *Chatuh-shataka*, a model of concision and lucidity.

The central tenet of the school is that every entity, whether atomic or macroscopic, is empty (*shunya*) of essence or 'own nature' (*svabhava*). This notion of *nih-svabhavata* is held to be a relativistic consequence of the fundamental Buddhist analysis of causation as interdependent genesis (***pratitya-samutpada***). If proliferated reality (*prapancha*) consists of entities that exist only in mutual dependence, there can be no immutable eternal substances. If essence is conceived in terms of an unchanging underlying core, a thing cannot undergo changes and this is contrary to experience. Nothing exists in its own right, everything being relative, but the constancy of linguistic forms generates the illusion of permanence. Because entities originate in dependence on causes and conditions, they lack inherent existence which is what the Madhyamika means by 'emptiness'. There is no source of origination, no subject of origination and no determinate identities of things that, like long and short, exist only in relation to counter-correlates. If distinctions are void of reality, it follows that there is no difference between the interdependent states of transmigratory existence (***samsara***) and **nirvana** (release). *Nirvana* is the radically altered perspective of the detached experient with insight into the way things really are. The enlightened one realizes that his sense of personal individuality is but a conventional conceptual and linguistic fiction with no basis in ultimate reality and acts accordingly. That is to say, removed from self-concern and cognizant of the relativity of all conditioned, impermanent and non-substantial phenomena to which he has become indifferent, he cultivates a compassionate attitude (*karuna*) to the unenlightened who are suffering due to the multifarious forms of attachment to the transitory. This is the syzygy of compassion and insight.

The Madhyamikas distinguish two aspects of truth or reality: the quotidian and conventional (*samvriti-satya*) that is bound up with discursive thought and language on the one hand and on the other the ultimate and inexpressible (*paramartha-satya*) which is the object of gnostic intuition and the truth realized by the enlightened individual who has insight into the universal **emptiness**. There can only be one reality but there are different modes of understanding.

The tradition bifurcated into what are called the Prasangika and Svatantrika schools. The principal representatives of the former are considered to be Buddhapalita (470–540 CE), who wrote a commentary on the *Mulamadhyamakakarikas*, and Chandrakirti (600–50 CE), author of the *Prasannapada* commentary on the *Karikas* and the *Madhyamakavatara*. Another major figure is **Shantideva**, author of the *Bodhicharyavatara* and *Shikshasamucchaya*.

Bhavya or Bhavaviveka (500–70 CE) is the most notable exponent of Svatantrika ideas. His works include the *Prajnapradipa* commentary on the *Karikas*, the *Madhyamakahridayakarika* and the auto-commentary *Tarkajvala*, the *Madhyamarthasamgraha* and the *Karatalaratna*.

Most Madhyamikas deny that their outlook involves the assertion of substantive, positive claims. In Quinean terms, their ontological commitment is zero (*shunya*). A basic argument schema (*chatushkoti*, 'tetralemma') deployed by Nagarjuna involves denying that an entity is F, nor not-F, nor both F and not-F, nor neither F and not-F. For instance, entities are not self-generated, nor other-generated, nor both self-generated and other-generated and not self-generated and not other-generated (uncaused). The Prasangikas are so called because they elaborate this schema in terms of *reductio ad absurdum* or *prasanga* arguments. They maintained that the auto-generation of the already extant would be pointless; if entities were other-generated, anything could be produced from anything; the third conjunction combines the defects of the former two and the fourth means that everything would exist forever.

The Svatantrikas thought that the words of the Buddha in the canonical *sutra* texts teach 'right views' accessible to human comprehension and that the mere attempt to convince the opponent of the falsity of his position by exposing its internal contradictions was too restrictive as a soteriology. They insisted on the use of standard categorical syllogisms (*svatantra-anumana*) to prove the tenet of *nih-svabhavata* or *shunyata*. Unlike the Prasangikas, they recognized the conventional or provisional existence of 'own-nature' (*svabhava*) and the possibility of existential truth-claims from this standpoint.

Later thinkers integrated elements of the idealist **Yogachara** school's philosophy with the Svatantrika outlook. The most significant figure is Shantarakshita (725–84 CE), author of the encyclopedic *Tattvasamgraha* which was the subject of the *Panjika* commentary by Kamalashila (740–97 CE). Shantarakshita subjected the epistemological and metaphysical realism about the macroscopic views of the **Sarvastivada** atomists and the representationalism of the Sautrantikas to trenchant criticisms (see **Sautrantika**). Dispensing with the postulate of a mind-independent domain, he held that reality could be accounted for in terms of continuous streams of ideas which themselves lack *svabhava*.

Further reading

de Jong, J. (1977) *Nagarjuna Mulamadhyamakakarikah*, Madras: Adyar Library and Research Centre.

Lamotte, E. (1944–80) *Le Traité de la grande vertu de sagesse de Nagarjuna*, 5 vols, Louvain: Publications de l'Institut Orientaliste de Louvain.

Lindtner, C. (1982) *Nagarjuniana*, Copenhagen: Akademisk Forlag.

Matilal, B. (1977) *The Logical Illumination of Indian Mysticism*, Oxford: Oxford University Press.

May, J. (1959) *Candrakirti, Prasannapada, Madhyamakavritti*, Paris: Adrien Maisonneuve.

Murti, T. (1955) *The Central Philosophy of Buddhism: A Study of the Madhyamika System*, London: George Allen and Unwin.

Ruegg, D. (1981) *The Literature of the Madhyamaka School of Philosophy in India*, Wiesbaden: Otto Harrassowitz.

Shackleton Bailey, D. (1952) *The Satapancasatka of Matrceta*, Cambridge: Cambridge University Press.

Warder, A. (1991) *Indian Buddhism*, Delhi: Motilal Banarsidass.

Williams, P. (1989) *Mahayana Buddhism*, London: Routledge.

—— (1998) *Altruism and Reality*, Richmond: Curzon Press.

CHRIS BARTLEY

Madhyamaka and thesislessness

The questions of whether or not the Madhyamaka has a thesis of its own, and if not, what exactly does it mean to say that it does not have a view, lie at the heart of much of the debates within the Tibetan philosophical discourse. Those who argue that the Madhyamaka literally does not have any views of its own base their claim on the literal reading of some of the critical passages from Indian Madhyamika philosophers like **Nagarjuna**, Aryadeva and Chandrakirti, especially the following passage from *Vigrahavyavartani*, 29:

> If I had posited any thesis, then I may be open to objections.
> As I do not have any thesis, I am entirely free of contradiction.

However, as to what exactly does this claim about thesislessness mean there is a great divergence of opinions among Tibetan thinkers. Some like Shang Thangsakpa appear to adopt a radical, literal view, which asserts that the Madhyamaka does not have any views of its own at all. On this view, Madhyamaka discourse acts as a parasite upon other's views and is aimed at putting an end to all discourse, including its own! Its purpose is literally to still the mind and destroy all views. It is thus said to be a cure against all views and can be abandoned when all views are eliminated.

Yet there are others like Takstang Lotsawa who do not subscribe to such a radical denial of views but confine the rejection only from the standpoint of ultimate truth. On this interpretation the denial of thesis has to do with the rejection of any views about the ultimate nature of reality, i.e. **emptiness**. According to this view, emptiness refers to the highest truth which can be said not to be is, or is not, or both is and is not, or neither is nor is not. Thus from the perspective of ultimate truth all propositions remain false with no factual content.

Both these versions of the thesislessness view contain an aspect of agnosticism, if not seeds of ontological nihilism. Epistemologically, the proponents of the 'no-thesis' view tend to reject any possibility of true knowledge, especially with regard to the nature of the ultimate. Thus they are on the whole epistemological sceptics. In linguistic terms they tend to hold the view that language has no bearing on reality, let alone any objective referential relation. Logic too, on this view, cannot access the ultimate truth, which is intuited only in a state of nonconceptual experience.

Tsongkhapa vehemently rejects this doctrine of thesislessness on the grounds that it leads to ontological nihilism and epistemological scepticism. He identifies what he sees as four key premises underlying the 'no-thesis' view and subjects them to intense critique. They are that (1) critical reasoning that enquires into the question of whether or not things exist in terms of their intrinsic natures negates all phenomena; (2) events such as origination, cessation and so on cannot be objects of true cognition for it has been stated in the scriptures that perceptions like the visual, auditory, olfactory and so on cannot be accepted as veridical; (3) events such as origination cannot be accepted as existent even at the conventional level; and (4) there is nothing which does not fall into the categories of is, is not, both is and is not, and neither is nor is not, but all these four possibilities have been shown to be untenable by the Madhyamaka dialectic.

For Tsongkhapa the proponents of the 'no-thesis' view, by rejecting existence, denigrate the world of dependent origination (see **dependent origination in Tibetan philosophy**); and since, according to the Madhyamaka school as he understands it, dependent origination is the meaning of emptiness, they also denigrate **emptiness**. He argues that not only is it possible for dependent origination and emptiness to have a common locus, but the very fact of dependence is the highest proof of the absence of intrinsic existence. So, to hold that a belief in dependent origination entails a belief in intrinsic being is to turn everything topsy-turvy. Thus, argues Tsongkhapa, the Madhyamaka does have theses, but no theses adhering to any notion of intrinsic existence. The Madhyamaka

rejects intrinsic existence, and the emptiness of intrinsic existence is their position.

Predictably, Tsongkhapa's influential intellectual heirs such as Khedrup have followed up on his critique of the 'no-thesis' view, which has compelled the subsequent upholders of the view to redefine their standpoints. We see this impact already being felt, for example, in Rongton's position on the issue of thesislessness. Rongton identifies three kinds of thesis: (1) the thesis that is accepted for the sake of others under special circumstances, (2) the thesis accepted both by oneself and others, and (3) the thesis accepted only by oneself, and develops a hermeneutics based on the assertion that the Madhyamaka does not have a thesis of its own. After the fifteenth century the debate seems to have remained dormant, perhaps because of the overwhelming domination of Tibet's philosophical scene by the **Geluk school**. Interestingly it was the publication of **Gendun Chophel**'s posthumous work on Madhyamaka which appeared to have revived the debate. In this work, Gendun Chophel argued that the 'no-thesis' doctrine could be read in a way that could be reconcilable with Tsongkhapa's Madhyamaka philosophy.

Further reading

Jinpa, T. (1997) 'Self, Persons and Madhyamaka Dialectics: A Study of Tsongkhapa's Middle Way Philosophy', PhD thesis, University of Cambridge, ch. 5.

Napper, E. (1989) *Dependent Arising*, London: Wisdom Publications, pt I, 54–66.

Ruegg, D. (1983) 'On Thesis and Assertion in the Madhyamaka/dBu ma', in E. Steinkellner and H. Tauscher (eds), *Contributions on Tibetan and Buddhist Religion and Philosophy*, Vienna: Universität Wien, vol. 2, 205–42.

THUPTEN JINPA

magic squares

Magic squares are part of numerology or the system of magical numbers. The 'River Writing' (*Lushu*) and the 'River Diagram' (*Hotu*) are the best-known examples in China. The former is built around the magic square of three, a 3×3 diagram with nine boxes filled with the numbers 1 to 9 and all rows, columns and diagonals adding up to 15.

4	9	2
3	5	7
8	1	6

Considered the perfect pattern of the cosmos – with *yin–yang* and the **Five Elements** in balance – it is used in **rites** of cosmic renewal in Daoism, at which time the priest does the dance of Yu by tracing the sequence from one to nine. This is a legendary pacing that the Sage-King Yu did after he tamed the Flood. In effect, he carved out the land into the Nine Continents, corresponding to the Chinese conception of the square Earth as portioned out into nine smaller squares. The magic square is that 3×3 box, marking out eight directions and the centre. Yu measured out the Earth, and his 'dance' is still performed by Daoist priests in a cosmic renewal ritual every sixty years. The priest dances on one-leg like Yu.

This perfectly balanced magic square is used anytime there is need to restore order after **chaos**. It also occurs as the 'nine provinces' of China; the plan behind troop formations in battle or in ritual dance; the hidden design embedded in Daoist talismans; the shape of the **well-field system**; and so on.

Further reading

Carmann, S. (1960) 'Evolution of Magic Squares in China', *Journal of the American Oriental Society* 80: 116–24.
—— (1961) 'The Magic Square of Three in Old Chinese Religion and Philosophy', *History of Religions* 1(1): 37–90.
—— (1962) 'Old Chinese Magic Squares', *Sinologica* 7: 14–53.
Lai, W. (1990) 'Looking for Mr. Ho Po: Unmasking the River God of Ancient China', *History of Religions* 20(4): 335–50.

WHALEN LAI

MAHABHARATA *see* Sanskrit epics

mahamudra

It was probably Gampopa, one of the founding fathers of the **Kagyu school** of Tibetan Buddhism, who initiated the usage of the term *mahamudra* (in Tibetan, *chak gya chen mo*), which literally means the 'great seal', as referring to a systematic doctrinal and philosophical standpoint. Gampopa distinguished between two levels of introducing the profound view of **emptiness**, one in the context of Mahayana *sutras* and the other in the context of Vajrayana Buddhism. In the first context, the 'great seal' refers to the absence of real existence of mind that is uncovered as a result of one's search into the nature of mind. In the Vajrayana context, the 'great seal' refers to the union of great bliss and emptiness that is experienced in states of what is called the clear light nature of mind. This is said to arise when the process of withdrawal of the energies into the central channel has reached its culmination through meditative practice. This 'great seal' is sometimes described as the 'single remedy for all ailments' (*karpo chik thup*), for it is said to be the innermost essence of all the Vajrayana teachings. The proponents of the 'single remedy' tend also to accept the doctrine of simultaneity whereby the mature individual is said to experience the ultimate nature of mind in a direct, unmediated manner without the need for a gradual approach.

Later interpreters of the 'great seal' appear to have emphasized the doctrine more as a meditative perspective than a philosophical view. A consequence of this is to associate the doctrine primarily with the idea of introducing the nature of one's mind, with a close correlation of mind with its diverse perceptions of the world. Also, the notion that all aspects of cognition, especially the various thought processes, are manifestations of some kind of basic, pristine mind called *dharmakaya* became dominant amongst the upholders of the 'great seal' doctrine. Some of the versions of the 'great seal' doctrine came under severe criticism by **Shakya Pandita**, who accused the proponents of the 'single remedy' idea of subscribing to what the Tibetans perceive to be the views of the heretical

Chinese master Hoshang. Interestingly, there has been a strong tradition of Geluk–Kagyu ecumenism on the theory and practice of the 'great seal'. The earliest figure in this lineage is most probably the Geluk master Khedrup Norsang Gyatso (1423–1513), who wrote a treatise on the 'great seal'. The tradition became further solidified with Panchen Lobsang Chogyen's (1570–1662) influential work on *mahamudra*.

Further reading

Jackson, R. (1982) 'Sa skya Pandita's Account of the bSam gyas Debate: History as Polemic', *Journal of the International Association of Buddhist Studies* 5: 89–99.

THUPTEN JINPA

Mahasamghika

Mahasamghika was one of the eighteen schools of Hinayana (Lesser Vehicle) Buddhism. Some of its ideas contributed to the development of the Mahayana (Great Vehicle) forms of Buddhism. At the Council of Vaishali or Vesali around the middle of the fourth century BCE, the Mahasamghikas separated from the Sthavira-vada (Tradition of the Elders) school as the result of an obscure controversy over aspects of monastic arrangements towards the end of the fourth century BCE. Later sources, which it must be admitted are not particularly reliable and probably reflect subsequent controversies, indicate that the Mahasamghikas were critical of the original ideal of the *arhat*, the detached and enlightened solitary individual in whom the fires of clinging, aversion and delusion have been extinguished, which they saw as an inferior goal of Buddhist praxis. They are traditionally held to have claimed that *arhats* were capable of erotic dreams, that they were subject to ignorance of matters of fact, that they may have doubts or anxieties, that they were susceptible of instruction and that they may fall away from the Path.

Another major point of difference, evidenced in a text called the *Mahavastu* which purports to be a biography of the Buddha, is found in their tendency to idealize the career of the historical Buddha as belonging to a level of apparent manifestation while exalting a supramundane (*lokottara*) conception of Buddhahood. The Mahasamghikas also anticipate the Mahayana traditions in holding that insight (*prajna*), rather than **meditation**, is the necessary and sufficient condition of liberation understood as the termination of the series of existences (*nirvana*).

The Lokottaravadin (Ekavyavaharika) sub-school appear to have emphasized the docetic character of the careers of the omniscient Buddhas, seeing them not as ordinary human beings but as pure spirits untainted by empirical conditions. Miraculous elements are introduced into the biographical accounts of the Buddha who is said to be asexually conceived and whose emergence from his mother's intact right side is painless.

The Prajnaptivada sect maintained the purely conceptual or nominal (*prajnapti*) nature of everything, including Buddhist doctrinal statements, in accordance with their tenet (which will be highlighted in the Madhyamaka traditions) that all of the basic constituents of reality (***dharma***) lack inherent existence or determinate substantial identity (*svabhava*) just like the macroscopic entities which are held to be reducible to them by the mainstream realistic and atomistic **Abhidharma** traditions. For them, insight (*prajna*) is the realization of the **emptiness** (*shunyata*) of all *dharmas* rather than the analytical awareness of the essentially composite and conditioned nature of every entity which we encounter.

Further reading

Bareau, A. (1955) *Les sectes bouddhiques du Petit Véhicule*, Saigon: Ecole Française d'Extrême-Orient.

Cousins, L. (1992) 'The "Five Points" and the Origins of the Buddhist Schools', in *The Buddhist Forum*, Vol. II, Seminar Papers: Delhi.

Lamotte, E. (1988) *History of Indian Buddhism: From the Origins to the Shaka Era*, trans. S. Webb-Boin, Louvain: Université Catholique de Louvain.

Warder, A. (1991) *Indian Buddhism*, Delhi: Motilal Banarsidass.

CHRIS BARTLEY

Mahayana Buddhism

The Mahayana or 'Great Vehicle' to enlightenment probably originated and developed in the northwest of the Indian sub-continent India in the century prior to the beginning of the Common Era, and during subsequent centuries spread to Central Asia, Nepal, Tibet, China, Mongolia, Vietnam, Korea and Japan. The continuity of Mahayana traditions with pre-existing Buddhist traditions (**Hinayana**), whose monastic and moral codes (*Vinaya*) they share, tends to be overlooked by Mahayanists themselves.

Mahayana schools are distinguished from the so-called 'Lesser Vehicle' Hinayana traditions, which regard the Buddhas as enlightened human teachers whose lives end in irreversible death, by the emphasis they place on the supernatural character of the many Buddhas and in regarding them as objects of devotion. This outlook is anticipated in the **Mahasamghika** school's docetic assignment of the career of the historical Gotama Buddha to the sphere of apparent phenomena. Mahayanists exalt the gradual path to enlightenment of the *bodhisattva* (future buddha), marked by kindness and compassion for all sentient beings, as a religious ideal. The Mahayana traditions tend to see enlightenment as a mode of being in the world. For example, according to the Madhyamika schools, *nirvana* and the transmigratory condition marked by unsatisfactoriness and suffering (*samsara*) are ontologically indistinguishable: what changes is the perspective of the detached experient with insight into the way things really are. The enlightened one realizes that his sense of personal individuality is but a conventional conceptual and linguistic fiction with no basis in ultimate reality and acts accordingly. That is to say, removed from self-concern and cognizant of the relativity of all conditioned, impermanent and non-substantial phenomena to which he has become indifferent, he cultivates a compassionate attitude (*karuna*) to the unenlightened who are suffering due to the multifarious forms of attachment to the transitory. This is the syzygy (union) of compassion and insight. According to the idealist (**Yogachara**) traditions, both *samsara* and *nirvana* are states of mind. One's inherent enlightened **buddha nat-**ure (**tathagatagarbha**) has become obscured by ignorance and moral defects. The underlying 'store-consciousness' (**alaya-vijnana**) that is the source of all experience has the potentiality for both unenlightened and enlightened outlooks. Buddhist praxis is a technique for clarifying and manifesting the Buddha-nature.

The earliest Mahayana scriptures (*sutra*) are those on the 'perfection of wisdom' (*prajna-paramita*) such as *Ashtasahashrika-prajnaparamita* (the 8,000 verse Sutra) probably completed in the first century CE. Somewhat later are the Diamond and Heart Sutras. The perfection of wisdom literature expanded to a vast extent. The basic nominalistic tenet to be realized, the truth about existence, is that everything which originates in dependence upon other factors is devoid (*shunya*) of essence (*svabhava*). Investing entities, which are really components of processes, with permanent identities is the work of ignorance (**avidya**) which reifies what are purely conventional conceptual and linguistic designations. Meditative insight into reality (*dharmata*; *tathata*) beyond proliferative categorization is the goal of the perfection of wisdom.

Mahayanists typically regard the aspiration of the Hinayana monks to *nirvana* (arhatship) understood as the extinction of the fires of passion, hatred and delusion coupled with insight (*prajna*) into the impermanence (*anitya*), and unsatisfactoriness (*duhkha*) and lack of substantiality of all macroscopic phenomena as an individualistic and selfish ideal. By contrast, the aspirant (*bodhisattva*) to complete buddhahood cultivates perfect enlightenment which commits him to the welfare of all suffering beings through a succession of lives and ten stages (*bhumi*) of spiritual development. During the first six stages, the *bodhisattva* retains ideas about individual conscious beings and objects. In the seventh, he no longer tries to perceive objects. In the eighth, he acquires the certainty that phenomena do not arise and that untroubled by thoughts and objects he is certain to follow an irreversible course to the achievement of buddhahood. In the ninth, he acquires the ability to change form and teach according to the dispositions of his audience. In the tenth, he receives from the Buddha the consecration in omniscience which will make him almost the equal of a buddha in terms of enlightenment. Not even mindful of his compassionate

nature and absorbed in mediation, he simultaneously ensures the welfare and happiness of all
beings in many worlds.

The path which brings the *bodhisattva* close to
final enlightenment involves the practice of the six
perfections (*paramita*) of generosity (*dana*), morality
(*shila*), patience (*kshanti*), vigour as opposed to moral
and intellectual sloth (*virya*), meditative absorption
(*dhyana*) and wisdom (*prajna*). It culminates in the
acquisition of supernatural powers, profound insight into the **emptiness** (*shunyata*) of conditioned
phenomena as existing only in relative dependence,
omniscience and universal compassion.

The interpretation of the basic Buddhist theory
of conditioned genesis (***pratitya-samutpada***),
which accounts for the organization of the
elements of existence and predictable ethical
consequentiality, as the idea that all entities (*dharma*)
are empty (*shunya*) of 'own-being' or essence
(*svabhava*) is a feature of most schools of Mahayana
even if there is no consensus about what it means.
This universal absence of essential identity which is
the object of the highest meditative insight is what
is called *dharmata* or *tathata*. The soteriological ideal
is construed as comprehension of the emptiness of
transmigratory existence. Although strictly ineffable, the truth can be taught by the Buddha's
employment of skilful pedagogical techniques
(*kushala-upaya*) appropriate to the level of understanding of the audience.

See also: expediency

Further reading

Bechert, H. and Gombrich, R. (eds) (1984) *The
World of Buddhism*, London: Thames and Hud-
son.
Conze, E. (1959) *Buddhist Scriptures*, Harmonds-
worth: Penguin.
—— (1967) *Buddhist Thought in India*, Ann Arbor,
MI: University of Michigan Press.
Dayal, H. (1932) *The Bodhisattva Doctrine in Buddhist
Sanskrit Literature*, London: Kegan Paul.
de Jong, J. (1977) *Nagarjuna Mulamadhyamakakarikah*,
Madras: Adyar Library and Research Centre.

Lamotte, E. (1944–80) *Le Traité de la grande vertu de
sagesse de Nagarjuna*, 5 vols, Louvain: Publications
de l'Institut Orientaliste de Louvain.
—— (1988) *History of Indian Buddhism: From the
Origins to the Shaka Era*, trans. S. Webb-Boin,
Louvain: Université Catholique de Louvain.
Murti, T. (1955) *The Central Philosphy of Buddhism, A
Study of the Madhyamika System.*, London: George
Allen and Unwin.
Ruegg, D. (1968) *La Théorie du tathagatagarbha et du
gotra, Etude sur la sotériologie et gnoséologie du
bouddhisme*, Paris: Publications de l'Ecole Fran-
çaise d'Extrême-Orient.
Shackleton Bailey, D. (1952) *The Satapancasatka of
Matrceta*, Cambridge: Cambridge University
Press.
Suzuki, D. (1930) *Studies in the Lankavatara Sutra*,
London: Eastern Buddhist Library.
—— (trans.) (1932) *Lankavatarasutra*, London: East-
ern Buddhist Library.
Warder, A. (1991) *Indian Buddhism*, Delhi: Motilal
Banarsidass.
Williams, P. (1989) *Mahayana Buddhism*, London:
Routledge.

CHRIS BARTLEY

Mahayana: the Sinitic schools

Four Chinese Buddhist schools rose between 500–
700 CE, based on the *sutras* but, unlike the
Madhyamika and Yogachara (*sastra*) schools, had
no institutional counterparts in India. These are

Tiantai, based on the *Lotus Sutra*;
Huayan, based on the *Flower Garland Sutra*;
Pure Land, based on the *Pure Land Sutra*;
Chan, supposedly outside the scriptures.

Philosophically, the best way to appreciate them
is to consider them as representing the combinations of two known set of variables concerning the
Buddha: that he is mundane or transmundane and
has wisdom and compassion. Mapped according to
that, we will find:

	wisdom	*compassion*	
Transmundane	Wreath	Pure Land	more
	Vairochana	Amitabha	Dharma-centric
Mundane	Lotus	Zen	more
	Shakyamuni	Patriarch	Man-centred

Tian-tai

Tiantai, the first Sinitic Mahayana school to rise, was largely built by Zhiyi (538–97), its third patriarch. It legitimized itself via the *Lotus Sutra*, which taught the One Vehicle subsuming the Three Vehicles. This is translated into a triune doctrine, 'One is Three; Three are One', and justified on the basis of Zhiyi's reading of **Nagarjuna**'s *Madhyamika-karika* (Middle Treatise). The lines in Kumarajiva's translation are as follows:

> What is produced by cause and condition
> Is what I mean by the Empty
> Also known as conditioned co-arising
> It is also what is meant by the Middle Path.

The lines – causation, **emptiness**, interdependence and the middle – are synonymous in Nagarjuna. Zhiyi read this as implying how (One) Reality is (Three) Empty, Real and Middle. So everything in the universe (the many) is a holistic unity (one) which is simultaneously Empty, Real and Neither. Enlightenment means seeing things from all sides; transcending their biases, grasping the One and finding perfection in 'every colour and aroma' as encompassed by the One Mind. The highest mystical vision is to telescope all facets of reality – a round count of 3,000 worlds – into one moment of thought. This is called the 'round and perfect' enlightenment.

Instead of talking about 'Chinese Buddhism' as sinicized Buddhism, the term 'Sinitic Mahayana' might grant the Chinese schools their independence and creative access to the Dharma they deserve. Just as Christian theology might be seen as a synthesis of the Jewish and the Greek tradition, of God and Logos, Sinitic Mahayana is marked by the same sort of combination of disparate points of view. It started with the Tiantai school which boldly claimed: 'It was said (by

others in authority) but I say unto you ...' concerning the true teaching of the *Lotus Sutra*. Previous readings are exegetical, but Zhiyi, who commented on 'words and sentences' (the letter of the Law), also claimed to have recovered the 'hidden meaning' (the spirit of the One *Dharma*). He found not just One Dharma-Mark in this *sutra*; he also disclosed all the principles of all *sutras*, upon which he distinguished the common 'essence' of a scripture from its specific 'principle'. The break with the past is marked off by having the first Tiantai patriarch enlightened without a teacher. Then, in the first meeting at Mount Great Awakening between Zhiyi, the third patriarch, and his master Huisi, both are supposedly transported back to their being in the presence of the Buddha when he first taught the *Lotus Sutra* at Vulture Peak in India. This kerygmatic myth guarantees that the masters had received the Truth directly from the Buddha's 'golden mouth' (that is, uncorrupted by any mediated transmission). With that, the school could discount even Sanskrit commentaries on this scripture as being not up to par. It even bypassed the much honored Kumarajiva, whose translation is the canonical one.

The form of this kerygmatic myth is no human invention; it is drawn from the very first chapter of the *sutra* where, during its own genesis as a new revelation, the scripture has Manjusri, the Mahayana **bodhisattva** and the guardian of wisdom, reminding Maitreya of the forgetful Hinayana *bodhisattva* whom they had personally heard this Lotus *dharma* teach aeons ago. The Tiantai school also claimed a direct transmission from Nagarjuna, so that the peculiar formula of the Three Truths in this school is the right reading of the Madhyamika philosophy. Truth needs no apology. After this historic breakthrough (probably datable to the leading disciple who codified the works of Zhiyi), the other Sinitic Mahayana schools followed suit.

They nearly always claimed similar direct or hidden transmission of the Truth.

Faxiang (Yogachara) School

Faxiang is not counted as a Sinitic Mahayana school because it is often regarded as too Indian, and it did not survive. It was denounced for not accepting universal **buddha nature** and for having a core consciousness that is still polluted and not pure. The name is given to this school to deride it for being still fixated with phenomenal *dharma*-characteristics and missing out on the noumenal *dharma*-essence.

The Indian school to which this Chinese body of thought is most closely connected is the Yogachara, and in particular the thought of Vasubandhu. It was established by Xuandang (600–64) and his disciple Kuiji (638–82), and its name means 'Signs of Existence School'. It analyses all forms of existence in terms of ideas, and distinguishes between the reliability of different categories of those ideas as varying indications of the reality which lies behind them. What sets this school up against the other Mahayana schools is its rather restrictive attitude to enlightenment. One of the features of the Mahayana which it regards as separating it from the Hinayana is precisely the fact that everyone is capable of achieving enlightenment, since everyone has the buddha nature, but the Faxiang school is sceptical about the universality of buddha nature. For example, those who do not set out to achieve enlightenment, and who may even deny the possibility of its attainment, are said by the Faxiang school not to have a buddha nature, which their Mahayana colleagues argued was unduly restrictive.

Huayan (Avatamshaka) School

Based on the *Flower Garland Sutra*'s vision of a *dharma*-realm in which every part reflects all the other parts, this school is known for a holist philosophy wherein 'One is All and All is One'. It rose in response to the importation of the Yogachara philosophy by Xuanzang. The important patriarch Fazang then relied on the **Awakening of Faith in Mahayana** to undercut Yogachara. This text postulates a pure suchness mind behind the tainted **alaya-vijnana** (storehouse consciousness) and provided a powerful metaphor to account for the state of the world and of the mind. It is due to the wind of ignorance and the suchness mind as ocean that all individuated consciousness and reality (the waves) came to be. But this means that:

1 the Mind is Pure; everything is generated out of this pure suchness mind;
2 the discrete forms of things in the world (the waves) may delude the unsuspecting but the wise know the waves are no less watery (suchness);
3 pure suchness being the substance of the mind, the forms of things and the essence of Mind are one; not only that but the characteristics of the things and the essence of things (*dharmata*) are also one;
4 finally, every particular characteristic (i.e., a wave) encapsulates totally the essence (the whole ocean). Each wave is all the water and the sum of all the waves. One is All. And All is One.

Chan

The most Chinese of all Buddhist schools, Chan is based allegedly on a secret transmission that cannot be verified by any Indian record. Legend has it that Bodhidharma brought this teaching to China in the early 500s. The basic teaching has been given as:

No reliance on words
Transmission outside the scriptures
Point directly at the minds of men
See your (Buddha) nature and be enlightened.

Pure Land School

Pure Land is a form of Buddhism based on the idea that there is a pure land or land of happiness which may be attained by calling on the appropriate buddha. Although this school originated in India and crystallized in China, it became very popular in Japan. It brings Buddhism close to personal belief in a deity, who comes to be identified with the Buddha Amitayus.

Further reading

Chang Chen-chi (Garma C.C. Chang) (1971) *The Buddhist Teaching of Totality: The Philosophy of Hwa Yen Buddhism*, University Park, PA: Pennsylvania State University Press.

Chappell, D. (ed.) (1983) *Tien-t'ai Buddhism: An Outline of the Fourfold Teachings*, Tokyo: Daiichi Shobo.

Cook, F. (1977) *Hua-yen Buddhism: The Jewel Net of Indra*, University Park, PA: Pennsylvania State University Press.

Henderson, J. (1991) *Scripture, Canon and Commentary: A Comparison of Confucian and Western Exegesis*, Princeton, NJ: Princeton University Press.

Lai, W. (1985) 'Why the Lotus Sutra? On the Historical Significance of Tendai', *Japanese Journal of Religious Studies* 14(2–3): 83–97.

Swanson, P. (1989) *Foundations of Tien-T'ai philosophy: The Flowering of the Two Truths Theory in Chinese Buddhism*, Berkeley, CA: Asian Humanities Press.

WHALEN LAI
OLIVER LEAMAN

Mandana Mishra

b. 650; d. 700

Philosopher

Mandana Mishra was a theorist of Mimamsa and non-dualist (**Advaita**) Vedanta. His works include *Mimamsanukramanika*, *Bhavanaviviveka* and *Vidhiviveka* (Mimamsa ritualism); *Sphotasiddhi* (philosophy of language); *Vibhramaviveka* (epistemology); and *Brahmasiddhi* (Vedantic). In Mandana's work, the Absolute (*Brahman*) is unitary and uniform being in general (*satta*): it is the simple fact of existence. He rejects the definitions of Being as that which is or can be known (*jneyatva* or *pramanasambandhayogyata*) or that which is causally effective (*arthakriyakaritva*).

Everything shares the undifferentiated form of Being (*sad-rupa*) which is perceived everywhere. There is a constant awareness of an undetermined, non-variant form of Being which is the core identity common to particular entities abstracted from their properties and relations. He identifies

Being without determinations as *Brahman*. Being is constant and real: difference, construed as the mutual non-existence of opposing forms, is false. The universal reality appears in every awareness as its objective ground but is mistaken for something else. Mandana accepts the *anyatha-khyati* theory of **cognitive error**, according to which a cognitive error has a real objective substrate (*alambana*) presented to the senses (see **cognitive error, classical Indian theories**). Misrepresentation of the object is due to superimposition on the perceived object (e.g., shell) of something else (e.g., silver). On the macrocosmic level, *Brahman*, a static conscious reality without properties and relations, is the substrate of diversity imagined by the transmigrating individual who superimposes it upon *Brahman*. The individual self (*jiva-atman*) is the locus (*ashraya*) of *avidya* whose object (*vishaya*) is *Brahman*.

Mandana appears to follow **Dignaga** in maintaining a distinction between perception qua pure sensation and conceptualized, propositional awareness. 'First, there is a non-conceptual perception (*avikalpaka-pratyaksha*) relating to the bare object. The ensuing constructive cognitions (*vikalpa-buddhi*) comprehend particularities (*vishesha*).' Difference (*bheda*) is not given in perception but is a mental construct (*vikalpa*) subsequent to the perception of the mere object (*vastu-matra*) in its true nature. The absolute *Brahman*, the supreme universal, which is pure, undifferentiated and non-specific reality (*sanmatra*; *satta*) is given in non-conceptual awareness.

Beginningless misconception (*avidya*) is responsible for all plurality of selves, cognitions and objects and the concomitant transmigration. *Avidya* is also connected with sorrow, delusion and passion and the predisposition to cognitive error. It conceals one's true nature, creating the illusion of an individual agent subject to ritual duties and transmigration.

The relationship between *Brahman* and *avidya* is inexpressible (*anirvachaniya*). Were *avidya* the same as *Brahman*, release would be impossible. If it is a positive entity (*bhava*) independent of *Brahman*, non-dualism is contradicted. Were it absolutely non-existent, there would be neither bondage nor worldly transactions (*vyavahara*). On the level of the familiar, cognitive errors (*vibhrama*) occur and have practical consequences but they may also be annulled. On the basis of these considerations, Mandana says that *avidya* is indefinable as being or non-being; a formulation which perhaps attempts to avoid the contradiction implicit in calling it both.

Scripture is the authoritative source of knowledge (*pramana*) about the trans-empirical *Brahman*. To the objection that language cannot reveal the non-empirical, since a word is only informative when its connection with its referent is established, Mandana replies that *Brahman* is already known in that it is given in cognition of particulars which are always accompanied by the form of the universal. Although we are in the sphere of misconception (*avidya*) where awareness involving reference to difference is actually erroneous, we can still grasp the truth of non-duality because pure Being (*Brahman*) is given in every perception even if it is usually misidentified. Negative scriptural statements teach the unreality of phenomenal diversity (*prapancha-abhava*) and eradicate *avidya* while positive ones affirm the sole reality of *Brahman* with which the Self (*atman*) is identical. Mandana ascribes a unique status to Vedic language which he elevates above the sphere of misconception (*avidya*).

Shankara and his radical renunciatory school maintain that the ritual actions enjoined in the Vedic *karma-kanda* are dispensable in the quest for liberation. By contrast, Mandana thinks that all Vedically enjoined action is purificatory and predisposes towards realization of one's true identity. He subscribes to the view that release from the series of births is produced by a combination of knowledge and ritual action (*jnana-karma-samucchaya-vada*), a way especially suited to householders in normal society. Renunciation of all ritual actions (*samnyasa*) is a possible path to self-realization but it is slow and difficult.

Shankara and his followers consider the knowledge of *Brahman* derived from reading the major Upanishadic statements (*Mahavakyas*) such as 'That thou art' (**Tat tvam asi**), which are held to reveal the identity of the inner self (**atman**) and *Brahman*, to be sufficient for liberation from rebirth. Mandana's view is that since knowledge produced by the Vedanta texts is relational because verbal and conceptual, it cannot directly generate realization of the *Brahman–atman* identity state. His view is

that the understanding gleaned from those statements must be intensified in the performance of prescribed ritual actions and contemplation (*upasana*) to counteract traces of misconception and remove discursive mental features prior to direct intuition into reality. There are three conceptions of *Brahman*: the first is based on scriptural language; after knowledge from language, a continuous stream of that conception called **meditation** (*dhyana*), realization (*bhavana*) and contemplation (*dhyana*); leading to a perfected conception which is a direct intuition (*aparoksha-brahma-sakshatkara*) in which all discursive thought is obliterated.

Further reading

Biardeau, M. (1954) *Theories de la Connaissance et Philosophie de la Parole dans le Brahmanisme Classique*, Paris and the Hague: Mouton.

—— (ed. and trans.) (1958) *Sphotasiddhi (La Demonstration du Sphota)*, Pondicherry: Publications de l'Institut Français d'Indologie.

—— (1969) *La Philosophie de Mandana Misra vue a partir de la Brahmasiddhi*, Paris: Publications de l'Ecole Française d'Extrême-Orient.

Iyer, K. (trans.) (1966) *The Sphotasiddhi of Mandana Misra*, Poona: Deccan College.

Potter, K. (1981) *Encyclopedia of Indian Philosophies, Vol.III; Advaita Vedanta up to Samkara and His Pupils*, Delhi: Motilal Banarsidass.

Schmithausen, L. (1965) *Mandana Misra's Vibhramavivekah, mit einer Studie zur Entwicklung der indischen Irrtummslehre*, Vienna: Hermann Bohlaus.

Thrasher, A. (1993) *The Advaita Vedanta of the Brahma-Siddhi*, Delhi: Motilal Banarsidass.

Vetter, T. (1969) *Mandanamisra's Brahmasiddhih, Brahmakandah: Übersetzung, Einleitung und Anmerkungen*, Vienna: Herman Bohlaus.

CHRIS BARTLEY

Mao Zedong

b. 1893; d. 1976

Political leader

Founder of the People's Republic of China, Mao Zedong (Mao Tse-tung) was of peasant stock.

Graduating from normal school in 1918, he became assistant librarian at Beijing University under the head librarian, who happened to be a Marxist. He cooperated with the Nationalists during the Sino-Japanese war of 1937–45. This pact then fell through, and by 1949 Mao had taken full control of mainland China. His bypassing of an urban proletariat revolution to rally the peasantry to his cause broke with Marxist dogma. A faith in the power of the People lay behind the Great Leap Forward in the 1950s, as if massive raw, human effort alone could compensate for modern technology and jumpstart a commune-based industrial revolution. Mao's assessment of continual contradictions in society led to his call for a perpetual revolution to help bring about a utopian equality and fanned the Great Cultural Revolution and the drafting of the Red Guards to do battle with the entrenched power structure.

The thought of Mao Zedong came to have considerable influence in China in his lifetime, and is theoretically rather interesting. Mao builds on a long period of discussion in Chinese philosophy on the relationship between action and theory, and in his *On Practice* advocated the synthesis of theory and practice in revolutionary behaviour. This is a replication of the traditional debate between the materialists who stress action as the basis to morality, as opposed to idealists, who often saw thought as the basis to action. For Mao, social practice was not just the basis to human knowledge but also the criterion of that knowledge's value. A dialectical process ensures that both practice and knowledge develop together, and reach ever higher levels of human attainment. It is the nature of everything to change, and these changes may be understood in terms of contradictions, where people and principles stand in contrast to each other. Understanding the contradictions which run through reality is a vital aspect of understanding reality as such. Knowledge is not a neutral access to reality. On the contrary, it is practice which permits us to approach the truth and at the highest level such knowledge leads to revolutionary practice, which is only possible when the knower has a grasp of the forces which govern society.

It is an error to see Mao as an orthodox Marxist thinker, and there is no doubt but that he used several long-standing themes of Chinese philoso-phy in his extensive theoretical writings. Like the **chuch'e philosophy** produced in North Korea, there was a disinclination to use communism as a total cultural replacement for national culture. But it has to be said that the arrival of the People's Republic did bring a very rich tradition of thought largely to an end within China itself, and one can only hope that this sad state of affairs will prove to be merely temporary.

Further reading

Mao Zedong (1977) *Selected Works of Mao Tse-tung*, Peking: Foreign Languages Press.
Schram, S. (1969) *The Political Thought of Mao Tse-tung*, New York: Praeger.

WHALEN LAI
OLIVER LEAMAN

materialism

Greek thought uses the notion of some primeval stuff (*hule*) or raw material which was moulded into form. Matter and form were later dissociated. Chinese cosmogony similarly postulates some primeval stuff, the unformed chaos that also emerged into and became discernible form. This is usually phrased as 'originally nothing, subsequently something'. Since material form came later and emerged out of an indefinite or indeterminate background, it is hard to find a philosophy of 'materialism' in Chinese thought. **Ether** can be deemed quasi-material, but since it covers everything 'from the sublime to the gross', it is not entirely materialistic either. Guo Xiang (Kuo Hsiang) (*c*.312 CE), who denied that Being can come out of **Non-being**, should qualify as a materialist, but his thesis that all things 'are just there' or 'are born (suddenly) in one lump' is as much a mystery as any other theory of origination, and can hardly claim to provide an explanation in terms of some original or basic matter.

WHALEN LAI

Mazu Daoyi

b. 709; d. 788

Buddhist patriarch

The eighth Chan patriarch, Mazu Daoyi (Ma-tsu Tao-i) or Patriarch Ma was *dharma* heir to the Sixth Patriarch **Huineng** (638–713), but could as well be described as the cornerstone of Chan. The four lines describing the essence of Zen describe him at his best:

> No reliance on words
> Transmission outside the scriptures
> Point directly at the mind of men
> See your nature and be enlightened

Known for teaching, 'Mind is Buddha', he also declared, 'Neither Mind nor Buddha'. This means that Chan is not dependent on words. He also kicked and slapped his disciples into enlightenment, timing the *dharma* (teaching) to fit the capacity of the person and the ripe moment. This translates into the 'mind to mind transmission' seeking to 'awake the **buddha nature** in the student'. Mazu claimed the first 'Recorded Sayings' telling of Chan encounters, collected and then retold to help **trigger** enlightenment. He taught an active form of Chan in which even a blink of an eye is the buddha nature in action. Remembered for saying 'The Everyday Mind is the *dao*' – with 'everyday' reading also 'peaceful and constant' – he headed the line that three generations later would produce Linji and **Koan** Zen.

Further reading

Cheng Chien (1992) *Bhiksu Sun Face Buddha: The Teachings of Ma-tsu*, Fremont, CA: Asian Humanities Press.

Iriya Yoshitaka (1984) *Basho no Goroku* (The Recorded Sayings of Ma-tsu), Kyoto: Zenbunka kenkyusho.

Lai, W. (1984) 'The Transmission Verses of the Ch'an Patriarchs,' *Chinese Studies* 1(2): 593–624.

—— (1985) 'Ma-tsu Tao-i and the Unfolding of Southern Zen', *Japanese Journal of Religious Studies* 12(4): 172–92.

Levens, B. (1987) *The Recorded Sayings of Ma-tsu*, trans. J. Pas, New York: Mellen.

WHALEN LAI

meaning

Meaning in the Chinese discourse has two aspects: the meaning of words (semantics) and the intention of mind (the ethics of good will). In modern Chinese, 'meaning' is usually rendered *yiyi*, a compound which conjoins 'intent' and 'meaning' to yield 'intended meaning'. But both the inward pre-verbal intent and the outward expressed meaning can be covered by the early philosophical usage of the second character *yi*, which also implies 'rightness' and 'duty'. That conflation of words and mind has a telling history. **Confucius** started this with his theory of 'right name', in which a word which represents a fact like 'father' implies the virtue of 'fatherliness'. **Mozi** persisted in this equation: he works out a logical definition (meaning) of words that would support his call to do what is right. Thus loyalty defined as 'love for the lord' would logically cause the retainer to 'seek to benefit the lord'. Linguistic meaning and moral action coincide. The trouble was that other thinkers did not agree with his moral logic; they chose to use words their own way. Faced with the fact that the meaning of words is not self-evident to everybody, he conceded that there are just too many different definitions of words when, ideally speaking, there should be just one meaning. He concluded then that the person who sees things more clearly and has the public good in mind should be the one who sets down the meaning and also enforces its proper, ethical usage. That role falls naturally upon the Mohist version of a philosopher-king. This strong-arm solution was later adopted by the Legalists for absolutist rule (see **Legalism**).

That problem of the relativity of names (linguistic standards) was confronted by **Zhuangzi** who exposed it as being due to the subjective nature of men's minds. He then taught a way of transcending the different positions which represent partial opinions. In the process, he denied any fixity of meaning, leading in turn to his denial of its perspicuity and to the argument that there is no point in trying to establish perfectly clear meanings. Discourse on truth has to be indirect, metaphoric or allegorical. Out of this came Zhuangzi's formula that a person 'upon catching the fish (the meaning), should leave behind the fish trap (the names)'. This severs for good any connection between the word that signifies and the thing being signified. The Neo-Daoist Wang Bi underscored this when, in his commentary on the *Book of Changes*, he confessed that 'once one understands the meaning [behind the trigrams], one can just as well forget the forms'. So when Zhuangzi tells us that 'speech cannot exhaust the meaning', or **Laozi** claims that 'words cannot describe the *dao*', those two propositions do not come under the same indictment (of failure to communicate reference). We sense and get what they mean – the communication of meaning does come through – by recognizing their place in the richness of the larger context of a total speech (*parole* instead of *langue*). Meaning here is a function of objective reference; it is being seduced by the poetics of a speech into a way of thinking and looking at reality.

Mencius faced the same problem, of too many thinkers using the same words differently for different ends. But unlike Zhuangzi, Mencius still believed that there is one absolute truth about the Good, and that there is a way to find the right meaning (*yi*). It is that which is morally right, **righteousness** (*yi*) itself; it is not 'outer' (not based on some relative societal standard) but rather it is rooted in the 'inner' self which when extended would merge with the *dao*. To unseat other theories of what is right, Mencius looked also for an 'inner' solution. What a man says is less important than what he intends by it. His speech and deportment, not the reference or even meaning of the words, call for a critical examination. Only a sincere intent ensures a sincere speech. 'Knowing speech' in Mencius amounts to 'reading the mind that makes that speech'. He had thus moved beyond semantics or the probing of meaning to **hermeneutics** or figuring out what a person truly meant.

Semantics and hermeneutics amounted to meta-reflections to **Xunzi**. A nominalist, he regards words as conventions, names tagged onto things: but 'dog' can and does refer and point to the animal 'dog'. Meaning is also socially constructed and agreed upon. Once set, meanings should be inviolable: calling 'black' later 'white' would not do. An empiricist, he believed that any disagreement can be checked against the facts and resolved in that way. The Legalists took this matter-of-fact approach one step further, and the Buddhists probed still more deeply, precisely on how contextual meaning might just as well be artificially generated as a whole; it could well be empty.

Ambiguity

The Chinese word for both ambiguity and contradiction is 'shield and spear', which goes back to a story of man trying to sell, on the one hand, an impenetrable shield and, on the other hand, an unstoppable spear. Philosophers are divided as to whether clear-headed thinking is preferable to nuanced poetic ambiguity. It is a fact that China rejected the Mohist philosophy which resembles the rationalism of the West, did not much appreciate the Logicians for exploiting the ambiguity of words, and applauded Zhuangzi for his uncanny language and inimitable style.

Hermeneutics and Mencius

Hermeneutics, the theory of interpretation is based upon the suspicion that a speech or a text is saying more or other than what it apparently says. Irony is hardly alien to Chinese speech but in Chinese philosophy, Mencius is the first thinker to become aware of the problem and the first to work out a method of interpretating texts. Faced with contradictions in the Classics (see **Classics and Books**), he said bluntly, 'If you believe everything in the *Book of History*, it would be better not to have the Book at all.' So he threw out a variant telling or reading that has **Sage-King** Shun judging his evil father, the Blind Man. That is not what a filial son like Shun would do, argues Mencius. Shun would rather resign from office and carry his father on his back (an act of devotion) to his retirement at some distant shore. But beyond this rather heavy handed, moralistic reading or redacting of the Classics, Mencius is also responsible for calling attention to the problem that speech (text too) might be distorted by intent of the speaker or reporter. An optimist, Mencius believes that the intention can be exposed and the truth be told.

Applied to literature, he has said, 'So the interpreter of a poem should not allow the words to obscure the sentence or the sentence to obscure the intention. The right way to go about it is to meet or match the intention of the poet by sympathetic understanding' (*Mencius* 5A3).

The Logicians, as scholars of names (nouns), made such a mockery of reference with their 'white horse is no horse' or 'north is south', that the Neo-Mohists turned their attention beyond names – language being more than a string of nouns – to the role of the sentence. A sentence, however defined in different languages, constitutes a unit of complete thought. Being a carrier of meaning, it moves the discussion beyond semiotics (signs and their reference) into semantics (thought and meaning). When it is spoken and communicated as speech between persons, or as a reported poem, the issue of sympathetic understanding ensues.

Mencius addressed that literary challenge. In philosophy, this becomes the more daunting problem of how to tell if a speaker is being untrue. On this, Mencius made the claim that he 'had a gift in knowing speech (*yan*)' so much so that 'were a **sage** to rise, he would surely agree with him' (2A2). The formula runs:

> From a biased address (*zi*, spoken sentences) I can see where the speaker is blind;
> from an immoderate address, where he is ensnared;
> from a heretical address, where he has strayed from the right path;
> from an evasive address, where he is at his wits' end.
> What rises in the mind will interfere with policy,
> and what shows itself in policy will interfere with practice.

This amounts to a growth and a shift beyond Confucius, who was concerned with 'rectifying names' and with 'the coherence between speech and deed' (promise and performance). Mencius now 'scrutinized speech' and worked to 'link spoken speech with unspoken intent'. This inward turn will have him not 'rectifying names' to accord with reality (which was left to Xunzi) but 'making the will sincere' to accord with the good mind.

Mencius's hermeneutics is positive; he believes that even distorted speech is transparent enough to allow him to 'read minds'. The Neo-Mohists were still working at 'knowing speech as speech' but Mencius, by doubting the truthfulness of speech on account of the possible deceptions precipitated by the mind that is making those speeches, moved the discussion to a different level, to a metaphysics of sincerity. This turn may signal an awareness that perhaps philosophical differences are not so easily resolved by logic alone. The four-line formula cited above is usually taken to be describing four types of linguistic malaise. But an alternative interpretation may read them as describing four stages in the unravelling of an attempt at deception, a cover-up that was doomed to fail. If so, it runs as follows:

> The blind man who does not know he is blind talks prejudicially;
> Waking slightly, he hastens to weave immodestly a tangled web;
> Feeling trapped, he looks for others to take the blame;
> But at his wits' end, he tries last-minute evasions – but ultimately fails.

This reading is offered to agree more accurately with the classical assumption that truth in the end is self-evident; that deception will in the end self-destruct; and that there is no liar who does not know he is lying. The modern malaise of radical 'self-deception' was unknown to Mencius.

Metaphor

Theories and types of metaphor vary in the West. Applying them to China causes controversies; because Chinese philosophy allows only certain correlations between things, some argue that it cannot entertain 'metaphor of dissemblance', i.e., a jarring phrase, which exploits dissonance through its unconventional or unexpected combination of terms. You can only liken longevity to 'the southern hills' because the sunny south is the direction of life. You cannot say 'longevity of the northern mountains' because death goes with the north. In fact, nothing is so fixed; original juxtapositions do appear. Zhuangzi, for example, lumped 'wine goblet' and 'speech' together to create 'goblet words' for inspired speech. Oxymorons also exist: 'unheard music is sweeter' has a Chinese counterpoint in 'At that moment, the absence of sound [from her zither] is sweeter than any sound', and Chan creates impossible scenes like 'an iron horse neighs into the wind'. Care must be exercised in translating literary theory into philosophical opinion. The thesis that classical Chinese poets do not even use analogies (A is like B) but simply present word-pictures (A and B) may be true. All later usages would be building on associations. An untrained first reader might be impressed by 'grass by the river'. There is a wealth of cultural associations embedded in the expression, with memories of fertility festivals conducted at rivers in spring in ancient China and girls and boys mating freely in the bushes; but any informed Chinese now would recognize it as a well-worn, sly way of calling someone a bastard.

Pointing and Thing

Gongsun Long, best-known for his thesis that 'white horse is not horse', was charged by Xunzi with 'mis-using names with total disregard for the real': the plain fact is that white horses are very much horses. But what the former did is to simply apply the law of the excluded middle in its negative form – as Buddhists also would – to tackle the issue of 'white' and 'horse'. He stated his argument in an essay on 'Pointing and Thing', showing how paradoxical the pointing as signifier is, even though it does not point directly at the thing or the signified, it nonetheless can locate the desired target. Pointing (reference) X is never directly to the thing X; it is always to the denial of Non-X, such that pointing to X fails to point (directly) at X. But since it points out the Non-X to discard, the end result is that we do find X. This exclusionary logic undermines the Mohist call to love all men. To love X, one must have Non-X to form the class of those not to be loved. But if X equals 'all men', then loving X would leave no man to exclude and there is then no way to find X to love (over non-X). Loving all amounts to loving and benefiting none.

Hui Shi proved to be Gongsun Long's nemesis. Hui Shi argued as follows: if finding X (horse) is possible only through excluding everything which is not X, that is, by eliminating all the non-horse shapes there is, we may never find it: because (1) there is an infinite number of other animal shapes

such that to eliminate them all would take infinite time, or else (2) the so-called 'horse shape' is such a rough approximation that a large greyhound might be mistaken for a small pony. But Hui Shi drew the opposite moral conclusion. He would 'love all things generously [because in the final say, opposites like] Heaven and Earth are basically the same'. Mozi trusted that the human species is distinct, so loving one's neighbour might entail giving him a pony. But in Hui Shi's world, you might as well give the man to the horse also. The pointing, the thing, the action all blend into an eternal shade of grey.

See also: logic in Chinese philosophy

Further reading

Lai, W. (1994) 'White Horse Not Horse: Making Sense of a Negative Logic', *Asian Philosophy*: 59–74.
Ricoeur, P. (1977) *The Rule of Metaphor: Multi-disciplinary Studies in the Creation of Meaning in Language*, trans. R. Czerny, Buffalo: University of Toronto Press.

WHALEN LAI

meditation

Meditation is regarded as a vital route to salvation in most Indian philosophy. Often linked with yoga, there is an emphasis on the proper preparation of the body, since unless one can control the body one is unlikely to be able to control the mind. Controlling the body is possible to certain degrees, and similarly with the mind. The Samkhya-Yoga school argues that controlling the mind is equivalent to fixing the mind on an object, contemplating it and then entering into a trance. There are two degrees of trance. The easier kind to undertake is where the thinker is absorbed in the object of thought, but is still aware that it is an object of thought. The stronger kind is where the immersion is so total that it is no longer regarded as just an object of thought, but as something identical with the thinker. As we lose ourselves in the object we achieve enlightenment, since through meditation the individual can become detached from ordinary thinking and feeling, and can merge mentally with an idea which dissipates the notion of self, the chief source of error and suffering. Buddhists in particular stress that it is through meditation that one can not only experience the absence of a fixed self but also what it is like to operate without such a self. On one version of Buddhism, what the meditator is doing is uniting with **emptiness**, the only plausible definition of reality. One of the chief functions of meditation is to bring about a calming and concentrating (*samatha*) effect, to weaken the power of desire or craving, while the sort of awareness produced through forms of meditation (*vipassana*) designed to produce a strong sense of one's mind can reduce both craving and ignorance.

Some Buddhists argued that the higher states of consciousness attained in meditation could lead to rebirth in a more spiritual and less corporeal state of existence. For example, Dogen *zazen* or seated meditation involves transcending the body/mind dichotomy. We all have the **buddha nature**, and we can realize it through meditation. We can attain enlightenment through riddles (*koan*) or paradoxical sayings which stimulate the mind to work out where the truth lies. Often Chinese approaches to meditation insist on the possibility of sudden enlightenment (see **enlightenment, sudden**), as compared with the tendency in Indian philosophy to stress a more gradual approach. The stages of meditation are seen as really states of mind which are to a degree always present. It was combined with a view of meditation which stressed the absence of attachment, allowing the mind to flow freely without being slowed down by the introduction of value judgements, judgements about whether the objects of the thoughts are true or not. This is not the absence of thought, though, but rather it is a process which restores the original clarity of the mind, and allows the agent to use the concepts which are in his mind without attachment. This view of meditation has the advantage that it is resolutely nondualistic, in that it does not see enlightenment as the goal and meditation as the means.

In the Chan tradition the key Indian principles of *samadhi* (concentration) and *prajna* (wisdom) were altered to make them fit in better with the Chinese orientation to sudden enlightenment. This is possible if these stages are seen as states of mind

as compared with types of practice, and they were often combined in one single experience in which the whole Buddhist path could be collapsed. The Chan emphasis on direct insight replaces the development of *samadhi* and *prajna*, and these came to be regarded as only useful to the less sophisticated meditators.

What replaced this more gradual approach is what came to be known as the no-mind (*wu xin*) or no-thought (*wu nian*) practice. The problem with thought is the erroneous belief that the concept of a thing is the thing itself, and using concepts is a way of projecting one's own view of the world on the world itself, assuming that point of view is an accurate picture of reality. Concepts are acceptable as sorting ideas to deal with experience, but they should be used without drawing any implications of their accuracy in capturing the nature of the world. The mind should flow freely, not being concerned about issues like validity or anything which interferes with spontaneity.

According to the Madhyamaka notion of meditation, the preparation starts with analysis into the notion of inherent existence. This analysis considers the arguments in favour of such existence, rejects them and then looks at the contrast between the notion of inherent existence and the notion of the everyday existence of objects in the world of experience. After this stage the meditator has to be careful to get the balance right between these different aspects of what might be seen as reality, and she has to appreciate that the concept which she considers is neither really existent nor non-existent. She will have in her mind the absence of real essence of the concept, and this is equivalent to the cognition of emptiness, since she realizes that the concept refers to emptiness. But this is not a direct awareness of emptiness, only a grasp of the concept of emptiness as being implied by the emptiness of the concept. Such direct awareness is a bit further along the process, and is equivalent to total meditative absorption. What the meditator needs to do here is place her mind without distraction and also without effort on the object. Of course, this is not easy, since the calmness which is part of the appropriate attitude may have been disrupted by the analysis which has gone into the construction of the concept of emptiness. Once the calmness is established, the meditator tries to alternate between analysis and calmness, until the analysis itself brings about the calmness. This level is known as that of insight, and if it has emptiness as its object it is called the path of preparation. Then there are four successive paths to follow, which result in the stage by stage removal of the conceptual elements on this concentration on emptiness. When a direct and non-conceptual insight is achieved one has a direct cognition of the ultimate. When this is combined with the unselfish compassion of the **bodhisattva**, the meditator is at the first of the ten *bodhisattva* stages. One might think that this was the end of the journey, but in fact it is just the beginning. Progress has been made, in that the meditator can now after her meditation appreciate that what looks like inherent existence is just an illusion, but she still has to purify her understanding of any fragments of such essences in her moral and conceptual life. The goal is to attain Buddhahood, and this means that the essences are replaced by emptiness in the perceptual act itself.

In **Yogachara** meditation, we start off by analysing the stream of consciousness as the only real factor in our experience, and then we proceed to dispense with the notion of the subject and concentrate on the notion of non-duality. This involves not the negation of the stream of experiences themselves, but rather of the mind as something distinct from those experiences. The experiences must be grasped in a non-dual manner, without distinction between knower and known, and this shows why consciousness is often identified with suchness or thatness. In so far as we see the experiences as the basis to real things we remain in the world of **samsara**, but if we manage to transcend that notion we can reach **nirvana**, since we have left duality behind.

Pure Land versions of Buddhism often see meditation as a vital aspect of preparation for death and a good rebirth, or transcendence of transmigration as a whole. The calmer the mind is in the approach to death, the more likely is one to escape the bounds of materiality and attain a high level of spiritual life.

Zhuangzi spoke of adepts who could appear in suspended 'animation' ('like dead wood'), reported on immortals who 'knew states of "no mind"' and described it as like 'sitting in forgetfulness'. The

'psychic chapters' in the *Guanzi* include a mapping of meditative ascent. Among religious Daoists, there was use of 'quiet rooms' and advocacy of 'keeping to the One', and later on, extensive use of visualization techniques. One Daoist term for meditation is 'inner alchemy'. This describes the manipulation of the elemental forces for realizing internal immortality or enlightenment. Regular outer alchemy involves use of actual materials (mercury and cinnabar, etc.) to prolong life. Inner alchemy internalized that process. The vocabularies are similar, and the two paths are not mutually exclusive. One can breathe in the early morning air as the embryonic breath of *yang* and then go on an astral journey entirely within the body.

Song Neo-Confucians were known for 'quiet sitting' as part of their moral self-cultivation. Han Confucians utilized the Five Classics (see **Classics and Books**) as social institutions for 'managing the world'. Song Neo-Confucians utilized the Four Books as realizing inner sagehood. If they learned certain forms of Chan sitting meditation, they borrowed more from a version of Daoist self-cultivation by way of Zhou Dunyi. The Daoist 'inner alchemy' had a programme of 'refining the essence into **ether** and transforming ether into spirit'. They used a diagram of the Former Heaven to help track a psychic reversal of a cosmogonic sequence, to return the fragmented Many to the original One. This diagram was converted by Zhou into the **Diagram of the Great Ultimate**, which forms the basis of Song Neo-Confucian metaphysics. The Daoists read the diagram 'from bottom up'; Zhou read his 'from top down'.

The Daoist understanding is explained in terms of the self, where collecting the present given, i.e. the body, and reversing the sequence of life as decay back to the origin is the process being recommended. When the five internal gods (who reside in the five internal organs) are channelled up into the *yin–yang* (phoenix and dragon) pair, one can unite *yin* and *yang* back into the One and be enlightened. In Daoism, 'essence' is dense; it is the male 'semen' located at the base of the spine (as in kundalini yoga). Essence needs to be made fluid, changed into 'ether' in order to circulate freely and be drawn upwards to the crown of the head. There it is transformed into the most *yang* of elements, the 'spirit'. One attains immortality or enlightenment at that point.

Neo-Confucians adopted the diagram for a different end. In their moral introspection, they target the first movement of mind, the incipient thought or intent, to make sure it wills the good and not the evil. Some even used black and white beans, one for good and the other for bad thoughts, to help mark their moral contemplative progress.

Further reading

de Bary, W. (1981) *Neo-Confucian Orthodoxy and the Learning of the Mind-and-Heart*, New York: Columbia University Press.

Lu Kuan Yu (1970) *Taoist Yoga: Alchemy and Immortality*, London: Rider.

Wong, E. (trans.) (1997) *Harmonizing Yin and Yang: The Dragon-Tiger Classic*, Boston: Shambhala.

WHALEN LAI
OLIVER LEAMAN

Meiroku zasshi

The *Meiroku zasshi* (Journal of Meiji 6) was the journal of the Meirokusha, the Meiji 6 Society, founded in February 1874, which aimed at spreading *bummei kaika* (civilization and enlightenment). Besides public lectures, the *Meiroku zasshi* was the society's most effective instrument for realizing this aim. Also, because of its rational, humane and progressive spirit, the enthusiasm of the contributors, the wide range and variety of the topics addressed and the lucid style, the *Meiroku zasshi* has remained the most instructive and impressive document of the vivid and free intellectual climate of early Meiji. Almost all the articles in it are of philosophical relevance.

The Meirokusha was established at the initiative of Mori Arinori (1846–89) who, on his return from his post as first Japanese ambassador to the United States (1871–3), was convinced that Japan must embrace 'civilization and enlightenment' if she wanted to reach the level of Western powers. To spread civilization and enlightenment, he suggested to **Nishimura** Shigeki (1828–1902) that leading

intellectuals should regularly discuss, and publicly lecture, on relevant topics, and that the best way to do this was to found a society similar to American intellectual societies. When the Meirokusha was established, Mori and Nishimura, Sugi Koji (1828–1917), **Nishi** Amane (1829–97), **Tsuda Mamichi** (1829–1903), Nakamura Masanao (1832–91), **Fukuzawa** Yukichi (1835–1901) and Kato Hiroyuki (1836–1916) belonged to the charter members. Altogether, the society had twenty-eight members, corresponding members included. Most of them had been educated in both Eastern and Western learning, had mastered at least one foreign language, and had been abroad. In the broad sense of the word, all were scholars though, in making their livelihood, they followed different professions. For instance, some were merchants, some officials, while Fukuzawa remained an independent scholar and educator. Though they were united in the idea that education, particularly the realization of civilization and enlightenment, was essential in order to improve Japan's socio-political and military situation, with regard to the details their views differed considerably.

When, in 1875, laws were passed that severely restricted freedom of the press, the Society decided to cease publication of the *Meiroku zasshi*. Some members continued to meet more or less regularly until about 1900, but with the end of the *Meiroku zasshi* the group's influence rapidly declined.

All contributors agreed that civilization and enlightenment required both moral as well as scientific education and competence. All were convinced that traditional Japanese rule was too authoritarian, and the traditional behaviour of the ruled too servile. Hence, they favoured at least a certain degree of individual freedom, with most of them even arguing for some kind of natural (human) rights and people's rights. Also, they agreed that neo-Confucian ontology provided no basis for empirical and logically consistent science and technology but even hindered scientific development. In particular, doctrines of *yin* and *yang* and the five elements (*inyo gogyo*) were attacked. However, while some contributors, such as Nishimura and Nakamura, believed that moral education was fundamental, others like Tsuda and Fukuzawa took a more balanced stance. Also, whereas the former advocated an ethics that combined what they regarded as the strong points of Western theories and classic Confucian doctrines, such as ideas of individual freedom *and* social obligation, Fukuzawa emphasized the spirit of individual independence. Further, the contributors disagreed regarding the question as to which kind of governmental system (monarchy, democracy, etc.) Japan should adopt, and when such a system should be adopted. As far as the last question was concerned, Nishimura was one of the few who argued for a popularly elected assembly, and in this respect was more progressive than Mori and Kato, and even Fukuzawa who, in spite of his anti-traditionalism, remained somewhat elitist and nationalist in his thought. Another hotly disputed issue was whether a scholar should work for, or within, the government, or independently of it, with Fukuzawa strongly arguing in favour of independence.

Almost all contributions to the *Meiroku zasshi* are characterized by rational and systematic argument and touch on important problems. One, Nakamura's essay 'An Outline of Western Culture', sketches Western intellectual history. Some clarify basic human rights concepts. Others argue against metaphysics and superstition. Perhaps the most impressive articles, however, are Mori's 'On Wives and Concubines', in which he champions the rights of women, Tsuda's essays against prostitution, torture and the death sentence, and Nishi's articles on religious freedom and the strict separation of religion and state.

With the publication of the last issue of the *Meiroku zasshi* in November 1875, one of the most lively and stimulating periods of public philosophical discourse in modern Japan came to an end.

See also: Japanese philosophy, post-Meiji; philosophy of human rights, Japanese

Further reading

Braisted, W. (ed. and trans.) (1976) *Meiroku zasshi*, Tokyo: University of Tokyo Press.

GREGOR PAUL

Melanesia, philosophy in

Melanesia is recognized as consisting of the Pacific island nations of Papua New Guinea, Vanuatu, the Solomon Islands and Fiji. It is generally understood that Indian traders, who traveled throughout the East, were the vehicles for the dissemination of central philosophic and religious traditions from the Indian sub-continent to the rest of Asia. But although Hinduism, Buddhism and Islam in different periods and at different times gained a devoted following among the people who inhabited the neighbouring Islands of Indonesia, the religious and philosophic ideas of these major world religions never penetrated the shores of Melanesia. Until visited by the European explorers of the nineteenth century, Melanesia remained physically and socially isolated from Europe and Asia, and intellectually isolated from the philosophies and religions which swept through Southeast Asia. This meant that Melanesian ideas on ethics, metaphysics and cosmology developed in isolation and were entirely uninfluenced by the major religious and scientific ideas, from either the great Western or Eastern traditions. Accordingly, in coming to understand Melanesian philosophy, one must be careful to distinguish Melanesian thought from the major Western and Eastern traditions.

It is also necessary to mention that Melanesian culture and ideas are embodied in an oral rather than a written tradition. This means that the ideas and philosophy of the Melanesians are not readily available or cited through identifiable written works, as for example, one might reference post-Vedic Indian philosophy through the *Bhagavad Gita*. In a presentation of Melanesian thought, it is best to follow the so-called 'hermaneutical' approach. This means that understanding of the central ideas, which animate Melanesian philosophy and cosmology and the intellectual leadership, demands an understanding of the so-called Melanesian 'cultural field'. Beginning with Dilthey through to Habermas and recent communitarians like Charles Taylor and Alasdair McIntyre there has developed a strong tradition of hermeneutical analysis, which offers an understanding, which departs from the epistemic models of simple empiricism based on detached observation. According to this view, the human subject cannot be completely understood independently of his cultural context, understanding will require a complete familiarity with a cultural tradition, including self-definition within the cosmic order.

This means understanding how the Melanesian views himself or herself in relation to the natural environment and available resources and within the greater universe which includes both spiritual and material realities. With reference to the literature one can articulate this cultural context as follows.

The Melanesian ideology recognizes society as the ultimate value through which individual satisfaction is achieved. With this recognition one observes the importance of relationships over actors. However, the community does not constitute the entirety of concern, the greater whole to which all social action is geared is society and universe combined. The whole consists of humans, ancestors, deities, plants, animals or things drawn from temporary conjunctions of different socio-cosmic combinations. In this context the Melanesian sees cyclical and not linear development in the universe and cosmological relations – things do not improve incrementally, rather phenomena are regenerated, renewed or restored in a cyclical movement. This is the motif suggested by the expressions found in the studies of anthropologists: 'regeneration of total society', 'renewal through time', 'life giving death', 'ronde des échanges', 'circulation' or 'ritual system'.

Melanesian identification with the community is intimately and inextricably connected with the parallel identification with the communal land holding. Finally, one needs to appreciate the transformation of and reaction of Melanesian culture and ideas in light of the encroachment of Western culture, including the introduction of Western industrial products and the cash economy initiated with the introduction of money.

A philosophy of renewal and regeneration

Absent from Melanesian philosophy is the Western concept of *telos* or purpose, that is, that individuals, nature and society develop towards a state of completion and/or fruition. Instead of the Western preference for lineal development with a definite terminus, there is a preference for seeing cyclical development. According to this thinking, things and events are restored, regenerated and even repeated in recurring cycles of renewal. This attitude is most famously symbolized in the Kula Ring Trade of the Trobriand Islands, as originally documented by Bronislaw Malinowsky. The Kula Ring system of exchange and transfer as it exists among the Trobriand Islanders off the southeast coast of Papua New Guinea involves two kinds of articles, red shell necklaces and white shell bracelets. These kinds of articles follow a ceremonial pattern and trade route. Each type of article travels in opposite directions around a rough geographical ring several hundred miles in circumference. The participants are permanent contractual partners who only keep each item for a relatively short time before passing it on to another partner, from whom he/she receives an opposite article in exchange. The items are not producer's capital, being neither consumables nor media of exchange outside the ceremonial system. The ultimate purpose of these partnerships is to effect a network of relationships linking many tribes for social and possible military purposes. Ultimately, there is no point of completion in this form of trade, as each article continues indefinitely, endlessly returning to its place of origin along the two hundred-mile ring. Entirely absent are the usual Western rationales for commerce and trade, which have as their goals personal enrichment or consumption. In contrast, the Kula ring trade is solely intended to renew and restore social and community relationships, through repeating cycles of trade for items which endow no permanent titles.

Another interesting aspect of this belief in cyclical renewal is found in the beliefs surrounding ancestral devotion and the return of the ancestors. Melanesians believe that death is not the end of individual existence, but their concepts of the afterlife differ profoundly from more familiar Christian and Eastern views on survival after death. Unlike Christian thinking, which regards death as a terminus of earthly existence and a passage to other worldly existence, in Melanesia, the human personality does not die and leave the world to dwell elsewhere (in an ontically distinct afterlife, like Heaven or Hell). At the same time, Melanesians do not see this continuation as 'return' in the sense envisioned in the great Hindu and Buddhist traditions. These Eastern religions understand that the souls of humans continue or are reborn after the death of the body. On this view we are reborn into different bodies, and different social and living contexts depending on past behaviour and the 'laws of *karma*'. Melanesians believe quite simply that the ancestors never leave and go somewhere else; they continue to exist as a presence in the community in which they were born. They do not change social and existential contexts. Often the dead are thought to live nearby maintaining a watchful presence over the affairs of the community. Usually they are regarded as continuing to live in definite spatial locations like nearby islands, valleys or proximate mountains. Many Melanesian groups continue to maintain 'spirit houses' in which food is left to sustain the ancestors. In fact they continue to be a recognized living presence and play a role in the affairs of the community; and according to this understanding, members of the community must not exhibit behaviour which displeases the ancestors, for they may react and bring harm upon individuals and the community.

One may conclude that these beliefs have important ethical and ontological implications. With respect to ethics, one sees the ancestors regarded as having an important role in maintaining the customs and ethical traditions of the community through their perceived capacity to sanction deviant behaviour. At the same time they are ontically part of the community, because the community is believed to consist of past as well as living members.

Cargo cults

The 'cargo cults' represented a singular response of the Melanesians to the arrival of the 'white man' and the products of his advanced technology. It is worthwhile to examine the beliefs and ideas which animated these movements in order to gain an insight into the shifting changes in contemporary Melanesian ideas and philosophy. An important component of this thinking was the belief that the modern products and the cargo, which the 'white man' possessed, had been sent by the ancestors, and intended for the indigenous people. Indeed some cultists taught that the white men were in fact the returning ancestors bringing gifts, intended for the indigenous Melanesians. P.M. Worsley summarized these events in the following terms. First, there was the adoption of new rituals – based on the behaviour of the whites – aimed at the control and acquisition of these modern goods and gadgets. Indigenous people came to regard the behaviour of the whites as ritual behaviour with a magical connection to the arrival of the desired cargo. Hence the Melanesians imitated the behaviour of the whites, dressing in western clothing, scribbling notations on bits of paper and passing them around. Second, there was a desertion of traditional ways and labouring activities in expectation of the arrival of the desired cargo. Associated with the latter were millenarian views, which carried expectations of the birth of a new age of peace and prosperity. But ultimately, the desired cargo never arrived, and the cultists reasoned that they had yet to master the rituals properly.

Among the movements best known to students of Melanesia are the 'Taro Cults' of New Guinea, the 'Vailala Madness' of Papua, the 'Naked Cult' of Espiritu Santo, the 'John From Movement' of the New Hebrides (Vanuatu) and the 'Tuka Cult' of Fiji. What is important about this phenomenon, in terms of contemporary political-social reality, is that these cults produced a new type of leadership, one whose prominent figures claimed charismatic magical powers which promised a healthy share of the white man's 'cargo' for the leader and his followers. Hans Martin-Schoell, writing in the *PNG Independent* (23 October 1998), notes that many of the first Papua New Guinean parliamentarians came from cargo cults or were even their leaders. (Papua New Guinea became independent in 1975.) The implication to be drawn is that the leadership of these first parliamentarians was built upon a perception that these individuals possessed special abilities to acquire vast amounts of cargo and distribute it to their followers. At time of writing, Francis Koimanrea, the Governor of East New Britain Province of Papua New Guinea, who was a former cargo cult leader for many years, later turned his followers to commercial enterprise and subsequently built his own political career from the same following. To this day he continues to exert a powerful influence over national politics.

The most significant attempt to articulate formally Melanesian philosophy was made in the 1980s by the leading lawyer and Papua New Guinean politician, Bernard Narokobi, who produced a controversial work entitled *The Melanesian Way.* Narokobi sought to develop the ideas of a Melanesian ethic based on cooperation and mutual support. He contrasted this perspective with the individualism of the West, and argued for the integration of customary law and Melanesian ways with the Western law and Western practices, rather than subsuming the former under the latter. On the other hand, many critics have seen Narokobi's work as simply a distillation of nostalgic yearnings, rather than a system which successfully integrates the modern Western social and philosophical ideas within the ideological traditions of Melanesia.

Wantokism

The character of Melanesian interpersonal relations is best understood through the phenomenon of 'wantokism'. 'Wantokism' refers to the mutual duties and responsibilities, which exist between those individuals who share the same language. 'Wantok' is a Melanesian pidgin English term which refers to all those who share this language. Collectively, they are called 'wantoks'. (But as in all lexical matters, this term has a shifting usage and is often applied to individuals who come from the same country or neighbourhood.) Responsibilities for those within the wantok system can be extremely demanding. Wantoks are always under heavy responsibility to help other wantoks in terms of providing food, shelter and cash. Essentially, its strictures prescribe mutual sharing of the advantages and benefits. To deny one's wantok is a grave matter which generates social repercussions which threaten one's place or standing within the community. This brings us to the cosmic view, which supports and buttresses the wantok system of social responsibility.

According to Melanesian cosmology, the individual always finds himself situated in a web of relationships. These relationships consist not only of relationships within the community, but also of connections with ancestors, with other communities and with the entire environment. One must maintain the proper attitude towards all these elements including one's ancestors. Individuals are not free to execute their plans according to chosen life styles; these linkages to ancestors, communal traditions and the other sentient and insentient creatures, which make up the environment, circumscribe their activities. Because one must carefully observe these relationships, individuals find themselves subject to very strong restraints.

The principal source of constraint is, of course, the community. Community existence is central to the Melanesian, to the point that life itself is not conceivable outside one's community. A community is thought to consist not simply of a particular aggregate of individuals, but individuals in a number of specified relationships. The Melanesian understands the community in terms of these relationships and, according to this understanding, these connections are seen to carry more importance than the individuals who are so related. As the community is thought to be made up of these relationships, the community and thus, life itself, may be disrupted or threatened if these relationships are ruptured. Clearly, the community can sustain the loss of certain individuals but if the appropriate relationships are not maintained the community itself may be destroyed and with it all the individual members. Thus, Melanesian cosmology expresses itself in an implicit Melanesian axiology, one which finds its basis in the idea of community and whose ethical implications will be seen to impose severe restrictions on the ideas of autonomous and self-interested behaviour.

Mantovani (1987), a cleric with extensive experience in the Highlands of Papua New Guinea, points out that in the traditional clans of the Highlands, individuals frequently put aside their most personal preferences (for example, marriage preferences) in favour of decisions which would be more advantageous to the group and the community. Furthermore, Mantovani indicates that since the community is the primary value, the ethical rules will respond to this primary value. In other words, what is considered bad behaviour in terms of the individual's actions is that which hurts the community. What does not hurt the community is not bad despite what the Western courts may say about individual guilt. Mantovani mentions the case of some villagers in Chimbu Province who were not much concerned about some petty crimes which some younger members were committing in another village, except that those crimes might affect the safe travel of their own villagers who had to pass by that village. The community thus responds to what the individual does as it is seen to bring harm upon the community.

It is not difficult to appreciate that these Melanesian attitudes contrast strongly with the Western cultural attitudes, which have been concomitant with the market economy and technological advance. Western thinking for over a hundred years has been dominated by liberal philosophy, which holds that the function of the community and civil society is to afford the maximum expression of individual freedom and autonomy. Liberals and libertarians from John Stuart Mill to Robert Nozick have often repeated this formula. In traditional Melanesian society, however, the established order of the cosmos and the ultimate value of the community impose themselves upon the individual and there is little room for individual planning which does not take account of the ends of the community.

Emphasis upon individualism may well have engendered a certain blindness in Western understanding of Melanesian culture. Certain anthropologists have remarked upon the impossibility of understanding indigenous Melanesian culture through the Western 'individualistic' paradigm, which pervades Western analysis. For example, the anthropologist Daniel de Coppet (1981, 1990) has asserted that our modern approach to society is exceptional in that it disregards society as an ultimate value, to the benefit of a quite opposite and non-social value, the individual. He argues that as the liberal ideology values nothing beyond the individual, the continuous move towards its expanding freedom discredits society as a value and makes understanding society even more difficult. De Coppet contrasts individualistic societies, like those of the Western world with holistic societies like the Melanesian, societies in which the ultimate value is society itself.

Furthermore, the religious dimensions of Melanesian culture have worked to maintain the ontological continuity and identity of the Melane-

sian community. Animism and the various forms of ancestral worship we associate with traditional Melanesian life, for example, have and had a local topology which, like the land base itself, maintains the identity of communities and clans over time and given space. It is noteworthy that various forms of animism and a topology of local spirits also characterized the life of pagan pre-Christian Europe. When Christianity replaced these spiritual realities with an exclusive focus upon the one universal Summum Bonum embodied in the three persons of the Trinity, responsibilities to those spirits and gods, who traditionally maintained the well-being of the community were thereby lost. This only served to vitiate and undermine an original profound sense of community.

Further reading

de Coppet, D. (1981) 'The Life Giving Death', in *Mortality and Immortality: The Anthropology and Archaeology of Death*, London: Academic Press.

—— (1990) 'The Society as the Ultimate Value and the Socio-Cosmic Configuration', *Ethnos* 55: 140–51.

Habermas, J. (1991) *The Philosophical Discourse of Modernity*, trans. F. Lawrence, Cambridge, MA: MIT Press.

Iteanu, A. (1983) *La Ronde des echanges: De les circulation aux valeurs chez Orokaiva*, Cambridge: Cambridge University Press.

Malinowski, B. (1961) *Argonauts of the Western Pacific: An Account of Native Enterprise and Adventure in the Archipelagoes of Melanesian New Guinea*, New York: E.P. Dutton, 81–95.

Mantovani, E. (1987) 'Traditional Values and Ethics', in S. Stratigos and P. Hughes (eds), *Ethics of Development: The Pacific in the Twentieth Century*, Port Moresby: U.P.N.G. Press.

McIntyre, A. (1981) *After Virtue*, Notre Dame, IN: Notre Dame Press.

—— (1988) *Whose Justice? Which Rationality?* Notre Dame, IN: Notre Dame Press.

Narokobi, B. (1980) *The Melanesian Way*, Fiji: Institute of Pacific Studies.

Taylor, C. (1985) *Philosophy and the Human Sciences: Philosophical Papers*, Cambridge: Cambridge University Press.

—— (1989) *Sources of Self: The Making of Modern*

Identity, Cambridge, MA: Harvard University Press.

Weiner, A. (1976) *Women of Value, Men of Renown: New Perspectives on Trobriand Exchange*, Austin, TX and London: University of Texas Press.

Worsley, P.M. (1975) 'Cargo Cults', in D. Hunter and P. Whitten (eds), *Anthropology, Contemporary Perspectives*, Boston: Little, Brown & Co., 290–7.

DAVID LEA

Mencius

b. 371 BCE; d. 289? BCE

Confucian philosopher

Mengzi (Meng Tzu, Master Meng) is often latinized as Mencius. He probably lived in the fourth century BCE, although different dates are often given also. He has been regarded as the spiritual heir to **Confucius** since the Song period. Called the second **sage**, next in line to the foremost sage Confucius, he displaced **Xunzi** from that position. Known for his thesis that human nature is good, Mencius in effect internalized the 'mandate of **heaven**'. After Yang Zhu had made the case that Heaven intended him to be selfish, Mencius restored the Zhou ideal and brought moral man and moral Heaven back into alliance. He has been claimed as a 'democrat' for supporting the people's right to revolt; indeed, those sections of his book that had put the welfare of the people ahead of the ruler have been regularly expunged by kings in imperial times. Because of his high standing, the amount of scholarship on the *Mencius* is formidable. Lampooned by a few (for his strict morals) in modern times, he remains revered by many more. The depth and subtlety of his thoughts continue to inspire. The spiritually uplifting hymn on the 'floodlike **ether**' in *Mencius* 2A2 is perhaps the most profound personal statement in the Confucian tradition. It is so dense and rich that it is still read differently by different people. Those disagreements go back to differences among Song dynasty Neo-Confucians; what is historically even more surprising is the fact that before the Song, that hymn went virtually unnoticed.

Mencius's great status in Chinese philosophy arises due to his role as the chief commentator and transmitter of the thought of Confucius. He set out to revive Confucius as a significant, indeed as the leading Chinese philosopher, in response to the attacks which had been made on the latter since his death. Mencius should not be regarded merely as a slavish follower of Confucius, however. On the contrary, he added a great deal to the Confucian tradition, and played an important role in formulating the tradition in such a way as to enable later thinkers to work much more comfortably with Confucianism.

Mencius's concentration on four key ethical qualities is particularly interesting. These are *ren* (benevolence), *li* (ritual), *yi* (propriety) and *zhi* (wisdom). What this is designed to do is to contrast with the lack of sophistication of the Mohist classification of ethics, which is based merely on benevolence. The other qualities are there to control *ren*, which needs to be applied in a graduated and discriminatory way, because it is only appropriate in particular cases and it is far from being a disposition which can be cultivated uncritically. The Mencian list of qualities represents the feelings which we feel quite naturally, and what we ought to do is to strengthen our natural feelings, but only in a balanced way and without upsetting the delicate relationship which exists between them. The Confucian notion of self-cultivation is profoundly realistic, since all it does is formalize the ways in which people think normally anyway, and allows them to organize how they are going to act in a more rational and less haphazard manner. The trouble with Mohism is that it sets as an ideal a level of general benevolence which is far beyond anyone except for the most exceptional individual. Mencius sees Confucianism establishing as an ideal a way of life which is eminently attainable and in line with our natural capacities and feelings.

Mencius extends this notion of self-cultivation into political philosophy by advocating that the leaders promote a similar policy of ethical self-improvement in themselves as in the ruled. If the moral rules which are followed by the rulers are embodied as norm, then they will serve to improve the political atmosphere in general, and there will be a genuine synchronicity between the thinking of the leaders and the led. The people are concerned with far more than just material benefits (in contrast to the views of Yang Zhu the Egoist), because we are all basically good. We are indeed naturally interested in our own welfare, but not to the exclusion of everything else, or at least not unless something has clouded that natural ethical light. When the state helps that ethical character develop it is pushing against an open door, as it were, but it could be that the door will not open because of the corrupt accretions which have affected the nature of the individual concerned. What needs to be done then is to set out to change those impediments by encouraging the individual to rejoin the rest of the community by responding in a natural way to the demands of others and, indeed, of himself. This rather optimistic analysis came to be criticized by Xunzi (third century BCE) but it was explored in greater detail by many in the Neo-Confucian school and developed into a highly sophisticated and plausible form of moral psychology.

See also: courage; hermeneutics; Mencius's mother

Further reading

Ames, R. (1991) 'The Mencian Conception of Ren Xing: Does it Mean "Human Nature"?', in H. Rosemont (ed.), *Chinese Texts and Philosophical Contexts: Essays dedicated to Angus C. Graham*, La Salle, IL: Open Court, 143–75.

Graham, A. (1989) *Disputers of the Tao: Philosophical Argument in Ancient China*, La Salle, IL: Open Court.

—— (1990) 'The Background of the Mencian Theory of Human Nature', in A. Graham, *Studies in Chinese Philosophy and Philosophical Literature*, Albany, NY: State University of New York Press, 7–66.

Nivison, D. (1996) *The Ways of Confucianism: Investigations in Chinese Philosophy*, La Salle, IL: Open Court.

Lau, D. (trans.) (1970) *Mencius*, Harmondsworth: Penguin.

WHALEN LAI
OLIVER LEAMAN

Mencius's mother

Mencius's mother came down in history as the Confucian ideal of what a mother should be. Widowed, she tutored her charge, the very young **Mencius**, into eventual sagehood. She moved her home twice, away from the market and from theatres (or funeral homes with their ritual theatre). She settled finally on living near a school house within earshot of books being recited, which afforded her child the best environment to learn. But it is said that one day Mencius played truant and came home early. Hearing that, his mother cut the cloth she was weaving. That being the family's livelihood, when the shocked child asked why, she noted that by one willful act, all past efforts could be lost. Mencius never missed class again.

This is 'teaching by example' and 'nurturing with environment'. Merchants were shunned because they live for material gain. A gentleman lives by **righteousness** alone. Theatre is considered frivolous sport; it runs contrary to the seriousness of study. But even more so, this is about getting a fun-loving child to behave by plucking at his heart strings, so that he could not bear to see his dear mother suffer for his unthinking misdeed. Mencius's mother is classified as a typical 'masochistic' mother by Freudian social psychologists like George de Vos. Instead of hurting the child (caning him), she turned the hurt against herself. This was meant to induce guilt in the child who, in order to please her, then complies with her will. Mencius's mother did appeal to the child's love for her; but significantly, there are no tears. A closer reading is here required. A widow, she had to play a double role, not just to coax a child emotionally as mothers would but also, to impart a lesson rationally and as impassively as a stoic father should. In this Mencian parable, she taught by personal example (her livelihood as weaver), by analogy (of cutting cloth and cutting class), and by inborn *ren* (the child's love for her). The story shows the Mencian 'mind of commiseration' at work.

Instead of avoiding the theatre, Mencius's mother might have avoided funeral homes. According to Kaji Nobuyuki, Confucius's mother officiated in such popular rites (as a female shaman would at unorthodox sessions) and **Confucius** as a child used to play at such games of ritual worship. Mencius departed from Confucius; he never played ritual games. Confucius stressed an education by ritual mimesis. Mencius saw moral education as bringing out the innate benevolence from within man; that is the mind that cannot bear to see another suffer. This is what Mencius's mother taught her son by her exemplary suffering. This is not unusual; in traditional patriarchal societies, Hindu or Islamic, the father canes and the mother coaxes. When a young child misbehaves, the father takes the mother aside and scolds her for failing in her charge. This explains why whereas a father canes a child coolly 'according to the books', a mother under pressure and driven to her wits' end (by a misbehaving charge) might lose all self-control and lash out wildly at the child. The distinction of Mencius's mother is that she was widowed and she combined both roles.

Further reading

deVos, G. (1994) 'Japanese Sense of Self', *Journal of Japanese Studies* 2(2): 587–95.

Kaji Nobuyuki (1990) *Jukyo wa nani ka?* (What is Confucianism?), Tokyo: Chuo Koron.

Lai, W. (1992) 'The Family as the Axis of Religion: Notes on the Dream of the Red Chambers', *Cheng Feng* 35(1): 44–56.

Lau, D. (trans.) (1970) *Mencius*, Middlesex: Penguin, Appendix 2.

Wolfe, M. (1978) 'Child Training and the Chinese Family', in A. Wolfe (ed.), *Studies in Chinese Society.* Stanford, CA: Stanford University, 221–46.

WHALEN LAI

mental perception

There is a great divergence of opinions amongst Tibetan epistemologists on the question of what is meant by 'mental perception' in the Indian Buddhist epistemological writings. Generally speaking, the Tibetan epistemologists characterize mental perception as (a) free of conceptualization, (b) perceiving an object subsequent to a preceding sensory perception and (c) having the mind as its dominant condition. In that the yogi's transcendent awareness of ultimate truth is a direct mental perception there is no dispute. The problem pertains to the identification of mental perceptions of an ordinary person. The Tibetan thinkers identify three conflicting Indian positions on this.

First is the view that mental perception occurs between the various instances of a sensory perception. For example when a visual perception of say a blue flower takes place, the first and the third instances of the perception are sensory, while what occurs in between is said to be purely mental. Second is the view that when such a perception occurs, the first instance is purely sensorial, but from the second instance onwards three perceptual events occur simultaneously; these being (1) instance of a visual perception, (2) an instance of mental perception and (3) an apperceptive experience that cognizes both the sensory and visual perception. The third position is the view that maintains that when a visual perception occurs it is only after the ceasing of the last instance of the sensory experience that an instance of mental perception occurs. In fact, on this view, it is argued that the duration of the mental perception is so minute that it is impossible for the person himself or herself to have any first person knowledge of the instance that could verify its presence. The event is said to occur within such a short moment that it is simply beyond the cognitive capacity of an ordinary person to register this act. Therefore, it is only on the basis of scripture that we can infer that such a mental perception does occur.

Many **Shakya school** thinkers including the great **Shakya Pandita** and, in the **Geluk school**, Khedrup subscribed to the second position. They reject the idea of there being a mental event that is totally uncognizable by the individual himself or herself, something whose existence can only be proven on the basis of a scriptural authority. Yet others like Gyaltsap and the first Dalai Lama, Gendun Drup (1391–1474), have convincingly argued in defence of the third position. This is also the standard Geluk position on the **Sautrantika** view of mental perception today. However given that most Tibetan schools claim to follow Chandrakirti's Prasangika-Madhyamaka the issue of whether or not one can accept any of the above characterizations of mental perceptions within one's own epistemology is problematic. For example, **Tsongkhapa** rejects the idea of only a momentary, fleeting occurrence of mental perception at the end of a sensory experience as purely fictitious. He argues that mental perception need not be purely a non-conceptual event, but a thought about an object or an event can also have the vividness of a perceptual experience. Furthermore, Tsongkhapa argues that there could be a mental perception occurring when, say, we experience a sensation. At that instance, he suggests that there could be (a) the 'sensation' that is experienced, (b) the 'perception' of the sensation and (c) the 'act' of experiencing the sensation. And the perception, which occurs within such a nexus, according to Tsongkhapa, is best described as mental as opposed to sensory.

This debate about the nature and identity of mental perception from the Madhyamaka point of view is part of a larger issue. It pertains to the problematic question of the interface in Tsongkhapa's thought between **Dharmakirti**'s epistemological theories and Chandrakirti's Prasangika non-essentialism. The Tibetan critics of Tsongkhapa's Madhyamaka have accused him of logocentric bias in his interpretation of Madhyamaka thought. Jamyang Shepa (1648–1722) has attempted to develop a systematic account of the contrasts between Prasangika-Madhyamaka's epistemology and that of the Dharmakirtian tradition.

Further reading

Dreyfus, G.B. (1997) *Dharmakarti's Philosophy and its Tibetan Interpretations*, Albany, NY: State University of New York, ch. 25.

Stcherbatsky, T. (1930–2) *Buddhist Logic*, Leningrad, vol. 2, appendix III.

Tillemans, T.F. (1989) 'Indian and Tibetan Madhyamikas on Manapratyakea', *The Tibet Journal* 14(1): 70–85.

THUPTEN JINPA

MICROCOSM *see* correlative thinking

Miki Kiyoshi

b. 1897; d. 1945

Marxist philosopher

A philosopher, humanitarian and existentialist interpreter of Marxism, from 1917 Miki studied at Kyoto University under **Nishida** Kitaro (1870–1945), Tanabe Hajime (1885–1962) and the philosopher of religion Hatano Seiichi (1877–1950). In 1922 he went to Europe, where he studied with Heinrich Rickert (1863–1936) and Martin Heidegger (1889–1976), and also took private lessons with other German scholars, among them Eugen Herrigel, Hermann Glockner, Karl Löwith, Robert Schinzinger and Hans-Georg Gadamer. (Löwith and Schinzinger later taught in Japan.) After his stay in Germany, Miki continued his studies in Paris. He returned to Japan in 1925. In 1927, he became professor of philosophy at Hosei University, but in 1930 was arrested and banned from his job because of his Marxist leanings. Though no radical opponent of Japanese imperialism, Miki was arrested again in 1945, and died in prison one month after the end of the Second World War.

In 1926, Miki published his *Pasukaru ni okeru ningen no kenkyu* (The Study of Man in Pascal). This early work already displays Miki's interest in existential philosophy and what can be called concrete human life and concrete humanity. Accordingly, in his *Kaishakuteki genshogaku no kisogainen* (Basic Concepts of Hermeneutical Phenomenology) (1927), he argues in favour of Heidegger's approach and against Husserl's (1859–1938) pure phenomenology. In Miki's view, *Dasein*, the simple fact of existence, is the most basic phenomenological concept. Similar to Pascal (1623–62) and Heidegger, Miki conceives of man, and man's life, as characterized by a kind of elementary fear (*fuan*), and constant anguish and worry ('Sorge', *kanshin*) to overcome, or escape from, this fear. In 1932, *Rekishi-tetsugaku* (A Philosophy of History) and *Shakaigaku genron* (An Outline of Social Science) appeared. In these studies again, Miki tried somehow to defend the importance of concrete and directly relevant knowledge against merely abstract and general science. In 1939, he brought out *Kosoryoku no ronri* (The Logic of the Power of

Imagination), in which he conceived of a notion of a human creativity that comprises both regularity and individuality, or sensibility. By 'logic', Miki does not mean (rules of) formal logic, but wants to refer to a fundamental and comprehensive creative mechanism, and/or set of rules which generates, and is reflected in, the structure of human culture as a whole, particularly 'myths', 'institutions' (morality, customs, laws, politics, arts) and 'techniques'. In this connection, Miki also speaks of a 'logic of form' (*katachi no ronri*), namely, the form of cultural products.

As to Miki's interpretation of Marx, it was also influenced by Heidegger. From among the contemporary European Marxists, Georg Lukács (1885–1971) had a certain impact on his thought. Published in 1928, *Yuibutsushikan to gendai no ishiki* (Historical Materialism and Modern Consciousness) comprised four essays, namely *Ningengaku no marukusuteki keitai* (Marxist Anthropology), *Marukusushugi to yuibutsuron* (Marxism and Materialism), *Puragumatizumu to marukishizumu no tetsugaku* (Pragmatism and Marxist Philosophy) and *Hēgeru to Marukusu* (Hegel and Marx). Miki conceived of the experience of the proletariat as 'fundamental experience' (*kiso keiken*) that had to be taken as the starting point for theorizing and politics, ultimately evolving into an 'anthropology', a theory and practice of how ideal human life ought to be. Miki also translated many European philosophical texts into Japanese, among them Marx and Engels's *German Ideology*.

Further reading

Kim, Y.M. (1974) 'Miki Kiyoshi: A Representative Thinker of his Times', Ph.D. thesis, University of California, Berkeley.

GREGOR PAUL

Mohism: moral logic

Logic was developed by **Mozi** as a rational tool to critique and reform tradition. That strict use of logic for philosophical disputation was defended by the Neo-Mohists. But coming after Mozi were Gongsun Long (b. 380 BCE) and Hui Shi (380–305 BCE), members of the School of Names, also called Logicians and Sophists. Mocked for abusing names or ignoring reality, they pushed logic into two different but unexpected conclusions. They affected moral discourse by challenging the Mohist theory of Universal Love, which argues that loving all will inevitably benefit all.

Gongsun Long argues that loving X is relative to not-loving the non-X. But since loving all men leaves none to disprivilege, universal love amounts to benefitting none. He was actually defending egoism against altruism, the self against the all. He endorsed the Mohist stand 'against aggression' to safeguard the sanctity of the self. He just found that 'universal love' equals 'not loving anyone'. Meanwhile, Hui Shi drew the opposite conclusion. He introduced the measure of the Infinite. Categories became thereby so indistinct – or the distinctions so relative – that a large dog can be mistaken for a small pony. The only certainty left is that everything as 'thing' is the same. It follows that in loving all (things), there is no reason to privilege human beings as exclusive objects of love.

WHALEN LAI

monism

The mystique of the One in Chinese thought runs through its whole history. It may go all the way back to the mystique of the Chinese **dragon**, the animal that is the sum of all other species, or to the *Taotie* animal mask on ancient ritual bronzes, which represents how the One splits into the Two. **Laozi** remembered that 'in former times, there were attainers of the One (whereby) Heaven became clear; earth became tranquil; the spirits became divine; the valley became full; the myriad things became luxuriant; and the rulers became able to bring order.' From this came the Daoist **meditation** known as 'keeping to the One', which centuries later reappeared in the teaching of Daoxin ('keeping to the one true mind') and influenced the direction of Chan Buddhist meditation.

Other classical thinkers spoke of the One. **Confucius** hinted at a One Thread running through his teachings. Hui Shi the Logician grasped the one basis common to **Heaven** and Earth. His friend **Zhuangzi** also levelled all distinctions and formed one body with the myriad realities. **Mencius** charged the Mohist Yizi with 'making two' of the one basis intended by Heaven. The **Yijing** spells out the cosmogonic sequence: 'From the (One) Great Ultimate came the Two Poles (of *yin–yang*); from the Two Poles came the Four Forms (or Emblems); and from the Four Forms the Eight Trigrams.' Han *Yijing* scholarship worked on the 'numbers and emblems' in a hexagram in order to chart the course of emerging events. Turning away from such prognostication, the Neo-Daoists noted the manifoldness of the subsequential Many (the chaotic post-Han world) and sought to revert to the original One. Wang Bi concluded, as Plotinus would, that the One being the source of all numbers cannot be itself a number, the numeral one. Commenting on Zhuangzi's statement that 'Where the One first rose, there is only the One; there is not yet any visible form', fellow Neo-Daoist thinker Guo Xiang characterized this One at the source of all beings as most subtle (*miao*). That is where 'there is then not yet the form that comes with the being of a thing'. *Miao*, which mediates non-being and being, is itself neither being nor **non-being**. This term would influence the Chinese appreciation of Mahayana **emptiness** which is also 'neither one nor different'.

The term was also used by Kumarajiva to render the title of the *Lotus Sutra*. Previously the *saddharma* (true **dharma**) of the *pundarika* (lotus) was rendered by Dharmaraksha with a philologically correct 'true law'. Kumarajiva, who learned Chinese during his long years of captivity in northwest China, chose instead *miao fa* to describe this Wondrous Teaching. This was the keener, semantic choice. Chinese Buddhist exegesis of this title did not lose sight of the magic of this term; **Jizang** of the Sanlun school and Zhiyi of the Tiantai school would both make much of *miao*. Henceforth, it stands for the 'mysterious being (yet) truly empty'. With the *Lotus Sutra* teaching the doctrine of this (wondrous) One Vehicle, Zhiyi would use this inexplicable 'wonder' to explicate the meaning of Ekayana, the One Vehicle. The One Vehicle that absorbs the Three Vehicles within itself is at once both One and Three and

neither One nor Three. This results in a triune formula that it is given, not in sequence but in the round. This arabesque of 'Three is One, One is Three' anticipated the Huayan formula of the 'All is One, One is All', which draws the One into the Infinity.

To the Neo-Confucians who came after (see **Neo-Confucianism, concepts**), the Buddhists talked too much of a transcendental unity at the expense of the very real world of social distinctions like 'ruler and minister' or 'father and son'. The key, said Cheng Yi, is to see the 'One Principle manifesting itself in the Many Divergences'. The One (Great Ultimate) is found fully in the Many without losing sight of the specifics of the varied roles and rules in the human world. This returns the indiscriminate Buddhist compassion to the Mencian standard of the 'one basis' with many 'graded loves'. But there being no way back to the Han monism of just One **ether** in the origin evolving into the many ends, **Zhu Xi** settled for a distinction between the One that is the metaphysical principle and the Many that are the permutations of the physical ether. That taming of the monistic pathos by a discerning, dualistic rationality has informed Chinese thinking ever since.

Further reading

Munro, D. (ed.) (1985) *Individualism and Holism: Studies in Confucian and Taoist Values*, Ann Arbor, MI: University of Michigan Center for Chinese Studies.

WHALEN LAI

moral failure

If the *dao* is one, it could well be a Way 'without crossroads' (Fingarette 1972). If there is a unity to the virtues, there are ultimately no competing claims about the nature of the good. But what of the proverbial contrary demands in China, such as family versus state? Although indeed at times '**filial piety** and loyalty cannot co-exist', the number of actual cases of conflict in the historical records are rare. The ideal of the 'family state' and the orthodoxy of 'filial piety and loyalty' had long reached mutual accommodation.

Mencius 4A17 poses a more tricky dilemma. **Mencius** had argued that any man would have an immediate urge to assist upon seeing a child about to fall into a well (2A6). He was quizzed about whether he would violate a ritual taboo to save a drowning sister-in-law by touching her. Using good judgement, Mencius readily complied with **humaneness** and suspended the **rites**. Love overrides law. But the question was then raised as to why one would not do as much to save the world? Mencius, who had mocked Yang Zhu the Egoist for 'not being willing to spare a single hair' to save the world, was mocked in turn here for not raising an arm to save the world. Mencius, a morally exacting individual, had refused to serve lords of questionable virtue. Mencius's answer is that the *dao* cannot be compromised. (Elsewhere, in the *Mencius*, he appears more flexible.)

There is a more insidious problem than moral conflict, namely, a moral failure due to a lack of will. In China, Mencius was the first thinker to recognize such a problem might exist. But for him, people who say 'I want to but I can't' really mean 'I won't'. This goes deeper than what Confucius had previously considered as a lack of moral **courage**, since Mencius is talking here about the possibility of self-deception. It is 'cheating oneself' as well as 'cheating others'. To Mencius, it is basically 'selling oneself short'. A moral optimist, Mencius believes that if you will something from an ethical point of view, you can carry out the action. The resource is inside you.

On the question of the source of the moral will, there were two earlier opinions. The Mohists were rationalists who assumed that knowledge is power. If you know what is good, you would naturally do what is good. Volition is subsumed under reason. And given the Mohist faith in the self-evidential nature of the common good, there is never reason to will against self-interest or egoism. The Daoists held the opposite view. Distrusting all human effort to promote the human good, **Laozi** repudiated all action and subverted the exercise of the human will. By renouncing assertion, the natural good of *wuwei* (non-action) will realize itself by itself. Although there is a repudiation of the human will, the term 'no will' or 'no mind' had not come up

yet; that appears only in **Zhuangzi**. Will is embedded in 'action', which is moved by 'desires'. Laozi pleaded for a lessening of desires.

Mencius had to contend with both the Mohist activist and the Daoist passivist legacy. Faced with the problem of the greater and the lesser good – caring for just oneself or caring for the larger community – Mencius fell back on a calculus of a 'greater and lesser self' within. The lesser self has a lesser supply of good will; it pursues more selfish ends. Enlarging that self by extending a natural empathy for fellow beings outwards, that larger self can draw on the greater will power to pursue the greater good. At its highest, one even sacrifices one's lesser self in order to bring fruition to that greater self. In that process of asserting a moral will by accumulating 'right deeds', the person is somehow swept up by an overwhelming force (the floodlike **ether**). He is told to 'be attentive' but 'not to assert himself' if he is to reach a union with the *dao*. However one might put it, the voluntarism at pursuing the greater good that Mencius took over from the Mohists somehow ends at that point; and the involuntarism that requires a resignation of the will takes over in line with Daoism.

Further reading

Fingarette, H. (1972) *Confucius: The Secular as Sacred*, New York: Harper Torchbook.
Lai, W. (1984) 'Kao-tzu and Mencius on Mind: Analyzing a Platonic Shift in Classical China', *Philosophy East and West* 34(2): 147–60.

WHALEN LAI

motivation

Mencius gave probably the most subtle analysis of motivation in *Mencius* 2A6. In the parable of the falling child – how any normal person would have the urge to save a small child crawling towards a well – he states that a person would do so 'not because he wanted to get in the good graces of the parents, nor because he wished to win the praise of his fellow villagers or friends, nor yet because he disliked the cry of the child'. This denial of other plausible reasons for so doing was crafted in such a way as to target for criticism (a) **Mozi**, who does good only after calculating the benefits (the good grace of the parents); (b) **Gaozi**, who does good out of a sense of a social obligation and social standing, honour and dishonour; and (c) Yang Zhu, who might save the child for purely egoistic reasons (he hated the racket the child was making). Implied in Mencius's thesis is that (d) the good will might be corrupted, i.e. someone may lose their humanity and not care about the child, (e) the good will might be checked by utilitarian reasons, and finally (f) by legitimate self-concern, if there is a justifiable chasm between the agent and the child.

Further reading

Nivision, D. (1996) 'Motivation and Moral Action in Mencius', in D. Nivison, *The Ways of Confucianism*, La Salle, IL: Open Court.

WHALEN LAI

Mozi

b. *c*.490 BCE; d. 403 BCE)

Philosopher

Mozi (Mo Tsu) created the school of Mohism, and is thus the founder of one of the most important Chinese schools of philosophy. He dealt with one of the recurrent issues in Chinese philosophy, the apparent relativity of ethics, and sought an objective standard of value. Utility seemed to him to be the solution, and those approaches to action which are most likely to result in general welfare are the ones to be pursued. The reason for preferring this system of value is that it is the general choice, he argues, the natural (*tian*) choice. Since *tian* also means 'heaven', it seemed an eminently sensible choice as a basis to value, and Mozi argued that not only does our natural choice have a basis in **heaven**, but that implies a certain constancy about it also. This is in marked contrast to the variety of traditions which exist and which can also serve as the basis of value. Mozi is here referring to one of the main advantages of utilitarianism, its apparent objectivity. It does not ask of the individual what he wants as an outcome,

or what he sees as the best outcome, but it rather presents a system of calculation in terms of which a certain option comes out as the best, entirely on the basis of measurement. We may not immediately be able to choose in line with general utility, of course, and this means that we have to work on our moral dispositions (*de*) to ensure that it is appropriate to keep us in line with the way, *dao*, of ethical life.

The advantage of this theory is that it takes seriously our participation in a society, since Mozi has as his ideal *ren*, or benevolence, but at the same time does not freeze the particular social relations in which we find ourselves as the context which defines precisely how we should act. That is not to say that he argued for very different forms of political organization as compared, say, with the Confucians, because this is not the case. But what is at the foundation of that organization, for Mozi, is the value of the system, and it has a value independently of the system and in terms of which the system may be assessed. He follows a tentative approach when considering what statements can be defended and which should be abandoned, especially in the area of ethics and political life. Some institutions are worth keeping since they have a genuine utility, while others are more dubious but still may be worth retaining since it is not clear that their replacement would be generally beneficial. Mozi takes the same rather conservative pragmatic approach to knowledge claims, where he often criticizes the sorts of things which people say but suggests that they should continue to produce those knowledge claims since they may well perform a valuable social and/or personal function. He does not take the same relaxed line on the sorts of institutions such as music and elaborate funerals and mourning ceremonies, which are so important a part of the Confucian notion of *li*, the appropriate rites. This form of criticism was felt to be shocking by the Neo-Confucians and frequently served as the object of attempted refutation.

Further reading

Graham, A. (1978) *Later Mohist Logic: Ethics and Science*, Hong Kong: Chinese University Press.
Hansen, C. (1989) 'Mozi: Language Utilitarianism. The Structure of Ethics in Classical China', *Journal of Chinese Philosophy* 16: 355–80.

Mozi (1929) *The Ethical and Political Works of Mo-tse*, London: Probsthain.

OLIVER LEAMAN

Mulla Sadra

b. 979–80 AH/1571–2 CE; d. 1050 AH/ 1640 CE

Philosopher

Sadr al-Din Muhammad ibn Ibrahim ibn Yahya al-Qawami al-Shirazi, often known as Mulla Sadra or Sadr al-Muta'allihin, comes as his name suggests from Shiraz, in Iran. He died in Basra. He is undoubtedly one of the most creative thinkers in Islamic philosophy. His main achievement is systematically linking the thought of **Ibn Sina**, **al-Suhrawardi** and **Ibn al-'Arabi**, which resulted in a very rich new philosophy. Unlike Ibn Sina and al-Suhrawardi (although interestingly like **Ibn Rushd**), Mulla Sadra regards existence as more central than essence, so central that it cannot even be regarded as a category. Existence is however an ambiguous factor in reality (*tashkik al-wujud*), occurring in everything but in different ways and degrees of strength. It is matched by a gradually changing or transubstantial motion (*al-haraka al-jawhariyya*) which replaces the Aristotelian notion of change. The latter suggests that change is a sudden and all-or-nothing process. For Mulla Sadra, by contrast, everything is in constant motion since existence is a matter of an eternal process of change and development. The ways in which we talk of things is a reflection of the ways in which our imagination breaks things up into individual essences, but in reality they are all part of one changing existence. This gives him a neat way of resolving the longstanding theological problem of explaining the eternity of the world. The world is continually coming into existence as a manifestation of the eternal unfolding of existence. Change may be constant, but it is constant in time, which is the measure of change. So the world is created both in time and is also eternal. It is eternal in the sense that it has no beginning or end, since time is not there for creation to occur within. Although it is eternal, the world is also a site of development of existence, and so is far from fixed.

Mulla Sadra extends the epistemology of al-Suhrawardi and Ibn Sina, the theory of the **active intellect** with that of knowledge by presence (*'ilm al-huduri*). The former leads us to come into contact with the formal principles of reality, while the latter explains why we are justified in thinking that our knowledge is certain and self-evident. As we progressively improve our understanding we come to identify with the ever higher levels of existence and ever more formal levels of thought. But we should not identify these levels of thought with more complex essences, on the contrary what happens is that we come into contact more directly with existence and realise that our ideas of that existence, the essences, are misleading and require replacement. Like Ibn al-'Arabi, he places considerable significance on the **imaginal realm** (*al-'alam al-mathal/al-khayal*), which is more than merely the faculty of working with images and corporeal ideas. This world is the source of understanding of issues such as human immortality and prophecy, since these notions are a combination of ideas from the ordinary world of generation and corruption and higher ideas from the spiritual world. So the implication that an imaginary realm is a realm of what does not really exist is misguided (and is the motive behind Corbin's translation of *khayali* as 'imaginal' and not 'imaginary'). There is nothing unreal about the imaginary if it borrows ideas from what is present to us in experience and also from what is at a theoretically higher level in intellectual thought.

See also: illuminationist philosophy; space and time in Islamic philosophy

Further reading

Nasr, S. (1996) *The Islamic Intellectual Tradition in Persia*, ed. M. Amin Razavi, Richmond: Curzon.

Rahman, F. (1976) *The Philosophy of Mulla Sadra*, Albany, NY: State University of New York Press.

Ziai, H. (1990) *Knowledge and Illumination*, Atlanta, GA: Scholars Press.

OLIVER LEAMAN

music

In both China and classical Greece, music educates by harmonizing the emotions, the classical view being that musical notes embody the emotions which are objective or societal. Although the *Classic of Music* was lost, the music chapter in the *Book of Rites* preserved a theoretical base. Music rose from within, when feelings were stirred by things without; voice produces sound, which when harmonized produces tones or notes and when orchestrated with instruments produces music. (And when the individual is inspired to move his limbs, there is dance.) Unlike **rites**, which came from without, music rose from within. Rites serve to differentiate; music to inculcate the mean. For that reason, music is calming while rites are patterned. The best of music is easy; the best of rites are simple. Where music spreads, there is no resentment, and where rites spread, there is no contention.

See also: Xi Kang

WHALEN LAI

mysticism

Calling Confucianism rational and Daoism mystical is of only limited value. **Laozi**'s *dao* can appear the very opposite of mystical, being defined sometimes as 'plain, simple and laughable'. The prophet's sense of feeling small and worthless before God was for the Daoist the sure sense of being one with the lowly and dusty *dao*. When the **Daodejing** speaks of the 'valley' of the 'mystic female', it turns out to be not just about the Earth (dust); it is not even about some generic feminine (like *yin*). The script for 'female' is animalian; it is a she-bovine; the cow is associated with the moon. It can be a mark for the goddess of the herd, or the mistress of the hunt before she became the symbol of earthly agrarian fertility.

Some, such as Wing-tsit Chan, have argued, for example, that classical Daoism is 'naturalistic' and not 'mystical' because there is no sharp distinction in it between the natural and the mysterious. If so, one can postulate a later heightening of the sense of the 'mysterious' among the Neo-Daoists speculating on this dark mystery. This was soon enhanced by the Mahayana introduction of a transcendental wisdom called *prajna* and a Two Truths theory from **Nagarjuna** distinguishing the mundane truth from the highest truth. If so, then at the end of the medieval Buddhist period, we can speak of a turning back to the 'natural' as Chan sanctifies the everyday. The pleroma of buddhas and *bodhisattvas* receded; the iconography of supernatural marks was no longer required.

If this view holds, then we will have to confront the problem stated in the beginning, of how to draw the line between Confucian rationality and Daoist mysticism. There is a strong mystical strand in Zhang Zai's *Western Inscriptions*, and yet he was an important link in the Neo-Confucian revival.

Further reading

Lai, W. (1977), 'Some Notes on Mystical Militancy', *Insight: A Journal of World Religions* 2(1): 37–46.
—— (1978) 'Innerworldly Mysticism, East and West', in H. Heifetz (ed.), *Zen and Hasidism*, Wheaton, IL: The Theosophical Society Publishing House, 186–207.

WHALEN LAI

myth of Laozi

The religious Daoist tradition depicts Laozi as having a fabled life similar to that of the Buddha. He is the incarnation of the *dao* after the *dao* changed into sun rays that changed into a pearl that, coming down on a chariot pulled by nine dragons, changed into a pill that entered into the womb of the Jade Maiden. After incubation for 81 (9 × 9) years, he came out of his mother's side (thus he is called the Old One) as she was holding on to a plum branch. With the four cardinal **animals** protecting him, he paced nine steps. The sun and moon bathed him in light; the nine dragons sprang from the earth and showered him with rain. He pointed up to **heaven** and down at earth, declared himself unsurpassed; having had compassion on the ignorant world, he had come down to show men the way, concocting an elixir to teach men how to cultivate immortality and demonstrating the goal by ascending to the sky from a cypress on the back of a deer. This happened during the reign of the Shang king Wu Ding. With nine transformations, Laozi produced the 81 major and 72 minor supernatural marks on his body. His mother then rose to heaven to be the Great Queen of Former Heaven. Laozi also ascended, with gods paying homage and protecting his future descendents, especially the Emperors of the Tang dynasty.

WHALEN LAI

Nagarjuna

*c.*150 CE

Buddhist philosopher

Nagarjuna was a Buddhist Madhyamika ('Middle Way') dialectician whose major works include the *Madhyamika-karika*, the *Yuktishashtika*, the *Shunyata-saptati*, the *Vaidalyaprakarana* and the *Vigrahavyavar-tani*. He is particularly concerned to demonstrate by rational analysis the essentially conditional and provisional nature of the phenomenalist-realist and atomic **dharma** theory (**Abhidharma**) of the Sarvastivadin Vaibhashikas. This is an aspect of Nagarjuna's general sceptical thesis about the necessarily provisional nature of any philosophical account of reality. He contended that the complex and holistic Abhidharma taxonomies, which purport to identify the irreducible building blocks of reality, are self-defeating in that the systematic inter-relations between the *dharmas* traced therein vitiate the thesis that they enjoy discrete and self-sufficient existence (*svabhava*). He understands *svabhava* to involve permanence, independence, numerical unity and self-generation. He argued that an entity lacks 'own-nature' (*svabhava*) or essence on both empirical and a priori grounds. Experience reveals the occurrence of events but not essences. If essence is conceived in terms of an unchanging underlying core, a thing cannot change and this is contrary to experience. Everything is empty (*shunya*) of own-nature because everything exists in relative dependence (***pratitya-samutpada***). Nothing exists in its own right, everything being relative. This relativity – A's

arising when B is present – is proposed as a deliverance of experience, while own-nature is a mere assumption. Because entities originate in dependence on causes and conditions, they lack inherent existence which is what the Madhyamika means by 'emptiness'. There is no source of origination, no subject of origination and no determinate identities of things that exist only in relation to counter-correlates.

Nagarjuna claims that the Abhidharmists in postulating fundamental *dharmas* with inherent natures do not go far enough down the road of reductive analysis to momentariness that is the true Buddhist path. In fact, the doctrine of *svabhava* undermines the Buddha's teaching. If unsatisfactoriness (*duhkha*) had essence, it would be uncaused and eternal. If the Buddha's teaching had own-nature, it could not be inculcated in an individual since its possession would be an all or nothing matter. **Nirvana** with own nature would be unattainable. In a world of entities with own-nature, change, becoming and activity would be impossible since everything would be static and eternal. But because everything is changeable and empty of own nature, moral improvement and spiritual growth are possible.

Nagarjuna thinks that people are moved to actions with inevitable retributive potencies (***karma***) by desires for the pleasant, avoidance of the unwelcome and mistaken beliefs in the non-transitoriness of things. These motive forces are generated by dichotomizing thought (*vikalpa*), ideas (*samkalpa*), opinions (*kalpana*), hypotheses (*parikalpa*) and dogmatic theories (*dristi*) all of which are instrumental in constructing the expanding circle of experience (*prapancha*). *Vikalpa* classifies experience into binary opposites such as cause and effect, subject and object, succession and simultaneity, substance and attribute, subject and predicate, short and long, near and far, presence and absence, is and is not, being and **non-being**. The operation of *vikalpa* can be eradicated through meditative practice and analytical insight (*prajna*) exposing through logical techniques, in particular the deployment of paradoxes to demonstrate inevitable contradictions in the way our minds work, the internal contradictions and undesirable implications (*prasanga*) of *vikalpa*-based world-views, especially the direct realism propounded in the systematizations of the Sarvastivadin Vaibhashikas who maintained that the *dharmas* existed in past, present and future.

Against the Vaibhashikas, Nagarjuna argued that it is impossible coherently to articulate the relation between present and future times in relation to time past. Any such relation would involve the compresence or simultaneity of present or future with the past. Thus everything would occur in the past and temporal sequentiality would be impossible. Parallel consequences can be derived if the notions of the present or the future are taken as focal.

This critique is related to that of the process of movement (*gamanam*, 'going') in *Mulamadhyamaka-karika* ch. 2. Nagarjuna says that the grammatical structure of the Sanskrit language allows for paths which (1) have been traversed (*gata* – 'gone'), (2) not yet been traversed (*agata*) and (3) currently being traversed (*gamyamanam*). Of the first two cases it is not possible to say that it is currently being travelled (*gamyate*). But there is no third kind of path apart from those two of which the expression 'currently being travelled' could be predicated. He next addresses the obvious case of someone walking along a road. *Gamyamanam* and *gamyate* denote an object relative to the act of going. Those terms are combined in the locution 'what is currently being traversed, that is being travelled' (*gamyamanam gamyate*) which would be usually understood as meaning a single act of going. If it is assumed that act is presently occurring on path type (3), it appears that two acts of going are happening on the one path. If one insists that there is only one act, the unwelcome implication or

prasanga follows that the referent of *gamyamanam* is not connected with going. Accordingly, one cannot explain going in the case of path type (3). Going can only be explained if there is an agent who goes. But if there are two acts of going expressed in *gamyamanam gamyate*, there is the *prasanga* that there would have to be two agents.

Having exposed the problems in the concept of going (*gamanam*), Nagarjuna next attempts to reveal those implicit in the notion of the agent of going (*ganta*). 'Goers' and 'goings' are interdependent. But if it cannot be said that path types (1) and (2) are currently being travelled and there is no third type of path, how can the notion of agency in this context be coherently specified? If one says 'a goer is going' (*ganta gacchati*) expresses an agent and an act in relation to the same path, there is the *prasanga* of two acts of going. If it expresses a single act in which the agent is the same as the action performed, Nagarjuna objects that the agent does not perform the same act (he does not go that going) in virtue of which he is called the agent of going. 'John is going to London' is a perfectly intelligible expression. But the concept of the agent in 'a goer is going' is not satisfied prior to the act of going itself. Moreover the agent here does not perform an act of going different from the one in virtue of which he is specified as the agent since there cannot be two acts of going in relation to the one goer.

Implicit in Nagarjuna's *prasanga* method of argumentation is a critique of the Brahminical *karaka*-analysis, developed in the *vyakarana* or grammatical tradition, of actions (*kriya*) and events into the determinate categories of 'starting-point', 'recipient', 'instrumental cause', 'locus', 'primary object' or 'effect' and 'agent' which Buddhist philosophers see as reifying or substantializing aspects of what are actually fluid processes. For the theorists of Brahminism, the agent, defined as independent, is the linchpin of an event. By contrast, Buddhists reduce agency to another equiparate factor in a causal process.

Nagarjuna's outlook is characterized by a low, one might say 'zero' (*shunya*), level of ontological commitment. He regards subscription to philosophical views as a dogmatic form of the attachment whose eradication is the purport of the doctrine discovered by the Buddha. In the *Vigraha-Vyavartani*,

Nagarjuna poses the question: if everything (including statements) is empty then the statement, 'everything is empty' is empty and thus loses its claim to truth. In other words, we are dealing with a self-referential paradox of the form, 'All statements are false'. Nagarjuna's reply is that since he is not positively proposing a thesis he cannot be convicted of self-contradiction. Indeed, if his statement is meaningless, it only exemplifies universal **emptiness**. The truth is ineffable, but silence is of no instructional value. The teacher must needs have recourse to the everyday conventions of discourse (*vyavahara*) if he is to communicate his message.

Nagarjuna's distinction between conventional truth (*vyavahara* or *samvriti-satya*) and ultimate truth (*paramartha-satya*) is not a distinction between two levels of objective reality but should be understood in a pedagogical context. The first refers to the practice of the teacher imparting instruction about the *buddha-dharma* to beginners using the conventions of everyday thought and language. The latter relates to insight into the emptiness of everything including the conventional categories previously employed by the teacher. *Nirvana*, the end of rebirth, is the coincidence of the cognition of emptiness of all phenomena and the exercise of compassion. Considering it as a sort of state analogous to the transmigratory condition (***samsara***) would be an example of unenlightened *vikalpa*.

Further reading

de Jong, J.W. (1977) *Nagarjuna Mulamadhyamakakarikah*, Madras: Adyar Library and Research Centre.

Lindtner, C. (1982) *Nagarjuniana*, Copenhagen: Akademisk Forlag.

Matilal, B. (1977) *The Logical Illumination of Indian Mysticism*, Oxford: Clarendon Press.

Murti, T. (1970) *The Central Philosophy of Buddhism*, London: George Allen and Unwin.

Ruegg, D. (1981) *The Literature of the Madhyamaka School of Philosophy in India*, Wiesbaden: Otto Harrassowitz.

Williams, P. (1989) *Mahayana Buddhism*, London: Routledge.

CHRIS BARTLEY

name and reality

The debate on name and reality followed the collapse of the Zhou feudal order, during which a man had been what his name and position (title and rank) said he was. When that order disintegrated, **Confucius** worked at restoring that equation with a thesis called the 'rectification of names'. Social harmony would ensue only if 'ruler is ruler (i.e. acts as a ruler would), minister is minister, father is father, son is son'. This is often taken to mean that 'name must correspond to reality', which is a position held later by **Xunzi**. But Confucius intended it as a theory of virtue. It is not name that has to comply with reality; it is reality that should be brought in line with the excellence implicated in the name. The line 'father be father, son be son' is not about each party having fixed ritual standards to live up to. It is confirming the intrinsic good of having father and son (i.e. a family) and a way to bring about its excellence by having both members strive after a common good. That good must be good for both, son as much as father. Likewise, the excellent state is one which is to the good of both ruler and subject.

Coming after Confucius, **Mozi** also trusted that the 'goodness' is there in the name and that there is a moral logic associated with the name. It is logical for man to love (all) men; the whole family of humanity benefits that way. But the right course of action should be based not on tradition but on reason. There is a test by the standard *yi* (right, **righteousness**). Does the action do the beloved good? Or will it only cause harm? A love that hurts the other can therefore never be right. Mozi never discounted the requisite of a good will; he only wanted to make sure that good intention does not, as it often can, bring about pain unintentionally. Up to this point, name and virtue, logic and ethics, the true and the good still coincided.

It was the two Logicians, Gongsun Long and Hui Shi, who brought that system down. Each pushed logic to a logical conclusion, but came up with opposite theses that cancel each other out. Gongsun Long concluded that you cannot love everybody; or loving all amounts to loving none. Hui Shi concluded that you can, except that you should then love everything, including dogs and rats.

WHALEN LAI

Navya-Nyaya

Navya-Nyaya (New Nyaya) is an Indian realistic school primarily concerned with logical and epistemological questions, dating from the time of the thirteenth-century philosopher Gangesha (whose magnum opus is the *Tattva-Chintamani*) to the present. Gangesha lived at a time when Buddhism, the principal adversary of old **Nyaya**, had almost disappeared in India, and he primarily directed his arguments against **Purva Mimamsa** and **Vedanta** theorists. Later important Navya-Naiyayikas include Jayadeva Pakshadhara (*c.*1425–1500 CE), Raghunatha Shiromani (*c.*1475–1550 CE) author of the *Padartha-tattva-nirupana* and the *Didhiti* commentary on the *Tattva-Chintamani*, and Mathuranatha Tarkavagisha (*c.*1600–75 CE), who wrote commentaries on works by Vallabha, **Udayana** and Gangesha.

Navya-Nyaya follows the old Nyaya in recognizing four types of valid cognition (*prama*): sensory perception (*pratyaksha*); inference (*anumana*); identification (*upamana*); and testimony (*shabda*). Fundamental to the school's logic and metaphysics is the relationship, based on an inductive generalization, of invariable concomitance (*vyapti*) between pervader (*vyapaka*) and pervaded (*vyapya*). One term pervades another when it occurs in all of or more than the places or loci of that other. From the fact that wherever there is smoke there is fire it follows that smoke is pervaded by fire. But fire may occur where there is no smoke, so fire is not pervaded by smoke.

A fully elaborated inference has the form:

Thesis: There is fire (*sadhya*) on the mountain (*paksha*).
Warrant: Because there is smoke (*hetu*).
Exemplification: Wherever there is smoke, there is fire (*vyapti*); like a kitchen (*sapaksha*), unlike a lake (*vipaksha*).
Application: There is smoke on the mountain.
Certain conclusion: There is fire on the mountain.

The instrumental cause in an inference is awareness of the pervasive concomitance (*vyapti*) of the probandum (*sadhya*) and the justificatory warrant (*hetu*); no smoke without fire. A successful inference should usually include citation of a positive supporting example (*sapaksha*) exemplifying the pervasive concomitance (*vyapti*) of warrant (*hetu*) and probandum (*sadhya*) in a sample locus (*sapaksha*, the kitchen) other than the actual subject of the inference and citation of a negative supporting example (*vipaksha*, the lake) illustrating the constant absence of both warrant and probandum in another locus. The operation of the inference involves a reflection that the pervasion occurs in the subject term ('the mountain possesses smoke which is pervaded by fire'). Since the major premise is explicitly inductively derived from experience, the Indian syllogism does not attract the empiricist objection that the conclusion cannot be deduced from the major premise since the major premise cannot be known to be true unless the truth of the conclusion is already known.

Navya-Nyaya espouses a form of direct epistemological realism. Sense-mediated information is assumed to provide an accurate picture of a mind-independent sphere save in those exceptional cases where there is some deficiency in the sense-organs. Entities are assigned to the categories (***padartha***) of substance (*dravya*) which comprises earth, water, fire, air, atmosphere, time, space, soul and mind; quality (*guna*) which comprises colours, forms, tastes and smells which inhere in material substances, pleasure and pain which inhere in the soul, and number and contact which inhere in all kinds of substances; actions (*kriya*) which are inherent only in substances; universals (*jati*) such as cowness and blueness in which inhere substances, qualities and actions and which occur in more than one locus; unique individuators (*vishesha*) resident in individual atoms; inherence (*samavaya*) relating substances to their parts, qualities and actions to substances and universals to substances, qualities and actions; absences (*abhava*) which are best construed as the referents of negative expressions.

The universal 'being' (*satta*) inheres in all substances, qualities and actions. In addition, there are the notions of 'presence' or 'actuality' (*bhava*) and its contradictory absence. While the universal humanity is spoken of as present in men, it is absent in horses.

In addition to *jatis*, which inhere in many individuals, there is another type of basic distinguishing factor or qualifier (*visheshana*) in cognitions known as 'imposed property' (*upadhi*). A *jati* must occur in more than one locus. When a particular individual is identified by a proper name, the name denotes a qualifier unique to that individual and this is an imposed property occurrent in its possessor, not by inherence but by a type of relation dubbed 'specific' (*svarupa-sambandha*; *visheshanata-vishesha-sambandha*). The same applies in the case of 'atmosphere-ness' (*akashatva*) since it does not group a plurality. A qualifier is an imposed property if it is the qualifier of a universal: potness is a *jati* but the second level abstraction potness-ness (expressing a unit class) is an imposed property characterizing potness. In addition, not every characteristic common to a group of individuals is a genuine universal. 'Cookness' for example may be applied to all cooks but it is classified as an imposed property.

Consistent with its realist stance, Navya-Nyaya maintains that all entities are knowable, if not by humans then by God. Perceptions are of two kinds: indeterminate (*nirvikalpaka-pratyaksha*) and determinate (*savikalpaka-pratyaksha*). The latter is a perception in which the object is distinguished from other similar and dissimilar things involving environment-relative identification. Where a cognition of a pot on the ground is concerned, its precondition is an informational input consisting in an ineffable indeterminate registration of a differentiating, isolating factor (potness in the case of pots) and a registration that the item presented to the senses possesses the differentiating factor in question. Indeterminate cognitions lie below the level of conscious awareness and can only be inferred. A determinate cognition which is present to the mind explicitly comprehends the relationship between the attribute (*visheshana*) potness and the pot which is the qualified substrate (*visheshya*), the pot in addition to specifying its object in relation to other entities.

The school recognizes three types of relation: contact (*samyoga*); inherence (*samavaya*); and specific or self-linking (*svarupa-sambandha*). Contact belongs to the category (*padartha*) quality (*guna*) and

temporarily inheres in pairs of substances. Universals inhere in substances, qualities and actions. Actions and qualities inhere in substances. Substances inhere in their parts. The eternal substances atmosphere, time, soul and space, do not inhere in anything. Specific or self-linking relations connect both imposed properties (*upadhi*) and relational abstracts and the places where they occur and absences and their loci.

There are two types of absence: mutual absence (*anyonya-abhava*) is the denial of identity; relational absence (*samsarga-abhava*) is the denial of relations other than identity. The latter is of three kinds: prior absence (*prag-abhava*), the absence of an entity prior to its creation; posterior absence (*dhvamsa-abhava*), the absence of an entity after it has been destroyed; constant absence (*atyanta-abhava*), the absence of an entity when this absence is not limited to a portion of time.

Key terms in the school's philosophical vocabulary are 'qualifier' (*visheshana*) and 'qualificand' (*visheshya*). The latter refers to what is expressed by the subject of the sentence. These expressions are particularly favoured where the entities expressed by subject and predicate are not related by contact or inherence. In the verbalized cognition, 'There is no pot on the ground', absence of pot is the qualificand, while in the cognition 'The ground has absence of pot' ground is the qualificand. In a cognition that there is a pot on the ground, the two terms have grammatical but not epistemological uses, the cognition being explained in terms of the relationships of contact between the visual sense organ, the ground and the pot. In most cases of valid inference, it is necessary to cite a negative supporting example (*vipaksha*) justifying the relationship of invariable concomitance by illustrating the constant absence of both warrant (*hetu*) and probandum (*sadhya*) in a locus other than the one under consideration. The stock example is the absence of both fire and smoke from a lake. There is a direct relation between the absence of fire and the lake. This relation cannot be contact for that is what is denied. Nor can it be inherence since that requires something which inheres. The Navya-Naiyayikas call this relation between an absence and its locus a relation of absential particular qualification (*abhaviya-visheshanata-vishesha-sambandha*) in which absence of fire is cognized as a qualifier of the lake.

Definitions (*lakshana*) have the purpose of demarcating their referents. Their particular utility consists in their acting as warrants (*hetu*) in negative forms of inference (*kevala-vyatirekin*) where it is impossible to cite a positive example (*sapaksha*) similar to but independent of the subject (*paksha*) under consideration which supports the statement of pervasive concomitance (*vyapti*) between the warrant (*hetu*) and probandum (*sadhya*) because the probandum is uniquely present in the subject (*paksha*). But we can cite a negative supporting example (*vipaksha*), i.e. a non-*paksha*, where neither warrant nor probandum occurs. A typical instance is: the living (*hetu*) body (*paksha*) cannot lack a soul (*sadhya*), for if it did, it would not be alive. If the probandum and the warrant express two properties which mutually imply each other such that the warrant can serve as the definition of the class of things possessing the probandum, the inference that the subject differs from what lacks the probandum because it has the warrant is valid.

Further reading

Ingalls, D. (1951) *Materials for the Study of Navya-Nyaya Logic*, Cambridge, MA: Harvard University Press.

Matilal, B. (1968) *The Navya-Nyaya Doctrine of Negation*, Cambridge, MA: Harvard University Press.

Mohanty, J. (1966) *Gangesha's Theory of Truth*, Santiniketan: University of Santiniketan.

—— (1991) *Reason and Tradition in Indian Thought*, Oxford: Oxford University Press.

Potter, K. (ed. and trans.) (1957) *The Padarthatattva-nirupanam of Raghunatha Siromani (A Demonstration of the True Nature of the Things to Which Words Refer)*, Cambridge, MA: Harvard University Press.

—— (1993) *Encyclopedia of Indian Philosophies, Vol. VI: Indian Philosophical Analysis Nyaya-Vaishesika from Gangesha to Raghunatha Shiromani*, Delhi: Motilal Banarsidass.

CHRIS BARTLEY

negation, double negative

Does a double negative make a positive? On that question, there is an interesting history in Chinese Madhyamaka. When the philosophy of **emptiness** was first introduced, it was mistaken for the Daoist notion of **non-being**. In time, the Buddhists realized the mistake. **Laozi** might have taught that 'being comes from non-being', but the purpose of *shunyata* is to 'empty both [concepts of] being and non-being'. But since emptiness also reconfirms **nirvana** as **samsara**, Chinese Buddhists took the 'double negation' in *shunyata-shunyata*, an emptiness that empties even itself, to imply a positive. Meanwhile the Daoists, seeking to catch up with that more sophisticated Buddhist dialectics, picked up on the last line in the first chapter of the **Daodejing** – 'Mystery of mysteries/ The gate to various wondrous subtleties' – and created its own 'double mystery' dialectics. Since the Daoists had a more 'ontological' reading of that double negative, their 'positivism' probably in turn rubbed off on the Buddhist exegetes.

Even in this century, after Stcherbatsky (1866–1942) rendered *shunyata* as 'relativity', there was a furore. The Kyoto School prefers to see its reading of emptiness as proposing an absolute **nothingness**; it absolves all opposites and relativities. That is partly in keeping with traditional Chinese reading of the double negative of *shunyata-shunyata* (that it affirms) and *atyanta shunyata* as 'emptying or terminating of both extremes' (an absolute emptiness). What the Kyoto School added to that is the history of the Japanese Buddhist appreciation of that legacy. The Chinese 'positive' reading of *tathata* as the True Suchness – the prefix 'true' is a Chinese addendum – was offset by the Japanese Zen appreciation of the resounding 'No' (*mu*) in the *Mumonkan*. The Kyoto School puts forward an absolute *mu* (nothingness), preferring *mu* to *ku* (emptiness).

Further reading

Robinet, I. (1977) *Les commentaires du Tao To King jusqu'au VIIeme siècle*, Paris: Collège de France, Institut des Hautes Etudes Chinoises.

Stcherbatsky, F. (1973) *The Conception of Buddhist Nirvana (Along With Sanskrit Text of Madhayamaka-karika)*, New York: Gordon Press.

WHALEN LAI

negation, forms of

The understanding of the nature and forms of negation is seen as crucial for logic and epistemology in Tibetan philosophy. Although the Tibetan understanding of the forms of negation is based on Indian sources, it is in Chapa Chokyi Senge's 'collected topics' system that these divisions are fully formalized. According to this system, there are two principal forms of negation, namely (1) non-implicative negation, a negation which is simple and leaves no room for any affirmation or implication in its aftermath, and (2) implicative negation, which makes an affirmation in place of the negation. A verse attributed to **Nagarjuna** succinctly illustrates this difference:

> Here, the existence is negated only;
> But its nonexistence not upheld.
> For when I say that it is not black,
> I do not assert that it is white!

Within the first category of negation, namely the non-implicative negation, there are two kinds, one whose object of negation does not exist even on the conventional level, and the other whose object of negation does exist in general. The following examples illustrate the two classes of non-implicative negation:

1 Object of negation is non-existent. Example: 'A horn of rabbit does not exist'.
2 Object of negation exists in general. Example: 'There are no yaks'.

The negation in both the statements is direct and final, but there is a difference in scope. In the first statement the negation is universal while in the second it is limited to spatio-temporal contexts. **Tsongkhapa** maintains that the negation involved in the Buddhist discourse on **emptiness** belongs to the first class of the non-implicative negation.

As regards implicative negation, the following fourfold division is identified based on Avalokitavrata's commentary on Bhavya's *Prajnapradipa*:

1 Affirmation by implication. Example: 'This fat person does not eat during the day'. The affirmative point that he eats during the night is implied by the negation of eating during the day.
2 Negation and affirmation both effected explicitly. Example: 'There is an absence of self'. This proposition both explicitly negates the self and also posits its absence.
3 Affirmation effected both explicitly and implicitly. Example: 'This fat person does not eat during the day time but does not lose any weight'. The affirmation that the person eats during night is not only implicit but also quite explicit because of the additional information given about the constancy of his weight.
4 Affirmation implied by the context. Example: 'This man is not a Brahmin', in the context where the person is known to be either a Brahmin or of a royal caste. Because of the context, when one possibility is rejected the other is automatically affirmed.

Tibetan epistemologists argue that the identification of these various forms of negation is critical to appreciate how inferences take place in argumentation. Interestingly, however, Tibetan thinkers do not seem to distinguish clearly between statements and their propositional contents when distinguishing between the various forms of negation. Often the discussion is conducted in terms of 'negative phenomena' as opposed to 'negations' as if they are objective features of reality rather than aspects of a meta-language.

Further reading

Dreyfus, G. (1997) *Dharmakarti's Philosophy and its Tibetan Interpretations*, Albany, NY: State University of New York, chs 2–5.

Hopkins, J. (1984) *Meditation on Emptiness*, London: Wisdom Publications, appendix 4.

Klein, A. (1991) *Knowing, Naming and Negation: A Sourcebook on Tibetan Sautrantika*, Ithaca, NY: Snow Lion, 90–113.

THUPTEN JINPA

negation, identifying its object

Of the various elements of **Tsongkhapa**'s Madhyamaka, his emphasis on the need for clear identification of the object of negation remains one of the most controversial and also innovative ideas. Some modern scholars refer to this as 'Tsongkhapa's doctrine of object of negation' (*gak jha ngo zin*). On the surface, the idea is rather simple. The principle states that it is crucial to have a clear conception of what is being negated when engaging in the Madhyamaka dialectic of **emptiness**. The premise for this is that if one goes too far in one's negation, it can result in a nihilistic position that denigrates the everyday world of valid experience. On the other hand, if the scope is too narrow, one may let certain residues of the reified categories slip through. So, what is required is a skilful path between the extremes of 'over-negation' and 'under-negation'. Although Tsongkhapa assumes that this principle is explicit in the writings of the Indian Madhyamika thinkers, the issue of Indian textual sources for the doctrine is somewhat problematic. Tsongkhapa and his followers cite *Bodhicharyavatara* IX: 139 to substantiate this point, but no commentator both in India and Tibet prior to Tsongkhapa appears to have ever associated this passage with the principle of identifying the object of negation.

What does it mean to say that one must have a clear identification of the object of negation in the context of the Madhyamaka discourse? It appears that, for Tsongkhapa, this 'correct identification' means developing a clear understanding of the meaning of the term 'ultimate' in the context of the Madhyamaka's rejection of ultimate ontological status to things and events. However, the principle is more than a linguistic analysis of the term 'ultimate'. In fact, it entails developing an insight into how we perceive things and events within our naive, normal, pre-philosophical ways of seeing the world. Tsongkhapa argues that there exists within each of us a natural belief, which leads us to perceive things and events as possessing some kind of intrinsic existence and identity. He calls this an innate apprehension of self-existence and argues that this is what the Buddhist texts are referring to when they speak of a fundamental ignorance (*avidya*). This relates to a deeply embedded pattern that lies at the most fundamental level of our unenlightened existence and creates a fundamentally flawed perception of our own existence and the world around us. So to have a clear understanding of the mechanism of this process is to have a clear identification of the object of negation.

This emphasis on identifying the object of negation is closely related to Tsongkhapa's overall project of delineating reason's scope for negation so that the Madhyamaka's emptiness cannot be construed as mere nothingness. Other key elements of the project are (1) distinguishing between the domains of 'conventional' and 'ultimate' discourses, (2) distinguishing between the various senses of the term 'ultimate' in the contexts of Madhyamaka dialectics, (3) logically distinguishing between that which is 'negated' and what is 'not established' by reason, and finally (4) understanding correctly the logical forms of negation involved in the Madhyamaka application of dialectic. In developing these, Tsongkhapa can be seen as logically determining the parameters of reason's scope for negation. For Tsongkhapa, the Madhyamaka doctrine of emptiness entails a rejection of the essentialist ontology, not existence of things *per se*. Of course, for those who wish to argue for a more literalist reading of the Madhyamaka dialectic, Tsongkhapa's project involves too much logocentricism. For them, the Madhyamaka dialectic literally involves the rejection of all views including any theory about the reality of our everyday world of experience.

Further reading

Jinpa, T. (1998) 'Delineating Reason's Scope for Negation: Tsongkhapa's Contribution to Madhyamaka's Dialectical Method', *Journal of Indian Philosophy* 26: 275–308.

Williams, P. (1998) *Altruism and Reality: Studies in the Philosophy of the Bodhicaryavatara*, Richmond: Curzon Press, ch. 4.

THUPTEN JINPA

Neo-Confucianism, concepts

Neo-Confucianism is sometimes represented as *Daoxue*, or the study of the *dao* or the way (to truth). One of the interesting developments which took place in this school is that it moved away from its original overwhelming concentration on exclusively moral and political issues to embrace interests in even wider metaphysical issues. To a certain extent, this was of course to try to meet the challenge thrown up by Daoism and Buddhism. So, for example, Zhang Zai argued that the ontological basis to all reality is ether or gas, and all objects are constituted of **ether** or gas, to some extent or another, and eventually return to gas. When this gas is transformed into the human body, it leads to the construction of human nature. One type of human nature shares in the nature of **heaven** and earth, which is equivalent to reason and which is positive, and the other is a nature which is full of temperament and as a consequence is impure and evil. The individual should seek to restrain temperament and develop the nature of heaven and earth through self-cultivation. Although it is true that Buddhism also argues for the control of the passions, what is being suggested here is very different. There is no suggestion that emptiness is a pervasive feature of reality; on the contrary, there is a stuff which is at the basis of reality, albeit a type of stuff which often appears rather similar to emptiness, given its nebulous nature when not informed by principle. We cannot seek to transcend the natural processes which make up our world, and what we need to do is to develop an attitude of respect to everything in the universe, since in this way we properly reflect the unity of existence, the fact that everything in the world is connected to everything else. We should also not seek to pursue the Daoist path of praising longevity, since that is to try to challenge the normal way of things with an unnatural demand. We should just accept a normal lifespan as appropriate and part of the pattern which makes up the whole of the universe.

For the Buddhist, what is important is achieving enlightenment, and this can involve abandoning society and its demands. For the Neo-Confucian, what is important is becoming a **sage**, and this can only come about through full participation in society. But we should not over-emphasize the distinctions between Neo-Confucianism and Buddhism; thinkers like Zhou Dunyi managed to identify the similarities between the two schools when he suggested that the route to becoming a sage is through having no desires which he also links to the principle of non-action (**wuwei**). An absence of desires leads to **emptiness** when the thinker is at rest, and to basic forms of activity when one is acting. Enlightenment which is achieved through such attitudes leads to knowledge, and actions based on simplicity to impartiality. Impartiality is a vital aspect of the path to universality, and that helps the development of the holist and unbiased view of the sage. One of the points which this approach stresses is the necessity to allow one's thoughts and actions to reflect one's natural goodness, whereas if we spend a lot of time reflecting on what we are going to do, all sorts of improper motives, emotions and feelings may intrude and corrupt what we do. The more we consider our action, the more selfish our thoughts become, whereas by contrast the less we think about what we do, the more natural our responses to situations, the more our inherent goodness can direct our activity. The conclusion which brings this close to Buddhism is that the overthrow of selfish and personal desires transforms the mind to a shining mirror which is capable of reflecting the truth clearly. Such a brilliant mirror is able to appreciate what each situation objectively requires without making discriminations based on personal and subjective ideas and wishes. Both Zhou and his successors made much use of the *Book of Changes* in their thought, which stresses the cyclical nature of reality and its ability to display an inherent structure despite such constant change, a structure which represents the principles of its operation as nature.

The *Li xue* school (literally, the school of principles) was established by the two brothers Cheng Yi and Cheng Hao. They argued that unity with everything is the basic principle of *ren* (benevolence). If one can keep this at the forefront of one's mind, and make it the basis of action, one will become even more firmly a part of everything, and it is a mistake to consider that this is something which is difficult and which requires great effort and concentration. This way of thinking should be developed in the personality as a disposition which can then be easily and naturally brought into action. There is a tendency for human beings to base their actions on selfishness, which interferes in the basic unity which links all nature. If we think of that unity, then that helps us in the conflict between selfishness and benevolence, and allows us to strengthen our natural desire to identify with everyone else and practice virtue. Of course, even the noblest of us may experience pleasure and pain, but this does not trouble the status of the sage. His mind is characterized by impartiality, universality and objectivity, so he observes these feelings as though they were unconnected to his self, from an attitude of genuine detachment. If he really is a sage, then when these feelings arise, they arise at the right sort of time and in line with the objective description of the world, not merely as reflections of his own emotions. All he does is reflect reality, which means that when the cause of the emotion – the object – goes, the emotion goes with it. So the sage has emotions but is not put into bondage through them. He controls them, they do not control him.

There is a reference in *The Analects* (6:3) to Yan Hui, a favourite pupil of Confucius not venting his anger on those who do not deserve it, and not repeating an error, and this is a passage made much of by the Neo-Confucians. Like a mirror, Yan Hui was affected by the objects in front of him, but once they went, he was not so taken up with those objects that he could not happily seem them go and the emotions which went with them. Once they go, the reflection and everything connected with them go as well, so the mirror like the sage is in charge of what is represented, in the sense that these representations will consist entirely of objective images of the truth. Yan Hui's anger was not connected to his self, so once what stimulated the anger went, the anger went also. Thinking that emotions are important and should persist is an aspect of error and of small-mindedness. The Confucian gentleman, and certainly the sage, does his best to transcend the emotions in so far as they are partial and biased representations of reality, which is most of the time.

It is because the sage can distinguish between the self and the emotions that he can be happy. He is happy because he takes pleasure in simple things,

and ultimately in himself, since he is a simple thing. Both as an agent and when not acting he lives in accordance with himself, with his authentic self, and since he has a self which is not occluded by the changing events of the world of experience he blends into the nature of heaven and earth. The sage certainly does not respect the opinions of others, and especially the ordinary conception that happiness consists in wealth and social position.

Zhu Xi constructed a metaphysical system in which *li* (principle) is the essence of reality. After all, everything has its own nature, which makes it the sort of thing it is. What makes things possible is the combination of ***li*** and ***qi*** (matter or energy), and the latter is shaped by the former into the objects of our world. The matter should not be thought of as passive, but in fact it embodies the ability to be transformed, and what transforms it, the *li*, is not itself anything different from the principle of form. It does not have any intentions or ideas about how the matter should be shaped, these are inherent in the matter itself. That is, the matter already has a certain orientation, which is given the push to instantiation by the presence of *li*, and this is how we can explain the fact that a common and undifferentiated principle can lead to the creation of so many different things in the world. To take a popular example of the time, before a father can have a son, which is an entirely material relationship, there must exist the idea of such a relationship, and that idea must exist before it is brought into physical existence. The idea, the suggestion is, leads to the material facts, Although *li* and *qi* have to work together, there is a certain priority of the former, but this is only an ontological priority. The *qi* in the universe is identified with *yin* (when it rests) and the *yang* (when it moves), while *li* remains unchanged behind these processes of change and rest.

For a human being to exist, he must be the result of a particular kind of matter, which is what distinguishes him from other people. The *li* or principle of humanity is the same for everyone. The latter is inherently good, so the evil in the universe must arise due to the matter, the way a particular thing was destined to be shaped. But the mind is also affected by *li*, since like everything else in existence it is a blend of *li* and *qi*. We are capable of acting nobly due to the presence of *li*, but this presence is affected by matter, and this explains the ways in which we as agents vary in our capacity to follow the correct actions demanded by the principles of justice. The political implications of this view fit in nicely with those of Confucius, since they suggest that there must be a *li* or principle of political life which would transform the state in such a way that it would be prosperous and harmonious. **Zhu Xi** argues that sadly most of the governments in China have followed the path of the selfish interests of its rulers, as opposed to being based on knowledge of how the state really ought to be run, its *li*. The *li* is not difficult to understand, since what needs to be done is to understand the nature of the material, which will produce a grasp of the principles which exist in the phenomenal world and within ourselves, since we will notice how the material is shaped in various ways and according to particular principles. As a result, the basis of the world's structure will become evident.

A different approach to the nature of reality was taken by Wang Shuren, who rejected the dualism of principle and matter for a theory according to which the world is an entirely spiritual entity. This spiritual entity which is equivalent to the universe is shared by everyone, and all we need to do to behave well is to follow our natural instincts. Anyone can be a sage, and everyone is potentially a sage. All that has to be done is to follow one's original nature and understand how to bring into action the basic knowledge of good and evil. This knowledge is the inner light of our mind, which represents and is at the same time part of the fundamental unity of reality. We return yet again to the idea of the mind as like a mirror, which reminds us again of the ease with which Neo-Confucians and Buddhists could accepts each others' ideas.

See also: Chong Che-du; Shingaku

Further reading

Chan Wing-tsit (1972) *A Source Book in Chinese Philosophy*, Princeton, NJ: Princeton University Press.

Creel, H. (1953) *Chinese Thought: From Confucius to Mao Tse-Tung*, Chicago: University of Chicago Press.

Fung Yu-lan (1952) *A History of Chinese Philosophy*,
trans. D. Bodde, Princeton, NJ: Princeton University Press.

Gardner, D. (1986) *Chu Hsi and the Ta-Hsueh*, Cambridge, MA: Harvard University Press.

Graham, A. (1989) *Disputers of the Tao: Philophical Arguments in Ancient China*, La Salle, IL: Open Court Press.

Tu Wei-ming (1985) *Confucian Thought: Selfhood as Creative Transformation*, Albany, NY: State University of New York Press.

OLIVER LEAMAN

Neo-Confucianism, history

The Song dynasty saw a coming together of three maturing teachings, from Confucianism, Daoism and Buddhism, each taking the best from the other two. The Neo-Confucian synthesis was just one of the emerging syntheses. It absorbed critically both Buddhist psychology and Daoist cosmology as it resurrected and single-mindedly championed the Confucian priority of social morality. If classical philosophy was generally this-worldly and medieval piety was overall otherworldly, then this classical renaissance mediated the two in being 'inner-worldly'.

First Han Yu (768–842) in the Tang dynasty launched a major moral attack on the Buddhist heresy; and then his student **Li Ao** (*fl.* 798) co-opted Buddhist ascetic denial for Confucian moral self-cultivation. Through the efforts of five major Northern Song masters in the eleventh century, Confucianism revamped its metaphysics and its analysis of mind, repudiated the acosmic height of Buddhist transcendence, restored faith in a basically benevolent universe, and worked to transform the self and improve society for a realizable future good. Thus would Zhou Dunyi (1017–73) track down the immanence of the Great Ultimate; **Shao Yong** (1011–77) uncover the numerical order in all things; **Zhang Zai** (1020–77) find personal communion with all things via a dynamic **ether**; and the two Cheng brothers, Cheng Hao (1032–85) and Cheng Yi (1033–1107), bear witness to the one principle embedded within all things.

Zhu Xi (1130–1200), following the more rationalistic Cheng Yi, then brought these various strands together and created a new system of thought with which the whole classical Confucian tradition could be thus reviewed and analysed. He opted for an investigation of things that would distinguish the higher principle and the lower material make-up of things. This then exposed a moral reason in the nature of all things. The dualism postulated for principle and ether in the external world ran parallel to a psychological tension within. The moral reason that is man's **heaven**-bestowed nature was developed in order to oversee his variable temperament. This moral metaphysics helped to mold the puritanical character of the mainstream Neo-Confucians. On this, Zhu Xi was opposed by Lu Xiangshan (1139–93), who regarded the mind as constructed in such a way that the principle makes feasible a more relaxed and intuitive approach.

After the Cheng–Zhu school became the official ideology of the Ming dynasty, it lost its power as a reformer of society and a critic of the state. The more intuitive approach then found a new spokesman in Wang Yangming (1472–1529). In Wang, practical reason had precedence over theoretical reason, and the call went out to 'change the world' instead of just understanding it. Unlike Zhu Xi, who saw the world as orderly and judged man as a potential deviant from the norm, Wang Yangming argued that it is man who is moral; it is the world that needs rectification. He called for 'rectifying (instead of just investigating) the world' in furtherance of 'the innate knowledge of the Good'. This activistic interpretation and implementation guided the left-wing followers of Wang Yangming known as the Taizhou school in the late Ming dynasty.

Further reading

Cheng Hao and Cheng Yi (1963) 'Erh-Ch'eng Ch'uan-shu/Ercheng quanshu' (Complete Works of the Two Ch'engs), trans. Wing-tsit Chan, *A Sourcebook in Chinese Philosophy*, Princeton, NJ: Princeton University Press, 523–71.

Graham, A. (1958) *Two Chinese Philosophers: Ch'eng Ming-tao and Ch'eng Yi-Ch'uan*, London: Lund Humphries.

WHALEN LAI

Neo-Daoism

The term is a modern coinage to describe a revival of Daoist thought after the fall of the Han dynasty (220 CE) and before the ascendancy of Buddhist thought (*c.*400 CE). The Chinese term is 'dark learning' and pertains to scholarship that investigated to the three mysteries of the *Yijing*, the *Laozi* and the *Zhuangzi*. Initial interest was based on scholars who admired Confucius. They ranked Confucius above Laozi because Confucius exemplified the wisdom of 'one who knows [and] does not speak'. He is wiser than Laozi, who did not discourse too openly on the Dao.

The Neo-Daoists were known for their witty language in social conversation and their 'pure talk' about the intangible. Such 'lofty discourse' was rooted in the 'pure or non-partisan criticism' of the later Han that evaluated individual worth and summed up personalities in sharp pithy phrases.

Neo-Daoism is generally divided into three phases. The first period (220–48) was headed by Ho Yan (d. 249) and Wang Bi (226–49). Ho suggested that sages be regarded as impassive, but he was defeated in argument by Wang, who noted how Confucius shed tears when his favourite disciple died. Sages do effuse outward feelings; it is only their inner composure that remains untouched by such emotional vicissitudes. Wang is best remembered for discussing the ground of **non-being** in the *Laozi*: the concrete arrangement of this text came from him. Ho and Wang had support from the rulers of Wei (one of the Three Kingdoms in the post-Han civil war). When the house of Jin usurped power in 249, the Confucian faction moved against the Neo-Daoists.

Under duress, Neo-Daoism entered its second phase. Under the leadership of Xi Gang (223–62) and Ruan Ji (219–53), the hitherto assumed Confucian–Daoist compatibility faltered as this pair 'repealed the teaching of names [Confucian rituals] and returned to being spontaneous Daoist [Daoist naturalness]'. However, they went separate ways. Xi was the stoic who 'for thirty years showed no sign of joy or sorrow'; he looked for a quietistic way of prolonging life. Ruan was the Epicurean, a crazed madman who could stay drunk for a month; he shamelessly claimed to be the 'great man' aligned with the sun, moon and stars. Both try to stay out of harm's way; Ruan survived, but Xi was executed by the new regime. This extravagant phase ended when the Jin gained full control and reunited China in 265.

The last creative phase was represented by Guo Xiang (d. 312) and the book *Liezi*. Guo edited and commented on the *Zhuangzi* and, in a tour de force, reconciled the man-made and the natural. It is, he argued, no less in the nature of things that herded cows should now have rings piercing their nostrils. And if cicadas cannot span the sky like a giant roc, they are no less free in their own small, spontaneous way. Scholars are still divided on whether Guo was not just bowing to necessity and so presenting slavery as freedom, or whether as a low-born person who got into the circle of the high-born Neo-Daoists by sheer talent, he was really giving the common man in his small station in life a share of life as a companion of the *dao*. The *Liezi* is similarly divided between an advocacy of hedonism in the Yang Zhu chapter and a resignation before fate elsewhere.

The heyday of Neo-Daoism ended with the barbarian invasion of 316. The highly refined and effeminate Neo-Daoist culture could not withstand the invading nomads and had no answer to offer their threat. The new era belonged to a new species of men, the Buddhist monks. A legend tells of this transition, showing also the poverty of Neo-Daoist philosophy. A group of gentlemen gathered at the White Horse temple in the old capital, spinning their 'pure talk' about how to 'rove freely' with the *dao*. It was proposed that freedom comes simply from following one's nature, a thesis derived from the case of the cicada and the roc. The monk **Zhi Dun** (314–66) happened upon the group and queried: 'Were that the case, would not the evil king who followed his evil impulses be a companion of the Way too?' The gentlemen had no rejoinder, and were silent.

The various schools of Chinese philosophy, including Neo-Daoism, are happy to borrow ideas and theories from other schools, and there is no doubt that aspects of Buddhism, and in particular the **emptiness** thesis in the sense of *wu*, entered Neo-Daoism. The Neo-Daoists set themselves against the Han Confucians by advocating *xuan xue* or the 'dark learning' as the way to approach the nature of reality, with its emphasis on the idea of non-being or emptiness as the source of all existence. This makes a nice contrast with the Neo-Confucian principle of the rectification of names, with its implication that once one manages to understand language properly one will know everything which needs to be known about the world. The idea that there is a fixed relationship between a word and that to which it refers ignores the fact of the emptiness which lies at the base of being, and the constancy of change. If there is nothing at the source of reality, then we are limited to claiming that all that exists are the beings of which we have experience. It could be said that this reveals the 'dark' nature of the learning, in that there is a marked absence of the sort of confidence in the underlying raionality and comprehensibility of the world which we find later in Neo-Confucianism.

This has a serious effect on how we study institutions, which again contrasts with Neo-Confucianism and its deep respect for ritual and public bodies. We need to be aware of the changing nature of such institutions, according to the Neo-Daoists, and adapt our attitude to them accordingly. For example, it is quite easy for an institution which initially was solidly based in nature to become over time artificial and no longer appropriate for us, and this even applies to the wise words of the **sage**. These words may sometimes lack the force they had initially, given the fact of changing circumstances, and even if the words are still relevant, it may be that their interpretation should change, since they were never meant to apply to an unchanging world. This brings out the significance of the doctrine of **wuwei**, of acting through non-action, of doing a lot by doing little. The idea here is that the more we try to act directly, the more likely we are to affect and change for the worse the situation within which we are working, and so the eventual aim we have in mind may become less likely to be achieved than otherwise. What we should do is try to bring about the result we want through doing as little as possible to bring it about, since in that way we may preserve the fragile nature of the structure within which we are acting and focus entirely on the desired result.

Another contrast with Neo-Confucianism is the acceptability for many Neo-Daoists of the emotions. Whereas the Neo-Confucian gentleman is calm and measured in everything he does, the Neo-Daoist looks on the emotions as perfectly acceptable ways of experiencing the world and parts of our lives. Many stories about them have them getting drunk and fighting as parts of living the good life, and there are clearly links here with particular kinds of Chan or zen Buddhism with its emphasis on shocks and surprises as routes to enlightenment.

It surprises some that the Neo-Daoists and the Legalists (see **Legalism**) often share the same views, but this is really because the Legalists emphasize the changing nature of society, and the importance as a result of changing what one does to regulate society. Again, the Legalist is suspicious of others, and certainly does not have the same trust in the basic rationality of human behaviour as compared, say, with the Confucian. There is also the important idea that human action is fragile, dangerous and difficult, and should only be employed when one has a reasonable confidence in attaining one's end and not making things even worse.

OLIVER LEAMAN
WHALEN LAI

Neo-Mohists

The Neo-Mohists were later followers of **Mozi** who developed Mohist thought in new directions. They sharpened, among other things, Mohist logic. They had to respond to Yang Zhu the Egoist, who would not love others, and the two Logicians, one who argued that universal love is illogical in practice and the other who ended up loving everything, horses and dogs no less than men. To repudiate their subversion of the Mohist thesis that universal love is logical, practical (utilitarian), properly anthropocentric and entirely in the interest of the self, the Neo-Mohists reacted with the following points:

In terms of the proper use of logic, they distinguish imperfect sense knowledge, like bad eyesight, from true understanding or clear sight. The instinctual desire for 'food and sex' is imperfect; it is not the same as liking which is

based on cool deliberation. Short-sighted over-eating, like excessive sex, can harm the self. To like (to prefer with discernment) means always to calculate the benefit and harm beforehand. The **sage** has that a priori knowledge of what is truly good and bad because he works this out on behalf of mankind or the common good.

Against the abuse of logic which says 'a puppy is not a [mature] dog', the answer is to admit that although a perfect circle may not be empirically drawable, yet names for things that change over time can be delimited by usage. At present a puppy defined as a canine age one to three is not a mature dog defined as three and above but it will cease to be a puppy and become a dog at age three. The term 'canine' can describe either a puppy or a dog, but not both ('two things') at the same time. (This thesis runs into problems with the Chinese compound-noun 'ox-horse' for generic 'cattle.') To avoid confusing 'dog' and 'horse' because when defined by shape alone, they may look alike, the answer is to distinguish 'total identity' (two straight lines taking up the same space between two points); 'same in kind' (*lei*, the equestrian species); and just 'partial identity' based on a partial standard (like shape) which is deemed not a sufficient standard.

A problem arises with infinity and the problem of infinite regress when applied to universal love for an infinite humanity, since to love an infinite number means to divide it up into infinite portions, which is impossible. The solution is to draw a space for the limitless. If mankind fills it, mankind has a limit. If mankind cannot fill it, mankind would also have a limit. This does not really work as a solution, since it refuses to accept the possibility of infinity.

There have been a number of modern attempts to decode the argument of the two Logicians. Feng thought Gongsun Long was a realist talking about universals; Graham concluded that 'white horse is not horse' involves a synecdoche and a part/whole logic; and Hansen came up with a theory of 'mass nouns', which he argued plays a large part in the actual phrasing of the issue.

One of the interesting features of Neo-Mohism is its critical attitude to tradition. **Confucius** honoured tradition, but Mozi repudiated feudally ascribed stations. He advocated meritocracy and 'selection of the worthy' to rule. Once those who could rule well are in power, there is a duty of compliance with superiors. Mozi is often called China's classical advocate of 'science and demoncracy', but he has been re-evaluated since for supporting China's past shift from feudalism into centralized, but not necessarily liberal, monolithic rule.

See also: logic in Chinese philosophy

Further reading

Fung Yu-lan (1952) *A History of Chinese Philosophy*, trans. D. Bodde, 2 vols, Princeton, NJ: Princeton University Press.

Graham, A. (1978) *Later Mohist Logic, Ethics, and Science*, London: School of Oriental and African Studies, University of London.

—— (1990) 'Three Studies on Kung-sun Lung', in A. Graham, *Studies in Chinese Philosophy and Philosophical Literature*, Albany, NY: State University of New York Press.

Hansen, C. (1983) *Language and Thought in Ancient China*, Ann Arbor, MI: University of Michigan Press.

WHALEN LAI

new religions in Korea

The new religions of Korea are those which developed since the middle of the nineteenth century. Some are syncretistic, some are nationalistic and some are millenarian. Many of them originated when the political and social situation of Korea was declining, and the traditional religions and philosophies lost vitality and lost touch with the masses. The new religions appealed mainly to those in lower socio-economic groups.

Ch'ondogyo

Ch'ondogyo (The Religion of the Heavenly Way) is the first new religion of Korea, founded by Ch'oe Che-u in 1860. It is a unique, humanistic and syncretistic religion, which has a philosophical system of thought. It synthesized some of the important Confucian, Daoist and Buddhist ideas. The founder is usually called by his honorific name, Suun, especially by his followers. Ch'ondo-gyo was originally called Tonghak (Eastern Learning), in reaction to Sohak (Western Learning), that is, Christianity. The name was changed to Ch'ondogyo in 1905 to signify the movement primarily as a religious one. In the Ch'ondogyo history, the positions of the founder, Ch'oe Che-u (1824–64), the second leader, Ch'oe Si-hyong (also known as Haewol, 1827–98), and the third leader, Son Pyong-hui (also known as Uiam, 1861–1922) are most important.

In Ch'ondogyo, God is called Hanullim, very similar to the common name of God in Korean tradition, Hanunim (see **Han and Hanunim**). Ch'ondogyo defines Hanullim as the supreme being of the universe, who is both transcendent and immanent. God in Ch'ondogyo is always self-evolving being, which is similar to the idea of God in the modern process philosophy and theology in the West. He is the object of faith and worship, and he has power to bless and inspire believers. However, there is little or no mention of his roles as the creator and judge of the world.

The Ch'ondogyo idea of God is monotheistic, but at the same time there is some pantheistic element. Recent Ch'ondogyo thinkers like Yi Ton-hwa and Paek Se-myong define Hanullim as the original substance of life (*ponch'e saengmyong*) or the totality of life (*chonch'e saengmyong*). According to them, all things evolve or emanate from God and all things are always connected to the life of God.

Chigi, which means the ultimate energy or ultimate vital force, is another important metaphysical idea in Ch'ondogyo. Chigi is the ultimate force and source of the universe, which is immanent in all things. It is the power of God, through which all things are made and evolve. All things are permeated and embraced by it. Chigi is one ultimate reality, in which spirit and matter, idea and actuality belong together as parts of harmony, complement and completeness.

One of the most important ideas in Ch'ondogyo is the concept of man. The Ch'ondogyo idea of human nature can be explained by two key phrases, namely *si ch'onju* (divinity in man) and *in nae ch'on* (man is God). *Si ch'onju* means literally 'bearing God (Heaven)' or 'serving God'. 'Bearing God' implies divinity in man. It means that God is within human heart and mind, and man serves God like parents with respect and reverence. Since man bears divine nature, he/she is the most spiritual being in the universe, according to Suun. *In nae ch'on* literally means 'man is Heaven (God)'. This idea is based on *si ch'onju* logically and historically. The idea of *si ch'onju* developed first, and then later, the idea of *in nae ch'on* developed. Since human nature bears divine nature and man is considered as a life individuated from God, who is the Totality of Life, Ch'ondogyo concludes that man is one with God in essence. It does not mean that at the present time every human being is identical with God. It means that in the original essence and in terms of potentiality man is divine. It also means that man can attain oneness with God through spiritual and moral training.

Both *si ch'onju* and *in nae ch'on* express the fundamental **monism** of Ch'ondogyo regarding man's relation to God. These ideas also indicate the high value Ch'ondogyo places on man in the universe. Man is considered the mostly highly developed being among all beings and things evolved from or made by God. According to Ch'ondogyo teaching, all beings and things are shaped by one energy, and man and heaven share the same spiritual essence.

In ethics, too, Ch'ondogyo displays a monistic tendency. *Hap ki dok*, which means 'unity with virtue', is an important ethical idea. It means that man in his conduct ought to attain oneness with divine virtue or divine will. In other words, human life itself should be the embodiment of universal virtue. Here again one finds the Ch'ondogyo emphasis on oneness between man and God.

The most important ethical idea in Ch'ondogyo is *sain yoch'on*, which means 'to treat man as **Heaven** (God)'. This idea is logically based on the ideas of *si ch'onju* (man supports God) and *in nae ch'on* (man is God). Since man is divine in nature, one ought to treat his fellow man as one would God, with the utmost concern, respect, sincerity, dignity and reverence. On the basis of this idea, Ch'ondogyo has emphasized the idea of equality of all men from its very beginning.

The Ch'ondogyo idea of man's essential divinity and its ethical idea of equality were quite new and revolutionary in the nineteenth century feudalistic society of Korea. In particular, the idea of 'treating man as God' presented a dynamic challenge to the feudalistic ethical system based on a corrupted form of Confucianism, which cultivated a discriminatory class ethics. Ch'ondogyo (Tonghak) rejected the traditional discrimination between the aristocrats (*yangban*) and the commoners, and emphasized treating all men on the basis of their inherent human dignity and character from a spiritual and moral standpoint. Ch'ondogyo also taught the radical transformation of the world through the idea of *kaebyok* (recreation). The old decayed world must end and the new world must be created through the transformation of humanity.

The most important historical contribution of Ch'ondogyo thought was the Tonghak Revolution of 1894, which was one of the most significant political and social reform movements in modern Korea toward democracy. The Tonghak Revolution contributed toward the eventual fall of the Choson dynasty, when political corruption, social injustice and moral decay reached a high level, and toward the modernization of Korean political and social systems.

During the leadership of Son Pyong-hui in the 1920s, Ch'ondogyo was one of the largest religions in Korea. In the March First Independence Movement of 1919, a nationwide protest against Japanese colonialism, Ch'ondogyo played a major role. Ch'ondogyo also played an important role in the modernization of Korean society through the new culture movement with the publication of influential journals and magazines. Ch'ondogyo was in the forefront of the modern women's movement and a youth movement, thereby contributing to the modernization of Korean society.

Chungsan'gyo

Chungsan'gyo was founded in 1901 by Chungsan (Kang Il-sun). In his youth, Chungsan was deeply influenced by Ch'ondogyo thought and the Tonghak Revolution. After several years of searching and pondering, he began to teach his 'truth' mainly to the lower classes.

Chungsan taught that the present world is corrupt and decayed, and therefore, the recreation and transformation of the world (*ch'onji kongsa*) is necessary to bring about the Kingdom of Heaven on earth. This idea is similar to the Tonghak idea, and both Tonghak and Chungsan'gyo have a millenarian outlook. Chungsan further claimed to be God incarnate, who came down to the world to recreate it by transforming humanity. Mankind must find love, cooperation and reconciliation, and must be liberated from oppression and injustice; then the Kingdom of Heaven on earth will arrive. His emphasis on the equality of all men and on giving hope to the oppressed masses was very similar to that of Ch'ondogyo.

Chungsan'gyo is divided into several sects, which use different names. It is not a major and significant force at present. However, in 1974 the Society for the Study of Chungsan's Thought was established, and several scholars are attempting to study Chungsan's thought as an important aspect of the national religions. There has been an increasing interest in Chungsan'gyo among some university students.

Taejonggyo

Taejonggyo (The Religion of Great God) is a school of Tan'gunism. It claims that Tan'gun, the legendary founder of Korea, is the original founder of Taejonggyo, which was revived by Nach'ol in 1909. It claims that it embodies the national spirit and philosophy. Tan'gun is believed to be the god-man and the founder of Korea, and he is the object of worship in Taejonggyo.

Taejonggyo was in the forefront of the anti-Japan independence movement during Japanese colonialism in Korea. As a result, its followers were persecuted severely by the Japanese authorities. Many of its leaders and members took refuge in Manchuria, where they continued the independence movement.

Taejonggyo initiated the idea of Kaech'onjol (Day of Opening Heaven, the founding of Korea) as a national holiday, which was adopted by the Korean government in 1948. It signifies that Tan'gun opened the door of heaven and descended on Mt Paekdu to establish the nation of Korea. Taejonggyo wants to strengthen the ideal of Tan'gun as the national ideology, but interest in it is limited to some scholars and to a relatively small number of the Korean people. Many educated Koreans, especially Christians, look upon the Tan'gun story as mythology, which has no substantial value for their lives and for the nation.

Hanolgyo

Hanolgyo (The Religion of Heavenly Spirits) is another type of Tan'gunism, founded by Shin Chong-il in 1965. It believes in Hanollim, which may be translated as Heavenly Spirit, Great Spirit or God. It claims that Tan'gun is the original founder of this religion and has a similar nationalistic tendency to Taejonggyo.

The main goal of Hanolgyo is to revive the idea of Han, meaning 'one' or 'great', which is the original essence of Korean thought, and to restore the consciousness of *hanol* (one, great, heavenly or Korean spirit). It wants to develop a movement honouring Tan'gun as the founder of the nation. There is some interest in this idea of Han among some scholars, but like Taejonggyo, this religion has no significant following in Korea today.

Won Buddhism

Won Buddhism (Won Pulgyo) was founded in 1916 by Sot'aesan (Pak Chung-bin) in Cholla province. It is a modern reformed type of Buddhism, which has over one million followers. Sot'aesan claimed that Buddhism is the best religion, but some good ideas from other religions also should be incorporated. He wanted to make a popular Buddhism, which can be understood and practiced easily by the masses in their daily life. Thus, Won Buddhism became a modern religion of the masses and not primarily for monks and nuns.

The term *won* means circle, which is a central symbol of Won Buddhism, and Irwonsang (one-circle-figure) is the essence of the truth in Won Buddhism. According to this religion, Irwon (one circle) is the origin of the universe and the original nature of all beings. Sang is 'figure' or 'shape' of all things. Both together constitute reality and its manifestations in the universe. The one circle also symbolizes the essential nature of Buddha. Therefore, in Won Buddhist temples there is no Buddha statue, image or picture as the object of worship, but the symbol of the one circle is enshrined clearly and noticeably to signify *Dharmakaya* (Body of Truth) or the Buddha Mind. Thus, Won Buddhist ritual is reformed and modernistic.

Won Buddhism also provides practical social

ethics. To solve social problems and human suffering, it teaches the cultivation of self-ability and self-reliance, the protection of the helpless, cooperation with others and the practice of justice. Women play an important role in Won Buddhism. About two-thirds of the over one thousand ministers of Won Buddhism are women. Such a proportion of female clergy over male clergy is a unique phenomenon among Korean religions (perhaps with the exception of shamanism (see **shamanism in Korea**). Most of the female ministers in this religion remain unmarried, so that they can devote all their energies and time to their work.

Education has been an important activity of Won Buddhism. It operates Wonkwang University, an important institution of higher learning, and junior and senior high schools. It also has organizations for charitable work. This has had a positive effect on many people of the underprivileged class in south-western Korea by providing education and by teaching classes in economic self-support. It aims at making all sentient beings into living buddhas. Thus, by becoming a modern, democratic and pragmatic religion of the masses, Won Buddhism contributed greatly to the improvement of the lives of the masses in modern Korean society.

The Unification Church

The Unification Church, founded in Korea by Sun Myong Moon shortly after the Second World War, is a new religion with a Christian background. The 'unification principle' that Moon advocates is the fundamental idea of this new religion, which has branches in many nations. The Unification Church teaches that Jesus is the Saviour and that He is to come again in Korea. It wants to build the Kingdom of God on earth by teaching Moon's unification principle, which is to unite all Christians and all religions under the principle of love. One of its key ideas is that Jesus was a failed Messiah, because he died on the cross, and the second Messiah to come in Korea is the perfect one. Because of this and other ideas of the Unification Church, it is rejected by the mainline Christian churches in Korea as a heretical movement.

One of the most interesting activities of the Unification Church is the large group wedding ceremony. Recently, many thousands of couples participated in several group wedding ceremonies. These ceremonies signify the building of ideal families, which will work for the unification philosophy in order to build an utopian world of love and peace. The Reverend and Mrs Moon are called the 'True Parents', for they nurture and guide their followers to live for God and His Kingdom. Unification Church members dedicate their lives entirely to the work of the Kingdom of God. However, the number of Moon's followers is relatively small and recent growth has been slow.

Because the Unification Church is financially strong, it has been sponsoring many academic conferences and seminars for university professors both in Korea and other countries in order to win sympathy and support. It has been also active in the ecumenical movement for all religions in Korea, sponsoring interreligious dialogues and conferences. It publishes several newspapers in Korea and the United States, and operates various levels and types of schools in Korea. However, its influence has been limited both in Korea and in other countries.

Further reading

Chung Bong-kil (1984) 'What is Won Buddhism?', *Korea Journal* May: 18–32.

—— (1987) 'The Concept of Dharmakaya in Won Buddhism: Metaphysical and Religious Dimensions', *Korea Journal* January: 4–15.

Durst, M. (1984) *To Bigotry, No Sanction: Reverend Sun Myung Moon and the Unification Church*, Chicago: Regnery Gateway.

Jeungsando (1997) *The Teachings of Jeungsan Do*, Taejon: Jeungsando Publication Center.

Kim T'ae-gon *et al.* (1973) *Han'guk Chonggyo* (Korean Religions), Iri: Wonkwang University Press.

Kim, Yong-choon (1975) 'Ch'ondogyo Thought and Its Significance in Korean Tradition', *Korea Journal* May: 47–53.

—— (1978) *The Ch'ondogyo Concept of Man*, Seoul: Pan Korea Book Corp.

—— (1997) 'Ch'ondogyo and Other New Religions of Korea', in L. Lancaster and R. Payne, *Religion and Society in Contemporary Korea*, Berkeley, CA: Institute of East Asian Studies, University of California, 252–6.

Lee, P. (ed.) (1996) *Sourcebook of Korean Civilization*, 2 vols, New York: Columbia University Press, 313ff, 500ff.

Pac Yong dok (1986) 'Chungsan'gyo', in *Chonhwan'giui Han'guk Chonggyo* (Korean Religions in a Changing Time), ed. Department of Religious Studies, Seoul National University, Seoul: Chipmundang, 69–108.

Park Kwang-soo (1997) *The Won Buddhism of Sot'aesan*, Bethesda, MD: International Scholars Publications.

Shin Chong-il (1986) 'Hanolgyo', in *Chonhwan'giui Han'guk Chonggyo* (Korean Religions in a Changing Time), ed. Department of Religious Studies, Seoul National University, Seoul: Chipmundang, 232–62.

Sontag, F. (1977) *Sun Myung Moon and the Unification Church*, Nashville, TN: Abingdon Press.

Wu Won-sang (1986) 'Taejonggyo', in *Chonhwan'giui Han'guk Chonggyo* (Korean Religions in a Changing Time), ed. Department of Religious Studies, Seoul National University, Seoul: Chipmundang, 109–50.

Yu Byong-dok (1974) *Han'guk Sinhung Chonggyo* (New Religions of Korea), Iri: Wonkwang University Press.

YONG-CHOON KIM

New Zealand philosophy

Philosophy in New Zealand has developed along the lines of that practised in the English-speaking world. The New Zealand professional association is a division of the Australasian Association of Philosophy, reflecting a close connection with philosophy in Australia. Karl Popper was a lecturer (1937–45) at the Canterbury College, Christchurch of the University of New Zealand when he wrote the *Open Society and its Enemies* (1945). The native New Zealander A.N. Prior read philosophy under J.N. Findlay at Otago, and succeeded Popper as a lecturer at Christchurch in 1946, holding the Chair from 1952 to 1959. John Passmore and J.L. Mackie held the Otago Chair in the 1950s. The study of modal logic has been prominent since the Second World War. George Hughes and Max Cresswell, both of the Victoria University of Wellington, are noted for their contributions in this field, and Pavel Tichy developed transparent intensional logic at Otago. There is a contemporary preoccupation with the philosophy of environmental and political issues.

Prior's initial, and abiding, interest was in the field of ethics (*Logic and the Basis of Ethics*, 1949) but by the 1950s his concentration had shifted to logic and he published *Formal Logic* in 1955. *Time and Modality* (1957) dealt with the relation between the logic of modality and that of past, present and future statements. He claimed that the propositions, 'It has been the case that p' and 'It is necessary that p' share the same syntax, as do 'It will be the case that p' and 'It is possible that p'. This was followed by *Past, Present and Future* and *Papers on Time and Tense*.

The upshot of Prior's logical analyses was that times and events are not to be regarded as 'basic particulars' and in common with facts, propositions and possible worlds are to be treated as logical constructions. Although not a strict Quinean extensionalist, he thought that truth would be preserved in intensional contexts if some other purely referential expression were substituted for a proper name. The truth value of the sentence would only change when some definite description applied *de dicto* was substituted for the name. Nevertheless, he found difficulty in deciding when an expression was really functioning as a name and came to the Russellian opinion that few of our thoughts are directly referential.

Maori culture

The Maoris traditionally conceive of reality dualistically in terms of the communicating spheres of the physical and the supernatural beings inhabiting the heavens and the underworld. Birth is the transition of human spirit from the spiritual sphere into that where spatio-temporal conditions obtain, and death is the return of the spirit to its previous habitation.

Gods or spiritual beings (*atuas*) visit and are active in the physical domain. Events lacking obvious physical causes are explained by invisible divine causation. *Tapu* is a state of possession or permeation, transmissible by contagion, on the part of humans or material entities by some spirit which may be either benevolent or malevolent. Maori religion consisted largely in the manipulation in human interests of the operations of the spirits in the physical world. The spirits are invoked through automatically effective magico-ritual incantations called *karakia*. The favour of the spirits can be secured by gifts, including the fruits of human sacrifice. Other rituals are used to expel evil spiritual influences.

Further reading

Best, E. (1924) *Maori Religion and Mythology*, Wellington: Dominion Museum.
—— (1954) *Some Aspects of Maori Myth and Religion*, Wellington: Dominion Museum.
—— (1954) *Spiritual and Mental Concepts of the Maori*, Wellington: Dominion Museum.
Copeland, J. (ed.) (1996) *Logic and Reality: Essays in Applied Logic in Memory of Arthur Prior*, Oxford: Oxford University Press.
Sylvan, R. (1985) 'Prospects for Regional Philosophies in Australasia', *Australasian Journal of Philosophy* 63(2): 188–204.

CHRIS BARTLEY

Ngok Loden Sherap

b. 1059; d. 1109

Buddhist philosopher

Loden Sherap is known as one of the two Ngok brothers (the other being Ngok Lekpai Sherap) and shared sectarian affiliation with the reforming Kadam school of Atisha and Dromtonpa. It is perhaps to Loden Sherap's authoritative translation of **Dharmakirti**'s *Pramanavarttika*, and **Shakya Pandita**'s influence, that the Tibetans owe the tradition of treating Dharmakirti's *Pramanavarttika* as the key text for the study of Buddhist logic and epistemology. Prior to this, Dharmakirti's other work, *Pramanavinishchaya*, appears to have been the principal text.

Though revered as an authoritative scholar on the study of Maitreya's *Abhisamayalamkara*, Loden Sherap's greatest philosophical contribution lies possibly in his attempt to develop a reading of

Chandrakirti's Prasangika-Madhyamaka ontology through a Dharmakirtian epistemological language. In this respect, Loden Sherap can be seen as a precursor to **Tsongkhapa** in that it was the latter that succeeded in systematically carrying out this philosophical project. Unfortunately, most of Loden Sherap's philosophical works are no longer extant.

THUPTEN JINPA

NICHIREN   *see* Buddhist philosophy in Japan

nirukta

Indian culture produced two traditions of linguistic analysis, *vyakarana* (grammar) and *nirukta* or *nirvachanashastra* (semantic analysis). Both are classed among the six *vedanga*s, the branches of knowledge designed to preserve the Veda and secure its correct application. This, however, did not prevent them from being widely resorted to also by non-Vaishika forms of Brahmanical religion, as well as by Buddhists and Jains. While the *vyakarana* tradition boasts a number of treatises, only one basic work of *nirvachanashastra* is known to us. This is the *Nirukta* of Yaska. From the *Nirukta* itself we know that Yaska was part of a longer tradition, but we know little of his predecessors apart from a few scanty remarks. In outline the *Nirukta* is a commentary on the *Nighantu* (*nighantuh*, singular, but frequently *nighantavah*, plural), the earliest lexicographical work that has survived in India. The words listed in the *Nighantu* are predominantly Vedic, most of them occurring in the *Rigveda*. From the *Nirukta* it is clear that already at Yaska's time there were difficulties in understanding Vedic words and passages, a fact that indicates a broken tradition when it comes to grasping the *meaning* of the Vedic hymns. Yaska set out to remedy this situation by laying down principles for a type of semantic analysis designed to make any word yield its meaning, in effect treating all nouns as information-invoking singular terms.

The date of Yaska is uncertain, but it seems likely that it falls around the third or fourth century BCE. There exist three Sanskrit commentaries on the *Nirukta*. The *Vritti* of Durga, known as the *Rijvartha*, is clearly earlier than the sixth century CE, but how much earlier is uncertain. The date of the *Niruktabhashyatika* attributed to Skandasvamin and Maheshvara is even more problematic, and its authorship raises difficulties too. It is later than Durga whom it quotes, and earlier than the *Niruktashlokavarttika* of Nilantha Gargya which echoes it. The latter commentary, in about 5,000 *shlokas* (verses), was composed in Kerala in the twelfth or thirteenth century. Finally, there is Devarajayajvan's commentary on the *Nighantu* which was probably written in the fourteeenth or fifteenth century. This serves to establish that there was a continuous tradition of *nirvachanashastra* which is distinct from the *vyakarana* tradition.

The methods and principles of interpretation laid down in Yaska's *Nirukta* remained very much alive in Indian philosophical and religious literature, and were put to particularly good use in the processing of Sanskrit texts. These methods have also left their traces in several Asian languages far beyond the Indian borders through the translations of Sanskrit texts which accompanied the spread of Buddhism. They have permeated the Tibetan translations from Sanskrit completely, and as recently as the eighteenth century these techniques were still alive in Manchuria when the Buddhist dictionary *Mahavyutpatti* was translated into Manchu.

Yaska divides the parts of speech into four classes of words: nouns (*naman*), verbs (*akhyata*), preverbs or prepositions (*upasarga*) and particles (*nipata*). He ascribes to his predecessor Shakatayana and the Nairuktas the view that nouns arise because of the actions denoted by verbs. Words in which the accent and grammatical formation would be in agreement with the meaning which is to be expressed and are accompanied by a phonetic quality which is in accordance with the grammatical derivation, should be analysed in a regular manner. But, Yaska tells us, when the meaning is not accompanied by a regular accent and grammatical formation and a phonetic modification is not in accordance with the grammatical derivation, one who is intent on a meaning should examine the word through some similarity with a phonetic formation accepted by the grammarians in other cases. He goes on to say

that even when such a similarity is not found, one should analyse on the basis of a possible similarity in syllables or in single sounds, and that never should one not analyse. He underlines this by adding that one should not pay attention to the grammatical formation, for phonetic changes possess a wide range of possibilities. In other words, one should try to stick to the rules of grammar as far as possible, but if this is of no avail in bringing out the hidden semantic content of a word one should abandon them and proceed by analysing on the basis of similarities in syllables and single sounds which should be interpreted according to meaning.

These are some of the basic principles laid down by Yaska, who characterizes his branch of knowledge as a complement to *vyakarana*, as well as something which is a means to its own end. Conversely, *vyakarana* authors do resort to *nirvachana* analysis. For example, the famous grammarian Patanjali makes use of it in his *Mahabhashya*, and the method is a design feature in the twelfth century Pali grammar *Saddaniti* of the Burmese monk Aggavamsa. With regard to the relationship between *vyakarana* and *nirukta*, the Tibetans speak of two traditions of linguistic analysis, *sgra bzin du* (according to sound) and *don bzin du* (according to meaning).

A fundamental feature of *nirvachana* analysis is that it regards all nouns as related to some activity which is considered the reason for a noun signifying that which it signifies. For example, Yaska analyses the word *ahar* (day) as follows: *ahah kasmat? upaharanty asmin karmani* (why (is it called) *ahar*? (because) one carries out (*upaharanti*) actions in the course of it). The word *grishma* (summer) is analysed: *grishmo grasyante 'smin rasah*, (*grishma* (is so called because) juices are devoured (*grasyante*) in the course of it). An example from outside the *Nirukta* is the following analysis of the term ***dharma***, which in Buddhism denotes the smallest ontological building blocks it saw itself able to operate with: *svalakshanadharanad dharmah* (on account of (its) holding (*dharanam*) (its) unique particular, (it is called) a *dharma*). Similarly, the term *diksha*, which denotes the Shaiva Tantric ritual of initiation, is analysed: 'through it knowledge is imparted (*diyate*), and the impression (of contraction) which characterizes (the consciousness of) the individual is destroyed (*kshiyate*); hence, in as much as it is connected with (these activities of) giving and destroying, it is termed *diksha* here (in this system)'.

The power of *nirvachanashastra* as a hermeneutic device can be illustrated by an example from the learned Sanskrit literature of Shaiva Kashmir. **Abhinavagupta** (*fl. c.*975–1025 CE) offers in his *Tantraloka* as many as six different analyses of the name of the deity Bhairava, a Tantric form of Shiva. One analysis runs as follows: '(Bhairava means) he who is manifest among those whose awareness is devoted to that trance which devours time, that is, in those who desiccate that essence of time which is the propellor of the celestial bodies'. Here the term 'Bhairava' has been divided up as follows: (((*bha* (= *nakshatra*) + *ira bhera*) + *va*) *bherava*) *bhairava*. The item *bha*, which is taken to mean *nakshatra* (celestial body/bodies; constellation; asterism), is combined with the item *ira* in the sense of *preraka* (motivator; propellor) (*vir* (move; rise; agitate)) to form the item *bhera* and hence a synonym of 'time'. From *bhera* we get *bherava* by adding the item *va*, obviously thought of as related to the verbal root *va* (blow; move). For these, *bheravah* are further specified as *samshoshakarinah*, the desiccators of *bhera* (time): as they blow on it they dry it out completely. They are the yogins who desiccate time by having their attention centred in that trance which is called the devouring of time. The master among them is Bhairava, the supreme Bherava, the supreme desiccator of time, being vividly manifest as that which devours time; the name *bhairava* thus derived by vowel-strengthening (*vriddhi*) of *bherava*.

When Rudolph Roth's *editio princeps* of Yaska's *Nirukta* was published in Göttingen in 1852, European scholars were completely immersed in the recent discoveries of comparative philology. The relation in *nirvachana* analysis between a noun and some activity, expressed by a finite verb or merely hinted at by the mention of a verbal root caused nineteenth-century scholars to refer to *nirvachanashastra* as 'the science of etymology' and treat Yaska as a primitive forerunner of historical linguistics. Later this interpretation was adopted also by Indian scholars, and it has kept its position up to the present day. Inevitably, such an approach imposed heavy presuppositions upon the interpretation of the *Nirukta*, and *nirvachana* analysis is

indeed not simply etymological in the sense that it does not reflect the findings of historical linguistics which probably is how we understand 'etymology' today. In fact, such an approach falls short of explaining both the acceptance of *nirvachanashastra* within the sophisticated tradition of *vyakarana* and its effective usage in the processing of Sanskrit texts. Some scholars refer to *nirvachana* analysis as 'hermeneutic etymology', but it is probably better to avoid the word etymology altogether and simply speak of 'semantic analysis'. The purpose and function of *nirvachana* analysis is to bring out the *meaning* of a word.

The method of *nirvachana* analysis is better understood in the light of a model of substitution, used at least since the time of the **Upanishads** and later refined in the technical literatures of grammar and ritual. According to this model, a substitute (*adesha*) takes the place (*sthana*) of the original placeholder (*sthanin*) under given circumstances. In *nirvachana* analysis, the term to be explained is the substitute we meet with in language for a fuller statement with the same semantic content. The *nirvachana* is an ideal rewording which is both explanatory and semantically equivalent. Prominent *vyakarana* authors interpret the term *sthana* (place) as *artha* (meaning). With this in mind, a *nirvachana* analysis is to be interpreted not only as 'X in the place of Y' but as 'X in the meaning of Y'. This implies that we have an ideal expression Y which is the place-holder in semantic space. This place, that is to say, this *meaning*, is instead occupied by the item X which replaces Y. Knowledge of that secret place or meaning and that secret entity Y is provided by experts who are in command of the tools of the tradition. The substitutional model also explains why authors can suggest more than one analysis for one and the same word without accepting a particular analysis as the 'correct' one. The various *nirvachanas* are simply alternative placeholders in semantic space. Now, one can give exactly the same truth conditions in a language by making systematic shifts in what the singular terms refer to and what satisfies the predicates. One gets a different thought if one gets a different sentence to represent it.

In *nirvachana* analysis the word that is explained embeds a sentence with most of its elements elided and replaced by zero. According to the *sthanivadb-*

hava principle met with in the literatures of grammar and ritual, the principle that the substitute retains the qualities of the substituend, it is still possible to treat the word we meet with in language like the original sentence it ultimately replaces. A look at one of the more technically phrased *nirvachanas* in the *Nirukta* may serve to highlight some of the philosophical underpinnings of this method of semantic analysis. Since the term *artha* frequently refers to that which is designated by a name as well as to the meaning of that name, it is less crucial whether we take *artha* in the sense of linguistic meaning or we take it in the sense of the thing meant. In the *Nirukta* (2.21) the term *megha* (cloud) is analysed: *megho mehatiti satah*. This can be interpreted: *meghah* occurs in the meaning of that which really exists such that it is true to say of it: it rains.

A *nirvachana* analysis works so that it establishes the truth-value of a sentence in the sense that if a true sentence can be established as an ideal version of a prevalent term, then that term is infused with the meaning of the true sentence. As such, *nirvachana* analysis is an empirical theory of what expressions mean by force of its appearance as a theory of truth. Whether we can say of any particular that it has necessary or contingent properties depends simply on the way it is described. The important feature of *nirvachana* analysis is that the attribution of properties happens *through* the name itself, for example 'Bhairava'. The analysis establishes an ideal expression which has the semantic power to identify the nature of that which a name signifies.

Further reading

Bronkhorst, J. (1981) 'Nirukta and Astadhyayi: Their Shared Presuppositions', *Indo-Iranian Journal* 23: 1–14.

—— (1984) 'Nirukta, Unadi Sutra, and Astadhyayi: A Review Article', *Indo-Iranian Journal* 27: 1–15.

Kahrs, E. (1983) 'Yaska's Use of *Kasmat*', *Indo-Iranian Journal* 25: 231–7.

—— (1986) 'Durga on *Bhava*', in E. Kahrs (ed.), *Kalyanamitraraganam: Essays in Honour of Nils Simonsson*, Oslo: Norwegian University Press, 115–44.

—— (1998) *Indian Semantic Analysis: The Nirvacana*

Tradition, University of Cambridge Oriental Publications 55, Cambridge: Cambridge University Press.

Mehendale, M. (1978) 'The Science of Etymology (Niruktashastra)', in M. Mehendale, *Nirukta Notes*, Series II, Pune: Deccan College Postgraduate and Research Institute, 63–80.

Sarup, L. (ed. and trans.) (1967) *The Nighantu and the Nirukta, the Oldest Indian Treatise on Etymology, Philology, and Semantics*, Delhi: Motilal Banarsidass.

EIVIND KAHRS

nirvana

Nirvana (in Pali, *nibbana*) is the *summum bonum* for Buddhists by whose multifarious schools and traditions both the means and the end are variously conceived. In the earliest substrata, it is described as the end of the series of unsatisfactory existences (*duhkha/***samsara**) through the extinction of the fires of craving, hatred and delusion which generate rebirth-causing actions. It is a selfless and detached state beyond sensory pleasures and all forms of clinging. The enlightened person has a profound grasp of the truth about existence (***dharma***; *dhamma* [p]): to wit, everything is unsatisfactory (*duhkha*) because transitory (*anitya*) and lacking essential identity (*anatma*; *anatta*). All the transient phenomena constitutive of existence are said to be conditioned (*samskrita*; *samkhara* [p]): they are both causes and caused. *Nirvana* transcends the chain of being, becoming and causation and is said to be unconditioned.

According to the **Sarvastivada** traditions there are two types of existential transformation: (a) cessation of suffering due to knowledge (*pratisankhya-nirodha*) which is disjunction from impure *dharma*s, that is, *nirvana* attained while alive through transformative insight (*prajna*) into the **Four Noble Truths**; and (b) cessation of suffering not due to knowledge (*apratisankhya-nirodha*) which is the prevention of the arising of future conditioned *dharma*s in a psycho-physical stream. It is so called because it is obtained not by the comprehension of the Truths, but by the impotency of the causes of arising. It is the attainment of ultimate extinction (*parinirvana*) at death. The idea is that the life in the world of the enlightened one (*Arhat*) continues until the five constituents of personality (matter and form, feelings, perceptions, dispositions and conscious acts) are expended or 'burnt out'. After the death of the enlightened one, there is no rebirth. *Nirvana* is the irreversible end of recognizable forms of human life.

The early traditions refer to the 'blowing out' or 'extinction' of the fires of clinging, hostility and delusion. The fires metaphor is not accidental. It refers to the three fires which the Hindu Brahminical householder was obliged to keep burning and which symbolized his life, responsibilities and attachments as a man in the world. The original sense of the metaphor was missed in developed Mahayana where craving, aversion and delusion are simply called the 'three defects'.

As formulated into the early traditions, *nirvana* can be categorized both as a psychological condition experienced by the enlightened person in the world and as a state (of extinction) beyond the realm of rebirth and unsatisfactoriness. The later Mahayana traditions tend to see enlightenment as a mode of being in the world. According to the Madhyamika schools, *nirvana* and *samsara* are ontologically indistinguishable: what changes is the perspective of the detached experient with insight into the way things really are. The enlightened one realizes that his sense of personal individuality is but a conventional conceptual and linguistic fiction with no basis in ultimate reality, and acts accordingly. That is to say, removed from self-concern and cognizant of the relativity of all conditioned, impermanent and non-substantial phenomena to which he has become indifferent, he cultivates a compassionate attitude (*karuna*) to the unenlightened who are suffering due to the multifarious forms of attachment to the transitory. This is the syzygy, or union, of compassion and insight.

According to the idealist (**Yogachara**) traditions, both *samsara* and *nirvana* are states of mind. One's inherent enlightened **buddha nature** (*tathagata-garbha*) has become obscured by ignorance and moral defects. The underlying 'store-consciousness' (**alaya-vijnana**) that is the source of all experience has the potentiality for both unenlightened and enlightened outlooks. Buddhist praxis is a technique for clarifying and manifesting the Buddha-nature.

Further reading

Gombrich, R. (1996) *How Buddhism Began: The Conditioned Genesis of the Early Teachings*, London: Athlone.

Nishitani Keiji (1985) *Religion and Nothingness*, trans. J. van Bragt, Berkeley, CA: University of California Press.

Welbon, G. (1968) *The Buddhist Nirvana and its Western Interpreters*, Chicago: University of Chicago Press.

CHRIS BARTLEY

Nirvana School of Chinese Buddhism

Nirvana School is a designation given to describe Buddhist monk scholars of the Mahayana *Nirvana Sutra*, who argued that 'all sentient beings have **buddha nature**'. Because the early Chinese Buddhists had trouble understanding the idea of **no-self**, they had assumed that there must be a soul that transmigrates from one life to the next. But soon after Kumarajiva exposed that wrong assumption and stressed universal **emptiness**, the *Nirvana Sutra* arrived and, without denying universal emptiness, reaffirmed the existence of this great 'self' called the buddha nature which is permanent, pure and blissful. This was welcomed by the Buddhists in the south. For the next two centuries, they speculated almost exclusively on buddha nature and on the doctrine of the **Two Truths**.

WHALEN LAI

Nishi Amane

b. 1829; d. 1897

Philosopher and government official

Nishi was born into a *samurai* family in Tsuwano, in present-day Shimane prefecture. His father worked as a physician. In his youth, Nishi received a comprehensive education in Confucianism, and was much impressed by the thought of the Kogakuha scholar Ogyu Sorai (1666–1728). Because of his brilliance, he was offered the opportunity to continue his studies in Edo, where he went in 1853. In a short time, he mastered Dutch and English. From 1857 Nishi was employed at the Bansho shirabe dokoro, the Office for the Investigation of Foreign Books, and found himself a teacher of foreign languages. Also, he translated Western texts. It was at this institute where he met **Tsuda Mamichi** (1821–1903). Both were interested in Western philosophy, and in 1862 they were permitted to go to Europe. In Leiden, Nishi studied under Johann Joseph Hoffmann (1805–78) and Simon Vissering (1818–88), becoming especially proficient in European jurisprudence, jurisdiction and philosophy of law. Back in Japan in 1865, he was appointed professor at his old institute, which had in the meantime been renamed. Later, it developed into the Tokyo Imperial University, and finally Tokyo University. After the Restoration, Nishi was employed by the Hyobusho, the Ministry for Military Affairs, and wrote the Conscription Ordinance of 1873 which made military service compulsory for all males.

Nishi taught on a wide range of subjects, including a large variety of philosophical topics. In 1873, he joined the Meirokusha and during the next years published a number of philosophically relevant essays and treatises. When freedom of thought was more and more restricted, Nishi continued his lectures and studies in private. In 1882, he was elected a member of the Upper House.

Nishi's philosophical achievements were impressive. First, he introduced Western philosophy in a comprehensive and systematic way. In his lectures *Hyaku gaku renkan* (The Relations Between the Hundred Sciences), with the English subtitle *Encyclopedia*, he distinguished between different kinds of science and philosophy and described their relationship to each other. His most general categories are 'general sciences' (*futsugaku*) and 'special sciences' (*shubetsugaku*), with the former including history and mathematics. Within the special sciences, Nishi distinguished between humanities, *Geisteswissenschaften* (*shinrijogaku*), and natural sciences (*butsurijogaku*). Though he regarded philosophy as a special science, namely a kind of

Geisteswissenschaft, he also saw it as fundamental for many other sciences. Nishi further distinguished particular philosophical disciplines, namely, logic, psychology, ontology, ethics, political philosophy, aesthetics, philosophy of history and positivist philosophy.

The *Encyclopedia* was not published during Nishi's lifetime. However, in his *Hyakuichi shinron* (A New Theory of the Unity of the Hundred [Sciences]), which appeared in 1874, he expressed most of its ideas again. Nishi also devoted separate studies to almost all philosophical disciplines, among them for example *Ronri shinsetsu* (A New Theory of Logic), published in 1884. Though Nishi's classification is strongly influenced by Western systematizations, especially Comte's (1798–1857), it is also the result of his own critique of Shushigaku and his approval of Sorai's and **Xunzi**'s (313?–238? BCE) doctrines about the differences between natural laws on one hand and moral, social and juridical laws on the other, and between 'is' and 'ought'. Contrary to a widespread opinion, these fundamental distinctions could be drawn within the tradition of classic Confucian philosophy. Also, these distinctions just reflect common sense. Thus, with regard to the very basis of the distinction between natural sciences and humanities, Western influence on Nishi should not be overestimated. Besides his own studies, Nishi also introduced Western philosophy by way of translation, the most important being his translations of Mill's *Utilitarianism* and Kant's *On Eternal Peace*. Others were his translations of Vissering and of Ihering's *Der Kampf ums Recht*. Also, Nishi coined many Japanese philosophical terms, among them the words for a priori, a posteriori, deduction, induction and philosophy itself. He achieved this by ingeniously combining Chinese characters.

In one of his explanations of philosophy, Nishi characterizes it as a discipline that covers both the explanation of natural and moral phenomena. Using Chinese philosophical terminology, he says that 'philosophy, which [he has] translated by *tetsugaku*, means the establishment of a teaching method to expound and make clear the way of heaven [the realm and principles of nature] and that morality which is manifest in the human spirit' [the principles of good behaviour].

Perhaps Nishi's ethics reflects best his philosophical views, for his ethical theory is also a result of his investigations in epistemological, logical and ontological questions. With his interest in ethics and practical philosophy in general, Nishi responded to what he perceived as the needs of his time. Nishi conceived of ethics as (the theory of) the way of man (*jindo*, or *hito no michi*). Contrary to Shushigaku, he held that this way is different from, and independent of, the way of **heaven** (*tendo*). This amounted to saying that one must distinguish between (right) principles of human behaviour and principles of nature. Nishi also chose the terms *shinri* and *butsuri* to differentiate between moral and natural principles. Similar to the *Xunzi*, Nishi emphasized the fact that natural disasters occur independently of whether a government rules well or otherwise. Further, he pointed out that while natural laws cannot be violated, moral norms can. Finally, whereas natural laws are not man-made and so in a sense are a priori, the principles of what is morally good, though grounded in human nature, are in a certain respect a product of human endeavour and therefore a posteriori.

These observations and notions also reflect Nishi's distinction between knowledge and faith (or belief), his opposition to superstition, and his critical view of religion. In agreement with positivism, but also with classic critical Confucianism, Nishi regarded empirical truth and logical consistency as necessary criteria of valid thought. Whereas religion is based on faith beyond human knowledge, philosophy, in his view, should be based on reason. Accordingly, Nishi criticized ontological speculations so characteristic to Shushigaku, as empty, and even nonsensical. By the phrase 'manifest in the human spirit', Nishi refers to a moral sense which, though grounded in human nature, needs development.

In his ethical theory, Nishi also emphasized the distinction between 'is' and 'ought', and the difference between morality and public law, or – respectively – ethics and legal theory. He indicated that law ought to concur with morality. Again, though these points signify a radical departure from Shushigaku, they are compatible with classic Confucianism. More important, they are favourable to a socio-political system which upholds such ideas as liberty, equality and other human rights.

Since these were much debated issues in early Meiji times, Nishi's contribution was extremely relevant. Like many others, Nishi criticized and deplored the despotism of traditional Japanese government and the resulting servility of the people. Speaking of the 'subservient character' and slave-like status and behaviour of the Japanese, he blamed in particular the governmental traditions like that of the Qin (221–206 BCE), the Mitogaku and its departure from classic Confucianism, and Motoori Norinaga's (1730–1801) **Kokugaku**. Arguing against traditionalism, Nishi emphasized that truth is independent of customs, traditions and ruling opinions, thus not only sticking to the distinction between 'is' and 'ought', but also implicitly distinguishing between the source of ideas and their validity. In human rights discourse, this is an important distinction. Nishi's criticism of despotism, servility and blind traditionalism implied an argument in favour of dignity, freedom, right to life and humane socio-political development. Explicitly, he argued for freedom, particularly religious freedom, equality and even for abolishing the death sentence. However, Nishi held that the conditions of Meiji Japan and the cultural level of her people did not yet permit for a full fledged democratic system, thus viewing democratization as – among other things – a function of socio-cultural development. In his later years, Nishi became rather more conservative but did not abandon his rational and critical method.

In his foundation of ethics, Nishi pointed out that man is by nature endowed with a moral sense but that this sense needs cultivation. This view comes close to the Mencian approach, though Nishi's emphasis on the deontological aspect of moral cultivation is influenced by Kant's philosophy. Further, Nishi took into account the European idea of natural rights. However, because of his clear distinction between 'is' and 'ought' and because of his agreement with Xunzi's and Sorai's view that rights, as morality in general, are also historical human achievements, his notion of human rights is not essentialist or biological. The pragmatic and positivist features of Nishi's ethics are most apparent in his *Jinsei sampo* (Three Human Treasures) in which he put forward a utilitarian theory. He argued that man should strive to realize the 'greatest happiness' of all people. This happiness, he held, consists of the three treasures, health (*mame*), wisdom (*chie*) and wealth (*tomi*). Since Nishi argued for the equal happiness of all people, individual pursuit of the treasures is limited by the legitimate interest of others. This also implies that, for example, individual freedom ought not violate the freedom of others. Referring to **Mencius**'s (372?–289? BCE) critique of extreme altruism and extreme egoism, and thus again making use of traditional Sino-Japanese philosophy, Nishi explained that it is not only natural but ultimately most beneficial for all to stick to a middle course. Though the three values are, at least in many respects, non-moral goods, Nishi tried to show that pursuing them necessarily implies the pursuit of such basic classic Confucian values as **humaneness** (*ren*; in Japanese, *jin*) and **righteousness** (*yi*; in Japanese *gi*), as well as the realization of such rights as equality and freedom.

The first four parts of *Jinsei sampo* (*setsu*) appeared in the ***Meiroku zasshi***. Among Nishi's other contributions to this journal, his articles 'Kyomonron' (On Religion), 'Chisetsu' (Knowledge) and on Japanese character are particularly important. As indicated, in his philosophy of religion, Nishi emphasized the difference between faith and knowledge. Also, he argued for religious freedom and a complete separation of church and government. Religion, in his opinion, is a private matter, and religious faith has nothing to do either with argument or with compulsion.

See also: Japanese philosophy, post-Meiji; philosophy of human rights, Japanese

Further reading

Braisted, W.R. (ed. and trans.) (1976) *Meiroku zasshi*, Tokyo: University of Tokyo Press.

Havens, T. (1970) *Nishi Amane and Modern Japanese Thought*, Cambridge, MA: Harvard University Press.

Nishi Amane (1976) *Kyomon-ron* (On Religion), trans. W.R. Braisted in *Meiroku zasshi*, Tokyo: University of Tokyo Press.

—— (1976) *Jinsei sambo* (The Three Human Treasures), Parts 1–4, trans. W.R. Braisted in *Meiroku zasshi*, Tokyo: University of Tokyo Press.

GREGOR PAUL

Nishida Kitaro

b. 1870; d. 1945

Philosopher of religion and culture

Nishida is often called the founder of the **Kyoto school**, though it was rather his early followers who established and formed this group. He was born in a village near the city of Kanazawa. His school education was rather irregular; after having visited local schools for several years, Nishida continued his studies in private. In 1886, he entered Kanazawa's higher school but, for unclear reasons, left it shortly before graduation in 1890. One of his school friends was Suzuki Daisetz (1870–1966). Because he had not formally finished higher school, Nishida was forced to pursue his studies at Tokyo University as a special student. Nevertheless he was successful, graduating in 1894. Among his teachers were L. Busse (1862–1907) and Raphael von Koeber (1841–1923).

From 1895 until 1909, Nishida taught at several schools, finally and for most of the time at his former higher school in Kanazawa. In 1909 he became professor at Gakushuin University in Tokyo, and in 1910 was appointed assistant professor at Kyoto University. In 1928 he retired, devoting himself for the rest of his life to developing further his basic philosophical ideas, the thrust of which had already been apparent in his first major publication *Zen no kenkyu* (A Study of Good), published in 1911.

Nishida's main interest was in what may be called ontological truth as a means to an existentially satisfactory life. More precisely, he held that man must know true reality, reality as it is, or, in other words, ultimate or absolute reality, to be able to lead the life he rightly longs for, namely a life that satisfies his soteriological or religious needs. Accordingly, Nishida tried to understand and characterize this reality, and also to characterize the way this reality can be known or realized. Among his most influential attempts to indicate true reality are his concepts of God, *mu* (**nothingness**), *zettai mu* (absolute nothingness) and *(zettai) mujunteki jiko doitsu* ([absolute] contradictory self-identity), whereas his notions of *junsui keiken* (pure experience), *bashoteki ronri* (logic of place) and *toyo no ronri* (Eastern logic) became the best known symbols of what he regarded as the epistemological methods for grasping ultimate reality. While 'God' and 'pure experience' are key-notions of *A Study of Good*, the concepts of 'absolute nothingness', 'logic of place' and 'Eastern logic', as well as such related concepts as 'concrete logic' and 'dialectical logic', are central to later writings, especially *Hataraku mono kara miru mono e* (From the Acting to the Seeing), *Zettai mujunteki jiko doitsu* (The Absolute Contradictory Self-Identity) and *Bashoteki ronri to shukyoteki sekai* (The Logic of Place and the Religious World), published in 1927, 1934, and 1945 respectively.

As the titles and key notions indicate, Nishida's thought was influenced by and took into account both Western and Eastern teachings of philosophy, religion and mysticism. In *A Study of Good*, Nishida utilized, among others, William James's (1842–1910) concept of pure experience, Jacob Böhme's (1575–1624) ideas of mystical experience, Nicholas of Cusa's (1401–64) negative theology, and certain Buddhist, especially Zen, doctrines to develop his own notion of *junsui keiken*. Later, Fichte (1762–1814), Hegel (1770–1831), Plato (427–347 BCE), and also particular interpretations of Buddhist ontology according to which ultimate reality is a state or realm of, or characterized by, *mu* (nothingness), became more influential. Nishida was also very well acquainted with Kant (1724–1804) and neo-Kantianism but because of his conviction that a realization of ultimate reality is indispensable for man, and must be possible, he could not agree with Kant's argument denying the possibility of such an ultimate grasp of reality by finite knowers.

Nishida's thought follows and expresses a rather general pattern of thinking, namely (1) that there exists a kind of ultimate reality, (2) that this ultimate reality is the basis and source of everyday or phenomenological reality, (3) that it cannot be realized by a reasoning that follows formal logical laws, but (4) only by ways of mystical experience or intuition, and methods of non-formal logic, and finally, (5) that this ultimate reality ought to be understood and realized, for then we would be able finally to understand the meaning of life and thus satisfy our existential and soteriological needs. This pattern of thought is common to, among other doctrines, Platonism, numerous mystical systems, *theologica negativa*, the doctrine of an inborn 'true'

buddha nature which must be realized to become enlightened and saved, and to the Shushigaku teaching that man must know the principle of fundamental and good reality and actualize his original nature, which is but a manifestation of this principle, if he wants to realize humanity. As with many such doctrines, it is also difficult to understand Nishida's distinctions between everyday and ultimate reality, for if one interprets his notion of 'absolute self-contradictory identity' as referring to everyday reality, it either makes no sense at all or must be understood as succinctly (though somewhat misleadingly) expressing insights achieved from different points of view. For example, Nishida's concept of the contradictory identity of the one and the many could mean that from a certain point of view an entity is conceived of as one, while from another perspective it is seen as a combination of many distinct elements. Interpreted in this way, the concept would be conceived of as logically consistent, simply expressing that one and the same entity can be regarded as both a unity and manifold. If 'absolute self-contradictory identity' is understood as referring to ultimate reality, however, it must be interpreted as a metaphor for something beyond logical description, or simply as a negation of the notion of (the properties of) everyday reality. Further, it is often difficult to understand whether Nishida, by his notions of non-formal logic, refers to ways of thought or to internal dynamics of reality. Finally, it is not clear whether the methods that, according to Nishida, enable man to realize ultimate reality, are mere epistemological means, or whether they also include an existential experience comparable to a *unio mystica*.

Nevertheless, even in his usage of the word *ronri* (logic), Nishida is clearer than Tanabe Hajime (1885–1962), Suzuki Daisetz (1870–1966) or Nishitani Keiji and many other thinkers, who believe that Nishida's thought is proof that there exists an almost mysteriously distinctive way of Eastern thinking, namely, Eastern logic. Also, Nishida is much less of a cultural relativist than almost all his followers. First of all, he expressly distinguished between formal, or abstract, and non-formal, or concrete, logic. In his *Nihon bunka no mondai* (Problems of Japanese Culture), a series of lectures delivered at Kyoto University in 1938 when the ultra-nationalist kokutai ideology was all-pervasive (see **kokutai ideology since Meiji times**), he emphasized that formal logic is the same everywhere, and that it is only concrete logic that differs according to cultural conditions and the field of application. Though Nishida did 'not deny that Japanese culture is a culture of emotion (*joteki bunka*)', he warned against conceiving of it as 'being only emotional, illogical and mystical'. Besides regarding Japanese culture as (though not illogical) a culture of emotion, Nishida's account of Japanese culture is characterized by his conviction that it is non-dual in the sense that in it 'man and nature have become one', and that subject and world are conceived of as identical. As part of Oriental culture, Japanese culture, according to Nishida, is also influenced by what he calls 'Buddhist logic', that is, interest in and methods of reflecting on the (workings) of the mind, or self, rather than on other objects. If adequately understood, such a way of using the term *ronri* (logic) does indeed not imply that formal logical rules are invalid.

However, in spite of his distinction between formal, or abstract, and concrete logic, Nishida never completely systematized his different usages of the term *ronri*. He employed the term to indicate at least the following ways of thought and structural development: (1) formal logic, (2) Kantian transcendental logic, (3) Hegelian dialectical logic, (4) non-formal epistemological methods of realizing reality, (5) internal dynamics of reality, (6) logic of place, (7) systematic reflection on the (workings of the) mind, (8) object logic, (9) Eastern logic and even (10) such specific structures of argument as Nagarjuna's logic of eightfold negation. Thereby, 'logic of place' seems to indicate both an epistemological method of realizing reality and an internal dynamics of reality, especially a process of specification, whereas 'Eastern logic' alludes to almost everything except for formal and transcendental logic.

Nishida's thought has been very influential. Besides constituting the basis for the developments of the Kyoto school, and influencing other Japanese philosophers (as for example **Watsuji Tetsuro**, 1889–1960), it has also met with much interest on the side of Western scholars, especially analysts of culture, those critical of so-called Western rationality, and religious thinkers. Most of them were particularly attracted by Nishida's notions of non-formal and Eastern logic and his rhetoric of absolute nothingness and the identity of contradictions. These expressions almost worked as catch words. However, usually their relevance as indications of something distinctively Eastern or Japanese is overestimated. Also, it is often simply overlooked that Nishida's thought is by no means exemplary of modern Japanese philosophy but only one example among others, and is criticized by Japanese Kantians, analytical philosophers, Buddhist scholars of *hetuvidya* and representatives of critical Buddhism. Another source of a possible misunderstanding of Nishida is insufficient distinction between his ideas and those of the Kyoto school which, as indicated, are often less sophisticated and balanced.

See also: Buddhist philosophy in Japan, post-Meiji; Japanese philosophy; logic; orientalism

Further reading

Nishida Kitaro (1958) *Intelligibility and the Philosophy of Nothingness: Three Philosophical Essays*, trans. R. Schinzinger, Tokyo: Maruzen.

—— (1960) *Zen no kenkyu* (A Study of Good), trans. V. Guglielmo, Tokyo.

—— (1970) *Tetsugaku no kompon mondai* (Fundamental Problems of Philosophy), trans. D. Dilworth, Tokyo: Sophia University Press.

—— (1973) *Geijutsu to dotoku* (Art and Morality), trans. D. Dilworth and V. Viglielmo, Honolulu, HA: The University Press of Hawaii.

—— (1987) *Jikaku ni okeru chokkan to hansei* (Intuition and Reflection in Self-Consciousness), trans. V. Viglielmo *et al.*, Albany, NY: State University of New York Press.

—— (1987) *Last Writings: Nothingness and the Religious Worldview*, trans. D. Dilworth, Honolulu, HA: University of Hawaii Press.

—— (1991) *Nihon bunka no mondai* (La culture Japonaise en question), trans. P. Lavelle, Paris: Publications Orientalistes de France.

—— (1999) *Logik des Ortes: Der Anfang der modernen Philosophie in Japan*, ed. and trans. R. Elberfeld, Darmstadt: Wissenschaftliche Buchgesellschaft.

GREGOR PAUL

Nishimura Shigeki

b. 1828; d. 1902

Philosopher and educator

Nishimura tried in a systematic and critically balanced way to combine what he regarded as the strong points of Western enlightenment ethics and Sino-Japanese Confucianism. The son of a *samurai* of high standing, he received an excellent traditional, especially Confucian, education, and also became acquainted with Mitogaku. In due course, he became aware of the difficult conditions of pre-Meiji Japan. The fact that his father was in the service of Hotta Masayoshi (1810–64), one of the progressive *daimyo* (feudal lords) of his time, and even experimented in Western military methods, determined the direction of this awareness. Convinced that the Japanese must know Western science, and particularly gunnery, to be able to cope with the foreign powers (although he was opposed to the vilification of foreigners), he went to Edo and in 1851 became a disciple of Sakuma Shozan (1811–64) the famous advocator of 'Eastern morality and Western technology', and one of the most competent scholars of *rangaku*. Following Shozan's advice, Nishimura soon began to study Dutch. But like **Fukuzawa** Yukichi (1834–1901), he later realized that English was more important, and from 1861 also studied English.

Nishimura served as a government official before and after the Restoration in 1868. In 1873, he accepted a leading post in the Ministry of Education, and in 1875 succeeded Kato Hiroyuki (1836–1916) as lecturer on Western books to the emperor. By the time of his death, he was a famous and highly respected personality. Nishimura is best remembered, however, as founding member of the Meirokusha (1874) and author of *Nihon dotoku ron* (On Japanese Morality), published in 1887, and his greatest philosophical achievements were this treatise and his contributions to the *Meiroku zasshi*.

As a promoter of enlightenment and civilization (*bummei kaika*), Nishimura, in articles for the *Meiroku zasshi*, provided elucidating 'expositions of foreign words', among them 'civilization' (which he translated as *bummei kaika*), 'liberty' and 'freedom' (*jishu* or *jiyu*), and 'right' (*kenri*). These articles can also be read as an argument for naturally endowed human rights. This is the more so since Nishimura, like Fukuzawa, always criticized servility and despotism, and since he was one of the few Meirokusha members who advocated establishing a popularly elected assembly, pointing out that the Japanese were at least as fit to do this as the English 600 years earlier. For many years, Nishimura continuously attacked what he regarded as the Asian and Japanese inclination to stick to tradition and to 'reform' by 'returning to antiquity' (*fukko*). As early as 1868, he remarked, 'In general, since opportunities in the world open up year by year, it cannot be that the ancient is superior to the present'. He also wrote that 'it is against the law of heaven to cling to old customs and never change'. However, he did not argue in favour of blind and abrupt changes but for conscious and well reasoned socio-political improvements which avoided social unrest. Facts, reason and universal moral norms should be the standards. Nishimura also, from about 1886, supported the myth of Japanese uniqueness, but nevertheless criticized Japanese chauvinism and aggression and Japan's politics toward Korea and China.

Nishimura was one of those scholars who were convinced that modernization, especially modern government and law, must be based on morality. This was perhaps the main reason for his interest in moral education. Though he became more conservative when he grew older, it may be said that he stuck to the principle that facts and reason had to be used to identify the right morality, and hence never overlooked what he considered the weak points of Eastern morality. Accordingly, in his *Nihon dotoku ron*, Nishimura criticized Confucianism on the grounds that it lacked precision, objectivity and consistency, emphasized prohibitions instead of encouraging people, unjustly favoured descent, age and position, discriminated against women, and venerated the past while denigrating the present. With regard to Western culture, he held that it overemphasized theory while neglecting practice, lacked techniques of self-control and self-cultivation, was too much inclined to attack tradition, especially traditional philosophy, not adequately honouring traditional doctrines, and lacked unity of thought, thus favouring one-sidedness and partiality. Though Nishimura praised loyalty and **filial piety**, he also warned against perverting them into subservience and blind obedience.

Nishimura wrote over 130 books and 200 articles and, in his philosophical contributions, often (though certainly not always) expressed himself in a critically discriminating manner. As indicated, over the course of his long life he also changed some of his philosophical positions. Both these factors make it difficult to provide a satisfactory final survey of his philosophical contributions.

See also: Japanese philosophy, post-Meiji; kokutai ideology since Meiji times; Meiroku zasshi; philosophy of human rights, Japanese

Further reading

Shively, D. (1982) 'Nishimura Shigeki: A Confucian View of Modernization', in M. Jansen (ed.), *Changing Japanese Attitudes Toward Modernization*, Tokyo: Tuttle, 193–241.

GREGOR PAUL

Noble Eightfold Path

The Noble Eightfold Path is the Buddhist path leading to the cessation of experience of unsatisfactoriness or dis-ease (*duhkha*) through the elimination of craving, attachment, aversions and delusions. The path (*marga*; *magga* [p]) is said to consist of right views, right thoughts, right speech, right action, right livelihood, right effort, right mindfulness and right concentration. Right views and thoughts are classified as mind-purifying wisdom (*prajna*) or insight into the transitory, unsatisfactory and non-substantial nature of the elements of conditioned existence; right speech, action and livelihood are classified as moral conduct (*shila*); right effort, mindfulness and concentration are classified as meditative cultivation (*samadhi*).

The condition of the transmigrating unenlightened person, for whose plight the path is the remedy, involves a belief in individuality, doubt convictions about the efficacy of religious vows and rites, sensual desires, malice, craving for existence

in subtle form, craving for formless existence, pride, restlessness and ignorance.

The path is held to be the 'middle way' between a life of luxurious self-indulgence and rigorous asceticism, neither of which are conducive to the attainment of release from the desire-fuelled series of existences whose termination requires the neutralization of potentially retributive and thus rebirth-causing actions through the elimination of the basic defects of craving, aversion and delusion. Buddhism claims to be a truly universal morality. In this respect it differs from caste-based Hinduism where what is right is relativized to individual circumstances. In Hinduism, the particular duty (*sva-dharma*) of a married farmer with a family differs significantly from that of a born Brahmin who has renounced his social and religious role.

Buddhists insist that virtuous conduct is a necessary condition for the cultivation of **meditation** and insight. In early Buddhism, intention (*chetana*) is understood as the crucial factor determining the moral quality of an action. Morality consists in deliberate abstention from murder, theft, sexual misconduct, false speech, slander, harsh words, frivolous talk, covetousness, malice and false views. Right livelihood would preclude such occupations as arms trading, dealing in drugs and alcohol, or butchering animals. Normative Buddhist lay ethics involves abstention from theft, lies, injury, sexual malpractice and intoxicants which occasion heedlessness and lead to the other four.

Samadhi involves fixing the mind on a single point. It is the achievement of tranquillity (*samatha*) through avoidance of distractions (*vikshepa*) and by suppression of sensory activity. It arises from the transcendence of lust, envy, apathy, anxiety, and scepticism. Emphasis is placed upon mindfulness, which may be understood as developing a controlling perspective upon one's physical, mental and emotional states. *Samadhi* may also involve the cultivation of the four states called *Brahma-viharas*: goodwill (*maitri*), compassion (*karuna*), sympathetic joy (*mudita*) and equanimity (*upeksha*). Practised to perfection, the *brahma-viharas* will take one to what are purely mind-states on the plane of formlessness proximate to the apex of existence.

Four meditative stages called *dhyana*s are correlated with heavens in the world of Brahma populated by higher beings that have been reborn in the supernatural sphere of subtle matter (*rupadhatu*). The first *dhyana* is a state of joy and happiness involving reasoning (*vitarka*) and discursive thought (*vichara*). It is achieved through suppression of sensory desires (*kama*) and destruction of hindrances to meditation which are covetousness, malice, apathy, regret and doubt. After transcending reasoning and thought, the meditator with his mind blissfully concentrated on one point enters the second *dhyana* of inner peace which is joy (*priti*) and happiness. Having renounced joy, he experiences equanimity (*upeksha*), mindful and fully aware. This is the third *dhyana*. The fourth *dhyana* is beyond happiness and suffering.

When he has left behind all thoughts about matter, he enters the domain of infinite space on the plane of formlessness (*arupyadhatu*) inhabited by beings reborn purely as 'mental streams'. Transcending the domain of infinite space, he successively enters the spheres of infinite consciousness, infinite nothingness and that of neither perception nor non-perception, the pinnacle of existence. Finally, he achieves the cessation of perception and feeling. His passions are now destroyed by knowledge and he has attained *nirvana* while still alive in the world. When *samadhi* is complemented by what is called *vipashyana*-meditation, the adept acquires magic powers, the far-reaching divine eye, telepathy, divine hearing, recall of previous existences and the destruction of all corruptions which might hinder spiritual progress. Wisdom (*prajna*; *vipashyana*) is profound and settled insight into the impermanence, unsatisfactoriness and insubstantiality of phenomena and the correlative peace of **nirvana**.

Further reading

Collins, S. (1982) *Selfless Persons: Imagery and Thought in Theravada Buddhism*, Cambridge: Cambridge University Press.

Harvey, P. (1990) *An Introduction to Buddhism*, Cambridge: Cambridge University Press.

Lamotte, E. (1988) *History of Indian Buddhism*, trans. S. Webb-Boin, Louvain: Publications de l'Institut Orientaliste de Louvain.

Rahula, W. (1969) *What the Buddha Taught*, London: Gordon Fraser.

Warder, A. (1991) *Indian Buddhism*, Delhi: Motilal Banarsidass.

CHRIS BARTLEY

nominalism and realism, universals

There are commentators who seriously doubt whether the idea of universals ever existed in Chinese thought, and whether, if that is the case, we can talk meaningfully of the presence of realism in China. Did not **Xunzi**, a firm nominalist, have the last word on the classical debate on '**name and reality**'? But when Huayan Buddhism made such claims as that the entire golden lion is contained in one hair of that lion, one has to suspect a functional realism is at work somewhere.

Culturally speaking, realism in Europe was an ideology that supported sacramentalism and sacerdotalism. It set the whole up as more than the sum of its parts. It made sense of the doctrine of transsubstantiation: that it is the substance (what subsists below the properties) of the bread that has been changed at the eucharist. We can observe a change from a concern with the supernatural in Huayan to the naturalistic in Chan Buddhism. The former supported the proto-Tantric mysteries at the court of Empress Wu; the latter found its patron among the regional military leaders. A comparison of Variochana's iconography on the one hand with an ink painting of the Sixth Patriarch tearing up the *sutra* in the other should illustrate that well. Vairochana is the Sun Buddha, the most magnificent of the Buddhas, the only one warranted to be called the Dharmakaya Buddha. Dharmakaya, the Law body, is shared by all Englightened Ones and, when equated with **emptiness** in Mahayana, should be formless. But the Sun Buddha's form can claim that status for the following iconographic reason. He has a flaming (dynamic) halo instead of the usual round (stable) one. The tongues of flame shooting up from that halo contain in each another buddha figure, except that when examined closely those other figures are none other than Vairochana himself.

This means that he is infinite in his magnitude, so that each part of him is another him. Such a view corresponds with realism, since now the universal is real and present in full in every member of a species.

In his sermon on the Golden Lion, Fazang claimed that in every hair of the golden lion is all the gold making up the whole statue as well as the totality of the lion form. This is his way of expressing the mystery of the part being the whole. Impossible according to nominalism, it can be justified on realist assumptions. It is continuous with the mystery of the Sun Buddha, namely, that on every tongue of flame in his flaming halo is another Sun Buddha with a flaming halo, and so on *ad infinitum*. The realist explanation is that the universal that is the lion and the universal that is the gold are somehow fully present and made accessible in that particular hair. For the sake of argument, Chan nominalism is the reverse. Instead of a multi-headed and multi-armed Buddha, it gave us the Sixth Patriarch who looked just like anyone else, i.e. unkempt and in rags, tearing up a sacred scripture in a setting as naturalistic as can be. This tradition would not confuse the finger (a nominal pointer, name) and the moon that it points to (reality).

See also: Huineng; language, Chinese philosophy of

Further reading

Getty, A. (1914) *The Gods of Northern Buddhism: Their History, Iconography and Progressive Evolution through the Northern Buddhist Countries*, Oxford: Clarendon Press.

WHALEN LAI

nominalism and realism: abstract, abstraction

There are currently scholars who dispute abstractions like universals or transcendental ideas beyond the particular, physically changing phenomenon. It is also sometimes argued that Chinese abstractions are tied to a system of **correlative thinking** that is non-reductive, and to a classification system that is holistic or has universals which are connected in accordance with a 'family resemblance' model. Chinese philosophy certainly understood the concept of abstraction. Any attempted intellectual grasp that moves beyond the sense object, any selection of focus, any inference of significance, would constitute abstraction. The issue is the degree of abstraction, the prejudice of focus, the mode of classification. The modern Chinese term for 'to abstract' is 'to extract [out of an object] its emblemic form (*xiang*)'. The term might be a translated neologism; the process described is not. The act of 'abstracting the form' is basic to the **Yijing**. After the two greater poles of *yin–yang* (sun and moon), there arose the four forms or *xiang* (add the two lesser intermediates), which helped constitute the eight trigrams (paired to eight natural phenomena) that multiply into the sixty-four hexagrams. 'Forms' and 'numbers' here may not be Platonic, but are no less fundamental to the Han exegesis of this Classic. The whole process involves abstraction, whether it be the reduction of the Many into the One; and the expansion from the four greater/lesser *yin–yang* set into the 'emblems' like hills and marshes, wind and thunder.

But it would be myopic to equate the *Book of Changes* with the Becoming of Heraclitus and against the Being of Parmenides, because *yi* (change) itself is said to be composed of three aspects: the unchanging, the changing, and the simplicity of it all. In other words, Being, Becoming and the principle of reducing the complex to the simple are all part of abstraction itself, and are familiar ideas in any metaphysics.

The Chinese pictogram is a rich and easy source for allegations about her attitude to the concrete. The peculiar semiotics and grammar of the Chinese language have inspired some interesting readings of the Way (*dao*). A more positive avenue may actually be myth. The myth of a cosmogonic **chaos** rooted probably in the south left a mark on Chinese metaphysics. Instead of having abstract ideas provide an idealist anchorage to reality, Daoism is more fascinated with the potency of a vague something that precedes the emergence of distinct name and form (logic and reality). Thus the *dao* is nameless and formless, defies classification and is capable of infinite transformations. Since it predates form, it is not abstract ideas but reversion to the *prima materia* that truly liberates. Within that continuum from the nebulous to the concretized, the term now used to render 'metaphysics' (which the Song dynasty Neo-Confucians took to be the immaterial principle that is 'above form'), that term 'above form' should be rendered as what is 'before form'. The **chaos myth** certainly informs Chinese thought, but it is not the only defining cosmogonic myth in China. It had to contend with a cosmographic myth in the north which was more interested in working out some kind of ideal placement of people and things in the Four Directions radiating from the Centre, making up a cross and informing the **Magic Square**. This is the model that would inform the classification system and the correlative thinking of China.

See also: numerology

Further reading

Girardot, N. (1983) *Myth and Meaning in Early Taoism*, Berkeley, CA and Los Angeles: University of California Press.

Graham, A. (1986) *Yin-Yang and the Nature of Correlative Thinking*, Singapore: Institute of East Asian Philosophies, National University of Singapore.

Hall, D. and Ames, R. (1995) *Anticipating China: Thinking Through the Narratives of Chinese and Western Cultures*, Albany, NY: State University of New York Press.

Neville, R. (1982) *The Tao and the Daemon*, Albany, NY: State University of New York Press.

Wilhelm, H. (1977) *Heaven, Earth, and Man in the Book of Changes*, Seattle, WA: Washington University Press.

Zhang Longxi (1992) *The Tao and the Logos: Literary Hermeneutics, East and West*, Durham, NC and London: Duke University Press.

WHALEN LAI

no-self

Together with the ideas of impermanence and suffering, the theory of 'no-self' is one of the three fundamental philosophical tenets of Buddhism.

The Tibetan thinkers, however, understand the meaning of 'no-self' differently in different contexts, thus developing a progressively subtle interpretation of the doctrine. For example, at the general level 'no-self' can be understood in terms of the rejection of a metaphysical self that is characterized as 'permanent', 'unitary' and 'autonomous'. This is the self that is thought to be postulated by many of the non-Buddhist ancient Indian schools and rejected by the Buddhists. Read thus, the doctrine relates only to the nature of personal identity and not universally to all phenomena. However, the Mahayana schools argue that the doctrine must embrace the whole spectrum of reality hence they posit 'no-self' of persons and 'no-self' of phenomena. According to **Tsongkhapa**, as far as the understanding of the doctrine of 'no-self' of person is concerned there is no difference between all four Buddhist schools (**Vaibhashika**, **Sautrantika**, Chittamatra and Madhyamaka) except for the Prasangika division of the Madhyamaka school. In their view, 'no-self' of persons is understood in terms of the rejection of the substantial reality of person. For, according to these Buddhists, the person is a construct designated on the basis of the physical and mental constituents that together constitute the individual's existence. Thus, it is argued, the person is real only in name and concept. Nevertheless, it is maintained that there is a real referent to the term 'person' that is real and exists substantially. Some take the mental consciousness to be this candidate, while for others it is a unique faculty called the **foundational consciousness**.

In contrast, the 'no-self' of phenomena is defined differently by the various schools according to their own basic metaphysical standpoints. For the Chittamatra school, the 'no-self' of phenomena refers to the ultimate nonduality of subject and its object. Our perception of the external world is revealed to be an illusion, what is real is the existence of the mind. This, according to them, lies at the heart of the Mahayana teachings on **emptiness**. Yet for the Madhyamaka school this is not the final doctrine. No metaphysical theory that dichotomizes between the mind and the material world is tenable. Just as the external world of objects is shown to be lacking in real existence so must we also accept the mental world to be devoid of real existence. And this absence of real, objective, independent existence of things is the final meaning of emptiness, and is also the 'no-self' of phenomena. Yet, according to Tsongkhapa, even the Svatantrika division of the Madhyamaka school which maintains this universal doctrine of emptiness fails to arrive at the final understanding of 'no-self' for they still harbour a residual belief in some form of intrinsic existence.

Prasangika-Madhyamaka does not posit any difference of subtlety between the two 'no-selves'. For them the difference lies only in the bases upon which the 'no-self' is defined. Thus, the emptiness of the intrinsic existence of person is the 'no-self' of persons, and the emptiness of the intrinsic being of phenomena is the 'no-self' of phenomena. On this view, any metaphysical concept that entails a belief in some form of intrinsic being is false and all concepts which could be judged to provide some kind of haven for this belief must be 'deconstructed'. Therefore, the rejection of intrinsic existence can be seen as the culmination of the whole Buddhist philosophical project of deconstruction that proceeds with the deconstruction of the self, *dharmas*, indivisible atoms, foundational consciousness, autonomous reason and so on. So, 'no-self' now equals emptiness of intrinsic being. It is in this sense the Tibetans understand the Prasangika-Madhyamaka view of the emptiness of intrinsic existence to be the final understanding of the Buddhist teaching on 'no-self'.

Further reading

Hopkins, J.P. (1983) *Meditation on Emptiness*, London: Wisdom Publications, part V, 307–17.

THUPTEN JINPA

no-thought/no-mind

These negative compounds are tropes, and have lured many into flights of mystical imagination as to what they really mean. But the poetics of negative thinking is such that what they mean depends on what 'thought' and 'mind' stand for. Do they mean rational thought, secondary reflection, superimposed ideation, just any sort of thinking, egoism, subjectivity or conscious intent? Only the context can tell. In China, **Zhuangzi** spoke of 'no-mind', and the *Platform Sutra* later declared 'no-thought' to be the principle of Southern Zen. D.T. Suzuki devoted an early book on this Zen philosophy of 'no-mind/thought'.

Whatever the Sanskrit root for that term might be, Han thought made a clearer distinction between mind and thought. 'Mind' as the basis of all thought is higher and claims priority and constancy. 'Thought' is a term for derivative mental events and pertains to a mutable succession of 'momentary presentations'. Because the term 'thought' happens also to be used to render Sanskrit *kshana*, the split-second unit of time, the Chinese word combines the meaning of both 'a moment of fleeing thought' and 'a fleeting thought of the moment'. Thereupon 'no-thought' can imply a severing of this samsaric chain of 'thought-moments' and a reverting to the pure mind of no-thought that transcends the subject–object dichotomy. It is that conflation we find in the ***Awakening of Faith in Mahayana*** and the *Platform Sutra*.

Further reading

Hall, D. (1994) 'To Be or Not to Be: the Postmodern Self and the Wu-Forms in Taoism', in R. Ames *et al.* (eds), *Self as Person in Asian Thought and Practice*, Albany, NY: State University of New York Press.

Lai, W. (1980) 'Hu-jan Nien-ch'i (Suddenly a Thought Rose): Chinese Understanding of Mind and Consciousness', *Journal of the International Association of Buddhist Studies* 3(1): 42–59.

—— (1986) 'The Early Chinese Understanding of the Psyche: Chen Hui's Commentary on the Yin chih ju ching', *Journal of the International Association for Buddhist Studies* 9(1): 85–103.

Suzuki, D. (1969) *The Zen Doctrine of No-Mind: The Significance of the Sutra of Hui-neng*, London: Rider & Co.

WHALEN LAI

non-being (*wu*)

The opposite of *you* for being, *wu* is also translated as **nothingness**. The Chinese terms mean 'to have not/to have' or 'there is not/there is'. Given the different Chinese semiotics, there have been objections to using non-being or nothingness to render *wu*. Many alternatives have been proposed.

The Neo-Daoist thinker Wang Bi started this when he proclaimed non-being to be the substance of being. Only then did these two words – now standing clearly for something of critical importance – become so divisive as to have two camps lined up one against the other. Wang Bi was perceived by his opponents as denying the reality of the world and was charged with being a nihilist. An opposing thesis titled *In Praise of Being* was composed to reaffirm the reality of the here-and-now. For the word 'reality', the reader might substitute 'significance' because the 'real' issue was over 'value': should we or should we not live up to the obligations of social living in the present? But since we always give to matters of 'value' this character of the 'real', the two sides were divided over the status of 'reality'. So the archaic semiotics of *you* and *wu* (have and have-not, etc.) did graduate into meaning what is real and what is not, i.e. something like being and non-being. We do not need to know Greek or archaic Chinese to appreciate the very human sentiments and generalizations involved here.

Wang Bi himself changed the meaning of those key words. He used the word *wu* in the abstract, standing alone, and was the first thinker to reduce it philosophically to a mathematical 'zero'. It is absolute nothing(ness), as compared with being just a mere deprivation of visible form or tangible substance (as in the *Huainanzi*). He apparently reached that conclusion independently, without first-hand knowledge of the *Emptiness Sutra* then available in translation, where **emptiness** or *shunyata* is the Sanskrit 'zero'. For Wang Bi, of course, the starting point is the thought of **Laozi**. Wang Bi would inspire the Neo-Confucians to take the two key words as 'nouns' instead of as 'adjectives', qualifying the next word 'name' and 'desire'.

> The Dao that can be talked about is not the invariable Dao,
> The Name that can be named is not the invariable name.
> Non-Being names [instead of 'Nameless is'] the

> Mother of all things,
> Being names [instead of 'Name is'] the beginnings of all things....
> Abide in a state of Non-being if you want to [instead of 'Free from desires'] see its subtle beginning.
> Abide in a state of Being if you want to [instead of 'With a measure of passion') see its stirring into becoming manifest.

The point is that you can look at the world with an emptied mind (no-mind) or with a regular mind. The former allows one to see the mysterious origin (the Nameless) while the latter only gets you as far as seeing the many (named things).

The current arrangement that sets the *dao* chapters ahead of the *de* (virtue) chapters came from Wang Bi. There is a late Han commentary from the **Taiping** religious Daoist circle, and another early one from a figure called Heshanggong (the Master Up the River). The latter is concerned with teaching ways of 'nurturing life'. Since Daoism regarded sex to be healthy, sexual intercourse (the mixing of *yin* and *yang*) is deemed therapeutic. So in this commentary, the text's reference to the 'mystic female' and to the (fertile) 'valley' is taken to be about the female sexual organ. Such physiological reading disappeared from Wang Bi, who equated the *dao* with a metaphysical non-being, making it the source and substance of being. Although he himself did not change the reading of the first chapter, the Neo-Confucians would later read four lines as follows:

> Non-being is used to name ...
> Being is used to name ...
> With non-being, one desires
> With being, one may

After Buddhism introduced the dialectics of **Nagarjuna** and claimed that 'both being and non-being are empty', the Daoists felt pressured to emulate that double negation. They found justification in the formula of a 'double mystery' hinted at in the second last line of Chapter 1. Han commentaries usually assumed an orderly cosmogonic sequence with the One (nameless *dao*) preceding the Two (of named **Heaven** and Earth) which then produced the Many. Wang Bi himself followed the old reading, but the Buddhists would foster that absolutization of non-being. No-mind is no longer just a careless mind, a non-egocentric or non-scheming mind; it is somehow a mind that has touched base with this poetic non/sense of an Absolute Nothingness.

See also: dao as nameless

Further reading

Chan, A. (1990) *Two Visions of the Way: A Study of the Wang Pi and the Ho-shang-kung Commentaries on the Lao-tzu*, Albany, NY: State University of New York Press.

Graham, A. (1959) 'Being in Western Philosophy compared with Shih/fei and Yu/wu in Chinese Thought', *Asia Major* 7: 76–112.

Hendrick, R. (trans.) (1989) *Lao-tzu Tao-te-ching: A New Translation Based on the Recently Discovered Ma-wang-tui Texts*, New York: Ballantine Books.

Lau, J. (trans.) (1982) *Tao Te Ching*, Hong Kong: Hong Kong University Press.

Rump, A. and Wing-tsit Chan (trans.) (1979) *Wang Pi's Commentary on the Lao-tzu*, Honolulu, HA: University of Hawaii Press.

Waley, A. (1934) *The Way and its Power*, London: George Allen & Unwin.

WHALEN LAI

non-dualism

There is a general consensus amongst Buddhist thinkers that the highest experience of the ultimate truth, i.e. **emptiness**, occurs within a state that is thoroughly free of any form of dualism. Such an experience is said to be 'fused' with its object as if 'water is poured onto water', and so far as the perspective of the 'experiencer' is concerned there is no distinction between the subjective experience and its object. This kind of 'insight' is characterized as 'the yogi's transcendent awareness of nonduality'. It is only from the perspective of a third person that one can speak of a subject and its object. It is important to bear in mind that in the Tibetan philosophical context the discourse on dualism versus non-dualism does not relate to the philo-sophical problem concerning the mind–body relation.

In defining what constitutes dualism we find different types of dualism identified in varying contexts. For example, when the Yogacharins assert that reflexive awareness, the self-cognizing, apperceptive faculty of cognition which is posited by every instance of a mental event is non-dualistic, then dualism is understood in terms of a perception of anything that is extraneous to the subjective experience. So, to say that reflexive awareness is a nondualistic experience is to say that it does not take on any object that is not in the nature of mere awareness. This is one meaning of non-dualism. There is, of course, a great divergence of opinions among Tibetan thinkers on the question of whether or not this concept of reflexive awareness is ultimately tenable.

There is, however, another meaning of non-dualism. For example, as stated above, when the yogi's direct, transcendent awareness of the ultimate truth is said to be non-dualistic, dualism in such a context is understood in terms of a sense of separateness between the subject and its object. On this view, it is believed that all our ordinary cognitive states such as our everyday sensory perceptions and our thoughts operate invariably through a dualistic mode of engagement. In these cognitive acts the sense of distinctness between the subject and its object is always present such that our experience tends to reinforce the belief in the existence of an objectively real, independent world 'out there'. Even the cognition of emptiness does not escape from this pervasive experience of dualism as long as the cognition remains on the level of thought. This is because thoughts by nature engage with their objects through concepts, and to a large extent through language as well. When one's insight into the truth has reached a profound level where it has become spontaneous, direct and non-conceptual then the experience is said to be free of dualism. This is then the second meaning of non-dualism.

The non-conceptual awareness of the ultimate truth is said to be non-dualistic in yet another sense. Such an experience is said to be also non-dualistic in that within its sphere there is no perception of any multiplicity for it is single-pointedly fused with emptiness. It is characterized as being in a 'meditative equipoise', thoroughly and exclusively absorbed in the experience of this mere absence, which is an absolute negation of intrinsic existence. From the perspective of such an experience, there is no 'origination', no 'cessation', no 'non-existence', no 'existence', no 'coming', no 'going', no 'identity' and no 'difference'. In brief, the world of multiplicity has been thoroughly calmed by the expanse of emptiness. This then is the third meaning of non-dualism. **Tsongkhapa** suggests that it is crucial to distinguish between a dualistic perception on the one hand and the dualistic manner in which an object is cognized on the other. For example, he would argue that an intellectual cognition of emptiness being a thought is necessarily dualistic but that does not entail that emptiness is perceived by that mind in a dualistic manner. So far as the perception is concerned, even to that thought it will appear only as a mere negation, i.e. a simple absence, rather than some extraneous objective entity.

One critical area of debate amongst Tibetan thinkers pertains to the question of how the Buddha's omniscient mind, which is non-dualistic in every sense, can be said to perceive the everyday world of multiplicity. Many argue that the buddhas do not perceive the world of multiplicity for this world is an illusion created by the deluded mind. When the mind is cleansed of its delusions, all perceptions created by such delusion must necessarily cease. Yet others like Tsongkhapa argue that the world of multiplicity cannot be accepted as mere illusion, for suffering sentient beings do exist and the buddhas must surely have compassion towards these beings. If this is true, the buddhas must perceive the everyday world of cause and effect, pain and pleasure, and so on. It is that the buddhas perceive the world totally free of any perception and assumption of the intrinsic existence of things.

Further reading

Lopez, D. (1987) *The Study of Svatrantika*, Ithaca, NY: Snow Lion, 192–217.

THUPTEN JINPA

nothingness

Nothingness as *xu* is an important concept, with affinity with **non-being** and **emptiness**. Vacuity

is generally regarded as being short of total nothingness. It also describes a mental state, a mind emptied of specific content (fixated particulars). It is discussed by **Zhuangzi** and **Xunzi**: an uncluttered mind can best comprehend all. The classic analogy is the hollow (inner) centre of the bamboo that imparts to the bamboo its very (outer) strength. It is the mark of the gentleman.

WHALEN LAI

numerology

There are many uses of mystical numbers in China. The following example is included here to explain how the Birth Series of the **Five Elements** works. Instead of '**magic squares**', this involves a cross:

$$6$$
$$1$$
$$9 \quad 4 \quad 10/5 \quad 3 \quad 8$$
$$2$$
$$7$$

There is a number '10' that overlaps with or rather surrounds the 5 in the centre. In this scheme, the numbers of Heaven are 1, 2, 3, 4, 5; they are found in the inner circle. These are prior and they start the process of change. The Earthly numbers are 6, 7, 8, 9, 10. These are in the outer circle. They are subsequent and they complete the process of change. The inner circle gives birth; the outer circle completes. North is placed at the bottom of the page following Chinese custom.

This diagram explains the birth sequence of the Five Elements which coincides with the succession of the seasons. For example, the numbers 1 and 6 make 7, which equals Water: direction North, solstice Winter. It is born of the 4 and 9 combination [to its right], total 13 which is the number for Metal: direction West, equinox Autumn, and so on. In this scheme, the sequence is Clockwise:

6	1	8
9	10/5	3
4	7	2

This scheme maps the Chinese cosmos; it puts a green dragon to the East, a red bird in the South, a white tiger in the West and a black tortoise to the North. It is what led the Emperor to wear green in spring; to play a particular musical note in the summer; to withdraw and retire in the autumn; and to schedule executions in the cruel months during the death of winter and in the north. It informs the placement of houses, the dishes served at festivals, the choice of colours on seasonal occasions and so on. It has poets seeing phoenixes on the western slopes, it leads painters to imagine emerald isles on the eastward sea, myth-makers to find black-skinned people in the north, and mystics to locate five gods in five colors in five organs within their bodies. And when all these things worked as they were supposed to, there was indeed harmony in the heavens, peace on earth and joy in men's heart.

Further reading

Graham, A. (1980) *Yin-Yang and the Nature of Correlative Thinking*, Singapore: Institute of East Asian Publications.

Henderson, J. (1984) *The Development and Decline of Chinese Cosmology*, New York: Columbia University Press.

WHALEN LAI

Nursi, Said

b. 1876; d. 1960

Theologian and philosopher

Often called 'Bediuzzaman' (the wonder of the age) Said Nursi was a Kurd who lived in a very difficult time for devout Muslims in Turkey; he both fought for his country and tried to resist the pressures of the Turkish state when it became fiercely secular. His writings consist mainly of theological works dealing with the Qur'an, and they have been enthusiastically taken up by many in Turkey itself and farther afield. Although his work is mainly theological, it is imbued with interesting philosophical ideas, and he was clearly influenced by the Ishraqi movement, which saw light as the basic ontological principle and sought to reinterpret our everyday world in terms of light and that which is lit up. He is close to **Sufism**, although he is rather suspicious of its subjectivity and antinomianism, and is clearly attracted to the significance of the personal relationship which we can establish with God, as mediated through Islam. The mixture of theory and vivid description in his writing has made him a popular writer, and he follows in the tradition of trying to reconcile Islam with modernity. One of the tasks which he set himself was showing how there is no incompatibility between Islam and science, and so Islam is just as relevant to modern life as any other system of belief.

See also: revival of Islam, theories of

Further reading

Mardin, S. (1989) *Religion and Social Change in Modern Turkey: The Case of Bediuzzaman Said Nursi*, Albany, NY: State University of New York Press.

OLIVER LEAMAN

Nyaya

In India, one of the six orthodox Brahminical schools (***darshana***) accepting the **Vaisheshika** pluralist and realistic ontological scheme and chiefly concerned with questions of logic and epistemology. Major works and theorists include Gautama Akshapada (*c.*150 CE), the author of the fundamental *Nyaya-Sutra*; Vatsyayana (350–400 CE) author of the *Nyaya-Bhashya*; Uddyotakara (550–600 CE) author of the *Nyayavarttika*; Vachaspati Mishra (800–50 CE) author of the *Tatparyatika*; Jayanta Bhatta (850–900 CE) author of the *Nyayamanjari*; Bhasarvajna (900–50 CE) author of the *Nyayasara*; and **Udayana** (1050–1110) author of the *Atmatattvaviveka, Kiranavali, Lakshanavali* and *Nyayakusumanjali*.

Naiyayika theorists espouse a form of direct realism and maintain that whatever exists is in principle humanly knowable. Cognitions (*jnana*) are always and only the manifestation of mind-independent entities, including perceptible universals and relations. A cognition is not intrinsically reflexive but requires a subsequent cognition (*anuvyavasaya*) to reveal it.

Perception (*pratyaksha*) is the basic form of knowledge and it is assumed to be reliable. It is of two kinds: primary sensory awareness in which specific characteristics are not explicitly recognized for what they are (*nirvikalpaka-pratyaksha*) and awareness saturated by concepts and language (*savikalpa-pratyaksha*) which identifies the given with a higher degree of specificity.

The former can never be invalid, but the second stage may become infected by error. Cognitive errors may result from defects in the sense-organs but they are more usually attributable to environmental factors, such as when a limpid crystal is misidentified as red due to reflections from proximate red objects. It is a feature of the Naiyayika's direct realism that he rejects attempts to analyse perceptual illusions by appeals to putative entities such as sense-data allegedly intervening between consciousness and what is given.

In the case of shell mistaken for silver, there is visual perception of a shiny white surface upon which revived memory traces of silver are superimposed due to similarity of the surfaces of the objects. That this is possible is illustrated by cases such as awareness of a seen but untouched piece of ice as cold. The content of erroneous cognition always derives from experience of something real and has an objective basis. Error results from a miscombination of what have been data of awareness with the immediate objective support of the present experience. Non-correspondence to immediate reality is manifested in unsuccessful activity and valid cognition in success.

Inference (*anumana*) is dependent upon the deliverances of perception and testimony and is of three types:

1 *purvavat*: this is based on resemblance to what has been previously seen as when we see smoke on a hill and infer the presence of fire on the basis of prior experience. In other words, this is inference from cause to effect.
2 *sheshavat*: inference from effect to cause as when heavy rain in the hills is inferred from swollen rivers.
3 *samanyatodrishta*: inference from general correlation as well as reasoning from the empirically given to the non-empirical as in the case of the inference of the existence of God on the basis of the considerations that the universe, because partite, is an effect and effects are invariably concomitant with causes adequate to their complexity.

A fully elaborated inference has the form:

Thesis: There is fire (*sadhya*: probandum) on the mountain (*paksha*).
Warrant: Because there is smoke (*hetu*:warrant).
Exemplification: Wherever there is smoke, there is fire (*vyapti*); like a kitchen (*sapaksha*) unlike a lake (*vipaksha*).
Application: There is smoke on the mountain.
Certain conclusion: There is fire on the mountain.

The instrumental cause in an inference is awareness of the pervasive concomitance (*vyapti*) of the probandum (*sadhya*) and the justificatory warrant (*hetu*); no smoke without fire. The operation of the inference involves a reflection that the pervasion occurs in the subject term (the mountain possesses smoke which is pervaded by fire). Since the major premise is explicitly inductively derived from experience, the Indian syllogism does not attract the empiricist objection that the conclusion cannot be deduced from the major premise since the major premise cannot be known to be true unless the truth of the conclusion is already known.

Conditions of a successful inference include citation of a positive supporting example (*sapaksha*) exemplifying the pervasive concomitance (*vyapti*) of warrant and probandum in a sample locus (*sapaksha*, the kitchen) other than the actual subject of the inference and citation of a negative supporting example (*vipaksha*, the lake) illustrating the constant absence of both warrant and probandum in another locus.

For these theorists, a statement of invariable concomitance is an inductive generalization free from falsifying counter-examples. An inferential form (termed *kevala-anvayin*) in which there is no *vipaksha* is valid. Such a case would be 'This is nameable because it is knowable.' There can be no *vipaksha* because according to the Nyaya system everything that is knowable is also expressible.

There is another valid form termed *kevala-vyatirekin* in which there can be no *sapaksha*. A typical instance is: the living body cannot lack a soul, for if it did, it would not be alive. The argument is that if a body (*paksha*) has the unique property of being alive (*hetu*) it must possess a soul (*sadhya*), otherwise it would not be alive. Since the *hetu* is a unique property of the *paksha* and since the presence of *sadhya* and *hetu* mutually imply each other, there is no *sapaksha*.

Nyaya philosophers provide many and various accounts to the ways in which inference may be vitiated due to the specious nature of the warrant (*hetvabhasa*). Basically, the warrant may be contradictory, unproved or doubtful. Examples of some of the major instances are:

1 Deviating or uncertain (*vyabhichara; anaikantika*): This covers a multitude of sins: the presence of the *hetu* in the absence of the *sadhya*, such as the attempt to infer smoke from the presence of fire since there can be fire without smoke. Also, where the universal applicability of the warrant renders it too general to justify the thesis; for example, 'there is fire on the mountain, because it is knowable'. Knowability occurs in the absence of fire so the *vyapti* fails. Lack of *sapaksha* (agreeing example) and *vipaksha* (disagreeing example): 'sound is eternal because it resonates'. Finally, there are cases where no negative exemplification is available because everything is included in the subject (*paksha*): 'all things are transient because they are knowable'. The warrant occurs in the absence of the probandum as well as in its presence, for example, that village is holy because it is close to the Ganges'. Proximity to the Ganges occurs in *vipaksha* cases such as corpses.

2 Unestablished (*asiddha* or *svarupa-asiddha*): the warrant is not true of the *paksha*, for example,

'the lake has fire because it has smoke', where mist is mistaken for smoke. Usually applies in cases where the *hetu*'s occurrence in the *paksha* is open to doubt.

3 Contradictory (*viruddha*): where the warrant is standardly the sign for the absence of the probandum or where it occurs in the *sapaksha* and the *vipaksha*.

The Naiyayikas recognize testimony of trustworthy people (*apta*) as a valid means of knowledge. The Vedic scriptures are valid because they have a divine author who is omniscient. Circularity is avoided because the existence of God is inferentially established.

The existence of the per se non-conscious self (**atman**) is inferred as that which has to be the enduring substrate of the transitory episodic cognitions, sensation and emotions with which it is contingently linked. Liberation (*moksha*) from rebirth (**samsara**) is negatively described as a state of irreversible non-consciousness in which the self is disjoined from contingent experiential features characteristic only of the embodied, transmigratory condition. Happiness is not an unalloyed ideal, since it is always pervaded by fear of its loss. The profound realization of this unappetizing truth is the soteriological goal of philosophical reflection. A person who grasps the truth will achieve release, understood as *apavarga* – escape – on dissociation from the physical body at death. Unhappily, this is also a state of unconsciousness, sentience being a property of carnal existence.

Further reading

Athalye, Y. and Bodas, M. (eds) (1974) *The Tarka-Samgraha of Annambhatta*, Poona: Bhandarkar Oriental Research Institute.

Matilal, B. (1971) *Epistemology, Logic and Grammar in Indian Philosophical Analysis*, The Hague/Paris: Mouton.

—— (1985) *Logic, Language and Reality: An Introduction to Indian Philosophical Studies*, Delhi: Motilal Banarsidass.

—— (1986) *Perception*, Oxford: Oxford University Press.

Potter, K. (ed.) (1977) *Encyclopedia of Indian*

Philosophies, Vol.II: The Tradition of Nyaya-Vaisheshika up to Gangesha, Delhi: Motilal Banarsidass.

CHRIS BARTLEY

Nyingma school

Although the Tibetan religious 'historians' present a linear account of the evolution of the Nyingma school by associating it with such historical figures as the Indian masters Padmasambhava, Shantarakshita, and the translator Vairochana, the history of its emergence as a distinct school within Tibetan Buddhism appears to be rather complex. As the name Nyingma, which literally means the 'old school', itself suggests, the identification of Nyingma as a distinct lineage of Tibetan school appears to be retroactive. Furthermore, the distinction between the 'old' and 'new' pertained explicitly with the phases during which many of the Indian Buddhist texts, especially those that belong to the Vajrayana teachings were translated into Tibetan. Therefore, in its early stages of development philosophy appears to have played a marginal role, if at all. It is in the person of the great master **Longchen Rabjampa** that Nyingma developed a systematic philosophy of its own, especially with its so-called distinct Dzokchen standpoint (see **Dzokchen thought**).

In so far as the scholarly study of Buddhist epistemology and Madhyamaka philosophy of **emptiness** are concerned, Nyingma appeared to have shared a similar lack of serious engagement with these disciplines. In fact, it was not until the end of the nineteenth and the beginning of the twentieth century that a major Nyingma figure, namely Ju Mipham Namgyal Gyatso (1847–1912), wrote substantive treatises based on the Indian Madhyamaka and epistemological writings. However, at least from the Longchenpa's time onwards, the Nyingma school have subscribed to the general Tibetan premise that the standpoints of the Prasangika-Madhyamaka represent the apex of the Mahayana philosophical thinking. Key figures in the development of this school are amongst others, the Indian master Padmasambhava (eighth century CE), the translator Vairochana (eighth century CE), Rongzom Pandita (eleventh century), Longchen Rabjampa, Jikme Lingpa (1729–98) and Ju Mipham Namgyal Gyatso.

Further reading

Karmay, Samten (1989) *The Great Perfection: A Philosophical and Meditative Teaching of Tibetan Buddhism*, Leiden: Brill, chs 7–8.

THUPTEN JINPA

One, Guarding the

Laozi has high praise for the One. To quote:

> Heaven graced by the One becomes clear.
> Earth graced by the One becomes tranquil.
> Spirits graced by the One become divine.
> Valleys graced by the One become full.
> Myriad things flourish because of it.
> Kings and barons rule well because of it.
>
> (*Laozi* 39)

Keeping to the One becomes a technique of **meditation** in Daoism. This blended into early Chinese Buddhist insight meditation where 'guarding the intention' was also 'keeping to the One'; it is so that the mind would not waver. It later entered into early Chan through the fourth patriarch, Daoxin, who taught 'keeping to the true mind and not ever wavering'. It involves being watchful of the positive flow of the pure mind into all the everyday senses. The method is identified with the *ekavyuha samadhi* in the **Awakening of Faith in Mahayana** based on original enlightenment. When the One is thus grafted onto **buddha nature**, it becomes a meditation focusing on the transcendental element within.

Further reading

Chang Chung-yuan (1970) *Creativity and Taoism: A Study of Chinese Philosophy, Art, and Poetry*, New York: Harper & Row.

Chappell, D. (1983) 'The Teachings of the Fourth Chían Patriarch Tao-hsin (580–651)', in L. Lancaster and W. Lai (eds), *Early Ch'an in China*

and Tibet, Berkeley, CA: Asian Humanities Press, 89–130.

Kohn, L. (ed.) (1989) *Taoist Meditation and Longevity Techniques*, New York: State University of New York Press.

WHALEN LAI

One Thread, The

The 'one' that 'threads' through **Confucius**'s teaching is that principle guiding all moral behaviour. It is identified with *zhongshu* (loyalty and forgiveness), and conscientiousness and altruism. *Zhong* is directed at oneself: it is being truthful to (centering upon) the benevolence in the mind-heart. It seeks naturally to actualize itself. *Shu* is directed at others: it is the extension of that same benevolence into caring for others. The two words also sum up the Golden Rule: 'Do not do unto others', says Confucius, 'what one would not wish for oneself'. Christian critics prefer the positive formulation by Jesus; Chinese defenders find the negative form more deferential and more considerate. But there is also a positive form of it in the *Analects*: 'To complete/fulfill in others what one would complete/fulfill of the self'. This line, however, has to do more with the demanding task of self-perfection and other-perfection. The rule informs the 'one thread' of *zhongshu*.

Mencius later attacked Mohism so strongly that the connection between Mohism and Confucianism has become obscured. After all, since no man in his right mind ever desires to be harmed,

Mozi could well have derived his formula for universal love from that idea (see **love in Chinese philosophy**). Thus to love another is to benefit the other as he desires to be benefited. But Mencius would insist that Mozi's thesis is antithetical to the Confucian norm.

One would expect that proponents of one Golden Rule would recognize easily another. But apparently that is not so. Mencius and Confucians thereafter would not treat Mozi kindly. The Nestorian translation of Jesus's Sermon on the Mount in a tract titled *The Lord on Charity* in Chinese during the Tang dynasty did not make so smooth a connection. Abraham the Elder was new to China and might not have known the *Analects* or the Chinese language well. He might have relied on a Chinese aide. At any rate 'Love thy neighbour as thyself' came out in a negative form and in long hand: 'What you need [is also] what others seek. What others need is also what you seek. If others ask of you and you give them, that is departing from evil.'

Further reading

Fingarette, H. (1979) 'Following the 'One Thread' of the Analects', in H. Rosemont and B. Schwartz (eds), *Studies in Classical Chinese Thought, Journal of the American Academy of Religions*, Thematic Issues 47(3): 373–406.

Tu Wei-ming (1989) *Centrality and Commonality: An Essay on Confucian Religiousness*, Albany, NY: State University of New York Press.

WHALEN LAI

Onishi Hajime

b. 1864; d. 1899

Philosopher

Critical and systematic philosopher who argued against positivism, evolutionism and materialism. Onishi was born in 1864 in Okayama. After graduating from the Christian university Doshisha, he entered the philosophy department of Tokyo University. Among other lectures, he attended those by **Inoue Tetsujiro** (1855–1944). In 1889,

he graduated and then worked as a teacher of philosophy and ethics at the school which later became Waseda University. In 1898, Onishi went to Germany to deepen his philosophical studies but fell so ill that he returned to Japan the next year, and died soon after.

Though influenced by Protestantism and much impressed by Kant (1724–1804), Onishi remained an independent mind, not only criticizing what he regarded as obscurantism and a confusion of facts and norms, but also what in his opinion was Kant's ethical formalism. Arguing against Inoue Enryo (1859–1919) and 'obscurity as a characteristic of philosophy', he emphasized the importance of logical consistency and epistemological critique, stressing that 'it is precisely philosophical speculation that must not be lacking in logic'. Also, he pointed out the relevance of logic as an independent philosophical discipline. Attacking Kato Hiroyuki's (1836–1916) evolutionist arguments against human rights, Onishi asserted that they were untenable since Kato had failed to distinguish between is and ought and natural and moral law. Relying on Kant, Onishi argued that man, because of his moral autonomy, possesses dignity and hence human rights. As to his criticism of Kantian ethics, Onishi raised the question of whether Kant's theory was realistic, particularly whether it did not neglect the relevance which feelings and desires have for human behaviour. Also, he expressed doubt with regard to Kant's postulate of a synthesis of virtue and happiness which, in Onishi's opinion, was not based on logic but hope. Onishi also criticized intuitionist, authoritarian, hedonist and altruist ethics. Finally, he argued against ideologically oriented philosophy. This is reflected for example in his critique of the *Imperial Edict on Education* and of Inoue Tetsujiro's commentary on the *Edict*.

Onishi's writings include *Hokon shisokai no yomu* (The Essential Duties of the Contemporary Intellectual World) (1889), in which he observed that Japan is a market place for an exchange of Eastern and Western culture; *Ryoshin kigen ron* (On the Origin of Conscience), his master's thesis of 1890; *Rinri shiso no nidai cho ryu* (Two Main Trends in Ethical Thought) (1895), in which he pointed out that 'the idealists' had not yet succeeded in clarifying the notion of a moral ideal, while the 'naturalists' had not been able 'to explain the *why* of moral oughtness'; *Ronrigaku* (Logic) (1893), in which he discussed deductive and inductive logic and compared Aristotelian and Buddhist theories of **logic**; *Seiyo tetsugaku shi* (History of Western Philosophy) (1895); and *Rinrigaku* (Ethics) (1903), in which he critically analysed different ethical systems. Perhaps Onishi's approach to philosophy is best expressed by a programmatic assertion he made in his *Hokon shisokai no yomu*: 'I feel that the first essential duty of the intellectual world is to compare, judge, criticize all thought, Western and Eastern, to recognize its trends and values. I venture to suggest that it is not necessary to be radical or conservative'.

See also: Buddhist philosophy in Japan, post-Meiji; philosophy of human rights, Japanese

GREGOR PAUL

orientalism

The term 'orientalism' has been in use for some time, but it really became important after Edward Said used it to characterize an intellectual approach to the Middle East of which he disapproved. Orientalism is a matter of treating the Orient as a single cultural entity with a distinctive and unique way of thinking and acting. Said criticized the ways in which Western scholars romanticized the East, and produced a body of knowledge which was part of the imperialist enterprise. Often this involved treating the East as inferior to the West, or premodern, or in many ways superior because more 'spiritual'. There can be no doubt that orientalism has led to a great deal of knowledge about the East, but it is problematic when it imposes on that knowledge cultural assumptions which misrepresent the situation. One of the features which Said criticizes is the ways in which people often reify apparent differences between ethnic and religious groups to argue that there are essential differences between them and their corresponding thought.

Orientalism has not really been considered a great deal when it comes to philosophy, but it certainly characterizes the subject. In Islamic philosophy, it occurs in the common belief that Islamic philosophy owes its existence and structure to Greek philosophy, as though it would have been impossible for Muslims to have developed philosophical ideas by themselves. It is also the case that Western thinkers have imposed on their understanding of Islamic philosophy the leading principles of Christian and Jewish thought, and have treated Islamic philosophy as though it was part of the same problematic. Sometimes it is, of course, but there is no reason to think that this is always the case, and the influence of orientalism in philosophy has often been to contrast an analytical Occident with a mystical Orient. In fact, this stereotype has often been internalized by thinkers from the East themselves. Yet these broad distinctions are caricatures of the very varied forms of thought which exist in both East and West, and it is of course often entirely arbitrary what counts as the East and West. Many of the Islamic philosophers worked in what is today Spain, while it has recently been argued that several twentieth century Western thinkers such as Heidegger were thoroughly influenced by Asian ideas. An examination of Indian philosophy, for example, makes it clear that there was just as much interest in logic and scientific method in India as has developed in Europe and the Americas. There is also a long and deep tradition in the West of mystical and religious thought, so the idea that there is a fixed distinction between the Eastern and Western mind is far too crude to bear even slight examination.

Further reading

Bhabha, H. (1994) *The Location of Culture*, London: Routledge.

Said, E. (1978) *Orientalism: Western Conceptions of the Orient*, London: Routledge and Kegan Paul.

Turner, B. (1994) *Orientalism, Postmodernism and Globalism*, London: Routledge.

OLIVER LEAMAN

orientalism: existential anxiety

Kierkegaard uncovered the psychology of angst (anxiety) as an objectless fear; it is objectless because it is so total as to threaten the fundamental being of man. By the time an anxiety is turned into a fear, it would have lost much of its punch and evolved into a mere problem. The authentic mood for a 'sickness unto death' is more than that; it is that which Heidegger takes to be **non-being** and Sartre to be death itself. Tillich enumerates it into a trinity of material 'fate and death', moral 'guilt and condemnation' and existential 'futility and meaninglessness'. Weber depicted Chinese philosophy and religion as anything but anxiety-driven. According to Weber, the **sage**, Daoist or Confucian, is mystically tuned into the world.

That token of a romantic Orientalism remains. Lin Yutang is perhaps the most consummate popularizer of this Chinese aspect of the Chinese psyche. He captures well the light-heartedness of *dao* and Zen, quite different from D.T. Suzuki's presentation. But Chang Taiyan, an imprisoned revolutionary who discovered Buddhism in prison, would read the same material differently. He rediscovered **Zhuangzi** as a man haunted by the frailty of the self and the prospect of death, a refreshing departure from much current appreciation. This strand has now been picked up in China by a Nietzschean existentialist reappraisal of the darker moods of the Neo-Daoist thinkers Ruanji and Xikang.

Meanwhile in the United States, Thomas Metzger, assimilating the New Neo-Confucian scholarship of Tang Junyi and Mou Zongsan, went against Weber and wrote on the Confucian sense of dilemma and the need to 'escape from that predicament'. But ironically, the anxiety is not due to sin and the uncertain state of grace; and the escape is not from the weight of freedom and responsibility. It is rather the reverse, a sense of cosmic optimism that underwrites the 'epistemological optimism' about human ability to be perfectly cognizant of the goodness of Heaven. It is that attitude which becomes problematic when faced with an imperfect reality. That mood of deep but melancholy concern has been well captured by Zhang Hao. It roughly translates into 'being worried about one's capacity' internally and being 'appropriately anxious about the state of the world (especially the nation)' externally.

Further reading

Chang Hao (1987) *Chinese Intellectual in Crisis: Search for Order and Meaning 1890–1911*, Berkeley, CA: University of California Press.

Lai, W. (1991) 'Tillich on Death and Suffering: A Key to Buddhist-Christian Dialogue', *Ecumenical Studies* 28(4): 566–80.

Lin Yu-t'ang (1959) *From Pagan to Christian*, Cleveland, OH: World Publishing.

Metzger, T. (1977) *Escape from Predicament: Neo-Confucianism and China's Evolving Political Culture*, New York: Columbia University Press.

Moore, C. (ed.) (1967) *The Chinese Mind: Essentials of Chinese Philosophy and Culture*, Honolulu, HA: East-West Center Press.

Tillich, P. (1942) *Courage to Be*, New Haven, CN: Yale University Press.

WHALEN LAI

orientalism: origin of Chinese culture

James Legge, the missionary and scholar who returned from China to hold the first chair of Sinology at Oxford, could still remember those who speculated on how China might be one of God's people who went east after the fall of the Tower of Babel. He had to write against a contemporary scholar who held that the Chinese writing is just a far-flung strand of the cuneiform script and her culture a Pan-Babylonian extension. Others held China to be a sideline that had spun off from the Indian end of the Indo-Europeans. Sinocentric pride meant that the Chinese scholars held out for a clear and unique, separate and distinct East Asiatic genesis. The discovery of Peking Man was the proof of China's prehistoric distinction. The recent discovery of a prehistoric Caucasian mummy on the Silk Road, indicative of early East/West contact, has reopened the old debate between the indigenists and the diffusionists.

National pride would see a single centre of a proto-Chinese culture, with traditionalists pushing for identifying a Xia culture at the neolithic site of

Erlitou. A recent report of a 60,000 year-old site in the Yangtse basin (away from the Yellow River cradle) might force still more revision. Evidence of a number of prehistoric local cultures, some surviving even to this day, favours not a singular root but heterogenous beginnings. Even the idea that major Han cultural traits were embedded in the late Shang archaeological findings is challenged by a thesis involving a dipolar dialectic of 'eastern Yi and western Xia'. (The Yi are the 'Eastern **barbarians**'; they migrated west to 'central Xia' and rose to become the Shang rulers.)

Occident and Orient still do not see eye to eye on this matter of Chinese origin. European scholars are more open to 'outside' presence; Chinese scholars prefer a 'single-line' development, and Japanese scholars have done well with a modified 'dipolar' compromise. Insider and outsider still find it hard to look at China objectively, whether it be in the dawn of history or in recent times.

Further reading

Giradot, N. (1999) 'Ritual Combat During the 'Babylonian Era of Sinology', in N. Giradot (ed.), *The Victorian Translation of China–James Legge: Missionary Tradition, Sinological Orientalism, and the Comparative Science of Religions in the 19th Century*, Berkeley, CA: University of California Press.

Madsen, R. (1995) *China and the American Dream*, Berkeley, CA and Los Angeles: University of California Press.

WHALEN LAI

orientalism: rational West, aesthetic East

A byproduct of the East–West encounter is the presentation of Western thought as rational while Chinese thought is more intuitive and aesthetic. This reduces modern Western thought to being singularly rational and analytical, predicated upon a subject–object dualism which then requires some theoretical resolution of its own. Against that, Chinese thought is credited with knowing a 'dynamic, harmonious, functioning whole'. What that indicates is that when different cultures meet,

some thinkers routinely see only those aspects which emphasize the differences, not the similarities. This is because we too often remake others after our own image or else into our antithesis. Currently, Roger Ames and David Hall are the most diligent in calling attention to the fundamental differences in Chinese and Western thought. From the Chinese side, we find similar emphasis on the antithetical. For example, much is made of the ideology of the **Yijing**. If life giving birth to life is the basis of change, then in this self-generative universe, the aesthetics of 'natural creativity' and 'dynamic becoming' is hailed as its distinctiveness.

WHALEN LAI

Ox-head School

The rage among 'higher critics' of early Chan, the Ox-head school is alleged by Yanagida Seizan to be the real inspiration behind the *Platform Sutra*, dedicated originally to its own Sixth Patriarch before it was coopted into being a record of **Huineng**. Mount Ox-head was the home base of its lineage head, a contemporary of Daoxin (the so-called Fourth Patriarch) who taught 'Pacifying (resting assuredly on the one true) Mind'. Mount Ox-head was in close proximity to the home base of the Sanlun (Three Treatises, Madhyamika) school that was known for undercutting all opponents' theses. The Ox-head school apparently applied that same methodology to undercut Daozin. In a treatise about *adrishti* (holding no view), a teacher of enlightenment instructed a novitiate (abiding with) conditionality thus:

> What is mind? What is pacifying mind?
> Posit no mind. Don't try to pacify.
> That is how it is pacified

The retrieval of the negative Ox-head dialectics is important, but the 'higher criticism' may have conflated skilled rhetoric with hard and fast dogmatics.

Further reading

Dumoulin, H. (1988) *Zen Buddhism: A History, India and China*, vol. 1, New York: Macmillan.

MacRae, J. (1986) *The Northern School and the Founding of Ch'an Buddhism*, Honolulu, HA: University of Hawaii Press.

Tokiwa, G. (trans.) (1973) *A Dialogue of the Contemplation-Extinguished*, Kyoto: Institute of Zen Studies.

WHALEN LAI

P

Padartha

Padartha means 'referent of a term': in Indian philosophical contexts it refers to 'category of existence', but in ordinary usage it may simply mean entity or thing. *Padartha* is often defined as that which is existent (*astitva*), knowable (*jneyatva*) and nameable (*abhidheyatva*). According to the important **Vaisheshika** theorist Prashastapada (*c*.500–50 CE), the *padarthas* include *dravya* (substance), *guna* (quality), ***karma*** (activity/motion), *samanya/jati* (universal/class-property), *vishesha* (individuator) and *samavaya* (inherence). The realistic and pluralistic syncretistic Nyaya-Vaisheshika school adds *abhava* (absence), a category interpretable as the referents of negative expressions.

The basic category substance (*dravya*) is defined as that in which a quality or activity inheres. This category encompasses the eternal, causeless non-sensible atoms (*paramanu*) underlying the manifest forms of earth, water, fire and air; the atmosphere or vehicle of sound (*akasha*), time, space, souls and minds. Atmosphere, space and time are non-atomic, non-composite, ubiquitous and eternal. The existence of atoms is deduced from the decomposability of macroscopic objects. The process of division must halt at some point on pain of infinite regress (*anavastha*). The atoms in combination are the irreducible uncaused causes of the impermanent, originated and effected components of the material environment.

The twenty-four *gunas* are colour, taste, smell, touch, number, size, separateness, conjunction, disjunction, remoteness, proximity, weight, fluidity, viscidity, sound, cognition, pleasure, pain, desire, aversion, intentional effort, merit, demerit and inherited tendencies. They are construed as particulars or unrepeatable instances individuated by their bearers. That is to say, the blue of a given blue pot is a different individual property from the blue of a given blue cloth. The weight of an elephant differs from that of a leaf. Merit and demerit are properties specific to individuals. Relational properties such as conjunction, disjunction and number which involve several related substances are understood as distributed over them. 'Blueness' is a universal, not a quality.

Motion inhering in macroscopic bodies is of five types: upward, downward, bending, stretching and locomotion. A universal or repeatable generic property (*samanya*) inheres or is inseparably present in the individual (*vyakti*) substances, qualities and motions comprising a class of entities (*jati*). It is defined as single (*eka*), eternal (*nitya*) and occurrent in many (*aneka-vritti*). These self-existent and indestructible mind-independent constituents of the universe are ontologically distinct or separable from their instances or possessors (*vyakti*; *dharmin*). They account for the fact that numerically distinct entities may be brought under a single concept and word and be treated as members of the same class. Universals are hierarchically arranged in accordance with their comprehensiveness. There is an all-inclusive supreme universal 'reality' (*satta*) which inheres in all substances, qualities and motions. It confers existence upon impermanent and causally dependent entities. Next in the hierarchy appear substance-ness, quality-ness and motion-ness. Lower universals (such as cowness and potness) have both an inclusive and an exclusive function.

A universal is involved both in the inclusive cognition 'cow' that recurs with reference to different individuals and in the cognition 'this cow differs from another one', which is mutually exclusive in respect of those individuals. (This is the orthodox interpretation of the statement in *Vaisheshika-Sutra* 1.2.3. to the effect that depending on the mode of cognition (*buddhi-apeksha*) the universal appears as a general or specific factor.) Universals may feature in the content (*vishayata*) of perceptions. The perception of concrete entities involves a simple awareness of universals as qualifiers (*visheshana*) even if their recurrent character is not recognized. Not every general term stands for a real universal. Examples of the latter are earthness, colour-types, types of movement, natural kinds and established artifact types. Other kinds of generality, such as 'being a cook' are classified as imposed characteristics (*upadhi*).

Features of universals differentiating them from impermanent entities in the categories of substance, quality and motion include their being self-existent (*svatmasattva*); their being neither effects nor causes; their not being the substrata of other universals or individuators (*vishesha*); their always being logically and linguistically classified as attributes (**dharma**). They cannot be treated as concrete objects (*artha*) or substrata (*dharmin*).

Individuators (*vishesha*) are the ultimate factors of individual identity occurrent in eternal non-composite substances (the atoms of earth, water, fire and air; mind; the unitary substances atmosphere, space and time) accounting for the irreducible identities of these entities. They are also the principles of individuation in the case of depersonalized, disembodied liberated individual selves (*jiva*).

Samavaya or inherence is a dyadic relation of 'asymmetrical inseparable presence in'. It is internal (*ayutasiddha*) and obtains between part and whole, substance and quality, motions and substrate, universals and their individual instances, individuators and eternal substances. *Samavaya* may be understood as the cement of the universe. Inherence is contrasted with contact or conjunction (*samyoga*) which is an external, separable (*yutasiddha*) relation. Later theorists formulate a third category, that of 'self-linking' relations

(*svarupa-sambandha*) where it is the essence of one or both of the terms to be related to the other.

Absences, the referents of negative expressions, are counted as existent, knowable and nameable. This is plausible when one considers that negative numbers are real numbers, that there are negative states of affairs such as doing or saying nothing and that the notion of negative facts is intelligible. There are four kinds of absence: prior absence (*pragabhava*) which expresses the relation between cause and effect in the context of the **asatkaryavada** theory of causation; the termination of what had existed (*dhvamsa*); absolute non-existence or impossibility (*atyanta-abhava*); reciprocal absence or difference (*anyonya-abhava*). Absences are held to have identity (*svarupa*). What is usually meant, except in the case of *atyanta-abhava*, is the identifiable absence of some positive entity and relates to something possible but unexemplified at a given time and place. As such it may be cognitively fruitful.

Further reading

Athalye, Y. and Bodas, M.S. (eds) (1974) *The Tarka-Samgraha of Annambhatta*, Poona: Bhandarkar Oriental Research Institute.

Halbfass, W. (1992) *On Being and What There Is*, Albany, NY: State University of New York Press.

Hiriyanna, M. (1993) *Outlines of Indian Philosophy*, Delhi: Motilal Banarsidass.

CHRIS BARTLEY

PAI-CHANG *see* Baizhang

Pak Un-sik

b. 1859; d. 1926

Political philosopher and historian

Pak Un-sik was one of the leading thinkers of the enlightenment movement in Korea at the end of Choson dynasty (see **Enlightenment, Korean**). He was a political philosopher, historian and novelist. After the Japanese annexation of Korea and the March First Independence Movement against Japanese colonialism, Pak Un-sik went to China and participated in the independence movement for Korea, and continued to write for and about Korea. He wrote several important books, including a history of Korea, as well as papers on Confucianism. His thought was progressive and modern, but also included some Confucian elements, since he had been educated in the Confucian tradition. Pak's Confucianism was relatively progressive, since it was based on the philosophical school of Wang Yangming. His thought was also influenced by the modern Chinese thinker, Kang Yuwei.

According to Pak Un-sik, the mind is the ruler of the body and the source of good and evil. When the mind is pure and bright, it correctly determines what is right or wrong. This idea is basically rooted in the Confucian idea of mind and virtue. On the basis of this idea of pure mind, he believed that it is the will of Heaven to oppose the feudalistic social system in Korea and to oppose the immoral Japanese colonialism in Korea.

Pak was greatly influenced by the French Enlightenment and Western political and scientific ideas. He tried to synthesize Eastern and Western thought. For example, according to Pak, the Western idea of evolution, which states that the fittest and healthiest survive while the weakest are eliminated, and the Confucian ethics of **humaneness** and justice can be harmonized because only wise, strong and courageous persons can possess such a morality.

Pak Un-sik believed that scientific knowledge and a fine national ethics are the two most important elements in building a strong independent nation. He thought that the development of progressive knowledge was essential for the elimination of the feudalistic social system and gaining independence of Korea from Japanese imperialism. He envisioned a free, modern, democratic society for Korea.

Further reading

Choi, Min-hong (1980) *A Modern History of Korean Philosophy*, Seoul: Seongmoon Sa, 222–6.

Lee, P. (ed.) (1996) *Sourcebook of Korean Civilization*, vol. 2, New York: Columbia University Press, 418–22, 426ff.

YONG-CHOON KIM

Pali Canon

The Pali Canon is the collection of Theravada Buddhist texts produced in Sri Lanka in the first century BCE, after a process of oral transmission over a period of at least three centuries. It consists of three 'baskets' (*ti-pitaka*):

Vinaya-pitaka (The Basket of Discipline, regulations for monks and nuns):

1 *Sutta-vibhanga*. This is an analysis of violations of the basic codes of rules (*Patimokkha*) for monks (227 rules) and nuns (311 rules). Monks should avoid murder; theft; sex; dishonesty; alcohol; eating after noon; dancing, music and entertainment; garlands, perfumes and unguents; soft beds, gold and silver.

2 *Khandaka*. Regulations (*kamma-vachana*) of organization of the monastic order (*sangha*).

3 Appendices including some history of the order.

Sutta-pitaka (The Basket of Discourses of Gotama Buddha):

1 *Digha-Nikaya*, Collection of Long Discourses.

2 *Majjhima Nikaya*, Collection of Middle Length Discourses.

3 *Samyutta Nikaya*, Collection of Connected Discourses.

4 *Anguttara Nikaya*, Various Discourses.

5 *Khuddaka Nikaya*, including the **Dhammapada** (ethical treatise); *Suttanipata* (various verses); *Theragatha* (accounts of early monks' enlightenment); *Therigatha* (accounts of early nuns' enlightenment); *Jatakas* (547 edifying 'birth stories' of previous lives of the Buddha, exemplifying moral conduct; and the *Buddhavamsa* about twenty-four previous Buddhas.

Abhidhamma-pitaka (systematizations of material presented more discursively in the Sutta-pitaka):

1 *Dhammasangani*

2 *Vibhanga*

3 *Dhatukatha*

(The above refine the analysis of personality into the five components (*khandha*), listing and characterizing the basic elements (*dhammas*) of phenomenal existence).

4 *Puggala-pannatti*, deals with character types and levels of spiritual development.

5 *Kathavatthu* (Points of Controversy), defends orthodox views against over two hundred opinions held in other schools of Buddhism.

6 *Yamakas* (Book of Pairs), to prevent terminological ambiguity.

7 *Patthana*, refines articulation of interdependent genesis (**pratitya-samutpada**) specifying the links between psycho-physical phenomena.

These texts represent the earliest layer of Theravada Buddhist writings and are claimed to be the actual words of the Buddha, Siddhartha Gotama. But since the Buddha probably lived in what is now Northeast India in the second half of the fifth century BCE and probably spoke another Middle Indo-Aryan Prakrit called Magadhi and since the canonical texts were not committed to writing in Pali, and thus to an extent stabilized, until the first century in Sri Lanka, some scepticism is appropriate. The Pali texts appear archaic and their often repetitive nature is indeed a sign of their origins in oral transmission of the teaching. But they are not primitive and often seem to reflect puritanical, world-renunciatory reform movements. While some of the material is of considerable antiquity and may go back to the Buddha Gotama, much of it reflects the various interests and beliefs of later generations of monks who were charged with spreading the message.

Editions and translations of the canon are published by the Pali Text Society.

CHRIS BARTLEY

PEI-TU *see* Beidu

perception, Indian theories of

The majority of Indian philosophers regarded perception (*pratyaksha*), whose causal conditions are contact between sense-organs (*indriya*) and objects (*artha*), as the fundamental means of knowledge (*pramana*) and the primary source of information about the world. Perceptual deliverances are the basis of inference (*anumana*).

From the second half of the fifth century CE, most non-Buddhist Indian philosophers draw a distinction between two types of perception or two stages in the perceptual process:

nirvikalpaka-pratyaksha, which is translatable according to context as 'indeterminate', 'non-constructive', 'pre-conceptual', 'non-qualificative' and 'non-classificatory'.

savikalpaka-pratyaksha; 'determinate', 'judgmental', 'conceptual', 'qualificative' and 'classificatory'.

Nirvikalpaka perception is usually understood as the bare awareness of the whole object in which the characteristics that are specific to it and those which it shares with others things are not explicitly identified for what they are. The later school of **Navya-Nyaya** defines it in terms of its not involving a grasp of the qualifier (*visheshana*) and qualificate (*visheshya*) relation between locus (*dharmin*) and properties (**dharma**).

The distinction between the two types of perception was elaborated in the realist traditions in response to the theories of the Buddhists **Dignaga** and **Dharmakirti**. Dignaga maintained that reality consists of momentary particulars (*svalakshana*) which elude linguistic and conceptual apprehension. He says that perception, produced by sense-object contact, is the mere awareness of an object unassociated with attributes (*visheshana*). He defines perception as a cognitive state that is free from conceptual construction (*kalpana*). The latter is the association of names, class-properties, quality-terms, etc. with the given. For Dignaga, language and conceptual construction are inextricably linked: 'Speech is born out of conceptual construction and conceptual construction is born out of speech.' When we apply a word expressing a class-property, we are probably wrongly superimposing a concept upon the momentary particulars. Substance-language and the imagination of persisting entities involves investing the particulars with a spatio-temporal continuity that they do not possess. Proper names generate the illusion of enduring personal identity. The organization of reality in terms of 'constants' cannot represent it truly.

The **Advaita** Vedantin Mandana Mishra (650–700 CE), who is followed in this respect by Prakashatman (c.900 CE), appears to follow Dignaga in maintaining a distinction between perception qua pure sensation and conceptualized, propositional awareness. 'First, there is a non-conceptual perception (avikalpaka-pratyaksha) relating to the bare object (artha-matra). The ensuing constructive cognitions (vikalpa-buddhi) comprehend particularities (vishesha).' Difference (bheda) is not given in perception but is a mental construct (vikalpa) subsequent to the perception of the mere object in its true nature. The absolute Brahman, the supreme universal, which is pure, undifferentiated and non-specific reality (san-matra; satta) is given in non-conceptual awareness.

By contrast, the followers of the **Nyaya** and **Vaisheshika** schools held that whatever falls under the categories (**padartha**) of substance (dravya), quality (guna), motion (karma), universal (samanya), particularity (vishesha), inherence (samavaya) and absence (abhava) is an ultimately real constituent of the universe. They maintain that there is some sort of correspondence between thought and language and mind-independent reality. They denied that a cognition of an object under categorical determinates involved conceptual construction – the addition or superimposition of mind-independent attributes – but was a case of a more complete, analytical representation of things as they really are.

The Vaisheshika philosopher Prashastapada (c.500 CE) refers to a type of perception that is the simple intuition (alochana) of the proper form (svarupa) of an entity. It is the apprehension of an undifferentiated whole arising from cognition of its specific universals. This mere observation with respect to objects with such features is perception as a means of knowing which effects a cognition which has substance and other categorical determinates as its object. Prashastapada thought that the object of this basic intuition was an entity, inclusive of its characteristics which are elements of the informational input derived from the 'given', taken as an undifferentiated (avibhaktam) whole. But the generic feature is not grasped qua generic feature and its other features are not grasped qua

specific features since that sort of identification requires comparison with other things. This initial stage in the perceptual process is a form of non-relational cognition in which the features of the entity are not grasped as qualifiers or attributes (visheshana).

This preliminary stage is followed by another type of perception: 'From the contact of self and mental organ there arises perception in dependence upon the qualifiers of generic property, specific features, substance, quality and action.'

That Prashastapada is distancing his position from that of Dignaga is obvious. For the Buddhist, the determinates of cognitions are subjective constructs imposed upon the given and constructive cognition is not perception. The realists' discussions centre around the question of what must belong to the unnoticed informational input if sense is to be made of the manifest content of a perceptual cognition. For a realist like Prashastapada, the determinates are objective constituents of reality and their conceptual correlates are not inter-subjective fictions. At the initial stage in the perceptual process, what will be identified as attributes are perceived together with the locus in which they occur. At the subsequent stage they are identified as located qualifiers (dharma and visheshana) distinguishable from their possessor (dharmin) which is the qualificate (visheshya) in the cognition.

The **Purva Mimamsa** realist **Kumarila Bhatta** (fl. 650) draws Prashastapada's distinction between types of perception more explicitly and introduces the terms nirvikalpaka and savikalpaka. He says that there is an initial non-qualificative perception which is mere observation of the thing itself and comparable to the cognitions of babies and the mute. For Kumarila, one aspect of non-qualificative perception is its lying below the level of linguistic expression. (In this he is followed by the Naiyayikas Jayanta Bhatta (850–900) and Bhasarvajna (900–50), who hold that whatever is grasped by perceptual judgment was also grasped by the prior non-constructive perception: the difference is that in the judgmental state what is seen is verbalized in propositional form. At the initial stage, neither the generic nor the specific features are knowingly experienced, only the pure form of the individual (vyakti) which is their locus (adhara) is apprehended. Still, the generic and specific features are components in the informational input albeit not explicitly identified as distinct elements. The object is not cognized in its precise individuality but we do form an idea of a determinate entity. It is not cognized under its generic aspect until we have definite ideas about its similarity to other objects. The subsequent cognition by which the object is analytically cognized along with its attributes is also to be considered as perceptual.

The Prabhakara Mimamsaka Shalikanatha (900–50) holds that non-qualificative perception relates to the generic and specific aspects. He says that there is an initial perception which produces an apprehension of the mere proper forms of substances, universals and qualities. He means that substances, etc. are cognized as they are in themselves and not in relation to other entities. The object of this perception is not a bare particular (*svalakshana*), since there is clear presentation of the forms such as the universal. Nor is the object only the generality (*samanya*), since difference is also directly cognized. Consequently, the initial perception yields an understanding of the general and specific aspects. But since there is no comparison in relation to other entities, they are not cognized as such. The generality is identified on the basis of its recurrence in many things and the specifics are identified on the basis of their absence from other things. It is not possible to identify the recurrence or the absence without comparisons. Still the general and specific features have been grasped as existents. The ensuing qualificative perception, in which thanks to memory impressions the perceived object is compared with other things, apprehends them as such. The distinct individuality of things is not known through their mere being but requires awareness of other things with other properties. At the qualificative stage, the qualifier–qualificate relation (*visheshana-visheshya-bhava*) between the universal and other properties (*dharma*) and their locus or possessor (*dharmin*) is understood.

Shalikanatha's views seem to have influenced Prashastapada's commentator Shridhara (991 CE) who says that indeterminate perception does not only grasp the generality, for difference also appears in it. Nor does it only grasp momentary particulars since there is cognition of generic form

and also because at the later stage there is comparison when other individuals are encountered. But although it grasps both the generic property and specific features, one does not understand the object as differentiated under the description 'This is the generality' and 'This is the specific' since there are no comparisons. The generality is discriminated through the apprehension of its recurrence and the specific from its absence. But their proper forms are aspects of the perceptual input since that process is not dependent upon comparisons. Non-qualificative perception does not involve the qualifier–qualificate relation between the generality, the differentia and the individual since that presupposes awareness of distinctions absent from it. The ensuing qualificative stage cognizes the generality and differentia as such.

In his lengthy refutation of the Advaita Vedantin view that reality as non-differentiated (*nirvishesha*) pure being is given in every perception while differences are not, the eleventh century theistic **Vishishtadvaita** theologian and philosopher **Ramanuja** insists that his opponents have no authoritative sources of knowledge (**pramana**) for the alleged non-differentiated reality. He contends that all *pramana*-based cognitions are necessarily of particularized and differentiated entities possessing identifiable features. Were reality non-differentiated, our accredited means of knowing could not operate. Ramanuja argues that *nirvikalpa-pratyaksha* must refer to what is differentiated since it is the causal condition of recognitional comparison (*pratisamdhana*) with similar entities at the subsequent classificatory stage where the repetition or recurrence (*anuvritti*) of shared properties is explicitly realized. Every cognition arises in virtue of some differentiating feature, and is expressed as 'this is a such and such' rather than the indeterminate 'this is a something'. The form of the verbalization itself reflects the nature of the referent. The difference between the two forms of perception – non-classificatory and classificatory – consists in the fact that the recurrence of, for example, the generic structure common to cows is not grasped in the apprehension of the singular object.

Further reading

Matilal, B. (1971) *Epistemology, Logic and Grammar in Indian Philosophical Analysis*, The Hague: Mouton.
—— (1986) *Perception: An Essay in Indian Theories of Knowledge*, Oxford: Oxford University Press.

CHRIS BARTLEY

perennial philosophy

Perennialists are those who hold that at heart all religions are the same, being informed by a mystical core of some direct unitary experience. Chinese history may or may not cast light on such an issue. The 'unity of the three teachings' is a popular catch phrase in Ming intellectual history; many supported it, and one group even called itself the 'Three (are) One Teaching'. (This school is still active today, even enjoying a revival in the People's Republic of China.) Proponents all assume that there is a common spiritual core to all three teachings. **Buddha nature**, human-nature and Dao-nature are aligned and seen as essentially seeking the same goal; any discursive difference is deemed superficial. A common judgment consequential to that is the familiar saying that, theory aside, in the area of practice, 'the three teachings all teach men to do good'. Out of that came the non-denominational 'Societies for Doing Good Together' that helped set up volunteer social welfare programmes. Where theoretical reason cannot settle (the perennialist claim), practical reason seems to find some measure of consensus.

Further reading

Berling, J. (1980) *The Syncretic Religion of Lin Chao-en*, New York: Columbia University.
Bharati, A. (1976) *The Light at the Center: Context and Pretext of Modern Mysticism*, Santa Barbara, CA: Ross-Erikson.
Katz, S. (ed.) (1978) *Mysticism and Philosophical Analysis*, New York: Oxford University Press.
—— (1983) *Mysticism and Religious Traditions*, Oxford: Oxford University Press.

Stace, W. (1961) *Mysticism and Philosophy*, London: Macmillan.

WHALEN LAI

perfect man, the

A key concept in Islamic mysticism is that of the perfect man (*al-insan al-kamil*). He is the paradigmatic example of all the virtuous moral qualities, which in turn represent the qualities which exist in God, albeit to a far stronger degree. What the concept of the perfect man represents is the greatest possible human development of understanding, compassion, charity and spiritual growth, and he serves as the bridge or mediator between humanity and what is higher than humanity. His task is to help others to cross the gap which exists between this world and the next world, the latter being the world of reality, and as one might expect the perfect man is often identified with the prophet, or the Prophet Muhammad, who has exactly this role. He is often also identified with the friends of God, the *wali*, since they enjoy a special relationship with the deity. This is because they are a microcosm of the perfection and balance of God himself, a state which enables them to remain unaffected by anything except God himself. The friend of God or the perfect man is the *barzakh* (isthmus, bridge) between us and God; he shares some of our qualities and also some of God's, and through his character he is able to lead us from where we are to where God is. He links the microcosm (us) with the macrocosm (the universe as a whole as an aspect of what is higher).

We have tremendous scope for independent action, in the sense that we can shape our lives in a variety of different ways. We can become perfect, or we can become corrupt and evil. But we are more than just a part of the universe, we are the spirit of the universe, because the universe has no meaning apart from its human beings. God brought us into existence with the intention that we should know him, and apart from us there is nothing in the universe which is capable of knowing him in the right sort of way, in accordance with his names. Everything in the universe may be said to reflect God in its particular way, and imperfect human beings can reflect and grasp him in a limited way. The perfect man is able to comprehend him through an awareness of how everything celebrates its origins in and dependency on God.

We should not think of our links with God as something very difficult to establish or understand, since we are all born with the natural tendency to worship him. He has set us up in the world to worship him, so it would be surprising were he to make this difficult. In the words of a famous *hadith* (saying of the Prophet), 'Every child is born with the original disposition, and then its parents make it a Christian, a Jew, or a Zoroastrian'. These religious systems are regarded as rather idolatrous, since these religions are not as monotheistic as Islam, in the opinion of the Prophet. What the mystic seeks to do is to return us to where we started, to our original disposition to feel a simple trust in the goodness and power of a single God. The sufis have a concept which they call *dhikr*, or remembering, to characterize the aim of their spiritual work (see **Sufism**). The influence of the deity shines on the world like light, and what we take to be reality is the result of this light. What we should do to understand the genuine nature of the world is to immerse ourselves as individuals in the macrocosm, through understanding that we are merely aspects of an immensely greater and divinely constituted whole. At the same time we should not seek to dismiss the diversity and particularity of our experience, since these are also aspects of reality, and they also have a divine source. Combining these two ways of looking at the same reality is not simple and involves the use of the allegorical and frequently difficult language of the mystic.

We need to incorporate these two ways of thinking in our efforts to understand, since it is not sufficient to immerse ourselves in the contemplation of God, nor is it enough to lose ourselves in the contemplation of the world of generation and corruption, including ourselves. We need to bring these seemingly opposed ideas into a synthesis, and the difficulty of doing this explains the paradoxical and puzzling terminology which characterizes the language of Sufism. If we are to use *kashf*, or unveiling of what confronts us, we may eventually arrive at the core of the truth. Yet our language to describe this tends to be limited to describing what happens at the superficial level of our experience, not as descriptive of what lies beneath the veils of that experience. What the Perfect Man tries to do is show us how to move from what we think we know to the basis of knowledge itself, and the language of prophecy is significant in that it helps to guide us in the appropriate direction, using ideas with which we are familiar but extending them gradually into the unfamiliar, until we manage to move over onto a deeper and more significant form of thought.

See also: Ibn al-'Arabi

Further reading

Leaman, O. (1999) *Brief Introduction to Islamic Philosophy*, Oxford: Polity.

OLIVER LEAMAN

perfection

There is a basic assumption in Christian anthopology that 'to err is human'. Chinese philosophy likewise understands very well how 'even sages make mistakes'. Chinese philosophical anthropology concentrates not on sinful people but rather on perfectible humanity, which causes no end of misunderstanding between present-day Augustinians and present-day Mencians. The Jewish tradition would be more understanding of the Mencian rhetoric, since Job was 'perfect and upright' in his time and context. There is no human–divine divide in Buddhism, and so in Mahayana there are six or ten *paramitas* (perfections) to pursue. The goal being higher, they are far more taxing than the eight noble paths of early Buddhism. For example, the perfection of *dana* (giving, charity) is not just being kind, generous and charitable; it means imitating the Buddha. In his second last rebirth, the Buddha gave up his kingdom, home, family, spouse and finally his own life as part of his trial as a sannyasin. Daoists lay out similar stages of ascent to becoming immortal, while the Neo-Confucians (see **Neo-Confucianism, concepts**) chart their inner progress with the *Doctrine of the Mean* and the outer kingship with the *Great Learning*.

One of the ironies of medieval piety and philosophy is that in a period when people were materially and temperamentally 'down', the aspiration and hope for perfection was 'up'. In the waning days of the medieval Buddhist era, an unstable ('up and down') time, direct access to the highest perfection became even more readily available.

In the Confucian tradition, the word '**sage**' came into focus with the Master; it was set on top of a ranking of perfection; and way above the 'gentleman' which was no easy or mean achievement. Throughout the Han, 'sages' were rare occurrences and sagehood not something a person could 'learn' and then 'become'. The idea that sagehood can be acquired through study – that 'to learn' is 'to learn to be a sage' – is a formula initiated by **Zhu Xi** in the Song dynasty. Before that, one could learn but not become a sage; or one could do neither. The Daoists, having a similar hierarchy of perfecting beings leading up to the highest, the immortal, also designed a path of that ultimate perfectability of self. Not many actually live long enough to achieve it. Actual immortals, like living sages, were rare. So it became part of the literary convention, in poetry as in hagiography, to relate close encounters with immortals and missed opportunities of becoming one.

The Buddhist tradition has long institutionalized authority and routinizes (away) charisma so that only those intent on mysteries who exist on the fringe would claim buddhahood. Otherwise, the six or ten *paramitas* or bodhisattvic perfections provided a more reasonable scheme for classifying 'saints' in their midst. A person known for his charity would be credited with the perfection of giving; an ascetic would be credited with the perfection of forbearance, and a master healer would be called Medicine Master incarnate. Perfections were multiple and varied; they were not homogeneous. It is a rare honour to be ranked at the seventh rank, a benchmark for realizing **emptiness** (insight into the unborn). Deference alone would prevent any men – kings excepted – from freely claiming full buddhahood, and attainment of the tenth rank is reserved only for the Samyaksambuddha, the fully enlightened one.

The situation changed in late medieval times. Chan claimed full Buddhahood for everyone,

possibly, as Garma Chang (Chang Chen-chi, 1920–) once noted about *satori*, conflating or short-circuiting *prajna* at the seventh with *jnana* at the tenth stage, initial awakening with omniscience. Daoists also democratized their pathway to immortality; it became more a 'state of mind' (emboding the *dao*) instead of actual physical longevity, a 'soaring insight' instead of rising on a cloud to the sky. Confucianism was the last to catch up with this good news of the perfectability of man. Now, anyone can be and should be a sage, and suddenly the innocent line in the *Great Learning* about extending knowledge so it may 'end in the ultimate good' – a teleology or virtue – was emphasized. The word 'to end or stop' took on the taste of Buddhist *samatva* ('stop', the calming of the senses) and the 'end good' took on the ascent to 'the highest good'. The 'bright virtue' that was the public light of social virtue finding the self-vindication of acclaim now becomes the perfect light within perfecting itself without.

See also: Noble Eightfold Path; spiritual ladders

Further reading

Garma Chang (1971) *The Buddhist Teaching of Totality: The Philosophy of Hwa Yen Buddhism*, University Park, PA: Pennsylvania State University Press.
Ray, R. (1994) *Buddhist Saints of India: A Study of Buddhist Values and Orientations*, Oxford: Oxford University Press.
Ricour, P. (1965) *Fallible Man*, trans. C. Kelbley, Chicago: Regnery.

WHALEN LAI

persons (theory of)

Tibetan philosophers, on the whole, do not appear to have felt the need to develop any systematic constructive theory of persons. Interestingly, the question of what is the person especially in the aftermath of the Madhyamaka's rejection of the intrinsic existence and identity does not appear to have been perceived as problematic. However **Tsongkhapa** remains an exception. He does address in some depth the two questions that are critical to a theory of persons: 'what is the person?'

and 'in what sense can it be said to exist?' Tsongkhapa is aware that unless there is a coherent notion of person, and also unless one accords a robust status of existence to persons, many of the ethical concepts like responsibility, accountability, and many of the soteriological questions become problematic. He is also keenly aware of the need to account for many of the empirical facts of our existence, which appear to suggest the presence of some kind of enduring subject. In other words, Tsongkhapa accepts that a coherent theory of the self or person must be able to account for such phenomenal facts as individuality, continuity and recollection.

The challenge for Tsongkhapa is to develop a theory of person that does not compromise the rejection of any concept of an underlying, un-changing self yet, at the same time, gives coherence to much of our conventional notions of personal identity. Simply stated, Tsongkhapa asserts that person is the intentional object of our instinctual sense of 'I' or the self, that is, our natural 'I'-consciousness. He argues that this person is a mere 'construct' that is contingent upon physical and psychological constituents of the individual. For example, if we are to examine the nature of a single instance of thought 'I am', we will find that it occurs only in reliance upon one or a composite of our physical and mental constituents. All thoughts such as 'I am going', 'I am happy', 'I am sick', etc. relate either to a physical or a mental state of ourselves. And the status of these elements being the basis of our designation of the thought 'I am' is relative. Yet underlying all this must be a presupposed unity that is the object of our natural sense of self. Tsongkhapa appears to be suggesting that personal identity is that unity that is presupposed when talking about the life of an individual, be it oneself or another person. In so far as this is so, Tsongkhapa's theory of person can be characterized as non-reductionist.

As can be inferred, Tsongkhapa's theory of person is heavily influenced by his theory of designation and its underlying nominalist ontology. It is also related to the Madhyamaka principle of dependent origination in that the identity of the person is contingent upon many factors and events. Based on the above theory of person Tsongkhapa attempts to account for the occurrence of our

natural 'I'-consciousness. He argues that there are both a 'general identity' (*nga tsam po pa*) and 'particular' identities (*khye par du jhe pa'i dak*) to an individual. For example, a single person can be a man, a Tibetan, a monk, a scholar and so on. These are all identities specific to particular contexts. However, underlying all this there must lie an identity that is simply the object of that individual's thought, 'I am'. This, he suggests, is the general identity of the individual. Tsongkhapa then develops a complex theory of memory that explains how it is this 'general' identity that connects the various stages of an individual when he or she experiences past recollections.

See also: pratitya-samutpada

THUPTEN JINPA

philosophical dictionaries and Japanese philosophy

From the very beginning of the Meiji era (1868–1912), Japanese scholars, to master the basics of the philosophical craft, consciously produced transla-tions, surveys and dictionaries. Translations like those of Rousseau (1712–78), J.S. Mill (1806–73) and Herbert Spencer (1820–1903) even influenced contemporary socio-political discourse, but the impact of the surveys and dictionaries was more or less restricted to academic business. Outstanding among the surveys were **Nishi** Amane's (1829–97) *Encyclopedia* and Nakamura Masanao's (1832–91) 'Outline of Western Culture'. In 1881, **Inoue** Tetsujiro (1855–1944) and Ariga Nagao (1860–1921) edited the *Tetsugaku jii* (Philosophical Dic-tionary), a dictionary based on William Fleming's *Vocabulary of Philosophy, Mental, Moral and Metaphysical* of 1856. In 1905, Miyake Setsurei (1860–1945) and Tokutani Toyonosuke edited *Futsu jutsugo jii* (Com-mon Technical Terms of Philosophy). In the same year, Tomonaga Sanjuro (1871–1951) published the *Tetsugaku jiten* (Philosophical Dictionary). In 1912 Inoue, together with other scholars, brought out a new edition of his dictionary of 1881. From 1909 until 1912, the *Tetsugaku daijiten* (Great Dictionary of Philosophy) appeared, and in 1922 Tomiyama Wakichi and others published another dictionary. Thus, the tools for professional philosophy were provided at an early stage.

Today there exist numerous philosophical dictionaries, many of which focus on philosophy of Western provenance. General encyclopedias also include articles on philosophy. Information about Confucianism, Buddhism and other kinds of non-Western philosophy is provided by an equally large number of special dictionaries and, again, within general encyclopedias. The English language Buddhist dictionaries compiled by Japanese scholars belong to the best such works available in English. Among them, the *Japanese–English Buddhist Dictionary*, published by Daito Shuppansha in 1979 is especially valuable.

There are of course also dictionaries which include both entries on so-called Western philosophy as well as on non-Western philosophy. An example is provided by the *Tetsugaku jiten* (Philosophical Dictionary) first published in 1971. Though this book comprises some 1700 pages it may be considered a handy one-volume-work useful for a large range of interested readers. Apart from general dictionaries, there exist also specialized dictionaries such as *rinrigaku jiten* (dictionaries of ethics).

See also: Meiroku zasshi

GREGOR PAUL

philosophy of human rights, Japanese

In the 1860s in Japan, human rights (*jinken*) questions, especially the question of whether government should be based on the idea of universal rights, became a much debated issue. The most important reason for these discussions was the question of whether the strength and welfare of Western powers was a function of their – alleged or actual – acknowledgement of human rights. Another reason was simply a disgust with despotism and, in the words of **Fukuzawa** Yukichi (1835–1901), 'worm-like servility'. Controversial human rights discourse continued until the ultimate victory of ultra-nationalism and imperialism in the 1930s made advocating human rights

impossible. After the Second World War, human rights became an important topic once more.

From around 1870, a large number of scholars, politicians and journalists engaged in the discourse. Thus different personal inclinations and views came into play. The influence of different theories on the discourse added to the diversity of the respective approaches, methods and results. For example, while certain scholars adduced relevant theories of Rousseau (1712–78), Mill (1806–73), and Kant (1724–1804) – but also **Mencius** (372?–289? BCE) and **Xunzi** (313?–238? BCE), in particular their justification of tyrannicide – to support human rights ideas, others relied on Social Darwinism, Shushigaku and Tennoism to argue against them. In such cases, the dispute was also about human rights as natural rights, which were often referred to by the Sino-Japanese metaphor of *tempu* (endowed by heaven). For instance, 'natural freedom (of man)' was rendered *tempu no jiyu* (heavenly endowed freedom). Also, actual political development, namely constitutional problems, the quest for the right form of government (democracy, absolute monarchy, constitutional monarchy and so on), and party strife had an impact on the discourse. As its name indicates, the Jiyu minken undo (Freedom and People's Rights Movement) in the 1870s and 80s fought for freedom (*jiyu*) and people's rights (*minken*), whereas other groups opposed it. More often than not, however, politicians employed the philosophy of human rights as ideological means to pursue private and elitist interests. With respect to these parties in the Movement for Freedom and People's Rights, critics spoke ironically of 'upper class people's rights' and 'former *samurai*(s') people's rights'.

But there were also cases in which the idea of naturally endowed human rights served as justification for rebellion and uprising, as for instance in the Fukushima incident of 1882 in which some thousand people protested against economic exploitation by the local government. Foreign politics too determined the discourse. Western discrimination against Japan and Japanese was utilized to demand racial equality but also employed to support nationalism. Unequal treaties forced on Japan, anti-immigration politics in the United States, and the refusal by Western powers to accept the Japanese proposal that the principle of racial equality be anchored in the covenant of the League of Nations were examples of this discrimination. It is a feature of the complexity of the human rights discourse especially from the 1860s until the 1930s that it was only in part expressly philosophical. Often, its philosophical relevance is only implicit, while the explicit discussion is on people's (not human) rights, the system of government, or such specific topics as capital punishment, torture, racism, *burakumin* (outcasts in Japan), freedom of speech, universal suffrage or the situation of women.

Among those who significantly contributed to the philosophical human rights discourse were Kato Hiroyuki (1836–1916), Nakamura Masanao (or Nakamura Keiu, 1822–91), **Nishimura** Shigeki (1828–1902), **Nishi** Amane (1829–97), **Tsuda Mamichi** (1829–1903), Fukuzawa Yukichi (1834–1901), Nakae Chomin (1847–1901), Yano Fumio (1850–1931), Baba Tatsui (1850–88), Ueki Emori (1856–92), **Onishi** Hajime (1864–1900), **Kotoku** Shusui (1871–1911), Yoshino Sakuzo (1878–1933), **Inoue** Tetsujiro (1855–1944), post-Second World War Marxists, Tanaka Kotaro (1890–1974) and Kaneko Takezo (1905–87).

Kato was the son of a *samurai*. He attended a local *samurai* school, and then went to Edo to engage in Western learning. Like Nishi and Tsuda, he was employed at the Bansho shirabe sho where he devoted much time to the studies of German books, and like them he joined the Meirokusha. Later he became president of Tokyo University and served in high government posts. In 1862, Kato published his *Tonarigusa* (Grass in the Neighbourhood) arguing for the universal validity of human rights as natural rights. His *Kokutai shinron* (A New Theory of National Polity) of 1875 included the sentence, 'The Emperor and the people are not different in kind: The Emperor is a man, the people too are men', thus stating the equality of men in an almost provocative way. Also, he deplored 'the vulgar [Japanese] tradition of servility'. After close studies of evolutionism, Darwinism and German statist theory, however, Kato radically changed his view and tried to suppress the book. In 1882, he wrote *Jinken shinsetsu* (A New Theory of Human Rights), in which he argued that man is not endowed with rights but acquires them, or receives them from the state

(*kokufu jinken*). He pointed out that rights are gained by way of competition and according to men's strength, with the outcome of this struggle determined by the universal law of the survival of the fittest. Kato tried to further strengthen his argument by using the rhetorical device that in recent years, because of scientific progress, the idea of human rights had become outdated in the West too. In 1893, Kato published *Kyosho no kenri no kyoso* (The Struggle for the Rights of the Strongest), of which he also prepared a German version, *Der Kampf ums Recht des Stärkeren und seine Entwicklung.* Kato's materialist and empiricist approach is also apparent from his *Kirisutokyo no gaidaku* (The Poison of Christianity), published in 1911.

Kato's critique of the idea of universal human rights was immediately countered by Yano Fumio (or Ryukei), Baba Tatsui and Ueki Emori. In 1882, Yano wrote *Jinken shinsetsu bakuron* (Refutation of the New Theory of Human Rights), pointing out that Kato had failed to distinguish between 'is' and 'ought', or natural and moral law. Yano also argued that one must distinguish between moral and legal laws, with moral laws being basic. As for instance Nishi Amane too, Yano supported his argument by stating that moral and legal laws can be violated, whereas natural laws are inviolable. In the following year, Baba published his *Tempu jinken ron* (On Natural [Heavenly Endowed] Human Rights) in which he criticized Kato's materialist and biological view of historical progress, and Ueki wrote *Tempu jinken ben* (Defence of Natural [Heavenly Endowed] Human Rights). Already in 1879, Ueki had published *Minken jiyu ron* (On People's Rights and Liberty) and expounded the idea of naturally endowed human rights. Another of his tracts was entitled *Genron jiyu ron* (On the Freedom of Speech and Opinion). As Kosaka Masaaki (1900–69) observed, Baba's and the others' notion of natural human rights was itself not simply a concept of existing facts but in some respect a normative notion.

Baba was a remarkable personality. After studying at the school established by Fukuzawa Yukichi, he twice went to England. After his return to Japan, he not only made himself a name as a scholar of human rights but also engaged in politics and criticized the government's conservative position. In 1885 he was imprisoned, but was released in 1886. Baba then emigrated to the United States where (in 1888) he wrote *The Political Condition of Japan, Showing the Despotism and Incompetency of the Cabinet and the Aims of the Popular Parties.*

Members of the Meirokusha like Nishi, Fukuzawa, Tsuda and Nakamura Masanao argued in several ways for human rights, especially the rights to dignity, freedom and life. As to human dignity, they deplored the 'servility' of the Japanese, variously blaming Shushigaku, **Kokugaku** and the feudalistic shogunate for this feature, and in many speeches and publications strongly emphasizing that man should have self-respect, and should not be forced into self-denigration. Sugi Koji (1828–1917), one of the less famous members, stated 'the responsibility' of the state 'to protect the lives of the people [and] to avoid injuring individual dignity'. Ueki Emori, a representative of the People's Rights Movement, in his *Minken jiyu ron* not only stressed governmental obligations, but also pointed to the self-responsibility of the people asserting that not to pursue their natural right to freedom is 'a great disgrace to themselves'.

Further, the right of the people to oppose, and even topple, a despotic government was invoked. In this connection, not only respective Western theories were used. Japanese scholars also referred quite often to Confucius's humanism and Mencius's (and at least implicitly Xunzi's) doctrines that the people are more important than the ruler, that government should be for the welfare of the people and that tyrannicide is justified. For instance, Tsuda Mamichi, though rather critical of Shushigaku and Yomeigaku, regarded Confucius's (551–479 BCE) and Mencius's teachings as still relevant for the promotion of human rights. Influenced by Christianity and Mencius, he held that 'all men' are 'descended from divinity' and hence ought be honoured, thus implying that the 'divine descent' of man is the source of a human dignity which requires that all human beings treat each other humanely. The word 'divine' must be taken in a loose sense. In the *Mencius*, the equivalent is the metaphorical 'heavenly'. Tsuda further affirmed the 'Chinese' view that 'the people are the foundation of the nation'. In his argument against torture and the death penalty, he referred to the 'old Chinese proverb' that 'it is better not to apply the law at all than to kill the innocent'.

Tsuda's extensive and detailed argument against torture and the death penalty is an exemplary argument for the rights to dignity, freedom and life. In his criticism of the death penalty, he makes the following points. (1) Nobody has the right to take human life for no man has 'the power to give life'. The death penalty is actually murder. (2) Punishment is for the purpose of correcting men. Hence the death penalty is actually no punishment. (3) The death penalty does not prevent people from 'misdeeds', cannot be justified as a means for revenge (which is 'properly forbidden' in a time 'of civilisation and enlightenment'), and is no acceptable instrument to protect the society against criminals. Tsuda's arguments are not only very rational and systematic but also impressive in their humane flavour.

As indicated, Nakamura Masanao also argued for human rights and against severe punishment. However, he did so mainly by translating Western writings and commenting on them. His translation of Mill's *On Liberty* was especially influential, and his 'Outline of Western Culture' an excellent introduction into Western philosophy. In this survey, he approvingly mentioned Michel de L'Hôpital as a fighter for religious freedom and Jean Bodin (1530–96) as a defender of civil liberty. Quoting from George Buchanan (1506–82), who argued against cruel punishment and justified tyrannicide, Nakamura remarked that Buchanan 'is honoured as a penetrating scholar' with modern views.

As to the realization of human rights by means of democratization, however, most Meirokusha members warned against what they regarded as untimely haste and radicalness, arguing that Japan and the Japanese were not yet sufficiently prepared for unrestricted democracy. Fukuzawa even took a somewhat elitist stance. A counter-argument was that the English had entered democracy at a stage of even lower socio-political development and enlightenment than the Japanese had reached by the Meiji era. Arguments and counter-arguments reflected different positions within what could also (besides being described as philosophy of human rights) be called a philosophy of moral norm and cultural tradition. The main results in this field were that tradition – as mere tradition – cannot justify its preservation; that the value of a tradition depends on its morality; and that necessary changes should be undertaken carefully, gradually, in a natural way, and by taking into account the particular conditions of the times. The last point refers to, for example, customs which simply because of their strength hinder abrupt changes.

Some representatives of the People's Rights Movement like Baba and Ueki, however, were more strident in their attitude. Ueki, who criticized Fukuzawa's position, even argued in favour of a *constitutional* right to resistance and rebellion. The most influential among these scholars and activists, however, was Nakae Chomin.

Chomin, whose original name was Nakae Tokusuke, was the son of a lower-ranking *samurai*. Born in the town of Kochi, he attended a local school. Chomin became well acquainted with Shushigaku and Yomeigaku but also engaged in *rangaku*. When he was about eighteen years old, he was sent to Nagasaki to study French. In 1871 the government ordered him to go to France, where he developed a particular interest in philosophy and became a convinced materialist and human rights advocate. He returned to Japan in 1874. Among Chomin's major achievements is his partial translation of Rousseau's *Social Contract* in 1882 which, like Mill's *On Liberty*, became one of the fundamental texts of human rights philosophy in Meiji Japan. Because of his admiration for the French advocate of enlightenment, Chomin earned the nickname 'the Eastern Rousseau'. Of similar importance was his *Rigaku kogen* (An Exploration of the Principles of Philosophy). When, in 1900, Chomei learned that he had only a short time to live, he wrote his philosophical diaries *Ichinen yuhan* (One Year and a Half) and *Zoku ichinen yuhan* (Sequel to One Year and a Half). In the first work, he asserted that there existed no philosophy in traditional Japan, namely no critically rational and principled thought. This, however, was probably rather meant as a critique of opportunism and servility. The subtitle of the *Zoku ichinen yuhan* is 'No God, No Spirit', thus poignantly expressing Chomin's materialist and secularist position.

As Kato Shuichi (1919–), one of the most rational and critical post-Second World War philosophers and cultural criticists in Japan, observed, for Chomin human rights, especially the right to freedom, were universal, and he sharply went against their restriction by the government. Also, Chomin argued against imperialism and ethnic discrimination, particularly the discrimination against the *burakumin*. The rigorous Kotoku Shusui, who was executed in 1911, became his follower. Like later Marxists, anarchists and communists, Kotoku emphasised the close relation between economic conditions and a dignified human life, maintaining that there was 'nothing in life so cruel as . . . the persistent unemployment' caused by the capitalist labour surplus for it turned men into thiefs and women into prostitutes depriving them of their dignity. 'Truth, justice and humanity' were thus completely neglected. According to Kotoku, the Japanese politicians had 'forgotten the original purpose of the [Meiji] revolution and its original spirit based on freedom, equality and fraternity'. Katayama Sen (1860–1933), a contemporary socialist and Marxist, in his *Waga shakaishugi* (My Socialism), voiced similar views. When, in the middle of Taisho (1912–26), democratic thought and Marxism gained influence again, scholars like Sakai Toshihiko, Yoshino Sakuzo, Hasegawa Nyozekan (1875–1969), **Kawakami Hajime** (1879–1946) and others further elaborated respective arguments.

Outside the Meirokusha, the People's Rights Movement, Marxism, anarchism and communism, radical opponents of human rights advanced traditionalist arguments to the effect that Japan was essentially different from the West, and that this difference ought be preserved and nourished. These opponents emphasized what they regarded as traditional Japanese virtues superior to 'Western' morality, especially unconditional loyalty and **filial piety**, often advocating Tennoism, nationalism and imperialism. To achieve their goals, they utilized almost everything they regarded as helpful, especially myths, historical legends and blunt lies. However, if one holds that philosophy demands a certain degree of evidence and logical consistency, and that blind faith, myth and defence of fundamental contradictions are unphilosophical, then their theories should not be called philosophical. From about 1933 through 1945, the anti-human rights ideology prevailed. Different voices were simply oppressed.

After the Second World War this ideology was sharply attacked, and soon philosophy of human rights in Japan did not differ significantly from human rights philosophy in the West. Among the more interesting Japanese contributions to the human rights issue are the investigations of Maruyama Masao (1914–96), an outstanding professor of political science, who analysed the history of the notion of resistance and revolution in traditional Japan. As indicated, this notion goes back to Mencius and Xunzi. Because of the critical spirit which Maruyama displays, his study is not only a history but also an argument in favour of rational humaneness. Another important contribution which addressed postwar problems more directly is Tanaka Kotaro's *Shinri to heiwa o motomete* (In Search of Truth and Peace), printed in 1950. Tanaka was not only a scholar, but also served Japan as minister of education and as chief justice of the Supreme Court. In *Shinri to heiwa*, he argued against any kind of moral relativism, be it historical, cultural or racial, and in favour of the value of the individual. According to him, morality is the criterion of a state and culture, and not vice versa. State and culture 'should exist for the sake of man and not man for the sake of culture. In the last analysis man's value as an individual comes first'. State and culture are acceptable only as far as they do not 'disregard morality'. In particular, denial of freedom is unacceptable for it 'completely deprives' man of his 'dignity'. Neither 'blind conformity to external authority' nor uncritical denial of it is justified, but regarding truth and 'the universal principle of morality' as the natural and ultimate norm is the right thing. This norm is the same in East and West. In his youth, Tanaka was a follower of **Uchimura Kanzo** (1861–1930). In 1926, he converted to Catholicism. But though he was a Christian and, in his *Shinri to heiwa* quoted from the Bible and referred to god as the only 'true authority', many of his views are also compatible with the ethics of Mencius and Xunzi. As in other countries, nationalist traditionalism continues to exist in Japan too but plays only a marginal role.

Perhaps the most apparent effect of the influence of human rights thought in Japan at the end of the twentieth century is the existence of university departments which focus on the problems of discrimination against *burakumin*, women and foreigners. Most members of the Meirokusha already discussed these problems.

See also: Confucian philosophy in Japan, post-Meiji; Japanese philosophy, post-Meiji; kokutai ideology since Meiji times; Kotoku Shusui; Kyoto school; Meiroku zasshi

Further reading

Abosch, D. (1964) 'Kato Hiroyuki and the Introduction of German Political Thought in Modern Japan', Ph. D. dissertation, University of California, Berkeley.

Kato Hiroyuki (1894) *Der Kampf ums Recht des Stärkeren und seine Entwicklung*, Berlin: Friedländer.

philosophy and religion in China
The terms 'philosophy' and 'religion'

China counts three philosophical traditions: Confucianism, Daosim and, originating outside China but developing within it, Buddhism. The modern term for 'philosophy' is the 'learning of wisdom', which originated as a modern Japanese coinage in response to the western term 'philosophy' as the love of wisdom. Traditionally the Chinese would refer to the three types of philosophy simply as 'teaching' or 'learning' and prefix them with scholar (for Confucian), way (for Daoism) and Buddha (for Buddhism). The idea is that such wisdom of the ancients can be taught and learned. Exclusive loyalty (faith) to one tradition is not necessary and a monopoly of truth by one is not assumed, although of course there are some purists in each camp. Belonging to a certain lineage and having a distinct teaching are important. So a Chan Buddhist text called the *Record of the Lineage Mirrors* has a preface which noted that to be regarded as valid and true, a teaching must have a lineage and a lineage must have a teaching.

The modern use of the compound 'lineage teaching' was adopted, again first by the Japanese in the Meiji period, to render the western category of 'religion'. The three teachings of China are now regularly called 'philosophy' or 'religion'. But whereas Indians, though wary of these Western terms, have less trouble with them – the two terms being close to each other in the Hindu context – Confucians do not mind philosophy as 'the study of wisdom' but still resist the label of 'religion'. Wary of superstitious beliefs, they can appreciate the thinkers **Laozi** and **Zhuangzi** but not the folk religious practices that claim to be the Daoist teaching. A distinction can be made between Daoist philosophy and Daoist religion. It is then argued that the distinction is already present in the native Chinese use of the term '*dao* learning' for the philosophical and '*dao* teaching' for the religious. But no such linguistic discriminative convention is observed for learning/teaching in Confucianism and Buddhism, and the idea that Daoist philosophy is totally other than Daoist religion is best seen as an elitist distinction, a truth that is self-evident only to the intellectuals. The majority of the people do not even realize that such a distinction exists.

Traditionally, the three teachings exist side by side. The average Chinese acquiesce in all three. Most live out all three teachings in their lives, some more and some less, often depending on the different stages and varying stations of their lives. A Chinese is born 'Daoist', that is, natural and free. A child is deemed innocent ('true-to-heaven') and incapable of guile; he or she is spoiled and goes virtually unpunished for the first two years of his or her life. At age six, however, he or she turns 'Confucian', graduating into learning the rites and recognizing his or her low position (the most junior) in the hierarchy of the family. Confucian ritualism is a norm of all family life and is a basic requisite of the life of the scholar official. Daoist naturalism is preserved for private life. It caters to the individual's place in nature and provides a frequent refuge for people away from home, in retirement and out of office. Buddhism, because of its promise of handling life after death, often proves attractive after sixty, at old age and at the twilight of this natural life.

WHALEN LAI

Platform Sutra of the Sixth Patriarch

The Bible of Southern Chan Buddhism, the *Platform Sutra* contains a biography of **Huineng** and a lecture he delivered, supposedly in a temple at Guangzhou. The former tells of his winning the

succession from the fifth patriarch Hongren by bettering his northern opponent in coming up with a Mind Verse:

> Bodhi originally has no tree.
> The mirror also has no stand.
> Buddha-nature being always clear and pure.
> Where is there room for dust to adhere?

The lecture is an initiation lecture for administering precepts on an elevated platform. Calling it a *sutra* is presumptuous, and amounts to declaring Huineng a buddha. The work set up '**no-thought**' as the Southern principle, and claimed a 'sudden enlightenment' based on seeing into one's **buddha nature**. More an ideological platform for carving out a southern school, this famous work has actually not been much used in Zen training.

Further reading

Yampolsky, P. (trans.) (1976) *The Platform Sutra of the Sixth Patriarch*, New York: Columbia University Press.

WHALEN LAI

pleasure

China has its share of hedonists, but supposedly the Yang Zhu chapter in the book *Liezi* (a third century compilation) exemplifies philosophical 'hedonism', as the book overall spoke up for '**fatalism**' in the rather unstable post-Han era. Some contemporary Neo-Daoist thinkers were known for their indulgence in emotions. Except for some famous drunkards, their idea of natural abandon turns out to be fairly quietistic, because it was thought that excessive emotional display hurts the *élan vitale*, and that is not considered conducive to the 'nurturing of life'. After the **barbarians** took North China in 317, the southern Chinese court then slid into infamous debauchery. Examples include a king boasting of a 'flesh curtain' (nude courtesans), a human 'spitoon' and a proud polygamous princess. That culture was reflected in the erotic poetry. Political order and more emotional balance returned with the Tang dynasty. A refined culture of the high-class 'pleasure quarters' developed, but unlike its *geisha* counterpart in Japan, a Confucian 'moral rearmament' helped to disestablish it. Displaced from the capital, the pleasure culture spread downward to the mercantile cities. It is best captured in the 'pornographic' novel *Jinpinmei*, which though counted as one of the four masterpieces of Chinese literature, is far from Rabelais.

In China, it was the landed gentry rather than the urban merchant that championed the puritan lifestyle. Even with the glorification of feeling and desires in seventeenth-century ('nascent capitalist') thought and literature, China did not pay tribute to any Marquis de Sade or know the decadent Romanticism experienced by Europe. The infamous foot fetish notwithstanding, China did not produce a literature of obsession as its neighbour, Japan, eventually would. Personal liberties in the Republican era unleashed one 'Professor of Sex', but even with the call for free love among the anarchists, the Chinese Communist Revolution soon became a notably puritanical revolution. Even Mao's indiscretions seem rather tame.

Further reading

Graham, A. (trans.) (1990) *The Book of Lieh-tzu*, New York: Columbia University Press.

WHALEN LAI

PO YI *see* Bo Yi and Shu Qi

Prabhakara Mishra

b. 625; d. 675

Philosopher

Prabhakara Mishra was a Hindu **Purva Mimamsa** theorist of ritualism and author of the *Brihati* commentary on Shabara's commentary on the Mimamsa sutras. He shares the basic Mimamsaka direct realist and empiricist epistemological stance and is best known for his '*akhyati*' theory of cognitive error, according to which an error such as that in which a piece of mother of pearl is mistaken for silver or a rope is seen as a snake is caused by

non-cognition of a lack of relation. The mind is the wholly passive recipient of perceptual information and all cognitions must therefore be considered intrinsically valid since no intra-mental concepts possibly leading to distorted perceptions can intervene between awareness and what is presented to it. But error occurs when a perception of present mother of pearl produces and is combined with a memory of silver encountered at a previous time and place. There is a failure to discriminate between the two mental events since their content is very similar in many respects.

Prabhakara and his school differ from the followers of **Kumarila Bhatta**, who deny the intrinsic reflexivity of consciousness and maintain the inferability of the soul (*atman*), in holding that the latter is revealed as the subject simultaneously with the object by a self-luminous, reflexive awareness (*samvit*) in every cognitive act. He also differs from Kumarila, who thinks that the Vedic imperatives (*vidhi*) are hypothetical, having motivational and reason-giving force only for people who have an interest in the promised results of enjoined actions, in espousing the deontological view that the Vedic injunctions (*niyoga*) have an intrinsic and automatic reason-giving force when heard by those (*adhikari*) whose ritual duty they command. They may thus be compared to categorical imperatives that are held to move to action regardless of the desires and interests of the agent.

Prabhakara restricts the cognitive authority (*pramanya*) of language to the injunctive statements found in the Vedic scriptures (*shastra*). Where language about existent objects and states of affairs (*siddha*) is concerned, its referents are already established by perception or inference. Since the Vedas are primarily concerned with enjoining ritual action, they cannot be an authoritative source of knowledge (*pramana*) for the existence and description of an entity such as the *Brahman* defined as the Absolute by the Vedantic schools. Vedic linguistic forms other than injunctions expressed in the optative mood, such as explanatory statements (*arthavada*) and incantations (*mantras*), have significance only in so far as they are connected with injunctions and assist in the accomplishment of ritual action.

Consonantly with his theory that language is only genuinely significant and informative when it is prescriptive and relating to an interconnected reality that has to be brought about (*sadhya*) in accordance with the dictates of Vedic injunction, Prabhakara, in opposition to Kumarila and his followers, advocates the related designation (*anvita-abhidhana*) theory of meaning, according to which it is only in the context of a sentence that a word means anything and that the fabric of linguistic understanding consists of sentences, not of words understood in isolation. Again in opposition to Kumarila and his followers, he holds that all meanings are related to the specific instantiations of universals, since the signification (*abhidhana*) of words is understood only with reference to the particular actions with which they are involved. This theory is supported by considerations derived from the way in which a child learns a language by observing the way in which its elders act upon it.

See also: grammar and the philosophy of language in India

Further reading

Jha, G. (1918) *The Prabhakara School of Purva Mimamsa*, Benares: Benares Hindu University.
Verpoorten, J. (1987) *Mimamsa Literature*, Wiesbaden: Otto Harrassowitz.

CHRIS BARTLEY

Prajna schools

The term Prajna schools is a reference to early Chinese attempts at interpreting **emptiness** before Kumarajiva introduced **Nagarjuna** to China after 401 CE. Up to six positions on this topic were staked out. The simplest is to reduce Mahayana emptiness to Daoist **non-being**. The counter-thesis was 'Mind as Empty', a minority opinion much disparaged. Upon a closer look, this is the first school to realize that emptiness is not reducible to nothingness. The world of form remains as it is; it is only the mind which is affected. To resolve that problem, it was then proposed that if the mind is emptied, then the world of form would appear empty. The school was also the first to push the point that there is no-soul (*anatman*, no-mind), which only antagonized its

opponents more. (The majority believed that there must be a soul that transmigrates and some spirit that attains **nirvana**.) Yet the 'Mind as Empty' proposition was well supported by the scriptures and not easy to refute, until the renowned monk Huiyuan (334–417) stepped in with a witty response mocking its proponent for speaking out of turn, citing the line 'without going ahead, it arrives; without making haste, it dashes forth'. That classic line is a description of the mind.

Further reading

Lai, W. (1982) 'Sinitic Speculation on Buddha-Nature: The Nirvana School (420–589)', *Philosophy East and West* 32(2): 135–49.
—— (1983) 'The Early Prajna Schools, especially Hsin-Wu, Reconsidered', *Philosophy East and West* 33(1): 61–76.

WHALEN LAI

pramana

In Indian epistemology, the concept of an informational method agreed upon as generating true cognitions or knowledge (*prama*). *Pramanas* are pragmatically validated in so far as they conduce to successful activity by producing knowledge of objects. The most important defining mark of a *pramana* is that in revealing something previously unknown it yields new information. In line with the generally empiricist epistemological stance of Indian philosophers, the primary method is sense-perception from whose deliverances inference proceeds. According to Mimamsa and **Vedanta** theories, infallible and non-falsifiable Vedic scripture is the sole *pramana* for whatever lies beyond the bounds of sense.

The three *pramana*s recognized by the Mimamsakas, Naiyayikas and Vedantins are:

1 *Pratyaksha* (perception), which is basically defined as a cognition arising when external objects are presented to sense-organs. Perceptions are classified as pre-linguistic and non-conceptual (*nirvikalpa*) and conceptual and linguistically saturated (*savikalpa*).
2 *Shabda* (language). In general, verbal testimony

(especially the words of the wise) and more specifically Vedic scriptural language (*shruti*) whose eternal sound units are regarded as infallible and unfalsifiable. Vedic *shabda* is held to be authorless and non-originated (*apaurusheya*, non-personal). The connection between Vedic words and their primary referents, the metaphysical forms (*akriti*) in which individual entities (*vyakti*) participate, is innate. Indeed a Vedic term enters into its referent's being, not a conventional label contingently attached to it. The cognitive authority (*pramanya*) of Vedic language is restricted to whatever lies beyond the range of sensory perception: thus it cannot be contradicted by those *pramana* whose operation is restricted to the empirical sphere. A well-formed, meaningful sentence generates a verbal cognition (*shabda-bodha*) if it satisfies the conditions of grammatical completeness (*akanksha*), semantic compatibility (*yogyata*) and spatio-temporal contiguity of utterance (*sannidhi*).

3 *Anumana* (inference) whose operation is dependent upon the deliverances of perception and testimony.

A fully elaborated inference has the form:

Thesis: There is fire (*sadhya*) on the mountain.
Reason: Because there is smoke (*hetu*).
Exemplification: Wherever there is smoke, there is fire (*vyapti*); like a kitchen (*sapaksha*) unlike a lake (*vipaksha*). There is smoke on the mountain. Therefore there is fire.

Inference involves (i) awareness of the invariable concomitance (*vyapti*) of the inferendum (*sadhya*) and the justificatory warrant (*hetu*) and the presence of the *hetu* in the subject-locus (*paksha*), and (ii) observation of co-existence of smoke and fire in at least one locus and no awareness of a counter-exemplary locus where the *hetu* is present and the *sadhya* absent.

A statement of *vyapti* is an inductive generalization free from falsifying counter-examples. Conditions of a successful inference include citation of positive supporting example (*sapaksha*) exemplifying compresence of warrant (*hetu*) and probandum (*sadhya*) in a sample locus (*paksha*) other than the actual subject of the inference and citation of negative supporting example (*vipaksha*) illustrat-

ing the absence of both warrant and probandum in another locus. Since the major premise is explicitly inductively derived from experience, the Indian syllogism does not attract the empiricist objection that the conclusion cannot be deduced from the major premise since the major premise cannot be known to be true unless the truth of the conclusion is already known.

There is an exceptional case (*kevalanvayin*) of inference where the *sadhya*'s non-existence is inconceivable (e.g. everything is nameable – because knowable) and so there can be no *vipaksha*.

An inference is fallacious if vitiated by one of the five pseudo-warrants (*hetvabhasa*) which are:

1 Deviating (*vyabhichara*): This covers a multitude of sins:

The presence of the *hetu* without the *sadhya*.
The attempt to infer smoke from the presence of fire since there can be fire without smoke.
Where the universal applicability of the warrant renders it too general to justify the thesis: for example, 'There is fire on the mountain, because it is knowable.' Knowability occurs in the absence of fire so the *vyapti* fails. Lack of *sapaksha* (agreeing example) and *vipaksha* (disagreeing example): 'Sound is eternal because it resonates.'
Cases where no *drstanta* (exemplification) is available because everything is included in the *paksha* (subject): 'All things are transient because they are knowable.'

2 Unestablished (*Asiddha*): where the warrant's existence is dubious.
3 Contradictory (*Viruddha*): where the warrant is standardly the sign for the absence of the probandum.
4 Futile (*Badhita*): the thesis precludes the possibility of adducing a sign as a warrant by virtue of its incompatibility with the thesis.

Philosophers of the **Purva Mimamsa** tradition of ritual exegesis recognize presumption or implication (*arthapatti*) as a means of knowledge in its own right. A popular example is that of fat Devadatta who does not eat during the day. So he must eat at night. The Naiyayikas classify *arthapatti* under *anumana*.

Further reading

Matilal, B. (1986) *Perception: An Essay in Indian Theories of Knowledge*, Oxford: Oxford University Press.

Mohanty, J. (1991) *Reason and Tradition in Indian Thought*, Oxford: Oxford University Press.

Potter, K. (ed.) (1977) *Encyclopedia of Indian Philosophies, Vol. II: The Tradition of Nyaya-Vaisheshika up to Gangesha*, Delhi: Motilal Banarsidass.

CHRIS BARTLEY

pratitya-samutpada

Pratitya-samutpada (in Pali, *Paticca-samuppada*) is rendered in English as interdependent genesis, conditioned co-production or dependent co-origination. It is part of the Buddhist theory of causal regularity in the physical, organic and psychological spheres and predictable consequentiality in the ethical realm. The process of conditioned genesis automatically governs the interactions and aggregations of the elements of existence (*dharma*). From the ethical point of view, such a principle has to be postulated given the absence of any persisting entity such as the soul (*atman*) that might serve as a principle of continuity through a series of lives and reap the future consequences of retributive actions (*karma*). More generally, interdependent genesis fundamentally involves a denial that there are any intrinsic causal powers. The most succinct, ancient and vague expression of the principle that everything occurs in dependence upon a complex of conditions is, 'This being, that becomes; from the arising of this, that arises. This not being, that becomes not, from the ceasing of this, that ceases.'

This view of causality is held to be the middle way between the denial of free will in the strict naturalistic determinism of the *Ajivakas* (*niyati-vada*) and the view that everything is random and without purpose (*yadriccha-vada*). It also involves a rejection of divine originative causality (*Ishvara-nirmana*). It differs from essentialist Upanishadic views of causation as the auto-transformation of a primal causal substrate (*Brahman*, the universal essence). This can be interpreted as the view designated *sat-karana-vada* or the doctrine that the

cause remains intrinsically the same, its effects lacking independent identities. Interpreted from a realist point of view as **satkaryavada**, what will be called the effect pre-exists in potentia as a germinal modality of a future state in its causal substrate prior to its entitative manifestation when it acquires determinate name and form. Effects enjoy the same degree of reality as the substrative causes from which they emerge. This is the idea that kinds of entities with determinate identity conditions have definite and specific causal powers. Also different is the view that effects are not contained in their causes but are novel products arising from a collocation of substrative and instrumental causes which are either destroyed or rendered inoperative upon their production (**asat-karyavada**). According to the theory of interdependent genesis, nothing is really originated as a novel product with a determinate identity.

A beginningless process of twelve mental and physical factors is held to organize the fluid and dynamic formations of the five components or *skandhas* (matter, feelings, perceptions, dispositions and awareness) constituting the transmigrating soulless individual stream of psycho-physical experiences.

The twelve-fold causal nexus is: spiritual ignorance (**avidya**) conditions karmic dispositions (*samskara*) which condition consciousness (*vijnana*) which conditions the psycho-physical matrix (*nama-rupa*) which conditions the six bases of consciousness (*sad-ayatana*) which condition sense–object interactions (*sparsha*) which condition feelings (*vedana*) which condition 'thirst' (*trishna*) which conditions craving (*upadana*) which conditions repeated existences (*bhava*) which condition births (*jati*) which condition old age and death (*jara-maranam*) and all our woe. This is proposed as an account of causal regularity, the repeatability of kinds and predictable ethical consequentiality given the absence of any persisting entity such as a soul (*atman*) that might serve as a principle of continuity. Ignorance and desire are the key factors propelling causal processes.

The first two elements are sometimes held to refer to the immediately previous life, the next eight to the present existence and the final two to the next life. While the process, propelled by ignorance and desire is beginningless, it is reversible and terminable by insight (*prajna*) into the fundamental unsatisfactoriness (*duhkha*), impermanence (*anitya*) and non-substantiality or non-essentiality (*anatman*, no-identity) of the constituents of transmigratory existence.

The theory may be expressed in terms of a non-temporal and non-generative relation of logical equivalence: p is a necessary and sufficient condition of q if and only if q is a necessary and sufficient condition of p. Buddhists deny that one entity really produces or influences another either intrinsically or with the help of other factors. Rather, there is a co-operation between moments constituting the uninterrupted flow of a stream of events. There being no duration, there are no stable entities with the time to produce one another. Since all forms of Buddhism deny the reality of individual personal identity, they must also deny that of individual agency. According to the mainstream Brahminical analysis of events, the agent (*karta*) is the independent (*svatantra*) item in a complex (*samagri*) consisting of six factors (*karakas*) which include: *karana* (instrument), *apadana* (point of departure), *sampradana* (recipient), *adhikarana* (locus) and *karman* (object). Buddhist philosophy does not ascribe any special significance to individual agency, reducing what is ordinarily and mistakenly understood as the agent to just another equal factor in a causal complex.

The Madhyamika school, founded by **Nagarjuna**, interprets *pratitya-samutpada* as ontological relativity. All the fundamental constituents of reality (*dharma*) are empty (*shunya*) of essence or own-nature (*svabhava*) in virtue of their ontic interdependence. Nothing exists in its own right, everything being relative.

Further reading

Collins, S. (1982) *Selfless Persons: Imagery and Thought in Theravada Buddhism*, Cambridge: Cambridge University Press.

Gombrich, R. (1996) *How Buddhism Began: The Conditioned Genesis of the Early Teachings*, London: Athlone Press.

Harvey, P. (1990) *An Introduction to Buddhism*, Cambridge: Cambridge University Press.

Kalupahana, D. (1975) *Causality: The Central Philosophy of Buddhism*, Honolulu, HA: Hawaii University Press.

Lamotte, E. (1988) *History of Indian Buddhism, From the Origins to the Saka Era*, trans. S. Webb-Boin, Louvain: Université Catholique de Louvain.

Murti, T. (1960) *The Central Philosophy of Buddhism: A Study of the Madhyamika System*, London: George Allen and Unwin.

Rahula, W. (1969) *What the Buddha Taught*, London: Gordon Fraser.

Warder, A. (1991) *Indian Buddhism*, Delhi: Motilal Banarsidass.

CHRIS BARTLEY

Pratyabhijna

Pratyabhijna (Recognition) is a Kashmiri school of philosophy articulating a monistic form of Shaivism and commencing with Somananda's (900–50) *Shivadristi*. He was followed by Utpaladeva (925–75), whose major works are the *Ishvarapratyabhijnakarika* (or Sutra) with an auto-commentary, and **Abhinavagupta**, author of the *Ishvarapratyabhijnavimarshini* and the *Ishvarapratyabhijnavivritivimarshini*. Kshemaraja (1000–50) wrote the useful compendium, the *Pratyabhijnahridayam*.

The school propounds a form of absolute idealism maintaining the identity of the individual self and the trans-individual consciousness known as Shiva that is the self-projecting basis, the efficient and substrative causes, of the universe of experience. Shiva is the sole reality both objectively and subjectively. It is not conceived as an abstract, quiescent, transcendental divinity but as the limitless creative activity of consciousness. Enlightenment consists not in suppressing mental activity but in the realization of the divine nature as self-transformation via the energies of consciousness expressed as the goddesses of the **Trika Shaivism** system of ritual and yoga. The supreme human good (*moksha*, liberation) is the recognition that, 'I am Shiva and this whole world is my self-expression.'

The school's philosophical articulation in the works of Utpaladeva and Abhinavagupta is of the utmost sophistication and cogency. It involves sustained critiques of the anti-essentialist Buddhist realists (Vaibhashikas), representationalists (Sautrantikas) and subjective idealists (Yogacharas), the illusionism of **Advaita** Vedanta and any ontology postulating the reality of an objective, in the sense of mind-independent, sphere.

The school's name derives from its tenet that the constantly experienced self within is none other than the transcendental self that is the substrate of all subjects, acts and objects of experience. The inner self is already known but must be recognized, scrutinized and continuously reflected upon in its full reality as the supreme.

Major Pratyabhijna theses include the following. First, whatever is experienced is simply a manifestation of one's self which is the divinity understood as trans-individual consciousness (*samvit*). Second, divinity, which is the same as the self when its powers of will, knowledge and action are at their fullest expansion, is autonomous and reflexive consciousness and will. It is intrinsically dynamic and active.

Third, trans-individual consciousness simultaneously and successively manifests all subjects (*pramatri*), acts (*pramana*) and objects (*prameya*) of awareness through its dual powers of cognition (*jnana-shakti*) and action (*kriya-shakti*). Experiential variety can only be accounted for if it derives from this process of auto-projection. It is an aspect of the perfect autonomy (*svatantrya*) of trans-individual consciousness that it manifests itself through a power called *maya-shakti* as limited individual self-conscious enduring centres of will (*iccha*) and agency. Were subjects and objects not constituents of a single, universal field of consciousness, the synthesis and analysis of different cognitions, the fact of memory, the intelligible order of the universe unified in space and time and the entire network of intersubjective communication would not be possible.

Fourth, only that which enters the content of consciousness can be considered real. The unreal does not enter the content of consciousness. The mind-independent is non-existent. What appear as external, physical objects are really constituted by consciousness because consciousness bears no relation to the insentient. If objectivity is defined in terms of independence of consciousness, how can it be experienced? Trans-individual consciousness causes phenomenal objects of awareness

(*abhasa*) to appear as if distinct from the limited subjects of experience.

Fifth, the cause–effect relation (*karya-karana-bhava*) obtains only between agents and the objects of action (*kartri-karma-bhava*). Causality is exclusively a property of conscious agents capable of volition. Thus causality and creativity on the part of the material or physical is impossible.

Further reading

Iyer, K. and Pandey, K. (1998) *Isvarapratyabhijnavimarshini: Doctrine of Divine Recognition*, 3 vols, Delhi: Motilal Banarsidass.

Singh, J. (1991) *Pratyabhijnahrdayam*, Delhi: Motilal Banarsidass.

CHRIS BARTLEY

primitivism

In their rejection of civilization and its artifice ('falsehood'), Daoists seek to return to a natural state and romanticize the primitive society. Thus **Laozi** called for a 'doing away with humaneness and righteousness' and a 'return to compassion and filiality'. **Humaneness** and **righteousness** are urban, civic values; compassion and filiality are ethos of a simpler time, care from elders and devotion from those who are younger. He called also for 'emptying the mind and filling the stomach', another attack on high culture and a return to the basics. Social fashions only breed social ills: 'treasure gold and silver and there are suddenly more robbers; value beauty and there is suddenly this perception of ugliness'. So abandon the sophisticated, he said, and embrace the unadorned. The learning of the Way is to unlearn what civilization has taught; it is daily attrition of what had been a daily growth in human knowledge. If Laozi idealized the 'small state with few men' and villages so self-sufficient as 'not even bothering to visit another one close by', then **Zhuangzi** went even further back, to the forest of hunters and gatherers, with footprints from unknown others, a time with no writing and no records, just people tying knots to aid memory.

See also: agrarianism

WHALEN LAI

puranas

The name *purana* has in the Sanskrit language the literal meaning of 'ancient, primeval', and the genre of literature to which it gives its name claims to recount ancient tales coming from an undefined period of Hindu civilization, unspecified except for being considered old. Several *puranas* are named after famous Indian gods such as Vishnu, Shiva, Brahma, Surya, Ganesha and Devi, and others after figures or symbols associated with these gods. These names are consistent with the strong theological imprint of the individual *puranas*, an imprint reflecting one of the significant features defining the genre as a whole. Traditionally, scholars of Indian literature have focused on individual specimens of the genre rather than focusing on the explicit and implicit generic conditions necessary for a text to be called a *purana*. This has created a sense of desperation in dealing with this literature because so many individual *puranas* appear to diverge radically from each other and certainly do not share the similarities that mark the two Sanskrit epics or other literary genres such as poetry or philosophical commentarial writing. Traditionally, the *puranas* are divided into the categories of *mahapurana* (larger) and *upapurana* (lesser) and eighteen texts are included in each according to the many lists found both inside and outside of the *puranas*. There are, however, hundreds of texts in many Indian languages claiming the name *purana*, and collectively they cover almost everything found in the culture over the past two millennia.

Of the eighteen *mahapuranas*, the verse total amounts to approximately 400,000 stanzas. Chronologically, they date from about the early centuries of the Christian era up until the present day, though specific dating is largely guesswork and has given rise to much dispute. While originally composed in the Sanskrit language, they have often been recited to popular audiences in vernacular summaries, and in the last four hundred years new *puranas* have been composed in most of the prominent Indian languages. *Puranas* continue to be recited at temples and festivals to the present day, especially popular ones like the *Bhagavatapurana*, which is central for the worship of the god Krishna.

At first sight, the *puranas* appear to be repositories of ancient myths, many to be traced back to Vedic literature, constituting a body certainly predating the extant *puranas* in absolute chronology. Yet deliberate preservation of an ambience of antiquity is a distinctive feature of the puranic narrative, and allows the texts to develop a complex temporality in relation to content because of their explicit mixture of new material with what is known, by the puranic audience, to be old. One example of this would be the juxtaposition of known Vedic myths with descriptions of rituals performed only in the medieval period when cults surrounding the great gods Vishnu and Shiva had developed enormously throughout India. Or, one could add the long section devoted to poetics in the *Agnipurana* or the sections of the *Vishnudharmottarapurana* dealing with methods of painting, the theoretical elaboration of which only dates from the fifth century CE. This impression of a mixed temporality is further complicated by the occurrence of many theological passages where the deity is depicted existing outside of time, thereby becoming a metaphor of the abstract **brahman** of the **Upanishads**. All of this is foreign to the earliest strata of Indian literature.

What is immediately apparent to anyone who reads an individual *purana* is the clear absence of a plot, extending the full length of the text. Such a plot would function as one frame to integrate the data found therein. Compounding the impression of disarray scholars sometimes find in *puranas*, due to the lack of a comprehensive plot, is the massive profusion of subjects treated in an individual text, covering anything from grammar, mineralogy, astronomy, devotional theology and ritual, politics, medicine and detailed rules of conduct pertaining to daily life. This has led to them being described as encyclopedic, a description accurate only to the extent of the entire body of *puranas* containing within them a hugely diverse range of content. And if they were only a repository of data, it would be difficult to reconcile them with their long acceptance within Indian culture as constituting a distinct genre of literature, separable from others such as the Sanskrit epics, drama and other specimens of narrative literature.

However, it has long been recognized traditionally and by Western scholars that the *puranas*, characterized as they are by a clear eclecticism, form a hybrid genre, stuck between the two related genres of *itihasa* (epic) and *dharmashastra* (formal treatises listing specific rules regulating all aspects of life). From the first, the puranic narrative takes a huge body of myths and a propensity to combine these myths with didactic material into larger literary units, but not large enough to encompass the entire puranic narrative within a single mythic frame. From the second it takes, by direct borrowing or minimal paraphrase, thousands of verses dealing with human conduct. This has led to the *puranas* being described as **Dharmashastras**, a judgement correct in its recognition of their link to the concerns of everyday life and their claim to offer a total view of what life can and could be.

Stylistically the *puranas* are composed primarily in the *shloka* metre, intermixed at various significant junctures of the narrative with longer, more elaborate, metres normally only found in poetry. This confers upon them a sense of monotony in recitation, but a shift to the longer metres heightens the tension already present in the content of the narrative when these verses are used. Each *purana* is presented as a collection of verses spoken by several different interlocutors each reaching forward in time to a later set of interlocutors, finishing finally with the reciter, Vyasa, who is traditionally said to have recited the *puranas* to a group of sages in Naimisha forest. Thus any given puranic narrative almost always starts from an imputed present and goes back interlocutory layer by interlocutory layer to a distant past. Their composition in verse, the occurrence of a standard interlocutory scheme and the movement from the present to past provides them with a kind of homogeneity against which is contrasted the high variability of content found even in an individual *purana*. If the content seems highly variable, the compositional features of the genre are substantially invariable.

Even if western scholars have been dismayed by what they consider to be the generic confusion of the *puranas*, the puranic tradition itself, embodied in individual *puranas*, has experienced no such doubts

and shows a real awareness in laying down some basic characteristics required of any text calling itself a *purana*. Because many *puranas* do not contain all of these characteristics – and some contain virtually none – certain scholars, especially H.H. Wilson, argued that they could not be called *puranas* at all. However, the fallacy here is to confuse the genre as a whole with individual texts within that genre. Merely by calling a text a *purana* means that it links in some way, or will be recognized as such by an audience of a puranic recitation, into the larger literary world identified with the genre as a category of literature defining both form and content. Even if most of the features of that literary world are absent in a given text, the presence of that world will be known, in the consciousness of an indigenous audience, as being relevant to the understanding of that text.

Two principal sets of formal characteristics are laid down in some *puranas*, and are simply called the 'five characteristics' and the 'ten characteristics'. The latter substantially embraces what is covered in the former and in doing so increases the dimensions of the world the puranic genre creates and implies. In combination they place a stamp of singularity upon the genre that distinguishes it from its other two related neighbours. They function as a loose guide to the frame in which the diverse contents of the *puranas* can be placed and though this guidance does not necessarily manifest itself in a specific sequence, it would make no sense to speak of the genre without making reference to these two sets of characteristics.

The five characteristics of the first scheme are uniformly listed as follows:

sarga, cosmogony
pratisarga, cosmogony and cosmology
vamsha, genealogy of kings
manvantara, histories of the world during a period of one patriarch
vamshanucharitam, legends of the reigns of kings

Considered collectively in terms of their actual narrative presentations in individual *puranas*, what results from the clusters of content surrounding these characteristics is the creation of a mythic/literary world containing its own measures of space and time, its own geography, its own society – dominated by the elite classes of brahmins and warriors and all sorts of marginal figures including ascetics, demons and outcastes – and its own history constructed on the descriptions of royal genealogies and the actions of their kings. This world mirrors the empirical world, though the exact relationship between the two is never spelled out with any certainty, nor was this absence a problem for the composers of the text and their audience.

What is achieved by the ordered collection of content based on the five characteristics is the representation of a universe viable in its own terms and close enough to the empirical world to be taken seriously as an environment for the working through of problems relevant to everyday life as well as the more metaphysical questions relating to the nature of the self and the absolute which transcended both space and time. Such is its closeness to the empirical world that there are many passages in the *puranas*, notably prescriptive rules for descriptions of widely performed rituals called *pujas*, lists of names of gods used in ritual and hymn singing and dharmashastric passages, where the empirical world actually penetrates the 'fictional world'. Such descriptions have been, and still are, used as guides to the contemporary performance of rituals, and hymns, called *stotras*, are also extracted from the *puranas* and used in a variety of practical contexts.

Where this five-character scheme differs from the kind of plots continually intruding across the narratives of the two Sanskrit epics, for example, is that it does not constantly intrude into the narrative of all the individual *puranas*. However, it does not need to, because even if a given *purana* (such as the *Vamanapurana* and the *Ganeshapurana*) gives only a minimal explicit portrayal of the subjects associated with the five characters, the fact that it is called *purana* will invoke this very scheme in the minds of an audience. This scheme is then a deliberate and successful attempt to provide a temporal and spatial anchorage point into which a wide variety of other unrelated literary material can be located.

The total silence within the *puranas* as to their precise literary function suggests that as a group the five characteristics were not intended to be a binding check on what should be included or excluded in a puranic recitation. This suggestion is confirmed by the actual contents of the extant *puranas* where so much space is given to subjects other than those dealing with the five characteristics. As soon as this material finds its way into the puranic fictional universe, however, it is given broad spatial and historical boundaries, yet without excluding a multiplicity of other meanings from being located in it. But there are limits to the interpretation of these meanings set by the *puranas* themselves. One cannot find anything and everything within them.

A prominent clue to the control that can be placed on interpretations comes from the huge amount of material relating to theology of important gods such as Vishnu, Shiva, Ganesha, Surya and a generic female divinity often just called Devi. Such theology is expressed through myths, often repeated several times in the same *purana*, telling of the interaction of these gods with other gods and humans, prescriptive descriptions of rituals to be performed to individual gods, lists of their names to be chanted, philosophical disquisitions about their identity with the abstract foundation of the universe: *brahman*, and explorations about the imputed metaphysical identity between god and his devotee, even when for the purposes of a devotional relationship they must be seen to be provisionally different. As with the content grouped around the five characteristics, this material is spread out across the narratives of individual *puranas*, not necessarily in a particular sequential order. Despite this, there is a logic governing its insertion into the narrative.

Besides the meaning derived from their plots, most of the myths occurring in any given *purana* are filled with information about what in the West would be considered as theological matters, accompanied by a large body of material – especially in medieval *puranas* – consisting simply of descriptions of how rituals should be performed. These sections of the *puranas* virtually mimic ritual handbooks and invite any audience of puranic recitation somehow to correlate the ritual material with the more abstract theological texts and, finally, with the huge body of myths, themselves open to a range of interpretations. Beneath all of this material, and performing an important unifying function, can be isolated what has been termed a *bhakti* semantic frame where *bhakti* can be translated as 'devotion'. This can best be understood as an abstract reconstruction of a pathway marking the transformation of a subject – human, animal or other – from a condition where his or her status is technically that of non-devotee, to a new status where the subject will regard himself/herself, and is regarded by the god, as the devotee of that particular god. The underlying mythic frame plots a change of status, a conversion from non-devotee to devotee, hence an acknowledged relationship between devotee and divinity. Equally, if recognized as a particular sequential scheme, the semantic frame can function as an implicit narrative grid according to which the contents of the *puranas* can be organized.

As an example of one such myth, and there are hundreds throughout the *puranas*, a brief summary of the myth of the demon Prahlada in the *Vamanapurana* (chs 7.22–8.72), a figure who becomes one of Vishnu's most famous devotees, will suffice. The god Vishnu had killed the demon Hiranyakashipu and his son, Prahlada, became king of the demons in succession. At this time the Earth was ruled by kings in absolute conformity with the normative order (*dharma*). A sage named Cyavana visits the underworld and is duly honoured by Prahlada, who asks the sage to tell him which are the most sacred pilgrimage places in heaven, Earth and the underworld. Having gained this information, Prahlada resolves to visit the sacred Naimisha forest with Cyavana for the purpose of gaining a vision of Narayana.

They leave, but Prahlada becomes suddenly angry when he sees the two ascetics named Nara and Narayana, beside whom are bows, near a Shala tree. He considers them to be hypocritical for practising exercises in austerity while also bearing weapons. He talks to them for some time during which the two ascetics declare themselves to be unconquerable in battle. Prahlada vows to defeat them.

A great battle ensues, but after one thousand years Prahlada is incapable of overcoming Narayana and consults Vishnu about what he should do. Vishnu says Narayana cannot be conquered in battle, but only by devotion (*bhakti*). Prahlada then renounces his kingdom in favour of Andhaka and proceeds to Badarika hermitage, where he gains a vision of Nara and Narayana. The latter asks

Prahlada why he is bowing down to him and he answers with a recitation of Vishnu's names, in the course of which he declares Vishnu to be the supreme being in the universe. Vishnu then declares himself conquered by this single-minded devotion and offers Prahlada a boon. He asks for three boons: any evil **karma** incurred while fighting Vishnu should be annulled, he should be perpetually devoted to Vishnu and he should acquire fame through his devotion to Vishnu. As well as these boons the gods confer invincibilty upon him and freedom from the effects of *karma*. Finally, Vishnu tells Prahlada to return to his own place of residence and there to be devoted to his duties and to rule over the kingdom as an adviser. However, he refuses to become king.

Following this example and dozens of others from different *puranas*, the myth can be divided into nine separate sequential stages, each of which implies a body of content that collectively has the potential to encompass every aspect of the devotional relationship as it has been actually practised and theorized upon in literary texts such as the *puranas*. These stages are manifested through the narrative of each myth on which the *bhakti* semantic has had a demonstrable influence. Each of the stages listed below is simply a summary of the common features of the narrative manifestation of a particular action (function) in the myth:

1 Introduction.
2 Spiritual ignorance of the future devotee.
3 Beginning of spiritual realization for the future devotee.
4 Demonstration of the god's grace.
5 'Conversion' of the devotee.
6 Demonstration of the devotee's devotion.
7 The god offers grace to his devotees.
8 The devotee reaffirms devotion by accepting the grace.
9 The devotee performs specific activities as an expression of devotion.

Not every myth in the *puranas* is a *bhakti* myth, and many of these functions exist individually in myths not demonstrably shaped by the *bhakti* semantic. However, no *purana* exists that does not contain at least one myth depicting one or several manifestations of the actions listed here and in the sequential configuration in which they are here summarized. Some, like the *Ganesha purana*, strongly reflect its influence in every myth it contains. Others, like the *Vamanapurana*, depict it in about forty per cent of their myths, whereas the *Vishnupurana* only contains a few versions. No individual *purana* lacks examples of this myth or explicit signs that devotional values have had an effect on the composition of the narrative.

The last four stages of the myth encompass the practical expression of the devotee's devotion and so include such topics as ritual, recitation of lists of names of the god, pilgrimage, recitation of *mantras* and so on, all of which are comprehensively represented in the puranic narrative outside of the actual myths themselves. Much of the non-mythological material in these texts is taken up with this kind of data. As well as covering the practical applications of devotion the final stages also require for the devotee the presentation of the maximum possible knowledge (theology) about the deity. Accordingly, they can produce theological statements, discussions about the functions performed by the god in the puranic creation myths or even biographies of deities like those of Krishna found in the *Vishnu* and the *Bhagavatapuranas* and of Ganesha in the *Brahmavaivartapurana*. The full textual manifestation of such a semantic frame requires a large narrative, though it is certainly possible for its presence to be made evident in small fragments. Given that it will normally generate mythic as well as didactic units, its shaping influence on a particular text will produce various kinds of sub-texts, including myths and more formal descriptions of rituals and rules of conduct in daily life.

Just as the five-character scheme is fundamental to the definition of the puranic genre and is explicitly acknowledged as such in all the *puranas*, so too does the *bhakti* semantic frame play an equivalent role in the establishment of the specificity of this genre. The five-character scheme has generic authority conferred upon it by virtue of its constant restatement in the *puranas*. But there is no explicit presentation of a set of propositions defining *bhakti* as a subject which should be dealt with in any text that is to be accorded the status of *purana*, even if definitions of *bhakti* itself are common in the *puranas*. Given the universality of devotional practices and theologies in Indian

culture since the fourth century BCE, however, meaning that it is too broad to be used as the basis for a generic classification of literature, the privileged position explicitly given to the five character scheme means that for analytical purposes it must be considered to operate as a surface structure, the *bhakti* semantic as a deep semantic structure. The latter opens the possibility for a large range of apparently heterogenous and distinct material – theology, myth, biography, descriptions of ritual and dharmashastric material – to be included in the bounds of a single text, not necessarily in a precise narrative order, and facilitates the maintenance of semantic coherence across the entire text. And it is narrative coherence which must be stressed, because it enables all this material to be included in the text, even if it is not done so in a way that follows a precise sequential order easily recognizable to the eye. The unique feature of the *puranas* is that they allow the possibility of a cohesive meaning to be found while encouraging a narrative capable of mixing together an enormous amount of literary material which superficially appears to have very little in common.

Some *puranas* (*Bhagavatapurana* 2.10.1, 12.7.9; *Naradapurana* 1.96.5) do combine the five-character scheme with another five characters; this makes up the ten-character scheme, one enabling a more comprehensive organization of the puranic genre. To the five-character scheme they add subjects such as:

6 *utaya*, karmic traces
7 *Ishanukatha*, tales about the Lord
8 *nirodha*, cessation
9 *mukti*, spiritual liberation
10 *ashraya*, refuge (*Bhagavatapurana* 2.10.1)

What results is a combination of both devotional and Vedantic themes, befitting the more philosophical nature of this *purana*. Its significance lies in its drawing together philosophical concepts into the devotional framework contained in the *puranas*. This is certainly not new, as a similar combination can be found in some *Upanishads* and in the twelfth book of the *Mahabharata*.

The devotional frame comes to encompass the cosmogonic and cosmological content, laid out in the five-character scheme. This emerges from the attribution to the deity, to whom devotion is offered, of the functions of creator and organizer of the spatial and temporal configuration of the universe. As well, the deity becomes the ultimate power to whom individuals, of any species, can appeal for the achievement of material and religious goals, the difference between these two goals being recognized in the texts as taking the individual on two different paths – dealing with asceticism/**meditation** and the performance of sacrificial rituals – that are not fundamentally incompatible because each can be seen as a practical approach to the expression of devotion to god or the goddess.

Function of the *puranas*

Many Indian scholars in particular have argued that the *puranas* performed, and continue to perform, an integrative or synthesizing role in Indian culture, synthesizing **Tantra** with brahmanical ritualism, devotionalism and proto-Vedantic philosophy in the early centuries of the Christian era. Working from a supposition that Indian culture really consists of many regional cultures loosely united by a pan-Indian veneer of brahmin teaching, they have sought to find instruments within the culture capable of allowing diversity and unity to co-exist without unbearable tension. The *puranas* have constituted one such instrument and their synthetic role has been demonstrated by the fact that different manuscripts of the same *purana* contain content that is often substantially different and that significant alterations can be discerned as having occurred over time. In certain cases these differences are concentrated in manuscript traditions coming from different parts of India. To this can be added a view, developed in particular by R.C. Hazra, that the extant *puranas* are considerably different from the same *puranas* when they were first composed in the early centuries of the Christian era. This means puranic composition must be regarded as a process rather than as an event completed many centuries ago, and that this process is ongoing.

To conceive of the *puranas* from this perspective is to highlight their historical role in cultural formation. Development of different genres has long been recognized as a partial reflection of changing socio-economic conditions and the emergence of a new genre is as much the emergence of a new cultural object as it is of a conduit for a particular set of contents reflecting items of cultural significance.

A potentially very fruitful way to investigate this historical function of the *puranas* as embodying a process of cultural synthesis is to take the important suggestion of V. Narayana Rao. He defines a kind of puranic culture where a distinct set of texts were produced that sum up culture in both a synchronic (i.e. as a set of rules defining traditionally sanctioned conduct at any given time in the puranic universe created within the five-character frame) and a diachronic sense insofar as any given *purana* demonstrates its heritage as Vedic, or traditional through reference back to an epic lineage, whilst attempting to maintain a continuity with its recitational present. This produces 'a text flexible in content but fixed in its ideological apparatus. *Purana* and *itihasa*...are such texts...' (Narayana Rao 1993: 93). The broad principle on which this is worked out is summarized by Narayana Rao in terms of a continuity created between myth and history: 'What is common to all the three cases [Puranic texts] ... is that all of them begin with what we call "myth" and move into what we call "history", with no dividing line between them. This is one continuous line of events...this continuity is what the Puranic worldview promotes, and that it results from the ideological frame of Puranas' (Narayana Rao 1993: 86–7). Whilst these sentences condemn us to the resolution of virtually insuperable problems – especially the attempt within the Indian context to locate the interrelationship between myth and history and their different epistemological bases – they firmly set the direction to be taken in any kind of serious interpretation of the integrative role of the *puranas* considered historically. Moreover, Narayana Rao's conceptualization of the problem focuses on the dual role of *puranas* as offering a process of transmission for change and authority and an ideological frame which is itself a product of particular socio-historical positionings yet to be defined with any accuracy.

In conclusion, the *puranas* present a collection of texts filled with symbols of the past mixed easily with startlingly new literary and cultural material incorporated at different times along the historical trajectory of their ongoing recitational tradition.

Whether there was any tension felt by reciters and audience alike about what is in truth a juxtaposition of traditional and new seems unlikely, yet the presence of such a juxtaposition compels interpretation of the *puranas* as a textual process successful in transforming whatever was new, and potentially radical, into a form acceptable to the present. This corresponds to a very ancient indigenous perception of the *puranas* where they are defined as preserving the old while constantly coming to terms with the new. Never should they be seen as static relics of a past frozen into the present. If they are anything they are signs of an ongoing process of cultural adaptation and transformation. One of the many conclusions drawn from this understanding of the *puranas* is that they can be read as a mirror of the changes occurring in Hinduism during the first two millennia of the Christian era, that is, given the production of new *puranas*, virtually up until the present. But this is a mirror which makes sense only within the frame of a 'fictional history' contextualizing human activity and sharing many resemblances to the empirical world. It implies a process that seeks to establish cultural cohesion and stability by cushioning the shock of the new with enframement within symbols and narratives from the past, so that the new is only ever seen as forming one new component consistent with a world whose credentials are impeccable because of the stamp of authority conferred upon them by virtue of an imagined antiquity.

Further reading

Bailey, G. (1995). *The Ganesha Purana, Vol. I The Upasanakhana*, Wiesbaden: Otto Harrassowitz.

Doniger, W. (ed.) (1993) *Purana Perennis. Reciprocity And Transformation in Hindu and Jaina, Texts*, Albany, NY: State University of New York Press.

Hazra, R.C. (1975) *Studies in the Puranic Records on Hindu Rites and Customs*, Delhi: Motilal Banarsidass.

Narayana Rao, V. (1993) 'Purana as Brahminic Ideology', in W. Doniger (ed.), *Purana Perennis. Reciprocity And Transformation in Hindu and Jaina, Texts*, Albany, NY: State University of New York Press, 85–100.

Rocher, L. (1986) *The Puranas*, Wiesbaden: Otto Harrassowitz.

Wilson, H.H. (1961) *The Vishnu Purana: A System of Hindu Mythology and Tradition*, Calcutta: Punthi Pustak.

GREG BAILEY

PURGATORY *see* afterlife in Chinese thought

purushartha

The four legitimate goals of life *purushartha* recognized by mainstream Hindu Brahminical orthodoxy and dealt with in the **Dharma-Shastra** literature. They are social and religious duty (*dharma*); economic prosperity (*artha*); aesthetic and sexual enjoyment (*kama*); and irreversible release from the series of births (*moksha*).

CHRIS BARTLEY

Purva Mimamsa

Purva Mimamsa (Previous Enquiry) is one of the six mainstream Indian *darshanas* (viewpoints) (see **darshana**), also called the *Karma Mimamsa* which prescribe and describe ritual. It is closely associated with the path of knowledge as leading to liberation from the series of births which is the concern of the **Vedanta** or the systematic exegesis of the Vedic 'knowledge portion' (*jnana kanda*), the **Upanishads**. When the latter enterprise was called the 'Later Enquiry' (*Uttara Mimamsa*), the ritualist enterprise acquired the designation 'Previous Enquiry' in so far as the path of action was seen as precedent and propaedeutic to the path of knowledge.

The Purva Mimamsakas were concerned with the interpretation and clarification of the portions of the eternal, authorless and infallible Vedas whose language is held to be the only source of knowledge (*pramana*) about the performance of ritual and the public and private duties of the twice-born members of the higher three castes (see **caste**). They insist (against the Vedantins in particular) that the purport of the Veda, whose most significant statements are of imperative form, is what has to be done (*karya*) in the spheres of primarily ritual and, derivatively, social duty (*dharma*). Prescription rather than description is regarded as the primary purpose of language from which its significative power is derived. The Mimamsaka outlook was atheistic in the sense that they believed that the gods (*devas*) existed only in name; that is to say, only in so far as the utterance of their names was part of the sacrificial mechanism. They maintained that the continued existence of the ordered universe depended upon the Vedic rituals and not upon divine sustenance. Exact performance being a necessary condition of ritual efficacy, precise understanding of the prescriptive formulae was essential. This led to an intense concern with the nature and functioning of words and sentences. The need to establish the infallible authority of the Veda led them into epistemological enquiries into the scope of the means of knowledge (*pramana*).

The school's basic text is the *Mimamsa Sutra* of Jaimini (*c.*100 CE) with the commentary by Shabara (fourth century CE). In the second half of the seventh century the school divided into the followers of **Kumarila Bhatta** and **Prabhakara Mishra**, the latter insisting that the Vedic injunctions (*vidhi*) incite action automatically, like categorical imperatives, while the former locate their motive force in the promise of rewards yielded by the rituals. The *Prakaranapanchika* of Prabhakara's disciple Shalikanatha (*c.*850 CE) is a noted philosophical work.

The Mimamsakas' enterprise is the investigation into the cosmic order (*dharma*) that is upheld by the ritual performances prescribed by the Vedic injunctions. The original view (which undergoes modifications in subsequent centuries) of the school is that the correct performance of ritual generates a new supernormal power (called *apurva*) which in turn produces the future result of the ritual, in particular the post mortem reward accruing to the patron (*yajamana*) of the sacrifice in paradise (*svarga*); the latter understood as the state of transitory felicity enjoyed by those transmigrating selves whose accumulated merit derived from ritual action has earned them a sojourn there. The qualification (*adhikara*) for patronage and performance of the Vedic rituals is restricted to physically intact male members of the Brahmin, Kshatriya and Vaishya castes (see caste).

Mimamsa epistemology is a form of direct realism and empiricism involving a *tabula rasa* account of the mind as the non-creative, passive recipient of data mediated by the senses. There is no inner realm of ideas and language intervening between the subject's awareness and the given, no possibility that the workings of conceptualization and language might generate a distorted representation of a mind-independent sphere in which all things, facts and values are external to consciousness. Cognitions are acts which are intrinsically valid (*svatah pramana*). Their function consists entirely in manifesting a mind-independent external world. Cognitive errors and illusions are attributable to extraneous factors such as defects in the sensory system which is the instrument of cognition or to the indistinctness of their objects. Cognitions being valid simply in virtue of their occurrence, the validity of the Veda which relates only to the supernatural was indubitable simply because the eternal and omnipresent phonemes (*varna*) comprising its injunctions are cognized. Their content, pertaining as it does to matters inaccessible to finite sensory modalities, is beyond the scope of contradiction by the empirical cognitive authorities of perception and inference. How would one falsify a statement that a person desiring heaven should sacrifice in such and such a way? Moreover, the Vedas being authorless (*apaurusheya*) and non-originated their authority could not be impugned by considerations bearing upon their author's reliability. What are only apparent internal discrepancies can be explained by intelligent exegesis, one of whose stated goals is harmonization.

Mimamsaka theses about language include:

1 The relation between a word and its referent (*shabdarthasambandha*) is innate (*autpattika*) and eternal (*nitya*).
2 The inherent word–object relation obtains between the phonemes comprising the word and the metaphysical form (*akriti*) common to the class of objects which it denotes.
3 Words participate in the substance of their referents.
4 Proper names of individuals are purely arbitrary conventional designations (*yadriccha-shabda*).

The Vedic statements are classified as injunctions (*vidhi*), descriptions and explanations (*artha-*

vada) and incantations (*mantra*) to be used in the rituals. Since the Veda teaches what must be done in the ritual sphere, injunctive statements have a primary status. *Arthavadas* are auxiliary statements whose function is that of motivating the hearer to perform the actions enjoined by *vidhis* and to explain their purpose by stating their fruits. The non-*vidhi* statements derive their significance from being accessory and supplementary to injunctions. The authority of scriptural statements is vested in their prescriptive function.

All the Vedic statements are held to be meaningful and non-repetitive and their literal senses to form an internally consistent whole. (In some circumstances it may behove the exegete to postulate a non-literal meaning (**lakshana**-*artha*) to make sense of the text.)

The Mimamsa conception of the soul is of an eternal omnipresent and inherently active spiritual essence whose location in finite environments is due to the workings of *karma*, the theory that motivated and intentional actions generate retributive potencies that develop into future experiences and which personalize and propel the agent from life to life. Once the aspiration to irreversible liberation (*moksha*) from rebirth had supplanted the transitory felicity of heaven (*svarga*) as the *summum bonum*, the purpose of ritual performance was transformed from the acquisition of benefits to the depersonalization of the individual through renunciatory detachment from the consequences of his binding actions. Through the disinterested performance of obligatory actions in a spirit of 'duty for duty's sake', he could look forward to liberation when his no longer increasing accumulated **karma** had been exhausted in a long but finite succession of lives passed in unmotivated conformity to social and religious duty (*dharma*).

Further reading

Biardeau, M. (1954) *Théories de la Connaissance et Philosophie de la Parole dans le Brahmanisme Classique*, Paris and the Hague: Mouton.

Hiriyanna, M. (1993) *Outlines of Indian Philosophy*, Delhi: Motilal Banarsidass.

CHRIS BARTLEY

Q

qi

There is no agreement on how this key term is best rendered: it can appear as **ether**, *élan vitale* or vital force, humour, breath or psychosomatic force. *Qi* (*ch'i*) (the pictogram shows 'stream rising from cooked rice'; the etymology is of 'air' or 'breath') encompasses both matter and spirit. To the extent that *yin* and *yang* are the two *qi* that inform the whole universe, it covers everything from the most sublime to the most gross. And since *yin* and *yang* (as substance) are passivity and activity (in motion) and can alternate as the hidden and the manifest (in phases of in/visibility), it is as much a moving force mediating the potential and the actual. It is no mere metaphysical abstraction, being the air we breathe in and out. But then, it is more than air as we now know it, for it circulated through the body in channels that western science cannot chart but whose nodal points acupuncture needles can pinpoint and stimulate for therapeutic ends. It can even be made to 'stay put' by *qigong* masters, making the person immovable to pushing or shoving by strong men. That centre of gravity called the 'cinnabar field' is located in the lower abdomen, the seat of the so-called deep (dia-phragm) breathing. Its significance for philosophy is because the whole *qi* dynamics and vocabulary appears in the Mencian discourse on the 'immove-able mind'. It influences Chinese lives through the homeopathic principle in Chinese medicine, phy-sical hygiene and the 'bedchamber arts' (the *dao* of sex).

To say the least, the origin of this *qi* ideology is murky. It may be buried in some archaic medical wisdom, orally transmitted and written down later in the ***Inner Classic of the Yellow Emperor***, a work judged by some to epitimize a Han philosophical synthesis. Some scholars speak of there being two regional inspirations to this *qi* ideology, a Lu Confucian source that is anthropo-centric and a *qi* Daoist root further east that is cosmocentric. In brief, the former holds that man has only a limited supply of an *élan vitale* at birth, which he must carefully keep intact within his body. If he dissipates this life force via eruption or exposure, such as bad temper, he risks shortening his life. The latter position may accept that too, but it also believes in a cosmic store of the same ether outside man, which can be tapped and channelled into the body to promote health and immortality. The *Analects* knew only the former anthropocentric usage; it speaks of 'blood and breath' and means by it what we would call a person's bearing and character. The 'psychic chapters' of the *Guanzi* preserve the latter, cosmocentric understanding. They teach a method of drawing on that cosmic store and flow of *qi* which, being also aligned with the various manifestations of the **Five Elements** on earth and in **heaven**, can bring the person (microcosm) in line with that (macrocosmic) structure. **Confucius**'s moral anthropology was originally based on the Zhou social charter; it did not require this other cosmocentric ideology.

Not unlike Plato drawing on a Pythagorean mystery to support the Socratic platform, it seems that **Mencius** defending Confucius also tapped into an 'eastern' tradition of a cosmic *qi*. In the feudal Zhou period, the state of Qi lay to the East (the present-day Shandong peninsula). This legendary home of the Daoist tradition may have inspired Mencius to adopt its Qi philosophy to defend Confucius (the two '*qi*s' are alike in sound but different characters). In his hymn on the floodlike ether, he reconstructed it as a moral force that 'fills the space between heaven and earth' that can animate and direct a personal life of moral **righteousness**. **Zhuangzi** was aware of the same cosmic psychology, but he used it to paint a much more casual relationship with the *dao*. A schematization of the ether, *yin–yang* and the Five Elements came later with Zou Yan, and that system formed the backbone of Chinese science, metaphysics and **correlative thinking** from Han times onward. The Han saw one ether informing everything in the cosmos. After the Buddhists demoted that cosmos to being *samsara*, an acosmic principle is postulated to go with the higher gnosis or *prajna*. When in the Song dynasty Neo-Confucians reconstituted the classical world-view, **Zhu Xi** would argue against the Han monism of one ether. A singular principle is postulated above the many manifestations of ethereal forms. Dissatisfied with this dualism, some seventeenth-century thinkers worked to erase it and redeem the world of the ether as the immediate arena for a freer expression of the human passions.

See also: Ch'oe Han-ki; Chong Che-du; Chong Yag-yong (Tasan); Neo-Confucianism, concepts of

Further reading

Lai, W. (1984) 'Kao-tzu and Mencius on Mind: Analyzing a Platonic Shift in Classical China', *Philosophy East and West* 34(2): 147–60.

Yasuyori, T. (1970) *The Tao of Sex*, New York: Harper & Row.

WHALEN LAI

R

Radhakrishnan, Sarvepalli

b. 1888; d. 1975

Philosopher

Sarvepalli Radhakrishnan was a philosopher and apologist for the consciousness-monist (**Advaita** Vedanta) variety of Hinduism which he saw as the unique representative of the highest religious aspirations of mankind. A native of South India, he was educated at Christian missionary schools, taking his first degrees in philosophy at Madras Christian College, where Hinduism was evaluated as ethically unsound because of the **caste** specificity of the notion of duty (***dharma***). This was still provoking a vehement reaction as late as 1939 in *Eastern Religions and Western Thought*. These European influences reinforced a pervasive sense of impotent desperation at the decline into moribundity and irrelevance to the scientific and humanistic modern world of once vital Hindu traditions of thought. In 1921 Radhakrishnan was appointed to the King George V Chair of Mental and Moral Science at Calcutta University. From 1936 to 1941 he held the Spalding Chair of Eastern Religions and Ethics at the University of Oxford, where he was a Fellow of All Souls College. He was also Indian ambassador to the Soviet Union, Vice-President of India from 1952 to 1962 and President from 1962 to 1967.

Radhakrishnan tended to understand his own Advaitic intellectualist tradition though the eyes of **Vivekananda**, who was a disciple of **Ramakrishna**. As an Advaitin, he understood ultimate reality as a single principle that is the ineffable and impersonal Brahman, defined as inactive consciousness and bliss, with which centres of consciousness, that temporarily misunderstand themselves as embodied individual agents, are identical. *Brahman* is the source of the non-illusory experienced world although the relation between *Brahman*, and its manifestation cannot be logically specified. He is concerned to understand the universe as the locus of value and opposed the dominant trend in his own tradition which dismissed it as ultimately illusory (*maya*). The multifarious Hindu deities of Hindu mythology are personifications of aspects of a commodious Absolute and worshipped as entities in their own right by people whose understanding does not stretch to the truth of impersonalist non-dualism.

Radhakrishnan understood the mechanism of ***karma*** in a positive light as affirming the possibility of free choice and self-improvement. Unselfish action (and social democracy) should follow from the realization of the spiritual unity of mankind. He interpreted the caste structure in terms of a necessary distribution of occupations suitable to types of personality at different stages of progressive evolutionary development.

The rationality of religious tolerance was a major theme of his work. Different religious expressions are relativized to the historical environments of their adherents. The spiritualism of Advaita, maintaining the non-dualistic experience of the impersonal Absolute and the true Self ('the consubstantiality of the spirit in man and God'), is the supreme truth providing an absolute perspective on other understandings of reality for whose occurrence as partial understandings it can give an account. Radhakrishnan was an exponent of the perennial philosophy view that there is a universal type of religious experience and drew widely on all manner of philosophies and faiths in his writings. He contrasts what he characterized as **faith** deriving from unitive mystical or spiritual experience (exemplified by that of the 'seers' who composed the authoritative Hindu scriptures or *shruti*) with beliefs which are the acceptance as true of traditional conflicting dogmas.

Further reading

Gopal, S. (1989) *Radhakrishnan*, Delhi: Oxford University Press.

Radhakrishnan, S. (1920) *The Reign of Religion in Contemporary Philosophy*, London: Macmillan.

—— (1923) *Indian Philosophy*, London: Allen and Unwin.

—— (1927) *The Hindu View of Life*, London: Allen and Unwin.

—— (1927) *An Idealist View of Life*, London: Allen and Unwin.

—— (1939) *Eastern Religions and Western Thought*, London: Oxford University Press.

—— (1947) *Religion and Society*, London: Allen and Unwin.

—— (trans.) (1948) *The Bhagavad Gita*, London: Allen and Unwin.

—— (1950) *The Dhammapada*, London: Oxford University Press.

—— (1953) *The Principal Upanishads*, London: Allen and Unwin.

CHRIS BARTLEY

Ramakantha

b. 950; d. 1000

Philosopher and theologian

Ramakantha was a Kashmiri philosopher and theologian belonging to the pluralistic and theistic **Shaiva Siddhanta** tradition of scriptural interpretation and ritual, which flourished in Kashmir from the eighth to the eleventh centuries CE. The son of Narayanakanthabhatta, author of a commentary on the *Mrigendra Agama*, Ramakantha

produced dualistic interpretations of scriptures such as the *Matangaparameshvara Agama* and wrote commentaries on the works of Sadyojyoti (*fl. c.*750), most notably the latter's *Nareshvarapariksha* (Enquiry into Man and God), his *Moksha-Karikas* (Verses on Liberation from Rebirth) and the *Paramokshanirasa-Karikas* (Verses Refuting Other Schools' Theories of Liberation).

The ethos of his philosophical stance can be appreciated from the introduction to the *Commentary on the Nareshvarapariksha*.

Knowledge of God, the source (*sara*) of every knowable entity, is the means to ultimate well-being. Only the Shaivas have an adequate conception of divinity as possessed of infinite powers. Some other schools, typically Vedantins and Pancharatra Vaishnavas, say that God is not only the instrumental but also the substantive cause (*upadana-karana*) of the universe. This view has the rather awkward implication that God is insentient like clay, the substantive cause of pots. According to the **Samkhya** school, agency being a property of material nature, God would not be an agent. Other schools make God subject to the periodic emanations and dissolutions of the cosmos. The **Yoga** school conceives of God as a special type of individual with pre-eminent mental faculties who is untouched by afflictions such as *karma*. But since the mental faculties are emergent products of material nature, they are also subject to destruction. Others say that Ishvara possesses conjunction with mind which is generally recognized to be a natural product. But mind being *per se* insentient, it is manifold and impermanent since it is an effect.

But the Enquiry into the nature of man precedes that into the nature of God because some atheistic ritualists say, 'Man is everything, so why postulate God?' Buddhists say that there is no supreme director given the spontaneous origination and destruction of entities in every moment. Materialists recommend enjoying oneself while one is alive. In the absence of just regulation by factors such as *karma*, why bother with God?

The second verse of the *Nareshvarapariksha* reads: 'He who is a cognizer and agent acts having perceived an object by a cognition. In this system the experiencer of the results of activity is called the individual person.' Ramakantha says that 'cognizer' means one who has the power of cognition.

The existence of this faculty is not inferred (the view of the Naiyayikas) because consciousness is self-illuminating or reflexive in that it is always the manifestor of objects. In addition, something cannot be the object of inference to itself. The non-ideal self is immediately and infallibly given in every act of awareness as the persisting subject. 'Agent' means possessed of the power of action evidenced by the experience of physical movement. The Samkhya view of essential non-agency runs counter to direct experience. Their denial that the self is really an agent and ascription of agency to the operations of material nature means that given the absence of a director, instruments and effects would operate spontaneously, like a drunkard out of control. The possession of these powers is not something produced or emergent because were the self ever to lack them, it would cease to be self. The individual is directly conscious of itself as a free agent. The objects of awareness are mind-independent entities with determinate identities and not merely ideas. The experiencer of the results of activity must be a persisting entity: were it momentary (the Buddhist view) the beneficial karmic fruits of a meritorious action would not redound to its instigator.

Ramakantha holds that the existence of God can be proved by an inferential cosmological argument that the complexity and organization of the conscious and non-conscious world presupposes an omnipotent and omniscient creator. Shiva is the efficient cause of the universe of worlds which he creates via recourse to *maya*, the real substantive cause of the material and mental domains. The divine power of occlusion (*tirodhana-shakti*) is understood positively as the compassionate provision of environments in which finite beings may experience the fruits of their *karma*, thereby depotentiating it.

See also: Nyaya

Further reading

Goodall, D. (1998) *Bhatta Ramakantha's Commentary on the Kiranatantra*, Pondicherry: Institut Française.

CHRIS BARTLEY

Ramakrishna

b. 1836; d. 1886

Philosopher and mystic

Ramakrishna was a Hindu mystic who maintained the essential unity of all religions. A priest at a Kali temple in Bengal, his exceptional devotion to that goddess resulted in the attainment of transic states so intense that he was prevented from performing his ritual duties. He thought himself to have experienced unity with the Absolute through the practice of profound meditative interiorization (*nirvikalpaka-samadhi*) in which experience of subject–object duality is obliterated. Subsequently, he followed the Vaishnava praxis of devotion (*bhakti*) to Krishna of whom he had a vision. There followed emotional and practical identifications with other religious traditions, each culminating in revelations of other deities and major religious figures, including Jesus and Muhammad. As a result of these experiences, he concluded that all religions are equal in that they are aspects of a quest for the One Absolute, which is a plenum of knowledge and bliss. His mystical experience of unity drew him to the **Advaita** Vedanta system of religious philosophy which asserts the identity of God and the soul. His inclusivist outlook attracted a number of educated disciples, the most significant of whom was **Vivekananda**, at one time an associate of the **Brahmo Samaj**, who came to regard him as a *guru* incarnating divinity.

Further reading

de Bary, W. (1958) *Sources of Indian Tradition*, New York: Columbia University Press.

CHRIS BARTLEY

Ramanuja

*fl. c.*1100

Theologian and philosopher

A Tamil based in Shrirangam, Ramanuja was a Shri Vaishnava theologian of theistic **Vedanta** resolutely opposed to the non-dualist (**Advaita**) traditions. Ramanuja sought to improve the credentials of the beliefs and practices of his Shri Vaishnava cult by demonstrating their conformity to mainstream Vedic orthodoxy represented by the **Brahma-Sutras**, the **Upanishads**, the **Bhagavad Gita** and the **Dharma-Shastra** literature. His principal works include the *Shri Bhashya* (his commentary on the *Brahma-Sutras*), the *Gita-Bhashya* and the *Vedarthasamgraha* (a non-commentatorial work). Many of the characteristic themes of **Vishishtadvaita** (Integral Unity of a Complex Reality) are anticipated in the works of his predecessor in the Shri Vaishnava tradition, **Yamuna**. But whereas the latter, in his *Agamapramanyam*, attempted to demonstrate the Veda-equivalence of the tantric sectarian Vaishnava Pancharatra system of theology and ritual, Ramanuja avoids reference to this embarrassing relative. Indeed, his overall conservatism must be emphasized. For example, devotional religion (*bhakti*) may be interpreted as having have egalitarian anti-caste implications (as it was by his Tamil Alvar precursors in the Shri Vaishnava tradition) since emotions are the common property of everyone and indifferent to **caste** status. Ramanuja exalts *bhakti* as a mode of relationship with the quasi-personally conceived deity Vishnu Narayana culminating in communion with God in heaven, but he insists that devotion belongs in a context of the observation of the strictly hierarchical caste and ritual obligations (*varna-ashrama-dharma*). Indeed, he identifies *bhakti* with the performance of the latter. He characterizes the experiential nature of *bhakti* in highly intellectualized terms as a form of hyper-lucid perception and a steady flow of contemplative concentration.

The term 'Vishishtadvaita' is interpreted in the tradition as meaning 'non-duality' of a differentiated reality: that is, reality is a single, structured, organic whole, ultimately intelligible while being internally complex. While the Advaitins regard the world including the individual agency that is crucial to the householder's *dharma* as an illusion concealing the static impersonality of a negatively conceived Absolute, Ramanuja sees it as the real self-differentiation of the Supreme Person. His metaphysic is organized in three basic categories of a personal deity; individual agent selves whose essential property is reflexive consciousness (*chit*)

and material entities (*achit*). The latter two depend upon the first and material bodies depend upon the selves which ensoul them. Entities falling into the three categories are essentially distinct. Taking his cue from the *Brihadaranyaka Upanishad* 3.7.3f., which refers to a self who is the inner self and inner controller of individual selves, he formulates the soul–body doctrine (*sharira-shariri-bhava*). The basic idea is that the Supreme Self is related to the individual selves (*jiva*) in a manner analogous to that in which they are related to their material bodies. He defines a body as a dependent and essentially distinct entity whose entire *raison d'être* consists in subserving the purposes of a self which controls it. The key elements here are essential dependence, intimate connection and distinctness. Individual selves and material things constitute the body of God in the senses that they are dependent upon God and exist to express his non-purposive actuality. But just as the essential distinction between the individual selves and their bodies means that they are unimpaired by physical imperfections to which the flesh is heir, likewise the difference between God and his body, the world, exempts him from the vicissitudes of finiteness. Ramanuja also expresses the relationship as that between a substrate (*adhara*) and attribute (*adheya*), controller and thing controlled and between principal (*sheshi*) and accessory or servant (*shesha*).

It is in the field of anti-Advaitic scriptural exegesis that the soul–body doctrine comes into its own. The Advaitins construe co-referential (**samanadhikaranya**) expressions such as 'That thou art' (**Tat tvam asi**; *Chandogya Up.* 6.2.1) as identity statements conveying the absolute non-difference of **atman** and *Brahman*. They tend to explain Upanishadic statements suggesting difference in non-literal senses. Through recourse to the soul–body doctrine, Ramanuja is able to construe statements suggestive of unity in those suggesting difference in their literal senses – one of the desiderata of satisfactory scriptural exegesis. Statements asserting non-difference are intelligible from the point of view that *Brahman* alone exists with everything as his body inseparably connected to him. Statements of difference and non-difference are intelligible when it is considered that the one *Brahman* exists as a plurality qualified by his modes, the conscious and non-conscious entities. Statements about difference make sense given that God, souls and matter are all distinct. The key text (*mahavakya*) '*Tat tvam asi*' is construed as conveying unity and essential difference. Since terms for bodies referentially extend to their souls (we may speak of people via their bodies) terms usually applied to aspects of the world (the body of God) may extend in their scope to the Supreme Person. The term '*Tat*' is thus applied directly and not in a secondary or apophatic sense to Vishnu.

Ramanuja subscribes to the **satkaryavada** theory of causation, according to which an effect pre-exists in its causal substrate as a germinal modality of a future state prior to its entitative manifestation. An effect is not a novel product: creation is not *ex nihilo*, and effects have the same degree of reality as their substrative causes. *Brahman* is said to be the cause of the universe when its body is in its causal mode, 'containing' in subtle form the various entities that comprise the universe. *Brahman* is said to be the effect when its body is in its effected mode, selves and matter being manifested as entities with determinate names and forms. Theorists of the Bhedabheda school such as **Bhaskara** and Yadavaprakasha conceptualized a real creative process as a transformation of *Brahman* (*Brahma-parinama-vada*). If this process is regarded as a transformation of the proper form of the Absolute, problems will obviously arise, especially if the ontic link between God and creation is a particularly strong one. For this reason, Ramanuja replaces *Brahma-parinama-vada* with *Brahma-sharira-parinama-vada*. According to this view, the cosmic transformation occurs in the sphere of *Brahman*'s body and the flawless integrity of the ultimate principle is protected. With a view to avoiding the attribution of means–end rationality to the perfect divinity, he characterizes the generation of the world process as *lila* (play) or non-purposive, unconstrained activity.

Ramanuja's metaphysic is one for the man in the world following the active religion of social and ritual duty (*pravrtti-dharma*). The active householder solves the problem of karmic consequentialism and concomitant bondage to rebirth by fostering an awareness that it is not he who acts but God who acts in him as inner controller (*antaryamin*). Perfecting himself through disinterested conformity to God's will manifested as his *dharma*, he acts not out of desire for the fruits of his prescribed actions but in a spirit of awareness of God as ultimate agent.

Ramanuja distances himself from Advaita by defining selves as enduring individual agents whose essential property is consciousness. The category consciousness is explicated in terms of reflexivity (**svayam prakasha**) and intentionality (*savishayata*). His claim that in the state of release the selves are qualitatively identical raises the problem of individuation. Ramanuja maintains that each uniquely knows itself: distinct individualities are privately known. Consistent with his claim that there is no consciousness without object, he also asserts that there is divine provision of supernatural bodies, environments and experiences for the released selves.

Ramanuja's epistemology is characterized by extreme realism. In his attempts to controvert the varieties of anti-realist arguments advanced by Advaitins and Buddhists of idealist or phenomenalist persuasion, he goes as far as denying the possibility of genuine cognitive error (see **cognitive error, classical Indian theories**). Cognitions are always intrinsically valid, and relate to a mind-independent sphere simply in virtue of their occurrence. Cognition never deviates from external, given reality (even in cases of apparent illusions) and in the case of objects whose appearance is 'private' to individuals, there is no purely subjective element intervening between awareness and the world. All cognitions correspond to present realities. Appealing to the ancient theory of quintuplication (*panchi-karana*) according to which material things have a compounded constitution containing all the five elements (*bhuta*: earth, water, fire, air and atmosphere) in different proportions, Ramanuja says that in the case of a mirage, we really do perceive water in the sands of the desert. When shell is mistaken for silver, we are actually apprehending scintillae of silver present in the shell and manifested in the lustrous similarity of their surfaces. Perhaps overwhelmed by avarice, the perceiver overlooks the preponderance of the less precious material.

Classical Indian epistemology centres on the status and scope of the authoritative means of knowledge (**pramana**), the three most important of which are sense-perception (*pratyaksha*), inference (*anumana*), which is based on the former, and testimony (*shabda*). In the case of the latter, only scriptural testimony, in so far as it bears on that which transcends the bounds of sense, is intrinsically and independently authoritative. Anything genuinely existent can in principle be established or validated by one or more of the means of knowledge.

The Advaitin, Ramanuja insists, has no means of establishing his thesis that reality is ultimately non-differentiated contentless consciousness. All *pramana*-based cognitions are necessarily of particularized and differentiated entities possessing identifiable features. It follows that if reality is non-differentiated, our recognized means of knowing could not operate. The Advaitin might claim that reflexive consciousness which is always the same in the turbid flux of mental states establishes a constant, non-differentiated reality. Ramanuja says that this is refuted by the fact that what is immediately given in the first personal perspective is experience of differentiated entities. Scriptural language cannot establish that reality is non-differentiated pure consciousness. The intrinsically composite and relational nature of the Sanskrit language reflects the complexity of that to which it refers.

According to Advaitins such as **Mandana Mishra**, the Absolute qua undifferentiated pure being manifests itself in the initial, preconceptual stage (*nirvikalpaka*) in the perceptual process:

> First, there is a non-conceptual perception (*avikalpaka-pratyaksha*) relating to the bare object. The ensuing constructive cognitions (*vikalpa-buddhi*) comprehend particularities (*vishesha*). 'Difference' (*bheda*) is not given in perception but is a mental construct (*vikalpa*) subsequent to the perception of the mere object (*vastu-matra*) in its true nature. The absolute *Brahman*, the supreme universal, which is pure, undifferentiated and non-specific reality (*san-matra; satta*) is given in non-conceptual awareness.

In common with most philosophers, Ramanuja accepts a distinction between two stages in the perceptual process, technically termed *nirvikalpaka-pratyaksha* and *savikalpaka-pratyaksha*. In accordance with his understanding of perception, the Sanskrit terms should be translated 'classificatory' and 'non-classificatory'. He denies that either can be a *pramana* for a non-differentiated reality. The object of classificatory perception is differentiated since it relates to that which is qualified by several categorial determinates (**padartha**) such as class-property and qualities. The object of non-classificatory perception is differentiated since it is the cause of the recognitional comparison (*pratisamdhana*) with similar things of an entity qualified by those determinates at the classificatory stage. Non-classificatory perception apprehends an entity as devoid of some differentia, but not of all differentia. Every cognition arises in virtue of some feature and is expressed as 'this is a particular thing' as opposed to 'this is a something'. Specifically, his view is that we grasp a complex entity having a generic structure (*samsthana*) in every act of awareness but in first-stage perception we do not appreciate the recurrence (*anuvritti*) of that feature in a class of entities.

Further reading

Abhyankar, V. (ed.) (1914) *Sribhasya of Ramanuja*, Bombay: Government Central Press.

Bartley, C. (2000) *Realism and Religion: Ramanuja's Vedanta*, Richmond: Curzon.

Carman, J. (1974) *The Theology of Ramanuja*, New Haven, CN and London: Yale University Press.

Dasgupta, S. (1940) *A History of Indian Philosophy*, vol. III, Cambridge: Cambridge University Press.

Lacombe, O. (1937) *L'Absolu selon le Vedanta*, Paris: Librairie Orientaliste Paul Geuthner.

—— (1938) *La Doctrine morale et métaphysique de Ramanuja*, Paris: Adrien-Maisonneuve.

Lester, R. (1976) *Ramanuja on the Yoga*, Madras: Adyar Library and Research Centre.

Lipner, J. (1986) *The Face of Truth: A Study of Meaning and Metaphysics in the Vedantic Theology of Ramanuja*, Albany, NY: State University of New York Press.

Lott, E. (1976) *God and the Universe in the Vedantic Theology of Ramanuja*, Madras: Ramanuja Research Society.

Thibaut, G. (1904) *Vedanta-Sutras with Ramanuja's Commentary*, Oxford: Oxford University Press.

van Buitenen, J. (1953) *Ramanuja on the Bhagavad Gita*, The Hague: Smits.

—— (ed. and trans.) (1956) *Ramanuja's Vedarthasamgraha*, 2 vols, Poona: Deccan College Postgraduate and Research Institute.

CHRIS BARTLEY

RAMAYANA *see* Sanskrit epics

Rammohan Roy

b. 1772; d. 1833

Philosopher and writer

Born into a Bengali Brahmin family, Rammohan was the first Indian whose thought was significantly influenced by exposure to post-Enlightenment Western European culture. His influence has been formative of the self-understanding of many educated modern Indians. After a remarkably comprehensive education which involved exposure to aniconic Islamic monotheism, in 1803 he entered the East India Company in which he attained high rank. Having retired at the age of forty-two, a substantial private income enabled him to found and edit English, Bengali and Persian newspapers, to establish secondary schools in which English was the medium of instruction, to promote campaigns against the practice of forcible widow-burning (*sati*) and to organize the **Brahmo Samaj** (founded 1828), which has exerted a considerable influence on the social and religious affairs of modern India. He engaged in controversies with Christian missionaries (producing the memorable epigram; 'It is not new, it is not true and it is not you') and those traditional Brahmins whom he regarded as polytheistic idolaters. For a period (1824–8) he considered himself a 'Hindu Unitarian'. Towards the end of his life (1830) he travelled to England, the supposed home of scientific rationalism, where he presented to a parliamentary committee a series of recommendations on the amelioration of British rule in India. Much admired by people of Unitarian theological persuasion, he died in Bristol.

In an early work (*A Gift for the Monotheists*), he argued that the natural light of human reason leads people to a belief in a supreme being who is the creator and sustainer of reality. A combination of custom, tradition and the wiles of religious leaders distracts men's minds from this pure conviction.

Rammohan's attitude to Christianity was ambivalent: while admiring the character of Jesus (as he pointed out, 'an Asiatic') and his humanitarian teachings 'tending evidently to the maintenance of the peace and harmony of mankind at large', he rejected what he regarded as distorting doctrinal accretions, in particular the notions of the Trinity, the divinity of Christ and the miraculous. (He translated the New Testament into Bengali.) Correlatively, he emphasized those Hindu scriptures (the **Upanishads**) which appeared to endorse ethical monotheism, which he contrasted with what he regarded as the superstitious and idolatrous degenerate beliefs and practices espoused by the majority of his Indian co-religionists and which attracted the contempt of the English rulers. Christianity and Hinduism both being equally incomprehensible sublime mysteries transcending the human understanding, one cannot be preferred to the other. This strategy had the effect of inhibiting the conversion of many Brahmin intellectuals to Christianity.

His defence of the status of Hindu women attracted death threats from ultra-traditionalist Brahmins. The immolation of widows was recommended ironically on the grounds:

that women are by nature of inferior understanding, without resolution, unworthy of trust, subject to passions, and void of virtuous knowledge; they according to the precepts of the *shastra* are not allowed to marry again after the demise of their husbands, and consequently despair at once of all worldly pleasure; hence it is evident that death to these unfortunate widows is preferable to existence for the great difficulty which a widow may experience by living a purely ascetic life as prescribed by the shastras is obvious; therefore if she does not perform concremation, it is probable that she may be guilty of such acts as may bring disgrace upon her maternal and paternal relations, and those that may be connected with her husband. Under these circumstances we instruct them from their early life in the idea of concremation, holding out to them heavenly enjoyments in company with their husbands, as well as the beatitude of their relations, both by birth and marriage, and their reputation in this world. From this many of them, on the death of their husbands, become desirous of accompanying them; but to remove every chance of their trying to escape from the blazing fire, in burning them we first tie them down to the pile.

(*English Works* 360)

Rammohan Roy replies that the faults imputed to women are not 'planted in their constitution by nature'. He pointed out that feminine inferiority in respect of understanding was hardly surprising in a society in which women were denied education. In terms of the capacity for duplicity, men and women are on an equal footing. The charge of lack of resolution could not be levelled against people who were prepared to die on their deceased husband's funeral pyre. Men who could practise polygamy were not in a position to accuse women of subjection to passion. Moreover, there is no shortage of examples of the exercise of 'virtuous knowledge' by women. Partly as a result of Rammohan Roy's efforts, *sati* was made illegal in 1829.

His attitude to indigenous traditions of scholarship and philosophy is expressed in his *Letter on Education* (1823) to the Governor General, registering opposition to the government's establishment of a new Sanskrit College in Calcutta under Hindu pandits and pleading for 'a more liberal and enlightened system of instruction' on the modern European model:

This seminary (similar in character to those which existed in Europe before the time of Lord Bacon) can only be expected to load the minds of youth with grammatical niceties and metaphysical distinctions of little or no practical use to the possessors or to society. The pupils will there acquire what was known two thousand years ago with the addition of vain and empty subtleties since then produced by speculative men such as is already commonly taught in all parts of India. The Sanskrit language, so difficult that almost a lifetime is necessary for its acquisition, is well known to have been for ages a lamentable check to the diffusion of knowledge, and the learning concealed under this almost impervious veil is far from sufficient to reward the labour of acquiring it... Neither can much improvement arise from such speculation as the following which are the themes suggested by the Vedanta: In what manner is the soul absorbed into the deity? What relation does it

bear to the Divine Essence? Nor will youths be fitted to be better members of society by the Vedantic doctrines which teach them to believe that all visible things have no real existence, that as father, brother etc have no real entity, they consequently deserve no real affection, and therefore the sooner we escape from them and leave the world the better.

(*English Works* 474)

Rammohan's influential contentions were adopted by Macaulay, whose *Minute on Education* (1835) recommended the development of a Western system of education. Macaulay wrote:

The question now before us is simply whether, when it is in our power to teach this language [English], we shall teach languages in which, by universal confession, there are no books on any subject which deserve to be compared to our own; whether, when we teach European science, we shall teach systems which, by universal confession, whenever they differ from those of Europe, differ for the worse; and whether, when we can patronise sound philosophy and true history, we shall countenance, at the public expense, medical doctrines which would disgrace an English farrier, astronomy which would move laughter in girls at an English boarding school, history abounding with kings thirty feet high and reigns thirty thousand years long, and geography, made up of seas of treacle and seas of butter.

He anticipated the rise of nationalist movements opposed to British rule consequent upon the development of the national character of a people who have had 'the advantage of being ruled by and associated with an enlightened nation, advocates of liberty and promoters of knowledge'; a nation which nevertheless disappointed by imposing degrading unjust and oppressive measures on its subjects.

Further reading

Killingley, D. (1993) *Rammohum Roy in Hindu and Christian Traditions*, Newcastle upon Tyne: Grevatt and Grevatt.

Kopf, D. (1979) *The Brahmosamaj and the Shaping of the*

Modern Indian Mind, Princeton, NJ: Princeton University Press.

Roy, R. (1906) *The English Works of Raja Rammohun Roy*, Allahabad: The Panini Office.

CHRIS BARTLEY

recluse and kings

The mode and the degree of world denial appears to be correlated to the degree of freedom available in a particular community. Indian **caste** society is so strait-jacketed that to rebel against the status quo, one has to renounce the world totally. This is quite unlike the Hebrew prophet, who works to change the system from within; he speaks on behalf of God with some effect because God happens to remain King to his people. Chinese society lies somewhere in between these two extremes of world-transcendence and world-transformation. Its Daoist recluse retires and does not renounce the world, while its Confucian ministers counsel but do not challenge. Recluse is *yin*, which means 'to hide', the antonymn of 'to manifest' (the pair 'hidden/manifest' is one shade subtler than *yin–yang*). The word for 'to hide' is *yin* ('to hide') but it is different from the script *yin* in *yin–yang*; the latter, meaning 'shadow', can also mean 'to hide'. *Yin* cannot turn into *yang* but the hidden can become the manifest. Han Confucians dealt well with the *yin–yang* distinction; Song Neo-Confucians discussed it rather better in terms of 'hidden/manifest'. That distinction is reflected in their metaphysics.

Politically, there is a similar dialectics. Early Han Daoist rulers honoured and imitated recluses; they intentionally stayed hidden from view, they ruled *wuwei*, *laissez-faire* style, by delegating authority to the prime minister. Under the Neo-Confucian Ming dynasty, the ruler made himself visible and publicized his fatherly concern; the scholar officials themselves refuse to honour the recluse, holding up the new ideal of 'inner sagehood and outer kingship' due the innerworldly ascetic; and imperial rule became proactive and, by taking away the power of the top ministers, has been called 'despotic'. The hands-on style of rule worked well with tireless and committed rulers, who took on the role of 'benevolent despots'. The system truly wrought havoc with the other extreme, the utterly indolent irresponsive and irresponsible monarch. The Ming dynasty began with the former and ended with the latter.

In between the Han and the Ming came the largely Buddhist era, which included all types of medieval religio-politics involving sinners and saints, kings and holy men, suicidal ascetics and armed monks, power and piety making strange bedfellows like strong-willed empresses and their Rasputin-like monk counsels. There were regular holy men at court and occasional 'prime ministers in black robes or in the hills' (king-making monks and recluses), apolitical 'mountain men' and political 'retirees'. In the Buddhist tradition, the forest monk who retired to the forest to meditate and to pursue the ascetic life represents the reclusive saint. He stands in opposition to the village monk who serves the lay public. The forest monk could often resist the power of the secular ruler better, since he was not part of the ordinary social structure.

Further reading

Ching, J. and Guisso, R. (eds) (1991) *Sages and Filial Sons*, Hong Kong: Chinese University of Hong Kong.

WHALEN LAI

recluse in Islam

There are contrasting arguments in Islamic philosophy on the desirability or otherwise of the recluse or solitary. Ibn Bajja argues that there are situations where the philosopher is regarded as making no useful contribution to society, as a weed, and in those circumstances he ought to abandon society and seek to preserve himself, and his thought, by going into seclusion. Many *sufis* also were attracted to the solitary life, to staying in particular places where they could contemplate without the interruptions inevitable in social life (see **Sufism**).

In the philosophical novel by Ibn Tufayl, *Hayy ibn Yaqzan*, a sort of philosophical Robinson Crusoe, a baby escapes a shipwreck by floating to an island, uninhabited by any other human beings. He is looked after by a deer, and works out by himself the main principles of science and the spiritual nature of reality, using reason and his own capacity for feeling alone. Eventually a stranger arrives on the island and is greeted enthusiastically by Hayy, and there follows a genuine dialogue of opinions and forms of knowledge. (One might contrast this treatment of the stranger with Robinson Crusoe's enslavement of Man Friday.) Hayy has the confidence of someone who has gone to the source of knowledge, and when someone comes he is eager to share his knowledge with the other and also learn from him. They both go to a large city, but are disappointed at the inability of the 'civilized' to listen to them or live according to rational and religious principles. When both are disappointed by life in 'civilization', they return to the island and seek to resume their simple yet perfect lives there. It would obviously be better for them to be able to participate in social life, since in that way they could influence others and possibly even be influenced by them in useful ways, but if society is so corrupt that there is no scope for such a result, the thinker and seeker after the truth is better off going elsewhere.

Further reading

Ibn Tufayl (1972) *Hayy ibn Taqzan: A Philosophical Tale*, trans. L. Goodman, New York: Twayne.

OLIVER LEAMAN

relative and absolute

The now standard Chinese terms for 'relative' and 'absolute' read literally 'mutually opposing' and 'terminating all opposings'. They go back to the Neo-Daoist pair 'with reliance' and 'without reliance', meaning the dependent and the independent (see **Neo-Daoism**). Things being caused are dependent; the *dao*, being the origin of all things, is independent, according to the argument of the Neo-Daoist Guo Xiang. Because the pair presumes a cosmogony, the Buddhist Sanlun (Madhyamika) masters changed it into a purely

logical pair of what is 'mutually dependent' and what 'terminates all dependences'. The latter describes the Middle Path. Japan probably coined the modern pair by substituting 'opposition' for 'dependent'. The **Kyoto school** of **Nishida** Kitaro then developed a complex system of metaphysics around this Absolute Nothingness.

Further reading

Waldenfels, H. (1980) *Absolute Nothingness: Foundations for a Buddhist-Christian Dialogue*, trans. J. Heisig, New York: Paulist Press.

WHALEN LAI

religious Daoism

Organized religious Daoism rose towards the end of the Han dynasty (late second century CE). The cultivation of the *dao* involved a 'quiet or pure room' used for **confession** and **meditation**. In liturgical Daoism, this spiritual space is created at the altar; at the same time, it is being visualized inside the body. The human body is the abode of the many gods; it is the landscape of the *dao* incarnate. The gods being actively manipulated ritually without are being visualized in **wuwei** (non-active) style within. **Laozi**, as *dao* personified, is that cosmic body of the *dao*. By meditatively 'keeping to the One', the primeval One **Ether** is being condensed through the breathing exercised, reintegrated and unified. The religious Daoists know also the ineffability of the *dao*, and to them the Neo-Daoist Wang Bi's reading of the *dao* is just woefully disembodied speculation.

Three other religious Daoist sects rose in early medieval China from the fourth century onward. The major one is the Great Purity tradition based at Mount Mao. Here, bodily visualization is detailed in the *Yellow Court Scripture* (symbol of the mind-heart), while the art of keeping to the One is told in the *Book of Great Profundity*. The latter has its own triune formula of uniting the Three into One. Immortality is the goal, achievable through the manipulation of a process of metamorphosis. Mystical journeys are taken among the stars; such 'pacing of the void' followed a detailed cosmographic course. Towards that end, a whole new vocabulary was developed. Though at heart esoteric, it was diffused sufficiently among a cultural elite as to inform the poetry of Tang down through the tenth century.

The rise of new, socially more broadly based sects in the Song–Yuan era eventually eclipsed the more refined Great Purity tradition. Of the new groups, that of the Complete Truth (or genuine essence) was and is still pre-eminent. A new style of meditation called 'inner alchemy' redirected the religious goal in the eleventh century. It made spiritual enlightenment the end, rather than physical **immortality** and, in the same way that the Zohar is related to the Kabbalah, it exchanged the clarity of the interior light for the arabesque of cosmic flights.

Currently in Taiwan, the orthodox 'black-head' Daoist priests are of the Complete Truth camp. Their liturgical magic relies on written summons, decreed talismans and official registers. Alongside them are the more folk shamanic 'red-head' village Daoists, who rely on personal charisma and serve often in the role of intermediaries on behalf of the unquiet dead.

Further reading

Robinet, I. (1993) *Taoist Meditation: The Mao-shan Tradition of Great Purity*, trans. J. Pas and N. Girardot, Albany, NY: State University of New York Press.
Schipper, K. (1993) *Taoist Body*, trans. K. Duval, Berkeley and Los Angeles: University of California Press.

WHALEN LAI

REN *see* humaneness

return to the root

A key Daoist concept, 'return to the root' is also an ideology that seeks to reverse the degenerative process of birth by a regression to the natal or even prenatal state. As a general term, it means keeping to the essentials. The metaphor of root (of a tree) and the tip (of a branch) make up 'origin and end'.

Where something comes from is primary, and better than where it is trying to go.

See also: Neo-Daoism; simplicity; substance and function

Further reading

Kohn, L. (1991) *Early Chinese Mysticism: Philosophy and Soteriology in the Taoist Tradition*, Princeton, NJ: Princeton University Press.

WHALEN LAI

reversal

A principle in **Laozi**'s view of nature, 'reversal' says that whenever a thing or situation reaches its limit, it will reverse itself. Change is more like the pendulum swing in the *Laozi* than an endless circle of transformation, as in the case of *Zhuangzi*. The hexagram for 'to return' or *fu* in the *Yijing* has five *yin* (broken) passive lines sitting on top of a *yang* (unbroken) moving line, the lowest line being counted as the first line. The commentator Ho Yan takes this to be about *yin* reaching its limit and *yang* beginning the whole process anew. Wang Bi, who followed Laozi, wrote instead:

> Return means reverting to the Origin. Heaven and Earth rests on it. Where movement ceases, there is quietude but quietude is not there to be its antithesis. When speech ceases, there is silence but silence is not there as the relative other to speech.

```
- - - - - - - - - - - - - - -        - - - - - - - - - - - - - - -
- - - - - - - - - - - - - - -        - - - - - - - - - - - - - - -
- - - - - - - - - - - - - - -        - - - - - - - - - - - - - - -
- - - - - - - - - - - - - - -        - - - - - - - - - - - - - - -
- - - - - - - - - - - - - - -        - - - - - - - - - - - - - - -
```

Silence is absolute; it is not in any ways relative to noise or speech. Similarly, **non-being** is not a privation of being in the same way that the One is not a number, i.e. a number among numbers, but it is instead the source of all numbers. In short, Wang

Bi absolutizes the negative, making non-being the foundation of being. Instead of reading the first (the bottom) *yang* line as marking 'a new dynamic beginning', he has it as it were 'upside down' by having all activities resting as it were on a singular *yin* base.

Further reading

Robinet, I. (1993) *Taoist Meditation*, trans. N. Girardot, Albany, NY: State University of New York Press.

WHALEN LAI

revival of Islam, theories of

There is a well-known *hadith* (saying of the Prophet) in which the Prophet predicts that during each century God will send someone to the community of Islam in order to revive religion. Reviving religion involves showing that religion is capable of doing something which any alternative system cannot, and that is providing spiritual guidance to its community. There is also the need to demonstrate that the arguments of those hostile to religion fail to get a grip on religion. Finally, it is important that the reviver can express himself in a way which is capable of resonating with the *umma* (community) as a whole, and not only with a part of it. Many Muslim philosophers have seen themselves as revivers of religion, in particular **al-Ghazali**, Muhammad **Iqbal** and Said **Nursi**. All three began by taking seriously the system of thought which is apparently opposed to faith, and they do not dismiss it merely as ungodly or blasphemous. On the contrary, they accept much of what it offers, and attempt to understand the structure and persuasiveness of what they are criticizing. Then they argue that whatever can be said in favour of that system of thought, it cannot replace religion since religion is trying to do something entirely different anyway. Finally, they write in ways which are designed to resonate with the public at large, and which are in fact capable of converting those who have largely turned away from God.

The epitome of this style is al-Ghazali's *Ihya' 'ulum al-din*, an extraordinary work consisting of four parts, each of which comprises ten books. In this encyclopedic work, he deals with every conceivable aspect of Islamic belief and practice. This must have been the model for Nursi's *Risale-i nur*. Al-Ghazali acknowledges strong links with **Sufism** in his *Ihya'*, and the text often becomes very personal. But it is in other works where his attempted refutation of philosophy and particular theological approaches occur. One of the strengths of al-Ghazali is that in his works other than the *Ihya'* he explores the arguments of his opponents with so much rigour and understanding that he was in the past, and is still today, often associated with those against whom he apparently argues.

Al-Ghazali's work as a whole does not amount to a rejection of what at the time might be identified with modernity, since he showed how aspects of philosophy such as Aristotelian logic might be profitably employed in theology, and argued that the *falasifa* themselves err in their use of the philosophical principles to which they are committed. His strategy in refuting philosophy is not to show that philosophy as a system is misguided, but that the philosophers themselves take it in directions which are not in accordance with the system itself.

This is very much a theme of *ihya'* literature, and it is strategically a very effective move. Instead of directly confronting the system of thought which one wishes to oppose, al-Ghazali and his successors explain the nature of that system and try to show what is wrong with it as a system of thought in its own terms. Al-Ghazali argues in his *Tahafut al-falasifa* that the sort of philosophy pursued by **al-Farabi** and **Ibn Sina** was not capable of drawing the conclusions which the *falasifa* argued could be drawn. In fact, he argued, if one were to pursue that system of thought rigorously one would come up with other conclusions, which would perhaps be more in accordance with faith. But the line of approach is important here, and it is not that the conclusions of *falsafa* are *kufr* (unbelief) or *bid'a* (innovation) and so must be rejected. On the contrary, the conclusions are indeed suspect from a religious point of view, but what is primarily wrong with them is that they are not properly derived from the premises; they are the results of poor and invalid arguments.

Muhammad Iqbal follows this approach closely. In his critique of what he saw as Western culture and science, he in no way wished to go back to an earlier time of ignorance. There is nothing wrong with science; indeed, there are tremendous intellectual and material benefits to be derived from it. So in criticizing Western material culture one is not criticizing the benefits which it can bring, but only the atheistic cultural forces which accompany it. Iqbal argues that it is a tragedy that empirical science has declined so markedly in the Islamic world in the last few centuries, since Islam is the paradigmatically empirical religion. This is a point which Nursi makes very frequently also. Unlike another-worldly faith like Christianity, Islam values involvement with the empirical world, and so there is nothing incompatible between Islam and science. Unfortunately, for a variety of political and historical reasons many Muslim communities became immured in ignorance and poor education, and the scholars were and often remain reluctant to explore intellectual issues at any depth.

The solution, according to Iqbal, is not to mimic the West. The West has made great material strides, but spiritually it is entirely impoverished. The answer for Muslims is to involve themselves in the best of material and scientific progress while rejecting the materialist theoretical framework which is often regarded as part and parcel of modernity. What often happens is that Islam is contrasted with Westernization, and appears to be antiquated and irrelevant in comparison. This is especially the case given the depressing state into which Islam had fallen during much of its history, when it was popularly restricted to only the sidelines of life and took up an entirely defensive attitude to the changing conditions of modern life. Iqbal contrasted what he saw as the ossified condition of Islamic thought during his lifetime with the early centuries of Islam, during which there was rich and diversified debate and intellectual development. Yet in just the same way as there is no reason to contrast Islam with science, so there is also no reason to contrast Islam with philosophy. There is much in Islam which is in accordance with philosophy, and Iqbal links Bergson and other contemporary thinkers with his rather *ishraqi* approach to the nature of reality. The major thesis of some philosophers, that the world operates

blindly and automatically, with no directing hand or guide, needs to be rejected by Muslims, but there is much else in apparently secular philosophical theories which can be incorporated within an Islamic view of the world. What is required is a revivification of Islam, a confident attitude to the modern world from an Islamic perspective. Then what is antagonistic to religion can be rejected at the same time as what is compatible with religion and useful is accepted.

By contrast with al-Ghazali, Iqbal and Said Nursi are suspicious of Sufism. Al-Ghazali himself is rather a strange *sufi*, since there is no evidence of any instruction by a *shaykh* or spiritual leader, but it is clear that he saw in Sufism a route to personal awareness (*dhawq*) or taste of the divine nature of reality. This might well be regarded as a problem in his *ihya'* project. The trouble with Sufism is its emphasis on the personal and the essential incommunicability of the sorts of experiences which the *sufi* evinces. Given the personal and private nature of the experiences which al-Ghazali describes, it is not clear how the individual reader is supposed to use his work to come closer to God. It is for this very reason that Iqbal and Nursi are dubious about Sufism as a necessary condition for revival. Sufism appears to be limited to only particular sections of the *umma*, and it seems inappropriate as part of a revival to present advice which can only apply to part of the community. Nursi sometimes compares Sufism with fruit, while simple faith is bread, and he suggests that one can easily get by with bread alone. He goes further, and implies that Sufism can easily mislead the seeker after truth, since he may mistake the nature of his experiences for the nature of reality. There is no doubt that Nursi respects the motives and the efforts of the *sufi*, but wonders whether *tasawwuf* (mysticism) is really effective or necessary.

The main route to *ihya'* is through an understanding of the rational nature of Islam, according to Nursi in the *Risale-i nur*. The text places considerable emphasis on the importance of knowledge and reason. Like the *Ihya' 'ulum al-din*, it is a complex mixture of topics and ways of dealing with topics, but written in a far more straightforward manner than al-Ghazali's great work. One line of approach which runs right through the text is the refusal to contrast Islam with reason. The Qur'anic passages and *ahadith* (sayings of the Prophet) which are considered are shown to be clear and far from mysterious, although religion itself is based on mystery, and Nursi explains simply what he thinks the meaning of these passages is. The basic approach is to counter the arguments of the materialists by attacking their suggestion that human beings are nothing more than material. This is actually his general strategy in dealing with all his opponents. He argues that they adopt a one-dimensional approach to humanity, and as such miss the point.

Nursi takes the normal steps of arguing that the Qur'an is a miraculous text as is evidenced by its style, and that the Prophet was a remarkable person, as evidenced by the accounts of him and by him. What is interesting is the overriding argument that we should start by analysing the nature of humanity itself. Where many thinkers go awry, he argues, is in adopting a notion of humanity which is impoverished. For example, the philosopher sees reason as the only important route to knowledge, rejecting any other attitude to the world as of no significance. The materialist (a general term really for all those committed to science as a total explanation of reality) fails to acknowledge our links with a creator. But what does Nursi do to disprove the theoretical bases of his opponents? The answer is that he looks to the Qur'an to provide evidence against them, and this is not as circular a strategy as it might seem. One might argue that if one assumes that the Qur'an is a veracious text, and that the Prophet really is a prophet, then it is an easy matter to argue against those with different views. But he does not adopt this uncritical stance. The excellence of the Qur'an is argued for, as is its comprehensiveness, and these are arguments, not assertions.

Let us take a particular example of how Nursi operates. He is very critical of philosophy when it is separated from prophecy, and he accuses Plato, Aristotle, al-Farabi and Ibn Sina of being 'immersed in Naturalism and being completely incapable of emerging from associating partners with God'. He also claims that this overdependence on reason creates a form of human identity which has no meaning higher than itself. He links this with an uncritical acceptance of power, and frequently links materialism with Pharaoh, by which he means the use of power for no other reason than to serve the interests of the strong. Now, at first sight this seems a strange set of criticisms to bring against this rather diverse group of thinkers. Naturalism is a difficult doctrine to identify with Plato, for example. But the broader point is quite persuasive. All these thinkers assume in their philosophical thought that reason alone is capable of working out the nature of reality. In politics, they start from the individual and work from there to the community, trying to base the interests of the former on association with the latter. The dependence on reason alone does indeed in all of them lead to a theory of God's relationship with the world, where there is such a theory, which is indirect. Since there is no reason to think that the world was created by God, they have to explain the nature of that creation in terms of connected processes which do indeed seem to come close to *shirk* (associating God with partners, idolatry). God is given a role in setting off the creative mechanism, but there are a number of steps before they are completed in our world, and were any of those steps not to be present, then creation would not take place. Similarly, the question of whether God chose to create or not is difficult to answer in a way acceptable to Islam, if it were to look as though he had to create the world, and had to create it in a particular way, because that was the best way, or the only logical form of creation.

Nursi argues against this view by contrasting two observers of the world, one who can observe no divine influence in it, and someone who can. The former just makes a mistake, he may be quite honest in what he is asserting, but he misses out on something real, the divine nature of the world. Were he to accept the Prophet he would have no difficulty seeing the way the world really is, and there is little excuse for not accepting the Prophet and the Qur'an, given the evidences provided for their veracity. The argument, and it is an argument, is based not on faith but on evidence, on rational evidence, and once one accepts that evidence and properly assesses it faith then one is provided with a secure grounding. Islam does not require anything unreasonable of its adherents, Nursi argues. On the contrary, it is unreasonable not to accept the evidence for the truth of Islam and the divinely inspired nature of the world.

The philosophers are accused of *shirk* because, as argued by al-Ghazali in his *Tahafut al-falasifa*, the *falasifa* do not give any real room for independent action to God. The question is whether God is really an agent, and to be a real agent means to act entirely as one wishes or intends. It means to have one's power to act unrestrained, in the case of an omnipotent agent, and to be able to do anything which is logically possible. Yet the God of the *falasifa* cannot do this, he is indeed in partnership with other principles or even beings, in his causal power. For Plato, God is co-existent with matter, for Aristotle and the *falasifa* he is co-existent with the universe itself, so he is far from being an entirely independent agent. Nursi suggests that this makes God a sort of creature in that God like everything else in the universe turns out to be, according to the *falasifa*, someone who acts through and with other things and agents.

Why are the philosophers and the materialists compared with Pharaoh and the cynical use of power? The philosophers tend to start from the principle of egoism, and work from that principle to some justification and explanation of the institution of community, an institution in which social and moral roles have force. Yet Nursi suggests that this is to put the cart before the horse, since unless we start by assuming that community is a natural state of affairs in which individuals flourish, we shall never come to an explanation of its significance. The point of moral life is not to limit as far as possible the potential conflicts between individuals, but to allow us to experience as much moral and spiritual growth as is appropriate for human creatures. The role of prophecy is crucial here, since the Prophet demonstrates the naturalness of community, how everything in the world works together with everything else as part of a divine plan. Looking at nature reveals how everything is part of a system, a rational process, and it is through our participation in such a pattern of being that we shall most appropriately live in accordance with our divinely formed essence. Assuming that we are naturally brutish leads to notions of community based on power and fear, on restraining the ability of others to persecute us and of us to persecute them. We can escape from this by observing how everything is part of a spiritual system in which harmony naturally reigns provided that we live in accordance with the plan which God has for us.

Further reading

al-Ghazali (1937–8) *Ihya' 'ulum al-din*, Cairo: Matba'a lajna nashr al-thaqafa al-islamiyya.
—— (1997) *Tahafut al-falasifa*, trans. M. Marmura, Provo, UT: Brigham Young University Press.
Iqbal, M. (1930) *The Reconstruction of Religious Thought in Islam*, Lahore: Ashraf (appropriately translated into Persian as *Ihya-yi fikr-i dini dar Islam*).
Leaman, O. (1999) *A Brief Introduction to Islamic Philosophy*, Oxford: Polity Press.
McIntyre, A. (1981) *After Virtue: A Study in Moral Theory*, London: Duckworth.
Nursi, S. *The Risale-i Nur Collection*, Istanbul: Sozler Nesriyat A.S.

OLIVER LEAMAN

revolution and reform

From the founding of the Zhou dynasty came two expressions that serve now as words for the Chinese 'revolution' and the Japanese Meiji 'restoration'. The Zhou claimed that the Mandate of **Heaven** is not permanent and can change, and that 'though the Zhou is an ancient state, its appointment or mission is new'. Henceforth, any dynastic change in China was seen as a change of mandate (to rule) and a moral revolution. It follows that under imperial China, no one but the Son of Heaven should sacrifice to Heaven. But that does not stop rebels from usurping that regal prerogative, claiming only to be 'implementing the *dao* on Heaven's behalf'. Since Liu Bang rose from peasant to become the first Han emperor after routing fellow peasant rebel Xiang Yu, cynics have concluded that 'the one who wins becomes emperor; the one who loses a bandit forever'. Imperial rule ended in 1911, but for decades supporters of **Mao Zedong** (Peoples Republic of China) and Chiang Kai-shek (Republic of China) routinely called each other 'bandits'.

One term for 'reform' is 'a revision of law'. The Han thought its institutions would last: 'Heaven does not change. Neither would the Way'. But Wang Mang usurped the throne, founded the New Dynasty, claimed a change of mandate and revised the institutions after the newly discovered Zhou Classics written in an ancient script (see **Classics and Books**). That appeal to a Zhou precedent was important, since precedent is highly useful for the pursuit of new policies. Wang Anshi used that pretext during the northern Song dynasty, and on a new reading of Confucius as a reformer, Kang Yuwei effected the 1898 reform and restoration movement. Far earlier, the *Book of Lord Shang* distinguishes 'emulating the old' and 'changing anew'. It was the Confucians who regularly sought to emulate the old, and the Legalists who consistently pushed for starting anew (see **Legalism**).

WHALEN LAI

Ricci, Matteo

b. 1552; d. 1610

Missionary

Matteo Ricci headed the Jesuit mission to China. He concluded that China once knew God as 'the Lord on High', but the country grew forgetful of that monotheistic past when the cult of **Heaven** superseded and masked a faith in the 'Lord of Heaven'. His mission was to restore that original monotheism, and Catholicism has been known in China ever since as the 'Teaching of the Lord of Heaven'. (Protestant Christianity would name itself the 'Teaching of Christ', and use 'Lord on High' for 'God'.) The Jesuits blamed the recent turn towards a naturalistic philosophy – Neo-Confucianism in particular – on the Buddhists, feeling that the Indian belief in *samsara* (rebirth) originated from Pythagoras and his belief in metempsychosis. China needed to set above her naturalistic philosophy the faith in God and a Thomistic upper tier superior to nature and including grace. Given the Aristotelian frame of reference, Ricci could well have misread Neo-Confucian thought and missed the immanent

holism of the Great Ultimate being present in all things. But he would not be the last to do so, and all intercultural understanding may well at first be metaphoric, translating what we do not know into that with which we are familiar.

WHALEN LAI

righteousness

Yi (righteousness, rightness, duty) was elevated by **Mencius** to be almost on a par with *ren* (**humaneness**). Although Mencius insisted that righteousness is an 'inner' quality of mind, it was for a long time an 'objective' standard of rightness. Though tied to the feudal ethos, it prescribes a general obligation independent of expressed commitments and is operative prior to anyone actually entering into a relationship. 'To know what is right (that is, the right thing to do) and yet not to act upon it', judges **Confucius**, 'shows a lack of courage'. This is often explained with a homophone: righteousness is what is appropriate (*yi*) to a situation. **Mozi**, having aligned *ren* with subjective love, defined *yi* as that which must benefit the beloved. An action is judged right when it does the intended recipient good. Too much harm has been caused by men of good intentions who do not think before they act. To think is to weigh the action's consequence. Confucius noted how 'the gentleman is motivated by righteousness; the inferior person by gain', and since Mozi linked the right and personal benefit, he has been regarded by Mencians as being inferior, or as valuing the inferior over the superior. Objecting to such a gross 'objective' standard, Mencius moved the 'right' inside man as an inner quality like *ren*.

Although the Confucian orthodoxy tied *yi* naturally to the requirement of **filial piety** and loyalty, *yi* as a general egalitarian virtue did survive. It appears as suffixes to compounds like 'good deeds', 'good-will charities', 'free school', 'adopted son' and 'voluntary labour', where it recalls its meaning of simply 'doing right by one another'. In defying traditional hierarchies, it operates well among the common folk and those on the fringe of proper society. The code of knight-errants as well as the honour among thieves, it is the norm that guides sworn brothers and mutual-aid associates. Peasant rebels who rejected the status quo will claim that they broke laws or revolted only so as to 'do right by the decree of **Heaven**'. This Chinese idea of 'right' is not about something being 'true to fact'; it is performative, demanding 'doing the right thing'. This might explain why questions of truth in China are not tied to verification of fact but are a matter of *xin* or 'trust', trusting in the testimony of another. This emphasis on interpersonal trust slides easily into the issue of *cheng* or 'sincerity', captured in the expressive language of the man-to-self relationship.

See also: Chong Che-du

Further reading

Bruce, E. and Takeo Brooks, A. (1998) *The Original Analects*, New York: Columbia University Press.

Chung-ying Cheng (ed. and trans.) (1971) *Tai Chen's Inquiry into Goodness*, Honolulu, HA: East-West Center Press

Shun Kwong-loi (1997) *Mencius and Early Chinese Thought*, Stanford, CA: Stanford University Press.

WHALEN LAI

rites

The Confucian ritual Classics were codified in the Han dynasty. As a social norm and a means of governance, they ruled traditional China. After the May Fourth liberals castigated rites for being a feudal burden, inhumane and cannibalistic, it has been customary to separate Confucius's discovery of a universal good – *ren* (**humaneness**) – from his conservative endorsement of the old, particularistic *li* (rites). Herbert Fingarette's positive evaluation of the rites has forced a re-examination of that premise. The dust has yet to settle on this revisionism.

The *Analects* have actually very little to say on specific rites. Since most of the rites were already lost (3.9) and the master was not tutored into the 'higher' rites of imperial sacrifice (3.11) at the Grand Temple (3.15), Confucius's ritual repertoire might be limited to the 'lower' rites of the family

and clan ancestral mourning and funerals. As he had distilled the 'six (aristocratic) arts' into moral principles, he could have boiled down the ritual code for the five human relationships to an ethics of 'reciprocity' supported by his theory of the 'rectification of names'.

Further reading

Fingarette, H. (1972) *Confucius: The Secular as Sacred*, New York: Harper & Row.

WHALEN LAI

rites and the rites controversy

The Jesuit mission in China ended with the rites controversy. Rome accepted the Franciscan report that Confucian ancestral worship (which the Jesuits condoned) was more than a social ritual, more than just honouring the father and the mother; it is pagan worship and idolatry, something that Chinese people should be converted away from. The Manchu rulers retaliated by banning the missions. Modern education has removed old superstitions and made irrelevant the Roman Catholic stigma about Chinese worshipping spirits, but the question of whether the rites are religious is still alive in academic discussion.

Xunzi is the theoretician of rites. He accepted that rites were created by past sages, and that social manners could change with time and that the rites serve not so much gods or ghosts but the good of communal life. He did not theorize to the same extent on **music**, which is just as well, because it is well recognized that **barbarians** have music; they just do not have the proper Chinese manners. Babies could make gurgling sounds and children could make up ditties, but that does not mean they do not have to learn ritual behaviour. Being a product of high culture, rites accept and inculcate social distinctions that music seeks to soothe by evoking shared sentiments.

The call for 'science and democracy' by the liberals of the May Fourth Movement had for a time doomed the rites as feudalistic hangovers. But as the West evolved modern theories of rituals, so a revaluation was forced. The functionalist anthropologist Radcliffe-Brown quotes the *Book of Rites* in support of the idea put forward by Durkheim, namely, that God is Society. The rites unite a community after a transcendental image of itself. The Chinese idea that rites were means for 'harmonizing human (social) emotions' supports that functionalist appreciation which in turn helps clarify statements in the *Book of Rites*. For example, the first section on 'explaining rites' notes that rites can also settle 'right and wrong' as well as dispel 'doubts and suspicion'. That now actually makes good social sense. The ritual code can adjudicate problems in those grey areas in social behaviour. For example, it is acceptable to grieve privately at the passing of a great man, but it is wrong to presume familiarity with the deceased by publicly writing something *in memoriam*, for that right and honour goes to his immediate disciples. Even good intentions might arouse suspicion that abiding by the code would dispel.

The pragmatics of 'speech-acts' from the linguistic philosopher Austin has also helped to redeem **Confucius**'s advocacy of rites. Instead of seeing rites as feudal, outdated and falsifiable (by the objective standards of modernity), his advocacy might serve to induce an acquired, effortless deportment that is, to wit, no sooner said than done (liveable in a shared life-world). Neo-traditionalists have adopted these modern and post-modern theories in their own defence of the viability of the Confucian rites. The old critics of rites might not agree. That is because Confucian rites were born of 'clan rules' and they are nothing like the 'civil law'. Members of the Greek *polis* could appeal to a justice, the *nomos*, that was higher than rules. Clan rules are by their nature particularistic, and are not civil law. So the 'rites controversy' then or now rests on how universaliz-able the rites, and ritual courtesy, may be understood as being.

The Chinese word for 'culture' is *wen*, which also means 'writing' or 'literature' and 'pattern'. China is culturo-centric; by acculturation, a barbarian can join the Han family. As China is more bibliocentric than logocentric, to do this requires knowing China's written culture. The word also covers the six arts, but rites and music would have priority over archery and chariot-driving. Rites create the orderliness of culture. Xunzi assigns it two functions: the economy of restraining the emotions and the beauty of giving it social form. One ensures utility, the other aesthetics. *Wen* is also contrasted with *wu* as the literary to the military. Since the Tang dynasty, but excluding the present, the weaker China became militarily *vis-à-vis* those that conquered her, the more conservative her ritual culture became.

Further reading

Hall, D. and Ames, R. (1999) *The Democracy of the Dead: Dewey, Confucius, and the Hope for Democracy in China*, Chicago: Open Court.

Minamiki, G. (1985) *The Chinese Rites Controversy: From Its Beginnings to Modern Times*, Chicago: Loyola University Press.

Mungello, D. (1994) *The Chinese Rites Controversy: Its History and Meaning*, Nettetal: Steyler Verlag.

Radcliffe-Brown, A. (1958) *Method in Social Anthropology: Selected Essays*, Chicago: University of Chicago Press.

WHALEN LAI

RU *see* scholar

S

sage

The expression 'inner sagehood and outer king-ship' is first used by **Zhuangzi**, the only time he used the terms 'sage' and 'king' closely together. The phrase was co-opted by the Song dynasty Neo-Confucians in order to describe their new project of realizing 'inner sagehood' so as to actualize 'outer kingship'. This was intended to fulfill the aim of the Great Learning, that is, moral self-cultivation as basis for social engagement and political transformation. This is a Neo-Confucian development coming after the medieval Buddhists, which took over the Buddhist search for enlightenment (Buddhahood) and re-directed it towards a Confucian reform of society.

Sagehood was rarely claimed in Han times, for the consensus then was that sages were born, not made. Being uncommon, sagehood is not something for everyone to emulate, even less to acquire entirely through learning, as **Zhu Xi** would hold. **Confucius** was considered a sage, but his foremost disciple Yan Hui was only a *xian*, a worthy, one grade below a sage. The Neo-Daoists known in English as the 'Seven Sages of the Bamboo Grove' were, to be correct, just called worthies, outstanding men but short of sagehood. While democratizimg sagehood as Chan did with Buddhahood, the Song Neo-Confucians sidelined Yan Hui and picked **Mencius** as their 'second sage' (next in rank or in line after Confucius). The Mencian idea that in theory 'everyone can be Yao or Shun' (legendary rulers who abdicated so that the next man of virtue, the sage, could rule) then became credal, and Mencius's other more qualified statements – about how in reality sages came only once perhaps every 500 years – were thus put aside. Even Mencius only hoped but never openly claimed that he was the overdue sage.

After Zhu Xi won his case, more Chinese claimed to realize sagehood than ever before, in particular those from the idealist wing constructed by Lu Xiangshan (1139–93) and Wang Yangming (1472–1529). Similar to the experience of Buddhists, this is marked usually by two episodes in their spiritual biography: the initial moment when the student of the Way realized that he could (and should) be a sage and the moment when he attained unity with **Heaven**. **Xunzi** had a simple response to this: it amounts, he mockingly said, to having 'the whole street full of sages'.

See also: education in China, philosophy of

Further reading

Creel, H. (1949) *Confucius: The Man and the Myth*, New York: J. Day.
Lai, W. (1991) 'The Spirituality of Confucian Humanism', *Journal of Humanism and Ethical Religion* 4(1): 63–76.

WHALEN LAI

sage-king

A 'sage-king' combines in himself the virtue of a **sage** and the power of a king, right and might rolled into one. In the narrow and ideal sense, the term refers only to Yao, Shun and Yu, who voluntarily abdicated the throne (power) in favour of the next sage (virtue). But the term has been lavished on and appropriated by less than perfect rulers. A synonym for sage-king is wise king or philosopher-king. **Mencius** probably considered **Confucius** as 'the sage who would be king'; the myth of Confucius as the 'uncrowned king of the Spring and Autumn dynasty' took shape soon after. The *Analects* do not use the compound 'sage-king', and the current *Book of History* (which begins with Yao) does not call him a 'sage-king' either. A quick check of the Harvard–Yenching Concordia turns up this frequency of usage among key thinkers of use of terms sage, sage-king and sage-man (wise man being just a synonym of sage). There are severe limitations to using statistics but it is interesting to see what they reveal:

	sage-king	sage	sage-man
Analects	0	4	4
Mozi	122	15	48
Mencius	1	48	0
Zhuangzi	0	22	111
Xunzi	38	18	80

The picture that emerges is as follows. Confucius is responsible for designating the sage as the highest example of humanity; before him, the word 'sage' was largely adjectival. The compound sage-king is primarily a creation of **Mozi** (who uses it a disproportionate 122 times). There is a reason for this; before Mozi, Confucius admired the ancients and called for a return to the Zhou model, but he did not 'rewrite (prior) history' as a pretext for remaking present society anew. Mozi did; unable to idealize Shang because of the bad publicity it had in the Zhou records, he looked one dynasty further back, to a legendary Xia dynasty founded by Sage-King Yu. This tamer of the Flood is the model Mohist ruler; he laboured long and hard to serve the people; so much so that he passed by his home three times and never once went in.

Within the Mohist canon, the chapters on **logic** and on warfare have no use for 'sage-king'. Of the pre-dynastic (non-hereditary) trio, Yu outnumbered Yao and Shun by two to one (60 to 30 times), and he appears by himself in the most authentic chapters of 'Universal Love' and 'Against Aggression'. Mozi used him as the paradigm to prove his own case: 'Universal Love benefits everyone; how do I know it is so? Because it happened under Sage-King Yu.' (This use of historical precedent as proof was later dropped by the Neo-Mohist logicians.) But for all his bold imagination, Mozi did not – nor did Mencius – question the legitimacy of 'hereditary rule'. The history of 'voluntary abdication' developed in the last chapter of the Analects is a later Mencian interpolation. Confucius never knew that anti-dynastic myth.

The Mohist use of the term 'sage-king' does not observe that mythic distinction either. The founders of the Three Dynasties were also, as a matter of routine, sage-(and-)kings. This so politicized sagehood that the later **Zhuangzi** would never use the compound 'sage-king'; for him, sages were better off without being ever kings. Mencius also shunned the compound; he mentioned 'sage' forty-eight times, but 'sage-king' only once. **Xunzi**, who had no use for voluntary abdication, basically followed the Mohists in a non-discriminative use of the term 'sage-king'. The Legalists showered the term on their immoral patrons even more indiscriminately. But once Mozi had used fictional history as a pretext to support his philosophy, other thinkers also began rewriting history; Mencius would glorify Shun to make his case for a rule based on **filial piety** and compare that against the Mohist hero Yu, and the Agriculturist school would spin myths about the Divine Peasant or the Fiery Emperor. The school of medicine would idolize the Yellow Emperor. Before long, the prehistoric myths purporting to be actual history mushroomed, until Xunzi gave up on these nebulous 'former kings' and turned to the models provided by the 'later (dynastic) ones'.

Further reading

Ching, J. (1997) *Mysticism and Kingship in China: The Heart of Chinese Wisdom*, Cambridge: Cambridge University Press.

Lai, W. (1985) 'A Brief Note: Who Used the Term "Sage-King" First?', *Cheng Feng* 27(4): 204–8.

WHALEN LAI

samanadhikaranya

In Indian logical contexts, *samanadhikaranya* means co-occurrence of two or more items (such as a substance and its properties) in the same locus. In grammatical usage, the reference is to one object of terms with the same case-ending having different grounds for their application (*pravritti-nimitta*). The latter notion may be interpreted in terms of a sense-reference distinction. The exegesis of co-referential Upanishadic statements such as **Tat tvam asi** (That thou art) and **Satyam jnanam anantam brahma** is central to Vedantic theology (see **Vedanta**) and thus to much Hindu thought. Non-dualist (**Advaita**) Vedantins such as **Shankara** emphasize the singularity of reference and construe co-referential constructions as identity statements conveying a featureless essence where the different grounds for the applications of the terms are subjective senses. His theological rival **Ramanuja**, and his followers, maintain that the differences between the modes of presentation imply objective differentiation: *samanadhikaranya* is thus the reference to one object of words denoting several properties.

Further reading

Bartley, C. (1986) 'Interpreting Satyam Jnanam Anantam Brahma', in N. Allen *et al.*, *Oxford University Papers on India*, Delhi: Oxford University Press, 103–15.

CHRIS BARTLEY

Samkhya

One of the six orthodox Indian soteriological systems and usually associated with **Yoga** which accepts the Samkhya metaphysic. This originally atheistic system receives its principal articulation in the Samkhya *Karikas* of Ishvarakrishna (*c.*400–500 CE), upon which the most significant commentaries are the *Yuktidipika* (*c.*700) and Vachaspati Mishra's *Tattvakaumudi* (*c.*850). Samkhya, which is basically a renunciatory system, propounds the duality of *purusha* – an infinity of isolated, inactive spiritual monads beyond space and time – and *pradhana* or

mula prakriti – from whose transformations (*parinama*) the cosmos of mental and material phenomena arises in accordance with the **satkaryavada** theory of causation which holds that an effect pre-exists in a subtle, undeveloped form in its causal substrate. The *pradhana* or raw material is analysed into three strands or qualities (*guna*): *sattva* (limpid serenity), *rajas* (dynamic energy) and *tamas* (tenebrous inertia). Prior to the transformational process, the three *gunas* repose in a state of equilibrium, cancelling out one another's properties. The *purushas* abide in splendid isolation as spectators, each illuminated by its own consciousness. With the commencement of the transformational process, held to be occasioned by the 'mere presence' of *purusha*, the disequilibriated *gunas* combine to form the basic material and psychological entities (*tattva*) comprising the universe. These are: *buddhi* (mind); *ahamkara* (ego); *manas* (sensory co-ordinator); the senses (*indriya*) of hearing, touch, sight, taste and smell; the organs of speech, holding, walking, excretion and procreation; the subtle elements of sound, touch, form, taste and smell (i.e. the sense-data perceived by the senses); and the gross elements of space, air, fire, water and earth, the perceived external substances.

The *purushas* become entangled in and misidentify themselves with aspects of the material environment, including the individual personality and body. Given the 'proximity' of the *purusha*-consciousness to the mind (*buddhi*), the latter is illuminated (the material *buddhi* becomes 'quasi-conscious') and the confusion is compounded when the activity of the *buddhi* is misattributed to the inactive *purusha*. Thus we have the origins of human personal individuality and the series of births marked by suffering ensues. Liberation (*kaivalya*; 'wholeness' or 'isolation') from the samsaric cycle of unsatisfactoriness and becoming results from the discriminating awareness, presupposing the discipline of the Yoga soteriology, that transcendental pure consciousness is distinct from the physical and mental sphere. With the advent of such insight and subsequent to the exhaustion of **karma** appropriate to the present embodied existence, 'generous *prakriti*' (whose development is said to have been for the sake of *purusha*, a controversial instance of non-conscious teleology) ceases to function in relation to the enlightened individual and withdraws like an entrancing dancer at the conclusion of her performance.

A standard criticism of Samkhya is that it is not clear why the process of bondage does not recommence given the tenet that it has been generated by the 'mere presence' of *purusha*. Some theistic Samkyha theorists (referred to by Shankara (*c*.700), Haribhadra (*c*.750) and Ramanuja (*c*.1100)) invoke divine efficient causality to account for the disequilibriation of the *gunas*.

Further reading

Hiriyanna, M. (1993) *Outlines of Indian Philosophy*, Delhi: Motilal Banarsidass.

Hulin, M. (1978) *Samkhya Literature*, Wiesbaden: Otto Harrassowitz.

Larson, G. and Bhattacharya, R. (1987) *Samkhya: A Dualist Tradition in Indian Philosophy*, Delhi: Motilal Banarsidass.

Wezler, A. and Motegi, S. (1998) *Yuktidipika*, Stuttgart: Franz Steiner.

CHRIS BARTLEY

samnyasa

Samnyasa or *sannyasa* is a Hindu institution, meaning the renunciation of social role, normatively that of the householder, and caste status which is formalized through a special type of initiation ritual. The practice represents a rejection of major aspects of the mainstream Brahminical ideology such as the life of active external ritual, **caste** hierarchy and the pivotal social role of the adult male householder with his duties of wealth generation, procreation and the performance and patronage of rituals. Accordingly, it was legitimated and integrated into the mainstream religion of the group by classification as the fourth stage of life (*ashrama*) additional to those of celibate studentship (*brahmacharya*), householdership (*grihastha*) and retirement or 'forest-dwelling' (*vanaprastha*). In parallel, the world-denying ideal of ultimate liberation from the series of births was sometimes defined as the religiously sanctioned specific duty (*svadharma*) of the renouncer. In the case of exceptionally detached and self-controlled individuals of unusual

virtue, it is recognized that they may renounce without having lived as householders.

Renouncers are peripatetic homeless mendicants committed to celibacy. This way of life devoted to individual salvation through gnosis must be understood both as an ascetic ideal and a symbolic rejection of the dominant social mores of the religion of the group as practised by the householder in the world.

The initiation ritual lasts for two days. On the first day, the aspirant performs nine oblations for the dead, the last of which he offers for himself. From a socio-legal point of view he is now irreversibly dead; his marriage is dissolved and his heirs succeed. On the second day, he performs his last sacrifice and gives away all his property. He then symbolically deposits his sacred fires within himself by inhaling their smoke, burns his sacrificial utensils and extinguishes his sacred fires. The renouncer understands himself as interiorizing ritual practice: he bears the fires within himself in the breaths (*prana*) and offers an internal sacrifice in these fires on each occasion of eating. He then repeats the formula, 'I have renounced', and donates the 'gift of safety' to all sentient beings with a commitment never to injure a living being. Finally, he acquires the requisites of saffron robe, begging bowl and staff.

The person of the renouncer is ambivalent in the sense that although from a theological point of view he represents the ideals of spiritual purity and detachment, within ritual contexts his presence is considered inauspicious. While the renouncer is ideally a solitary individual, most founders of sects have been renouncers. Indeed, there are settled communities of a monastic type (*matha*) traditionally held to have been founded by **Shankara**. In a paper of enormous influence, Louis Dumont has argued that the key to understanding Hinduism as a unified phenomenon is to be found in the dialogue between the renouncer and the householder.

Further reading

Dumont, L. (1980) 'World Renunciation in Indian Religions', in L. Dumont, *Homo Hierarchicus*, Chicago: Chicago University Press.

Olivelle, P. (1992) *Samnyasa Upanishads: Hindu*

Scriptures on Asceticism and Renunciation, New York: Oxford University Press.

CHRIS BARTLEY

samsara

Samsara (wandering) in many Indian soteriologies is the negative evaluation of the world and human life as the sphere of becoming characterized by impermanence, dis-ease and transmigration. This state is propelled by individuals' **karma** and is contrasted with its contrary, *moksha* or liberation from the series of births in the here and now due to the annihilation of *karma*. The 'here and now' encompasses spheres of existence other than the human: one may also be reincarnated in a variety of heavens or hells in accordance with the overall quality of the accumulated *karma*-stock. There is a range of minority views holding that reincarnation as insects, plants or inanimate objects is possible. These ideas do not find much acceptance in that such states preclude intentional actions which are the conditions of the improvement of one's lot and thus conflict with the ethical thrust of the ideology.

According to Hindu traditions, the essential inner soul (**atman**) is actually immune from *karma*. It has, however, somehow become associated with and trapped in a transmigrating entity (*jiva-atman*) consisting of a gross, perceptible physical frame and a 'subtle body', the latter being the repository of karmic residues. The gnostic non-dualist (**Advaita**) school insists that insight into the identity of the essentially non-agentive conscious soul and the Supreme Soul or *Brahman* generates a disinterested attitude, as a result of which no fresh *karma* is produced. Another family of views (predominantly Shaiva and Shakta ritualisms) see the ceremony of cultic initiation as obliterating all *karma* save that appropriate to the present existence. Diligent cultic practice on the part of the votary prevents the acquisition of fresh *karma*. Devotional theists maintain that a self-understanding of oneself as an instrument, servant and devotee of god and the consequent attribution of one's agency and its consequences to him prevents the accrual of *karma* to the self. In some of these devotional traditions, the *samsara–moksha* dichotomy is implicitly eroded

in so far as the essential character of the relationship of loving service and obedience to god in this world is identical with that enjoyed by the released soul in heaven.

Further reading

O'Flaherty, W. (ed.) (1980) *Karma and Rebirth in Classical Indian Traditions*, Berkeley, CA: University of California Press.

CHRIS BARTLEY

samsara in China

The Buddhist system of *samsara* involves six possible paths of rebirth, only some of which have pre-Buddhist Chinese counterparts.

India	China
gods	gods
atmospheric spirits	–
man	man
animals	–
hungry ghosts	hungry ghosts
hell	earth prisons

Understandably, those with native counterparts struck a chord with the Chinese. Chinese favour being reborn as a god in heaven, but to live again as a human is not that bad a prospect. Much less is made of the path of angry spirits. Animal rebirths are recounted more in didactic retrospect, and they do not seem to be regarded very seriously. But because the Chinese regularly feed their dead, they became more obsessed with hungry ghosts. That and rebirth in hell became the major features of the afterlife in the Ghost Festival. In this Chinese version of the Halloween, there is generous feasting of monks, beggars and ghosts in order to extend aid to parents who might suffer those two purgatory fates. By the Ming dynasty, the majority of registered monks were specialists in the 'Yogachara rite for opening up the burning mouth' of the hungry ghosts. The grandest of Buddhist public liturgy then was the 'Water and Land Assembly' for delivering those who died unmourned at sea and on land.

See also: afterlife in Chinese thought

WHALEN LAI

Sanskrit epics

Of all the texts produced within South Asian culture over the last two and a half thousand years, the two great Sanskrit epics, the *Mahabharata* and the *Ramayana*, are arguably the most well known and have been the most significant in shaping South-Asian culture and reflecting historical change within that culture. Though both are traditionally called epics, a word still lacking a universally accepted definition in Western literary theory, the traditional Sanskrit term for them is *itihasa*, literally meaning 'that which was said'. As such, Indian scholars have sometimes regarded them as constructing a particular view of history on the basis of past utterances, though not in the same way as the ***puranas***, another related genre, which has traditionally claimed to narrate 'ancient tales'. Above all, both texts are concerned with genealogy and the problems of regal succession and it is in their treatment of these problems and the structuring of divine and human lineage that their 'historical' dimension comes forth. The *Mahabharata* contains considerable philosophical speculation in its twelfth book, but apart from this these are not texts designed to present technical philosophical argumentation in the same style as can be found in later Hindu philosophical texts composed in Sanskrit. However, consistent with their narrative style, both epics do present a complex world-view in both theoretical and practical terms. They lay down a particular position in a didactic style, well known from other genres, and explore it in a series of case studies presented in self contained myths, sub-genres such as the ***Bhagavad Gita*** as well as through the principal plot extending across the entire narrative.

By any standards the two Sanskrit epics are huge, and have grown substantially since their earliest renditions appeared perhaps around 400 BCE. Differing in size in its many distinct versions, the *Mahabharata* is generally reckoned at about one hundred thousand verses divided into eighteen books; the *Ramayana* has about thirty thousand verses and seven books. Although they are still occasionally recited in their entirety and exist today in many different forms, it is likely that most Indians would know the epics from certain famous episodes recounted in them and from summaries of them that must have been continually recited. Their frequent citation and summary in other texts, including Buddhist literature, means that both epics were almost certainly widely known from the early centuries of the Christian era, if not before, and that they influenced and continue to influence the shape of Indian culture. Both epics contain perceptible plots extending across their entire narrative, plots which can be summarized to a size sufficient to allow the epic to be recapitulated in a text of a mixed genre such as a *purana* or narrative poem or to be recited orally in a vernacular language for ritual performances. Equally important, this plot provides a constant reference point for an audience to anchor its own comprehension of the epic and to make recollections back to previous episodes in the plot.

Both epics contain features which must have made them accessible to a larger audience than texts whose function was intended to be much more specific, such as ritual and philosophical texts, for example. The presence of a clearly perceptible plot, a partial resolution of the fundamental problems raised in it and the use of many role models in its development meant that the epics were able to be interpreted in terms of the conditions of everyday life. Crucially, they can also be read as comments upon subjects of universal significance such as the nature of the self, the person, the body, the relationship between God and the world, and other subjects which are developed in a more technical manner in later Hindu philosophical schools. Both are sufficient to guarantee their popularity. There are many signs that both epics are the products of the social and political elite. They show a pronounced bias towards showcasing the ideologies of the priestly and warrior groups respectively, who constituted the highest classes in terms of military and intellectual prestige in ancient and medieval Indian society. Yet the emphasis they also place on kingship, on models of marriage and, especially in the case of the *Mahabharata*, on role models designed to offer guidance as to the most appropriate form of expression of devotion towards a deity, means that their many messages quickly extended beyond elite circles.

The *Mahabharata*

The plot of this epic focuses on thwarted claims to regal succession, a war between the Pandavas and the Kauravas over the claims of this succession, the ultimate victory of the family (the Pandavas) entitled to the crown, and the adventures of the Pandavas after they have won the war. This basic content is shaped by two mythic frames perceptible across the entire narrative. The first is the myth of the *avatara*, where the god Vishnu manifests himself on Earth in the form of Krishna to re-establish the correct cosmic order (***dharma***) when the Earth is under threat of being overrun by the forces of evil and disorder. This frame is duplicated on the human plane, where the king plays the role of the *avatara* in his obligation to uphold his subjects' commitment to adhere to *dharma* in all of their actions (Biardeau 1976: 217). Second, there is a mythic scheme of creation, encompassing the origins of the universe and the establishment of its geographical and pseudo-historical order, the latter pictured especially in the genealogies contained in the first book of the *Mahabharata*. Both mythic frames occur in texts outside of the *Mahabharata* and the relation between the myths in their extra epic (especially in the *puranas*) form and their epic versions is not one of historical difference, but rather involves a variation on one fundamental set of mythic structures. Many of the individual episodes, for example, the famous series of individual duels narrated in the battle books (6–9) contain distinctive textual signs and symbols, indicating they are reworkings of the myths dealing with the destruction of the triple world (Earth/atmosphere/heaven) as it is described in the puranic creation myths. So too does the content of the eleventh book, the *Sauptikaparvan*, contain traces of a very early Indo-European eschatological myth whilst mirroring the narrative sequence of stages in the puranic myth of cosmic destruction. However, it is the *avatara* myth, with its simply defined structure of descent and re-ascent of a portion of the deity, which provides the main structuring element of the central narrative

One of the most prominent themes in the *Mahabharata* is the question of the validity of a particular world order and the capacity of this world order to guarantee both long-term and short-term happiness for the individual and stability for the universe. This concept of world order is named *dharma* and is most accurately defined as 'the socio-cosmic order, which can be said to be desirable simply inasmuch as it is necessary to the maintenance of the happy existence of the world constituted by the "three worlds"...' (Biardeau 1997: 40). Much of the twelfth and thirteenth books of the *Mahabharata* is concerned with setting out in considerable detail very specific rules about conduct as it pertains to kings, members of different social classes – especially the priestly and warrior classes – husband and wife and the so-called four stages of life that a brahmin ideally should lead when he reaches a particular age. All of this is *dharma*, and much of it is found in the different, but somewhat related, genre of *dharma* literature called *Dharmashastra*. What results is a particular position on the thrust of *dharma* which is portrayed as extensively as possible.

However, the epic recitational tradition is not content simply to present an idealized picture of the successful working out of *dharma* across a narrative incorporating a multitude of life situations and a huge battle confronting the forces of *dharma* against those of its opposite, *adharma*. If it did just this, it would not have lasted for as long as it has. Instead, it constantly depicts *dharma* as a concept of great subtlety and ambiguity, portraying many situations where individuals acting in an adharmic manner appear to defeat those whose actions are wholly motivated by concerns to preserve *dharma*. Attention has been paid to the unethical or non-dharmic killings of the four Kaurava field-marshals, all of whom had fought with absolute conformity to *dharma*; the propriety of the acts involved in these killings is heavily debated at the end of each of the battle books. While perhaps the most spectacular instance of the ambiguity of *dharma*, there is much more material in the *Mahabharata* pointing to the operative ambiguity of this concept and the subtlety, if not desperation, of interpretation in respect of those whom it affects. Mention need only made of the number of times the word *dharma* is used during the famous dice game (especially 2, 59–64) and the rhetorical debates conducted there about whether it is consistent with *dharma* that the Pandavas' wife Draupadi be used as a stake in a gambling match, as well as the massive amount of didactic material about *dharma* contained in the third, twelfth and thirteenth books of the epic. There is even one section in the twelfth book which deals with *dharma* in times of cosmic and social reversal, a time when all correct forms of behaviour are transgressed and people are allowed to act in such a way as to ensure their physical survival rather than with a view primarily to maintaining *dharma*. The theme of the decline and fall of *dharma* is central in the *avatara* myth, one of the most prominent mythic frames in the epic. Given this centrality of *dharma* in the *Mahabharata*, it is likely that the epic may be exploring the very capacity of a concept like *dharma* to function comprehensively as world-view and practical guide for regulating complex forms of social interaction.

Reading through the colourful narrative with its many descriptions of battles, episodes where ascetics perform many different kinds of magical feats, myths of creation and of gods in conflict with one another, we can see in the *Mahabharata* an extended reflection on a culture coming to terms with a variety of *dharmas*, even if *dharma* is often only used in the singular in the epic. The normative view of culture must be built up from a reading of the long twelfth and thirteenth books in particular, whereas the potential irruption of divergent cultural forces comes out of the constant references to tribal peoples, who live outside of the area of the *aryas* who practise the correct *dharma*, peoples frequently met with during the wanderings of the Pandavas in the forest as narrated in the first and third books of the epic. Another source of divergence from the norm comes from the host of ascetic figures who populate the pages of the *Mahabharata*, figures whose claim to notoriety is their withdrawal from society into the forest to practise austerities in order to gain social power when they do finally return to society, or to attain enlightenment if their austerities involve meditation on the nature of the self. Ultimately, the *Mahabhar-*

ata allowed these figures and the lifestyle they promoted, one originally considered subversive towards a dharmically ordered society, to be brought back into the fold and subsumed under the realm of *dharma* from which it had originally fled. At least, this is how it worked in an ideological sense. What actually happened in practice must have been far more messy than this, and some of this messiness is reflected in situations where ascetic figures appear who range from extremely austere power seekers, to sexual adventurers and even advisers to kings. The *Mahabharata* countenances the possibility of several ways leading towards individual contentment and tranquillity. Yet in the final analysis, all of these will be unified under the devotional relationship with the deity, developed at such length in the sixth and twelfth books of the epic.

The *Ramayana*

Although considerably shorter than the *Mahabharata*, the *Ramayana* shares many of the thematic unities found in the former and replicates in some measure some of the features of its narrative. It too involves the banishment of a hero into the forest, the mistreatment (abduction) of the hero's wife, a compromise on the part of the hero who is forced to perform an adharmic act, and a climactic battle between the forces of *dharma* and those of *adharma*, with all the accompanying ambiguities in the behaviour of characters produced by this. In many respects the plot is simpler than that of the *Mahabharata*, focusing on a palace intrigue where Rama, the rightful heir to the throne, is denied the kingship in favour of his younger brother, Bharata; Rama's subsequent banishment to the forest with his wife Sita; Sita's abduction by the brahmin demon Ravana; Rama's alliance with the monkey king Sugriva; the search by Hanuman (Rama's ally) for Sita and the discovery of her in Ravana's kingdom in Lanka; the battle between the forces of Rama and Ravana; Rama's killing of Ravana; and the re-uniting and subsequent separation of Rama and Sita. Within this convoluted plot the themes of regal succession, denial of primogeniture, adharmic betrayal of allies and the conflict between good and evil are worked out in a multitude of variations.

At another level, emphasis is placed on the relationship between Rama and his wife Sita, which extends across the entire narrative and is especially heightened during her absence from Rama in the latter half of the third and the fourth books, and Rama from her in the fifth book. Both as the expression of a love story and as an exploration of the ideal relation of husband and wife, the *Ramayana* has continued to attract audiences over the last two millennia. In the end, when Rama twice publicly humiliates Sita, believing false rumours of sexual infidelity made about her, she finally disappears into the Earth, of which she is a living symbol, leaving this aspect of the epic to conclude without any real narrative closure.

Like the *Mahabharata*, there is a 'duplication' of the plot in the narrative, where one exemplification of it concerns the earthly adventures of Rama, Sita and Ravana, the other the means by which the gods act to clean out the Earth of evil and its excessive number of humans. One recent view, focusing on the third book of the *Ramayana*, sees it like this:

> What had appeared to be a localized, circum-scribed, self-contained set of social and political problems in 'Ayodhya' is now seen to be part of a divine initiative made necessary by the periodic crudesence of demonic evil. The *Ayodhyakanda*, given the peculiar focus of its social vision, was an inappropriate arena for anything more than fragmentary revelations. The present book, where Rama finds himself in a realm that transcends the human world to the same degree that it descends to the demonic, is quite different. The gods themselves acknowledge the heavenly plan that the hero's sufferings advance; and the demons present themselves to permit the plan's advancement.
>
> (Pollock 1991: 31–2)

Thus there are two distinct but related expressions of the same plot running the length and breadth of the epic. This enables the *Ramayana* to be read as a palace intrigue about regal succession with its accompanying working out through political manoeuvring, and the relationship between the king and the Earth as exemplified in the close, but varying relationship between Rama (the king) and Sita (the Earth). In ancient Indian political theory the king is required, metaphorically speaking, to guard the Earth and to guarantee her fertility, the analogy between a husband and a wife being immediately obvious. The lengthy period of absence of Sita from Rama and her imprisonment in the court of Ravana as described in the fifth book, the *Sundarakanda*, is a direct instance of a king not fulfilling his proper function in respect of the Earth and can be understood thus on the political level. But the domestic analogy should never be underestimated, and the anguish Rama and Sita feel, and the loyalty the latter shows towards the former even when publicly repudiated by him, is easily understood by a popular audience even where the political and mythological message may be lost.

Like the *Mahabharata* the *Ramayana* also reinterprets much that comes from India's ancient Vedic culture. In both texts, symbols of the Vedas are used explicitly to produce an impression of antiquity in the content of what is being narrated. But more than this, it is the application of an implicit mythic frame derived from Vedic mythology that has been highlighted as having an important shaping significance on the *Ramayana* narrative. The narrative function is fulfilled, it is argued by one scholar, by the poet Valmiki's appropriation of the three faults of the warrior (where Rama killed Ravana, a brahmin, and Valin, a kshatriya, and repudiates Sita, who represents the mercantile/farmer class), to provide a kind of narrative frame forming the basis of a legend about Rama. Recognition of these three episodes as privileging an interpretation of the entire epic goes hand in hand with the view that they give semantic coherence to the whole because they represent the transformation into an extended narrative of a prior mythic structure, first reconstructed by Georges Dumézil who termed it 'the three faults of the warrior'. In addition, it is likely that the relationship between Rama and his brother Lakshmana, one of many significant relationships in the *Ramayana*, mirrors an earlier relationship between the gods Indra and Vishnu as they occurred in Vedic literature (Dubuisson 1986: 193). This is another instance of how the divine plane of events is transferred onto the human plane in the sphere of epic, where the fundamental problems of human existence – fatalism versus human effort as determinative factors in life, theories of personal and group identity and the tensions between each, the tension between acceptance of a deep self which stands in opposition to all of the surface parts of the mind and identity required to live in the social world – are displayed though never definitely resolved. Perhaps resolution only occurs in the kind of devotional dependence on God taught in the *Mahabharata*, but only hinted at in the *Ramayana*.

In conclusion, both Sanskrit epics together, but especially the *Mahabharata*, should be seen as defining a total vision of a particular order of culture and as exposing the conditions under which this order could be compromised if not subverted. This subversion could take two forms. Firstly, and most obviously, it would involve the perpetual defeat of order by disorder, an option which is never allowed as both epics only allow for the overthrow to be temporary and cyclical in a repetitive sense. Ultimately, right order will always be preserved even if, during much of the scheme of world history which gives these epics their quality of grandeur and expanse, it appears to be under constant attack and serious abuse, and therefore productive of great personal and social distress. Secondly, an individual ensconced within the socio-cultural system based on *dharma* can make a decision to become an ascetic who explicitly leaves society for the purpose of living a life on the outskirts of civilization in order to engage in a form of contemplative meditation leading to enlightenment. While initially this life style was considered as undermining *dharma*, the synthesizing function of both epics was sufficiently strong to be able to draw together the anti-social ideology of the ascetic into the embrace of *dharma*, treating it as just another method of achieving the fulfilment of *dharma* and therefore domesticating the threat to absolute order it may have represented.

Any civilization must confront the problem of the disjunction between order and disorder. Indeed, one could not comprehend how there could be a civilizational consciousness in the absence of such dichotomies. So fundamental are these themes that they can be used to enframe other subjects such as death, evil, fate, free will, the idea of an absolute beyond time and the subservience of humans to some higher force. As a genre epic is wonderfully suited to taking up these subjects and enframing them within the context of order/disorder and this may well be the fundamental contribution the two Sanskrit epics have made to South Asian culture. Not only do they extensively display both extremes, they also do not shy away from the kind of play that makes both such ambiguous categories and even go to the brink of abandoning both – in the transcendence of the soul – without going right over the edge. And they do this in a typical Indian context, for by focusing on kingship and genealogy, they have focused on two powerful symbols of socio-cosmic order.

Further reading

Biardeau, M. (1976) 'Études De Mythologie Hindoue. IV Bhakti et Avatara', *Bulletin de l'Ecole Française d'Extrême Orient* 63: 111–263.

—— (1997) *Hinduism: The Anthropology of a Civilization*, Delhi: Oxford University Press.

Brockington, J. (1998) *The Sanskrit Epics*, Leiden: Brill.

Dubuisson, D. (1986) *La légende royale dans l'Inde ancienne: Rama et le Ramayana*, Paris: Economica.

Hiltebeitel, A. (1976) *The Ritual of Battle: Krishna in the Mahabharata*, Ithaca, NY: Cornell University Press.

Matilal, B. (1989) *Moral Dilemmas in the Mahabharata*, Shimla: Indian Institute of Advanced Studies and Motilal Banarsidass.

Pollock, S. (trans.) (1991) *The Ramayana of Valmiki: An Epic of Ancient India*, vol. III, *Aranyakanda*, Princeton, NJ: Princeton University Press.

GREG BAILEY

Sarvastivada

Sarvastivada, 'Everything exists', is one of the eighteen schools (*nikaya*, 'ordination tradition') of early Buddhism flourishing in the Northwest, from Mathura to Afghanistan and into Central Asia, from about the middle of the third century BCE to the seventh century CE. As a branch of the Sthavira-vada (Doctrine of the Elders) purporting to perpetuate original Buddhist teaching, the

Sarvastivada is related to the Dharmaguptaka and Theravada schools. The **Sautrantika**, **Vaibhashika** and Mulasarvastivadin schools developed from the Sthaviravada.

The name of the school is derived from its theory that the fundamental elements or principles of existence (*dharma*) underlying every type of process subsist in all three temporal dimensions of past, present and future. Actualization and causal efficacy (*karitram*) in the present is one phase in the existence of a *dharma*. Prior to that, it had existed in a potential future mode. When appropriate conditions or circumstances (*pratyaya*) occur, it becomes the momentary (*kshanika*) present, after which it becomes past. What has been present continues to exist when it has become the past and is really continuous with the future. A conditioned (*samskrita*) *dharma* at the moment of its actualization has the characteristics of arising (*utpada*), stasis (*sthiti*), entropy (*jara*) and disappearance due to ultimate impermanence (*anityata*). There are three types of unconditioned **dharma**: space (**akasha**); cessation due to knowledge (*pratisankhya-nirodha*) which is disjunction from impure *dharmas*, that is, **nirvana** attained while alive through transformative insight (*prajna*) into the **Four Noble Truths**; and cessation not due to knowledge (*apratisankhya-nirodha*) which is the prevention of the arising of future *samskrita dharmas* in a psycho-physical stream. It is so called because it is obtained not by the comprehension of the Truths, but by the impotency of the causes of arising. It is the attainment of ultimate extinction (*parinirvana*) at death.

The rationale behind the doctrine of the eternal subsistence of the *dharmas* is that of explaining structural regularities in the non-human sphere and, most importantly, justifying the continuity within the series (*samtana*) of experiences to which persons are reduced between morally significant actions and their consequences in the face of the doctrines of momentariness (*anitya*) and no-soul (*anatman*). The basic constituents of reality are *per se* unconditioned, enduring and substantial (*dravya sat*); it is their mutually conditioned macroscopic aggregations that are characterized by impermanence.

In the absence of an enduring soul qua agent that would serve as a principle of metaphysical and moral continuity, the Vaibhashikas held that intentional (*chetana*) actions condition the *dharma*-based constituents of soulless personality through the operation of a *dharma* called 'possessive action' (*prapti*) which governs the karmic continuity of a series (*santana*) of psycho-physical experiences upon which substantial continuity is mistakenly superimposed. The Sautrantikas, who insisted on a radical momentariness doctrine, were opposed to this school in that they denied the existence of permanent *dharmas*. In particular, they classified the karmically crucial *prapti* as enjoying notional (*prajnapti sat*) rather than real (*dravya sat*) existence.

Further reading

Frauwallner, E. (1995) *Studies in Abhidharma Literature and the Origins of Buddhist Philosophical Systems*, trans. S. Kidd, Albany, NY: State University of New York Press.

Lamotte, E. (1988) *History of Indian Buddhism: From the Origins to the Shaka Era*, trans. S. Webb-Boin, Publications de l'Institut Orientaliste de Louvain, Louvain: Université Catholique de Louvain.

Potter, K. (1993) *Encyclopedia of Indian Philosophies*, vol. VII, Delhi: Motilal Banarsidass.

Stcherbatsky, T. (1970) *The Central Conception of Buddhism and the Meaning of the Word 'Dharma'*, Delhi: Motilal Banarsidass.

CHRIS BARTLEY

satkaryavada

Satkaryavada is an Indian theory of causation, propounded by the **Samkhya** and **Vedanta** traditions, according to which what will be called the effect (*karya*) pre-exists in a subtle form in its causal substrate (*upadana-karana*; identified as primordial nature – *prakriti* or *pradhana*) as a modality of a future state prior to its manifestation or actualization as an identifiable entity with determinate name and form. This is exemplified by the case of clay which is the substantive cause containing the pot where the causal process involves a transformation (*parinama*) of a stable underlying reality, not the generation of a totally novel product. So this is a version of the metaphysical theory that kinds of entities with determinate identity conditions have definite and specific intrinsic causal powers. Five considerations are adduced in favour of this theory: the non-existent cannot be produced or *creatio ex nihilo* is impossible; the effect requires a substrative cause; specific types of cause give rise to specific types of effect; causes have specific potentialities; the effect shares the nature of the cause.

Further reading

Halbfass, W. (1992) *On Being and What There Is*, Albany, NY: State of New York Press.

CHRIS BARTLEY

satyam jnanam anantam brahma

Satyam jnanam anantam brahma (The Absolute is reality, knowledge, infinite) (*Taittiriya Upanishad* 2.1.1) is an Upanishadic characterization of the Absolute (see **Upanishads**). The statement is of co-referential form (*samanadhikaranya*): the reference to one object of several words with different grounds for their applications. Conflicting exegeses of this major Upanishadic statement illustrate the centrality of the interpretation of co-referential statements to Vedantic theological dialectic (see **Vedanta**). The **Advaita**-Vedantin **Shankara** emphasizes the singularity of reference and construes co-referential statements as identity statements conveying a featureless essence where the different grounds for the applications of the terms are subjective senses. His theological rival **Ramanuja** and his followers maintain that the differences between the terms imply objective differentiation: *samanadhikaranya* is the reference to one object of words denoting several properties.

Shankara thinks that the statement is a definition (*lakshana*) of *Brahman* intimating a non-active, immutable, non-relational and featureless conscious essence. The notion of definition is congenial to his apophatic approach to transcendent predication since in Indian logic a definition has an exclusivist force, identifying the definiendum through demarcation while not offering a comprehensive enumeration of its properties. Shankara observes that the three predicates (reality, consciousness, infinite) are in a grammatical relationship of co-referentiality with the subject and distinguish *Brahman* from other subjects. Shankara rejects the objection that predicates have informative force only when applied to individuals belonging to the same class (as a blue lotus is singled out by the implicit exclusion of the predicate red and vice versa) and not to unique entities, on the grounds that the predicates have predominantly definitional senses. Predominantly qualifying terms, he claims, distinguish a subject from other entities belonging to the same class, but a definition demarcates it from everything else.

Shankara analyses the Taittiriya formula into three distinct identity statements. Each predicate is related to the term *Brahma* independently of the others. Each non-synonymous term has a different subjective sense in that each negates different empirical determinations of *Brahman* without implying internal differentiation in the ultimate reality. He thinks that each predicate has an extra-ordinary, analogical sense when applied to *Brahman*. 'Reality' distinguishes *Brahman* from modifications, unreality being associated with mutability and instability of form according to Advaita. *Jnana* differentiates *Brahman* from whatever is insentient and, in this context, means 'static awareness' and not cognitive agency, objecthood or instrumentality. Taken together in these special senses, the three predicates generate a concept of objectless, immutable awareness devoid of limitations.

Brahman is not a cognitive agent; it cannot be expressed by the everyday scope of the term 'knowledge'. It is defined by the term which usually refers to properties of finite minds that are phenomenal manifestations of the absolute consciousness. It is not directly designated by the word, since it lacks properties which are the grounds for the application of words. Likewise with the term 'reality'; since *Brahman* essentially lacks differentiating features, it is defined by the term *satya* which denotes the highest generic property (*satta*) occurrent in external things. But *Brahman* is not the direct referent of the term. The three identity statements in juxtaposition controlling and being controlled by one another, differentiate *Brahman* from what it is not and have definitional forces since *Brahman* is not directly expressible by the terms 'reality' and so on.

Ramanuja, Shankara's later theological oppo-nent, understands the Taittiriya formula as belong-ing to the corpus of **shruti** texts stating that *Brahman* is possessed of characteristics (*saguna*). He contends that the Advaitin exegetical procedure entails taking the three predicates non-literally (in most cases, an exegetical defect) since they lose their primary senses when they have the force of conveying the essence of an entity distinct from whatever is contrary to their proper, conventional senses. Interpreting co-referentiality as reference to a single object qualified by several distinct proper-ties, he denies that the Taittiriya formula refers to a non-differentiated entity. An uncompromising rea-list, Ramanuja holds that there is a structural isomorphism between knowledge and the known and between language and its referents. The language of scripture is the sole source of our knowledge of the transcendent *Brahman*. If scrip-tural language is complex, its object must be correspondingly complex. The term *satya* denotes *Brahman* as possessed of unconditioned existence and distinguishes it from both insentient matter that is the substrate of modifications and from conscious entities implicated in matter. Those two categories do not enjoy unconditioned existence since they are connected with different states designated by different names. The term *jnana* expresses uniform and permanently uncontracted consciousness and distinguishes *Brahman* from liberated selves whose consciousness is sometimes contracted. The term *ananta* expresses a proper form devoid of spatio-temporal limitations. As *Brahman*'s proper form has qualities, infinity applies to both proper form and qualities. By this term are excluded the permanently released selves, distinct from the two categories of selves excluded by the previous two terms, whose qualities and natures are superior to the other two types.

Further reading

Bartley, C. (1986) 'Interpreting Satyam Jnanam Anantam Brahma', in N. Allen *et al.*, *Oxford University Papers on India*, Delhi: Oxford Univer-sity Press, 103–15.

CHRIS BARTLEY

Sautrantika

Sautrantika is a Buddhist school deriving from the **Sarvastivada**, which differentiated itself from the Vaibhashikas by re-emphasising the radical mo-mentariness doctrine (*kshanika-vada*) and rejecting the view that the irreducible constituents of reality (*dharma*) subsist in past, present and future; a view which is condemned as an essentialist and eternalist heresy. The conservative Sautrantikas regarded only the sutras of the Vinaya and *Sutta Pitakas* in the **Pali Canon** as authoritative and rejected the **Abhidharma** doctrinal systematiza-tions.

The Sautrantikas held that reality consists of instantaneous, featureless particulars with unique causal efficacies. They reason that if a putative entity A endures (that is, persists by being wholly present at more than one time) for, say, three moments, it must be causally effective at each of them and thus productive of three effects because the same effect cannot be thrice generated. It follows that A has disintegrated into three mo-mentary realities. But if we construe persistence as perdurance (the possession of different temporal parts or stages at different times with no one part being present for more than one time) and say that tri-momentary A lies dormant, awaiting auxiliary factors, for its first two moments and is causally effective at the third (as the seed in the granary awaits soil and rain), then it is only the terminal condition that is real, the previous temporal parts or stages being either non-entities or distinct entities, one generating the other.

The school holds that reality, construed as causally effective point-instants, is given only in immediate sensation. The existence of the mind-independent sphere of instantaneous (*kshanika*) atoms inaccessible to sensory perception is infer-entially established. What is apprehended as form or content (*akara*) in perceptual awareness is a representation that is internal to consciousness although causally related to temporary configura-tions of atoms. Perception involves the occurrence of mental images or representations that stand in a relation of conformity (*sarupya*) to their causal basis. The Sautrantika view is a type of critical realism about the macroscopic world which is construed as a construction produced by an inferential and imaginative process of abstraction in which thought and language are inextricably interwoven. Verbalized cognitions (*vikalpa*) involving classificatory concepts are analysed as quasi-inferences from what is given in immediate sensation. Individual cognitions are held to be intrinsically reflexive. That is to say, an object-cognition is simultaneously and in virtue of the same act cognized by itself, just as a lamp illuminates itself while illuminating an object. Words refer through generalizing modes of presentation, but can never capture particulars and certainly do not express real essences.

The Sautrantikas reduce individual personality to a flux of psycho-physical elements (**dharma**) aggregated from moment to moment, under the influence of **karma**, spiritual ignorance and craving. The elements comprise the five constituents (*skandhas*) that make up the human being: matter and form (*rupa*), feelings (*vedana*), perceptions (*samjna*), volitions (*samskara*) and acts of consciousness (*vijnana*).

The denial of any permanent entity such as an enduring soul and the belief in the momentariness (*kshanikatva*) of phenomena raises problems where moral agency and responsibility are concerned. There was a widespread Sarvastivadin Abhidharmika belief that all bad (*akushula*) intentions derive from one or other of the basic defects (*klesha*) of grasping or greed (*lobha*), hatred or aversion (*dvesha*) and delusion (*moha*) while all good intentions derive from their contraries. The operations of the two classes of the springs of action are mutually exclusive. The basic passions operate until the time of full enlightenment. There thus arises the question of the *modus operandi* of the bases of virtuous dispositions with which the three fundamental enduring corrupt passions are incompatible. They cannot operate simultaneously. Nor can they act successively since succession requires homogeneity between preceding and succeeding instants. It would also involve an admission that good can arise from evil, and vice versa.

To explain the serial occurrence of heterogeneous mental states, the Vaibhashikas postulate two non-mental forces (*chitta-viprayukta-samskara*) called *prapti* (possession), which governs the aggregation of particular types of *dharma* and locates them in a particular experiential stream, and another termed *aprapti*, which precludes such combination. When a morally wrong state of mind is followed by a virtuous one, the latter is activated by the intervention of *prapti* of virtuous (*kushala*) *dharmas*. The Sautrantika insistence that only the momentary present exists leads them to reject the Vaibhashika theory of *karma* according to which actions are causally effective in the past, present and future through the operation of *prapti* which produces the combination of *dharmas* into the stream or process that is individual personality with a stable diachronic identity. They argue that the operation of *prapti* and *aprapti* would require prior cases of *prapti* and *aprapti* as their causal basis which involves an infinite regress. They explain the occurrence of virtuous and vicious states of mind by postulating a metaphorical theory of 'seeds' (*bija* = *shakti* (potency) = *vasana* (perfume)). There are seeds of evil, seeds of good and seeds which are morally neutral. The correlative dispositions co-exist in a mental series but only one can be operative at a given time. The mind is a storehouse of good and bad seeds producing fresh results in a mental series (*chitta-samtana*). This anticipates the 'storehouse conscious' (**alaya-vijnana**) theory of the Yogacharins (see **Yogachara**). The Vaibhashikas question the ontic status of the *bijas*. Are they identical with or different from the mind? If the latter, we have the *prapti* theory under another name. If identical, the compresence of different kinds of seeds in one storehouse appears to rule out determinate moral identities for particular intentions.

Where the operation of *karma* is concerned, the Vaibhashikas distinguished between the intention (*chetana*) behind an action and its subsequent public manifestation (*vijnapti*, 'information'). The potential future effects of acts remain with the agent at a sort of subconscious quasi-physical level (*avijnapti*). It follows that people are subject to forces over which they have no conscious control. But the Sautrantikas exclusively identified karmic efficacy with intention and rejected *prapti* and *aprapti* as theoretical fictions. They claim that the maturation of *karma* as the fruit of volitional and therefore morally significant actions is as follows: although mental, physical and verbal intentional actions lack duration, they leave a residue of tendencies which, as it were, 'perfumes' (*vasana*) the mental series (*chitta-samtana*) which is the mind of the agent and experiencer in which they originated, just as the scent of a flower persists after the bloom has perished. The impregnated series develops over time and culminates in experiences or dispositions of character which are the fruits of prior deeds.

Further reading

Hattori, M. (1968) *Dignaga on Perception*, Cambridge, MA: Harvard University Press.

Jaini, P. (1959) 'The Vaibhashika Theory of Words and Meanings', *Bulletin of the School of Oriental and African Studies* 22: 95–107.

—— (1959) 'The Sautrantika Theory of Bija', *Bulletin of the School of Oriental and African Studies* 22: 235–49.

—— (1959) 'Origin and Development of the Theory of Viprayukta-Samskaras', *Bulletin of the School of Oriental and African Studies* 22: 531–47.

—— (1959) *Abhidharmadipa*, Patna.

Lamotte, E. (1988) *History of Indian Buddhism: From the Origins to the Shaka Era*, trans. S. Webb-Boin, Louvain: Université Catholique de Louvain.

—— (1988) *Karmasiddhiprakarana: The Treatise on Action by Vasubandhu*, trans. L. Pruden, Berkeley, CA: Asian Humanities Press.

Matilal, B. (1986) *Perception: An Essay in Indian Theories of Knowledge*, Oxford: Clarendon Press.

Stcherbatsky, T. (1970) *The Central Conception of Buddhism and the Meaning of the Word 'Dharma'*, Delhi: Motilal Banarsidass.

CHRIS BARTLEY

scholar

Confucians are referred to as *ru*, 'scholars' or 'literati'. *Déclassé* knights, they traded in their swords for the pen or the Chinese brush to become clerical administrators, the scholar officials of the imperial bureaucracy. The term also connotes 'weaklings', and could be how these 'men of letters' were first perceived by their knightly peers. **Confucius** himself and an early circle of his disciples apparently taught the importance of ritual performance and plied their trade as master ritualists. By **Mencius**'s time, a distinction was made between the superior and the lowly – the true

and the lesser – *ru*. Mencius held himself to a higher moral than the 'village worthy' type, who was clearly looked up to by the public but who did only what society expected and no more. True moral courage comes defiantly from within.

It was the Song dynasty that truly made China into a 'kingdom of scholars' who ruled all under **Heaven**. The civil service examination created a gentry class of scholar officials, and the state openly 'elevated the literati and subordinated the military (under it)'.

WHALEN LAI

self

The 'self' is one of the most elusive concepts and controversial philosophical topics at the moment, due to the unravelling of the assumptions of the Enlightenment. Western scholars sympathetic to and native thinkers redefining the Chinese distinction *vis-à-vis* the West have gone beyond simply presenting Daoist **mysticism** as the reverse of Western rationality. The esoteric tradition of one culture always affords an easier contrast to the exoteric tradition of another. But the current debate about the nature of the Chinese 'self' is focused more on Confucian moral personhood. Instead of presenting the Chinese self as falling short of the rational, democratic individualism of the West or as some ready-made antithesis, some aesthetical continuum or communion with nature (such readings still exist), the new focus is either on retrieving the original genius that is **Confucius** or reinterpreting Neo-Confucianism in postmodern discourse, or both.

An unexpected impetus came earlier from the philosopher Herbert Fingarette, whose book *Confucius: The Secular as Sacred* (1972) jolted Sinologists by arguing that Confucius knew neither 'inner self' nor 'inner conflict' (they go together); that his Way was straight and was no 'cross road' requiring the weighing of options or choices by a deliberating mind; and that '**rites**' were the real cornerstone of *ren* (**humaneness**, benevolence). The last item reverses the judgment of the May Fourth liberals, who found the rites 'feudalistic', a judgement that left modern defenders of Confucianism to hold that the rites were from the Zhou but that Confucius himself created the higher virtue of *ren*. The latter being as 'universalistic' as humanism anywhere, it could reform or contravene the 'particularism' of the inherited rites. But with postmodernists now putting that claim to universality by modern humanism on hold, such liberal apologetics became suspect. Fingarette's positive reappraisal of rites opened up a whole new avenue for the neo-traditionalists to explore

Basing his argument on the methodology of J.L. Austin, Fingarette presents Confucius's teaching on the rites as that of speech-acts calling forth a performance so very smoothly that a life of ritual can be as effortless and as selfless as a consummate Kabuki dance. The performer follows that singular path of the Dao. Fingarette also presents Confucius, who felt called by **Heaven**, as a man with a mission. All of life now being a ritual performance, the secular is sacred. The book is an extension of Fingarette's earlier investigation into other constructions of the self – other than the modernist autonomous subject – in his post-Freudian tract, *The Self in Transformation*. He continues that pursuit in *Self-Deception*. Fingarette had originally intended his thesis about the absence of an 'inner (and divided) self' to apply only to Confucius. Once the debate on human nature surfaced in **Mencius**, once Mencius had to weigh the claims of egoism and altruism, 'inner' life began and 'choice of option' among the many philosophical ways would be necessary. That assessment has been revised by the current proponents of Neo-Confucianism, who hold that Mencius and Mencians since could, in their advanced moral state, be as single-minded as Confucius. Meanwhile, Fingarette's redemption of the pre-modern rites as near-magical moral speech-acts opens the door for a neo-traditionalist rebuttal of modern Western 'rational individualism'.

Philosophical reconstitution and interpretation of the Chinese 'self' in its own terms or as filtered through new insights became a preoccupation now too diverse to recount. The old, outward contrast stands. The Chinese self accepts the positive 'human feelings' defining the dyadic relationships; it is not an abstract, self-contained and self-sufficient individual entity. The new, more inward analysis focuses on spiritual progress. Tu Wei-ming sees it as an emerging third wave of global Confucianism. Roger Ames and David Hall renewed a sharpened East–West contrast in a series of books, beginning with their new exposition of Confucius's intellectual biography. It began with his 'love of learning at age fifteen' to his 'following his heart-mind without ever erring (from the Way)' in *Thinking Through Confucius*. Tu settles for the relational model in an expanding set of concentric circles drawn from the Great Learning; Ames employs an aesthetic array of 'focus and field', and Hall develops a Meadian symbolic interactionism and Whiteheadian process. The framework of discussion in the United States has thus moved away from the vocabulary of Kant and Hegel, Heidegger and Nietzche that the Hong Kong and Taiwan spokesmen used. Of great interest to philosophers, the discussion seems a bit removed from the reality of the modern Chinese self caught up in the market economy or the reality of the traditional rites and the political institutions as recounted by more hard-nosed historians.

See also: atman

Further reading

Fingarette, H. (1963) *The Self in Transformation: Psychoanalysis, Philosophy, and the Life of the Spirit*, New York: Harper & Row.

—— (1972) *Confucius: The Secular as Sacred*, New York: Harper & Row.

Hall, D. and Ames, R. (1987) *Thinking Through Confucius*, Albany, NY: State University of New York Press

Munro, D. (1969) *The Concept of Man in Early China*, Stanford, CA: Stanford University Press.

Northrop, F. (1947) *The Logic of Science and the Humanities*, New York: World Publishing.

Tu Wei-ming (1979) *Harmony and Self-Cultivation: Essays in Confucian Thought*, Berkeley, CA: Asian Humanities Press.

WHALEN LAI

Sengzhao

b. 384?; d. 414

Buddhist philosopher

Tutored by Kumarajiva into the dialectics of **Nagarjuna**, Sengzhao (Seng-chao) was the first to master Madhyamaka. He then reviewed the prior *prajna* scholarship and found it wanting. He rejected the thesis of original nothingness for being nihilist, the mind-as-empty thesis for its subjective bias, and argued with Zhi Dun, charging him with failing to see that **emptiness** simply describes the unreality (of the given reality). Well received in his time, he was actually sidelined soon after and excluded from the Sanlun lineage. In mediating a conflict between his royal patrons, he used the *Wisdom Sutra* to defend 'gradual enlightenment' and to oppose the *Lotus Sutra* which was the original source for the 'sudden enlightenment' thesis.

Further reading

Richardson, R. (1967) *Early Madhyamika in India and China*, London: University of Wisconsin Press.

WHALEN LAI

sense perception

A general consensus in early Chinese thought is that the five senses are correlated to the five separate kinds of sense data: the eyes see colour, the nose recognizes smell, and so on. Behind them, the mind controls the senses and integrates the information received. An empty (uncluttered) mind works best. But as **Laozi** says, the five colours can make the eyes go blind, meaning that seduction by objects and an overload of ever-changing sensations may confuse the eyes and in turn muddle the mind. Other thinkers are more positive towards such inputs of sense data which may strengthen body and soul, and these positivists do not subscribe to the idea that to acquire the *dao*, one should unlearn or erase the accretion of information.

When the eyes see an object, is it the eyes 'reaching out' to apprehend the thing or the sights

'coming in' to get our attention? In the end, a compromise is reached; it is by *ganying* or 'stimulus and response' that the process is realized. That had become standard by Han times, and in English it sounds almost behaviourist; but linking the inner to the outer the direction is not just from matter to mind but both ways. The direction relies on a correlative logic, a symbiosis between different categories of thing. No physical contact and no time lapse need even be assumed. For the Chinese Buddhists, sense perception is not one thing but two. Sensation and perception are two of the five *skandhas* (the factors which make up a person) which are quite distinct from the physical form (object) and yet fall short of the inner workings of consciousness and will.

But if a treatise attributed to the Logician Gongsun Long entitled 'On Hard and White' is to be trusted, then China had also hit upon a version of the Buddhist analysis of the eighteen *dhatus* (elements). Briefly stated, this goes as follows. We can never know if or prove that 'hard' and 'white' (picture a piece of marble) take up the same space. Gongsung Long himself argues for their being separate as categories and as realities. That is because hard is to touch as white is to sight. These are two different sense data hitting two separate sense organs. These two discrete 'sensations' would not even be 'perceived' (be known) distinctly unless and until the related 'spirit' (consciousness, the eye and the touch consciousness) is working. This is nearly identical with the Buddhist analysis, which breaks it down to a full count of eighteen elements, three for each of the five senses plus another trio for the sixth sense (mind, mental object and mental consciousness). The Buddhist system gained currency during China's medieval period.

The Neo-Confucians (see **Neo-Confucianism, concepts**) who came afterwards reverted, as did the Vedantins in India, to a more classical mode of monistic intuition or organic sympathy. A term they often used that would correspond roughly to the English 'experience' seems at first to be equivalent to 'sense perception'; but it is not. The term reads literally 'body verification', but by body (literally, the torso) is meant the 'full person' and by verification is meant, not separate sensation and perception but 'what is attested to be true and concrete personal experience'. This was used by the Neo-Confucians to describe the actualization of virtue through actual practice. It accords not with British empiricism nor American pragmatism, but with the classic *arete* (virtue) of Aristotelianism, or 'living out the truth of an inherent excellence'.

Further reading

Gongsun Lung (1964) 'Essay on Hard and White', in Wing-tsit Ch'an (ed.), *A Sourcebook of Chinese Philosophy*, Princeton, NJ: Princeton University Press, 240–2.

Paul, D. (1984) *Philosophy of Mind in Sixth-Century China: Paramartha's 'Evolution of Consciousness'*, Stanford, CA: Stanford University Press.

Kasulis, T., Ames, R. and Dissanayake, W. (eds) (1993) *Self as Body in Asian Theory and Practice*, Albany, NY: State University of New York Press.

—— (1994) *Self as Person in Asian Theory and Practice*, Albany, NY: State University of New York Press.

—— (1998) *Self as Image in Asian Theory and Practice*, Albany, NY: State University of New York Press.

WHALEN LAI

Shaiva Siddhanta

Shaiva Siddhanta is a pluralistic, realistic and theistic Tantric but Veda-congruent system of scriptural (*agamic*) interpretation and ritual. It flourished in Kashmir from the eighth to the eleventh centuries CE, after which time its influence was supplanted by forms of monistic Shaivism. It survives to this day in Tamilnadu in significantly different emotional *bhakti*-centred form.

Important Kashmiri theorists include Sadyojyoti (700–800), Narayanakanthabhatta (925–75) and his son Ramakanthabhatta (950–1000). In the debate with non-dualism, the latter is a writer of considerable significance. His major works are the *Nareshvaraparikshaprakasha* and the *Matangaparameshvaragamavrtti*. Mention should also be made of the southerner Aghorashivacharya from Chidambaran (*fl.* 1157–8), who wrote philosophical treatises and a ritual handbook widely used today in South Indian temples.

Whereas the visionary idealist and anti-Vedic Kaula theorists of the monistic **Trika Shaivism**

and Karma schools emphasized the salvific efficacy of gnosis in a yogic context, the Siddhantins insisted on the indispensability of a life of ritual action, subsequent to initiation into the cult, on the part of enduring individual centres of consciousness and agency as the means to the elimination of an innate defect (*mala*) which suppresses their innate capacities for universal knowledge and omniagency and which is also ultimately responsible for their susceptibility to the acquisition of the merit and demerit (good and bad **karma**) that brings about bondage to a series of births in the here and now. Salvation is understood as Shivaequality, meaning qualitative but not numerical identity with Shiva, in which the selves's innate faculties of omniscience and omnipotence are realized. (In order to avoid a clash of purposes, the non-competitive released selves voluntarily refrain from the exercise of omnipotence.) It is a significant feature of this tradition, differentiating it from the more radical and ancient Pashupata forms of Shaivism, that the properties characterizing the released selves are not imparted or transferred (*guna-samkranti-vada* or *avesha*) by the deity, a view whose origins in possession cults is perhaps discernible. The Saiddhantika view reflects a belief in the integral and impermeable nature of personal identity consonant with orthodox Brahminical emphasis on self-control as a virtue.

Mala, the quintessential disability, is characterized as a kind of substance (*dravya*) which can be removed only by action. Knowledge of its presence is not enough. *Mala* is likened to an ocular cataract, mere awareness of whose presence does not impair its efficacy and whose removal requires the action of the surgeon's instrument. Whereas the extreme Tantric votaries of the ferocious deities Bhairava and Kali believe that sectarian initiation annuls one's former **caste**, Shaiva Siddhantin initiation leaves caste, understood as an intrinsic physical property, intact. The Siddhantin is thus able to fulfil his Brahminical social and ritual duties. His exacting life of ritual duty, combining both *smarta* and extra-*smarta* commitments, is consistent with mainstream orthodox Brahminical duty and caste purity (*varnashramadharma*).

The school recognizes three distinct categories of existents:

1   *Pati*, a category that particularly concerns

the divine in relation to the created spheres of existence or worlds (*loka*). There is divine efficient causation of the cyclical emanation, maintenance in existence and reabsorption of the universe. The divine power of occlusion (*tirodhana-shakti*) is understood positively as the compassionate provision of environments in which finite beings may experience the fruits of their *karma*, thereby depotentiating it. Salvific grace (*anugraha-shakti*) is primarily operative in the cult's initiation rituals. God is the efficient cause of the universe of worlds which he creates via recourse to *maya*, the real substantive cause of the material and mental domains. The Saiddhantikas differ from Shaivas of a more radical anti-caste persuasion by accepting the anthropocentric orthodox view that divine originative causality and the structuring of created worlds or spheres of experience occurs in accordance with the accumulated *karma* of individuals. Indeed, divine creation is a compassionate act for the sake of bound souls who need spheres of experience in which they may be freed from *mala* and *karma*.

That Shiva is the creator is inferred from the fact the universe is an effect because it is comprised of parts. Such an effect, it is argued, requires an omniscient and omnipotent producer adequate to its infinite complexity. This category also includes liberated souls of various kinds some of whom act as intermediaries in the creative process.

2 *Pashu*, irreducibly individual selves, understood as stable continuants beyond space and time, with essential properties of cognition (defined in terms of reflexivity and intentionality) and reflexively known agency. Potentially omniscient and omnipotent, some of them (*sakalas*) have become enmeshed in physical and mental existences due to:

3 *Pasha*, bonds which include the real substrative cause of the inferior worlds of material and mental phenomena from which they are emanated and into which they are re-absorbed (*maya*), *karma*, *mala* and the occlusory power of Shiva.

Shiva, the efficient cause, activates *maya* in order to produce universes where individuals may experience the fruits of and thus exhaust their *karma*. The products of *maya* are time (*kala*); causal regularity ensuring that the results of his actions will accrue to the agent (*niyati*); limited agency and cognitive power (*kala*) bestowed upon selves who would otherwise be paralyzed by *mala*; an interest

in the objects of experience on the part of the otherwise apathetic *mala*-afflicted selves (*raga*); basic, unformed matter (*prakriti/avyakta*) consisting of the three *guna*s; *buddhi* (mind); *ahamkara* (ego); *manas* (sensory co-ordinator); the senses of hearing, touch, sight, taste and smell; the organs of speech, holding, walking, excretion and procreation; the subtle elements of sound, touch, form, taste and smell (i.e. the sense-data perceived by the senses); and the gross elements – space, air, fire, water and earth – the perceived external substances.

Mala, represented as a type of substance in its own right, is a defect beginninglessly and thus inexplicably attached to selves which radically limits their potentially infinite innate capacities for knowledge and action. The postulation of *mala* serves the purpose of providing a non-circular answer to the question of why human beings have *karma* and are bound to a series of births. *Mala* is thought of as 'ripening': at a critical point in this process, the aspirant will be moved to approach the guru for initiation. Since *mala* is categorized as a 'substance' it can only be removed, in classical Indian terms, by an action, specifically the ritual action of initiation.

There are various types of initiation involving temporary entheosis (deification) through the descent of divine grace (*shakti-pata*), including *samaya-diksha* is admission to the sect, conferring the right to learn the Agamas; the *mantras* or the sonic form of supernatural entities whose incantatory repetition invokes their 'bearers' and deifies the reciter; and the ritual practices of the cult. *Nirvana-diksha*, the liberation seeker's (*mumukshu* or *putraka*) initiatory ritual, qualifies the votary for participation in the cult. It destroys the matured *mala* and accumulated (*sanchita*) *karma* that would otherwise have caused future incarnations. The disinterested performance of the rituals for which one is now qualified brings about the diminution of that remaining impurity which sustains one's current physical and mental existence.

Initiation at the hands of the *guru* or *acharya* who, after a ceremony of deifying *mantra*-infusion, incarnates Shiva, annihilates the latent *karma* that would otherwise have propelled one onto and conditioned future modes of existence, while leaving the *karma* appropriate to the current life (*prarabdha karma*) intact. Allowance is made for the exceptional case of an initiatory ritual (*sadyonirva-nadiksha*) involving an extremely intense infusion (lit. descent) of divine power (*tivratara-shakti-pata*) by which all *karma* is obliterated. The initiate dies in the course of the ritual. Subsequent to the normal procedure of *nirvana-diksha*, a lifetime of unmotivated observance of daily and occasional rites, Shaiva and Vedic, prevents the production of fresh *karma* and liberation occurs at death.

Acharya-abhisheka is the highest form of initiation, open only to *putrakas*. It confers the right to teach, to initiate votaries and to preside at public rituals.

Sadhaka-abhisheka is for the aspirant to mundane well-being (*bubhukshu*) seeking supernatural powers (*siddhi*) through the mastery of mantras. This type of initiate has usually already undergone the preceding two initiations. He is described as a perpetual student and celibate (*naisthika*). The types of supernatural powers, whose magical origins are patent, specified in the Shaiva scriptures are *anima* (physical minuteness, non-obstructibility and indetectability); *laghima* (weightlessness); *mahima* (unrestricted physical expansion); *prapti* (the capacity to go wherever one wants); *prakamya* (ability to create and enjoy incomparably beautiful female forms); *ishitva* (subjection of enemies); *vashitva* (mundane domination); and *kamavasayitva* (the capacity to do as one wishes). This type of initiate may also seek various forms of enjoyment (*bhukti*) as a denizen of worlds superior to this.

Further reading

Brunner, H. (1981) 'Un Chapitre du Sarvadarsanasamgraha: Le Saivadarsana', in *Mélanges Chinois et Bouddhiques*, vol. XX, Brussels.
Goodall, D. (1998) *Bhatta Ramakantha's Commentary on the Kiranatantra*, Pondicherry: Institut Français.

CHRIS BARTLEY

Shakya Chokden

b. 1428; d. 1507

Buddhist philosopher

Arguably one of the most original and certainly one of the most controversial thinkers of the classical period of Tibet, Shakya Chokden Serdok Panchen's place within the overall history of Tibetan philosophy was somewhat ambigious. Formally, his sectarian affiliation lies with the **Shakya school**, and it was with great Shakya masters like Rongton Shakya Gyaltsen (1367–1449) that Shakya Chokden studied many of the subjects of Tibetan Buddhist scholarship. However, as he gained scholarly maturity Shakya Chokden began to depart from the Shakya orthodoxy, and in fact wrote a highly critical commentary to **Shakya Pandita**'s (1182–1251) *A Thorough Differentiation of the Three Vows*. In his Madhyamaka writings, Shakya Chokden struggles to reclaim the authenticity of many of the early Tibetan interpretations against the influential reading of **Tsongkhapa** and his immediate followers. In fact, the whole of *A Definite Ascertainment of the Middle Way*, Shakya Chokden's key work on Madhyamaka philosophy, is a systematic critique of many aspects of Tsongkhapa's Madhyamaka. Like Taktsang Lotsawa (b. 1405), Shakya Chokden's central criticism of Tsongkhapa's interpretation relates to the allegation that it is logo-centric. Furthermore, he claims that by making the absence of intrinsic existence as the final **emptiness**, Tsongkhapa remains caught within the boundaries of language and conceptualization. Hence, he argues, Tsongkhapa's emptiness does not represent a total transcendence of all boundaries of conceptual elaboration. The **Geluk school** thinker Jetsun Chokyi Gyaltsen (1469–1544) has responded to this critique in defence of Tsongkhapa.

In his later years, Shakya Chokden's thought underwent a radical shift as his views moved closer to **Shentong philosophy**. Shakya Chokden came to think that the purely negative characterization of emptiness as found in **Nagarjuna**'s *Mulamadhyamakakarika*, especially as read by Chandrakirti, represents only a partial picture of the Madhyamaka's highest truth of emptiness. According to him, it was the thoughts of Maitreya, Asanga and **Vasubandhu** which represent the ultimate view of emptiness, which Shakya Chokden called 'the great Middle Way'. And he argued that this great middle way is in greater concordance with Vajrayana teachings. We can thus detect a progressive reading of history in Shakya Chokden's understanding of the Madhyamaka philosophy. It is this kind of shift in Shakya Chokden's views which made the Tibetan doxographer Thukan Chokyi Nyima (1737–1802) assert that Shakya Chokden was first a **Yogachara**, then a Madhyamika, and in his later age a proponent of Shentong. Perhaps, it is because of such complexity that it is difficult to determine the impact of Shakya Chokden's works on Tibetan philosophy as a whole. His own Shakya school seems to have literally disowned his writings when they were deliberately left out from the well-known anthology *The Collected Works of the Masters of the Shakya Sect of Tibetan Buddhism*.

THUPTEN JINPA

Shakya Pandita

b. 1182; d. 1251

Buddhist philosopher

Shakya Pandita Kunga Gyaltsen was one of the greatest thinkers of Tibet and one of the five founding fathers of the Shakya school of Tibetan Buddhism. Highly eclectic in his interests, his writings cover a wide spectrum of scholarship including one of the earliest scholarly treatises on music and aesthetics. He was also instrumental in introducing Sanskrit poetics into the Tibetan language. In writing *The Gateway to Being a Learned Scholar*, Shakya Pandita can be perceived as having established a systematic academic classification of higher education that remains to this day a model of scholarship for the Tibetan academia. Furthermore, with the composition of *A Thorough Differentiation of the Three Vows* and *An Elucidation of the Buddha's Thought*, Shakya Pandita embarked on a highly polemical project of cleansing what he perceived as distorted understanding of some of the fundamental Buddhist tenets in Tibet.

In philosophy, Shakya Pandita's greatest contribution lies in the development of the studies of Buddhist logic and epistemology in Tibet. His influential treatise on logic and epistemology entitled *Treasury of Knowledge* remains to this day a masterpiece and the primer on the subject in the Shakya school. His interpretation of **Dharmakirti** represents a restoration of a non-realist reading based on a literal interpretation of the Buddhist logician's classics. Thus Shakya Pandita's epistemological views, especially following their defence by Gorampa and **Shakya Chokden**, served as a counterpoint to the realist epistemology of Chapa Chokyi Senge and its influential heirs, the **Geluk school** writers like Gyaltsap and Khedrup.

Further reading

Dreyfus, G. (1997) *Dharmakarti's Philosophy and its Tibetan Interpretations*, Albany, NY: State University of New York Press, ch. 8.

Jackson, D. (1987) *The Entrance Gate for the Wise: Sa skya Pandita on Indian and Tibetan Traditions of Pramana and Philosophical Discourse*, Vienna: Arbeitskreis für Tibetische und Buddhistische Studien Universität Wien, introduction.

THUPTEN JINPA

Shakya school

The Shakya school is named after a monastery founded in the eleventh century by Khon Konchok Gyalpo (1034–1102) in central Tibet. It was under the influence of the great **Shakya Pandita**, fourth amongst what are known as the five great masters of Shakya, that this monastery became a major centre of learning in the thirteenth century. Thus Shakya and Sangphu became the two most important seats of philosophical learning in central Tibet. As such, the Shakya school's role in the establishment of a full-fledged tradition of the disciplines of logic and epistemology based on **Dharmakirti**'s works has been highly critical. Ironically, it was perhaps after the founding of the **Geluk school** and the emergence of the highly influential realist epistemology of **Gyaltsap Dharma Rinchen** and Khedrup in the fifteenth century that Shakya Pandita's non-realist epistemological tradition was fully appreciated even by the Shakya school itself. It was thanks to Yakton Sangye Pal (1348–1414) and Rongton Shakya Gyaltsen (1367–1449) that Shakya Pandita's non-realist interpretation of Dharmakirti's epistemology was brought into sharp relief, perhaps partly in response to Bodong Chokle Namgyal's (1376–

1451) critique of Shakya Pandita's non-realism. Later, the writing of the influential Shakya thinkers Gorampa and **Shakya Chokden** led to the formation of a distinct Shakya epistemology, based on the works of Shakya Pandita, which represented a powerful counterpoint to the Geluk epistemology. Today the Shakya school remain, in the realm of epistemology, the upholders of Shakya Pandita's non-realism, while the Geluk school are the upholders of Chapa's somewhat moderate realism.

The position of the Shakya school appears to be less clear with respect to the second major Tibetan philosophical discipline, namely the study of the Madhyamaka philosophy of **emptiness**. This may be due partly to the ambiguity of Shakya Pandita's final standpoint on the reading of **Nagarjuna** amongst the influential Indian interpreters. Interestingly, again it appears that it was only after the emergence of the influential Madhyamaka writings of **Tsongkhapa** and his immediate students such as Gyaltsap and Khedrup that a distinct Shakya reading of Madhyamaka evolved. In fact, some of the influential early Shakya thinkers such as Sasang Mati Panchen (fourteenth century CE) and Nyapon Kunga Pal (1300–80) seemed to have espoused the so-called 'extrinsic emptiness' view of Shentong philosophy. An important exception to this was Rendawa Shonu Lodro (1348–1412), but his works may have been judged to be too close to the emerging new Geluk school of Tsongkhapa and his followers. Therefore, it is thanks to Rongton, perhaps the earliest critic of Tsongkhapa's Madhyamaka, and his two influential students, Gorampa and Shakya Chokden, that a self-conscious, distinct Madhyamaka reading of the Shakya school seemed to have emerged. Key figures in the development of the philosophy of this school are, in addition to the five great Shakya masters, Yakton Sangye Pal, Rendawa Shonu Lodro, Rongton Shakya Gyaltsen, Gorampa Sonam Senge and Shakya Chokden.

Further reading

Dreyfus, G. (1997) *Dharmakarti's Philosophy and its Tibetan Interpretations*, Albany, NY: State University of New York Press, introduction.

THUPTEN JINPA

shamanism in Korea

Shamanism, the earliest religion of Korea, is as old as the history of the Korean people. Shamanism is a religion centered on the shaman, who is a priest or medicine man. A shaman is a spiritual leader, who has the mystical and supernatural power to communicate with the deity, and fulfills the needs and desires of the members of the community. Most Korean shamans are called *mudang*. A shaman has special gifts to perform the functions of the healing ceremony, fortune telling and other various rituals for the well-being of individuals and the community.

The idea of god in shamanism is basically polytheistic and animistic. There are several hundred deities in Korean shamanism: there are nature-related deities, and there are deities who are closely related to the daily life of people, namely, the deities of earth, mountains, water and heaven. In shamanism, all these deities have personal characteristics and superhuman powers. They are objects of fear and awe, for they can bring punishment in the form of suffering. Korean shamanism believes that life and death, fortune and misfortune, health and sickness, and all human affairs and destiny are dependent upon divine will. Shamanism is basically a pragmatic religion, seeking benefits for earthly life, praying for one's wishes to have good fortune and blessing, and to remove misfortune and sickness.

Shamanism is still widely practised in Korea, mainly in agricultural and fishing villages. Since the arrival of Buddhism and Confucianism in Korea around the fourth century, and Christianity in the eighteenth century, shamanism has been practised mainly among the poorer people, who felt more at home with shamanism than the so-called higher religions, because they believed that shamanism was their traditional way, offering them simple, visual and concrete rituals for immediate benefits and because the simple and less educated people have a tendency to feel close to nature deities in which shamanism believed, while higher religions have a tendency to be intellectual and abstract in ideas and beliefs.

Further reading

Covell, A. (1983) *Ecstasy: Shamanism in Korea*, Elizabeth, NJ: Hollym International Corp.

Kendall, L. (1985) *Shamans, Housewives, and Other Restless Spirits*, Honolulu, HA: University of Hawaii Press.

Kim T'ae-gon *et al.* (1973) *Han'guk Chonggyo* (Korean Religions), Iri: Wonkwang University Press, 13ff.

Lee, P. (ed.) (1993) *Sourcebook of Korean Civilization*, vol. 1, New York: Columbia University Press, 94ff, 443ff.

Yu Chai-shin and Guisso, R. (eds) (1988) *Shamanism: The Spirit World of Korea*, Berkeley, CA: Asian Humanities Press.

YONG-CHOON KIM

shame and guilt

China has been called a shame culture, in contrast to the guilt culture that characterizes the Christian West. Shame is outer as guilt is inner; it is other-oriented instead of self-directed. Such sweeping characterizations are useful only to a degree, for shame and guilt are present in all societies. An observer often assumes greater inner integrity to his own culture and attributes more consensual mores to the unfamiliar Other he observes.

With that said, it should first be noted that the Chinese have two words for 'shame'. One describes the shyness natural to children and young maidens. That shyness due to a lack of social contact is never deemed becoming in the adult male. The other Chinese word for 'shame' is anything but other-directed; its 'self-accusation' causes no end of remorse in private. More than just doing wrong according to society (the superego), it is falling short of one's personal integrity (the ego ideal). It is the code of the gentleman **scholar** who strives to be 'broad in learning and outlook, while in all his dealings, be guided by (this self-critical) shame'. This is as 'inner directed' as any Christian sense of guilt. The guilt due to sinning against God, violating his interdicts, and being motivated by pride and self-idolatry looks, to a defender of that 'inner shame', are all too 'outer directed'. However, this merely goes to show that there are significant problems when different cultures come to appreciate the moral language of the other.

Further reading

Eberhard, W. (1967) *Guilt and Sin in Traditional China*, Berkeley, CA: University of California Press.

WHALEN LAI

Shankara

b. *c.*650; d. *c.*700

Philosopher

Shankara was a renouncer (*samnyasin*) and major theorist of non-dualistic (**Advaita**) Vedanta. Of the many texts attributed to him, genuine ascriptions of authorship include: the commentary on the *Brahma-sutras*; commentaries on the *Isha*, *Aitareya*, *Katha*, *Kena*, *Chandogya*, *Taittiriya*, *Prashna*, *Brihadaranyaka*, *Mundaka* and *Shvetasvatara Upanishads*; the commentary on the *Bhagavad Gita*; the commentary on the *Mandukya Upanishad* with the *Gaudapadiyakarika*; and the *Upadesasahashri*.

In common with all Vedantins, he held that transpersonal scripture (**shruti**) is the only means of knowledge (**pramana**) about whatever lies beyond the empirical sphere. It is as a Vedantic exegete seeking to legitimate his non-dualist convictions by demonstrating their conformity to the Upanishadic texts that he must be understood. The many 'biographical' accounts are later hagiographies of little historical value, and there is no evidence independent of tradition for the frequently cited dates of 788–820. There is some agreement that dates in the range 650–700 CE are probable.

Shankara's major theses are:

1 Reality (*Brahman*, the Absolute all-encompassing entity) is undifferentiated, relationless, static, contentless consciousness and bliss. Nevertheless, due to primal ignorance (**avidya**) it somehow becomes the substratum of experienced diversity.

2 The self-revealing (*sva-samvedana*) and self-established (*svatah siddha*) 'inner self' or soul

(*atman/pratyagatman*) which is the constant witness (*sakshin*) of all conscious states is essentially identical with *Brahman*.

3 Differentiation and change, albeit experienced, are ultimately unreal. All plurality of selves, mental events, objects, causes and effects is a function of beginningless ignorance or misconception (*avidya*) generating the misapprehension of the self as a personalized individual agent and experient subject to Vedic social and ritual duties (*varnashramadharma*) and transmigration (**samsara**). The human person is a composite of spirit (**atman**) and matter (non-*atman*). Such a composite has experiences and is subject to the illusion that it is an agent due to an ultimately unreal centre of individual awareness, a congenital conflation of spirit and matter.

4 Non-discursive, gnostic insight (*jnana*), preceded by the renunciation (**samnyasa**) of all ritual action (*karma*) and caste duty, into the identity of the non-agentive core self and *Brahman* negates *avidya* and is a necessary and sufficient condition of release (*mukti*) from the series of births propelled by intentional and motivated actions.

5 Salvific knowledge concerning the nature of the *Brahman–atman* state can only be derived from the accredited scriptures (*shruti*) which are the only means of knowledge about trans-empirical realities. Liberating insight is expressed in Upanishadic major statements (*mahavakyas*) such as 'That thou art' (**Tat tvam asi**) allegedly asserting the identity of the individual self (*jiva/jivatman*) and the Absolute.

6 Ritual action (*karman*) and devotion (*bhakti*), while purifying the mind, cannot of themselves produce release since they presuppose that differences are real and thus belong in the sphere of ignorance. In short, any form of action binds one to *samsara*. This denial of the agentive notion of the self is crucial to Advaita.

7 The human life of the enlightened and liberated individual (*jivanmukta*) continues until what is termed the *prarabdha-karman* appropriate to the final existence has been exhausted. No fresh *karman* is being generated given the renunciation of all ritually and ethically significant actions.

8 Misconception or ignorance (*avidya/ajnana*) of the true identity of the soul and the nature of reality as undifferentiated is the root cause of bondage to the series of births (*samsara*).

Given the view of the nature of the Absolute as undifferentiated, non-agentive awareness, accounting for the origin and nature of the world-appearance and the experience of diversity will inevitably be problematic. How does the empirical, differentiated material manifold come about?

The introduction to the commentary on the *Brahma-Sutras* reads:

When it is established that a real relation of the subject and object which pertain to the concepts of the 'I' and the 'Thou' and which are essentially opposed like light and darkness is impossible and that all the more impossible is a real relation of their properties, then it is correct to say that what is false (*mithya*) is: (a) the superimposition (*adhyasa*) of the objective (viz the psycho-somatic complex) and its properties, which falls under the concept of the 'not-self' on the subject, whose essence is consciousness, which falls under the concept of subjectivity and (b), the reverse of the preceding, the superimposition of the subject and its properties on the object. Even so, after combining the real and the unreal and failing to discriminate between two aspects that are absolutely distinct both as property-possessors and in terms of their properties and having superimposed upon each the characteristic nature and properties of the other, there arises the congenital matrix of mundane transactions whose basis is misconception and which is manifest in thoughts such as 'I am this' and 'this is mine'. Superimposition is the appearance, whose form is memory, of something previously encountered elsewhere. The learned think that superimposition thus defined is *avidya*. The reciprocal superimposition (*itaretara-adhyasa*) of the subjective and the objective, called *avidya*, is the precondition of thought and language about objects and means of knowledge, of secular and religious activities and of all the scriptures concerned with ritual injunctions, prohibitions and ultimate liberation from the series of births.

So Shankara thinks that there is a beginningless process of misconception termed 'reciprocal superimposition' (*itaretara adhyasa*) in which consciousness misidentifies itself as an individual experiencer and agent and misattributes to itself the objective circumstances of its embodied life, mind, senses and caste which are putatively located in a causally ordered spatio-temporal framework. It should be noted that while Shankara clearly equates *avidya*, *mithyajnana* and *itaretara-adhyasa*, his successors in the Advaitin tradition view *avidya* as a cosmic force that is the substrative cause of all errors and of the manifold universe. But for Shankara it is the confusion of consciousness with what it is not, an association of the real and the unreal occasioned by misconception. One aspect of the mechanism is that when the *atman*-consciousness somehow comes into relation with the active and material mind (*buddhi*) which is an evolute of primal nature (*prakriti*), the latter is illuminated (the material *buddhi* becomes 'quasi-conscious') and confusion is compounded when the activity of the *buddhi* is misattributed to the inactive *atman*. It is this process of superimposition that is *avidya* and it is the precondition of all thought, language and action and of scriptural teaching.

On the one hand, the Vedic scriptures belong to the sphere of *avidya* while on the other, Shankara, as a Vedantin, is committed to the view that scripture (*shruti*) is the sole means of knowing (*pramana*) about the transcendental Brahman. Shankara makes a sharp distinction between *shruti* texts concerned with action (*karma-kanda*) and those concerned with spiritual insight (*jnana-kanda*). The Purva Mimamsakas (see **Purva Mimamsa**) classify the Vedic statements as injunctions (*vidhi*), descriptions and explanations (*arthavada*) and incantations (*mantra*) to be used in the rituals. They hold that since the Veda teaches what has to be done (*karya*) predictive statements have a primary status. *Arthavadas* are auxiliary statements whose function is that of motivating the hearer to perform the actions enjoined by *vidhis* and to explain their purpose by stating their fruits. Shankara rejects this relegation of *arthavadas*, which category of course includes statements on *Brahman* and the soul, to an auxiliary status. He says that the statements comprising the *karma-kanda* pertain to this worldly social and religious duties (*dharma*), means and ends, causes and effects, and are the special concern of the Purva Mimamsa schools of exegesis. The statements of the *jnana-kanda* are concerned

with the absolute *Brahman* and are the field of Vedanta or Uttara Mimamsa. Shankara says that the desire-based practices associated with the *karma-kanda* have as their fruit a state of transitory felicity subject to the workings of *karma* while the product of the *jnana-kanda* is eternal and irreversible release from rebirth.

There is a key difference between the types of statement found in the two sections: *karma-kanda* statements are primarily injunctive prescribing what must be done while the fact-asserting indicative statements of the *jnana-kanda* are descriptive of what is the case. From Shankara's point of view, the fact that the former belong to the matrix of differentiated agents, actions and results that is the sphere of *avidya* is unproblematic. At best, ritual actions have a propaedeutic function in so far as they may purify the mind and predispose it to knowledge of *Brahman*. But what is the nature of the authority of those texts which are held to bear upon the Absolute? What is the role of scripture in relation to the knowledge of *Brahman* whose comprehension constitutes release? There is no problem in connection with those Upanishadic texts dealing with topics such as the originative causality of the universe; but what of those which purport to refer to the literally inexpressible *Brahman* and speak of its relation to the soul (*atman*)? Shankara thinks that the descriptive Upanishadic statements should not be regarded as conveying salvific knowledge about *Brahman* and the self descriptively: they do not impart information. Intuitive realization of the identity of the *atman* and *Brahman*, which is in any case already known at a profound level of self-conscious awareness, cannot arise from hearing and reflecting upon scriptural utterances since that is an activity involving discursive thought belonging to the sphere of *avidya* and involved with all sorts of differences. Rather, the function of the descriptive scriptures is twofold: they both strip away misconceptions about the soul and *Brahman* and direct our attention away from absorption in the concerns of everyday life to the Self that is to be realized.

As a Vedantin, Shankara subscribes to the **Satkaryavada** theory of causation, according to which what will be called the effect (*karya*) pre-exists in a subtle form in its casual substrate (*upadana-*

karana; identified as primeval nature – *prakriti* or *pradhana*) as a modality of a future state prior to its manifestation or actualization as an identifiable entity with determinate name and form. Taking his cue from passages in the *Chandogya Upanishad*, Shankara calls the 'raw material' from which the universe unfolds 'unevolved name and form' which he understands as the undifferentiated and hence indescribable (*anirvachaniya*) substrative cause of the manifestation of the differentiated universe and from which objects and individual observers are generated. Since name and form, the sphere of *avidya*, differ from *Brahman* they are, from the ultimate point of view, illusory and may be characterized as *maya* although, unlike the later Advaitin traditions, he attaches no particular significance to this conceptuality except when comparing the creator God Ishvara conceived in quasi-personal terms to a magician producing a show. Ishvara (*saguna-Brahman*) is the impersonal absolute *Brahman* understood and described as an omnipotent and omniscient divinity who may be the object of meditation and worship rather than as an abstract (*nirguna*) principle.

As a Vedantin, it behoved Shankara to demonstrate the conformity of his doctrine with *shruti* and *smriti*. He is thus confronted with statements that purport to be about the inexpressible *Brahman*. Since the *Brahman* is ineffable, Shankara must adopt an apophatic approach to transcendent predication. The *locus classicus* of this apophaticism is his commentary on *Brihadaranyaka Upanishad* 2.3.6: 'Now there is the teaching "not...", "not...".' There is no better description than 'not'. The designation of it is 'the fundamental reality'. Shankara says that the statement conveys the fundamental reality by eliminating all specific limiting conditions. It refers to something that per se has no distinguishing features; either name, form, action, difference, class-property, or qualities which are the grounds for the application of words. *Brahman* has no distinguishing features. Therefore it is not possible to describe it positively as 'this' or 'that'. *Brahman* can be described by means of name, form and action superimposed upon it but when it comes to describing its proper form which is devoid of determinate conditions, then it is impossible to describe it in any way. There is only one way left,

the designation 'not', 'not', the negation of all possible descriptions.

Brahman, the universal source, cannot be spoken of as existent in the same way in which everyday objects are. We cannot say that *Brahman* and empirical objects exist in the same sense of 'exist'. It stands to reason that *Brahman* cannot be directly expressed by words such as 'existent' and 'nonexistent' for every word is used to reveal an object and on being heard conveys its object through the conventional word-object relation by referring to class, action, property, or relation. Words such as 'cow' and 'horse' refer to generic forms; the expressions 'he cooks', 'he studies' refer on the basis of actions; 'white' and 'black' refer via properties and 'wealthy' and 'cow-owner' are relational. But *Brahman* belongs to no class so it cannot be the referent of words such as 'existent'. Nor, since it is featureless, does it possess properties through which it would be expressible by propertyterms, likewise with action-words. Since it is nonrelational, non-dual, non-objectifiable transcendental subject, it is correct to say that it cannot be denoted by any word.

There is no evidence for the conventional supposition that Shankara was a **Shaiva Siddhanta** votary. That he was a renouncer from a Vaishnava milieu is clear from the theistic *Commentary on the Bhagavad Gita* which propounds (for the unenlightened) specifically Vaishnava forms of devotion to a personal deity (*Ishvara-bhakti*). But the overall commentatorial framework is definitely renunciatory (*nivritti-dharma*).

It is unlikely that the text styled the *Yogasutrabhashyavivarana* ascribed to Shankarabhagavatpada is by the great Advaitin. The suggestion that it is largely relies on acceptance as factual of the story in some biographies that Shankara was a Yogin convert to the Advaitic point of view. We have here a literary trope epitomized by the accounts that Gautama Buddha in his progressive quest for enlightenment had experimented with Yoga practices which he subsequently rejected.

The canard that Shankara was a crypto-Buddhist (*pracchana-bauddha*) may safely be dismissed. Contrary to Buddhism, he maintains that there is a single, non-dual, permanent, static reality consisting of pure consciousness. Arguing the need for a permanent witness of the stream of cognitions and the irrefragable nature of our experience of externality, he rejects both the views of the idealist **Yogachara** Buddhists and also those of the Sarvastivadins who accept a mind-independent world consisting of momentary atomic constituents (see **Sarvastivada**). The Madhyamika relativists, who reject the *pramana* system, he simply dismisses as not worth arguing with.

See also: Gaudapada

Further reading

Halbfass, W. (1995) *Philology and Confrontation*, Albany, NY: State University of New York Press.
Mayeda, S. (1979) *A Thousand Teachings*, Tokyo: Tokyo University Press.

CHRIS BARTLEY

Shantideva

b. 685; d. 763

Buddhist philosopher

Shantideva was the Buddhist Mahayanist author of the *Bodhicharyavatara* (Entering the Path of Enlightenment) and *Shikshasamucchaya* (Compendium of Teaching). He was a noted exponent of the Madhyamika school, stressing the perfection of wisdom (*prajna-paramita*) as co-incident with the **emptiness** (*shunyata*) of all phenomena which lack independent essence. The attainment of perfection by the truly enlightened being (***bodhisattva***) presupposes the elimination of all desires, the achievement of a state of calm and the transcendence of the sphere of the knower and known. Insight (*prajna*) is a condition beyond all forms of discursive thought in which the *bodhisattva* is liberated from the chain of cause and effect (***pratitya-samutpada***) and thus enters ***nirvana*** which transcends even emptiness.

Further reading

Shantideva (1996) *The Bodhicaryavatara*, trans. K.

Crosby and A. Skilton, Oxford: Oxford University Press.

CHRIS BARTLEY

Shao Yong

b. 1012; d. 1077

Neo-Confucian philosopher

A major figure in Northern Song Neo-Confucianism, Shao Yong (Shao Yung) was later sidelined by **Zhu Xi**. This urbane 'Recluse of Loyang' sided with the anti-reformist faction in the new capital, Gaifeng. A **Yijing** (Book of Changes) numerologist, he was the source for the Diagram of the Former Heaven, attributed to Fu Xi as paired to the Diagram of the Later Heaven of King Wen. His **numerology** was most intricate, beginning with the binary combinations. In opposition to Buddhist idealists who meditated on the mind, he turned back to the world and meditated on things. The cosmos evolved from the Great Ultimate, through the liminal spirit, to the numbers, and finally to the myriad things of the world of our experience. Thinking backwards, the one principle is recovered in the midst of the many; thinking forward, future events can be predicted. A legendary prognosticator, Shao Yong was instrumental in subverting Buddhist **emptiness** by constructing a metaphysics of concrete particulars. In the end, Zhu Xi, who designed a moral metaphysics with a sharper 'is/ought' distinction between the moral principle above form and the material realities below it, had little use for the numerological infrastructure of the continuum of cosmic evolution.

Further reading

Wyatt, D. (1996) *The Recluse of Loyang: Shao Yung and the Moral Evolution of Early Sung Thought*, Honolulu, HA: University of Hawaii Press.

WHALEN LAI

Shentong philosophy

Shentong (spelt *gzhan stong*) literally means 'empti-ness of the other' or 'extrinsic emptiness' (see **emptiness**) and refers to an interpretation of the Madhyamaka doctrine of emptiness that is distinct from the Prasangika–Madhyamaka's notion of the emptiness of intrinsic existence. On this view, all dependent phenomena, namely the things and events that are causally produced, and imputed phenomena, i.e. the world of mental constructs, are literally empty of themselves and possesses no identity and existence of their own. The world of multiplicity is not only false but must also be discarded by the seeker of truth. What is truly real is the consummate phenomenon (the ultimate truth), which is not empty of its own intrinsic being but is empty of all phenomena of depen-dence and construction. Hence the term 'emptiness of the other'. This ultimate truth is said to be the non-dual wisdom as opposed to the **foundational consciousness**; it is thus true **buddha nature** and also the primordial basis. Although this wisdom of nonduality is said to be ever present, it is not perceptible by an ordinary consciousness. It is characterized as permanent, unchanging, trans-cendent, pristinely pure, and endowed with all the enlightened attributes and it pervades the entire universe. This ultimate truth is not cognizable through language or through reason; rather it must be intuited through a higher faculty attained once language and thought are discarded. This empti-ness is said to be not the emptiness of intrinsic being as presented in the *Mulamadhyamakakarika* and other logical texts, but the higher emptiness presented in the works of Maitreya and Asanga, and found also in **Nagarjuna**'s hymns.

The principal proponent of this view was **Dolpopa Sherap Gyaltsen**, whose composition of *Ocean of Definitive Meaning* systematized this lineage of thought as a comprehensive philosophi-cal position. One can detect three principal influences in the development of Shentong philo-sophy. First, at least in its epistemology and usage of philosophical language, Shentong appears to be deeply indebted to the Indian **Yogachara** school. Shentong uses extensively the Yogachara schema of 'three natures' to articulate much of its ontological views, and also the Yogachara idea of foundational consciousness appears to play a crucial role in its philosophy of mind. The second major source of influence appears to be the scriptures and Indian literature related to the doctrine of buddha nature. To a large extent, it could be argued that Shentong represents an attempt to develop a literalist reading of the buddha nature theory whereby the highest truth or ultimate reality is conceived of in affirmative terms as eternal, unchanging, unitary, in short, as the absolute. The third source of influence seems to be Vajrayana Buddhism. It is evident, at least in Dolpopa's writings, that the Shentong view perceives this absolute also in terms of the Vajrayana concept of *dharmakaya* (*trikaya*). Some Tibetan critics of Shentong have argued that Shentong's conception of the absolute shares affinities with **Vedanta** thought as well.

Many influential thinkers such as **Buton Rinchen Drup**, Rendawa (1349–1412), **Tsong-khapa, Gyaltsap Dharma Rinchen**, Khedrup (1385–1438), Rongton (1367–1449) and Taktsang Lotsawa (b. 1405) have subjected Shentong philo-sophy to vehement criticism. However others like **Shakya Chokden**, Karmapa Mikyo Dorje (1507–54) and Druk Pema Karpo (1527–96) have espoused versions of Shentong thought. It is perhaps in Shakya Chokden's later thought that we see the most systematic and coherent philoso-phical attempt to vindicate the basic tenets of Shentong philosophy. One of the darkest periods in the history of Tibetan philosophy relates to the state-enforced ban on the Shentong school and its activity during the seventeenth century, leading to the closure of many of its monasteries and important libraries. Today, however, some form of the Shentong view appears to be widely embraced as representing the highest doctrinal position by many in the **Kagyu school** and **Nyingma school**. This is particularly true in the light of the so-called 'non-partisan' (*ri me*), a somewhat syncretist movement that began at the beginning of the nineteenth century to counter the dominance of **Geluk school** tradition.

Further reading

Ruegg, D. (1963) 'The Jo nang pas: A School of Buddhist Ontologists According to the Brub mtha' shel gyi me long', *Journal of American Oriental Society* 83: 73–91.

Williams, P. (1989) *Mahayana Buddhism*, New York: Routledge, ch. 5.

THUPTEN JINPA

Shingaku

Shingaku is the Japanese pronunciation of Chinese *xinxue*, and means 'Learning of the Mind'. This term originated with the Neo-Confucianism of the Song dynasty (960–1280), where it referred to the discipline of cultivating the originally good 'human nature' with which each human being is endowed from birth. This human nature was thought to be at one with the moral principle that underlies the cosmic order, also known as 'the Way', and Neo-Confucian thinkers taught that through reverent introspection into one's own mind, one will be able to attain a state of harmony with this Way. By holding fast to the 'mind of the Way' that is innate in all human beings, and by asserting its command over one's selfish desires, man can reach a state of perfect morality, and then proceed to benefit society by providing good leadership by virtuous example.

In Japan, the term 'Shingaku' gained popularity during the early Edo period (1600–1868). It was used to refer to Neo-Confucian theories about the mind, or to the school of Wang Yangming (1472–1529), a Ming period Confucianist who stressed the cultivation of the innate goodness of human nature even more strongly than the Neo-Confucians of the Song. In modern writings on Japanese intellectual history, however, the term is more readily associated with a popular movement of mass education begun by students of Ishida Baigan (1685–1744). To distinguish between the various usages of the term Shingaku, Baigan's school is often referred to as Sekimon Shingaku (Ishida's Shingaku school).

Baigan was a clerk working for a Kyoto merchant, conspicuous only for his singular dedication to self-improvement and enlightenment. Although initially he aspired to become a Shinto preacher, his way towards enlightenment was a Neo-Confucian one: he strove to attain unity with his human nature by means of meditation and introspection. Under the guidance of Oguri Ryoun (*fl.* 1729), a Neo-Confucian scholar who was also well-versed in Buddhist and Daoist teachings, Baigan had two experiences of Zen-like enlightenment. Baigan wrote that these experiences allowed him to attain a state in which he was in perfect harmony with his human nature, a state in which his personal emotions coincided perfectly with his social and moral obligations. After Ryoun's death in 1729, Baigan began to give regular lectures at his house in Kyoto, and somewhat later he also started sessions in which he and his students questioned each other on the attainment of the Way. Lectures, mutual questioning sessions and sitting meditation defined Baigan's teaching and remained the backbone of Shingaku practice.

Baigan's audience remained small but included a number of committed disciples, of whom Teshima Toan (1718–86) was to become the most influential. Under Toan's leadership, Shingaku developed into an extremely popular religious movement, centring on 'meeting houses' (*kosha*) where sermons were delivered, questions and answers were exchanged, and group meditation sessions took place. Toan made a special effort to convey his message to all layers of the population, and published materials aimed specifically at the less educated, women and even children. The nationwide popularity of the movement made it one of the prime channels through which Confucian ideals such as **filial piety**, frugality, etiquette and hard work were inculcated among commoners.

At the basis of Shingaku teaching was the notion of the 'original mind' that is in harmony with the Way. The movement mainly used texts from the Neo-Confucian canon: the Four Books (the *Great Learning, Doctrine of the Mean, Analects* and *Mencius*), the *Reflections on Things at Hand* and *Elementary Learning*, adding to these standard classics only the writings of Baigan and other Shingaku teachers. However, Toan mixed this Neo-Confucian fundament with a considerable portion of Zen ideas and practices. The exchange of questions and answers at Shingaku meeting houses, for example, owed much to the use of **koan** (enigmatic statements used for meditative purposes, aiming to press the meditator's mind beyond everyday rationality, into a non-discursive state of consciousness) in Zen.

Similarly, the sitting meditation practised by Shingaku followers drew not only on the Neo-Confucian practice of quiet sitting (*seiza*), but also on Zen sitting (*zazen*), which, as in Shingaku, was practised in groups. Perhaps even more importantly, popular Zen sermons served as an example for the Neo-Confucian preaching of Shingaku teachers. Zen preachers had for centuries made use of Neo-Confucian terms in addressing lay audiences, and did in fact play a major role in introducing Neo-Confucianism to Japan (see **Buddhist philosophy in Japan**); in a similar way, Toan did not hesitate to use Zen terminology to illuminate the meaning of Neo-Confucian concepts. Thus, he referred to the 'original mind' that is the key to self-improvement also as the 'Buddha-mind' or as 'no-self', and stressed that cultivation of one's original mind led to a Zen-like experience of sudden enlightenment, a flash of insight in which all contradictions will be solved and in which one's life will be changed for ever.

Like the various Zen schools, Shingaku institutionalized the experience of enlightenment by officially checking and recognizing the genuineness of the enlightenment reached by Shingaku disciples, a practice that clearly set Shingaku apart from more orthodox Neo-Confucian schools in Japan. Shingaku, then, is perhaps best described as a popular mixture of Neo-Confucian and Zen ideas about the mind and practices of contemplation on the mind. As such, it was a direct continuation of the amalgamation of Zen and Neo-Confucianism that had been at the centre of warrior culture during the medieval period.

However, while during the medieval period the syncretic teachings on which Shingaku drew had been regarded as supremely authoritative in an intellectual sense, they had been displaced as such by a more orthodox, anti-Buddhist Neo-Confucianism in the course of the early Edo period. But the purer Neo-Confucian (or otherwise Confucian) schools that dominated intellectual reflection during the Edo period were rather inaccessible for the less well-educated common man, let alone woman. These schools stressed that the basis of government lay in virtuous conduct by those who rule, but had rather little to say to those who are ruled. Shingaku's emphasis was different in that it taught that all human beings, regardless of

class, status, or education, were endowed by birth with an 'original mind' that bore within it the possibility of enlightenment and moral perfection. While most Neo-Confucian schools frowned upon the activities of merchants, whom they placed at the bottom of society for the reason that they are 'non-productive', Shingaku actively argued that the daily business of merchants was potentially as ethical as that of the ruling class, as long as it was conducted with the aim of providing a service to society as a whole, and not to enrich oneself and satisfy one's selfish desires. Similarly, Shingaku offered peasants, women and even children, to whom neither the Neo-Confucian academies nor most Buddhist organizations had much to offer, a basic moral education and, to the more committed, even the potential of achieving the grand aim of enlightenment through one's own efforts.

This is not to say, however, that Shingaku teachings were in any way subversive in the sense that they empowered those below to aspire to political influence. Shingaku taught its adepts to improve themselves by exerting themselves within their given occupation or station in life, by becoming the perfect merchant, peasant, wife, or child. The movement did not argue that merchants, peasants or women should be allowed to wield political power, but simply that they be admitted to the human race, and regarded as moral beings. The shogunate saw Shingaku not as a threat but as an ally, and during the early nineteenth century repeatedly supported and endorsed Shingaku preaching as a means to further the 'moral edification of commoners'.

Shingaku declined rapidly after the Meiji Restoration (1868), partly because of its former association with the now discredited shogunate, partly because of the vigorous condemnation of all syncretic teachings that characterized the early Meiji period, and partly due to the establishment of a public schooling system that filled the educational lacuna that had been Shingaku's domain. Its influence remained tangible within Japanese society not only in the field of moral education, but also in the form of widely shared ethical attitudes. In particular, its legacy lives on through its early influence on new religions, which to this day share Shingaku's religious quest for a Neo-Confucian set of ethical norms through purification of one's own mind.

See also: Buddhist philosophy in Japan; Confucianism in Japan; Folk Chan

Further reading

Bellah, R. (1985) *Tokugawa Religion: The Cultural Roots of Modern Japan*, New York: The Free Press.
Sawada, J. (1993) *Confucian Values and Popular Zen*, Honolulu, HA: University of Hawaii Press.

MARK TEEUWEN

SHINGON *see* Buddhist philosophy in Japan

SHINRAN *see* Buddhist philosophy in Japan

Shinto

'Shinto' is commonly used as a term for Japan's indigenous religion. As such, it is employed to refer to a wide range of Japanese practices and ideas that centre on *kami* (Japan's indigenous deities) and their cults, and especially to those that cannot readily be identified as Chinese or otherwise of foreign origin (whether Buddhist, Daoist or Confucian). In this sense, 'Shinto' refers to a large variety of popular practices surrounding *kami*, often with the implication that these multifarious practices all represent different aspects of a single cultic system. Used in this way, the term reflects a theological ideal advocated by Shintoist thinkers of different guises since the medieval period: the ideal that all Japanese are united by their participation in a single communal cult. This ideal has been superimposed on a very different reality, in which *kami* cults are highly locale-specific and are characterized by local differences rather than communalities.

From the medieval period onwards, the term 'Shinto' has served as a focus for theories about Japan's national identity, as opposed to China, India, and, later, the West. Such theories invariably focused on the ancestral *kami* of the Imperial House, as well as a few other *kami* that were integrated into the state cult at an early date. Shinto thinkers, in the medieval as in the modern period, looked for evidence for their ideas to the myths about these deities that were laid down in *Record of Ancient Matters* (*Kojiki*) (712) and *Chronicles of Japan* (*Nihon shoki*) (720), rather than to local *kami* cults. These two works were national histories, compiled following the example of Chinese dynastic histories, as part of the transformation of Japan's political structure from a coalition of 'clans' (*uji*) headed by the Yamato clan, into a Chinese-style centralized state, headed by an emperor (in Japan, the head of the Yamato clan), and governed by a bureaucracy appointed by him from among allied clans. The national histories recorded the history of Japan from the origin of the universe, through the 'Age of the Gods' (*kamiyo, jindai*), to the acts of the human ancestors of the Imperial House. Their aim was to legitimize imperial rule by transposing its origins into the Age of the Gods: both works recount how rule over Japan was handed down from Amaterasu and/or Takami-musubi (the Imperial clan deities) to their grandson Ninigi, the ancestor of the imperial lineage. Moreover, the relations between the Imperial House and its allied clans were defined by integrating the myths of these clans into a storyline that focuses on the imperial lineage, and by incorporating the deities of these clans in the role of servants or family relations of this lineage.

One possible definition of Shinto, then, is as 'a series of successive theories about the sanctity of the Japanese state, as embodied by the Imperial House'. Shinto teachings of this kind were first pioneered in the fourteenth century, but were moved to the centre stage first in the eighteenth century, by Confucian and nativist scholars. Many Shintoist scholars have consistently blurred the distinction between Shinto in this sense on the one hand, and popular *kami* cults on the other, implying that Shinto theories as here defined have been at the heart of Japan's 'national, indigenous religion'. However, it is worth repeating that local *kami* cults reflect a huge variety of locale-specific beliefs and concerns, and do not constitute in any sense a shared, Japan-wide belief system, let alone one focusing on the emperor. Therefore, a strict distinction should be maintained between the terms 'Shinto' and '*kami* cults'.

Another possible definition of the term Shinto is as 'theories that give universal meaning to *kami* cults and myths – whether formulated by *kami* priests, Buddhist monks, Confucian scholars, or others'. This definition too is based on a distinction between Shinto, now defined as an historical succession of universalistic theories of various backgrounds, and *kami* cults of purely local significance. If one follows this definition, it becomes possible to discuss as part of the Shinto tradition interpretations of *kami* cults and myths that stress topics other than the state and imperial rule. Perhaps the most important topic of this kind was the interpretation of *kami* worship (and, especially, purification) as a universal method to attain salvation, immortality or moral perfection and sainthood. Shinto theories in this sense were first formulated in the late twelfth and early thirteenth centuries, and predated the formulation of Shinto teachings focusing on the state and the emperor.

Most medieval traditions of Shinto thought combined both strains of Shinto theology (theories about the state and imperial rule, and theories about salvation or sainthood); but a swell of anti-Buddhism that reached its peak in the eighteenth century led Kogaku and nativist scholars to reject the latter as 'syncretic' teachings based on Buddhist ideas about 'the mind', and to accept only the former as 'pure Shinto'.

See also: Confucianism in Japan; Kokugaku; Shinto, Buddhist; Shinto, Confucian

Further reading

Aston, W. (1956) *Nihongi: Chronicles of Japan from the Earliest Times to A.D. 697*, London: Kegan Paul, Trench, Trubner & Co.

Breen, J. and Teeuwen, M. (eds) (1999) *Shinto in History: Ways of the Kami*, Richmond: Curzon Press.

Chamberlain, B. (1981) *The Kojiki: Records of Ancient Matters*, Tokyo: Tuttle.

Kuroda Toshio (1981) 'Shinto in the History of Japanese Religion', trans. J. Dobbins and S. Gray, *The Journal of Japanese Studies* 7–1.

Muraoku Tsunetsugu (1988) *Studies in Shinto Thought*, New York: Greenwood.

Naumann, N. (1988) 'Die einheimische Religion Japans. Teil 1. Bis zum Ende der Heian-Zeit', *Handbook of Oriental Studies* V.4.1.1, Leiden: Brill.

MARK TEEUWEN

Shinto, Buddhist

When Buddhism first arrived in Japan, it functioned within the context of and alongside a native system of *kami* cults. Throughout the early period, Buddhist and *kami* cults co-existed as parallel but separate ritual systems. Gradually, Buddhist influence transformed *kami* cults and incorporated them into Buddhist thought and practice.

The amalgamation of *kami* cults and Buddhism is usually described as a process in three stages. First, the eighth century saw the appearance of the first 'shrine-temples' (*jinguji*), founded by itinerant mountain ascetics at the request of provincial lords and village heads, whose local *kami* asked to be saved from their *kami* state by means of Buddhist ritual. The idea behind these shrine-temples was that *kami* could be rendered both more beneficent and more powerful when served a menu of Buddhist services. The building of temples at shrines resulted in integrated temple-shrine complexes that became hothouses of the amalgamation process. Towards the end of the same century, this process entered a second stage with the identification of the *kami* Hachiman as a protector-deity of the Buddhist Law, and (somewhat later) even as a **bodhisattva**. This was followed by the adoption of tutelary *kami* (*chinju*) by temples all over the country. Now, shrines were built at temples, taking the institutional amalgamation of *kami* cults and Buddhism an important step further. The third stage of the process began in the ninth century, which saw the origin of the notion that some *kami* are skilful means, emanations of buddhas, *bodhisattvas* or *devas* who 'soften their light and mingle with the dust' (*wako dojin*) in order to lead us to the Buddhist Way. This notion is known as *honji suijaku*, '[Buddhist] original source and [*kami*] emanations.' Between the ninth and eleventh centuries, an increasing number of *kami* were 'promoted', in Buddhist terms, from potentially dangerous spirits whose character should be improved through contact with the Buddhist Law, to localized emanations of buddhas and *bodhisattvas*, embodying their wisdom or compassion. By worshipping such *kami*, it was now possible to unleash the magical powers (*riyaku*) of Buddhist divinities ranging from Shakyamuni to Fudo Myoo (in Sanskrit, Acalanatha), or to escape to the Pure Lands of Amida (Amitayus or Amitabha), Kannon (Avalokiteshvara) or Yakushi (Bhaishajyaguru).

However, these notions did not yet give rise to a 'Buddhist Shinto'; they merely served to include the *kami* in the scope of Buddhist ritual. From the late Heian period (twelfth century) onwards, however, Buddhist interest in the *kami* grew rapidly as political power shifted from the imperial court to the leaders of the rising warrior class, who established the first shogunate in Kamakura in 1185. The great changes of this period brought about a new interest in the myths of origin that sanctified the remains of the old system; at the same time, the notion that the Buddhist Law had entered into its phase of final decline (*mappo*) led many to place their faith in the local deities. The Mongol invasions of 1274 and 1281 and the struggles for the throne between various branches of the Imperial House in the fourteenth century further strengthened this interest.

In the course of the thirteenth and fourteenth centuries, various teachings were developed that regarded the *kami* (or a few specific *kami*) as embodiments of the Buddha's compassion, and therefore as vehicles to salvation superior to the Buddha himself. Worship of the *kami* was seized upon as a way out of the eschatological denial of the efficacy of Buddhist practice. Some *kami*, notably Amaterasu, then gradually evolved from embodiments of compassion into embodiments of the Absolute itself, and came to be seen as paragons of the natural, inherent enlightenment of this world (*hongaku*) that is superior to the acquired, secondary enlightenment (*shigaku*) that is the province of Buddhism.

The primary focus of these theories was Amaterasu, who was identified as the 'spirit', or even the 'original source' of the World-Buddha Dainichi (Vairochana). This association was elaborated upon by identifying the two shrines of Ise as manifestations of the Diamond Realm *mandala* and the Womb *mandala*, which according to Shingon thought depict Dainichi's twin aspects of wisdom

and compassion. Theories based on this association were developed at many temples (Ninnaji, Daigoji, Onjoji and others), where they were handed down as tangled webs of secret transmissions. This body of transmissions is often referred to in one word as Ryobu Shinto, the 'Shinto of the Two Mandalas'. Ryobu theory was also adopted at the shrine-temple complex of Miwa, where 'Miwa Shinto' took shape during the same period. This Shinto lineage identified the *kami* of Miwa as both Amaterasu and the two Shingon *mandalas*. Tendai monks, moreover, developed a teaching that identified the *kami* of the Hie shrines, tutelary deities of the Tendai headquarters at Mount Hiei, both as Amaterasu and as the embodiment of the 'natural' enlightenment inherent in every particle of the universe: the universal enlightenment of Dainichi. These teachings were given expression in esoteric ordinations (*kanjo*), in which a master revealed to his disciple (or to a fellow master) the 'three secrets' (*mantra*, *mudra* and *samadhi*) of the *kami* in question and taught him how to accomplish various ends by attaining union with the *kami*, and, through the *kami*, with Dainichi or other Buddhist divinities.

The notion that lay at the basis of all the Buddhist Shinto schools here mentioned was that the *kami* represent the natural, inherent enlightenment of Dainichi, and are therefore superior to, or 'more fundamental' than the historical Buddha. Shakyamuni figures in these schools as a provisional 'helpful means' emanating from Dainichi, who taught the method of attaining 'acquired enlightenment'. In contrast, the *kami* were the very 'spirits' of Dainichi, and their non-Buddhist and often violent nature represented the insight that this unperfect world, just as it is, is inherently enlightened. While the Buddha represents the (inferior) 'acquired enlightenment' of exoteric Buddhism, the *kami* embody the (superior) 'inherent enlightenment' of esoteric Buddhism.

In this discourse, *kami* were given precedence over the Buddha, and this idea gave rise to the theory of 'inverted *honji suijaku*' according to which the *kami* are the source of the various buddhas, rather than the reverse. Thus the *kami* were for the first time presented as religious forces in their own right, rather than as secondary 'traces' of Buddhist divinities. This represented a first tentative step towards the non-Buddhist Shinto of later ages.

See also: Buddhist philosophy in Japan; expediency

Further reading

Breen, J. and Teeuwen, M. (eds) (2000) *Shinto in History: Ways of the Kami*, Richmond: Curzon Press.

Grapard, A. (1987) 'Linguistic Cubism: A Singularity of Pluralism in the Sanno Cult', *Japanese Journal of Religious Studies* 14–23.

—— (1992) *The Protocol of the Gods: A Study of the Kasuga Cult in Japanese History*, Berkeley, CA: University of California Press.

Naumann, N. (1994) 'Die einheimische Religion Japans. Teil 2. Synkretistische Lehren und religiöse Entwicklungen von der Kamakura- bis zum Beginn der Edo-Zeit', *Handbook of Oriental Studies* V.4.1.2, Leiden: Brill.

Tyler, S. (1989) 'Honji Suijaku Faith', *Japanese Journal of Religious Studies* 16–23.

MARK TEEUWEN

Shinto, Confucian

Confucian texts were used in a fragmentary way for the interpretation of *kami* myths from the medieval period onwards – for example, by Watarai Ieyuki (1256–1351?), Kitabatake Chikafusa (1293–1354) and Yoshida Kanetomo (1435–1511) – but only in a rather superficial manner, reflecting these scholars' limited knowledge of Confucian thought. It was only in the seventeenth century, when Song Neo-Confucianism became a defining element of Japanese intellectual life, that more systematic attempts were made at integrating *kami* practice and *kami* myths into a Confucian worldview. The most important pioneer in this respect was Hayashi Razan (1583–1657), a scholar of Neo-Confucianism and a *bakufu* clerk, who, in an attempt to relate his studies to Japan, drew parallels between Confucian teachings and Shinto myth and argued that 'Shinto' and Confucianism are 'ultimately one', two expressions of the same universal 'Way'.

Razan's ideas were picked up by traditional priestly lineages, such as the Yoshida and the Kiyowara at the Imperial Court, by the mid-seventeenth century; but they became part of the mainstream of intellectual life only after the emergence of private 'academies' in the latter part of that century. These academies, which were as a rule one-man enterprises, became popular among *samurai* and merchants alike in the cities of the late seventeenth and early eighteenth centuries. They allowed scholars to gain an income from lecturing to private students, while, in many cases, at the same time trying to put their views to the ruling elite. Their curriculum centred on the study of the Chinese classics and the composition of Chinese prose and poetry. The development of these academies had a profound impact on the nature of Japanese scholarship. They recruited a large new audience, and brought a new openness to many fields of learning that before had been the jealously defended monopolies of lineages of professional scholars, who guarded their secrets as their prime source of income and status.

Epoch-making in opening up the study of Shinto to the general public was the school of Suika (or Suiga) Shinto, founded by the Confucian scholar Yamazaki Ansai (1618–82) in the 1670s. Although this school established its own system of initiations into secret traditions, limiting access to some of its teachings, it nevertheless greatly stimulated wider scholarly interest in Shinto. Students of Ansai's school set up their own 'academies' throughout Japan and dominated Shinto scholarship for nearly a century, until the 1760s.

While there were subtle differences between the various schools of Confucian Shinto, they were sufficiently similar to allow Ansai's teaching to serve as a representative example. Key concepts in Ansai's thought were 'the unity of Heaven and man', 'reverence' (*jing*; in Japanese, *kei* or *tsutsushimi*), and 'the centre' or 'harmony' (*zhong*; in Japanese, *chu*). In Ansai's thought, man and **Heaven** are at one in the sense that the inborn virtues that constitute human nature are identical to the virtues that govern the universe. These virtues find their expression in the five relationships (*wulun*; in Japanese, *gorin*) first defined by Mencius, and foremost among them, in the relation between 'ruler and minister'. The term 'minister' in this phrase should be understood to refer to all subjects of a ruler, and not just those who assist his government as his magistrates. Ansai argued that the mind is the source of these virtues in man and rules his body and conduct through reverence, a state of constant mental watchfulness fostered by the awareness that even the slightest deviation from the Way will lead to total disaster. What is needed is a constant effort to maintain a state of unity with the 'centre', a concept discussed in the *Doctrine of the Mean* (*Zhongyong*; in Japanese, *Chuyo*) and signifying pure good and total **harmony**.

These ideas were linked to Shinto myth in a number of ways. Drawing on medieval Shinto theology (and most heavily on Yoshida Shinto), Ansai identified the first deity to appear in the *Chronicles of Japan* (*Nihon shoki*) (720), who is variously known as Ame no Minakanushi (Heavenly Lord of the Centre) or Kuni no Tokotachi ([Lord of the] Eternal Stability of the Land), as the embodiment of 'the centre'. This deity was not only regarded as the foundation of the universe, but also as the source of man's human nature: every man was said to carry within his body a 'mind-god' (*shinshin*) who is a spirit of Ame no Minakanushi/Kuni no Tokotachi. Shinto practice (and ritual purification in particular) was redefined as a mental exercise with the aim of attaining union with one's mind-god, automatically leading to union with the 'centre'. According to Ansai, the practitioner who maintained this union achieved permanent reverence, activated the virtues embedded in his mind, and displayed a perfect mastery of conduct according to the five relationships.

Moreover, Ansai stated (again following medieval examples) that Japan has its own 'Way of ruler and minister', fundamentally different from its Chinese counterpart. He argued that whereas the emperors of China receive the Mandate of Heaven because of their superior virtue, and lose it when they cease to be virtuous, in Japan, imperial rule is as absolute as Heaven itself. The emperors of Japan rule the country because they are the descendants of Amaterasu, who is at the same time the sun in Heaven and the source of virtue in human society. Thus virtue is embodied in the emperor, irrespective of his moral conduct; he is more akin to Heaven itself than to the Chinese emperors who served Heaven.

As most other schools of Shinto thought in the seventeenth century, Ansai's Shinto thought was based on the Neo-Confucianism of the Cheng brothers (Cheng Hao (1032–85) and Cheng Yi (1033–1107)) and **Zhu Xi** (1130–1200). This school had dominated Confucian learning since the medieval period. However, from the late seventeenth century onwards, Neo-Confucianism was challenged by a new stream of Confucian scholarship, usually referred to as 'Ancient Learning' (see **Confucianism in Japan**). This school took a totally different attitude towards Shinto, ranging from indifference to derision. Ansai's school proved unable to defend itself from criticism by Kogaku and, later, **Kokugaku** scholars. As a result, Confucian Shinto lost its domination over Shinto scholarship in the mid-eighteenth century.

See also: Shinto, Buddhist

Further reading

Muraoku Tsunetsugu (1988) *Studies in Shinto Thought*, New York: Greenwood.
Nosco, P. (1984) 'Masuho Zanko (1655–1742): A Shinto Popularizer between Nativism and National Learning', in P. Nosco (ed.), *Confucianism and Tokugawa Culture*, Princeton, NJ: Princeton University Press.
Ooms, H. (1985) *Tokugawa Ideology: Early Constructs, 1570–1680*, Princeton, NJ: Princeton University Press.
Teeuwen, M. (1996) *Watarai Shinto: An Intellectual History of the Outer Shrine in Ise*, Leiden: CNWS Publications.

MARK TEEUWEN

Shri Harsha

b. 1125; d. 1180

Philosopher

Shri Harsha was the Indian exponent *par excellence* of the method of negative dialectic (*vitanda*), who attempted in his *Khandanakhandakhadya* to establish the philosophical tenets of the **Advaita** Vedanta tradition. This argued that the non-dual absolute reality, self-established and reflexive consciousness called Brahman, is featureless and ineffable by means of destructive criticism of the definitions of the logical and epistemological concepts propounded by the realistic **Nyaya** and **Vaisheshika** schools whose basic stance on ontological questions is that what is, is knowable and nameable. He argues that the epistemological and metaphysical categories that the realist regards as having a well-defined real existence are in fact indefinable and of a provisional nature relative to human conventions. In the history of Indian philosophy his particular importance consists in the fact that his negative criticisms of the definitions proposed by thinkers such as Vachaspati Mishra and **Udayana** prompted the often highly technical and sophisticated reformulations developed by the **Navya-Nyaya** school.

In Indian logic, a definition (*lakshana*) has the purpose of discriminating its referent from whatever lacks the nature of that referent. Definitions are liable to three faults:

1 overextension (*ativyapti*), where the definition is so wide that it covers more than the definiendum; 'Cattle are horned animals'.
2 under-extension (*avyapti*), where the definition is too narrow so that part of the definiendum is not covered; 'Cattle have spots'.
3 impossibility (*asambhava*), where the definition misses the point altogether; 'Cattle are solid-hoofed animals'.

Shri Harsha's objective is to show that nothing is definable. His method is to examine the definitions proposed by his opponents and to demonstrate that they suffer from the above defects. He does not attempt to prove any theses of his own, being content to show that his opponents' accounts of differentiated reality are incoherent and their epistemological techniques inadequate to what they seek to establish. The only certainty is the Cartesian one that reflexive (*svayam prakasha*) consciousness exists.

The first chapter of his *Khandanakhandakhadya* is a sustained critique of a range of definitions of valid cognition (*prama*) and its instruments (*pramana*: perception, inference, presumption, non-awareness and testimony) propounded in the various realist and non-realist schools, in particular those proposed by correspondence theorists. Taking a definition such as 'Valid cognition is experience

of an existent object', he denies that it excludes invalid cognitions. According to Nyaya theory, validity being a quality determined by the type of the object of cognition, if an object of a cognition exists in nature, then the cognition is valid. When a piece of shell is mistaken for silver, an object, silverness and the inherence relation between them feature in the content of awareness. In the case of shell mistaken for silver, there is visual perception of a shiny white surface upon which revived memory traces of silver from another context of experience are superimposed due to similarity of the surfaces of the objects. The content of erroneous cognition always derives from experience of something real and has an objective basis. Silverness is a naturally occurrent reality. The three elements actually appear in their natural form: it is irrelevant that silverness does not exist in the shell actually presented to the senses. So the definition is over-extended in that it covers false cognitions. Moreover, since the expression 'existent object' in the definition lacks explicit reference (something admitted by Udayana), it is indeterminate and vacuous. If it is replaced by a specific referent, the definition will be under-extended.

The Naiyayika is allowed to relativize the truth-conditions of the cognition to a particular time and place. The cognition of a shell as silver would then be excluded from the definition. But this procedure is contradicted by another Nyaya tenet: time and space are single, they cannot exist in other times and places. The Naiyayika cannot say that the silverness component of the invalid cognition relates to silverness existing at a time and place other than the present context. So the reformulated definition is under-extended. Shri Harsha continues by exposing the internal contradictions in Nyaya attempts to define experience as a factor distinct from memory and recognition. He directs his attention to a Buddhist definition: valid cognition is undisputed experience where the latter means having as its object something which leads to successful activity. But the fact that false cognitions may co-incidentally generate successful activity means that the definition is overextended.

As a prelude to demolishing definitions of individual alleged authoritative means of knowledge (*pramana*), he rejects definitions of instrumental causality. For example, in the expression, 'He cooks with fire by means of his hands', the hand would be considered the instrumental cause of the act of cooking. But could we not equally say that the fire, the utensils and above all the agent are the instrumental causes of the activity? A definition such as 'perception is knowledge in the soul produced by contact between the senses and something present', is overextended because in the shell–silver illusion something is present, namely the shell. 'Perception is immediate experience' is obviously useless because error and dreams are as immediate as truth.

Shri Harsha makes a particularly telling criticism of an aspect of Udayana's method. The latter tends to employ negative definitions such as, 'Substance is that which lacks the constant absence of qualities' and 'Immediate knowledge is that which is not produced by the unique causes of inferential cognitions etc which are to be excluded from the present type, perception'. It is a cardinal tenet of the Nyaya-Vaishesika realism (although the tenet could be construed anti-realistically) that everything falling under the categories of reality (**padartha**) is existent, knowable and nameable. Shri Harsha points out that the negative properties such as 'not being produced' and 'lacking constant absence' are serving as sufficient causes for the identification of positive entities. He says that this amounts to acceptance of the Buddhist *apoha* nominalist theory of meaning according to which words and concepts are not applied on the basis of repeatable general properties actually possessed by classes of entities but upon the exclusion of differences. For any given term, it is possible to frame an exclusion class consisting of all those things for which it does not stand. The feature common to cows that serves as the grounds for the application of the term 'cow' is simply difference from all those things that are not conventionally designated as cows.

Another objection to the realists' procedure is that a relationship of invariable concomitance requires prior knowledge of a universal. If a universal is necessary to establish a definition, then the definition is unnecessary.

Philosophers opposed to non-dualism will object that it is contradicted by experience of difference. Shri Harsha says that difference may be variously defined either as (1) the essence of an object, (2) reciprocal absence (*anyonya-abhava*: the otherness of the pot from the cloth), (3) the possession of some specific property (*vaidharmya*) or (4) intrinsic individuality. From the definition of difference as essence the conclusion that everything is identical with everything else may be derived. The proper form (*svarupa*) of an entity is supposed to be independent and 'self-contained'. Difference (*bheda*) is always difference from something: it is specified in terms of correlatives (*pratiyogin*). If proper form and difference were identical, the proper form of an entity would consist solely in its differing from other entities. The entity would then exist only in virtue of its relations to others. Moreover,

if *x-svarupa = y-pratiyogika-bheda & y-svarupa = x-pratiyogika-bheda*

then x & y are identical.

In response to the second possibility which says that difference is the reciprocal absence of two entities (*anyonya-abhava*), he argues that difference as *reciprocal* absence needs to be described in terms of some correlative which in this case must be identity. If it is said that 'The absence of the pot is the very nature of the cloth', and vice versa, the above reasoning applies. If the opponent tries to avoid the difficulty by claiming that the proper form of the cloth's differing from the proper form of the pot is to be construed as referring to the difference between potness and clothness, Shri Harsha contends that this will entail the identity of clothness and potness. If what is denied is potness in the cloth and vice versa, there would have to be a further property, potness-ness, occurrent in potness which can be denied of clothness and vice versa. No one admits the existence of such properties since universals have no distinguishing characteristics inhering in them. In the absence of such differentia which are being held to constitute difference, potness and clothness must be identical. So denying potness of the cloth will also involve denying it of the pot.

In response to the third option that difference is the possession of a specific individuating property (*vaidharmya*), he says that this leads to an infinite regress on two fronts: the properties would have to possess further properties to distinguish them *ad infinitum*. Where their distinctness from their substrata is concerned, those differences would require different relations connecting them to their substrata and so on.

In response to one version of the fourth interpretation that difference means 'proper form absent from the one and the other and vice versa', the argument is that since 'proper form' is an indeterminate general expression, the opponent is simply asserting the non-existence of proper form or inherent nature. The opponent can only render the expression specific by applying it to a class and claiming that the nature of pots is absent from cloths and the nature of cloths is absent from pots. But this would not enable him to distinguish a particular pot from a particular cloth. If the opponent appeals to unique individuating features, he is admitting an extreme nominalism which is wholly repugnant to the realist and which would render impossible the use of language. Shri Harsha does not deny that we experience differences: the point is that this experience is purely conventional and a function of misunderstanding or *avidya*.

Further reading

Dasgupta, S. (1932) *A History of Indian Philosophy*, vol. II, Cambridge: Cambridge University Press.
Granoff, P. (1978) *Philosophy and Argument in Late Vedanta: Shri Harsha's Khandanakhandakhadya*, Dordrecht: Reidel.

CHRIS BARTLEY

shruti

Shruti, or 'accredited scripture', is a tenet of the Indian systems of ritual interpretation and scriptural exegesis such as the **Purva Mimamsa** and **Vedanta** (Uttara Mimamsa) that non-originated and unfalsifiable Vedic language is the only means of knowledge (*pramana*) about whatever lies beyond the bounds of sense perception. **Shankara** is representative of Vedanta in holding that *shruti*'s cognitive authority (*pramanya*) applies not in the spheres of perception and inference but to matters such as the performance and results of the *agnihotra* sacrifice which are beyond the cognitive scope of perception and inference. Even if a hundred scriptural texts were to say that fire is cold or that it is not bright, they would have no cognitive authority. If scripture were to say that fire is cold or that it is not bright, we would have to assume that it intended some other meaning, otherwise it would cease to have cognitive authority. Such statements cannot be understood as opposed either to the other authoritative sources of knowledge or to themselves.

Whereas Mimamsa is the hermeneutic of the primarily injunctive portions of the **Veda** dealing with the performance of ritual (*karma-kanda*), Vedanta is the systematic interpretation of fact-asserting statements forming the knowledge portion (*jnana-kanda*); in effect, the **Upanishads**.

The Purva-Mimamsakas classify the Vedic statements as injunctions (*vidhi*), descriptions and explanations (*arthavada*) and incantations (*mantra*) to be used in the rituals. They hold that since the Veda teaches what has to be done (*karya*) prescriptive statements have a primary status. *Arthavadas* are auxiliary statements whose function is that of motivating the hearer to perform the actions enjoined by *vidhis* and to explain their purpose by stating their fruits. This relegation of *arthavadas*, which of course include statements about Brahman and the soul, to a subsidiary status is opposed by all Vedantins.

What is classed as Vedically derived *Smriti* ('remembered', 'traditional') literature, which has the exegetical function of corroborating and elucidating *shruti*, includes the **Bhagavad Gita**, the **puranas** and the **Dharma-Shastras**. In the case of a conflict between *shruti* and *smriti*, the former should prevail.

Further reading

Halbfass, W. (1991) *Tradition and Reflection*, Albany, NY: State University of New York Press.

CHRIS BARTLEY

shunyata

Shunyata (**emptiness**) is a Buddhist concept particularly associated with **Nagarjuna** and the Madhyamika school and referring to the non-substantiality or lack of essence or 'own-nature' (*svabhava*) of the fundamental elements of existence (*dharma*) postulated by the realistic Sarvastivadin **Vaibhashika** school of Buddhist philosophy, which is characterized as their 'emptiness'. The view is that everything encountered exists in dependence on causes and conditions (*pratitya-samutpada*) and is inter-related. The relative cannot enjoy self-sufficient, independent reality. Understanding life from this point of view, the sage achieves detachment from what are only temporary items and states of affairs. This outlook coincides with an attitude of compassion towards all sentient beings whose suffering (*duhkha*, **Four Noble Truths**) derives from attachment to what will not last and is itself equivalent to *nirvana*.

CHRIS BARTLEY

Siming Zhili

b. 959; d. 1028

Buddhist philosopher

Unlike Japan, where Zen and Jodo (Pure Land) are polarized as the two paths of reliance on faith (other powers) and power over the self (self power), in China wisdom and faith joined hands with Chan meditation and Amitabha's name-chanting combined. The argument is that 'The (Chan) Mind is Pure Land'; and 'Who is chanting Amitabha?' is a *koan*. However, such a cerebral explanation fades before a personal testimony from the Song dynasty Tiantai master Siming Zhili (Ssu-ming Chih-li). This most erudite monk had decided to undertake a *Lotus Sutra* confession lasting three years; after that he would 'abandon the self' (set himself aflame) to go to the Pure Land. He was deterred by anxious supplicants. Asked why, if the Mind is the Pure Land, he should seek that fiery end, he explained that the wisdom in seeing the world in all its three aspects – as empty, as real, as both/neither – ensures a total knowledge of reality. And although there is 'Pure Land of the Mind', the weight of **karma** and the potential lack of pure roots might hinder self-effort. A submission to the demanding confession and to the fiery purgation was a real counter-measure.

In his pious devotion, Zhili headed the first massive (10,000 strong) mixed (monk and lay) Pure Land Association in the Song dynasty. Others then followed his example; the society founded by Mou Ziyuan would later mutate into the militant White Lotus movement that inspired peasant rebellions in the subsequent dynasties.

See also: faith

Further reading

Lai, W. (1981) 'Faith and Wisdom in the T'ien-t'ai Buddhist Tradition: A Letter by Ssu-ming Chih-li', *The Journal of Dharma (India)* 6(3): 281–98.

WHALEN LAI

simplicity

Unadorned simplicity, *po* is characteristic of the *dao*. It is the 'plain timber' that has not been carved. It is equivalent to the *dao* as the 'uncarved block' (of stone). **Laozi** used it as a metaphor for the 'natural state', *dao* uncontaminated by human handling. Adopted by Ge Hong as part of his Daoist name, Baopozi (the Master who Embraces Simplicity), it describes a concept simlar to the Biblical idea that 'blessed are the poor in spirit'.

Further reading

Sailey, J. (1978) *The Master who Embraces Simplicity: A Study of the Philosophy of Ho Hung (A.D. 283–343)*, San Francisco: Chinese Materials Center.
Ware, J. (trans.) (1966) *Alchemy, Medicine, Religion in the China of A.D. 320: The nei-p'ien of Ko Hung*, Cambridge, MA: MIT Press.

WHALEN LAI

Sirhak

Sirhak became a very important school of philosophy in Korea after the Japanese invasion of Korea in 1592, the *Imjin waeran*. Before then, Neo-Confucianism was the dominant philosophy in Korea, which controlled politics, economy, social system and all areas of culture. Following the Japanese invasion, society was in chaos; the metaphysical debate of Neo-Confucian philosophy offered no practical solution or comfort to the suffering masses. Sirhak emerged in such a situation to criticize and reform what were seen as the impractical ideas of Neo-Confucianism, and offered in its place a practical philosophy; hence the name 'Sirhak', the 'School of Practical Learning'.

Sirhak was an important intellectual movement of Korea, especially between the seventeenth and nineteenth centuries, and represented a new spirit of enquiry among many Confucian scholars, who were outside the mainstream of political power. They were urban intellectuals, who were acutely aware of the newly introduced Western Learning (Roman Catholicism) and Western science and political ideas, and they addressed progressively the social, political and economic issues of the time. The school started with the following rationale and ideas. First, it realized the impractical and abstract nature of Neo-Confucian metaphysics and the endless unproductive debate of the different interpretations among the Neo-Confucian philosophers, which led to political conflict between the ruling aristocrats. Second, Sirhak scholars did not agree with the dogmatism of the Neo-Confucian philosophers, and they challenged the orthodoxy of the Neo-Confucian interpretation of the Confucian Classics (see **Classics and Books**) and offered alternative interpretations of the Confucian texts. Third, the Sirhak philosophers wanted to reform the idea and status of labour. At that time, the Neo-Confucian scholars were in positions of political, economic and social power. In order to preserve their privileged positions, they used Neo-Confucianism as the ideological tool for controlling the masses, without giving proper credit to the productive labour of the commoners in agriculture and commerce. Sirhak scholars wanted to recognize the value of labour.

Sirhak scholars emphasized the practical values for life such as economic sufficiency, while Neo-Confucianism emphasized metaphysical theories. Sirhak gave more value to the material things and practical ethics than did Neo-Confucianism. Unlike the Neo-Confucian scholars, Sirhak scholars criticized the evils of slavery. However, like Neo-

Confucianism, Sirhak emphasized the essential Confucian virtues of **humaneness**, justice, propriety and wisdom.

Sirhak scholars were deeply interested in the study of geography, economics, politics, military affairs, language and customs, and especially in the scientific technology of the West and Roman Catholicism, which were introduced to Korea from China. Their purpose was to improve the living condition of the masses and to strengthen the nation. Sirhak favored empirical science, which ascertained truth by examining facts in history, geography and literature. Important Sirhak philosophers included **Yu Hyong-won** (1622–73), Yi Ik (1681–1763), Hong Tae-yong (1731–83), Pak Chi-won (1737–1805), **Chong Yag-yong** (1762–1836) and **Ch'oe Han-ki** (1803–79).

See also: Christianity, Korean

Further reading

Ch'oi Min-hong (1980) *A Modern History of Korean Philosophy*, Seoul: Sungmun Sa, 149ff.

Kum Chang-t'ae (1987) *Han'guk Sirhak Sasang Yon'gu* (A Study of Korean Sirhak Thought), Seoul: Chipmundang.

Lee, P. (ed.) (1993) *Sourcebook of Korean Civilization*, vol. 2, New York: Columbia University Press, 12, 337ff.

YONG-CHOON KIM

Song Xing

fl. late 4th c. BCE

Philosopher

Song Xing (Sung Hsing) was an early Chinese thinker between **Confucius** and **Mencius**, now conveniently classified as a proto-Daoist. He could be responsible for the 'Psychic Chapters' in the text *Guanzi*. These chapters may represent the earliest Chinese reflection on the inner workings of the mind so as to foster a systematic programme of **meditation**. The discussion there has cast light on similar discourses on mind, spirit and vital breath in **Zhuangzi** and Mencius.

The word 'spirit' in English describes both a spirit out there and a spirit inside us. The same complex meaning applies to the Chinese word *shen*. At the time of the Shang oracle bones, the script *shen* was not yet used to describe a 'spirit' inside man. Confucius and **Mozi** still used *shen* primarily in the 'outer' sense. The vocabulary for gods and ghosts, form and spirit, mind and intelligence, was however quite extensive in other texts of this period and was well developed within the medical sector where spirit, wind and breath functioned as key concepts of health and illness.

Among early philosophers, Song Xing was able to merge the two meanings of *shen*, namely by connecting the ritual invitation of the 'god' (to come down to the altar) to the indwelling of the god now as the 'spirit' in the human mind. As one should keep the altar clean lest the god would not descend, so one should clear the mind so that the spirit, the hyper-intelligence called the 'mind within the mind', might abide. Zhuangzi later called that 'inner cleansing' the 'washing of the mind'. That shift in meaning may be compared with the shift from *Rig Veda* to the **Upanishads**. In India, the sacrifice to the god was also being internalized so as to become eventually the **atman** or self in man.

By eliminating gross desires, the mind gains yogic control of the passions: 'The mind in the body is like the ruler; the nine apertures are like the various officials. When the mind is in tune with the *dao*, the nine (officials) will follow the principle. But if desires are allowed to flourish, then [confusion ensues and] the eyes cannot see colours nor can the ears hear sounds. Therefore, should the superior depart from the Way, those below him would fail in their tasks.' Inner composure is a prelude to outer control: 'The Way is not far away'. One begins with ascetic self-control; one ends with being god-like: 'Men are ruled by passions. But by eliminating the desires, a person penetrates. Thus free from confusion, there is quiescence. Thus impassive, there is concentration of essence. Heightened thus in ability, there is singularity. Being one-pointed or whole, there is illumination. Illuminated, there is *shen* or spiritedness'. Since it is most precious, the residence of the mind must be swept clean so that the honoured guest, the god, will abide. 'If the form of the body is not correct, virtue will not come. If it is not quintessential, the mind cannot rule. There-fore make the body correct, adorn it with virtue, then all things may be attained and (the spirit) will come flying to you (on its own accord)'. Like the Upanishadic sages rising above the need of the brahmanical sacrifice to the gods, the pneumatic, what pertains to the soul, can now do without the gods: 'Focus your will. Integrate your mind. Let the ears and eyes penetrate clear and far. Can you focus? Can you integrate? Can you see into the future without divinatory means? Can you know without consulting (the gods)? It is said: think and think again. The spirits cannot teach you. Their powers cannot inform. It is ultimately by the virtue of the refined **qi** (ether, life force, vital force) that you know.'

Song Xing further speculated on how this **ether** may be so expansive as to fill and animate the universe:

> This sublime essence in things is their reason for being. It is what is born as the five cereals (wheat, beans, panicled millet, hemp, millet) below and as the five stars above. It is what moves freely between **Heaven** and Earth as ghosts and gods. It is that which is hidden in the breast of men as his sage wisdom. Therefore is this breath in man broad as Heaven and deep as the Abyss, wide as the ocean and minute as the inner self. Not bendable by force, it can be coaxed by virtue. No sound can summon it; but music may court it. Preserve it with reverence and never lose it – this is the way to complete virtue.

As a result, the person may then find communion with the universe.

Further reading

Lai, W. (1988) 'Interiorization of the Gods', *Taoist Resources* 1(2): 1–10.

Onozawa Sei'ichi (ed.) (1978) *Kī no shiso* (The Philosophy of Qi), Tokyo: Tokyo University Press.

Rickett, A. (1965) *Kuan Tzu: A Repository of Early Chinese Thought, A Translation and Study of Twelve Chapters*, Hong Kong: Hong Kong University Press.

Roth, H. (forthcoming) *Inward Training; The First Daoist Text on Self-Cultivation*, New York: Ballantine.

Shigehisa Kuriyama (1994) 'The Imagination of

Winds and the Development of Chinese Conception of the Body', in A. Zito and T. Barlow (eds), *Body, Subject and Power in China*, Chicago: University of Chicago Press.

WHALEN LAI

SPACE *see* akasha; space and time, Indian theories of

space and time, Indian theories of

The philosophers of the **Nyaya** and **Vaisheshika** traditions consider space (*dik*) and time (*kala*) to be distinct substances (*dravya*) or objective realities in their own right. They are unitary, infinite, impartite and imperceptible. Temporal instants and spatial points are conventional divisions. Expressions such as 'past', 'present' and 'future', and 'remote' and 'proximate', are only to be applied in a secondary, figurative sense (*upachara*). Time can only be humanly measured by formed products with parts, such as the movements of the sun or by reference to actions with duration. Vatsyayana says that the present is apprehended in two ways: as dissociated from the past as the future and secondly as associated with them. The first kind of apprehension is made possible by the existence of an object, the second by the serial nature of actions. Space can only be demarcated by reference to determinate objects such as the stars and directions such as left and right, north, south, east and west. This conception of time is realistic in the sense that if A is later than B, the characteristic of 'being later than' (*paratva*, 'farness') is determinate and non-relativistic (*niyata*) in the sense that if A is later than B, it is later for all subjects of experience. That temporal proximity and remoteness are independent of spatial proximity and remoteness is exemplified by the case of a youth and an old man who are respectively more distant and closer in space to a young person to whom they are known to be less and more removed in time. In addition, the two realities are distinguished by the fact that spatial farness is indeterminate: my right is your left. Divisions into past, present and future are

accepted because while sensory perception only refers to what is presently existence, inference relates to past, present and future. Neither category is essentially defined nor really affected by any system of calibrations. The basic atoms comprising the primary elements (*bhuta*), earth, water, fire and air are outside space and time while the macroscopic objects built from them are contained in space and time. Space is filled by the atmosphere (**akasha**) which is a primary element that is defined as the vehicle of sounds.

Time is held to be the grounds of the possibility or occasioning cause (*nimitta-karanatva*) of concepts such as priority, posteriority, simultaneity and successiveness. It is also the causal basis of our conventional references to measured temporal units. Both time and space are the grounds of the possibility of everything subject to origination (*utpatti*), perdurance (*sthiti*) and destruction (*vinasha*). Their causal role is not generative but distributive and organizational of already produced entities having other causal factors. Although time and space are uniform, diversity is figuratively (*upacharika*) ascribed to them due to the different conditions (*upadhi*) of the finite, produced entities and their actions with which they are associated.

Concepts such as priority, posteriority and simultaneity are indicators (*linga*) of imperceptible time in that they are its specific effects. In this context, the expressions 'origination', 'perdurance' and 'destruction' can be correlated with notions such as spring, summer and winter; morning, noon and night. For the realist Naiyayikas and Vaisheshikas, the sequential ordering of experience is explained by its having an extra-mental, objective basis (*nimitta-karana*). All causal processes occur in time and space. Time and space exercise a special sort of regulative causality which guarantees that the fruit of an action (**karma**) with a retributive potentiality occurs at a particular time and place.

For definitional purposes, time and space are said to have five qualities (*guna*): number (*samkhya*) in the sense of numerical unity, dimension (*parinama*) in the sense of infinite extension, separability from entities and events (*prithaktva*), conjunction (*samyoga*) and disjunction (*vibhaga*). Cognition grasps spatial regions between the observer and the object. Accordingly, the latter is experienced as near (*aparatva*) or remote (*paratva*). Temporal priority and posteriority are explained analogously. The connection and lack thereof of the observer with temporal instants and spatial regions is probably what is meant by conjunction and disjunction. Time and space *per se* cannot be conjoined with or disjoined from anything since they are infinite and all-pervasive. These qualities are also associated with the origination and destruction of persisting spatio-temporal continuants.

The Naiyayika Bhasarvajna (*c.*900) denies that real, absolute time can be established as the necessary condition of cognitive and linguistic phenomena or as a universal cause. God alone causes mental and non-mental effects. He underpins realism by holding that entities exist in virtue of their association with divine cognition. His denial that it can be the substrate of qualities implies that it cannot be a substance (*dravya*).

The Navya-Naiyayika philosopher Raghunatha Shiromani (1475–1550) also denied that time was a substance or an independent reality in is own right. He identified space, time and the atmosphere with phases of the divine being. Raghunatha defined the supreme universal Being (*satta*) occurrent in all substances, qualities and actions as 'relatedness to time in the mode of being present' or simply 'relatedness to time'. The standard Navya-Naiyayika view is that everything finite occurs in time by a temporal relation (*kalika-sambandha*). Time and space are the substrata of all finite entities. All of the latter reside directly in a portion of time. A portion of time is an imposed property (*upadhi*) on time, a calibration provided by actions, contacts and disjunctions. Shivaditya, another Navya-Naiyayika, controversially held that the atmosphere, time and space are really one and that they appear to be different due to their being associated with different functions and imposed properties (*upadhi*).

The Nyaya-Vaisheshikas reject the predominantly Vedic and Upanishadic doctrine that time is a supreme cosmic creative power (see **Veda**; **Upanishads**). The Maitri *Upanishad* 6.15 says that there are two forms of *Brahman* (ultimate reality): time and not time and that 'time cooks all things' (*kalah pachati bhutani*). For a later version of this conceptuality we must go to the grammarian **Bhartrihari**, whose philosophical outlook is a form of non-dualism. He understands time as the principal autonomous power (*svatantrya-shakti*) of

the Absolute *Brahman*. It is the initial phase in the development of the illusion of cosmic diversity, the appearance of the pluriformity of sequential temporal phenomena from original unity. Bhartrihari accepts the view that time is a single, eternal, all-pervading substance, independent of processes (*vyapara*), the measure (*parimana*) of entities involved in actions. This substance is the efficient cause (*nimitta*) of the origin, perdurance and destruction of finite entities and of sequentiality through its self-differentiation. It is the wire-puller (*sutra-dharah*) of the world machine, differentiating and regulating the universe. Time differentiates the universe through its inhibiting and permitting the occurrence of particular acts. The supreme reality (*satta*), which is understood as eternal act or process (*kriya*), is manifested in lower universals (*jati*) which are the prototypes of particular modes of existence (*vyakti*). In this process, time is the principle of organizational power. Although immutable, it appears to acquire the characteristics of past, present and future and divisions into moments, hours, days, months, seasons and so on, and to participate in the processes that it controls. Incidentally, he rejects the cyclical view, often mistakenly attributed to Indian philosophers, that reality will repeat itself.

According to the non-dualist school of **Advaita** Vedanta, time is a parallel phenomenon to *maya*, the ontologically indeterminable causal basis of experienced cosmic diversity that is somehow associated with the Absolute *Brahman*. Space is understood as a primary emergent phenomenon of *maya*. Apart from space, all products originate in time and space but space is only in time.

Buddhist ideas

The realist Sarvastivadin (everything exists) Buddhists maintain that reality consists of irreducible elements or *dharmas* which possess essential identities (*svabhava*) (see **Sarvastivada**). They underlie all processes and subsist in past, present and future. The basic constituents are *per se* unconditioned, enduring and substantial (*dravya sat*); it is their mutually conditioned macroscopic aggregations that are characterized by impermanence. Some early Sarvastivadin realists, called Darstantikas and Vibhjyavadins, postulated time (*kala*) as an eternal entity in its own right. According to them, conditioned states of affairs (*samskara*) pass through the stages of time (*adhvana*).

The Vaibhashika theorist Vasumitra (*c.*140 CE), whose views were subsequently endorsed by **Vasubandhu** and developed by Samghabhadra, formulated the normative interpretation of the central thesis about the eternal endurance of the fundamental constituents (*dharma*). Prior to him, Dharmatrata (*c.*100 CE) had argued that when a *dharma* passes from one time to another, its substance (*dravya*) is unaltered while its state (*bhava*) changes. This theory, which was negatively compared to the transformationist **satkaryavada** theory of the Samkhyas, was seen as associating change too closely with essence. Another theory, developed by Ghoshaka (*c.*125 CE), construed temporal progression in terms of the different conditions (*samskrita-lakshana*) connected with essentially immutable entities participating in impermanent processes. But Ghoshaka also taught that when something is connected with present characteristics, it is not completely dissociated from past and future ones. This would appear to preclude any real temporal successiveness.

Vasumitra argued that actualization and causal efficacy (*karitram*) in the present is one phase (*avastha*) in the existence of a substantially self-identical *dharma* which itself remains unchanged. He attributed trans-temporal differences exclusively to connections with external circumstances which were seen as occasioning efficacy. Prior to its present phase, the *dharma* had existed in a potential future mode. When appropriate external circumstances occur, it becomes the momentary present. Once the circumstantial efficacy has been expended, it becomes past. On this view, past, present and future are different designations of *dharmas* with persisting, immutable identities. Thus there is the basis of a real continuum. Temporal sequence is a phenomenon relative to human experience. Accordingly, the Vaibhashikas do not include time as an independent category in their taxonomies of reality, temporal stages being reductively identified with the occurrence of conditioned events (*samskaras*).

The central rationale behind the doctrine is that of guaranteeing a strong continuity within the series (*samtana*) of experiences to which persons are reduced between morally significant actions and their consequences in the face of the doctrines of momentariness (*anitya*) and no-soul or absence of essential identity (*anatman*). This Sarvastivadin outlook of the Vaibhashikas is the primary target of the relativism of **Nagarjuna**'s Madhyamika philosophy. Nagarjuna argues that the *dharmas* are empty (*shunya*) of own-nature (*svabhava*) (see **emptiness**). He draws attention to the problems in reconciling the claims that on the one hand the *dharmas* are independent and self-existent and on the other that they are actualized through the operations of causes and conditions (**pratitya-samutpada**) and thus are relative (like long and short) and interdependent. He thinks that the Abhidharmists in postulating fundamental *dharmas* with inherent natures (*svabhava*) do not go far enough down the road of reductive analysis to momentariness that is the true Buddhist path. He maintains that in a world of entities with permanent identities in all three temporal dimensions, change, becoming and activity would be impossible since everything would be static and eternal. But because everything is empty of own nature, moral improvement and spiritual growth are possible.

Nagarjuna argued that it is impossible coherently to articulate the relation between present and future times in relation to time past. Any such relation would involve the compresence or simultaneity of present or future with the past. Thus everything would occur in the past and temporal sequentiality would be impossible. Parallel consequences can be derived if the notions of the present or the future are taken as focal.

The **Sautrantika** Buddhists, who are representationalists, also criticized the Sarvastivadins for introducing eternal principles into Buddhist metaphysics. They held that reality consists of instantaneous, featureless particulars with unique causal efficacies. Only the strictly instantaneous present exists substantially (*dravyatas*), the percepts, concepts and words (*akara*, mental representations) comprising a world-view which is a matrix of representations (*akara*) at least one remove from the given being but convenient fictions. They reason that if a putative entity A endures (i.e., persists by being wholly present at more than one time) for, say, three moments, it must be causally effective at each of them and thus productive of three effects because the same effect cannot be thrice generated.

It follows that A has disintegrated into three momentary realities. But if we construe persistence as perdurance (the possession of different temporal parts or stages at different times with no one part being present for more than one time) and say that tri-momentary A lies dormant, awaiting auxiliary factors, for its first two moments and is causally effective at the third (as the seed in the granary awaits soil and rain), then it is only the terminal condition that is real, the previous temporal parts or stages being either non-entities or distinct entities, one generating the other.

Their critique of the various Sarvastivadin attempts to characterize the relationship between stable, immutable essences and change is encapsulated in the verse: 'The essence (*svabhava*) always exists, but you do not want actualizations (*bhava*) to be eternal; nor do you suppose that actualization is other than essence – this is clearly acting in a high-handed manner'.

The strict insistence on instantaneity obviously produces problems where moral consequentiality is concerned. A morally significant action, which is by definition momentary, is characterized as 'perfuming' the stream of instantaneous mental events in which it occurs, creating in it a specific potentiality. They also appeal to the analogy of 'seed' and the production subsequent to intermediate stages of fruit although the seed has ceased to exist.

Further reading

Balslev, A. (1983) *A Study of Time in Indian Philosophy*, Wiesbaden: Otto Harrassowitz.

Cardona, G. (1991) 'A Path Still Taken: Some Early Indian Arguments Concerning Time', *Journal of the American Oriental Society* 3(3): 445–63.

Frauwallner, E. (1995) *Studies in Abhidharma Literature and the Origins of Buddhist Philosophical Systems*, trans. S. Kidd, Albany, NY: State University of New York Press.

Halbfass, W. (1992) *On Being and What There Is*, Albany, NY: State University of New York Press.

Potter, K. (1993) *Encyclopedia of Indian Philosophies*, vol. 6, Delhi: Motilal Banarsidass.

CHRIS BARTLEY

space and time in Islamic philosophy

A protracted debate arose within Islamic philosophy over the nature of creation, and the link between creation and space and time. According to many understandings of the Qur'an, God created the world out of nothing, at whatever time he wished and in whichever way he wanted. It ended up being created at a certain time, but could have been created at a different time, had he wished to create at a different time. Similarly, the space which it came to occupy could well be very different, had God wished it to be very different. As **al-Ghazali** puts it, at first God existed by himself, and then he existed with the world, a world which he had created. Yet there are difficulties with this model. For one thing, if the world was worth creating, why would God delay his creation? It is not as though like us he is contrained by a lack of power or indecisiveness. Similarly, if the world occupies a certain space, surely it must be the right sort of space for the world, and God would not (or perhaps even could not?) go against the rational principles of space by producing a different space. In any case, if time is regarded as a measure of change, as it often was by the *falasifa*, then were the world to be created, it would literally have been created at no time at all, since before there was change there was no time. For these reasons, and many more, the *falasifa* tended to argue that the world is eternal and its structure is pre-established, in the sense that it could not have a different form than that which it does have.

Al-Ghazali wonders whether we could not imagine a time before time, strange though that form of words might look, during which God exists alone, and then he brings ordinary time into being when he creates the world. The problem with this theory is that two contrasting notions of time are in operation here, the notion of time as a measure of change, which constitutes ordinary time, and the notion of time as a sort of framework or container, which can exist with nothing in it. We need some explanation as to how these two conflicting theories can co-exist in the way in which al-Ghazali suggests.

The other issue which the *falasifa* find difficult to accept is that of a perfect creator delaying his creation. Al-Ghazali argues that this is not a problem since we understand how someone can delay his action, even though he has decided to act, since it is an aspect of being an agent that one can decide when an action will take place. He gives examples from our ordinary behaviour to suggest that this is something we do all the time, and if we can do it, then God can certainly do it. It might be suggested that we have to delay, since we are imperfect and often have to wait, or wait until we see what happens. God is not in this position, all times are the same for him, and so what need has he for delay? Al-Ghazali throws this question back, and asks what is wrong with delay. We often make arbitrary decisions, and that is what is involved in being an agent.. He gives the example of a hungry man being offered two identical dates, where he has to choose which one to eat. Since there is nothing to distinguish the dates from each other, this is a suitable analogy for the decision which God made about the time at which to create the world. In just the same way that we can choose one date over another, when there is nothing different about one as compared with another, so God can choose one time over another.

Ibn Rushd argues that what the hungry individual is deciding is not primarily which date to eat, but whether to eat or not, so it does not matter to him which date he selects. They are really identical in so far as satisfying his hunger goes, and this brings out a problem with the analogy, the idea that an agent wants or needs something to be achieved through his action. This idea is not one we can apply to God, who does not need or want anything and who acts through pure grace. What al-Ghazali would argue in response to such an objection is that if God is a real agent then there must be a real similarity between what he does and what we do. If we can choose between two identical things, as we can, then so can he. If what we mean by God's agency is to have any relevance to the notion of God as a powerful being, then his acting must resemble our acting. Of course, his action is far greater than ours, but it must still be the same sort of activity. If we can make arbitrary choices, then so can God, and it

follows that he could have created the world at any time, and in any way, that he wished.

A linked issue which al-Ghazali has to discuss is why God would delay a decision to create the world. If God could create the world at any time, and if the world is worth creating, which presumably it is since it was created, what point is there in waiting? Al-Ghazali interprets this question as a challenge to the ability of God to wait, and suggests that if God wants to wait, he will wait. The problem is, as the *falasifa* often point out, that they can see no circumstances in which it would be appropriate to wait, unless of course one had to wait, which can hardly apply to God. This is different from the previous problem of explaining how God could decide between two identical alternatives. The decision here is between creating or not creating at all. Although in a sense both alternatives are the same for God, after all, he is not creating to satisfy some purpose he has, we clearly need some explanation why something which should be done and could be done is not done. Al-Ghazali suggests that just as we can delay our actions, God can do the same. This surely will not work in exactly the same way, since when we delay we have some reason for the delay. God cannot have such a reason, since before the world is created, there is nothing else in existence which could explain delay.

Mulla Sadra and his theory of change tries to resolve this apparent dilemma. **Ibn Sina** and Ibn Rushd argue that there are two kinds of change, there is essential change from one substance to another which is sudden, and a kind of gradual change which takes place when the accidents like quantity or quality alter. Mulla Sadra rejects this theory of change, arguing by contrast that when something moves from potentiality to actuality we need to refer both to an abstract mental idea and also a material thing which is in constant flux. He called this substantial movement (*al-haraka al-jawhariya*), and it is perpetually operating, bringing into existence the phenomena of the world. For Mulla Sadra, there is no connection between the essences of the world, the ideas we have of what goes on in the world, but only between those things which actually exist. We tend to ignore the small changes which occur in what actually exists since they are so small and gradual as hardly to be noticed, and we create ideas which represent a type of stability which is more mental than real. By contrast, substantial motion operates constantly, so that something is never the same at two separate moments. We create out of this movement the concept of time, which in itself is not real, and also a concept of space as an independent thing, whereas in reality it is nothing more than a reflection of our imagination. Time is itself a measure of change, it is a feature of ideas which we construct, and so is like the notion of space. We tend to identify things in our imagination, but in reality we abstract over what is in fact constantly changing, so that what we regard as things are really just aspects of motion. Time is the measure of this continual change, and not an independent space-like dimension in which change takes place. As a consequence, the world is eternal in the sense that it represents the continual bringing of things into existence. On the other hand, there is continual change and movement, and everything which comes about is produced at a particular time. The world consists of events which can be registered in time, and yet it is also eternal since it has no beginning or end. Time is not something independent of the world of change, and so we cannot speak of a time before the time when the changes started. Nor can we give any independent status to the notion of time.

Muhammad **Iqbal** used this theory to produce an interesting theory of the self. He starts by noting the Christian idea of humanity being excluded from Paradise through sin, and suggests in contrast that the symbol of Adam is a concept of self-conscious humanity, not a particular individual who went awry. The Fall is a matter of the transition from 'a primitive state of instinctive appetite to the conscious possession of a free self, capable of doubt and disobedience' (Iqbal 1930: 85). Human beings are a mixture of matter and spirit, and given the variety of these two constituents, it is not surprising that conflict can arise when our materiality comes into conflict with our spirituality. What we need to do is evolve and strengthen our notion of who we are, at the same time recognizing that we are dependent upon God. We can increase in our knowledge of ourselves and other beings, including nature, and we then become progressively self-conscious; the notion of God is that of a being who is completely self-conscious, without any restrictions on his understanding and awareness of himself, since he is without any material limitations.

It is an error to think of the creation of the world as being something which happened in the past, and so represents a past action of God. For Iqbal, God is always acting and the creation is an ongoing project, not something which was started and left to itself. It is also a mistake to think of ourselves as finished products, since we are constantly changing and developing. This is even the case at the level of our ordinary activities, since we have all the time to work out our relationship with what is around us in the material world, and this is not a finished and completed matter. At a higher level, there is the self which is abstracted from the empirical world, and which embodies the pure notion of our individuality or essential self.. This is the pure self, the self which concentrates on who we really are, as compared with our empirical selves, and which can operate almost independently of the body. Iqbal makes this distinction clearer by contrasting two different concepts of time, ordinary serial time and what he calls pure duration. Serial time is experienced as the ordinary flow of events, often represented in a spatialized form, so that we experience the changing nature of the world and of ourselves as physical beings in the world. Yet there is also a more profound notion of time, according to which everything has some form of eternal and constant being, and is not merely a feature of our experience. This is like the attitude which we may achieve during **meditation**, in which the whole of reality is seen as being present all at the same time, in the sense that its main features are observed all at once. God might well be thought of seeing the world in this way, since what for us is change and chance is for him the constant repetition of themes and patterns. In meditation, we have the feeling that what we otherwise regard as in motion is fixed, and this is the deeper self and the more perfect notion of time which is available to us, at least in principle, through the development of our spiritual capacities to see at a deeper level than is available to us in our everyday experience.

Iqbal draws rather challenging conclusions from this theory. One conclusion attacks the position of the *salafi* thinkers who glorify the past, who attempt, in Iqbal's view, to 'freeze' Islam in a certain political and theological position. He points out that there existed in the past a vast variety of legal and theological points of view, and rich and vigorous debates within the Islamic world about the appropriate understanding of the most important aspects of the faith. Those who might be called 'fundamentalists' often regard the world as a finished product, and the question now is how to return to an earlier and purer state of affairs, to a more fundamental understanding of Islam. Iqbal spent much of his time arguing for and even trying to revive Islam, in particular defending its continuing relevance in a period of modernity, and yet he was opposed to the harking back to a 'golden age' when everything was clear and perfect. He offers as an alternative looking back to a past when Islam was tolerant and interested in other ideas and in particular in scientific ideas and theories. While certain fundamental truths have to be acknowledged as eternally true, it is a mistake to try to fix them forever within a particular political and legal structure, since the main principle of reality is that it changes all the time. This principle of constant change even affects us when we are dead and in heaven (if we are successful in getting there, of course) where we shall still not be able to relax, since even heaven is not a holiday. Even there we shall be obliged to change and develop our selves and use the others who are with us to come to growing awareness of what and who we are. Different accounts of the nature of time play a vital part in understanding the nature of the world.

Ibn Rushd also tries to reconcile the views that the world is eternal with the idea that it was created. He claims that there are things which are brought about through the actions of other things and which take place in time. Then there is a being which is not brought about through something else and which may be said to be outside time, and that is God. Finally, there are beings which come between these two extremes, and these are not made from anything nor in time, and this is the world as a whole. It certainly cannot be made from anything since there is nothing to make it out of, since the world is all that there is. It is not in time since time is the measure of its changes, and without the world there cannot be change. The world looks both as though it has been brought about by something else, and also seems to be eternal. Yet if it is brought about through something else it must be finite, and if it exists out of time then there is nothing to bring it into existence, and so it is infinite. Ibn Rushd suggests that the theologians – and here he means the Ash'arites – differ from the philosophers only over the issue of the origin of time. The theologians argue that time is finite while the philosophers argue that it is infinite. But really there is no contradiction in holding both that the world is infinite, since it is not produced in time, and that it is originated, since the philosophers do suggest that it is in some unspecified way dependent on God.

Mulla Sadra and Ibn Rushd have the scope to produce these sorts of arguments, since there is no clear statement in the Qur'an that the world is finite and was created out of nothing at a particular time. The world can be seen as eternal if this does not rule out its dependence on God. On the principle of emanation, which was resisted by Ibn Rushd but was firmly part of the Neo-Platonic curriculum of the time, there is no time at which God exists and then brings the world into existence later. God always exists and is always thinking, and these facts bring about a number of different levels of reality and existence which finally end up in our world. Since time is the measure of change, and change involves matter according to Ibn Rushd, we can claim that our world is later than God, since what led up to the creation of our world did not occur in time, since it did not initially take place with matter.

We get the same possibility of reconciliation of the two positions on time in Mulla Sadra, since he suggests that change occurs right from the start of the creative process, and does not require matter, and that time has always been in operation. Time and the world are infinite, and the world is infinite in the sense that there has always been change. And yet the world is also finite in the sense that all the changes which take place in it occur in time, and the world is itself characterized by finitude. These sophisticated theories of time make possible a range of answers to theological and philosophical questions which arise in relation to the creation of the world and what it means for God to be an agent.

See also: Ash'ariyya and Mu'tazila; revival of Islam, theories of

Further reading

Al-Ghazali (1997) *The Incoherence of the Philosophers*, trans. M. Marmura, Provo, UT: Brigham Young University Press.

Iqbal, M. (1930) *The Reconstruction of Religious Thought in Islam*, London: Oxford University Press.

Leaman, O. (1997) *Averroes and his Philosophy*, Richmond: Curzon.

Mulla Sadra (1967) *Al-Hikma al-Muta'aliya fi'l Asfar al-'Aqliyya al-Arba'a* (Transcendental Wisdom about the Four Intellectual Journeys), ed. R. Lutfi, Tehran: Shirkat Dar al-Ma'arif al-Islamiyya.

OLIVER LEAMAN

spanda

Spanda is the Kashmiri theological articulation of the view that God is ultimately to be understood as integrated, emanative and dynamic consciousness. This outlook is one of the components of **Abhinavagupta**'s syncretistic **Trika Shaivism**. The *Concise Verses on Oscillation* (*Spanda Karika*) are alternatively considered to have been composed by Vasugupta (850–900) or by his pupil Kallata. They are the subject of a commentary (*Spanda Nirnaya*) by the Trika theorist Kshemaraja (1000–50). There is also a commentary (*Spanda Pradipika*) from a sectarian Vaishnava point of view by Utpala Vaishnava (925–75).

The *Spanda-Karikas* propound the doctrine that the deity Shiva exists as everything in that it is a single, all-inclusive trans-individual reflexive consciousness spontaneously flashing forth as all subjects, acts and objects of awareness by virtue of its intrinsic, eternal power of oscillation (*spanda*). A limiting condition called *anava mala* reduces trans-individual consciousness to limited subjects of experience embodied in particular circumstances (*mayiya-mala*) where they acquire a burden of good and bad **karma** which propels them into further spheres of experience. Liberation on the part of the fully enlightened *yogi* or adept is understood as the realization of one's identity as the *spanda* principle which is the nature of all forms of experience.

Further reading

Dyczkowski, M. (1987) *The Doctrine of Vibration*, Albany, NY: State University of New York Press.

—— (1992) *The Stanzas on Vibration*, Albany, NY: State University of New York Press.

Singh, J. (1980) *Spanda Karikas*, Delhi: Motilal Banarsidass.

CHRIS BARTLEY

SPIRITS *see* afterlife in Chinese thought

spiritual ladders

The topics of knowledge and action in the Chinese Buddhist discussion would translate neatly into the 'ladders of speculation' and of works in medieval Christianity. The ladders from one realm of reality to another are supported by a Great Chain of Being. The Neoplatonic chain is one way to resolve the tension of the One and the Many, namely, to have the One at the apex of a pyramid emanating into the Many at the base. In medieval spirituality, the chain is the rational way to bring some hierarchic order to the sudden explosion of the pleroma (fullness of Being) that ended the 'finite cosmos' of classical thought as a whole. Pleroma is a mark of Gnostic thought on the Silk Road (see **gnosticism**), but it can also be found in medieval Hinduism, Buddhism and Daoism. A suitable example for East/West comparison are the systems of Pseudo-Dionysius for the West and the Three Realms in Buddhism for the East.

Pseudo-Dionysius set up the following ranks in the heavenly and the early ecclesiastical hierarchy:

Heavenly hierarchy

1 seraphim
  cherubim
  thrones

2 dominions
  powers
  authorities

3 principalities
   archangels
   angels

Ecclesiastical hierarchy

4 bishops
   priests
   deacons

5 monks
   baptized Christians
   cathechisms

The Buddhist has the set of Three Realms: of Desires, where the six paths of rebirth would be found, of Form for the higher gods, and of Formlessness, where no perceivable personality exists.

1 Realm of Formlessness
   neither perception nor non-perception
   nothing at all
   infinite space
   infinite consciousness

2 Realm of Form
   pure abodes
   splendour gods
   radiant gods
   creator gods

3 Realm of Desires
   six classes of heavenly beings
   men
   angry spirits
   animals
   hungry spirits
   eight levels of hells

To approach or to gain communion with God, the contemplative ascends the spiritual hierarchy in the Christian series. To realize ***nirvana***, one ascends two sets of four trance states to go with the upper two realms. It is from the last rung of the ladder that a meditator would break off 'with no gradation' (i.e. suddenly) from ***samsara*** and realize (discontinuously) *nirvana*. One scheme is theistic with Being at the top; the other is atheistic with Non-Being (extinction) at the top instead.

Spiritual ladders were eventually brought down by the nominalists, who questioned the concept's realist assumptions. The question about the possibility of 'leaping' across many of the rungs on the ladder, as against gradually ascending (or descending) came to be a significant issue. Various kinds of 'leap philosophy' which short-circuited the chain appeared in the East. In Hinduism, this appears in **Shankara**; in China, there is the sudden enlightenment of Chan, and in Japan there is the leap of **faith** in Amida.

Further reading

de la Vallée Poussin, L. (trans.) (1952) *L'Abhidharmakosa de Vasubandhu*, Paris: Paul Guethner.

Lai, W. (1992) 'The Sectarian Beginning of Jodoshu: Honen's Senchaku Nembutsu Shu', *The Pacific World* New Series 8: 1–17.

Lovejoy, A. (1930) *The Great Chain of Being*, Cambridge, MA: Harvard University Press.

Nygren, A. (1969) *Agape and Eros*, New York: Harper & Row.

Potter, K. (1983) *The Presuppositions of India's Philosophies*, Englewood Cliffs, NJ: Prentice Hall.

Tatz, M. and Kent, J. (1977) *Rebirth*, New York: Doubleday Anchor.

WHALEN LAI

subject and object

Modern European philosophy started with Descartes, who is now criticized for perpetuating a body–mind and a subject–object dichotomy. So much has been made of the need to overcome that dichotomy, and so often non-Western philosophies are rallied to support that cause, that in some circles it is denied there existed an idea of 'subject' and 'object' in Chinese thought. Yet we do not need to evoke the Romantics who created the anti-Cartesian rhetoric; it is a myth to hold modernity responsible for an all-pervasive and homogenous subject–object dualism. The simpler fact is that human beings everywhere negotiate a range of cognitive distance and of emotional resonance between self and objects. Some persons and things are close at hand; some others are farther away. Some relationships are more personal while others are more impersonal, and only a totally disinterested natural scientist might be so Cartesian as to objectify and dehumanize all reality into a consistent 'it'.

In classical discourse, the issue in Chinese philosophy is framed as '**self**' and 'thing'. The terms *wo* and *wu* were common words. When they are juxtaposed, one against the other, they become aspects of a subject–object discourse. The first Chinese thinker who played up this dialectic was **Zhuangzi**; we do not see that tension between 'things' and the 'self' in **Confucius**. Of the two leading Logicians who confronted the problem of part and whole, Gongsun Long sided with the discrete and distinct while Hui Shi went with the shared and encompassing. An essay attributed to the former recognized that to see an object, there must be the sense organ (eye), the object of sight (a thing) and a working consciousness. A paradox proposed by the latter recognized that 'the moment you live, that moment you die'. Neither personalized these into an existential problem, a 'life and death' issue of the self dying and the world continuing on; that task was left to Zhuangzi. But we tend to remember Zhuangzi for overcoming precisely that *wu-wo* (things and self) dichotomy so much that we fail to credit him with discovering the divide in the first place. We often admire the flight of his spirit, but we forget his text is filled with the pathos of one who bemoaned the very opposite: 'People said there is no death, but, alas, the body decays and the mind goes with it', which perhaps goes to show that it is only with seeing the problem that one could transcend it. Only when subject and object, self and world, life and death seem hopelessly apart does the self clinging to life drop off and the boundary of subjectivity dissolves and one becomes one with the One. Zhuangzi had to struggle to find that solace. He seems to have been sad initially when his wife died; he first cried, then he stopped, then he reflected, and only then did he soar above his particular problems and put them within a far more elevated perspective.

The problem of self and thing became in Buddhism the issue of mind and realm. Buddhism is more aware of and has a sharper vocabulary for delineating the subject-mind and object-field. Perhaps the words 'subject' and 'object' are again

too Cartesian to describe the 'no-self' and the conditioned environment of its 'field', but in any case a rhetorical dichotomy is postulated. The overcoming of this dichotomy took a Chinese twist at the end of the medieval Buddhist era when Linji rephrased the pair as 'man' and 'realm'. With a Daoist flare but a sound Madhyamika 'four-cornered' negative dialectics, this Chan master would sometimes snatch away the subject (man), sometimes the object (realm), sometimes both, and sometimes neither. That is, he would try to dismantle the certainties and apparent stability of the subject–object relationship. The case demonstrates how in Chinese thought, subject–object reality may arise into consciousness as apparent dichotomies so as to work towards its own erasure. For Cartesians, the divide is absolute not because of the divide (the distancing) but the consequent nature of the two entities; they have no common ground to stand on. In the Chinese set, the bipolarity is real. The cognitive distance might be shorter, but there is no reason to presume Chinese minds are naturally constructed according to some mystique of intuitive participation. It is the 'common ground' upon which both self and object stand that makes possible that ultimate overcoming.

The metaphor of 'host and guest' or 'lord and client' was borrowed to render the modern concepts of 'subjective versus objective' imported from the West. The result is that subjective is the 'perspective of the host' and objective is the 'perspective of the guest'. Objectivity now being prized over subjectivity, the view of the guest is being ranked above the host, a reverse of traditional priority. The host was once primary, and his view judged the fuller and more comprehensive one. Now that regal host has to play second fiddle to the dependent guest.

Further reading

Lai, W. (1990) 'Tanabe and the Dialectics of Mediation', in Taisetsu Unno and J. Heisig (eds), *The Religious Philosophy of Tanabe Hajime*, Berkeley, CA: Asian Humanities, 256–76.

Lenk, H. and Paul, G. (1993) *Epistemological Issues in*

Classical Chinese Philosophy, Albany, NY: State University of New York Press.

WHALEN LAI

substance and function

The Neo-Daoist Wang Bi (226–49 CE) originated the first philosophical usage of this pair of concepts, although not actually in the same passage. Prior to this, the standard metaphor would be 'origin and end': the root of a tree and the tip of a branch. Part of a larger biogenerative worldview, it describes how from the one origin came many consequences. There is in this process a material continuity and a temporal development. Wang Bi developed a rather different way of understanding the process.

The Neo-Daoist substance and function

On this approach, substance is regarded as what subsists and sustains function; there is no temporal priority involved. Substance is 'body', while as a verb, function means 'to use'. Their relationship is likened to that of body and limb. The limbs are anchored in the body; the body needs the limbs to function. If that suggests essence and attribute, it deviates from that Western pair in that function, being a material extension of the body, is 'one in substance' with the body, even though, in terms of passivity and activity, substance and function are 'two'. This produces an interesting ambiguity. Wang Bi used this pair to subvert the idea of Being as substance. For him, **non-being** is substance and being is its function. Though he derived this from **Laozi**'s saying that 'Being comes from Non-being,' he also reversed his prior explanation for function or utility. Using the analogy of a room, Laozi had argued that the four walls are real, but then notes how it is the empty space enclosed by the walls that is actually useful. In this case substance is real (being) while function is empty (non-being). But Wang Bi turned that around: substance is empty while function is visibly real. A wheel is real and useful, but it is the empty hub hole that makes the active movement possible.

The Buddhist Two Truths and a Third

Chinese Buddhists soon used the substance/function paradigm to explain the Two Truths. **Nagarjuna** originally intended the distinction of the Two Truths as two modes of discourse: the mundane truth is for living in the world, while the highest truth points to nirvanic liberation. A conflation by the Chinese of the ontologic and the epistemic led to their assuming that the Two Truths were two levels or aspects of the One (the non-dual) Reality. Applying the substance/function paradigm to the Two Truths led some to seeing the Two Truths as being 'one in substance but two in function'. This brought the negative Madhyamika dialectics dangerously close to the *bhedhabheda* (difference in identity) position of Hindu **Vedanta**. With the 'being' that is the **buddha nature** furthermore equated with the 'highest truth' (promising **nirvana**), the *samsara* generated by ignorance can be attributed to being the function of the buddha nature. That structure is visible in Emperor Wu's essay defending the 'immortality of the soul'. He made mind or spirit the permanent substance behind the function of a changing stream of consciousness. The resultant structure is shown below:

mind	permanent	nirvana	true
consciousness	momentary	samsara	unreal

The deluded consciousness is here grounded in the wisdom of the Buddha-mind. Its ignorance in turn serves as the substance upon which the illusion of life and death (*samsara*) rests. This structure of thought was found later in the *Awakening of Faith in Mahayana*, which expands the substance/function paradigm into the trio of substance/form/function. Using the analogy of 'the wind of ignorance ruffling up the water of the Suchness Mind into the waves of subject–object consciousness', this text argues that even though the mind is perturbed (lured into samsaric consciousness) like water is churned into waves, both water and wave (*nirvana* and *samsara*) are essentially the same, both remain alike in being wet, wetness being the 'form' or 'characteristics' linking up substance (water) and function (waves). The Huayan school used this metaphor to defeat the Consciousness Only school.

The Neo-Confucian aftermath

Huayan went further; it collapsed the qualitative distinction between substance and function, origin and end, essence and manifestation. So in the infinite realm of the *Dharmadhatu*, the individual wave is said to contain the whole ocean. Part is Whole. One is All. Any part of the ocean is dynamically generating itself, all other parts, and the whole, in an endless matrix of totalistic interpenetration. When the Neo-Confucians built their metaphysics, they took over some of the Huayan worldview, though they also cut back on its extravagance and reverted back to the more stable model of the One substance with Many functions or manifestations. They saw the Principle or the Great Ultimate as being present in all particulars; they just did not think that that presence is reversible. The substance/function paradigm continues to permeate Chinese discourse: Zhang Zhitong used it for his modernizing slogan that China should retain 'Eastern learning as substance' while adopting 'Western learning (science) as function'.

Further reading

Lai, W. (1979) 'Chou Yung vs Chang Jung: The pen-mo yu-wu Controversy in Fifth-Century China', *The Journal of the International Association of Buddhist Studies* 1(2): 23–44.

—— (1995) 'T'i-Yung: Substance and Function: Clarifying the History of an Idea', *The Journal of Religious Studies* 26(1–2): 83–98.

WHALEN LAI

suffering

Buddhism makes suffering (*duhkha*) the first noble truth and the fundamental reality. To look at life as painful and as the ground for philosophical reflection represents a sharp departure from Vedic thought and classical thought in general. Modern-day apologists routinely qualify it as meaning not suffering but 'being awry; feeling un-ease; a general state of dissatisfaction'. But the Buddha first encountered it, so the legend goes, as the unpleasant sights of old age, sickness and death, and Chinese Buddhists have known it in translation as physical 'hardship' and mental 'anguish'. Literally leaving a 'bitter' taste, it is the reverse of its antonym, *suhkha*, 'bliss' as in the 'land of bliss'. (Wary of confusion with Daoist paradises, though, early Chinese Buddhists chose to render that more officially as Pure Land.) As a harsh reality, suffering should not perhaps be intellectualized away.

Warrior cultures accept physical pain and the lesson it might inflict; classical civil society usually has less use for it. Buddhism tackles it head on. Of the three limitations and existential anxiety facing man, suffering belongs to the arena of 'fate and death', the other two being 'guilt and condemnation' and 'futility and meaninglessness'. It may be translated into and resolved at a higher levels, perhaps as a consequence of the fall (from an Edenic 'land of bliss') and a punishment for sin in the Biblical account. Early Buddhism, though accepting the **karma** of retribution, chose not to so 'sublimate' the physics of suffering into an ethics of guilt or a semantics of a Fall. To illustrate the difference of the early Buddhist solution, we may retell the story in Genesis as follows. For Buddhists, it is not Adam eating the forbidden fruit and disobeying God that brought about the Fall into suffering the pains of mortal life; rather, it is the desire (the craving) for the fruit, an object of pleasure with a misplaced presumption of permanence (a lasting pleasure) that is the root (cause) of suffering. That is what created the self (the **atman** as a false self-identity on the part of the subject, Adam) that then drives the wheel of rebirth around.

At their core, the Abrahamic traditions (Judaism, Christianity, Islam) operate at the level of 'moral anxiety' because their fundamental premise is community life and social justice. Buddhism originally – not consequentially – operates on a premise derived from the level of 'psycho-physical anxiety'. The question, 'Why do innocent children suffer?' is worrisome for theists who presume the existence of a just God; but for the Buddha, the question is not a karmic 'why?' The answer 'because of the evils it did in a past life', is like the cold comfort afforded Job by his friends who were not suffering; it begs the real question. The real issue for the Buddhist begins with the 'that' of the first Noble Truth: that there is the fact of suffering. Moses's sense of injustice was aroused when he saw a soldier of the Pharaoh beating up a poor Hebrew slave, a case of man's inhumanity to man. The young Sidhartha saw none of that. He saw the fact of old age, sickness and death, and realized that these are his own and everyone else's inevitable fate. Some theologians charged him with narcissism for his seeming lack of a social concern (justice), but this is not true. This is the Buddhist basic sense of common humanity or sentience from which an ethics of profound commiseration – yes, even of redemptive suffering through a bodhisattvic surrogate – would rise. It has been pointed out by Tillich how at the end of the ancient civilizations ontic anxiety (about fate and death) was predominant, at the end of the Middle Ages there was moral anxiety, and at the end of the modern period there is spiritual anxiety. Stoicism has its modern European counterpart which may well account for some of the modern appeal of Buddhism to those post-Christian pantheists.

Further reading

Bemporak, J. (1987) 'Suffering', in M. Eliade (ed.), *Encyclopedia of Religions*, New York: Macmillan.

Bowker, J. (1970) *The Problem of Suffering in Religion of the World*, Cambridge: Cambridge University Press.

Burke, K. (1961) *The Rhetoric of Religion: Studies in Logology*, Boston: Beacon Press.

Lai, W. (1976) 'Suffering in the Buddhist Consciousness', *Ohio Journal of Religious Studies* 4(1): 73–7.

—— (1981) 'From Shakyamuni to Amitabha: The Logic behind the Pure Land Devotion', *Ching Feng* 24(3): 156–74.

—— (1991) 'Tillich on Death and Suffering: A Key to Buddho-Christian Dialogue', *Journal of Ecumenical Studies* 28(4): 566–80.

Tillich, P. (1942) *Courage to Be*, New Haven, CN: Yale University Press.

WHALEN LAI

Sufism

Sufism is an Islamic form of mysticism, the name of which probably comes from the word *suf*, which means wool. This is appropriate, as it captures the simple lifestyle of the original mystics. Sufism has developed into very complex and different schools of thought, but if there is anything which can be said to hold them together, it is the notion of *tawhid* or divine unity as a theme. All Muslims believe in the oneness of God, of course, and it is part of the declaration of faith, but the *sufis* develop this notion in often very radical ways, some of them even downplaying the reality of the variety of the world of generation and corruption. This became a point of contention between the *sufis* themselves, with those emphasizing the unity of God and the ability of human beings to become one with God contrasting with those who had doubts about how far that sort of unity was possible and even acceptable from a religious point of view.

One of the points of the simple and solitary life which many *sufis* live is to enable them to experience God in an almost physical way; hence the use of the term *dhawq* or taste for the sort of relationship which they want to establish with that which is higher than them. This often brought them into conflict with the religious and political authorities, and even today there are often rather difficult relationships between groups of *sufis* and the secular authorities. In many ways, though, their practices reflect those of orthodox Islam, in that they generally insist on the need for a teacher, a *shaykh*, to guide them in their spiritual development. Their **meditation** is normally on a Qur'anic or linked text, and they refer to many of their activities as *dhikr* or remembrance, based on the idea that in seeking to achieve an understanding of the nature of the link between God and the world all we are doing is finding again the very natural grasp we had of this link when we were much younger.

One of the issues which Sufism raises dramatically is over the significance of *shari'a* or Islamic law and the various rules and rituals of formal religion. Some *sufis* such as **al-Ghazali** (but he may well not have been a very orthodox Sufi, if there can be such a thing) insisted on the significance of the mystic adhering strictly to the ordinary practices of public religion. Others implied, or acted as if, the latter was not important, and it certainly seems rather unimportant when compared with the direct awareness of divine reality which is available to the mystic. In this way there arose again the problem of reconciling formal religion with the more sophisticated and/or direct understanding of the philosopher and the mystic. If the philosopher could come into contact with the **active intellect**, is there really any need for him to adhere to the ordinary beliefs and rules of Islam? After all, through his philosophical work he can attain a much better (at least intellectually) understanding of the nature of reality, and does not have to rely on the stories and highly metaphorical language of religion. The *sufi* could also wonder why, if he is capable of attaining a high level of awareness of the nature of reality through his mystical activities, he should take part in activities which seem to be designed for those unable to reach such heights.

Further reading

Leaman, O. (1992) 'Philosophy vs. Mysticism: An Islamic Controversy', in M. McGhee (ed.), *Philosophy, Religion and the Spiritual Life*, Cambridge: Cambridge University Press, 177–88.

Lewisohn, L. (ed.) (1991–9) *The Heritage of Sufism*, vols 1–3, Oxford: Oneworld.

OLIVER LEAMAN

Al-Suhrawardi

b. 549 AH/1154 CE; d. 587 AH/1191 CE

Illuminationist philosopher

Shihab al-Din Yahya ibn Habash Abu'l-Futuh al-Suhrawardi was born in Suhraward, Iran, and was executed for reasons which are now not clear. He is very much the founder of *ishraqi* or **illuminationist philosophy**, hence his title *shaykh al-ishraq*, which sought to discover the third way in philosophy between Peripatetic (*mashsha'i*) thought and mysticism (**Sufism**). This philosophy rejects some of the main principles of Aristotelianism in favour of a metaphysics based on light. The traditional distinction between existence and essence is replaced by a distinction between what is illuminated and what does the illuminating. The ultimate source of light is God, the Light of Lights, and there is a consequent hierarchy of lights stemming from him and ending up in our own capacity to have perfect knowledge of ourselves in so far as we can assimilate our knowledge to self-knowledge. Existence is nothing more than an idea, and is unreal in itself.

Al-Suhrawardi also attacks the Aristotelian notion of definition, which is the basis of the Aristotelian notion of science. Definition cannot reveal to us everything about an idea, he argues, since the properties are infinite and the attempt to differentiate between essential and inessential properties fails since it presupposes that we understand what these properties are. But we cannot until they have been defined, and so on *ad infinitum*. In any case, how could we ever know that we had grasped all the essential properties unless we already know the definition, which the knowledge of the essential properties is supposed to make possible. The categories are also criticized and replaced by the notion of intensity, as one might expect of a system based on light.

This part of al-Suhrawardi's system is analytical in nature, and is balanced by a more mystical interpretation. There is between our world and the higher world the realm of what has come to be known as the imaginal realm (*'alam al-mithal*) which is the intermediary (*barzakh*) between what we can experience around us and the source of the reality which is best understood by us through imaginative stories and symbolic experiences. There is in fact in the system an enormous number of categories of light and complex links between the different levels of light and darkness.

Al-Suhrawardi got *ishraqi* thought off the ground, and so created one of the main schools of thought in Islamic philosophy. It came to be very popular in the Persian-speaking world, and in particular had a very powerful effect on **Mulla Sadra**, who both sought to counter many of al-Suhrawardi's theses while at the same time accepting much of his system.

Further reading

Amin Razavi, M. (1997) *Suhrawardi and the School of Illumination*, Richmond: Curzon.

Ziai, H. (1990) *Knowledge and Illumination*, Atlanta, GA: Scholars Press.

OLIVER LEAMAN

Sun Yat-sen

b. 1866; d. 1925

Political leader

Called the 'father of modern China', Sun Wen was born near Macau. He went to Hawaii, but returned to Hong Kong to finish high school, and then entered the medical college there to become a doctor in 1892. He gave up his medical career to organize the Revolutionary Society (later renamed the Nationalist Party or KMT), and finally succeeding in overthrowing the Qing government on 10 October 1911. He is best known for his Three People's Principle: a right to livelihood, basic liberties and democratic self-rule. He preached equality of opportunity and, though following the United States in recognizing the division of the legislative, judiciary and executive, added two more branches of government, namely the selective (election to civil examinations) and the supervisory (to audit and investigate the government). He supported the socialist programme of land redistribution, but not the class struggle theory of the communists. In the long tradition of philosophical debate on knowledge and action, he reversed an ancient proverb about 'knowing is easy, acting is hard' into 'acting is easy, knowing is hard'. People act as a matter of custom and routine without knowing why they do what they do. A new society needs new citizens who do not simply follow old practice; they need first to know what ideals to promote in the first place.

Further reading

Cheng Chi-yun (ed.) (1989) *Sun Yat-sen's Doctrine in the Modern World*, Boulder, CO and London: Westview Press.

Wu, J. (1979) 'Contemporary Chinese Philosophy Outside Mainland China', *International Philosophical Quarterly* 19(4): 415–67.

WHALEN LAI

svayam prakasha

Svayam prakasha (self-illumination, reflexivity of consciousness) is the Indian view that when a subject cognizes a thing or fact, simultaneously and in virtue of the same act, he is aware of himself cognizing that entity. For Buddhists such as **Vasubandhu**, **Dignaga** and **Dharmakirti**, who deny that there is an enduring self which is the permanent background to experiences which it 'possesses', it is individual mental states which are characterized by self-awareness.

The self-luminosity theory is opposed by Nyaya-Vaisheshikas and Bhatta Mimamsakas (**Kumarila Bhatta**) who deny that conscious states, which are essentially defined in terms of intentionality, are intrinsically reflexive or self-revealing. The Naiyayikas hold that a perceptual state may be retrospectively revealed by another perceptual state (*anuvyavasaya*). The standard objections to this position are that it involves an infinite regress and that dependence upon an extraneous factor for illumination is a common characteristic of the inert. The ultra-realist Bhatta Mimamsakas say that cognitions, in themselves formless and receptive, are acts (*kriya*) which produce the temporary property of being known (*jnatata*) in the external object. We know that cognition has occurred by inference from this effect, and not by introspection. This invites the objection that everything would be cognized at all times.

Further reading

Matilal, B. (1986) *Perception: An Essay in Indian Theories of Knowledge*, Oxford: Clarendon Press.

Mohanty, J. (1991) *Reason and Tradition in Indian Thought*, Oxford: Clarendon Press.

CHRIS BARTLEY

synchronicity

A theory proposed by Carl Jung to account for the working of the **Yijing**, synchronicity is antithetical to the temporal sequence presumed in 'cause and effect' analysis in Western science. The basis of the idea came from the canonical view that the stalks used in the divination are moved by spirits in direct response to shifts in remote reality. This 'stimulus and response' requires no physical contact and can be instantaneous. Jung was looking for an alternative to temporal causality, and he found the *Yijing* to be exactly that. When one casts lots (or stalks),

the way the roll of the dice comes up as a mark of fortune is that the result is an immediate reflection of the cosmic structure. It is a synchronic response. The idea is that the instruments of divination reflect the structure of reality. How much one should make of synchronicity as a general theory is however another matter. It does not necessarily preclude the presence of temporal causality in the sacred text.

See also: yin–yang harmony

Further reading

Aziz, R. (1990) *C.G. Jung's Psychology of Religion and Synchronicity*, Albany, NY: State University of New York Press.

WHALEN LAI

T

Taiping

Chinese history was often characterized by violence. The Shang and the Zhou rode their chariots roughshod over farmers who became their subjects. The royal hunt (over 'rice fields') was an archaic survival, like the English fox hunt. During the Warring States period, there was a resurgence of the philosophy of war (the military classics) and even peace-loving Mohists apparently turned into architects of aggressive warfare for the new conquerors. For all its talk of civilian virtues, the Confucian courtiers were often divided between war and peace. 'Enrich the nation and strengthen the army' is a slogan of a modernizing China that has a long history, and a recent study of the military classics might have dispelled all the romantic notions about Daoist principles of 'defence' and 'yielding' which are used in them.

On the brighter side, most Chinese prefer order to chaos, compromise to conflict. Peace in Chinese is written as 'harmony and level-ness', with Confucians making more of '**harmony**' and Daoists more of the 'even-ness' or even 'un-eventful-ness'. Harmony as warranted by the Confucian **rites** presumes distinction; the function of rites is to differentiate superior and inferior, older and younger, close kin and all those farther removed. The Daoists prefer the equality that comes with the 'level-ness' of justice and the 'even-ness' of the distribution of goods. This is enshrined in their ideal of the Great Peace or Taiping. The Confucians approximate that with a mythic age of the Great Equanimity or Daitong. The dream of a coming peace, however, dovetails into peasant rebellions seeking to establish that eschatological kingdom. But in this history of war and peace, the traditional idea of harmony would be severely challenged in the Maoist revolution by Mao's idea of an inherent 'contradiction' in any society requiring an endless and hence permanent revolution.

Further reading

Burkert, W., Girard, R. and Smith, J. (1987) *Violent Origins: Ritual Killing and Cultural Formation*, Stanford, CA: Stanford University Press.

Griffith, S. (trans.) (1963) *Sun Tzu bing-fa (Sun Tzu's Art of War)*, London: Oxford University Press.

Johnston, A. (1995) *Cultural Realism: Strategic Culture and Grand Strategy in Chinese History*, Princeton, NJ: Princeton University Press.

Lewis. M. (1990) *Sanctioned Violence in Early China*, Albany, NY: State University of New York Press.

Sagan, E. (1979) *The Lust to Annihilate: A Psychoanalytic Study of Violence in Ancient Greek Culture*, New York: The Psychohistorical Press.

WHALEN LAI

Taiwan

An island off the China coast, Taiwan (Formosa) was settled by immigrants from the mainland from the fifteenth century on, and was formally annexed in 1683 but then ceded to Japan in 1895. It was restored to China after the Second World War in 1945. The indigenous native cultures remain disprivileged. Knowledge of Japanese survives among the older generation, who remember these overlords more kindly than do the mainlanders. Taiwan did not suffer the kind of brutality of Japanese rule that was present on the mainland. The withdrawal of the KMT (Kuomingtang) under Chiang Kai-shek to this outpost in 1949 turned this island into the home base of the RoC (Republic of China), which dreamed of retaking the mainland from **Mao Zedong** and the PRC (People's Republic of China). The military rule by these newcomers was especially frustrating for the long-settled, native Taiwanese who agitated for self-rule. The government of Taiwan has kept alive Confucian learning such as the Four Books, has made studying Dr **Sun Yat-sen**'s 'Three People's Principle' mandatory, and repudiates Hu Shih's more liberal criticism of China's feudal tradition.

WHALEN LAI

Taixu

b. 1890; d. 1947

Buddhist leader

Leader of the modern Chinese Buddhist revival, Taixu (T'ai-hsu) was born just after the failed 1898 constitutional monarchy reform. From a poor background, he entered a Buddhist order and went through the usual routine of buddha name chanting, **meditation** and so on, until a more informed monk introduced him to the writings of the 1898 reformers and modern thought in general. Then the activist monk Jiyun brought him into contact with the revolutionary circle in Guangzhou. He avoided persecution from the authorities only through his ties to the literary circle (he was himself a poet and a painter). With the founding of the Republic in 1911, he planned a similar revolution for Buddhism. Committed to monkhood, he set up a national association of Buddhists and sought to reform the Sangha from within: doctrinally by evoking a Mahayana commitment to this world and calling for active lay participation in the larger Sangha; socially by setting up centres of learning with a new curriculum that included modern science and by

publishing a series of journals; and politically by replicating **Sun Yat-sen**'s 'Three Principles of the People' in his 'Three Principles of the Buddha' for the Sangha. However, he failed to persuade the traditional elements to endorse his radical monastic reform, especially as related to land holdings and property ownership. A successful propagandist, his vision of a rebirth of Chinese Buddhism is however utopian; his command of the world situation is limited, and he was outdone by some of his students in terms of Buddhist scholarship.

Further reading

Fa Chu Academy (1989) *Proceedings of the International Centennial Conference Commemorating the Birthday of Master T'ai-hsu*, Hong Kong: Fa Chu Academy (in Chinese).

Welch, H. (1968) *The Buddhist Revival in China*, Cambridge, MA: Harvard University Press.

WHALEN LAI

Tan Sitong

b. 1854; d. 1898

Reformer

Third and youngest member of the three leaders of the 1898 Reform, Tan Sitong (T'an Ssu-t'ung) was impressed by the Christian notion of *agape* before meeting **Liang Qichao**. Liang introduced him to the Buddhist teachings and to the utopian vision of Kang Yuwei. Kang had compared **Confucius**, the Buddha and Christ, all reformers who lived during a transition from an age of chaos in relative proximity to the time of ascending peace. A hot-blooded youth with many friends among swordsmen, Tan believed that successful reform movements demand heroic self-sacrifice. Though he had a chance to escape the purge initiated against the reformers by the Empress Dowager, he chose to stay and fight and offer himself up to be a martyr. His *Study of Humaneness* takes the Confucian concept of *ren* to its most universal level. He equated *ren* with what holds the universe together; it is interpreted as the European scientific notion of **ether**. In that, he updated the Chinese monistic *qi* (ether, breath) moral cosmology. He notes, among other things, that sex would be less of a taboo topic were it to be more public: social attitudes would be different if the genitalia were found, not hidden between the legs but growing on the forehead.

Further reading

Chan Sin-wei (1980) *T'an Ssu-t'ung: An Annotated Bibliography*, Hong Kong: Hong Kong University Press.

T'an Ssu-t'ung (1984) *An Exposition of Benevolence: the Jen-hsueh of T'an Ssu-t'ung*, trans. Chan Sin-wei, Hong Kong: Chinese University.

WHALEN LAI

Tan'gun mythology in Korean thought

Tan'gun mythology is a theory of the origin of Korea as a nation. According to this story, Tan'gun founded the Old Choson, the name of the Old Korea, in 2333 BCE. The story is recorded in *Samguk Yusa* (The Events of the Three Kingdoms) authored by Ilyon, a renowned Buddhist monk in the thirteenth century CE. The oral tradition of the Tan'gun mythology may have existed from the ancient past of Choson, probably since about 2000 BCE.

The Tan'gun story is regarded as mythology by many scholars, but it is also regarded by many Koreans as a real and factual history of their origins. According to this story, there was a Heavenly king called Hanin, who sent his son Hanung to rule the world. Hanung descended upon T'aebaek Mountain in the northernmost part of Korea and founded the Heavenly City, and with the assistance of the ministers of wind, rain and cloud, he ruled and judged all human affairs. Hanung married a woman who had changed from a bear to a female form, and bore a son called Tan'gun, who became the founder of Choson (the name of Old Korea).

Tan'gun was both the political and religious head of the nation, in which there was no separation of state and religion; he was both king and priest (shaman). Tan'gun was a divine–human

being. Thus, in this mythology there is an implication of the pride and glory of Korea as a unique nation, since its founder was the son of God. Tan'gun mythology shows the primitive form of Korean thought concerning the origin of its nation and people. This mythology is an old and common belief on the part of most Korean people.

See also: shamanism in Korea

Further reading

Grayson, J. (1997) 'The Myth of Tan'gun: A Dramatic Structural Analysis of a Korean Foundation Myth', *Korea Journal* (Spring): 35–52.

Han'guk Ch'orhak Sasang Yon'guhoe (Korean Institute of Philosophical Thought) (ed.) (1996) *Iyagi Han'guk Ch'orhak* (Korean Philosophical Story), vol. 1, Seoul: P'ulbit Press, 51–8.

Lee, P. (ed.) (1993) *Sourcebook of Korean Civilization*, vol. 1, New York: Columbia University Press, 4–7.

YONG-CHOON KIM

Tantra

Literally 'weaving' or 'thread', Tantra is the name for a variety of esoteric Hindu and Buddhist texts. These texts often work on the principle that the microcosm which we are is representative of the macrocosm of higher reality, and that we can work out from our own situation what the nature of that higher reality is. In addition, we can affect that higher reality by acting on ourselves, provided that we understand the precise links between our world and the higher world and appreciate what the mechanisms of contact actually are.

One of the interesting aspects of Tantra as compared with, say, Vedic practices is that the former tend to be more inclusive. They are not restricted to a particular gender nor to members of a particular **caste** or even religion. Through **meditation** and other linked practices the individual can, if properly guided by a teacher or guru, tap into the basic processes which underlie the world, and as a result can benefit both physically and spiritually. Actually, it is an error to distinguish between the physical and the spiritual, since the material emerges from the higher realms and maintains contact with it, albeit a contact which is clouded by the obfuscatory influence of the matter itself. Many of the books on Tantra go into great detail on how the material can affect the spiritual and vice versa, but the important thing about this contact is that it represents a holistic view of the world as an integrated and entirely interrelated entity.

One of the problems which arises within Tantra is that it is often difficult to distinguish between what is acceptable and what is not, a problem with many systems of thought based on mysticism. The Mahayana adhere to the view that **nirvana** is **samsara**, that enlightenment and liberation are in essence empty, and this had led to some Tantrists believing that anything goes as far as the route to liberation is concerned, since that route is characterized as empty. On the other hand, many others place severe restrictions on what may be done, and how it may be done, and would also restrict tantra as a means of liberation to only a fairly low level of such enlightenment.

OLIVER LEAMAN

Tantra, kundalini

Kundalini in Indian Tantra refers to the 'coiled serpent' at the end of the spinal cord, a power awaiting to be released. That snake is an ancient and widespread symbol, being a mark of chthonic deities such as Medusa prior to the rise in Greece of Zeus and the sky gods. In the Bible it was Satan, the fallen angel, in the garden of Eden. In the Babylonian genesis myth, it guarded the Tree of Life. In China, the serpent was one Ur-form of the Dragon. Pangu (P'an-ku), the first man, could be its alias; the name reads 'the coiled ancient'. **Zhuangzi** remembers it as Weituo (Wei-t'o), literally 'coiled serpent' but described as being 'as big as a wheel hub, as tall as a carriage shaft'. It wears 'a purple robe and a vermilion hat and, as creatures go, is very ugly. When it hears the sound of thunder, it grabs its head and stands up. Anyone who sees it will soon become a dictator. The hub and the shaft refer to parts of the sun chariot which when driven across the plain of heaven produces

the sound of rolling thunder. Once a regal figure (purple is the color of royalty; vermilion goes with the sun-bird), this demigod had fallen from high and is now an ugly monstrosity. With Heaven now supporting the good kings of Zhou, this demigod is aligned with the evil rulers (of Shang). Though the name is serpentine, its manifest form here is the frog. Frogs pick up their heads when storm approaches. They open their mouths to drink in the rain. Their rumbling, drum-like bellies call down the rolling thunder, a seasonal summons to the rice farmers in South China to start spring planting.

Further reading

Avalon, A. (1919) *The Serpent Power: The Secrets of Tantric and Shaktic Yoga*, London: Luzac.

Lai, W. (1994) 'Recent PRC Scholarship on Chinese Myth', *Asian Folklore Studies* 53(1): 156–61.

WHALEN LAI

Tantrayana in China

Tantrayana, or to be exact, Mantrayana flourished in Tang China but faded out afterwards. Japanese legend has it that the true transmission had been diverted by the gifted Kukai to Japan for founding the Shingon school in Heian. The less esoteric explanation is that perhaps Chinese Huayan coopted much of the aura of Indian Tantrayana, and that religious Daoism could supply the native versions of its claim to magic and power, especially at the folk level. Far from gone for good, its Lamastyle form attracted the patronage of non-Chinese rulers from the Mongols through the Ming to the Manchus. Thus a Lama headquarters and monastery was installed within the grounds of the imperial palace in Beijing. Among the general population, miscellaneous Tantric rites are actually the mainstay of many of the Buddhist liturgies in use. To cite one example found in a package prepared for guiding the laity through funeral services currently in use in Taiwan, here is a diluted, Daoistic form of the *Tibetan Book of the Dead*. To predict a person's path of rebirth in the next life, locate the spot on the body where the body heat of the dying remains longest:

> Top of the head for sagehood [in Pure Land], eyes for rising to heaven [as god];
> The heart for [rebirth as] human, the stomach for a hungry ghost;
> The knee caps for falling into the wayside as animals;
> And from the sole of the feet, hell.

Of the signs noted, the eyes stand for a clinging consciousness, still hoping to stay in the rounds of rebirth; the bent knees go with the fate of kneeling four-legged animals; and the soles like the feet in the Purusha Hymn in the Vedas connote the lowliest fate. Legs however are not always so associated with the lowly. At one time and it is still the case in many texts, Daoist contemplatives valued a circulation of energy or the vital breath coming up through the potent, earth-touching soles.

See also: afterlife in Chinese thought

WHALEN LAI

Tao Qian

b. 365; d. 427

Poet

First and foremost of the 'farm and orchard' poets, Tao Qian (T'ao Ch'ien) is famous for refusing to bend his back (bow) any more just to keep the meagre income of his office. He resigned, returned home and wrote on the quiet delights of a simple life back on the farm. Well loved for that authentic life after the Tang poet Wang Wei helped to rediscover him, Tao had been unsung until then in part because he never made the circle of the highborn Neo-Daoists who made a cult of retiring as hermits in very comfortable locations. In the history of ideas, one poem of Tao captures well the then current debate on the soul or what constitutes one's true nature and destiny. 'Form, Shadow, and Soul' is meant to render a conversation among this trio. Faced with the transience of life, physical form (the body self) opts for an Epicurean repast, a call to 'eat, drink, and be merry; for tomorrow we die'.

Shadow disagrees. Conceding that name (personal identity) perishes with body, Shadow defends the need to leave a legacy, a shadow of a social memory. Soul chips in at this point, noting how man has a place, not just in society but also in the universe. Wine may be bad for your health; virtue needs no social reward; but like the Stoic who found a home into the universe (a cosmopolitan), still better just to 'surrender yourself to (nature's) Great Transformation' and just go when it is time to go. Tao stopped short of the Buddhist desire to leave the world for **nirvana** and did not care much for Daoist immortality, being one of the last clear and unassuming voices upholding a quickly disappearing classical ideal.

See also: Body, Shadow and Soul

Further reading

Hightower, J. (1970) *The Poetry of T'ao Ch'ien*, Oxford: Clarendon Press.

WHALEN LAI

taotie

A famous animal mask on early Chinese ritual bronzes, the *taotie* is at once the upper mask of a frontal animal (without the lower jaw) or two animals (tigers or leopards) facing one another in profile. As identified by scholars, it is supposed to be a glutton, a monster of such rapacious appetite that it ended up swallowing its own tail, then its body until only its face is left. Interpretations abound. At one end of the controversy, there are art historians who see no meaning in it; it is just a geometric design, a decor and space filler, perhaps for comic effect. On the other, Jungians like Joseph Campbell see this as another symbol of the Round, the Mask of Eternity as with a snake biting its own tail, linked with the Hindu temple guardian and the Church gargoyle. The iconography of two animals standing on their hind legs and facing each other holding a man's head between their jaws has been traced to ritual (execution, sacrificial) axes in the south, though a Shang bronze in the north also shows such a similar 'mother cat holding a man in her mouth'. It could be a symbol of death/rebirth, the animal (tiger, leopard) being the animal in the west that can serve as the guardian at the gate of hell (similar to Cerberus). Down to the Tang dynasty, we find such tomb guardian animals. Philosophers might be more interested in the structuralist observation that this animal mask represents the One splitting into the Two, thus qualifying as a precursor to the one Great Ultimate evolving into the two of *yin* and *yang*.

See also: Chiyou; dragon

Further reading

Lai, W. (1990) 'Looking for Mr. Ho Po: Unmasking the River God of Ancient China', *History of Religions* 29: 335–50.

Napier, A. (1986) *Masks, Transformation, and Paradox*, Berkeley, CA and Los Angeles: University of California Press.

WHALEN LAI

tat tvam asi

Tat tvam asi, 'That thou art', is a statement of the relationship between the absolute *Brahman* and the individual self (*jiva-atman*) which recurs in the sixth chapter of the *Chandogya Upanishad*. The immediate context is, 'That which is the subtle essence, all this has for its self, that is the real, that is the self, that thou art'. The pronoun *tat* denotes the subtle essence, the Real, the *Brahman*. The pronoun *tvam* stands for an ordinary person. The statement has the grammatical form of co-referentiality (**samanadhikaranya**), which is defined as the reference to one object of words having different grounds for their application. The terms differ in sense but have the same case-ending and denote one thing. The interpretation of co-referential scriptural statements is central to Vedantic theological dialectic.

Philosophers of the non-dualist **Advaita** Vedanta tradition construe co-referential statements found in scripture as expressive of identity. They interpret the expression 'one object' in the definition of co-referentiality as meaning the simple unity of the essential nature of an entity devoid of properties and relations. The different grounds for the application of the different words are purely subjective modes of presentation. They belong to the level of understanding but not to that of being. In the case of 'That thou art', this procedure involves denials of the essential individuality of the self and of its difference from the Supreme Being. Interpreting the text in the context to which it belongs, they hold that the related cosmographical statement, 'In the beginning this was being alone, one without a second', teaches that *Brahman*, the sole reality, is non-differentiated since it lacks all heterogenous and homogeneous distinctions. According to them, the text reveals the identity of the core, inner self (*pratyag-atman*) with the undifferentiated conscious reality that is its causal substrate. From the Advaitic point of view, the usual reference of the term *tvam* is an embodied transmigrating psychosomatic matrix in which the reflection of the universal consciousness is said to be captured generating the illusion of individual consciousness and agency. But in co-referentiality with *tat*, the term cannot denote the empirical individual. Rather, it refers to the undifferentiated proper form of the 'core self' which is contentless, static consciousness.

'*Tat*' does not refer to a *Brahman*-with-qualities that is in some sense the causal basis of the experienced cosmos but to the non-differentiated, quality-less *Brahman* that is pure consciousness with which the core self is identical and upon which plurality is wrongly projected. Taken together, the terms convey the *Brahman–atman* identity state. The Advaitic method is one of semantic purification. *Tvam* has to be purged of its usual connotations of empirical limitations in order to render it semantically compatible with *tat*. When the experiences associated with transmigration and agency are abstracted from the sense of the word 'I', the inner self is discriminated. *Tat* must be purified of connotations that the Absolute is in some sense really a creator.

The anti-Advaitic philosopher **Ramanuja** objects that his opponents' procedure involves construing the terms in non-literal senses and that it abolishes the actual, objective differences that are required as grounds for the application of the terms. His rival exegesis of the statement seeks to establish that *Brahman* is characterized by properties and that there is a real difference between

Brahman and the essentially individual agent self. In his panentheistic theology, the relationship between God and the world is to be conceived as intrinsically analogous to that between soul and body, where bodies are understood as essentially dependent and distinct attributes subservient to controlling selves. Whereas the Advaitins maintain that co-referentiality expresses identity, Ramanuja holds that it is the application of two terms to one entity on the basis of two of its attributes. It expresses the unity of distinct items. The attributive relation is such that the referential scope of terms denoting essentially dependent entities extends to the attribute-possessor. This applies in the case of terms for body and soul. He interprets *tat tvam asi* thus: the 'thou' which has previously understood itself as the controller of a body, is an attribute of the Supreme Self, since it constitutes his body, existentially culminating in him. The term *tvam* denotes the inner ruler of the individual self who is qualified by the latter as its attribute. *Brahman* is the referent of the terms *tat* and *tvam* operating co-referentially. The term *tat* refers to *Brahman* as the cause of the universe, comprising every exalted quality, flawless and immutable.

Tvam refers to the same *Brahman* in the form of the inner ruler of the individual, qualified by that as its attribute. Thus the words denote the one *Brahman* by having different grounds for their application. *Brahman*'s perfection, possession of every excellent quality and the fact of being the cause of the universe are not contradicted. The statement expresses the unity of the *Brahman*, the universal cause, with the individual self dependent upon it.

CHRIS BARTLEY

tathagatagarbha

Literally, *tathagatagarbha* links the term *tathagata*, which means the 'thus gone', referring to the individual who has reached complete enlightenment, with the embryo or womb of buddhahood. The idea is a specifically Mahayana one, that the **buddha nature** lies in the individual like a seed waiting for the right conditions in which it can develop and flourish. Here the buddha nature is

equivalent to *tathata*, sometimes translated as suchness or thusness, by which is meant the ways things really are. Since everything is potentially the Buddha, enlightened, and bears within itself the seeds to becoming enlightened (literally, to wake up), there is no need for a monastic community to monopolize the route to enlightenment, nor even for a transcendence of the world. It may even be that there is no need for a slow and gradual development into buddhahood, since every sentient being is already a buddha, and all that one would need in order to realize this inherent buddha-nature is to take the sudden step into enlightenment.

But of course the main problem which this school has to resolve is how to explain the nature of our failure to live and think as buddhas. If we already are buddhas, what stops us from appreciating this? According to the Yogachara school, the problem here is the effect of the **alaya-vijnana** (the storehouse consciousness) from which all problematic **dharma**s emerge. What needs to be done is to bring about the destruction of these aspects of **avidya** or ignorance, and then the buddha can emerge. Within Chinese Buddhism this was often seen rather differently, not as a project of negating ignorance but of removing it temporarily from clouding the pure nature of the buddha itself. The central paradox is how someone can become enlightened in the future if they are already (potentially) enlightened at the moment.

Further reading

Abe, M. (1992) *A Study of Dogen: His Philosophy and Religion*, ed. S. Heine, Albany, NY: State University of New York Press.

Chan Wing-Tsit (1972) *A Source Book in Chinese Philosophy*, Princeton, NJ: Princeton University Press.

Creel, H. (1953) *Chinese Thought: From Confucius to Mao Tse-Tung*, Chicago: University of Chicago Press.

Dreyfus, G. (1997) *Recognizing Reality: Dharmakirti's Philosophy and its Tibetan Interpretations*, Albany, NY: State University of New York Press.

Fung Yu-lan (1952) *A History of Chinese Philosophy*, trans. D. Bodde, Princeton, NJ: Princeton University Press.

Griffiths, P. (1994) *On Being Buddha: The Classical Doctrine of Buddhahood*, Albany, NY: State University of New York Press.

Jackson, R. (1993) *Is Enlightenment Possible? Dharmakirti and rGyal-tshab-rje on Mind and Body, No-Self and Freedom*, Ithaca, NY: Snow Lion Publications.

King, S. (1991) *Buddha Nature*, Albany, NY: State University of New York Press.

LaFleur, W. (ed.) (1985) *Dogen Studies*, Honolulu, HA: University of Hawaii Press.

Williams, P. (1989) *Mahayana Buddhism: The Doctrinal Foundations*, London: Routledge.

OLIVER LEAMAN

TEAISM *see* aesthetics in Japan, post-Meiji

TENDAI *see* Buddhist philosophy in Japan

Theravada Buddhism

The Singhalese Theravada (dating from *c.*250 BCE) or 'tradition of the elders' (which is also the form of Buddhism found in Burma, Thailand and Cambodia) derives from the Vibhajyavada school of early Buddhism. They used originally the north Indian Middle Indo-Aryan language called Pali. The **Pali Canon**, committed to writing in the first century BCE, is claimed to preserve the original discourses of the Buddha in what is called the *Sutta Pitaka*. The rules for monastic discipline binding on monks and nuns are collected in the *Vinaya Pitaka*, and scholastic elaborations of the Doctrine in the *Abhidhamma Pitaka*. Most Hinayanist Buddhist schools, but not the Sautrantikas, developed their own systematic **Abhidharma** philosophical literature, while the substance of the books of Discourses (*Suttas*) and Discipline (*Vinaya*) are common to every tradition.

The Pali Canon of the Sinhalese Theravada consists of:

Vinaya-pitaka (The Basket of Discipline, i.e. regulations for monks and nuns):

1 *Sutta-vibhanga*. This is an analysis of violations of the basic codes of rules (*Patimokkha*) for monks (227 rules) and nuns (311 rules). Monks should avoid murder; theft; sex; dishonesty; alcohol; eating after noon; dancing, music and entertainment; garlands, perfumes and unguents; soft beds, gold and silver.

2 *Khandaka*. These are regulations (*kamma-vachana*) of the organization of the monastic order (*sangha*).

3 appendices including some history of the order.

Sutta-pitaka (The Basket of Discourses of Gotama Buddha):

1 *Digha-Nikaya*, Collection of Long Discourses.

2 *Majjhima Nikaya*, Collection of Middle Length Discourses

3 *Samyutta Nikaya*, Collection of Connected Discourses

4 *Anguttara Nikaya*, Various Discourses

5 *Khuddaka Nikaya*, including the **Dhammapada** (ethical treatise); *Suttanipata* (various verses); *Theragatha* (accounts of early monks' enlightenment); *Therigatha* (accounts of early nuns' enlightenment); *Jatakas* (547 edifying 'birth stories' of previous lives of the Buddha, exemplifying moral conduct; and the *Buddhavamsa*, about 24 previous Buddhas.

Abhidhamma-pitaka (systematizations of material presented more discursively in the *Sutta-pitaka*). Its contents include:

1 *Dhammasangani*. Book One deals with factors conducive to the arising of ethically positive awareness, including various meditative techniques and states. It has sections describing bad and neutral kinds of awareness. Book Two analyses the constitution of the material sphere including the body. The third book deals with the three roots of good **karma**; absence of grasping, absence of hate and absence of delusion and their respective consequences and their contraries.

2 *Vibhanga*. Book One analyses conditioned entities and processes. Book Two deals with the operation of the sensory modalities. Book Three treats of the basic psycho-physical principles (*dharmas*). Book Four is an explication of the Four Noble Truths. There are also treatments of the doctrine of conditioned genesis (**pratityasamutpada**), mindfulness, meditative states and discriminative knowledge.

3 *Dhatukatha*. Topics include the five aggregates to which personal identity is reduced, namely matter, feelings, perceptions, dispositions of character and conscious events; the operations of the senses; the Four Noble Truths; conditioned genesis, mindfulness; meditative stages; factors conducive to enlightenment; and the **Noble Eightfold Path**.

4 *Puggala-pannatti*. This is concerned with various personality-types and levels of spiritual attainment. It analyses phenomenal existence in terms of six types of conventional designations (*prajnapti*): aggregates; senses; bases; basic elements; the Four Noble Truths; and cognitive and affective faculties and personalities.

5 *Kathavatthu* (Points of Controversy). This defends orthodox views against over two hundred opinions held in other schools of Buddhism.

6 *Yamakas* (Book of Pairs). Designed to prevent terminological ambiguity.

7 *Patthana*. Refines articulation of interdependent genesis (*pratitya-samutpada*) specifying the links between psycho-physical phenomena.

These texts represent the earliest layer of Theravada Buddhist writings and are claimed to be the actual words of the Buddha, Siddhartha Gotama. But since the Buddha probably lived in what is now North East India in the second half of the fifth century BCE, and probably spoke another Middle Indo-Aryan Prakrit called Magadhi, and since the canonical texts were not committed to writing in Pali, and thus to an extent stabilized, until the first century in Sri Lanka, such claims must be treated with caution. The Pali texts appear archaic, and their often repetitive style is indicative of their origins in oral transmission of the teaching. But they are not truly primitive and often seem to reflect puritanical, world-renunciatory trends followed by people beset by world-weariness and aspiring to an ideal of individual self-sufficiency. While some of the material is of considerable antiquity and may go back to the Buddha Gotama, much of it expresses the various interests and beliefs of later generations of monks who were charged with spreading the message.

It is not known how and when the north Indian language Pali came to Sri Lanka. It was perhaps brought by missionaries sent by the third king of the Mauryan dynasty, Ashoka (*c*.269–*c*.231 BCE) who ruled over a large area of North India from his capital Pataliputra (now Patna in Bihar State).

See also: Hinayana (Lesser Vehicle) Buddhism

Further reading

Bareau, A. (1955) *Les sectes bouddhiques du Petit Véhicule*, Saigon École Française d'Extrème Orient.

Bechert, H. and Gombrich, R. (1984) *The World of Buddhism*, London: Thames and Hudson.

Collins, S. (1982) *Selfless Persons*, Cambridge: Cambridge University Press.

Conze, E. (1959) *Buddhist Scriptures*, Harmondsworth: Penguin.

Cousins, L. (1991) 'The "Five Points" and the Origins of the Buddhist Schools', in T. Skorupski (ed.), *The Buddhist Forum, Vol.II, Seminar Papers, 1988–90*, London: School of African and Oriental Studies.

—— (1996) 'The Dating of the Historical Buddha: A Review Article', *Journal of the Royal Asiatic Society* 114: 57–63.

Gombrich, R. (1988) *Theravada Buddhism: A Social History from Ancient Benares to Modern Colombo*, London: Routledge.

—— (1996) *How Buddhism Began: The Conditioned Genesis of the Early Teachings*, London: Athlone.

Lamotte, E. (1988) *History of Indian Buddhism: From the Origins to the Shaka Era*, trans. S. Webb-Boin, Louvain: Université Catholique de Louvain.

Rahula, W. (1969) *What the Buddha Taught*, London: Gordon Fraser.

Warder, A. (1980) *Indian Buddhism*, Delhi: Motilal Banarsidass.

CHRIS BARTLEY

things

Matter is distinguished from form in Aristotle, but the word 'matter' shares the same root as 'metre', and (mathematical) 'measure' is a prime property of Platonic form. In Chinese, the generic term for 'things' is *wu*, which is now associated with inanimate objects or dead things. But in its most archaic script from Shang times, *wu* meant 'spirit'.

The Japanese use of this script as *mono* preserves that early sense; *mono*, for 'things', is also the word for 'ghosts'. In ancient China and Japan, things were considered to be 'alive', to contain spirits or to be spirits. That outlook half-survives into the Chinese philosophical distinction between 'thing' and 'spirit'. Things are 'what is passive and not moving or else what is moving and passive'. Spirit (*shen*, the daemonic) 'what is active and yet not active; passive but also not passive'. The **Yijing** confirms this: 'One *yin* and one *yang* (alternate spells of passivity and activity) constitutes the *dao*; when you cannot tell *yin* and *yang* apart, that is called spirit or daemon'. What this passage says is that a 'thing' is either absolutely still like a rock, or else it is constantly moving like a stream. A rock, once set down, cannot move unless someone kicks it; a stream, unless impeded, should be in perpetual motion. What contradicts that law of motion is a show of 'spirit'. So a tiger on the prowl – at first moving but then it stops still, staying absolutely motionless before suddenly leaping on an unsuspecting prey – is a demonstration of the daemonic from this most 'spirited' of land animals. This Chinese understanding of 'thing' and 'spirit' does not prioritize (unmoving) Being over (moving) Becoming, but neither does it mean that contrary to the West, China tends to prioritize Becoming (change, Whiteheadian Process).

See also: Shinto

Further reading

Bonifazi, C. (1976) *A Theology of Things: A Study of Man in his Physical Environment*, Westport, CN: Greenwood Press.

WHALEN LAI

Three Truths

The theory of **Two Truths** is fundamental to Indian Madhyamaka, but China went beyond this to evolve a Three Truths formula. The Chinese interpreters mistook the Two Truths for two realities, as if the mundane truth (everyday speech) equals **samsara** and the highest truth (wisdom speech) is **nirvana**. Since '*samsara* is *nirvana*, *nirvana*

is *samsara*', the Chinese felt obliged to postulate a Third Truth that is the 'unity of the Two Truths'. Jizang of the Three Treatises (Madhyamika) school exposed this as an error, the result of a confusion of the epistemic with the ontological. He turned the Middle Path philosophy back on track, into being a dialectical critique in which **emptiness** as the 'middle path' is not some positive mean uniting the two extremes. It should just be a neither/nor, an eternal nay-saying, denying both extremes. However, Zhiyi of the Tiantai school responded to this corrective, absorbing it into a new dialectics of the Three Truths.

See also: trinity and triune

Further reading

Lai, W. (1979) 'Nonduality of the Two Truths in Sinitic Mahayna: Origin of the Third Truth', *The Journal of the International Association of Buddhist Studies* 2(2): 45–65.

WHALEN LAI

time and being

In Japan, Dogen wrote an essay entitled *Yuji* (Being-Time). In typical Zen fashion, he troped the line 'There is time' (or 'Time exists') to yield 'Time = Is' (Time is Being). The **Kyoto school** has connected this with Heidegger's discussion of Being and Time.

The **Sarvastivada** proposed that 'everything exists'. A form of conceptualism, it equates the logical with the real, in effect postulating that 'everything conceivable exists'. For anything to exist independently thus requires it to be logically separate and discrete and irreducible. When applied to time then, past, present and future being conceptually distinct, have also to be equally real. Freezing time thus made it hard to account for how things change or pass through the three times. **Nagarjuna** used this point to attack the reality of the Three Times, exposing them as a logico-linguistic convention, empty of self-nature. Before this, **Confucius** had understood time as a flowing stream. He too pointed out that 'one does not step into the same stream twice'. Hui Shi echoed the

Heraclitian sentiment that, 'the moment you live, that moment you die'. The Sarvastivada thesis which froze the three times was not really known in China, and Seng Zhao misappropriated it in his essay on how 'things do not move'. (What he meant to say is that things seem to move, yet they do not; and in truth, movement and non-movement are non-dual.) Nagarjuna's declaration of the three times as empty eventually had an impact, but it was Zhiyi who came up with the formula of 'the three times are one moment'. Past, present and future may merge into an eternal now. It is this instantiation of the all into the one that Dogen later deconstructed in his *Yuji*.

See also: trinity and triune

Further reading

Heine, S. (1994) *Dogen and the Koan Tradition: A Tale of Two Shobogenzo Texts*, Albany, NY: State University of New York Press.

WHALEN LAI

totalism

The term totalism is used as a shorthand for the Huayan philosophy, which holds that 'all is one; one is all'. 'All' here is the word 'total', which etymologically reads 'one slicing across' (the bone at its joint), and connotes 'taken all together'. It is not so much a numerical 'all' as a quality of the total, the one essential thing that 'cuts across' everything.

The use of the concept of 'all' presumes a knowledge of 'everything' there is to know. **Confucius** uses the metaphor of 'a hundred things', while the later standard is 'ten thousand things'; both presume a finite totality. When **Mozi** presumes to love all men, he does not anticipate the problem of an infinite regression in the division of benefits for an infinite count of people. He might however have solved the problem in the paradox of infinity in terms of 'the direction south having both a limit and no limit'. Indians count far beyond 'ten thousand', and the Buddhists use impossible metaphors like 'the sand of the Ganges' or 'grounding down Mount Sumeru into dust'.

Chinese Huayan exegetes employ crisp negatives like 'non-stop' as in 'non-stop or continuous, minute-to-minute causation'.

· How the individual thinker handles the 'all' may be telling. Confucius' notion of *ren ren* is descriptive of being humane (benevolent) towards (all) humanity. Mozi taught 'universal love' or *qian'ai*, which is technically 'love for/among members of the same class'. Mozi does not love horses as he loves man. Hui Shi, however, professed *fan'ai* (generously loving) [all] 'ten thousand things' on the basis of their being 'one in substance'. His opponent, Gongsun Long, who believed there were real differences among things, just as logically provided arguments to vindicate his attitude that one should not love all things. Loving the common whole and safeguarding the unique particular thus part company. **Mencius** worked out a compromise, an extension of the principle from the near to the far, from kin to kind, from family to all under **Heaven**. He taught that 'all men have this heart of commiseration', but actually he might have said, 'Men irrespective of rank or standing are alike in having this heart of commiseration'. **Zhuangzi** followed his friend Hui Shi in 'loving equally all things' – but only after he equalizes things, that is, erases the many apparent differences/oppositions. But the verb 'to equal' (*qi*) need not imply a total aggregation of opposites. One can line up pencils and pens of different lengths and thickness on the same base line, and that would constitute *qi*. If so, the common thread running through many of these thinkers remains a search for a common ground. The expression 'self and things' (**subject and object**) is as such 'one' or 'one in being thus', or *ru*, which later Chinese Buddhists use to translate *tathata* (suchness). It seems that Huayan totalism is still heir to this Chinese way of handling the All.

Further reading

Chang, G. (1971) *The Buddhist Teaching of Totality: The Philosophy of Hwa Yen*, University Park, PA and London: Pennsylvania State University Press.

Cook, F. (1977) *Hua-yen Buddhism: The Jewel Net of Indra*, University Park, PA and London: Pennsylvania State University Press.

WHALEN LAI

totemism

Most Sinologists influenced by either Confucian humanism or modern liberal humanism accepted the popular thesis that the ancient Chinese worshipped (as Chinese still do) gods who were basically deified men. They then set out to discount the theory of totemism as applied to ancient China. But there is possible evidence that the zoomorphic designs on the early ritual bronzes represented such animalian deities and totemic ancestors. The Russian folklorist Boris Livovich Riftin (1932–) is an exception; he takes those figures seriously as tribal totems.

By the Han dynasty, as China shook off her animalian ancestry, the Queen Mother of the West – once a tigress and a guardian of the portal of death in the west, and like the Sphinx probably a devourer of men – had become a fully human empress dowager. However, Buddhism soon injected another rich animal lore into China from India, where man and animals regularly crossed their rebirth paths. As a result, medieval China would still regularly describe human personality and physiognomy with animalian metaphors. And in popular religion born out of such folklore, the Monkey King in the novel *Journey to the West* demonstrated not just full humanity but advanced to being worshipped at his temples as god, saint, protector of pilgrims (like the Dog-Man that became St Christopher) and all-round destroyer of evil.

See also: animals

Further reading

Lai, W. (1994) 'From Protean Ape to Handsome Saint: The Monkey King', *Asian Folklore Studies* 53(1): 30–65.
White, G. (1991) *The Myth of the Dog-Man*, Chicago: University of Chicago Press.

WHALEN LAI

trigger

Chan Buddhism made famous the use of *ji*, this 'triggering' of someone to enlightenment at the 'ripe or most opportune moment'. The concept covers both the 'trigger mechanism' as well as the opportune moment. This apocryphal anecdote of **Mazu Daoyi** may illustrate the concept. The uncle of Patriarch Ma had been pestering his nephew for the *dharma*. Unable to shake him off, the patriarch told him to 'get it from the well' (like 'go jump in the lake' in English.) The patriarch's word being law, the uncle had to comply. And so daily he sat by the well and requested from it the *dharma*. Months passed by and the uncle felt only more ridiculous as time went on. One wintry morning when Mazu saw the 'moment was ripe', he took a bucket of cold water there in the courtyard, chilled thoroughly from the night, and dumped its contents over the poor old man. In that moment, it is said, the uncle was triggered to enlightenment.

The concept has a rich history. The Chinese pictogram shows a soldier on guard, alert to the slightest of movements. The word described the trigger mechanism on an ancient Chinese crossbow. By extension, it describes any mechanical device. Meaning 'incipient motion', it mediates the passive and the active, the *yin* and the *yang*. For that, the **Yijing** described its hexagrams as what could disclose incipient movement so that the gentleman may act accordingly, accomplishing affairs all day without ever tiring. Because this trigger mediates non-action and action, judgement which follows it can go either way. Thus in the **Zhuangzi**, the centipede could coordinate all its many feet without conscious thought; it simply lets this 'heavenly trigger' operate, and they move as one. Yet the same book would charge that people who use mechanical devices are in danger of acquiring and developing a mechanical (scheming) mind. Joseph Needham translates this term as 'germ', and cites *Zhuangzi* on this cycle of life: 'everything comes out of this germ at birth and returns to it at death'. An evolution of species is described in the story of maggots coming out of the rotting human dead and mutating until, in the end, from the horse a human being comes again.

The concept of trigger also provides a perfect exegesis for **wuwei**. Non-action is 'putting only so little effort on this end' (touching the trigger) and 'setting off such an impact far away' (when the arrow hits the target). For the Legalists, it signals being in the right place in the right time. So Cao Cao is said to be 'most talented and skillful in strategy, able to decide on the spur of the moment and act with no second thought'.

The Buddhists gave new life to the concept. It was chosen by Zhiyi of the *Lotus Sutra* school for reading the import of *upayakaushalya* (system of **expediency**) as the Buddha teaching according to the capacity (the trigger) of the audience; a central theme in this *sutra*. From his powerful exegesis came the dialectics between the objective Truth (*dharma*) and the subjective proclivity (trigger), universal truth and timely expediency. When Mazu relativized the objective *dharma* (the formula goes, 'Mind is Buddha' or 'No Mind, No Buddha'), he also absolutized the subjective 'trigger': either you seize the moment or else you lose the opportunity for good. Everything has to rise to the occasion before that sudden enlightenment would occur. It is of course presumed that master and disciple were so familiar with one another as to be able to read the signs and catch the cues. As Mazu also said, 'Every day is a good day'.

See also: Zhu Xi

Further reading

Lai, W. (1985) 'Ma-tzu Tao-i and the Unfolding of Southern Zen', *Japanese Journal of Religious Studies* 12(4): 173–92.

WHALEN LAI

Trika Shaivism

Trika is a Shaiva system of ritual originating and developing in Kashmir, the goal of which is the appropriation by the votary, who has undergone a caste-obliterating initiation ritual, of the supernatural powers of a triad (*trika*) of female deities, Para, Parapara and Apara, of whom the first is benevolent and the second two wild and intimidating. Associated with this cult was that of the eight mother goddesses and their expressions in families (*kula*; hence the term Kaula for forms of Shaivism cognate with the Trika) of female spirits called *yoginis*. They may be invoked and pacified, most auspiciously in the cremation ground, with offerings of maximally impure and hence potent substances such as blood, flesh, wine and sexual fluids by adepts whose affinity with one of the families had been divined at the time of initiation into the cult, seeking their powers for themselves through a process of controlled possession. At some point the cult assimilated the horrific, all-devouring Kalasamkarshini form of the goddess Kali into its pantheon, and she became seen as the unifying ground of the original three, absorbing all forms of conscious experience in an abyss of light.

From 900 CE the Trika was in competition with the dualistic system of ritual and theology known as **Shaiva Siddhanta** for the allegiance of worshippers of Shiva in Kashmir. But, articulated in the sophisticated **Pratyabhijna** philosophy whose chief proponent is **Abhinavagupta**, it was able to respond to and ultimately defeat the various challenges posed by dualism, Vedantic illusionism and anti-essentialist Buddhism. Its rituals, some of which verged towards the socially unacceptable, underwent a process of domestication and internalization. The latter trend is represented in the Trika Kaulism of Abhinavagupta, where orgasm with a female partner is thought to manifest the expansion of blissful self-awareness that is none other than the trans-individual consciousness that is the ground of all phenomena which are its projections, annihilating the confining self-centredness of the votary. Likewise, impure substances are not consumed for their supposedly inherent magical powers but as a means of intensifying experience to the point of ecstasis, a sense of antinomian freedom arising from violation of the taboo. For the Trika votaries, there is no bondage other than the state of ignorant self-limitation which regards the values of purity and impurity, central to the **caste** ideology of mainstream orthodoxy, as objectively inherent in a consciousness-independent sphere. The enlightened person realizes that the data of consciousness are non-different from one another and from the subject. They all appear in his consciousness as merged into a unity. The opposite is the case with the unenlightened, who are immersed in and untroubled by the experiences of diversity and externality. Anxious concern with caste and related values such as one's Vedic learning, family's status, conventional conduct, virtues and wealth, all sanctioned by orthodoxy, are aspects of a false identity. Fears of participation in non-Vedic rites, Tantric *mantras* (see **Tantra**), forbidden substances and types of people, deeds, places and dangerous supernatural forces all represent contraction of an identity that is potentially infinite in its fullest expansion.

The outlook of the developed Trika includes a number of triads:

1 the unity of the individual self, cosmic power (*shakti*) and its ground, Shiva;
2 the psychologistic equation of the three goddesses (which become assimilated to Kali as her aspects) with liberating awareness of the unity in trans-individual consciousness of will (*iccha*), cognition (*jnana*) and action (*kriya*); the epistemological identification of the three female deities with the objects of knowledge (*prameya*), media of knowledge (*pramana*) and subjects of knowledge (*pramatri*); their cosmogenetic reinterpretation as the projection of, immersion in and retraction of the contents of consciousness;
3 a threefold soteriology for the votary including:

Anava-upaya, which involves external rituals and yogic practices;
Shakta-upaya, the intensification of a single thought (for example, 'I am both transcendent to and immanent in the universe') culminating in its dissolution in non-discursive awareness;
Shambhava-upaya, spontaneous realization, unmediated by thought, of the self as all-inclusive, reflexive trans-individual consciousness.

Further reading

Flood, G. (1993) *Body and Cosmology in Kashmir Shaivism*, San Francisco: Mellen Research University Press.

Sanderson, A. (1986) 'Mandala and the Agamic Identity of the Trika of Kashmir', in A. Padoux (ed.), *Mantras et diagrammes rituels dans l'hindouisme*, Paris: Centre National de la Recherche Scientifique.

—— (1988) 'Shaivism and the Tantric Traditions', in S. Sutherland *et al.* (eds), *The World's Religions*, London: Routledge.

—— (1990) 'The Visualisation of the Deities of the Trika', in A. Padoux (ed.), *L'Image divine: culte et meditation dans l'Hindouisme*, Paris: Centre National de la Recherche Scientifique.

CHRIS BARTLEY

trinity and triune

Both Europe and China in their medieval period placed emphasis on the triune formula. A 'three in one' formula often helps to resolve the tension between the two (dualism) and the one (**monism**). Dualism is basic to the medieval worldview, but it invites a transcending. The triune formula moderates the radical divide of man and God (via Christ) or **samsara** and **nirvana** (via the **bodhisattva**). In China, the Tiantai Buddhist school is best known for a 'triple truth'.

Early Buddhism rejected both the monism of the **Upanishads** and the dualism of **Samkhya** and postulated instead a plurality of elements in dependent co-origination. But the dualism of *samsara* and *nirvana* remained and the Chinese mistakenly aligned them with the Two Truths of the mundane and the transmundane. That led them to envisage a third member to reunite the two. This deviated from Indian Madhyamaka's idea of an eternal neither/nor and risked a relapse into the Vedantic both/and (*bhedabheda*, 'the world is both different from and rooted in Brahman'). **Nagarjuna** had used a Two Bodies theory to handle the distinction between the physical form of Gautama and the formless Law Body or *dharmakaya* that is realized in *bodhi* (enlightenment). **Yogachara** in India had expanded this into a Three Bodies theory so as to better handle the transmundane and salvific buddhas and *bodhisattvas* who are neither of the physical world nor simply empty of form; they somehow mediate the two.

Chinese Buddhists inherited the problem – they wondered if the Buddhist Pure Land is a 'real' refuge or a mere 'fiction', meant for some or for all? – and in the process of reconciling the **Two Truths** to the Three Bodies came up with their own 'triune' formula. Although religious Daoists had worked out their own 'three–one' mysteries, Zhiyi of the Tiantai school developed the most advanced solution to the problem. His key inspiration was the *Lotus Sutra*, which calls itself the One Vehicle that subsumed the Three Vehicles. This supplied him with a 'three-in-one' teleology. The *sutra* also declares the Buddha to be continually present in a transcendental yet personal body (it does not use or know the term *dharmakaya*). In his exegesis, Zhiyi equates the *dharmakaya* with the Wondrous Law (*saddharma*) of the *Lotus Sutra*; the Ekeyana (one vehicle absorbing the three vehicles) is the doctrine of the *Lotus Sutra*. This three-in-one crowns the Buddha as the One Reality. The three vehicles of the dependently enlightened (*arhat sravaka*), the self-enlightened (*pratyekabuddha*) and the other-enlightening (*bodhisattva*) are the three ways to enlightenment. The **Hinayana** emphasized the first two, the Mahayana the last.

The *Lotus Sutra*, however, represented the Buddhayana in terms of devotion to the Buddha instead of the *Dharma* as ways to enlightenment. This path to the Buddha is outside the three traditional routes, when it subsumes them under its own One Vehicle, it basically crowns the Buddha, because now everybody can be a Buddha by simply being devoted to the Buddha. Upon this One (real, concrete) Reality, Zhiyi crafts the dialectics of a Threefold Truth. This translates into seeing the world as real, as empty, and as in the middle between these extremes (both/neither) in an endless round of affirmation/negation. The goal is to blend these three perspectives on truth, all true but none absolutely, into one 'round' (perfect, all-embracing) vision. Everything is then being captured fully from all three angles resulting in 'every colour and aroma (the objects of sense) being immediately the perfect round (Middle Path)'. This multi-focus approach yields the knowledge of the One Reality which is then telescoped into the One Mind with its corresponding triad of meditative outlooks. This dialectics of 'three in one; one in three' – in shorthand, the 'Three/One' teaching – anticipates the Huayan formula of 'all is one, one is all' (shorthand, 'Many/One').

Unlike Christian Trinitarianism, there here is no ontological priority or temporal procession (the son proceeds from the Father, and the Holy Spirit from both). Any one of the three perspectives can lead or can follow. There is no historical economy of salvation (such as the age of the father, the son and then the holy ghost); at any moment, the Three Times (past, present, future) can become the Eternal Now. The scheme marks a triumph of reason at domesticating the elusive mystery. Other triadic solutions to metaphysical problems followed, but the term 'Three/One' – short for the syncretism of the Three Teachings (Confucianism, Daoism and Buddhism) being One – is now more often tied to the movement founded by Lin Zhao'en (1527–92).

Further reading

Berling, J. (1980) *The Syncretic Religion of Lin Chao-an*, New York: Columbia University Press.

Lai, W. (1987) 'Why the Lotus Sutra? The Historical Significance of Tendai', *Japanese Journal of Religious Studies* 14(2–3): 83–99.

Swanson, P. (1989) *Foundations of T'ien-t'ai Philosophy: The Flowering of the Two Truths Theory in Chinese Buddhism*, Berkeley, CA: Asian Humanities Press.

WHALEN LAI

truth as sincerity

There is some debate as to whether propositional truth is the driving concern in Chinese philosophy. The Chinese may ask, not so much 'what is the Truth?' but 'what is the Way?' Among the Confucians, the issue of truth is primarily that of moral truth. It is less about objective reality (real or false) and more about a personal stand (right or wrong). Thus the Chinese words for yes and no (affirmation and negation) double as approval and disapproval. When compounded, this connotes contention ('pros and cons'), and by extension, gossip and scandal. In the harsh Chinese legal system, a 'man of ay and nay' is a trouble-maker and a wrongdoer. Little wonder that the Daoists hated contention and sought to rise above ay and nay.

Despite its rhetoric, the Confucian theory of 'rectification of names' has less to do with getting names to accord with reality as with seeing to roles living up to its *arete* (excellence). 'A son is called a son' translates into 'a son is worthy to be called a son if and only if he fulfills his filial duty as son'. **Mozi** worked at tying name to reality, and a concern for propositional truth by observing rules of logical proof is the Mohist forte. However, Mohism did not survive long. Of the two logicians who came after Mozi, one supported his 'non-aggression' and the other extended his 'universal love', but together they subverted his logical ethics. It was left to **Xunzi** later to salvage the objectivity of moral truths.

The preferred Chinese word for saying something is 'true' is *zhen*, best rendered as 'genuine', and not *shi* or what is the 'concrete' as with the 'hard' fact of the matter. When compounded, it is the word for truth as 'true to fact', but it was not until the seventeenth century that being 'concrete' (as in 'practical learning') was valued. Its opposite, the *xu* or 'vacuous', was often deemed more 'genuine'. This has to do with the fact that practical science has always played second fiddle to the wisdom of the gentleman. The word 'genuine', though ancient, is not at all pivotal in the Five Classics. Before **Mencius** and **Zhuangzi** used the term, Yang Zhu was dedicated to 'preserving the genuine'. For this Egoist, one must be 'true to this precious life given us'. Mencius remade this authentic gift into the moral good, and Zhuangzi made it into the natural *dao*.

For Confucius, human truth or *xin*, is about truth-telling and promise-keeping. Paired with the word *shi* for 'concrete', it depicts a man who is 'trustworthy and honest'. When Mencius shifted the issue of truth from the domain of speech and deed (promise-keeping) to the inner dynamic of mind, then before the gentleman can even be truthful to others, he must first *chengyi* (make sincere the will). In the *Doctrine of the Mean*, sincerity as the standard of the good became the measure of the authentic and the real.

For this conjoining of goodness and truth, the Buddhists may take some indirect credit. In the operation of the **Noble Eightfold Path**, the first and the last involves a loop. 'Right view' is verified as indeed 'right and true' by the final 'right **meditation**'. To see the light, one must first have the right information, the process can be described as like a loop or circle; one must have 'faith' in the truth of the report. **Faith** is rendered as *xin* in Chinese. But when that faith is verified, it is truth (also *xin*) itself. That double entendre is found in the late sixth-century Chinese text, the **Awakening of**

Faith in Mahayana. What is awakened is not just a weak-kneed 'belief' in some propositional truth; it is also the arousing of the **bodhichitta** or the 'aspiration for enlightenment' which, by the time of the *Mahavairochana Sutra* is equivalent to realizing the buddha mind. Condensing that first and last step is this Chan couplet: 'The mind of faith is not-two (never wavering)/Not two (fully identical) is that Mind and that Truth'. Initial trust and final truth mesh as one. Chan provided the Neo-Confucians with the technique of 'quiet sitting', wherein the sincerity of the will would be brought in line with the sincerity of heaven and earth itself.

Sincerity, when generalized into a social virtue as being 'truthful to the truth', restores trust in human intercourse. It is blended into the *samurai* spirit of loyalty and 'true mind', but it also informs the 'honesty' and 'reliability' of mercantile ethics.

Further reading

Fukuyama, F. (1995) *Trust: The Social Virtues and the Creation of Prosperity*, New York: Free Press.

Hall, D. and Ames, R. (1998) *Thinking from the Han: Self, Truth, and Transcendence in Chinese and Western Culture*, Albany, NY: State University of New York Press.

Tu Wei-ming (1976) *Centrality and Commonality: An Essay on Chung-yung*, Honolulu, HA: University of Hawaii Press.

WHALEN LAI

Tsongkhapa

b. 1357; d. 1419

Buddhist philosopher

Undisputedly one of Tibet's greatest philosophers, Tsongkhapa's writings cover a wide range of classical Buddhist and Tibetan scholarship. However two areas remain the central focus: the Middle Way philosophy of Buddhism and the *annutara* class of Vajrayana Buddhism. In the latter case, Tsongkhapa's authoritative writings have contributed towards a highly systematic interpretation of the central teachings of Vajrayana that is consonant within an overall vision of the Mahayana Buddhist path to enlightenment.

Philosophically, Tsongkhapa's greatest contribution lies in his novel interpretation of **Nagarjuna**'s thought as read through the works of Chandrakirti. His extensive critique of the early Tibetan interpretations of Madhyamaka especially the so-called thesislessness, his systematic attempts to delineate reason's scope so that the Madhyamaka dialectic cannot be seen as negating everything, his emphasis on the need to develop a coherent and robust basis for the validity of our conventional experience of the everyday world, and his insistence on understanding the doctrine of **emptiness** thoroughly in apophatic terms, all gave rise to an entirely new lineage of Madhyamaka thought in Tibet. For Tsongkhapa, there is not even a minute atom which can be said to possess some kind of intrinsic being, a mode of being that is independent of thought, language and convention. Yet this is not to say that nothing exists; the fact that things do exist is attested to by our own everyday experience. Therefore, according to Tsongkhapa, the crux of the Madhyamaka philosophical endeavour is to reconcile the essentially empty nature of things and their empirical, conventional reality. These ideas were developed extensively in many of Tsongkhapa's Madhyamaka works such as *Essence of Eloquence*, the extensive and abridged versions of 'Special Insight', and his commentaries on Nagarjuna's *Mulamadhyamakakarika* and Chandrakirti's *Madhyamakavatara*.

Tsongkhapa's Madhyamaka philosophy has attracted substantial critiques from many notable thinkers, most prominent of whom were Taktsang Lotsawa (b. 1405), Goram Sonam Senge (1429–89), **Shakya Chokden** and Karmapa Mikyo Dorje (1507–54).

Further reading

Jinpa, T. (1999) 'Tsongkhapa's Qualms about Early Tibetan Interpretations of Emptiness', *The Tibet Journal*, XXIV (2): 3–28.

Thurman, R. (ed.) (1981) *Life and Teachings of Tsongkapa*, Dharamsala: Library of Tibetan Works and Archives.

THUPTEN JINPA

TSOU YEN *see* Zou Yan

Tsuda Mamichi

b. 1829; d. 1903

Scholar and government official

One of the outstanding representatives of the Civilisation and Enlightenment Movement, Tsuda was born in Okayama. The son of a *samurai*, he first received a traditional education but then also studied Western science and military technology. After having completed his studies in Tokyo, where he had gone in 1847, Tsuda became an instructor at the Office for the Investigation of Foreign Books, and in 1862, together with his colleague **Nishi** Amane (1829–97), was sent to Leiden. At Leiden University he studied, among other things, law and philosophy. His most important teacher was the professor of law Simon Vissering (1818–88). After his return to Japan in 1865, Tsuda resumed his work as an instructor and, under the titles *Taisei kokuho ron* (On Western Public Law) and *Bankoku koho* (International Public Law), published adapted versions of Vissering's lectures. After the Meiji Restoration (1868) he occupied various important official posts. When the Meirokusha was founded in 1874, Tsuda became one of the leading and most active members, contributing more articles to the *Meiroku zasshi* than any other member.

Tsuda's philosophical outlook was positivist and humanistic. Impressed by Mill (1806–73) and Comte (1798–1857), he strongly argued for human rights and against superstition and metaphysics, insisting on the necessity of trying to 'implant a spirit of freedom in' the Japanese people 'and teach them that they have the right to deny even unreasonableness in government degrees'. Oppression of freedom of speech he regarded as a source of unrest. In particular, Tsuda published articles against prostitution, torture and the death penalty, and characterized Shushigaku, Yomeigaku, *yin–yang* doctrines and religious Buddhism as 'empty studies' (*kyogaku*), confronting them with 'practical studies (*jitsugaku*) that solely explain factual principles through actual observation and verification'. He also attacked **Zhu Xi**'s (Shushi's) denouncement of human desires, pointing out that, for example, the desire for 'relishing liberty' is a 'fine human aspiration' and 'essential to human nature'. While he was thus rather critical of conservative and metaphysical Neo-Confucianism, he several times referred to Confucius (551–479 BCE), Mencius (372?–289? BCE) and pre-Qin (before 221 BCE) thought in general to support his views. When Tsuda died in 1903, his spirit of independence and his humane philosophy had earned him widespread respect.

See also: philosophy of human rights, Japanese

GREGOR PAUL

TWO SOULS *see* afterlife in Chinese thought

two truths

The notion of two levels of reality, namely the 'conventional' versus the 'ultimate', is familiar in Indian Mahayana Buddhist thought. Given that the theory pertains to the disparity between reality and our perception of it, some version of the theory can be found in many other ancient Indian philosophical schools of thought. On the whole, the Madhyamika thinkers, whose reading of the theory Tibetans uphold, tend to understand the two truths in terms of two 'dimensions' or 'aspects' of one and the same world. In other words, they are thought to be two different natures of one and the same world albeit attained from two different perspectives. The nature that is attained from the non-deluded perspective of the enlightened beings is said to be the 'ultimate truth', while the nature that is attained from the deluded perspectives of an unenlightened mind is the 'conventional' or 'relative' truth. For instance, in the case of a jar, all the characteristics of the jar that can be described coherently at the level of the everyday world of multiplicity are its conventional truths. In contrast, the **emptiness** of the jar's intrinsic existence is its ultimate truth. There is thus a strong epistemic aspect to the theory of two truths as understood by the Tibetan Madhyamikas.

There is, however, an ontological dimension to the theory, which is most extensively explored perhaps in Tibetan philosophy, especially in **Tsongkhapa**'s thought. In this sense, the theory pertains to the notion of existence, especially with respect to the question of 'in what sense can one say that things and events exist?' Madhyamika philosophers, on the whole, reject any notion of existence on the ultimate level, for nothing can be said to possess such an ultimate ontological status. So, the argument goes, if things and events exist, they must do so on the conventional level.

Further reading

Lopez, D. (1987) *The Study of Svatrantika*, Ithaca, NY: Snow Lion, 192–217.
Newland, G. (1994) *The Two Truths*, Ithaca, NY: Snow Lion.

THUPTEN JINPA

U

Uchimura Kanzo

b. 1861; d. 1930

Theologian and missionary

Uchimura was born in Edo, the son of a *samurai*. At an early age, he began to learn English, and in 1877 went to Sapporo where he studied biology at the Sapporo Agricultural College. Since most lectures were in English, he further improved his language abilities. In 1878 Uchimura was baptized, and from after his graduation in 1881 devoted much of his life and thought to interpreting and spreading Christianity. From 1885 until 1888 Uchimura lived in the USA, continuing his biological studies but also studying theology. Back in Japan, he worked as a high school teacher. However, in January 1891, Uchimura refused to 'bow' to the Imperial signature affixed to the *Imperial Edict on Education*, until he was assured that 'the *bow*' did 'not mean *worship*', and that by bowing he was merely '*conform[ing] to the custom* of the nation'. This caused such a scandal that he gave up his job. Uchimura related the incident in a letter to a friend.

After having resigned from his post, he engaged in publishing comments on various ethical, religious and socio-political issues. First he supported Japanese nationalism, and even defended the Japanese aggression against China (in 1894), but later became critical of Japanese politics and turned pacifist. By the time of the Russo-Japanese War, Uchimura had sided with the socialist **Kotoku** Shusui (1871–1911) in condemning Japanese imperialism. Besides publishing articles

and books, Uchimura lectured on the Bible, sometimes addressing several hundred people. Critical of institutionalized religion, he started a *mukyokai undo*, a 'no Church movement' which earned him many followers. The epitaph on his tombstone reads 'The Self for Japan, Japan for the World, the World for Christ, and all for God!'

Uchimura's main publications are related to Christianity and include *Kyuanroku* (Search after Peace), *Kirisuto shinto no nagusame* (Consolations of a Christian) and *How I became a Christian*, all published around 1893; *Shitsubo to kibo* (Despair and Hope), published in 1903; and *Japan and the Japanese*, brought out in 1894. Though a theologian and preacher rather than a philosopher, Uchimura's life and works are conventionally regarded as being not without philosophical significance, and he is hence a standard topic in studies on modern Japanese philosophy. His views that religion should not be modelled on and practised within church institutions, and that religious truth is beyond description and revelation is relevant to philosophy of religion, while his conviction that man must rely on God since he is unable to free himself, is a religious, or theological, position.

Indicative, however, of an important feature of Japanese philosophy was the scandal aroused by Uchimura's 'refusal to bow'. This scandal reflected the conviction that there exists no transcendent, or transworldly, powers superior to worldly powers, particularly governmental power. Also, men ought not recognize any power above state power, for this would endanger public order and peace: it would permit men, in the name of the supreme power, to rebel and revolt. This argument has been a continuous and generally accepted argument in Japan from early times, and was also widely acknowledged after the Restoration in 1868. It indicates the epistemological, ethical and socio-political criticism any doctrine of a superior transcendental power, and in particular, of an almighty god, encountered, and encounters, in a rational and this-worldly Sino-Japanese culture.

See also: kokutai ideology since Meiji times

GREGOR PAUL

Udayana

b. *c.*1050; d. *c.*1100

Realist philosopher

Udayana was an Indian philosopher who combined the **Nyaya** tradition of logic and epistemology with the **Vaisheshika** system of categories in the course of refuting a wide range of Buddhist theories. His major works include the *Atmatattvaviveka*, in which he attacks the ideas propounded by various schools of Buddhism. He rejects the view that everything is momentary as a prelude to establishing the reality of eternally enduring omnipresent souls distinct from the body. He argues for the existence of a mind-independent sphere. He maintains that the possessor of properties is a reality actually and logically distinct from those properties (otherwise the soul would be ontologically inseparable from the stream of transitory experiences), and controverts the theory of the Madhyamikas that everything is relative and therefore empty (*shunya*) of own-nature (*svabhava*) (see **emptiness**). Finally he refutes the anti-realist theory that what is not perceived, does not exist. The Kiranavali and the Lakshanavali belong to the Vaisheshika tradition of defining the fundamental categories of reality. The *Nyayavarttikatatparyaparishuddhi* is a contribution to logic and epistemology. The *Lakshanamala* synthesizes Nyaya and Vaisheshika doctrines and techniques. The *Nyayakusumanjali* attempts inferential proofs of the existence of God as an omniscient creator.

As a descriptive metaphysician, Udayana sought to classify the fundamentally real cognizable components of the world and their relations. The term ***dharma*** stands for the components: things, properties, relations and states. In a more restricted usage, the term means 'property' which is related to a logically and actually distinct substrate or property-possessor (*dharmin*) either by inherence (*samavaya*) or conjunction (*samyoga*). *Dharma* and *dharmin* have determinate identities in logic and actuality. A property may be termed a 'qualifier' (*visheshana*) of its possessor which is the qualificate (*visheshya*). Individuals are manifestations (*vyakti*) of real universals or class-properties (*jati*) inherent in them. Nothing inheres in class-properties, and they are necessarily instantiated by inherence in more than one individual. Accordingly, since space is unique, it has no class-property.

Udayana defines a category of existence (*padartha*) as that which is nameable. The categories are substances (*dravya*), qualities (*guna*), motions (***karma***), universals (*samanya*), inherence (*samavaya*) ultimate differentia (*vishesha*) and absences or the referents of negative expressions (*abhava*). Decomposable impermanent macroscopic substances, qualities, motions, universals and ultimate differentia inhere in other things. Permanent substances (the basic atoms underlying earth, water, fire and air; omnipresent and eternal souls; atmosphere; time; space and mind), inherence and absence do not inhere in anything. Substances, qualities and motions are substrata of inherence, while universals, ultimate differentia, inherence and absences have nothing inhering in them.

The notion of substance (*dravya*) is fundamental to Udayana's ontology since substance alone is the vehicle of material or substrative causation. The categories of quality (*guna*), motion (*karma*) and universal (*jati*) rest upon substances. He defines substance as 'that which is not the locus of the constant absence of qualities', and says that the category has nine types: earth, water, fire, air, atmosphere (the medium of sounds), time, space or direction, omnipresent and eternal souls (finitely, the contingent locus of cognitions and infinitely: God who never lacks the property of omniscience) and minds which are instruments in the production of mental events such as anger, pleasure and pain in the self which is their substrate.

Quality (*guna*) is defined as exclusive of substance and action. There are twenty qualities: colour, taste, smell, touch, number, size, separateness, conjunction, disjunction, remoteness, proximity, weight, fluidity, viscidity, sound, cognition, pleasure, pain, desire, aversion, intentional effort, merit, demerit and inertia. *Gunas* are construed as particulars or unrepeatable instances individuated by their bearers. The blue of a given blue pot is a different individual property from the blue of a given blue cloth. The weight of an elephant differs from that of a leaf. Merit and demerit are properties specific to individuals. Relational properties such as conjunction, disjunction and number which involve several related substances are understood as distributed over them. 'Blueness' is classified as a universal, not a quality.

Amongst universals (*samanya*), Udayana distinguishes objective universals (*jati*) which are either metaphysical or natural kinds from nominal universals called 'imposed property' (*upadhi*). The former are hierarchically arranged in accordance with their scope.

Objective universals are eternally subsistent perceptible entities, but they are apprehensible only via the instances in which they are fully present. An objective universal property occurs in and thus groups a plurality of instances. Skyness and the state of being the man Devadatta must be imposed properties since they are applied to unique entities. Cookness is an imposed property since it is an arbitrary and non-simple characteristic, not a metaphysical or natural kind. (Universals characterizing artifacts such as pots are treated as natural since pots are causally related to earth atoms.) An attribute is an imposed property if it is treated as the qualifier of an objective universal on pain of infinite regress: potness is a *jati*, but the second level non-perceptible abstraction potness-ness (expressing a unit class) is an imposed property.

The concept of inherence, the relation between things that are inseparably connected, is central to the Vaisheshika system. It is the cement of the universe. *Samavaya* obtains between wholes and their parts; impermanent substances (aggregates of atoms) and their properties; permanent substances and their impermanent qualities; and substances and their movements. The preceding exemplify a causal relation. Cases where the entities are not related as cause and effect are those of permanent substances and their qualities, substances and universals, substances and ultimate differentia.

Udayana says that the terms of the *dharma–dharmin* relation are causally related just in case one inheres in the other. This covers the relation of a whole pot to its components. Since the whole inheres in each part, it is a *dharma* of each part. In this case the parts are the material cause of the pot.

Udayana defines the category absence as the concept expressed by the negative particle. Absence of an entity prior to origination is an absence that has a later temporal limit. Absence of an entity after its disappearance is an absence that has a prior temporal limit. Mutual absence, the difference of a pot from a cloth, is the denial of identity. Constant absence is the absence of all types of relation and lacks temporal limits.

The *Nyayakusumanjali* is a major piece of theological apologetics: 'This logical investigation of the Lord, which has the designation reflection and which follows from the acceptance of scripture, I make as an act of worship'. The scriptures speak of God, but they are insufficient to prove his existence. Human authorship is fraught with pitfalls and dubiety, whereas the postulate of divine authorship (which Udayana accepts) involves circularity if allowed to stand alone as probative of divine existence. He thus adduces a battery of arguments purporting to demonstrate the existence of an omniscient divinity who is the originative creator, preserver and destroyer of the repetitive cosmic process to which he is compassionately disposed. The basic inferential argument is: 'Earth, etc., have a maker as their cause; because they are effected'. (There is a lemma that the familiar macroscopic realities are effects because they are partite.) The complexity and extent of the effected cosmos is such that only an eternal, omniscient and omnipotent maker will suffice. There must be a conscious agent that directs, at the moment of creation, the activity of the non-conscious causal factors (atoms, space and time) contributing to the production of the universe. A supremely intelligent agent is required to unite the eternal disembodied selves, which are *per se* unconscious according to this system, with their bodies and a fortiori the quality of cognition so that they may enjoy experiences appropriate to their stock, accumulated over many lives, of merit and demerit (*karma*). Moreover, the organization of the worlds into environments justly consonant with the inherited *karma* of living beings presupposes an all-knowing superintendent. In addition, physical regularities are adduced to indicate a controller.

Further reading

Chemparathy, G. (1972) *An Indian Rational Theology*, Vienna: Publications of the De Nobili Research Library.

Laine, J. (1998) 'Udayana's Refutation of the Buddhist Thesis of Momentariness in the Atmatattvaviveka', *Journal of Indian Philosophy* 26: 51–97.

Potter, K. (1977) *The Encyclopedia of Indian Philosophies*, vol. 2, Delhi: Motilal Banarsidass.

Tachikawa, M. (1981) *The Structure of the World in Udayana's Realism*, Dordrecht: Reidel.

CHRIS BARTLEY

Uich'on

b. 1055; d. 1101

Buddhist philosopher

Uich'on (1055–1101) was an eminent Korean Buddhist philosopher. His title was Taegak kuksa, the National Master of the Great Enlightenment. He contributed significantly to the growth of Buddhism during the Koryo dynasty, which adopted Buddhism as the state philosophy and religion. He established a new type of Ch'on-t'ae (Tiantai, in Chinese) by unifying the schools of Kyo (Doctrinal or Scriptural Study) and Son (Meditation) on the basis of Ch'on-t'ae philosophy. Tiantai, the most influential Chinese school of Buddhism during the Tang dynasty was founded by Chih I (538–97) in a famous monastery in the Tiantai mountains of southeast China. Its basic text is the *Lotus Sutra*, which teaches that Shakyamuni (Gautama) Buddha is but an earthly manifestation of the Eternal Buddha, and totality is identical with its parts.

Uich'on was a son of a king of the Koryo dynasty. At the age of eleven he became a monk in accordance with his father's wishes. After first studying Buddhism in Korea, he went to China for further study, where he studied the Huayan and Tiantai philosophies under the great Chinese masters of that time. Upon returning to Korea, Uich'on produced many Buddhist scriptures. Uich'on was influenced by **Wonhyo**, the great Buddhist philosopher of the Silla dynasty, and desired to inherit Wonhyo's tradition of unifying the different schools of Buddhism. He emphasized the combined practice of both Buddha's teaching of important doctrines and **meditation**.

Further reading

Han'guk Ch'orhak Sasang Y'onguhoe (Korean Institute of Philosophical Thought) (ed.) (1996) *Iyagi Han'guk Ch'orhak* (Korean Philosophical Story), vol. 1, Seoul: P'ulbit Press, 108–10.

Lee, P. (ed.) (1993) *Sourcebook of Korean Civilization*, vol. 1, New York: Columbia University Press, 389–92.

YONG-CHOON KIM

Uisang

b. 625; d. 702

Buddhist philosopher

Uisang (625–702) was a distinguished Buddhist philosopher during the Silla dynasty in Korea. He is regarded as the founder of the Hwa-um (in Chinese, Huayan, the Flower Garland) school in Korea. Uisang studied Buddhism both in Korea and China. After studying the Flower Garland philosophy under the famous Chinese master Zhi Yan (602–68), he returned to teach in Korea. Uisang emphasized the practice of the Flower Garland Buddhism and monastic life, while his famous Chinese colleague Fazang (643–712) emphasized the metaphysical aspect of Huayan philosophy. Uisang and his disciples concentrated on the interpretation of the Buddhist scripture for the purpose of practice to attain Buddhahood. With three thousand disciples, Uisang helped develop the Flower Garland school as the most influential in the Silla dynasty.

According to the Flower Garland philosophy, principle or noumenon and phenomenon, the two aspects of the *dharma* realm are interfused without obstruction, and all things are mutually identified with one another. This philosophy affirms the interpenetration of all the *dharmas* and the ultimate identification of all things with Buddha.

Uisang wrote *Popkye toso in* (Diagram Seal of the *Dharmadhatu*), which emcompasses the essentials of the One Vehicle, that is, the non-dualistic nature of the Buddhist **dharma** (law or truth). He expounded the philosophy of the Flower Garland school as follows:

> The *dharma* nature is perfectly interfused; it has no duality.
> All *dharma*s are unmoving; by nature they are quiescent;
> They have no names or characters; all distinctions are severed.
> It is known through realization wisdom and not by any other means.
> It is the one in the all, the one in the many.
> The one is the all, the many are the one.
> A mote of dust contains the ten directions;
> All the motes are thus.
> The immeasurably distant cosmic age is the same as a single thought-moment,
> A single thought-moment is the same as the immeasurably distant cosmic age.
> The first production of the thought of enlightenment is the same as true enlightenment.
> *Samsara* and *nirvana* are always in harmony.
> ...the practioner...must return to the original source...
> Finally, seated on the throne of the Middle Way of Ultimate Reality,
> From times long past he has not moved – hence his name is Buddha.
>
> (Lee 1993: 163).

According to Uisang, the world is a totality which cannot exist without individual units, but when individuality of units is emphasized, totality is lost. He emphasized that parts must be moulded into a unified identity, and the totality must seek harmony of the individual parts. This idea was applied to the relationship between the state and individual citizens, and became an important idea for the unification of the Three kingdoms (Silla, Koguryo, and Paekche) by Silla.

Further reading

Lee, P. (ed.) (1993) *Sourcebook of Korean Civilization*, vol. 1, New York: Columbia University Press, 159–65.

The Korean Buddhist Research Institute (ed.) (1993) *The History and Culture of Buddhism in Korea*, Seoul: Dongguk University Press, 88ff.

YONG-CHOON KIM

Upanishads

The *Upanishads*, which where originally composed orally, are parts of the Vedic revelation (see **Veda**), the sound units of which are characterized by Purva Mimamsaka ritual theorists as authorless (*apaurusheya*) and eternal (*nitya*). Of the hundreds of works seeking to establish their authority by calling themselves 'Upanishad', there are thirteen composed probably in the seventh to the fourth centuries BCE which are accepted as authoritative by most traditions claiming to represent mainstream orthodoxy. These are the *Brihad-Aranyaka, Chandogya, Taittiriya, Aitareya, Kaushitaki, Kena, Katha, Isha, Shvetashvatara, Mundaka, Prashna, Maitri* and *Mandukya*. They represent the more abstract and esoteric aspects of the Vedic corpus. The *Rig Veda, Sama Veda, Yajur Veda* and *Atharva Veda* consist of hymns to and evocations of the Vedic pantheon. To these collections are attached texts called *Brahmanas*, largely comprising instructions for the performance of large-scale rituals (called *shrauta*) by priests and their householder patrons. They also include explanations of the occult significances of the ritual actions and words and explore correspondences between aspects of ritual and the cosmos, understanding of which was held to be a kind of power. Cognate texts called *aranyakas* (forest books) were composed by people detached from the actual performance of the Vedic rituals who chose to reflect upon what they saw as their real significance. It was from the latter trend that the more generally metaphysical Upanishadic speculations arose in world-renunciatory milieux. It should, however, be noted that there is a measure of overlap in the contents of texts described as *Brahmana, Aranyaka* and *Upanishad*, illustrated by the fact that the earliest member of the latter genre is called the *Brihad Aranyaka* or 'Great Forest Book'.

The composers of the *Upanishads* were concerned with finding interiorized, hidden meanings of whatever is publicly manifest. This tendency culminates in the radical interiorization of the ritual; the view that its 'internal performance' by the enlightened individual is just as effective as its public enactment. The Vedic deities come to be understood as personifications of aspects of what is humanly experienced rather than objective realities.

The central themes of the *Upanishads* include:

samsara, the negative evaluation of one's embodied human existence as belonging to a series of births confined to the non-ultimate physical conditions of space, time and causation. *Samsara* is a bewildering jungle, a place of disease and discontent, the sphere of mere Becoming rather than true Being, an endless cycle of repetitions through which one wanders aimlessly.

Karma, the correlative notion that motivated and intentional ritual actions generate a latent potential which redounds to the agent in the form of future consequences and propels him through a series of births in mundane and supramundane temporary spheres of existence (*loka*). Punctilious performance of the Vedic rituals will lead to rebirth in superior spheres and their neglect leads to existences in inferior realms. The performance of rituals is ultimately meaningless in that their time-bound beneficial consequences will become exhausted.

Brahman (The Ultimate Truth and Universal Essence). Originally standing for the power immanent in the ritual, this term came to express the more general idea that underlying the turbid flux of empirical experience there is a static, atemporal, all-pervasive, animating yet immutable reality that is immanent in the cosmos in that it is identical with the essence of everything including human beings. It is sometimes characterized in relation to the manifest cosmos as possessing properties chief amongst which are consciousness, bliss and infinity (*saguna Brahman*, or '*Brahman* with qualities') and as being the 'inner controller'

(*antaryamin*) of all. But there is also a conception of a wholly transcendent and featureless (*nirguna*) *Brahman* which can only be specified negatively (It is not this, not this).

Atman (soul), an impermeable, inactive identity beyond **space and time** which underlies and transcends finite human forms of experience and which is identical with *Brahman*. This centre of consciousness is contingently associated with the matrix of body, ego, mind and senses. Thus burdened by karmic residues, it has been reduced to the status of the transmigrator.

Irreversible release (*moksha*) from the series of births is possible through gnostic realization, consequent upon study of these texts and **meditation** upon their significance, of the nature of the fundamental realities of *Brahman* and the essential soul as transcending transmigratory existence. The more one is removed from physically mediated experience of the external, through the practice of contemplative progressive interiorization, to increasingly profound levels of being, the more one reverts to the true centre of one's identity, presently only accessible in dreamless sleep.

The compilers of the *Upanishads* sought connections between three spheres: the ritual that is central to the Vedic outlook, the cosmos and the embodied human person. The assumption is that while the universe forms a unified totality, the connections are occult ('Upanishad' may mean 'connection' and 'secret') but revealed by esoteric gnosis implicit in the *Upanishads*. Knowledge of what is hidden is related to the attainment of *post mortem* felicity which tends to be construed as the ultimate, irreversible end to the series of births rather than as the temporary (and thus samsaric) paradises that are the goals of the ritualist enterprise. The connections are often traced in homologies or phonetic similarities between words superficially standing for different things but related at a fundamental level. The link between sameness of sound and sameness of being derives from the principle that an entity's designation is an aspect of its identity and not merely a label attached to it. Accordingly, the terms associated with the *Brahman* (primarily the sound *Om*) relate us to the basic reality.

There were different traditions (*shakha*) of Vedic interpretation, perpetuated by exogamous clans (*gotra*) of priestly Brahmin families who were specialists in particular types and aspects of the highly complex sacrificial *shrauta* rituals. Each of the major Upanishads is aligned with a Vedic *sakha* and included in its textual corpus.

The *Brihad-Aranyaka Upanishad* concludes the *Shatapatha Brahmana* of the *White Yajur Veda*. Predominantly dialogical in form, its themes include the significance of the horse sacrifice; cosmogenesis; speculations about the nature of the soul (*atman*), the impersonal *Brahman* as the support of phenomena such as speech, the vital breath, the eye, the mind and the heart with which it had been variously identified; the relation between the *Brahman* and the *atman*; and the possible *post mortem* destinies of transmigrating beings.

The *Chandogya Upanishad* is a section of the *Brahmana* of the same name and belongs to the Tandya school of the Samaveda. Its themes include the significance of the ritual and cosmic correspondences of the Samavedic chant in the Soma sacrifice, in particular the High Chant (Udgitha) which is identified with the mystic sound *Om*, the universal essence; *Brahman* as one's fundamental identity; *Brahman* as the cosmos; the superiority of breath (*prana*) over other vital functions; possible *post mortem* destinies and the causal factors; the emergence of the cosmos as a modification of a real, self-conscious pre-existing substrate; the pervasion of the manifest cosmos of entities possessing 'name and form' by the universal self; and 'that which is the subtle essence, all this has for its self: that is the real, that is the soul and That Thou Art (***Tat tvam asi***)'.

The *Taittiriya Upanishad* is identical with chapters 7–9 (the tenth being the *Mahanarayana Upanishad*) of the *Taittiriya Aranyaka* which is itself a coda to the *Taittiriya Brahmana* of the *Black Yajurveda*. Its themes include correspondences between the body and the cosmos; the universe as the sound *Om*; the cruciality and moral supremacy of the public and private recitation of the Veda; a person who knows

Brahman attains the summum bonum; *Brahman* is reality, consciousness, infinite (***Satyam jnanam anantam brahma***); *Brahman* as food; vital breath; mind; perception; and bliss.

The above three plus the *Kaushitaki Upanishad* (Books 3–6 of the *Kaushitaki* (or *Shankhayana*) *Aranyaka* which is part of the *Kaushitaki Brahmana* of the *Rig Veda*; the *Aitareya* (Chapters 4–6 of Book 2 of the *Aitareya Aranyaka* which is part of the Aitareya school of the *Rig Veda*); and the *Kena* (belonging to the Jaiminiya branch of the *Sama Veda*) are the earliest extant examples of the genre and pre-date the rise of Buddhism. The *Katha, Isha, Shvetashvatara* and *Mundaka Upanishads* are later and sometimes reflect developments in **Samkhya** and Yoga and in theistic sectarianism.

Many incompatible interpretations may be derived from the frequently ambiguous and cryptic Upanishad texts which are one of the primary authorities (***shruti***), along with the ***Brahma-Sutras*** and ***Bhagavad Gita*** for **Vedanta**. Vedantic philosophical theologians categorize the *Upanishads* as comprising the 'knowledge portion' (*jnana-kanda*) of the Vedic corpus, in contradistinction to the 'ritual action portion' (*karma-kanda*) which is largely the object of Purva Mimamsaka exegesis.

Further reading

Hanfeld, E. (1976) *Philosophische Haupttexte der alteren Upanishaden*, Wiesbaden: Otto Harrassowitz.

Hume, R. (1949) *The Thirteen Principal Upanishads*, Oxford: Oxford University Press.

Olivelle, P. (1996) *Upanishads*, Oxford: Oxford University Press.

Radhakrishnan, S. (1953) *The Principal Upanishads*, London: George Allen and Unwin.

Rocher, L. (ed.) (1988) *J.A.B. van Buitenen, Studies in Indian Literature and Philosophy; Collected Articles of J.A.B. van Buitenen*, Delhi: Motilal Banarsidass.

CHRIS BARTLEY

V

Vaibhashika

Vaibhashika is a Buddhist school belonging to the **Sarvastivada** (Everything exists) tradition, which bases itself not only on the canonical sutras of the *Vinaya*, *Sutta* and **Abhidharma** *Pitakas* but also on the comprehensive Sarvastivadin taxonomic work from Kashmir, the *Mahavibhasha* (second century CE), which is in turn the model for **Vasubandhu**'s (fourth century CE) **Sautrantika** works *Abhidharmakosha* and *Abhidharmakoshabhashya*.

This school understands the spheres of the inanimate, the organic and the experiential as a flux of seventy-two conditioned (*samskrita*) or interrelated eternal, imperceptible atomistic types of mental and physical elements (**dharma**). The interplay and aggregation into the macroscopic of the irreducibly real factors is ordered by the law of interdependent genesis (**pratitya-samutpada**) which guarantees causal regularity and ethical consequentiality. Vaibhashikas also recognize the existence of three unconditioned eternal and immutable states independent of the law of interdependent origination governing phenomenal existence. The *dharmas* are the irreducible units of identification and are held to possess *svabhava* (literally, 'own being') which is interpreted as essential existence in their own right in the past, present and future. They are said to support their own identity and distinctness (*svalakshana*).

The developed position of the school is that actualization and causal efficacy (*karitram*) in the present is one phase (*avastha*) in the existence of a *dharma* which itself remains unchanged. Transtemporal differences are attributed exclusively to connections with external circumstances which were seen as occasioning efficacy. Prior to its present phase, the *dharma* had existed in a potential future mode. When appropriate external circumstances occur, it becomes the momentary present. Once the circumstantial efficacy has been expended, it becomes past. On this view, past, present and future are different designations of *dharmas* with persisting, immutable identities. Thus there is the basis of a real continuum. Temporal sequence is a phenomenon relative to human experience. Accordingly, the Vaibhashikas do not include time as an independent category in their taxonomies of reality, temporal stages being reductively identified with the occurrence of conditioned events (*samskaras*).

The tenet of the eternal existence of the elements can be seen as the basis of a defence of karmic causality or just moral consequentiality, given the doctrine of atomistic impersonality. Ontologically speaking, the Vaibhashikas are realists about the microscopic and, epistemologically, phenomenalists where knowledge of the macroscopic emergent products of the combinations of tokens of the dharmic types is concerned. An expanse of colour, for example, is a conventionally existent (*samvriti-sat*) synthetic mental phenomenon (*prajnapti-sat*) reducible to ultimately real (*paramartha-sat*) atomic constituents (*dravya-sat*).

The school's proliferative taxonomies are elaborated in its Abhidharma texts. While in respect of essence the fundamental entities exist immutably and eternally, they are actualized in the present. The present mode of macroscopic existence (*bhava*) is composite and conditioned, undergoing origination, temporary duration and withdrawal into latency pending re-emergence in new karmically determined formations. Actualization of the *dharmas* is brought about by the karmic process under the sway of ignorance about the real nature of things (*avidya*) and their suppression under the influence of intuitive insight into reality (*prajna*) is **nirvana**. Rebirth-generating **karma** can be neutralized through insight (*prajna*) into the aggregations of the *dharmas* which are causally responsible for our perceptual awareness of the macroscopic. This form of analytical insight eliminates the corruptions (*asrava*) which are integral to the cosmic process.

The irreducible elements underlie the five constituents of personality (*skandhas*) – matter (*rupa*), feelings (*vedana*), perceptions (*samjna*), karmic formations and volitions (*samskara*) and consciousness (*vijnana*) – into which human lives are analytically reduced without reference to a stable, enduring entity such as the soul (**atman**) which is central to the orthodox Brahminical outlook. Neither collectively nor singly do the components amount to an enduring, substantial essential self or soul. The latter terms, and the proper names supposedly designating them, may be understood as abbreviated definite descriptions for bundles of causally related momentary experiences. Enduring selfhood is a fiction which the experiential fluxes conventionally called persons superimpose upon themselves.

The interactions of the *dharmas* are also analysed in two other classifications:

a 'base' (*ayatana*) account postulating the five sensory modalities plus mind and six kinds of data that are their objective correlates;
a 'base-element' (*dhatu*) which adds to the twelve 'bases' six types of awareness; visual, auditory, olfactory, gustatory, tactile and non-sensory.

The seventy-five types of *dharmas* are either mutually conditioned (*samskrita*), impermanent and 'defiled' (*sasrava*) (seventy-two types), or unconditioned, changeless and 'undefiled' (*anasrava*). The former are classified into four major categories:

1 Material (*rupa*); five sense organs and corresponding physical and non-physical sense-data plus subtle matter which is the repository of karmic potencies (*avijnapti-rupa*).
2 Contentless mind or awareness (*chitta*).

3 Forty-six mental elements or faculties (*chaitta-dharma*) combinable with *chitta*, which receive a sixfold classification:

Class A: feelings; perceptions; intentions; sensations; desires; intelligence; memory; attention; ascertainment; concentration.
Class B: virtues of faith; courage in performing good
    actions; equanimity; modesty; remorse; lack of greed; non-malevolence; non-violence; practical wisdom; attentiveness.
Class C: defects of delusion; negligence; intellectual idleness; unbelief; apathetic sloth; addiction to pleasure.
Class D: disrespect to the virtuous and lack of remorse.
Class E: secondary defects of anger; hypocrisy; meanness; jealousy; emulation; violence; resentment; deceit; fraudulence; complacency.
Class F: faculties of remorse; deliberation; reflectiveness; investigation; determination; mental attachment; hatred; arrogance.

4 Fourteen forces (*chitta-viprayukta-samskara*, conditioned factors dissociated from mind) which elude classification as physical or mental: a force governing the aggregation of particular types of *dharma* and linking experiences with their substrata (*prapti*, 'acquisition'), and another preventing such aggregation; a force producing homogeneity of existences; a force transporting an individual into unconscious trance; a force stopping consciousness and producing the annihilation trance; another producing the non-ideational supreme trance state; life energy; the force of origination; the force of stasis; the force of decay; the force of extinction; the force of naming; the force conferring meaning on sentences; and the force conferring meaning on phonemes.

The three immutable, unconditioned and undefiled factors are: space; the extinction (*nirvana*) of the manifestations of elements through discriminative knowledge; and extinction through lack of productive causes, not through discriminative knowledge.

According to the fully developed metaphysics of the school, which synthesizes a multiplicity of previous analyses and thus tends towards over-elaboration, the actualization of *dharmas* into macroscopic aggregations and psycho-physical experiential streams is analysed in terms of the operation of six types of originating cause (*hetu*) and four types of conditions (*pratyaya*) which contribute to and further processes. Causes were sometimes treated as internal to a particular series, whereas conditions are external and shared by other series.

The *hetus*, with some possible exemplifications, are:

1 efficient cause (*karana-hetu*): for example, the eye in visual awareness or the production of soil, etc. from earth.
2 simultaneous cause (*sahabhu-hetu*): operates when things co-occur, for example, awareness is a simultaneous cause of acts of awareness.
3 homogeneous cause (*sabhaga-hetu*): dispositions from previous births generate like dispositions; good actions produce good consequences.
4 associated cause (*samprayukta-hetu*): patterns of feelings coincident with particular types of thought.
5 pervading cause (*sarvatraga-hetu*): dispositional tendencies may act upon both the material and immaterial spheres.
6 cause of maturation (*vipaka-hetu*): the maturation of karmic dispositions in the present and future lives.

The *pratyayas* are:

1 Causal condition (*hetu-pratyaya*).
2 An immediately prior/contiguous homogeneous condition (*samanantara-pratyaya*).
3 A basis or object for each of the six forms of consciousness (*alambana-pratyaya*).
4 A decisive condition (*adhipati-pratyaya*).

For example, a red visual sensation is caused by the temporary co-ordination of the visual sense, the external red patch, the preceding moment of consciousness, perhaps something heard or smelled, and light. To take an external causal process, the seed is the cause of the origin of the sprout since the seed arises in immediate sequence to it whereas soil and rain are contributory conditions in the process.

Buddhist philosophers deny that one entity really produces or influences another either intrinsically or with the help of other factors. Rather, there is a co-operation between moments constituting the uninterrupted flow of a stream of events. There being no duration, there are no stable entities with the time to produce one another. Nothing is really originated as a novel product with a determinate identity. In this respect the Buddhist view is at odds with the Brahminical *asatkarya* and *satkarya* essentialist theories.

According to the mainstream Brahminical analysis of events, the agent (*karta*) is the independent (*svatantra*) item in a complex (*samagri*) consisting of six factors (*karakas*) which include *karana* (instrument), *apadana* (point of departure), *sampradana* (recipient), *adhikarana* (locus) and *karman* (direct object). By contrast, Buddhist philosophy does not ascribe any special significance to individual agency, reducing what is ordinarily and mistakenly understood as the impermeable agent to just another equiparate factor in a complex event.

The denial of the soul and the belief in the momentariness (*kshanika*) of phenomena raises problems about moral agency and responsibility. According to the Vaibhashikas, individual personality is reducible to a process or stream (*samtana*) of real psycho-physical elements conditioned by *karma*. There was a widespread Sarvastivadin Abhidharmika belief that all bad (*akushula*) intentions derive from one or other of the basic defects (*klesha*) of grasping or greed (*lobha*), hatred or aversion (*dvesha*) and delusion (*moha*), while all good intentions derive from their contraries. The operations of the two classes of the springs of action are mutually exclusive. The basic passions operate until the time of full enlightenment. There thus arises the question of the *modus operandi* of the bases of virtuous dispositions with which the three fundamental enduring corrupt passions are incompatible. They cannot operate simultaneously. Nor can they act successively since succession requires homogeneity between preceding and succeeding instants. It would also involve an admission that good can arise from evil and vice versa. To explain the serial occurrence of heterogeneous mental states, the Vaibhashikas postulate two non-material but non-mental forces (*chitta-viprayukta-samskara*): one called *prapti* (acquisition) which governs the aggregation of particular types of *dharma* and locates them in a particular stream of personality, and another termed *aprapti*, which precludes such combination. When a morally wrong state of mind is followed by a virtuous one, the latter is activated by the intervention of *prapti* of virtuous (*kushala*) *dharmas*. *Prapti* is understood as a force which invests the stream of individual personality with a stable diachronic identity in that it imposes latent continuity on experiential sequences, remanifesting itself when in an appropriate combination with other elements it produces the consequence of the particular action within the appropriate stream.

The Vaibhashikas distinguished between intention and its subsequent public manifestation (*vijnapti*, information) as operative elements in the karmic matrix. The potential future effects of acts remain with the agent at a sort of subconscious quasi-physical level (*avijnapti*). It follows that people may be subject to inherited forces over which they have no conscious control.

The conservative Sautrantikas exclusively identified karmic efficacy with the intention (*chetana*) with which actions are performed. They denied the reality of *avijnapti* and any karmic quality to the physical. They regarded the notion of *prapti* as purely fictional. This Sarvastivadin outlook of the Vaibhashikas is the primary target of the relativism of **Nagarjuna**'s Madhyamika philosophy. Nagarjuna argues that the *dharmas* are empty (*shunya*) of own-nature (*svabhava*). He draws attention to the problems in reconciling the claims that on the one hand the *dharmas* are independent and self-existent and on the other that they are actualized through the operations of causes and conditions (*pratitya-samutpada*) and thus are relative (like long and short) and interdependent. He thinks that the Abhidharmists in postulating fundamental *dharmas* with inherent natures (*svabhava*) do not go far enough down the road of reductive analysis to momentariness that is the true Buddhist path. In fact, according to Nagarjuna, the doctrine of *svabhava* undermines the Buddha's teaching. If unsatisfactoriness (*duhkha*) had essence, it would be uncaused and eternal. If the Buddha's teaching had own-nature, it could not be inculcated in an individual since its possession would be an all or nothing matter. *Nirvana* with own nature would be unattainable. In a world of entities with own-nature,

change, becoming and activity would be impossible since everything would be static and eternal. But because everything is empty of own nature, moral improvement and spiritual growth are possible.

See also: space and time, Indian theories of

Further reading

Frauwallner, E. (1995) *Studies in Abhidharma Literature and the Origins of Buddhist Philosophical Systems*, trans. S. Kidd, Albany, NY: State University of New York Press.

Jaini, P. (1959) 'The Vaibhashika Theory of Words and Meanings', *Bulletin of the School of Oriental and African Studies* 22: 95–107.

—— (1959) 'The Sautrantika Theory of Bija', *Bulletin of the School of Oriental and African Studies* 22: 235–49.

—— (1959) 'Origin and Development of the Theory of viprayukta-samskaras', *Bulletin of the School of Oriental and African Studies* 22: 531–47.

Lamotte, E. (1988) *History of Indian Buddhism: From the Origins to the Shaka Era*, trans. S. Webb-Boin, Louvain: Université Catholique de Louvain.

—— (1988) *Karmasiddhiprakarana: The Treatise on Action by Vasubandhu*, trans. L. Pruden, Berkeley, CA: Asian Humanities Press.

Matilal, B. (1986) *Perception: An Essay in Indian Theories of Knowledge*, Oxford: Clarendon Press.

Stcherbatsky, T. (1970) *The Central Conception of Buddhism and the Meaning of the Word 'Dharma'*, Delhi: Motilal Banarsidass.

CHRIS BARTLEY

Vaisheshika

One of the six orthodox Hindu philosophical outlooks (***darshana***), the Vaisheshika school is concerned with the taxonomic mapping of the constituents (***padartha***) of the universe. Principal theorists and works include Prashastapada (*c*.500 CE, whose commentary *Padarthadharmasamgrah* on the legendary founder Kanada's ur-text the *Vaisheshika-Sutra* is the major authority; Vyomashiva's *Vyomavati* on Prashastapada's work, *c*.800; Shridhara's *Nyayakandali* (991); and **Udayana**'s *Kiranavali* (*c*.1075).

The six basic categories are substances (*dravya*); particular qualities (*guna*); motions (*karman*); universals (*samanya*); individuators (*vishesha*); and inherence (*samavaya*). Later theorists add absence (*abhava*) which is perhaps best construed as the referent of negative expressions. Entities belonging to the categories are characterized by existence or objectivity (*astitva*), knowability (*jneyatva*) and nameability (*abhidheyatva*).

The basic category substance is defined as that in which a quality or activity inheres. This category encompasses the eternal, causeless non-sensible atoms (*paramanu*) underlying the macroscopic forms of earth, water, fire and air; the atmosphere which is the vehicle of sound (*akasha*); time; space; eternal and ubiquitous souls which may or may not be substrata of the property of cognition, and minds which are instruments in the production of mental events such as anger, pleasure and pain in the self, which are their substrate.

Atmosphere, space and time are non-atomic, non-composite, ubiquitous and infinite. The existence of atoms is deduced from the decomposability of macroscopic objects. The process of division must halt at some point on pain of infinite regress (*anavastha*). The atoms in combination are the irreducible uncaused causes of the impermanent, originated and effected components of the material environment.

The twenty-four qualities (*gunas*) are colour, taste, smell, touch, number, size, separateness, conjunction, disjunction, remoteness, proximity, weight, fluidity, viscidity, sound, cognition, pleasure, pain, desire, aversion, intentional effort, merit, demerit and inherited tendencies. They are construed as particulars or unrepeatable instances individuated by their bearers. That is to say, the blue of a given blue pot is a different individual property from the blue of a given blue cloth. The weight of an elephant differs from that of a leaf. Merit and demerit are properties specific to individuals. Relational properties such as conjunction, disjunction and number which involve several related substances are understood as distributed over them. 'Blueness' is a universal, not a quality.

Motion inhering in macroscopic bodies is of five types: upward, downward, bending, stretching and locomotion. A universal or repeatable generic property (*samanya*) inheres or is inseparably present in the individual (*vyakti*) substances, qualities and motions comprising a class of entities (*jati*). It is defined as single (*eka*), eternal (*nitya*) and occurrent in many (*aneka-vritti*). These self-existent and indestructible mind-independent constituents of the universe are ontologically distinct or separable from their instances (*vyakti*; *dharmin*). They account for the fact that numerically distinct entities may be brought under a single concept and word and be treated as members of the same class. Universals are hierarchically arranged in accordance with their comprehensiveness. There is an all-inclusive supreme universal 'reality' (*satta*) which inheres in all substances, qualities and motions. It confers existence upon impermanent and causally dependent entities. Lower universals (for example, cowness and potness) have both an inclusive and an exclusive function. A universal is involved both in the inclusive cognition 'cow' that recurs with reference to different individuals and in the cognition 'this cow differs from another one', which is mutually exclusive in respect of those individuals. (This is the orthodox interpretation of the statement in *Vaisheshika-Sutra* 1.2.3. to the effect that depending on the mode of cognition (*buddhi-apeksha*) the universal appears as a general or specific factor.) Universals may feature in the content (*vishayata*) of perceptions. The perception of concrete entities involves a simple awareness of universals as qualifiers (*viseshana*) even if their recurrent character is not recognized. Not every general term stands for a real universal. Examples of the latter are earthness, colour-types, types of movement, natural kinds and established artifact types. Other kinds of generality grouping a collection of individuals, such as 'being a cook', are classified as imposed characteristics (*upadhi*).

Features of universals differentiating them from impermanent entities in the categories of substance, quality and motion include their being self-existent (*svatmasattva*); their being neither effects nor causes; their not being the substrata of other universals or individuators (*vishesha*); and their always being logically and linguistically classified as attributes (*dharma*). They cannot be treated as concrete objects (*artha*) or substrata (*dharmin*).

Individuators (*vishesha*) are the ultimate factors of individual identity occurrent in eternal non-composite substances (the atoms of earth, water, fire and air; mind; the unitary substances atmosphere, space and time) accounting for the irreducible identities of these entities. They are also the principles of individuation in the case of depersonalized, disembodied liberated individual selves (*jiva*).

Samavaya or inherence is a dyadic relation of 'asymmetrical inseparable presence in'. It is internal (*ayutasiddha*) and obtains between part and whole, substance and quality, motions and substrate, universals and their individual instances, individuators and eternal substances. It is the cement of the universe. Inherence is contrasted with contact or conjunction (*samyoga*) which is an external, separable (*yutasiddha*) relation. Later theorists formulate a third category, that of 'self-linking' relations (*svarupa-sambandha*) where it is the essence of one or both of the terms to be related to the other.

Absences, the referents of negative expressions, are counted as existent, knowable and nameable. This is plausible when one considers that negative numbers are real numbers, that there are negative states of affairs such as doing or saying nothing and that the notion of negative facts is intelligible. There are four kinds of absence: prior absence (*pragabhava*) which expresses the relation between cause and effect in the context of the **asatkaryavada** theory of causation; the termination of what had existed (*dhvamsa*); absolute non-existence or impossibility (*atyanta-abhava*); and reciprocal absence or difference (*anyonya-abhava*). Absences are held to have identity (*svarupa*). What is usually meant, except in the case of *atyanta-abhava*, is the identifiable absence of some positive entity and relates to something possible but unexemplified at a given time and place. As such, it may be cognitively fruitful.

The system is realistic in that the entities falling under the categories (*padarthas*) are not artifacts of human conceptual schemes and language. They are discovered, not invented. But if reality is that which is independent of human subjective standpoints or that which would exist in the absence of observers, the realist doctrine may be threatened by the definition of the *padarthas* in terms of the three predicates, 'objectivity' (*astitva*), cognizability (*jneyatva*) and nameability (*abidheyatva*), if the latter are construed as necessarily involving anthropocentric reference.

The non-eternal spatio-temporal continuants,

real substrates (*ashraya*) of real properties, that furnish the world of everyday experience are integrated whole things (*avayavin*) over and above their constituent parts (*avayava*) with identities of their own. The Vaisheshikas subscribe to the *asatkaryavada* theory of causation, according to which the effect is held to arise from its antecedent causal conditions as a whole (*avayavin*) new product over and above its parts. This involves the denial that an effect pre-exists *in potentia* in subtle or germinal form in a causal substrate of which it is a modification or transformation (**satkaryavada**). The combination of homogeneous types of eternal substances (earth, water, fire, air and their atoms) by both the relations of conjunction (*samyoga*) and inherence (*samavaya*) brings about a novel product (such as a cloth). The relation of conjunction on its own simply yields an aggregate (such as a bundle of threads). Effects inhere in their parts and substrative causes whose aggregation produces them.

A cause is defined as an invariably concomitant, temporally immediate and indispensable antecedent condition of an effect. There are three factors in a causal complex (*karana-samagri*): the inherent (*samavayi-karana*) which is always a substance (*dravya*), for example, the threads (parts, *avayava*) comprising the cloth (the whole, *avayavin*); the non-inherent (*asamavayi*) which is always a quality (*guna*) or activity (*karma*), for example, the interconnection and colour of the threads; and the efficient (*nimitta*), for example, the weaver (conscious agent), shuttle and other instruments.

The eternal, unitary and omnipresent substances space (*dik*) and time (*kala*) are conceptualized as containers exercising a regulative causality over everything that has an origin which would otherwise be merely random process. Time is the basis of the notions of priority, simultaneity and posteriority and the different systems of measurement such as moments, days, months, seasons, years and cosmic cycles. Although unitary, it acquires a semblance of multiplicity due to its involvement with the different stages of existence of finite entities.

The existence of the eternal and omnipresent soul substance (**atman**) is inferred, rather than reflexively or introspectively revealed, as that which must be the substratum of cognitions, feelings and effort. The phenomenon of dreamless sleep is adduced to establish the persistence of personal identity in the absence of conscious experience. Cognition, volition and effort are only contingently connected with the *per se* non-conscious soul. Those three properties are exhaustively defined and explicated in terms of their intentionality. The view is an 'externalist' one, maintaining that the content of what is experienced, thought and said is essentially, and not just causally, dependent upon relations to an extra-mental environment. The implication that the state of irreversible release from rebirth (*apavarga*, 'escape') is not characterized by consciousness attracted severe criticism.

The existence of deity (*Ishvara*) – the omniscient, omnipotent and eternal supreme self – is inferred from the fact that the universe's complexity implies that it is a product requiring a creator, qua efficient cause of the initial dispositions of the primal atoms, whose power and knowledge are adequate to that complexity. *Ishvara* organizes initial conditions of the newly created universe in accordance with the accumulated **karma** of finite beings.

See also: padartha; space and time, Indian theories of

Further reading

Frauwallner, E. (1953–6) *Geschichte der indischen Philosophie*, 2 vols, Salzburg: Otto Muller.

Halbfass, W. (1992) *On Being and What There Is: Classical Vaisheshika and the History of Indian Ontology*, Albany, NY: State University of New York Press.

Potter, K. (ed.) (1977) *Encyclopedia of Indian Philosophies, Vol.II: The Tradition of Nyaya-Vaisheshika up to Gangesha*, Delhi: Motilal Banarsidass.

CHRIS BARTLEY

VARNA *see* caste

Vasubandhu

*fl. c.*400 CE

Buddhist philosopher

Vasubandhu was traditionally held to be the younger brother of the Mahayana master Asanga, who wrote the *Mahayanasamgraha* and *Abhidharmasamucchaya*. Initially ordained in the **Hinayana** Sarvastivadin (Everything exists) school, he subsequently converted to Mahayana. Vasubandhu departed from the atomistic reductionist realism about the microscopic of the Sarvastivadin Vaibhashikas (see **Vaibhashika**) to the critical realism or representationalism of the Sautrantikas (see **Sautrantika**), finally aligning himself with the idealist **Yogachara**–Vijnanavada school. His most influential work is the *Abhidharmakosha* (with auto-commentary), which is a critical survey from a Sautrantika point of view of Buddhist realist schools. This work summarizes the second century CE *Mahavibhasha* (hence the term 'Vaibhashika'), which is a voluminous commentary on the Kashmiri Sarvastivadin Abhidharmika literature. Other major works include the *Karmasiddhiprakarana*, which is a Sautrantika critique of realist notions of karmic causation and an attempt to reconcile atomistic impersonality with moral responsibility and consequentiality; the *Madhyantavibhagashastra* (idealist); the *Trisvabhavanirdesha* (idealist); the *Trimshika* (idealist); the *Vadavidhi* (on logic, superseded by **Dignaga**); and the *Vimshatika* with auto-commentary (idealist).

The *Abhidharmakosha* expounds an event or process ontology whose basic constituents are properties (**dharma**) rather than substances (*dharmin*). Its burden is that the complex entities, including human beings, to which we are attached in everyday life are impermanent and that the seeker after truth, mental equanimity, dispassionate detachment and ultimately escape from rebirth should develop a facility in analytically reducing them to their components. The work catalogues the *dharmas* that form the content of experience, as well as its subjects, and the faculties through which it is mediated. The universe is understood as a product of the interactive **karma** or inherited habitual tendencies of sentient beings. Skill in **meditation** leads to correct understanding, which engenders superiority of character in which negative and destructive habits of mind and conduct have been eliminated.

Earlier philosophers in the realist Abhidharmika traditions had inferred the real existence of atoms as the fundamental building blocks of macroscopic reality. As a proponent of idealism (*vijnaptimatra*, understanding only), Vasubandhu rejects this conceptuality as internally inconsistent. If an atom is of the smallest possible size, it must be impartite. Therefore its putative spatial location has no sub-regions. So it lacks spatial relations or position. If a single atom is non-spatial, so is a putative atomic aggregation. Thus the notion of macro-entities is incoherent.

Vasubandhu's developed position is that unen-lightened people inhabit a maelstrom of craving, aversions and delusions. Enlightened people who are detached from the objects of sense realize that the world is a fabric of appearances and are free from desires, aversions and delusions; in particular the delusion that one is fundamentally an enduring, substantial soul, a 'further fact' over and above the stream of one's psycho-physical continuity. Aware-ness of a mind-independent physical sphere is the product of habitual inferential construction rather than direct cognition. People are individualized not through relations to external circumstances but by a 'mind-set' consisting of their inherited traits, attitudes, moods, emotions and memories. Decon-struction of these purely subjective factors incul-cates detachment from all forms of experience.

The contents of awareness, perceptions of an external world, memories and dreams are held to derive from a beginningless supply of residual traces of experience (*vasana*, literally 'perfume') in the form of mental states and dispositions of character preserved in an underlying unconscious level of mind termed the 'storehouse consciousness' (***alaya-vijnana***) which also generates the illusion of a real stable, individual subject confronting a world of objects. The *alaya-vijnana* consisting of a series of thoughts and karmic 'seeds' accounts for the continuity of individual personality through death and the transition between lives and in spells of unconsciousness. When the traces of experience operate as moral and psychological conditions, the effect of such 'perfuming' by prior unenlightened actions of a series of experiences temporarily constituting an individual personality is to predis-pose the mind to perform further actions condi-tioned and motivated by craving, aversion and delusion.

In their exhaustive reductive identification of extra-mental entities to elements of awareness, Vasubandhu and his followers oppose the repre-sentationalist's view that the existence of a momentary mind-independent sphere may be inferentially established on the basis of the fact that mental representations occur. They draw attention to the dissimilarity between the imper-ceptible, microscopic purported causes and their supposed phenomenal effects. They point to the indistinguishability from the phenomenological point of view of dream and waking states; the former demonstrating the possibility of experience without objective or extra-mental supports, which is also evidenced by hallucinations. If experience without contemporaneous objective reference or extra-mental support (*alambana*) is possible in one case, it is possible in all. Awareness (*vijnana*) and its contents or objects (*vishaya*) are inseparable. If there are no grounds for assuming their distinctness, they may be understood as two aspects of a single factor (mind).

Integral to the idealist theory is the view that form or content is internal to awareness. The object-form apprehended in awareness is not caused by mind-independent object or states of affairs. It is only when object-forms are projected outside or externalized that there is experience interpretable as that of external to the mind. The individual cognitions in a mental series (*samtana*) are held to be intrinsically reflexive. That is to say, an object-cognition is simultaneously and in virtue of the same act self-cognized, just as a lamp illuminates itself while illuminating an object. The tenet of the reflexivity of consciousness is central to the idealist outlook in that it illustrates the fact that consciousness adopting a perspective upon itself may be aware of its own contents as if they were objects external to it.

Further reading

Anacker, S. (1984) *Seven Works of Vasubandhu, the Buddhist Psychological Doctor,* Delhi: Motilal Ba-narsidass.

de la Vallée Poussin, L. (ed. and trans.) (1923–31) *L'abhidharmakosha de Vasubandhu,* 6 vols, Paris and Louvain: Institut Belge des Hautes Etudes Chinois.

Lamotte, E. (trans.) (1936) 'Le Traité de l'acte de Vasubandhu: karmasiddhiprakarana', *Mélanges chinois et Bouddhiques* 4: 151–288; English transla-

tion by L. Pruden, Berkeley, CA: Asian Humanities Press, 1988

Levi, S. (1925) *Vijnaptimatratasiddhi: deux traités de
Vasubandhu*, Paris: Bibliotheques des Hautes
Etudes.

—— (1932) *Un système de philosophie bouddhique:
Matériaux pour l'etude du system Vijnaptimatra*, Paris:
Bibliothèque de l'Ecole des Hautes Etudes.

CHRIS BARTLEY

Veda

In the latter half of the second millennium BCE,
pastoralist nomads calling themselves Aryans,
representing the eastern branch of the Indo-
Iranians whose original homeland appears to have
been the area north of the Caucasus between the
Black and Caspian Seas, began migrating to and
settling in Northern India from the region of
Central Asia around the Aral Sea. They brought
with them a quadripartite hierarchical social
structure, an Old Indo-Aryan language called
Vedic Sanskrit and a religion focusing on sacrificial
rituals. The latter is expressed in the *Rig, Sama, Yajur*
and *Atharva* Vedas, whose sound units came to be
regarded by mainstream orthodox Hindus as an
authorless (*apaurusheya*), timeless and infallible
repository of all knowledge. They were held to
have been received and promulgated by seven
primordial 'seers' (*rishi*).

The Veda achieved its present form thanks to
Vyasa. The tradition was orally preserved by
priestly Brahmin families specializing in particular
aspects of the corpus. The basic component of each
of the four Vedas is its collection (*samhita*) of verses
(*mantra*), evocative of the divinities in whose natures
they participate, used in the rituals called 'Vedic'
and 'Shrauta'. Attached to each *samhita* are texts
called *brahmanas*, which prescribe, describe and
elucidate the purposes of the sacrificial rituals.
They posit correspondences (*bandhu*) between
aspects of the rites and features of the macrocosm,
the social structure and the human body. These
correspondences are not accidental analogies. It
was believed that ritual performance orders,
sustains and perpetuates the universe, creating
new time and ensuring the regular succession of the

seasons. The operation of most rituals is regarded
as automatic and mechanical. If correctly performed, they could not fail to produce their
appropriate results. The priests and patron are
simply aspects of a ritual complex, although the
intention (*kratu*) with which the ritual is performed
is of determinative significance. Crucially, the
success of the rituals came to be understood as
independent of the favour of capricious deities.
Indeed, the latter came to be understood not as
independent, objective existences but as identical
with their names which are mentioned in the
course of the rites.

Cognate with the *brahmanas* are the *aranyakas*
(forest books) which speculate about the 'inner'
meaning of the rituals and are closely associated
with the **Upanishads**, which are in turn themselves classified as belonging to the Vedic corpus.
Texts called *Shrauta-Sutras* dealing with large-scale
public rituals and others (*Grihya-Sutras*) concerned
with domestic (*grihya*) rituals are sometimes included in this literary taxonomy despite their
acknowledged human composition.

The *Rig Veda* consists of ten books of 1,028
hymns addressed to a pantheon including Indra,
Varuna, Surya the sun, Ushas the dawn, Agni the
fire and Rudra the storm. It was compiled in a pre-
classical form of Sanskrit during the two or three
centuries after 1200 BCE. Each of the ten books was
composed by sages belonging to different families.
The *Sama Veda* is a collection of melodies derived
from the *Rig Veda* with instructions on their
recitation (*gana*). The *Yajur Veda*, of which there
are two major recensions called 'Black' and
'White', comprises brief prose and verse formulae
recited by an officiating priest. The for the most
part later *Atharva Veda* includes verses and magical
spells and is only tangentially related to the other
three. The classical *Upanishads* were probably
compiled between the seventh and third centuries
BCE. All these texts are classified as **shruti**, or
'what has been heard', as opposed to *smriti* which is
recognized as arising from human traditions.

There were schools (*shakha*) of Brahmins specializing in particular aspects of the rituals. The social
identity of a Brahmin is determined by his
affiliation to one of these schools. They maintained
the continuity and integrity of the ritual traditions
through disciplined recitation of the Vedas, even

when the original meanings of the words had been forgotten.

The original religious practice of the Aryans centred upon the making of offerings into a specially consecrated fire by which the gods (*devas*) were propitiated, benefits such as sons, cattle and longevity received from them and the social status, power or purity of the wealthy patron (*yajamana*) augmented. It is he who has the priests perform the sacrifice on his behalf. Prior to the sacrifice he undergoes a ceremonial consecration (*diksha*) which sets him apart from other people for the duration of the rite. It is essential that the *yajamana* be a married man. These rituals were not tied to particular sacred locations. All that was required were priests cognizant of the ritual formulae and acts, temporary constructs such as fire-altars made from bricks as well as animal victims, vegetables, milk and ghee offered into the fire. These immolated substances would be transported through the fire to the world of the gods that had been invoked. Fire was a pivotal symbol in the world-view of the ritualists, representing the link between the human and divine spheres. It later came to be seen as a metaphor for the repetitive nature of transmigratory existence (**samsara**). As such, it featured in the early Buddhists' symbolic articulations of their analysis of mundane life as unsatisfactory (*duhkha*) and transient process (*aniccha*), ablaze with cravings, aversion and delusion. **Nirvana**, the end of rebirth, is the extinction of just those fires.

The major public rites were termed *shrauta*. The *shrauta* observances were largely focused on the fire god Agni and the plant god Soma, to whom vegetable offerings were made. In consonance with the view that the rituals do not just mark or measure time but create it anew, rites were performed at the junctions of the days and seasons, and at the new and full moons. It should be mentioned that although provision is made for human sacrifice (*purusha-medha*) this was purely symbolic and did not involve harm to anyone.

Although the basic principle behind the operation of the ritual was simple and involved making offerings into the fire which will be transported to the world of the gods, the elaborated rituals acquired considerable complexity. For example, in the offering of the *soma* plant, whose identity is

mysterious, four priests were needed, each being an expert in one of the four Vedic Samhitas. The chief priest (*hotar*) would recite verses from the *Rig Veda* while the Udgatar priest would chant verses (*stotra*) set to the melodies of the *Sama Veda*. The Adhvaryu priest would chant verses from the *Yajur Veda* and perform many of the ritual actions including the preparation of the sacrificial ground, building the fire pits, killing the sacrificial victim and throwing the offerings onto the fire. Another priest associated with the *Atharva Veda*, called the Brahman, would sit in silence and be alert to and correct errors of omission and commission.

There were three fires: the householder's fire (*garhapatya*) in the west, the fire of oblation (*ahavaniya*) in the east and a southern fire (*dakshina-agni*). The altar (*vedi*) was a shallow pit, narrow in the centre and strewn with grass. For more elaborate rites, it was a brick structure between the eastern and western fires. The construction, from 2,000 bricks, of this fire altar in the *agnichayana* ceremony lasted several days and involved the co-operation of many people. Overall, the expensive major public rituals can be seen as conducive to social cohesion.

There are seven types of sacrifice involving the *soma* plant. The most important is called the *Agnistoma*, performed in spring during a single day. The *soma* plants are pressed and the juices offered to the gods in the fire and consumed by the priests. The identity of the plant is unknown. It has been supposed to have hallucinogenic properties, and there have been speculations that it was the mushroom *amanita muscaria*, but John Brough (1971, 1973) demonstrated the unlikelihood of this.

In addition to the *shrauta* rituals there were also domestic (*grihya*) rites (*yajna*) and various rites of passage. Brahmins perform the obligatory (*nitya*) daily domestic rites, such as the *agnihotra* fire sacrifice, for themselves and on behalf of members of the other twice-born castes (Kshatriyas and Vaishyas). Texts called *Grihya-Sutras* contain instructions on maintaining the domestic fire which must be kept alight at all times in Brahmin households in addition to rules about ritual purity and the occasional (*naimittika*) rites of passage: birth, initiation into caste, marriage and death.

The Vedic universe is populated with both beneficent and potentially hostile supernatural beings ranging from personifications of natural forces, celestial phenomena and representatives of cosmic and social order to spirits immanent in rivers and trees. There is no supreme deity.

Some Rig Vedic hymns contain speculations of a cosmological and metaphysical nature. *Rig Veda* 10.129 asks what there was before existence (*sat*) and non-existence (*asat*) prior to death and immortality, light and dark. The hymn conveys a sense of genuine philosophical perplexity and awe: 'Whence this creation has arisen – perhaps it formed itself, or perhaps it did not – the one who looks down on it, in the highest heaven, only he knows – or perhaps he does not know' (O'Flaherty 1981). Such inquiries come to fruition in the *Upanishads*.

The *Purusha-Sukta* (Hymn to the Cosmic Man; *Rig Veda* 10.90) expresses a homology between the human body, the universe and society. It describes the creation of the world by the gods who sacrifice and dismember a primeval man from whose parts the cosmos, the quadripartite social order and also the Vedas are formed. The Brahmins, who utter the rituals and recite the Vedas, emerged from his mouth; the rulers and warriors (*rajanya*, *kshatriya*), symbolizing society's strength, came from his arms; the agriculturalists (*vaishya*), society's support, came from his thighs and the peasants (*shudra*), on whom society stands, from his feet. The human hierarchical social structure is thus legitimated by being defined as a microcosmic manifestation of cosmic order.

It is a tenet of mainstream Brahminical orthodoxy that the Vedas are the source of our knowledge about social and religious duty in accordance with the natural universal order (**dharma**). The **Purva Mimamsa** theorists of ritual say that *dharma* is that which is indicated by Vedic ritual predictions (*vidhi*). Indeed, the infallible and unfalsifiable Vedas are our only means of knowledge (**pramana**) for whatever lies beyond the bounds of sense such as the categorical obligation to sacrifice and the acquisition of types of merit from optional, fructiferous rituals.

In addition to the ritual *sutras* and **Dharma-Shastras**, there are texts defined as ancillary to the Vedas *strictu sensu* whose subjects are other facets of *dharma*. These are called Vedangas and are instructional treatises (*shastra*) on the correct pronunciation of Vedic texts (*shiksha*); the correct performance of the ritual (*kalpa*); Sanskrit grammar (*vyakarana*); Sanskrit etymology (**nirukta**); Sanskrit prosody (*chandas*); and astrology (*jyotisha*).

Further reading

Biardeau, M. and Malamoud, C. (1976) *Le Sacrifice dans l'Inde ancienne*, Paris: Presses Universitaires de France.

Brough, J. (1971) 'Soma and Amanita Muscaria', *Bulletin of the School of Oriental and African Studies* 34(2): 331–62; reprinted in M. Hara and J. Wright (eds), *J. Brough: Collected Papers*, London: School of Oriental and African Studies, 1996.

—— (1973) 'Problems of the "Soma-mushroom" Theory', *Indologica Taurinensia* I: 21–32; reprinted in M. Hara and J. Wright (eds), *J. Brough: Collected Papers*, London: School of Oriental and African Studies, 1996.

Flood, G. (1996) *An Introduction to Hinduism*, Cambridge: Cambridge University Press.

Geldner, K. (1951) *Der Rigveda: Aus dem Sanskrit ins Deutsche übersetzt und mit einem laufenden Kommentar versehen*, 3 vols, Harvard Oriental Series, Cambridge, MA: Harvard University Press.

Gonda, J. (1975) *Vedic Literature*, Wiesbaden: Otto Harrassowitz.

—— (1977) *The Ritual Sutras*, Wiesbaden: Otto Harrassowitz.

Heesterman, J. (1985) *The Inner Conflict of Tradition: An Essay in Indian Ritual, Kingship and Society*, Chicago: University of Chicago Press.

—— (1993) *The Broken World of Sacrifice: Essays in Ancient Indian Ritual*, Chicago: University of Chicago Press.

Keith, A. (1925) *The Religion and Philosophy of the Veda and Upanishads*, Cambridge, MA: Harvard University Press.

Muller, M. and Oldenberg, H. (1973) *Vedic Hymns*, 2 vols, Sacred Books of the East 32 and 46, Delhi: Motilal Banarsidass.

O'Flaherty, W. (1981) *The Rig Veda*, Harmondsworth: Penguin.

Wasson, R. (1968) *Soma, the Divine Mushroom of Immortality*, New York: Harcourt, Brace.

Witzel, M. (1987) 'On Localisation of Vedic Texts and Schools', in G.Pollet (ed.), *India and the Ancient*

World: History, Trade and Culture before A.D.650, Leuven: Orientalia Lovaniensia Analecta.

CHRIS BARTLEY

Vedanta

Vedanta (literally, 'end of the Veda', meaning the **Upanishads**) or Uttara Mimamsa is the systematic interpretation of the *Upanishads* either by direct commentary upon them or by elucidation of the aphoristic summaries of their contents in the **Brahma-Sutras** of Badarayana (*c.*200 CE) The **Bhagavad Gita** is also a key authority. The theological context of Vedanta is basically Vaishnava. There are three major schools: **Advaita** (Non-dualism), **Vishishtadvaita** (Integral Unity of Complex Reality) and **Dvaita** (Dualism). What they have in common is a recognition of non-originated, authorless, transpersonal scripture (**shruti**) as the sole means of knowledge (**pramana**) for that which transcends the domains of sensory perception and inference. Vedantins hold that it is the *Upanishads* (the knowledge portion or *jnana-kanda* of the Veda) which provide information about the ultimate reality (Brahman), the soul (**atman**) and the relation between the two, the origin of the universe from *Brahman*, retributive causality (**karma**), transmigration (**samsara**) and the means to and nature of ultimate liberation from rebirth (**moksha**). Vedantins seek a systematic interpretation of the *Upanishads* in accordance with the principles of their harmony of import and predominantly literal meaning.

Whereas the predominantly atheistic ritual theorists (Purva Mimamsakas) were concerned with and upheld the primary significance of injunctive Vedic *karma-kanda* texts (*vidhi*) bearing on ritual actions, Vedantins focus upon the category of fact-asserting or descriptive texts (*arthavada*) referring to already existent entities or states of affairs rather than 'things to be done' (*karya*) whose paramount authority they are concerned to defend against their ritualist rivals. Both schools developed sophisticated techniques of textual exegesis and engaged in lengthy controversies frequently centring upon the salvific efficacy of prescribed ritual actions (in contradistinction to

knowledge (*jnana*), devotion (*bhakti*) and divine grace) and the intrinsic meaningfulness of non-injunctive statements.

Further reading

Hiriyanna, M. (1993) *Outlines of Indian Philosophy*, Delhi: Motilal Banarsidass.

Lipner, J. (1986) *The Face of Truth: A Study of Meaning and Metaphysics in the Vedantic Theology of Ramanuja*, Albany, NY: State University of New York Press.

Lott, E. (1980) *Vedantic Approaches to God*, London: Macmillan.

CHRIS BARTLEY

Vimalakirti

Vimalakirti is the hero of the *Vimalakirti Sutra*. The way of the householder **bodhisattva**, as exemplified in this *sutra*, and his teaching of the non-dual **dharma** by staying silent were both of interest to followers of **Neo-Daoism**. Chinese Buddhist **hermeneutics** sometimes placed the non-dual between the negative **emptiness** of the Wisdom Sutras and the One Vehicle doctrine of the *Lotus Sutra*.

Further reading

Lu K'uan Yu (Charles Luk) (trans.) (1972) *The Vimalakirti nirdesa sutra*, Berkeley, CA: Shambala.

WHALEN LAI

Vishishtadvaita

Vishishtadvaita, 'Integral Unity of Complex Reality', is a system of Vedantic theological philosophy (see **Vedanta**), intimately associated with the South Indian Shri Vaishnava cult. Its foremost representative is the systematizer **Ramanuja** (*fl.* 1100) who was himself substantially influenced by the work of **Yamuna** (966–1038). The term 'Vishishtadvaita' is interpreted in the tradition as meaning 'non-duality of a differentiated reality'; that is, reality is a single, structured organic whole, ultimately intelligible while being internally complex.

Vedanta is the systematic exegesis of the 'knowledge portions' (*jnana-kanda*) of the Vedic scriptures usually known as the **Upanishads**, the **Brahma-Sutras** and the **Bhagavad Gita**. Shri Vaishnava teachers such as Nathamuni (900–50), Yamuna and Ramanuja are notable for integrating aspects of the popular emotional *bhakti* or theistic devotion expressed in the hymns of Tamil Alvars whose object is a compassionate personal deity; the non-Vedic Pancharatra temple ritual and theology which stresses divine immanence in the universe and in the individual selves with mainstream classical Vedantic or Upanishadic elements. The school's principal philosopher after Ramanuja is Vedantadeshika or Venkatanatha, who flourished in the thirteenth century.

According to this school, the universe is the real self-differentiation of the Supreme Person. Its metaphysic is organized in three basic categories of a personal deity; individual agentive selves whose essential property is reflexive consciousness (*chit*) and material entities (*achit*). The latter two depend upon the first and material bodies depend upon the selves which ensoul them. Entities falling into the three categories are essentially distinct. *Brihadaranyaka Upanishad* 3.7.3f. refers to a self who is the inner self and inner controller of individual selves. This is the crucial scriptural support for the school's soul-body doctrine (*sharira-shariri-bhava*). The Supreme Self is held to be related to the individual selves (*jiva*) in a manner analogous to that in which they are related to their material bodies. A 'body' receives a specialized definition as a dependent and essentially distinct entity whose entire *raison d'être* consists in subserving the purposes of a self which controls it. The key elements here are essential dependence, intimate connection and distinctness. Individual selves and material things constitute the body of God in the senses that they are dependent upon God and exist to express his non-purposive actuality. But just as the essential distinction between the individual selves and their bodies means that they are unimpaired by physical imperfections, likewise the difference between God and his body, the world, exempts him from the vicissitudes of finiteness. The relation is also expressed as that between a substrate (*adhara*) and attribute (*adheya*), controller or moral guide and thing guided and between principal (*sheshi*) and accessory or servant (*shesha*).

If the process of cosmic emanation is regarded as a transformation of the proper form or essential nature of the Absolute, problems will obviously arise, especially if the ontic link between God and creation is a particularly strong one. For this reason, the school insists that the real transformation occurs in the sphere of Brahman's body which has been defined as essentially distinct while essentially dependent on it. Thus the flawless integrity of the ultimate principle is protected.

At some point in the thirteenth century, the Shri Vaishnava tradition split into two schools, effectively undermining the synthesis achieved by Yamuna and Ramanuja. The northern Vatakalai school emphasized the socially exclusive high Brahminical Sanskritic culture and specified the *yoga* of devotion (*bhakti*) towards the temple icon (*archa-avatara*) as the soteriological path. The southern Tenkalai school emphasized the ecstatic *bhakti* expressed in the popular Tamil scriptures, and insisted on total self-surrender (*prapatti*) to Lord Vishnu as the means for prompting unmerited divine grace (*sharanagati*). The two outlooks were designated the 'monkey' and the 'cat' schools. According to the Vatakalai, salvation is achieved through a combination of human effort and divine grace, the baby monkey clinging to its receptive mother. The Tenkalai claimed that grace alone is the necessary and sufficient cause of salvation, the mother cat picking up her young without any effort on their part.

Further reading

Bartley, C. (2000) *Realism and Religion: A Study in the Theology of Ramanuja*, Richmond: Curzon.

Carman, J. (1974) *The Theology of Ramanuja*, New Haven, CN and London: Yale University Press.

Dasgupta, S. (1940) *A History of Indian Philosophy*, vol. 3, Cambridge: Cambridge University Press.

Lacombe, O. (1937) *L'Absolu selon le Vedanta*, Paris: Librairie Orientaliste Paul Geuthner.

—— (1938) *La Doctrine morale et metaphysique de Ramanuja*, Paris: Adrien Maisonneuve.

Lipner, J. (1986) *The Face of Truth: A Study of Meaning*

and Metaphysics in the Vedantic Theology of Ramanuja, Albany, NY: State University of New York Press.

Lott, E. (1976) God and the Universe in the Vedantic Theology of Ramanuja, Madras: Ramanuja Research Institute.

Thibaut, G. (1904) Vedanta-Sutras with Ramanuja's Commentary, Oxford: Oxford University Press.

van Buitenen, J. (1953) Ramanuja on the Bhagavad Gita, The Hague: Smits.

—— (ed. and trans.) (1956) Ramanuja's Vedarthasamgraha, 2 vols, Poona: Deccan College Postgraduate and Research Institute.

CHRIS BARTLEY

Vivekananda

b. 1863; d. 1902

Philosopher

The most significant disciple of the mystic **Ramakrishna**, Vivekananda (Narendra Nath Datta) received a Western style education imbued with post-Enlightenment scientific rationalism at Presidency College and Scottish Churches College, Calcutta. He also acquired a knowledge of Sanskrit. As a young man, Vivekananda was associated with the **Brahmo Samaj**. After his encounter with Ramakrishna, whom he came to regard as a quasi-divine figure, he renounced normal social life and travelled throughout India for a period of seven years, in the course of which he not only realized for himself an experience of unity with the Absolute beyond differentiation, but was also exposed to the humiliating poverty endured by most of his fellow-countrymen. He internalized Ramakrishna's visionary message of the unity of all religions and the solidarity of humanity as incarnations of an impersonal divinity. In Vivekananda's thought, there is a confluence of enlightened, modern Western notions of social welfare and universal education: 'The chief cause of India's ruin has been the monopolising of the whole education and intelligence of the land . . .

among a handful of men. If we are to rise again we shall have to do it in the same way [as the West], i.e. by spreading education among the masses'. There is a sense of national identity as the necessary context of social progress and the indigenous Indian tradition of spiritual monism (**Advaita Vedanta**).

At the World Parliament of Religions held in Chicago in 1893, Vivekananda influentially preached the unity of religions and tolerance of diversity in opposition to the work of Christian missionary attempts to convert Indians to their faith. Against the traditional Christian tenet that there is no salvation outside the Church, he propounded a neo-Advaitic concept of Hinduism as essentially unitary and inclusivist in its recognition of all religions as approximate and partial expressions of a single truth.

His visit to America, which lasted until 1896 (with intermissions in England and the rest of Europe), was partially motivated by his concern to constitute a pan-Indian national identity. He wrote that, 'We must see how the engine of society works in other countries, and keep free and open communication with what is going on in the minds of other nations, if we really want to be a nation again'. He thought that the unifying factor in the case of India would have to be religion: specifically a form of Advaita Vedanta which identified the multitudinous diverse forms of religious belief and practice as relatively valid approaches to the supreme truth. His convictions acquired concrete and institutional expression in 1896 with the establishment of the Ramakrishna Mission, a philanthropic organization which promotes education and social welfare.

Further reading

Halbfass, W. (ed.) (1995) Philology and Confrontation: Paul Hacker on Traditional and Modern Vedanta, Albany, NY: State University of New York Press.

CHRIS BARTLEY

W

WANDERING GHOSTS *see* afterlife in Chinese thought

Wang Chong

b. 27 CE; d. 100 CE

Philosopher

Wang Chong (Wang Ch'ung) was a rationalist thinker from the Later Han period, rediscovered by Marxist scholars as China's foremost materialist. Reacting to the excesses of *yin–yang* Confucianism that had devolved into competing political prophesies, auspices, omenology and popular supernaturalism, Wang subjects them to a sceptical critique. He turned **Heaven** back into impersonal nature, **Confucius** back to being a wise counsel, fortunes and misfortunes to just chance and accident, and offered a reasoned treatise to prove the non-existence of ghosts.

Though often presented as an atheist thesis, Wang was actually open to the existence of some universal spirit and the treatise only addresses ghosts, not gods. Ghosts are the human dead, but Wang disputed the possibility of the human dead turning into and coming back as ghosts. Why? Because to die means to be without life; a 'live' ghost is an oxymoron. We do not expect an insentient thing like a tree to die and become a ghost, and if all men turn into ghosts at death, there being so many generations before our time, there would be more ghosts than men in the world now. Furthermore, dead ashes cannot be rekindled. It is in the nature of life that it begins and ends with

an individuated consciousness; before and after that, he is part of the universal spirit.

Further reading

Forke, A. (trans.) (1907–11) *Wang Ch'ung's Lun-Hung*, London: Luzac.

WHALEN LAI

WANG YANGMING *see* enlightenment experience and religious biography

WAR *see* Taiping

Watsuji Tetsuro

b. 1889; d. 1960

Philosopher of ethics and culture

Watsuji was born in the village of Nibuno, which later became part of the city of Himeiji. In 1909, he entered the philosophical department of Tokyo University, where he became one of the students of Raphael von Koeber (1848–1923). He also joined a literary circle around Natsume Soseki (1867–1916), frequented by such talents as Abe Jiro (1883–1959) and Tanizaki Jun'ichiro (1886–1965). In 1913, he published *Nichie kenkyu*, a study on Nietzsche, and graduated with a thesis on Schopenhauer. Two years later, he brought out *Zēren Kierukegoru* (Søren Kierkegaard). However, his sympathetic view of Western philosophy, particularly the individualist and existentialist ideas of Nietzsche and Kierkegaard, soon gave way to a more critical assessment. His *Guzo saiko* (Resurrecting Idols), published in 1918, also documented a renewed interest in Eastern culture and arts. In 1925, Watsuji became assistant professor of ethics at Kyoto University. Two years later he was sent to Germany and also visited Italy and Greece. Back in Japan, he continued teaching in Kyoto until 1934; from then until 1949, he taught at Tokyo University.

Watsuji was well acquainted with both Western and Eastern forms of thought. Besides his early studies on Nietzsche, Schopenhauer and Kierkegaard, he also wrote *Genshi kiristokyo non bunkashiteki igi* (The Culturo-Historical Significance of Primitive Christianity), *Homerus hihan* (A Critique of Homer) and *Porisuteki ningen no rinrigaku* (The Ethics of the Man of the Polis), published in 1926, 1948 and 1946 respectively, which testify to his knowledge of traditional Western culture. Though the essays on Homer and the ethics of the polis were published after the Second World War, they are founded on studies that go back to the 1920s and 1930s. Watsuji was also thoroughly familiar with German philosophy, particularly Kant, Hegel, Herder, Dilthey, Husserl and Heidegger. As to Eastern culture, publications such as *Koji junrei* (A Pilgrimage to Old Buddhist Temples) (1919), *Nihon kodai bunka* (Ancient Japanese Culture) (1920), *Genshi bukkyo no jissen tetsugaku* (The Practical Philosophy of Primitive Buddhism) (1927), *Nihon seishin-shi kenkyu* (Studies in the History of the Japanese Spirit) (1926, 1934), *Sakoku Nihon no higeki* (Japan's Tragedy of National Seclusion) (1951) and *Nihon rinri shisoshi* (History of Japanese Ethical Thought) (1952) document his interests.

In his ethics, as it is best known from his works *Fudo* (A Climate) (1935) and *Rinrigaku* (Ethics) (1937–49), Watsuji criticized what he regarded as Western individualism, egoism, materialism and dualism (namely, a distinction between subject and object, man and nature), and extolled communalist and culturalist ideas. Watsuji utilized Buddhist and Confucian traditions to argue for his convictions, and also employed some of **Nishida** Kitaro's (1870–1945) key concepts. Further, he simply asserted a normative quality of concrete cultural tradition. Arguing from what he regarded as fundamental Buddhist positions, Watsuji empha-

sized that everything, man included, exists in dependence on other things, or beings, and that thus everything is originally without substance or self. In Buddhist terms, Watsuji held that everything is *ku* (empty) and *muga* (selfless). This implied the view that men are originally selfless parts of an all-comprising whole of interdependent human relations. Conceiving of this alleged original state of human existence as a value, Watsuji argued further that men ought to strive to realize their original and, so to say, true, state of being. Making use of one of Nishida's favourite terms, namely *mu* (nothingness), Watsuji tried to give his conviction an even deeper ontological foundation. According to such an approach, **nothingness**, **emptiness**, selflessness (or lack of substantiality) are not only the characteristics of ultimate, or true, reality but also the highest ethical goals. Men who achieve these goals are not only altruistic but also realize non-duality, overcoming all distinctions between themselves and the others, and objects in general.

Watsuji tried to support his position further by reference to Confucian role ethics and other examples of what he conceived of as Eastern communitarism. He even advanced communitarian interpretations of such Sino-Japanese notions as *ningen* (man, human being), claiming that they refer to the character of human beings in their 'betweenness', that is, basic mutual relatedness to each other. In *Fudo*, he further tried to demonstrate that *fudo* – the concrete natural and cultural environment of human beings – determines such ethical positions as anthropomorphism, that is, the dualism constituted by man's interest in dominating nature. For instance, Watsuji maintained that what he called European rationality and will to conquer nature resulted from the influence of 'Europe's meadow climate'. Finally, Watsuji argued on an empirical and commonsensical level, pointing out that men are actually both individuals and social beings.

It was probably his study of Heidegger's *Being and Time* that motivated Watsuji to distinguish sharply between what he conceived of as Western overemphasis on being, individualism and – a fortiori – self-assertion on the one hand, and Buddhist and Confucian doctrines of emptiness, selflessness and social roles on the other. Watsuji interpreted Heidegger's concept of time as more or less implying individualism, and introduced as an alternative, or at least necessary complement, a concept of space. By this concept, or metaphor, Watsuji wanted to indicate that embeddedness within a concrete extensional realm of relations is a necessary condition of human existence which hence, again, must be understood as a basically dependent existence.

In his explications of his concept of ultimate reality, reality as a whole, or the basis of reality, Watsuji developed a concept of the state as an actualization of this reality. In this context, he conceived of man as an integral element of the state, namely, a being that, in the first place, ought to fulfil his obligations toward the whole constituted by the state. Since this approach amounted to a justification of totalitarianism, Watsuji was severely criticized after the Second World War. This, in turn, led him to alter his views. As to the question of whether Watsuji's concept of ultimate reality as emptiness and nothingness is largely a religious notion, scholars disagree. But it seems quite clear that to him, in distinction to Nishida and members of the **Kyoto school**, metaphysical and soteriological problems were of less interest and importance than socio-political and cultural issues.

Watsuji interpreted *mu*, nothingness, as an indication of fundamental differences between Western and Eastern ways of thought, and on this he agreed with Nishida and the Kyoto school. Also, he shared with them the conviction that Western culture was more rational, and logocentric, while Eastern culture was more intuitive. With regard to this point, he went perhaps further than Nishida (who in some publications explicitly maintained the universal validity of formal logical laws) though not as far as, for example, Daisetz Suzuki (1870–1966). Watsuji even borrowed Nishida's concept of *mujun doitsu* (the identity of self-contradiction) to describe what he regarded as the fundamental features of human existence and reality in general. Nevertheless, in spite of such concurrences, Watsuji, when speaking of nothingness, emptiness or wholeness, seems to refer to a dynamic socio-political world of humans rather than to an independent, or even transcendent, realm or foundation of being. Every decisive judgement, however, is difficult for one also may suspect that – against his own

intention – Watsuji's notion of an authentic person, i.e. a person realizing his selflessness, logically implies an idea of an absolute and soteriologially relevant ground of existence.

Watsuji's ethics has remained an issue of controversy. While many scholars continue criticizing its dangerous ideological implications, some communitarians value him as a philosopher who succeeded in offering an alternative to what they – as Watsuji himself did – regard as Western egoism and materialism.

Further reading

Carter, R. and Yamamoto Seisaku (trans.) (1996) *Watsuji Tetsuro's Rinrigaku*, Albany, NY: State University of New York Press.

Watsuji Tetsuro (1961) *Fudo* (A Climate), trans. G. Bownas, Tokyo: Japanese Government printing Bureau.

GREGOR PAUL

well-field system

Idealized by **Mencius** as a policy of Sage rule, the 'well-field system' is where eight households would each farm their own private plots of land but together would farm a ninth public plot, the produce of which would go to the lord. This is a variant of the Magic Square, the central square being the 'public' plot (see **magic squares**). (The word 'public' is the word for 'lord'; the king in theory owns all land.) The Chinese pictogram for 'well' – two parallel vertical and horizontal lines crossing – yields the ninefold division. Whether there was ever such a system, the proposal attests to a situation in the Warring States period where there was still land open to be claimed and where virtuous rulers by their generosity could still attract willing and mobile peasants to live and farm under them. If true, it means that the peasants were not serfs and were not tied to the land, as the Marxists held.

WHALEN LAI

Western learning in Japan

With the establishment of contact with Western powers (Portugal, Spain, Britain and Holland) in the sixteenth century, Japan made its first acquaintance with Western technology, and Western firearms, clocks and navigation aids were adopted, copied and even refined by Japanese craftsmen. The Japanese also showed a great interest in Western medicine (especially surgery) and science. Will Adams (1564–1620), for example, who had arrived in Japan on the Dutch vessel *De Liefde* in 1600, was retained by Shogun Tokugawa Ieyasu as his adviser not only on foreign politics and diplomacy but also on astronomy, cartography and shipbuilding.

During the first decades of the seventeenth century, however, contacts with the West were increasingly limited by law, until by 1639 only the Dutch were allowed to trade with Japan. This trade took place under strict shogunal supervision, from 1641 at a specially constructed trading post on Dejima, a tiny manmade islet in the harbour of Nagasaki. For more than two centuries, Dejima served as Japan's only gateway to the West. From this time onwards the study of things Western, which had before been known as 'Learning of the Southern Barbarians' (*nanbangaku*), came to be called 'Dutch Learning' (*rangaku*). Only in the mid-nineteenth century, when Japanese scholars once more gained access to materials in other Western languages, did the term 'Western Learning' (*yogaku*) come into common use.

By its very nature, Western Learning covered a wide range of topics. The most important of these were medicine, astronomy, geography, language and, especially towards the end of the Edo period (1600–1868), military science (notably ballistics). Less important subjects studied by the Japanese were botany, mathematics, physics, chemistry and Western law and art (especially Western-style painting). Rather than list the achievements of scholars of Western Learning in introducing knowledge of these various fields to Japan, it is worth examining some aspects of the impact Western Learning had on Japanese philosophy and intellectual history.

Perhaps the most valued and influential branch of Western Learning was the study of Western medicine. From an early date, the Dutch East India Company was aware of the high regard the Japanese had for Western medicine, and took special care to select their best physicians for service on Dejima. Some of these physicians accompanied the head of the trading post on his annual visits to Edo and taught Dutch medicine to shogunal doctors. They also shared their knowledge with the Japanese Nagasaki interpreters, who compiled works on Western surgical techniques on the basis of their notes. The first such works appeared around 1700. Translations of Dutch medical works became more frequent and accurate during the second half of the eighteenth century. The publication of *Kaitai shinsho* (A New Book of Anatomy) by Sugita Genpaku (1733–1817) and Maeno Ryotaku (1723–1803) in 1774 is widely regarded as a milestone in this process, and rightly so: it seems that while at the time of this book's publication only a handful of physicians had an interest of Western medicine, Western anatomical knowledge had become familiar to most by 1800.

The increased interest in Western medicine both led to and was spurred on by the adoption of Western techniques such as the dissection of corpses by Japanese physicians of Chinese medicine. At the time, Japanese medicine was dominated by two schools: the 'New School' (Gosei-ha, or Rishu-ha) and the 'Old School' (Koho-ha). The first theorized about the causes of illness in terms of *yin* and *yang* and the Five Phases of matter (wood, fire, earth, metal and water), but failed to establish a solid link between such theories and medical practice. Followers of the Old School, which was directly inspired by the Confucian school of Ancient Learning, rejected what they called the New School's 'useless sophistry' and advocated complete reliance on medical texts compiled by the sages of ancient China (Han dynasty texts such as the *Shanghanlun*), and on trial and error. It was a physician of this Old School, Yamawaki Toyo (1704–62), who in 1754 gained permission to perform the first anatomical dissection, and as a result disproved the ancient Chinese theory that the body contains 'five organs and six viscera'. Sugita Genpaku attended a dissection in Edo in 1771, and was so impressed by the accuracy of his Western anatomical tables that he decided to translate what was to become the *Kaitai shinsho*.

The translators of Dutch medical works, who were (mostly Old School) physicians themselves, criticized both the New and the Old Schools of Chinese medicine. A good example is Genpaku's student Otsuki Gentaku (1757–1827), who criticized the New School for producing good scholars but bad doctors, and the Old School for trying to link illnesses with treatments without a proper understanding of the functioning of the body. Gentaku called for a strictly empirical approach, which stood in contrast to the traditional theoretical and philological methods. On the one hand, this constituted a break with the methodologies of both Neo-Confucianism and Ancient Studies, which dominated all intellectual endeavour at the time; on the other hand, Gentaku described the empirical method with the term *kyuri*, 'investigating principle [as it manifests itself in the world]'. This Confucian term indicates how, by means of gaining insight in the workings of the moral 'principle' that governs both the natural world and the world of man, all human beings can improve themselves and ultimately become sages. As this choice of terminology indicates, scholars such as Gentaku did not regard their study of Western science as in any way incompatible with a Confucian world view, which saw the world as built on moral principles. While *yin* and *yang* and the **Five Elements** were sidelined very early on, *li* and *qi* (a term for energy or matter, governed by *li* or 'principle') remained central concepts in Japanese Western Learning.

Another aspect of Western Studies that would seem to indicate that even this form of scholarship remained Confucian in nature was the fact that in spite of some attempts at independent empirical research, scholars largely confined themselves to the translation of Dutch-language works. Gentaku, again, was of great importance in lifting the knowledge of the Dutch language to a new level. He compiled and published a Dutch grammar and vocabulary list (*Rangaku kaitei* (A Ladder to Dutch Learning), completed in 1783 and printed in 1788), and in 1786 founded the first academy specializing in the teaching of Dutch, the Shirando in Edo. The first Dutch-Japanese dictionary (*Haruma wage* (Halma Explained in Japanese) (1796), based on François Halma's *Woordenboek der Nederduitsche en Fransche Talen*) was compiled by one of Gentaku's

students, Inamura Sanpaku (1758–1811). Notable here, though, is that while scholars of Ancient Studies and National Studies (see **Kokugaku**) regarded ancient Chinese, or ancient Japanese, as receptacles of profound wisdom in themselves, and sought self-improvement through mastering these languages, Dutch was never seen as more than a morally indifferent code that needed to be cracked in order to access the information conveyed in the language.

Western knowledge of geography also had an impact on the Japanese view of the world and Japan's position in it. Western maps, which became known to the Japanese as early as the sixteenth century, dealt a blow both to the Confucian world view which placed China at the centre of the world, and also to the Buddhist conception of the world as centring on a giant mythical mountain known in Japanese as Mount Sumi (in Sanskrit, Sumeru). Knowledge of such maps, and of Western customs, led to a relativization of Chinese culture. To scholars of Western learning, it seemed obvious that 'the Way is not something established by the sages of China; it is the universal Way of Heaven and Earth' (as Sugita Genpaku put it), and that this Way is present in different countries in the form of different sets of customs. Some scholars of Western Learning even held that what they saw as the superior accomplishments of Western culture were rooted in a superior morality, grounded first of all in a superior practice of 'investigating principle'. Needless to say, this invited vigorous criticism from Confucians and Kokugaku scholars alike.

During the early nineteenth century, Western powers such as Russia and Britain increasingly came to be perceived as a threat to Japanese independence. This led, on the one hand, to an increased interest in Western knowledge on the part of both shogunal and domainal authorities, and to a growing suspicion of practitioners of Western Learning, who faced the accusation of being 'pro-Western'. On the one hand, institutes for the translation of Dutch books were set up by the shogunate (most importantly the Ransho yakukyoku (Bureau for the Translation of Dutch Books), set up in 1811, and the Yogakusho (Centre for Western Learning), founded in 1855 and in the following year renamed Bansho shirabesho (Centre for the Investigation of Barbarian Books), and at these places Western Learning progressed at a great pace. On the other hand, there were periodic bouts of repressive measures against Western Learning. After it was found that Philipp Franz von Siebold (1796–1866), a German physician in Dutch employment, had attempted to smuggle restricted information (such as maps) out of the country in 1828, some fifty of his Japanese students and contacts were arrested and punished. Another incident in 1839 ended in the exile of one scholar and the imprisonment of another, whose writings were thought to display pro-Western sympathies and anti-*bakufu* criticism. After both incidents, measures were taken to restrict access to Western books and translations thereof, and to limit the study of the West to only topics deemed of direct value to the Japanese government. However, such measures did no more than temporary and local damage to Western Learning as a whole. The 1839 incident seems to have had little effect on the fortunes of, for example, the Osaka scholar Ogata Koan (1810–63), who founded an academy of Western studies (mainly medicine and military studies) in 1838 and in the course of the 1840s and 1850s went on to train more than 600 students, many with positions in shogunal and domainal authorities.

After the shogunate was forced to open the country to foreign trade in 1854, and especially in the wake of the Opium Wars in China (1840–2 and 1856–60), the acquisition of Western military science came to be regarded as a matter of great urgency, and in 1855 the shogunate founded a Naval Institute (Kaigun denshujo) where Dutch navy officers instructed students in naval techniques. Two years later, a Medical Institute (Igaku denshujo) was set up, where Dutch doctors trained Japanese physicians, and after the founding of a hospital in 1861 also treated Japanese patients. Scholars of Western Studies were employed by many domains, and the subject became part of the curriculum at educational institutions for retainers. In 1862 the first two Japanese students (both staff of the Centre for the Investigation of Barbarian Books) were sent abroad to study in the Netherlands. After the opening of ports for trade, English, German and French also came to be studied, and finally, foreigner specialists and technicians were

hired in increasing numbers to work and teach in Japan.

During the last decades of the Edo period, Western Learning functioned in an environment that was torn between extreme anti-foreignism on the one hand, and an urgent need for modernization on the basis of Western Learning on the other. This period saw an increasing understanding not only of Western science, but also of Western society and culture. Awe for Western achievements was offset by a staunch resolve to stand up to the West and secure the independence of the Japanese empire. Many political thinkers were fascinated by Western institutions such as established Christianity, and in the light of their new knowledge of the West saw Japan's own cultural institutions in a different and often unflattering light. The result was a push for 'modernization' of Japan's own institutions, with the aim of rendering them equally powerful as their Western counterparts. These institutions, the imperial house and its Shinto rituals, were singled out as of particular importance. Many argued that teachings about the sacredness of the imperial lineage, backed up by Neo-Confucian ethics such as loyalty and filial piety, should be instilled in the Japanese people to prevent the Christianization of the populace, which would ultimately lead to colonization (see **Confucianism in Japan**). This led to a widely shared consensus *vis-à-vis* Western Learning that stressed that while it was essential to import Western techniques, this should not lead Japanese subjects away from Japanese ethics. In this indirect manner, Western Learning thus played some part in bringing about the restoration of imperial rule in 1867–8. It certainly made a major contribution to the successful modernization and industrialization of the Japanese state after the Meiji Restoration of 1868, by supplying Japan with a long tradition of adopting and adapting Western ideas and techniques.

Further reading

Keene, D. (1969) *The Japanese Discovery of Europe, 1720–1830*, Palo Alto, CA: Stanford University Press.

Krieger, C. (1940) *The Infiltration of European*

Civilization into Japan during the 18th Century, Leiden: E.J. Brill.

Numato, J. (1992) *Western Learning*, Tokyo: Japan-Netherlands Institute.

MARK TEEUWEN

Wonhyo

b. 617; d. 686

Buddhist philosopher

Wonhyo is often regarded as the outstanding philosopher in Korean Buddhist history. He had a vast knowledge of both Mahayana and **Hinayana** Buddhist philosophies and scriptures, and wrote many volumes of books. The ideas of One Mind and the harmonization of disputes were central to his philosophy.

According to Wonhyo, One Mind is the basis of all truth, all beings, and all things. Nothing in the phenomenal world can be conceived without One Mind. All the phenomena of the universe can be understood and explained by One Mind. One Mind transcends all the relative discriminations. It transcends all the dualities of eternity and time, existence and non-existence, and form and formlessness. It is not an object and cannot be conceived of as an object.

One Mind is the foundation of Wonhyo's philosophy. It is non-discriminatory and non-dualistic. All things are originally equal from the point of view of One Mind. In the present world all things appear in various different forms and shapes, but they are one in ultimate nature. The cycle of birth and death (*samsara*) and Suchness (*tathata*) are not two, when viewed from the ultimate standpoint of One Mind. There is no distinction between *samsara* and *tathata*, nor distinction between the sacred and secular, but they are identical in One Mind. In One Mind many different ideas are not different from One Truth (*dharma*). This identification is possible, because One Mind encompasses dualities and discriminations. On the basis of this idea, Wonhyo practised his Buddhism for the salvation of all sentient beings.

This idea is essentially similar to the Mahayana Buddhist idea of *shunyata* (**emptiness**), in which there is no discrimination between yes and no, affirmation and negation, existence and non-existence. *Shunyata* is a non-discriminatory and non-dualistic state of mind, the absolute state of mind, the state of Enlightenment and Suchness.

Another important aspect of Wonhyo's thought is the idea of 'harmonization of disputes' (*hwajaeng*). He thought that the constant disputes among various thinkers because of different theories are based on attachment to their own views and interpretations of the Buddhist truth, and thus he tried to reconcile and harmonize the various theories and views. He believed that all the disputes are discriminatory and contrary to Buddha's teaching. The harmonization of disputes is the harmonization of theories as they are expressed in language. Therefore, it is important to understand language. Often disputes develop because of the misunderstanding of language. Wonhyo characterized the nature of language as follows. First, language and truth are interdependent; second, truth can be expressed by language, but language has limits, because not all truth can be fully expressed by language; therefore, we cannot attach absolute value to language.

According to Wonhyo, the method for the harmonization of disputes can be carried out only on the basis of such an understanding of language. There are three levels for the method of the harmonization of disputes. First, in order to be free from attachment, all the theories must be denied. Furthermore, one must not be attached even to the denial. The second level is explaining ideas as they are without affirming or denying. In other words, one must give sincere and truthful explanation of ideas and issues without bias or discrimination. Third, one needs to have a broad and comprehensive understanding of the content of the sacred texts.

The idea of the harmonization of disputes characterizes Wonhyo's thought. He recognized the value of various Buddhist theories and tried to bring harmony to them. There is a clear connection between the ideas of the harmonization of disputes and One Mind. The goal of the harmonization of disputes is to return to One Mind. When one has One Mind, the harmonization of disputes results.

Wonhyo's special emphasis on the above ideas is

his unique contribution to Korean and Asian Buddhism. It clearly belongs to Mahayana Buddhist tradition, where one can find similar ideas of non-duality and non-discrimination as the central ideas of Buddhism. The Buddha Mind, *tathata* (Suchness) and *shunyata* (emptiness) are all Mahayana ideas concerning non-duality and non-discrimination. Probably Wonhyo emphasized these ideas more clearly than anyone else in the Korean Buddhist tradition through his concepts of One Mind and the harmonization of disputes, and thereby made an outstanding contribution to Korean philosophy.

Further reading

Chung Byong-jo (1996) 'Korean Buddhism: Harmonizing the Contradictory', in *Korean Cultural Heritage, Vol. II: Thought and Religion*, ed. J. Kim, Seoul: Korea Foundation, 50ff.

Lee, P. (ed.) (1993) *Sourcebook of Korean Civilization*, vol. 1, New York: Columbia University Press, 135–58.

Park Sung Bae (1983) *Buddhist Faith and Sudden Enlightenment*, Albany, NY: State University of New York Press.

Rhi Ki-yong (1977) 'Wonhyo and His Thought', in *Korean and Asian Religious Tradition*, ed. C. Yu, Toronto: Korean and Related Studies Press, 197–207.

YONG-CHOON KIM

wuwei

The term *wuwei* (non-action) does not mean total inactivity, but rather no conscious, artificial, unnatural, humanly-imposed activity. It is letting nature take its course by either riding on the crest of change or giving it just a slight push (as in *judo*). The model is **Heaven**, which by not acting nonetheless gets everything done. Once that idea is broken down into smaller parts, one can come up with different levels of *wuwei*. It has a mystical use, and also an application to politics and in the martial arts. That is where one can witness degrees of human intervention at abating or maximizing the so-called natural flow of events. There too the art of doing something/nothing artifcial/natural is put to the test; and the original ideal can be totally abused.

More contextually subtle are a series of Chinese words describing 'incipient movement' mediating inactivity and activity in a number of different contexts: the daemonic spirit in cosmogony, the first stirring of life, the wondrously subtle that is 'truly empty but mysteriously there', the **trigger** point and mechanism used in Chan, the first thought or intent, the threshold between the pre-aroused and aroused, the penumbra between shadow and reality, and the hidden yet manifest.

Further reading

Wu Kuang-ming (1990) *The Butterfly as Companion: Meditations on the First Three Chapters of the Chuang Tzu*, Albany, NY: State University of New York Press.

WHALEN LAI

xenophobia

Culturocentric China, confident of her superiority, welcomes outsiders who emulate her way. Han China was condescending towards **barbarians** and treated the nomads who chose to live inside its borders as second-class citizens, but Tang China (whose rulers were not the purest of Chinese) was cosmopolitan enough to make foreigners and all kinds of foreign religions welcome. Han Yu, who protested at the worship of the barbaric Buddhist relic, aired anti-foreign sentiments not in keeping with the time. The Song dynasty Neo-Confucians (see **Neo-Confucianism, concepts**) would take pride in 'this culture of ours', so much so as to reject everything foreign. The state, by prizing the literati over the military, weakened its own defensive capability; China fell to the Mongols after protracted warfare with two other barbaric enemies. The Mongols ruled all of China; an unprecedented disaster. And unlike earlier barbarian rulers, the Mongols were not so ready to be absorbed or sinicized; they looked down on the weak-kneed Confucian scholars (ranked 'one grade above the beggars'). They ruled a world empire that spanned Asia and acquired a multi-cultural realm from Persia to India, from Europe to China.

Although the civil examination system was later reinstated, China remembered the dark days of a non-Confucian China. The Ming dynasty that followed was devoted to a policy of preserving Confucian orthodoxy, eventually closing the country to all foreign contact and hoping to curb the disruptive forces of mercantilism. Fear of foreign contamination led India under Mughal rule to freeze the **caste** system, and the same fear led Ming China to keep its women indoors. When China fell under foreign rule again, this time that of the Manchu, Han pride ('to restore the Ming') fostered the more recent Chinese inclination towards being anti-foreign. European imperialism and Christian missions aggravated that attitude.

See also: kokutai ideology since Meiji times; orientalism

Further reading

Bol, P. (1992) *'This Culture of Ours': Intellectual Transition in T'ang and Sung China*, Stanford, CA: Stanford University Press.
Johnston, A. (1995) *Cultural Realism: Strategic Culture and Grand Strategy in Chinese History*, Princeton, NJ: Princeton University Press.

WHALEN LAI

Xi Kang

b. 223; d. 262

Neo-Daoist philosopher

The song of a new dynasty is always exuberant; the song of one in decline is naturally sad. This is the classical theory of **music**: that music by embodying objectively the social feelings and doing so properly (without excess) may serve well to inculcate the moral sentiments and moderate souls (avoid over-celebration/grieving). Thus music unites emotionally what the rites distinguish rationally.

The classical view seems reasonable as a theory of communication: we expect a sad person or people to vocalize a sad tune so that hearing the sad outer tune, we can infer the sadness inside him or them. Then by resonating with it inside us, we feel sad ourselves and learn to empathize.

However, this theory was challenged and over-thrown by Neo-Daoist thinker Xi Kang (Hsi K'ang), himself a superb zither player, in the political (and emotional) chaos following the fall of the Han dynasty. In a difficult thesis titled *There is Neither Joy or Sadness in Music*, he offered what appears on the surface to be a Romantic theory of music: namely, that feeling is purely subjective. It belongs solely to the person (the artist and the audience) and not to the musical score. There is then no way the correlative theory is right, that the five individual notes capture the five corresponding human feelings, one to one, unambiguously. Such a theory of correspondence would be naive. Music is more complex than that, as any musician knows. Notes are combined to create the necessary harmonies, and so on. But to conclude that only man has feelings and a sheet of music has not is just as naive. It begs the point of how we communicate our feelings, and it misses the real point of Xi Kang's thesis.

The classical theory and classical rationality fail to address the very real possibility of people having 'mixed emotions', feelings so deep and troubled that the person might not even know their import, as when a person feels overwhelmed, sobs uncon-trollably and yet cannot honestly tell why. Xi Kang struggled with this phenomenon, tried hard to give it expression and came closest to explaining it when he cited the case of drunken musicians. A number of them were at first playing the same tune, but after they became intoxicated with wine their continual playing aroused in each player a very different emotion. Some laughed or became agitated, while others cried or became sedated. That the same piece of music could stir up these different reactions proved his point: that the order of musical notes does not embody a fixed emotion as to evoke a singular reaction from everyone who hears or plays it. If the same music can stir conflicting feelings and if the result is an unbecom-ing display – people sobbing and giggling or a person laughing one minute and crying the next

and neither have any idea why – then the situation is contrary to and effectively defeats the classical theory and its assumptions. Such a crazed display in any public performance utterly disrupts the sense of ritual propriety. Xi Kang in fact shifted the blame to the wine (to intoxicating wine instead of intoxicating music or being responsible for the dissonance). In that, he himself remained a classical zither player who was known to love its 'pure and aloof' tune. He avoided 'crass and licentious' songs, although like most of his contemporaries he was drawn to the music of Chu, 'southern dirges' famous for their depth of sorrow, a pathos that the orderly music of Central China shunned.

What Xi Kang shows is that music, instead of being always 'socially harmonizing', could just as well be personally cathartic. It cleanses the soul by releasing all these pent-up feelings, these mixed emotions hitherto unexpressed, ambiguous moods (like love-hate relationships) not admitted into and not admissible by the conscious standard of classical forms. In one master-stroke, Xi Kang, who was famous for subverting Confucian 'teach-ing of names' in order to retrieve the Daoist 'freedom and spontaneity', rewrote the classical formula on the social use of **rites** and music. Rites that justify social divisions rationally and music that unites emotionally were seen by him to be rites which repress unreasonably and music which liberates inexplicably. Thus, in a sense, he brought the classical era to an end. With that, he exposed what is a historical case of 'ritual civilization and its belated musical discontent'.

Further reading

Mather, R. (trans.) (1976) *Shih-shuo Hsin-yu: A New Account of the Tales of the World*, Minneapolis, MN: University of Minnesota.

WHALEN LAI

Xie Lingyun

b. 385; d. 433

Poet

One of the earliest and finest Chinese nature

('mountains and waters') poets, Xie Lingyun (Hsieh Ling-yum) is remembered in the history of ideas for coming to the defense of the monk **Daosheng** (*c*.360–434), who shocked the Buddhist community with his untested thesis that 'enlightenment has to be sudden' (see **enlightenment, sudden**). This subitist thesis, made famous later by Chan, went against all available records at the time. Xie tried to mediate the difference of opinion in his essay *Distinguishing the Principles*:

> In the discourse of Shakyamuni
> Though the Way of the Sage [the goal of enlightenment] be remote
> By accumulated learning, it can nonetheless be reached
> Still it is only when the (karmic) burdens are lifted and (final) insight begins to dawn
> Would one gradually come to be enlightened.
> (But) in the discourse of Confucius
> Because the Way of the Sage is subtle
> Even Yan Hui could only approximate it.
> But when one does experience Nonbeing and the insight shines through totally
> Then all principles revert [all of a sudden] to the One Ultimate.

Without intending it, Xie, by presenting the difference of opinion as a cultural one, in effect credited sudden enlightenment to a peculiarly Chinese proclivity. In so doing, he actually exposed as non-canonical the subitist thesis of Daosheng.

The passage cited above adheres to the Neo-Daoist view (see **Neo-Daoism**) according to which **Confucius** is rated higher than **Laozi**. By embodying in his person this ultimate **non-being**, which is ineffable, Confucius lived the Truth and never had to talk about it. By failing to so incarnate non-being in his person, Laozi actually talked about it. As for Yan Hui, Confucius's favourite disciple, he is rated a Worthy, one grade lower than the **Sage** but clearly above Laozi. Tradition interprets his poverty (that he had 'nothing' in his often empty rice bin) as a mark of his intimacy with non-being.

Further reading

Lai, W. (1987) 'Tao-sheng's Theory of Sudden Enlightenment Re-examined', in P. Gregory

(ed.), *Sudden and Gradual: Approaches to Enlightenment in Chinese Buddhist Thought*, Honolulu, HA: University of Hawaii Press, 169–200.

WHALEN LAI

xin

The Chinese word *xin* here covers what would be rendered as both 'mind' and 'heart' in English. It has been suggested that China knew a heart-mind of both reason and emotion, thought and feeling, in contradistinction to the rational mind of the Greek or the modern West (as if that exhausts the concepts of European psychology). Throughout China's history, Chinese thinkers themselves had known different shades of this mind-heart. **Mencius** knew that emotive and righteous mind-heart, but **Mozi** prioritized the rational mind. **Zhuangzi** probed the psychic depth and discovered a 'vacuous, luminous, spirited, self-knowing mind', a person who turns inwards and suspends for the duration the active working of the senses would discover this pre-subject-object and holistic mind. **Xunzi** is credited with a synthesis of all three modes above: he too knew how to 'empty his mind' to find his 'moral centre', and thereupon also be disinterested so as to exercise 'rational analysis'.

Speaking generally, despite a deep-rooted suspicion of 'selfish desires', Han dynasty thinkers had yet to fully polarize reason and emotion into the good and the evil. The word *qing*, which is now easy to read as 'feeling', described then a larger matrix of both objective 'situation' and subjective 'dispositions'. It was the Buddhists, with their denunciation of desires and their ascetic practices, that truly divided the (**buddha nature**) mind which is good and the (grossly and subtly defiled) emotions. That dichotomy of nature and emotion was taken over unwittingly by the anti-Buddhist critic **Li Ao**, a mistake which was not corrected until the Song dynasty Neo-Confucians (see **Neo-Confucianism, concepts**). Although **Zhu Xi** would not deem the mind-heart singularly rational and therefore feelingless, yet it is also evident that he stressed the rational functions more. Later, Wang Yangming pushed for a singular mind-heart in a mode closer to the original Mencian conception, but even then, Wang privileged the Mencian mind in its seminal mode of 'knowing instinctively right and wrong'. The more romantic followers of his took it one step further in glorifying the 'good feelings' and the 'good mind'.

Further reading

Lai, W. (1983) 'The Pure and the Impure: The Mencian Problematik in Chinese Buddhism', in W. Lai and L. Lancaster (eds), *Early Ch'an in China and Tibet*, Berkeley, CA: University of California, Buddhist Studies Series, 299–326.

Moore, C. (ed.) (1967) *The Chinese Mind: Essentials of Chinese Philosophy and Culture*, Honolulu, HA: East–West Center.

WHALEN LAI

xing

The mainstream of Chinese philosophy may be broadly defined as moral philosophy, and much of that discussion is framed by the debate on the nature of humanity. That debate affects choices over the mode of moral education. **Mencius** held that men are born good, and saw the role of education to be one of simply and naturally drawing out that seminal good towards its fruition. **Xunzi**, who held that human nature is evil or inclining towards selfishness, conceived of education as curbing evil. **Gaozi** held human nature to be liable to be either good or evil, while Mohist anthropology saw men being guided by likes and dislikes and counted on man being so reasonable as to act upon the recognition that concern for others brings naturally many returns (likeable benefits). Of the metaphors of education used by these classical thinkers, the good should be nursed organically while the evil should be trimmed mechanically. 'Trim and nurse' is the compound for moral cultivation.

By the Han dynasty, **Dong Zhongshu** aligned the good with the *yang* element in man and the evil with the *yin* element, while Yang Xiong proposed that human nature is a mix of good and evil; both reflect a syncretic compromise. The later Han development towards a social gradation of human

nature – the three or the nine grades – privileged the status quo and tended to subvert the ideal of a common humanity. The Buddhist period saw both trends, the presence of the Three Vehicles and the nine grades as well as the universal **buddha nature**. Han Yu kept a three-grade distinction, while **Li Ao** unwittingly took over a Buddhist ascetic division of '(human) nature being good; the (desirous) feelings being evil'.

The Song dynasty Neo-Confucians (see **Neo-Confucianism, concepts**) corrected this and reverted to a Mencian premise. Although these Mencians spoke of moral self-cultivation as 'nurturing the good in men', these 'innerworldly ascetics' in effect opted for perpetual vigilance and self-imposed hardship. This was in order to 'build up character' (independence), but also required keeping the emotions in check. It is not truly the classical way of education via 'music and rites', since the Neo-Confucians held poetry suspect and put theatre and operas off limits for the young. The liberal wing of Wang Yangming's circle revolted against such strictures in the late Ming dynasty.

WHALEN LAI

Xiong Shili

b. 1883; d. 1968

Philosopher

Xiong Shili (Hsiung Shih-li) was a modern Chinese philosopher, best known for his 'New Consciousness Only' philosophy, and considered by some to be the most profound thinker of his generation. Xiong took up the study of the **Yogachara** (Consciousness Only) philosophy, which had long been discontinued in China but had recently been re-imported from Japan. Presented as a highly logical and scientific probing of the human consciousness, it was deemed the Eastern 'inner learning' on the same level and as well placed to compete with the modern West's 'outer science'. Xiong modified Yogachara philosophy, making it more positive, dynamic and monistic. Basically, he used an updated version of Huayan Totalism. This is new in the sense that historically Huayan had simply displaced Yogachara philosophy without bothering to work out a synthesis and taking its detailed analysis to heart. Huayan had developed the idea that the world is full of buddhas, which was thought to be more fruitful than the sort of introverted analysis championed by the subjectivity of Yogachara. Thus the study of Yogachara was discontinued in China, even though it was kept formally alive as one of the 'old schools' in Nara, Japan.

Unlike the **Kyoto school** in Japan, there is in China no university chair and no official successors to Xiong. The Kyoto school used the **emptiness** theory (now called the absolute nothingness of pure experience) to engage Western philosophy by attacking its ontological assumptions and by raising the stakes in its romantic quest for unitary intuition. This proved enticing to the West. By contrast, Xiong and Chinese philosophy concentrated on Yogachara instead, confident that this rational no-self form of thought would outdo European egocentric ways of thinking. But in insisting that it is rational and autonomous, the Chinese ended up with a closed system that does not compare at all with the West.

Further reading

Wang Shou-ch'eng (1987) *A Study of Hsiung Shih-li,* Singapore: Institute of East Asian Philosophies, National University of Singapore.

WHALEN LAI

Xunzi

b. 340 BCE; d. 245 BCE

Confucian philosopher

Xunzi was the Confucian thinker who opposed **Mencius** in holding that humans are naturally inclined towards evil. Because the Song dynasty Neo-Confucians (see **Neo-Confucianism, concepts**) proclaimed a Mencian orthodoxy, Xunzi has been slighted though it can be argued that he was once the more influential Confucian spokesman, being the tutor of the Legalists (see **Legalism** and the theoretician for ritual educa-

tion who finalized the debate on Name and Reality. Marxists have tried to make him out as a materialist; others classify him as a 'naturalist' thinker for not holding **Heaven** responsible for the rise and fall of dynasties. Heaven no more acts with approval or disapproval than prayers could effect or impede downpours. When it rains, it rains, irrespective of human wish or divine will. On the same note, Xunzi would find that humans are born selfish and, given the availability of limited resources, would naturally enter into conflict and competition. Whatever is good is not innate or due to nature; it is the 'doing of man' (*renwei*). More specifically, it is the standard set down with the wisdom of foresight by past sages. For *homo politicus*, that social good is based on the ritual norms of proper behaviour that all citizens should be socialized into. Moral education is learning the rites and being habituated into the good like wood being bent into a useful form.

Though he respected tradition (the way of prior sages), Xunzi, who saw the demise of the Zhou state and the failure of feudal rule, accepted the Mohist premise of a bold, centralized rule. He thus recognized that as times change, institutions too may change, a concept later advanced further by the Legalists. At a time when the myths of the predynastic **sage-king** were gaining currency, Xunzi chose to disregard their unrealistic model. He accepted only the standard of the later (i.e., the dynastic) sage-kings. He also denigrated the *yin–yang* speculation and the cult of omens and auspices.

A nominalist who regarded names to be social conventions, he made Reality the standard for measuring the truthfulness of such appellations. In that, he helped to conclude the debate on names and voided a number of linguistic confusions. Two different words such as 'dog' and 'canine' still describe the same animal. Chinese just happened to have two such words like the English, and one word with two possible meanings should not be allowed to confuse the issue just because it is ambivalent. 'Dark' and 'heavy' are two antonyms to 'light', but that does not mean a hard (heavy: not-light) stone cannot be white (not-dark: light in colour). In this, Xunzi was successful in his campaign against the Logicians. For him, common sense would dictate that a horse is a horse, no matter what additional colour predicate a 'white horse' might have. Social convention or the normal meaning of words would ensure that mountains are higher than valleys. To register how a valley up the Himalayas is demonstrably higher than a hill next to the Dead Sea is an abuse of different contexts. Therefore, names should always comply with the truth of reality (hard fact).

Xunzi however also adopted this idea for a defence of moral values, in which case a person in a given social role (carrying the name of 'son') should live up to the standard of **filial piety** by being truthfully and factually a good son. For him, that standard (called the 'teaching of names' which designates Confucianism) is objective, pre-set, and has to be acquired through the learning of the rites, because it was set down by the foresight of former sages.

Regarded by many as a no-nonsense thinker, there is an aspect of Xunzi that may not be so mystery-free. He has an understanding of the inner workings of the mind that resonates with the Daoist mind. For him, a rationally discerning mind has to be vacuous, empty, unperturbed and free from the passions that drove other thinkers to being one-sided in their philosophies.

Xunzi could deliberate means and ends as coolly as any Mohist, but he also claimed for himself a unique trait, a comprehensive vision that rose above all prior partial viewpoints and was rooted in this psychic detachment and selflessness. This rhetoric of the inner self is very much in the Daoist strand. As the other end to this self, Xunzi had a concept of the cosmos that may not be some direction-less sky. This harsh critic of any myth involving a personified Heaven subscribed to a cosmic order. He spoke of a *li* or principle in the universe, and clearly assumed that the 'good' that is due to human effort and as set forth as ritual norms by the sages is in compliance with that Principle. He set up a triad of Heaven, Earth and Man in a terse formula: Heaven has its seasons, Earth its benefits and Man his sociability. Nothing lasting is ever accomplished without the proper alignment of the timely opportunities provided from above; the material advantage offered by the environment; and both of these could only be maximized by humanity through a basic quality of social life: harmony or commensurability.

The opposition of nature and culture in China was spelled out by the Daoists in terms of *wuwei* (non-action) and *renwei* (human action). The latter, as 'of human artifice', is synonymous with 'false, artificial, man-made' and is thus 'unnatural'. It signifies the purposive doings of culture as contrasted to the spontaneity of nature. But **Confucius** did not know this dichotomy. Education was for him a matter of socializing a child of nature (or acculturating **barbarians**) into acquiring a 'second nature'. Thus he spoke in a metaphor of 'polishing jade', turning a rough diamond into a true gem. The compound for moral 'cultivation' was literally as much about 'trimming' (the deviant offshoots) as about 'nurturing' (the proper growth). From the Mohists, urban artisans whose rhetoric preferred the carpentry metaphors of 'chisel and square', there was a reaction. Mencius too would prefer the organic metaphors of 'nursing the sprouts of virtue' according to their natural growth, and **Gaozi**, who spoke in terms of 'channelling whirling water and molding pliant wood', stopped short of retreating into the farming vocabulary. He knew better than simply to let water seek its own level, for morally the gentleman should always 'look up' (aspire to heights) and not 'flow down' (behave badly, a mark of the uncultured low-born person). Mencius, who argued in favour of letting water flow naturally down and against splashing it up would elsewhere recognize the need to 'hedge in' any flooding torrent; Gaozi was simply addressing how best to divert such energy into the good forms of social behaviour.

Because Xunzi in his social engineering adopted the imagery of the carpenter using the square and casting the mold, it is often assumed that he and Gaozi were alike in their assessment of man and society. However, according to Bruce Brooks, the extirpation of the state of Song in 286 BCE was such an earthshaking event that the revulsion against the course of civilization among some led to social dropouts and a primitivist idealization of the natural society as with the Agrarian utopians. So whereas Gaozi was more akin to Confucius, Xunzi was more akin to the Daoists. Gaozi held that human nature is morally neutral but malleable for good or bad; he still both 'trims' and 'nurtures' the human garden. But born into anarchy, Xunzi accepted the Daoist dichotomy of nature and culture but came out on the opposite side of the dreamy-eyed primitivists. He equated the natural state (at any time in history) with amorality, and banked on the good that human culture creates. But to counter chaos, Xunzi gave up on any possible connection between man's 'innate nature' (evil) and the socially-imposed standard of good or his normative 'second nature'. Thus unlike Gaozi, Xunzi, who effected the final Confucian synthesis in the classical period, incorporated into his system Daoist psychology, Mohist instrumentalism and the Logicians' problematic.

Xunzi followed the Confucian line on the significance of ritual (*li*) as the leading method to produce, maintain and foster **harmony** in the state. The important aspect of ritual is that it allows the desires of the individual to be restrained by something objective and independent, thus allowing him to find an explanation for his curbing of his behaviour in sources which seem to him to be satisfactory. Again, the differences in hierarchy and status are solidly based if they are felt to reflect ritual differences between people. **Music** has a special role here, since it can affect our emotions as well as our reason, and the playing of music can lead us to control our feelings and channel them in appropriate ways. In listening to music we fit in with the harmony of the universe, and align our behaviour with that greater harmony, which can only be helpful to the harmony of the state. It is the **sage** who is capable of bringing harmony both to himself and to the community, and sage-kings are heartily to be recommended, according to Xunzi. He manages to control his feelings and then institutes rituals which help maintain that control, and make it available to the public at large. When the state is built around the principles established by the sage, and where the community at large follows those principles, everything goes well.

Xunzi is neither optimistic nor pessimistic when it comes to discussing human nature, he accepts it as part of a morally neutral nature, a reflection of the influence of a heaven which operates according to natural principles and without any intentions behind its operations. If left to ourselves, we are capable of great evil, and yet we might also do good. What is required is regulation, both political and intellectual, in that a rectification of names should be instituted which would make clear to each successive generation what ideas were held to be important by the ruler and their connection with the facts which they name. Xunzi's systematization of key Confucian concepts played an impressive part in the development of Confucianism as a philosophical system in Asia.

See also: category

Further reading

Cua, A. (1985) *Ethical Argumentation: a Study of Hsun-Tzu's Moral Epistemology*, Honolulu, HA: University of Hawaii Press.

Machle, E. (1993) *Nature and Heaven in the Xunzi*, Binghamton, NY: State University of New York Press.

Taeko Brooks, B. and Taeko Brooks, A. (1998) *The Original Analects*, New York: Columbia University Press.

Ts'ai Jen-hou (1987) *A Comparative Study of Hsin and Hsing in the Philosophy of Hsun Tzu and Chu Tzu*, Singapore: Institute of East Asian Philosophies, National University of Singapore.

Watson, B. (1963) *Hsun-tzu: Basic Writings*, New York: Columbia University Press.

WHALEN LAI
OLIVER LEAMAN

Y

Yamuna

b. 966; d. 1038

Philosopher

Yamuna was a South Indian Tamil Shri Vaishnava philosopher of theistic devotionalism (*bhakti*) whose works include the *Siddhitraya* (*Atmasiddhi, Samvitsiddhi* and *Ishvarasiddhi*), the *Agamapramanya*, the *Gitarthasamgraha* (Summary of the Meaning of the Bhagavad Gita) and the *Kashmiragama*. He was instrumental in the formulation of what came to be known as the **Vishishtadvaita Vedanta** theological philosophy of qualified non-dualism whose foremost representative is his successor **Ramanuja** upon whom Yamuna's works, in particular the *Siddhitraya* and *Gitarthasamgraha*, exercised a considerable influence. Shri Vaishnava teachers such as Nathamuni (900–950), Yamuna and Ramanuja are notable for integrating aspects of the popular emotional *bhakti* expressed in the hymns of Tamil Alvars whose object is a personal deity; the non-Vedic Pancharatra temple ritual and theology stressing divine immanence in the universe and the individual selves and mainstream classical Vedantic or Upanishadic elements (see **Upanishads**; **Vedanta**).

Yamuna maintained the existence of three real and distinct basic categories of existents: God, individual conscious selves and a mind-independent material domain. He argues for the existence of God (*Ishvara*) on the **Nyaya**-style grounds that the universe must be an effect since it is comprised of parts. The organization of the parts and the distribution of experiences in accordance with the accumulated merit and demerit of human beings presupposes an omniscient and omnipotent agentive cause. God is understood in personal terms, interacting with his votaries or servants with whom He is intimately connected, albeit distinct from them.

Every first personal, *cogito*-type act of awareness refers directly to the individual self as a disembodied subject distinct from its environments. The subject is immediately and reflexively (**svayam prakasha**) given in all cognitive and affective acts of awareness, be they intransitive or object-directed. In fact, all conscious states, even those that are predominantly concerned with external objects, include an element of reflexivity. Consciousness, defined in terms of its dual aspects of intentionality and reflexivity or self-luminosity, is categorized as an essential property of the permanent substantial self which is the constant witness of its transitory experiences. The body is a contingent property of the self thus understood, relating it to external environments. The essential self is 'this self-luminous one that reveals its proper form without beginning and end.

In the *Agama-pramanya*, he extended the scope of the Vedantic tradition in arguing that the Tantric (non-Vedic) sectarian scriptures (*Agama* or *Samhita*) (see **Tantra**) which form the basis of the Pancharatra temple ritual were equal in validity to the orthodox Vedic scriptures on the grounds that they are the utterances of God.

In the *Gitarthasamgraha*, he maintained that the chief purport of the **Bhagavad Gita** is the inculcation of *bhakti*, the proper context of any form of religious observance, as the sole means of attaining release (*moksha*) which he understands as an adoring personal relationship with God in heaven in which the self retains its individuality.

Further reading

Neevel, W. (1977) *Yamuna's Vedanta and Pancaratra: Integrating the Classical and the Popular*, Montana: Scholars Press.

van Buitenen, J. (1953) *Ramanuja on the Bhagavadgita*, The Hague: Smits (for the *Gitarthasamgraha*).

—— (1971) *Yamuna's Agama Pramanya, or, Treatise on the Validity of the Pancaratra*, Madras: Adyar Library and Research Centre.

—— (1988) 'On the Archaism of the Bhagavata Purana', in L. Rocher (ed.), *Studies in Indian Literature and Philosophy: Collected Articles of J.A.B. van Buitenen*, Delhi: Motilal Banarsidass.

CHRIS BARTLEY

Yan Fu

b. 1853; d. 1920

Philosopher

The introduction by Yan Fu (Yen Fu) of Huxleyian (Darwinian) evolutionism and survival of the fittest was remade in translation into a Legalist argument for the pursuit of wealth and power (see **Legalism**). Chinese intellectuals recognized fully the alien autonomy of the West, enough for a thesis of 'total Westernization' to arise. A public debate on the relative merit of science and philosophy highlights that issue. It is a familiar scene, typical of the envy/unease with the modern advance of the truth of the natural sciences versus the more subjective truth of the life of the spirit. Europe went through that soul searching before, but of course did not have to face science as an alien force.

Further reading

Schwartz, B. (1964) *In Search of Wealth and Power: Yen Fu and the West*, Cambridge: Harvard University Press.

WHALEN LAI

The Yellow Emperor

Legendary first ruler of China, the Yellow Emperor was a figure unknown to **Confucius**. He was an ideological creation placed before the three Sage-Kings. His myth rose in the Warring States period, being the model of those looking forward to a powerful ruler to reunite China. He represented strong, militant, centralized, bureaucratic rule, with all facets of cultures allegedly invented under him. His brother or half-brother, the Red Emperor (alias the Divine Peasant), represented the hope of those looking backward to a primitive, agrarian, classless, war-less utopia. In the myth, the Red Emperor lost; the Yellow Emperor won, going on to subdue the people in all four directions. From that came a legend that he had four faces, which could mean he faces down people of the 'four directions'.

The Grand Historian began Chinese history with him, making him the ancestor of all Chinese (the *Classics of Mountains and Seas* made him the ancestor even of the other non-Han people). The Grand Historian was an official title for the court chronicler, and the *Historical Record* was begun by Sima Tan (d. 110 BCE) and completed under his son Sima Qian (145?–90? BCE). The work began with the Yellow Emperor and came all the way down to the current reign of Han Emperor Wu. The text includes a summary of the six major schools from the age of the philosophers, and traces their social origins: the six are the *yin–yang*, Confucian, Mohist, Logical, Legalist and Daoist, with Qian's obvious preference being the last. The book also lays out an objective method of historiography. The *Historical Record* is often praised for its balance and breadth of coverage, and compared with the *Spring and Autumn Annal* attributed to Confucius.

See also: history, concept of

WHALEN LAI

YI *see* righteousness

Yi Hang-no

b. 1792; d. 1868

Confucian philosopher

Yi Hang-no, whose pen name was Hwa-so, was an important Korean Confucian scholar. He followed **Zhu Xi**'s Neo-Confucianism as his model and ideal. He was one of the key leaders in the movement known as *ch'oksa wijong*, which means 'to oppose heterodoxy and defend orthodoxy'. Heterodoxy in this sense meant the Western ideology represented by Roman Catholicism, and orthodoxy was the Neo-Confucianism of Zhu Xi and **Yi T'oegye**.

Yi Hang-no believed that the Western learning represented by Roman Catholicism was a dangerous threat to the preservation of the Neo-Confucian orthodoxy in Korea. He regarded Western ideas of the relationships between parents and children and between king and ministers as ideas of **barbarians**. He believed that Western ethics lacked filial respect for parents, and Western ideas of human relationships were contrary to the Confucian idea of proper order. Yi was a strong representative of the defenders of tradition against the modern Western culture in general, and Western philosophy and religion in particular.

Yi understood the universe and various natural and human systems on the basis of Zhu Xi's metaphysics. According to Yi, the common and fundamental essence of all things and all beings and their relationships is *i* (*li* in Chinese, meaning principle). He also elevated principle over material force (*ki* in Korean, *qi* in Chinese). *I* is the ultimate reality of all things in the universe and of human nature and morality. Central to Yi's philosophy was the primacy and priority of *i* in human nature, society and the universe.

See also: Christianity, Korean

Further reading

Choi Min-hong (1980) *A Modern History of Korean Philosophy*, Seoul: Songmunsa, 192–6.

Chung Chai-sik (1995) *A Korean Confucian Encounter with the Modern World: Yi Hang-no and the West*, Berkeley, CA: Institute of East Asian Studies, University of California, Berkeley.

Lee, P. (ed.) (1996) *Sourcebook of Korean Civilization*, vol. 2, New York: Columbia University Press, 156ff, 266ff.

YONG-CHOON KIM

Yi T'oegye

b. 1501; d. 1570

Neo-Confucian philosopher

T'oegye is the honorific pen name of Yi Hwang. He is one of the greatest Neo-Confucian philosophers in Korean history (see **Neo-Confucianism, concepts**). He belongs to the Cheng–Zhu school, which is also known as **Zhu Xi** school or the school of human nature and principle (*songnihak*). He studied Zhu Xi's philosophy thoroughly and developed his own unique interpretation of it. T'oegye's thought was well known among the Neo-Confucian scholars in Japan and made a significant impact on them.

One of the most important issues developed in the Korean Neo-Confucianism is the idea of 'the four beginnings and the seven emotions'. There was a long period of debates among the Neo-Confucian scholars in Korea on understanding and interpreting not only the textual meanings and philosophical questions about the Confucian idea of the 'four beginnings of virtue' and the 'seven emotions', but also their moral and psychological meanings and implications for the practice of self-cultivation, which had not been clearly articulated in Chinese Confucianism.

The Confucian term 'four beginnings' (*sadan*) of virtues originally comes from a famous passage in *The Book of Mencius*:

> The feeling of commiseration is the beginning of humanity; the feeling of shame and dislike is the beginning of righteousness; the feeling of deference and compliance is the beginning of propriety; and the feeling of right and wrong is the beginning of wisdom. Men have these Four Beginnings just as they have their four limbs.
>
> (*Mencius* 2A:6, in Chan 1963: 65)

The 'seven emotions' (*ch'ilchong*), according to the Confucian classic, *The Book of Rites*, are pleasure, anger, sorrow, fear, love, hatred and desire, which are the basic feelings not acquired through learning but innate.

An issue was how to interpret the four beginnings and the seven emotions in terms of principle (*i* in Korean; **li** in Chinese) and material force (*ki* in Korean; **qi** in Chinese). The Korean thinkers were divided on the issue of interpreting Zhu Xi's statement, 'The four beginnings are issuances (manifestations) of *i* and the seven emotions are issuances of *ki*' (Chung 1995: 50). T'oegye interpreted these ideas dualistically in the dichotomous system of *i* and *ki*, while others like Yulgok interpreted them non-dualistically in terms of the inseparability and the oneness of *i* and *ki*.

According to T'oegye, the four beginnings can be identified with the mind and heart of man which one has from the time of birth, and the seven emotions can be identified with all the feelings of man whether good or bad. T'oegye said that with regard to the four beginnings, *i* issues and *ki* follows, and with regard to the seven emotions, *ki* issues and *i* rides on it. T'oegye thought that *i* is active, and he distinguished the four beginnings as the perfect good and the seven emotions as a combination of both good and evil.

Zhu Xi emphasized *i* (*li*) as actionless, motionless metaphysical reality and *ki* (*qi*) as an active, moving agent. But T'oegye gave *i* the characteristics of activity and movement, because he reasoned that for *i* to be the source of goodness, it must be alive and active. However, following Zhu Xi's tradition, T'oegye emphasized the primacy of *i*, stating that *i* is more precious than *ki*, and *i* is the master of *ki*.

T'oegye's main concern was to find the source of good and evil in human nature and to provide a solid moral philosophy. Thus, T'oegye's philosophy was really the philosophy of human nature (*songnihak*). This was an important characteristic of the Korean Neo-Confucianism of Choson dynasty, as the followers of T'oegye all emphasized basically the same issue.

For a concrete method of moral cultivation, T'oegye emphasized 'reverence' or 'reverential seriousness' (*kyong*). It is a key moral concept in T'oegye's thought. According to him, one must be centered on a moral standard whatever one does or wherever one is. T'oegye's idea of studying the mind and heart focuses on learning reverential seriousness. It is an inner-directed method of self-cultivation, which suppresses desires and preserves Heaven's principle. Through this practice, one must remove selfish and materialistic desires.

T'oegye emphasized a contemplative way of self-cultivation more than Zhu Xi. He emphasized the realization of sagehood through **meditation** and the cultivation of reverence. T'oegye's emphasis on the self-realization of principles inherent in human nature is a difference from Zhu Xi's emphasis on the intellectual understanding of principles. Although T'oegye was a great follower and promoter of Zhu Xi's metaphysics in Korea, T'oegye emphasized human nature and ethics probably more than did Zhu Xi.

Further reading

Chan Wing-tsit (ed.) (1963) *A Sourcebook in Chinese Philosophy*, Princeton, NJ: Princeton University Press.

Chung, E. (1995) *The Korean Neo-Confucianism of Yi T'oegye and Yi Yulgok*, Albany, NY: State University of New York Press.

Kalton, M. (1988) *To Become a Sage: The Ten Diagrams on Sage Learning by Yi T'oegye*, New York: Columbia University Press.

Yun, Sasoon (1990) *Critical Issues in Neo-Confucian Thought: The Philosophy of Yi T'oegye*, Seoul: Korea University Press.

YONG-CHOON KIM

Yi Yulgok

b. 1536; d. 1584

Confucian philosopher

Yulgok is the honorific name of Yi I. He and **Yi T'oegye** are regarded as the two greatest philosophers in Korean Confucianism. Yulgok was a scholar, educator and statesman, an original thinker who advocated practical learning and political and social reform. He not only mastered the Chinese Confucian classics at an early age, but also studied Buddhist scriptures and Daoist classics, especially the writings of **Laozi** and **Zhuangzi**.

Like T'oegye, Yulgok was dedicated to Neo-Confucianism, specifically the **Zhu Xi** school or the school of human nature and principle (*songni-hak*). He advocated Confucian ethics for self-cultivation and moral society. Yulgok possessed a balanced and liberal attitude toward other philosophies such as Buddhism, Daoism and the Yangming school of Neo-Confucianism, while T'oegye had a critical and negative attitude toward them.

Like T'oegye, Yulgok was a major figure in the sophisticated philosophical debate on the issue of 'the four beginnings' of the virtues (**humaneness**, **righteousness**, propriety and knowledge) and 'the seven emotions' (pleasure, anger, sorrow, fear, love, hatred and desire) in relation to the ideas of principle (in Korean, *i*; in Chinese, *li*) and material force (in Korean, *ki*; in Chinese, *qi*). There were some important differences of view between T'oegye and Yulgok on these ideas and their relationships. Yulgok disagreed with T'oegye's view that *i* has movement. According to Yulgok, *i* is a metaphysical principle and therefore has no form or movement. *Ki*, on the other hand, has form and movement, and it is the material force of *i*. Yulgok interpreted all the phenomena of the universe according to the relationship of principle and material force.

Yulgok rejected T'oegye's view that the 'four beginnings' (of virtues) issue from *i* and the 'seven emotions' issue from *ki*. According to T'oegye, the four beginnings are the issuances of *i*, while *ki* follows thereafter; the seven emotions are the issuances of *ki*, while *i* rides on it. By rejecting T'oegye's theory of 'alternate issuances of *i* and *ki*' (*ikihobal*), Yulgok developed 'the theory of *ki* issues and *i* rides' (*kibalisungiltosol*). Yulgok thought that T'oegye's view of the 'alternate issuances of *i* and *ki*' is improper for understanding of the 'Four–Seven' relationship, because it implies that *i* and *ki* are two separate entities. In other words, for Yulgok, T'oegye's thesis is dualistic. Yulgok believed that *i* and *ki* are inseparable in phenomena, and this view of Yulgok represents his non-dualistic approach regarding man and all things (Ro 1989: 52ff).

Yulgok developed a sophisticated interpretation of human nature and the mind. He accepted Zhu Xi's view that the mind has substance and function; the substance of the mind is nature and the function of the mind is feeling. But Yulgok also interpreted the mind in the following way: the state of the mind which has not been issued is nature, and the state of the mind which has already been issued is feeling. According to Yulgok, nature has two aspects, namely, the 'nature of original disposition' and the 'nature of physical disposition'. The nature of original disposition basically means reason and the nature of physical disposition means sense or feeling. This does not mean, however, that there are two natures in man. They are merely two different aspects of the unitary nature, which is endowed by **Heaven**. Here Yulgok's view is essentially non-dualistic.

Yulgok had an original interpretation of the issue of the 'four beginnings and the seven emotions' and the 'universal mind of the way' (*tosim*) and 'privatized mind of man' (*insim*). He made the following statement concerning the issue:

> The mind is originally one. The distinction between the universal mind of the way and the privatized mind of man is from the distinction between the 'Heaven-endowed nature' and the 'physical form of the material force'. The feelings are emotions. The distinction between the four beginnings and the seven feelings derives from the fact that there is the difference when we say only *i* aspect and when we say *i* and *ki* aspects altogether.
>
> Therefore, it is not possible that the universal mind of the way and the private mind of man exist alongside each other. It is, however, possible to say that one becomes a starting point while the other becomes an ending point. The four beginnings do not contain the seven feelings, but the seven feelings do contain the four beginnings. Zhu Xi made a complete explanation on the statement; the universal mind of the way is subtle, and the privatized mind of man is precarious. However, I would say, the four beginnings are not as complete as the seven feelings while these seven feelings are not as pure as the four beginnings. This is my humble view.

(*Yulgok chonso*, in Ro 1989: 47)

As noted, Yulgok's vision of human nature and mind is basically non-dualistic. He did not wish to make any sharp division between the universal mind of the way and the private mind of man and between the four beginnings and the seven emotions. The 'privatized mind of man' is the physical, material and sensual aspect of mind, while the 'universal mind of the way' is the rational and moral state of mind. These two states or characteristics can be altered by the influence of each other. In other words, the mind can change from one state to another. Ontologically there is only one mind, but phenomenologically there are two states of the mind. These two states of mind are two different phenomena; they cannot exist concurrently. In other words, the privatized mind of man cannot be, at the same time, the universal mind of the way. There are no two separate minds, but only two different states or aspects of one mind. One may become the other, or vice versa.

Yulgok's interpretations of human nature and mind as well as his interpretations of *i* and *ki* and the four beginnings of virtue and the seven emotions are highly original and unique. Such an original and sophisticated philosophical interpretation with the non-dualistic vision of man and the universe made a significant contribution to the enrichment of the Korean philosophical tradition. In Yulgok's thought, as well as in T'oegye's thought, the above ideas of metaphysics and human nature were important. But both always emphasized these ideas for the moral cultivation of self and for the ethico-spiritual self-cultivation for the ultimate goal of realizing sagehood and also self-cultivation for the moral government and the peaceful world.

See also: Confucianism in Korea

Further reading

Chung, E. (1995) *The Korean Neo-Confucianism of Yi T'oegye and Yi Yulgok*, Albany, NY: State University of New York Press.

Ro Young-chan (1989) *The Korean Neo-Confucianism of Yi Yulgok*, Albany, NY: State University of New York Press.

YONG-CHOON KIM

YI ZHI *see* funerals

Yijing

The *Yijing* (Book of Changes) is shrouded, even now, with an aura of mystery. Structured by the sixty-four hexagrams, it is supposed to capture all possible elemental configurations of change in the cosmos. Its reliance on a binary system of broken and unbroken lines has both the beauty of simplicity and the comprehensiveness of modern calculus, supposedly inspiring Leibniz.

Tradition assigns the eight trigrams to a mythic progenitor of mankind, who created them after observing the patterns of nature. As a divinatory text, it is associated with the Zhou, replacing the earlier form of divination in the Shang dynasty which was built around observing the cracks of a heated tortoise shell. The *Yijing* relies instead on the numerical valence in casting the stalks for constructing the six lines of the hexagram. It is said: 'The stalks, at once quiet and not moving, are suddenly moved by the spirit to reveal or penetrate completely.' The principles of Change are three: the *yi* as the transforming, as the unchanging, and as the very simplicity of it all. Therein the world is deemed eminently intelligible: there is only a finite number of combinations of these elemental iconic metaphors possible for encoding reality.

The gentleman is one who by noting, in the revealed patterns, the incipient movement (of changing into the next configuration), would be able to accomplish much without having to exert effort. He is riding on the momentum of that *ji* or **trigger** to maximize the situations to his own advantage. That describes the practical use of this text. There is then the theoretical structure itself and then a self-cultivational aspect, for as the 'explanation to the (eight) trigrams' notes: 'In ancient times, the **sage** created the *Yijing* in order to track man's nature and destiny (his beginning and end). He set up *yin* and *yang* as the Way of **Heaven**; the yielding and the unyielding as the Way of Earth; and the humane and the righteous as the Way of Man'. These three are somehow to be aligned. And before the Neo-Daoist Wang Bi turned the logic upside down – for him, silence is golden – the text clearly says this: the sage of old 'sets up the (eight) trigrams in order to give full expression to the (pre-verbal) intent or the (hidden) meaning'. He then 'appended remarks to help fully disclose what he intends to say (in speech)'. This tops a tripartite set of materials: (1) the hexagrams and the cryptic comments for divining fortune and misfortune, the practical; (2) the binary structure in geometric progression from 2, 4, 8, to 64, the beauty of reality; and (3) the reflective philosophical appendix that speculates on the One that is the Great Ultimate or the *dao* and the spirit.

Historically, the *Book of Changes* went through three distinct periods of commentatorial interpretation, each with its own focus and style:

1 the focus on emblems and numbers in Han;
2 the focus on the dark principle in Wei-Jin;
3 the focus on the diagrammatical in Song.

The emblems refer to the eight basic forms of the trigrams for heaven, earth, mountain, marsh, fire, water, thunder and wind; and the numbers refer to the value and the position of the six lines, each line being correlated to social class and other categories. The hexagrams are supposed to mutate according to sequence. The Han focused on the minutiae of their practical application.

The Neo-Daoists subverted that utility. They gave up 'the end' of use for 'the origin' of intent. They sought out the sublime principle behind the myriad emblems. No longer is this a handbook for fortune-telling; it is now the 'dark instruction' concerning the One, the **Non-Being**, the Quiescent, the Silence beyond words, some Substance proud to rise above gross utility. After the Buddhists contributed a mandalic arrangement of the hexagrams, adopted its structure of progression for a Huayan philosophy and remade the 'fire and water' trigram into a diagram of the human mind, came the Song dynasty Neo-Confucians, who used the *Book of Changes* to support a new and moral metaphysics. They reunited the Han interest in the Many and the Neo-Daoist interest in the One. Now the One Principle divides itself into the many manifestations, and doing so – quite unlike the Neo-Daoist reading – with no diminishing of virtue, power or reality. In another synthesis of all three prior approaches, the Classic now became a map of the mind (inner) but a mind that emanates out into the real world (outer), with the point of

transition being at the old 'trigger' point (*ji*). This trigger point is morally redefined; it is where incipient intentions of good or evil part company. The new Song 'inner, moral self-cultivation' targets this critical point for what they call vigilance and stopping at the ultimate good (their reading of the Chinese terms for Buddhist *samata-vipasana*, the two steps of 'calming down/ending the sensory inputs' and 'focused concentration'). The Neo-Confucians used the Buddhist idiom of 'stop and meditate' but changed it to mean meditating on one's inner intent, the motive behind the action, and stopping at the ultimate good. In this new exercise, the Neo-Confucians relied on a number of mandalic diagrams that probably originated from among religious Daoist circles.

Further reading

Ching, J. and Oxtoby, W. (eds) (1992) *Moral Enlightenement: Leibniz and Wolfe on China*, Nettetal: Steyler Verlag.

Lai, W. (1980) 'The I Ching and the Formation of Chinese Hua-yen Philosophy', *Chinese Philosophy* 7: 245–58.

Lynn, R. (trans.) (1994) *The Classic of Changes: A New Translation of the I Ching*, Princeton, NJ: Princeton University Press.

Smith, K., Bol, P., Adler, J. and Wyatt, D. (1990) *Sung Dynasty Uses of the I Ching*, Princeton, NJ: Princeton University Press.

Usaburo, I. (1958) *Sodai Ekigaku no Kenkyu* (Study on Sung/Song Dynasty I Ching/Yijing Scholarship), Tokyo: Meiji.

Wilhelm, H. (1977) *Heaven, Earth, and Man in the Book of Changes*, Seattle, WA: University of Washington Press.

WHALEN LAI

yin–yang harmony

Everything in the universe is classifiable into *yin* and *yang*, female and male. Unlike the conflict dualism that originated with **Zarathushtra** in Persia, where Good is pitted against Evil and Light against Darkness, there is strictly speaking nothing that is totally black (*yin*) or totally white (*yang*) in *yin–yang*. In the darkest hour of night (midnight) there is already hidden the germ of morning light. In the brightest hour of day (midday), the seed of darkness is likewise planted. The truth is as ancient as time itself: the moment we are born, we are already dying – and vice versa. The rejection of absolute conflict in this system means that as a complementary pair, *yin–yang* seeks out cosmic harmony instead of cosmic conflict. *Yin*, although lower in status to *yang*, is not evil *per se*. Evil is regarded as nothing more than the imbalance of the elements. There is no call for an apocalyptic battle to ensure that Good would ultimately triumph over Evil; and little cause to imagine an acosmic transcendence like **nirvana** that is 'beyond good and evil'. The overall outlook has been telescoped into the well-known *yin–yang* circle.

The outer circle stands for the primal unity of the Great Ultimate; the whirling blobs – they should be seen as being in perpetual counter-clockwise motion – are the duality of *yin* and *yang* that emerged out of the one Ultimate. The *yin–yang* schema is open to finer and finer subsets. Take a tree: the tree above ground is *yang*; the roots below are *yin*. The tree is *yang*; its shadow is *yin*. The main trunk is *yang*; the branches are *yin*. A branch is *yang*; the foliage is *yin*. The upper side of a leaf, usually lighter in colour, is *yang*; the darker underside is *yin* – and so on.

The *yin–yang* circle as we know it now appeared relatively late. It first appeared in the miscellaneous writings of the tenth-century Daoist Zhen Duan, who might have collected it from an earlier source. A known precursor is the Likan Circle. *Li* is the trigram for fire in the **Yijing**. *Kan* is the trigram for water. The trigram for fire is two unbroken *yang* lines sandwiching a broken *yin* line. That for water

is its reverse. These patterns were used to construct a circle with three concentric rings divided vertically in the middle: the white/black/white semicircles on one side is then Water; the black/white/black semicircle on the other is then Fire. The diagram was used by the Buddhist monk Zongmi (780–841) to render the **alaya-vijnana** (storehouse consciousness). That dual-semicircle design was later changed into a roving blob design, with the white eye whirling in the midst of the black blob being a new rendition of the black/white/back sandwich and so on. That *yang* 'fire' should sandwich *yin* 'water' and *yin* 'water' should sandwich *yang* 'fire' might appear odd, but the paradox could go back to early mythopoeic observations. The sun is the Great Yang (three unbroken lines); the moon is the Great Yin (three broken lines). The sun rises out of and sinks back into the sea; so when underground it is enveloped by water. That subterranean water can circulate upward into the sky (to be a source of rain) and envelope the moon which may function as the 'bright of night'.

See also: Five Elements

Further reading

Lai, W. (1984) 'Before the Yin-Yang Circle was Created: Individuation in the Soto Zen Circle Series', *Anima: An Experiential Journal* 10(2): 136–42.

WHALEN LAI

Yoga

In Indian culture, any discipline of physical and mental self-control with a soteriological intent. The normative text of the classical Yoga School (**darshana**) is Patanjali's *Yoga Sutra* variously dated between 200 BCE and 400 CE. Vedavyasa's commentary is probably a sixth-century work. Other important works are Shankarabhagavatpada's *Yogasutrabhasyavivarana*, controversially attributed to the Advaitin **Shankara** but probably posterior to Vachaspati Mishra's *Tattvavaisharadi* (*c*.850). The *Yoga Sutra* defines its subject as the restraint of all mental modifications – that is to say, the suppression of all forms of thought and feeling (*chitta-vritti-nirodha*). Classical Yoga presupposes the truth of the **Samkhya** dualism of primal matter (*prakriti*) and featureless, transcendental conscious entities (*purusha*), but accepts the existence of God (*Ishvara*, who is a conscious individual unique in that it is never subject to the operation of retributive action (***karma***)) as the entity exemplifying maximal greatness in respect of every property. God also initiates the world process by associating the featureless conscious subjects and matter with each other.

A Purusha, entangled in an environment of mental and material phenomena, recovers its transcendental proper form (*svarupa*) as pure consciousness on the cessation of the modifications of the personalizing, matter-derived (prakritic) mind (*buddhi*), ego (*ahamkara*) and the organ of sensory co-ordination (*manas*), collectively termed *chitta*. To this end, the psycho-somatic complex, prey to passions, current impressions and accumulated memories, should be disciplined and focused upon a single point. The Yogic practices of asceticism (*tapas*), *mantra*-recitation and the study of scriptures on liberation (*svadhyaya*), the direction of the mind to *Ishvara* conduce to intensification of contemplation (*samadhi-bhavana*) and the attenuation of the defects (*klesha*) of ignorance, egoism, desires, dislikes and obsessive attachments. Ignorance (***avidya***) consisting in the apprehension of the impermanent as permanent, the impure as the pure, pain as pleasure and non-self as self is the ground of the rest.

The eight stages (*ashtanga*) of the physical, moral and mental discipline that form classical yoga are:

Self-restraint (*yama*): non-violence, honesty in thought, word and deed, sexual continence and lack of greed.

Discipline (*niyama*): interiorization, tranquillity, asceticism, *mantra* recitation and the study of doctrinal texts on liberation, and attention to God.

Physical postures (*asana*); exercising control over the psychosomatic complex.

Breath-control (*pranayama*): regulation and reduction of the processes of inhalation and exhalation.

Withdrawal of the senses from their objects (*pratyahara*) with a consequent redirection of attention to the inner self.

Attention (*dharana*); fixing the mind on a single locus (i.e. an object of **meditation**).

Meditation (*dhyana*): the uninterrupted continuity of thought concerning the locus.

Profound contemplative absorption (*samadhi*) culminating in oblivion of the body and the environment. In the stage called *samprajnata samadhi*, the individual absorbed in the object of meditation is still aware of the object as an object. In *asamprajnata samadhi*, the individual can no longer be said to be aware of anything, a condition compared to deep sleep.

The state of liberation from transmigration is understood as one of wholeness and isolation (*kaivalya*) where unconditioned consciousness experiences only itself.

A somewhat different tradition of thought present in the Sutras (ch. 3) sees the triad consisting of attention, meditation and concentration as constituting a discipline (*samyama*) which yields various magical and supernatural accomplishments (*siddhi*) for the practitioner. Examples of the types of supernatural powers are: *anima* (physical minuteness and indetectability); *laghima* (weightlessness and levitation); *mahima* (vastly increasing one's physical size); *prapti* (the ability to reach remote objects and locations); *prakamya* (complete satisfaction of one's wishes); *ishitritva* (the capacity to create, destroy and arrange the constituent elements of the universe); *vashitva* (mastery of the elements); *kamavasayitva* (the capacity to determine matters in accordance with one's wishes). The attainment of *siddhis* represents an optional lower goal additional to that of ultimate perfection (*kaivalya*).

Further reading

Woods, J. (1927) *The Yoga Sutras*, Cambridge, MA: Harvard University Press.

CHRIS BARTLEY

Yogachara

Yogachara, 'the practice of meditation', is a Buddhist Mahayana school asserting the unreality of objective duality and denying the mind-independence of the material sphere. Yogacharins hold that while consciousness is the only genuine existent, it has the constructive capacity to bifurcate itself into experience of subjects and objects (*vikalpa*). The school is also known as Chittamatra (Mind Only), Vijnaptimatra (Understanding Only) and Vijnanavada (Consciousness Doctrine). Significant theorists include Asanga (*fl. c.*400 CE), whose works include the *Madhyantavibhaga*, the *Dharmadharmatavibhaga*, the *Mahayanasutralamkara*, the *Mahayanasamgraha* and the *Abhidharmasamucchaya*. His younger brother **Vasubandhu** composed the *Abhidharmakoshabhashya* which is a critical survey from a **Sautrantika** representationalist point of view of various theories adumbrated in the Buddhist realist schools. He also wrote the idealist *Vimshatika* (Twenty Verses) with auto-commentary, *Trimshika* (Thirty Verses) and *Trisvabhavanirdesha* (Statement of the Three Natures), in addition to commentaries on the *Madhyantavibhaga* and the *Dharmadharmatavibhaga*. Sthiramati (*c.*550 CE) composed commentaries on the *Trimshika* and *Madhyantavibhaga*.

In common with Madhyamaka, the Yogachara school recognizes the Mahayanist 'Perfection of Wisdom' texts (*Prajnaparamita Sutras*) as authorities. The earliest Yogachara scripture is the third century CE *Sandhinirmochanasutra*. This text propounds the view that the Buddha turned the 'wheel of doctrine' (*Dharma-chakra-pravartana*) three times. Initially he taught the **Four Noble Truths**, which is the Hinayana path to arhatship. According to Yogachara, this refers to the Sarvastivadin **Abhidharma** doctrine which was thought by some to have wandered from the truth of impermanence into an eternalist doctrine maintaining that the fundamental constituents underlying transient processes possess permanent, essential identities (*svabhava*). Thus in the Second Turning, he taught the universal **emptiness** (*shunyata*) of all phenomena (**dharma**). The Third Turning was definitive, rendering explicit (*nitartha*) what was only implicit (*neyartha*) in the Buddha's earlier teachings. This is the Yogachara doctrine.

Another early work, the *Yogacharabhumi*, describes the seventeen states (*bhumi*) to be accomplished by the practitioner of Yoga. Beginning with the stages involving sensory perception, it proceeds through many levels of **meditation** leading to the progressive statuses of the Hinayanist 'individual enlightened ones' (*pratyeka-buddha*), the all-compassionate Mahayanist *bodhisattvas* who have insight into emptiness and who are working for the welfare of all sentient, suffering beings, and finally those who are fully enlightened. The text introduces the notion of a 'storehouse-consciousness' (**alaya-vijnana**) from which all experience derives.

The *Madhyantavibhaga* provides a Yogachara interpretation of the Madhyamaka notion that all phenomena (*dharma*) are empty (*shunya*) of identity (*svabhava*). It propounds the middle way between the comprehensive relativistic scepticism of the Madhyamikas and atomistic reductionist realism about the constituents (*dharma*) of the Sarvastivadin Abhidharmists. The occurrence of phenomenal existence is explained by reference to a principle called *abhuta-parikalpa* (imagination of the unreal), which brings about proliferative language-impregnated experience structured in terms of object and subject (*grahya-grahaka-kalpana* = *vikalpa*). Meditative reinforcement (*abhyasa*) of insight into the fact that the constituents of existence are internal to consciousness and lack determinate identities (*dharma-nairatmya*) effects the annihilation of both mental corruptions (*asrava*) and the objects of cognition and their causal antecedents. Emptiness (*shunyata*) is construed as the absence of duality in consciousness which is an irreducible existent positively characterizable as essence (*dharmata*; *tathata*), perfected and self-sufficient (*parinishpanna*), final truth and ultimate reality (*paramartha-satya*), pure and luminous (*parisuddhi*) and supramundane (*lokottara*). Such a mind is free from the afflictions (*klesha*) of self-deception (*atma-moha*), belief in the endurance of personal identity (*atma-drishti*), self-regard (*atma-mana*) and self-love (*atma-sneha*) from which all rebirth-and-suffering generating effects (**karma**) evolve.

In the *Sandhinirmochanasutra* the Buddha is asked whether the images produced by meditative practice and experienced as external to the *yogin* are different or non-different from the mind. He replies that they are non-different, and that the same is true of what are ordinarily thought of as extra-mental material objects. Central to Yogachara soteriology is the conviction that unenlightened people preoccupied with the ephemeral and quotidian inhabit a maelstrom of karmic desires, aversions and delusions. Enlightened people who are detached from the objects of sense realize that the world is a fabric of representations and are consequently free from desires, aversions and delusions. On this view, experience of a mind-independent physical sphere is the product of habitual inferential construction rather than something derived from cognition of the external. People are individualized not through relations to external circumstances but by a 'mind-set' consisting of their inherited traits, attitudes, moods, emotions and memories. Deconstruction of these purely subjective factors inculcates detachment from all forms of experience. Both the transmigratory condition (**samsara**) and **nirvana** are states of mind. One's inherent enlightened **buddha nature** (*tathagata-garbha*) has become obscured by ignorance and moral defects. The underlying 'storehouse-consciousness' (*alaya-vijnana*) that is the source of all experience has the potentiality for both unenlightened and enlightened outlooks. Buddhist praxis is a technique for clarifying and manifesting the buddha nature.

The school differentiates itself from the universal emptiness teaching (*shunya-vada*) of the Madhyamikas in asserting the irreducible reality of constructive consciousness. Mind, which imagines or constructs duality (the non-existent), exists in its own right. Yogacharins also reject the **Vaibhashika**s' extreme realism about the fundamental constituents. Their arguments here centre upon the difficulties in providing a coherent account of the constitution of the alleged atomistic reality and its aggregation or extension into macroscopic formations. The atoms being of the smallest possible size are held to be indivisible and impartite. But if, say, six atoms combine and touch a central atom, it would have six parts, which is a contradiction. If it is supposed that they occupy the same spatial location, a 'gross' macroscopic entity would never be produced since there would be no increase in size. It is argued that if atoms have extension they are divisible but if they lack extension, they also lack solidity and resistance (for example, to light)

and spatial location. If a single atom is non-spatial, so is a putative atomic aggregation. Thus the notion of macro-entities is incoherent.

In their exhaustive reductive identification of extra-mental entities to elements of awareness, the Yogacharins oppose the representationalist's view that the existence of a momentary mind-independent sphere may be inferentially established on the basis of the fact that mental representations occur. They draw attention to the dissimilarity between the imperceptible, microscopic causes and their supposed phenomenal effects. They point to the indistinguishability from the phenomenological point of view of dream and waking states, the former demonstrating the possibility of experience without objective or extra-mental supports, which is also evidenced by hallucinations. If experience without contemporaneous objective reference or extra-mental support (*alambana*) is possible in one case, it is possible in all. Individual mindsets are karmically co-conditioned in such a way as to produce something analogous to a collective hallucination which is the experience of a common world.

Integral to the idealist theory is the view that form or content is internal to awareness (*sakara-jnana-vada*). The object-form apprehended in awareness does not derive from extra-mental factors. It is only when object-forms are projected outside or externalized that there is experience interpretable as that of mind-independent objects. Individual cognitions in a mental series (*samtana*) are held to be intrinsically reflexive. That is to say, an object-cognition is simultaneously and in virtue of the same act self-cognized, just as a lamp illuminates itself while illuminating an object. The tenet of the reflexivity of consciousness is central to the idealist outlook in that it illustrates the fact that consciousness adopting a perspective upon itself may be aware of its own contents as if they were objects external to it.

The contents of awareness, perceptions of an external world, memories and dreams are held to derive from a beginningless supply of residual traces of experience (*vasana*, literally 'perfume') in the form of mental states and dispositions of character preserved in an underlying unconscious level of mind termed the 'storehouse-consciousness' (*alaya-vijnana*) which also generates the illusion of a permanent, substantial, individual subject confronting a world of objects. The *alaya-vijnana* consisting of a series of thoughts and karmic 'seeds' accounts for the continuity of individual personality through death and spells of unconsciousness. When the traces of experience operate as moral and psychological conditions, the effect of such 'perfuming' by prior unenlightened actions of a series of experiences temporarily constituting an individual personality is to predispose the mind to perform further actions conditioned and motivated by craving, aversion and delusion. Needless to say, the idealists identify *karma* exclusively with intentional (*chetana*) actions.

Central to Yogachara thought is the doctrine of the Three Natures (*trisvabhava*) of phenomena. First is *parikalpita-svabhava*, the constructed or imagined nature which is intimately connected with the operation of language. This refers to the experience of unenlightened people subject to the four kleshas. It involves consciousness positing persisting objects (*grahya*) with essences (*svabhava*) as external to itself and a concomitant misunderstanding of the series of mental states as a permanent individual perceiver (*grahaka*). This process is termed *abhuta-parikalpa* or 'the imagination of the unreal', and it is this that is empty (*shunya*). Second is *paratantra-svabhava*, the 'dependent nature', the stream of inter-dependently originating (**pratitya-samutpada**) momentary experiences acting as the substrate of our conditioned conceptual and linguistic constructions which mistakenly presuppose the ultimate validity of the subject–object polarity. The dependent nature is the condition for either enlightenment or non-enlightenment relative to one's perspective. It is either the basis (*ashraya*) of *parikalpita*-type experience or the basis purified, *klesha*-free, insight into the way things really are. Third, re-orientation of consciousness (*ashraya-paravritti*) leads to *parinishpanna-svabhava*, the nature of reality in and of itself as perfect 'suchness' (*tathata*) unconditioned by dichotomizing and self-externalizing conceptualization. This is the truth realized by the enlightened meditator that ultimately there are neither objects nor enduring subjects.

Further reading

Levi, S. (1925) *Vijnaptimatratasiddhi: deux traités de Vasubandhu*, Paris: Bibliothèques des Hautes Etudes.

—— (1932) *Un système de philosophie bouddhique: Matériaux pour l'étude du système Vijnaptimatra*, Paris: Bibliothèque de l'Ecole des Hautes Etudes.

Lindtner, C. (1986) 'Bhavya's Critique of Yogacara in the Madhyamakaratnapradipa', ch. 4 in B. Matilal and R. Evans (eds), *Buddhist Logic and Epistemology*, Dordrecht: Reidel.

Matilal, B. (1986) *Perception: An Essay in Indian Theories of Knowledge*, Oxford: Clarendon Press.

Stcherbatsky, T. (trans.) (1970) *Madhyanta-vibhanga: Discourse on Discrimination between Middle and Extremes, Ascribed to Maitreyanatha and Commented by Vasubandhu and Sthiramati*, Osnabrück: Biblio Verlag Osnabruck.

Williams, P. (1989) *Mahayana Buddhism*, London: Routledge.

—— (1998) *Altruism and Reality*, Richmond: Curzon.

CHRIS BARTLEY

Yu Hyong-won

b. 1622; d. 1673

Sirhak philosopher

Yu Hyong-won was one of the greatest thinkers of **Sirhak** (the School of Practical Learning). He had a wide variety of interests and studied politics, economics, history, geography and literature as well as Neo-Confucianism. Yu criticized the economic system of his time, as he saw that the wealthy people had too much land while the poor had too little – in his view, the rich had become richer and the poor had become poorer – and that the poor masses had become servants of the rich.

In the semi-feudal society of Korea at that time, most people were farmers. In theory, all the land belonged to the nation. But in practice, the *yangban* (aristocrat) class held most of the land, and the farmers worked for the *yangban* class. According to Yu Hyong-won, farmers were the most important group in the nation and agriculture was the heart of the nation's economy, and therefore all farmers should have at least a minimum amount of land to provide a decent living for the whole family. Yu's idea of land reform became a model for the Sirhak idea of the reform of the land system.

Further reading

Choi Min-hong (1980) *A Modern History of Korean Philosophy*, Seoul: Seongmoon Sa, 150ff.

Lee, P. (ed.) (1993) *Sourcebook of Korean Civilization*, vol. 2, New York: Columbia University Press, 47ff, 74ff, 179ff.

YONG-CHOON KIM

Z

Zarathushtra

*fl. c.*11th century BCE

Prophet and sage

Zarathushtra is the prophet of one of the most ancient religious traditions surviving to this day and which takes his name for its own, Zoroastrianism. He was known to classical antiquity by the hellenized form of his name, Zoroastres, and thereafter in the West as Zoroaster, the Persian prophet; he was then, as nowadays, usually associated with the Persian Magi, a priestly class of Western Iran known to Herodotus in the fifth century BCE. Zarathushtra (his original name in the Iranian language of the Avestan scriptures) in fact lived many centuries before, probably, as scholars generally now agree, around 1,000 BCE or earlier, in an area to the northeast of present-day Iran. The Zoroastrian religion continues today among minority communities of Zartushtis in Iran and Parsis ('Persians') of India. Considerable numbers of both communities have emigrated to the West in modern times, yet Zoroastrians remain united by a reverence for their prophet Asho Zarathushtra (Righteous Zarathushtra). The religious tradition he founded is perhaps more properly to be known as 'Mazdaism', the worship of Ahura Mazda (Avestan *mazdayasna*).

The prophet's visionary hymns, the *Gathas*, are the most ancient core of the greater canon of Avestan scriptures; they are thought to have been revolutionary in promoting a new stage of religious development among the ancient Iranians. The *Gathas* are believed by Zoroastrians to be the original words of their prophet, and they are held as supremely sacred *manthras*, inspired utterances of intense power. The seventeen hymns are contained within the *Yasna* liturgy of the religion, one of the sections of the Avesta; like the Indian *Vedas*, these texts were composed long before writing existed among the Indo-Iranians. For centuries they were transmitted orally by generations of priests, whose first duty was to commit the whole body of Avestan scriptures to memory. The *Avesta* was finally committed to writing in the sixth century CE, in an elaborate script of forty-four letters modified from the Pahlavi alphabet to accommodate the verbal and consonantal subtleties of the different phases of the Avestan language. Only one-fifth of the *Avesta* has survived from antiquity.

Ancient as they are, the *Gathas* have survived into the modern age preserving distinctive linguistic features which identify them as much older than the Avestan texts of the rest of the *Yasna*. The *Avesta* was unknown to Western scholarship until the end of the eighteenth century, when the French traveller A.H. Anquetil du Perron published a French translation of the *Avesta*. In the past two hundred years, it has been possible to study the *Gathas* in the light of other later texts of the tradition, from the Achaemenian, Parthian, Sasanian and Islamic Persian periods in Iran. Similarly, the cultic life of the Zoroastrian tradition has been studied in texts and observed in practice, both in the Iranian and Parsi Indian traditions. The question of how much light later texts and practices can shed upon the enigmas of the *Gathas* is still controversial, both among scholars and in the modern religious community.

Zarathushtra's *Gathas* are written in an Iranian language known as Gathic Avestan, which is closely akin to Vedic Sanskrit of the second millennium BCE. They are among the most enigmatic of any known religious texts, full of archaic imagery, linguistic obscurities and *hapax legomena* which have presented problems of interpretation to scholars for over two hundred years. The *Gathas* give voice to a series of encounters and dialogues with the deity whom Zarathushtra recognizes as supreme: Ahura Mazda, 'the Wise Lord'. Zarathushtra's religious vision is fundamentally different from that of other primary religious figures such as Buddha, Jesus, Moses or Muhammad. Both priest and sage, throughout the tradition he has been seen primarily as the epitome of holiness and heroic virtue; he embodies the sage's human aspiration towards wisdom, justice, goodness and truth along with the priest's concern for purity of the cult and ritual efficacy. He is champion against the onrush of evil upon the world. His role as priest of a highly elaborate sacrificial and liturgical cult is balanced in the tradition with that of enlightened proto-philosopher of the life of virtue. In the *Gathas* his discourse is characterized by intimacy and friendliness with Ahura Mazda: either he is asking questions of the Creator or, as he comes to understand Ahura Mazda's nature, pledging his devotion and commitment to him. Yet, the tone of human friendship with Ahura Mazda does not dilute the strength of reverence expressed, but rather reflects an original conception: that material reality is not diminished and overwhelmed by some essentially superior spiritual world. Materiality coexists with the spiritual world, and so human and divine beings must work in a cooperative relationship. Ahura Mazda is himself aided by human righteousness, worship and goodness in the cosmic plan to annihilate the opposing principle of evil from existence. An individual's life of virtue and piety results in a personal eschatology of happiness and salvation in heaven: this contributes to the greater eschatology of the world's 'healing' at the end of time. Deliverance from suffering is therefore conceived not just in human but also in cosmic terms. The religion professes an optimistic and life-affirming philosophy for individual and society, one that is not intimidated either by monstrous demon or titanic deity: evil is beneath

contempt as 'the Lie'. Zarathushtra's God is the Wise Lord, neither overweening jealous god, nor angry, paternalistic tyrant.

His vision is of a perfection which will be fully drawn into the physical world, once the corruption of evil has been overcome. He teaches the need for rational reflection by the individual human being, in the quest for the perfecting of wisdom, goodness, truth and moral principles; these are not philosophical abstractions, but rather spiritual beings which must be cared for with actual worship and service. Later, popular texts ornament the prophet's own persona hagiographically, elevating him to the status of a miraculously born, superhuman figure akin to the Buddha of the *Jataka* stories or the Muhammad of popular Muslim tradition. The figure of the prophet plays an exemplary and unifying role in the religious tradition, from the sober genre of philosophical theology to fantastical representations in legendary texts. Though in the *Gathas* Zarathushtra's voice is a solitary one from the remote past, his appeal to modernity endures by the very fact that his rationality seems ageless in pointing out a path of virtue through a world afflicted with evil and suffering.

The *Gathas* are typical of archaic, oral religious performance texts: they are cast in complex metrical form, replete with formulaic utterances and epithets, often referring to cultural contexts which the modern reader can only strain to imagine. Their poetic form does not diminish their philosophical power, though the metaphorical language has often perplexed modern translators who have laboured to find an appropriate terminological vocabulary. The *manthras* are sincere, sometimes almost desperate strivings after truth; sometimes they are resounding statements of clear vision of that truth received from Ahura Mazda.

To what extent can the later theological, legal and other religious works of the Zoroastrian tradition help us to understand the *Gathas* better? It is now more generally thought that they do provide a key to interpret the *Gathas*, though this must be used judiciously. An example is found in the interpretation of the abstract nouns *asha vahishta* 'best righteousness', *vohu manah* 'good mind' and so on. In the later tradition these terms describe fully formed divine beings who are worshipped and revered alongside Ahura Mazda. Some scholars have insisted on the merely philosophical abstraction of these terms in the *Gathas*, while others have followed the later Zoroastrian tradition of regarding them as actual divine beings, known as the *Amesha Spentas*, 'Blessed Immortals' (even though this precise term is not found in the *Gathas*). It has been argued that to regard them as merely philosophical abstractions is anachronistic, since personification of what are perceived to be living realities is clearly widespread in Vedic and other ancient texts of this genre (Boyce 1975: 200, following Lommel 1970: 257). In this key passage of the *Gathas* it is said that there are two, not one, fundamental spirits in the universe, utterly irreconcilable and opposite in nature, namely the virtuous or most holy spirit, the author of all life, and the deceitful, evil spirit. This is probably not so much a metaphysical statement, as it has been interpreted by some modern readers, but rather part of a teaching about the nature of good and evil as understood by Zarathushtra.

Such is the antiquity of Zarathushtra's age that no historical facts can be established with any certainty: yet in consideration of his religious and philosophical message, this turns out to be less relevant than might be thought. There is no reason to doubt that the Gathic teachings were the realization of a single human mind inquiring into the nature of truth and goodness. These are the very terms Zarathushtra uses. In several of the verses Zarathushtra asks a series of fundamental questions about the nature of reality (for example, *Yasna* 44 and 48). He even inquires of the ability of Ahura Mazda to fulfil his own divine plan. These questions may be seen as rhetorical in function, being a device to define and elaborate his teachings, but they sprang nevertheless from a searching inquiry. Zarathushtra, as we know from his words, was a priest of the ethnic Indo-Iranian religion which was based on votive offering, liturgical ritual and reverence to a great range of gods and titans. In statements in the *Gathas*, we hear that Zarathushtra had to struggle for support and recognition during his own lifetime, until he was accepted as a true visionary prophet by his patron, a nobleman called Vishtaspa. He frequently laments that he was spurned by all levels of society, and that no one would listen to his teachings. Zarathushtra's visions

brought him to question the old ways of thinking and to find a single focus of his devotions in Ahura Mazda, the creator and supreme being among a number of beneficent spiritual powers; Ahura Mazda is identified with the holiest spirit, and is opposed by the separate principle of evil, 'the worst spirit'. From this vision Zarathushtra formulated a creedal faith, based upon worship of the beneficent spiritual powers and the uncompromising rejection of the old gods of violence and aggression who had previously been appeased with placatory offerings and devotions. With them he rejected all the evil forces of darkness and fury, who are summed up in his concept of Angra Mainyu, the 'Hostile Spirit'. Zarathushtra instructs that each man must listen to his words and 'reflect with a clear mind – man by man for himself – upon the two choices of decision, being aware to declare yourselves to Him before the great retribution' (*Yasna* 30.2, in Insler 1975: 33).

Six great, beneficent spirits are alongside Ahura Mazda, the 'Blessed Immortals' (*amesha spentas*). These and other spiritual beings 'worthy of worship' (*yazata*) are repeatedly mentioned by Zarathushtra, often in groups, in terms of praise and as powers to be internalized into man's own spiritual being. The most often mentioned spiritual being and overarching supreme deity is Ahura Mazda and his Holiest Spirit, Spenishta Mainyu. This hypostasis of Ahura Mazda's beneficent power is able to enter into the human being if invited to do so by the human will which has been strengthened and purified by Truth (*Asha*) and the Good Mind (*Vohu Manah*) and the spiritual attributes represented by the other Blessed Immortals. The tone of Zarathushtra's message is urgent, warning of the cosmic, social and moral violence with which titanic forces of evil threaten the creation. He pledges himself as leader in this struggle and exhorts humankind to struggle with him. The opponent is the hostile, evil spirit which produced 'the worst things' and is conceived as 'the deceitful one of evil doctrine', or 'lie' (*draoga*). Whereas Ahura Mazda created life, this 'hostile spirit' Angra Mainyu is the anti-creator of its opposite, death, termed 'not-life'. The rewards of which he speaks, for those who struggle for the sake of the truth, are virtue itself, and the progress towards justice and happiness in this world in the future. Zarathushtra asks for the power of good dominion (*Khshathra*

Vairya), and for instruction from Ahura Mazda on how 'the foremost existence' of perfection shall come about. Ahura Mazda is called the father of good thinking and the creator of truth, and is identified with the spirit of goodness: those who are obedient to his will must always choose truth and goodness in preference to the way of the evil spirit. Sinners, who have chosen to worship the hostile spirit, who follow him in his fury and deception, suffer punishment in the hereafter as a result of their evil actions.. Zarathushtra teaches that those who follow him should, like him, heal the world of the affliction of the evil spirit.

The gods of the Indo-Iranian pantheon who had been associated with the warrior class, and thus with violence, are referred to as *daeva* (later *dew*, which comes to mean 'devil'). They were rejected by Zarathushtra as the offspring of evil thinking, deceit, tyranny and disrespect, and they are reviled and ritually cursed by Zoroastrians as enemies of the truth. Zarathushtra asks for the same immortality, truth, self-perfection and other divine attributes of Ahura Mazda to be given to him. In return, such perfection and immortality are declared to be for the sustenance of Ahura Mazda himself. He asks earnestly to know the will of Ahura Mazda, just as he declares his wish to heal the world. Zarathushtra identifies himself closely with his Wise Lord and demonstrates the interdependency of the power of God and the actions of those who believe in Him.

Zarathushtra speaks of a final judgment for all mankind. Actions as well as words will have their results at the end of time. He refers to a figure called the *daena*, which is to be understood as a kind of eschatological soul, made virtuous by good actions, or alternatively foul and ugly by sinful deeds. Human choice is at the very centre of eschatology, as in a sense man judges himself by his actions. Ahura Mazda is said to be the greatest of all spiritual beings, not only because he created the world in perfection and then redeemed it from destruction by the evil spirit, but also because he created the possibility of ultimate salvation and perfection in a physical world. The *Gathas* have a doctrine comparable to that of the Orthodox Christian 'deification' (in Greek, *theosis*) through the incorporation of the powers represented in Ahura Mazda and the other beneficent immortals,

as in the affirmation 'through the determination of his good thinking, he shall be someone like Thee, Wise One'. Zarathushtra puts humankind into a pivotal position in that human choice can affect the fulfilment or destruction of the benevolent creation. Zarathushtra links moral action directly to philosophical principles: 'Let fury be stopped. Cut away cruelty, ye who wish to attract the attention of Good Thinking along with that of truth. The virtuous man indeed is its companion' (*Gathas*, *Yasna* 48.7, in Insler 1975: 93).

Philosophical as they may seem, Zarathushtra's words are not merely theoretical conclusions, but rather the results of a visionary apprehension of a transformed world and the moral imperatives which he discovered in that vision. His certainty is that of one assured of the inevitability of the good prevailing over evil through the rational choice. From the viewpoint of the Western philosophical tradition this may seem to be an act of merely religious faith, and indeed a long surviving religious tradition hallows Zarathushtra as its founder. Yet his own reflections, as recorded in the *Gathas*, may be seen as the first recorded philosophical reflections in dialogue, albeit in 'religious' language, yet laying bare the fundamentals of philosophical questioning. Its problems and questions are still central in Western thought: that of the individual and responsibility for action; of human free will and choice between alternatives; of what is the good, and what is evil; of the human capability of virtue, making a positive choice of the greater good and the will to be as against a selfish preference for evil and the denial of being itself. The Zoroastrian religion enshrined Zarathushtra's Gathic utterances as sacred truths. However much the religion became crystallized into doctrinal forms, hierarchies and ecclesiastical institutions, conforming to social and cultural constraints over centuries of development, it continued to refer to and include the central elements of Zarathushtra's teachings, always modelling them as various types of theological, mythological and ritual representations. These representations changed according to circumstances which varied from pastoral subsistence, to cosmopolitan power under the imperial patronage of Achaemenians and Sasanians, then in Islamic times as a minority faith in Iran, latterly in exile abroad in India, and recently in the secularized context of Indian and Western urban milieus.

Zarathushtra, both the visionary teacher in the ancient texts and later religious prophet of a developed tradition, deliberated the twin question of the problem of evil and the nature of the human existential situation in the world. The answers to his question came as revelations from a supernatural source: henceforward he proclaimed the Wise Lord as creator of the world and all that is good in it, who offered salvation through the appropriation of wisdom, holiness, righteousness, good mind and the other divine virtues. As his religion teaches, by this path of virtuous stewardship of the world, the world may progress towards rehabilitation, when evil will be destroyed and the realms of spiritual and physical beings will coalesce in a state of perfection in multiplicity.

Further reading

Boyce, M. (1975) *A History of Zoroastrianism*, *Handbuch der Orientalistik*, Leiden: Brill.
—— (1979) *Zoroastrians, Their Religious Beliefs and Practices*, London: Routledge.
Humbach, H. (ed. and trans.) (1991) *The Gathas of Zarathushtra*, 2 vols, Heidelberg.
Insler, S. (ed. and trans.) (1975) *The Gathas of Zarathushtra*, Acta Iranica 8, Leiden: Brill.
Kellens, J. and Pirart, E. (1988) *Les textes vieil-avestiques*, Wiesbaden: Dr Ludwig Reichert Verlag.
Lommel, H. (1970) in B. Schlerath, *Zarathustra, Wege der Forschung*, Bd CLXIX, Darmstadt ed. Schlerath, Wissenschaftliche Buchgesellschaft: Wege der Forschung.

ALAN WILLIAMS

ZEN *see* Buddhism in China, origins and development; Buddhist philosophy in Japan

Zhang Zai

b. 1020; d. 1077

Neo-Confucian philosopher

Zhang Zai (Chang Tsai) was a Northern Sung Neo-Confucian best known for his piece titled *Western Inscription*, in which he voiced his sense of being united with the One **Ether** that activates all things in the universe. By recalling this monistic ethereal base, he reaffirmed the reality of this world against the Buddhist denial of it as empty (see **emptiness**). He also thus restored the physical base to the discourse on human nature, and put corporeal habituation to the **rites** back on the agenda of moral self-cultivation. He did so without denying the aspiration for a metaphysical unity of the human mind with the cosmic principle and without falling into a dualistic split of mind and matter. Socially he was a conservative, part of the school holding that sages are born and not self-created (see **sage**). Learning can only bring one up to be a 'great man'. And since the material base of human character does vary, not everyone can study the classics (see **Classics and Books**) and not everyone is meant to be great. His programme of habituating the self into virtue is meant for the gentry class and his revival of family rituals was meant to rebuild an ancient ideal, the **well-field system**, an agrarian system designed for rural self-sufficiency.

Zhang was the uncle of the two Cheng brothers, Cheng Hao and Cheng I, who went on to develop an idealist interpretation of Confucianism. Zhang's own account was more materialist, according to which both *qi* and *li*, matter and principle, are irretrievably connected in the structure of the universe and its consequent harmony. Change occurs when *yin* and *yang* causes matter (*qi*) to rise or sink, which means to become solid or to dissipate into the general environment. It is not clear what role *li* has here, sometimes it looks as though it is directing the changes in matter, and sometimes it seems to be reflecting changes in *yin* and *yang* which are operating on *qi*. Where he is quite clear is in his claim that whatever happens to *qi*, it cannot become nothing, there is no such thing as a total vacuum, and so the Buddhists and the Daoists, with their notions of **Non-Being** and emptiness/**nothingness**, cannot find in the universe anything physical to corroborate their theories. In fact, they are misled by the etiolated state of *qi* when it is dispersed by *yang* into thinking that it has disappeared, but this is wrong; it is still there, albeit in a very different form.

The ethical implications of this theory are interesting. We are essentially good, but our actual character is strongly affected by the ways in which our matter or *qi* is affected by external forces and by its original character. We go awry when our *qi* is occluded and gets in the way of our proper selection of actions and our understanding of our motives. In the appropriate Confucian manner, Zhang recommends that we try to establish control over our moral character by considering that character, controlling our personal desires and ambitions, and fitting our behaviour with the *dao* or way which represents reality. This process should be distinguished both from Daoism, with its emphasis on the significance of long life, and Buddhism with its commitment to liberation from the world. What Zhang seeks to do is explain how one should accept the sort of life in which human beings inevitably find themselves, while also trying to improve our ability to align with the underlying principles of that life and the universe of which it is merely a part.

Further reading

de Bary, W. (1990) *The Message of the Mind in Neo-Confucian Thought*, New York: Columbia University Press.

Fung Yu-lan (1953) *A History of Chinese Philosophy*, Princeton, NJ: Princeton University Press, 477–99.

Tu Wei-ming (1971) 'The Neo-Confucian Concept of Man', *Philosophy East and West* 21(1): 79–87.

Zhang Zai (1963) *Cheng-meng/Zhengmeng (Correcting Youthful Ignorance)*, trans. Chan Wing-tsit, *A Sourcebook in Chinese Philosophy*, Princeton, NJ: Princeton University Press, 500–17.

WHALEN LAI
OLIVER LEAMAN

Zhang Zhidong

b. 1886; d. 1962

Philosopher

Known best for calling for an '(inner) eastern essence; (outer) western function', Zhang Zhidong

(Chang Chih-tung) sought a modernization of China while keeping alive the traditional spirit. The formula of 'inner Daoism, outer Confucianism' was produced during the Han by Ke Hung and others; it could work because of a shared cosmology. The updated paradigm has been criticized as highly problematical in the new setting, since Western science carries certain metaphysical implications that seem to be incompatible with the 'eastern spirit'. Yet 'total westernization' that totally renounces the past is just as questionable. Such crude alternatives between choosing to go entirely with the West or the East hardly addresses properly the complex nature of culture, society and personality. Post-modernism has placed under suspicion the imperialist project of looking to the inevitable demise of Eastern traditions, and has also pointed to the absence of independent justification of the processes implicit in Western ways of reasoning and arguing. Hardly surprisingly, Neo-Traditionalists have latched onto that Western self-criticism for their own ends.

Further reading

Chang Hao (1987) *Chinese Intellectuals in Crisis: Search for Order and Meaning 1890–1911*, Berkeley, CA: University of California Press.

WHALEN LAI

zhengming

A theory of virtue attributed to **Confucius**, *zhengming* (rectification of names) is based on the formula, 'let the ruler be ruler, the minister a minister, the father a father, the son a son' (*Analects* 12:11). It is usually read through the interpretation of **Xunzi**, who insisted that 'name must comply with reality'. So a nominal ruler ought to act as a normative ruler would, the 'ought' being what the rites had set down. But in *Analects* 13:3, the logic of the theory is given as follows: 'When names are not right, then speech does not accord; when speech does not accord, affairs cannot be conducted; when affairs cannot be conducted, rites and music will not flourish; when rites and music do not flourish, punishments will not be fitting; and when punishments do not fit, then the common people will not know even where to put their hands and feet'. Whether this passage is original or interpolated later, it is clear that the intent is not to 'make name conform to reality' but to 'have reality accord with the excellence of the name'. In short, this is a classic theory of virtue (*arete*, excellence) inscribed in the name so that one rectifies the imperfect reality according to the excellence of the name. Thus the virtue of stone is its hardness by which all stones are to be judged. So diamond qualifies as a very good stone but sandstone does not. This admits of an intrinsic good to 'father-hood', the excellence of being a father that is empirically verifiable. The Good is not subjective, not an Ought contrary to the Is; it is a fact deducible from observing a sufficient number of good and bad family lives. Far from being feudal, Confucius's formula eliminated all reference to feudal ranks and speaks in terms of the two relationships basic to all developed societies: the family (father/son) and the state (ruler/minister). These two are intrinsic goods, for the simple reason that having a family is better than having none, living in a state is better than being stateless. Once that is acknowledged, the common good is the good that is good for both parties. That would disqualify anything that is only good for father or ruler and not son and subject.

Further reading

Confucius (1979) *The Analects*, trans. D. Lau, Harmondsworth: Penguin.

Lai, W. (1990) 'Rectifying the Theory of the "Rectification of Names", *Journal of Humanism and Ethical Religion* 3(1): 124–40.

MacIntyre, A. (1981) *After Virtue*, Notre Dame, IN: Notre Dame University Press.

WHALEN LAI

Zhi Dun

b. 314; d. 366

Neo-Daoist philosopher

Foremost of the 'Neo-Daoist' monks, Zhi Dun

(Chih Tun), also known as Zhi Daolin (Chih Tao-lin) synthesized Daoist **non-being** and Mahayana **emptiness** in a three-stepped dialectic. He first ontologically reduced being to non-being after the manner of Laozi; then he epistemologically traced the distinction of being and non-being to a discriminating mind, as **Zhuangzi** did; then, emptying the distinction by emptying that mind, he had his refined mind or spirit become one with the *dao*. With that, the **sage** could spiritually rove in emptiness while abiding physically in the world of form. 'Neo-Daoist' monks were often retired gentlemen with independent wealth. They had money to buy up mountains for their retreat. The monk Zhi Dun even clipped the wings of cranes so they would stay longer around his hermitage.

WHALEN LAI

Zhou Yong

fl. 5th century CE

Buddhist philosopher

Zhou Yong (Chou Yung), who wrote on 'Three Schools of **Two Truths**', initiated the 'Three Truths' discourse. **Nagarjuna** taught only Two Truths, but the Chinese assumed that there should be a union of the two, leading to a postulation of a 'third and highest truth'. In the next generation, to explain how reality could be both real and empty, the Chinese used metaphors like 'rolling and unrolling a lotus leaf', 'bobbing a melon in and out of water' or 'flipping a coin front to back'.

Further reading

Lai, W. (1979) 'Chou Yung vs. Chang Jung (on Sunyata): The Pen-wu Mo-yu Controversy in Fifth-Century China', *The Journal of the International Association of Buddhist Studies* 1(2): 23–44.

WHALEN LAI

Zhu Xi

b. 1130; d. 1200

Neo-Confucian philosopher

The systemizer of Neo-Confucian metaphysics (see **Neo-Confucianism, concepts**), Zhu Xi (Chu Hsi) is responsible for setting up the apparent dualism of principle and **ether**. Principle is 'above form' and non-material; it is the Great Ultimate. Ether is 'below form' and encompasses the material realm of *yin–yang*. Principle underwrites the moral norms; it is one with the goodness of human nature. Accessible to the minds of man through a patient, rational investigation into the principle of things, the self-evidency of the principle may be clouded by the accidents of ether. (But even if a flower blooms out of season 'in October snow', it is not without reason, i.e. principle.) Likewise the goodness of human nature may be distorted by inappropriate private feelings. However, by granting Principle logical priority over Ether while acknowledging their being coterminous, Zhu Xi was criticized for being an inconsistent 'dualist'.

Actually Zhu Xi had confronted that problem head on, and he came up with a solution in the formula: 'The principle rides on the **trigger** point of the ether (material force)' even as 'the mind unites nature and emotion'. Prior to that, he had set the moral principle 'above form' and the material ether 'below form', and considered nature to be 'before the arousal' of the four emotions and the emotions to be 'after the arousal'. He made a distinction between the materiality of the spatially placed *yin–yang* (i.e. earth and **heaven**) which is encompassed within the Great Ultimate and 'one *yin* one *yang*' (an expression describing a temporal succession of *yin* passivity and *yang* movement). The union of principle and ether is then understood as the principle riding on the 'trigger' point directing the alternating movement. On the human end of this equation, the mind rises above and is placed in charge of the emotions, seeking a synthesis of nature and emotion, reason and passion. There is a subtle and crucial distinction. The principle of nature, all accidental distortions notwithstanding, functions 'divinely' by itself. Nature is blameless; it is without error and requires no supervision.

Unlike nature, man is fallible; he may err when swayed by his selfish desires; for that reason, the mind rises to supervise, unite and bring in line his nature and emotion. Analysts who point to there being still 'two minds' in Zhu Xi's writings, the mind of moral principle and the mind of material ether, a necessary distinction, miss the point of that higher synthesis.

See also: li as principle

Further reading

Chan Wing-tsit (ed.) (1986) *Chu Hsi and Neo-Confucianism*, Honolulu, HA: University of Hawaii Press.

de Bary, W. (1991) *Learning for One's Self: Essays on the Individual in Neo-Confucian Thought*, New York: Columbia University Press.

Lai, W. (1984) 'How the Principle Rides on the Chi [trigger point] of the Ether: Chu Hsi's Non-Buddhist solution of Nature and Emotion', *Journal of Chinese Philosophy* 11: 31–66.

WHALEN LAI

Zhuangzi

*fl. c.*360 BCE

Zhuangzi (Chuang-tzu) used to be classified as a Daoist, and was indeed counted as the second major Daoist thinker. However, this identification is now much more questionable. Zhuangzi's philosophical position is elusive; his 'Daoist' association' came late, and the book written and given his name has many strata. The chapter entitled 'Equalization of Things' was thought to be his way of finding unity where others see only differences. But now it is unclear whether he actually proposed a thesis about 'things being equal', or merely laid out the various current theories about reality. Interpretation is currently divided. Is Zhuangzi a mystic with transcendental wisdom, or just a sceptic finding all knowledge to be relative? Or both? Is he a perspectival relativist, or a perspectival realist? Did he merely register the mutability of all things, or point ahead to a way out by achieving 'no-mind'?

Zhuangzi has a poetic style which makes precise decisions on this sort of topic difficult to make, and unlike many other Chinese philosophers he seems to have concentrated as much on style as on exactly what he wanted to communicate. There is an exciting dialectical tone to his work; he seems to be constantly challenging the reader, and just at the stage where one feels one has understood his point, he will question what he himself appears to have been arguing. One reason for this approach is that he makes a close link between language and the reality which the language sets out to describe. It is a mistake, he thinks, to portray language as a less authentic guide to reality than reality itself, since words can be seen as just as real as the natural phenomena themselves. On the other hand, Zhuangzi is happy to defend nature, and he is far more complimentary about it than about the sorts of concepts which the Confucians proffer as appropriately in charge of nature, such as the heart-mind (**xin**). This has the role of establishing how we should behave, and is best constructed when it is found in the **sage**. Zhuangzi is suspicious of the idea that there could be one answer to ethical problems which everyone is supposed to follow, one dao which is perfectly captured by the Confucian xin. It is certainly the case that there are a lot of views by different people on how we should behave, and there is much debate about the best way to resolve such disputes, and we want to present some sort of argument to show that one resolution of the issue is better than the others. But neither the Confucian reliance on an appeal to tradition, nor Mohist utilitarianism (aiming at beneficial consequences of moral action) can represent the 'final' position on how we should act. How could there be just one acceptable view on such an issue?

This is the sort of approach which Zhuangzi follows throughout, challenging comfortable truths and established positions by identifying their subjective roots. He attacks the notion of the sage by arguing that the latter's constant appeals to **heaven** (*tian*) are no more than a projection of his own beliefs on some supposedly independent and more authoritative source. Rather than looking somewhere else for a resolution of our theoretical problems, we should look those problems straight in the eye and consider the language in which they are fomulated. That language is no less 'real' than the reality which it purports to represent, it is part and parcel of our view of the world, and is something which we should celebrate, not try to replace with something surer and better based. This relativism is present in the analogy for which he is famous, where he dreams of being a butterfly and then wonders what the difference is between dreaming he is a butterfly, or a butterfly dreaming he is Zhuangzi! Of course there is a problem with this defence of the relative, since such a defence in itself offends the principle of relativity itself, and perhaps that is why Zhuangzi is rather hesitant about specifying clearly his conclusions. Another reason to be dubious about knowing something completely is his thesis that there is no such thing as doing something perfectly or completely, since even if we do manage to do one activity perfectly, there will be others which are less satisfactory, whether they are intellectual or practical. This brings out nicely the general modesty which Zhuangzi thinks should be applied to any philosophical theories, which can only, however acute they are, represent the truth partially.

Further reading

Giles, H. (ed.) (1981) *Zhuangzi, Mystic, Moralist and Social Reformer,* London: Allen & Unwin.

Graham, A. (ed.) (1981) *Chuang Tzu: The Inner Chapters,* London: Allen & Unwin.

Mair, V. (ed.) (1983) *Experimental Essays on Chuang-tzu,* Honolulu, HA: University of Hawaii Press.

Watson, B. (ed.) (1964) *Zhuangzi: Basic Writings,* New York: Columbia University Press.

WHALEN LAI
OLIVER LEAMAN

Zongmi

b. 780; d. 841

Buddhist patriarch

Zongmi (Tsung-mi), a patriarch of both the Huayan and Chan schools, is the last of the Tang dynasty schematizers of the Buddhist teaching, whose *Enquiry into the Origin of Man* also bridged

Buddhist and Neo-Confucian anthropology (see **Neo-Confucianism, concepts**). His abridged reading of the ***Awakening of Faith in Mahayana*** became the Chinese standard, and his use of a series of circular diagrams for depicting stages of enlightenment and delusion in the ***alaya-vijnana*** anticipated the *yin–yang* circle. However, his summation of the Chan schools is too neat to be true, on top of which it is ideologically self-serving. By setting the three religions of China on a comparable platform, i.e., the depth of the 'origin of man', he also unknowingly paved the way for the Neo-Confucians to 'overcome' Buddhism later by making the social being of man, not the depth of the mind, the new moral standard.

Further reading

Gregory, P. (1991) *Tsung-mi and the Sinification of Buddhism*, Princeton, NJ: Princeton University Press.

WHALEN LAI

Zoroastrian philosophy in the Denkard

The most complete account of Zoroastrian philosophical theology is to be found in the compendious ninth century CE text *Denkard* (Acts of the Religion). It is a vast work, made up of different genres of religious writing, comprising nearly 170,000 words, in the Middle Persian language known as 'Book Pahlavi'. Much of it is written in a complicated, sometimes almost impenetrable, style. Unfortunately, perhaps because of the size and difficulty of the text, no complete translation of the *Denkard* has ever been made into any European language; versions of single books, or even single chapters, have appeared at different times in scholarly translations. In English we have E.W. West's translation of the last three books in the Sacred Books of the East series (now much outdated), selective translations by R.C. Zaehner, and S. Shaked's edition and translation of Book VI.

In ninth-century Iran the Persian language was written in the Arabic script of the Muslim conquerors and the older Pahlavi writing system,

which had been derived from the Aramaic alphabet, was already almost completely obscure to all except Zoroastrians: an important reason for the Zoroastrian priests to maintain its use in their works. The compilation of the *Denkard* was begun by the High Priest/scholar Adurfarnbag, son of Farrokhzad, in the first part of the ninth century and was completed in the latter part of the century by a successor, Adurbad son of Emed, two hundred years after Islam had become dominant in Iran with the defeat of the Sasanian king Yazdegird III in the mid-seventh century CE. Only seven of the nine books of the original work survive, namely III–IX, the first two books having been lost within the first hundred and fifty years after its completion.

The work as a whole was described by the Iranist Père Jean De Menasce, whose scholarship on the *Denkard* is unsurpassed, as 'une encyclopédie mazdéenne'. Its principal purpose is constantly reaffirmed: the exposition of the religion. It is part of what is known in Zoroastrian tradition as the *Zand*, the 'explanation' of the *Avesta* (the primary scriptural canon). Thus, neither compiler makes any claim to original composition but rather emphasizes that it has been handed down to him from the 'ancient sages' (*portyotkeshan*). Of the seven books extant, Book III is the most concentrated and the most interesting philosophically and theologically; although it has received much attention from scholars, the only complete modern translation is the French of De Menasce. Book IV is a very short compendium of religious 'sayings' taken from another book by Adurfarnbag Farrokhzadan. Book V is another exposition of the discourses of the same writer and a series of responses to Christian criticisms of Zoroastrian doctrines. Book VI is the largest known collection of gnomic aphorisms (*handarz*). There are other collections of *handarz* in other texts of this period, but that of the *Denkard* is elevated above the popular, moralizing level of most other *handarz* texts to a higher intellectual dimension. The aphorisms combine the theological sophistication of the earlier books with a psychological subtlety seldom met in other Zoroastrian texts outside the *Gathas* of Zarathushtra. The remaining three books are of less interest in regard to philosophical thought. Book VII tells of the life of Zarathushtra, adorned with miraculous embellishments reminiscent of hagiographical accounts of prophets in other religions. Book VIII is a uniquely informative document in Zoroastrian literature as it provides a resumé of the divisions (*nasks*) of the original *Avesta*, four-fifths of which have been lost. The last book is a paraphrase of three *nasks* of the *Avesta* which comment on the *Gathas* of Zarathushtra.

The third book of the *Denkard* examines the dogmatic and moral principles of the Zoroastrian religion from the perspective of a rational systematic exposition. It is an energetic inquiry into the true faith in an *apologia*, which is at the same time self-defensive and aggressive towards other systems of belief. The underlying argument is arranged around two central foci: (1) elaboration of the rational arguments of Zoroastrian dualism and correction of errors made by Judaism, Christianity and Islam; and (2) an explanation of the cosmogony and anthropology of Zoroastrian lore, which is intended to integrate the current understanding of physical nature into the dualistic metaphysics of the religious tradition. In spite of the writer's insistence on the traditional nature of this exposition from ancient sages, passages in *Denkard* III appear to be a vigorous rearguard action and response to attacks on specific Zoroastrian doctrines by Muslim clerics and theologians. Muslims were not mentioned by name in the *Denkard*, nor in other Zoroastrian books in Pahlavi, for fear of reprisal and punishment under Islamic law. They and those of other faiths are referred to as '(other) religious teachers' (*keshdaran*), and '(members of) other religions' (*juddenan*). Questions of dualism and the nature of God and the nature of evil are central in this discussion. Throughout this book the foundation upon which everything is said to rest is the principle of the Good Religion (*weh den*), revealed to Zarathushtra and transmitted through the ages by the Ancient Sages (*poryotkeshan*). The arrangement of chapters is apparently *ad hoc*, moving through a series of themes of fundamental theological significance. Central to the philosophy of the *Denkard*, is the unity of three notions prized as quintessentially Zoroastrian: the Good Religion (*weh den*), 'right measure' (*payman*), i.e, the mean between excess and deficiency, and 'innate wisdom' (*asn khrad*).

Paradoxically, in view of the closed nature of the Pahlavi language to outsiders, the discussions of the *Denkard* seem to be addressed to the circumspectly named *keshdaran*, i.e., the 'religious teachers' of the other faiths. This, however, is a rhetorical device. Most energetically disputed are Islamic doctrines, without direct reference, of course, either to the name of Islam or to Muslims. For example the author attacks the Qur'anic notion that Muhammad is said to be the last of the prophets. The *Denkard* objects that in the very terms of the Muslim doctrine of prophecy, the last of the prophets would announce and inaugurate an age of immortality and justice. But such is not the case, since Islam has inaugurated a regime of conquests and violence. The main targets for the *Denkard*'s attack are the Islamic doctrines of divine omniscience and omnipotence in connection with human sin and their chastisement in the fires of hell. The Zoroastrian argument of the *Denkard* (which tends, like much religious polemic, to simplify and vulgarize the logic of the theology under attack) is that if man must suffer eternal hell for the sake of his conduct which is within the foreknowledge of God, then God is effectively the cause of what has led man to his downfall if God is, as Zoroastrians understood Muslim belief, the author of the evil desire (*varan*) as much as of its contrary, wisdom. The alleged illogicality of the Muslim belief is that the ruin of men seems to have been brought about by the divine will itself. As the author of the *Denkard* sees it, in Islam God seems to allow evil to exist and thus participates in it, which is incompatible with the Zoroastrian understanding of the supreme creator-divinity.

According to Zoroastrianism, wisdom is innate in human beings but attains its fullness in the Wise Lord (Avestan, *Ahura Mazda*; Pahlavi, *Ohrmazd*). For Zoroastrians, there is little wisdom in the Jewish, Christian and Islamic conceptions of God. Their God appears to be a torturer lacking the most elementary mercy, which is itself well-established in the human experience of fatherhood and motherhood of children. That God is believed by these religions to punish those who would not know how to act otherwise is seen by the *Denkard* tradition as a cruel act of injustice and inhumanity. The *Denkard* does not refrain from finding such a doctrine guilty of making God the supreme and eminent cause of evil; such a god cannot be God for, in the Zoroastrian view, he lacks all the very attributes which are of the order of good and which define God: it better describes that which is in Zoroastrianism deemed to be the antagonist of God, Ahreman.

Nor does the *Denkard* tolerate the Islamic doctrine of eternal punishment in hell. The Zoroastrian view is, first, that God himself does not punish, but that sinful human action itself results in chastisement in a hellish realm because it damages and disfigures the human soul: God is not responsible for, nor is he involved in, such a process. Second, this hell is not eternal: to admit this would be to deny Zoroastrian belief in the eschatological transfiguration of the world (*frashegird*) by which the physical world is promised to be rid of the demonically originated evil and imperfection which entered it while it was still in its pristine state of original perfect creation. Since then the world has been in a condition known as the 'mixed state' (*gumezishn*); it is promised by Zoroastrian tradition, from Zarathushtra onwards, that it will be re-established in perfection through the cooperation of the spiritual beings of Ohrmazd's creation and the efforts of humankind. Moreover, hell has nothing to do with fire as in the Qur'anic depiction of hell (Arabic *nar*, 'the fire'): no true God would ever in any case chastise sinners with this pure element. Zoroastrians strictly maintained the purity of the physical elements, especially fire, water and earth, and for them hell is darkness, the absence of the sacred element of fire and its light.

The author of the *Denkard* makes it plain that there is no similarity or even common ground between the Zoroastrian and the Islamic, Christian or Jewish views of God, most obviously in the Zoroastrian doctrine of dualism. Theological dualism has been mistakenly interpreted as a great theological stumbling block by outsiders to the Good Religion. In the *Denkard*, it is handled with utmost confidence and adroitness: misunderstanding of dualism arises from too sensual an understanding of things. A purely sensual appreciation of reality never grasps the Zoroastrian doctrine of first principles, which can only be clearly perceived by one who is able to see *beyond* appearances, through innate wisdom. This supreme spiritual and intellectual human faculty is damaged and eventually destroyed by a surfeit of sensuality and by other vices (ch. 294).

Wisdom (*khrad*) and sensuality (*az*, also translated 'lust' and 'concupiscence') are opposites in the spiritual psychology of the *Denkard*, just as the blessed immortals (*amahraspands*) and demons (*dews*) are opposed in the cosmology of the religion. Through the notion of human 'innate wisdom', the *Denkard* bridges the apparent divide between such a spiritual psychology and religious cosmology, depicting the benevolent and malevolent spiritual entities as participating in an eschatological drama which is both individual and cosmic in scale. As the *Denkard* puts it:

> men know God by their power and their perseverance in their struggle against the Lie (*drug*) and in saving from it their souls and their bodies, and by their power of governing the other creatures of the visible world (*getig*) according to the project of the creator who has given to men to govern them and endowed them with power. Concupiscence to another principle is the contrary of the innate intellect, conjoins men to sin and throws them to the demons... the innate intellect is at once the greatest and the most sure messenger from the creator to the creatures of the visible world. It is by it that men know the creator, see God as God, demons as demons...
>
> (ch. 77)

Excess of sensual, as opposed to spiritual, understanding in the minds of those of other religions, however righteous and theologically sophisticated they might consider themselves to be, absolutely prevents their knowledge and understanding of God, because it makes them incapable of differentiating good from evil. *Denkard* III renders an ancient Zoroastrian doctrine, namely that the Blessed Immortals are helpers of the Wise Lord, Ohrmazd, and human kind: human understanding of reality and human power to oppose the titanic powers of evil is effected by incorporation of the spiritual power of the good spiritual beings through worship, service and the conscious choice of virtue in the world. The virtues recognized by human thinkers are instruments of the innate wisdom *asn khrad*, a gift of Ohrmazd, the origin and essence of all wisdom; all the vices of this world are instruments of the opposite of wisdom – that is, sensuality – epitomized in the hostile spirit Angra

Mainyu/Ahreman. The *Denkard* repeatedly emphasizes the parallelism between the agencies of the invisible spiritual world, the intermediate psychological realm of our human nature, and the external visible world of physical creatures. At all levels of reality, the same struggle between order and chaos takes place, and always Ohrmazd is seen as the source of all spiritual and material good in the world.

Men of virtue are said to resemble the good spiritual beings who alone are 'worthy of worship' (*yazads*), whereas evil men become like the demons (*dews*). In the mixed state of the present world the resemblance to either the *yazads* or *dews* is only partial, in proportion to their wisdom and virtue or ignorance and vice. Human nature is perfectible, but only when evil has been completely purged from the world at the end of time. An aphorism in the sixth book of the *Denkard* sums up the direct connection between human physical and psychological purity and the eschatology of the cosmos:

> The beneficent divinities (*yazads*) should be made to inhabit that place which if they inhabit, they are made to inhabit the whole of this world. For when Ahreman is put out of the body of men he is annihilated from the whole world, and the *yazad*s, when they are made rulers over the bodies of men they are rulers over the whole world.
>
> (Shaked 1979: 103)

The beneficent powers of the Blessed Immortals and the *yazads* are present in the visible world both as spiritual presence and as the physical elements. Again, humankind has a central role, as the 'righteous man' is said to be the manifestation of Ohrmazd and his holiest spirit. In other texts the term 'righteous man' (*mard i ahlaw, arda*) usually refers specifically to the Zoroastrian priest, but in *Denkard* III it seems to denote a spiritual ideal of human attainment. The Blessed Immortals are seen not as disembodied, celestial entities remote from the human world, but rather as entering and dwelling in that world, in the human body and mind, especially in response to human righteousness, performed in ritual or other virtuous acts.

According to a passage in *Denkard* III, the Blessed Immortals and other good spiritual beings come to the aid of human beings in the physical world when they abstain from sin and accomplish virtuous deeds: the demons (see **demons in Zoroastrianism**) are repelled and the creatures of the world experience safety and happiness. Conversely, when men abstain from virtue and turn towards sin, the demons return and the way is closed for the coming of any goodness from the powers of Ohrmazd. The same passage goes on to say that the benefit or, *mutatis mutandis*, damage to human happiness takes place not just for the individual but can affect whole realms and epochs of history. Thus the vicissitudes of history are explained as being occasioned according to human pursuit of virtue or vice: the incentives to righteousness and direction towards the perfection of human happiness are made plain.

Practical aspects of religious teaching are not overlooked in the exposition of the *Denkard*. As one would expect in a religion which has such a highly developed culture of ritual practice and codes of purity, human action in ordinary day to day living is valued as contributing towards the eschatological purpose. The ritual act of purification is the principal technique of enabling virtue to predominate over evil. So it is said that by the purification, of the place, of the body and of the clothes, from all dirt and odour, the power of the evil spirit, is smitten. By invocation of the *yazads*, by worship, by cultivation of plants, and by beautifying the world with luminous, pure and perfumed things through the Good Religion, the man of good renown is, as the text puts it, 'completely conformed to divinity and distanced from devilry'. The body and the mind, therefore, like the world at large, are the battle ground for the warring forces of good and evil powers: the prize is the world itself. From the earliest texts, the *Gathas*, the religion taught that Ahura Mazda/Ohrmazd and his righteous creation will in the end prevail over the Hostile Spirit, Angra Mainyu/Ahreman, so that he will be annihilated in the spiritual as well as in the material world. Through the *Denkard*'s explanation of a wisdom innate in human nature (*asn khrad*) this eschatological optimism is worked into a theory of spiritual psychology. The *Denkard* also speaks in the traditional language of eschatological myth about the end of things; however, by having supplied also a psychological interpretation for the gods and demons, it sets out a clear rationale and incentive

for virtue in the individual. The *Denkard* says that
when the time of Frashegird comes, the demon of
sensuality/concupiscence (Az), who is the counter-
creation of the evil spirit Gannag Menog (a term
used interchangeably with Ahreman), will return to
attack Gannag Menog himself, and will devour,
overcome and destroy all his own counter-
creations. The good Creator Ohrmazd has fore-
seen this through his omniscience, and the demons
which still exist at the moment of the Frashegird
will destroy the very essence of the demonic power,
without which they cannot come back into
existence, and they will attack the primordial
'Lie' without his being able to get up again. Thus,
evil is demonstrated to be ultimately futile and self-
destructive. The eschatological vision of Zarathushtra in the *Gathas* is thus given the benefit of
a philosophical exegesis which explains why the
doctrine of dualism, the identification of a principle
of evil which is absolutely separate from God is not
an aberrant theology, but a philosophical and
psychological necessity for the practice of virtue
and the pursuit of happiness.

Further reading

de Menasce, J. (1958) *Une encyclopédie mazdéenne le
Denkart*, Paris: Presses Universitaires de France.
Denkard (1892, 1895), Books VIII and IX trans.
E.W. West, in F. Max Müller (ed.), *Sacred Books of
the East*, Oxford, Clarendon Press, vol. VII,
1892; Book VII in *ibid.*, vol. XLVII, 1895.
—— (1973) *Le troisième livre du Denkart traduit du
pehlvi*, Paris: Librairie C. Klincksieck.
Shaked, S. (1979) *The Wisdom of the Sasanian Sages
Denkard VI*, Boulder, CO: Westview Press.
West, E. (1974) 'Pahlavi Literature', in C. Bartho-
lomae (ed.), *Grundriss der iranischen Philologie*, vol.
II, 91 ff.

ALAN WILLIAMS

Zoroastrianism

Zoroastrianism traces its religious tradition back to
the ancient Iranian visionary prophet **Zarathushtra**, author of the *Gathas* in the canon of their
scripture called the *Avesta*. The *Gathas* were written

in a northeast Iranian language related to Vedic
Sanskrit, *c.*1200–1000 BCE. This religion is traditionally known to itself as *mazdayasna* 'worshipping
(*Ahura*, 'Lord') *Mazda* (wise)', the Creator God and
source of all goodness, and *vi daeva* 'against the
demons'. Zarathushtra's message in the *Gathas* is
strongly ethical and rationalistic, rejecting violence,
tyranny and injustice, and advocating the life of
active virtue in thought, word and deed. Throughout its long history, the Zoroastrian tradition has
been founded on two principles: one the affirmation of virtue, through worship of Ahura Mazda
and his spiritual powers, and the other the denial of
evil, through the rejection of Angra Mainyu, the
Hostile Spirit and his demonic powers. The
tradition runs from the prophet's words in the
Gathas onwards, that worship of Ahura Mazda is
performed through service to seven cardinal,
Beneficent Immortal spirits (Avestan *amesha spenta*,
Pahlavi *amahraspand*): Ahura Mazda himself, who is
thought of as the creative 'holiest spirit' (*spenishta
mainyu*); 'Sublime Truth' (*asha vahishta*); 'Virtuous
Power' (*khshathra vairya*); 'Good Mind' (*vohu manah*);
Holy Piety (*spenta armaiti*); Wholeness (*haurvatat*),
and Immortality (*ameretat*). The second principle,
the avoidance of evil, demands the ability to
discriminate between good and evil. Therefore evil
is characterized as originating neither from God
nor from his creatures, but from a wholly other
source, personified as Angra Mainyu, who is
deemed to have no real existence. Real existence
is the creation and preserve of Ahura Mazda alone.
The charge, made by opponents of this 'dualistic'
religion, that it is tantamount to ditheism or
polytheism and is not truly monotheistic, is a
misunderstanding of the Zoroastrian doctrine of
good and evil. Evil has no existence, but has
attacked existence in order to gain it for himself.
The influence which Zoroastrianism may have had
upon other religions on the nature of evil, human
responsibility, and eschatological consequences,
among other things, is being reappraised by
scholars in modern times.

Zoroastrianism survives to this day in one of the
world's smallest and most widely dispersed ethnic
minority communities, the Zartushtis in the Islamic
Republic of Iran and their 'Parsi' co-religionists in
India. In the Classical world and in pre-modern
Europe the figure of Zoroaster has been associated,

in esoteric and popular circles, with a mysterious prophet of wisdom; the religious communities who continue to uphold his name are generally ignored or underestimated as to their historical importance. Yet Zoroastrianism was the principal religion of the Iranians under the Achaemenian, Parthian and Sasanian empires from the sixth century BCE for a thousand years; as the state church of the Sasanian kings in their wars against Rome, it directly opposed Christianity. It was brought down by the Islamic conquest of Iran in the seventh century CE, and since then Zoroastrians have been a religious minority in their own homeland. A number of them migrated to northwest India in the eighth century CE, as a result of religious persecution, and established the Parsi ('Persian') community. Their descendants made their home in the caste-conscious milieu of Gujarat, first as agriculturalists, then as traders, merchants and entrepreneurs in the colonial and post-colonial periods. Like Judaism, Zoroastrianism has for many centuries been an 'ethnic' religion which generally does not accept converts, and largely remains so. In modern times the problems of the community's demographic decline have worsened through intermarriage, secularization and emigration from the Indian subcontinent and from post-revolutionary Iran to Western countries. The total number of Zoroastrians worldwide is reckoned to be less than 120,000.

The holiest texts of the faith, the *Gathas*, are the oldest stratum of a much larger scripture, the *Avesta*, of which only one-fifth has survived. There is also an accompanying exegetical body of texts known as the *Zand*. This *Zand* once existed in several Iranian languages, but today is preserved only in the Middle Persian language of the Sasanian and early Islamic periods (fourth–tenth centuries CE), known as Pahlavi. If taken on their own, without the help of the greater Avestan and Pahlavi tradition, the *Gathas* are difficult to interpret satisfactorily, because of their archaic, prehistoric context and symbolism. The study of the *Gathas* continues to divide modern scholars, with regard to dating, geography and the precise nature of Zarathushtra's teachings. Nevertheless, a preponderance of opinion, led chiefly by the work of Mary Boyce, credits the later Zoroastrian tradition as having preserved in the Avestan and

Pahlavi texts a genuine picture of the prophet and his mission. Zarathushtra had been trained as a priest in his ancestral religion: he was skilled in its ritual and lore. However he felt a calling to seek a higher object of worship and the principles of a more just human society, rid of the oppression of marauders and tyrants. According to tradition, after years spent wandering, he received his first visions from Ahura Mazda at the age of thirty. His prophetic mission lasted the rest of his life, transmitting the divine message to those who would listen, until, it is said, in his old age he was slain by an assassin.

The principles of Zoroastrian doctrine are founded in elaborate ideas of cosmogony and eschatology. Before all existence there were two spirits, one good, creative of life, and beneficent: the other one evil, inimical to life, evil and malevolent. The two spirits are eternally opposed to one another. Ahura Mazda is identified in the tradition as the 'holiest spirit' of goodness. Ahura Mazda created the spiritual, then the physical worlds as a means of combatting and finally annihilating the Evil Spirit. This world, which was originally created in a state of perfection by the good, wise Ahura Mazda, was afflicted by the Evil/Hostile Spirit, also known as the 'Lie'. Man is urged to choose goodness and to reject the Hostile Spirit, to smite evil and align himself with Ahura Mazda, his Blessed Immortals and 'beings worthy of worship' (*yazatas*). Human beings have a soul while in this physical world, which is originally a part of an eternal spiritual nature which remains in the spiritual world. The human soul is affected by (that is, it records) a person's acts of virtue and wickedness which will be, consequently, rewarded or atoned for in a spiritual state after one life in the physical state. The religion advocates purity in thought, word and deed, as Angra Mainyu benefits from all polluting and defiling acts against Ahura Mazda's creation. Human life is a relentless struggle for goodness and purity against evil. Towards the end of human history a saviour will come to lead the righteous to victory over the forces of evil. Time will end, there will be a resurrection of all the dead and a last judgment of all souls. There will be made a new, spiritually and physically perfect world here on earth, no longer afflicted by evil, which will have been banished for eternity from the universe. There will be a return to the pristine perfection of the original creation, but with the fullness of physical and spiritual multiplicity of forms unafflicted by evil in a state called *Frashokereti* (Renovation, Re-establishment). The religion is thus based on a vision which is primarily soteriological and eschatological, promising a deliverance from imperfection by human effort aligned with the divine will.

The eschatological scale of time according to the developed Zoroastrian tradition may be drawn out as below, starting from a pre-temporal condition of parallel, but exclusively separate, equilibrium of Ahura Mazda and the Evil Spirit:

0–3000. Ahura Mazda dwells in Endless Light and is aware of the Evil Spirit, from which he is separated by a void, lurking in the depths of darkness. With his foreknowledge of future events, Ahura Mazda knows he must destroy this Evil Spirit and so brings his creation into being in an invisible or spirit (Pahlavi, *menog*) state. The Evil Spirit rises from the depth and sees this creation. Out of enviousness, the Evil Spirit fashions his own demonic creation in the spiritual state. The Evil Spirit is cast down by Ahura Mazda's recitation of a sacred prayer, the Ahuna Vairya.

3000–6000. For three thousand years the Evil Spirit remains unconscious. Ahura Mazda gives a prototype material (Pahlavi *getig*) existence to manifest his spiritual creation, in which each element of creation exists in singular form: one plant, one animal, one human being. The world proceeds according to the will of Ohrmazd. This is the time called 'Creation' (in Pahlavi, *bundahishn*).

6000–9000. The Evil Spirit breaks into and pollutes the material world, destroying the plant, animal and human creations. From their seeds Ahura Mazda manages to create all existing plants, animals and human beings. The events of human history begin to take place, in which evil continues to afflict this world in the time of 'mixture' (Pahlavi, *gumezishn*) when the world is open to the wills of both Ohrmazd and Ahriman.

8970. Birth of Zarathushtra.

9000. Beginning of the millennium of Zar-

athushtra, as he receives his revelation and teaches humankind. The myth speaks from the 'now' of this millennium, for though Zarathushtra himself dies and returns to the spiritual world Zoroastrians await the coming of the first of three Saviours who will lead the world towards the final victory over evil.

10,000. The millennium of the first saviour, Hushedar.

11,000. The millennium of the second saviour, Hushedarmah.

11,943. Birth of the Soshyans.

11,973. Like Zarathushtra, at the age of thirty the Soshyans will begin his mission to lead those of the Good Religion in the final struggle towards the restoration of perfection, Frashokereti (Pahlavi, *frashegird*). From all ages the souls of the dead will be recalled from heaven and hell, both good and evil, and will be resurrected in their reconstituted *getig* bodies. The final judgement will take place and the Evil Spirit and all his brood of demons will be utterly annihilated.

12,000. Time ends. The kingdom of Ahura Mazda will reign eternally on earth; physical and spiritual *getig* and *menog* worlds coalesce in an unprecedented state of spiritual perfection manifested in the fullness of physical multiplicity. It is called *Wizarishn* ('Separation', of good from evil).

Zarathushtra's vision became embedded in a sacramental and liturgical tradition which is a modified continuation and elaboration of the pre-Zoroastrian cult. It is generally thought by scholars that in remote antiquity an Indo-Iranian civilization of Central Asia comprised one cultural and linguistic whole, living a semi-nomadic pastoral existence probably in the area of Kazakhstan on the inner Asian steppes. It is thought that their common religious tradition was formed in the fourth to third millennia BCE, and thus when, around 1800 BCE, the Indians and Iranians separated and began to move to what are now their respective homelands, they took with them the basis of what became the related religious cultures of Brahmanism and Zoroastrianism. Over time they articulated their religious cult and beliefs in distinctive ways, but both continued to share an understanding of the world as needing maintenance through human action of renewal and reconsecration of the elements of the cosmos. The central religious act was the rite called *yasna* in Avestan, *yajna* in Vedic Sanskrit, literally 'act of worship'. It was performed in order to re-enact the great cosmic sacrifice by which the universe was created. In Zoroastrianism, though it is an elaborate ceremony, it is in principle an act of reconsecration of the symbolic elements of the created world: metal, water, earth, plant, animal, human and fire. The common basis of the Indian and Iranian religious traditions is best exemplified by the cognate words of Vedic Sanskrit *rta* and Zoroastrian Avestan *asha*, both of which mean 'order, law, truth', divinely sanctioned as the highest principle in the universe. The term *asha* also means spiritual and moral righteousness, and Zarathushtra urges his followers to become 'possessors of righteousness' *ashavan*, as distinct from those who adhere to evil (Avestan, *dregvant*).

Zarathushtra transformed and developed the old Indo-Iranian religion, by making paramount the *human* ethical and practical role in the maintenance of the world and in the fight against the forces of disorder. The beliefs and practices of Zoroastrianism all aim at achieving a harmony of the human world with that of nature, both physical, spiritual and divine. The Blessed Immortals mentioned by name in the *Gathas* were associated with the elements of the physical world, not as merely symbolic correspondences, but as the spiritual realities which protect and inhabit, and from which originate, the elements of the physical world. In this way the Zoroastrian has a fundamentally different attitude towards the physical, natural world from that of the western, monotheistic religions of semitic origin. The living world of plants and animals, and the rest of the natural world, is felt to be alive with divinity, not in a pantheistic sense of nature-worship, but because the physical world is seen as the visible manifestation of the spiritual world. Damage to the physical creation is thus hurtful to the spiritual beings which, mysteriously to us mortals, lie behind physical reality. This is the theological basis of the moral and physical code of purity in Zoroastrianism. Fire, for example, is revered not in itself but as 'truth-strong fire', i.e., the physical manifestation of the Blessed Immortal whose name Asha Vahishta is

translated as 'Best Righteousness'. The dubbing of Zoroastrians as 'fire-worshippers' is an old and slanderous misunderstanding of the religion, as crude as calling Christians 'cannibals'.

Zoroastrian understanding of purity is not merely moral but physical also, as it is part of an apprehension that the mortal human condition is a perilously vulnerable one, which is attacked on all sides by inimical conditions. The body and the physical world, it must be emphasized, are not considered to be intrinsically polluted or substantially inferior to the spiritual state. Although the regime of purity for laity and particularly the priesthood seem strenuous to non-Zoroastrians, there have never been any tendencies towards ascetic practices of self-mortification found in almost all other major religions of the world. Little has been said here of the complex ritual and liturgical practices. Reformers in the contemporary Zoroastrian community question the value of the traditional forms of practice, while conservatives adhere to them as essentially important in the form they preserve them. Underlying all forms of Zoroastrianism, however, is the belief that the example of Zarathushtra and his *spenta daena* 'virtuous conception' of humanity expresses a true human potentiality to reflect the divine nature.

Further reading

Boyce, M. (1979) *Zoroastrians, Their Religious Beliefs and Practices*, London: Routledge.

ALAN WILLIAMS

Zou Yan

b. 305 BCE; d. 240 BCE

Philosopher

A late Warring States period philosopher, Zou Yan (Tsou Yen) is credited with codifying the *yin–yang* and **Five Elements** theory that became the backbone of Chinese **correlative thinking**. He used the 'conquest series' of the Five Elements to explain the law of dynastic succession. The first dynasty is of Earth (Yellow) under the **Yellow Emperor**. It was conquered by the virtue of Wood

(Green), the emblem of the Xia; which was overtaken by the Metal (White) virtue of the Shang; which was superseded by the Fire (Red) element of the Zhou. Writing in the demise of Zhou during the Warring States period, he foresaw on the horizon the dawning of the age of Aquarius, Chinese style; that is, the rise of the Water element under a coming Black Emperor who would be coming from the North (or northeast). Working at the academy at the state of Qi in the northeast, he probably intended that role for his own patron.

Further reading

Schwartz, B. (1973) 'On the Absence of Reductionism in Chinese Thought', *Journal of Chinese Philosophy* 1(1).

WHALEN LAI

Zurvanism

Zurvanism is a strain of Zoroastrian religious thought which, for most of the twentieth century, was thought of as being a separate organized religious system which rivalled that of so-called 'orthodox' forms of **Zoroastrianism**, and which was even believed to be the more genuine and original form of Zarathushtra's religious heritage. Scholarly debate culminated in R.C. Zaehner's monumental, but now largely discredited, *Zurvan: A Zoroastrian Dilemma* (1955), and it is now generally thought that 'Zurvanism' was not practised by 'Zurvanite' heretics as such, but was one of several varieties of religious interpretation by Zoroastrians themselves. The figure of 'Zurvan' and the mythology which surrounds him were popular sporadically from the fifth/fourth centuries BCE until the twelfth century CE. This phenomenon may now be understood as a theological variant of the Zoroastrian religion which corresponded to certain internal and external pressures. It is notable that it has largely been outsiders to the Zoroastrian religion (Syrian and Armenian Christians, and Muslims) who relished the details of a purported 'Zurvanite' cosmogony which differed so radically from that given in the extant Zoroastrian texts, and which they (and modern scholars) held up as an original and profound challenge to Zoroastrianism. The Avestan Zrvan ('time') is only a minor divinity in the *Avesta*.

In the 'Zurvanite' heresy, which some scholars think dates back to the late Achaemenian period, 'Zurvan' was elevated to the ultimate source of all. In the Syriac and Armenian Christian sources he appears as a *deus otiosus* who, in a picturesque myth, left his supposed sons Ahura Mazda and Angra Mainyu to fight over the world (with the outcome that Ahura Mazda would win). The evidence for 'Zurvanism' is almost all late, but the scriptural justification which is deployed in these late foreign sources seems to be a mocking, literalistic interpretation of the most ancient Zoroastrian text, the *Gathas* (*Yasna* 30.3): 'Truly there are two primal spirits, twins renowned to be in conflict'. Even though this is a clearly metaphorical statement, especially given the genre and context of the original, the 'Zurvanite' reading is a case of *cherchez le père*, who is identified as 'Zurvan'.

'Zurvanism' is, as J. de Menasce has put it, 'a pseudo-monism, which envisages evil as a substance'. In the Sasanian period, when there was much strife within Iran itself between the Zoroastrian and Christian churches 'Zurvanism' became useful to the Christian enemies of the Iranian religion as an easy target for ridicule. Its mythological and theological vocabulary was that of a crude theism in which Ahura Mazda was reduced from being the original creator to being merely a created thing. This interpretation of Zoroastrian teachings disabled the vitally important body of dualistic ethical and philosophical thinking at the core of its theology, and was portrayed by Christian and Muslim critics as no more than a decadent form of idolatrous paganism in monistic guise. Ahura Mazda, the Wise Lord of Zarathushtra's *Gathas*, could thus be dismissed as merely a created being who was, after all (as the Christian polemicists of the Syriac Martyrdom texts put it), 'the brother of Satan' and offspring of a heartless god of fate. For modern scholars, if 'Zurvanism' had indeed been the preferred interpretation of the Zoroastrian scriptural tradition by the Sasanian church, it could be explained by the fact that the kings often behaved as if they themselves were, like 'Zurvan', above and beyond good and evil, wielding an amoral authority over their sovereign realm. Long after the downfall of the Sasanians, polemic continued against 'Zurvanite' mythology.

There is one great stumbling block to the whole theory of 'Zurvanite' religion. In spite of the assertions of ancient and modern Christian critics, 'Zurvanite' myth is absent from all Zoroastrian texts, so far from its ever being found as a coherent theology. The voluminous ninth-century CE Zoroastrian books in Pahlavi did not devote a single line of polemic against 'Zurvanism', as they do, for example, against the organized religion of 'the accursed Mani'. 'Zurvanism' was then, in Sasanian and early Islamic times, as it became in the nineteenth century, a polemical tool of opponents of Zoroastrianism.

While it is true that in the course of the next thousand years, under Islamic influence in Iran and under Hindu influence in India, the theological expression of the dualism at the heart of Zarathushtra's old tradition was de-emphasized, there was never any recourse to any 'Zurvanite' theology or mythology within Zoroastrianism. In the nineteenth century a new form of 'quasi-Zurvanism' took hold of some Zoroastrians and western scholars, which posited that the two spirits of the *Gathas* were co-equals under a higher omnipotent divinity. This alien interpretation once again had the effect of misrepresenting Zoroastrian teaching, in that evil was thereby made a necessary part of the divine plan, originating from one source. As Shaked has put it: 'Zurvanism as an organized religious system is a scholarly invention which lacks historical substance'.

Further reading

de Jong, A. (1996) *Traditions of the Magi: Zoroastrianism in Greek and Latin Literature*, Leiden: Brill, 330–8.

Shaked, S. (1992) 'The Myth of Zurvan: Cosmogony and Eschatology', in I. Gruenwald, S. Shaked and G.G. Stroumsa (eds), *Messiah and Christos. Studies in the Jewish Origins of Christianity*, TSAJ 32, Tubingen: Mohr.

Williams, A. (1986) 'The Real Zoroastrian Dilemma', in V.C. Hayes (ed.), *Identity Issues and World Religions*, Selected Papers from the XVth Congress of the International Association for the Study of Religion, Sydney, Australia, 1985, Sturt Campus, S. Australia, Australian Association for the Study of Religions, 93–103.

—— (1997) 'Zoroastrians and Christians in Sasanian Iran', *Bulletin of the John Rylands University Library of Manchester* 78(3): 37–53.

ALAN WILLIAMS

Name index

Subject index

shame **488**
Shao Yong **492**
Shu Qi **65**
Siming Zhili **504**
simplicity **504**
Song Xing **505–7**
spirit 532
spiritual ladders 514
subject/object **515–16**
substance/function relationship **517–18**
sudden enlightenment **182**
Sun Yat-sen **521**
Taiping **523**
Taixu **524**
Tan Sitong **524–5**
Tantrayana **526–7**
Tao Qian **527**
taotie **527–8**
things **531–2**
Three Truths **532**
time **532–3**
totalism **533**
totemism **534**
trigger **534–5**
trinity and triune **536–7**
truth as sincerity **537–8**
universals **398–9**
Wang Chong **562**
well-field system **564**
Western thought distinction 413
wuwei **569**
xenophobia **570**
Xi Kang **570–1**
Xie Lingyun **571–2**
xin **572–3**
xing **573**
Xiong Shili **573–4**
Xunzi **574–6**
Yan Fu **578**
Yellow Emperor **578**
Yijing (Book of Changes) **582–3**
yin-yang **583–4**
Zhang Zai **594–5**
Zhang Zhidong **595**
zhengming **595–6**
Zhi Dun **596**
Zhou Yong **596**
Zhu Xi **597**
Zhuangzi **597–8**

Zongmi **598–9**
Zou Yan **606–7**
Chittamatra *see* Yogachara Buddhism
Chogye School of Buddhism 75, 76, 113
Ch'on-t'ae 544
    see also Tiantai Buddhism
Ch'ondogyo 381–2
    see also Tonghak
Christianity 48, 72, 89, 91, 92–3, 355
    Averroism 54, 55
    charity 106
    China **122–3**
    evangelical 244
    heavenly hierarchy 514–15
    Hong Xiuquan 241
    idols 254
    India 561
    Japan 277, 278
    Korea **117–22**, 143, 187–8, 228, 298–9, 384, 487
    Liang Fa 317–18
    love 329
    Rammohan Roy 454
    trinitarianism 537
    Uchimura Kanzo 541
    Zoroastrian opposition 600, 604, 607, 608
    Zurvanism 607, 608
    see also Jesuits; Protestantism; Roman Catholicism
chuch'e philosophy 121, **124–6**, 343
Chungsan'gyo 382–3
Chunqiu **126**
civil religion **126**
Classics **126–7**, 144, 145, 254, 289, 463
    Dai Zhen 157
    Dong Zhongshu 174
    dragon 176
    education 179, 180, 186–7
    Han Confucians 349
    Han Learning 229, 230
    hermeneutics 345
    Japanese Confucianism 134, 138
    Kokugaku 293
    rites 464
    Sirhak 505
    Tasan 116
co-apprehension 170
cognition
    Advaita Vedanta 13–14